Collins easy learning

French
Dictionary

HarperCollins Publishers
Westerhill Road
Bishopbriggs
Glasgow
G64 2QT

HarperCollins Publishers
Macken House, 39/40 Mayor Street Upper
Dublin 1, D01 C9W8, Ireland

Ninth Edition 2024

10 9 8 7 6 5 4 3 2 1

ISBN 978-0-00-869519-4

A catalogue record for this book is available from the British Library

Typeset by Sharon McTeir Creative Publishing Services and Davidson Publishing Solutions, Glasgow

Printed in India

Acknowledgements
We would like to thank those authors and publishers who kindly gave permission for copyright material to be used in the Collins Corpus. We would also like to thank Times Newspapers Ltd for providing valuable data.

Collins gratefully acknowledge the help of the examining boards, whom we have consulted throughout this project, and whose word lists and exam papers we carefully studied when compiling this dictionary in order to ensure appropriate coverage and support for GCSE and other exams of a similar level.

EDITOR
Gina Macleod

CONTRIBUTORS
Gaëlle Amiot-Cadey, Marie Olivier-Caudray, Maurane Prezelin, Maggie Seaton, Anna Stevenson

FOR THE PUBLISHER
Maree Airlie, Gerry Breslin, Kerry Ferguson, Evangeline Sellers

TECHNICAL SUPPORT
Ruth O'Donovan, Agnieszka Urbanowicz

Contents

Glossary of grammar terms

Adjective

a 'describing' word that tells you more about a person or thing, such as their appearance, colour, size or other qualities, for example, *pretty*, *blue*, *big*, and, in French, grand, alphabétique, génial.

> une solution **éventuelle** a **possible** solution
> l'équipe **irlandaise** the **Irish** team

Adverb

a word usually used with verbs, adjectives or other adverbs that gives more information about when, where, how or in what circumstances something happens or to what degree something is true, for example, *quickly*, *happily*, *now*, *extremely*, *very*. Some adverbs in French are: mieux, naturellement, ainsi.

> Il l'a fait **autrement**. He did it **differently**.
> Je suis **très** fatiguée. I'm **very** tired.

Article

a word like *the*, *a* and *an*, which is used in front of a noun. In French the words le, la, un or une are articles.

> **les** filles **the** girls
> **un** journal **a** newspaper

Conjunction

a word such as *and*, *because* or *but* that links two words or phrases of a similar type or two parts of a sentence, for example, *Diane <u>and</u> I have been friends for years; I left <u>because</u> I was bored*. Common French conjunctions are donc, ou, mais.

> la voiture **et** la maison the car **and** the house
> Réfléchis bien **car** c'est important. Think carefully **because** it's important.

Noun

a 'naming' word for a living being, thing or idea, for example, *woman*, *desk*, *happiness*, *Andrew* and, in French, maison, chien, ville.

> la **capitale** the **capital**
> le **chocolat** **chocolate**

Preposition

a word such as *at*, *for*, *with*, *into* or *from*, which is usually followed by a noun, pronoun or, in English, a word ending in *-ing*. Prepositions show how people and things relate to the rest of the sentence, for example, *She's at home*; *a tool for cutting grass*; *It's from Nadia*. Some French prepositions are contre, dans, de.

> **dès** le début **right from** the start
> Il marchait **devant**. He was walking **in front**.

Pronoun

a word which you use instead of a noun, when you do not need or want to name someone or something directly, for example, *it*, *you*, *none* and, in French, elle, leur, même.

> Ce vélo-là, c'est le **mien**. That bike's **mine**.
> Prends **ceci**, tu en auras besoin. Take **this**, you'll need it.

Verb

a 'doing' word which describes what someone or something does, is, or what happens to them, for example, *be*, *sing*, *live*. Some common verbs in French are aimer, prendre, être.

> Elle **n'a pas** beaucoup **changé**. She **hasn't changed** much.
> Je **cherche** mes clés. I**'m looking** for my keys.

In order to provide additional practice with pronunciation and dictionary skills, free downloadable resources are now available for teachers and learners of French at **www.collins.co.uk/pages/free-easy-learning-language-resources**

Guide to entries

Numbers in brackets refer to verb tables at the back of the book

Shading indicates core vocabulary

Verb tables for common irregular verbs

Translations underlined to find them quickly

Examples show how the translation is used

Important phrases set out separately

Numbers clearly point out different senses

Look at the main verb to find out about common irregular verb forms

Less common plural forms given for nouns

Cultural notes offer additional information

Articles show whether a noun is masculine and/or feminine

devoir VERB [26]

PRESENT TENSE	
je dois	nous devons
tu dois	vous devez
il/elle doit	ils/elles doivent
PAST PARTICIPLE	
dû	

▷ see also **devoir** NOUN

1 to have to
□ Je dois partir. I've got to go.
2 must
□ Tu dois être fatigué. You must be tired.
3 to be due to
□ Le nouveau centre commercial doit ouvrir en mai. The new shopping centre is due to open in May.
■ **devoir quelque chose à quelqu'un** to owe somebody something □ Combien est-ce que je vous dois ? How much do I owe you?

le **devoir** MASC NOUN
▷ see also **devoir** VERB
1 exercise
■ **les devoirs** homework
■ **un devoir sur table** a written test
2 duty
□ Aller voter fait partie des devoirs du citoyen. Voting is part of one's duty as a citizen.

disent, disiez, disions VERB ▷ see dire

le **drapeau** (PL les **drapeaux**) MASC NOUN
flag
□ le drapeau français the French flag □ le drapeau tricolore the French flag

DID YOU KNOW...?
le drapeau tricolore is the French flag: its three colours are blue, white and red.

le **débutant** MASC NOUN
beginner
la **débutante** FEM NOUN
beginner
le/la **dentiste** MASC/FEM NOUN
dentist

Guide to entries

nice ADJECTIVE

1 gentil (FEM gentille) (*kind*)
□ Your parents are very nice. Tes parents sont très gentils. □ It was nice of you to remember my birthday. C'était gentil de ta part de te souvenir de mon anniversaire.
■ **to be nice to somebody** être [35] gentil avec quelqu'un

2 joli (FEM jolie) (*pretty*)
□ That's a nice dress! Qu'est-ce qu'elle est jolie, cette robe ! □ Aix is a nice town. Aix est une jolie ville.

> **WORD POWER**
> You can use a number of other words instead of **nice** to mean 'pretty':
> **attractive** séduisant
> □ an attractive girl une fille séduisante
> **beautiful** beau
> □ a beautiful painting un beau tableau
> **lovely** charmant
> □ a lovely surprise une charmante surprise
> **pretty** joli
> □ a pretty dress une jolie robe

to **depart** VERB
partir [57ᴱ]

doubt NOUN
▷ *see also* **doubt** VERB
le doute *masc*
□ I have my doubts. J'ai des doutes.

to **doubt** VERB
▷ *see also* **doubt** NOUN
douter [28] de
■ **I doubt it.** J'en doute.
■ **to doubt that** douter [28] que

> **douter que** has to be followed by a verb in the subjunctive.

□ I doubt he'll agree. Je doute qu'il soit d'accord.

ashamed ADJECTIVE
■ **to be ashamed** avoir [8] honte □ You should be ashamed of yourself! Tu devrais avoir honte !

Shading indicates core vocabulary

Word classes written out in full

Feminine form of adjectives shown

Words in brackets identify the meaning given

Word Power boxes help build vocabulary

English text always in black

French text always in blue

'E' indicates verbs that use être in the perfect tense

Reminder to check other word classes of the same word

Language Tip notes give key grammar points

Entries may show phrases or examples rather than a main translation to illustrate most common usages

Abbreviations used in this dictionary

aux   =   auxiliary (for verbs that use être in the perfect tense)

E   =   indicates that a verb uses être in the perfect tense

fem   =   feminine

masc   =   masculine

pl   =   plural

sing   =   singular

Prefixes and suffixes in French

In French, as in English, it is useful to know how words can change their meaning or part of speech when they have certain prefixes or suffixes added to them. Understanding how French words are grammatically related helps to develop and expand vocabulary.

Prefix/ Suffix	Add to...	...to create...	Examples
in- / im-	Adjectives (e.g. **possible**) Abverbs (e.g. **également**) Nouns (e.g. **sécurité**)	New adjective	possible → impossible également → inégalement sécurité → insécurité
-ième	Ordinal numbers (e.g. **trois, quatre**)	Cardinal numbers	trois → troisième quatre → quatrième
-able/ -eable	Verb stem (e.g. **chang**er, **soutenir**)	Adjective	changer → changeable soutenir → soutenable
-ion / -ation	Verb stem (e.g. **progress**er, **continuer**)	Noun	progresser → progression continuer → continuation
-ment/ -emment	Feminine form of adjective (e.g. **première**) Stem of adjective ending -ant(e)/-ent(e) (e.g. **pati**ent)	Adverb	première → premièrement patient → patiemment
-eur/ -ateur	Verb stem (e.g. **chant**er, **consomm**er)	Agent noun	chanter → chanteur consommer → consommateur

French pronunciation guide: sound-symbol correspondence

This pronunciation guide has been compiled to help learners pronounce French with greater confidence. The tables below focus on key differences between French and English, and should not be understood as a comprehensive guide of all of the different sounds that are possible in French; letters (or combinations of letters) pronounced in approximately the same way in French as in English are not listed.

The use of hyphens indicates the position of the letters in a word, when position is relevant to the sound: xx- (at the beginning of a word); -xx- (in the middle of a word); -xx (at the end of a word).

Table 1 focuses on sounds that can be illustrated with equivalent or near-equivalent sounds in English.

French sound	French examples	Similar sounds in English
a	aller, avec	apple, bat
i/y	vie, physique	bead, sheep
eu	deux, bleu	hurt, work
e	le, je	over, favour
au/eau/closed o/ô	sauf, bateau, mot, hôtel	hope
ou	sous, bouche	full, boom
u	dur, menu	zoo, too
é, -er, -ez	moitié, parler, chez	fiancé
è/ê/ai	très, êtes, mai	ten, respect
oi/oy	moi, voyage	wag, wacky
ch	chose, chercher	shout, bash
ç/soft c	français, cinéma	so, rice
qu	quelle, chaque	kiss, rock
j	jeune, projet	beige, leisure
-gn-	campagne, mignon	canyon
open eu/œu	leur, sœur	bird, word
open o	donner, objet	honour, oblong
-s-	raison, visage	raise, zero
th	bibliothèque, thé	late, eight
-ill-/-ille	papillon, fille	yet, million
-aill-/-ail	taille, travail	tyre, inspire
r	rue, mardi	*'gargled' r; close to Scottish 'loch'*

Table 2 gives information on letters and types of letters that are usually silent in French – note that sometimes these letters are pronounced as a result of liaison (see **Table 3**).

Silent letters	French examples
silent final consonant	pa**s**, for**t**
silent final e	jeun**e**, visit**e**
h-	**h**omme, **h**istoire

Table 3 looks at common liaisons in French – liaison occurs when a consonant that would normally be silent is pronounced because it is followed by a vowel or a mute 'h'. An equivalent or near-equivalent example of an English sound is given to illustrate the pronunciation of the normally silent consonant.

Liaison	French examples	Similar sounds in English
s-liaison	me**s** animaux, le**s** enfants	rai**s**e, **z**ero
t-liaison	peti**t** ami, c'es**t** elle	la**t**e, eigh**t**
n-liaison	e**n** hiver, mo**n** oncle	mi**n**e, ca**nn**on
x-liaison	deu**x** heures, yeu**x** ouverts	rai**s**e, **z**ero

Finally, **Table 4** looks at nasalised vowels, common in French but not used in English. A nasalised vowel is produced by allowing air out of the nose as well as the mouth as you speak. Vowels followed by a single 'n' or 'm' are generally nasalised. The 'n' and 'm' are not pronounced, but instead affect the sound of the vowel before them, meaning the vowel sounds the same whether it is non or nom.

Nasalised vowel sounds	French examples
un	l**un**di, br**un**
en/em/an/am	**en**s**em**ble, t**an**t, ch**am**bre
on/om	c**om**bien, d**on**c
ain/ein/in/aim/im	b**ain**, pl**ein**, f**aim**
-ion	direct**ion**, nat**ion**
-ien	r**ien**, b**ien**

Numbers

1	un(e)	21	vingt et un(e)
2	deux	22	vingt-deux
3	trois	30	trente
4	quatre	40	quarante
5	cinq	50	cinquante
6	six	60	soixante
7	sept	70	soixante-dix
8	huit	71	soixante et onze
9	neuf	72	soixante-douze
10	dix	80	quatre-vingts
11	onze	81	quatre-vingt-un(e)
12	douze	90	quatre-vingt-dix
13	treize	91	quatre-vingt-onze
14	quatorze	100	cent
15	quinze	101	cent un(e)
16	seize	300	trois cents
17	dix-sept	301	trois cent un(e)
18	dix-huit	1,000	mille
19	dix-neuf	2,000	deux mille
20	vingt	1,000,000	un million

Examples

Il habite au dix.	He lives at number ten.
à la page dix-huit	on page eighteen
au chapitre sept	in chapter seven
neuf fois sur dix	nine times out of ten

Years

1764	mille sept cent soixante-quatre
1988	mille neuf cent quatre-vingt-huit
2022	deux mille vingt-deux

Fractions

½	un(e) demi(e)
⅓	un tiers
⅔	deux tiers
¼	un quart
⅕	un cinquième

0.5	zéro virgule cinq (0,5)
3.4	trois virgule quatre (3,4)
10%	dix pour cent
100%	cent pour cent
1st	premier (1er), première (1re)
2nd	deuxième (2e)
3rd	troisième (3e)
4th	quatrième (4e)
5th	cinquième (5e)
6th	sixième (6e)
7th	septième (7e)
8th	huitième (8e)
9th	neuvième (9e)
10th	dixième (10e)
11th	onzième (11e)
12th	douzième (12e)
13th	treizième (13e)
14th	quatorzième (14e)
15th	quinzième (15e)
16th	seizième (16e)
17th	dix-septième (17e)
18th	dix-huitième (18e)
19th	dix-neuvième (19e)
20th	vingtième (20e)
21st	vingt et unième (21e)
22nd	vingt-deuxième (22e)
30th	trentième (30e)
100th	centième (100e)
101st	cent unième (101e)
1000th	millième (1000e)

Examples

Il habite au cinquième (étage).	He lives on the fifth floor.
Il est arrivé troisième.	He came in third.
C'est la deuxième fois que je viens en France.	It's the second time I've been to France.

Time

Quelle heure est-il ? Il est ...   **What time is it? It's ...**

une heure

une heure dix

une heure et quart

une heure et demie

deux heures moins vingt

deux heures moins le quart

À quelle heure ?   **At what time?**

à minuit

à midi

à une heure (de l'après-midi)

à huit heures (du soir)

à 11h15 *or* onze heures quinze

à 20h45 *or* vingt heures quarante-cinq

In French times are often given in the twenty-four hour clock.

Aa

a VERB ▷ *see* **avoir**

> **a** should not be confused with the preposition **à**.

■ **Il a beaucoup d'amis.** He has a lot of friends.
■ **Il a mangé des frites.** He had some chips.
■ **Il a neigé pendant la nuit.** It snowed during the night.
■ **il y a** 1 there is □ Il y a un bon film à la télé. There's a good film on TV. 2 there are □ Il y a beaucoup de monde. There are lots of people. 3 ago □ Je l'ai rencontré il y a deux ans. I met him two years ago.
■ **il y en a** □ Combien y a-t-il de pommes ? — Il y en a trois. How many apples are there? — There are three.
■ **Qu'est-ce qu'il y a ?** What's the matter?
■ **Il n'y a qu'à partir plus tôt.** We'll just have to leave earlier.

à PREPOSITION

> **à** should not be confused with the verb form **a**.

1 at
□ être à la maison to be at home □ à trois heures at 3 o'clock
2 in
□ être à Paris to be in Paris □ habiter au Portugal to live in Portugal □ habiter à la campagne to live in the country □ au printemps in the spring □ au mois de juin in June
3 to
□ aller à Paris to go to Paris □ aller au Portugal to go to Portugal □ aller à la campagne to go to the country □ donner quelque chose à quelqu'un to give something to somebody □ Cette veste appartient à Marie. This jacket belongs to Marie. □ Je n'ai rien à faire. I've got nothing to do.
■ **Ce livre est à Paul.** This book is Paul's.
■ **Cette voiture est à nous.** This car is ours.

> **à** changes when followed by **le** or **les**, but when followed by **la** or **l'**, it stays the same:
> à + le = <u>au</u>   à + les = <u>aux</u>
> à + la = <u>à la</u>   à + l' = <u>à l'</u>

4 by
□ à bicyclette by bicycle □ être payé à l'heure to be paid by the hour
■ **à pied** on foot
■ **C'est à côté de chez moi.** It's near my house.

■ **C'est à dix kilomètres d'ici.** It's 10 kilometres from here.
■ **C'est à dix minutes d'ici.** It's 10 minutes from here.
■ **cent kilomètres à l'heure** 100 kilometres an hour
■ **À bientôt !** See you soon!
■ **À demain !** See you tomorrow!
■ **À samedi !** See you on Saturday!
■ **À tout à l'heure !** See you later!

abandonner VERB [28]

1 to abandon
□Il a abandonné son chien. He abandoned his dog.
2 to give up
□ J'ai décidé d'abandonner la natation. I've decided to give up swimming.

l'abeille FEM NOUN
bee

abîmer VERB [28]
to damage
■ **s'abîmer** to get damaged

l'abonnement MASC NOUN

1 season ticket
2 subscription (*to magazine*)

s'**abonner** VERB [28]
■ **s'abonner à une revue** to take out a subscription to a magazine
■ **être abonné sur Instagram** to be on Instagram

l'abord MASC NOUN
■ **d'abord** first □ Je vais rentrer chez moi d'abord. I'll go home first.

aboyer VERB [53]
to bark

l'abri MASC NOUN
shelter
■ **être à l'abri** to be under cover
■ **se mettre à l'abri** to shelter

l'abricot MASC NOUN
apricot

s'**abriter** VERB [28]
to shelter

l'absence FEM NOUN
absence
■ **Il est passé pendant ton absence.** He came while you were away.

absent (FEM **absente**) ADJECTIVE
absent

a

absolument - acheter

absolument ADVERB
absolutely

l'**abus** MASC NOUN
abuse
- **abus de confiance** breach of trust
- **abus de pouvoir** abuse of power
- **abus sexuels** sexual abuse

l'**accélérateur** MASC NOUN
accelerator

accélérer VERB [34]
to accelerate

l'**accent** MASC NOUN
accent
□ Il a l'accent de Marseille. He has a Marseille accent.
- **un accent aigu** an acute accent
- **un accent grave** a grave accent
- **un accent circonflexe** a circumflex

accentuer VERB [28]
to stress

accepter VERB [28]
to accept
- **accepter de faire quelque chose** to agree to do something

l'**accès** MASC NOUN
access
□ avoir accès à quelque chose to have access to something
- **« Accès aux quais »** 'To the trains'

l'**accessoire** MASC NOUN
1 accessory
□ les accessoires de mode fashion accessories
2 prop

l'**accident** MASC NOUN
accident
□ un accident de la route a road accident
□ Elle a eu un accident de ski. She had a skiing accident.
- **par accident** by chance

accompagner VERB [28]
to accompany

accomplir VERB [38]
to carry out
□ Il n'a pas réussi à accomplir cette tâche. He didn't manage to carry out this task.

l'**accord** MASC NOUN
agreement
- **être d'accord** to agree □ Tu es d'accord avec moi ? Do you agree with me?
- **se mettre d'accord** to come to an agreement
- **D'accord !** OK!

l'**accordéon** MASC NOUN
accordion
□ Mathieu joue de l'accordéon. Mathieu plays the accordion.

l'**accoudoir** MASC NOUN
armrest

l'**accrochage** MASC NOUN
collision

accrocher VERB [28]
- **accrocher quelque chose à 1** to hang something on □ Il a accroché sa veste au portemanteau. He hung his jacket on the coat rack. **2** to hitch something up to □ Ils ont accroché la remorque à leur voiture. They hitched the trailer up to their car.
- **s'accrocher à quelque chose** to get caught on something □ Sa jupe s'est accrochée aux ronces. Her skirt got caught on the brambles.

s'**accroupir** VERB [38]
to squat down

l'**accueil** MASC NOUN
welcome
□ Il nous a remerciés de notre accueil. He thanked us for our welcome.
- **Elle s'occupe de l'accueil des visiteurs.** She's in charge of looking after visitors.
- **« Accueil »** 'Reception'

accueillant (FEM **accueillante**) ADJECTIVE
welcoming
□ Ses parents ont été très accueillants. Her parents were very welcoming.

accueillir VERB [22]
to welcome

accumuler VERB [28]
to accumulate
- **s'accumuler** to pile up

l'**accusation** FEM NOUN
accusation

l'**accusé** MASC NOUN
accused
□ L'accusé a déclaré que ... The accused stated that ...
- **un accusé de réception** an acknowledgement of receipt

l'**accusée** FEM NOUN
accused

accuser VERB [28]
to accuse
□ accuser quelqu'un de quelque chose to accuse somebody of something

l'**achat** MASC NOUN
purchase
- **faire des achats** to do some shopping

acheter VERB [1]
to buy
□ J'ai acheté des gâteaux à la pâtisserie. I bought some cakes at the cake shop.
- **acheter quelque chose à quelqu'un**
1 to buy something for somebody □ Qu'est-ce que tu lui as acheté pour son anniversaire ? What did you buy him for his birthday? **2** to buy something from somebody □ J'ai acheté des œufs au fermier. I bought some eggs from the farmer.

acide (FEM **acide**) ADJECTIVE
▷ *see also* **acide** NOUN
acid
□ Ce pamplemousse est trop acide. This grapefruit is too acid.

l'**acide** MASC NOUN
▷ *see also* **acide** ADJECTIVE
acid

l'**acier** MASC NOUN
steel

l'**acné** FEM NOUN
acne
□ Il a de l'acné. He has acne.

acquérir VERB [2]
to acquire

acquis VERB ▷ *see* **acquérir**

acquitter VERB [28]
to acquit
□ L'accusé a été acquitté. The accused was acquitted.

l'**acte** MASC NOUN
act
■ **un acte de naissance** a birth certificate

l'**acteur** MASC NOUN
actor
□ Il est acteur. He's an actor. □ un acteur de cinéma a film actor

actif (FEM **active**) ADJECTIVE
active
■ **la population active** the working population

l'**action** FEM NOUN
action
■ **une bonne action** a good deed

s'**activer** VERB [28]
1 to bustle about
□ Elle s'activait à préparer le repas. She bustled about preparing the meal.
2 to get moving
□ Allez ! Active-toi ! Come on! Get moving!

l'**activité** FEM NOUN
activity

l'**actrice** FEM NOUN
actress
□ Elle est actrice. She's an actress. □ une actrice de cinéma a film actress

l'**actualité** FEM NOUN
current events
■ **un problème d'actualité** a topical issue
■ **les actualités** the news

actuel (FEM **actuelle**) ADJECTIVE
present
□ le système actuel the present system
■ **à l'heure actuelle** at the present time

BE CAREFUL!
actuel does not mean **actual**.

actuellement ADVERB
at present

BE CAREFUL!
actuellement does not mean **actually**.

l'**adaptateur** MASC NOUN
adaptor

adapter VERB [28]
to adapt
■ **s'adapter à quelque chose** to get used to something □ Je me suis adapté au collège. I've gotten used to secondary school

l'**addition** FEM NOUN
1 addition
□ l'addition et la soustraction addition and subtraction
2 bill
□ L'addition, s'il vous plaît ! Can we have the bill, please?

additionner VERB [28]
to add up

l'**adhérent** MASC NOUN
member

l'**adhérente** FEM NOUN
member

adhésif (FEM **adhésive**) ADJECTIVE
■ **le ruban adhésif** sticky tape

adieu EXCLAMATION
farewell!

l'**adjectif** MASC NOUN
adjective

admettre VERB [47]
1 to admit
□ Il refuse d'admettre qu'il s'est trompé. He won't admit that he made a mistake.
2 to allow
□ Les chiens ne sont pas admis dans le restaurant. Dogs are not allowed in the restaurant.

l'**administration** FEM NOUN
administration
■ **l'Administration** the Civil Service

admirable (FEM **admirable**) ADJECTIVE
admirable

l'**admirateur** MASC NOUN
admirer

l'**admiratrice** FEM NOUN
admirer

admirer VERB [28]
to admire

admis VERB ▷ *see* **admettre**

l'**ado** MASC/FEM NOUN
teenager
■ **un camp d'ados** a youth camp

l'**adolescence** FEM NOUN
adolescence

l'**adolescent** MASC NOUN
teenager

adolescente - afin de

l'adolescente FEM NOUN
teenager

adopter VERB [28]
to adopt

adorable (FEM **adorable**) ADJECTIVE
lovely

adorer VERB [28]
to love
□ Elle adore le chocolat. She loves chocolate.
□ J'adore jouer au tennis. I love playing tennis.

l'adresse FEM NOUN
address
■ **une adresse web** a Web address
■ **mon adresse électronique** my email
address

adresser VERB [28]
■ **adresser la parole à quelqu'un** to speak to
someone
■ **s'adresser à quelqu'un** **1** to speak to
somebody □ C'est à toi que je m'adresse. It's
you I'm speaking to. **2** to go and see somebody
□ Adressez-vous au patron. Go and see the boss.
□ Adressez-vous aux renseignements. Ask at
the enquiry desk.
3 to be aimed at somebody □ Ce film s'adresse
surtout aux enfants. This film is aimed mainly
at children.

l'ADSL MASC NOUN (= *asymmetric digital
subscriber line*)
ADSL
■ **On a l'ADSL à la maison.** We have
broadband at home.

l'adulte MASC/FEM NOUN
adult

l'adverbe MASC NOUN
adverb

l'adversaire MASC/FEM NOUN
opponent

aérien (FEM **aérienne**) ADJECTIVE
■ **une compagnie aérienne** an airline

l'aérobic MASC NOUN
aerobics
□ Teresa fait de l'aérobic. Teresa does aerobics.

l'aérogare FEM NOUN
terminal

l'aéroglisseur MASC NOUN
hovercraft

l'aéroport MASC NOUN
airport

l'affaire FEM NOUN
▷ *see also* **affaires** NOUN
1 case
□ une affaire de drogue a drugs case
2 business
□ Son affaire marche bien. His business is doing
well.
■ **une bonne affaire** a real bargain

■ **Ça fera l'affaire.** This will do nicely.
■ **avoir affaire à quelqu'un** to deal with
somebody

les affaires FEM PL NOUN
▷ *see also* **affaire** NOUN
1 things
□ Va chercher tes affaires ! Go and get your
things!
2 business
□ Les affaires marchent bien en ce moment.
Business is good at the moment. □ Mêle-toi de
tes affaires. (*informal*) Mind your own business.
■ **un homme d'affaires** a businessman
■ **le ministre des Affaires étrangères** the
Foreign Secretary

l'affection FEM NOUN
affection

affectueusement ADVERB
affectionately

affectueux (FEM **affectueuse**) ADJECTIVE
affectionate

l'affiche FEM NOUN
poster

afficher VERB [28]
to put up
□ Ils ont affiché les résultats dehors. They've put
the results up outside.
■ **« Défense d'afficher »** 'Post no bills'

affilée
■ **d'affilée** ADVERB at a stretch □ Il a travaillé
douze heures d'affilée. He worked 12 hours at
a stretch.

l'affirmation FEM NOUN
assertion

affirmer VERB [28]
to claim
□ Il a affirmé que c'était la vérité. He claimed it
was the truth.
■ **s'affirmer** to assert oneself □ Il est trop
timide, il faut qu'il s'affirme. He's too shy, he
should assert himself.

l'affluence FEM NOUN
■ **les heures d'affluence** the rush hour

s'affoler VERB [28]
to panic
□ Ne t'affole pas ! Don't panic!

affranchir VERB [38]
to stamp

affreux (FEM **affreuse**) ADJECTIVE
awful

affronter VERB [28]
to face
□ L'Allemagne affrontera l'Italie en finale.
Germany will face Italy in the final.

afin de CONJUNCTION
■ **afin de faire quelque chose** so as to do
something □ Je me suis levé très tôt afin d'être

prêt à temps. I got up very early so as to be ready on time.

afin que CONJUNCTION
so that

> **afin que** is followed by a verb in the subjunctive.

□ Il m'a téléphoné afin que je sois prêt à temps. He phoned me so that I'd be ready on time.

africain (FEM **africaine**) ADJECTIVE, NOUN
African
- **un Africain** an African (*man*)
- **une Africaine** an African (*woman*)

l'Afrique FEM NOUN
Africa
- **en Afrique 1** in Africa **2** to Africa
- **l'Afrique du Sud** South Africa

agacer VERB [12]
- **agacer quelqu'un** to get on somebody's nerves □ Tu m'agaces avec tes questions ! You're getting on my nerves with all your questions!

l'âge MASC NOUN
age
- **Quel âge as-tu ?** How old are you?

âgé (FEM **âgée**) ADJECTIVE
old
□ Son père est âgé. His father's old. □ Il est âgé de dix ans. He's 10 years old.
- **les personnes âgées** the elderly

l'agence FEM NOUN
1 agency
□ l'agence pour l'emploi the employment agency
- **une agence de voyages** a travel agency
2 office
□ l'agence de Londres the London office
- **une agence immobilière** an estate agent's

l'agenda MASC NOUN
diary
□ J'ai perdu mon agenda. I have lost my diary.

> **BE CAREFUL!**
> The French word **agenda** does not mean **agenda**.

s'**agenouiller** VERB [28]
to kneel down

l'agent MASC NOUN
- **un agent de police** a police officer
- **un agent d'entretien** a cleaner

l'agglomération FEM NOUN
town
- **l'agglomération parisienne** Greater Paris

aggraver VERB [28]
to make worse
- **s'aggraver** to worsen

agir VERB [38]
to act

□ Il a agi par vengeance. He acted out of vengeance.
- **Il s'agit de ...** It's about ... □ Il s'agit du club de sport. It's about the sports club. □ De quoi s'agit-il ? What is it about?
- **Il s'agit de faire attention.** We must be careful.

agité (FEM **agitée**) ADJECTIVE
1 restless
□ Les élèves sont agités. The pupils are restless.
2 rough
□ La mer est agitée. The sea is rough.
- **un sommeil agité** broken sleep

agiter VERB [28]
to shake
□ Agitez la bouteille. Shake the bottle.

l'agneau (PL les **agneaux**) MASC NOUN
lamb

l'agrafe FEM NOUN
staple (*for papers*)

l'agrafeuse FEM NOUN
stapler

agrandir VERB [38]
1 to enlarge
□ J'ai fait agrandir mes photos. I've had my photos enlarged.
2 to extend
□ Ils ont agrandi leur jardin. They've extended their garden.
- **s'agrandir** to expand □ Leur magasin s'est agrandi. Their shop has expanded.

agréable (FEM **agréable**) ADJECTIVE
nice

agréer VERB [18]
- **Veuillez agréer, Monsieur, l'expression de mes sentiments les meilleurs. Jean Ormal.** Yours sincerely, Jean Ormal.

agressif (FEM **agressive**) ADJECTIVE
aggressive

l'agressivité FEM NOUN
aggression
- **faire preuve d'agressivité envers quelqu'un** to be aggressive to somebody
- **l'agressivité au volant** road rage

agricole (FEM **agricole**) ADJECTIVE
agricultural
□ le matériel agricole agricultural machinery
- **une exploitation agricole** a farm

l'agriculteur MASC NOUN
farmer
□ Il est agriculteur. He's a farmer.

l'agricultrice FEM NOUN
farmer

l'agriculture FEM NOUN
farming

ai VERB ▷ *see* **avoir**
- **J'ai deux chats.** I have two cats.
- **J'ai bien dormi.** I slept well.

Aïd – ajouter

l'Aïd MASC NOUN
Eid

l'aidant MASC NOUN
carer
□ les jeunes aidants young carers

l'aidante FEM NOUN
carer
□ Delphine est aidante. Delphine is a carer.

l'aide FEM NOUN
1 help
□ J'ai besoin de ton aide. I need your help.
□ appeler quelqu'un à l'aide to call to somebody for help
■ À l'aide ! Help!
2 aid
□ une aide financière financial aid
■ à l'aide de using □ J'ai réussi à ouvrir la boîte à l'aide d'un couteau. I managed to open the tin using a knife.

aider VERB [28]
to help
■ aider quelqu'un à faire quelque chose to help someone to do something □ Alix a aidé son père à laver la voiture. Alix helped her father wash the car.

l'aide-soignant (PL les **aides-soignants**)
MASC NOUN
auxiliary nurse
□ Il est aide-soignant. He's an auxiliary nurse.

l'aide-soignante (PL les **aides-soignantes**)
FEM NOUN
auxiliary nurse
□ Léa est aide-soignante. Léa is an auxiliary nurse.

aie VERB ▷ see **avoir**

aïe EXCLAMATION
ouch!

aigre (FEM **aigre**) ADJECTIVE
sour

aigu (FEM **aiguë**) ADJECTIVE
sharp (pain)
□ une douleur aiguë a sharp pain
■ e accent aigu e acute

l'aiguille FEM NOUN
needle
□ une aiguille à tricoter a knitting needle
■ les aiguilles d'une montre the hands of a watch

l'ail MASC NOUN
garlic

l'aile FEM NOUN
wing

aille VERB ▷ see **aller**

ailleurs ADVERB
somewhere else
■ partout ailleurs everywhere else
■ nulle part ailleurs nowhere else
■ d'ailleurs besides

aimable (FEM **aimable**) ADJECTIVE
kind

l'aimant MASC NOUN
magnet

aimer VERB [28]
1 to love
□ Elle aime ses enfants. She loves her children.
2 to like
□ Tu aimes le chocolat ? Do you like chocolate?
□ J'aime bien ce garçon. I like this boy. □ J'aime bien jouer au tennis. I like playing tennis.
□ J'aimerais aller en Grèce. I'd like to go to Greece.
■ J'aimerais mieux ne pas y aller. I'd rather not go.

aîné (FEM **aînée**) ADJECTIVE
▷ see also **aîné** NOUN
elder
□ mon frère aîné my big brother

l'aîné MASC NOUN
▷ see also **aîné** ADJECTIVE
oldest child
□ C'est l'aîné. He's the oldest child.

l'aînée FEM NOUN
▷ see also **aîné** ADJECTIVE
oldest child
□ C'est l'aînée. She's the oldest child.

ainsi ADVERB
in this way
□ Il faut faire ainsi. This is the way to do it.
■ C'est ainsi qu'il a réussi. That's how he succeeded.
■ ainsi que as well as
■ et ainsi de suite and so on

l'air MASC NOUN
1 air
□ l'air chaud warm air
■ prendre l'air to get some fresh air
2 tune
□ Elle a joué un air au piano. She played a tune on the piano.
■ Elle a l'air fatiguée. She looks tired.
■ Il a l'air d'un clown. He looks like a clown.

l'aire de jeux FEM NOUN
playground

l'aire de repos FEM NOUN
rest area (on motorway)

l'aise FEM NOUN
■ être à l'aise to be at ease □ Elle est à l'aise avec tout le monde. She's at ease with everybody.
■ être mal à l'aise to be ill at ease
■ se mettre à l'aise to make oneself comfortable

ait VERB ▷ see **avoir**

ajouter VERB [28]
to add

l'**alarme** FEM NOUN
alarm
□ donner l'alarme to raise the alarm

l'**Albanie** FEM NOUN
Albania

l'**album** MASC NOUN
album

l'alcool MASC NOUN
alcohol
□ Je ne bois pas d'alcool. I don't drink alcohol.
■ **les alcools forts** spirits

alcoolisé (FEM **alcoolisée**) ADJECTIVE
alcoholic
■ **une boisson non alcoolisée** a soft drink

les **alentours** MASC PL NOUN
■ **dans les alentours** in the area
■ **aux alentours de Paris** in the Paris area
■ **aux alentours de cinq heures** around
5 o'clock

l'**algèbre** FEM NOUN
algebra

Alger NOUN
Algiers

l'Algérie FEM NOUN
Algeria

algérien (FEM **algérienne**) ADJECTIVE, NOUN
Algerian
■ **un Algérien** an Algerian (*man*)
■ **une Algérienne** an Algerian (*woman*)

l'**algue** FEM NOUN
seaweed

l'**aliment** MASC NOUN
food

l'**alimentation** FEM NOUN
1 groceries
□ le rayon alimentation du supermarché the
grocery department in the supermarket
2 diet
□ Elle a une alimentation saine. She has a
healthy diet.

l'**allée** FEM NOUN
1 path
□ les allées du parc the paths in the park
2 drive (*in street names*)
■ **les allées et venues** comings and goings

allégé (FEM **allégée**) ADJECTIVE
low-fat
□ un yaourt allégé a low-fat yoghurt

l'**Allemagne** FEM NOUN
Germany
■ **en Allemagne 1** in Germany **2** to Germany

allemand (FEM **allemande**) ADJECTIVE, NOUN
German
□ Elle parle allemand. She speaks German.
■ **un Allemand** a German (*man*)
■ **une Allemande** a German (*woman*)
■ **les Allemands** the Germans

aller VERB [3, *aux* être]

PRESENT TENSE	
je vais	nous allons
tu vas	vous allez
il/elle va	ils/elles vont
PAST PARTICIPLE	
allé	

▷ *see also* **aller** NOUN
to go
□ Je suis allé à Londres. I went to London. □ Je
dois y aller. I've got to go. □ Elle ira le voir. She'll
go and see him. □ Je vais me fâcher. I'm going
to get angry.
■ **s'en aller** to go away □ Je m'en vais demain.
I'm going tomorrow.
■ **aller bien à quelqu'un** to suit somebody
□ Cette robe te va bien. This dress suits you.
■ **Allez ! Dépêche-toi !** Come on! Hurry up!
■ **Comment allez-vous ? — Je vais bien.**
How are you? — I'm fine.
■ **Comment ça va ? — Ça va bien.** How are
you? — I'm fine.
■ **aller mieux** to be better

l'aller MASC NOUN
▷ *see also* **aller** VERB
1 outward journey
□ L'aller nous a pris trois heures. The journey
there took us three hours.
2 single (*ticket*)
□ Je voudrais un aller pour Angers. I'd like a
single to Angers.
■ **un aller simple** a single
■ **un aller retour 1** a return ticket □ Je
voudrais un aller retour pour Londres. I'd like a
return to London. **2** a round trip □ Il a fait l'aller
retour en dix heures. He did the round trip in
ten hours.

allergique (FEM **allergique**) ADJECTIVE
■ **allergique à** allergic to □ Je suis allergique
aux poils de chat. I'm allergic to cat hair.

allô EXCLAMATION
hello!
□ Allô ! Je voudrais parler à Monsieur Simon.
Hello! I'd like to speak to Mr Simon.

allô is only used when talking to someone on
the phone.

l'**allocation** FEM NOUN
allowance
■ **les allocations chômage** unemployment
benefit

s'**allonger** VERB [45]
to lie down
□ Il s'est allongé sur son lit. He lay down on his
bed.

allumer VERB [28]
1 to switch on
□ Tu peux allumer la lumière ? Can you switch the
light on? □ Allume la radio. Switch on the radio.

2 to light

□ Elle a allumé une cigarette. She lit a cigarette.
■ **s'allumer** (*light*) to come on □ La lumière s'est allumée. The light came on.

l'**allumette** FEM NOUN

match
□ une boîte d'allumettes a box of matches

l'**allure** FEM NOUN

1 speed
□ à toute allure at top speed
2 look
□ avoir une drôle d'allure to look odd

l'**allusion** FEM NOUN

reference

alors ADVERB

1 then
□ Tu as fini ? Alors je m'en vais. Have you finished? I'm going then.
2 so
□ Alors je lui ai dit de partir. So I told him to leave.
■ **Et alors ?** So what?
3 at that time
□ Il habitait alors à Paris. He was living in Paris at that time.
■ **alors que 1** as □ Il est arrivé alors que je partais. He arrived just as I was leaving.
2 while □ Alors que je travaillais dur, lui se reposait. While I was working hard, he was resting.

les **Alpes** FEM PL NOUN

Alps
□ dans les Alpes in the Alps

l'**alphabet** MASC NOUN

alphabet

alphabétique (FEM alphabétique) ADJECTIVE

alphabetical
□ par ordre alphabétique in alphabetical order

l'**alpinisme** MASC NOUN

mountaineering

l'**alpiniste** MASC/FEM NOUN

mountaineer

l'**Alsace** FEM NOUN

Alsace

l'**amande** FEM NOUN

almond
■ **la pâte d'amande** marzipan

l'**amant** MASC NOUN

lover

amateur (FEM amatrice) ADJECTIVE

▷ *see also* **amateur** NOUN
amateur
□ Elle est pianiste amateur. She's an amateur pianist.

l'**amateur** MASC NOUN

▷ *see also* **amateur** ADJECTIVE
amateur
■ **en amateur** as a hobby □ Il fait de la photo en amateur. He takes photos as a hobby.

■ **C'est un amateur de musique.** He's a music lover.

l'**amatrice** FEM NOUN

▷ *see also* **amateur** ADJECTIVE
amateur

l'**ambassade** FEM NOUN

embassy

l'**ambassadeur** MASC NOUN

ambassador

l'**ambiance** FEM NOUN

atmosphere
□ Je n'aime pas l'ambiance ici. I don't like the atmosphere here. □ Il y a de l'ambiance dans ce café. This café has a lively atmosphere.
■ **la musique d'ambiance** background music

ambitieux (FEM ambitieuse) ADJECTIVE

ambitious

l'**ambition** FEM NOUN

ambition
□ Il a l'ambition de devenir Premier ministre. His ambition is to be Prime Minister.
■ **Il a beaucoup d'ambition.** He's very ambitious.

l'**ambulance** FEM NOUN

ambulance

l'**âme** FEM NOUN

soul

l'**amélioration** FEM NOUN

improvement

améliorer VERB [28]

to improve
■ **s'améliorer** to improve □ Le temps s'améliore. The weather's improving.

l'**amende** FEM NOUN

fine
□ une amende de cinquante euros a 50 euro fine

amener VERB [43]

to bring
□ Qu'est-ce qui t'amène ? What brings you here? □ Est-ce que je peux amener un ami ? Can I bring a friend?

amer (FEM amère) ADJECTIVE

bitter

américain (FEM américaine) ADJECTIVE, NOUN

American
■ **un Américain** an American (*man*)
■ **une Américaine** an American (*woman*)

l'**Amérique** FEM NOUN

America
■ **en Amérique 1** in America **2** to America
■ **l'Amérique du Nord** North America
■ **l'Amérique du Sud** South America

l'**ami** MASC NOUN

friend
■ **C'est son petit ami.** He's her boyfriend.
■ **ajouter quelqu'un à sa liste d'amis** to friend somebody (*social networks*)

■ **supprimer quelqu'un de sa liste d'amis** to unfriend somebody (*social networks*)

amical (FEM **amicale**, MASC PL **amicaux**) ADJECTIVE
friendly

amicalement ADVERB
in a friendly way
■ **Amicalement, Pierre.** (*in letter*) Best wishes, Pierre.

l'**amie** FEM NOUN
friend
■ **C'est sa petite amie.** She's his girlfriend.

l'**amitié** FEM NOUN
friendship
■ **Fais mes amitiés à Paul.** Give my regards to Paul.
■ **Amitiés, Lucie.** (*in letter*) Best wishes, Lucie.

l'**amour** MASC NOUN
love
■ **faire l'amour** to make love

amoureux (FEM **amoureuse**) ADJECTIVE
in love
□ être amoureux de quelqu'un to be in love with somebody

l'**amour-propre** MASC NOUN
self-esteem

l'**amphithéâtre** MASC NOUN
lecture theatre

amplement ADVERB
■ **Nous avons amplement le temps.** We have plenty of time.

l'**ampoule** FEM NOUN
1 light bulb
2 blister
□ J'ai une ampoule au pied. I've got a blister on my foot.

amusant (FEM **amusante**) ADJECTIVE
amusing

les **amuse-bouches** MASC PL NOUN
party nibbles

amuser VERB [28]
to amuse
■ **s'amuser** 1 to play □ Les enfants s'amusent dehors. The children are playing outside. 2 to enjoy oneself □ On s'est bien amusés. We really enjoyed ourselves.

l'**an** MASC NOUN
year
■ **le premier de l'an** New Year's Day
■ **le nouvel an** New Year

l'**analyse** FEM NOUN
1 analysis
2 test (*medical*)
□ une analyse de sang a blood test

l'**ananas** MASC NOUN
pineapple

l'**ancêtre** MASC/FEM NOUN
ancestor

l'**anchois** (PL les **anchois**) MASC NOUN
anchovy

ancien (FEM **ancienne**) ADJECTIVE
1 former
□ C'est une ancienne élève. She's a former pupil.
2 old
□ notre ancienne voiture our old car
3 antique
□ un fauteuil ancien an antique chair

l'**ancre** FEM NOUN
anchor

Andorre FEM NOUN
Andorra

l'**âne** MASC NOUN
donkey

l'**ange** MASC NOUN
angel
■ **être aux anges** to be over the moon

l'**angine** FEM NOUN
throat infection

anglais (FEM **anglaise**) ADJECTIVE, NOUN
English
□ Est-ce que vous parlez anglais ? Do you speak English?
■ **un Anglais** an Englishman
■ **une Anglaise** an Englishwoman
■ **les Anglais** the English

l'**angle** MASC NOUN
1 angle
□ un angle droit a right angle
2 corner
□ à l'angle de la rue at the corner of the street

l'**Angleterre** FEM NOUN
England
■ **en Angleterre** 1 in England □ J'habite en Angleterre. I live in England. 2 to England □ Je suis allée en Angleterre le mois dernier. I went to England last month.

anglo- PREFIX
anglo-
■ **les îles Anglo-Normandes** the Channel Islands

anglophone (FEM **anglophone**) ADJECTIVE
English-speaking

angoissé (FEM **angoissée**) ADJECTIVE
stressed
□ Il a l'air angoissé. He looks stressed.

l'**animal** (PL les **animaux**) MASC NOUN
animal

l'**animateur** MASC NOUN
1 host
□ Il est animateur à la télé. He's a TV host.
2 youth leader
□ Pierre est animateur au centre sportif. Pierre is a youth leader at the sports centre.

animatrice – appareil

l'**animatrice** FEM NOUN

1 host
  □ Elle est animatrice à la télé. She's a TV host.

2 youth leader
  □ Cécile est animatrice au centre sportif. Cécile is a youth leader at the sports centre.

animé (FEM **animée**) ADJECTIVE
  lively
  □ Cette rue est très animée. This is a very lively street.
  ■ un dessin animé a cartoon

l'**anis** MASC NOUN
  aniseed

l'**anneau** (PL les **anneaux**) MASC NOUN
  ring

l'**année** FEM NOUN
  year
  □ l'année dernière last year □ l'année prochaine next year □ une année de césure a gap year

l'**anniversaire** MASC NOUN

1 birthday
  □ C'est l'anniversaire de Marion. It's Marion's birthday.

2 anniversary
  □ un anniversaire de mariage a wedding anniversary

l'**annonce** FEM NOUN
  advert
  □ J'ai lu votre annonce dans le journal. I saw your advert in the newspaper. □ passer une annonce to place an advert
  ■ les petites annonces the small ads

annoncer VERB [12]
  to announce
  □ Ils ont annoncé leurs fiançailles. They've announced their engagement.

l'**annuaire** MASC NOUN
  phone book

annuel (FEM **annuelle**) ADJECTIVE
  annual

annuler VERB [28]
  to cancel

anonyme (FEM **anonyme**) ADJECTIVE
  anonymous

l'**anorak** MASC NOUN
  anorak

l'**Antarctique** MASC NOUN
  Antarctic

l'**antenne** FEM NOUN

1 aerial
  ■ antenne parabolique satellite dish
  ■ être à l'antenne to be on the air

2 antenna

l'**antibiotique** MASC NOUN
  antibiotic

l'**antidépresseur** MASC NOUN
  antidepressant

□ Elle est sous antidépresseurs depuis un mois. She's been on antidepressants for a month.

l'**antigel** MASC NOUN
  antifreeze

les **Antilles** FEM PL NOUN
  West Indies
  ■ aux Antilles 1 in the West Indies 2 to the West Indies

antipathique (FEM **antipathique**) ADJECTIVE
  unpleasant
  □ Je le trouve plutôt antipathique. I find him rather unpleasant.

antipelliculaire (FEM **antipelliculaire**) ADJECTIVE
  ■ shampooing antipelliculaire anti-dandruff shampoo

l'**antiquaire** MASC/FEM NOUN
  antique dealer
  □ Elle est antiquaire. She's an antique dealer.

l'**antiquité** FEM NOUN
  antique
  □ un magasin d'antiquités an antique shop
  ■ pendant l'Antiquité in classical times

antiseptique (FEM **antiseptique**) ADJECTIVE
  ▷ see also **antiseptique** NOUN
  antiseptic

l'**antiseptique** MASC NOUN
  ▷ see also **antiseptique** ADJECTIVE
  antiseptic

antivirus MASC NOUN
  antivirus (program)

l'**antivol** MASC NOUN

1 lock (on bike)

2 steering lock (on car)

anxieux (FEM **anxieuse**) ADJECTIVE
  anxious
  ■ Il est anxieux de nature. He's a born worrier.

août MASC NOUN
  August
  ■ en août in August

apercevoir VERB [67]
  to see
  □ J'aperçois la côte. I can see the shore.
  ■ s'apercevoir de quelque chose to notice something
  ■ s'apercevoir que ... to notice that ...

l'**apéritif** MASC NOUN
  aperitif
  □ Venez donc prendre l'apéritif ce soir ! Come round for drinks this evening!

apparaître VERB [56]
  to appear

l'**appareil** MASC NOUN
  device
  ■ un appareil dentaire a brace (for teeth)
  ■ les appareils ménagers domestic appliances
  ■ un appareil photo a camera

Numbers in brackets refer to verb tables on pages 650 to 658

■ **Qui est à l'appareil ?** Who's speaking? *(on phone)*

apparemment ADVERB
apparently

l'**apparence** FEM NOUN
appearance

l'**apparition** FEM NOUN
appearance
□ Il n'a fait qu'une brève apparition. He only appeared briefly.

l'**appartement** MASC NOUN
flat

appartenir VERB [83]
■ **appartenir à quelqu'un** to belong to somebody

apparu VERB ▷ *see* **apparaître**

l'**appel** MASC NOUN
1 cry
□ un appel au secours a cry for help
2 phone call
□ un appel vidéo a video call
■ **faire appel à quelqu'un** to appeal to somebody
■ **faire l'appel** to call the register *(in school)*
■ **faire un appel de phares** to flash one's headlights

appeler VERB [4]
to call
□ Elle a appelé le médecin. She called the doctor.
□ J'ai appelé Richard à Londres. I called Richard in London.
■ **s'appeler** to be called □ Comment ça s'appelle ? What is it called?
■ **Elle s'appelle Muriel.** Her name's Muriel.
■ **Comment tu t'appelles ?** What's your name?

l'**appendicite** FEM NOUN
appendicitis

appétissant (FEM **appétissante**) ADJECTIVE
appetizing

l'**appétit** MASC NOUN
appetite
■ **Bon appétit !** Enjoy your meal!

applaudir VERB [38]
to clap *(applaud)*

les **applaudissements** MASC PL NOUN
applause *sing*

l'**appli** FEM NOUN *(informal)*
app

l'**application** FEM NOUN
application

appliquer VERB [28]
1 to apply
2 to enforce
□ appliquer la loi to enforce the law
■ **s'appliquer** to apply oneself

apporter VERB [28]
to bring

apprécier VERB [19]
to appreciate

appréhender VERB [28]
to dread
□ J'appréhende cet examen. I'm dreading this exam.

apprendre VERB [65]
1 to learn
□ apprendre quelque chose par cœur to learn something by heart
■ **apprendre à faire quelque chose** to learn to do something □ J'apprends à faire la cuisine. I'm learning to cook.
2 to hear
□ J'ai appris son départ. I heard that she had left.
■ **apprendre quelque chose à quelqu'un**
1 to teach somebody something □ Ma mère m'a appris l'anglais. My mother taught me English.
2 to tell somebody something □ Vincent m'a appris la nouvelle. Vincent told me the news.
■ **apprendre à quelqu'un à faire quelque chose** to teach someone to do something □ Elle lui a appris à conduire. She taught him to drive.

l'**apprenti** MASC NOUN
apprentice

l'**apprentie** FEM NOUN
apprentice

l'**apprentissage** MASC NOUN
learning
□ On dit que l'apprentissage de l'arabe est très difficile. Learning Arabic is said to be very difficult.

appris VERB ▷ *see* **apprendre**

l'**approbation** FEM NOUN
approval
□ donner son approbation to give one's approval

approcher VERB [28]
■ **approcher de** to approach □ Nous approchons de Paris. We are approaching Paris.
■ **s'approcher de** to come closer to □ Ne t'approche pas, j'ai la grippe ! Don't come too close to me, I've got flu!

approprié (FEM **appropriée**) ADJECTIVE
suitable
□ une tenue appropriée suitable clothes

approuver VERB [28]
to approve of
□ Je n'approuve pas ses méthodes. I don't approve of his methods.

approximatif (FEM **approximative**) ADJECTIVE
1 approximate
□ un prix approximatif an approximate price
2 rough
□ un calcul approximatif a rough calculation

appui – armoire

l'appui MASC NOUN
support
□ J'ai besoin de votre appui. I need your support.

appuyer VERB [53]
1 to press
□ appuyer sur un bouton to press a button
2 to lean
□ Elle a appuyé son vélo contre la porte. She leaned her bike against the door.
■ **s'appuyer** to lean □ Elle s'est appuyée contre le mur. She leaned against the wall. □ Il s'est appuyé sur la table. He leaned on the table.

après PREPOSITION, ADVERB
1 after
□ après le déjeuner after lunch □ après son départ after he had left □ après qu'il est parti after he left
■ **après avoir** □ Nous viendrons après avoir fait la vaisselle. We'll come after we've done the dishes.
2 afterwards
□ aussitôt après immediately afterwards
■ **après coup** afterwards □ J'y ai repensé après coup. I thought about it again afterwards.
■ **d'après** according to □ D'après lui, c'est une erreur. According to him, that's a mistake.
■ **après tout** after all

après-demain ADVERB
the day after tomorrow

l'après-midi MASC/FEM NOUN
afternoon

l'après-rasage MASC NOUN
aftershave

l'aquarium MASC NOUN
aquarium

arabe (FEM **arabe**) ADJECTIVE, NOUN
1 Arab
□ les pays arabes the Arab countries
2 Arabic
□ la littérature arabe Arabic literature □ Il parle arabe. He speaks Arabic.
■ **un Arabe** an Arab (*man*)
■ **une Arabe** an Arab (*woman*)

l'Arabie Saoudite FEM NOUN
Saudi Arabia

l'araignée FEM NOUN
spider

l'arbitre MASC NOUN
1 referee
2 umpire

l'arbre MASC NOUN
tree
■ **un arbre généalogique** a family tree

l'arbuste MASC NOUN
shrub

l'arc MASC NOUN
bow

□ son arc et ses flèches his bow and arrows

l'arc-en-ciel (PL les **arcs-en-ciel**) MASC NOUN
rainbow

l'archéologie FEM NOUN
archaeology

l'archéologue MASC/FEM NOUN
archaeologist
□ Elle est archéologue. She's an archaeologist.

l'archipel MASC NOUN
archipelago

l'architecte MASC/FEM NOUN
architect
□ Elle est architecte. She's an architect.

l'architecture FEM NOUN
architecture

l'Arctique MASC NOUN
Arctic

l'ardoise FEM NOUN
slate

l'arène FEM NOUN
bullring
■ **des arènes romaines** a Roman amphitheatre
■ **l'arène politique** the political arena

l'arête FEM NOUN
fish bone

l'argent MASC NOUN
1 silver
□ une bague en argent a silver ring
2 money
□ Je n'ai plus d'argent. I haven't got any more money.
■ **l'argent de poche** pocket money
■ **l'argent liquide** cash

argentin (FEM **argentine**) ADJECTIVE, NOUN
Argentinian
■ **un Argentin** an Argentinian (*man*)
■ **une Argentine** an Argentinian (*woman*)

l'Argentine FEM NOUN
Argentina

l'argile FEM NOUN
clay

l'argot MASC NOUN
slang

l'argument MASC NOUN
argument

l'arme FEM NOUN
weapon
■ **une arme à feu** a firearm

l'armée FEM NOUN
army
■ **l'armée de l'air** the Air Force

l'armistice MASC NOUN
armistice

l'armoire FEM NOUN
wardrobe

Numbers in brackets refer to verb tables on pages 650 to 658

l'**armure** FEM NOUN
armour
◻ un chevalier en armure a knight in armour

arnaquer VERB [28] (*informal*)
to con

l'**arobase** FEM NOUN
@ symbol
■ **Mon adresse e-mail, c'est « lola arobase europost point fr ».** My email address is 'lola@europost.fr'.

aromatisé (FEM **aromatisée**) ADJECTIVE
flavoured

l'**arôme** MASC NOUN
1 aroma
2 flavouring (*added to food*)

arpenter VERB [28]
to pace up and down
◻ Il arpentait le couloir. He was pacing up and down the corridor.

arrache-pied
■ **d'arrache-pied** ADVERB furiously ◻ travailler d'arrache-pied to work furiously

arracher VERB [28]
1 to take out
◻ Le dentiste m'a arraché une dent. The dentist took one of my teeth out.
2 to tear out
◻ Arrachez la page. Tear the page out.
3 to pull up
◻ Elle a arraché les mauvaises herbes. She pulled up the weeds.
■ **arracher quelque chose à quelqu'un** to snatch something from somebody

arranger VERB [45]
1 to arrange
◻ arranger des fleurs dans un vase to arrange flowers in a vase
2 to suit
◻ Ça m'arrange de partir plus tôt. It suits me to leave earlier.
■ **s'arranger** to come to an agreement
◻ Arrangez-vous avec le patron. You'll have to come to an agreement with the boss.
■ **Je vais m'arranger pour venir.** I'll organize things so that I can come.
■ **Ça va s'arranger.** Things will work themselves out.

l'**arrestation** FEM NOUN
arrest
◻ en état d'arrestation under arrest

l'**arrêt** MASC NOUN
stop
◻ un arrêt de bus a bus stop
■ **sans arrêt** 1 non-stop ◻ Elle travaille sans arrêt. She works non-stop. 2 continually ◻ Ils se disputent sans arrêt. They quarrel continually.

arrêter VERB [28]
1 to stop
■ **Arrête !** Stop it!
■ **arrêter de faire quelque chose** to stop doing something
2 to switch off
◻ Il a arrêté le moteur. He switched the engine off.
3 to arrest
◻ Mon voisin a été arrêté. My neighbour's been arrested.
■ **s'arrêter** to stop ◻ Elle s'est arrêtée devant une vitrine. She stopped in front of a shop window.
■ **s'arrêter de faire quelque chose** to stop doing something ◻ Il s'est arrêté de fumer. He stopped smoking.

les **arrhes** FEM PL NOUN
deposit *sing*
◻ verser des arrhes to pay a deposit

l'**arrière** MASC NOUN
▷ *see also* **arrière** ADJECTIVE
back
◻ l'arrière de la maison the back of the house
■ **à l'arrière** at the back
■ **en arrière** behind ◻ Ils sont restés en arrière. They stayed behind.

arrière (FEM+PL **arrière**) ADJECTIVE
▷ *see also* **arrière** NOUN
back
◻ le siège arrière the back seat ◻ les roues arrière the rear wheels

l'**arrière-grand-mère** (PL les **arrière-grands-mères**) FEM NOUN
great-grandmother

l'**arrière-grand-père** (PL les **arrière-grands-pères**) MASC NOUN
great-grandfather

l'**arrivée** FEM NOUN
arrival

arriver VERB [5, *aux* être]
1 to arrive
◻ J'arrive à l'école à huit heures. I arrive at school at 8 o'clock.
2 to happen
◻ Qu'est-ce qui est arrivé à Thomas ? What happened to Thomas?
■ **arriver à faire quelque chose** to manage to do something ◻ J'espère que je vais y arriver. I hope I'll manage it.
■ **Il m'arrive de dormir jusqu'à midi.** I sometimes sleep till midday.

arrogant (FEM **arrogante**) ADJECTIVE
arrogant

l'**arrondissement** MASC NOUN
district

DID YOU KNOW...?
Paris, Lyon and Marseille are divided into numbered districts called **arrondissements**.

arroser - assistante

arroser VERB [28]
to water
□ Daphné arrose ses tomates. Daphné is watering her tomatoes.
■ **Ils ont arrosé leur victoire.** They had a drink to celebrate their victory.

l'**arrosoir** MASC NOUN
watering can

l'**art** MASC NOUN
art

l'**artère** FEM NOUN
1 artery
2 thoroughfare
■ **les grandes artères de Paris** the main roads of Paris

l'**artichaut** MASC NOUN
artichoke

l'**article** MASC NOUN
1 article
□ un article de journal a newspaper article
2 item
□ les articles en promotion items on special offer

l'**articulation** FEM NOUN
joint
□ l'articulation du genou the knee joint

articuler VERB [28]
to pronounce clearly

artificiel (FEM **artificielle**) ADJECTIVE
artificial

l'**artisan** MASC NOUN
self-employed craftsman

l'**artiste** MASC/FEM NOUN
1 artist
2 performer

artistique (FEM **artistique**) ADJECTIVE
artistic

as VERB ▷ see **avoir**
▷ see also **as** NOUN
■ **Tu as de beaux cheveux.** You've got nice hair.

l'**as** MASC NOUN
▷ see also **as** VERB
ace
□ l'as de trèfle the ace of clubs

l'**ascenseur** MASC NOUN
lift

l'**Ascension** FEM NOUN
Ascension

asiatique (FEM **asiatique**) ADJECTIVE
Asiatic
■ **la cuisine asiatique** Oriental cooking
■ **le Sud-Est asiatique** South East Asia

l'**Asie** FEM NOUN
Asia
■ **en Asie 1** in Asia **2** to Asia

l'**aspect** MASC NOUN
appearance

l'**asperge** FEM NOUN
asparagus

l'**aspirateur** MASC NOUN
vacuum cleaner
■ **passer l'aspirateur** to vacuum

l'**aspirine** FEM NOUN
aspirin

assaisonner VERB [28]
to season

l'**assassin** MASC NOUN
murderer

assassiner VERB [28]
to murder

assembler VERB [28]
to assemble
■ **s'assembler** to gather □ Une foule énorme s'était assemblée. A huge crowd had gathered.

s'**asseoir** VERB [6]
to sit down
□ Asseyez-vous ! Sit down! □ Assieds-toi ! Sit down!

assez ADVERB
1 enough
□ Nous n'avons pas assez de temps. We don't have enough time. □ Est-ce qu'il y a assez de pain ? Is there enough bread?
■ **J'en ai assez !** I've had enough!
2 quite
□ Il faisait assez beau. The weather was quite nice.

assied, assieds VERB ▷ see **s'asseoir**

l'**assiette** FEM NOUN
plate
□ une assiette creuse a soup plate □ une assiette à dessert a dessert plate
■ **une assiette anglaise** assorted cold meats

assis (FEM **assise**) ADJECTIVE
sitting
□ Il est assis par terre. He's sitting on the floor.

assis VERB ▷ see **s'asseoir**

l'**assistance** FEM NOUN
1 audience
□ Y a-t-il un médecin dans l'assistance ? Is there a doctor in the audience?
2 aid
□ l'assistance humanitaire humanitarian aid
3 assistance
□ avec l'assistance de quelqu'un with the assistance of somebody

l'**assistant** MASC NOUN
assistant
□ Il était assistant d'anglais à Tourcoing. He was an English assistant in Tourcoing.
■ **un assistant social** a social worker

l'**assistante** FEM NOUN
assistant

□ Elle est assistante de français à Oxford. She's a French assistant in Oxford.
■ **une assistante sociale** a social worker

assister VERB [28]
to assist
■ **assister à un cours** to attend a class
■ **assister à un accident** to witness an accident

l'**association** FEM NOUN
association

l'**associé** MASC NOUN
partner (in business)

l'**associée** FEM NOUN
partner (in business)

s'**associer** VERB [19]
to go into partnership

assommer VERB [28]
to knock out
□ Il l'a assommé avec une bouteille. He knocked him out with a bottle.

l'**Assomption** FEM NOUN
Assumption

assorti (FEM **assortie**) ADJECTIVE
1 matching
□ des couleurs assorties matching colours
2 assorted
□ des chocolats assortis assorted chocolates
■ **être assorti à quelque chose** to match something □ Son sac est assorti à ses chaussures. Her bag matches her shoes.

l'**assortiment** MASC NOUN
assortment

l'**assurance** FEM NOUN
1 insurance
□ une assurance maladie medical insurance
2 confidence
□ parler avec assurance to speak with confidence

assurer VERB [28]
1 to insure
□ La maison est assurée. The house is insured.
□ être assuré contre quelque chose to be insured against something
2 to assure
□ Je t'assure que c'est vrai ! I assure you it's true!
■ **s'assurer de quelque chose** to make sure of something □ Il s'est assuré que la porte était fermée. He made sure the door was shut.

l'**asthme** MASC NOUN
asthma
□ une crise d'asthme an asthma attack

l'**astronaute** MASC/FEM NOUN
astronaut

l'**astronomie** FEM NOUN
astronomy

astucieux (FEM **astucieuse**) ADJECTIVE
clever

l'**atelier** MASC NOUN
1 workshop
2 studio (artist's)

Athènes NOUN
Athens

l'**athlète** MASC/FEM NOUN
athlete

l'**athlétisme** MASC NOUN
athletics
□ un championnat d'athlétisme an athletics championship

l'**Atlantique** MASC NOUN
Atlantic

l'**atlas** MASC NOUN
atlas

l'**atmosphère** FEM NOUN
atmosphere

atomique (FEM **atomique**) ADJECTIVE
atomic
□ la bombe atomique the atomic bomb

l'**atout** MASC NOUN
1 asset
□ L'atout principal de ce joueur, c'est sa vitesse. This player's main asset is his speed.
2 trump card
□ J'avais quatre atouts dans mon jeu. I had four trump cards in my hand.

atroce (FEM **atroce**) ADJECTIVE
terrible

attachant (FEM **attachante**) ADJECTIVE
lovable

attacher VERB [28]
to tie up
□ Elle a attaché ses cheveux avec un élastique. She tied her hair up   n elastic band.
■ **s'attacher à quelqu'un** to become attached to somebody
■ **une poêle qui n'attache pas** a non-stick frying pan

l'**attaque** FEM NOUN
attack

attaquer VERB [28]
to attack

atteindre VERB [60]
to reach

attendant
■ **en attendant** ADVERB in the meantime

attendre VERB [7]
to wait
□ attendre quelqu'un to wait for someone
□ J'attends d'avoir un appartement à moi. I'm waiting until I've got a flat of my own.
□ Attends qu'il ne pleuve plus. Wait until it's stopped raining.
■ **attendre un enfant** to be expecting a baby

■ **s'attendre à** to expect □ Je m'attends à une surprise. I'm expecting a surprise.

BE CAREFUL!
attendre does not mean **to attend**.

l'attentat MASC NOUN
■ **un attentat à la bombe** a terrorist bombing

l'attente FEM NOUN
wait
□ deux heures d'attente two hours' wait
■ **la salle d'attente** the waiting room

attentif (FEM **attentive**) ADJECTIVE
attentive

l'attention FEM NOUN
attention
□ à l'attention de for the attention of
■ **faire attention** to be careful
■ **Attention !** Watch out! □ Attention, tu vas te faire écraser ! Watch out, you'll get run over!

attentionné (FEM **attentionnée**) ADJECTIVE
thoughtful

atterrir VERB [38]
to land

l'atterrissage MASC NOUN
landing (of plane)

attirant (FEM **attirante**) ADJECTIVE
attractive

attirer VERB [28]
to attract
□ attirer l'attention de quelqu'un to attract somebody's attention
■ **s'attirer des ennuis** to get into trouble
□ Si tu continues, tu vas t'attirer des ennuis. If you keep on like that, you'll get yourself into trouble.

l'attitude FEM NOUN
attitude

l'attraction FEM NOUN
■ **un parc d'attractions** an amusement park

attraper VERB [28]
to catch

attrayant (FEM **attrayante**) ADJECTIVE
attractive

attrister VERB [28]
to sadden

au PREPOSITION ▷ see **à**

au is the contracted form of **à + le**.

□ au printemps in the spring

l'aube FEM NOUN
dawn
□ à l'aube at dawn

l'auberge FEM NOUN
inn
■ **une auberge de jeunesse** a youth hostel

l'aubergine FEM NOUN
aubergine

aucun (FEM **aucune**) ADJECTIVE, PRONOUN
1 no
□ Il n'a aucun ami. He's got no friends. □ Aucun enfant ne pourrait le faire. No child could do that.
2 none
□ Aucun d'entre eux n'est venu. None of them came. □ Aucune de mes amies n'aime le foot. None of my female friends like football. □ Tu aimes ses films ? — Je n'en ai vu aucun. Do you like his films? — I haven't seen any of them.
■ **sans aucun doute** without any doubt

au-delà ADVERB
■ **au-delà de** beyond □ Votre ticket n'est pas valable au-delà de cette limite. Your ticket is not valid beyond this point.

au-dessous ADVERB
1 downstairs
□ Ils habitent au-dessous. They live downstairs.
2 underneath
■ **au-dessous de** under □ au-dessous du pont under the bridge
■ **dix degrés au-dessous de zéro** ten degrees below zero

au-dessus ADVERB
1 upstairs
□ J'habite au-dessus. I live upstairs.
2 above
■ **au-dessus de** above □ au-dessus de la table above the table

audiovisuel (FEM **audiovisuelle**) ADJECTIVE
audiovisual

l'auditeur MASC NOUN
listener (to radio)

l'auditrice FEM NOUN
listener (to radio)

l'augmentation FEM NOUN
rise

augmenter VERB [28]
to increase

aujourd'hui ADVERB
today
□ Il travaille aujourd'hui. He's working today.

auparavant ADVERB
first
□ Vous pouvez utiliser l'ordinateur, mais auparavant vous devez taper le mot de passe. You can use the computer, but first you have to key in the password.

auquel (MASC PL **auxquels**, FEM PL **auxquelles**) PRONOUN

auquel is the contracted form of **à + lequel**.

□ l'homme auquel j'ai parlé the man I spoke to

aura, aurai, aurais, aurait, auras, aurez, aurons, auront VERB
▷ see **avoir**

l'**aurore** FEM NOUN
daybreak

aussi ADVERB

1 too
□ Dors bien. — Toi aussi. Sleep well. — You too.
□ Lui aussi parle espagnol. He speaks Spanish too.

2 also
□ J'aimerais aussi que tu achètes le journal. I'd also like you to get the paper. □ Je parle français et aussi allemand. I speak French and also German.
■ **aussi ... que** as ... as □ Son fils est aussi grand qu'elle. Her son is as tall as her.

aussitôt ADVERB
straight away
□ aussitôt après son retour straight after his return
■ **aussitôt que** as soon as □ aussitôt que tu auras fini as soon as you've finished

l'**Australie** FEM NOUN
Australia
■ **en Australie 1** in Australia **2** to Australia

australien (FEM **australienne**) ADJECTIVE, NOUN
Australian
■ **un Australien** an Australian (*man*)
■ **une Australienne** an Australian (*woman*)

autant ADVERB
■ **autant de 1** so much □ Je ne veux pas autant de gâteau. I don't want so much cake. **2** so many □ Je n'ai jamais vu autant de monde. I've never seen so many people.
■ **autant que** as much as □ Elle travaille autant que moi. She works as much as I do.
■ **autant ... que 1** as much ... as □ J'ai autant d'argent que toi. I've got as much money as you have. **2** as many ... as □ J'ai autant d'amis que lui. I've got as many friends as he has.
■ **d'autant plus que** all the more since □ Elle est d'autant plus déçue qu'il le lui avait promis. She's all the more disappointed since he had made her a promise.
■ **d'autant moins que** even less since
□ C'est d'autant moins pratique pour lui qu'il doit changer deux fois de train. It's even less convenient for him since he has to change trains twice.

l'**auteur** MASC NOUN
author

l'**autisme** MASC NOUN
autism

autiste (FEM **autiste**) ADJECTIVE
autistic

l'**auto** FEM NOUN
car

l'**autobus** MASC NOUN
bus
□ en autobus by bus

l'**autocar** MASC NOUN
coach
□ en autocar by coach

autocollant (FEM **autocollante**) ADJECTIVE
▷ see also **autocollant** NOUN
self-adhesive
□ une étiquette autocollante a self-adhesive label
■ **une enveloppe autocollante** a self-seal envelope

l'**autocollant** MASC NOUN
▷ see also **autocollant** ADJECTIVE
sticker

l'**auto-école** FEM NOUN
driving school

automatique (FEM **automatique**) ADJECTIVE
automatic

l'**automne** MASC NOUN
autumn
■ **en automne** in autumn

automobile (FEM **automobile**) ADJECTIVE
▷ see also **automobile** NOUN
■ **une course automobile** a motor race

l'**automobile** FEM NOUN
▷ see also **automobile** ADJECTIVE
car

l'**automobiliste** MASC/FEM NOUN
motorist

l'**autoradio** MASC NOUN
car radio

l'**autorisation** FEM NOUN

1 permission
□ Il m'a donné l'autorisation de sortir ce soir. He's given me permission to go out tonight.

2 permit
□ Il faut une autorisation pour camper ici. You need a permit to camp here.

autoriser VERB [28]
to give permission for
□ Il m'a autorisé à en parler. He's given me permission to talk about it.

autoritaire (FEM **autoritaire**) ADJECTIVE
authoritarian

l'**autorité** FEM NOUN
authority

l'**autoroute** FEM NOUN
motorway

l'**auto-stop** MASC NOUN
■ **faire de l'auto-stop** to hitchhike

l'**auto-stoppeur** MASC NOUN
hitchhiker

l'**auto-stoppeuse** FEM NOUN
hitchhiker

autour ADVERB
around
□ autour de la maison around the house

autre – avant-dernier

autre (FEM **autre**) ADJECTIVE, PRONOUN
other
□ Je viendrai un autre jour. I'll come some other day. □ J'ai d'autres projets. I've got other plans.
■ **autre chose** something else
■ **autre part** somewhere else
■ **un autre** another □ Tu veux un autre morceau de gâteau ? Would you like another piece of cake?
■ **l'autre** the other □ Non, pas celui-ci, l'autre. No, not that one, the other one.
■ **d'autres** others □ Je t'en apporterai d'autres. I'll bring you some others.
■ **les autres** the others □ Les autres sont arrivés plus tard. The others arrived later.
■ **ni l'un ni l'autre** neither of them
■ **entre autres** among other things □ Nous avons parlé, entre autres, de nos projets de vacances. We talked about our holiday plans, among other things.

autrefois ADVERB
in the old days

autrement ADVERB
1 differently
□ Il l'a fait autrement. He did it differently.
2 otherwise
□ Je n'ai pas pu faire autrement. I couldn't do otherwise.
■ **autrement dit** in other words

l'**Autriche** FEM NOUN
Austria
■ **en Autriche 1** in Austria **2** to Austria

autrichien (FEM **autrichienne**) ADJECTIVE, NOUN
Austrian
■ **un Autrichien** an Austrian (*man*)
■ **une Autrichienne** an Austrian (*woman*)

l'**autruche** FEM NOUN
ostrich

aux PREPOSITION ▷ *see* **à**

> **aux** is the contracted form of **à** + **les**.

□ J'ai dit aux enfants d'aller jouer. I told the children to go and play.

auxquelles PL PRONOUN

> **auxquelles** is the contracted form of **à** + **lesquelles**.

□ les revues auxquelles il est abonné the magazines to which he subscribes

auxquels PL PRONOUN

> **auxquels** is the contracted form of **à** + **lesquels**.

□ les enfants auxquels il a parlé the children he spoke to

avaient, avais, avait VERB ▷ *see* **avoir**
■ **Il y avait beaucoup de monde.** There were lots of people.

l'**avalanche** FEM NOUN
avalanche

avaler VERB [28]
to swallow

l'**avance** FEM NOUN
■ **être en avance** to be early
■ **à l'avance** beforehand □ réserver longtemps à l'avance to book well beforehand
■ **d'avance** in advance □ payer d'avance to pay in advance

avancé (FEM **avancée**) ADJECTIVE
advanced
□ à un niveau avancé at an advanced level
■ **bien avancé** well under way □ Les travaux sont déjà bien avancés. The work is already well under way.

avancer VERB [12]
1 to move forward
□ Il avançait prudemment. He was moving forward cautiously.
2 to bring forward
□ La date de l'examen a été avancée. The date of the exam has been brought forward.
3 to put forward
□ Il a avancé sa montre d'une heure. He put his watch forward an hour.
4 to be fast (*watch*)
□ Ma montre avance d'une heure. My watch is an hour fast.
5 to lend
□ Peux-tu m'avancer dix euros ? Can you lend me 10 euros?

avant (FEM+PL **avant**) PREPOSITION, ADJECTIVE
▷ *see also* **avant** NOUN
1 before
□ avant qu'il ne pleuve before it rains
■ **avant de** □ Avant de partir, Marie demande à le voir. Before leaving, Marie asks to see him.
2 front
□ la roue avant the front wheel □ le siège avant the front seat
■ **avant tout** above all

l'**avant** MASC NOUN
▷ *see also* **avant** PREPOSITION, ADJECTIVE
front
□ l'avant de la voiture the front of the car
■ **à l'avant** in front
■ **en avant** forward □ Il a fait un pas en avant. He took a step forward.

l'**avantage** MASC NOUN
advantage

l'**avant-bras** (PL les **avant-bras**) MASC NOUN
forearm

avant-dernier (FEM **avant-dernière**, MASC PL **avant-derniers**) ADJECTIVE
last but one
□ l'avant-dernière page the last page but one

□ Ils sont arrivés avant-derniers. **They arrived last but one.**

avant-hier ADVERB
the day before yesterday
□ Il est arrivé avant-hier. **He arrived the day before yesterday.**

avare (FEM **avare**) ADJECTIVE
▷ see also **avare** NOUN
miserly

l'**avare** MASC/FEM NOUN
▷ see also **avare** ADJECTIVE
miser

avec PREPOSITION
with
□ avec mon père **with my father**
■ Et avec ça ? **Anything else?** (*in shop*)

l'**avenir** MASC NOUN
future
■ à l'avenir **in future** □ À l'avenir, essayez d'être à l'heure. **Try to be on time in future.**
■ dans un proche avenir **in the near future**

l'**aventure** FEM NOUN
adventure

l'**avenue** FEM NOUN
avenue

l'**averse** FEM NOUN
shower (*of rain*)

avertir VERB [38]
to warn
■ avertir quelqu'un de quelque chose **to warn somebody about something**

l'**avertissement** MASC NOUN
warning

aveugle (FEM **aveugle**) ADJECTIVE
blind

avez VERB ▷ see **avoir**

l'**avion** MASC NOUN
plane
■ aller en avion **to fly** □ Il est allé en Italie en avion. **He flew to Italy.**
■ par avion **by airmail**

l'**aviron** MASC NOUN
rowing

l'**avis** MASC NOUN
1 opinion
□ J'aimerais avoir ton avis. **I'd like to have your opinion.**
■ à mon avis **in my opinion**

2 notice
□ jusqu'à nouvel avis **until further notice**
■ changer d'avis **to change one's mind** □ J'ai changé d'avis. **I've changed my mind.**

l'**avocat** MASC NOUN
1 lawyer
□ Il est avocat. **He's a lawyer.**
2 avocado

l'**avocate** FEM NOUN
lawyer
□ Elle est avocate. **She's a lawyer.**

l'**avoine** FEM NOUN
oats
□ les flocons d'avoine **porridge oats**

avoir VERB [8]

PRESENT TENSE	
j'ai	nous avons
tu as	vous avez
il/elle a	ils/elles ont
PAST PARTICIPLE	
eu	

1 to have
□ Ils ont deux enfants. **They have two children.**
□ Il a les yeux bleus. **He's got blue eyes.** □ J'ai déjà mangé. **I've already eaten.** □ Est-ce que tu as vu ce film ? **Have you seen this film?**
■ Je lui ai parlé hier. **I spoke to him yesterday.**
■ On t'a bien eu ! (*informal*) **You've been had!**

2 to be
□ Il a trois ans. **He's three.** □ J'avais dix ans quand je l'ai rencontré. **I was ten when I met him.**
■ il y a **1** there is □ Il y a quelqu'un à la porte. **There's somebody at the door. 2** there are □ Il y a des chocolats sur la table. **There are some chocolates on the table. 3** ago □ Je l'ai rencontré il y a deux ans. **I met him two years ago.**
■ Qu'est-ce qu'il y a ? **What's the matter?**
■ Il n'y a qu'à partir plus tôt. **We'll just have to leave earlier.**

avons VERB ▷ see **avoir**

l'**avortement** MASC NOUN
abortion

avouer VERB [28]
to admit

avril MASC NOUN
April
■ en avril **in April**

ayant, ayez, ayons VERB ▷ see **avoir**

Bb

b

le **baby-foot** MASC NOUN
table football
□ jouer au baby-foot to play table football

le **baby-sitting** MASC NOUN
■ faire du baby-sitting to babysit

le **bac** MASC NOUN = baccalauréat

le **baccalauréat** MASC NOUN
A levels
□ Elle a passé son baccalauréat l'année dernière. She did her A levels last year.

> **DID YOU KNOW...?**
> The French **baccalauréat**, or **bac** for short, is taken at the age of 17 or 18. Students have to sit a few compulsory classes, but are otherwise free to choose any combination of subjects they want. If you pass you have the right to a place at university.

bâcler VERB [28]
to botch up
□ Je déteste le travail bâclé ! I hate botched work!

le **bagage** MASC NOUN
luggage
■ faire ses bagages to pack
■ les bagages à main hand luggage □ un bagage à main a piece of hand luggage

la **bagarre** FEM NOUN
fight
□ Une bagarre a éclaté à la fermeture du pub. A fight broke out when the pub closed.

se **bagarrer** VERB [28]
to fight
□ Il s'est encore bagarré avec son frère. He's been fighting with his brother again.

la **bagnole** FEM NOUN (*informal*)
car

la **bague** FEM NOUN
ring

la **baguette** FEM NOUN
1 stick of French bread
2 chopstick
□ manger avec des baguettes to eat with chopsticks
■ une baguette magique a magic wand

la **baie** FEM NOUN
bay

la **baignade** FEM NOUN
■ « baignade interdite » 'no swimming'

se **baigner** VERB [28]
to go swimming
□ Si on allait se baigner ? Shall we go swimming?

la **baignoire** FEM NOUN
bath (*bathtub*)

bâiller VERB [28]
to yawn

le **bain** MASC NOUN
bath
□ prendre un bain to take a bath
■ prendre un bain de soleil to sunbathe

le **baiser** MASC NOUN
kiss

la **baisse** FEM NOUN
fall
□ la baisse du taux de chômage the fall in the unemployment rate
■ être en baisse to be falling
■ revoir les chiffres à la baisse to revise figures downwards

baisser VERB [28]
1 to turn down
□ Il fait moins froid, tu peux baisser le chauffage. It's not so cold, you can turn down the heating.
2 to fall
□ Le prix des jeux vidéo a baissé. The price of video games has fallen.
■ se baisser to bend down □ Il s'est baissé pour ramasser son mouchoir. He bent down to pick up his handkerchief.

le **bal** MASC NOUN
dance
□ un bal populaire a local dance

la **balade** FEM NOUN (*informal*)
walk
□ faire une balade to go for a walk

se **balader** VERB [28] (*informal*)
to wander around
□ J'adore me balader dans les rues de Paris. I love to wander around the streets of Paris.

le **baladeur** MASC NOUN
■ un baladeur numérique an MP3 player

le **balai** MASC NOUN
broom

- **Je vais donner un coup de balai dans la cuisine.** I'm going to sweep the kitchen.

la **balance** FEM NOUN
scales pl (for weighing)
- **la Balance** Libra □ Todd est Balance. Todd is Libra.

se **balancer** VERB [12]
to swing

la **balançoire** FEM NOUN
swing

balayer VERB [59]
1 to sweep
□ Clément a balayé la cuisine. Clément swept the kitchen.
2 to sweep up
□ Va balayer les feuilles sur la terrasse. Go and sweep up the leaves on the terrace.

le **balayeur** MASC NOUN
roadsweeper

balbutier VERB [19]
to stammer

le **balcon** MASC NOUN
balcony

la **baleine** FEM NOUN
whale

la **balle** FEM NOUN
1 ball
□ une balle de tennis a tennis ball
2 bullet

la **ballerine** FEM NOUN
1 ballet dancer
2 ballet shoe
□ une paire de ballerines rouges a pair of red ballet shoes

le **ballet** MASC NOUN
ballet

le **ballon** MASC NOUN
1 ball
□ lancer le ballon to throw the ball
- **un ballon de foot** a football
2 balloon

balnéaire (FEM **balnéaire**) ADJECTIVE
- **une station balnéaire** a seaside resort

banal (FEM **banale**) ADJECTIVE
1 commonplace
□ La violence est devenue banale à la télévision. Violence has become commonplace on television.
2 hackneyed
□ L'intrigue du film est très banale. The plot of the film is very hackneyed.

la **banane** FEM NOUN
1 banana
2 bumbag
□ Mes clés sont dans ma banane. My keys are in my bumbag.

le **banc** MASC NOUN
bench

bancaire (FEM **bancaire**) ADJECTIVE
- **une carte bancaire** a bank card

le **bandage** MASC NOUN
bandage

la **bande** FEM NOUN
1 gang
□ une bande de voyous a gang of louts
2 bunch
□ C'est une bande d'idiots ! They are a bunch of idiots!
3 bandage
□ une bande Velpeau® a crepe bandage
- **une bande dessinée** a comic strip

> **DID YOU KNOW...?**
> Comic strips are very popular in France with people of all ages.

- **une bande magnétique** a tape
- **la bande sonore** the sound track
- **Elle fait toujours bande à part.** She always keeps to herself.

le **bandeau** (PL les **bandeaux**) MASC NOUN
headband

bander VERB [28]
to bandage
□ L'infirmière lui a bandé la jambe. The nurse bandaged his leg.

le **bandit** MASC NOUN
bandit

la **banlieue** FEM NOUN
suburbs
□ Pauline habite en banlieue. Pauline lives in the suburbs.
- **les lignes de banlieue** suburban lines
- **les trains de banlieue** commuter trains

la **banque** FEM NOUN
bank
- **une banque alimentaire** a food bank

le **banquet** MASC NOUN
dinner

la **banquette** FEM NOUN
seat
□ la banquette arrière de la voiture the back seat of the car

le **banquier** MASC NOUN
banker

la **banquière** FEM NOUN
banker

le **baptême** MASC NOUN
christening
□ le baptême de notre fille our daughter's christening
- **C'était mon baptême de l'air.** It was the first time I had flown.

bar – basque

le bar MASC NOUN
bar

la baraque FEM NOUN (*informal*)
house
□ Elle habite dans une belle baraque. She lives in a beautiful house.

barbant (FEM **barbante**) ADJECTIVE (*informal*)
boring
□ Il est vraiment barbant ! He's so boring!

barbare (FEM **barbare**) ADJECTIVE
barbaric

la barbe FEM NOUN
beard
□ Il porte la barbe. He's got a beard.
■ **Quelle barbe !** (*informal*) What a drag!
■ **la barbe à papa** candyfloss

le barbecue MASC NOUN
barbecue

barbouiller VERB [28]
to daub
□ Les murs étaient barbouillés de graffitis. The walls were daubed with graffiti.
■ **J'ai l'estomac barbouillé.** (*informal*) I'm feeling queasy.

barbu (FEM **barbue**) ADJECTIVE
bearded
□ un grand barbu a big, bearded man

barder VERB [28] (*informal*)
■ **Ça va barder !** There's going to be trouble!

le baromètre MASC NOUN
barometer

la barque FEM NOUN
rowing boat
■ **Ils sont allés faire une promenade en barque.** They've gone for a row.

le barrage MASC NOUN
dam
■ **un barrage de police** a police roadblock

la barre FEM NOUN
bar (*metal*)
□ une barre de fer an iron bar

le barreau (PL les **barreaux**) MASC NOUN
bar (*on window*)
□ Il s'est retrouvé derrière les barreaux. He ended up behind bars.

barrer VERB [28]
to block
□ Il y a un tronc d'arbre qui barre la route. There's a tree trunk blocking the road.
■ **se barrer** (*informal*) to clear off □ Barre-toi ! Clear off!

la barrette FEM NOUN
hair slide

la barrière FEM NOUN
fence

le bar-tabac (PL les **bars-tabacs**) MASC NOUN

> **DID YOU KNOW...?**
> A bar-tabac is a bar which also sells cigarettes, lottery tickets and sometimes stamps; you can tell a **bar-tabac** by the red diamond-shaped sign outside it.

bas (FEM **basse**) ADJECTIVE, ADVERB
▷ *see also* **bas** NOUN
low
□ parler à voix basse to speak in a low voice
■ **en bas 1** down □ Ça me donne le vertige de regarder en bas. I get dizzy if I look down.
2 (down) at the bottom □ Son nom est tout en bas. His name is down at the bottom. □ Il y a un supermarché en bas de la rue. There's a supermarket at the bottom of the street.
3 downstairs □ Elle habite en bas. She lives downstairs.

le bas MASC NOUN
▷ *see also* **bas** ADJECTIVE, ADVERB
1 bottom
□ en bas de la page at the bottom of the page
□ en bas de l'escalier at the bottom of the stairs
□ Le bas de mon pantalon est plein de boue. The bottom of my trousers is full of mud.
2 stocking
□ une paire de bas a pair of stockings

le bas-côté MASC NOUN
verge
□ Il s'est garé sur le bas-côté de la route. He parked his car on the verge.

la bascule FEM NOUN
■ **un fauteuil à bascule** a rocking chair

la base FEM NOUN
base
□ la base de la pyramide the base of the pyramid
■ **de base** basic □ Le pain et le lait sont des aliments de base. Bread and milk are basic foods.
■ **à base de** made from □ des produits de beauté à base de plantes cosmetics made from plants
■ **une base de données** a database

le basilic MASC NOUN
basil

le basket MASC NOUN
basketball
□ jouer au basket to play basketball

les baskets FEM PL NOUN
trainers
□ une paire de baskets a pair of trainers

> **BE CAREFUL!**
> The French word **baskets** does not mean **baskets**.

basque ADJECTIVE, NOUN
Basque

□ Elle parle basque. **She speaks Basque.**
■ un Basque a Basque (*man*)
■ une Basque a Basque (*woman*)

basse FEM ADJECTIVE ▷ *see* bas

la **basse-cour** (PL les **basses-cours**) FEM NOUN
farmyard

le **bassin** MASC NOUN
1 pond
□ Il y a un bassin à poissons rouges dans le parc. **There's a goldfish pond in the park.**
2 pelvis
□ une fracture du bassin **a fractured pelvis**

la **bassine** FEM NOUN
bowl (*for washing*)

le **bas-ventre** MASC NOUN
lower abdomen
□ Elle se plaint de douleurs dans le bas-ventre. **She is complaining of pains in her lower abdomen.**

la **bataille** FEM NOUN
battle

le **bateau** (PL les **bateaux**) MASC NOUN
boat

le **bateau-mouche** (PL les **bateaux-mouches**) MASC NOUN
pleasure boat

bâti (FEM **bâtie**) ADJECTIVE
■ bien bâti well-built

le **bâtiment** MASC NOUN
building

bâtir VERB [38]
to build

le **bâton** MASC NOUN
stick
□ un coup de bâton **a blow with a stick**

le **battement** MASC NOUN
■ J'ai dix minutes de battement. **I've got ten minutes free.**

la **batterie** FEM NOUN
1 battery
□ La batterie est à plat. **The battery is flat.**
2 drums
□ jouer de la batterie **to play the drums**
■ la batterie de cuisine the pots and pans

le **batteur** MASC NOUN
drummer

battre VERB [9]
to beat
□ Quand je le vois, mon cœur bat plus vite. **When I see him, my heart beats faster.**
■ se battre to fight □ Je me bats souvent avec mon frère. **I fight a lot with my brother.**
■ battre les cartes to shuffle the cards
■ Battre les blancs en neige. Beat the egg whites until stiff.
■ battre son plein to be in full swing □ A minuit,

la fête battait son plein. **At midnight, the party was in full swing.**

bavard (FEM **bavarde**) ADJECTIVE
talkative

bavarder VERB [28]
to chat

baver VERB [28]
to dribble

baveux (FEM **baveuse**) ADJECTIVE
runny
□ une omelette baveuse **a runny omelette**

la **bavure** FEM NOUN
blunder
□ une bavure policière **a police blunder**

le **bazar** MASC NOUN
general store
■ Quel bazar ! (*informal*) What a mess!

BCBG (FEM+PL **BCBG**) ADJECTIVE (= *bon chic bon genre*)
posh

la **BD** (PL les **BD**) FEM NOUN (= *bande dessinée*)
comic strip
□ Marguerite adore les BD. **Marguerite loves comic strips.**

béant (FEM **béante**) ADJECTIVE
gaping
□ un trou béant **a gaping hole**

beau (FEM **belle**, MASC PL **beaux**) ADJECTIVE, ADVERB

> The masculine singular form beau changes to bel before a vowel and most words beginning with 'h'.

1 lovely
□ un bel été **a lovely summer** □ une belle journée **a fine day**
2 beautiful
□ C'est une belle femme. **She is a beautiful woman.**
3 good-looking
□ C'est un beau garçon. **He is a good-looking boy.**
4 handsome
□ un bel homme **a handsome man**
■ Il fait beau aujourd'hui. It's a nice day today.
■ J'ai beau essayer, je n'y arrive pas. However hard I try, I just can't do it.

beaucoup ADVERB
1 a lot
□ Il travaille beaucoup. **He works a lot.**
2 much
□ Elle n'a pas beaucoup d'argent. **She hasn't got much money.** □ Louise est beaucoup plus grande que moi. **Louise is much taller than me.**
■ beaucoup de a lot of □ Il y avait beaucoup de monde au concert. **There were a lot of people at the concert.** □ Elle fait beaucoup de fautes. **She makes a lot of mistakes.**

■ **J'ai eu beaucoup de chance.** I was very lucky.

le **beau-fils** (PL les **beaux-fils**) MASC NOUN
1 son-in-law
2 stepson

le **beau-frère** (PL les **beaux-frères**) MASC NOUN
brother-in-law

le **beau-père** (PL les **beaux-pères**) MASC NOUN
1 father-in-law
2 stepfather

la **beauté** FEM NOUN
beauty

les **beaux-arts** MASC PL NOUN
fine arts

les **beaux-parents** MASC PL NOUN
in-laws

le **bébé** MASC NOUN
baby

le **bec** MASC NOUN
beak

la **bécane** FEM NOUN (*informal*)
bike

la **bêche** FEM NOUN
spade

bêcher VERB [28]
to dig
□ Il bêchait son jardin. He was digging the garden.

bégayer VERB [59]
to stammer

beige (FEM **beige**) ADJECTIVE
beige

le **beignet** MASC NOUN
1 fritter (*savoury or sweet batter*)
□ les beignets aux pommes apple fritters
2 donut (*sweet dough*)

bel MASC ADJECTIVE ▷ *see* **beau**

belge (FEM **belge**) ADJECTIVE, NOUN
Belgian
■ **un Belge** a Belgian (*man*)
■ **une Belge** a Belgian (*woman*)

la **Belgique** FEM NOUN
Belgium
■ **en Belgique 1** in Belgium **2** to Belgium

le **bélier** MASC NOUN
ram
■ **le Bélier** Aries □ Marine est Bélier. Marine's Aries.

belle FEM ADJECTIVE ▷ *see* **beau**

la **belle-famille** (PL les **belles-familles**) FEM NOUN
in-laws

la **belle-fille** (PL les **belles-filles**) FEM NOUN
1 daughter-in-law
2 stepdaughter

la **belle-mère** (PL les **belles-mères**) FEM NOUN
1 mother-in-law
2 stepmother

la **belle-sœur** (PL les **belles-sœurs**) FEM NOUN
sister-in-law

la **bénédiction** FEM NOUN
blessing

le **bénéfice** MASC NOUN
profit
□ La société réalise de gros bénéfices. The company is making big profits.

bénéficier VERB [19]
■ **bénéficier de 1** to receive □ Les élèves bénéficieront de coaching personnel. The students will receive personal coaching.
2 to enjoy □ Il a bénéficié d'un important soutien. He has enjoyed huge support.

bénévole (FEM **bénévole**) ADJECTIVE
voluntary
□ du travail bénévole voluntary work

le/la **bénévole** MASC/FEM NOUN
volunteer

bénir VERB [38]
to bless

bénit (FEM **bénite**) ADJECTIVE
consecrated
■ **l'eau bénite** holy water

la **béquille** FEM NOUN
crutch
□ Il marche avec des béquilles. He walks on crutches.

le **berceau** (PL les **berceaux**) MASC NOUN
cradle

bercer VERB [12]
to rock

la **berceuse** FEM NOUN
lullaby

le **béret** MASC NOUN
beret

la **berge** FEM NOUN
bank (*of river*)

le **berger** MASC NOUN
shepherd

la **bergère** FEM NOUN
shepherdess

le **besoin** MASC NOUN
need
■ **avoir besoin de quelque chose** to need something □ J'ai besoin d'argent. I need some money. □ J'ai besoin d'y réfléchir. I need to think about it.
■ **une famille dans le besoin** a needy family

le **bétail** MASC NOUN
livestock

Numbers in brackets refer to verb tables on pages 650 to 658

bête (FEM **bête**) ADJECTIVE
▷ *see also* **bête** NOUN
stupid

la **bête** FEM NOUN
▷ *see also* **bête** ADJECTIVE
animal

la **bêtise** FEM NOUN
■ **faire une bêtise** to do something stupid □ J'ai fait une bêtise. I've done something stupid.
■ **dire des bêtises** to talk nonsense □ Tu dis des bêtises ! You're talking nonsense!

le **béton** MASC NOUN
concrete
■ **un alibi en béton** a cast-iron alibi

la **betterave** FEM NOUN
beetroot
□ la salade de betterave beetroot salad

le/la **beur** MASC/FEM NOUN (*informal*)

> DID YOU KNOW...?
> A **beur** is a young person of North African origin born in France.

le **beurre** MASC NOUN
butter
□ une sauce au beurre a sauce made with butter

beurrer VERB [28]
to butter

Beyrouth NOUN
Beirut

bi (FEM **bi**, +PL **bis**) ADJECTIVE (*informal*)
bi
□ Il est bi. He is bi.

le **bibelot** MASC NOUN
ornament

le **biberon** MASC NOUN
baby's bottle

la **Bible** FEM NOUN
Bible

le/la **bibliothécaire** MASC/FEM NOUN
librarian

la **bibliothèque** FEM NOUN
1 library
□ emprunter un livre à la bibliothèque to borrow a book from the library
2 bookcase
□ une bibliothèque en chêne massif a bookcase made of solid oak

le **bic**® MASC NOUN
Biro®

la **biche** FEM NOUN
doe

la **bicyclette** FEM NOUN
bicycle

le **bidet** MASC NOUN
bidet

le **bidon** MASC NOUN
▷ *see also* **bidon** ADJECTIVE
can
□ un bidon d'essence a can of petrol

bidon (FEM+PL **bidon**) ADJECTIVE (*informal*)
▷ *see also* **bidon** NOUN
phoney
■ **Son histoire est complètement bidon.** His story is a complete load of rubbish.

le **bidonville** MASC NOUN
shanty town

la **Biélorussie** FEM NOUN
Belarus

bien (FEM+PL **bien**) ADJECTIVE, ADVERB
▷ *see also* **bien** NOUN
1 well
□ Marie travaille bien. Marie works well. □ Je me sens bien. I feel fine. □ Je ne me sens pas bien. I don't feel well.
2 good
□ Ce restaurant est vraiment bien. This restaurant is really good.
3 quite
□ bien assez quite enough
■ **Je veux bien le faire.** I'm quite willing to do it.
■ **bien mieux** much better
■ **J'espère bien y aller.** I very much hope to go.
4 right
□ Ce n'est pas bien de dire du mal des gens. It's not right to say nasty things about people. □ Il croyait bien faire. He thought he was doing the right thing.
■ **C'est bien fait pour lui !** It serves him right!

le **bien** MASC NOUN
▷ *see also* **bien** ADJECTIVE, ADVERB
1 good
□ le bien et le mal good and evil □ Jean m'a dit beaucoup de bien de toi. Jean told me a lot of good things about you. □ C'est pour son bien. It's for his own good.
■ **faire du bien à quelqu'un** to do somebody good □ Ses vacances lui ont fait beaucoup de bien. His holiday has done him a lot of good.
2 possession
□ son bien le plus précieux his most treasured possession

le **bien-être** MASC NOUN
well-being
□ une sensation de bien-être a feeling of well-being

la **bienfaisance** FEM NOUN
charity
■ **une œuvre de bienfaisance** a charity

bien que CONJUNCTION
although

> **bien que** is followed by a verb in the subjunctive.

□ Il fait assez chaud bien qu'il n'y ait pas de soleil. It's quite warm although there's no sun.

bien sûr ADVERB
of course

bientôt ADVERB
soon
■ **A bientôt !** See you soon!

le **bienvenu** MASC NOUN
■ **Vous êtes le bienvenu !** You're welcome!
□ Vous êtes tous les bienvenus ! You're all welcome!

la **bienvenue** FEM NOUN
welcome
■ **Bienvenue !** Welcome! □ Bienvenue à Paris ! Welcome to Paris!

la **bière** FEM NOUN
beer
■ **la bière blonde** lager
■ **la bière brune** brown ale
■ **la bière pression** draught beer

le **bifteck** MASC NOUN
steak

le **bijou** (PL les **bijoux**) MASC NOUN
jewel

la **bijouterie** FEM NOUN
jeweller's

le **bijoutier** MASC NOUN
jeweller

la **bijoutière** FEM NOUN
jeweller
□ Elle est bijoutière. She's a jeweller.

le **bilan** MASC NOUN
■ **faire le bilan de quelque chose** to assess something □ Il faut faire le bilan de la situation. We need to assess the situation.

bilingue (FEM **bilingue**) ADJECTIVE
bilingual

le **billard** MASC NOUN
billiards
■ **le billard américain** pool

la **bille** FEM NOUN
marble (*toy*)
□ jouer aux billes to play marbles

le **billet** MASC NOUN
1 ticket
□ un billet d'avion a plane ticket □ un billet électronique an e-ticket
2 banknote
□ un billet de dix euros a 10 euro note

bio (FEM+PL **bio**) ADJECTIVE
organic
□ Je préfère les produits bio. I prefer organic produce.

le **biocarburant** MASC NOUN
biofuel

biodégradable ADJECTIVE
biodegradable

la **biographie** FEM NOUN
biography

la **biologie** FEM NOUN
biology

biologique (FEM **biologique**) ADJECTIVE
1 organic
□ des légumes biologiques organic vegetables
2 biological
□ des armes biologiques biological weapons

le **bip** MASC NOUN
beep
■ **bip sonore** tone □ Veuillez laisser votre message après le bip sonore. Please leave your message after the tone.

la **Birmanie** FEM NOUN
Burma

bis ADVERB
▷ *see also* **bis** NOUN
■ **Il habite au douze bis rue des Fleurs.** He lives at 12A rue des Fleurs.

le **bis** MASC NOUN
▷ *see also* **bis** ADVERB
encore

la **biscotte** FEM NOUN
toasted bread (*sold in packets*)

le **biscuit** MASC NOUN
biscuit
■ **un biscuit de Savoie** a sponge cake

la **bise** FEM NOUN (*informal*)
kiss
□ Grosses bises de Bretagne. Love and kisses from Brittany.
■ **faire la bise à quelqu'un** to give somebody a kiss on the cheek □ Elle m'a fait la bise. She gave me a kiss on the cheek.

> **DID YOU KNOW...?**
> Between friends and family members, the normal French way of saying hello and goodbye is with two kisses, usually one on each cheek, but sometimes three or even four depending on the region. Men and boys often shake hands instead.

bisexuel (FEM **bisexuelle**) ADJECTIVE
bisexual

le **bisou** MASC NOUN (*informal*)
kiss
□ Viens faire un bisou à maman ! Come and give Mummy a kiss!

bissextile (FEM **bissextile**) ADJECTIVE
■ **une année bissextile** a leap year

le **bistrot** MASC NOUN (*informal*)
café

> **DID YOU KNOW...?**
> Cafés in France sell both alcoholic and non-alcoholic drinks.

bizarre (FEM bizarre) ADJECTIVE
strange

la blague FEM NOUN (*informal*)
1 joke
  □ raconter une blague to tell a joke
  ■ Sans blague ! No kidding!
2 trick
  □ Antoine nous a encore fait une blague !
  Antoine has played a trick on us again!

blaguer VERB [28] (*informal*)
to joke

le blaireau (PL les blaireaux) MASC NOUN
1 badger
2 shaving brush

blâmer VERB [28]
to blame

blanc (FEM blanche) ADJECTIVE
  ▷ *see also* blanc NOUN
1 white
  □ un chemisier blanc a white blouse
2 White
  □ Elle est blanche. She is White.
3 blank
  □ une page blanche a blank page

le blanc MASC NOUN
  ▷ *see also* blanc ADJECTIVE
1 white
  □ habillé tout en blanc dressed all in white
2 white wine
  □ un verre de blanc a glass of white wine
3 blank
  □ S'il vous plaît, remplissez les blancs.
  Please fill in the blanks.
  ■ un blanc d'œuf an egg white
  ■ un blanc de poulet a chicken breast

blanche FEM ADJECTIVE ▷ *see* blanc

la blanchisserie FEM NOUN
laundry

le blé MASC NOUN
wheat

blessé (FEM blessée) ADJECTIVE
  ▷ *see also* blessé NOUN, blessée NOUN
injured

le blessé MASC NOUN
  ▷ *see also* blessé ADJECTIVE
injured person
  □ L'accident a fait trois blessés. Three people
  were injured in the accident.

la blessée FEM NOUN
  ▷ *see also* blessé ADJECTIVE
injured person

blesser VERB [28]
1 to injure
  □ Il a été blessé dans un accident de voiture.
  He was injured in a car accident.
2 to hurt

□ Il a fait exprès de le blesser. He hurt him on
purpose.
  ■ se blesser to hurt oneself □ Geneviève s'est
  blessée à la cheville. Geneviève has hurt her
  ankle.

  BE CAREFUL!
  blesser does not mean **to bless**.

la blessure FEM NOUN
injury

bleu (FEM bleue) ADJECTIVE
  ▷ *see also* bleu NOUN
1 blue
  □ une veste bleue a blue jacket
  ■ bleu marine navy blue
2 very rare (*steak*)

le bleu MASC NOUN
  ▷ *see also* bleu ADJECTIVE
1 blue
  □ J'aime le bleu. I like blue.
2 bruise
  □ Il a un bleu au front. He's got a bruise on
  his forehead.

le bleuet MASC NOUN
cornflower

le bloc MASC NOUN
pad
  □ un bloc de papier à lettres a pad of writing
  paper
  ■ le bloc opératoire the operating theatre

le bloc-notes (PL les blocs-notes) MASC NOUN
note pad

le blog MASC NOUN
blog

le bloggeur MASC NOUN
blogger

bloguer VERB [28]
to blog

le blogueur MASC NOUN
blogger

la blogueuse FEM NOUN
blogger

blond (FEM blonde) ADJECTIVE
blond
  ■ blond cendré ash blond □ Simon a les
  cheveux blond cendré. Simon has ash blond hair.

bloquer VERB [28]
to block
  □ bloquer le passage to block the way
  ■ être bloqué dans un embouteillage to be
  stuck in a traffic jam

se blottir VERB [38]
to huddle
  □ Ils étaient blottis l'un contre l'autre. They were
  huddled together.

la blouse FEM NOUN
overall

le **blouson** MASC NOUN
jacket
□ un blouson en cuir a leather jacket

le **bob** MASC NOUN
cotton sunhat

la **bobine** FEM NOUN
reel
□ une bobine de fil a reel of thread

le **bocal** (PL les **bocaux**) MASC NOUN
jar

le **bœuf** MASC NOUN
1 ox
2 beef
□ un rôti de bœuf a joint of beef

bof EXCLAMATION (*informal*)
■ **Le film t'a plu ? — Bof ! C'était pas terrible !** Did you like the film? — Well … it wasn't that great!
■ **Comment ça va ? — Bof ! Pas terrible.** How is it going? — Oh … not too well actually.

le **bohémien** MASC NOUN
Gipsy

la **bohémienne** FEM NOUN
Gipsy

boire VERB [10]
to drink
■ **boire un coup** (*informal*) to have a drink

le **bois** MASC NOUN
▷ *see also* **bois** VERB
wood
■ **en bois** wooden □ une table en bois a wooden table
■ **avoir la gueule de bois** (*informal*) to have a hangover

bois VERB ▷ *see* **boire**
▷ *see also* **bois** NOUN
■ **Je bois du lait.** I drink milk.

la **boisson** FEM NOUN
drink
□ une boisson chaude a hot drink □ une boisson non alcoolisée a soft drink

boit VERB ▷ *see* **boire**

la **boîte** FEM NOUN
1 box
□ une boîte d'allumettes a box of matches
■ **une boîte aux lettres** a letter box
■ **une boîte postale** a PO Box
■ **une boîte vocale** voice mail
2 tin
□ une boîte de sardines a tin of sardines
■ **une boîte de conserve** a tin
■ **en boîte** tinned □ des petits pois en boîte tinned peas
■ **une boîte de nuit** a night club
■ **sortir en boîte** to go clubbing

boiter VERB [28]
to limp

le **bol** MASC NOUN
bowl
■ **en avoir ras le bol** (*informal*) to be fed up
□ J'en ai ras le bol de ce boulot. I'm fed up with this job.

bombarder VERB [28]
to bomb

la **bombe** FEM NOUN
1 bomb
2 aerosol
□ du déodorant en bombe aérosol deodorant

bon (FEM **bonne**) ADJECTIVE, ADVERB
▷ *see also* **bon** NOUN
1 good
□ un bon restaurant a good restaurant □ Le tabac n'est pas bon pour la santé. Smoking isn't good for you. □ être bon en maths to be good at maths
■ **sentir bon** to smell nice
■ **Bon anniversaire !** Happy birthday!
■ **Bon courage !** Good luck!
■ **Bon voyage !** Have a good trip!
■ **Bon week-end !** Have a nice weekend!
■ **Bonne chance !** Good luck!
■ **Bonne journée !** Have a nice day!
■ **Bonne nuit !** Good night!
■ **Bonne année !** Happy New Year!
■ **Bonnes vacances !** Have a good holiday!
2 right
□ Il est arrivé au bon moment. He arrived at the right moment. □ Ce n'est pas la bonne réponse. That's not the right answer.
■ **Il fait bon aujourd'hui.** It's nice today.
■ **de bonne heure** early
■ **bon marché** cheap □ Les fraises ne sont pas bon marché en hiver. Strawberries aren't cheap in winter.
■ **Ah bon ?** Really? □ Je pars aux États-Unis la semaine prochaine. — Ah bon ? I'm going to the States next week. — Really?
■ **J'aimerais vraiment que tu viennes ! — Bon, d'accord.** I'd really like you to come! — OK then, I will.
■ **Est-ce que ce yaourt est encore bon ?** Is this yoghurt still OK?

le **bon** MASC NOUN
▷ *see also* **bon** ADJECTIVE, ADVERB
voucher
□ un bon d'achat a voucher
■ **pour de bon** 1 for good □ Il est parti pour de bon. He's gone for good. 2 for real □ Cette fois, on le fait pour de bon. Let's do it for real this time.
■ **Il est fâché pour de bon.** He's really angry.

le **bonbon** MASC NOUN
sweet

bondé (FEM **bondée**) ADJECTIVE
crowded

Numbers in brackets refer to verb tables on pages 650 to 658

bondir VERB [38]
to leap

le **bonheur** MASC NOUN
happiness
- **porter bonheur** to bring luck

le **bonhomme** (PL les **bonshommes**) MASC NOUN
- **un bonhomme de neige** a snowman

bonjour EXCLAMATION
1 hello!
 □ Donne le bonjour à tes parents de ma part. Say hello to your parents for me.
2 good morning!
3 good afternoon!

> bonjour is used in the morning and afternoon; in the evening **bonsoir** is used instead.

- **C'est simple comme bonjour !** It's easy as pie!

bonne FEM ADJECTIVE ▷ see **bon**

le **bonnet** MASC NOUN
hat
 □ un bonnet de laine a woolly hat
- **un bonnet de bain** a bathing cap

bonsoir EXCLAMATION
good evening!

la **bonté** FEM NOUN
kindness

le **bord** MASC NOUN
1 edge
 □ le bord de la table the edge of the table
2 side
 □ Jeanne a garé sa voiture au bord de la route. Jeanne parked her car on the side of the road.
- **au bord de la mer** at the seaside
- **au bord de l'eau** by the water
- **monter à bord** to go on board
- **être au bord des larmes** to be on the verge of tears

le **bordeaux** MASC NOUN
 ▷ see also **bordeaux** ADJECTIVE
Bordeaux wine
- **du bordeaux rouge** claret

bordeaux (FEM+PL **bordeaux**) ADJECTIVE
 ▷ see also **bordeaux** NOUN
burgundy
 □ une jupe bordeaux a burgundy skirt

border VERB [28]
1 to line
 □ une route bordée d'arbres a tree-lined street
2 to trim
 □ un col bordé de dentelle a collar trimmed with lace
3 to tuck in
 □ Sa mère vient la border tous les soirs. Her mother comes and tucks her in every night.

la **bordure** FEM NOUN
border

- **une villa en bordure de mer** a villa right by the sea

la **borne** FEM NOUN
terminal (of computer)

la **Bosnie** FEM NOUN
Bosnia
- **la Bosnie-Herzégovine** Bosnia-Herzegovina

la **bosse** FEM NOUN
bump
 □ Nicolas a une grosse bosse au front. Nicolas has got a big bump on his forehead.
- **La route est pleine de bosses.** The road is very bumpy.

bosser VERB [28]
to work (informal)
- **bosser un examen** to study for an exam

le **bossu** MASC NOUN
hunchback

la **bossue** FEM NOUN
hunchback

botanique (FEM **botanique**) ADJECTIVE
 ▷ see also **botanique** NOUN
botanic
 □ le jardin botanique the botanic gardens

la **botanique** FEM NOUN
 ▷ see also **botanique** ADJECTIVE
botany

la **botte** FEM NOUN
1 boot
 □ une paire de bottes a pair of boots
- **les bottes en caoutchouc** Wellington boots
2 bunch
 □ une botte de radis a bunch of radishes

le **bottin**® MASC NOUN
phone book

le **bouc** MASC NOUN
1 goatee beard
2 billy goat
- **un bouc émissaire** a scapegoat

la **bouche** FEM NOUN
mouth
- **le bouche à bouche** the kiss of life
- **une bouche d'égout** a manhole
- **une bouche de métro** an entrance to the underground

la **bouchée** FEM NOUN
mouthful
- **une bouchée à la reine** a chicken vol-au-vent

boucher VERB [28]
 ▷ see also **boucher** NOUN
1 to fill
 □ boucher un trou to fill a hole
2 to block
 □ L'évier est bouché. The sink is blocked. □ J'ai le nez bouché. My nose is blocked.

b

le **boucher** MASC NOUN
▷ see also **boucher** VERB
butcher
□ Il est boucher. **He's a butcher.**

la **bouchère** FEM NOUN
butcher
□ Elle est bouchère. **She's a butcher.**

la **boucherie** FEM NOUN
butcher's

le **bouchon** MASC NOUN
1 top (of plastic bottle)
2 cork (of wine bottle)
3 hold-up
□ Il y avait beaucoup de bouchons sur l'autoroute. **There were a lot of hold-ups on the motorway.**

la **boucle** FEM NOUN
curl (of hair)
■ **une boucle d'oreille** an earring □ une paire de boucles d'oreille **a pair of earrings**

bouclé (FEM **bouclée**) ADJECTIVE
curly

le **bouclier** MASC NOUN
shield

bouddhiste (FEM **bouddhiste**) ADJECTIVE, NOUN
Buddhist
■ **un bouddhiste** a Buddhist (man)
■ **une bouddhiste** a Buddhist (woman)

bouder VERB [28]
to sulk

le **boudin** MASC NOUN
■ **le boudin noir** black pudding
■ **le boudin blanc** white pudding

la **boue** FEM NOUN
mud

la **bouée** FEM NOUN
buoy
■ **une bouée de sauvetage** a life buoy

boueux (FEM **boueuse**) ADJECTIVE
muddy

la **bouffe** FEM NOUN (informal)
food
□ La bouffe est infecte à la cantine. **The food in the canteen is revolting.**

la **bouffée** FEM NOUN
■ **une bouffée d'air frais** a breath of fresh air

bouffer VERB [28] (informal)
to eat

le **bougeoir** MASC NOUN
candlestick

bouger VERB [45]
to move

la **bougie** FEM NOUN
candle

la **bouillabaisse** FEM NOUN
fish soup

bouillant (FEM **bouillante**) ADJECTIVE
1 boiling
□ Faites cuire les pâtes à l'eau bouillante. **Cook the pasta in boiling water.**
2 piping hot
□ La soupe est bouillante. **The soup is piping hot.**

bouillir VERB [11]
to boil
□ L'eau bout. **The water's boiling.**
■ **Je bous d'impatience.** I'm bursting with impatience.

la **bouilloire** FEM NOUN
kettle

le **bouillon** MASC NOUN
stock
□ du bouillon de légumes **vegetable stock**

la **bouillotte** FEM NOUN
hot-water bottle

le **boulanger** MASC NOUN
baker
□ Il est boulanger. **He's a baker.**

la **boulangère** FEM NOUN
baker
□ Elle est boulangère. **She's a baker.**

la **boulangerie** FEM NOUN
baker's

la **boule** FEM NOUN
ball
□ une boule de cristal **a crystal ball**
■ **une boule de neige** a snowball
■ **jouer aux boules** to play bowls

DID YOU KNOW...?
boules is played on rough ground, not smooth grass. The balls are smaller than those used in bowls, and are made of metal.

le **boulevard** MASC NOUN
boulevard

bouleverser VERB [28]
1 to move deeply
□ Cette histoire déchirante m'a bouleversée. **This heartbreaking story moved me deeply.**
2 to shatter
□ La mort de son ami l'a bouleversé. **He was shattered by the death of his friend.**
3 to turn upside down
□ Cette rencontre a bouleversé sa vie. **This meeting turned his life upside down.**

le **boulot** MASC NOUN (informal)
1 job
□ Anita a trouvé du boulot. **Anita has found a job.**
2 work
□ J'ai beaucoup de boulot en ce moment. **I've got a lot of work to do at the moment.**

Numbers in brackets refer to verb tables on pages 650 to 658

la **boum** FEM NOUN (*informal*)
party

le **bouquet** MASC NOUN
bunch of flowers
▫ un bouquet de roses a bunch of roses

le **bouquin** MASC NOUN (*informal*)
book

bouquiner VERB [28] (*informal*)
to read

bourdonner VERB [28]
to buzz

le **bourg** MASC NOUN
small market town

bourgeois (FEM **bourgeoise**) ADJECTIVE
middle-class
▫ un quartier bourgeois a middle-class area

le **bourgeon** MASC NOUN
bud

la **Bourgogne** FEM NOUN
Burgundy

bourré (FEM **bourrée**) ADJECTIVE
■ **bourré de** stuffed with ▫ un portefeuille
bourré de billets a wallet stuffed with banknotes
■ **être bourré** (*informal*) to be plastered ▫ Il
était complètement bourré. He was completely
plastered.

le **bourreau** (PL les **bourreaux**) MASC NOUN
executioner
■ **C'est un véritable bourreau de travail.**
He's a real workaholic.

bourrer VERB [28]
to stuff
▫ bourrer une valise de vêtements to stuff
clothes into a case

la **bourse** FEM NOUN
grant
■ **la Bourse** the Stock Exchange

bous VERB ▷ *see* **bouillir**

la **bousculade** FEM NOUN
crush
▫ la bousculade dans les grands magasins au
moment des soldes the crush in the big stores
at sale time

bousculer VERB [28]
1 to jostle
▫ être bousculé par la foule to be jostled by the
crowd
2 to rush
▫ Je n'aime pas qu'on me bouscule. I don't like
to be rushed.

la **boussole** FEM NOUN
compass

bout VERB ▷ *see* **bouillir**

le **bout** MASC NOUN
1 end
▫ Elle habite au bout de la rue. She lives at

the end of the street. ▫ Marie est assise
en bout de table. Marie is sitting at the end of
the table.
2 tip
▫ le bout du nez the tip of the nose
3 bit
▫ un petit bout de fromage a bit of cheese
■ **un bout de papier** a scrap of paper
■ **au bout de** after ▫ Au bout d'un moment,
il s'est endormi. After a while he fell asleep.
■ **Elle est à bout.** She's at the end of her
tether.

la **bouteille** FEM NOUN
bottle
▫ une bouteille d'eau gazeuse a bottle of
sparkling water
■ **une bouteille de gaz** a gas cylinder

la **boutique** FEM NOUN
shop

le **bouton** MASC NOUN
1 button
2 spot (*on skin*)
▫ J'ai un bouton sur le nez. I've got a spot on
my nose.
3 bud
▫ un bouton de rose a rosebud
■ **un bouton d'or** a buttercup

le **bowling** MASC NOUN
1 tenpin bowling
2 bowling alley

la **boxe** FEM NOUN
boxing

le **boxeur** MASC NOUN
boxer

le **bracelet** MASC NOUN
bracelet

le **bracelet-montre** (PL les **bracelets-
montres**) MASC NOUN
wristwatch

le **brancard** MASC NOUN
stretcher

le **brancardier** MASC NOUN
stretcher-bearer

la **branche** FEM NOUN
branch

branché (FEM **branchée**) ADJECTIVE (*informal*)
trendy
▫ avoir un look branché to look trendy

brancher VERB [28]
1 to connect
▫ Le téléphone est branché ? Is the phone
connected?
2 to plug in
▫ L'aspirateur n'est pas branché. The hoover
isn't plugged in.

le **bras** MASC NOUN
arm

brasse – brocante

la **brasse** FEM NOUN
breaststroke
□ nager la brasse to do the breaststroke

la **brasserie** FEM NOUN
café-restaurant

brave (FEM **brave**) ADJECTIVE
nice
□ C'est un brave type. He's a nice enough fellow.

bravo EXCLAMATION
bravo!

le **break** MASC NOUN
estate car

la **brebis** FEM NOUN
ewe
■ le fromage de brebis sheep's cheese

bref (FEM **brève**) ADJECTIVE, ADVERB
short
□ Sa lettre était brève. His letter was short.
■ en bref in brief □ l'actualité en bref the news in brief
■ Bref, ça s'est bien terminé. To cut a long story short, it turned out all right in the end.

le **Brésil** MASC NOUN
Brazil

la **Bretagne** FEM NOUN
Brittany

la **bretelle** FEM NOUN
strap
□ La bretelle de son soutien-gorge dépasse. Her bra strap is showing.
■ les bretelles braces □ Il porte des bretelles. He's wearing braces.

breton (FEM **bretonne**) ADJECTIVE, NOUN
Breton
□ Ils parlent breton. They speak Breton.
■ un Breton a Breton (*man*)
■ une Bretonne a Breton (*woman*)
■ les Bretons the Bretons

brève FEM ADJECTIVE ▷ *see* bref

le **brevet** MASC NOUN
certificate

le **brevet des collèges** MASC NOUN

> **DID YOU KNOW...?**
> The **brevet des collèges** is an exam you take at the end of **collège**, at the age of 15.

le **bricolage** MASC NOUN
DIY
□ Elle aime le bricolage. She likes doing DIY.
□ un magasin de bricolage a DIY shop

la **bricole** FEM NOUN (*informal*)
■ J'ai acheté une bricole pour le bébé de Sabine. I've bought a little something for Sabine's baby.
■ J'ai encore quelques bricoles à faire avant de partir. I've still got a few things to do before I go.

bricoler VERB [28]
to do DIY
□ Pascal aime bricoler. Pascal loves doing DIY.

le **bricoleur** MASC NOUN
DIY enthusiast

la **bricoleuse** FEM NOUN
DIY enthusiast

le **bridge** MASC NOUN
bridge (*game*)
□ Guillaume adore jouer au bridge. Guillaume loves playing bridge.

brièvement ADVERB
briefly
□ Expliquez-moi brièvement ce qui s'est passé. Tell me briefly what happened.

la **brigade** FEM NOUN
squad (*of police*)
□ la brigade des stups (*informal*) the drugs squad

brillamment ADVERB
brilliantly
□ Il a réussi brillamment à son examen. He did brilliantly in the exam.

brillant (FEM **brillante**) ADJECTIVE
1 brilliant
□ une brillante carrière a brilliant career □ Ses notes ne sont pas brillantes. His marks aren't brilliant.
2 shiny
□ des cheveux brillants shiny hair

briller VERB [28]
to shine

le **brin** MASC NOUN
■ un brin d'herbe a blade of grass
■ un brin de muguet a sprig of lily of the valley

la **brindille** FEM NOUN
twig

la **brioche** FEM NOUN
brioche bun

la **brique** FEM NOUN
brick

le **briquet** MASC NOUN
cigarette lighter

la **brise** FEM NOUN
breeze

se **briser** VERB [28]
to break
□ Le vase s'est brisé en mille morceaux. The vase broke into a thousand pieces.

le/la **Britannique** MASC/FEM NOUN
Briton
■ les Britanniques the British

britannique (FEM **britannique**) ADJECTIVE
British

la **brocante** FEM NOUN
junk

□ un magasin de brocante **a junk shop**

le **brocanteur** MASC NOUN
dealer in second-hand goods

la **brocanteuse** FEM NOUN
dealer in second-hand goods

la **broche** FEM NOUN
brooch
□ une broche en argent **a silver brooch**
■ **à la broche** spit-roasted □ un poulet à la
broche **a spit-roasted chicken**

la **brochette** FEM NOUN
skewer
■ **les brochettes d'agneau** lamb kebabs

la **brochure** FEM NOUN
brochure

broder VERB [28]
to embroider

la **broderie** FEM NOUN
embroidery

la **bronchite** FEM NOUN
bronchitis
□ avoir une bronchite **to have bronchitis**

le **bronze** MASC NOUN
bronze

bronzer VERB [28]
to get a tan
□ Il est bien bronzé. **He's got a good tan.**
■ **se faire bronzer** to sunbathe

la **brosse** FEM NOUN
brush
■ **une brosse à cheveux** a hairbrush
■ **une brosse à dents** a toothbrush
■ **Il est coiffé en brosse.** He's got a crew cut.

brosser VERB [28]
to brush
■ **se brosser les dents** to brush one's teeth
□ Je me brosse les dents tous les soirs. **I brush
my teeth every night.**

la **brouette** FEM NOUN
wheelbarrow

le **brouillard** MASC NOUN
fog
■ **Il y a du brouillard.** It's foggy.

le **brouillon** MASC NOUN
first draft
□ Ce n'est qu'un brouillon. **It's just a first
draft.**

les **broussailles** FEM PL NOUN
undergrowth *sing*

brouter VERB [28]
to graze *(animals)*

broyer VERB [53]
to crush
■ **broyer du noir** to be down in the dumps

le **brugnon** MASC NOUN
nectarine

le **bruit** MASC NOUN
1 noise
□ J'ai entendu un bruit. **I heard a noise.** □ faire
du bruit **to make a noise**
■ **sans bruit** without a sound
2 rumour
□ Des bruits circulent à son sujet. **There are
rumours going round about him.**

brûlant (FEM **brûlante**) ADJECTIVE
1 blazing
□ un soleil brûlant **a blazing sun**
2 boiling hot
□ Marie boit son café brûlant. **Marie drinks her
coffee boiling hot.**

le **brûlé** MASC NOUN
smell of burning
□ Ça sent le brûlé. **There's a smell of burning.**

brûler VERB [28]
to burn
■ **se brûler** to burn oneself

la **brûlure** FEM NOUN
burn
■ **des brûlures d'estomac** heartburn

la **brume** FEM NOUN
mist

brumeux (FEM **brumeuse**) ADJECTIVE
misty

brun (FEM **brune**) ADJECTIVE
brown
■ **Elle est brune.** She's got dark hair.

le **brushing** MASC NOUN
blow-dry
□ une coupe et un brushing **a cut and blow-dry**

brusque (FEM **brusque**) ADJECTIVE
abrupt
■ **d'un ton brusque** brusquely

brusquer VERB [28]
to rush
□ Il ne faut pas la brusquer. **You mustn't rush
her.**

brut (FEM **brute**) ADJECTIVE
■ **le champagne brut** dry champagne
■ **le pétrole brut** crude oil
■ **son salaire brut** his gross salary

brutal (FEM **brutale**, MASC PL **brutaux**) ADJECTIVE
brutal

brutaliser VERB [28]
to knock about
□ Il a été brutalisé par la police. **He was knocked
about by the police.**

Bruxelles NOUN
Brussels

bruyamment ADVERB
noisily

bruyant (FEM **bruyante**) ADJECTIVE
noisy

bruyère – buvard

la **bruyère** FEM NOUN
heather

bu VERB ▷ *see* boire

la **bûche** FEM NOUN
log
■ la bûche de Noël the Yule log

> **DID YOU KNOW...?**
> la bûche de Noël is what is usually eaten in France instead of Christmas pudding.

le **bûcheron** MASC NOUN
woodcutter

le **budget** MASC NOUN
budget

le **buffet** MASC NOUN
1 sideboard
☐ un buffet en chêne an oak sideboard
2 buffet
☐ un buffet froid a cold buffet

le **buisson** MASC NOUN
bush

la **Bulgarie** FEM NOUN
Bulgaria

la **bulle** FEM NOUN
bubble
☐ une bulle de savon a soap bubble

le **bulletin** MASC NOUN
1 bulletin
■ le bulletin d'informations the news bulletin
2 report
☐ Ton bulletin n'est pas fameux. Your school report isn't very good.
■ le bulletin météorologique the weather report
■ un bulletin de salaire a pay slip
■ un bulletin de vote a ballot paper

le **bureau** (PL les **bureaux**) MASC NOUN
1 desk
☐ Posez le dossier sur mon bureau. Put the file on my desk.
2 office
☐ Il vous attend dans son bureau. He's waiting for you in his office.
■ un bureau de change a bureau de change
■ le bureau de poste the post office
■ le bureau de tabac the tobacconist's
■ le bureau de vote the polling station

bus VERB ▷ *see* boire

le **bus** MASC NOUN
bus

le **buste** MASC NOUN
bust

but VERB ▷ *see* boire

le **but** MASC NOUN
1 aim
☐ Ils n'ont pas de but dans la vie. They have no aim in life.
■ Quel est le but de votre visite ? What's the reason for your visit?
■ dans le but de with the intention of ☐ Je suis venue dans le but de vous aider. I came with the intention of helping you.
2 goal
☐ marquer un but to score a goal

le **butane** MASC NOUN
Calor gas®

le **butin** MASC NOUN
loot
☐ Les cambrioleurs se sont partagé le butin. The burglars shared the stolen goods.

buvais, buvait VERB ▷ *see* boire

le **buvard** MASC NOUN
blotter

Cc

c' PRONOUN ▷ *see* **ce**

ça PRONOUN

1 this
□ Est-ce que vous pouvez me donner un peu de ça ? **Can you give me a bit of this?**

2 that
□ Regarde ça là-bas. **Look at that over there.**

3 it
□ Ça ne fait rien. **It doesn't matter.**
■ **Comment ça va ?** How are you?
■ **Ça alors !** Well, well!
■ **C'est ça.** That's right.
■ **Ça y est !** That's it!

çà ADVERB
■ **çà et là** here and there

la **cabane** FEM NOUN
hut

le **cabillaud** MASC NOUN
cod

la **cabine** FEM NOUN
cabin (*on a ship*)
■ **une cabine d'essayage** a fitting room

le **cabinet** MASC NOUN
surgery (*of doctor, dentist*)
■ **une chambre avec cabinet de toilette** a room with washing facilities

les **cabinets** MASC PL NOUN
toilet *sing*

le **câble** MASC NOUN
cable
■ **la télévision par câble** cable television

cabosser VERB [28]
to dent

la **cacahuète** FEM NOUN
peanut
■ **le beurre de cacahuète** peanut butter

le **cacao** MASC NOUN
cocoa
■ **le beurre de cacao** cocoa butter

cache-cache MASC NOUN
■ **jouer à cache-cache** to play hide-and-seek

le **cachemire** MASC NOUN
cashmere

le **cache-nez** (PL les **cache-nez**) MASC NOUN
long woollen scarf

cacher VERB [28]
to hide
□ J'ai caché les cadeaux sous le lit. **I hid the presents under the bed.** □ Tu me caches quelque chose ! **You're hiding something from me!**
■ **se cacher** to hide □ Elle s'est cachée sous la table. **She's hidden under the table.**

le **cachet** MASC NOUN

1 tablet
■ **un cachet d'aspirine** an aspirin

2 fee (*for performer*)
□ Il a touché un gros cachet pour ce concert. **He got a big fee for the concert.**
■ **le cachet de la poste** the postmark

la **cachette** FEM NOUN
hiding place
■ **en cachette** on the sly □ Il est sorti en cachette sans réveiller ses parents. **He crept out on the sly without waking his parents.**

le **cachot** MASC NOUN
dungeon

le **cactus** MASC NOUN
cactus

le **cadavre** MASC NOUN
corpse

le **Caddie**® MASC NOUN
supermarket trolley

le **cadeau** (PL les **cadeaux**) MASC NOUN
present
□ un cadeau d'anniversaire **a birthday present**
□ un cadeau de Noël **a Christmas present**
■ **faire un cadeau à quelqu'un** to give somebody a present

le **cadenas** MASC NOUN
padlock

cadet (FEM **cadette**) ADJECTIVE
▷ *see also* **cadet** NOUN, **cadette** NOUN

1 younger (*brother, sister*)
□ ma sœur cadette **my younger sister**

2 youngest (*son, daughter*)
□ son fils cadet **his youngest son**

le **cadet** MASC NOUN
▷ *see also* **cadet** ADJECTIVE
youngest
□ C'est le cadet de la famille. **He's the youngest of the family.**

cadette - calme

la **cadette** FEM NOUN
▷ *see also* **cadet** ADJECTIVE
youngest
□ C'est la cadette de la famille. She's the youngest of the family.

le **cadre** MASC NOUN
1 frame
□ un cadre en bois a wooden frame
2 surroundings
□ L'hôtel est situé dans un très beau cadre. The hotel is set in beautiful surroundings.
3 executive
□ un cadre supérieur a senior executive

le **cafard** MASC NOUN
cockroach
■ **avoir le cafard** (*informal*) to be feeling down
□ J'ai le cafard. I'm feeling down.

le **café** MASC NOUN
1 coffee
□ un café au lait a white coffee □ un café crème a strong white coffee
2 café

> **DID YOU KNOW...?**
> Cafés in France sell both alcoholic and non-alcoholic drinks.

le **café-tabac** (PL les **cafés-tabacs**) MASC NOUN

> **DID YOU KNOW...?**
> A café-tabac is a bar which also sells cigarettes, lottery tickets and sometimes stamps; you can tell a café-tabac by the red diamond-shaped sign outside it.

la **cafétéria** FEM NOUN
cafeteria

la **cafetière** FEM NOUN
1 coffee maker
2 coffeepot

la **cage** FEM NOUN
cage
■ **la cage d'escalier** the stairwell

la **cagoule** FEM NOUN
balaclava

le **cahier** MASC NOUN
exercise book
□ mon cahier de brouillon my rough book

la **caille** FEM NOUN
quail

le **caillou** (PL les **cailloux**) MASC NOUN
pebble

la **caisse** FEM NOUN
1 box
□ une caisse à outils a tool box
2 till
□ le ticket de caisse the till receipt
3 checkout
□ J'ai dû faire la queue à la caisse. I had to queue at the checkout.

le **caissier** MASC NOUN
cashier

la **caissière** FEM NOUN
cashier

le **cake** MASC NOUN
fruit cake

le **calcul** MASC NOUN
1 calculation
□ Je me suis trompé dans mes calculs. I made a mistake in my calculations.
2 arithmetic
□ Je ne suis pas très bon en calcul. I'm not very good at arithmetic.

la **calculatrice** FEM NOUN
calculator

calculer VERB [28]
to work out
□ J'ai calculé combien ça allait coûter. I worked out how much it was going to cost.

la **calculette** FEM NOUN
pocket calculator

la **cale** FEM NOUN
wedge

calé (FEM **calée**) ADJECTIVE (*informal*)
■ **Elle est calée en histoire.** She's really good at history.

le **caleçon** MASC NOUN
boxer shorts

le **calendrier** MASC NOUN
calendar

le **calepin** MASC NOUN
notebook

caler VERB [28]
to stall
□ La voiture a calé dans une côte. The car stalled on a hill.

câlin (FEM **câline**) ADJECTIVE
▷ *see also* **câlin** NOUN
cuddly

le **câlin** MASC NOUN
▷ *see also* **câlin** ADJECTIVE
cuddle
□ faire un câlin à quelqu'un to give somebody a cuddle

le **calmant** MASC NOUN
tranquillizer

calme (FEM **calme**) ADJECTIVE
▷ *see also* **calme** NOUN
1 quiet
□ un endroit calme a quiet place
2 calm
□ Elle est restée très calme. She stayed very calm.

le **calme** MASC NOUN
▷ *see also* **calme** ADJECTIVE
peace and quiet

□ J'ai besoin de calme pour travailler. I need peace and quiet to work.

calmer VERB [28]
to soothe
□ Cette pommade calme les démangeaisons. This ointment soothes itching.
■ **se calmer** to calm down □ Calme-toi ! Calm down!

la **calorie** FEM NOUN
calorie

le/la **camarade** MASC/FEM NOUN
friend
■ **un camarade de classe** a school friend

le **cambriolage** MASC NOUN
burglary

cambrioler VERB [28]
to burgle

le **cambrioleur** MASC NOUN
burglar

la **cambrioleuse** FEM NOUN
burglar

la **camelote** FEM NOUN (informal)
junk
□ C'est vraiment de la camelote. It's absolute junk.

la **caméra** FEM NOUN
camera (cinema, TV)
■ **une caméra numérique** a digital camera

le **caméscope**® MASC NOUN
camcorder

le **camion** MASC NOUN
lorry

la **camionnette** FEM NOUN
van

le **camionneur** MASC NOUN
lorry driver

la **camomille** FEM NOUN
camomile tea

le **camp** MASC NOUN
camp
□ un camp de prisonniers a prison camp □ un camp de vacances a holiday camp

la **campagne** FEM NOUN
1 country
■ **à la campagne** in the country □ Nous passons nos vacances à la campagne. We spend our holidays in the country.
2 campaign
□ une campagne de marketing a marketing campaign

camper VERB [28]
to camp

le **campeur** MASC NOUN
camper

la **campeuse** FEM NOUN
camper

le **camping** MASC NOUN
camping
□ faire du camping to go camping
■ **un (terrain de) camping** a campsite

le **Canada** MASC NOUN
Canada
■ **au Canada** 1 in Canada 2 to Canada

canadien (FEM **canadienne**) ADJECTIVE, NOUN
Canadian
■ **un Canadien** a Canadian (man)
■ **une Canadienne** a Canadian (woman)

le **canal** (PL les **canaux**) MASC NOUN
canal

le **canapé** MASC NOUN
1 sofa
2 open sandwich

le **canard** MASC NOUN
duck

le **canari** MASC NOUN
canary

le **cancer** MASC NOUN
cancer
□ le cancer du poumon lung cancer
■ **le Cancer** Cancer □ Sabine est Cancer. Sabine's Cancer.

le **candidat** MASC NOUN
1 candidate (in exam, election)
2 applicant (for job)

la **candidate** FEM NOUN
1 candidate (in exam, election)
2 applicant (for job)

la **candidature** FEM NOUN
■ **poser sa candidature à un poste** to apply for a job □ Il a posé sa candidature à des dizaines de postes. He has applied for dozens of jobs.

le **caneton** MASC NOUN
duckling

la **canette** FEM NOUN
■ **une canette de bière** a small can of beer

le **caniche** MASC NOUN
poodle

la **canicule** FEM NOUN
scorching heat

le **canif** MASC NOUN
penknife

le **caniveau** (PL les **caniveaux**) MASC NOUN
gutter

la **canne** FEM NOUN
walking stick
■ **une canne à pêche** a fishing rod

la **cannelle** FEM NOUN
cinnamon

le **canoë** MASC NOUN
1 canoe
2 canoeing
□ faire du canoë to go canoeing

le canon MASC NOUN
1 gun
2 cannon

le canot MASC NOUN
dinghy
□ un canot pneumatique a rubber dinghy
■ un canot de sauvetage a lifeboat

la cantatrice FEM NOUN
opera singer

la cantine FEM NOUN
canteen

le caoutchouc MASC NOUN
rubber
■ des bottes en caoutchouc Wellington
boots

le cap MASC NOUN
cape (land)

capable (FEM capable) ADJECTIVE
■ Elle est capable de marcher pendant des
heures. She can walk for hours.
■ Il est capable de changer d'avis au
dernier moment. He's capable of changing his
mind at the last minute.

la cape FEM NOUN
cape (garment)

le capitaine MASC NOUN
captain

la capitale FEM NOUN
capital
□ la capitale de la France the capital of France

le capot MASC NOUN
bonnet (of car)

la capote FEM NOUN (informal)
condom

la câpre FEM NOUN
caper (food)

le caprice MASC NOUN
■ faire des caprices to make a fuss □ Il n'aime
pas les enfants qui font des caprices. He doesn't
like children who make a fuss.

capricieux (FEM capricieuse) ADJECTIVE
■ un enfant capricieux an awkward child

le Capricorne MASC NOUN
Capricorn
□ Hélène est Capricorne. Hélène's Capricorn.

captivant (FEM captivante) ADJECTIVE
fascinating

la captivité FEM NOUN
captivity
□ en captivité in captivity

capturer VERB [28]
to capture

la capuche FEM NOUN
hood
□ un manteau à capuche a coat with a hood
■ un pull à capuche a hoodie

le capuchon MASC NOUN
cap (of pen)

la capucine FEM NOUN
nasturtium

le car MASC NOUN
▷ see also **car** CONJUNCTION
coach
■ un car scolaire a school bus

car CONJUNCTION
▷ see also **car** NOUN
because
□ Réfléchis bien car c'est important. Think
carefully because it's important.

la carabine FEM NOUN
rifle

le caractère MASC NOUN
personality
□ Il a le même caractère que son père. He's got
the same personality as his father.
■ Il a bon caractère. He's good-natured.
■ Elle a mauvais caractère. She's bad-
tempered.
■ Il n'a pas un caractère facile. He isn't easy
to get on with.

caractéristique (FEM caractéristique)
ADJECTIVE
▷ see also **caractéristique** NOUN
characteristic

la caractéristique FEM NOUN
▷ see also **caractéristique** ADJECTIVE
characteristic

la carafe FEM NOUN
jug
□ une carafe d'eau a jug of water

les Caraïbes FEM PL NOUN
Caribbean Islands

le caramel MASC NOUN
1 caramel
□ la crème caramel crème caramel
2 toffee

la caravane FEM NOUN
caravan

carbonique (FEM carbonique) ADJECTIVE
■ le gaz carbonique carbon dioxide

le carburant MASC NOUN
fuel

cardiaque (FEM cardiaque) ADJECTIVE
■ une crise cardiaque a heart attack
■ Ma tante est cardiaque. My aunt has heart
trouble.

le cardigan MASC NOUN
cardigan

le/la cardiologue MASC/FEM NOUN
heart specialist

le carême MASC NOUN
Lent

la **caresse** FEM NOUN
stroke
▫ faire des caresses à un chat **to stroke a cat**

caresser VERB [28]
to stroke

la **carie** FEM NOUN
tooth decay
■ J'ai une carie. **I've got a hole in my tooth.**

caritatif (FEM **caritative**) ADJECTIVE
■ une association caritative **a charity**

le **carnaval** MASC NOUN
carnival

le **carnet** MASC NOUN
1 notebook
2 book
▫ un carnet d'adresses **an address book** ▫ un carnet de chèques **a cheque book** ▫ un carnet de timbres **a book of stamps** ▫ un carnet de tickets **a book of tickets**

> **DID YOU KNOW...?**
> In the Paris metro you can buy a virtual carnet of tickets for cheaper travel.

■ mon carnet de notes **my school report**

la **carotte** FEM NOUN
carrot
▫ les carottes râpées **grated carrots**

carré (FEM **carrée**) ADJECTIVE
▷ *see also* **carré** NOUN
square
■ un mètre carré **a square metre**

le **carré** MASC NOUN
▷ *see also* **carré** ADJECTIVE
square

le **carreau** (PL les **carreaux**) MASC NOUN
1 check
▫ une chemise à carreaux **a checked shirt**
2 tile (*on floor, wall*)
▫ des carreaux de terre cuite **terracotta tiles**
3 pane
▫ Il a cassé un carreau. **He broke a windowpane.**
4 diamonds (*cards*)
▫ l'as de carreau **the ace of diamonds**

le **carrefour** MASC NOUN
junction

le **carrelage** MASC NOUN
tiled floor

carrément ADVERB
1 completely
▫ C'est carrément impossible. **It's completely impossible.**
2 straight out
▫ Dis-lui carrément ce que tu penses. **Tell him straight out what you think.**

la **carrière** FEM NOUN
career
■ un militaire de carrière **a professional soldier**

la **carrure** FEM NOUN
build
▫ Il a une carrure d'athlète. **He has an athletic build.**

le **cartable** MASC NOUN
satchel

la **carte** FEM NOUN
1 card
■ une carte d'anniversaire **a birthday card**
■ une carte postale **a postcard**
■ une carte de vœux **a Christmas card**

> **DID YOU KNOW...?**
> The French send greetings cards (les cartes de vœux) in January rather than at Christmas, with best wishes for the New Year.

■ une carte de vœux électronique **an e-card**
■ une carte bancaire **a cash card**

> **DID YOU KNOW...?**
> Carte Bleue is a major French debit card.

■ une carte de crédit **a credit card**
■ une carte de fidélité **a loyalty card**
■ une carte d'embarquement **a boarding card**
■ une carte d'identité **an identity card**
■ une carte de séjour **a residence permit**
■ un jeu de cartes **1** a pack of cards **2** a card game
2 map
▫ une carte de France **a map of France** ▫ une carte routière **a road map**
3 menu
▫ la carte des vins **the wine list**
■ manger à la carte **to eat à la carte** ▫ Nous allons manger à la carte. **We'll choose from the à la carte menu.**

le **carton** MASC NOUN
1 cardboard
▫ un morceau de carton **a piece of cardboard**
2 cardboard box
■ un carton à chaussures **a shoe box**

la **cartouche** FEM NOUN
cartridge
■ une cartouche de cigarettes **a carton of cigarettes**

le **cas** (PL les **cas**) MASC NOUN
case
▫ plusieurs cas **several cases**
■ ne faire aucun cas de **to take no notice of**
■ en aucun cas **on no account**
■ en tout cas **at any rate**
■ au cas où **in case** ▫ Prends un sandwich au cas où la cantine serait fermée. **Take a sandwich in case the canteen's closed.**
■ en cas de **in case of** ▫ En cas d'incendie, appelez ce numéro. **In case of fire, call this number.**

la **cascade** FEM NOUN
waterfall

le **cascadeur** MASC NOUN
stuntman

la **case** FEM NOUN
1 square (in board game)
2 box (on form)

la **caserne** FEM NOUN
barracks

cash ADVERB
■ **payer cash** to pay cash

le **casier** MASC NOUN
locker

le **casque** MASC NOUN
1 helmet
2 headphones

la **casquette** FEM NOUN
cap

cassant (FEM **cassante**) ADJECTIVE
■ **Il m'a parlé d'un ton cassant.** He spoke to me curtly.

le **casse-croûte** (PL les **casse-croûte**, les **casse-croûtes**) MASC NOUN
snack

le **casse-noix** (PL les **casse-noix**) MASC NOUN
nutcrackers

casse-pieds (FEM+PL **casse-pieds**) ADJECTIVE (informal)
■ **Il est vraiment casse-pieds !** He's a real pain in the neck!

casser VERB [28]
to break
□ **J'ai cassé un verre.** I've broken a glass.
■ **se casser** to break □ **Il s'est cassé la jambe au ski.** He broke his leg when he was skiing.
■ **se casser la tête** (informal) to go to a lot of trouble □ **Ne te casse pas la tête pour le dîner.** Don't go to a lot of trouble over dinner.

la **casserole** FEM NOUN
saucepan

le **casse-tête** (PL les **casse-têtes**) MASC NOUN
■ **C'est un vrai casse-tête !** It's a real headache!

le **cassis** MASC NOUN
blackcurrant

le **castor** MASC NOUN
beaver

le **catalogue** MASC NOUN
catalogue

la **catastrophe** FEM NOUN
disaster

le **catch** MASC NOUN
wrestling

le **catéchisme** MASC NOUN
catechism

la **catégorie** FEM NOUN
category

catégorique (FEM **catégorique**) ADJECTIVE
firm
■ **un refus catégorique** a flat refusal

la **cathédrale** FEM NOUN
cathedral

catholique (FEM **catholique**) ADJECTIVE, NOUN
Catholic
■ **un catholique** a Catholic (man)
■ **une catholique** a Catholic (woman)

le **cauchemar** MASC NOUN
nightmare
□ **faire un cauchemar** to have a nightmare

la **cause** FEM NOUN
cause
■ **à cause de** because of □ **Je suis puni à cause de toi.** I've been punished because of you.

causer VERB [28]
1 to cause
□ **La tempête a causé beaucoup de dégâts.** The storm caused a lot of damage.
2 to chat
□ **Nous n'avons pas beaucoup eu le temps de causer.** We didn't have much time to chat.

la **caution** FEM NOUN
1 bail
2 deposit

le **cavalier** MASC NOUN
1 rider
2 partner (at dance)

la **cavalière** FEM NOUN
rider

la **cave** FEM NOUN
cellar

la **caverne** FEM NOUN
cave

le **CD** (PL les **CD**) MASC NOUN
CD

le **CDD** MASC NOUN (= contrat de durée déterminée)
temporary contract

le **CDI** MASC NOUN (= contrat de durée indeterminée)
permanent contract

le **CD-ROM** (PL les **CD-ROM**) MASC NOUN
CD-ROM

ce (FEM **cette**, PL **ces**) ADJECTIVE
▷ see also **ce** PRONOUN

> The masculine singular form **ce** changes to **cet** before a vowel and most words beginning with 'h'.

1 this
□ **Tu peux prendre ce livre.** You can take this book. □ **cet après-midi** this afternoon □ **cet hiver** this winter

- **ce livre-ci** this book
- **cette voiture-ci** this car

2 that

□ Je n'aime pas du tout ce film. I don't like that film at all.

- **ce livre-là** that book
- **cette voiture-là** that car

ce PRONOUN

▷ *see also* **ce** ADJECTIVE

> **ce** changes to **c'** before the vowel in **est, était** and **étaient**.

it

□ Ce n'est pas facile. It's not easy.

- **c'est 1** it is □ C'est vraiment trop cher. It's really too expensive. □ Ouvre, c'est moi ! Open the door, it's me! **2** he is □ C'est un peintre du début du siècle. He's a painter from the turn of the century. **3** she is □ C'est une actrice très célèbre. She's a very famous actress.
- **ce sont** they are □ Ce sont des amis de mes parents. They're friends of my parents.
- **Qui est-ce ?** Who is it?
- **Qu'est-ce que c'est ?** What is it?
- **ce qui** what □ C'est ce qui compte. That's what matters.
- **tout ce qui** everything that □ J'ai rangé tout ce qui traînait par terre. I've tidied up everything that was on the floor.
- **ce que** what □ Je vais lui dire ce que je pense. I'm going to tell him what I think.
- **tout ce que** everything □ Tu peux avoir tout ce que tu veux. You can have everything you want.

ceci PRONOUN

this

□ Prends ceci, tu en auras besoin. Take this, you'll need it.

céder VERB [34]

to give in

□ Elle a tellement insisté qu'il a fini par céder. She went on so much that he eventually gave in.

- **céder à** to give in to □ Je ne veux pas céder à ses caprices. I'm not going to give in to her whims.

le **cédérom** MASC NOUN

CD-ROM

la **cédille** FEM NOUN

cedilla

la **ceinture** FEM NOUN

belt

□ une ceinture en cuir a leather belt

- **une ceinture de sauvetage** a lifebelt
- **votre ceinture de sécurité** your seatbelt

cela PRONOUN

1 it

□ Cela dépend. It depends.

2 that

□ Je n'aime pas cela. I don't like that.

- **C'est cela.** That's right.
- **à part cela** apart from that

célèbre (FEM **célèbre**) ADJECTIVE

famous

célébrer VERB [34]

to celebrate

la **célébrité** FEM NOUN

celebrity

□ Il y avait quelques célébrités au concert. There were a few celebrities at the concert.

le **céleri** MASC NOUN

- **le céleri-rave** celeriac
- **le céleri (en branche)** celery

célibataire (FEM **célibataire**) ADJECTIVE

▷ *see also* **célibataire** NOUN

single

le/la **célibataire** MASC/FEM NOUN

▷ *see also* **célibataire** ADJECTIVE

single person

- **un célibataire** a bachelor
- **une célibataire** a single woman

celle PRONOUN ▷ *see* **celui**

celles PRONOUN ▷ *see* **ceux**

la **cellule** FEM NOUN

cell

celui (FEM **celle**, MASC PL **ceux**, FEM PL **celles**) PRONOUN

the one

□ Prends celui que tu préfères. Take the one you like best. □ Je n'ai pas d'appareil photo mais je peux emprunter celui de ma sœur. I haven't got a camera but I can borrow my sister's. □ Je n'ai pas de webcam mais je peux emprunter celle de mon frère. I haven't got a webcam but I can borrow my brother's.

- **celui-ci** this one
- **celle-ci** this one
- **celui-là** that one
- **celle-là** that one

la **cendre** FEM NOUN

ash

le **cendrier** MASC NOUN

ashtray

censé (FEM **censée**) ADJECTIVE

- **être censé faire quelque chose** to be supposed to do something □ Vous êtes censé arriver à l'heure. You're supposed to get here on time.

cent NUMBER

a hundred

□ cent euros a hundred euros

> **cent** is spelt with an -s when there are two or more hundreds, but not when it is followed by another number, as in 'four hundred and two'.

□ trois cents ans three hundred years □ cent deux kilomètres a hundred and two kilometres

□ trois cent cinquante kilomètres **three hundred and fifty kilometres** □ trois cent mille kilomètres **three hundred thousand kilometres**

la **centaine** FEM NOUN

about a hundred

□ Il y avait une centaine de personnes. **There were about a hundred people.**

■ **des centaines de** hundreds of □ Des centaines de réfugiés se sont présentés à l'ambassade. **Hundreds of refugees came to the embassy.**

le **centenaire** MASC NOUN

centenary

centième (FEM **centième**) ADJECTIVE

hundredth

le **centilitre** MASC NOUN

centilitre

le **centime** MASC NOUN

cent (*one hundredth of a euro*)

□ un centime d'euro **a euro cent**

> **DID YOU KNOW...?**
> The euro is divided into 100 **centimes**.

le **centimètre** MASC NOUN

centimetre

central (FEM **centrale**, MASC PL **centraux**) ADJECTIVE

central

la **centrale** FEM NOUN

power station

□ une centrale nucléaire **a nuclear power station**

le **centre** MASC NOUN

centre

■ **un centre commercial** a shopping centre

■ **un centre d'appels** a call centre

■ **un centre de recyclage** a recycling centre

le **centre-ville** (PL les **centres-villes**) MASC NOUN

town centre

cependant ADVERB

however

le **cercle** MASC NOUN

circle

□ Entourez d'un cercle la bonne réponse. **Put a circle round the right answer.**

■ **un cercle vicieux** a vicious circle

le **cercueil** MASC NOUN

coffin

la **céréale** FEM NOUN

cereal

□ un bol de céréales **a bowl of cereal**

■ **un pain aux cinq céréales** a multigrain loaf

la **cérémonie** FEM NOUN

ceremony

le **cerf** MASC NOUN

stag

le **cerf-volant** (PL les **cerfs-volants**) MASC NOUN

kite

la **cerise** FEM NOUN

cherry

le **cerisier** MASC NOUN

cherry tree

cerné (FEM **cernée**) ADJECTIVE

■ **avoir les yeux cernés** to have shadows under one's eyes □ Elle avait les yeux cernés. **She had shadows under her eyes.**

cerner VERB [28]

■ **J'ai du mal à le cerner.** I can't figure him out.

certain (FEM **certaine**) ADJECTIVE

1 certain

□ Je suis certain que je l'ai remis en place. **I'm certain that I put it back.** □ Ce n'est pas certain. **It's not certain.**

2 some

□ Certaines personnes n'aiment pas la crème. **Some people don't like cream.**

■ **un certain temps** quite some time □ Ça m'a pris un certain temps. **It took me quite some time.**

certainement ADVERB

1 definitely

□ C'est certainement le meilleur film que j'ai vu cette année. **It's definitely the best film I've seen this year.**

2 of course.

□ Est-ce que je peux t'emprunter ton stylo ? — Mais certainement ! **Can I borrow your pen? — Of course!**

certains (FEM **certaines**) PL PRONOUN

1 some

□ certains d'entre vous **some of you** □ certaines de ses amies **some of his friends**

2 some people

□ Certains pensent que le film est meilleur que le roman. **Some people think that the film is better than the novel.**

certes ADVERB

certainly

□ Nous nous connaissons, certes, mais nous ne sommes pas amis. **We know each other, certainly, but we are not friends.**

le **certificat** MASC NOUN

certificate

le **cerveau** (PL les **cerveaux**) MASC NOUN

brain

la **cervelle** FEM NOUN

brain

■ **se creuser la cervelle** (*informal*) to rack one's brains

le **CES** MASC NOUN (= *collège d'enseignement secondaire*)

secondary school

ces PL ADJECTIVE

1 these

□ Tu peux prendre ces photos si tu veux. **You can have these photos if you like.**
■ **ces photos-ci** these photos
2 those
□ Ces montagnes sont dangereuses en hiver. **Those mountains are dangerous in winter.**
■ **ces livres-là** those books

cesse
■ **sans cesse** ADVERB continually □ Elle me dérange sans cesse. She continually interrupts me.

cesser VERB [28]
to stop
□ **cesser de faire quelque chose** to stop doing something

le **cessez-le-feu** (PL les **cessez-le-feu**) MASC NOUN
ceasefire

c'est-à-dire ADVERB
that is
□ Nous partons lundi prochain, c'est-à-dire le quinze. We're leaving next Monday, that's the 15th.

cet ADJECTIVE ▷ see **ce**

cette ADJECTIVE ▷ see **ce**

ceux (FEM PL **celles**) PL PRONOUN
the ones
□ **Prends ceux que tu préfères.** Take the ones you like best. □ Je n'ai pas de skis mais je peux emprunter ceux de ma sœur. I haven't got any skis but I can borrow my sister's. □ Je n'ai pas de jumelles mais je peux emprunter celles de mon frère. I haven't got any binoculars but I can borrow my brother's.
■ **ceux-ci** these ones
■ **celles-ci** these ones
■ **ceux-là** those ones
■ **celles-là** those ones

chacun (FEM **chacune**) PRONOUN
1 each
□ Il nous a donné un cadeau à chacun. He gave us each a present. □ Nous avons chacune donné dix euros. We each gave 10 euros.
2 everyone
□ Chacun fait ce qu'il veut. Everyone does what they like.

le **chagrin** MASC NOUN
■ **avoir du chagrin** to be very upset □ Elle a eu beaucoup de chagrin à la mort de sa tante. She was terribly upset by the death of her aunt.

le **chahut** MASC NOUN
bedlam
□ Il y avait du chahut dans la classe. There was bedlam in the classroom.

la **chaîne** FEM NOUN
1 chain
□ **une chaîne en or** a gold chain

2 channel (on TV)
□ Le film passe sur quelle chaîne ? **Which channel is the film on?**
■ **une chaîne hi-fi** a hi-fi system
■ **une chaîne stéréo** a music centre
■ **travailler à la chaîne** to work on an assembly line

la **chair** FEM NOUN
flesh
■ **en chair et en os** in the flesh □ J'ai vu Kate Winslet en chair et en os. I saw Kate Winslet in the flesh.
■ **avoir la chair de poule** to have goose pimples

la **chaise** FEM NOUN
chair
■ **une chaise longue** a deckchair

le **châle** MASC NOUN
shawl

la **chaleur** FEM NOUN
1 heat
2 warmth

chaleureux (FEM **chaleureuse**) ADJECTIVE
warm
□ **un accueil chaleureux** a warm welcome

se **chamailler** VERB [28] (informal)
to squabble
□ Elle se chamaille sans cesse avec son frère. She's always squabbling with her brother.

la **chambre** FEM NOUN
1 bedroom
□ Il y a trois chambres. There are three bedrooms.
2 room
□ C'est la chambre de Camille. This is Camille's room.
■ **une chambre d'amis** a spare room
■ **une chambre simple** a single room
■ **une chambre pour une personne** a single room
■ **une chambre double** a double room
■ **une chambre pour deux personnes** a double room
■ **une chambre de famille** a family room
■ « **Chambres d'hôte** » 'Bed and Breakfast'

le **chameau** (PL les **chameaux**) MASC NOUN
camel

le **champ** MASC NOUN
field

le **champagne** MASC NOUN
champagne

le **champignon** MASC NOUN
mushroom
□ **une omelette aux champignons** a mushroom omelette
■ **un champignon de Paris** a button mushroom

le **champion** MASC NOUN
champion

le **championnat** MASC NOUN
championship
□ le championnat du monde the world
championship

la **championne** FEM NOUN
champion

la **chance** FEM NOUN
1 luck
 ■ **Bonne chance !** Good luck!
 ■ **par chance** luckily
 ■ **avoir de la chance** to be lucky □ Tu as de la
 chance de partir au soleil ! You're lucky, going off
 to the sun!
2 chance
 □ Il n'a aucune chance. He's got no chance. □ Il
 a des chances de réussir son examen. He's got a
 good chance of passing his exam.

le **change** MASC NOUN
exchange
□ le taux de change the exchange rate

le **changement** MASC NOUN
change
□ Il n'aime pas le changement. He doesn't like
change.
 ■ **le changement climatique** climate change

changer VERB [45]
to change
□ Il n'a pas beaucoup changé. He hasn't
changed much. □ J'ai changé les draps ce matin.
I changed the sheets this morning. □ J'ai changé
trois cents euros. I changed 300 euros.
 ■ **se changer** to get changed □ Je vais me
 changer avant de sortir. I'm going to get changed
 before I go out.
 ■ **changer de** to change □ Je change de
 chaussures et j'arrive ! I'll change my shoes and
 then I'll be ready!
 ■ **changer d'avis** to change one's mind
 □ Appelle-moi si tu changes d'avis. Give me a
 ring if you change your mind.
 ■ **changer de chaîne** to change the channel

la **chanson** FEM NOUN
song

le **chant** MASC NOUN
singing
□ des cours de chant singing lessons
 ■ **un chant de Noël** a Christmas carol

le **chantage** MASC NOUN
blackmail
□ faire du chantage à quelqu'un to blackmail
somebody

chanter VERB [28]
to sing

le **chanteur** MASC NOUN
singer

la **chanteuse** FEM NOUN
singer

le **chantier** MASC NOUN
building site

la **chantilly** FEM NOUN
sweetened whipped cream

chantonner VERB [28]
to hum

le **chapeau** (PL les **chapeaux**) MASC NOUN
hat

la **chapelle** FEM NOUN
chapel

le **chapitre** MASC NOUN
chapter

chaque (FEM **chaque**) ADJECTIVE
1 every
 □ chaque année every year
2 each
 □ Ces verres coûtent cinq euros chaque. These
 glasses cost 5 euros each.

le **char** MASC NOUN
tank (military)

le **charabia** MASC NOUN (informal)
gibberish
□ Je n'y comprends rien : c'est du charabia.
I don't understand any of it: it's gibberish.

la **charade** FEM NOUN
1 riddle
2 charade
 □ jouer aux charades to play charades

le **charbon** MASC NOUN
coal
 ■ **le charbon de bois** charcoal

la **charcuterie** FEM NOUN
1 pork butcher's

> **DID YOU KNOW...?**
> A **charcuterie** sells cuts of pork and pork
> products such as sausages, salami and
> pâté, as well as various cooked dishes and
> salads.

2 cold meats

le **charcutier** MASC NOUN
pork butcher

la **charcutière** FEM NOUN
pork butcher

le **chardon** MASC NOUN
thistle

charger VERB [45]
to load
 ■ **charger quelqu'un de faire quelque
 chose** to tell somebody to do something □ Paul
 m'a chargé de vous dire que la clé est sous le
 paillasson. Paul told me to tell you that the key's
 under the mat.

le **chargeur** MASC NOUN
charger

le **chariot** MASC NOUN
trolley (at supermarket)

charmant (FEM **charmante**) ADJECTIVE
charming

le **charme** MASC NOUN
charm

charmer VERB [28]
to charm

la **charrue** FEM NOUN
plough

la **chasse** FEM NOUN
1 hunting
  □ un chien de chasse a hunting dog
2 shooting
  □ la chasse au canard duck shooting
  ■ tirer la chasse d'eau to flush the toilet

le **chasse-neige** (PL les **chasse-neiges**,
les **chasse-neige**) MASC NOUN
snowplough

chasser VERB [28]
1 to hunt
  □ Mon père chasse le lapin. My father hunts
  rabbits.
2 to chase away
  □ Ils ont chassé les cambrioleurs. They chased
  away the robbers.
3 to get rid of
  □ Ouvre donc la fenêtre pour chasser les odeurs
  de cuisine. Open the window to get rid of the
  cooking smells.

le **chasseur** MASC NOUN
hunter

le **chat** MASC NOUN
1 cat
  ■ appeler un chat un chat to call a spade a
  spade
2 chat

This word has two pronunciations. **chat**
meaning **cat** is pronounced 'shah', and the
internet one is pronounced the same as in
English.

la **châtaigne** FEM NOUN
chestnut

le **châtaignier** MASC NOUN
chestnut tree

châtain (FEM **châtain**, PL **châtains**) ADJECTIVE
brown
  □ J'ai les cheveux châtains. I've got brown hair.

le **château** (PL les **châteaux**) MASC NOUN
1 castle
  ■ un château fort a castle
2 palace
  □ le château de Versailles the palace of
  Versailles

le **chaton** MASC NOUN
kitten

chatouiller VERB [28]
to tickle

chatouilleux (FEM **chatouilleuse**) ADJECTIVE
ticklish

la **chatte** FEM NOUN
cat (female)

chatter VERB [28]
to chat (on the internet)

chaud (FEM **chaude**) ADJECTIVE
1 warm
  □ des vêtements chauds warm clothes
  ■ avoir chaud to be warm □ J'ai assez chaud.
  I'm warm enough.
2 hot
  □ Il fait chaud aujourd'hui. It's hot today. □ un
  plat chaud a hot dish □ Attention, c'est chaud !
  Mind, it's hot! □ J'ai trop chaud ! I'm too hot!

le **chauffage** MASC NOUN
heating
  □ Le chauffage est en panne. The heating isn't
  working.
  ■ le chauffage central central heating

le **chauffe-eau** (PL les **chauffe-eau**, les
chauffe-eaux) MASC NOUN
water heater

chauffer VERB [28]
to heat
  □ Je vais mettre de l'eau à chauffer pour faire
  du thé. I'm going to heat some water to
  make tea.

le **chauffeur** MASC NOUN
driver
  □ un chauffeur de taxi a taxi driver

le **chaume** MASC NOUN
  ■ un toit de chaume a thatched roof

la **chaussée** FEM NOUN
road surface
  □ « Attention ! Chaussée déformée » 'Uneven
  road surface'

chausser VERB [28]
  ■ Vous chaussez du combien ? What size
  shoe do you take?

la **chaussette** FEM NOUN
sock

le **chausson** MASC NOUN
slipper
  ■ un chausson aux pommes an apple turnover

la **chaussure** FEM NOUN
shoe
  ■ les chaussures de ski ski boots

chauve (FEM **chauve**) ADJECTIVE
bald

la **chauve-souris** (PL les **chauves-souris**)
FEM NOUN
bat (animal)

c

le chef MASC NOUN

1 head
  □ le chef de famille the head of the family
  ■ **le chef de l'État** the Head of State

2 boss
  □ Je dois demander la permission à mon chef.
  I have to get permission from my boss.
  ■ **un chef d'entreprise** a company director

3 chef
  □ la spécialité du chef the chef's speciality
  ■ **un chef d'orchestre** a conductor

le chef-d'œuvre (PL les **chefs-d'œuvre**)
MASC NOUN
  masterpiece

la cheffe FEM NOUN

1 head
  ■ **la cheffe de l'État** the Head of State

2 boss
  □ J'ai une réunion avec ma cheffe. I have a
  meeting with my boss.

3 chef
  □ Elle est cheffe dans un restaurant célèbre.
  She's a chef in a famous restaurant.

le chemin MASC NOUN

1 path
  □ un chemin de montagne a mountain path

2 way
  □ Quel est le chemin le plus court pour aller
  à l'aéroport ? What's the quickest way to the
  airport?
  ■ **en chemin** on the way □ Je mangerai mon
  sandwich en chemin. I'll eat my sandwich on
  the way.
  ■ **le chemin de fer** the railway

la cheminée FEM NOUN

1 chimney
2 fireplace

la chemise FEM NOUN

1 shirt
  □ une chemise à carreaux a checked shirt
  ■ **une chemise de nuit** a nightdress

2 folder
  □ une chemise en plastique a plastic folder

le chemisier MASC NOUN
  blouse

le chêne MASC NOUN
  oak
  □ une armoire en chêne an oak wardrobe

le chenil MASC NOUN
  kennels

la chenille FEM NOUN
  caterpillar

le chèque MASC NOUN
  cheque
  ■ **les chèques de voyage** traveller's
  cheques

le chéquier MASC NOUN
  cheque book

cher (FEM **chère**) ADJECTIVE, ADVERB

1 dear
  □ Chère Mélusine ... Dear Mélusine ...

2 expensive
  □ C'est trop cher. It's too expensive. □ coûter
  cher to be expensive

chercher VERB [28]

1 to look for
  □ Je cherche mes clés. I'm looking for my keys.

2 to look up
  □ chercher un mot dans le dictionnaire to look
  up a word in the dictionary
  ■ **aller chercher** 1 to go to get □ Elle est allée
  chercher du pain. She's gone to get some bread.
  2 to pick up □ J'irai te chercher à la gare. I'll pick
  you up at the station.

le chercheur MASC NOUN
  scientist

la chercheuse FEM NOUN
  scientist

chère FEM ADJECTIVE ▷ see **cher**

chéri (FEM **chérie**) ADJECTIVE
  ▷ see also **chéri** NOUN, **chérie** NOUN
  darling
  □ ma petite fille chérie my darling daughter

le chéri MASC NOUN
  ▷ see also **chéri** ADJECTIVE
  darling
  ■ **mon chéri** darling

la chérie FEM NOUN
  ▷ see also **chéri** ADJECTIVE
  darling
  ■ **ma chérie** darling

le cheval (PL les **chevaux**) MASC NOUN
  horse
  ■ **un cheval de course** a racehorse
  ■ **à cheval** on horseback
  ■ **faire du cheval** to go riding

le chevalier MASC NOUN
  knight

la chevalière FEM NOUN
  signet ring

chevalin (FEM **chevaline**) ADJECTIVE
  ■ **une boucherie chevaline** a horsemeat
  butcher's

les chevaux MASC PL NOUN ▷ see **cheval**

le chevet MASC NOUN
  ■ **une table de chevet** a bedside table
  ■ **une lampe de chevet** a bedside lamp

les cheveux MASC PL NOUN
  hair *sing*
  □ Elle a les cheveux courts. She's got short hair.

la cheville FEM NOUN
  ankle
  □ Il s'est foulé la cheville. He sprained his ankle.

la **chèvre** FEM NOUN
goat
■ le fromage de chèvre goat's cheese

le **chevreau** (PL les **chevreaux**) MASC NOUN
kid (*animal, leather*)

le **chèvrefeuille** MASC NOUN
honeysuckle

le **chevreuil** MASC NOUN
1 roe deer
2 venison
□ un rôti de chevreuil roast venison

le **chewing-gum** MASC NOUN
chewing gum

chez PREPOSITION
■ chez Pierre 1 at Pierre's house 2 to Pierre's house
■ chez moi 1 at my house □ Mes amis sont restés chez moi. My friends stayed at my house. 2 to my house □ Allons chez moi. Let's go to my house.
■ Je rentre chez moi. I'm going home.
■ chez le dentiste 1 at the dentist's □ J'ai rendez-vous chez le dentiste demain matin. I've got an appointment at the dentist's tomorrow morning. 2 to the dentist's □ Je vais chez le dentiste. I'm going to the dentist's.

chic (FEM+PL chic) ADJECTIVE
1 smart
□ une tenue chic a smart outfit
2 nice
□ C'est chic de ta part de m'avoir invité. (*informal*) It was nice of you to invite me.

la **chicorée** FEM NOUN
endive

le **chien** MASC NOUN
dog
■ « Attention, chien méchant » 'Beware of the dog'

la **chienne** FEM NOUN
bitch (*dog*)

le **chiffon** MASC NOUN
cloth

chiffonner VERB [28]
to crease
□ Ma robe est toute chiffonnée. My dress is all creased.

le **chiffre** MASC NOUN
figure
□ en chiffres ronds in round figures
■ les chiffres romains Roman numerals

le **chignon** MASC NOUN
bun (*in hair*)
□ Elle s'est fait un chignon. She put her hair in a bun.

le **Chili** MASC NOUN
Chile

la **chimie** FEM NOUN
chemistry
□ un cours de chimie a chemistry lesson

chimique (FEM chimique) ADJECTIVE
chemical
□ une réaction chimique a chemical reaction
■ les produits chimiques chemicals

la **Chine** FEM NOUN
China

chinois (FEM chinoise) ADJECTIVE, NOUN
Chinese
□ Il apprend le chinois. He's learning Chinese.
■ un Chinois a Chinese (*man*)
■ une Chinoise a Chinese (*woman*)
■ les Chinois the Chinese

le **chiot** MASC NOUN
puppy

les **chips** FEM PL NOUN
crisps
□ un paquet de chips a packet of crisps

chirurgical (FEM chirurgicale, MASC PL chirurgicaux) ADJECTIVE
■ une intervention chirurgicale an operation

la **chirurgie** FEM NOUN
surgery
■ la chirurgie esthétique plastic surgery

le **chirurgien** MASC NOUN
surgeon

le **choc** MASC NOUN
shock
□ Ça m'a fait un sacré choc de le voir comme ça. It gave me a terrible shock to see him in that state.
■ Elle est encore sous le choc. She's still in shock.

le **chocolat** MASC NOUN
chocolate
■ un chocolat chaud a hot chocolate
■ le chocolat à croquer dark chocolate
■ le chocolat au lait milk chocolate

le **chœur** MASC NOUN
choir

choisir VERB [38]
to choose

le **choix** MASC NOUN
1 choice
■ avoir le choix to have the choice
2 selection
□ Il n'y a pas beaucoup de choix dans ce magasin. There's not a very wide selection of things in this shop.

le **chômage** MASC NOUN
unemployment
■ être au chômage to be unemployed

le **chômeur** MASC NOUN
unemployed person
□ Il est chômeur. He's unemployed.

c

c

la **chômeuse** FEM NOUN
unemployed woman
□ Elle est chômeuse. She's unemployed.

choquer VERB [28]
to shock
□ Cette remarque m'a choqué. I was shocked by that remark.

la **chorale** FEM NOUN
choir

la **chose** FEM NOUN
thing
□ J'ai des tas de choses à te raconter. I've got loads of things to tell you.
■ C'est peu de chose. It's nothing really.

le **chou** (PL les **choux**) MASC NOUN
cabbage
■ les choux de Bruxelles Brussels sprouts
■ un chou à la crème a choux bun

le **chouchou** MASC NOUN (informal)
teacher's pet

la **chouchoute** FEM NOUN (informal)
teacher's pet

la **choucroute** FEM NOUN
sauerkraut (with sausages and ham)

la **chouette** FEM NOUN
▷ see also **chouette** ADJECTIVE
owl

chouette (FEM **chouette**) ADJECTIVE (informal)
▷ see also **chouette** NOUN
brilliant
□ Chouette alors ! Brilliant!

le **chou-fleur** (PL les **choux-fleurs**) MASC NOUN
cauliflower

chrétien (FEM **chrétienne**) ADJECTIVE
Christian
□ Il est chrétien. He's a Christian.

le **Christ** MASC NOUN
Christ

chronologique (FEM **chronologique**) ADJECTIVE
chronological

le **chronomètre** MASC NOUN
stopwatch

chronométrer VERB [34]
to time

le **chrysanthème** MASC NOUN
chrysanthemum

DID YOU KNOW...?
Chrysanthemums are strongly associated with funerals in France and it is customary to lay them on graves on All Saints' Day (1 November). Because of this association they are never given as gifts.

chuchoter VERB [28]
to whisper

chut EXCLAMATION
shh!

la **chute** FEM NOUN
fall
■ faire une chute to fall
■ une chute d'eau a waterfall
■ la chute des cheveux hair loss
■ les chutes de neige snowfalls

Chypre NOUN
Cyprus

-ci ADVERB
■ ce livre-ci this book
■ ces bottes-ci these boots

la **cible** FEM NOUN
target

la **ciboulette** FEM NOUN
chives

la **cicatrice** FEM NOUN
scar

se **cicatriser** VERB [28]
to heal up
□ Cette plaie s'est vite cicatrisée. This wound has healed up quickly.

ci-contre ADVERB
opposite
□ la page ci-contre the opposite page

ci-dessous ADVERB
below
□ la photo ci-dessous the picture below

ci-dessus ADVERB
above

le **cidre** MASC NOUN
cider

le **ciel** MASC NOUN
1 sky
□ un ciel nuageux a cloudy sky
2 heaven
□ être au ciel to be in heaven

le **cierge** MASC NOUN
candle (in church)

la **cigale** FEM NOUN
cicada

le **cigare** MASC NOUN
cigar
□ Il fume le cigare. He smokes cigars.

la **cigarette** FEM NOUN
cigarette

la **cigogne** FEM NOUN
stork

ci-joint ADVERB
attached
□ Veuillez trouver ci-joint mon curriculum vitae. Please find attached my CV.

le **cil** MASC NOUN
eyelash

le **ciment** MASC NOUN
cement

le **cimetière** MASC NOUN
cemetery

le/la **cinéaste** MASC/FEM NOUN
film-maker

le **cinéma** MASC NOUN
cinema

cinq NUMBER
five
□ Il est cinq heures du matin. It's five in the morning. □ Il a cinq ans. He's five.
■ **le cinq février** the fifth of February

la **cinquantaine** FEM NOUN
about fifty
□ Il y avait une cinquantaine de personnes. There were about fifty people there.
■ **Il a la cinquantaine.** He's in his fifties.

cinquante NUMBER
fifty
□ Il a cinquante ans. He's fifty.
■ **cinquante et un** fifty-one
■ **cinquante-deux** fifty-two

cinquième (FEM **cinquième**) ADJECTIVE
▷ see also **cinquième** NOUN
fifth
□ au cinquième étage on the fifth floor

la **cinquième** FEM NOUN
▷ see also **cinquième** ADJECTIVE
year 8
□ Mon frère est en cinquième. My brother's in year 8.

DID YOU KNOW...?
In French secondary schools, years are counted from the **sixième** (youngest) to **première** and **terminale** (oldest).

le **cintre** MASC NOUN
coat hanger

le **cirage** MASC NOUN
shoe polish

circonflexe (FEM **circonflexe**) ADJECTIVE
■ **un accent circonflexe** a circumflex

la **circonstance** FEM NOUN
circumstance
□ dans les circonstances actuelles in the present circumstances

la **circulation** FEM NOUN
1 traffic
□ Il y avait beaucoup de circulation. There was a lot of traffic.
2 circulation
□ Elle a des problèmes de circulation. She has bad circulation.

circuler VERB [28]
to run

□ Il n'y a qu'un bus sur trois qui circule. Only one bus in three is running.

la **cire** FEM NOUN
wax

le **ciré** MASC NOUN
oilskin jacket

cirer VERB [28]
to polish (shoes, floor)

le **cirque** MASC NOUN
circus

les **ciseaux** MASC PL NOUN
■ **une paire de ciseaux** a pair of scissors

le **citadin** MASC NOUN
city dweller

la **citation** FEM NOUN
quotation

la **cité** FEM NOUN
estate
□ J'habite dans une cité. I live on an estate.
■ **une cité universitaire** halls of residence
■ **une cité-dortoir** a dormitory town

citer VERB [28]
to quote

le **citoyen** MASC NOUN
citizen

la **citoyenne** FEM NOUN
citizen

la **citoyenneté** FEM NOUN
citizenship

le **citron** MASC NOUN
lemon
■ **un citron vert** a lime
■ **un citron pressé** a freshly squeezed lemon juice

la **citronnade** FEM NOUN
still lemonade

la **citrouille** FEM NOUN
pumpkin

le **civet** MASC NOUN
stew
□ du civet de lapin rabbit stew

civil (FEM **civile**) ADJECTIVE
civilian
■ **en civil** in civilian clothes

la **civilisation** FEM NOUN
civilization

civique (FEM **civique**) ADJECTIVE
■ **l'instruction civique** citizenship

clair (FEM **claire**) ADJECTIVE, ADVERB
1 light
□ vert clair light green □ C'est une pièce très claire. It's a very light room.
2 clear (water)
■ **voir clair** to see clearly
■ **le clair de lune** moonlight

clairement ADVERB
clearly

la **clairière** FEM NOUN
clearing

clandestin (FEM **clandestine**) ADJECTIVE
■ un passager clandestin a stowaway

la **claque** FEM NOUN
slap
□ Elle m'a donné une claque. She gave me a slap.

claquer VERB [28]
1 to bang
□ On entend des volets qui claquent. You can hear shutters banging.
2 to slam
□ Elle est partie en claquant la porte. She left, slamming the door behind her.

les **claquettes** FEM PL NOUN
■ faire des claquettes to tap-dance

la **clarinette** FEM NOUN
clarinet

la **classe** FEM NOUN
1 class
□ C'est la meilleure élève de la classe. She's the best pupil in the class. □ voyager en première classe to travel first class
2 classroom

classer VERB [28]
to arrange
□ Les livres sont classés par ordre alphabétique. The books are arranged in alphabetical order.

le **classeur** MASC NOUN
ring binder

classique (FEM **classique**) ADJECTIVE
1 classical
□ de la musique classique classical music
2 classic
□ un style classique a classic style

le **clavier** MASC NOUN
keyboard (of computer, typewriter)

la **clé** FEM NOUN
1 key
□ une clé de voiture a car key
2 clef
□ la clé de sol the treble clef □ la clé de fa the bass clef
■ une clé USB a USB stick

la **clef** FEM NOUN = **clé**

le **client** MASC NOUN
customer

la **cliente** FEM NOUN
customer

la **clientèle** FEM NOUN
customers

cligner VERB [28]
■ cligner des yeux to blink

le **clignotant** MASC NOUN
indicator
□ Il a mis son clignotant à gauche. He's indicating left.

le **climat** MASC NOUN
climate

climatique (FEM **climatique**) ADJECTIVE
climate
■ le réchauffement climatique global warming

la **climatisation** FEM NOUN
air conditioning

climatisé (FEM **climatisée**) ADJECTIVE
air-conditioned
□ L'hôtel est climatisé. The hotel is air-conditioned.

le **clin d'œil** (PL les **clins d'œil**) MASC NOUN
wink
■ en un clin d'œil in a flash

la **clinique** FEM NOUN
private hospital

cliquer VERB [28]
to click
□ cliquer sur une icône to click on an icon

le **clochard** MASC NOUN
tramp

la **cloche** FEM NOUN
bell

le **clocher** MASC NOUN
1 church tower
2 steeple

le **clone** MASC NOUN
clone

cloner VERB [28]
to clone

le **clou** MASC NOUN
nail
■ un clou de girofle a clove

le **clown** MASC NOUN
clown

le **club** MASC NOUN
club

le **cobaye** MASC NOUN
guinea pig

le **coca** MASC NOUN
Coke®

la **coccinelle** FEM NOUN
ladybird

cocher VERB [28]
to tick
□ Cochez la bonne réponse. Tick the right answer.

cochon (FEM **cochonne**) ADJECTIVE (informal)
▷ see also cochon NOUN
dirty
□ une histoire cochonne a dirty story

le **cochon** MASC NOUN
▷ *see also* **cochon** ADJECTIVE
pig
■ **un cochon d'Inde** a guinea pig

le **cocktail** MASC NOUN
1 cocktail
2 cocktail party

le **coco** MASC NOUN
■ **une noix de coco** a coconut

cocorico EXCLAMATION
1 cock-a-doodle-doo!
2 three cheers for France!

> **DID YOU KNOW...?**
> The symbol of France is the cockerel and so **cocorico !** is sometimes used as an expression of French national pride.

la **cocotte** FEM NOUN
casserole (*pan*)
■ **une cocotte-minute**® a pressure cooker

le **code** MASC NOUN
code (*also computing*)
■ **le code de la route** the highway code
■ **le code postal** the postcode

coder VERB [28]
to code (*computing*)

le **cœur** MASC NOUN
heart
■ **avoir bon cœur** to be kind-hearted
■ **la dame de cœur** the queen of hearts
■ **avoir mal au cœur** to feel sick
■ **par cœur** by heart □ **apprendre quelque chose par cœur** to learn something by heart

le **coffre** MASC NOUN
1 boot (*of car*)
2 chest (*furniture*)

le **coffre-fort** (PL les **coffres-forts**) MASC NOUN
safe

le **coffret** MASC NOUN
■ **un coffret à bijoux** a jewellery box

le **cognac** MASC NOUN
brandy

se **cogner** VERB [28]
■ **se cogner à quelque chose** to bang into something □ Je me suis cogné à la table. I banged into the table. □ Je me suis cogné la tête contre la porte du placard. I banged my head on the cupboard door.

coiffé (FEM **coiffée**) ADJECTIVE
■ **Tu es bien coiffée.** Your hair looks nice.

coiffer VERB [28]
■ **se coiffer** to do one's hair
■ **se faire coiffer** to have one's hair done

le **coiffeur** MASC NOUN
hairdresser

la **coiffeuse** FEM NOUN
hairdresser

la **coiffure** FEM NOUN
hairstyle
□ Cette coiffure te va bien. That hairstyle suits you.
■ **un salon de coiffure** a hairdresser's

le **coin** MASC NOUN
corner
□ au coin de la rue on the corner of the street
■ **Tu habites dans le coin ?** Do you live near here?
■ **Je ne suis pas du coin.** I'm not from here.
■ **le bistrot du coin** the local pub

> **BE CAREFUL!**
> The French word **coin** does not mean **coin**.

coincé (FEM **coincée**) ADJECTIVE
1 stuck
□ La clé est coincée dans la serrure. The key is stuck in the keyhole.
2 stuffy
□ Il est un peu coincé. (*informal*) He's a bit stuffy.

coincer VERB [12]
to jam
□ La porte est coincée. The door's jammed.

la **coïncidence** FEM NOUN
coincidence

le **col** MASC NOUN
1 collar
2 pass (*of mountain*)

la **colère** FEM NOUN
anger
■ **Je suis en colère.** I'm angry.
■ **se mettre en colère** to get angry

le **colin** MASC NOUN
hake

la **colique** FEM NOUN
diarrhoea

le **colis** MASC NOUN
parcel

collaborer VERB [28]
to collaborate

collant (FEM **collante**) ADJECTIVE
▷ *see also* **collant** NOUN
1 sticky
2 clingy
□ Je le trouve un peu collant. (*informal*) I find him a bit clingy.

le **collant** MASC NOUN
▷ *see also* **collant** ADJECTIVE
tights
□ un collant en laine woollen tights

la **colle** FEM NOUN
1 glue
□ un tube de colle a tube of glue
2 detention
□ J'ai une heure de colle samedi prochain. I've got an hour's detention next Saturday.

■ Je n'en sais rien : tu me poses une colle.
I really don't know: you've got me there.

la **collecte** FEM NOUN
collection (*of money*)
□ On a fait une collecte au profit des victimes.
There was a collection for the victims.

la **collection** FEM NOUN
collection
□ une collection de timbres a stamp collection

collectionner VERB [28]
to collect

le **collège** MASC NOUN
secondary school

DID YOU KNOW...?
In France, pupils go to a **collège** between the ages of 11 and 15, and then to a **lycée** until the age of 18.

le **collégien** MASC NOUN
schoolboy

la **collégienne** FEM NOUN
schoolgirl

le/la **collègue** MASC/FEM NOUN
colleague

coller VERB [28]
1 to stick
□ Il y a un chewing-gum collé sous la chaise.
There's a bit of chewing gum stuck under the chair. □ Ce timbre ne colle plus. This stamp won't stick on.
2 to press
□ J'ai collé mon oreille au mur. I pressed my ear against the wall.

le **collier** MASC NOUN
1 necklace
□ un collier de perles a pearl necklace
2 collar (*of dog, cat*)

la **colline** FEM NOUN
hill

la **collision** FEM NOUN
crash

la **colombe** FEM NOUN
dove

la **colonie** FEM NOUN
■ aller en colonie de vacances to go to summer camp

la **colonne** FEM NOUN
column
■ la colonne vertébrale the spine

le **colorant** MASC NOUN
colouring

le **coloris** MASC NOUN
colour

le **coma** MASC NOUN
coma
□ être dans le coma to be in a coma

le **combat** MASC NOUN
fighting
□ Les combats ont repris ce matin. Fighting started again this morning.
■ un combat de boxe a boxing match

le **combattant** MASC NOUN
■ un ancien combattant a war veteran

combattre VERB [9]
to fight

combien ADVERB
1 how much
□ Vous en voulez combien ? Un kilo ? How much do you want? One kilo? □ C'est combien ? How much is that? □ Combien est-ce que ça coûte ? How much does it cost? □ Combien ça fait ? How much does it come to?
2 how many
□ Tu en veux combien ? Deux ? How many do you want? Two?
■ **combien de** 1 how much □ Combien de purée est-ce que je vous sers ? How much mashed potato shall I give you? 2 how many □ Combien de personnes as-tu invitées ? How many people have you invited?
■ **combien de temps** how long □ Combien de temps est-ce que tu seras absente ? How long will you be away?
■ **Il y a combien de temps ?** How long ago? □ Il est parti il y a combien de temps ? How long ago did he leave?
■ **On est le combien aujourd'hui ? — On est le vingt.** What's the date today? — It's the 20th.

la **combinaison** FEM NOUN
1 combination
□ J'ai changé la combinaison de mon antivol.
I've changed the combination on my bike lock.
2 slip (*petticoat*)
■ une combinaison de plongée a wetsuit
■ une combinaison de ski a ski suit

le **comble** MASC NOUN
■ **Alors ça, c'est le comble !** That's the last straw!

la **comédie** FEM NOUN
comedy
■ une comédie musicale a musical

le **comédien** MASC NOUN
actor

la **comédienne** FEM NOUN
actress

comestible (FEM **comestible**) ADJECTIVE
edible

comique (FEM **comique**) ADJECTIVE
▷ *see also* **comique** NOUN
comical

le/la **comique** MASC/FEM NOUN
▷ *see also* **comique** ADJECTIVE
comedian

le **comité** MASC NOUN
committee

le **commandant** MASC NOUN
captain (*of ship*, *plane*)

la **commande** FEM NOUN
order
□ un bon de commande an order form
■ être aux commandes to be at the controls

commander VERB [28]
1 to order
□ J'ai commandé une robe sur Internet. I've
ordered a dress on the internet.
2 to give orders
□ C'est moi qui commande ici, pas vous ! I give
the orders here, not you!
■ commander à quelqu'un de faire quelque
chose to order someone to do something

comme CONJUNCTION, ADVERB
1 like
□ Il est comme son père. He's like his father.
□ Je voudrais un manteau comme celui de la
photo. I'd like a coat like the one in the picture.
2 for
□ Qu'est-ce que tu veux comme dessert ? What
would you like for dessert?
3 as
□ J'ai travaillé comme serveuse cet été. I worked
as a waitress this summer. □ Faites comme vous
voulez. Do as you like.
■ comme ça like this □ Ça se plie comme ça.
You fold it like this.
■ C'était un poisson grand comme ça. The
fish was this big.
■ comme il faut properly □ Mets le couvert
comme il faut ! Set the table properly!
■ Comme tu as grandi ! How you've grown!
■ Regarde comme c'est beau ! Look, isn't it
lovely!
■ comme ci comme ça so-so □ Comment est-
ce que tu as trouvé le film ? — Comme ci comme
ça. What did you think of the film? — So-so.

le **commencement** MASC NOUN
beginning

commencer VERB [12]
to start
□ Les cours commencent à huit heures. Lessons
start at 8 o'clock.
■ commencer à faire (quelque chose) to
start to do (something) □ Il a commencé à
pleuvoir. It started raining. □ J'ai commencé à
réviser pour les examens. I've started revising for
the exams.

comment ADVERB
how
□ Comment arrives-tu à travailler dans ce bruit ?
How can you possibly work with this noise?
■ Comment allez-vous ? How are you?
■ Comment dit-on « pomme » en anglais ?

How do you say 'pomme' in English?
■ Comment s'appelle-t-il ? What's his name?
■ Comment ? What did you say?

le **commentaire** MASC NOUN
comment

les **commérages** MASC PL NOUN
gossip *sing*

le **commerçant** MASC NOUN
shopkeeper

le **commerce** MASC NOUN
1 trade
□ le commerce extérieur foreign trade
■ le commerce électronique e-commerce
2 business
□ Il fait des études de commerce. He's studying
business.
3 shop
□ tenir un commerce to have a shop
■ On trouve ça dans le commerce. You can
find it in the shops.

commercial (FEM **commerciale**, MASC PL
commerciaux) ADJECTIVE
■ un centre commercial a shopping centre

commettre VERB [47]
to commit
□ Il a commis un crime grave. He has committed
a serious crime.

le/la **commissaire** MASC/FEM NOUN
police superintendent

le **commissariat** MASC NOUN
police station

les **commissions** FEM PL NOUN
shopping *sing*
□ J'ai quelques commissions à faire. I've got
some shopping to do.

la **commode** FEM NOUN
▷ *see also* **commode** ADJECTIVE
chest of drawers

commode (FEM **commode**) ADJECTIVE
▷ *see also* **commode** NOUN
handy
□ Ce sac est très commode pour les voyages.
This bag is very handy for travelling.
■ Son père n'est pas commode. His father is
a difficult character.

commun (FEM **commune**) ADJECTIVE
shared
□ une salle de bain commune a shared
bathroom
■ Nous avons des intérêts communs. We
have interests in common.
■ en commun in common □ Ils n'ont rien en
commun. They've got nothing in common.
■ les transports en commun public transport
■ mettre quelque chose en commun to
share something □ Nous mettons tous nos
livres en commun. We share all our books.

C

la **communauté** FEM NOUN
community

la **communication** FEM NOUN
communication
- **une communication téléphonique** a
telephone call

la **communion** FEM NOUN
communion
□ faire sa première communion to make one's
first communion

communiquer VERB [28]
to communicate

communiste (FEM **communiste**) ADJECTIVE
communist
□ le Parti communiste the Communist Party

compact (FEM **compacte**) ADJECTIVE
compact
- **un disque compact** a compact disc

la **compagne** FEM NOUN
1 companion
2 partner (living together)

la **compagnie** FEM NOUN
company
□ J'aime avoir de la compagnie. I like to have
company. □ Je viendrai te tenir compagnie. I'll
come to keep you company.
- **une compagnie d'assurances** an insurance
company
- **une compagnie aérienne** an airline

le **compagnon** MASC NOUN
1 companion
2 partner (living together)

la **comparaison** FEM NOUN
comparison
□ en comparaison de in comparison with

comparer VERB [28]
to compare

le **compartiment** MASC NOUN
compartment (on train)

le **compas** MASC NOUN
compass (for drawing circles)

compatible (FEM **compatible**) ADJECTIVE
compatible

la **compétence** FEM NOUN
1 competence
2 skill
□ les compétences clés pour cet emploi the key
skills for this job

compétent (FEM **compétente**) ADJECTIVE
competent

compétitif (FEM **compétitive**) ADJECTIVE
competitive

la **compétition** FEM NOUN
competition
- **avoir l'esprit de compétition** to be
competitive

complet (FEM **complète**) ADJECTIVE
▷ see also **complet** NOUN
1 complete
□ les œuvres complètes de Shakespeare the
complete works of Shakespeare
2 full
□ L'hôtel est complet. The hotel is full.
- **« complet »** 'no vacancies'
- **le pain complet** wholemeal bread

le **complet** MASC NOUN
▷ see also **complet** ADJECTIVE
suit (for man)

complètement ADVERB
completely
□ J'avais complètement oublié que tu venais.
I'd completely forgotten that you were coming.

compléter VERB [34]
to complete
□ Complétez les phrases suivantes. Complete
the following sentences.

complexe (FEM **complexe**) ADJECTIVE
complex

complexé (FEM **complexée**) ADJECTIVE
hung up

la **complication** FEM NOUN
complication

le/la **complice** MASC/FEM NOUN
accomplice

le **compliment** MASC NOUN
compliment
- **faire un compliment** to compliment
□ Il m'a fait un compliment sur ma robe. He
complimented me on my dress.

compliqué (FEM **compliquée**) ADJECTIVE
complicated
□ C'est une histoire compliquée. It's a
complicated story.

le **complot** MASC NOUN
plot

le **comportement** MASC NOUN
behaviour

comporter VERB [28]
1 to consist of
□ Le château comporte trois parties. The castle
consists of three parts.
2 to have
□ Ce modèle comporte un écran couleur. This
model has a colour screen.
- **se comporter** to behave □ Il s'est comporté
de façon odieuse. He behaved atrociously.

composer VERB [28]
to compose (music, text)
- **composer un numéro** to dial a number
- **se composer de** to consist of □ L'uniforme
se compose d'une veste, d'un pantalon et
d'une cravate. The uniform consists of a jacket,
trousers and a tie.

le **compositeur** MASC NOUN
composer

la **composition** FEM NOUN
test
□ Nous avons une composition de français cet après-midi. We've got a French test this afternoon.

la **compositrice** FEM NOUN
composer

le **compostage** MASC NOUN
date stamping

composter VERB [28]
to punch
□ N'oublie pas de composter ton billet. Remember to punch your ticket.

la **compote** FEM NOUN
stewed fruit
■ **la compote de prunes** stewed plums

compréhensible (FEM **compréhensible**) ADJECTIVE
understandable

compréhensif (FEM **compréhensive**) ADJECTIVE
understanding

> **BE CAREFUL!**
> **compréhensif** does not mean **comprehensive**.

la **compréhension** FEM NOUN
1 comprehension
□ la compréhension orale listening comprehension
2 sympathy
□ Elle a fait preuve de beaucoup de compréhension à mon égard. She showed a lot of sympathy for me.

comprendre VERB [65]
1 to understand
□ Je ne comprends pas ce que vous dites. I don't understand what you're saying.
2 to include
□ Le forfait ne comprend pas la location des skis. The price doesn't include ski hire.

le **comprimé** MASC NOUN
tablet
■ **un comprimé d'aspirine** an aspirin

compris (FEM **comprise**) ADJECTIVE
included
□ Le service n'est pas compris. Service is not included.
■ **y compris** including □ Ils ont tout vendu, y compris leur voiture. They sold everything, including their car.
■ **non compris** excluding □ un menu à vingt euros, vin non compris a set menu for 20 euros, excluding wine
■ **cent euros tout compris** 100 euros all-inclusive

compromettre VERB [47]
to compromise

le **compromis** MASC NOUN
compromise
□ Ils sont parvenus à un compromis. They came to a compromise.

la **comptabilité** FEM NOUN
accounting
□ un cours de comptabilité a course in accounting

le/la **comptable** MASC/FEM NOUN
accountant
□ Il est comptable. He's an accountant.

comptant ADVERB
■ **payer comptant** to pay cash

le **compte** MASC NOUN
account
□ J'ai déposé le chèque sur mon compte. I've paid the cheque into my account.
■ **Le compte est bon.** That's the right amount.
■ **tenir compte de 1** to take into account □ Ils ont tenu compte de mon expérience. They took my experience into account. **2** to take notice of □ Il n'a pas tenu compte de mes conseils. He took no notice of my advice.
■ **travailler à son compte** to be self-employed
■ **en fin de compte** all things considered
□ Le voyage ne s'est pas mal passé, en fin de compte. The journey wasn't bad, all things considered.

compter VERB [28]
to count

le **compte rendu** (PL les **comptes rendus**) MASC NOUN
report

le **compteur** MASC NOUN
meter

le **comptoir** MASC NOUN
bar
□ au comptoir at the bar

se **concentrer** VERB [28]
to concentrate
□ J'ai du mal à me concentrer. I find it hard to concentrate.

la **conception** FEM NOUN
design

concernant PREPOSITION
regarding
□ Concernant notre nouveau projet, je voudrais ajouter que … Regarding our new project, I would like to add that …

concerner VERB [28]
to concern
□ en ce qui me concerne as far as I'm concerned
■ **Je ne me sens pas concerné.** I don't feel it's anything to do with me.

le concert MASC NOUN
concert

le/la concierge MASC/FEM NOUN
caretaker

conclure VERB [13]
to conclude

la conclusion FEM NOUN
conclusion

le concombre MASC NOUN
cucumber

concorder VERB [28]
to tally
□ Les dates concordent. The dates tally.

le concours MASC NOUN
1 competition
□ un concours de chant a singing competition
2 competitive exam (*for a job or a place in a school*)

concret (FEM **concrète**) ADJECTIVE
concrete

conçu VERB
designed
□ Ces appartements sont très mal conçus.
These flats are very badly designed.

la concurrence FEM NOUN
competition
□ La concurrence est vive sur ce marché.
There's a lot of competition in this market.

le concurrent MASC NOUN
competitor

la concurrente FEM NOUN
competitor

condamner VERB [28]
1 to sentence
□ Il a été condamné à deux ans de prison.
He was sentenced to two years in prison.
□ condamner à mort to sentence to death
2 to condemn
□ Le gouvernement a condamné cette décision.
The government condemned this decision.

la condition FEM NOUN
condition
□ Je le ferai à une condition ... I'll do it, on one
condition ...
■ **à condition que** provided that □ Je viendrai
à condition qu'il me le demande. I'll come
provided he asks me to.
■ **les conditions de travail** working
conditions

le conditionnel MASC NOUN
conditional tense

le conducteur MASC NOUN
driver

BE CAREFUL!
The French word **conducteur** does not mean
conductor.

la conductrice FEM NOUN
driver

conduire VERB [23]
to drive
□ Est-ce que tu sais conduire ? Can you drive?
□ Je te conduirai chez le docteur. I'll drive you to
the doctor's.
■ **se conduire** to behave □ Il s'est mal conduit.
He behaved badly.

la conduite FEM NOUN
behaviour

la conférence FEM NOUN
1 lecture
□ donner une conférence to give a lecture
2 conference
□ une conférence internationale an
international conference

se confesser VERB [28]
to go to confession

les confettis MASC PL NOUN
confetti

la confiance FEM NOUN
1 trust
■ **avoir confiance en quelqu'un** to trust
somebody □ Je n'ai pas confiance en lui. I don't
trust him.
■ **faire confiance à quelqu'un** to trust
somebody □ Tu ne me fais pas confiance ? Don't
you trust me?
2 confidence
■ **Tu peux avoir confiance. Il sera à l'heure.**
You don't need to worry. He'll be on time.
■ **confiance en soi** self-confidence □ Elle
manque de confiance en elle. She lacks self-
confidence.

confiant (FEM **confiante**) ADJECTIVE
confident

les confidences FEM PL NOUN
■ **faire des confidences à quelqu'un** to
confide in someone □ Elle me fait quelquefois
des confidences. She sometimes confides in me.

confidentiel (FEM **confidentielle**) ADJECTIVE
confidential

confier VERB [19]
■ **se confier à quelqu'un** to confide in
somebody □ Elle s'est confiée à sa meilleure
amie. She confided in her best friend.

le confinement MASC NOUN
lockdown (*of city, country*)

confirmer VERB [28]
to confirm

la confiserie FEM NOUN
sweet shop

confisquer VERB [28]
to confiscate

confit (FEM **confite**) ADJECTIVE
■ **des fruits confits** crystallized fruits

la **confiture** FEM NOUN
jam
▢ la confiture de fraises strawberry jam
■ **la confiture d'oranges** marmalade

le **conflit** MASC NOUN
conflict

confondre VERB [69]
to mix up
▢ On le confond souvent avec son frère.
People often mix him up with his brother.

le **confort** MASC NOUN
comfort
■ **tout confort** with all mod cons ▢ un
appartement tout confort a flat with all mod cons

confus (FEM **confuse**) ADJECTIVE
1 unclear
▢ J'ai trouvé ses explications confuses. I thought
his explanation was unclear.
2 embarrassed
▢ Il avait l'air confus. He looked embarrassed.

la **confusion** FEM NOUN
1 confusion
2 embarrassment
▢ rougir de confusion to go red with
embarrassment

le **congé** MASC NOUN
holiday
▢ une semaine de congé a week's holiday
■ **en congé** on holiday ▢ Je serai en congé la
semaine prochaine. I'll be on holiday next week.
■ **un congé de maladie** sick leave ▢ Il est en
congé de maladie. He's on sick leave.

le **congélateur** MASC NOUN
freezer

congeler VERB [1]
to freeze

la **conjonction** FEM NOUN
conjunction

la **conjonctivite** FEM NOUN
conjunctivitis

la **conjugaison** FEM NOUN
conjugation

connais VERB ▷ see **connaître**

la **connaissance** FEM NOUN
1 knowledge
▢ ... pour approfondir vos connaissances ... to
increase your knowledge
2 acquaintance
▢ Ce n'est pas vraiment une amie, juste une
connaissance. She's not really a friend, just an
acquaintance.
■ **perdre connaissance** to lose consciousness
■ **faire la connaissance de quelqu'un** to

meet somebody ▢ J'ai fait la connaissance de
son frère. I met her brother.

connaît VERB ▷ see **connaître**

connaître VERB [14]
to know
▢ Je ne connais pas du tout cette région. I don't
know this area at all. ▢ Je le connais de vue.
I know him by sight.
■ **Ils se sont connus à Nantes.** They first met
in Nantes.
■ **s'y connaître en quelque chose** to know
about something ▢ Je ne m'y connais pas
beaucoup en musique classique. I don't know
much about classical music.

connecté (FEM **connectée**) ADJECTIVE
online (computer)

se **connecter** VERB [28]
to log on
▢ Je me suis connecté sur Internet il y a dix minutes.
I logged onto the internet ten minutes ago.

connu (FEM **connue**) ADJECTIVE
▷ see also **connu** VERB
well-known
▢ C'est un acteur connu. He's a well-known
actor.

connu VERB ▷ see **connaître**
▷ see also **connu** ADJECTIVE
■ **Je l'ai connu autrefois.** I knew him once.

conquérir VERB [2]
to conquer

consacrer VERB [28]
to devote
▢ Il consacre beaucoup de temps à ses enfants.
He devotes a lot of time to his children.
■ **Je suis désolé, je n'ai pas beaucoup de
temps à vous consacrer.** I'm afraid I can't
spare much time for you.

la **conscience** FEM NOUN
conscience
▢ avoir mauvaise conscience to have a guilty
conscience
■ **prendre conscience de** to become aware of
▢ Ils ont fini par prendre conscience de la gravité
de la situation. They eventually became aware of
the seriousness of the situation.

consciencieux (FEM **consciencieuse**)
ADJECTIVE
conscientious

conscient (FEM **consciente**) ADJECTIVE
conscious

consécutif (FEM **consécutive**) ADJECTIVE
consecutive

le **conseil** MASC NOUN
advice
▢ Est-ce que je peux te demander conseil ? Can I
ask you for some advice?
■ **un conseil** a piece of advice

conseiller VERB [28]
▷ *see also* **conseiller** NOUN
1 to advise
  □ Il a été mal conseillé. He has been badly advised.
  ■ **conseiller à quelqu'un de faire quelque chose** to advise someone to do do something □ Elle lui a conseillé de se reposer. She advised him to take a rest.
2 to recommend
  □ Il m'a conseillé ce livre. He recommended this book to me.

le **conseiller** MASC NOUN
  ▷ *see also* **conseiller** VERB
1 councillor (*political*)
  □ un conseiller municipal a town councillor
2 adviser
  □ le conseiller d'orientation the careers adviser

le **consentement** MASC NOUN
  consent
  □ le consentement des parents the parents' consent

consentir VERB [77]
  to agree
  □ consentir à quelque chose to agree to something

la **conséquence** FEM NOUN
  consequence
  ■ **en conséquence** consequently

conséquent (FEM **conséquente**) ADJECTIVE
  ■ **par conséquent** consequently

le **conservatoire** MASC NOUN
  school of music
  □ Elle fait du piano au conservatoire. She's learning the piano at the school of music.

la **conserve** FEM NOUN
  tin
  □ Je vais ouvrir une conserve. I'll open a tin.
  ■ **une boîte de conserve** a tin
  ■ **les conserves** tinned food □ Il n'est pas bon de manger tous les jours des conserves. It's not healthy to eat tinned food every day.
  ■ **en conserve** tinned □ des petits pois en conserve tinned peas

conserver VERB [28]
  to keep
  □ J'ai conservé toutes ses lettres. I've kept all her letters.
  ■ **se conserver** to keep □ Ce pain se conserve plus d'une semaine. This bread will keep for more than a week.

considérable (FEM **considérable**) ADJECTIVE
  considerable
  □ Il a fait des progrès considérables. He's made considerable progress.

la **considération** FEM NOUN
  ■ **prendre quelque chose en considération** to take something into consideration

considérer VERB [34]
  ■ **considérer que** to believe that □ Je considère que le gouvernement devrait investir davantage dans l'éducation. I believe that the government should invest more money in education.

la **consigne** FEM NOUN
  left-luggage office
  ■ **une consigne automatique** a left-luggage locker

consistant (FEM **consistante**) ADJECTIVE
  substantial
  □ un petit déjeuner consistant a substantial breakfast

consister VERB [28]
  ■ **consister à** to consist of □ Mon travail consiste à répondre au téléphone et à recevoir les clients. My job consists of answering the phone and welcoming the customers.
  ■ **En quoi consiste votre travail ?** What does your job involve?

la **console de jeu** FEM NOUN
  games console

consoler VERB [28]
  to console

le **consommateur** MASC NOUN
1 consumer
2 customer (*in café*)

la **consommation** FEM NOUN
1 consumption
  □ la consommation d'électricité electricity consumption
2 drink
  □ Le billet d'entrée donne droit à une consommation gratuite. The ticket entitles you to one free drink.

la **consommatrice** FEM NOUN
1 consumer
2 customer (*in café*)

consommer VERB [28]
1 to use
  □ Ces grosses voitures consomment beaucoup d'essence. These big cars use a lot of petrol.
2 to have a drink
  □ Est-ce qu'on peut consommer à la terrasse ? Can we have drinks outside?

la **consonne** FEM NOUN
  consonant

constamment ADVERB
  constantly
  □ Elle se plaint constamment. She's constantly complaining.

constant (FEM **constante**) ADJECTIVE
  constant

constater VERB [28]
  to notice

constipé (FEM **constipée**) ADJECTIVE
  constipated

constitué (FEM **constituée**) ADJECTIVE
- **être constitué de** to consist of

constituer VERB [28]
to make up
□ les États qui constituent la Fédération russe the states which make up the Russian Federation

la construction FEM NOUN
building
□ des matériaux de construction building materials
- **une maison en construction** a house being built

construire VERB [23]
to build
□ Ils font construire une maison neuve. They're having a new house built.

le consulat MASC NOUN
consulate
□ le consulat de France the French consulate

la consultation FEM NOUN
- **les heures de consultation** surgery hours

consulter VERB [28]
1 to consult
□ Il vaut toujours mieux consulter un médecin. It's always best to consult a doctor.
2 to see patients
□ Le docteur ne consulte pas le samedi. The doctor doesn't see patients on Saturdays.

le contact MASC NOUN
contact
□ les contacts humains human contact
- **Il a le contact facile.** He's very approachable.
- **garder le contact avec quelqu'un** to keep in touch with somebody
- **le paiement sans contact** contactless payment

contacter VERB [28]
to get in touch with
□ Je te contacterai dès que j'aurai des nouvelles. I'll get in touch with you as soon as I have some news.

contagieux (FEM **contagieuse**) ADJECTIVE
infectious
□ une maladie contagieuse an infectious disease □ Je suis peut-être contagieux. I might have something infectious.

contaminer VERB [28]
to contaminate

le conte de fées (PL les **contes de fées**) MASC NOUN
fairy tale

contempler VERB [28]
to gaze at

contemporain (FEM **contemporaine**) ADJECTIVE
contemporary
- **un auteur contemporain** a modern writer

contenir VERB [83]
to contain
□ un portefeuille contenant de l'argent a wallet containing money

content (FEM **contente**) ADJECTIVE
glad
□ Je suis content que tu sois venu. I'm glad you've come.
- **content de** pleased with □ Elle est contente de mon travail. She is pleased with my work.

contenter VERB [28]
to please
□ Il est difficile à contenter. He's hard to please.
- **Je me contente de peu.** I can make do with very little.

le contenu MASC NOUN
1 contents
□ le contenu de la boîte the contents of the box
2 content
□ le contenu du message the content of the message

contesté (FEM **contestée**) ADJECTIVE
controversial
□ Cette décision est très contestée. This is a very controversial decision.

le contexte MASC NOUN
context

le continent MASC NOUN
continent

continu (FEM **continue**) ADJECTIVE
continuous
- **faire la journée continue** to work without taking a full lunch break

continuellement ADVERB
constantly

continuer VERB [28]
to carry on
□ Continuez sans moi ! Carry on without me!
□ Il ne veut pas continuer ses études. He doesn't want to carry on studying.
- **continuer à faire quelque chose** to go on doing something □ Ils ont continué à regarder la télé sans me dire bonjour. They went on watching TV without saying hello to me.
- **continuer de faire quelque chose** to keep on doing something □ Il continue de fumer malgré son asthme. He keeps on smoking, despite his asthma.

contourner VERB [28]
to go round
□ La route contourne la ville. The road goes round the town.

le contraceptif MASC NOUN
contraceptive

la contraception FEM NOUN
contraception

le **contractuel** MASC NOUN
traffic warden

la **contractuelle** FEM NOUN
traffic warden

la **contradiction** FEM NOUN
contradiction
- **par esprit de contradiction** just to be
awkward □ Il a refusé de venir par esprit de
contradiction. He refused to come, just to be
awkward.

le **contraire** MASC NOUN
opposite
□ Il a fait le contraire de ce que je lui avais
demandé. He did the opposite of what I asked
him.
- **au contraire** on the contrary

contrarier VERB [19]
1 to annoy
□ Il avait l'air contrarié. He looked annoyed.
2 to upset
□ Est-ce que tu serais contrariée si je ne venais
pas ? Would you be upset if I didn't come?

le **contraste** MASC NOUN
contrast

le **contrat** MASC NOUN
contract
□ un contrat de travail an employment contract

la **contravention** FEM NOUN
parking ticket

contre PREPOSITION
1 against
□ Ne mets pas ton vélo contre le mur. Don't
put your bike against the wall. □ Tu es pour ou
contre ce projet ? Are you for or against this
plan?
2 for
□ échanger quelque chose contre quelque
chose to swap something for something
- **par contre** on the other hand

la **contrebande** FEM NOUN
smuggling
- **des produits de contrebande** smuggled
goods

la **contrebasse** FEM NOUN
double bass

contrecœur
- **à contrecœur** ADVERB reluctantly □ Il est
venu à contrecœur. He came reluctantly.

contredire VERB [27]
to contradict
□ Il ne supporte pas d'être contredit. He can't
stand being contradicted.

la **contre-indication** FEM NOUN
- « Contre-indication en cas d'eczéma »
'Not to be used by people with eczema'

le **contresens** MASC NOUN
mistranslation

le **contretemps** MASC NOUN
- Désolé d'être en retard : j'ai eu un
contretemps. Sorry I'm late: I was held up.

contribuer VERB [28]
- **contribuer à** to contribute to □ Est-ce que tu
veux contribuer au cadeau pour Marie ? Do you
want to contribute to Marie's present?

le **contrôle** MASC NOUN
1 control
□ le contrôle des passeports passport control
2 check
□ un contrôle d'identité an identity check
- **le contrôle des billets** ticket inspection
3 test
□ un contrôle antidopage a drugs test
- **le contrôle continu** continuous assessment

contrôler VERB [28]
to check
□ Personne n'a contrôlé mon billet. Nobody
checked my ticket.

le **contrôleur** MASC NOUN
ticket inspector

la **contrôleuse** FEM NOUN
ticket inspector

controversé (FEM **controversée**) ADJECTIVE
controversial

convaincre VERB [86]
1 to persuade
□ Il a essayé de me convaincre de rester. He
tried to persuade me to stay.
2 to convince
□ Tu n'as pas l'air convaincu. You don't look
convinced.

la **convalescence** FEM NOUN
convalescence

convenable (FEM **convenable**) ADJECTIVE
decent
□ un hôtel convenable a decent hotel
- **Ce n'est pas convenable.** It's bad manners.

convenir VERB [89]
- **convenir à** to suit □ Est-ce que cette date te
convient ? Does this date suit you? □ J'espère
que cela vous conviendra. I hope this will suit you.
- **convenir de** to agree on □ Nous avons
convenu d'une date. We've agreed on a date.

conventionné (FEM **conventionnée**)
ADJECTIVE
- **un médecin conventionné** a Health Service
doctor

> **DID YOU KNOW...?**
> All doctors in France charge for treatment,
> but patients of Health Service doctors
> get most of their money refunded by the
> government.

convenu (FEM **convenue**) ADJECTIVE
agreed
□ au moment convenu at the agreed time

la **conversation** FEM NOUN
conversation

la **convocation** FEM NOUN
notification

convoquer VERB [28]
■ **convoquer quelqu'un à une réunion**
to invite somebody to a meeting
■ **Le directeur m'a convoqué dans son bureau.** The headteacher asked me into his office.

cool (FEM+PL **cool**) ADJECTIVE (*informal*)
cool

la **coopération** FEM NOUN
co-operation

coopérer VERB [34]
to co-operate

les **coordonnées** FEM PL NOUN
contact details
□ As-tu ses coordonnées ? Do you have his contact details?

le **copain** MASC NOUN (*informal*)
1 friend
□ C'est un bon copain. He's a good friend.
2 boyfriend
□ Elle a un copain. She's got a boyfriend.

la **copie** FEM NOUN
1 copy
□ Ce tableau n'est qu'une copie. This picture is only a copy.
2 paper
□ Il a des copies à corriger ce week-end. He's got some papers to mark this weekend.

copier VERB [19]
1 to copy
2 to burn (*CD, DVD*)
■ **copier-coller** to copy and paste

copieux (FEM **copieuse**) ADJECTIVE
hearty
□ un repas copieux a hearty meal

la **copine** FEM NOUN (*informal*)
1 friend
□ Je sors avec une copine ce soir. I'm going out with a friend tonight.
2 girlfriend
□ Il a une copine. He's got a girlfriend.

le **coq** MASC NOUN
cockerel

la **coque** FEM NOUN
hull (*of boat*)
■ **un œuf à la coque** a soft-boiled egg

le **coquelicot** MASC NOUN
poppy

la **coqueluche** FEM NOUN
whooping cough

le **coquillage** MASC NOUN
1 shellfish
2 shell

□ Nous avons ramassé des coquillages sur la plage. We picked up some shells on the beach.

la **coquille** FEM NOUN
shell
■ **une coquille d'œuf** an eggshell
■ **une coquille Saint-Jacques** a scallop

coquin (FEM **coquine**) ADJECTIVE
cheeky
□ Il m'a regardé d'un air coquin. He gave me a cheeky look.

le **cor** MASC NOUN
horn
□ Je joue du cor. I play the horn.

le **corbeau** (PL les **corbeaux**) MASC NOUN
crow

la **corbeille** FEM NOUN
1 basket
□ une corbeille de fruits a basket of fruit
2 recycle bin (*of a computer*)
■ **une corbeille à papier** a wastepaper basket

la **corde** FEM NOUN
1 rope
2 string (*of violin, tennis racket*)
■ **une corde à linge** a clothes line
■ **il pleut des cordes** it's bucketing down

la **cordonnerie** FEM NOUN
shoe repair shop

le **cordonnier** MASC NOUN
cobbler

coriace (FEM **coriace**) ADJECTIVE
tough

la **corne** FEM NOUN
horn

la **cornemuse** FEM NOUN
bagpipes
□ jouer de la cornemuse to play the bagpipes

le **cornet** MASC NOUN
■ **un cornet de frites** a bag of chips
■ **un cornet de glace** an ice cream cone

le **cornichon** MASC NOUN
gherkin

la **Cornouailles** FEM NOUN
Cornwall

le **coronavirus** MASC NOUN
coronavirus

le **corps** MASC NOUN
body

correct (FEM **correcte**) ADJECTIVE
1 correct
□ Ce n'est pas tout à fait correct. That's not quite correct.
2 reasonable
□ un salaire correct a reasonable salary □ Le repas était tout à fait correct. The meal was quite reasonable.

C

correction - couchette

la correction FEM NOUN
correction

la correspondance FEM NOUN
1 correspondence
  ■ **un cours par correspondance** a correspondence course
2 connection (*train, plane*)
  □ Il y a une correspondance pour Toulouse à dix heures. There's a connection for Toulouse at ten o'clock.

le correspondant MASC NOUN
penfriend

la correspondante FEM NOUN
penfriend

correspondre VERB [69]
to correspond
  ■ **Faites correspondre les phrases.** Match the sentences together.

le corridor MASC NOUN
corridor

corriger VERB [45]
to mark
  □ Vous pouvez corriger mon test ? Can you mark my test?

le corsage MASC NOUN
blouse

la Corse FEM NOUN
Corsica

corse (FEM **corse**) ADJECTIVE, NOUN
Corsican
  ■ **un Corse** a Corsican (*man*)
  ■ **une Corse** a Corsican (*woman*)

la corvée FEM NOUN
chore
  □ Quelle corvée ! What a chore!

costaud (FEM **costaude**) ADJECTIVE
brawny

le costume MASC NOUN
1 suit (*man's*)
  □ Il porte toujours un costume. He always wears a suit.
2 costume (*theatre*)
  □ de superbes costumes superb costumes

la côte FEM NOUN
1 coastline
  □ La route longe la côte. The road follows the coastline.
  ■ **la Côte d'Azur** the French Riviera
2 hill
  □ J'ai grimpé la côte. I went up the hill.
3 rib
  □ Il s'est cassé une côte en tombant. He broke a rib when he fell.
4 chop
  □ une côte de porc a pork chop
  ■ **une côte de bœuf** a rib of beef
  ■ **côte à côte** side by side

le côté MASC NOUN
side
  ■ **à côté de** 1 next to □ Le café est à côté du sucre. The coffee's next to the sugar. 2 next door to □ Il habite à côté de chez moi. He lives next door to me.
  ■ **de l'autre côté** on the other side □ La pharmacie est de l'autre côté de la rue. The chemist's is on the other side of the street.
  ■ **de chaque côté** □ Il y avait des voitures garées de chaque côté de la rue. There were cars parked on both sides of the street.
  ■ **De quel côté est-il parti ?** Which way did he go?
  ■ **mettre quelque chose de côté** to save something □ J'ai mis de l'argent de côté. I've saved some money.
  ■ **d'un côté … de l'autre côté** on the one hand … on the other hand

la côtelette FEM NOUN
chop
  □ une côtelette d'agneau a lamb chop

la cotisation FEM NOUN
1 subscription (*to club, union*)
2 contributions (*to pension, national insurance*)
  ■ **cotisations sociales** social security contributions

le coton MASC NOUN
cotton
  □ une chemise en coton a cotton shirt
  ■ **le coton hydrophile** cotton wool

le Coton-tige® (PL les **Cotons-tiges**) MASC NOUN
cotton bud

le cou MASC NOUN
neck

couchant ADJECTIVE
  ■ **le soleil couchant** the setting sun

la couche FEM NOUN
1 layer
  □ la couche d'ozone the ozone layer
2 coat (*of paint, varnish*)
3 nappy

couché (FEM **couchée**) ADJECTIVE
1 lying down
  □ Il était couché sur le tapis. He was lying on the carpet.
2 in bed
  □ Il est déjà couché. He's already in bed.

le coucher MASC NOUN
  ▷ see also **coucher** VERB
  ■ **un coucher de soleil** a sunset

se coucher VERB [28]
  ▷ see also **coucher** NOUN
1 to go to bed
  □ Je me suis couché tard hier soir. I went to bed late last night.
2 to set (*sun*)

la couchette FEM NOUN
1 couchette (*on train*)
2 bunk (*on boat*)

le **coude** MASC NOUN
elbow

coudre VERB [15]
1 to sew
□ J'aime coudre. I like sewing.
2 to sew on
□ Il ne sait même pas coudre un bouton. He can't even sew a button on.

la **couette** FEM NOUN
duvet

les **couettes** FEM PL NOUN
bunches
□ la petite fille avec les couettes the little girl with her hair in bunches

couler VERB [28]
1 to run
□ Ne laissez pas couler les robinets. Don't leave the taps running. □ J'ai le nez qui coule. My nose is running.
2 to flow
□ La rivière coulait lentement. The river was flowing slowly.
3 to leak
□ Mon stylo coule. My pen's leaking.
4 to sink
□ Le bateau a coulé. The boat sank.

la **couleur** FEM NOUN
colour
□ De quelle couleur est leur voiture ? What colour is their car? □ une pellicule couleur a colour film
■ **Tu as pris des couleurs.** You've got a tan.

la **couleuvre** FEM NOUN
grass snake

les **coulisses** FEM PL NOUN
wings (in theatre)
■ **dans les coulisses** behind the scenes

le **couloir** MASC NOUN
corridor

le **coup** MASC NOUN
1 knock
□ donner un coup à quelque chose to give something a knock
2 blow
■ **Il m'a donné un coup !** He hit me!
■ **un coup de pied** a kick
■ **un coup de poing** a punch
3 shock
□ Ça m'a fait un coup de le voir comme ça ! (informal) It gave me a shock to see him like that!
■ **un coup de feu** a shot
■ **un coup de fil** (informal) a ring □ Je te passerai un coup de fil demain. I'll give you a ring tomorrow.
■ **donner un coup de main à quelqu'un** to give somebody a hand □ Je viendrai te donner un coup de main. I'll come and give you a hand.
■ **un coup d'œil** a quick look □ jeter un coup d'œil to have a quick look

■ **attraper un coup de soleil** to get sunburnt
■ **un coup de téléphone** a phone call
■ **un coup de tonnerre** a clap of thunder
■ **boire un coup** (informal) to have a drink
■ **après coup** afterwards □ Après coup j'ai regretté de m'être mis en colère. Afterwards I was sorry I'd got angry.
■ **à tous les coups** (informal) every time □ Je me trompe de rue à tous les coups. I get the street wrong every time.
■ **du premier coup** first time □ Il a été reçu au permis du premier coup. He passed his driving test first time.
■ **sur le coup** at first □ Sur le coup je ne l'ai pas reconnu. I didn't recognize him at first.

coupable (FEM **coupable**) ADJECTIVE
▷ see also **coupable** NOUN
guilty

le/la **coupable** MASC/FEM NOUN
▷ see also **coupable** ADJECTIVE
culprit

la **coupe** FEM NOUN
cup (sport)
□ la coupe du monde the World Cup
■ **une coupe de cheveux** a haircut
■ **une coupe de champagne** a glass of champagne

le **coupe-ongle** (PL les **coupe-ongles**) MASC NOUN
nail clippers

couper VERB [28]
1 to cut
2 to turn off
□ couper le courant to turn off the electricity
3 to take a short-cut
□ On peut couper par la forêt. We could take a short-cut through the woods.
■ **couper l'appétit** to spoil one's appetite
■ **se couper** to cut oneself □ Je me suis coupé le doigt avec une boîte de conserve. I cut my finger on a tin.
■ **couper la parole à quelqu'un** to interrupt somebody

le **couple** MASC NOUN
couple

le **couplet** MASC NOUN
verse
□ le premier couplet the first verse

la **coupure** FEM NOUN
cut
■ **une coupure de courant** a power cut

la **cour** FEM NOUN
1 yard
□ la cour de l'école the school yard
2 court
□ la cour de Louis XIV the court of Louis XIV
□ la cour d'assises the criminal court

le courage MASC NOUN
courage

courageux (FEM **courageuse**) ADJECTIVE
brave

couramment ADVERB

1 fluently
□ Elle parle couramment japonais. She speaks Japanese fluently.

2 commonly
□ C'est une expression que l'on emploie couramment. It's a commonly used phrase.

courant (FEM **courante**) ADJECTIVE
▷ see also **courant** NOUN

1 common
□ C'est une erreur courante. It's a common mistake.

2 standard
□ C'est un modèle courant. It's a standard model.

le courant MASC NOUN
▷ see also **courant** ADJECTIVE

1 current (of river)
■ **un courant d'air** a draught

2 power
□ une panne de courant a power cut
■ **Je le ferai dans le courant de la semaine.** I'll do it some time during the week.
■ **être au courant de quelque chose** to know about something □ Je n'étais pas au courant de l'accident. I didn't know about the accident.
■ **mettre quelqu'un au courant de quelque chose** to tell somebody about something
■ **Tu es au courant ?** Have you heard about it?
■ **se tenir au courant de quelque chose** to keep up with something □ J'essaie de me tenir au courant de l'actualité. I try to keep up with the news.

le coureur MASC NOUN
runner
■ **un coureur à pied** a runner
■ **un coureur cycliste** a racing cyclist
■ **un coureur automobile** a racing driver

la coureuse FEM NOUN
runner

la courgette FEM NOUN
courgette

courir VERB [16]
to run
□ Elle a traversé la rue en courant. She ran across the street.
■ **courir un risque** to run a risk

la couronne FEM NOUN
crown

courons, courez VERB ▷ see courir

le courriel MASC NOUN
email

le courrier MASC NOUN
mail
□ Est-ce qu'il y avait du courrier ce matin ? Was there any mail this morning?
■ **N'oublie pas de poster le courrier.** Don't forget to post the letters.
■ **le courrier électronique** email

> **BE CAREFUL!**
> The French word **courrier** does not mean **courier**.

cours VERB ▷ see courir
▷ see also **cours** NOUN
■ **Tu cours vite !** You run fast!

le cours MASC NOUN
▷ see also **cours** VERB

1 lesson
□ un cours d'espagnol a Spanish lesson □ des cours particuliers private lessons

2 course
□ un cours intensif a crash course

3 rate
□ le cours du change the exchange rate
■ **au cours de** during □ Il a été réveillé trois fois au cours de la nuit. He was woken up three times during the night.

la course FEM NOUN

1 running
□ la course de fond long-distance running

2 race
□ une course hippique a horse race

3 shopping
□ J'ai juste une course à faire. I've just got a bit of shopping to do.
■ **faire les courses** to go shopping □ Elle est partie faire les courses de la semaine. She's gone to do her weekly shopping.

court VERB ▷ see courir
▷ see also **court** ADJECTIVE, NOUN
■ **Elle court jusqu'à sa maison.** She is running to her house.

court (FEM **courte**) ADJECTIVE
▷ see also **court** VERB, NOUN
short

le court MASC NOUN
▷ see also **court** VERB, ADJECTIVE
■ **un court de tennis** a tennis court

couru VERB ▷ see courir

le couscous MASC NOUN
couscous

> **DID YOU KNOW...?**
> **couscous** is a spicy North African dish made with meat, vegetables and steamed semolina.

le cousin MASC NOUN
cousin

la cousine FEM NOUN
cousin

le **coussin** MASC NOUN
cushion

le **coût** MASC NOUN
cost
□ le coût de la vie the cost of living

le **couteau** (PL les **couteaux**) MASC NOUN
knife

coûter VERB [28]
to cost
□ Est-ce que ça coûte cher ? Does it cost a lot?
■ **Combien ça coûte ?** How much is it?

coûteux (FEM **coûteuse**) ADJECTIVE
expensive

la **coutume** FEM NOUN
custom

la **couture** FEM NOUN
1 sewing
□ Je n'aime pas la couture. I don't like sewing.
■ **faire de la couture** to sew
2 seam
□ La couture de mon pantalon s'est défaite.
The seam of my trousers has come undone.

le **couturier** MASC NOUN
fashion designer
□ un grand couturier a top designer

la **couturière** FEM NOUN
1 dressmaker
2 designer (fashion)

le **couvercle** MASC NOUN
1 lid (of pan)
2 top (of tube, jar, spray can)

couvert (FEM **couverte**) ADJECTIVE
▷ see also **couvert** NOUN
1 covered
■ **couvert de** covered with □ Cet arbre est
couvert de fleurs au printemps. This tree is
covered with blossom in spring.
2 overcast (sky)

couvert VERB ▷ see **couvrir**

le **couvert** MASC NOUN
▷ see also **couvert** ADJECTIVE
■ **mettre le couvert** to lay the table

les **couverts** MASC PL NOUN
cutlery sing
□ Les couverts sont dans le tiroir de gauche.
The cutlery is in the left-hand drawer.

la **couverture** FEM NOUN
blanket

le **couvre-lit** MASC NOUN
bedspread

couvrir VERB [55]
to cover
□ Le chien est revenu couvert de boue. The dog
came back covered with mud.
■ **se couvrir 1** to wrap up □ Couvre-toi bien :
il fait très froid dehors. Wrap up well: it's very

cold outside. **2** to cloud over □ Le ciel se couvre.
The sky's clouding over.

le **COVID** MASC NOUN
COVID

le **covoiturage** MASC NOUN
car sharing

le **crabe** MASC NOUN
crab

cracher VERB [28]
to spit

le **crachin** MASC NOUN
drizzle

la **craie** FEM NOUN
chalk

craindre VERB [17]
to fear
□ Tu n'as rien à craindre. You've got nothing
to fear.

la **crainte** FEM NOUN
fear
■ **de crainte de** for fear of □ Il n'ose rien dire de
crainte de la vexer. He daren't say anything for
fear of upsetting her.

craintif (FEM **craintive**) ADJECTIVE
timid

la **crampe** FEM NOUN
cramp
□ J'ai une crampe au mollet. I've got a cramp in
my calf.

le **cran** MASC NOUN
hole (in belt)
■ **avoir du cran** (informal) to have guts

le **crâne** MASC NOUN
skull

crâner VERB [28] (informal)
to show off

le **crapaud** MASC NOUN
toad

craquer VERB [28]
1 to creak
□ Le plancher craque. The floor creaks.
2 to burst
□ Ma fermeture éclair a craqué. My zip's burst.
3 to crack up
□ Je vais finir par craquer ! (informal) I'm going to
crack up at this rate!
■ **Quand j'ai vu cette robe, j'ai craqué !**
(informal) When I saw that dress, I couldn't
resist it!

la **crasse** FEM NOUN
filth

la **cravate** FEM NOUN
tie

le **crawl** MASC NOUN
crawl
□ nager le crawl to do the crawl

le **crayon** MASC NOUN
pencil
□ un crayon de couleur a coloured pencil
■ un crayon feutre a felt-tip pen

la **création** FEM NOUN
creation

la **crèche** FEM NOUN
1 nursery
□ Elle dépose son fils à la crèche à huit heures.
She leaves her son at the nursery at 8 o'clock.
2 nativity scene

le **crédit** MASC NOUN
credit

créer VERB [18]
to create

la **crémaillère** FEM NOUN
■ pendre la crémaillère to have a house-warming party

la **crème** FEM NOUN
▷ see also **crème** NOUN
cream
■ la crème anglaise custard
■ la crème Chantilly sweetened whipped cream
■ la crème fouettée whipped cream
■ une crème caramel a crème caramel
■ une crème au chocolat a chocolate dessert

le **crème** MASC NOUN
▷ see also **crème** NOUN
white coffee
□ un grand crème a large white coffee

la **crémerie** FEM NOUN
cheese shop

crémeux (FEM **crémeuse**) ADJECTIVE
creamy

la **crêpe** FEM NOUN
pancake

la **crêperie** FEM NOUN
pancake restaurant

le **crépuscule** MASC NOUN
dusk

le **cresson** MASC NOUN
watercress

la **Crète** FEM NOUN
Crete

creuser VERB [28]
to dig (a hole)
■ Ça creuse ! That gives you a real appetite!
■ se creuser la cervelle (informal) to rack one's brains

creux (FEM **creuse**) ADJECTIVE
hollow

la **crevaison** FEM NOUN
puncture

crevé (FEM **crevée**) ADJECTIVE
1 punctured
□ un pneu crevé a puncture

2 knackered
□ Je suis complètement crevé ! (informal) I'm completely knackered!

crever VERB [43]
1 to burst (balloon)
2 to have a puncture (motorist)
□ J'ai crevé sur l'autoroute. I had a puncture on the motorway.
■ Je crève de faim ! (informal) I'm starving!
■ Je crève de froid ! (informal) I'm freezing!

la **crevette** FEM NOUN
prawn
■ une crevette rose a prawn
■ une crevette grise a shrimp

le **cri** MASC NOUN
1 scream
□ J'ai entendu un cri. I heard a scream. □ pousser des cris de douleur to scream with pain
2 call
□ Il sait reconnaître les cris des oiseaux. He can identify the calls of birds.
■ C'est le dernier cri. It's the latest fashion.
□ Ce haut est du dernier cri. This top is the latest fashion.

criard (FEM **criarde**) ADJECTIVE
garish (colours)

le **cric** MASC NOUN
jack (for car)

crier VERB [19]
to shout
■ crier de douleur to scream with pain

le **crime** MASC NOUN
1 crime
□ un crime de guerre a war crime
2 murder
□ Un crime a été commis ici. There was a murder here.

le **criminel** MASC NOUN
1 criminal
□ un criminel de guerre a war criminal
2 murderer

la **criminelle** FEM NOUN
1 criminal
2 murderer

le **crin** MASC NOUN
horsehair

la **crinière** FEM NOUN
mane

le **criquet** MASC NOUN
grasshopper

la **crise** FEM NOUN
1 crisis
□ la crise climatique climate crisis
■ la crise économique the recession
2 attack
□ une crise d'asthme an asthma attack □ une crise cardiaque a heart attack

- **une crise de foie** an upset stomach
- **piquer une crise de nerfs** to go hysterical
- **avoir une crise de fou rire** to have a fit of the giggles

le cristal (PL les **cristaux**) MASC NOUN
crystal
□ **un verre en cristal** a crystal glass

le critère MASC NOUN
criterion

critique (FEM **critique**) ADJECTIVE
▷ *see also* **critique** NOUN
critical

le critique MASC NOUN
▷ *see also* **critique** NOUN, ADJECTIVE
critic
□ **un critique de cinéma** a film critic

la critique FEM NOUN
▷ *see also* **critique** NOUN, ADJECTIVE
1 criticism
□ **Elle ne supporte pas les critiques.** She can't stand being criticized.
2 review
□ **Le film a reçu de bonnes critiques.** The film's had good reviews.

critiquer VERB [28]
to criticize

la Croatie FEM NOUN
Croatia

le crochet MASC NOUN
1 hook
2 detour
□ **faire un crochet** to make a detour
3 crochet
□ **un pull au crochet** a crocheted sweater

le crocodile MASC NOUN
crocodile

croire VERB [20]
to believe
□ **Il croit tout ce qu'on lui raconte.** He believes everything he's told.
- **croire que** to think that □ **Tu crois qu'il fera meilleur demain ?** Do you think the weather will be better tomorrow?
- **croire à quelque chose** to believe in something
- **croire en Dieu** to believe in God

crois VERB ▷ *see* **croire**

croîs VERB ▷ *see* **croître**

le croisement MASC NOUN
crossroads
□ **Tournez à gauche au croisement.** Turn left at the crossroads.

croiser VERB [28]
- **J'ai croisé Anne-Laure dans la rue.** I bumped into Anne-Laure in the street.
- **croiser les bras** to fold one's arms
- **croiser les jambes** to cross one's legs

- **se croiser** to pass each other □ **Nous nous croisons dans l'escalier tous les matins.** We pass each other on the stairs every morning.

la croisière FEM NOUN
cruise

la croissance FEM NOUN
growth

le croissant MASC NOUN
croissant
□ **un croissant au beurre** a butter croissant

croit VERB ▷ *see* **croire**

croître VERB [21]
to grow

la croix FEM NOUN
cross
- **la Croix-Rouge** the Red Cross

le croque-madame (PL les **croque-madame**) MASC NOUN
toasted ham and cheese sandwich with fried egg on top

le croque-monsieur (PL les **croque-monsieur**) MASC NOUN
toasted ham and cheese sandwich

croquer VERB [28]
to munch
□ **croquer une pomme** to munch an apple
- **le chocolat à croquer** dark chocolate

le croquis MASC NOUN
sketch

la crotte FEM NOUN
□ **une crotte de chien** dog dirt

le crottin MASC NOUN
1 manure
□ **du crottin de cheval** horse manure
2 small goat's cheese

croustillant (FEM **croustillante**) ADJECTIVE
crusty

la croûte FEM NOUN
1 crust (*of bread*)
- **en croûte** in pastry
2 rind (*of cheese*)
3 scab (*on skin*)

le croûton MASC NOUN
1 crust (*end of loaf*)
2 crouton
□ **des croûtons frottés d'ail** garlic croutons

croyons, croyez VERB ▷ *see* **croire**

les CRS MASC PL NOUN
French riot police

cru (FEM **crue**) ADJECTIVE
raw
□ **la viande crue** raw meat
- **le jambon cru** Parma ham

cru VERB ▷ *see* **croire**

crû VERB ▷ *see* **croître**

la cruauté FEM NOUN
cruelty

C

cruche - cuvette

la **cruche** FEM NOUN
jug

les **crudités** FEM PL NOUN
assorted raw vegetables

cruel (FEM **cruelle**) ADJECTIVE
cruel

les **crustacés** MASC PL NOUN
shellfish

le **cube** MASC NOUN
cube
■ **un mètre cube** a cubic metre

la **cueillette** FEM NOUN
picking
□ la cueillette des champignons mushroom picking

cueillir VERB [22]
to pick (*flowers, fruit*)

la **cuiller** FEM NOUN
spoon
■ **une cuiller à café** a teaspoon
■ **une cuiller à soupe** a soup spoon

la **cuillère** FEM NOUN
spoon
■ **une cuillère à café** a teaspoon
■ **une cuillère à soupe** a soup spoon

la **cuillerée** FEM NOUN
spoonful

le **cuir** MASC NOUN
leather
□ un sac en cuir a leather bag
■ **le cuir chevelu** the scalp

cuire VERB [23]
to cook
□ cuire quelque chose à feu vif to cook something on a high heat
■ **cuire quelque chose au four** to bake something
■ **cuire quelque chose à la vapeur** to steam something
■ **faire cuire** to cook □ « Faire cuire pendant une heure » 'Cook for one hour'
■ **bien cuit** well done
■ **trop cuit** overdone

la **cuisine** FEM NOUN
1 kitchen
2 cooking
□ la cuisine française French cooking
■ **faire la cuisine** to cook

cuisiné (FEM **cuisinée**) ADJECTIVE
■ **un plat cuisiné** a ready-made meal

cuisiner VERB [28]
to cook
□ J'aime beaucoup cuisiner. I love cooking.

le **cuisinier** MASC NOUN
cook

la **cuisinière** FEM NOUN
1 cook

2 cooker
□ une cuisinière à gaz a gas cooker

la **cuisse** FEM NOUN
thigh
■ **une cuisse de poulet** a chicken leg

la **cuisson** FEM NOUN
cooking
□ « une heure de cuisson » 'cooking time: one hour'

cuit VERB ▷ *see* cuire

le **cuivre** MASC NOUN
copper

le **culot** MASC NOUN (*informal*)
cheek
□ Quel culot ! What a cheek! □ Il a un sacré culot ! He's got a damn cheek!

la **culotte** FEM NOUN
knickers

la **culpabilité** FEM NOUN
guilt

le **cultivateur** MASC NOUN
farmer

la **cultivatrice** FEM NOUN
farmer

cultivé (FEM **cultivée**) ADJECTIVE
cultured
□ Il est très cultivé. He's very cultured.

cultiver VERB [28]
to grow
□ Il cultive la vigne. He grows grapes.
■ **cultiver la terre** to farm the land

la **culture** FEM NOUN
1 farming
□ les cultures intensives intensive farming
2 education
□ une bonne culture générale a good general education
■ **la culture physique** physical education

culturel (FEM **culturelle**) ADJECTIVE
cultural

le **culturisme** MASC NOUN
body-building

le **curé** MASC NOUN
parish priest

le **cure-dent** MASC NOUN
toothpick

curieux (FEM **curieuse**) ADJECTIVE
curious

la **curiosité** FEM NOUN
curiosity

le **curriculum vitae** MASC NOUN
CV

le **curseur** MASC NOUN
cursor

la **cuvette** FEM NOUN
bowl
□ une cuvette en plastique a plastic bowl

le **CV** MASC NOUN (= *curriculum vitae*)
CV

la **cyberattaque** FEM NOUN
cyberattack

le **cybercafé** MASC NOUN
internet café

le **cybercrime** FEM NOUN
cyber crime

le **cyberharcèlement** MASC NOUN
cyber bullying

cyclable (FEM **cyclable**) ADJECTIVE
■ une piste cyclable a cycle lane

le **cycle** MASC NOUN
cycle

le **cyclisme** MASC NOUN
cycling

le/la **cycliste** MASC/FEM NOUN
cyclist

le **cyclomoteur** MASC NOUN
moped

le **cyclone** MASC NOUN
hurricane

le **cygne** MASC NOUN
swan

Dd

d' PREPOSITION, ARTICLE ▷ see **de**

la **dactylo** FEM NOUN

1 typist
  □ Elle est dactylo. She's a typist.

2 typing
  □ Je prends des cours de dactylo. I'm taking typing lessons.

le **daim** MASC NOUN
  suede
  □ une veste en daim a suede jacket

la **dame** FEM NOUN

1 lady

2 queen (*in cards, chess*)

les **dames** FEM PL NOUN
  draughts

le **Danemark** MASC NOUN
  Denmark

le **danger** MASC NOUN
  danger
  ■ **être en danger** to be in danger
  ■ **« Danger de mort »** 'Extremely dangerous'

dangereux (FEM **dangereuse**) ADJECTIVE
  dangerous

danois (FEM **danoise**) ADJECTIVE, NOUN
  Danish
  □ Il parle danois. He speaks Danish.
  ■ **un Danois** a Dane (*man*)
  ■ **une Danoise** a Dane (*woman*)
  ■ **les Danois** the Danish

dans PREPOSITION

1 in
  □ Il est dans sa chambre. He's in his bedroom.
  □ dans deux mois in two months' time

2 into
  □ Il est entré dans mon bureau. He came into my office.

3 out of
  □ On a bu dans des verres en plastique. We drank out of plastic glasses.

la **danse** FEM NOUN

1 dance
  □ la danse moderne modern dance □ des danses folkloriques folk dances
  ■ **la danse classique** ballet

2 dancing
  □ des cours de danse dancing lessons

danser VERB [28]
  to dance

le **danseur** MASC NOUN
  dancer

la **danseuse** FEM NOUN
  dancer

la **date** FEM NOUN
  date
  □ votre date de naissance your date of birth
  □ la date limite de vente the sell-by date
  ■ **un ami de longue date** an old friend

dater VERB [28]
  ■ **dater de** to date from □ Cette coutume date du Moyen Âge. This custom dates from the Middle Ages.

la **datte** FEM NOUN
  date (*fruit*)

le **dauphin** MASC NOUN
  dolphin

davantage ADVERB
  ■ **davantage de** more □ Il faudrait davantage de stages de formation. There should be more training courses.

de PREPOSITION, ARTICLE

> **de** changes to **d'** before a vowel and some words beginning with 'h'. **de** also changes when followed by **le** or **les**, but stays the same when followed by **la** or **l'**:
> **de + le = du**   **de + les = des**
> **de + la = de la**   **de + l' = de l'**

1 of
  □ le toit de la maison the roof of the house □ la voiture de Paul Paul's car □ la voiture de mes parents my parents' car □ la voiture d'Hélène Hélène's car □ deux bouteilles de vin two bottles of wine □ un litre d'essence a litre of petrol
  ■ **un bébé d'un an** a one-year-old baby
  ■ **un billet de cinquante euros** a 50-euro note

2 from
  □ de Londres à Paris from London to Paris
  □ Il vient de Londres. He comes from London.
  □ une lettre de Victor a letter from Victor

3 by
  □ augmenter de dix euros to increase by ten euros

You use **de** to form expressions with the meaning of 'some' and 'any'.

- **Je voudrais de l'eau.** I'd like some water.
- **du pain et de la confiture** bread and jam
- **Il n'a pas de famille.** He hasn't got any family.
- **Il n'y a plus de biscuits.** There aren't any more biscuits.

le **dé** MASC NOUN
1 dice
2 thimble

le **dealer** MASC NOUN (*informal*)
drug-pusher

déballer VERB [28]
to unpack

le **débardeur** MASC NOUN
tank top

débarquer VERB [28]
to disembark
□ Nous avons dû débarquer à Marseille. We had to disembark at Marseille.
- **débarquer chez quelqu'un** (*informal*) to descend on somebody □ Ils ont débarqué chez nous à dix heures du soir. They descended on us at ten o'clock at night.

le **débarras** MASC NOUN
junk room
- **Bon débarras !** Good riddance!

débarrasser VERB [28]
to clear
□ Tu peux débarrasser la table, s'il te plaît ? Can you clear the table please?
- **se débarrasser de quelque chose** to get rid of something □ Je me suis débarrassé de mon vieux frigo. I got rid of my old fridge.

le **débat** MASC NOUN
debate

se **débattre** VERB [9]
to struggle

débile (FEM **débile**) ADJECTIVE
crazy
□ C'est complètement débile ! (*informal*) That's totally crazy!

débordé (FEM **débordée**) ADJECTIVE
- **être débordé** to be snowed under

déborder VERB [28]
to overflow (*river*)
- **déborder d'énergie** to be full of energy

le **débouché** MASC NOUN
job prospect
□ Quels débouchés y a-t-il après ces études ? What are the job prospects after this course?

déboucher VERB [28]
1 to unblock (*sink, pipe*)
2 to open (*bottle*)
- **déboucher sur** to lead into □ La rue débouche sur une place. The street leads into a square.

debout ADVERB
1 standing up
□ Il a mangé ses céréales debout. He ate his cereal standing up.
2 upright
□ Mets les livres debout sur l'étagère. Put the books upright on the shelf.
3 up
□ Tu es déjà debout ? Are you up already?
- **Debout !** Get up!

déboutonner VERB [28]
to unbutton

débraillé (FEM **débraillée**) ADJECTIVE
sloppily dressed

débrancher VERB [28]
to unplug

le **débris** MASC NOUN
- **des débris de verre** bits of glass

débrouillard (FEM **débrouillarde**) ADJECTIVE
streetwise

se **débrouiller** VERB [28]
to manage
□ C'était difficile, mais je ne me suis pas trop mal débrouillé. It was difficult, but I managed OK.
- **Débrouille-toi tout seul.** Sort things out for yourself.

le **début** MASC NOUN
beginning
□ au début at the beginning
- **début mai** in early May

le **débutant** MASC NOUN
beginner

la **débutante** FEM NOUN
beginner

débuter VERB [28]
to start

décaféiné (FEM **décaféinée**) ADJECTIVE
decaffeinated

le **décalage horaire** MASC NOUN
time difference (*between time zones*)
□ Il y a une heure de décalage horaire entre la France et la Grande-Bretagne. There's an hour's time difference between France and Britain.

décalquer VERB [28]
to trace

décapiter VERB [28]
to behead

décapotable (FEM **décapotable**) ADJECTIVE
convertible

décapsuler VERB [28]
- **décapsuler une bouteille** to take the top off a bottle

le **décapsuleur** MASC NOUN
bottle-opener

d

décéder – décolorer

décéder VERB [34, *aux* être]
to die
□ Son père est décédé il y a trois ans. His father died three years ago.

décembre MASC NOUN
December
■ **en décembre** in December

décemment ADVERB
decently

décent (FEM **décente**) ADJECTIVE
decent

la **déception** FEM NOUN
disappointment

décerner VERB [28]
to award

le **décès** MASC NOUN
death

décevant (FEM **décevante**) ADJECTIVE
disappointing
□ Ses résultats sont plutôt décevants. His results are rather disappointing.

décevoir VERB [67]
to disappoint

> **BE CAREFUL!**
> **décevoir** does not mean **to deceive**.

décharger VERB [45]
to unload

se **déchausser** VERB [28]
to take off one's shoes

les **déchets** MASC PL NOUN
waste *sing*
□ les déchets nucléaires nuclear waste □ les déchets toxiques toxic waste

déchiffrer VERB [28]
to decipher

déchirant (FEM **déchirante**) ADJECTIVE
heart-rending

déchirer VERB [28]
1 to tear (*clothes*)
2 to tear up
□ déchirer une lettre to tear up a letter
3 to tear out
□ déchirer une page d'un livre to tear a page out of a book
■ **se déchirer** to tear □ se déchirer un muscle to tear a muscle

la **déchirure** FEM NOUN
tear (*rip*)
■ **une déchirure musculaire** a torn muscle

décidé (FEM **décidée**) ADJECTIVE
determined
■ **C'est décidé.** It's decided.

décidément ADVERB
certainly
□ Décidément, je n'ai pas de chance aujourd'hui. I'm certainly not having much luck today.

décider VERB [28]
to decide
■ **décider de faire quelque chose** to decide to do something □ Ils ont décidé de rester. They decided to stay.
■ **se décider** to make up one's mind □ Elle n'arrive pas à se décider. She can't make up her mind.
■ **se décider à faire quelque chose** to make up one's mind to do something □ Il s'est décidé à partir. He made up his mind to leave.

décisif (FEM **décisive**) ADJECTIVE
decisive

la **décision** FEM NOUN
decision

la **déclaration** FEM NOUN
statement
□ Je n'ai aucune déclaration à faire. I have no statement to make.
■ **faire une déclaration de vol** to report something as stolen

déclarer VERB [28]
to declare
□ déclarer la guerre à un pays to declare war on a country
■ **se déclarer** to break out □ Le feu s'est déclaré dans la cantine. The fire broke out in the canteen.

déclencher VERB [28]
to set off (*alarm, explosion*)
■ **se déclencher** to go off

le **déclic** MASC NOUN
click

décoiffé (FEM **décoiffée**) ADJECTIVE
■ **Elle était toute décoiffée.** Her hair was in a real mess.

déçois, déçoit VERB ▷ see **décevoir**

le **décollage** MASC NOUN
takeoff (*of plane*)

décollé (FEM **décollée**) ADJECTIVE
■ **avoir les oreilles décollées** to have sticking-out ears

décoller VERB [28]
1 to unstick
□ décoller une étiquette to unstick a label
■ **se décoller** to come unstuck
2 to take off
□ L'avion a décollé avec dix minutes de retard. The plane took off ten minutes late.

décolleté (FEM **décolletée**) ADJECTIVE
▷ see also **décolleté** NOUN
low-cut

le **décolleté** MASC NOUN
▷ see also **décolleté** ADJECTIVE
■ **un décolleté plongeant** a plunging neckline

se **décolorer** VERB [28]
to fade

□ Ce T-shirt s'est décoloré au lavage. This T-shirt has faded in the wash.

■ **se faire décolorer les cheveux** to have one's hair bleached

les **décombres** MASC PL NOUN
rubble *sing*

se **décommander** VERB [28]
to cry off
□ Elle devait venir mais elle s'est décommandée à la dernière minute. She was supposed to be coming, but she cried off at the last minute.

déconcerté (FEM **déconcertée**) ADJECTIVE
disconcerted

décongeler VERB [1]
to thaw

se **déconnecter** VERB [28]
to log out

la **déconnection** FEM NOUN
disconnection

déconseiller VERB [28]
■ **déconseiller à quelqu'un de faire quelque chose** to advise somebody not to do something
□ Je lui ai déconseillé d'y aller. I advised him not to go.
■ **C'est déconseillé.** It's not recommended.

décontenancé (FEM **décontenancée**)
ADJECTIVE
disconcerted

décontracté (FEM **décontractée**) ADJECTIVE
relaxed
■ **s'habiller décontracté** to dress casually

se **décontracter** VERB [28]
to relax
□ Il est allé faire du footing pour se décontracter. He went jogging to relax.

le **décor** MASC NOUN
décor

le **décorateur** MASC NOUN
interior decorator

la **décoration** FEM NOUN
decoration

la **décoratrice** FEM NOUN
interior decorator

décorer VERB [28]
to decorate

les **décors** MASC PL NOUN
1 scenery *sing* (*in play*)
2 set (*in film*)

décortiquer VERB [28]
to shell
■ **des crevettes décortiquées** peeled prawns

découdre VERB [15]
to unpick
■ **se découdre** to come unstitched

découper VERB [28]
1 to cut out
□ J'ai découpé cet article dans le journal. I cut

this article out of the paper.
2 to carve (*meat*)

décourageant (FEM **décourageante**)
ADJECTIVE
discouraging

décourager VERB [45]
to discourage
■ **se décourager** to get discouraged
■ **Ne te décourage pas !** Don't give up!

décousu (FEM **décousue**) ADJECTIVE
unstitched
□ L'ourlet est décousu. The hem's come unstitched.

découvert VERB ▷ *see* **découvrir**
▷ *see also* **découvert** NOUN
■ **On a découvert la formule.** They discovered the formula.

le **découvert** MASC NOUN
overdraft

la **découverte** FEM NOUN
discovery

découvrir VERB [55]
to discover

décrire VERB [30]
to describe

le **décrochage** MASC NOUN
■ **le décrochage scolaire** truancy

décrocher VERB [28]
1 to take down
□ Tu peux m'aider à décrocher les rideaux ? Can you help me take down the curtains?
2 to pick up the phone
□ Il a décroché et a composé le numéro. He picked up the phone and dialled the number.
■ **décrocher le téléphone** to take the phone off the hook

déçu VERB ▷ *see* **décevoir**
disappointed

dédaigneux (FEM **dédaigneuse**) ADJECTIVE
disdainful
□ d'un air dédaigneux disdainfully

le **dédain** MASC NOUN
disdain
□ avec dédain with disdain

dedans ADVERB
inside
□ C'est une jolie boîte : qu'est-ce qu'il y a dedans ? That's a nice box: what's in it?
■ **là-dedans 1** in there □ J'ai trouvé les clés là-dedans. I found the keys in there. **2** in that □ Il y a du vrai là-dedans. There's some truth in that.

dédicacé (FEM **dédicacée**) ADJECTIVE
■ **un exemplaire dédicacé** a signed copy

dédier VERB [19]
to dedicate

déduire VERB [23]
to take off

□ Tu as déduit les vingt euros que je te devais ? Did you take off the twenty euros I owed you?

■ **J'en déduis qu'il m'a menti.** That means he must have been lying.

défaire VERB [36]

to undo

■ **défaire sa valise** to unpack

■ **se défaire** to come undone

la **défaite** FEM NOUN

defeat

le **défaut** MASC NOUN

fault

défavorable (FEM **défavorable**) ADJECTIVE

unfavourable

défavorisé (FEM **défavorisée**) ADJECTIVE

underprivileged

■ **personnes défavorisées** underprivileged people

défectueux (FEM **défectueuse**) ADJECTIVE

faulty

défendre VERB [88]

1 to forbid

■ **défendre à quelqu'un de faire quelque chose** to forbid somebody to do something

□ Sa mère lui a défendu de le revoir. Her mother forbade her to see him again.

2 to defend

□ défendre ses idées to defend your ideas

□ défendre quelqu'un to defend somebody

défendu (FEM **défendue**) ADJECTIVE

forbidden

□ C'est défendu. It's forbidden.

la **défense** FEM NOUN

1 defence

■ **prendre la défense de quelqu'un** to back somebody up

■ « **défense de fumer** » 'no smoking'

2 tusk (*of elephant*)

le **défi** MASC NOUN

challenge

■ **d'un air de défi** defiantly

■ **sur un ton de défi** defiantly

défier VERB [19]

1 to challenge

□ Je te défie de trouver un meilleur exemple. I challenge you to find a better example.

2 to dare

□ Il m'a défié d'aller à l'école en pyjama. He dared me to go to school in my pyjamas.

défigurer VERB [28]

to disfigure

le **défilé** MASC NOUN

1 parade

■ **un défilé de mode** a fashion show

2 march

défiler VERB [28]

to march

définir VERB [38]

to define

définitif (FEM **définitive**) ADJECTIVE

final

■ **en définitive** in the end □ En définitive, ils ont décidé de rester. In the end, they decided to stay.

la **définition** FEM NOUN

definition

définitivement ADVERB

for good

□ Elle s'est définitivement installée en Écosse en 2004. She settled in Scotland for good in 2004.

déformer VERB [28]

to stretch

□ Ne tire pas sur ton pull, tu vas le déformer. Don't pull at your sweater, you'll stretch it.

■ **se déformer** to stretch □ Ce T-shirt s'est déformé au lavage. This T-shirt has stretched in the wash.

se **défouler** VERB [28]

to unwind

□ Je fais de l'aérobic pour me défouler. I do aerobics to unwind.

dégagé (FEM **dégagée**) ADJECTIVE

■ **d'un air dégagé** casually

■ **sur un ton dégagé** casually

dégager VERB [45]

1 to free

□ Ils ont mis une heure à dégager les victimes. They took an hour to free the victims.

2 to clear

□ des gouttes qui dégagent le nez drops to clear your nose

■ **Ça se dégage.** (*weather*) It's clearing up.

se **dégarnir** VERB [38]

to go bald

les **dégâts** MASC PL NOUN

damage

le **dégel** MASC NOUN

thaw

dégeler VERB [1]

to thaw

□ faire dégeler un poulet congelé to thaw out a frozen chicken

dégivrer VERB [28]

1 to defrost

2 to de-ice

dégonfler VERB [28]

to let down

□ Quelqu'un a dégonflé mes pneus. Somebody let down my tyres.

■ **se dégonfler** (*informal*) to chicken out

dégouliner VERB [28]

to trickle

dégourdi (FEM **dégourdie**) ADJECTIVE
smart (clever)
□ Il n'est pas très dégourdi. He's not very smart.

dégourdir VERB [38]
■ **se dégourdir les jambes** to stretch one's legs

le **dégoût** MASC NOUN
disgust
□ une expression de dégoût a disgusted expression
■ **avec dégoût** disgustedly

dégoûtant (FEM **dégoûtante**) ADJECTIVE
disgusting

dégoûté (FEM **dégoûtée**) ADJECTIVE
disgusted
■ **être dégoûté de tout** to be sick of everything

dégoûter VERB [28]
to disgust
□ Ce genre de comportement me dégoûte. That kind of behaviour disgusts me.
■ **dégoûter quelqu'un de quelque chose** to put somebody off something □ Ça m'a dégoûté de la viande. That put me off meat.

se **dégrader** VERB [28]
to deteriorate

le **degré** MASC NOUN
degree
■ **de l'alcool à 90 degrés** surgical spirit

dégringoler VERB [28]
1 to rush down
□ Il a dégringolé l'escalier. He rushed down the stairs.
2 to collapse
■ **Elle a fait dégringoler la pile de livres.** She knocked over the stack of books.

le **déguisement** MASC NOUN
disguise

déguiser VERB [28]
■ **se déguiser en quelque chose** to dress up as something □ Elle s'était déguisée en vampire. She was dressed up as a vampire.

la **dégustation** FEM NOUN
tasting

déguster VERB [28]
1 to taste (food, wine)
2 to enjoy

dehors ADVERB
outside
□ Je t'attends dehors. I'll wait for you outside.
■ **jeter quelqu'un dehors** to throw somebody out
■ **en dehors de** 1 apart from □ En dehors de lui, tout le monde était content. Apart from him, everybody was happy. 2 outside □ en dehors des heures de cours outside school hours

déjà ADVERB
1 already
□ J'ai déjà fini. I've already finished.
2 before
□ Tu es déjà venu en France ? Have you been to France before?

déjeuner VERB [28]
▷ see also **déjeuner** NOUN
to have lunch

le **déjeuner** MASC NOUN
▷ see also **déjeuner** VERB
lunch

le **délai** MASC NOUN
1 extension
□ J'ai demandé un délai d'une semaine. I've asked for a week's extension.
2 time limit
□ être dans les délais to be within the time limit

> **BE CAREFUL!**
> **délai** does not mean **delay**.

délasser VERB [28]
to relax
□ La lecture délasse. Reading's relaxing.
■ **se délasser** to relax □ J'ai pris un bain pour me délasser. I had a bath to relax.

délavé (FEM **délavée**) ADJECTIVE
faded
□ un jean délavé a pair of faded jeans

le **délégué** MASC NOUN
representative
□ les délégués de classe the class representatives

> **DID YOU KNOW...?**
> In French schools, each class elects two representatives or **délégués de classe**.

la **déléguée** FEM NOUN
representative

déléguer VERB [34]
to delegate

délibéré (FEM **délibérée**) ADJECTIVE
deliberate

délicat (FEM **délicate**) ADJECTIVE
1 delicate
□ avoir la peau délicate to have delicate skin
2 tricky
□ une situation délicate a tricky situation
3 tactful
□ Il est toujours très délicat. He's always very tactful.
4 thoughtful
□ C'est une attention délicate de sa part. That was thoughtful on his part.

délicatement ADVERB
1 gently
2 tactfully

d

le **délice** MASC NOUN
delight
□ Vivre ici est un vrai délice. Living here is a real delight.
■ Ce gâteau est un vrai délice. This cake's a real treat.

délicieux (FEM **délicieuse**) ADJECTIVE
delicious

la **délinquance** FEM NOUN
crime
□ de nouvelles mesures pour combattre la petite délinquance new measures to fight petty crime
■ la délinquance juvénile juvenile delinquency

le **délinquant** MASC NOUN
criminal

la **délinquante** FEM NOUN
criminal

délirer VERB [28]
■ Mais tu délires ! (informal) You're crazy!

le **délit** MASC NOUN
criminal offence

délivrer VERB [28]
to set free (prisoner)

le **deltaplane** MASC NOUN
hang-glider
■ faire du deltaplane to go hang-gliding

demain ADVERB
tomorrow
□ demain matin tomorrow morning
■ A demain ! See you tomorrow!

la **demande** FEM NOUN
request
■ une demande en mariage an offer of marriage
■ « demandes d'emploi » 'situations wanted'

demandé (FEM **demandée**) ADJECTIVE
■ très demandé very much in demand

demander VERB [28]
1 to ask for
□ J'ai demandé la permission. I've asked for permission.
■ demander à quelqu'un to ask someone
□ On a demandé notre chemin à un chauffeur de taxi. We asked a taxi driver the way. □ Je lui ai demandé de m'aider. I asked him to help me.
2 to require
□ un travail qui demande beaucoup de temps a job that requires a lot of time
■ se demander to wonder □ Je me demande à quelle heure il va venir. I wonder what time he'll come.

> BE CAREFUL!
> demander does not mean to demand.

le **demandeur d'asile** MASC NOUN
asylum seeker

le **demandeur d'emploi** MASC NOUN
job-seeker

la **demandeuse d'asile** FEM NOUN
asylum seeker

la **demandeuse d'emploi** FEM NOUN
job-seeker

la **démangeaison** FEM NOUN
itching

démanger VERB [45]
to itch
□ Ça me démange. It itches.

le **démaquillant** MASC NOUN
make-up remover

démaquiller VERB [28]
■ se démaquiller to remove one's make-up

la **démarche** FEM NOUN
1 walk
□ Il a une drôle de démarche. He's got a funny walk.
2 step
□ faire les démarches nécessaires pour obtenir quelque chose to take the necessary steps to obtain something

démarrer VERB [28]
to start (car)

démêler VERB [28]
to untangle

le **déménagement** MASC NOUN
move
□ C'était le jour de notre déménagement. It was the day we moved house.
■ un camion de déménagement a removal van

déménager VERB [45]
to move house

le **déménageur** MASC NOUN
removal man

dément (FEM **démente**) ADJECTIVE
crazy

démentiel (FEM **démentielle**) ADJECTIVE
insane

demeurer VERB [28]
to live

demi (FEM **demie**) ADJECTIVE, ADVERB
▷ see also **demi** NOUN
half
□ Il a trois ans et demi. He's three and a half.
■ Il est trois heures et demie. It's half past three.
■ Il est midi et demi. It's half past twelve.
■ à demi endormi half-asleep

le **demi** MASC NOUN
▷ see also **demi** ADJECTIVE, ADVERB
half pint of beer
■ Un demi, s'il vous plaît ! A beer please!

la **demi-baguette** FEM NOUN
half a baguette

le **demi-cercle** MASC NOUN
semicircle

la **demi-douzaine** FEM NOUN
half-dozen
□ une demi-douzaine d'œufs half a dozen eggs

la **demie** FEM NOUN
half-hour
□ Le bus passe à la demie. The bus comes by on
the half-hour.

demi-écrémé (FEM **demi-écrémée**)
ADJECTIVE
semi-skimmed

la **demi-finale** FEM NOUN
semi-final

le **demi-frère** MASC NOUN
half-brother

la **demi-heure** FEM NOUN
half an hour
□ dans une demi-heure in half an hour □ toutes
les demi-heures every half an hour

la **demi-journée** FEM NOUN
half-day
□ On peut louer un parasol à la demi-journée.
You can hire a sun umbrella for a half-day.

le **demi-litre** MASC NOUN
half litre
□ un demi-litre de lait half a litre of milk

la **demi-livre** FEM NOUN
half-pound
□ une demi-livre de tomates half a pound of
tomatoes

la **demi-pension** FEM NOUN
half board
□ Cet hôtel propose des tarifs raisonnables en
demi-pension. This hotel has reasonable rates
for half board.

le/la **demi-pensionnaire** MASC/FEM NOUN
■ être demi-pensionnaire to have school
lunches

demi-sel (FEM+PL **demi-sel**) ADJECTIVE
■ du beurre demi-sel slightly salted butter

la **demi-sœur** FEM NOUN
half-sister

la **démission** FEM NOUN
resignation
■ donner sa démission to resign

démissionner VERB [28]
to resign

le **demi-tarif** MASC NOUN
1 half-price
□ un billet à demi-tarif a half-price season
ticket
2 half-fare
□ voyager à demi-tarif to travel half-fare

le **demi-tour** MASC NOUN
■ faire demi-tour to turn back □ La nuit
commence à tomber ; il est temps de faire demi-
tour. It's getting dark; it's time we turned back.

la **démocratie** FEM NOUN
democracy

démocratique (FEM **démocratique**)
ADJECTIVE
democratic

démodé (FEM **démodée**) ADJECTIVE
old-fashioned

la **demoiselle** FEM NOUN
young lady
■ une demoiselle d'honneur a bridesmaid

démolir VERB [38]
to demolish

le **démon** MASC NOUN
devil

démonter VERB [28]
1 to take down (tent)
2 to take apart (machine)

démontrer VERB [28]
to show

dénoncer VERB [12]
to denounce
■ se dénoncer to give oneself up □ Il s'est
dénoncé à la police. He gave himself up to the
police.

le **dénouement** MASC NOUN
outcome

la **densité** FEM NOUN
density

la **dent** FEM NOUN
tooth
□ une dent de lait a baby tooth □ une dent de
sagesse a wisdom tooth

dentaire (FEM **dentaire**) ADJECTIVE
dental

la **dentelle** FEM NOUN
lace
□ un chemisier en dentelle a lacy blouse

le **dentier** MASC NOUN
denture

le **dentifrice** MASC NOUN
toothpaste

le/la **dentiste** MASC/FEM NOUN
dentist

le **déodorant** MASC NOUN
deodorant

le **dépannage** MASC NOUN
■ un service de dépannage a breakdown
service

dépanner VERB [28]
1 to fix
□ Il a dépanné la voiture en cinq minutes. He
fixed the car in five minutes.

d

Core vocabulary is shaded.

2 to help out

□ Il m'a prêté dix euros pour me dépanner. (*informal*) He lent me 10 euros to help me out.

la **dépanneuse** FEM NOUN

breakdown lorry

le **départ** MASC NOUN

departure

□ Le départ est à onze heures. The departure is at 11.

■ **Je lui téléphonerai la veille de son départ.** I'll phone him the day before he leaves.

le **département** MASC NOUN

1 department

□ le département d'anglais à l'université the English department at the university

2 administrative area

□ le département du Vaucluse the Vaucluse region

> **DID YOU KNOW...?**
> France is divided into 96 **départements**, administrative areas rather like counties.

dépasser VERB [58]

1 to overtake

□ Il y a une voiture qui essaie de nous dépasser. There's a car trying to overtake us.

2 to pass

□ Nous avons dépassé Dijon. We've passed Dijon.

3 to exceed (*sum, limit*)

dépaysé (FEM **dépaysée**) ADJECTIVE

■ **se sentir un peu dépaysé** to feel a bit lost

se **dépêcher** VERB [28]

to hurry

□ Dépêche-toi ! Hurry up!

dépendre VERB [88]

■ **dépendre de** to depend on □ Ça dépend du temps. It depends on the weather.

■ **dépendre de quelqu'un** to be dependent on somebody

■ **Ça dépend.** It depends.

dépenser VERB [28]

to spend (*money*)

dépensier (FEM **dépensière**) ADJECTIVE

■ **Il est dépensier.** He's a big spender.

■ **Elle n'est pas dépensière.** She doesn't spend a lot of money.

dépilatoire (FEM **dépilatoire**) ADJECTIVE

■ **une crème dépilatoire** a hair-removing cream

le **dépit** MASC NOUN

■ **en dépit de** in spite of □ Il y est allé en dépit de mes conseils. He went in spite of my advice.

déplacé (FEM **déplacée**) ADJECTIVE

uncalled-for

□ C'était une remarque déplacée. That remark was uncalled-for.

le **déplacement** MASC NOUN

trip

□ Ça vaut le déplacement. It's worth the trip.

déplacer VERB [12]

1 to move

□ Tu peux m'aider à déplacer la table ? Can you help me move the table?

2 to put off

□ déplacer un rendez-vous to put off an appointment

■ **se déplacer 1** to travel around □ Il se déplace beaucoup pour son travail. He travels around a lot for his work. **2** to get around □ Il a du mal à se déplacer. He has difficulty getting around.

■ **se déplacer une vertèbre** to slip a disc

déplaire VERB [62]

■ **Cela me déplaît.** I dislike this.

déplaisant (FEM **déplaisante**) ADJECTIVE

unpleasant

le **dépliant** MASC NOUN

leaflet

déplier VERB [19]

to unfold

déposer VERB [28]

1 to leave

□ J'ai déposé mon sac à la consigne. I left my bag at the left-luggage office.

2 to put down

□ Déposez le paquet sur la table. Put the parcel down on the table.

■ **déposer quelqu'un** to drop somebody off

dépourvu (FEM **dépourvue**) ADJECTIVE

■ **prendre quelqu'un au dépourvu** to take somebody by surprise □ Sa question m'a pris au dépourvu. His question took me by surprise.

la **dépression** FEM NOUN

depression

■ **faire de la dépression** to be suffering from depression

■ **faire une dépression** to have a breakdown

déprimant (FEM **déprimante**) ADJECTIVE

depressing

déprimer VERB [28]

to get depressed

□ Il déprime tout le temps. He gets depressed all the time. □ Ce genre de temps me déprime. This kind of weather makes me depressed.

depuis PREPOSITION, ADVERB

1 since

□ Il habite Paris depuis 2013. He's been living in Paris since 2013. □ Je ne lui ai pas parlé depuis. I haven't spoken to him since.

■ **depuis que** since □ Il a plu tous les jours depuis qu'elle est arrivée. It's rained every day since she arrived.

2 for

□ Il habite Paris depuis cinq ans. He's been living in Paris for five years.

■ **Depuis combien de temps ?** How long? □ Depuis combien de temps est-ce que vous le connaissez ? How long have you known him?

■ **Depuis quand ?** How long? □ Depuis quand est-ce que vous le connaissez ? How long have you known him?

le **député** MASC NOUN
Member of Parliament

la **députée** FEM NOUN
Member of Parliament

déraciner VERB [28]
to uproot

le **dérangement** MASC NOUN
■ **en dérangement** out of order □ Le téléphone est en dérangement. The phone's out of order.

déranger VERB [45]
1 to bother
□ Excusez-moi de vous déranger. I'm sorry to bother you.
■ **Ne vous dérangez pas, je vais répondre au téléphone.** You stay there, I'll answer the phone.
2 to mess up
□ Ne dérange pas mes livres, s'il te plaît. Don't mess up my books, please.

déraper VERB [28]
to skid

le/la **dermatologue** MASC/FEM NOUN
dermatologist
□ Elle est dermatologue. She's a dermatologist.

dernier (FEM **dernière**) ADJECTIVE
1 last
□ Il est arrivé dernier. He arrived last. □ la dernière fois the last time
2 latest
□ le dernier film de Spielberg Spielberg's latest film
■ **en dernier** last □ Ajoutez le lait en dernier. Put the milk in last.

dernièrement ADVERB
recently

dérouler VERB [28]
1 to unroll
2 to unwind
■ **se dérouler** to take place □ L'action se déroule dans les années vingt. The action takes place in the 1920s.
■ **Tout s'est déroulé comme prévu.** Everything went as planned.

derrière ADVERB, PREPOSITION
▷ see also **derrière** NOUN
behind

le **derrière** MASC NOUN
▷ see also **derrière** ADVERB, PREPOSITION

1 back
□ la porte de derrière the back door
2 backside
□ un coup de pied dans le derrière a kick up the backside

des ARTICLE

des is the contracted form of **de** + **les**.

1 some
□ Tu veux des chips ? Would you like some crisps?

des is sometimes not translated.

□ J'ai des cousins en France. I have cousins in France. □ pendant des mois for months
2 any
□ Tu as des frères ? Have you got any brothers?
3 of the
□ la fin des vacances the end of the holidays
■ **la voiture des Durand** the Durands' car
■ **Il arrive des États-Unis.** He's arriving from the United States.

dès PREPOSITION
as early as
■ **dès le mois de novembre** from November
■ **dès le début** right from the start
■ **Il vous appellera dès son retour.** He'll call you as soon as he gets back.
■ **dès que** as soon as □ Il m'a reconnu dès qu'il m'a vu. He recognized me as soon as he saw me.

désabusé (FEM **désabusée**) ADJECTIVE
disillusioned

le **désaccord** MASC NOUN
disagreement

désagréable (FEM **désagréable**) ADJECTIVE
unpleasant

désaltérer VERB [34]
■ **L'eau gazeuse désaltère bien.** Sparkling water is very thirst-quenching.
■ **se désaltérer** to have a drink □ Nous sommes allés dans un café pour nous désaltérer. We went into a café to have a drink.

désapprobateur (FEM **désapprobatrice**) ADJECTIVE
disapproving
□ un regard désapprobateur a disapproving look

le **désastre** MASC NOUN
disaster

le **désavantage** MASC NOUN
disadvantage

désavantager VERB [45]
■ **désavantager quelqu'un** to put somebody at a disadvantage □ Cette nouvelle loi va désavantager les femmes. The new law will put women at a disadvantage.

descendre VERB [24, aux avoir or être]
1 to go down
□ Je suis tombé en descendant l'escalier. I fell as I was going down the stairs.

2 to come down
□ Attends en bas ; je descends ! Wait downstairs; I'm coming down!

3 to get down
□ Vous pouvez descendre ma valise, s'il vous plaît ? Can you get my suitcase down, please?

4 to get off
□ Nous descendons à la prochaine station. We're getting off at the next stop.
■ **descendre d'une voiture** to get out of a car

The verb **descendre** uses **être** in the perfect tense when talking about moving downwards. It uses **avoir** in the perfect tense when talking about moving an object down from somewhere else.

la **descente** FEM NOUN
way down
■ **Je t'attendrai au bas de la descente.** I'll wait for you at the bottom of the hill.
■ **une descente de police** a police raid

la **description** FEM NOUN
description

déséquilibré (FEM déséquilibrée) ADJECTIVE
unbalanced

déséquilibrer VERB [28]
■ **déséquilibrer quelqu'un** to throw somebody off balance □ Le coup de poing l'a déséquilibré. The punch threw him off balance.

désert (FEM déserte) ADJECTIVE
▷ see also **désert** NOUN
deserted
□ Le dimanche, le centre commercial est désert. On Sundays, the shopping centre is deserted.
■ **une île déserte** a desert island

le **désert** MASC NOUN
▷ see also **désert** ADJECTIVE
desert

déserter VERB [28]
to desert

désertique (FEM désertique) ADJECTIVE
desert
□ une région désertique a desert region

désespéré (FEM désespérée) ADJECTIVE
desperate

désespérer VERB [34]
to despair
□ Il ne faut pas désespérer. Don't despair.

le **désespoir** MASC NOUN
despair

déshabiller VERB [28]
to undress
■ **se déshabiller** to get undressed

déshériter VERB [28]
to disinherit
■ **les déshérités** the underprivileged

déshydraté (FEM déshydratée) ADJECTIVE
dehydrated

désigner VERB [28]
to choose
□ On l'a désignée pour remettre le prix. She was chosen to present the prize.
■ **désigner quelque chose du doigt** to point at something

le **désinfectant** MASC NOUN
disinfectant
■ **le désinfectant pour les mains** hand sanitizer

désinfecter VERB [28]
to disinfect

désintéressé (FEM désintéressée) ADJECTIVE
1 unselfish
□ un acte désintéressé an unselfish action
2 impartial
□ un conseil désintéressé impartial advice

désintéresser VERB [28]
■ **se désintéresser de quelque chose** to lose interest in something

le **désir** MASC NOUN
1 wish
□ Vos désirs sont des ordres. Your wish is my command.
2 will
□ le désir de réussir the will to succeed
3 desire
□ Ses yeux brillaient de désir. Her eyes were shining with desire.

désirer VERB [28]
to want
□ Vous désirez ? (in shop) What would you like?

désobéir VERB [38]
■ **désobéir à quelqu'un** to disobey somebody

désobéissant (FEM désobéissante) ADJECTIVE
disobedient

désobligeant (FEM désobligeante) ADJECTIVE
unpleasant
□ faire une remarque désobligeante to make an unpleasant remark

le **désodorisant** MASC NOUN
air freshener

désolé (FEM désolée) ADJECTIVE
sorry
□ Je suis vraiment désolé. I'm very sorry.
■ **Désolé !** Sorry!

désopilant (FEM désopilante) ADJECTIVE
hilarious

désordonné (FEM désordonnée) ADJECTIVE
untidy

le **désordre** MASC NOUN
untidiness
■ **Quel désordre !** What a mess!
■ **en désordre** untidy □ Sa chambre est toujours en désordre. His bedroom is always untidy.

d

Numbers in brackets refer to verb tables on pages 650 to 658

désormais ADVERB
from now on
□ Désormais, je boirai de l'eau. From now on I'll drink water.

desquelles PL PRONOUN

desquelles is the contracted form of **de** + **lesquelles**.

□ des négociations au cours desquelles les patrons ont fait des concessions negotiations during which the employers made concessions

desquels PL PRONOUN

desquels is the contracted form of **de** + **lesquels**.

□ les lacs au bord desquels nous avons campé the lakes on the banks of which we camped

dessécher VERB [34]
to dry out
□ Le soleil dessèche la peau. The sun dries your skin out.

desserrer VERB [28]
to loosen

le dessert MASC NOUN
pudding
□ Qu'est-ce que vous désirez comme dessert ? What would you like for pudding?

le dessin MASC NOUN
drawing
□ C'est un dessin de ma petite sœur. It's a drawing my little sister did.
■ **un dessin animé** (film) a cartoon
■ **un dessin humoristique** (drawing) a cartoon

le dessinateur MASC NOUN
■ **un dessinateur industriel** a draughtsman

dessiner VERB [28]
to draw

dessous ADVERB
▷ see also **dessous** NOUN
underneath
■ **en dessous** underneath □ Soulève le pot de fleurs, la clé est en dessous. Lift the flowerpot, the key's underneath.
■ **par-dessous** underneath □ Le grillage ne sert à rien, les lapins passent par-dessous. The fence is useless, the rabbits get in underneath.
■ **là-dessous** under there □ Il s'est caché là-dessous. He hid under there.
■ **ci-dessous** below □ Complétez les phrases ci-dessous. Complete the sentences below.
■ **au-dessous de** below □ vingt degrés au-dessous de zéro 20 degrees below zero

le dessous MASC NOUN
▷ see also **dessous** ADVERB
underneath
■ **les voisins du dessous** the downstairs neighbours
■ **les dessous** underwear □ des dessous en soie silk underwear

le dessous-de-plat (PL les **dessous-de-plat**) MASC NOUN
tablemat

dessus ADVERB
▷ see also **dessus** NOUN
on top
□ un gâteau avec des bougies dessus a cake with candles on top
■ **par-dessus** over □ Nous avons sauté par-dessus la barrière. We jumped over the gate.
■ **au-dessus** above □ la taille au-dessus the size above □ au-dessus du lit above the bed
■ **là-dessus** 1 on there □ Tu peux écrire là-dessus. You can write on there. 2 with that □ « Je démissionne ! » Là-dessus, il est parti. 'I resign!' With that, he left.
■ **ci-dessus** above □ l'exemple ci-dessus the example above

le dessus MASC NOUN
▷ see also **dessus** ADVERB
top
■ **les voisins du dessus** the upstairs neighbours
■ **avoir le dessus** to have the upper hand

le/la destinataire MASC/FEM NOUN
addressee

la destination FEM NOUN
destination
■ **les passagers à destination de Paris** passengers travelling to Paris

destiné (FEM **destinée**) ADJECTIVE
intended
□ Ce livre est destiné aux enfants. This book is intended for children.
■ **Elle était destinée à faire ce métier.** She was destined to go into that job.

la destruction FEM NOUN
destruction

le détachant MASC NOUN
stain remover

détacher VERB [28]
to undo
■ **se détacher** 1 to come off □ La poignée de la porte s'est détachée. The door handle came off. 2 to break away □ Un wagon s'est détaché du reste du train. A carriage broke away from the rest of the train.

le détail MASC NOUN
detail
■ **en détail** in detail

le détective MASC NOUN
detective
□ un détective privé a private detective

déteindre VERB [60]
to fade (in wash)

détendre VERB [88]
to relax
□ La lecture, ça me détend. I find reading relaxing.

détente - devoir

■ **se détendre** to relax □ Il est allé prendre un bain pour se détendre. He's gone to have a bath to relax.

la **détente** FEM NOUN
relaxation

le **détenu** MASC NOUN
prisoner

la **détenue** FEM NOUN
prisoner

se **détériorer** VERB [28]
to deteriorate

déterminé (FEM **déterminée**) ADJECTIVE
1 determined
□ C'est un homme déterminé. He's a determined man.
2 specific
□ un but déterminé a specific aim

détestable (FEM **détestable**) ADJECTIVE
horrible

détester VERB [28]
to hate

la **détonation** FEM NOUN
bang
□ J'ai entendu une détonation. I heard a bang.

le **détour** MASC NOUN
detour
■ **Ça vaut le détour.** It's worth the trip.

le **détournement** MASC NOUN
■ **un détournement d'avion** a hijacking

détrempé (FEM **détrempée**) ADJECTIVE
waterlogged

les **détritus** MASC PL NOUN
litter *sing*

détruire VERB [23]
to destroy

la **dette** FEM NOUN
debt

le **deuil** MASC NOUN
■ **être en deuil** to be in mourning

deux NUMBER
two
□ Il était deux heures. It was two o'clock. □ Elle a deux ans. She's two.
■ **deux fois** twice
■ **deux-points** colon
■ **tous les deux** both □ Nous y sommes allées toutes les deux. We both went.
■ **le deux février** the second of February

deuxième (FEM **deuxième**) ADJECTIVE
second
□ au deuxième étage on the second floor

deuxièmement ADVERB
secondly

devais, devait, devaient VERB ▷ *see* **devoir**

dévaliser VERB [28]
to rob

devant ADVERB, PREPOSITION
▷ *see also* **devant** NOUN
1 in front
□ Il marchait devant. He was walking in front.
2 in front of
□ Il était assis devant moi. He was sitting in front of me.
■ **passer devant** to go past □ Nous sommes passés devant chez toi. We went past your house.

le **devant** MASC NOUN
▷ *see also* **devant** ADVERB, PREPOSITION
front
□ le devant de la maison the front of the house
■ **les pattes de devant** the front legs

le **développement** MASC NOUN
development
■ **les pays en voie de développement** developing countries
■ **le développement durable** sustainable development

développer VERB [28]
to develop
■ **se développer** to develop

devenir VERB [25, *aux* **être**]
to become

devez VERB ▷ *see* **devoir**

la **déviation** FEM NOUN
diversion

deviez VERB ▷ *see* **devoir**

deviner VERB [28]
to guess

la **devinette** FEM NOUN
riddle
□ poser une devinette à quelqu'un to ask somebody a riddle

devions VERB ▷ *see* **devoir**

dévisager VERB [45]
■ **dévisager quelqu'un** to stare at somebody

la **devise** FEM NOUN
currency
□ les devises étrangères foreign currency

dévisser VERB [28]
to unscrew

dévoiler VERB [28]
to unveil

devoir VERB [26]

PRESENT TENSE	
je dois	nous devons
tu dois	vous devez
il/elle doit	ils/elles doivent
PAST PARTICIPLE	
dû	

▷ *see also* **devoir** NOUN

Numbers in brackets refer to verb tables on pages 650 to 658

1 to have to
  □ Je dois partir. I've got to go.
2 must
  □ Tu dois être fatigué. You must be tired.
3 to be due to
  □ Le nouveau centre commercial doit ouvrir en mai. The new shopping centre is due to open in May.
  ■ **devoir quelque chose à quelqu'un** to owe somebody something □ Combien est-ce que je vous dois ? How much do I owe you?

le **devoir** MASC NOUN
  ▷ see also **devoir** VERB
1 exercise
  ■ **les devoirs** homework
  ■ **un devoir sur table** a written test
2 duty
  □ Aller voter fait partie des devoirs du citoyen. Voting is part of one's duty as a citizen.

devons VERB ▷ see **devoir**

dévorer VERB [28]
  to devour

dévoué (FEM **dévouée**) ADJECTIVE
  devoted

devra, devrai, devras, devrez, devrons, devront VERB ▷ see **devoir**

le **diabète** MASC NOUN
  diabetes

diabétique (FEM **diabétique**) ADJECTIVE
  diabetic
  □ Je suis diabétique. I'm diabetic.

le **diable** MASC NOUN
  devil

le **diabolo** MASC NOUN
  fruit cordial and lemonade
  ■ **un diabolo menthe** a mint cordial and lemonade

diagonal (FEM **diagonale**, MASC PL **diagonaux**) ADJECTIVE
  diagonal

la **diagonale** FEM NOUN
  diagonal
  ■ **en diagonale** diagonally

le **diagramme** MASC NOUN
  diagram

le **dialecte** MASC NOUN
  dialect

le **dialogue** MASC NOUN
  dialogue

le **diamant** MASC NOUN
  diamond

le **diamètre** MASC NOUN
  diameter

la **diapo** FEM NOUN (*informal*)
  slide (*image*)

la **diapositive** FEM NOUN
  slide

  □ projeter des diapositives to show some slides

la **diarrhée** FEM NOUN
  diarrhoea
  □ avoir la diarrhée to have diarrhoea

le **dictateur** MASC NOUN
  dictator

la **dictature** FEM NOUN
  dictatorship

la **dictée** FEM NOUN
  dictation

dicter VERB [28]
  to dictate

le **dictionnaire** MASC NOUN
  dictionary

le **dièse** MASC NOUN
  hash (# *sign*)
  □ Pour plus d'options, appuyez sur la touche dièse. For more options, press the hash key.

diététique (FEM **diététique**) ADJECTIVE
  ■ **un magasin diététique** a health food shop

le **dieu** (PL les **dieux**) MASC NOUN
  god
  ■ **Dieu** God □ Mon Dieu ! Oh my God!

le **différé** MASC NOUN
  ■ **une émission en différé** a recording

la **différence** FEM NOUN
  difference
  ■ **la différence d'âge** the age difference
  ■ **à la différence de** unlike

différent (FEM **différente**) ADJECTIVE
1 different
  □ pour des raisons différentes for different reasons
2 various
  □ pour différentes raisons for various reasons
  ■ **différent de** different from □ Son point de vue est différent du mien. His point of view is different from mine.

difficile (FEM **difficile**) ADJECTIVE
  difficult
  □ C'est difficile à comprendre. It's difficult to understand.

difficilement ADVERB
  ■ **faire quelque chose difficilement** to have trouble doing something □ Ma grand-mère se déplace difficilement. My grandmother has trouble getting around.
  ■ **Je pouvais difficilement refuser.** It was difficult for me to refuse.

la **difficulté** FEM NOUN
  difficulty
  □ avec difficulté with difficulty
  ■ **élève en difficulté (scolaire)** a student who is struggling

diffuser VERB [34]
1 to diffuse

digérer - directrice

2 to broadcast
□ Les émissions étaient diffusées en français. The programmes were broadcast in French.

digérer VERB [34]
to digest

le **digestif** MASC NOUN
after-dinner liqueur

digne (FEM digne) ADJECTIVE
■ **digne de** worthy of □ digne de confiance trustworthy

la **dignité** FEM NOUN
dignity

le **dilemme** MASC NOUN
dilemma
□ être devant un dilemme to be faced with a dilemma

diluer VERB [28]
to dilute

le **dimanche** MASC NOUN
1 Sunday
□ Aujourd'hui, on est dimanche. It's Sunday today.
2 on Sunday
□ Dimanche, nous allons déjeuner chez mes grands-parents. On Sunday we're having lunch at my grandparents'.
■ **le dimanche** on Sundays □ Le dimanche, je fais la grasse matinée. I have a lie-in on Sundays.
■ **tous les dimanches** every Sunday
■ **dimanche dernier** last Sunday
■ **dimanche prochain** next Sunday
■ **À dimanche !** See you on Sunday!

diminuer VERB [28]
to decrease
□ Le chômage a un peu diminué le mois dernier. Unemployment fell slightly last month.

le **diminutif** MASC NOUN
pet name

la **diminution** FEM NOUN
1 reduction
2 decrease

la **dinde** FEM NOUN
turkey (*meat*)
□ la dinde de Noël the Christmas turkey

le **dindon** MASC NOUN
turkey (*bird*)

le **dîner** MASC NOUN
▷ *see also* **dîner** VERB
dinner (*evening meal*)

dîner VERB [28]
▷ *see also* **dîner** NOUN
to have dinner (*evening meal*)

dingue (FEM dingue) ADJECTIVE (*informal*)
crazy

diplomate (FEM diplomate) ADJECTIVE
▷ *see also* **diplomate** NOUN
diplomatic

le/la **diplomate** MASC/FEM NOUN
▷ *see also* **diplomate** ADJECTIVE
diplomat

la **diplomatie** FEM NOUN
diplomacy

le **diplôme** MASC NOUN
qualification

diplômé (FEM diplômée) ADJECTIVE
qualified

dire VERB [27]
1 to say
□ Il a dit qu'il ne viendrait pas. He said he wouldn't come.
■ **on dit que ...** they say that ... □ On dit que la nourriture est excellente là-bas. They say that the food is excellent there.
2 to tell
■ **dire quelque chose à quelqu'un** to tell somebody something □ Elle m'a dit la vérité. She told me the truth. □ Il nous a dit de regarder cette émission. He told us to watch this programme.
■ **dire à quelqu'un de faire quelque chose** to tell someone to do something □ Dis à ton frère de mettre la table. Tell your brother to set the table.
■ **On dirait qu'il va pleuvoir.** It looks as if it's going to rain.
■ **se dire quelque chose** to think something □ Quand je l'ai vu, je me suis dit qu'il avait vieilli. When I saw him, I thought that he'd aged.
■ **Est-ce que ça se dit ?** Can you say that?
■ **Ça ne me dit rien.** **1** That doesn't appeal to me. **2** It doesn't ring a bell.

direct (FEM directe) ADJECTIVE
direct
■ **en direct** live □ une émission en direct a live broadcast

directement ADVERB
straight
□ Il est rentré directement chez lui. He went straight home.

le **directeur** MASC NOUN
1 headteacher
□ Il est directeur. He's a headteacher.
2 manager
□ Il est directeur du personnel. He's a personnel manager.

la **direction** FEM NOUN
1 management
□ la direction et les ouvriers the management and the workers
2 direction
□ « toutes directions » 'all directions'

la **directrice** FEM NOUN
1 headteacher
□ Elle est directrice. She's a headteacher.

2 manager
  □ Elle est directrice commerciale. She's a sales manager.

dirent VERB ▷ *see* **dire**

le **dirigeant** MASC NOUN
  leader

la **dirigeante** FEM NOUN
  leader

diriger VERB [45]
  to manage
  □ Il dirige une petite entreprise. He manages a small company.
  ■ **se diriger vers** to head for □ Il se dirigeait vers la gare. He was heading for the station.

dis VERB ▷ *see* **dire**
  ■ **Dis-moi la vérité !** Tell me the truth!
  ■ **dis donc** hey □ Il a drôlement changé, dis donc ! Hey, he's really changed! □ Dis donc, tu te souviens de Sam ? Hey, do you remember Sam?

disaient, disais, disait VERB ▷ *see* **dire**

la **discothèque** FEM NOUN
  disco (*club*)

le **discours** MASC NOUN
  speech

discret (FEM **discrète**) ADJECTIVE
  discreet

la **discrimination** FEM NOUN
  discrimination
  □ la discrimination raciale racial discrimination
  □ la discrimination sexuelle sex discrimination

la **discussion** FEM NOUN
  discussion

discutable (FEM **discutable**) ADJECTIVE
  debatable

discuter VERB [28]
1 to talk
  □ Nous avons discuté pendant des heures. We talked for hours.
  ■ **discuter de** to talk about □ Nous avons discuté de nos jeux vidéo préférés. We talked about our favourite video games.
2 to argue
  □ C'est ce que j'ai décidé, alors ne discutez pas ! That's what I've decided, so don't argue!

disent, disiez, disions VERB ▷ *see* **dire**

disons VERB ▷ *see* **dire**
  let's say
  □ C'est à, disons, une demi-heure à pied. It's half an hour's walk, say.

disparaître VERB [56]
  to disappear
  ■ **faire disparaître quelque chose 1** to make something disappear □ Il a fait disparaître le lapin dans son chapeau. He made the rabbit disappear in his hat. **2** to get rid of something □ Ils ont fait disparaître tous les documents compromettants. They got rid of all the incriminating documents.

la **disparition** FEM NOUN
  disappearance
  ■ **une espèce en voie de disparition** an endangered species

disparu (FEM **disparue**) ADJECTIVE
  ■ **être porté disparu** to be reported missing

le **dispensaire** MASC NOUN
  community clinic

dispensé (FEM **dispensée**) ADJECTIVE
  ■ **être dispensé de quelque chose** to be excused something □ Elle est dispensée de gymnastique. She's excused gym.

disperser VERB [28]
  to break up
  □ La police a dispersé les manifestants. The police broke up the demonstrators.
  ■ **se disperser** to break up □ Une fois l'ambulance partie, la foule s'est dispersée. Once the ambulance had left, the crowd broke up.

disponible (FEM **disponible**) ADJECTIVE
  available

disposé (FEM **disposée**) ADJECTIVE
  ■ **être disposé à faire quelque chose** to be willing to do something □ Il était disposé à m'aider. He was willing to help me.

disposer VERB [28]
  ■ **disposer de quelque chose** to have access to something □ Je dispose d'un ordinateur. I have access to a computer.

la **disposition** FEM NOUN
  ■ **prendre ses dispositions** to make arrangements □ Est-ce que vous avez pris vos dispositions pour partir en France ? Have you made arrangements to go to France?
  ■ **avoir quelque chose à sa disposition** to have something at one's disposal □ J'ai une voiture à ma disposition pour la semaine. I have a car at my disposal for the week. □ Je tiens ces livres à votre disposition. The books are at your disposal.
  ■ **Je suis à votre disposition.** I am at your service.

la **dispute** FEM NOUN
  argument

se disputer VERB [28]
  to argue

le **disquaire** MASC NOUN
  record dealer

le **disque** MASC NOUN
  record
  ■ **un disque compact** a compact disc
  ■ **le disque dur** hard disk

disséminé (FEM **disséminée**) ADJECTIVE
  scattered

disséquer - documentaire

disséquer VERB [34]
to dissect

la **dissertation** FEM NOUN
essay

dissimuler VERB [28]
to conceal

se **dissiper** VERB [28]
to clear
□ Le brouillard va se dissiper dans l'après-midi. The fog will clear during the afternoon.

le **dissolvant** MASC NOUN
nail polish remover

dissoudre VERB [70]
to dissolve
■ **se dissoudre** to dissolve

dissuader VERB [28]
■ **dissuader quelqu'un de faire quelque chose** to dissuade somebody from doing something □ Elle m'a dissuadé d'aller voir ce film. She dissuaded me from going to see the film.

la **distance** FEM NOUN
distance

la **distillerie** FEM NOUN
distillery

distingué (FEM **distinguée**) ADJECTIVE
distinguished

distinguer VERB [28]
to distinguish

la **distraction** FEM NOUN
entertainment
□ Il lit beaucoup : c'est sa seule distraction. He reads a lot: it's his only form of entertainment.

distraire VERB [85]
■ **Va voir un film, ça te distraira.** Go and see a film, it'll take your mind off things.

distrait (FEM **distraite**) ADJECTIVE
absent-minded

distribuer VERB [28]
1 to give out
□ Distribue les livres, s'il te plaît. Give out the books, please.
2 to deal (*cards*)

le **distributeur** MASC NOUN
■ **un distributeur automatique** a vending machine
■ **un distributeur de billets** a cash machine

dit (FEM **dite**) ADJECTIVE
known as
□ Pierre, dit Pierrot Pierre, known as Pierrot

dit VERB ▷ *see* dire

dites VERB ▷ *see* dire
■ **Dites-moi ce que vous pensez.** Tell me what you think.
■ **dites donc** hey □ Dites donc, vous, là-bas ! Hey, you there!

divers (FEM **diverse**) ADJECTIVE
diverse
■ **pour diverses raisons** for various reasons

la **diversité** FEM NOUN
diversity

se **divertir** VERB [38]
to enjoy oneself

divin (FEM **divine**) ADJECTIVE
divine

diviser VERB [28]
to divide
□ Quatre divisé par deux égale deux. 4 divided by 2 equals 2.

le **divorce** MASC NOUN
divorce

le **divorcé** MASC NOUN
divorcee

la **divorcée** FEM NOUN
divorcee

divorcer VERB [12]
to get divorced

dix NUMBER
ten
□ Elle a dix ans. She's ten. □ à dix heures at ten o'clock
■ **le dix février** the tenth of February

dix-huit NUMBER
eighteen
□ Elle a dix-huit ans. She's eighteen. □ à dix-huit heures at 6 p.m.

dixième (FEM **dixième**) ADJECTIVE
tenth
□ au dixième étage on the tenth floor

dix-neuf NUMBER
nineteen
□ Elle a dix-neuf ans. She's nineteen. □ à dix-neuf heures at 7 p.m.

dix-sept NUMBER
seventeen
□ Elle a dix-sept ans. She's seventeen. □ à dix-sept heures at 5 p.m.

la **dizaine** FEM NOUN
about ten
□ une dizaine de jours about ten days

le **do** MASC NOUN
1 C
□ en do majeur in C major
2 do
□ do, ré, mi ... do, re, mi ...

le **docteur** MASC NOUN
doctor
□ Elle est docteur. She's a doctor.

le **document** MASC NOUN
document

le **documentaire** MASC NOUN
documentary

le/la **documentaliste** MASC/FEM NOUN
librarian

la **documentation** FEM NOUN
documentation

documenter VERB [28]
■ **se documenter sur quelque chose** to gather information on something

dodu (FEM **dodue**) ADJECTIVE
plump

le **doigt** MASC NOUN
finger
■ **les doigts de pied** the toes

dois, doit, doivent VERB ▷ see **devoir**

le **domaine** MASC NOUN
1 estate
□ Il possède un immense domaine en Normandie. He owns a huge estate in Normandy.
2 field
□ La chimie n'est pas mon domaine. Chemistry's not my field.

domestique (FEM **domestique**) ADJECTIVE
▷ see also **domestique** NOUN
domestic
■ **les animaux domestiques** pets

le/la **domestique** MASC/FEM NOUN
▷ see also **domestique** ADJECTIVE
servant

le **domicile** MASC NOUN
place of residence
■ **à domicile** at home □ Il travaille à domicile. He works at home.

domicilié (FEM **domiciliée**) ADJECTIVE
■ « **domicilié à : ...** » 'address: ...'

dominer VERB [28]
to dominate
■ **se dominer** to control oneself

les **dominos** MASC PL NOUN
dominoes
□ jouer aux dominos to play dominoes

le **dommage** MASC NOUN
damage
□ La tempête a causé d'importants dommages. The storm caused a lot of damage.
■ **C'est dommage.** It's a shame. □ C'est dommage que tu ne puisses pas venir. It's a shame you can't come.

dompter VERB [28]
to tame

le **dompteur** MASC NOUN
animal tamer

la **dompteuse** FEM NOUN
animal tamer

le **don** MASC NOUN
1 donation
2 gift
□ avoir un don pour quelque chose to have a gift for something

■ Elle a le don de m'énerver. She's got a knack of getting on my nerves.

donc CONJUNCTION
so

le **dongle** MASC NOUN
dongle

le **donjon** MASC NOUN
keep (of castle)

les **données** FEM PL NOUN
data

donner VERB [28]
1 to give
■ **donner quelque chose à quelqu'un** to give somebody something □ Elle m'a donné son adresse. She gave me her address.
■ **Ça m'a donné faim.** That made me feel hungry.
2 to give away
□ Tu as toujours ta veste en daim ? — Non, je l'ai donnée. Have you still got your suede jacket? — No, I gave it away.
■ **donner sur quelque chose** to overlook something □ une fenêtre qui donne sur la mer a window overlooking the sea

dont PRONOUN
1 of which
□ deux livres, dont l'un est en anglais two books, one of which is in English □ le prix dont il est si fier the prize he's so proud of
2 of whom
□ trois candidats, dont deux parlent italien three candidates, two of whom speak Italian □ la fille dont je t'ai parlé the girl I told you about

doré (FEM **dorée**) ADJECTIVE
golden
□ une étoile dorée a golden star

dorénavant ADVERB
from now on
□ Dorénavant, tu feras attention. From now on, you'll be careful.

dorloter VERB [28]
to pamper

dormir VERB [29]
1 to sleep
□ Tu as bien dormi ? Did you sleep well?
2 to be asleep
□ Tu dors ? Are you asleep?

le **dortoir** MASC NOUN
dormitory

le **dos** MASC NOUN
back
□ dos à dos back to back
■ **faire quelque chose dans le dos de quelqu'un** to do something behind somebody's back □ Elle me critique dans mon dos. She criticizes me behind my back.
■ **de dos** from behind

■ **nager le dos crawlé** to swim backstroke
■ **« voir au dos »** 'see over'

la **dose** FEM NOUN
dose
□ Ne pas dépasser la dose prescrite. Do not exceed the stated dose.

le **dossier** MASC NOUN
1 file
□ une pile de dossiers a stack of files
2 report
□ un bon dossier scolaire a good school report
3 feature (in magazine)
4 back (of chair)

la **douane** FEM NOUN
customs

le **douanier** MASC NOUN
customs officer

le **double** MASC NOUN
■ **le double** twice as much □ Il gagne le double. He earns twice as much.
■ **le double du prix normal** twice the normal price
■ **en double** in duplicate
■ **Garde cette photo, je l'ai en double.** Keep this photo, I've got a copy of it.
■ **le double messieurs** (tennis) the men's doubles

le **double-clic** (PL les **double-clics**) MASC NOUN
double-click

double-cliquer VERB [28]
to double-click
□ double-cliquer sur une icône to double-click on an icon

doubler VERB [28]
1 to double
□ Le prix a doublé en dix ans. The price has doubled in 10 years.
2 to overtake
□ Il est dangereux de doubler sur cette route. It's dangerous to overtake on this road.
■ **un film doublé** a dubbed film

douce FEM ADJECTIVE ▷ see **doux**

doucement ADVERB
1 gently
□ Il a frappé doucement à la porte. He knocked gently at the door.
2 slowly
□ Roulez doucement ! Drive slowly! □ Je ne comprends pas, parle plus doucement. I don't understand, speak more slowly.

la **douceur** FEM NOUN
1 softness
□ Cette crème maintient la douceur de votre peau. This cream keeps your skin soft.
2 gentleness
□ parler avec douceur to speak gently

■ **L'avion a atterri en douceur.** The plane made a smooth landing.

la **douche** FEM NOUN
shower
■ **les douches** the shower room
■ **prendre une douche** to have a shower

se **doucher** VERB [28]
to have a shower

le **doudou** MASC NOUN (informal)
1 comfort blanket (piece of fabric)
2 cuddly toy (toy)

doué (FEM **douée**) ADJECTIVE
talented
■ **être doué en quelque chose** to be good at something □ Il est doué en maths. He's good at maths.

douillet (FEM **douillette**) ADJECTIVE
1 cosy
□ un anorak douillet a cosy anorak
2 soft
□ Je ne supporte pas la douleur : je suis très douillette. I can't stand pain: I'm a real softie.

la **douleur** FEM NOUN
pain

douloureux (FEM **douloureuse**) ADJECTIVE
painful

le **doute** MASC NOUN
doubt
■ **sans doute** probably

douter VERB [28]
to doubt
■ **douter de quelque chose** to have doubts about something □ Je doute de sa sincérité. I have my doubts about his sincerity.
■ **se douter de quelque chose** to suspect something □ Je ne me doutais de rien. I didn't suspect anything.
■ **Je m'en doutais.** I suspected as much.

douteux (FEM **douteuse**) ADJECTIVE
1 dubious
□ une plaisanterie d'un goût douteux a joke in dubious taste
2 suspicious-looking
□ un individu douteux a suspicious-looking person

Douvres NOUN
Dover

doux (FEM **douce**, MASC PL **doux**) ADJECTIVE
1 soft
□ un tissu doux soft material □ les drogues douces soft drugs
2 sweet
□ du cidre doux sweet cider
3 mild
□ Il fait doux aujourd'hui. It's mild today.
4 gentle
□ C'est quelqu'un de très doux. He's a very gentle person.

■ **en douce** on the quiet □ Il m'a donné dix euros en douce. He slipped me 10 euros on the quiet.

la **douzaine** FEM NOUN
dozen
□ une douzaine d'œufs a dozen eggs
■ **une douzaine de personnes** about twelve people

douze NUMBER
twelve
□ Il a douze ans. He's twelve.
■ **le douze février** the twelfth of February

douzième (FEM **douzième**) ADJECTIVE
twelfth
□ au douzième étage on the twelfth floor

la **dragée** FEM NOUN
sugared almond

draguer VERB [28] (informal)
■ **draguer quelqu'un** to chat somebody up
□ Il est en train de la draguer. He's chatting her up.
■ **se faire draguer** to get chatted up □ Il aime se faire draguer. He likes getting chatted up.

le **dragueur** MASC NOUN (informal)
flirt (person)

la **dragueuse** FEM NOUN (informal)
flirt (person)

dramatique (FEM **dramatique**) ADJECTIVE
tragic
□ une situation dramatique a tragic situation
■ **l'art dramatique** drama

le **drame** MASC NOUN
drama (incident)
■ **Ça n'est pas un drame si tu ne viens pas.** It's not the end of the world if you don't come.

le **drap** MASC NOUN
sheet (for bed)

le **drapeau** (PL les **drapeaux**) MASC NOUN
flag
□ le drapeau français the French flag □ le drapeau tricolore the French flag

> **DID YOU KNOW...?**
> **le drapeau tricolore** is the French flag: its three colours are blue, white and red.

dressé (FEM **dressée**) ADJECTIVE
trained
□ un chien bien dressé a well-trained dog

dresser VERB [28]
1 to draw up
□ dresser une liste to draw up a list
2 to train
□ dresser un chien to train a dog
■ **dresser l'oreille** to prick up one's ears
□ Quand elle a dit ça, il a dressé l'oreille. When she said that, he pricked up his ears.

la **drogue** FEM NOUN
drug

□ le problème de la drogue the drugs problem
□ la lutte contre la drogue the war against drugs
■ **les drogues douces** soft drugs
■ **les drogues dures** hard drugs

le **drogué** MASC NOUN
drug addict

la **droguée** FEM NOUN
drug addict

droguer VERB [28]
■ **droguer quelqu'un** to drug somebody
■ **se droguer** to take drugs

la **droguerie** FEM NOUN
hardware shop

droit (FEM **droite**) ADJECTIVE, ADVERB
▷ see also **droit** NOUN, **droite** NOUN
1 right
□ le bras droit the right arm □ le côté droit the right-hand side
2 straight
□ une ligne droite a straight line □ Tiens-toi droite ! Stand up straight!
■ **tout droit** straight on

le **droit** MASC NOUN
▷ see also **droit** ADJECTIVE, ADVERB
1 right
□ les droits de l'homme human rights
■ **avoir le droit de faire quelque chose** to be allowed to do something □ On n'a pas le droit de fumer à l'école. We're not allowed to smoke at school.
2 law
□ faire son droit to study law □ un étudiant en droit a law student

la **droite** FEM NOUN
▷ see also **droit** ADJECTIVE, ADVERB
right
□ sur votre droite on your right
■ **à droite 1** on the right □ la troisième rue à droite the third street on the right **2** to the right □ à droite de la fenêtre to the right of the window
■ **Tournez à droite.** Turn right.
■ **la voie de droite** the right-hand lane
■ **la droite** (in politics) the right
■ **Elle est très à droite.** She's very right-wing.

droitier (FEM **droitière**) ADJECTIVE
right-handed
□ Elle est droitière. She's right-handed.

drôle (FEM **drôle**) ADJECTIVE
funny
□ Ça n'est pas drôle. It's not funny.
■ **un drôle de temps** funny weather

drôlement ADVERB (informal)
really
□ C'est drôlement bon. It's really good.

le **drone** MASC NOUN
drone

d

du ARTICLE

> du is the contracted form of **de** + **le**.

1 some
  □ Tu veux du fromage ? Would you like some cheese?

2 any
  □ Tu as du chocolat ? Have you got any chocolate?

3 of the
  □ la porte du garage the door of the garage □ la femme du directeur the headmaster's wife

dû (FEM **due**, MASC PL **dus**) ADJECTIVE
  ▷ *see also* **dû** VERB
  ■ **dû à** due to □ un retard dû au mauvais temps a delay due to bad weather

dû VERB ▷ *see* **devoir**
  ▷ *see also* **dû** ADJECTIVE
  ■ **Nous avons dû nous arrêter.** We had to stop.

le **duc** MASC NOUN
  duke

la **duchesse** FEM NOUN
  duchess

dupe (FEM **dupe**) ADJECTIVE
  ■ **Elle me ment mais je ne suis pas dupe.** She lies to me but I'm not taken in by that.

duquel (MASC PL **desquels**, FEM PL **desquelles**) PRONOUN

> duquel is the contracted form of **de** + **lequel**.

  □ l'homme duquel il parle the man he is talking about

dur (FEM **dure**) ADJECTIVE, ADVERB
  hard
  □ travailler dur to work hard □ être dur avec quelqu'un to be hard on somebody

durable (FEM **durable**) ADJECTIVE
  sustainable (*development*)

durant PREPOSITION
1 during
  □ durant la nuit during the night

2 for
  □ durant des années for years □ des mois durant for months

la **durée** FEM NOUN
  length
  □ Quelle est la durée des études d'ingénieur ? How long does it take to train as an engineer?
  ■ **pour une durée de quinze jours** for a period of two weeks
  ■ **de courte durée** short □ un séjour de courte durée a short stay
  ■ **de longue durée** long □ une absence de longue durée a long absence

durement ADVERB
  harshly

durer VERB [28]
  to last

la **dureté** FEM NOUN
  harshness
  □ traiter quelqu'un avec dureté to treat somebody harshly

le **DVD** MASC NOUN
  DVD

dynamique (FEM **dynamique**) ADJECTIVE
  dynamic

la **dyslexie** FEM NOUN
  dyslexia

dyslexique (FEM **dyslexique**) ADJECTIVE
  dyslexic

Ee

l'eau (PL les **eaux**) FEM NOUN
water
- **l'eau minérale** mineral water
- **l'eau plate** still water
- **tomber à l'eau** to fall through □ Nos projets sont tombés à l'eau. Our plans have fallen through.

ébahi (FEM **ébahie**) ADJECTIVE
amazed

éblouir VERB [38]
to dazzle

l'éboueur MASC NOUN
dustman

ébouillanter VERB [28]
to scald

l'écaille FEM NOUN
scale (of fish)

s'écailler VERB [28]
to flake

l'écart MASC NOUN
gap
- **à l'écart de** away from □ Ils se sont assis à l'écart des autres. They sat down away from the others.

écarté (FEM **écartée**) ADJECTIVE
remote
- **les bras écartés** arms outstretched
- **les jambes écartées** legs apart

écarter VERB [28]
to open wide (arms, legs)
- **s'écarter** to move □ Ils se sont écartés pour le laisser passer. They moved to let him pass.

l'échafaudage MASC NOUN
scaffolding

l'échalote FEM NOUN
shallot

l'échange MASC NOUN
exchange
□ en échange de in exchange for

échanger VERB [45]
to swap
□ Je t'échange ce jeux contre celui-là. I'll swap you this game for that one.

l'échantillon MASC NOUN
sample

échapper VERB [28]
- **échapper à** to escape from □ Le prisonnier a réussi à échapper à la police. The prisoner managed to escape from the police.
- **s'échapper** to escape □ Il s'est échappé de prison. He escaped from prison.
- **l'échapper belle** to have a narrow escape □ Nous l'avons échappé belle. We had a narrow escape.

l'écharde FEM NOUN
splinter of wood

l'écharpe FEM NOUN
scarf

s'échauffer VERB [28]
to warm up (before exercise)

l'échec MASC NOUN
failure

les échecs MASC PL NOUN
chess sing
□ jouer aux échecs to play chess

l'échelle FEM NOUN
1 ladder
2 scale (of map)

échevelé (FEM **échevelée**) ADJECTIVE
dishevelled

l'écho MASC NOUN
echo

échouer VERB [28]
- **échouer à un examen** to fail an exam

éclabousser VERB [28]
to splash

l'éclair MASC NOUN
flash of lightning
- **un éclair au chocolat** a chocolate éclair

l'éclairage MASC NOUN
lighting

l'éclaircie FEM NOUN
bright interval

éclairer VERB [28]
- **Cette lampe éclaire bien.** This lamp gives a good light.

l'éclat MASC NOUN
1 piece (of glass)
□ La vase a volé en éclats. The vase smashed into pieces.

2 brightness (of sun, colour)
- **des éclats de rire** roars of laughter

éclatant (FEM **éclatante**) ADJECTIVE
brilliant
□ des dents d'une blancheur éclatante brilliant white teeth

éclater VERB [28]
1 to burst (tyre, balloon)
- **éclater de rire** to burst out laughing
- **éclater en sanglots** to burst into tears
2 to break out
□ La Seconde Guerre mondiale a éclaté en 1939. The Second World War broke out in 1939.

écœurant (FEM **écœurante**) ADJECTIVE
sickly

écœurer VERB [28]
- **Tous ces mensonges m'écœurent.** All these lies make me sick.

l'école FEM NOUN
school
□ aller à l'école to go to school □ une école privée a private school □ une école publique a state school □ une école maternelle a nursery school

DID YOU KNOW...?
The **école maternelle** is a state school for 2–6 year-olds.

l'écolier MASC NOUN
schoolboy

l'écolière FEM NOUN
schoolgirl

l'écologie FEM NOUN
ecology

écologique (FEM **écologique**) ADJECTIVE
ecological
□ une lessive écologique an ecological washing powder

l'économie FEM NOUN
1 economy
□ l'économie de la France the French economy
2 economics
□ un cours d'économie an economics class

les économies FEM PL NOUN
savings
- **faire des économies** to save up □ Je fais des économies pour partir en vacances. I'm saving up for my holidays.

économique (FEM **économique**) ADJECTIVE
1 economic
□ une crise économique an economic crisis
2 economical
□ Il est plus économique d'acheter une grande boîte de lessive. It's more economical to buy a big box of washing powder. □ Cette petite voiture est économique. This little car is economical.

économiser VERB [28]
to save

l'économiseur d'écran MASC NOUN
screen saver

l'écorce FEM NOUN
1 bark (of tree)
2 peel (of orange, lemon)

s'**écorcher** VERB [28]
- **Je me suis écorché le genou.** I've grazed my knee.

écossais (FEM **écossaise**) ADJECTIVE, NOUN
1 Scottish
□ Elle est écossaise. She's Scottish.
- **un Écossais** a Scot (man)
- **une Écossaise** a Scot (woman)
- **les Écossais** the Scots
2 tartan
□ une jupe écossaise a tartan skirt

l'Écosse FEM NOUN
Scotland
- **en Écosse 1** in Scotland □ Il a passé une semaine en Écosse. He spent a week in Scotland. **2** to Scotland □ Nous allons en Écosse l'été prochain. We're going to Scotland next summer.

l'écotourisme MASC NOUN
ecotourism

s'**écouler** VERB [28]
1 to flow out (water)
2 to pass
□ Le temps s'écoule trop vite. Time passes too quickly.

écouter VERB [28]
to listen to
□ J'aime écouter de la musique. I like listening to music.
- **Écoute-moi !** Listen!

les écouteurs MASC PL NOUN
headphones

l'écran MASC NOUN
screen
- **le petit écran** television
- **un écran tactile** a touchscreen
- **l'écran total** sunblock

écraser VERB [28]
1 to crush
□ Écrasez une gousse d'ail. Crush a clove of garlic.
2 to run over
□ Mon chien s'est fait écraser par une voiture. My dog got run over by a car.
- **s'écraser** to crash □ L'avion s'est écrasé dans le désert. The plane crashed in the desert.

écrémé (FEM **écrémée**) ADJECTIVE
skimmed
□ le lait écrémé skimmed milk

l'écrevisse FEM NOUN
crayfish

écrire VERB [30]

to write

□ Nous nous écrivons régulièrement. We write to each other regularly.

■ Ça s'écrit comment ? How do you spell that?

écris, écrit VERB ▷ see **écrire**

▷ see also **écrit** NOUN

■ Chantal a écrit la pièce. Chantal wrote the play.

l'**écrit** MASC NOUN

written paper

□ L'écrit d'anglais a lieu la semaine prochaine. The written paper in English is next week.

■ par écrit in writing

l'**écriteau** (PL les **écriteaux**) MASC NOUN

notice

l'**écriture** FEM NOUN

writing

□ J'ai du mal à lire son écriture. I can't read his writing.

l'**écrivain** MASC NOUN

writer

□ Elle est écrivain. She's a writer.

l'**écrou** MASC NOUN

nut (metal)

s'**écrouler** VERB [28]

to collapse

écru (FEM **écrue**) ADJECTIVE

off-white

l'**écureuil** MASC NOUN

squirrel

l'**écurie** FEM NOUN

stable

Édimbourg NOUN

Edinburgh

éditer VERB [28]

to publish

□ On vient d'éditer un nouveau dictionnaire. A new dictionary has just been published.

l'**éditeur** MASC NOUN

publisher

l'**édition** FEM NOUN

1 edition

□ une édition de poche a paperback edition

2 publishing

□ Il travaille dans l'édition. He works in publishing.

l'**édredon** MASC NOUN

eiderdown

l'**éducateur** MASC NOUN

teacher (of people with special needs)

éducatif (FEM **éducative**) ADJECTIVE

educational

□ un jeu éducatif an educational game

l'**éducation** FEM NOUN

1 education

□ l'éducation physique physical education

■ Il n'a pas beaucoup d'éducation. He's not very well educated.

2 upbringing

□ Il a reçu une éducation très stricte. He had a very strict upbringing.

l'**éducatrice** FEM NOUN

teacher (of people with special needs)

éduquer VERB [28]

to educate

effacer VERB [12]

1 to rub out

2 to delete (file)

effarant (FEM **effarante**) ADJECTIVE

amazing

□ Il a mangé une quantité effarante de pain. He ate an amazing amount of bread.

effectivement ADVERB

indeed

□ Il est effectivement plus rapide de passer par là. It is indeed quicker to go this way. □ Oui, effectivement. Yes, indeed.

> **BE CAREFUL!**
> effectivement does not mean **effectively**.

effectuer VERB [28]

1 to make

□ Ils ont effectué de nombreux changements. They have made a lot of changes.

2 to do

□ On vient d'effectuer des travaux dans le bâtiment. They have just done some work in the building.

effervescent (FEM **effervescente**) ADJECTIVE

effervescent

□ un comprimé effervescent an effervescent tablet

l'**effet** MASC NOUN

effect

■ faire de l'effet to take effect □ Ce médicament fait rapidement de l'effet. This medicine takes effect quickly.

■ Ça m'a fait un drôle d'effet de le revoir. It gave me a strange feeling to see him again.

■ en effet yes indeed □ Je ne me sens pas très bien. — En effet, tu as l'air pâle. I don't feel very well. — Yes, you do look pale.

efficace (FEM **efficace**) ADJECTIVE

1 efficient

□ C'est une femme efficace. She's an efficient woman.

2 effective

□ un médicament efficace an effective medicine

s'**effondrer** VERB [28]

to collapse

Core vocabulary is shaded.

93 at bottom right

efforcer - élever

s'**efforcer** VERB [12]
■ **s'efforcer de faire quelque chose** to
try hard to do something □ Il s'efforce d'être
aimable avec la clientèle. He tries hard to be
polite to the customers.

l'**effort** MASC NOUN
effort
□ faire un effort to make an effort

effrayant (FEM **effrayante**) ADJECTIVE
frightening

effrayer VERB [59]
to frighten

effronté (FEM **effrontée**) ADJECTIVE
cheeky
□ Ce gamin est vraiment effronté. This kid's
really cheeky.

effroyable (FEM **effroyable**) ADJECTIVE
horrifying

égal (FEM **égale**, MASC PL **égaux**) ADJECTIVE
equal
□ une quantité égale de farine et de sucre an
equal quantity of flour and sugar
■ **Ça m'est égal. 1** I don't mind. □ Tu préfères
du riz ou des pâtes ? — Ça m'est égal. Would
you rather have rice or pasta? — I don't mind.
2 I don't care. □ Fais ce que tu veux, ça m'est
égal. Do what you like, I don't care.

également ADVERB
also

égaler VERB [28]
to equal

l'**égalité** FEM NOUN
equality
■ **être à égalité** to be level □ Maintenant les
deux joueurs sont à égalité. The two players are
now level.

l'**égard** MASC NOUN
■ **à cet égard** in this respect

égarer VERB [28]
to mislay
□ J'ai égaré mes clés. I've mislaid my keys.
■ **s'égarer** to get lost □ Ils se sont égarés dans
la forêt. They got lost in the forest.

l'**église** FEM NOUN
church
□ aller à l'église to go to church

l'**égoïsme** MASC NOUN
selfishness

égoïste (FEM **égoïste**) ADJECTIVE
selfish

l'**égout** MASC NOUN
sewer

l'**égratignure** FEM NOUN
scratch

l'**Égypte** FEM NOUN
Egypt

égyptien (FEM **égyptienne**) ADJECTIVE
Egyptian

eh EXCLAMATION
hey!
■ **eh bien** well

l'**élan** MASC NOUN
■ **prendre de l'élan** to gather speed

s'**élancer** VERB [12]
to hurl oneself

élargir VERB [38]
to widen

l'**élastique** MASC NOUN
rubber band

l'**électeur** MASC NOUN
voter (*man*)

l'**élection** FEM NOUN
election
□ les élections présidentielles the presidential
election

l'**électrice** FEM NOUN
voter (*woman*)

l'**électricien** MASC NOUN
electrician

l'**électricité** FEM NOUN
electricity
□ une facture d'électricité an electricity bill

électrique (FEM **électrique**) ADJECTIVE
electric
□ le courant électrique the electric current

électronique (FEM **électronique**) ADJECTIVE
▷ *see also* **électronique** NOUN
electronic

l'**électronique** FEM NOUN
▷ *see also* **électronique** ADJECTIVE
electronics

élégant (FEM **élégante**) ADJECTIVE
smart

élémentaire (FEM **élémentaire**) ADJECTIVE
elementary

l'**éléphant** MASC NOUN
elephant

l'**élevage** MASC NOUN
cattle rearing
□ faire de l'élevage to rear cattle
■ **un élevage de porcs** a pig farm
■ **un élevage de poulets** a chicken farm
■ **les truites d'élevage** farmed trout

élevé (FEM **élevée**) ADJECTIVE
high
□ Le prix est trop élevé. The price is too high.
■ **être bien élevé** to have good manners
■ **être mal élevé** to have bad manners

l'**élève** MASC/FEM NOUN
pupil

élever VERB [43]
1 to bring up

□ Il a été élevé par sa grand-mère. He was brought up by his grandmother.

2 to breed

□ Son oncle élève des chevaux. His uncle breeds horses.

■ **élever la voix** to raise one's voice

■ **s'élever à** to come to □ À combien s'élèvent les dégâts ? How much does the damage come to?

l'**éleveur** MASC NOUN

breeder

éliminatoire (FEM **éliminatoire**) ADJECTIVE

■ **une note éliminatoire** a fail mark

■ **une épreuve éliminatoire** (sport) a qualifying round

éliminer VERB [28]

to eliminate

élire VERB [44]

to elect

elle PRONOUN

1 she

□ Elle est ingénieur. She is an engineer.

2 her

□ Vous pouvez avoir confiance en elle. You can trust her.

3 it

□ Prends cette chaise : elle est plus confortable. Take this chair: it's more comfortable.

elle is also used for emphasis.

□ Elle, elle est toujours en retard ! Oh her, she's always late!

■ **elle-même** herself □ Elle l'a choisi elle-même. She chose it herself.

■ **à elle** hers □ C'est un collègue à elle. He's a colleague of hers.

elles PL PRONOUN

they

□ Où sont Anne et Rachel ? — Elles sont allées au cinéma. Where are Anne and Rachel? — They've gone to the cinema.

■ **elles-mêmes** themselves

élogieux (FEM **élogieuse**) ADJECTIVE

complimentary

□ Ton professeur a été très élogieux à propos de ton travail. Your teacher was very complimentary about your work.

éloigné (FEM **éloignée**) ADJECTIVE

distant

s'**éloigner** VERB [28]

to go far away

□ Ne vous éloignez pas : le dîner est bientôt prêt ! Don't go far away: dinner will soon be ready!

■ **Vous vous éloignez du sujet.** You are getting off the point.

élu VERB ▷ see **élire**

▷ see also **élu** ADJECTIVE

■ **Le conseil a élu une nouvelle présidente.** The council elected a new president.

élu (FEM **élue**) ADJECTIVE

▷ see also **élu** VERB

elected

□ le parti élu the elected party

l'**Élysée** MASC NOUN

Élysée Palace

DID YOU KNOW...?
The **Élysée** is the residence of the French president.

l'**e-mail** MASC NOUN

email

l'**emballage** MASC NOUN

■ **le papier d'emballage** wrapping paper

emballer VERB [28]

to wrap

■ **s'emballer** (informal) to get excited □ Il s'est emballé pour ce projet. He got really excited about this plan.

l'**embarquement** MASC NOUN

boarding

□ « embarquement immédiat » 'now boarding'

□ L'embarquement des passagers n'a pas encore été annoncé. Passenger boarding has not been announced yet.

l'**embarras** MASC NOUN

embarrassment

□ Votre question me met dans l'embarras. It's difficult for me to answer your question.

■ **Vous n'avez que l'embarras du choix.** The only problem is choosing.

embarrassant (FEM **embarrassante**) ADJECTIVE

embarrassing

embarrasser VERB [28]

to embarrass

□ Cela m'embarrasse de vous demander encore un service. I feel embarrassed to ask you to do something more for me.

embaucher VERB [28]

to take on

□ L'entreprise vient d'embaucher cinquante ouvriers. The firm has just taken on fifty workers.

embêtant (FEM **embêtante**) ADJECTIVE

annoying

les **embêtements** MASC PL NOUN

trouble sing

embêter VERB [28]

to bother

■ **s'embêter** to be bored □ Qu'est-ce qu'on s'embête ici ! Isn't it boring here!

l'**embouteillage** MASC NOUN

traffic jam

embrasser – empresser

embrasser VERB [28]

to kiss

□ Ils se sont embrassés. They kissed each other.

s'**embrouiller** VERB [28]

to get confused

□ Il s'embrouille dans ses explications. He gets confused when he explains things.

émerveiller VERB [28]

to dazzle

l'**émeute** FEM NOUN

riot

émigrer VERB [28]

to emigrate

l'**émission** FEM NOUN

programme

□ une émission de télévision a TV programme

s'**emmêler** VERB [28]

to get tangled

□ Ma laine s'est emmêlée. My wool has got tangled.

emménager VERB [45]

to move in

□ Nous venons d'emménager dans une nouvelle maison. We've just moved into a new house.

emmener VERB [43]

to take

□ Ils m'ont emmené au cinéma pour mon anniversaire. They took me to the cinema for my birthday.

l'**émoji** MASC NOUN

emoji

émotif (FEM **émotive**) ADJECTIVE

emotional

□ Il est très émotif. He's very emotional.

l'**émotion** FEM NOUN

emotion

émouvoir VERB [31]

to move

□ Sa lettre l'a beaucoup émue. She was deeply moved by his letter.

emparer VERB [28]

■ s'emparer de to grab □ Il s'est emparé de ma valise. He grabbed my case.

l'**empêchement** MASC NOUN

■ Nous avons eu un empêchement de dernière minute. We were held up at the last minute.

empêcher VERB [28]

to prevent

■ empêcher quelqu'un de faire quelque chose to prevent someone from doing something

□ Le café le soir m'empêche de dormir. Coffee at night keeps me awake.

■ Il n'a pas pu s'empêcher de rire. He couldn't help laughing.

l'**empereur** MASC NOUN

emperor

s'**empiffrer** VERB [28] (*informal*)

to stuff one's face

□ Arrête de t'empiffrer ! Stop stuffing your face!

empiler VERB [28]

to pile up

empirer VERB [28]

to worsen

□ La situation a encore empiré. The situation got even worse.

l'**emplacement** MASC NOUN

site

□ Un panneau indique l'emplacement du château. A sign shows the site of the castle.

l'**emploi** MASC NOUN

1 use

□ prêt à l'emploi ready for use

■ le mode d'emploi directions for use

2 job

□ la création d'emplois job creation

■ un emploi du temps a timetable

l'**employé** MASC NOUN

employee

■ un employé de bureau an office worker

l'**employée** FEM NOUN

employee

■ une employée de banque a bank clerk

employer VERB [53]

1 to use

□ Quelle méthode employez-vous ? What method do you use?

2 to employ

□ L'entreprise emploie dix ingénieurs. The firm employs ten engineers.

l'**employeur** MASC NOUN

employer

empoisonner VERB [28]

to poison

emporter VERB [28]

to take

□ N'emportez que le strict nécessaire. Only take the bare minimum.

■ plats à emporter take-away meals

■ s'emporter to lose one's temper □ Je m'emporte facilement. I'm quick to lose my temper.

l'**empreinte** FEM NOUN

footprint

■ l'empreinte carbone carbon footprint

■ une empreinte digitale a fingerprint

s'**empresser** VERB [28]

■ s'empresser de faire quelque chose to be quick to do something □ Ils se sont empressés de nous annoncer la nouvelle. They were quick to tell us the news.

emprisonner VERB [28]
to imprison

l'**emprunt** MASC NOUN
loan

emprunter VERB [28]
to borrow
■ **emprunter quelque chose à quelqu'un**
to borrow something from somebody □ Je peux
t'emprunter dix euros ? Can I borrow ten euros
from you?

EMT FEM NOUN (= *éducation manuelle technique*)
technology

ému (FEM **émue**) ADJECTIVE
touched
□ J'ai été très ému par sa gentillesse. I was very
touched by her kindness.

en PREPOSITION, PRONOUN
1 in
□ Il habite en France. He lives in France. □ La
mariée est en blanc. The bride is in white. □ Je le
verrai en mai. I'll see him in May.
2 to
□ Je vais en France cet été. I'm going to France
this summer.
3 by
□ C'est plus rapide en voiture. It's quicker by car.
4 made of
□ C'est en verre. It's made of glass. □ un collier
en argent a silver necklace
5 while
□ Il s'est coupé le doigt en ouvrant une boîte de
conserve. He cut his finger while opening a tin.
■ **Elle est sortie en courant.** She ran out.

> When **en** is used with **avoir** and **il y a**, it is
> not translated in English.

□ Est-ce que tu as un dictionnaire ? — Oui, j'en
ai un. Have you got a dictionary? — Yes, I've got
one. □ Combien d'élèves y a-t-il dans ta classe ?
— Il y en a trente. How many pupils are there in
your class? — There are 30.

> **en** is also used with verbs and expressions
> normally followed by **de** to avoid repeating
> the same word.

□ Si tu as un problème, tu peux m'en parler. If
you've got a problem, you can talk to me about
it. □ Est-ce que tu peux me rendre ce livre ? J'en
ai besoin. Can you give me back that book? I
need it. □ Il a un beau jardin et il en est très fier.
He's got a beautiful garden and is very proud
of it.
■ **J'en ai assez.** I've had enough.

encaisser VERB [28]
to cash (*money*)

enceinte FEM ADJECTIVE
pregnant
□ Elle est enceinte de six mois. She's 6 months
pregnant.

enchanté (FEM **enchantée**) ADJECTIVE
delighted
□ Ma mère est enchantée de sa nouvelle
voiture. My mother's delighted with her new
car.
■ **Enchanté !** Pleased to meet you!

encombrant (FEM **encombrante**) ADJECTIVE
bulky

encombrer VERB [28]
to clutter

encore ADVERB
1 still
□ Il est encore au travail. He's still at work.
□ Il reste encore deux morceaux de gâteau.
There are still two bits of cake left.
2 even
□ C'est encore mieux. That's even better.
3 again
□ Il m'a encore demandé de l'argent. He asked
me for money again.
■ **encore une fois** once again
■ **pas encore** not yet □ Je n'ai pas encore fini.
I haven't finished yet.

encourager VERB [45]
to encourage
■ **encourager quelqu'un à faire quelque
chose** to encourage someone to do something
□ Il m'a encouragé à persévérer. He encouraged
me to keep going.

l'**encre** FEM NOUN
ink

l'**encyclopédie** FEM NOUN
encyclopaedia

l'**endive** FEM NOUN
chicory

endommager VERB [45]
to damage

endormi (FEM **endormie**) ADJECTIVE
asleep

endormir VERB [29]
to deaden
□ Cette piqûre sert à endormir le nerf. This
injection is to deaden the nerve.
■ **s'endormir** to go to sleep

l'**endroit** MASC NOUN
place
□ C'est un endroit très tranquille. It's a very
quiet place.
■ **à l'endroit 1** the right way out **2** the right
way up

endurant (FEM **endurante**) ADJECTIVE
tough (*person*)

endurcir VERB [38]
to toughen up
□ Ces exercices servent à endurcir les soldats.
These exercises are to toughen up the soldiers.
■ **s'endurcir** to become hardened

endurer – ennui

endurer VERB [28]
to endure

l'énergie FEM NOUN
1 energy
□ Je n'ai pas beaucoup d'énergie ce matin. I haven't got much energy this morning.
2 power
□ l'énergie nucléaire nuclear power
■ **avec énergie** vigorously □ Il a protesté avec énergie. He protested vigorously.

énergique (FEM **énergique**) ADJECTIVE
energetic
■ **des mesures énergiques** strong measures

énerver VERB [28]
■ **Il m'énerve !** He gets on my nerves!
■ **Ce bruit m'énerve.** This noise gets on my nerves.
■ **s'énerver** to get worked up
■ **Ne t'énerve pas !** Take it easy!

l'enfance FEM NOUN
childhood
□ Je le connais depuis l'enfance. I've known him since I was a child.

l'enfant MASC/FEM NOUN
child

l'enfer MASC NOUN
hell

s'enfermer VERB [28]
■ **Il s'est enfermé dans sa chambre.** He shut himself up in his bedroom.

enfiler VERB [28]
1 to put on
□ J'ai rapidement enfilé un pull avant de sortir. I quickly put on a sweater before going out.
2 to thread
□ J'ai du mal à enfiler cette aiguille. I am having difficulty threading this needle.

enfin ADVERB
at last
□ J'ai enfin réussi à le joindre. I have at last managed to contact him.

enflé (FEM **enflée**) ADJECTIVE
swollen

enfler VERB [28]
to swell

enfoncer VERB [12]
■ **Il marchait, les mains enfoncées dans les poches.** He was walking with his hands thrust into his pockets.
■ **s'enfoncer** to sink □ Les roues de la voiture s'enfonçaient dans la boue. The wheels of the car were sinking into the mud.

s'enfuir VERB [39]
to run off

l'engagement MASC NOUN
commitment

engager VERB [45]
to take on (*person*)
□ engager quelqu'un to take somebody on

s'engager VERB [45]
to commit oneself
□ Le Premier ministre s'est engagé à combattre le chômage. The Prime Minister has committed himself to fighting unemployment.
■ **Il s'est engagé dans l'armée à dix-huit ans.** He joined the army when he was 18.

les engelures FEM PL NOUN
chilblains

l'engin MASC NOUN
device

> **BE CAREFUL!**
> The French word **engin** does not mean **engine**.

s'engourdir VERB [38]
to go numb
□ Mes doigts se sont engourdis avec le froid. My fingers have gone numb with the cold.

engueuler VERB [28] (*informal*)
■ **engueuler quelqu'un** to tell somebody off
□ Tu vas te faire engueuler ! You're going to get told off!

l'énigme FEM NOUN
riddle

s'enivrer VERB [28]
to get drunk

enjamber VERB [28]
to stride over
□ enjamber une barrière to stride over a fence

l'enlèvement MASC NOUN
kidnapping

enlever VERB [43]
1 to take off
□ Enlève donc ton manteau ! Take off your coat!
2 to kidnap
□ Un groupe terroriste a enlevé la femme de l'ambassadeur. A terrorist group has kidnapped the ambassador's wife.

enneigé (FEM **enneigée**) ADJECTIVE
snowed up
□ Les routes sont encore enneigées. The roads are still snowed up.

l'ennemi MASC NOUN
enemy

l'ennemie FEM NOUN
enemy

l'ennui MASC NOUN
1 boredom
□ C'est à mourir d'ennui. It would make you die of boredom.
2 problem
□ avoir des ennuis to have problems

Numbers in brackets refer to verb tables on pages 650 to 658

ennuyer VERB [53]

to bother

□ J'espère que cela ne vous ennuie pas trop. I hope it doesn't bother you too much.

■ **s'ennuyer** to be bored

ennuyeux (FEM **ennuyeuse**) ADJECTIVE

1 boring
2 awkward

□ Tu ne peux pas venir plus tôt ? C'est bien ennuyeux. You can't come any earlier? That's rather awkward.

énorme (FEM **énorme**) ADJECTIVE

huge

énormément ADVERB

■ **Il a énormément grossi.** He's put on an awful lot of weight.

■ **Il y a énormément de neige.** There's an enormous amount of snow.

l'**enquête** FEM NOUN

1 investigation

□ La police a ouvert une enquête. The police have begun an investigation.

2 survey

□ une enquête parmi les étudiants a montré que ... a survey of students has shown that ...

enquêter VERB [28]

to investigate

□ La police enquête actuellement sur le crime. The police are currently investigating the crime.

enrageant (FEM **enrageante**) ADJECTIVE

infuriating

enrager VERB [45]

to be furious

□ J'enrage de n'avoir pas pu profiter de cette occasion. I'm furious I wasn't able to take advantage of this opportunity.

l'**enregistrement** MASC NOUN

recording

■ **l'enregistrement des bagages** baggage check-in

enregistrer VERB [28]

1 to record

□ Ils viennent d'enregistrer un nouvel album. They've just recorded a new album.

2 to check in

□ Vous pouvez enregistrer plusieurs valises. You can check in several cases.

s'**enrhumer** VERB [28]

to catch a cold

□ Je suis enrhumé. I've got a cold.

s'**enrichir** VERB [38]

to get rich

enrouler VERB [28]

to wind

□ Enroulez le fil autour de la bobine. Wind the thread round the bobbin.

l'**enseignant** MASC NOUN

teacher

l'**enseignante** FEM NOUN

teacher

l'**enseignement** MASC NOUN

1 education

□ les réformes de l'enseignement education reforms

■ **l'enseignement à distance** remote learning

2 teaching

□ l'enseignement des langues étrangères the teaching of foreign languages

enseigner VERB [28]

to teach

□ Mon père enseigne les maths dans un lycée. My father teaches maths in a secondary school.

■ **enseigner à quelqu'un à faire quelque chose** to teach someone to do something

ensemble ADVERB

▷ see also **ensemble** NOUN

together

□ tous ensemble all together

l'**ensemble** MASC NOUN

▷ see also **ensemble** ADVERB

outfit

□ Elle portait un ensemble vert. She was wearing a green outfit.

■ **l'ensemble de** the whole of □ L'ensemble du personnel est en grève. The whole workforce is on strike.

■ **dans l'ensemble** on the whole

ensoleillé (FEM **ensoleillée**) ADJECTIVE

sunny

ensuite ADVERB

then

□ Nous sommes allés au cinéma et ensuite au restaurant. We went to the cinema and then to a restaurant.

entamer VERB [28]

to start

□ Qui a entamé le gâteau ? Who's started the cake?

s'**entasser** VERB [28]

to cram

□ Ils se sont tous entassés dans ma voiture. They all crammed into my car.

entendre VERB [88]

1 to hear

□ Je ne t'entends pas. I can't hear you.

■ **J'ai entendu dire qu'il est dangereux de nager ici.** I've heard that it's dangerous to swim here.

2 to mean

□ Qu'est-ce que tu entends par là ? What do you mean by that?

■ **s'entendre (avec)** to get on (with) □ Paul et

Isabelle ne s'entendent pas. Paul and Isabelle don't get on. □ Il s'entend bien avec sa sœur. He gets on well with his sister.

entendu (FEM **entendue**) ADJECTIVE

■ **C'est entendu !** Agreed! □ Je passerai te prendre à sept heures, c'est entendu. That's agreed then, I'll pick you up at 7 o'clock.

■ **bien entendu** of course

l'**enterrement** MASC NOUN
funeral (*burial*)

enterrer VERB [28]
to bury

entêté (FEM **entêtée**) ADJECTIVE
stubborn

s'**entêter** VERB [28]
to persist
□ Il s'entête à refuser de voir le médecin. He persists in refusing to go to the doctor.

l'**enthousiasme** MASC NOUN
enthusiasm

s'**enthousiasmer** VERB [28]
to get enthusiastic
□ Il s'enthousiasme facilement. He gets very enthusiastic about things.

entier (FEM **entière**) ADJECTIVE
whole
□ Il a mangé une quiche entière. He ate a whole quiche. □ Je n'ai pas lu le livre en entier. I haven't read the whole book.

■ **le lait entier** full fat milk

entièrement ADVERB
completely

l'**entorse** FEM NOUN
sprain
□ Il s'est fait une entorse à la cheville. He's sprained his ankle.

entourer VERB [28]
to surround
□ Le jardin est entouré d'un mur de pierres. The garden is surrounded by a stone wall.

l'**entracte** MASC NOUN
interval

l'**entraînement** MASC NOUN
training

entraîner VERB [28]

1 to lead
□ Il se laisse facilement entraîner par les autres. He's easily led.

2 to train
□ Il entraîne l'équipe de France depuis cinq ans. He's been training the French team for five years.

3 to involve
□ Un mariage entraîne beaucoup de dépenses. A wedding involves a lot of expense.

■ **s'entraîner** to train □ Il s'entraîne au foot tous les samedis matins. He does football training every Saturday morning.

l'**entraîneur** MASC NOUN
trainer

entre PREPOSITION
between
□ Il est assis entre son père et son oncle. He's sitting between his father and his uncle.

■ **entre eux** among themselves

■ **l'un d'entre eux** one of them

l'**entrecôte** FEM NOUN
rib steak

l'**entrée** FEM NOUN

1 entrance

2 starter (*of meal*)
□ Qu'est ce que vous prenez comme entrée ? What would you like for the starter?

entreprendre VERB [65]
to start on
□ Elle a entrepris des démarches pour adopter un enfant. She's started on the procedures for adopting a child.

l'**entrepreneur** MASC NOUN
contractor

l'**entreprise** FEM NOUN
firm

entrer VERB [32, *aux* **avoir** or **être**]

1 to come in
□ Entrez donc ! Come on in!

2 to go in
□ Ils sont tous entrés dans la maison. They all went into the house.

■ **entrer à l'hôpital** to go into hospital

■ **entrer des données** to enter data □ J'ai entré toutes les adresses de mon agenda sur mon ordinateur. I've entered all the addresses in my diary onto my computer.

> The verb **entrer** uses **être** in the perfect tense when talking about going into a place. It uses **avoir** in the perfect tense when it describes keying in information.

entre-temps ADVERB
meanwhile

l'**entretien** MASC NOUN

1 maintenance
□ un contrat d'entretien a maintenance contract

2 interview
□ On m'a convoqué à un entretien pour un travail. I've been called for a job interview.

l'**entrevue** FEM NOUN
interview
□ une entrevue avec le ministre an interview with the minister

entrouvert (FEM **entrouverte**) ADJECTIVE
half open
□ La porte était entrouverte. The door was half open.

envahir VERB [38]
to invade

l'**enveloppe** FEM NOUN
envelope

envelopper VERB [28]
to wrap

envers PREPOSITION
▷ *see also* **envers** NOUN
towards
☐ Il est bien disposé envers elle. He's well disposed towards her. ☐ son attitude envers moi his attitude towards me

l'**envers** MASC NOUN
▷ *see also* **envers** PREPOSITION
■ **à l'envers** inside out ☐ Je dois repasser ce chemisier à l'envers. I have to iron this blouse inside out.

l'**envie** FEM NOUN
■ **avoir envie de faire quelque chose** to feel like doing something ☐ J'avais envie de pleurer. I felt like crying. ☐ J'ai envie d'aller aux toilettes. I want to go to the toilet.
■ **Cette glace me fait envie.** I fancy some of that ice cream.

BE CAREFUL!
The French word **envie** does not mean **envy**.

envier VERB [19]
to envy

environ ADVERB
about
☐ C'est à soixante kilomètres environ. It's about 60 kilometres.

l'**environnement** MASC NOUN
environment

les **environs** MASC PL NOUN
area *sing*
☐ les environs de Nantes the Nantes area ☐ Il y a beaucoup de choses intéressantes à voir dans les environs. There are a lot of interesting things to see in the area.
■ **aux environs de dix-neuf heures** around 7 p.m.

envisager VERB [45]
to consider
☐ Est-ce que vous envisagez de travailler à l'étranger ? Are you considering working abroad?

s'**envoler** VERB [28]
1 to fly away
☐ Le papillon s'est envolé. The butterfly flew away.
2 to blow away
☐ Toutes mes feuilles de cours se sont envolées. All my lecture notes blew away.

envoyer VERB [33]
to send
☐ Ma tante m'a envoyé une carte pour mon anniversaire. My aunt sent me a card for my birthday.

■ **envoyer quelqu'un chercher quelque chose** to send somebody to get something ☐ Sa mère l'a envoyé chercher du pain. His mother sent him to get some bread.
■ **envoyer un e-mail à quelqu'un** to send somebody an email
■ **envoyer un message à quelqu'un** to message somebody ☐ Il m'a envoyé un message hier soir. He messaged me last night.

l'**éolienne** FEM NOUN
wind turbine

épais (FEM **épaisse**) ADJECTIVE
thick

l'**épaisseur** FEM NOUN
thickness

épatant (FEM **épatante**) ADJECTIVE (*informal*)
great
☐ C'est un type épatant. He's a great guy.

l'**épaule** FEM NOUN
shoulder

l'**épée** FEM NOUN
sword

épeler VERB [4]
to spell
☐ Est-ce que vous pouvez épeler votre nom, s'il vous plaît ? Can you spell your name, please?

l'**épice** FEM NOUN
spice

épicé (FEM **épicée**) ADJECTIVE
spicy
☐ un plat épicé a spicy dish

l'**épicerie** FEM NOUN
grocer's shop

l'**épicier** MASC NOUN
grocer

l'**épicière** FEM NOUN
grocer

l'**épidémie** FEM NOUN
epidemic

épiler VERB [28]
■ **s'épiler les jambes** to wax one's legs
■ **s'épiler les sourcils** to pluck one's eyebrows

les **épinards** MASC PL NOUN
spinach *sing*

l'**épine** FEM NOUN
thorn

l'**épingle** FEM NOUN
pin
■ **une épingle de sûreté** a safety pin

l'**épisode** MASC NOUN
episode

éplucher VERB [28]
to peel

l'**éponge** FEM NOUN
sponge

époque - Espagne

l'époque FEM NOUN

time

□ à cette époque de l'année at this time of year □ **à l'époque** at that time □ À l'époque, beaucoup de gens n'avaient pas l'eau courante. At that time a lot of people didn't have running water.

l'épouse FEM NOUN

wife

épouser VERB [28]

to marry

épouvantable (FEM **épouvantable**)
ADJECTIVE

awful

l'épouvante FEM NOUN

terror

■ **un film d'épouvante** a horror film

épouvanter VERB [28]

to terrify

l'époux MASC NOUN

husband

■ **les nouveaux époux** the newly-weds

l'épreuve FEM NOUN

1 test

□ une épreuve orale an oral test □ une épreuve écrite a written test

2 event (*sport*)

éprouver VERB [28]

to feel

□ Qu'est-ce que vous avez éprouvé à ce moment-là ? What did you feel at that moment?

l'EPS FEM NOUN (= *éducation physique et sportive*)

PE (= *physical education*)

épuisé (FEM **épuisée**) ADJECTIVE

exhausted

épuiser VERB [28]

to wear out

□ Ce travail m'a complètement épuisé. This job has completely worn me out.

■ **s'épuiser** to wear oneself out □ Il s'épuise à garder un jardin impeccable. He wears himself out keeping his garden immaculate.

l'Équateur MASC NOUN

Ecuador

l'équateur MASC NOUN

equator

l'équation FEM NOUN

equation

l'équerre FEM NOUN

set square

l'équilibre MASC NOUN

balance

□ J'ai failli perdre l'équilibre. I nearly lost my balance.

équilibré (FEM **équilibrée**) ADJECTIVE

well-balanced

l'équipage MASC NOUN

crew

l'équipe FEM NOUN

team

équipé (FEM **équipée**) ADJECTIVE

■ **bien équipé** well-equipped

l'équipement MASC NOUN

equipment

les équipements MASC PL NOUN

facilities

□ les équipements sportifs sports facilities

l'équitation FEM NOUN

riding

□ faire de l'équitation to go riding

l'équivalent MASC NOUN

equivalent

l'erreur FEM NOUN

mistake

■ **faire erreur** to be mistaken

es VERB ▷ *see* être

■ **Tu es très gentille.** You're very kind.

l'escabeau (PL les **escabeaux**) MASC
NOUN

stepladder

l'escalade FEM NOUN

climbing

□ faire de l'escalade to go climbing

escalader VERB [28]

to climb

l'escale FEM NOUN

■ **faire escale** to stop off

l'escalier MASC NOUN

stairs

□ un escalier roulant an escalator

l'escargot MASC NOUN

snail

l'esclavage MASC NOUN

slavery

l'esclave MASC/FEM NOUN

slave

l'escrime FEM NOUN

fencing

l'escroc MASC NOUN

crook

l'espace MASC NOUN

space

■ **espace de travail** workspace

■ **les espaces verts** green spaces

s'espacer VERB [12]

to become less frequent

□ Ses visites se sont peu à peu espacées. His visits became less and less frequent.

espadrille FEM NOUN

rope-soled sandal

l'Espagne FEM NOUN

Spain

■ **en Espagne 1** in Spain **2** to Spain

espagnol (FEM **espagnole**) ADJECTIVE, NOUN
Spanish
□ J'apprends l'espagnol. I'm learning Spanish.
■ **un Espagnol** a Spaniard (*man*)
■ **une Espagnole** a Spaniard (*woman*)

l'**espèce** FEM NOUN
1 sort
□ Elle portait une espèce de cape en velours.
She was wearing a sort of velvet cloak.
2 species
□ une espèce en voie de disparition an
endangered species
■ **Espèce d'idiot !** You idiot!

les **espèces** FEM PL NOUN
cash *sing*
□ payer en espèces to pay cash

espérer VERB [34]
to hope
■ **J'espère bien.** I hope so. □ Tu penses avoir
réussi ? — Oui, j'espère bien. Do you think
you've passed? — Yes, I hope so.

espiègle (FEM **espiègle**) ADJECTIVE
mischievous

l'**espion** MASC NOUN
spy

l'**espionnage** MASC NOUN
spying
■ **un roman d'espionnage** a spy novel

l'**espionne** FEM NOUN
spy

l'**espoir** MASC NOUN
hope

l'**esprit** MASC NOUN
mind
□ Ça ne m'est pas venu à l'esprit. It didn't cross
my mind.
■ **avoir de l'esprit** to be witty □ Il a beaucoup
d'esprit. He's very witty.

l'**esquimau**® (PL les **esquimaux**) MASC NOUN
ice lolly

l'**essai** MASC NOUN
attempt
□ Ce n'est pas mal pour un coup d'essai. It's not
bad for a first attempt.
■ **prendre quelqu'un à l'essai** to take
somebody on for a trial period

essayer VERB [59]
1 to try
■ **essayer de faire quelque chose** to try to do
something □ Essaie de rentrer de bonne heure.
Try to come home early.
2 to try on
□ Essaie ce pull : il devrait bien t'aller. Try this
sweater on: it ought to look good on you.

l'**essence** FEM NOUN
petrol

essentiel (FEM **essentielle**) ADJECTIVE
essential
■ **Tu es là : c'est l'essentiel.** You're here: that's
the main thing.

s'**essouffler** VERB [28]
to get out of breath

l'**essuie-glace** MASC NOUN
windscreen wiper

essuyer VERB [53]
to wipe
■ **essuyer la vaisselle** to dry the dishes
■ **s'essuyer** to dry oneself □ Vous pouvez vous
essuyer les mains avec cette serviette. You can
dry your hands on this towel.

est VERB ▷ *see* **être**
▷ *see also* **est** ADJECTIVE, NOUN
■ **Elle est merveilleuse.** She's marvellous.

est is pronounced 'ay' when it comes from
the verb **être**.

est (FEM+PL **est**) ADJECTIVE
▷ *see also* **est** VERB, NOUN
1 east
□ la côte est des États-Unis the east coast of the
United States
2 eastern
□ dans la partie est du pays in the eastern part
of the country

est is pronounced 'ayst' when it means **east**
or **eastern**.

l'**est** MASC NOUN
▷ *see also* **est** VERB, ADJECTIVE
east
□ Je vis dans l'est de la France. I live in the East
of France.
■ **vers l'est** eastwards
■ **à l'est de Paris** east of Paris
■ **l'Europe de l'Est** Eastern Europe
■ **le vent d'est** the east wind

est is pronounced 'ayst' when it means **east**
or **eastern**.

est-ce que ADVERB
■ **Est-ce que c'est cher ?** Is it expensive?
■ **Quand est-ce qu'il part ?** When is he
leaving?

l'**esthéticienne** FEM NOUN
beautician

l'**estime** FEM NOUN
■ **J'ai beaucoup d'estime pour elle.** I think a
lot of her.

estimer VERB [28]
■ **estimer quelqu'un** to have great respect for
somebody □ Mon père l'estime beaucoup. My
father has a lot of respect for him.
■ **estimer que** to consider that □ J'estime
que c'est de sa faute. I consider that it's
his fault.

e

l'**estivant** MASC NOUN
holiday-maker

l'**estivante** FEM NOUN
holiday-maker

l'**estomac** MASC NOUN
stomach

l'**Estonie** FEM NOUN
Estonia

l'**estrade** FEM NOUN
platform

et CONJUNCTION
and
□ toi et moi you and me
■ Et toi, qu'est-ce que tu en penses ?
What about you? What do you think?

établir VERB [38]
to establish
■ s'établir à son compte to set up in
business

l'**établissement** MASC NOUN
establishment
■ un établissement scolaire a school

l'**étage** MASC NOUN
floor
□ au premier étage on the first floor
■ à l'étage upstairs

l'**étagère** FEM NOUN
shelf

étaient VERB ▷ see être

l'**étain** MASC NOUN
tin

étais, était VERB ▷ see être
■ Il était très jeune. He was very young.

l'**étalage** MASC NOUN
display

étaler VERB [28]
to spread
□ Il a étalé la carte sur la table. He spread the
map on the table.

étanche (FEM **étanche**) ADJECTIVE
1 watertight
□ Le toit n'est pas étanche. The roof isn't
watertight.
2 waterproof (watch)

l'**étang** MASC NOUN
pond

étant VERB ▷ see être
■ Mes revenus étant limités ... My income
being limited ...

l'**étape** FEM NOUN
stage
□ une étape importante de la vie an important
stage in life
■ faire étape to stop off

l'**État** MASC NOUN
state (nation)
□ un chef d'État a head of state

l'**état** MASC NOUN
condition
□ en bon état in good condition □ en mauvais
état in poor condition
■ remettre quelque chose en état to repair
something
■ le bureau d'état civil the registry office

les **États-Unis** MASC PL NOUN
United States
■ aux États-Unis 1 in the United States
2 to the United States

été VERB ▷ see être
▷ see also **été** NOUN
■ Il a été licencié. He's been made redundant.

l'**été** MASC NOUN
▷ see also **été** VERB
summer
■ en été in the summer

éteindre VERB [60]
1 to switch off
□ Éteins la lumière. Switch the light off.
2 to put out (cigarette)

étendre VERB [88]
to spread
□ Elle a étendu une nappe propre sur la table.
She spread a clean cloth on the table.
■ étendre le linge to hang out the washing
■ s'étendre to lie down □ Je vais m'étendre
cinq minutes. I'm going to lie down for five
minutes.

l'**éternité** FEM NOUN
■ J'ai attendu une éternité chez le médecin.
I waited for ages at the doctor's.

éternuer VERB [28]
to sneeze

êtes VERB ▷ see être
■ Vous êtes en retard. You're late.

étiez VERB ▷ see être

étinceler VERB [4]
to sparkle

étions VERB ▷ see être

l'**étiquette** FEM NOUN
label
□ L'étiquette du pot de confiture s'est décollée.
The label has come off the jam pot.

s'**étirer** VERB [28]
to stretch
□ Elle s'est étirée paresseusement. She
stretched lazily.

l'**étoile** FEM NOUN
star
■ une étoile de mer a starfish
■ une étoile filante a shooting star
■ dormir à la belle étoile to sleep under the
stars

étonnant (FEM **étonnante**) ADJECTIVE
amazing

étonner VERB [28]

to surprise

□ Cela m'étonnerait que le colis soit arrivé. I'd be surprised if the parcel had arrived.

étouffer VERB [28]

■ **On étouffe ici : ouvre donc les fenêtres.** It's stifling in here: open the windows.

■ **s'étouffer** to choke □ Ne mange pas si vite : tu vas t'étouffer ! Don't eat so fast: you'll choke!

l'**étourderie** FEM NOUN

absent-mindedness

■ **une erreur d'étourderie** a slip

étourdi (FEM **étourdie**) ADJECTIVE

scatterbrained

l'**étourdissement** MASC NOUN

■ **avoir des étourdissements** to feel dizzy

étrange (FEM **étrange**) ADJECTIVE

strange

étranger (FEM **étrangère**) ADJECTIVE

▷ *see also* **étranger** NOUN

foreign

□ un pays étranger a foreign country

■ **une personne étrangère** a stranger

l'**étranger** MASC NOUN

▷ *see also* **étranger** ADJECTIVE

1 foreigner

2 stranger

■ **à l'étranger** abroad

l'**étrangère** FEM NOUN

1 foreigner

2 stranger

étrangler VERB [28]

to strangle

■ **s'étrangler** to choke □ s'étrangler avec quelque chose to choke on something

l'**être** MASC NOUN

▷ *see also* **être** VERB

■ **un être humain** a human being

être VERB [35]

PRESENT TENSE	
je suis	nous sommes
tu es	vous êtes
il/elle est	ils/elles sont
PAST PARTICIPLE	
été	

▷ *see also* **être** NOUN

1 to be

□ Je suis heureux. I'm happy. □ Mon père est instituteur. My father's a primary school teacher. □ Il est dix heures. It's 10 o'clock.

■ **il est … de** □ Il est impossible de le faire. It is impossible to do it.

2 to have

□ Il n'est pas encore arrivé. He hasn't arrived yet.

les **étrennes** FEM PL NOUN

■ **Nous avons donné des étrennes à la gardienne.** We gave the caretaker a New Year gift.

étroit (FEM **étroite**) ADJECTIVE

narrow

■ **être à l'étroit** to be cramped □ Nous sommes un peu à l'étroit dans cet appartement. We're a bit cramped in this flat.

l'**étude** FEM NOUN

study

□ une étude de cas a case study

■ **faire des études** to be studying □ Il fait des études de droit. He's studying law.

l'**étudiant** MASC NOUN

student

l'**étudiante** FEM NOUN

student

étudier VERB [19]

to study

l'**étui** MASC NOUN

case

□ un étui à lunettes a glasses case

eu VERB ▷ *see* **avoir**

■ **J'ai eu une bonne note.** I got a good mark.

euh EXCLAMATION

er

□ Euh … je ne m'en souviens pas. Er … I can't remember.

l'**euro** MASC NOUN

euro

l'**Europe** FEM NOUN

Europe

■ **en Europe** 1 in Europe 2 to Europe

européen (FEM **européenne**) ADJECTIVE, NOUN

European

■ **un Européen** a European (*man*)

■ **une Européenne** a European (*woman*)

eux PL PRONOUN

them

□ Elle parle beaucoup d'eux. She talks about them a lot.

■ **à eux** theirs □ La maison n'est pas à eux. The house is not theirs.

eux is also used for emphasis.

□ Elle a accepté l'invitation, mais eux, ils ont refusé. She accepted the invitation, but THEY refused.

■ **eux-mêmes** themselves

évacuer VERB [28]

to evacuate

s'**évader** VERB [28]

to escape

l'**évangile** MASC NOUN

gospel

s'**évanouir** VERB [38]

to faint

s'**évaporer** VERB [28]

to evaporate

évasif - exagérer

évasif (FEM **évasive**) ADJECTIVE
evasive

l'**évasion** FEM NOUN
escape
□ Ils ont préparé leur évasion pendant des mois. They spent months planning their escape.

éveillé (FEM **éveillée**) ADJECTIVE
1 awake
□ Il est resté éveillé toute la nuit. He stayed awake all night.
2 bright
□ C'est un enfant très éveillé pour son âge. He's very bright for his age.

s'**éveiller** VERB [28]
to awaken

l'**événement** MASC NOUN
event

l'**éventail** MASC NOUN
fan (hand-held)
■ un large éventail de prix a wide range of prices

l'**éventualité** FEM NOUN
■ dans l'éventualité d'un retard in the event of a delay

éventuel (FEM **éventuelle**) ADJECTIVE
possible
□ une solution éventuelle a possible solution
□ les conséquences éventuelles the possible consequences

> **BE CAREFUL!**
> éventuel does not mean **eventual**.

éventuellement ADVERB
possibly
□ Nous pourrions éventuellement avoir besoin de vous. We may possibly need you. □ les difficultés que vous pourriez éventuellement rencontrer the difficulties that you might possibly have

> **BE CAREFUL!**
> éventuellement does not mean **eventually**.

l'**évêque** MASC NOUN
bishop

évidemment ADVERB
1 obviously
□ Les tomates sont évidemment chères en cette saison. Tomatoes are obviously expensive at this time of year.
2 of course
□ Est-ce que je peux utiliser ton téléphone ? — Évidemment, tu n'as pas besoin de demander. Can I use your phone? — Of course, you don't need to ask.

l'**évidence** FEM NOUN
■ C'est une évidence. It's quite obvious.
■ de toute évidence obviously □ De toute évidence, il ne veut pas nous voir. Obviously he doesn't want to see us.
■ être en évidence to be clearly visible □ La lettre était en évidence sur la table. The letter was clearly visible on the table.
■ mettre en évidence to reveal

évident (FEM **évidente**) ADJECTIVE
obvious

l'**évier** MASC NOUN
sink

éviter VERB [28]
to avoid
■ éviter de faire quelque chose to avoid doing something

évolué (FEM **évoluée**) ADJECTIVE
advanced

évoluer VERB [28]
to progress
□ La chirurgie esthétique a beaucoup évolué. Cosmetic surgery has progressed a great deal.
■ Il a beaucoup évolué. He has come on a great deal.

l'**évolution** FEM NOUN
1 development
□ une évolution rapide rapid development
2 evolution
□ la théorie de l'évolution the theory of evolution

évoquer VERB [28]
to mention
□ Il a évoqué divers problèmes dans son discours. He mentioned various problems in his speech.

exact (FEM **exacte**) ADJECTIVE
1 right
□ Avez-vous l'heure exacte ? Have you got the right time? □ Votre voiture est garée dehors, n'est-ce pas ? — C'est exact. Your car's parked outside, isn't it? — That's right.
2 exact
□ Est-ce que vous pouvez m'indiquer le prix exact du billet ? Can you tell me the exact price of the ticket?

exactement ADVERB
exactly
□ C'est exactement ce que je cherchais. That's exactly what I was looking for.

ex aequo (FEM+PL **ex aequo**) ADJECTIVE
■ Ils sont arrivés ex aequo. They finished neck and neck.

exagérer VERB [34]
1 to exaggerate
□ Vous exagérez ! You're exaggerating!
2 to go too far
□ Ça fait trois fois que tu arrives en retard : tu exagères ! That's three times you've been late: you really go too far sometimes!

l'**examen** MASC NOUN

exam

□ Nous allons passer l'examen d'anglais vendredi matin. We're doing our English exam on Friday morning. □ un examen de français a French exam

■ **un examen médical** a medical

examiner VERB [28]

to examine

exaspérant (FEM **exaspérante**) ADJECTIVE

infuriating

exaspérer VERB [34]

to infuriate

l'**excédent** MASC NOUN

■ **l'excédent de bagages** excess baggage

excéder VERB [34]

to exceed

□ un contrat dont la durée n'excède pas deux ans a contract for a period not exceeding two years

■ **excéder quelqu'un** to drive somebody mad □ Les cris des enfants l'excédaient. The noise of the children was driving her mad.

excellent (FEM **excellente**) ADJECTIVE

excellent

excentrique (FEM **excentrique**) ADJECTIVE

eccentric

excepté PREPOSITION

except

□ Toutes les chaussures excepté les sandales sont en solde. All the shoes except sandals are reduced.

l'**exception** FEM NOUN

exception

■ **à l'exception de** except

exceptionnel (FEM **exceptionnelle**) ADJECTIVE

exceptional

l'**excès** MASC NOUN

■ **faire des excès** to overindulge □ On fait souvent des excès à la période de Noël. People often overindulge around Christmas.

■ **les excès de vitesse** speeding

excessif (FEM **excessive**) ADJECTIVE

excessive

excitant (FEM **excitante**) ADJECTIVE

▷ see also **excitant** NOUN

exciting

l'**excitant** MASC NOUN

▷ see also **excitant** ADJECTIVE

stimulant

□ Le thé et le café sont des excitants. Tea and coffee are stimulants.

l'**excitation** FEM NOUN

excitement

exciter VERB [28]

to excite

□ Il était tout excité à l'idée de revoir ses cousins. He was all excited about seeing his cousins.

■ **s'exciter** (informal) to get excited □ Ne t'excite pas trop vite : ça ne va peut-être pas marcher ! Don't get excited too soon: it may not work!

l'**exclamation** FEM NOUN

exclamation

exclu (FEM **exclue**) ADJECTIVE

■ **Il n'est pas exclu que ...** It's not impossible that ...

exclusif (FEM **exclusive**) ADJECTIVE

exclusive

l'**excursion** FEM NOUN

1 trip

□ faire une excursion to go on a trip

2 walk

□ une excursion dans la montagne a walk in the mountains

l'**excuse** FEM NOUN

1 excuse

□ une bonne excuse a good excuse

2 apology

□ présenter ses excuses to offer one's apologies

■ **un mot d'excuse** a note □ Vous devez apporter un mot d'excuse signé par vos parents. You have to bring a note signed by your parents.

excuser VERB [28]

to excuse

■ **Excusez-moi. 1** Sorry. □ Excusez-moi, je ne vous avais pas vu. Sorry, I didn't see you. **2** Excuse me. □ Excusez-moi, est-ce que vous avez l'heure ? Excuse me, have you got the time?

■ **s'excuser** to apologize

■ **s'excuser de** to apologize for □ Il s'est excusé de son retard. He apologized for being late.

exécuter VERB [28]

1 to execute

□ Le prisonnier a été exécuté à l'aube. The prisoner was executed at dawn.

2 to perform

□ Le pianiste va maintenant exécuter une valse de Chopin. The pianist is now going to perform a waltz by Chopin.

l'**exemplaire** MASC NOUN

copy

l'**exemple** MASC NOUN

example

□ donner l'exemple to set an example

■ **par exemple** for example

s'**exercer** VERB [12]

to practise

l'**exercice** MASC NOUN

exercise

exhiber VERB [28]

to show off

exhibitionniste - exposer

□ Il aime bien exhiber ses décorations. He likes showing off his medals.
■ **s'exhiber** to expose oneself

l'**exhibitionniste** MASC NOUN
flasher

exigeant (FEM **exigeante**) ADJECTIVE
hard to please
□ Elle est vraiment exigeante. She's really hard to please.

exiger VERB [45]
1 to demand
□ Le propriétaire exige d'être payé immédiatement. The landlord is demanding to be paid immediately.
2 to require
□ Ce travail exige beaucoup de patience. This job requires a lot of patience.

l'**exil** MASC NOUN
exile

exister VERB [28]
to exist
□ Ça n'existe pas. It doesn't exist.
■ **Ce manteau existe également en rose.** This coat is also available in pink.

exotique (FEM **exotique**) ADJECTIVE
exotic
□ une plante exotique an exotic plant
■ **un yaourt aux fruits exotiques** a tropical fruit yoghurt

expédier VERB [19]
to send
□ expédier un colis to send a parcel

l'**expéditeur** MASC NOUN
sender

l'**expédition** FEM NOUN
expedition
■ **l'expédition du courrier** the dispatch of the mail

l'**expéditrice** FEM NOUN
sender

l'**expérience** FEM NOUN
1 experience
□ Elle a plusieurs années d'expérience. She's got several years' experience.
2 experiment
□ une expérience de chimie a chemistry experiment

experimenté (FEM **experimentée**)
ADJECTIVE
experienced
□ un plongeur très experimenté a very experienced diver

expérimenter VERB [28]
to test
□ Ces produits de beauté n'ont pas été expérimentés sur des animaux. These cosmetics have not been tested on animals.

l'**expert** MASC NOUN
expert

l'**experte** FEM NOUN
expert

expirer VERB [28]
1 to expire (document, passport)
2 to run out (time allowed)
3 to breathe out (person)

l'**explication** FEM NOUN
explanation
■ **une explication de texte** a critical analysis (of a text)

expliquer VERB [28]
to explain
□ Il m'a expliqué comment faire. He explained to me how to do it.
■ **Ça s'explique.** It's understandable.

l'**exploit** MASC NOUN
achievement

l'**exploitation** FEM NOUN
exploitation
□ C'est de l'exploitation. It's exploitation.
■ **une exploitation agricole** a farm

exploiter VERB [28]
to exploit
□ Il se fait exploiter par son patron. He gets exploited by his boss.

explorer VERB [28]
to explore

exploser VERB [28]
to explode
□ La bombe a explosé en pleine rue. The bomb exploded in the middle of the street.

l'**explosif** MASC NOUN
explosive

l'**explosion** FEM NOUN
explosion

l'**exportateur** MASC NOUN
exporter

l'**exportation** FEM NOUN
export

l'**exportatrice** FEM NOUN
exporter

exporter VERB [28]
to export

l'**exposé** MASC NOUN
talk
□ un exposé sur l'environnement a talk on the environment

exposer VERB [28]
1 to show
□ Il expose ses peintures dans une galerie d'art. He shows his paintings in a private art gallery.
2 to expose
□ N'exposez pas la pellicule à la lumière. Do not expose the film to light.

3 to set out

□ Il nous a exposé les raisons de son départ.
He set out the reasons for his departure.

■ **s'exposer au soleil** to stay out in the sun
□ Ne vous exposez pas trop longtemps au soleil.
Don't stay out too long in the sun.

l'**exposition** FEM NOUN
exhibition
□ une exposition de peinture an exhibition of
paintings

exprès ADVERB

1 on purpose
□ Il l'a fait exprès. He did it on purpose.

2 specially
□ J'ai fait ce gâteau exprès pour toi. I made this
cake specially for you.

l'**express** MASC NOUN

1 espresso (*coffee*)

2 fast train
□ Il a décidé de prendre l'express de dix heures.
He decided to catch the fast train at 10 o'clock.

l'**expression** FEM NOUN

1 expression

2 phrase

exprimer VERB [28]
to express
■ **s'exprimer** to express oneself □ Il s'exprime
très bien pour un enfant de huit ans. For a child
of 8, he expresses himself very well.

exquis (FEM **exquise**) ADJECTIVE
exquisite

extérieur (FEM **extérieure**) ADJECTIVE
▷ *see also* **extérieur** NOUN
outside

l'**extérieur** MASC NOUN
▷ *see also* **extérieur** ADJECTIVE
outside

■ **à l'extérieur** outside □ Les toilettes sont à
l'extérieur. The toilet is outside.

l'**externat** MASC NOUN
day school

l'**externe** MASC/FEM NOUN
day pupil

l'**extincteur** MASC NOUN
fire extinguisher

extra (FEM+PL **extra**) ADJECTIVE
excellent
□ Ce fromage est extra ! This cheese is excellent!

extraire VERB [85]
to extract

l'**extrait** MASC NOUN
extract

extraordinaire (FEM **extraordinaire**)
ADJECTIVE
extraordinary

extravagant (FEM **extravagante**) ADJECTIVE
extravagant

extrême (FEM **extrême**) ADJECTIVE
▷ *see also* **extrême** NOUN
extreme
□ l'extrême droite et l'extrême gauche the far
right and the far left

l'**extrême** MASC NOUN
▷ *see also* **extrême** ADJECTIVE
extreme

extrêmement ADVERB
extremely

l'**Extrême-Orient** MASC NOUN
the Far East

l'**extrémité** FEM NOUN
end
□ La gare est à l'autre extrémité de la ville.
The station is at the other end of the town.

Ff

F ABBREVIATION
franc (*currency in Switzerland and many former French colonies*)

le **fa** MASC NOUN
F

la **fabrication** FEM NOUN
manufacture

fabriquer VERB [28]
to make
□ fabriqué en France made in France
■ **Qu'est-ce qu'il fabrique ?** (*informal*) What's he up to?

la **fac** FEM NOUN (*informal*)
university
■ **à la fac** at university

la **face** FEM NOUN
■ **face à face** face to face
■ **en face de** opposite □ Le bus s'arrête en face de chez moi. The bus stops opposite my house.
■ **faire face à quelque chose** to face something
■ **Pile ou face ? — Face.** Heads or tails? — Heads.

facebooker VERB [28]
to Facebook

fâché (FEM **fâchée**) ADJECTIVE
angry
■ **être fâché contre quelqu'un** to be angry with somebody □ Elle est fâchée contre moi. She's angry with me.
■ **être fâché avec quelqu'un** to be on bad terms with somebody □ Elle est fâchée avec sa sœur. She's on bad terms with her sister.

se **fâcher** VERB [28]
■ **se fâcher contre quelqu'un** to lose one's temper with somebody
■ **se fâcher avec quelqu'un** to fall out with somebody □ Il s'est fâché avec son frère. He's fallen out with his brother.

facile (FEM **facile**) ADJECTIVE
easy
■ **facile à faire** easy to do

facilement ADVERB
easily

la **facilité** FEM NOUN
■ **un logiciel d'une grande facilité**

d'utilisation a very user-friendly piece of software
■ **Il a des facilités en langues.** He has a gift for languages.

> **BE CAREFUL!**
> facilité does not mean **facility**.

la **façon** FEM NOUN
way
□ De quelle façon ? In what way?
■ **de toute façon** anyway

le **facteur** MASC NOUN
postman
□ Il est facteur. He's a postman.

la **factrice** FEM NOUN
postwoman
□ Elle est factrice. She's a postwoman.

la **facture** FEM NOUN
bill
□ une facture de gaz a gas bill

facultatif (FEM **facultative**) ADJECTIVE
optional

la **faculté** FEM NOUN
faculty
■ **avoir une grande faculté de concentration** to have great powers of concentration

fade (FEM **fade**) ADJECTIVE
tasteless
□ La soupe est un peu fade. The soup is a bit tasteless.

faible (FEM **faible**) ADJECTIVE
weak
□ Je me sens encore faible. I still feel a bit weak.
■ **Il est faible en maths.** He's not very good at maths.

la **faiblesse** FEM NOUN
weakness

la **faïence** FEM NOUN
pottery

faillir VERB [12]
■ **J'ai failli tomber.** I nearly fell down.

la **faillite** FEM NOUN
bankruptcy
■ **une entreprise en faillite** a bankrupt business
■ **faire faillite** to go bankrupt

la **faim** FEM NOUN
hunger
  ■ **avoir faim** to be hungry

fainéant (FEM **fainéante**) ADJECTIVE
lazy

faire VERB [36]

PRESENT TENSE	
je fais	nous faisons
tu fais	vous faites
il/elle fait	ils/elles font
PAST PARTICIPLE	
fait	

1 to make
  □ Je vais faire un gâteau pour ce soir. I'm going to make a cake for tonight. □ Ils font trop de bruit. They're making too much noise. □ Je voudrais me faire de nouveaux amis. I'd like to make new friends.
2 to do
  □ Qu'est-ce que tu fais ? What are you doing? □ Il fait de l'italien. He's doing Italian. □ Je fais du kayak dans mon temps libre. I do kayaking in my spare time. □ Qui veut faire la vaisselle ? Who'll do the dishes?
3 to play
  □ Il fait du piano. He plays the piano.
4 to be
  □ Il fait chaud. It is hot. □ Espérons qu'il fera beau demain. Let's hope it'll be nice weather tomorrow.
  ■ **Ça ne fait rien.** It doesn't matter.
  ■ **Ça fait cinquante-trois euros en tout.** That makes fifty-three euros in all.
  ■ **Ça fait trois ans qu'il habite à Paris.** He's lived in Paris for three years.
  ■ **faire tomber** to knock over □ Le chat a fait tomber le vase. The cat knocked over the vase.
  ■ **faire faire quelque chose** to get something done □ Je dois faire réparer ma voiture. I've got to get my car repaired.
  ■ **Je vais me faire couper les cheveux.** I'm going to get my hair cut.
  ■ **Ne t'en fais pas !** Don't worry!

fais, faisaient, faisais, faisait VERB
▷ see **faire**

le **faisan** MASC NOUN
pheasant

faisant, faisiez, faisions, faisons, fait VERB ▷ see **faire**

le **fait** MASC NOUN
fact
  □ Le fait que … The fact that …
  ■ **un fait divers** a news item
  ■ **au fait** by the way □ Au fait, tu as aimé le film d'hier ? By the way, did you enjoy the film yesterday?
  ■ **en fait** actually □ En fait je n'ai pas beaucoup de temps. I haven't got much time actually.

faites VERB ▷ see **faire**

la **falaise** FEM NOUN
cliff

falloir VERB [37] ▷ see **faut, faudra, faudrait**

famé (FEM **famée**) ADJECTIVE
  ■ **un quartier mal famé** a rough area

fameux (FEM **fameuse**) ADJECTIVE
  ■ **Ce n'est pas fameux.** It's not great.

familial (FEM **familiale**, MASC PL **familiaux**) ADJECTIVE
family
  □ une atmosphère familiale a family atmosphere
  ■ **les allocations familiales** child benefit

familier (FEM **familière**) ADJECTIVE
familiar

la **famille** FEM NOUN
1 family
  □ une famille nombreuse a big family □ Nous passons Noël en famille. We have a family Christmas.
2 relatives
  □ Il a de la famille à Paris. He's got relatives in Paris.

la **famine** FEM NOUN
famine

le/la **fan** MASC/FEM NOUN (informal)
fan
  □ Je suis fan de tennis. I'm a tennis fan.

fanatique (FEM **fanatique**) ADJECTIVE
  ▷ see also **fanatique** NOUN
fanatical

le/la **fanatique** MASC/FEM NOUN
  ▷ see also **fanatique** ADJECTIVE
fanatic

la **fanfare** FEM NOUN
brass band

fantaisie (FEM+PL **fantaisie**) ADJECTIVE
  ■ **des bijoux fantaisie** costume jewellery

fantastique (FEM **fantastique**) ADJECTIVE
fantastic

le **fantôme** MASC NOUN
ghost

la **farce** FEM NOUN
1 stuffing (for chicken, turkey)
2 practical joke
  □ Il aime faire des farces. He likes to play practical jokes.

farci (FEM **farcie**) ADJECTIVE
stuffed
  □ des tomates farcies stuffed tomatoes

la **farine** FEM NOUN
flour

fascinant (FEM **fascinante**) ADJECTIVE
fascinating

fasciner VERB [28]
to fascinate

le **fascisme** MASC NOUN
fascism
fasse, fassent, fasses, fassiez, fassions VERB ▷ *see* **faire**
■ **Pourvu qu'il fasse beau demain !** Let's hope it'll be fine tomorrow!
le **fast-food** MASC NOUN
fast food
fatal (FEM **fatale**) ADJECTIVE
fatal
■ **C'était fatal.** It was bound to happen.
la **fatalité** FEM NOUN
fate
fatigant (FEM **fatigante**) ADJECTIVE
tiring
la **fatigue** FEM NOUN
tiredness
fatigué (FEM **fatiguée**) ADJECTIVE
tired
se **fatiguer** VERB [28]
to get tired
fauché (FEM **fauchée**) ADJECTIVE (*informal*)
hard up
faudra VERB
> faudra is the future tense of **falloir**.
■ **Il faudra qu'on soit plus rapide.** We'll have to be quicker.
faudrait VERB
> faudrait is the conditional tense of **falloir**.
■ **Il faudrait qu'on fasse attention.** We ought to be careful.
se **faufiler** VERB [28]
■ **Il s'est faufilé à travers la foule.** He made his way through the crowd.
la **faune** FEM NOUN
wildlife
fausse FEM ADJECTIVE ▷ *see* **faux**
faut VERB
> faut is the present tense of **falloir**.
■ **Il faut faire ...** You have to do ...
■ **Il faut faire attention.** You've got to be careful.
■ **Nous n'avons pas le choix, il faut y aller.** We've no choice, we've got to go.
■ **Il faut que je parte.** I've got to go.
■ **Il faut du courage pour faire ce métier.** It takes courage to do that job.
■ **Il me faut de l'argent.** I need money.
la **faute** FEM NOUN
1 mistake
□ faire une faute to make a mistake
2 fault
□ Ce n'est pas de ma faute. It's not my fault.
■ **sans faute** without fail □ Je t'appellerai sans faute. I'll phone you without fail.

le **fauteuil** MASC NOUN
armchair
■ **un fauteuil roulant** a wheelchair
faux (FEM **fausse**) ADJECTIVE, ADVERB
> *see also* **faux** NOUN
untrue
□ C'est entièrement faux. It's totally untrue.
■ **faire un faux pas** to trip
■ **Il chante faux.** He sings out of tune.
le **faux** MASC NOUN
> *see also* **faux** ADJECTIVE, ADVERB
fake
□ Ce tableau est un faux. This painting is a fake.
la **faveur** FEM NOUN
favour
favori (FEM **favorite**) ADJECTIVE
favourite
favoriser VERB [28]
to favour
□ Ce système d'examen favorise ceux qui ont de la mémoire. This exam system favours people with good memories.
le **fax** MASC NOUN
fax
faxer VERB [28]
to fax
■ **faxer un document à quelqu'un** to fax somebody a document
la **fée** FEM NOUN
fairy
feignant (FEM **feignante**) ADJECTIVE (*informal*)
lazy
les **félicitations** FEM PL NOUN
congratulations
□ Félicitations à vous, Jérémy ! Congratulations, Jérémy!
féliciter VERB [28]
to congratulate
la **femelle** FEM NOUN
female (*animal*)
féminin (FEM **féminine**) ADJECTIVE
1 female
□ les personnages féminins du roman the female characters in the novel
2 feminine
□ Elle est très féminine. She's very feminine.
3 women's
□ Elle joue dans l'équipe féminine de France. She plays in the French women's team.
féministe (FEM **féministe**) ADJECTIVE
feminist
la **femme** FEM NOUN
1 woman
2 wife
□ la femme du directeur the headmaster's wife
■ **une femme au foyer** a housewife
■ **une femme de ménage** a cleaner

■ **une femme de chambre** a chambermaid
■ **une femme politique** a politician

se **fendre** VERB [88]
to crack

la **fenêtre** FEM NOUN
window

le **fenouil** MASC NOUN
fennel

la **fente** FEM NOUN
slot

le **fer** MASC NOUN
iron
■ **un fer à cheval** a horseshoe
■ **un fer à repasser** an iron

fera, ferai, ferais, ferait, feras, ferez
VERB ▷ see **faire**

férié (FEM **fériée**) ADJECTIVE
■ **un jour férié** a public holiday

feriez, ferions VERB ▷ see **faire**

ferme (FEM **ferme**) ADJECTIVE
▷ see also **ferme** NOUN
firm
□ Elle s'est montrée très ferme à mon égard.
She was very firm with me.

la **ferme** FEM NOUN
▷ see also **ferme** ADJECTIVE
farm

fermé (FEM **fermée**) ADJECTIVE
1 closed
□ La pharmacie est fermée. The chemist's is
closed.
2 off
□ Est-ce que le gaz est fermé ? Is the gas off?

fermer VERB [28]
1 to close
□ Ferme la fenêtre. Close the window.
2 to turn off
□ As-tu bien fermé le robinet ? Have you turned
the tap off?
■ **fermer à clé** to lock □ N'oublie pas de fermer
la porte à clé ! Don't forget to lock the door!

la **fermeture** FEM NOUN
■ **les heures de fermeture** closing times
■ **une fermeture éclair®** a zip

le **fermier** MASC NOUN
farmer

la **fermière** FEM NOUN
1 farmer (*woman*)
2 farmer's wife

féroce (FEM **féroce**) ADJECTIVE
fierce

ferons, feront VERB ▷ see **faire**

les **fesses** FEM PL NOUN
buttocks

le **festival** MASC NOUN
festival

les **festivités** FEM PL NOUN
festivities

la **fête** FEM NOUN
1 party
□ On organise une petite fête pour son
anniversaire. We're having a little party for his
birthday.
■ **faire la fête** to party
2 name day
□ C'est sa fête aujourd'hui. It's his name day
today.
■ **bonnes fêtes !** happy holidays!
■ **une fête foraine** a funfair
■ **la Fête Nationale** Bastille Day
■ **les fêtes de fin d'année** the festive season
■ **la Fête des Mères** Mother's Day
■ **la Fête du Travail** May Day

> **DID YOU KNOW...?**
> **La Fête du Travail** is on 1 May and
> traditionally people give each other small
> bunches of lily of the valley. In many towns
> and cities, there is no public transport and
> shops and restaurants close.

■ **la Fête de la Musique**

> **DID YOU KNOW...?**
> **La Fête de la Musique** takes place on 21
> June across France and in many other French-
> speaking countries. The events are free, with
> all kinds of music by groups and soloists,
> young and old, amateur and professional.
> The venues are as varied as the music.

fêter VERB [28]
to celebrate

le **feu** (PL les **feux**) MASC NOUN
1 fire
□ prendre feu to catch fire □ faire du feu to
make a fire
■ **Au feu !** Fire!
■ **un feu de joie** a bonfire
2 traffic light
□ un feu rouge a red light □ le feu vert the green
light □ Tournez à gauche aux feux. Turn left at
the lights.
■ **Avez-vous du feu ?** Have you got a light?
3 heat
□ ... mijoter à feu doux ... simmer over a gentle
heat
■ **un feu d'artifice** a firework display

le **feuillage** MASC NOUN
leaves

la **feuille** FEM NOUN
1 leaf
□ des feuilles mortes fallen leaves
2 sheet
□ une feuille de papier a sheet of paper
■ **une feuille de maladie** a claim form for
medical expenses

f

feuilleté – fin

feuilleté (FEM **feuilletée**) ADJECTIVE
- **de la pâte feuilletée** flaky pastry

feuilleter VERB [41]
to leaf through

le **feuilleton** MASC NOUN
serial

le **feutre** MASC NOUN
felt
- **un stylo-feutre** a felt-tip pen

la **fève** FEM NOUN
broad bean

février MASC NOUN
February
- **en février** in February

fiable (FEM **fiable**) ADJECTIVE
reliable

les **fiançailles** FEM PL NOUN
engagement *sing*

fiancé (FEM **fiancée**) ADJECTIVE
- **être fiancé à quelqu'un** to be engaged to somebody

se **fiancer** VERB [12]
to get engaged

la **ficelle** FEM NOUN
1 string
  □ Passe-moi un bout de ficelle. Give me a piece of string.
2 thin baguette (*bread*)

la **fiche** FEM NOUN
form
  □ Remplissez cette fiche, s'il vous plaît. Fill in this form, please.

se **ficher** VERB [28] (*informal*)
- **Je m'en fiche !** I don't care!
- **Quoi, tu n'as fait que ça ? Tu te fiches de moi !** You've only done that much? You can't be serious!

le **fichier** MASC NOUN
file

fichu (FEM **fichue**) ADJECTIVE (*informal*)
- **Ce parapluie est fichu.** This umbrella's knackered.

fidèle (FEM **fidèle**) ADJECTIVE
faithful

fier (FEM **fière**) ADJECTIVE
proud

la **fierté** FEM NOUN
pride

la **fièvre** FEM NOUN
fever
- **avoir de la fièvre** to have a temperature □ J'ai de la fièvre. I've got a temperature. □ Il a trente-neuf de fièvre. He's got a temperature of 39ºC.

fiévreux (FEM **fiévreuse**) ADJECTIVE
feverish

la **figue** FEM NOUN
fig

la **figure** FEM NOUN
1 face
  □ Il a reçu le ballon en pleine figure. The ball hit him smack in the face.
2 figure (*illustration*)
  □ Voir figure 2.1, page 32. See figure 2.1, page 32.

le **fil** MASC NOUN
thread
  □ le fil à coudre sewing thread
- **le fil de fer** wire
- **un coup de fil** a phone call

la **file** FEM NOUN
line (*of people*, *objects*)
- **une file d'attente** a queue □ se mettre à la file to join the queue
- **à la file** one after the other
- **en file indienne** in single file

filer VERB [28]
to speed along
  □ Les voitures filent sur l'autoroute. The cars are speeding along the motorway.
- **File dans ta chambre !** Off to your room with you!

le **filet** MASC NOUN
net

la **fille** FEM NOUN
1 girl
  □ C'est une école de filles. It's a girls' school.
2 daughter
  □ C'est leur fille aînée. She's their oldest daughter.

la **fillette** FEM NOUN
little girl

le **filleul** MASC NOUN
godson

la **filleule** FEM NOUN
goddaughter

le **film** MASC NOUN
film
- **un film policier** a thriller
- **un film d'aventures** an adventure film
- **un film d'épouvante** a horror film
- **le film alimentaire** Clingfilm®

le **fils** MASC NOUN
son

la **fin** FEM NOUN
▷ *see also* **fin** ADJECTIVE
end
  □ à la fin du film at the end of the film □ À la fin, il a réussi à se décider. In the end he managed to make up his mind.
- **« Fin »** 'The End'
- **Il sera en vacances fin juin.** He'll be on holiday at the end of June.
- **en fin de journée** at the end of the day
- **en fin de compte** when all's said and done
- **sans fin** endless

fin (FEM **fine**) ADJECTIVE
▷ *see also* **fin** NOUN
fine
■ **des fines herbes** mixed herbs

final (FEM **finale**) ADJECTIVE
final
□ le résultat final the final result

la **finale** FEM NOUN
final
□ les quarts de finale the quarter finals

finalement ADVERB
1 at last
□ Nous sommes finalement arrivés. At last we arrived.
2 after all
□ Finalement, tu avais raison. You were right after all.

fini (FEM **finie**) ADJECTIVE
finished

finir VERB [38]
to finish
□ Le cours finit à onze heures. The lesson finishes at 11 o'clock. □ Je viens de finir ce livre. I've just finished this book.
■ **Il a fini par se décider.** He made up his mind in the end.
■ **finir de faire quelque chose** to finish doing something. □ Elle a fini d'écrire son autobiographie. She has finished writing her autobiography.

finlandais (FEM **finlandaise**) ADJECTIVE, NOUN
Finnish
□ Ils parlent finlandais. They speak Finnish.
■ **un Finlandais** a Finn (*man*)
■ **une Finlandaise** a Finn (*woman*)
■ **les Finlandais** the Finns

la **Finlande** FEM NOUN
Finland

la **firme** FEM NOUN
firm

fis VERB ▷ *see* **faire**

la **fissure** FEM NOUN
crack

fit VERB ▷ *see* **faire**

fixe (FEM **fixe**) ADJECTIVE
1 steady
□ Il n'a pas d'emploi fixe. He hasn't got a steady job.
2 set
□ Il mange toujours à heures fixes. He always eats at set times.
■ **un menu à prix fixe** a set menu

fixer VERB [28]
1 to fix
□ Les volets sont fixés avec des crochets. The shutters are fixed with hooks. □ Nous avons fixé une heure pour nous retrouver. We fixed a time to meet.

2 to stare at
□ Ne fixe pas les gens comme ça ! Don't stare at people like that!

le **flacon** MASC NOUN
bottle
□ un flacon de parfum a bottle of perfume

le **flageolet** MASC NOUN
small haricot bean

flamand (FEM **flamande**) ADJECTIVE, NOUN
Flemish
□ Il parle flamand chez lui. He speaks Flemish at home.
■ **les Flamands** the Dutch-speaking Belgians

flambé (FEM **flambée**) ADJECTIVE
■ **des bananes flambées** flambéed bananas

la **flamme** FEM NOUN
flame
■ **en flammes** on fire

le **flan** MASC NOUN
baked custard

flâner VERB [28]
to stroll

la **flaque** FEM NOUN
puddle (*of water*)

le **flash** (PL les **flashes**) MASC NOUN
flash (*of camera*)
■ **un flash d'information** a newsflash

flatter VERB [28]
to flatter

la **flèche** FEM NOUN
arrow

les **fléchettes** FEM PL NOUN
darts
□ jouer aux fléchettes to play darts

la **fleur** FEM NOUN
flower

fleuri (FEM **fleurie**) ADJECTIVE
1 full of flowers
□ Son jardin était très fleuri. Her garden was full of flowers.
2 flowery
□ un papier peint fleuri flowery wallpaper

fleurir VERB [38]
to flower
□ Cette plante fleurit en automne. This plant flowers in autumn.

le/la **fleuriste** MASC/FEM NOUN
florist

le **fleuve** MASC NOUN
river

le **flic** MASC NOUN (*informal*)
cop

le **flipper** MASC NOUN
pinball machine

flirter VERB [28]
to flirt

f

le **flocon** MASC NOUN
flake

flotter VERB [28]
to float

flou (FEM **floue**) ADJECTIVE
blurred

le **fluor** MASC NOUN
■ **le dentifrice au fluor** fluoride toothpaste

la **flûte** FEM NOUN
flute
□ Je joue de la flûte. I play the flute.
■ **une flûte à bec** a recorder
■ **Flûte !** (*informal*) Heck!

la **foi** FEM NOUN
faith

le **foie** MASC NOUN
liver
■ **une crise de foie** a stomach upset

le **foin** MASC NOUN
hay
■ **le rhume des foins** hay fever

la **foire** FEM NOUN
fair

la **fois** FEM NOUN
time
□ la première fois the first time □ à chaque
fois each time □ À chaque fois que je vais à la
bibliothèque, j'oublie ma carte. Every time I go
to the library, I forget my card. □ Deux fois deux
font quatre. 2 times 2 is 4.
■ **une fois** once
■ **deux fois** twice □ deux fois plus de gens twice
as many people
■ **une fois que** once □ Tu te sentiras mieux une
fois que tu auras mangé. You'll feel better once
you've had something to eat.
■ **à la fois** at once □ Je ne peux pas faire deux
choses à la fois. I can't do two things at once.

fol MASC ADJECTIVE ▷ *see* **fou**

la **folie** FEM NOUN
madness
□ C'est de la folie pure ! It's absolute madness!
■ **faire une folie** to be extravagant

folklorique (FEM **folklorique**) ADJECTIVE
folk
□ de la musique folklorique folk music

folle FEM ADJECTIVE ▷ *see* **fou**

foncé (FEM **foncée**) ADJECTIVE
dark
□ bleu foncé dark blue

foncer VERB [12] (*informal*)
■ **Je vais foncer à la boulangerie.** I'm just
going to dash to the baker's.

la **fonction** FEM NOUN
function
■ **une voiture de fonction** a company car

le/la **fonctionnaire** MASC/FEM NOUN
civil servant

fonctionner VERB [28]
to work

le **fond** MASC NOUN
1 bottom
□ Mon porte-monnaie est au fond de mon sac.
My purse is at the bottom of my bag.
2 end
□ Les toilettes sont au fond du couloir. The
toilets are at the end of the corridor.
■ **dans le fond** all things considered □ Dans le
fond, ce n'est pas si grave. All things considered,
it's not that bad.

fonder VERB [28]
to found

fondre VERB [69]
to melt
□ La tablette de chocolat a fondu dans ma
poche. The bar of chocolate melted in my
pocket.
■ **fondre en larmes** to burst into tears

fondu (FEM **fondue**) ADJECTIVE
■ **du beurre fondu** melted butter

font VERB ▷ *see* **faire**

la **fontaine** FEM NOUN
fountain

le **foot** MASC NOUN
football

le **football** MASC NOUN
football
□ jouer au football to play football

le **footballeur** MASC NOUN
footballer

le **footing** MASC NOUN
jogging
□ faire du footing to go jogging

forain (FEM **foraine**) ADJECTIVE
▷ *see also* **forain** NOUN
■ **une fête foraine** a funfair

le **forain** MASC NOUN
▷ *see also* **forain** ADJECTIVE
fairground worker

la **force** FEM NOUN
strength
□ Je n'ai pas beaucoup de force dans les bras.
I haven't got much strength in my arms.
■ **à force de** by □ Il a grossi à force de manger
autant. He got fat by eating so much.
■ **de force** by force □ Ils lui ont enlevé son
pistolet de force. They took the gun from him
by force.

forcé (FEM **forcée**) ADJECTIVE
forced
□ un sourire forcé a forced smile
■ **C'est forcé.** (*informal*) It's inevitable.

forcément ADVERB
- ■ Ça devait forcément arriver. That was bound to happen.
- ■ pas forcément not necessarily

la **forêt** FEM NOUN
forest

le **forfait** MASC NOUN
all-in price
- ■ C'est compris dans le forfait. It's included in the price.
- ■ perdre par forfait to lose by forfeit
- ■ un forfait téléphonique a contract (*mobile phone*)

le **forgeron** MASC NOUN
blacksmith

la **formalité** FEM NOUN
formality
- □ Ce n'est qu'une simple formalité. It's just a formality.

le **format** MASC NOUN
size

la **formation** FEM NOUN
training
- □ la formation professionnelle vocational training
- ■ la formation continue continuing education
- ■ Il a une formation d'ingénieur. He is a trained engineer.

la **forme** FEM NOUN
shape
- ■ être en forme to be in good shape
- ■ Je ne suis pas en forme aujourd'hui. I'm not feeling too good today.
- ■ Tu as l'air en forme. You're looking well.

formellement ADVERB
strictly
- □ Il est formellement interdit de fumer dans les couloirs. It is strictly forbidden to smoke in the corridors.

former VERB [28]
1 to form
2 to train

formidable (FEM **formidable**) ADJECTIVE
great

le **formulaire** MASC NOUN
form

fort (FEM **forte**) ADJECTIVE, ADVERB
1 strong
- □ Le café est trop fort. The coffee's too strong.
2 good
- □ Il est très fort en espagnol. He's very good at Spanish.
3 loud
- □ Est-ce vous pouvez parler plus fort ? Can you speak louder?
- ■ frapper fort to hit hard

le **fortifiant** MASC NOUN
tonic (*medicine*)

la **fortune** FEM NOUN
fortune
- ■ de fortune makeshift □ un radeau de fortune a makeshift raft

le **forum** MASC NOUN
chat room

le **forum de discussion** MASC NOUN
forum (*for discussion*)

le **fossé** MASC NOUN
ditch

fou (FEM **folle**) ADJECTIVE

> The masculine singular form fou changes to fol before a vowel or most words beginning with 'h'.

mad
- ■ Il y a un monde fou sur la plage ! (*informal*) There are loads of people on the beach!
- ■ attraper le fou rire to get the giggles

la **foudre** FEM NOUN
lightning
- □ Il a été frappé par la foudre. He was struck by lightning.

foudroyant (FEM **foudroyante**) ADJECTIVE
instant
- □ un succès foudroyant an instant hit

le **fouet** MASC NOUN
whisk

la **fougère** FEM NOUN
fern

fouiller VERB [28]
to rummage

le **fouillis** MASC NOUN
mess
- □ Il y a du fouillis dans sa chambre. His bedroom is a mess.

le **foulard** MASC NOUN
scarf
- □ un foulard en soie a silk scarf

la **foule** FEM NOUN
crowd
- ■ une foule de masses of □ J'ai une foule de choses à faire ce week-end. I've got masses of things to do this weekend.

se **fouler** VERB [28]
- ■ se fouler la cheville to sprain one's ankle

le **four** MASC NOUN
oven
- □ un four à micro-ondes a microwave oven

la **fourchette** FEM NOUN
fork

la **fourmi** FEM NOUN
ant
- ■ avoir des fourmis dans les jambes to have pins and needles

f

fourneau - fredonner

le **fourneau** (PL les **fourneaux**) MASC NOUN
stove

fourni (FEM **fournie**) ADJECTIVE
thick (*beard, hair*)

fournir VERB [38]
to supply

le **fournisseur** MASC NOUN
supplier
■ **un fournisseur d'accès à Internet** an internet service provider

les **fournitures** FEM PL NOUN
■ **les fournitures scolaires** school stationery

fourré (FEM **fourrée**) ADJECTIVE
filled
□ un gâteau fourré à la confiture d'abricot a cake filled with apricot jam

fourrer VERB [28] (*informal*)
to put
□ Où as-tu fourré mon sac ? Where have you put my bag?

le **fourre-tout** (PL les **fourre-tout**) MASC NOUN
holdall

la **fourrure** FEM NOUN
fur
□ un manteau de fourrure a fur coat

le **foyer** MASC NOUN
home
□ dans la plupart des foyers français in most French homes
■ **un foyer de jeunes** a youth club

la **fracture** FEM NOUN
fracture

fragile (FEM **fragile**) ADJECTIVE
fragile
□ Attention, c'est fragile ! Be careful, it's fragile!

la **fragilité** FEM NOUN
fragility

fraîche FEM ADJECTIVE ▷ see **frais**

la **fraîcheur** FEM NOUN
1 cool
□ la fraîcheur du soir the cool of the evening
2 freshness
□ Je ne suis pas sûre de la fraîcheur du poisson. I'm not sure about the freshness of the fish.

frais (FEM **fraîche**) ADJECTIVE
▷ see also **frais** NOUN
1 fresh
□ des œufs frais fresh eggs □ Cette salade n'est pas très fraîche. This lettuce isn't very fresh.
2 chilly
□ Il fait un peu frais ce soir. It's a bit chilly this evening.
3 cool
□ des boissons fraîches cool drinks
■ « servir frais » 'serve chilled'
■ **mettre au frais** to put in a cool place

les **frais** MASC PL NOUN
▷ see also **frais** ADJECTIVE
expenses

la **fraise** FEM NOUN
strawberry
□ une fraise des bois a wild strawberry

la **framboise** FEM NOUN
raspberry

franc (FEM **franche**) ADJECTIVE
▷ see also **franc** NOUN
frank

le **franc** MASC NOUN
▷ see also **franc** ADJECTIVE
franc

DID YOU KNOW...?
The **franc** is the unit of currency in Switzerland and many former French colonies.

français (FEM **française**) ADJECTIVE, NOUN
French
□ Il parle français couramment. He speaks French fluently.
■ **un Français** a Frenchman
■ **une Française** a Frenchwoman
■ **les Français** the French

la **France** FEM NOUN
France
■ **en France** 1 in France □ Je suis né en France. I was born in France. 2 to France □ Je pars en France pour Noël. I'm going to France for Christmas.
■ **la France d'outre-mer** overseas France

franche FEM ADJECTIVE ▷ see **franc**

franchement ADVERB
1 frankly
□ Il m'a parlé franchement. He spoke to me frankly.
2 really
□ C'est franchement mauvais. It's really bad.

franchir VERB [38]
to get over

la **franchise** FEM NOUN
frankness

francophone (FEM **francophone**) ADJECTIVE
French-speaking

la **francophonie** FEM NOUN
French-speaking world

la **frangipane** FEM NOUN
almond cream

frapper VERB [28]
to strike
□ Il l'a frappée au visage. He struck her in the face. □ Son air fatigué m'a frappé. I was struck by how tired she looked.

fredonner VERB [28]
to hum

Numbers in brackets refer to verb tables on pages 650 to 658

le **freezer** MASC NOUN
freezing compartment

le **frein** MASC NOUN
brake
■ **le frein à main** handbrake

freiner VERB [28]
to brake

frêle (FEM **frêle**) ADJECTIVE
frail

le **frelon** MASC NOUN
hornet

frémir VERB [38]
shudder
□ Cette idée me fait frémir. The idea makes me shudder.

fréquemment ADVERB
frequently

fréquent (FEM **fréquente**) ADJECTIVE
frequent

fréquenté (FEM **fréquentée**) ADJECTIVE
busy
□ une rue très fréquentée a very busy street
■ **un bar mal fréquenté** a rough pub

fréquenter VERB [28]
to see (person)
□ Je ne le fréquente pas beaucoup. I don't see him often.

le **frère** MASC NOUN
brother

le **friand** MASC NOUN
■ **un friand au fromage** a cheese puff

la **friandise** FEM NOUN
sweet

le **fric** MASC NOUN (informal)
cash

le **frigidaire**® MASC NOUN
refrigerator

le **frigo** MASC NOUN (informal)
fridge

frileux (FEM **frileuse**) ADJECTIVE
■ **être frileux** to feel the cold □ Je suis très frileuse. I really feel the cold.

frimer VERB [28] (informal)
to show off

les **fringues** FEM PL NOUN (informal)
clothes

fripé (FEM **fripée**) ADJECTIVE
crumpled

frire VERB [80]
■ **faire frire** to fry □ Faites frire les boulettes dans de l'huile très chaude. Fry the meatballs in very hot oil.

frisé (FEM **frisée**) ADJECTIVE
curly
□ Elle est très frisée. She's got very curly hair.

le **frisson** MASC NOUN
shiver

frissonner VERB [28]
to shiver

frit (FEM **frite**) ADJECTIVE
fried
□ du poisson frit fried fish

frite FEM NOUN
chip
□ Elle mange des frites. She's eating chips.

les **frites** FEM PL NOUN
chips

la **friture** FEM NOUN
1 fried food
□ On lui a conseillé d'éviter les fritures. He's been advised to avoid fried food.
2 fried fish
□ Nous allons faire une friture ce soir. We are going to have fried fish tonight.

froid (FEM **froide**) ADJECTIVE
▷ see also **froid** NOUN
cold
□ Ça me laisse froid. It leaves me cold. □ de la viande froide cold meat

le **froid** MASC NOUN
▷ see also **froid** ADJECTIVE
cold
■ **Il fait froid.** It's cold.
■ **avoir froid** to be cold □ Est-ce que tu as froid ? Are you cold?

se **froisser** VERB [28]
1 to crease
□ Ce tissu se froisse très facilement. This material creases very easily.
2 to take offence
□ Paul se froisse très facilement. Paul's very quick to take offence.
■ **se froisser un muscle** to strain a muscle

frôler VERB [28]
1 to brush against
□ Le chat m'a frôlé au passage. The cat brushed against me as it went past.
2 to narrowly avoid
□ Nous avons frôlé la catastrophe. We narrowly avoided disaster.

le **fromage** MASC NOUN
cheese

le **froment** MASC NOUN
wheat
■ **une crêpe de froment** a pancake (made with wheat flour)

froncer VERB [12]
■ **froncer les sourcils** to frown

le **front** MASC NOUN
forehead

la **frontière** FEM NOUN
border

frotter VERB [28]

to rub
- □ se frotter les yeux to rub one's eyes
- ■ frotter une allumette to strike a match

le **fruit** MASC NOUN

fruit
- ■ un fruit a piece of fruit □ Est-ce que vous voulez manger un fruit ? Would you like some fruit?
- ■ les fruits de mer seafood

fruité (FEM **fruitée**) ADJECTIVE

fruity

frustrer VERB [28]

to frustrate

la **fugue** FEM NOUN
- ■ faire une fugue to run away

fuir VERB [39]

1 to flee
- □ fuir devant un danger to flee from danger

2 to drip
- □ Le robinet fuit. The tap's dripping.

la **fuite** FEM NOUN

1 leak
- □ Il y a une fuite de gaz. There is a gas leak.

2 flight (escape)
- ■ être en fuite to be on the run

fumé (FEM **fumée**) ADJECTIVE
- ▷ see also **fumée** NOUN

smoked
- □ du saumon fumé smoked salmon

la **fumée** FEM NOUN
- ▷ see also **fumé** ADJECTIVE

smoke

fumer VERB [28]

to smoke

le **fumeur** MASC NOUN

smoker

la **fumeuse** FEM NOUN

smoker

le **fur** MASC NOUN
- ■ au fur et à mesure as you go along □ Je vérifie mon travail au fur et à mesure. I check my work as I go along.
- ■ au fur et à mesure que as □ Je réponds à mon courrier au fur et à mesure que je le reçois. I answer my mail as I receive it.

le **furet** MASC NOUN

ferret

la **fureur** FEM NOUN

fury
- ■ faire fureur to be all the rage □ Ce genre de sac fait fureur actuellement. This sort of bag is all the rage at the moment.

furieux (FEM **furieuse**) ADJECTIVE

furious

le **furoncle** MASC NOUN

boil (on skin)

fus VERB ▷ see être

le **fuseau** (PL les **fuseaux**) MASC NOUN

ski pants

la **fusée** FEM NOUN

rocket

le **fusil** MASC NOUN

gun

fut VERB ▷ see être

futé (FEM **futée**) ADJECTIVE

crafty

le **futur** MASC NOUN

future

Gg

gâcher VERB [28]

to waste

□ Je n'aime pas gâcher la nourriture. I don't like to waste food.

le **gâchis** MASC NOUN

waste

la **gaffe** FEM NOUN

■ **faire une gaffe** to do something stupid

■ **Fais gaffe !** (*informal*) Watch out! □ Fais gaffe : la peinture est encore humide ! Watch out: the paint's still wet!

le **gage** MASC NOUN

forfeit (*in a game*)

□ recevoir un gage to pay a forfeit

le **gagnant** MASC NOUN

winner

la **gagnante** FEM NOUN

winner

gagner VERB [28]

to win

□ Qui a gagné ? Who won?

■ **gagner du temps** to save time

■ **Il gagne bien sa vie.** He makes a good living.

gai (FEM **gaie**) ADJECTIVE

cheerful

□ Elle est très gaie. She's very cheerful.

la **gaieté** FEM NOUN

cheerfulness

la **galerie** FEM NOUN

gallery

□ une galerie de peinture an art gallery

■ **une galerie marchande** a shopping arcade

■ **une galerie de jeux d'arcade** an amusement arcade

le **galet** MASC NOUN

pebble

la **galette** FEM NOUN

1 round flat cake

■ **une galette de blé noir** a buckwheat pancake

2 biscuit

□ des galettes pur beurre shortbread biscuits

■ **la galette des Rois**

DID YOU KNOW…?

A **galette des Rois** is a cake eaten on Twelfth Night (6 January) containing a figurine. The person who finds it is the king (or queen) and gets a paper crown. They then choose someone else to be their queen (or king).

Galles FEM NOUN

■ **le pays de Galles** Wales

■ **le prince de Galles** the Prince of Wales

gallois (FEM **galloise**) ADJECTIVE, NOUN

Welsh

□ un peintre gallois a Welsh painter

■ **un Gallois** a Welshman

■ **une Galloise** a Welshwoman

■ **les Gallois** the Welsh

le **galop** MASC NOUN

gallop

galoper VERB [28]

to gallop

le **gamin** MASC NOUN (*informal*)

kid

la **gamine** FEM NOUN (*informal*)

kid

la **gamme** FEM NOUN

scale (*in music*)

□ faire des gammes to do scales

■ **une gamme de produits** a range of products

gammée (FEM **gammée**) ADJECTIVE

■ **la croix gammée** the swastika

le **gant** MASC NOUN

glove

□ des gants en laine woollen gloves

■ **un gant de toilette** a face cloth

le **garage** MASC NOUN

garage

le/la **garagiste** MASC/FEM NOUN

1 garage owner

2 mechanic

la **garantie** FEM NOUN

guarantee

garantir VERB [38]

to guarantee

le **garçon** MASC NOUN

boy

■ **un vieux garçon** a bachelor

g

le **garde** MASC NOUN
▷ see also **garde** NOUN
1 warder (in prison)
2 guard (officer)
■ **un garde du corps** a bodyguard

la **garde** FEM NOUN
▷ see also **garde** NOUN
1 guarding
□ Il est chargé de la garde des prisonniers. He's responsible for guarding the prisoners.
2 guard (surveillance)
□ la relève de la garde the changing of the guard
■ **un chien de garde** a guard dog
■ **être de garde** to be on duty □ Mon père est de garde ce soir. My father is on duty tonight.
□ La pharmacie de garde ce week-end est ... The duty chemist this weekend is ...
■ **mettre en garde** to warn □ Elle m'a mis en garde contre les pickpockets. She warned me about pickpockets.

le **garde-côte** (PL les **garde-côtes**) MASC NOUN
coastguard

garder VERB [28]
1 to keep
□ Tu as gardé toutes ses lettres ? Have you kept all his letters?
2 to look after
□ Je garde ma nièce samedi après-midi. I'm looking after my niece on Saturday afternoon.
3 to guard
□ Ils ont pris un gros chien pour garder la maison. They got a big dog to guard the house.
■ **garder le lit** to stay in bed
■ **se garder** to keep □ Ces crêpes se gardent bien. These pancakes keep well.

la **garderie** FEM NOUN
nursery

la **garde-robe** FEM NOUN
wardrobe (clothes)
□ Elle a une garde-robe bien fournie. She's got an extensive wardrobe.

le **gardien** MASC NOUN
1 caretaker
2 attendant (in a museum)
■ **un gardien de but** a goalkeeper
■ **un gardien de la paix** a police officer

la **gardienne** FEM NOUN
1 caretaker
2 attendant (in a museum)

la **gare** FEM NOUN
▷ see also **gare** EXCLAMATION
station
□ la gare routière the bus station

gare EXCLAMATION
▷ see also **gare** NOUN
■ **Gare aux serpents !** Watch out for snakes!

garer VERB [28]
to park

■ **se garer** to park □ Où t'es-tu garé ? Where are you parked?

garni (FEM **garnie**) ADJECTIVE
■ **un plat garni** a dish served with accompaniments (vegetables, chips, rice etc)

le **gars** MASC NOUN (informal)
guy

gaspiller VERB [28]
to waste

le **gâteau** (PL les **gâteaux**) MASC NOUN
cake
■ **les gâteaux secs** biscuits

gâter VERB [28]
to spoil
□ Il aime gâter ses petits-enfants. He likes to spoil his grandchildren.
■ **se gâter** to go bad □ Les pommes vont se gâter si on ne les mange pas ce soir. The apples will go bad if we don't eat them tonight.
■ **Le temps va se gâter.** The weather's going to break.

gauche (FEM **gauche**) ADJECTIVE
▷ see also **gauche** NOUN
left
□ le bras gauche the left arm □ le côté gauche the left-hand side

la **gauche** FEM NOUN
▷ see also **gauche** ADJECTIVE
left
□ sur votre gauche on your left
■ **à gauche** 1 on the left □ la deuxième rue à gauche the second street on the left 2 on the left □ à gauche de l'armoire to the left of the cupboard
■ **Tournez à gauche.** Turn left.
■ **la voie de gauche** the left-hand lane
■ **la gauche** (in politics) the left
■ **Il est de gauche.** He's left-wing.

gaucher (FEM **gauchère**) ADJECTIVE
left-handed

la **gaufre** FEM NOUN
waffle

la **gaufrette** FEM NOUN
wafer

le **Gaulois** MASC NOUN
Gaul
□ Astérix le Gaulois Asterix the Gaul

gaulois (FEM **gauloise**) ADJECTIVE
Gallic

gay (FEM **gay**) ADJECTIVE
gay
□ la communauté gay the gay community

le **gaz** MASC NOUN
gas
■ **les gaz à effet de serre** greenhouse gases

gazeux (FEM **gazeuse**) ADJECTIVE
■ **une boisson gazeuse** a fizzy drink
■ **de l'eau gazeuse** sparkling water

le **gazole** MASC NOUN
diesel (*fuel*)

le **gazon** MASC NOUN
lawn

le **géant** MASC NOUN
giant

le **gel** MASC NOUN
frost

la **gelée** FEM NOUN
1 jelly
2 frost

geler VERB [43]
to freeze
■ Il a gelé cette nuit. There was a frost last night.

la **gélule** FEM NOUN
capsule (*containing medicine*)

les **Gémeaux** MASC PL NOUN
Gemini
□ Nicolas est Gémeaux. Nicolas's Gemini.

gémir VERB [38]
to moan

gênant (FEM **gênante**) ADJECTIVE
awkward
□ un silence gênant an awkward silence

la **gencive** FEM NOUN
gum (*in mouth*)

le **gendarme** MASC NOUN
police officer

la **gendarmerie** FEM NOUN
1 police force
2 police station
□ Vous devriez porter plainte à la gendarmerie.
You should go to the police station and report it.

le **gendre** MASC NOUN
son-in-law

gêné (FEM **gênée**) ADJECTIVE
embarrassed

gêner VERB [28]
1 to bother
□ Je ne voudrais pas vous gêner. I don't want to
bother you.
2 to feel awkward
□ Son regard la gênait. The way he was looking
at her made her feel awkward.

général (FEM **générale**, MASC PL **généraux**)
ADJECTIVE
▷ *see also* **général** NOUN
general
■ en général usually

le **général** (PL les **généraux**) MASC NOUN
▷ *see also* **général** ADJECTIVE
general

généralement ADVERB
generally

le/la **généraliste** MASC/FEM NOUN
GP

la **génération** FEM NOUN
generation

généreux (FEM **généreuse**) ADJECTIVE
generous

la **générosité** FEM NOUN
generosity

le **genêt** MASC NOUN
broom (*bush*)

la **génétique** FEM NOUN
genetics

génétiquement ADVERB
genetically
□ génétiquement modifié genetically-modified
□ les aliments génétiquement modifiés GM
foods □ un organisme génétiquement modifié a
genetically-modified organism

Genève NOUN
Geneva

génial (FEM **géniale**, MASC PL **géniaux**) ADJECTIVE
(*informal*)
great
□ Le film d'hier soir était génial. The film last
night was great.

le **genou** (PL les **genoux**) MASC NOUN
knee
□ Elle est à genoux. She's on her knees. □ se
mettre à genoux to kneel down

le **genre** MASC NOUN
kind
□ C'est un genre de gâteau à la crème. It's a kind
of cream cake.

les **gens** MASC PL NOUN
people

gentil (FEM **gentille**) ADJECTIVE
1 nice
□ Nos voisins sont très gentils. Our neighbours
are very nice.
2 kind
□ C'était très gentil de votre part. It was very
kind of you.

BE CAREFUL!
gentil does not mean **gentle**.

la **gentillesse** FEM NOUN
kindness
□ Je l'ai remerciée de sa gentillesse. I thanked
her for her kindness.
■ C'est un homme d'une grande
gentillesse. He is a very nice man.

gentiment ADVERB
1 nicely
□ Demande-le lui gentiment. Ask him nicely.
2 kindly
□ Ils nous ont gentiment proposé de rester
dîner. They kindly invited us to stay for dinner.

la **géographie** FEM NOUN
geography

g

la **géolocalisation** FEM NOUN
geolocation

la **géométrie** FEM NOUN
geometry

le **gérant** MASC NOUN
manager

la **gérante** FEM NOUN
manager

gérer VERB [34]
to manage

germain (FEM germaine) ADJECTIVE
■ un cousin germain a first cousin

le **geste** MASC NOUN
gesture
□ Il a voulu faire un geste. He wanted to make a gesture.
■ Ne faites pas un geste ! Don't move!

la **gestion** FEM NOUN
management

le/la **gestionnaire de site** MASC/FEM NOUN
webmaster

la **gifle** FEM NOUN
slap across the face

gifler VERB [28]
to slap across the face

gigantesque (FEM gigantesque) ADJECTIVE
gigantic

le **gigot** MASC NOUN
leg of lamb

le **gilet** MASC NOUN
1 waistcoat
□ un gilet en cuir a leather waistcoat
2 cardigan
□ un gilet tricoté main a hand-knitted cardigan
■ un gilet de sauvetage a life jacket

le **gingembre** MASC NOUN
ginger

la **girafe** FEM NOUN
giraffe

le **gitan** MASC NOUN
Gipsy

la **gitane** FEM NOUN
Gipsy

le **gîte** MASC NOUN
■ un gîte rural a holiday house

la **glace** FEM NOUN
1 ice
□ L'étang est recouvert de glace. The pond is covered with ice.
2 ice cream
□ une glace à la fraise a strawberry ice cream
3 mirror
□ Il se regarde souvent dans la glace. He often looks at himself in the mirror.

glacé (FEM glacée) ADJECTIVE
1 icy
□ un vent glacé an icy wind
2 iced
□ un thé glacé an iced tea

glacial (FEM glaciale, MASC PL glaciaux) ADJECTIVE
icy

le **glaçon** MASC NOUN
ice cube

glissant (FEM glissante) ADJECTIVE
slippery

glisser VERB [28]
1 to slip
□ Il a glissé sur une peau de banane. He slipped on a banana skin.
2 to be slippery
□ Attention, ça glisse ! Watch out, it's slippery!

global (FEM globale, MASC PL globaux) ADJECTIVE
total
□ la somme globale the total amount

les **glucides** MASC PL NOUN
carbohydrates

le **gluten** MASC NOUN
gluten
■ sans gluten gluten-free

la **godasse** FEM NOUN (informal)
shoe

le **goéland** MASC NOUN
seagull

le **golf** MASC NOUN
1 golf
□ Il joue au golf. He plays golf.
2 golf course
□ un golf dix-huit trous an 18-hole golf course

le **golfe** MASC NOUN
gulf
■ le golfe de Gascogne the Bay of Biscay

la **gomme** FEM NOUN
rubber

gommer VERB [28]
to rub out

gonflé (FEM gonflée) ADJECTIVE
1 swollen (arm, finger, stomach)
□ Elle a les pieds gonflés. Her feet are swollen.
2 inflated (ball, tyre)
□ Le ballon de foot était mal gonflé. The football wasn't properly inflated.
■ Il est gonflé ! (informal) He's got a nerve!

gonfler VERB [28]
1 to blow up
□ gonfler un ballon to blow up a balloon
2 to pump up
□ gonfler un pneu to pump up a tyre

googler VERB [28]
to google

la gorge FEM NOUN

1 throat
- □ J'ai mal à la gorge. I've got a sore throat.

2 gorge
- □ les gorges du Tarn the Tarn gorges

la gorgée FEM NOUN
sip
- □ une gorgée d'eau a sip of water

le gorille MASC NOUN
gorilla

le/la gosse MASC/FEM NOUN (*informal*)
kid

le goudron MASC NOUN
tar

le gouffre MASC NOUN
chasm
- ■ Cette voiture est un vrai gouffre ! This car eats up money!

la gourde FEM NOUN
water bottle

gourmand (FEM **gourmande**) ADJECTIVE
greedy

la gourmandise FEM NOUN
greed

la gousse FEM NOUN
- ■ une gousse d'ail a clove of garlic

le goût MASC NOUN
taste
- □ Ça n'a pas de goût. It's got no taste. □ Elle a très bon goût. She's got very good taste.

goûter VERB [28]
▷ *see also* **goûter** NOUN

1 to taste
- □ Goûte ce fromage. Taste this cheese.

2 to have a snack (*in the afternoon*)
- □ Les enfants goûtent généralement vers quatre heures. The children usually have a snack around 4 o'clock.

le goûter MASC NOUN
▷ *see also* **goûter** VERB
afternoon snack

la goutte FEM NOUN
drop

le gouvernement MASC NOUN
government

gouverner VERB [28]
to govern

la grâce FEM NOUN
- ■ grâce à thanks to □ Je suis arrivé à l'heure grâce à toi. I arrived on time thanks to you.

gracieux (FEM **gracieuse**) ADJECTIVE
graceful

les gradins MASC PL NOUN
terraces (*in stadium*)

graffiti MASC PL NOUN
graffiti *sing*

les graffitis MASC PL NOUN
graffiti *sing*

le grain MASC NOUN
grain
- □ un grain de sable a grain of sand
- ■ un grain de beauté a beauty spot
- ■ un grain de café a coffee bean
- ■ un grain de raisin a grape

la graine FEM NOUN
seed

la graisse FEM NOUN
fat

la grammaire FEM NOUN
grammar

le gramme MASC NOUN
gram

grand (FEM **grande**) ADJECTIVE, ADVERB

1 tall
- □ Il est grand pour son âge. He's tall for his age.

2 big
- □ une grande valise a big suitcase □ C'est sa grande sœur. She's his big sister.
- ■ une grande personne a grown-up

3 long
- □ un grand voyage a long journey
- ■ les grandes vacances the summer holidays

4 great
- □ C'est un grand ami à moi. He's a great friend of mine.
- ■ un grand magasin a department store
- ■ une grande surface a hypermarket
- ■ les grandes écoles top ranking colleges (*at university level*)
- ■ au grand air out in the open air □ Ça te fera beaucoup de bien d'être au grand air. It'll be very good for you to be out in the open air.
- ■ grand ouvert wide open

grand-chose PRONOUN
- ■ pas grand-chose not much □ Je n'ai pas acheté grand-chose au marché. I didn't buy much at the market. □ Voici un petit cadeau : ce n'est pas grand-chose. Here's a little present: it's nothing much.

la Grande-Bretagne FEM NOUN
Britain

la grandeur FEM NOUN
size

grandir VERB [38]
to grow
- □ Il a beaucoup grandi. He's grown a lot.

la grand-mère (PL les **grands-mères**) FEM NOUN
grandmother

grand-peine
- ■ à grand-peine ADVERB with great difficulty

le grand-père (PL les **grands-pères**) MASC NOUN
grandfather

les grands-parents MASC PL NOUN
grandparents

la grange FEM NOUN
barn

la grappe FEM NOUN
■ **une grappe de raisin** a bunch of grapes

gras (FEM **grasse**) ADJECTIVE
1 fatty (*food*)
□ Évitez les aliments gras. Avoid fatty foods.
2 greasy
□ des cheveux gras greasy hair
3 oily
□ une peau grasse oily skin
■ **faire la grasse matinée** to have a lie-in

gratis (FEM+PL **gratis**) ADJECTIVE, ADVERB
free
□ J'ai eu ce stylo gratis. I got this pen free.

le gratte-ciel (PL les **gratte-ciels**, les **gratte-ciel**) MASC NOUN
skyscraper

gratter VERB [28]
1 to scratch
□ Ne gratte pas tes piqûres de moustiques ! Don't scratch your mosquito bites!
2 to be itchy
□ C'est épouvantable comme ça gratte ! It's terribly itchy!

gratuit (FEM **gratuite**) ADJECTIVE
free
□ entrée gratuite entrance free □ J'ai deux places gratuites pour le film. I've got two free tickets for the film.

grave (FEM **grave**) ADJECTIVE
1 serious
□ une maladie grave a serious illness □ Il avait l'air grave. He was looking serious.
2 deep
□ Il a une voix grave. He's got a deep voice.
■ **Ce n'est pas grave.** It doesn't matter.
□ J'ai oublié ma clé. — Ce n'est pas grave, j'ai la mienne. I've forgotten my key. — It doesn't matter, I've got mine.

gravement ADVERB
seriously
□ Il a été gravement blessé. He was seriously injured.

le graveur MASC NOUN
■ **un graveur de CD** a CD burner

grec (FEM **grecque**) ADJECTIVE, NOUN
Greek
□ J'apprends le grec. I'm learning Greek.
■ **un Grec** a Greek (*man*)
■ **une Grecque** a Greek (*woman*)
■ **les Grecs** the Greeks

la Grèce FEM NOUN
Greece
■ **en Grèce** 1 in Greece 2 to Greece

la grêle FEM NOUN
hail

grêler VERB [28]
■ **Il grêle.** It's hailing.

grelotter VERB [28]
to shiver

la grenade FEM NOUN
1 pomegranate
2 grenade

la grenadine FEM NOUN
grenadine

> **DID YOU KNOW...?**
> **grenadine** is a bright pink drink which is very popular with children in France.

le grenier MASC NOUN
attic

la grenouille FEM NOUN
frog

la grève FEM NOUN
1 strike
■ **en grève** on strike □ Ils sont en grève depuis dix jours. They have been on strike for ten days.
■ **faire grève** to be on strike
2 shore
□ Nous nous sommes promenés le long de la grève. We went for a walk along the shore.

le/la gréviste MASC/FEM NOUN
striker

grièvement ADVERB
■ **grièvement blessé** seriously injured

la griffe FEM NOUN
1 claw
■ **donner un coup de griffe** to scratch □ Le chat m'a donné un coup de griffe. The cat scratched me.
2 label
□ la griffe d'un grand couturier the label of a top designer

griffer VERB [28]
to scratch
□ Le chat m'a griffé. The cat scratched me.

grignoter VERB [28]
to nibble

la grillade FEM NOUN
grilled food
□ une grillade d'agneau grilled lamb

la grille FEM NOUN
1 wire fence
□ L'usine est entourée d'une haute grille. The factory is surrounded by a high wire fence.
2 metal gate
□ Le facteur a sonné à la grille du jardin. The postman rang at the garden gate.

g

Numbers in brackets refer to verb tables on pages 650 to 658

3 grid
□ Complétez la grille. Complete the grid.

le **grille-pain** (PL les **grille-pains**) MASC NOUN
toaster

griller VERB [28]
1 to toast
■ **du pain grillé** toast
2 to grill
□ des saucisses grillées grilled sausages

la **grimace** FEM NOUN
■ **faire des grimaces** to make faces

grimper VERB [28]
to climb

grincer VERB [12]
to creak

grincheux (FEM **grincheuse**) ADJECTIVE
grumpy

la **grippe** FEM NOUN
flu
■ **avoir la grippe** to have flu □ J'ai eu une
mauvaise grippe l'hiver dernier. I had a bad bout
of flu last winter.
■ **la grippe A** swine flu
■ **la grippe aviaire** bird flu

grippé (FEM **grippée**) ADJECTIVE
■ **être grippé** to have flu

gris (FEM **grise**) ADJECTIVE
grey

le **Groenland** MASC NOUN
Greenland

grogner VERB [28]
1 to growl
□ Le chien a grogné quand je me suis approché
de lui. The dog growled when I went near it.
2 to complain
□ Arrête donc de grogner ! Stop complaining!

gronder VERB [28]
to tell off
□ Si ma mère l'apprend, elle va me gronder.
If my mother finds out, she'll tell me off.
■ **se faire gronder** to get a telling-off □ Tu vas
te faire gronder par ton père ! You're going to get
a telling-off from your father!

gros (FEM **grosse**) ADJECTIVE
1 big
□ une grosse pomme a big apple
2 fat
□ Je suis trop grosse pour porter ça ! I'm too fat
to wear that!

la **groseille** FEM NOUN
■ **la groseille rouge** redcurrant
■ **la groseille à maquereau** gooseberry

la **grossesse** FEM NOUN
pregnancy

grossier (FEM **grossière**) ADJECTIVE
rude

□ Ne sois pas si grossier ! Don't be so rude!
■ **une erreur grossière** a bad mistake

grossir VERB [38]
to put on weight
□ Il a beaucoup grossi. He's put on a lot of
weight.

grosso modo ADVERB
roughly
□ Dis-moi grosso modo ce que tu en penses.
Tell me roughly what you think of it.

la **grotte** FEM NOUN
cave

le **groupe** MASC NOUN
group
□ votre groupe sanguin your blood group

grouper VERB [28]
to group
□ On nous a groupés selon notre niveau. We
were grouped according to our level.
■ **se grouper** to gather □ Nous nous sommes
groupés autour du feu. We gathered round the
fire.

le **guépard** MASC NOUN
cheetah

la **guêpe** FEM NOUN
wasp

guérir VERB [38]
to recover
□ Il est maintenant complètement guéri. He's
now completely recovered.

la **guérison** FEM NOUN
recovery

la **guerre** FEM NOUN
war
□ en guerre at war □ une guerre civile a civil war
□ la Deuxième Guerre mondiale the Second
World War

guetter VERB [28]
to look out for
□ Elle guette l'arrivée du facteur tous les
matins. She looks out for the postman every
morning.

la **gueule** FEM NOUN
mouth
□ Le chat a ramené une souris dans sa gueule.
The cat brought in a mouse in its mouth.
■ **Ta gueule !** (*rude*) Shut your face!
■ **avoir la gueule de bois** (*informal*) to have a
hangover

> **gueule** is an impolite way of talking about a
> person's mouth but it is the correct term for
> an animal's.

gueuler VERB [28] (*informal*)
to bawl

le **guichet** MASC NOUN
counter (*in bank, booking office*)

g

le **guide** MASC NOUN
guide
guider VERB [28]
to guide
le **guidon** MASC NOUN
handlebars
les **guillemets** MASC PL NOUN
inverted commas
□ entre guillemets in inverted commas
la **guirlande** FEM NOUN
tinsel
□ Nous avons décoré le sapin de Noël avec des guirlandes. We decorated the Christmas tree with tinsel.
■ **des guirlandes en papier** paper chains

la **guitare** FEM NOUN
guitar
□ Sais-tu jouer de la guitare ? Can you play the guitar?
la **gym** FEM NOUN (*informal*)
PE
le **gymnase** MASC NOUN
gym
□ Le lycée a un nouveau gymnase. The school's got a new gym.
la **gymnastique** FEM NOUN
gymnastics
□ Elle fait de la gymnastique. She does gymnastics.
■ **faire sa gymnastique** to do one's exercises

g

Numbers in brackets refer to verb tables on pages 650 to 658

Hh

habile (FEM **habile**) ADJECTIVE
  skilful
  □ Il est très habile de ses mains. He is very clever with his hands.

habillé (FEM **habillée**) ADJECTIVE
1 dressed
  □ Il n'est pas encore habillé. He's not dressed yet.
2 smart
  □ Cette robe fait très habillé. This dress looks very smart.

s'**habiller** VERB [28]
1 to get dressed
  □ Je me suis rapidement habillé. I got dressed quickly.
2 to dress up
  □ Est-ce qu'il faut s'habiller pour la réception ? Do you have to dress up to go to the party?

l'**habitant** MASC NOUN
  inhabitant
  ■ **les habitants du quartier** the local people

l'**habitante** FEM NOUN
  inhabitant

habiter VERB [28]
  to live
  □ Il habite à Montpellier. He lives in Montpellier.

les **habits** MASC PL NOUN
  clothes

l'**habitude** FEM NOUN
  habit
  □ une mauvaise habitude a bad habit
  ■ **avoir l'habitude de quelque chose** to be used to something □ Elle a l'habitude des enfants. She's used to children. □ Je n'ai pas l'habitude de parler en public. I'm not used to speaking in public.
  ■ **d'habitude** usually
  ■ **comme d'habitude** as usual

habituel (FEM **habituelle**) ADJECTIVE
  usual

s'**habituer** VERB [28]
  ■ **s'habituer à quelque chose** to get used to something □ Il faudra que tu t'habitues à te lever tôt. You'll have to get used to getting up early.

le **hachis** MASC NOUN
  mince
  ■ **le hachis Parmentier** cottage pie

la **haie** FEM NOUN
  hedge

la **haine** FEM NOUN
  hatred

haïr VERB [40]
  to hate

l'**haleine** FEM NOUN
  breath
  □ avoir mauvaise haleine to have bad breath
  □ être hors d'haleine to be out of breath

les **halles** FEM PL NOUN
  covered market *sing*

la **halte** FEM NOUN
  stop
  □ faire halte to make a stop
  ■ **Halte !** Stop!

l'**haltérophilie** FEM NOUN
  weightlifting

le **hamburger** MASC NOUN
  hamburger

l'**hameçon** MASC NOUN
  fish hook

le **hamster** MASC NOUN
  hamster

la **hanche** FEM NOUN
  hip

le **handball** MASC NOUN
  handball
  □ jouer au handball to play handball

le **handicap** MASC NOUN
1 disability (*medical condition*)
2 handicap (*in sport*)

handicapé (FEM **handicapée**) ADJECTIVE
  disabled

le **handicapé** MASC NOUN
  disabled man

la **handicapée** FEM NOUN
  disabled woman

le **harcèlement** MASC NOUN
1 bullying
2 harassment
  □ le harcèlement sexuel sexual harassment

h

harceler VERB
to bully

le **hareng** MASC NOUN
herring
- **un hareng saur** a kipper

le **haricot** MASC NOUN
bean
- **les haricots verts** runner beans
- **les haricots blancs** haricot beans
- **C'est la fin des haricots.** (*informal*) It's the last straw.

l'**harmonica** MASC NOUN
mouth organ

la **harpe** FEM NOUN
harp

le **hasard** MASC NOUN
coincidence
□ C'était un pur hasard. It was pure coincidence.
- **au hasard** at random □ Choisis un numéro au hasard. Choose a number at random.
- **par hasard** by chance □ rencontrer quelqu'un par hasard to meet somebody by chance
- **à tout hasard** 1 just in case □ Prends un parapluie à tout hasard. Take an umbrella just in case. 2 on the off chance □ Je ne sais pas s'il est chez lui, mais je vais l'appeler à tout hasard. I don't know if he's at home, but I'll phone on the off chance.

la **hâte** FEM NOUN
- **à la hâte** hurriedly □ Elle s'est habillée à la hâte. She got dressed hurriedly.
- **J'ai hâte de te voir.** I can't wait to see you.

la **hausse** FEM NOUN
1 increase
□ la hausse des prix price increase
2 rise
□ On annonce une légère hausse de température. The forecast is for a slight rise in temperature.

hausser VERB [28]
- **hausser les épaules** to shrug one's shoulders

haut (FEM **haute**) ADJECTIVE, ADVERB
▷ *see also* **haut** NOUN
1 high
□ une haute montagne a high mountain
2 aloud
□ penser tout haut to think aloud

le **haut** MASC NOUN
▷ *see also* **haut** ADJECTIVE, ADVERB
top
□ un haut à bretelles a strappy top
- **un mur de trois mètres de haut** a wall 3 metres high
- **en haut** 1 upstairs □ La salle de bain est en haut. The bathroom is upstairs. 2 at the top □ Le nid est tout en haut de l'arbre. The nest is right at the top of the tree.

la **hauteur** FEM NOUN
height

le **haut-parleur** (PL les **haut-parleurs**) MASC NOUN
loudspeaker

l'**hebdomadaire** MASC NOUN
weekly (*magazine*)

l'**hébergement** MASC NOUN
accommodation

héberger VERB [45]
to put up
□ Mon cousin a dit qu'il nous hébergerait. My cousin said he would put us up.

hein ? EXCLAMATION
eh?
□ Hein ? Qu'est-ce que tu dis ? Eh? What did you say?

hélas ADVERB
unfortunately
□ Hélas, il ne restait plus de billets. Unfortunately there were no tickets left.

l'**hélicoptère** MASC NOUN
helicopter

l'**hémorragie** FEM NOUN
haemorrhage

l'**herbe** FEM NOUN
grass
- **les herbes de Provence** mixed herbs

le **hérisson** MASC NOUN
hedgehog

hériter VERB [28]
to inherit

l'**héritier** MASC NOUN
heir

l'**héritière** FEM NOUN
heiress

hermétique (FEM **hermétique**) ADJECTIVE
airtight

l'**héroïne** FEM NOUN
1 heroine
□ l'héroïne du roman the heroine of the novel
2 heroin (*drug*)

le **héros** MASC NOUN
hero

l'**hésitation** FEM NOUN
hesitation

hésiter VERB [28]
to hesitate
□ Il n'a pas hésité à nous aider. He didn't hesitate to help us.
- **J'ai hésité entre le pull vert et le cardigan jaune.** I couldn't decide between the green pullover and the yellow cardigan.
- **Est-ce que tu viens ce soir ? — J'hésite.** Are you coming this evening? — I'm not sure.
- **sans hésiter** without hesitating

Numbers in brackets refer to verb tables on pages 650 to 658

hétéro (FEM **hétéro**) ADJECTIVE (*informal*)
straight (*heterosexual*)

l'heure FEM NOUN
1 hour
□ Le trajet dure six heures. The journey lasts six hours.
2 time
□ Vous avez l'heure ? Have you got the time?
■ **Quelle heure est-il ?** What time is it?
■ **À quelle heure ?** What time? □ À quelle heure arrivons-nous ? What time do we arrive?
■ **deux heures du matin** 2 o'clock in the morning
■ **il est ... heure(s)** it is ... (o'clock) □ Il est six heures. It is six o'clock. □ Il est six heures moins le quart. It is quarter to six.
■ **être à l'heure** to be on time
■ **une heure de français** a period of French

heureusement ADVERB
luckily
□ Heureusement qu'il n'a pas été blessé. Luckily he wasn't hurt.

heureux (FEM **heureuse**) ADJECTIVE
happy

heurter VERB [28]
to hit

l'hexagone MASC NOUN
hexagon
■ **l'Hexagone** France

DID YOU KNOW...?
France is often referred to as **l'Hexagone** because of its six-sided shape.

le **hibou** (PL les **hiboux**) MASC NOUN
owl

hier ADVERB
yesterday
■ **avant-hier** the day before yesterday

la **hi-fi** FEM NOUN
stereo
■ **une chaîne hi-fi** a stereo system

hippique (FEM **hippique**) ADJECTIVE
■ **un club hippique** a riding centre
■ **un concours hippique** a horse show

l'hippopotame MASC NOUN
hippopotamus

l'hirondelle FEM NOUN
swallow (*bird*)

l'histoire FEM NOUN
1 history
□ un cours d'histoire a history lesson
2 story
□ C'est l'histoire de deux enfants. It's the story of two children.
■ **Ne fais pas d'histoires !** Don't make a fuss!

historique (FEM **historique**) ADJECTIVE
historic

□ un monument historique a historic monument

l'hiver MASC NOUN
winter
■ **en hiver** in winter

le/la **HLM** MASC/FEM NOUN (= *habitation à loyer modéré*)
council flat
■ **des HLM** council housing

le **hockey** MASC NOUN
hockey
■ **le hockey sur glace** ice hockey

hollandais (FEM **hollandaise**)
ADJECTIVE, NOUN
Dutch
□ J'apprends le hollandais. I'm learning Dutch.
■ **un Hollandais** a Dutch man
■ **une Hollandaise** a Dutch woman
■ **les Hollandais** the Dutch

la **Hollande** FEM NOUN
Holland
■ **en Hollande** 1 in Holland 2 to Holland

le **homard** MASC NOUN
lobster

homéopathique (FEM **homéopathique**)
ADJECTIVE
homeopathic

l'hommage MASC NOUN
tribute

l'homme MASC NOUN
man
■ **un homme d'affaires** a businessman
■ **un homme politique** a politician

homoparental (FEM **homoparentale**, MASC PL **homoparentaux**) ADJECTIVE
■ **une famille homoparentale** a same-sex-parent family

homosexuel (FEM **homosexuelle**) ADJECTIVE
homosexual

la **Hongrie** FEM NOUN
Hungary

hongrois (FEM **hongroise**) ADJECTIVE, NOUN
Hungarian
□ Il parle le hongrois. He speaks Hungarian.
■ **un Hongrois** a Hungarian (*man*)
■ **une Hongroise** a Hungarian (*woman*)
■ **les Hongrois** the Hungarians

honnête (FEM **honnête**) ADJECTIVE
honest

l'honnêteté FEM NOUN
honesty

l'honneur MASC NOUN
honour

la **honte** FEM NOUN
shame
■ **avoir honte de quelque chose** to be ashamed of something

h

l'**hôpital** (PL les **hôpitaux**) MASC NOUN
hospital

le **hoquet** MASC NOUN
- **avoir le hoquet** to have hiccups

l'**horaire** MASC NOUN
timetable
- **les horaires de train** the train timetable

l'**horizon** MASC NOUN
horizon

horizontal (FEM **horizontale**, MASC PL **horizontaux**) ADJECTIVE
horizontal

l'**horloge** FEM NOUN
clock

l'**horreur** FEM NOUN
horror
□ un film d'horreur a horror film
- **avoir horreur de** to hate □ J'ai horreur du chou. I hate cabbage.

horrible (FEM **horrible**) ADJECTIVE
horrible

hors PREPOSITION
- **hors de** out of □ Elle est hors de danger maintenant. She's out of danger now.
- **hors taxes** duty-free

le **hors-d'œuvre** (PL les **hors-d'œuvre**) MASC NOUN
starter (food)

hospitalier (FEM **hospitalière**) ADJECTIVE
hospitable
□ Ils sont très hospitaliers. They're very hospitable.
- **les services hospitaliers** hospital services

l'**hospitalité** FEM NOUN
hospitality

hostile (FEM **hostile**) ADJECTIVE
hostile

l'**hôte** MASC/FEM NOUN
1 host
□ N'oubliez pas de remercier vos hôtes. Don't forget to thank your hosts.
2 guest
□ Cette ferme accueille des hôtes payants. This farm takes paying guests.

l'**hôtel** MASC NOUN
hotel
- **l'hôtel de ville** the town hall

l'**hôtesse** FEM NOUN
hostess
- **une hôtesse de l'air** a stewardess

la **housse** FEM NOUN
cover
□ une housse de couette a duvet cover □ une housse de téléphone a phone cover

le **houx** MASC NOUN
holly

l'**huile** FEM NOUN
oil
- **l'huile solaire** suntan oil

huit NUMBER
eight
□ Il est huit heures du matin. It's eight in the morning. □ Il a huit ans. He's eight.
- **le huit février** the eighth of February
- **dans huit jours** in a week's time

la **huitaine** FEM NOUN
- **une huitaine de jours** about a week □ Nous serons de retour dans une huitaine de jours. We'll be back in about a week.

huitième (FEM **huitième**) ADJECTIVE
eighth
□ au huitième étage on the eighth floor

l'**huître** FEM NOUN
oyster

humain (FEM **humaine**) ADJECTIVE
▷ see also **humain** NOUN
human

l'**humain** MASC NOUN
▷ see also **humain** ADJECTIVE
human being

l'**humanité** FEM NOUN
humanity

l'**humeur** FEM NOUN
mood
□ Il est de bonne humeur. He's in a good mood.
□ Elle était de mauvaise humeur. She was in a bad mood.

humide (FEM **humide**) ADJECTIVE
damp
□ L'herbe est humide. The grass is damp. □ un climat humide a damp climate

humilier VERB [19]
to humiliate

humoristique (FEM **humoristique**) ADJECTIVE
humorous
- **des dessins humoristiques** cartoons

l'**humour** MASC NOUN
humour
□ Il n'a pas beaucoup d'humour. He hasn't got much of a sense of humour.

hurler VERB [28]
1 to howl
2 to scream

la **hutte** FEM NOUN
hut

hydratant (FEM **hydratante**) ADJECTIVE
- **une crème hydratante** a moisturizing cream

l'**hygiène** FEM NOUN
hygiene

hygiénique (FEM **hygiénique**) ADJECTIVE
hygienic

- une serviette hygiénique a sanitary towel
- le papier hygiénique toilet paper

l'**hymne** MASC NOUN
- l'hymne national the national anthem

l'**hyperlien** MASC NOUN
  hyperlink

l'**hypermarché** MASC NOUN
  hypermarket

hypermétrope (FEM hypermétrope)
  ADJECTIVE
  long-sighted

hypocrite (FEM hypocrite) ADJECTIVE
  hypocritical
  □ Il est hypocrite. He's a hypocrite.

l'**hypothèse** FEM NOUN
  hypothesis

h

I i

l'**IA** FEM NOUN (= *intelligence artificielle*)
AI
□ les progrès de l'IA advances in AI

l'**iceberg** MASC NOUN
iceberg

ici ADVERB
here
□ Les assiettes sont ici. The plates are here.
■ **La mer monte parfois jusqu'ici.** The sea sometimes comes in as far as this.
■ **Jusqu'ici nous n'avons eu aucun problème avec la voiture.** So far we haven't had any problems with the car.

l'**icône** FEM NOUN
icon

idéal (FEM **idéale**, MASC PL **idéaux**) ADJECTIVE
ideal
□ C'est l'endroit idéal pour faire un pique-nique. It's an ideal place to have a picnic.

l'**idée** FEM NOUN
idea
□ C'est une bonne idée. It's a good idea.

l'**identifiant** MASC NOUN
login (*on a computer*)

identifier VERB [19]
to identify
□ La police a identifié le meurtrier. The police have identified the murderer.

identique (FEM **identique**) ADJECTIVE
identical
□ Ils ont obtenu des résultats identiques. They obtained identical results.

l'**identité** FEM NOUN
identity
■ **une pièce d'identité** a form of identification
□ Avez-vous une pièce d'identité ? Have you got any form of identification?

idiot (FEM **idiote**) ADJECTIVE
▷ *see also* **idiot** NOUN, **idiote** NOUN
1 stupid
□ une plaisanterie idiote a stupid joke
2 silly
□ Ne sois pas idiot ! Don't be silly!

l'**idiot** MASC NOUN
▷ *see also* **idiot** ADJECTIVE
idiot

l'**idiote** FEM NOUN
▷ *see also* **idiot** ADJECTIVE
idiot

ignoble (FEM **ignoble**) ADJECTIVE
horrible
□ Il a été ignoble avec elle. He was horrible to her.

ignorant (FEM **ignorante**) ADJECTIVE
ignorant

ignorer VERB [28]
1 not to know
□ J'ignore son nom. I don't know his name.
2 to ignore
□ Il m'a complètement ignoré. He completely ignored me.

il PRONOUN
1 he
□ Il est parti ce matin de bonne heure. He left early this morning.
2 it
□ Méfie-toi de ce chien : il mord. Be careful of that dog: it bites. □ Il pleut. It's raining.

l'**île** FEM NOUN
island
■ **les îles Anglo-Normandes** the Channel Islands
■ **les îles Britanniques** the British Isles
■ **les îles Féroé** the Faroe Islands

illégal (FEM **illégale**, MASC PL **illégaux**) ADJECTIVE
illegal

l'**illettrisme** MASC NOUN
illiteracy

illimité (FEM **illimitée**) ADJECTIVE
unlimited

illisible (FEM **illisible**) ADJECTIVE
illegible
□ une écriture illisible illegible handwriting

illuminer VERB [28]
to floodlight
□ Le château est illuminé tous les soirs pendant l'été. The castle is floodlit every night in the summer.

l'**illusion** FEM NOUN
illusion
■ **Tu te fais des illusions !** You're deluding yourself!

l'**illustration** FEM NOUN
illustration

illustré (FEM illustrée) ADJECTIVE
▷ see also **illustré** NOUN
illustrated

l'**illustré** MASC NOUN
▷ see also **illustré** ADJECTIVE
comic

illustrer VERB [28]
to illustrate
□ Vous pouvez illustrer votre rédaction avec des exemples. You may illustrate your essay with examples.

ils PL PRONOUN
they
□ Ils nous ont appelés hier soir. They phoned us last night.

l'**image** FEM NOUN
picture
□ Les films donnent une fausse image de l'Amérique. Films give a false picture of America.

l'**imagination** FEM NOUN
imagination
□ Elle a beaucoup d'imagination. She's got a vivid imagination.

imaginer VERB [28]
to imagine

l'**imam** MASC NOUN
imam

l'**imbécile** MASC/FEM NOUN
idiot

l'**imitation** FEM NOUN
imitation

imiter VERB [28]
to imitate

l'**immatriculation** FEM NOUN
■ une plaque d'immatriculation a numberplate (of car)

l'**immédiat** MASC NOUN
■ dans l'immédiat for the moment □ Je n'ai pas besoin de ce livre dans l'immédiat. I don't need this book for the moment.

immédiatement ADVERB
immediately

immense (FEM immense) ADJECTIVE
1 huge
□ une immense fortune a huge fortune
2 tremendous
□ un immense soulagement a tremendous relief

l'**immeuble** MASC NOUN
block of flats

l'**immigration** FEM NOUN
immigration

l'**immigré** MASC NOUN
immigrant

l'**immigrée** FEM NOUN
immigrant

immobile (FEM immobile) ADJECTIVE
motionless

immobilier (FEM immobilière) ADJECTIVE
■ une agence immobilière an estate agent's

immobiliser VERB [28]
to immobilize

immunisé (FEM immunisée) ADJECTIVE
immunized

l'**impact** MASC NOUN
impact

impair (FEM impaire) ADJECTIVE
odd
□ un nombre impair an odd number

impardonnable (FEM impardonnable) ADJECTIVE
unforgivable

l'**impasse** FEM NOUN
cul-de-sac

l'**impatience** FEM NOUN
impatience

impatient (FEM impatiente) ADJECTIVE
impatient

impeccable (FEM impeccable) ADJECTIVE
1 immaculate
□ Elle est toujours impeccable. She's always immaculate.
2 perfect
□ Il a fait un travail impeccable. He's done a perfect job. □ C'est impeccable ! That's perfect!

l'**imper** MASC NOUN (informal)
mac

l'**impératif** MASC NOUN
imperative

l'**impératrice** FEM NOUN
empress

l'**imperméable** MASC NOUN
raincoat

impertinent (FEM impertinente) ADJECTIVE
cheeky
□ Ne sois pas impertinent ! Don't be cheeky!

impitoyable (FEM impitoyable) ADJECTIVE
merciless

impliquer VERB [28]
to mean
□ Son silence implique qu'il est d'accord. His silence means he agrees.
■ être impliqué dans to be involved in □ Il est impliqué dans un scandale financier. He's involved in a financial scandal.

impoli (FEM impolie) ADJECTIVE
rude

l'**importance** FEM NOUN
importance
■ C'est sans importance. It doesn't matter.

important (FEM **importante**) ADJECTIVE
1 important
  □ un rôle important an important role
2 considerable
  □ une somme importante a considerable sum

l'**importation** FEM NOUN
import
  □ Les importations de pétrole ont baissé. Oil imports have fallen.

importer VERB [28]
  ▷ see also n'**importe**
1 to import (goods)
2 to matter
  □ Peu importe. It doesn't matter.

imposant (FEM **imposante**) ADJECTIVE
imposing

imposer VERB [28]
to impose
  ■ La direction leur impose des horaires impossibles. The managers are making them work ridiculous hours.

impossible (FEM **impossible**) ADJECTIVE
  ▷ see also impossible NOUN
impossible

l'**impossible** MASC NOUN
  ▷ see also impossible ADJECTIVE
  ■ Nous ferons l'impossible pour finir à temps. We'll do our utmost to finish on time.

l'**impôt** MASC NOUN
tax

imprécis (FEM **imprécise**) ADJECTIVE
imprecise

l'**impression** FEM NOUN
impression
  □ Il a fait bonne impression à ma mère. He made a good impression on my mother.

impressionnant (FEM **impressionnante**) ADJECTIVE
impressive

impressionner VERB [28]
to impress

imprévisible (FEM **imprévisible**) ADJECTIVE
unpredictable

imprévu (FEM **imprévue**) ADJECTIVE
unexpected

l'**imprimante** FEM NOUN
printer (for computer)

imprimé (FEM **imprimée**) ADJECTIVE
printed
  □ un tissu imprimé a printed fabric □ C'est imprimé en grandes lettres. It's printed in large letters.

imprimer VERB [28]
to print

impropre (FEM **impropre**) ADJECTIVE
  ■ impropre à la consommation unfit for human consumption

improviser VERB [28]
to improvise

improviste ADVERB
  ■ arriver à l'improviste to arrive unexpectedly

l'**imprudence** FEM NOUN
carelessness
  ■ Ne fais pas d'imprudences ! Don't do anything silly!

imprudent (FEM **imprudente**) ADJECTIVE
1 unwise
  □ Il serait imprudent de prendre la voiture aujourd'hui. It would be unwise to take the car today.
2 careless
  □ un conducteur imprudent a careless driver

impuissant (FEM **impuissante**) ADJECTIVE
helpless
  □ Elle se sentait complètement impuissante. She felt completely helpless.

impulsif (FEM **impulsive**) ADJECTIVE
impulsive

inabordable (FEM **inabordable**) ADJECTIVE
prohibitive
  □ des prix inabordables prohibitive prices

inaccessible (FEM **inaccessible**) ADJECTIVE
inaccessible
  □ Cette plage est inaccessible par la route. This beach is inaccessible by road.

inachevé (FEM **inachevée**) ADJECTIVE
unfinished

inadmissible (FEM **inadmissible**) ADJECTIVE
intolerable
  □ Ce type de comportement est inadmissible ! This sort of behaviour is intolerable!

inanimé (FEM **inanimée**) ADJECTIVE
unconscious
  □ On l'a retrouvé inanimé sur la route. He was found unconscious on the road.

inaperçu (FEM **inaperçue**) ADJECTIVE
  ■ passer inaperçu to go unnoticed

inattendu (FEM **inattendue**) ADJECTIVE
unexpected

l'**inattention** FEM NOUN
  ■ une faute d'inattention a careless mistake

inaugurer VERB [28]
to open (an exhibition)

incapable (FEM **incapable**) ADJECTIVE
incapable
  □ être incapable de faire quelque chose to be incapable of doing something

incassable (FEM **incassable**) ADJECTIVE
unbreakable

l'**incendie** MASC NOUN
fire
  □ un incendie de forêt a forest fire

incertain (FEM **incertaine**) ADJECTIVE
1 uncertain

□ Son avenir est encore incertain. His future is still uncertain.

2 unsettled

□ Le temps est incertain. The weather is unsettled.

l'incident MASC NOUN
incident

inciter VERB [28]

■ **inciter quelqu'un à faire quelque chose** to encourage somebody to do something □ J'ai incité mes parents à partir en voyage. I encouraged my parents to go on a trip.

inclure VERB [13]

1 to enclose

□ Veuillez inclure une enveloppe timbrée libellée à votre adresse. Please enclose a stamped addressed envelope.

2 to include

inclus VERB ▷ see **inclure**
▷ see also **inclus** ADJECTIVE
■ Ils m'ont toujours inclus. They always included me.

inclus (FEM **incluse**) ADJECTIVE
▷ see also **inclus** VERB
included
■ **jusqu'au dix mars inclus** until 10th March inclusive

incohérent (FEM **incohérente**) ADJECTIVE
incoherent

incollable (FEM **incollable**) ADJECTIVE
■ **être incollable sur quelque chose** (*informal*) to know everything there is to know about something
■ **le riz incollable** non-stick rice

incolore (FEM **incolore**) ADJECTIVE
colourless

incompétent (FEM **incompétente**) ADJECTIVE
incompetent

incompris (FEM **incomprise**) ADJECTIVE
misunderstood

l'inconnu MASC NOUN
stranger
□ Ne parle pas à des inconnus. Don't speak to strangers.
■ **l'inconnu** the unknown □ la peur de l'inconnu the fear of the unknown

l'inconnue FEM NOUN
stranger

inconsciemment ADVERB
unconsciously

inconscient (FEM **inconsciente**) ADJECTIVE

1 unconscious
□ Il est resté inconscient quelques minutes. He was unconscious for several minutes.

2 unaware
□ Elle est inconsciente des risques que cela comporte. She is unaware of the risks involved.

incontestable (FEM **incontestable**)
ADJECTIVE
indisputable

incontournable (FEM **incontournable**)
ADJECTIVE
inevitable
□ l'incontournable petite robe noire the inevitable little black dress

l'inconvénient MASC NOUN
disadvantage
■ **si vous n'y voyez pas d'inconvénient** if you have no objection

incorrect (FEM **incorrecte**) ADJECTIVE

1 incorrect
□ une réponse incorrecte an incorrect answer

2 rude
□ Il a été incorrect avec la voisine. He was rude to the woman next door.

incroyable (FEM **incroyable**) ADJECTIVE
incredible

inculper VERB [28]
■ **inculper de** to charge with □ Il a été inculpé de meurtre. He was charged with murder.

l'Inde FEM NOUN
India

indécis (FEM **indécise**) ADJECTIVE

1 indecisive
□ Il est constamment indécis. He's always indecisive.

2 undecided
□ Je suis encore indécis. I'm still undecided.

indéfiniment ADVERB
indefinitely

indélicat (FEM **indélicate**) ADJECTIVE
tactless

indemne (FEM **indemne**) ADJECTIVE
unharmed
□ Il s'en est sorti indemne. He escaped unharmed.

indemniser VERB [28]
to compensate
□ Les victimes demandent maintenant à être indemnisées. The victims are now demanding compensation.

indépendamment ADVERB
independently
■ **indépendamment de** irrespective of
□ Les allocations familiales sont versées indépendamment des revenus. Child benefit is given irrespective of income.

l'indépendance FEM NOUN
independence

indépendant (FEM **indépendante**) ADJECTIVE
independent

l'index MASC NOUN

1 index finger

2 index (*in book*)

i

indicatif (FEM **indicative**) ADJECTIVE
▷ *see also* **indicatif** NOUN
■ **à titre indicatif** for your information

l'**indicatif** MASC NOUN
▷ *see also* **indicatif** ADJECTIVE
1 dialling code
2 indicative (*of verb*)
3 theme tune (*of TV programme*)

les **indications** FEM PL NOUN
instructions
□ Il suffit de suivre les indications. You just have to follow the instructions.

l'**indice** MASC NOUN
clue
□ La police cherche des indices. The police are looking for clues.

indien (FEM **indienne**) ADJECTIVE, NOUN
Indian
■ **un Indien** an Indian (*man*)
■ **une Indienne** an Indian (*woman*)

l'**indifférence** FEM NOUN
indifference

indifférent (FEM **indifférente**) ADJECTIVE
indifferent

l'**indigène** MASC/FEM NOUN
native

indigeste (FEM **indigeste**) ADJECTIVE
indigestible

l'**indigestion** FEM NOUN
indigestion

indigne (FEM **indigne**) ADJECTIVE
unworthy

indigner VERB [28]
■ **s'indigner de quelque chose** to get indignant about something

indiqué (FEM **indiquée**) ADJECTIVE
advisable
□ Ce n'est pas très indiqué. It's not really advisable.

indiquer VERB [28]
to point out
□ Il m'a indiqué la mairie. He pointed out the town hall.

indirect (FEM **indirecte**) ADJECTIVE
indirect

indiscipliné (FEM **indisciplinée**) ADJECTIVE
unruly

indiscret (FEM **indiscrète**) ADJECTIVE
indiscreet

indispensable (FEM **indispensable**) ADJECTIVE
indispensable

indisposé (FEM **indisposée**) ADJECTIVE
indisposed
■ **être indisposée** to be having one's period

l'**individu** MASC NOUN
individual

individuel (FEM **individuelle**) ADJECTIVE
individual
□ une portion individuelle an individual portion
■ **une chambre individuelle** a single room (*in hotel*)
■ **Vous aurez une chambre individuelle.** You'll have a room of your own.

indolore (FEM **indolore**) ADJECTIVE
painless

l'**Indonésie** FEM NOUN
Indonesia

indulgent (FEM **indulgente**) ADJECTIVE
indulgent
■ **Elle est trop indulgente avec son fils.** She's not firm enough with her son.

l'**industrie** FEM NOUN
industry

industriel (FEM **industrielle**) ADJECTIVE
▷ *see also* **industriel** NOUN
industrial

l'**industriel** MASC NOUN
▷ *see also* **industriel** ADJECTIVE
industrialist

inédit (FEM **inédite**) ADJECTIVE
unpublished

inefficace (FEM **inefficace**) ADJECTIVE
1 ineffective (*treatment*)
2 inefficient
□ un service de transports publics inefficace an inefficient public transport system

inégal (FEM **inégale**, MASC PL **inégaux**) ADJECTIVE
1 unequal
□ un combat inégal an unequal struggle
2 uneven
■ **La qualité est inégale.** The quality varies.

inévitable (FEM **inévitable**) ADJECTIVE
unavoidable
■ **C'était inévitable !** That was bound to happen!

inexact (FEM **inexacte**) ADJECTIVE
inaccurate

in extremis ADVERB
■ **Il a réussi à attraper son train in extremis.** He just managed to catch his train.
■ **Ils ont évité un accident in extremis.** They avoided an accident by the skin of their teeth.

l'**infarctus** MASC NOUN
coronary

infatigable (FEM **infatigable**) ADJECTIVE
indefatigable
□ Il est infatigable. He's indefatigable.

infect (FEM **infecte**) ADJECTIVE
revolting (*meal*)

s'**infecter** VERB [28]
to go septic

Numbers in brackets refer to verb tables on pages 650 to 658

□ La plaie s'est infectée. The wound has gone septic.

l'**infection** FEM NOUN
infection

inférieur (FEM **inférieure**) ADJECTIVE
lower
□ les membres inférieurs the lower limbs
□ C'est moins cher, mais de qualité inférieure. It's cheaper but of lower quality.

infernal (FEM **infernale**, MASC PL **infernaux**)
ADJECTIVE
terrible
□ Ils faisaient un bruit infernal. They were making a terrible noise.

l'**infini** MASC NOUN
■ à l'infini indefinitely □ On pourrait en parler à l'infini. We could discuss this indefinitely.

l'**infinitif** MASC NOUN
infinitive

l'**infirme** MASC/FEM NOUN
disabled person

l'**infirmerie** FEM NOUN
medical room
□ Elle est à l'infirmerie. She's in the medical room.

l'**infirmier** MASC NOUN
(male) nurse

l'**infirmière** FEM NOUN
(female) nurse

inflammable (FEM **inflammable**) ADJECTIVE
inflammable

l'**influence** FEM NOUN
influence

influencer VERB [12]
to influence

l'**influenceur** MASC NOUN
influencer
□ les influenceurs des réseaux sociaux influencers on social media

l'**influenceuse** FEM NOUN
influencer

l'**informaticien** MASC NOUN
computer scientist

l'**informaticienne** FEM NOUN
computer scientist

les **informations** FEM PL NOUN
1 news (on TV)
□ les informations de vingt heures the 8 o'clock news
2 information
□ Je voudrais quelques informations, s'il vous plaît. I'd like some information, please.
■ une information a piece of information

l'**informatique** FEM NOUN
computing

informer VERB [28]
to inform
■ s'informer to find out □ Je vais m'informer des heures de fermeture. I'm going to find out when they close.

infuser VERB [28]
1 to brew (tea)
2 to infuse (herbal tea)

l'**infusion** FEM NOUN
herbal tea

l'**ingénieur** MASC/FEM NOUN
engineer

ingrat (FEM **ingrate**) ADJECTIVE
ungrateful

l'**ingrédient** MASC NOUN
ingredient

inhabituel (FEM **inhabituelle**) ADJECTIVE
unusual

l'**inhalateur** MASC NOUN
inhaler

inhumain (FEM **inhumaine**) ADJECTIVE
inhuman

initial (FEM **initiale**, MASC PL **initiaux**)
ADJECTIVE
▷ see also **initiale** NOUN
initial

l'**initiale** FEM NOUN
▷ see also **initial** ADJECTIVE
initial

l'**initiation** FEM NOUN
introduction
□ un stage d'initiation à la planche à voile an introductory course in windsurfing

l'**initiative** FEM NOUN
initiative
□ avoir de l'initiative to have initiative

injecter VERB [28]
to inject

l'**injection** FEM NOUN
injection

l'**injure** FEM NOUN
1 insult
□ Il a pris ça comme une injure. He took this as an insult.
2 abuse
□ lancer des injures à quelqu'un to hurl abuse at somebody

BE CAREFUL!
The French word **injure** does not mean **injury**.

injurier VERB [19]
to insult

injurieux (FEM **injurieuse**) ADJECTIVE
abusive (language)

injuste (FEM **injuste**) ADJECTIVE
unfair

innocent (FEM **innocente**) ADJECTIVE
innocent

innombrable (FEM **innombrable**) ADJECTIVE
innumerable

innover VERB [28]
to break new ground

inoccupé (FEM **inoccupée**) ADJECTIVE
empty
□ un appartement inoccupé an empty flat

inoffensif (FEM **inoffensive**) ADJECTIVE
harmless

l'**inondation** FEM NOUN
flood

inoubliable (FEM **inoubliable**) ADJECTIVE
unforgettable

inoxydable (FEM **inoxydable**) ADJECTIVE
■ **l'acier inoxydable** stainless steel

inquiet (FEM **inquiète**) ADJECTIVE
worried

inquiétant (FEM **inquiétante**) ADJECTIVE
worrying

inquiéter VERB [34]
to worry
□ Son comportement m'inquiète beaucoup.
His behaviour really worries me.
■ **s'inquiéter** to worry □ Ne t'inquiète pas !
Don't worry!

l'**inquiétude** FEM NOUN
anxiety

insatisfait (FEM **insatisfaite**) ADJECTIVE
dissatisfied

l'**inscription** FEM NOUN
registration (for school, course)

inscrire VERB [30]
to write down
□ J'ai inscrit mon nom. I wrote down my name.
■ **s'inscrire à 1** to join □ Je me suis inscrit au
club de tennis. I've joined the tennis club. **2** to
register □ N'attends pas trop pour t'inscrire à
la fac. Don't leave it too long to register at the
university.

l'**insecte** MASC NOUN
insect

insensible (FEM **insensible**) ADJECTIVE
insensitive
□ Il la trouve insensible. He thinks she's
insensitive.

l'**insigne** MASC NOUN
badge

insignifiant (FEM **insignifiante**) ADJECTIVE
insignificant

insister VERB [28]
to insist
■ **N'insiste pas !** Don't keep on!

l'**insolation** FEM NOUN
sunstroke

insolent (FEM **insolente**) ADJECTIVE
cheeky

insouciant (FEM **insouciante**) ADJECTIVE
carefree

insoutenable (FEM **insoutenable**) ADJECTIVE
unbearable
□ une douleur insoutenable an unbearable pain

inspecter VERB [28]
to inspect

l'**inspecteur** MASC NOUN
inspector

l'**inspection** FEM NOUN
inspection

l'**inspectrice** FEM NOUN
inspector

inspirer VERB [28]
1 to inspire
■ **s'inspirer de** to take one's inspiration from
□ Le peintre s'est inspiré d'un poème. The
painter took his inspiration from a poem.
2 to breathe in
□ Inspirez ! Expirez ! Breathe in! Breathe out!

instable (FEM **instable**) ADJECTIVE
1 unsteady (piece of furniture)
2 unstable (person)

les **installations** FEM PL NOUN
facilities
□ Cet appartement est pourvu de toutes les
installations modernes. This flat has all modern
facilities.

installer VERB [28]
1 to put up (shelves)
2 to install (gas, telephone)
■ **s'installer** to settle in □ Nous nous sommes
installés dans notre nouvel appartement. We've
settled into our new flat.
■ **Installez-vous, je vous en prie.** Have a seat,
please.

l'**instant** MASC NOUN
moment
□ pour l'instant for the moment
■ **dans un instant** in a moment □ Le dîner sera
prêt dans un instant. Dinner will be ready in a
moment.

instantané (FEM **instantanée**) ADJECTIVE
instant
□ du café instantané instant coffee

l'**instinct** MASC NOUN
instinct

l'**institut** MASC NOUN
institute

l'**instituteur** MASC NOUN
primary school teacher

l'**institution** FEM NOUN
institution

l'**institutrice** FEM NOUN
primary school teacher

l'instruction FEM NOUN
1 instruction
  □ J'ai suivi ses instructions. I followed his instructions.
2 education
  □ Il n'a pas beaucoup d'instruction. He's not very well-educated.

s'**instruire** VERB [23]
  to educate oneself

instruit (FEM instruite) ADJECTIVE
  educated

l'instrument MASC NOUN
  instrument
  □ un instrument de musique a musical instrument

insuffisant (FEM insuffisante) ADJECTIVE
  insufficient
  ■ « travail insuffisant » (on school report) 'must try harder'

l'insuline FEM NOUN
  insulin

insultant (FEM insultante) ADJECTIVE
  insulting
  □ Il s'est montré insultant avec elle. He was insulting to her.

l'insulte FEM NOUN
  insult

insulter VERB [28]
  to insult

insupportable (FEM insupportable) ADJECTIVE
  unbearable

intact (FEM intacte) ADJECTIVE
  intact

intégral (FEM intégrale, MASC PL intégraux) ADJECTIVE
  ■ le texte intégral unabridged version
  ■ un remboursement intégral a full refund

intégrer VERB [34]
1 to incorporate
  □ Essaie d'intégrer cette citation dans ta dissertation. Try to incorporate this quote in your essay.
2 to join
  □ J'ai intégré l'entreprise en 2022. I joined the company in 2022.
  ■ s'intégrer à to fit in □ Elle s'est facilement intégrée à l'université. She fitted in easily at university.

l'intégrisme MASC NOUN
  fundamentalism

l'intelligence FEM NOUN
  intelligence

intelligent (FEM intelligente) ADJECTIVE
  intelligent

intense (FEM intense) ADJECTIVE
  intense

intensif (FEM intensive) ADJECTIVE
  intensive
  ■ un cours intensif a crash course

l'intention FEM NOUN
  intention
  ■ avoir l'intention de faire quelque chose to intend to do something □ J'ai l'intention de lui en parler. I intend to speak to him about it.

l'interdiction FEM NOUN
  ■ « interdiction de stationner » 'no parking'
  ■ « interdiction de fumer » 'no smoking'

interdire VERB [27]
  to forbid
  ■ interdire à quelqu'un de faire quelque chose to forbid someone to do something □ Ses parents lui ont interdit de sortir. His parents have forbidden him to go out.

interdit (FEM interdite) ADJECTIVE
  forbidden
  □ Il est interdit de fumer dans les couloirs. Smoking in the corridors is forbidden.

intéressant (FEM intéressante) ADJECTIVE
  interesting
  □ un livre intéressant an interesting book
  ■ On lui a fait une offre intéressante. They made him an attractive offer.
  ■ On trouve des CD à des prix très intéressants dans ce magasin. You can get very cheap CDs in this shop.

intéresser VERB [28]
  to interest
  ■ s'intéresser à to be interested in □ Est-ce que vous vous intéressez à la politique ? Are you interested in politics?

l'intérêt MASC NOUN
  interest
  ■ avoir intérêt à faire quelque chose to do well to do something □ Tu as intérêt à accepter. You'd do well to accept.

l'intérieur MASC NOUN
  inside
  □ à l'intérieur de la maison inside the house

l'interlocuteur MASC NOUN
  ■ son interlocuteur the man he's speaking to

l'interlocutrice FEM NOUN
  ■ son interlocutrice the woman he's speaking to

l'intermédiaire MASC NOUN
  intermediary
  ■ par l'intermédiaire de through □ Je l'ai rencontré par l'intermédiaire de sa sœur. I met him through his sister.

l'internat MASC NOUN
  boarding school

international (FEM internationale, MASC PL internationaux) ADJECTIVE
  international

l'**internaute** MASC/FEM NOUN
internet user

l'**interne** MASC/FEM NOUN
boarder

l'**Internet** MASC NOUN
internet
□ sur Internet on the internet

l'**interphone** MASC NOUN
intercom

l'**interprète** MASC/FEM NOUN
interpreter

interpréter VERB [34]
to interpret

interrogatif (FEM **interrogative**) ADJECTIVE
interrogative

l'**interrogation** FEM NOUN
1 question
2 test
□ une interrogation écrite a written test □ une interrogation orale an oral test

l'**interrogatoire** MASC NOUN
questioning
■ **C'est un interrogatoire ou quoi ?** Am I being cross-examined?

interroger VERB [45]
to question

interrompre VERB [75]
to interrupt

l'**interrupteur** MASC NOUN
switch

l'**interruption** FEM NOUN
interruption
■ **sans interruption** without stopping □ Il a parlé pendant deux heures sans interruption. He spoke for two hours without stopping.

l'**intervalle** MASC NOUN
interval
■ **dans l'intervalle** in the meantime

intervenir VERB [89, *aux* être]
1 to intervene
2 to take action
□ La police est intervenue. The police took action.

l'**intervention** FEM NOUN
intervention
□ une intervention militaire a military intervention
■ **une intervention chirurgicale** an operation (*surgical*)

l'**interview** FEM NOUN
interview (*on radio, TV*)

l'**intestin** MASC NOUN
intestine

intime (FEM **intime**) ADJECTIVE
intimate
■ **un journal intime** a diary

intimider VERB [28]
to intimidate

l'**intimité** FEM NOUN
■ **dans l'intimité** in private □ Ce que vous faites dans l'intimité ne m'intéresse pas. What you do in private doesn't interest me.
■ **Le mariage a eu lieu dans l'intimité.** The wedding ceremony was private.

intitulé (FEM **intitulée**) ADJECTIVE
entitled

intolérable (FEM **intolérable**) ADJECTIVE
intolerable

l'**intoxication** FEM NOUN
■ **une intoxication alimentaire** food poisoning

l'**Intranet** MASC NOUN
intranet

intransigeant (FEM **intransigeante**) ADJECTIVE
uncompromising

l'**intrigue** FEM NOUN
plot (*of book, film*)

l'**introduction** FEM NOUN
introduction

introduire VERB [23]
to introduce

l'**intuition** FEM NOUN
intuition

inusable (FEM **inusable**) ADJECTIVE
hard-wearing

inutile (FEM **inutile**) ADJECTIVE
useless
■ **Il est inutile d'attendre.** There's no point in waiting.

l'**invalide** MASC/FEM NOUN
person with a disability

l'**invasion** FEM NOUN
invasion

inventer VERB [28]
1 to invent
2 to make up
□ inventer une excuse to make up an excuse

l'**inventeur** MASC NOUN
inventor

l'**invention** FEM NOUN
invention

inverse (FEM **inverse**) ADJECTIVE
▷ *see also* **inverse** NOUN
■ **dans l'ordre inverse** in reverse order
■ **en sens inverse** in the opposite direction

l'**inverse** MASC NOUN
▷ *see also* **inverse** ADJECTIVE
reverse
■ **Tu t'es trompé, c'est l'inverse.** You've got it wrong, it's the other way round.

l'**investissement** MASC NOUN
investment

invisible (FEM **invisible**) ADJECTIVE
invisible

l'**invitation** FEM NOUN
invitation

l'**invité** MASC NOUN
guest

l'**invitée** FEM NOUN
guest

inviter VERB [28]
to invite

involontaire (FEM **involontaire**) ADJECTIVE
unintentional
□ C'était tout à fait involontaire. It was quite
unintentional.

invraisemblable (FEM **invraisemblable**)
ADJECTIVE
unlikely
□ une histoire invraisemblable an unlikely story

ira, irai, iraient, irais, irait VERB ▷ *see*
aller
■ J'irai demain au supermarché. I'll go to the
supermarket tomorrow.

l'**Irak** MASC NOUN
Iraq

l'**Iran** MASC NOUN
Iran

iras, irez VERB ▷ *see* aller

irlandais (FEM **irlandaise**) ADJECTIVE, NOUN
Irish
■ un Irlandais an Irishman
■ une Irlandaise an Irishwoman
■ les Irlandais the Irish

l'**Irlande** FEM NOUN
Ireland
■ en Irlande 1 in Ireland 2 to Ireland
■ la République d'Irlande the Irish Republic
■ l'Irlande du Nord Northern Ireland

l'**ironie** FEM NOUN
irony

ironique (FEM **ironique**) ADJECTIVE
ironical

irons, iront VERB ▷ *see* aller
■ Nous irons à la plage cet après-midi.
We'll go to the beach this afternoon.

irrationnel (FEM **irrationnelle**) ADJECTIVE
irrational

irréel (FEM **irréelle**) ADJECTIVE
unreal

irrégulier (FEM **irrégulière**) ADJECTIVE
irregular

irrésistible (FEM **irrésistible**) ADJECTIVE
irresistible

irritable (FEM **irritable**) ADJECTIVE
irritable

irriter VERB [28]
to irritate

islamique (FEM **islamique**) ADJECTIVE
Islamic

l'**Islande** FEM NOUN
Iceland

isolé (FEM **isolée**) ADJECTIVE
isolated
□ une ferme isolée an isolated farm

Israël MASC NOUN
Israel

israélien (FEM **israélienne**) ADJECTIVE, NOUN
Israeli
■ un Israélien an Israeli (*man*)
■ une Israélienne an Israeli (*woman*)
■ les Israéliens the Israelis

l'**issue** FEM NOUN
■ une voie sans issue a dead end
■ l'issue de secours emergency exit

l'**Italie** FEM NOUN
Italy
■ en Italie 1 in Italy 2 to Italy

italien (FEM **italienne**) ADJECTIVE, NOUN
Italian
□ J'apprends l'italien. I'm learning Italian.
■ un Italien an Italian (*man*)
■ une Italienne an Italian (*woman*)
■ les Italiens the Italians

l'**itinéraire** MASC NOUN
route

l'**IUT** MASC NOUN (= *Institut universitaire de
technologie*)
institute of technology (*at university level*)

ivre (FEM **ivre**) ADJECTIVE
drunk

l'**ivrogne** MASC/FEM NOUN
drunkard

i

Jj

j' PRONOUN ▷ *see* **je**

la **jalousie** FEM NOUN
jealousy

jaloux (FEM **jalouse**) ADJECTIVE
jealous

jamais ADVERB
■ **ne ... jamais** never
□ Ils ne vont jamais au cinéma. They never go to the cinema.
■ **Il va souvent en vacances ? — Non, jamais.** Does he go on holiday often? — No, never.

Phrases with **jamais** meaning 'ever' use a verb in the subjunctive.

□ C'est la plus belle chose que j'aie jamais vue. It's the most beautiful thing I've ever seen.

la **jambe** FEM NOUN
leg

le **jambon** MASC NOUN
ham
■ **le jambon cru** Parma ham

le **jambonneau** (PL les **jambonneaux**) MASC NOUN
knuckle of ham

janvier MASC NOUN
January
■ **en janvier** in January

le **Japon** MASC NOUN
Japan
■ **au Japon** **1** in Japan **2** to Japan

japonais (FEM **japonaise**) ADJECTIVE, NOUN
Japanese
□ Elle parle japonais. She speaks Japanese.
■ **un Japonais** a Japanese (*man*)
■ **une Japonaise** a Japanese (*woman*)
■ **les Japonais** the Japanese

le **jardin** MASC NOUN
garden
□ un jardin potager a vegetable garden

le **jardinage** MASC NOUN
gardening

le **jardinier** MASC NOUN
gardener

la **jardinière** FEM NOUN
gardener

jaune (FEM **jaune**) ADJECTIVE
▷ *see also* **jaune** NOUN
yellow

le **jaune** MASC NOUN
▷ *see also* **jaune** ADJECTIVE
yellow
■ **un jaune d'œuf** an egg yolk

jaunir VERB [38]
to turn yellow

la **jaunisse** FEM NOUN
jaundice

Javel NOUN
■ **l'eau de Javel** bleach

le **jazz** MASC NOUN
jazz

J.-C. ABBREVIATION= **Jésus-Christ**
■ **44 avant J.-C.** 44 BC
■ **115 après J.-C.** 115 AD

je PRONOUN

je changes to j' before a vowel and most words beginning with 'h'.

I
□ Je t'appellerai ce soir. I'll phone you this evening.
□ J'arrive ! I'm coming! □ J'hésite. I'm not sure.

le **jean** MASC NOUN
jeans

la **jeannette** FEM NOUN
Brownie
□ Elle est jeannette. She's a Brownie.

Jésus-Christ MASC NOUN
Jesus Christ

le **jet** MASC NOUN
1 jet (*of water*)
■ **un jet d'eau** a fountain
2 jet plane

jetable (FEM **jetable**) ADJECTIVE
disposable

la **jetée** FEM NOUN
jetty

jeter VERB [41]
1 to throw
□ Il a jeté son sac sur le lit. He threw his bag onto the bed.
2 to throw away
□ Ils ne jettent jamais rien. They never throw anything away.
■ **jeter un coup d'œil** to have a look

Numbers in brackets refer to verb tables on pages 650 to 658

le **jeton** MASC NOUN
counter (*in board game*)

le **jeu** (PL les **jeux**) MASC NOUN
game
□ Les enfants jouaient à un jeu. The children were playing a game.
- **un jeu d'arcade** an arcade video game
- **un jeu de cartes** 1 a pack of cards 2 a card game
- **un jeu de mots** a pun
- **un jeu de société** a board game
- **un jeu électronique** an electronic game
- **les jeux sur ordinateur** computer gaming
- **les jeux sur téléphone portable** mobile gaming
- **les jeux vidéo** video games
- **en jeu** at stake □ Des vies humaines sont en jeu. Human lives are at stake.

le **jeudi** MASC NOUN
1 Thursday
□ Aujourd'hui, nous sommes jeudi. It's Thursday today.
2 on Thursday
□ Il arrivera jeudi matin. He's arriving on Thursday morning.
- **le jeudi** on Thursdays □ Le musée est fermé le jeudi. The museum is closed on Thursdays.
- **tous les jeudis** every Thursday
- **jeudi dernier** last Thursday
- **jeudi prochain** next Thursday
- **À jeudi !** See you on Thursday!

jeun
- **à jeun** ADVERB on an empty stomach □ à prendre à jeun to be taken on an empty stomach □ Il faut être à jeun pour la prise de sang. You shouldn't have eaten anything before giving a blood sample.

jeune (FEM **jeune**) ADJECTIVE
▷ *see also* **jeune** NOUN
young
□ un jeune homme a young man □ une jeune femme a young woman
- **une jeune fille** a girl

le/la **jeune** MASC/FEM NOUN
▷ *see also* **jeune** ADJECTIVE
young person
□ les jeunes young people

la **jeunesse** FEM NOUN
youth

le **job** MASC NOUN (*informal*)
job

le **jogging** MASC NOUN
1 jogging
□ Il fait du jogging. He goes jogging.
2 tracksuit
□ un jogging rose a pink tracksuit

la **joie** FEM NOUN
joy

joindre VERB [42]
1 to put together
□ On va joindre les deux tables. We're going to put the two tables together.
2 to contact
□ Vous pouvez le joindre chez lui. You can contact him at home.

joint (FEM **jointe**) ADJECTIVE
- **une pièce jointe** (*in email*) an attachment

joli (FEM **jolie**) ADJECTIVE
pretty
□ un joli village a pretty village

le **jonc** MASC NOUN
rush

la **jonquille** FEM NOUN
daffodil

la **joue** FEM NOUN
cheek

jouer VERB [28]
1 to play
□ Viens jouer avec nous. Come and play with us.
- **jouer de** to play (*instrument*) □ Il joue de la guitare et du piano. He plays the guitar and the piano.
- **jouer à** to play (*sport, game*) □ Elle joue au tennis. She plays tennis. □ jouer aux cartes to play cards
- **jouer aux jeux vidéo** to game
2 to act
□ Je trouve qu'il joue très bien dans ce film. I think he acts very well in this film.
- **On joue Hamlet au Théâtre de la Ville.** Hamlet is on at the Théâtre de la Ville.

le **jouet** MASC NOUN
toy

le **joueur** MASC NOUN
player
- **un joueur sur ordinateur** a computer gamer
- **être mauvais joueur** to be a bad loser

la **joueuse** FEM NOUN
player

le **jour** MASC NOUN
day
□ J'ai passé trois jours chez mes cousins. I stayed with my cousins for three days.
- **Il fait jour.** It's daylight.
- **mettre quelque chose à jour** to update something
- **le jour de l'An** New Year's Day
- **un jour de congé** a day off
- **un jour férié** a public holiday
- **dans huit jours** in a week
- **dans quinze jours** in a fortnight

le **journal** (PL les **journaux**) MASC NOUN
1 newspaper
- **le journal télévisé** the television news

2 diary

□ Elle tient un journal depuis l'âge de douze ans. She has been keeping a diary since she was 12.

journalier (FEM **journalière**) ADJECTIVE

daily

le **journalisme** MASC NOUN

journalism

le/la **journaliste** MASC/FEM NOUN

journalist

□ Elle est journaliste. She's a journalist.

la **journée** FEM NOUN

day

joyeux (FEM **joyeuse**) ADJECTIVE

happy

■ **Joyeux anniversaire !** Happy birthday!

■ **Joyeux Noël !** Merry Christmas!

le **judo** MASC NOUN

judo

le **juge** MASC NOUN

judge

juger VERB [45]

to judge

juif (FEM **juive**) ADJECTIVE, NOUN

Jewish

□ la cuisine juive Jewish cooking

■ **un Juif** a Jew (*man*)

■ **une Juive** a Jew (*woman*)

juillet MASC NOUN

July

■ **en juillet** in July

juin MASC NOUN

June

■ **en juin** in June

le **jumeau** (PL les **jumeaux**) MASC NOUN

twin

□ des frères jumeaux twin brothers

jumeler VERB [4]

to twin

□ Saint-Brieuc est jumelée avec Aberystwyth. Saint-Brieuc is twinned with Aberystwyth.

la **jumelle** FEM NOUN

twin

□ des sœurs jumelles twin sisters

les **jumelles** FEM PL NOUN

binoculars

la **jument** FEM NOUN

mare

la **jungle** FEM NOUN

jungle

la **jupe** FEM NOUN

skirt

jurer VERB [28]

to swear

□ Je jure que c'est vrai ! I swear it's true!

juridique (FEM **juridique**) ADJECTIVE

legal

le **jury** MASC NOUN

jury

le **jus** MASC NOUN

juice

■ **un jus de fruit** a fruit juice

jusqu'à PREPOSITION

1 as far as

□ Nous avons marché jusqu'au village. We walked as far as the village.

2 until

□ Il fait généralement chaud jusqu'à la mi-août. It's usually hot until mid-August.

■ **jusqu'à ce que** until □ Tu peux rester ici jusqu'à ce qu'il cesse de pleuvoir. You can stay here until it stops raining.

■ **jusqu'à présent** so far

jusque PREPOSITION

as far as

□ Je l'ai raccompagnée jusque chez elle. I went with her as far as her house. □ Jusqu'ici nous n'avons pas eu de problèmes. So far we've had no problems. □ Jusqu'où es-tu allé ? How far did you go?

juste (FEM **juste**) ADJECTIVE, ADVERB

1 fair

□ Il est sévère, mais juste. He's strict but fair.

2 tight

□ Cette veste est un peu juste. This jacket is a bit tight.

■ **juste assez** just enough

■ **chanter juste** to sing in tune

justement ADVERB

just

□ C'est justement pour cela qu'il est parti ! That's just the reason he left!

la **justesse** FEM NOUN

■ **de justesse** only just □ Il a eu son permis de justesse. He only just passed his driving test.

la **justice** FEM NOUN

justice

justifier VERB [19]

to justify

juteux (FEM **juteuse**) ADJECTIVE

juicy

juvénile (FEM **juvénile**) ADJECTIVE

youthful

Kk

kaki (FEM+PL **kaki**) ADJECTIVE
khaki

le **kangourou** MASC NOUN
kangaroo

le **karaté** MASC NOUN
karate

la **kermesse** FEM NOUN
fair

kidnapper VERB [28]
to kidnap

kiffer VERB [28] (*informal*)
to be into
□ Il kiffe le foot. He's into football.

le **kilo** MASC NOUN
kilo

le **kilogramme** MASC NOUN
kilogram

le **kilomètre** MASC NOUN
kilometre

le/la **kiné** MASC/FEM NOUN
physio

le/la **kinésithérapeute** MASC/FEM NOUN
physiotherapist

le **kiosque** MASC NOUN
■ un kiosque à journaux a news stand

le **kit** MASC NOUN
kit
□ en kit in kit form □ un kit mains libres a hands-free kit □ un kit piéton a hands-free kit

le **klaxon** MASC NOUN
horn (*of car*)

klaxonner VERB [28]
to sound the horn

km ABBREVIATION (= *kilomètre*)
km (= *kilometre*)

km/h ABBREVIATION (= *kilomètres/heure*)
kph (= *kilometres per hour*)

KO (FEM+PL **KO**) ADJECTIVE
knocked out
■ mettre quelqu'un KO to knock somebody out □ Il l'a mis KO au troisième round. He knocked him out in the third round.
■ Je suis complètement KO. (*informal*) I'm completely knackered.

le **K-way**® MASC NOUN
cagoule

k

l' ARTICLE, PRONOUN ▷ *see* **la, le**

la ARTICLE, PRONOUN
▷ *see also* **la** NOUN

> **la** changes to **l'** before a vowel and most words beginning with 'h'.

1 the
  □ la maison the house □ l'actrice the actress
  □ l'herbe the grass
2 her
  □ Je la connais depuis longtemps. I've known her for a long time. □ C'est une femme intelligente : je l'admire beaucoup. She's an intelligent woman: I admire her very much.
3 it
  □ C'est une bonne émission : je la regarde tous les jours. It's a good programme: I watch it every day.
4 one's
  ■ **se mordre la langue** to bite one's tongue
  □ Je me suis mordu la langue. I've bitten my tongue.
  ■ **six euros la douzaine** six euros a dozen

le la MASC NOUN
▷ *see also* **la** ARTICLE, PRONOUN
1 A
  □ en la bémol in A flat
2 la
  □ sol, la, si, do so, la, ti, do

là ADVERB
1 there
  □ Ton livre est là, sur la table. Your book's there, on the table.
2 here
  □ Elle n'est pas là. She isn't here.
  ■ **C'est là que ...** **1** That's where ... □ C'est là que je suis né. That's where I was born.
  2 That's when ... □ C'est là que j'ai réalisé que je m'étais trompé. That's when I realized that I had made a mistake.

là-bas ADVERB
  over there
  □ Ma maison est là-bas. My house is over there.

le labo MASC NOUN (*informal*)
  lab

le laboratoire MASC NOUN
  laboratory

labourer VERB [28]
  to plough

le labyrinthe MASC NOUN
  maze

le lac MASC NOUN
  lake

lacer VERB [12]
  to do up (*shoes*)

le lacet MASC NOUN
  lace
  ■ **des chaussures à lacets** lace-up shoes

lâche (FEM **lâche**) ADJECTIVE
▷ *see also* **lâche** NOUN
1 loose
  □ Le nœud est trop lâche. The knot's too loose.
2 cowardly
  ■ **Il est lâche.** He's a coward.

le lâche MASC/FEM NOUN
▷ *see also* **lâche** ADJECTIVE
  coward

lâcher VERB [28]
1 to let go of
  □ Il n'a pas lâché ma main de tout le film. He didn't let go of my hand until the end of the film.
2 to drop
  □ Il a été tellement surpris qu'il a lâché son verre. He was so surprised that he dropped his glass.
3 to fail
  □ Les freins ont lâché. The brakes failed.

la lâcheté FEM NOUN
  cowardice

lacrymogène (FEM **lacrymogène**) ADJECTIVE
  ■ **le gaz lacrymogène** tear gas

la lacune FEM NOUN
  gap

là-dedans ADVERB
  in there
  □ Qu'est-ce qu'il y a là-dedans ? What's in there?

là-dessous ADVERB
1 under there
  □ Mon carnet d'adresses est quelque part là-dessous. My address book is under there somewhere.

2 behind it
□ Il y a quelque chose de louche là-dessous.
There's something fishy behind it.

là-dessus ADVERB
on there

là-haut ADVERB
up there

la **laïcité** FEM NOUN
secularism

laid (FEM **laide**) ADJECTIVE
ugly

la **laideur** FEM NOUN
ugliness

le **lainage** MASC NOUN
woollen garment

la **laine** FEM NOUN
wool
□ un pull en laine a wool jumper
■ une laine polaire a fleece (*jacket*)

laïque (FEM **laïque**) ADJECTIVE
■ une école laïque a non-denominational
state school

la **laisse** FEM NOUN
lead
□ Tenez votre chien en laisse. Keep your dog on
a lead.

laisser VERB [28]
1 to leave
□ J'ai laissé mon parapluie à la maison. I've left
my umbrella at home.
2 to let
□ Laisse-le parler. Let him speak.
■ Il se laisse aller. He's letting himself go.

le **laisser-aller** MASC NOUN
carelessness

le **lait** MASC NOUN
milk
■ un café au lait a white coffee

la **laitue** FEM NOUN
lettuce

les **lambeaux** MASC PL NOUN
■ en lambeaux tattered

la **lame** FEM NOUN
blade
□ une lame de rasoir a razor blade

la **lamelle** FEM NOUN
thin strip

lamentable (FEM **lamentable**) ADJECTIVE
appalling

se **lamenter** VERB [28]
to moan

le **lampadaire** MASC NOUN
standard lamp

la **lampe** FEM NOUN
lamp
■ une lampe de poche a torch

la **lance** FEM NOUN
spear

le **lancement** MASC NOUN
launch

lancer VERB [12]
▷ *see also* **lancer** NOUN
1 to throw
□ Lance-moi le ballon ! Throw me the ball!
2 to launch
□ Ils viennent de lancer un nouveau modèle.
They've just launched a new model.
■ se lancer dans to embark on □ Il s'est lancé
là-dedans sans bien réfléchir. He embarked on it
without thinking properly.

le **lancer** MASC NOUN
▷ *see also* **lancer** VERB
■ le lancer de poids putting the shot

lancinant (FEM **lancinante**) ADJECTIVE
■ une douleur lancinante a shooting pain

le **landau** MASC NOUN
pram

la **lande** FEM NOUN
moor

le **langage** MASC NOUN
language

la **langouste** FEM NOUN
crayfish

la **langue** FEM NOUN
1 tongue
□ Il m'a tiré la langue. He stuck out his tongue
at me.
2 language
□ une langue étrangère a foreign language
■ les langues vivantes modern languages
■ sa langue maternelle his mother tongue

la **lanière** FEM NOUN
strap

le **lapin** MASC NOUN
rabbit

le **laps** MASC NOUN
■ un laps de temps a space of time

la **laque** FEM NOUN
hair spray

laquelle (PL **lesquelles**) FEM PRONOUN
1 which
□ Laquelle de ces photos préfères-tu ? Which of
these photos do you prefer? □ À laquelle de tes
sœurs ressembles-tu ? Which of your sisters do
you look like?
2 whom
□ la personne à laquelle vous faites référence
the person to whom you are referring

⎡ **laquelle** is often not translated in English. ⎤

□ la personne à laquelle je pense the person I'm
thinking of

le **lard** MASC NOUN
streaky bacon

les **lardons** MASC PL NOUN
chunks of bacon

large (FEM **large**) ADJECTIVE, ADVERB
▷ *see also* **large** NOUN
wide
■ **voir large** to allow a bit extra □ Achète un autre pain : il vaut mieux voir large. Buy another loaf of bread: it's better to have a bit extra.

le **large** MASC NOUN
▷ *see also* **large** ADJECTIVE, ADVERB
■ **cinq mètres de large** 5 m wide
■ **le large** the open sea
■ **au large de** off the coast of □ Le bateau est actuellement au large du Portugal. The boat is off the coast of Portugal at the moment.

> **BE CAREFUL!**
> The French word **large** does not mean **large**.

largement ADVERB
■ **Vous avez largement le temps.** You have plenty of time.
■ **C'est largement suffisant.** That's ample.

la **largeur** FEM NOUN
width

la **larme** FEM NOUN
tear
□ être en larmes to be in tears

la **laryngite** FEM NOUN
laryngitis

le **laser** MASC NOUN
laser
■ **une platine laser** a compact disc player
■ **un disque laser** a compact disc

lasser VERB [28]
■ **se lasser de** to get tired of □ Tu vas te lasser de cette couleur. You're going to get tired of this colour.

le **latin** MASC NOUN
Latin

le **laurier** MASC NOUN
laurel tree
□ une feuille de laurier a bay leaf

lavable (FEM **lavable**) ADJECTIVE
washable

le **lavabo** MASC NOUN
washbasin

le **lavage** MASC NOUN
wash
□ Ce pull a rétréci au lavage. This jumper has shrunk in the wash.

la **lavande** FEM NOUN
lavender

le **lave-linge** (PL les **lave-linges**, les **lave-linge**) MASC NOUN
washing machine

laver VERB [28]
to wash
■ **se laver** to wash □ se laver les mains to wash one's hands

la **laverie** FEM NOUN
■ **une laverie automatique** a launderette

le **lave-vaisselle** (PL les **lave-vaisselles**, les **lave-vaisselle**) MASC NOUN
dishwasher

le ARTICLE, PRONOUN

> **le** changes to **l'** before a vowel and most words beginning with 'h'.

1 the
□ le livre the book □ l'arbre the tree
□ l'hélicoptère the helicopter

2 him
□ Martin est un vieil ami : je le connais depuis plus de vingt ans. Martin is an old friend: I've known him for over 20 years.

3 it
□ Où est mon stylo ? Je ne le trouve plus. Where's my pen? I can't find it. □ Où est le fromage ? — Je l'ai mis au frigo. Where's the cheese? — I've put it in the fridge.

4 one's
■ **se laver le visage** to wash one's face □ Évitez de vous laver le visage avec du savon. Avoid washing your face with soap.
■ **dix euros le kilo** 10 euros a kilo
■ **Il est arrivé le douze mai.** He arrived on 12 May.

le **leader** MASC NOUN
leader
□ le leader mondial de l'industrie automobile the world leader in the car industry

lécher VERB [34]
to lick

le **lèche-vitrine** MASC NOUN
■ **faire du lèche-vitrine** to go window-shopping

la **leçon** FEM NOUN
lesson

le **lecteur** MASC NOUN
1 reader
2 foreign language assistant (*at a university*)
■ **un lecteur de CD** a CD player
■ **un lecteur de DVD** a DVD player
■ **un lecteur MP3** an MP3 player

la **lectrice** FEM NOUN
1 reader
2 foreign language assistant (*at a university*)

la **lecture** FEM NOUN
reading

> **BE CAREFUL!**
> The French word **lecture** does not mean **lecture**.

légal (FEM **légale**, MASC PL **légaux**) ADJECTIVE
legal

la **légende** FEM NOUN
1 legend
2 key (of map)
3 caption (of picture)

léger (FEM **légère**) ADJECTIVE
1 light
2 slight
□ un léger retard a slight delay
■ **à la légère** thoughtlessly □ Il a agi à la légère. He acted thoughtlessly.

légèrement ADVERB
1 lightly
□ Habille-toi légèrement : il va faire chaud. Wear light clothes: it's going to be hot.
2 slightly
□ Il est légèrement plus grand que son frère. He's slightly taller than his brother.

les **leggings** MASC PL NOUN
leggings

les **législatives** FEM PL NOUN
general election sing

le **légume** MASC NOUN
vegetable

le **lendemain** MASC NOUN
next day
■ **le lendemain de son arrivée** the day after he arrived
■ **le lendemain matin** the next morning

lent (FEM **lente**) ADJECTIVE
slow

lentement ADVERB
slowly

la **lenteur** FEM NOUN
slowness

la **lentille** FEM NOUN
1 contact lens
□ Est-ce que tu portes des lentilles ? Do you wear contact lenses?
2 lentil
□ un rôti de porc aux lentilles roast pork with lentils

le **léopard** MASC NOUN
leopard

le **LEP** MASC NOUN (= lycée d'enseignement professionnel)
vocational school

lequel (FEM **laquelle**, MASC PL **lesquels**, FEM PL **lesquelles**) PRONOUN
1 which
□ Lequel de ces films as-tu préféré ? Which of the films did you prefer?
2 whom
□ l'homme avec lequel elle a été vue pour la

dernière fois the man with whom she was last seen

| **lequel** is often not translated in English. |

□ le garçon avec lequel elle est sortie the boy she went out with

les ARTICLE, PRONOUN
1 the
□ les arbres the trees
2 them
□ Elle les a invités à dîner. She invited them to dinner.
3 one's
■ **se brosser les dents** to brush one's teeth
□ Elle s'est brossé les dents. She brushed her teeth.
■ **dix euros les cinq** 10 euros for 5

la **lesbienne** FEM NOUN
lesbian

lesquels (FEM **lesquelles**) PL PRONOUN
1 which
□ Lesquelles de ces photos préfères-tu ? Which of the photos do you prefer?
2 whom
□ les personnes avec lesquelles il est associé the people with whom he is in partnership

| **lesquels** is often not translated in English. |

□ les gens chez lesquels nous avons dîné the people we had dinner with

la **lessive** FEM NOUN
1 washing powder
□ une marque de lessive a brand of washing powder
2 washing (laundry)
□ Il y a beaucoup de lessive à faire. There's a lot of washing to do.
■ **faire la lessive** to do the washing

leste (FEM **leste**) ADJECTIVE
nimble

la **Lettonie** FEM NOUN
Latvia

la **lettre** FEM NOUN
letter
□ écrire une lettre to write a letter
■ **une lettre de motivation** a covering letter (with CV)

les **lettres** FEM PL NOUN
arts
□ la faculté de lettres the Faculty of Arts

leur (FEM **leur**) ADJECTIVE, PRONOUN
1 their
□ leur ami their friend
2 them
□ Je leur ai dit la vérité. I told them the truth.
3 to them
□ Je le leur ai donné. I gave it to them.
■ **le leur** theirs □ mon camion et le leur my

truck and theirs □ Ma voiture est rouge, la leur est bleue. My car's red, theirs is blue.

leurs (FEM **leurs**) PL ADJECTIVE, PL PRONOUN
their
□ leurs amis their friends
■ **les leurs** theirs □ tes livres et les leurs your books and theirs

levé (FEM **levée**) ADJECTIVE
▷ see also **levé** NOUN
■ **être levé** to be up □ Il est levé ? Is he up?

la **levée** FEM NOUN
▷ see also **levé** ADJECTIVE
collection (of mail)
□ Prochaine levée : 17 heures Next collection: 5 p.m.

lever VERB [43]
▷ see also **lever** NOUN
to raise
□ Levez vos verres ! Raise your glasses!
■ **Levez la main !** Put your hand up!
■ **lever les yeux** to look up
■ **se lever** **1** to get up □ Il se lève tous les jours à six heures. He gets up at 6 o'clock every day. □ Lève-toi ! Get up! **2** to rise □ Le soleil se lève actuellement à cinq heures. At the moment the sun rises at 5 o'clock. **3** to stand up □ Levez-vous ! Stand up!

le **lever** MASC NOUN
▷ see also **lever** VERB
■ **le lever du soleil** sunrise

le **levier** MASC NOUN
lever

la **lèvre** FEM NOUN
lip

le **lévrier** MASC NOUN
greyhound

la **levure** FEM NOUN
yeast
■ **la levure chimique** baking powder

le **lexique** MASC NOUN
word list

le **lézard** MASC NOUN
lizard

LGBTQ (FEM+PL **LGBTQ**) ADJECTIVE (= *lesbienne, gay, bisexuel, transgenre, queer/en questionnement*)
LGBTQ
□ la communauté LGBTQ the LGBTQ community

la **liaison** FEM NOUN
affair
□ Ils ont eu une liaison dans leur jeunesse. They had an affair when they were younger.

la **libellule** FEM NOUN
dragonfly

libéral (FEM **libérale**, MASC PL **libéraux**)
ADJECTIVE
liberal

la **libération** FEM NOUN
1 liberation
□ la libération de Paris en août 1944 the liberation of Paris in August 1944
2 release
□ la libération des prisonniers the release of prisoners

libérer VERB [34]
to free
□ Les otages ont été libérés hier soir. The hostages were freed last night.
■ **se libérer** to find time □ Essaie de te libérer demain. Try to find time tomorrow.

la **liberté** FEM NOUN
freedom
■ **mettre en liberté** to release □ Il a été mis en liberté au bout d'un an de prison. He was released after a year in prison.

le/la **libraire** MASC/FEM NOUN
bookseller

la **librairie** FEM NOUN
bookshop

BE CAREFUL!
librairie does not mean **library**.

libre (FEM **libre**) ADJECTIVE
1 free
□ Tu es libre de faire ce que tu veux. You are free to do as you wish. □ Est-ce que cette place est libre ? Is this seat free?
■ **Avez-vous une chambre de libre ?** Have you got a free room?
2 clear
□ La route est libre : vous pouvez traverser. The road is clear: you can cross.

le **libre-service** (PL les **libres-services**) MASC NOUN
self-service store

la **Libye** FEM NOUN
Libya

la **licence** FEM NOUN
1 degree
□ une licence de droit a law degree
2 licence
□ une licence d'exportation an export licence

le **licencié** MASC NOUN
graduate

la **licenciée** FEM NOUN
graduate

le **licenciement** MASC NOUN
redundancy

licencier VERB [19]
to make redundant
□ Ils viennent de licencier sept employés. They've just made 7 employees redundant.

le **liège** MASC NOUN
cork
■ **un bouchon en liège** a cork (*for bottle*)

le lien MASC NOUN
1 connection
□ Il n'y a aucun lien entre ces deux événements. There's no connection between these two events.
■ **un lien de parenté** a family tie
2 link (*in computing*)

lier VERB [19]
■ **lier conversation avec quelqu'un** to get into conversation with somebody
■ **se lier avec quelqu'un** to make friends with somebody □ Je ne me lie pas facilement. I don't make friends easily.

le lierre MASC NOUN
ivy

le lieu (PL les **lieux**) MASC NOUN
place
□ votre lieu de travail your place of work
■ **avoir lieu** to take place □ La cérémonie a eu lieu dans la salle des fêtes. The ceremony took place in the village hall.
■ **au lieu de** instead of □ J'aimerais une pomme au lieu de la glace. I'd like an apple instead of ice cream.

le lièvre MASC NOUN
hare

la ligne FEM NOUN
1 line (*phone, train*)
□ La ligne est mauvaise. It's a bad line.
■ **la ligne de bus numéro six** the number 6 bus
■ **en ligne** (*computing*) online
■ **mettre en ligne** (*computing*) to upload
■ **une ligne fixe** a landline □ Je t'appelle sur ta ligne fixe ? Shall I ring you on your landline?
2 figure
□ C'est mauvais pour la ligne. It's bad for your figure.

ligoter VERB [28]
to tie up

la ligue FEM NOUN
league

le lilas MASC NOUN
lilac

la limace FEM NOUN
slug

la lime FEM NOUN
■ **une lime à ongles** a nail file

la limitation FEM NOUN
■ **la limitation de vitesse** the speed limit

la limite FEM NOUN
1 boundary (*of property, football pitch*)
2 limit
□ Est-ce qu'il y a une limite d'âge ? Is there an age limit?
■ **À la limite, on pourrait prendre le bus.** At a pinch we could go by bus.

■ **la date limite** the deadline
■ **la date limite de vente** the sell-by date

limiter VERB [28]
to limit
□ Le nombre de billets est limité à deux par personne. The number of tickets is limited to two per person.

la limonade FEM NOUN
lemonade

le lin MASC NOUN
linen
□ une veste en lin a linen jacket

le linge MASC NOUN
1 linen
□ le linge sale dirty linen
2 washing
□ laver le linge to do the washing
■ **du linge de corps** underwear

la lingerie FEM NOUN
underwear (*women's*)

le lion MASC NOUN
lion
■ **le Lion** Leo □ Louise est Lion. Louise is Leo.

la lionne FEM NOUN
lioness

la liqueur FEM NOUN
liqueur

liquide (FEM **liquide**) ADJECTIVE
▷ *see also* **liquide** NOUN
liquid

le liquide MASC NOUN
▷ *see also* **liquide** ADJECTIVE
liquid
■ **payer quelque chose en liquide** to pay cash for something

lire VERB [44]
to read
□ Tu as lu « Madame Bovary » ? Have you read 'Madame Bovary'?

lis, lisent, lisez VERB ▷ *see* **lire**
■ Je lis beaucoup. I read a lot.

lisible (FEM **lisible**) ADJECTIVE
legible

lisse (FEM **lisse**) ADJECTIVE
smooth

le lisseur MASC NOUN
hair straighteners

la liste FEM NOUN
list
■ **faire la liste de** to make a list of □ J'ai fait la liste de tout ce dont j'ai besoin. I've made a list of all the things I need.

le lit MASC NOUN
bed
□ un grand lit a double bed □ lits jumeaux twin beds □ aller au lit to go to bed

■ **faire son lit** to make one's bed □ Il ne fait jamais son lit. He never makes his bed.

■ **un lit de camp** a campbed

lit VERB ▷ *see* lire

la **literie** FEM NOUN
bedding

la **litière** FEM NOUN
1 litter (*for cat*)
2 bedding (*of caged pet*)

le **litre** MASC NOUN
litre

littéraire (FEM **littéraire**) ADJECTIVE
■ **une œuvre littéraire** a work of literature

la **littérature** FEM NOUN
literature

le **littoral** (PL les **littoraux**) MASC NOUN
coast

la **Lituanie** FEM NOUN
Lithuania

la **livraison** FEM NOUN
delivery
■ **la livraison des bagages** baggage reclaim

le **livre** MASC NOUN
▷ *see also* **livre** NOUN
book
■ **un livre numérique** an e-book
■ **un livre de poche** a paperback

la **livre** FEM NOUN
▷ *see also* **livre** NOUN
pound

DID YOU KNOW...?
The French **livre** is 500 grams.

□ une livre de beurre a pound of butter
■ **la livre sterling** the pound sterling □ Ce jouet coûte trois livres. This toy costs £3.

livrer VERB [28]
to deliver

le **livret** MASC NOUN
booklet
■ **le livret scolaire** the school report book

le **livreur** MASC NOUN
delivery man

local (FEM **locale**, MASC PL **locaux**) ADJECTIVE
▷ *see also* **local** NOUN
local

le **local** (PL les **locaux**) MASC NOUN
▷ *see also* **local** ADJECTIVE
premises
□ Nous cherchons un local pour les répétitions. We are looking for premises to rehearse in.

le/la **locataire** MASC/FEM NOUN
1 tenant
2 lodger
□ Ils ont décidé de prendre un locataire. They have decided to take a lodger.

la **location** FEM NOUN
■ **location de voitures** car rental
■ **location de skis** ski hire

BE CAREFUL!
The French word **location** does not mean **location**.

la **locomotive** FEM NOUN
locomotive

la **loge** FEM NOUN
dressing room

le **logement** MASC NOUN
1 housing
2 accommodation

loger VERB [45]
to stay
□ Elle loge chez sa cousine quand elle revient dans la région. She stays with her cousin when she comes back to the area.
■ **trouver à se loger** to find somewhere to live □ J'ai eu du mal à trouver à me loger. I had difficulty finding somewhere to live.

le **logiciel** MASC NOUN
software

logique (FEM **logique**) ADJECTIVE
▷ *see also* **logique** NOUN
logical

la **logique** FEM NOUN
▷ *see also* **logique** ADJECTIVE
logic

la **loi** FEM NOUN
law

loin ADVERB
1 far
□ La gare n'est pas très loin d'ici. The station is not very far from here.
2 far off
□ Noël n'est plus tellement loin. Christmas isn't far off now.
3 a long time ago
□ Les vacances paraissent déjà tellement loin ! The holidays already seem such a long time ago!
■ **au loin** in the distance □ On aperçoit la mer au loin. You can see the sea in the distance.
■ **de loin 1** from a long way away □ On voit l'église de loin. You can see the church from a long way away. **2** by far □ C'est de loin l'élève la plus brillante. She is by far the brightest pupil.
■ **C'est plus loin que la gare.** It's further on than the station.

lointain (FEM **lointaine**) ADJECTIVE
▷ *see also* **lointain** NOUN
distant
□ un pays lointain a distant country □ C'est un lointain parent de ma mère. He's a distant relation of my mother.

le **lointain** MASC NOUN
▷ see also **lointain** ADJECTIVE
- **dans le lointain** in the distance

le **loir** MASC NOUN
dormouse
- **dormir comme un loir** to sleep like a log

les loisirs MASC PL NOUN
1 free time sing
□ Qu'est-ce que vous faites pendant vos loisirs ? What do you do in your free time?
2 hobby
□ Le ski et l'équitation sont des loisirs coûteux. Skiing and riding are expensive hobbies.

le **Londonien** MASC NOUN
Londoner

la **Londonienne** FEM NOUN
Londoner

Londres NOUN
London
□ le métro de Londres the London underground
- **à Londres 1** in London **2** to London

long (FEM **longue**) ADJECTIVE
▷ see also **long** NOUN, **longue** NOUN
long

le **long** MASC NOUN
▷ see also **long** ADJECTIVE
- **un bateau de trois mètres de long** a boat 3 m long
- **tout le long de** all along □ Il y a des chemins de randonnée tout le long de la côte. There are footpaths all along the coast.
- **marcher de long en large** to walk up and down

longer VERB [45]
- **La route longe la forêt.** The road runs along the edge of the forest.
- **Nous avons longé la Seine à pied.** We walked along the Seine.

longtemps ADVERB
a long time
□ J'ai attendu longtemps chez le dentiste. I waited a long time at the dentist's.
- **pendant longtemps** for a long time □ On a cru pendant longtemps que la Terre était plate. For a long time people thought the Earth was flat.
- **mettre longtemps à faire quelque chose** to take a long time to do something □ Il a mis longtemps à répondre à ma lettre. He took a long time to answer my letter.

la **longue** FEM NOUN
▷ see also **long** ADJECTIVE
- **à la longue** in the end □ Elle a fini par agacer tout le monde à la longue. In the end she got on everybody's nerves.

longuement ADVERB
at length

□ Elle m'a longuement parlé de ses projets d'avenir. She talked to me at length about her plans for the future.

la **longueur** FEM NOUN
length
- **à longueur de journée** all day long □ Elle mâche du chewing-gum à longueur de journée. She chews gum all day long.

le **look** MASC NOUN
look
□ Il a un look d'enfer. He looks so cool.

les loques FEM PL NOUN
- **être en loques** to be torn to bits □ Sa chemise était en loques. His shirt was torn to bits.

lors de PREPOSITION
during
□ Je l'ai rencontré lors de mon stage en entreprise. I met him during my work placement.

lorsque CONJUNCTION
when
□ J'allais composer ton numéro lorsque tu as appelé. I was about to dial your number when you called.

le **lot** MASC NOUN
prize
- **le gros lot** the jackpot

la **loterie** FEM NOUN
1 lottery
□ la loterie nationale the National Lottery
2 raffle
□ J'ai gagné cet ours en peluche dans une loterie. I won this teddy in a raffle.

la **lotion** FEM NOUN
lotion
□ une bouteille de lotion solaire a bottle of suntan lotion
- **une lotion après-rasage** aftershave
- **une lotion démaquillante** cleansing milk

le **lotissement** MASC NOUN
housing estate

le **loto** MASC NOUN
lottery
- **le loto sportif** the pools

le **loubard** MASC NOUN (informal)
lout

louche (FEM **louche**) ADJECTIVE
▷ see also **louche** NOUN
fishy
□ une histoire louche a fishy story

la **louche** FEM NOUN
▷ see also **louche** ADJECTIVE
ladle

loucher VERB [28]
to squint

louer VERB [28]
1 to let
□ Ils louent des chambres à des étudiants. They let rooms to students.
■ « **à louer** » 'to let'

2 to rent
□ Je loue un petit appartement au centre-ville. I rent a little flat in the centre of town.

3 to hire
□ Est-ce que vous louez des vélos ? Do you hire bikes? □ Nous allons louer une voiture. We're going to hire a car.

4 to praise
□ Les journaux ont loué le courage des pompiers. The newspapers praised the courage of the firefighters.

le **loup** MASC NOUN
wolf
■ **J'ai une faim de loup !** I'm ravenous!

la **loupe** FEM NOUN
magnifying glass

louper VERB [28] (*informal*)
to miss
□ J'ai loupé mon bus. I've missed my bus.

lourd (FEM **lourde**) ADJECTIVE
▷ *see also* **lourd** ADVERB
heavy
□ Mon sac est très lourd. My bag's very heavy.

lourd ADVERB
▷ *see also* **lourd** ADJECTIVE
close (*weather*)
□ Il fait très lourd aujourd'hui. It's very close today.

la **loutre** FEM NOUN
otter

la **loyauté** FEM NOUN
loyalty

le **loyer** MASC NOUN
rent

lu VERB ▷ *see* **lire**

la **lucarne** FEM NOUN
skylight

la **luge** FEM NOUN
sledge

lugubre (FEM **lugubre**) ADJECTIVE
gloomy

lui PRONOUN
1 him
□ Il a été très content du cadeau que je lui ai offert. He was very pleased with the present I gave him. □ C'est bien lui ! It's definitely him! □ J'ai pensé à lui toute la journée. I thought about him all day long.

2 to him
□ Mon père est d'accord : je lui ai parlé ce matin. My father said yes: I spoke to him this morning.

3 her
□ Elle a été très contente du cadeau que je lui ai offert. She was very pleased with the present I gave her.

4 to her
□ Ma mère est d'accord : je lui ai parlé ce matin. My mother said yes: I spoke to her this morning.

5 it
□ Qu'est-ce que tu donnes à ton chat ? — Je lui donne de la viande crue. What do you give your cat? — I give it raw meat.

lui is also used for emphasis.

□ Lui, il est toujours en retard ! Oh him, he's always late!
■ **lui-même** himself □ Il a construit son bateau lui-même. He built his boat himself.
■ **à lui** his □ Ce n'est pas à lui, ce sac ? This isn't his bag, is it?

la **lumière** FEM NOUN
light
■ **la lumière du jour** daylight

lumineux (FEM **lumineuse**) ADJECTIVE
■ **une enseigne lumineuse** a neon sign

lunatique (FEM **lunatique**) ADJECTIVE
temperamental
□ Il est plutôt lunatique. He's rather temperamental.

le **lundi** MASC NOUN
1 Monday
□ Aujourd'hui, nous sommes lundi. It's Monday today.

2 on Monday
□ Ils sont arrivés lundi. They arrived on Monday.
■ **le lundi** on Mondays □ Le lundi, je vais à la piscine. I go swimming on Mondays.
■ **tous les lundis** every Monday
■ **lundi dernier** last Monday
■ **lundi prochain** next Monday
■ **le lundi de Pâques** Easter Monday
■ **À lundi !** See you on Monday!

la **lune** FEM NOUN
moon
■ **la lune de miel** honeymoon

les **lunettes** FEM PL NOUN
glasses
■ **des lunettes de soleil** sunglasses
■ **des lunettes de plongée** swimming goggles

la **lutte** FEM NOUN
1 fight
□ la lutte contre le racisme the fight against racism

2 wrestling
□ une épreuve de lutte a wrestling bout

lutter VERB [28]
to fight

le **luxe** MASC NOUN
luxury
■ **de luxe** luxury □ un hôtel de luxe a luxury hotel

luxueux (FEM **luxueuse**) ADJECTIVE
luxurious

le **lycée** MASC NOUN
secondary school
■ **lycée technique** technical college

le **lycéen** MASC NOUN
secondary school pupil

la **lycéenne** FEM NOUN
secondary school pupil

Mm

M. ABBREVIATION (= *Monsieur*)
Mr
□ M. Bernard Mr Bernard

m' PRONOUN ▷ *see* me

ma FEM ADJECTIVE
my
□ ma mère my mother □ ma montre my watch

les **macaronis** MASC PL NOUN
macaroni *sing*

la **Macédoine** FEM NOUN
Macedonia

la **macédoine** FEM NOUN
■ **la macédoine de fruits** fruit salad
■ **la macédoine de légumes** mixed vegetables

mâcher VERB [28]
to chew

le **machin** MASC NOUN (*informal*)
thingy
□ Passe-moi le machin pour râper les carottes.
Pass me the thingy for grating carrots. □ Qu'est-
ce que c'est que ce vieux machin ? What's this
old thing?

machinalement ADVERB
■ **Elle a regardé sa montre machinalement.**
She looked at her watch without thinking.

la **machine** FEM NOUN
machine
■ **une machine à laver** a washing machine
■ **une machine à écrire** a typewriter
■ **une machine à coudre** a sewing machine
■ **une machine à sous** a fruit machine

le **machiste** MASC NOUN
male chauvinist

le **macho** MASC NOUN (*informal*)
male chauvinist pig

la **mâchoire** FEM NOUN
jaw

mâchonner VERB [28]
to chew

le **maçon** MASC NOUN
builder

Madagascar MASC NOUN
Madagascar

Madame (PL **Mesdames**) FEM NOUN
1 Mrs
□ Madame Legall Mrs Legall

2 lady
□ Occupez-vous de Madame. Could you look
after this lady?

3 Madam
□ Madame, ... Dear Madam, ... (*in letter*)
■ **Madame ! Vous avez oublié votre
parapluie !** Excuse me! You've forgotten your
umbrella!

Mademoiselle (PL **Mesdemoiselles**) FEM
NOUN
1 Miss
□ Mademoiselle Martin Miss Martin

2 Madam
□ Mademoiselle, ... Dear Madam, ... (*in letter*)

le **magasin** MASC NOUN
shop
□ Les magasins ouvrent à huit heures. The
shops open at 8 o'clock.
■ **faire les magasins** to go shopping

le **magazine** MASC NOUN
magazine

le **magicien** MASC NOUN
magician

la **magicienne** FEM NOUN
magician

la **magie** FEM NOUN
magic
□ un tour de magie a magic trick

magique (FEM **magique**) ADJECTIVE
magic
□ une baguette magique a magic wand

magistral (FEM **magistrale**, MASC PL
magistraux) ADJECTIVE
■ **un cours magistral** a lecture (*at university*)

magnétique (FEM **magnétique**) ADJECTIVE
magnetic

le **magnétoscope** MASC NOUN
video recorder

magnifique (FEM **magnifique**) ADJECTIVE
superb

mai MASC NOUN
May
■ **en mai** in May

maigre (FEM **maigre**) ADJECTIVE
1 skinny

Numbers in brackets refer to verb tables on pages 650 to 658

□ Ma mère me trouve trop maigre. **My mother says I'm too skinny.**
2 lean (*meat*)
3 low-fat (*cheese, yoghurt*)

maigrir VERB [38]
to lose weight
□ Il fait un régime pour essayer de maigrir. **He's on a diet, to try to lose weight.** □ Elle a maigri de deux kilos en un mois. **She's lost two kilos in a month.**

le mail MASC NOUN
email

le maillot de bain MASC NOUN
1 swimsuit
2 swimming trunks

la main FEM NOUN
hand
□ Donne-moi la main ! **Give me your hand!**
■ **serrer la main à quelqu'un** to shake hands with somebody
■ **se serrer la main** to shake hands □ Les deux présidents se sont serré la main. **The two presidents shook hands.**
■ **sous la main** to hand □ Est-ce que tu as son adresse sous la main ? **Have you got his address to hand?**

la main-d'œuvre FEM NOUN
workforce
□ la main-d'œuvre de l'usine **the workforce of the factory**
■ **la main-d'œuvre immigrée** immigrant labour

maintenant ADVERB
1 now
□ Qu'est-ce que tu veux faire maintenant ? **What do you want to do now?** □ C'est maintenant ou jamais. **It's now or never.**
2 nowadays
□ Maintenant la plupart des gens font leurs courses au supermarché. **Nowadays most people do their shopping at the supermarket.**

maintenir VERB [83]
to maintain
□ Il maintient qu'il est innocent. **He maintains he is innocent.**
■ **se maintenir** to hold □ Espérons que le beau temps va se maintenir pour le week-end ! **Let's hope the good weather will hold over the weekend!**

le maire MASC NOUN
mayor

la mairie FEM NOUN
town hall

mais CONJUNCTION
but
□ C'est cher mais de très bonne qualité. **It's expensive, but very good quality.**

le maïs MASC NOUN
1 maize
2 sweetcorn

la maison FEM NOUN
▷ *see also* **maison** ADJECTIVE
house
□ C'est la maison de Julie. **It's Julie's house.**
■ **une maison des jeunes** a youth club
■ **une maison individuelle** a detached house
■ **une maison jumelée** a semi-detached house
■ **une maison mitoyenne** a terraced house
■ **une maison de retraite** a retirement home
■ **à la maison 1** at home □ Je serai à la maison cet après-midi. **I'll be at home this afternoon.**
2 home □ Elle est rentrée à la maison. **She's gone home.**

maison (FEM+PL **maison**) ADJECTIVE
▷ *see also* **maison** NOUN
home-made
□ Je préfère les tartes maison à celles qu'on achète. **I prefer home-made pies to bought ones.**

le maître MASC NOUN
1 teacher (*in primary school*)
2 master (*of dog*)
■ **un maître d'hôtel** a head waiter (*in restaurant*)
■ **un maître nageur** a lifeguard

la maîtresse FEM NOUN
1 teacher (*in primary school*)
2 mistress
□ Il paraît qu'il a une maîtresse. **They say he's got a mistress.**

la maîtrise FEM NOUN
master's degree
□ Elle a une maîtrise d'anglais. **She's got a master's degree in English.**
■ **la maîtrise de soi** self-control

maîtriser VERB [28]
■ **se maîtriser** to control oneself □ Il se met facilement en colère et a du mal à se maîtriser. **He loses his temper easily and finds it hard to control himself.**

majestueux (FEM **majestueuse**) ADJECTIVE
majestic

majeur (FEM **majeure**) ADJECTIVE
■ **être majeur** to be 18 □ Tu feras ce que tu voudras quand tu seras majeure. **You can do what you like once you're 18.** □ Elle sera majeure en août. **She will be 18 in August.**
■ **la majeure partie** most □ la majeure partie de mon salaire **most of my salary**

la majorité FEM NOUN
majority
□ dans la majorité des cas **in the majority of cases**

Majorque – malheureux

■ **la majorité et l'opposition** the government and the opposition

Majorque FEM NOUN
Majorca

la **majuscule** FEM NOUN
capital letter
□ un M majuscule a capital M

mal (FEM+PL **mal**) ADVERB, ADJECTIVE
▷ *see also* **mal** NOUN

1 badly
□ Ce travail a été mal fait. **The work was badly done.**
■ **Il a mal compris.** He misunderstood.

2 wrong
□ C'est mal de mentir. **It's wrong to tell lies.**
■ **aller mal** to be ill □ Son grand-père va très mal. **His grandfather is very ill.**
■ **pas mal** quite good □ Je te trouve pas mal sur cette photo. **I think you look quite good in this photo.**

le **mal** (PL les **maux**) MASC NOUN
▷ *see also* **mal** ADVERB, ADJECTIVE

1 ache
□ J'ai mal à la tête. **I've got a headache.** □ J'ai mal aux dents. **I've got toothache.**
■ **J'ai mal au dos.** My back hurts.
■ **Est-ce que vous avez mal à la gorge ?** Have you got a sore throat?
■ **Ça fait mal.** It hurts.
■ **Où est-ce que tu as mal ?** Where does it hurt?
■ **faire mal à quelqu'un** to hurt somebody □ Attention, tu me fais mal ! **Be careful, you're hurting me!**
■ **se faire mal** to hurt oneself □ Je me suis fait mal au bras. **I hurt my arm.**
■ **se donner du mal pour faire quelque chose** to go to a lot of trouble to do something □ Il s'est donné beaucoup de mal pour que cette soirée soit réussie. **He went to a lot of trouble to make the party a success.**
■ **avoir le mal de mer** to be seasick
■ **avoir le mal du pays** to be homesick

2 evil
□ le bien et le mal good and evil
■ **dire du mal de quelqu'un** to speak ill of somebody

malade (FEM **malade**) ADJECTIVE
▷ *see also* **malade** NOUN
ill
■ **tomber malade** to fall ill

le/la **malade** MASC/FEM NOUN
▷ *see also* **malade** ADJECTIVE
patient

la **maladie** FEM NOUN
illness

maladif (FEM **maladive**) ADJECTIVE
sickly
□ C'est un enfant maladif. **He's a sickly child.**

la **maladresse** FEM NOUN
clumsiness

maladroit (FEM **maladroite**) ADJECTIVE
clumsy

le **malaise** MASC NOUN
■ **avoir un malaise** to feel faint □ Elle a eu un malaise après le déjeuner. **She felt faint after lunch.**
■ **Son arrivée a créé un malaise parmi les invités.** Her arrival made the guests feel uncomfortable.

la **malchance** FEM NOUN
bad luck

mâle (FEM **mâle**) ADJECTIVE
male

la **malédiction** FEM NOUN
curse

mal en point (FEM+PL **mal en point**) ADJECTIVE
■ **Il avait l'air mal en point quand je l'ai vu hier soir.** He didn't look too good when I saw him last night.

le **malentendu** MASC NOUN
misunderstanding

le **malfaiteur** MASC NOUN
criminal

mal famé (FEM **mal famée**, MASC PL **mal famés**) ADJECTIVE
■ **un quartier mal famé** a seedy area

malgache (FEM **malgache**) ADJECTIVE
from Madagascar
□ Sa mère est malgache. **His mother's from Madagascar.**

malgré PREPOSITION
in spite of
□ Il est toujours généreux malgré ses problèmes d'argent. **He's always generous in spite of his financial problems.**
■ **malgré tout** all the same □ Il faisait mauvais mais nous sommes sortis malgré tout. **The weather was bad but we went out all the same.**

le **malheur** MASC NOUN
tragedy
□ Elle a eu beaucoup de malheurs dans sa vie. **She's had a lot of tragedy in her life.**
■ **faire un malheur** (*informal*) to be a smash hit □ Leur dernier album a fait un malheur. **Their latest album was a smash hit.**

malheureusement ADVERB
unfortunately

malheureux (FEM **malheureuse**) ADJECTIVE
miserable
□ Il a l'air malheureux. **He looks miserable.**

Numbers in brackets refer to verb tables on pages 650 to 658

malhonnête (FEM **malhonnête**) ADJECTIVE
dishonest

la malice FEM NOUN
mischief
□ Son regard était plein de malice. His eyes were full of mischief.

malicieux (FEM **malicieuse**) ADJECTIVE
mischievous

> **BE CAREFUL!**
> malicieux does not mean **malicious**.

malin (FEM **maligne**) ADJECTIVE
crafty
■ **C'est malin!** (*informal*) That's clever! □ Ah c'est malin! Nous voilà enfermés à cause de toi! That's clever! You've got us locked in!

la malle FEM NOUN
trunk

malsain (FEM **malsaine**) ADJECTIVE
unhealthy

Malte MASC NOUN
Malta

maltraiter VERB [28]
to ill-treat
□ Il maltraite son chien. He ill-treats his dog.
■ **des enfants maltraités** battered children

malveillant (FEM **malveillante**) ADJECTIVE
malicious
□ des rumeurs malveillantes malicious rumours

la maman FEM NOUN
mum

la mamie FEM NOUN
granny

le mammifère MASC NOUN
mammal

la manche FEM NOUN
▷ *see also* **manche** NOUN
1 sleeve (*of clothes*)
2 leg (*of game*)
□ Ils ont gagné la première manche du match. They won the first leg of the match.
■ **la Manche** the Channel

le manche MASC NOUN
▷ *see also* **manche** NOUN
handle (*of pan*)

la mandarine FEM NOUN
mandarin orange

le manège MASC NOUN
merry-go-round

la manette FEM NOUN
lever

mangeable (FEM **mangeable**) ADJECTIVE
edible
□ C'est à peine mangeable! It's practically inedible!

manger VERB [45]
to eat

la mangue FEM NOUN
mango

maniaque (FEM **maniaque**) ADJECTIVE
fussy

la manie FEM NOUN
1 obsession
■ **avoir la manie de** to be obsessive about □ Il a la manie du rangement. He's obsessive about tidying up.
2 habit
□ J'essaie de respecter ses petites manies. I try to go along with her little ways.

manier VERB [19]
to handle

la manière FEM NOUN
▷ *see also* **manières** NOUN
way
■ **de manière à** so as to □ Nous sommes partis tôt de manière à éviter la circulation. We left early so as to avoid the traffic.
■ **de toute manière** in any case □ Je n'aurais pas pu venir de toute manière. I couldn't have come in any case.

maniéré (FEM **maniérée**) ADJECTIVE
affected

les manières FEM PL NOUN
▷ *see also* **manière** NOUN
1 manners
□ apprendre les bonnes manières to learn good manners
2 fuss
■ **Ne fais pas de manières : prends le dernier morceau!** Don't be shy, take the last bit!

le manifestant MASC NOUN
demonstrator

la manifestante FEM NOUN
demonstrator

la manifestation FEM NOUN
demonstration
□ une manifestation pour la paix a peace demonstration

manifester VERB [28]
to demonstrate

manipuler VERB [28]
1 to handle
□ Ce vase doit être manipulé avec soin. This vase must be handled with care.
2 to manipulate
□ Tous les partis essaient de manipuler l'opinion publique. All the parties are trying to manipulate public opinion.

le/la mannequin MASC/FEM NOUN
model
□ Elle est mannequin. She's a model.

manœuvrer VERB [28]
to manœuvre

m

le manque MASC NOUN
- **le manque de** lack of □ Le manque de sommeil peut provoquer toutes sortes de troubles. Lack of sleep can cause all sorts of problems.
- **un drogué en état de manque** a drug addict suffering withdrawal symptoms

manqué (FEM **manquée**) ADJECTIVE
- **un garçon manqué** a tomboy

manquer VERB [28]
to miss
□ Tu n'as rien manqué : c'était nul. You didn't miss anything: it was rubbish. □ Il manque des pages à ce livre. There are some pages missing from this book.
- **manquer à quelqu'un.** □ Tu me manques. I miss you. □ Leurs parents leur manquent. They miss their parents. □ Georges manque à Lucas. Lucas misses Georges.
- **Il manque encore dix euros.** We are still 10 euros short.
- **manquer de** to lack □ La quiche manque de sel. The quiche lacks salt.
- **Je trouve qu'il a manqué de tact.** I don't think he was very tactful.
- **Il a manqué se tuer.** He nearly got killed.

le manteau (PL les **manteaux**) MASC NOUN
coat

manuel (FEM **manuelle**) ADJECTIVE
▷ see also **manuel** NOUN
manual

le manuel MASC NOUN
▷ see also **manuel** ADJECTIVE
1 textbook
2 handbook

le maquereau (PL les **maquereaux**) MASC NOUN
mackerel

la maquette FEM NOUN
model
□ une maquette de bateau a model boat

le maquillage MASC NOUN
make-up

se maquiller VERB [28]
to put on one's make-up
□ Je vais me maquiller en vitesse. I'll just quickly put on my make-up.

le marais MASC NOUN
marsh

le marbre MASC NOUN
marble
□ une statue en marbre a marble statue

le marchand MASC NOUN
1 shopkeeper
- **un marchand de journaux** a newsagent
2 stallholder (in market)

la marchande FEM NOUN
1 shopkeeper
- **une marchande de fruits et de légumes** a greengrocer
2 stallholder (in market)

marchander VERB [28]
to haggle

la marchandise FEM NOUN
goods

la marche FEM NOUN
1 step
□ Fais attention à la marche ! Mind the step!
2 walking
□ La marche me fait du bien. Walking does me good.
- **être en état de marche** to be in working order □ Cette voiture est en parfait état de marche. This car is in perfect running order.
- **Ne montez jamais dans un train en marche.** Never try to get onto a moving train.
- **mettre en marche** to start □ Comment est-ce qu'on met la machine à laver en marche ? How do you start the washing machine?
- **la marche arrière** reverse gear
- **faire marche arrière** to reverse
3 march
□ une marche militaire a military march

le marché MASC NOUN
market
- **un marché aux puces** a flea market
- **le marché noir** the black market

marcher VERB [28]
1 to walk
□ Elle marche cinq kilomètres par jour. She walks 5 kilometres every day.
2 to run
□ Le métro marche normalement aujourd'hui. The underground is running normally today.
3 to work
□ Est-ce que l'ascenseur marche ? Is the lift working?
4 to go well
□ Est-ce que les affaires marchent actuellement ? Is business going well at the moment?
- **Alors les études, ça marche ?** (informal) How are you getting on at school?
- **faire marcher quelqu'un** to pull somebody's leg □ Il essaie de te faire marcher. He's pulling your leg.

le marcheur MASC NOUN
walker

la marcheuse FEM NOUN
walker

le mardi MASC NOUN
1 Tuesday
□ Aujourd'hui, nous sommes mardi. It's Tuesday today.

2 on Tuesday
☐ Ils reviennent mardi. They're coming back on Tuesday.
■ **le mardi** on Tuesdays ☐ Le mardi, je vais à la gym. I go to the gym on Tuesdays.
■ **tous les mardis** every Tuesday
■ **mardi dernier** last Tuesday
■ **mardi prochain** next Tuesday
■ **À mardi !** See you on Tuesday!
■ **Mardi gras** Shrove Tuesday

la **mare** FEM NOUN
pond

le **marécage** MASC NOUN
marsh

la **marée** FEM NOUN
tide
☐ la marée haute high tide ☐ la marée basse low tide ☐ la marée montante the rising tide ☐ la marée descendante the ebb tide
■ **une marée noire** an oil slick

la **margarine** FEM NOUN
margarine

la **marge** FEM NOUN
margin

le **mari** MASC NOUN
husband
☐ son mari her husband

le **mariage** MASC NOUN
1 marriage
2 wedding
☐ un mariage civil a registry office wedding
☐ un mariage religieux a church wedding
■ **le mariage du même sexe** same-sex marriage

marié (FEM **mariée**) ADJECTIVE
▷ see also **marié** NOUN, **mariée** NOUN
married

le **marié** MASC NOUN
▷ see also **marié** ADJECTIVE
bridegroom
■ **les mariés** the bride and groom

la **mariée** FEM NOUN
▷ see also **marié** ADJECTIVE
bride

se **marier** VERB [19]
to marry
☐ Elle s'est mariée avec un ami d'enfance. She married a childhood friend.

marin (FEM **marine**) ADJECTIVE
▷ see also **marin** NOUN, **marine** NOUN, ADJECTIVE
sea
☐ l'air marin the sea air
■ **un pull marin** a sailor's jersey

le **marin** MASC NOUN
▷ see also **marin** ADJECTIVE
sailor

marine (FEM+PL **marine**) ADJECTIVE
▷ see also **marine** NOUN, **marin** ADJECTIVE
■ **bleu marine** navy-blue ☐ un pull bleu marine a navy-blue sweater

la **marine** FEM NOUN
▷ see also **marin** ADJECTIVE, **marine** ADJECTIVE
navy
■ **la marine nationale** the French navy

la **marionnette** FEM NOUN
puppet

le **marketing** MASC NOUN
marketing

la **marmelade** FEM NOUN
stewed fruit
■ **la marmelade de pommes** stewed apples
■ **la marmelade d'oranges** marmalade

la **marmite** FEM NOUN
cooking pot

marmonner VERB [28]
to mumble

le **Maroc** MASC NOUN
Morocco

marocain (FEM **marocaine**) ADJECTIVE, NOUN
Moroccan

la **maroquinerie** FEM NOUN
leather goods shop

marquant (FEM **marquante**) ADJECTIVE
significant
☐ un événement marquant a significant event

la **marque** FEM NOUN
1 mark
☐ des marques de doigts fingermarks
2 make
☐ De quelle marque est ton jean ? What make are your jeans?
3 brand
☐ une grande marque de cognac a well-known brand of cognac
■ **l'image de marque** the public image
☐ Le ministre tient à son image de marque. The minister cares about his public image.
■ **une marque déposée** a registered trademark
■ **À vos marques ! Prêts ! Partez !** Ready, steady, go!

marquer VERB [28]
1 to mark
☐ Peux-tu marquer sur la carte où se trouve le village ? Can you mark where the village is on the map?
2 to score
☐ L'équipe irlandaise a marqué dix points. The Irish team scored ten points.
3 to celebrate
☐ On va sortir au restaurant pour marquer ton anniversaire. We'll eat out to celebrate your birthday.

m

marraine - maternelle

la **marraine** FEM NOUN
godmother

marrant (FEM **marrante**) ADJECTIVE (*informal*)
funny

marre ADVERB (*informal*)
■ **en avoir marre de quelque chose** to be
fed up with something □ J'en ai marre de
faire la vaisselle. I'm fed up with doing the
dishes.

se **marrer** VERB [28] (*informal*)
to have a good laugh
□ On s'est bien marrés. We had a good laugh.

le **marron** MASC NOUN
▷ *see also* **marron** ADJECTIVE
chestnut
□ la crème de marrons chestnut purée

marron (FEM+PL **marron**) ADJECTIVE
▷ *see also* **marron** NOUN
brown
□ des chaussures marron brown shoes

le **marronnier** MASC NOUN
chestnut tree

mars MASC NOUN
March
■ **en mars** in March

le **marteau** (PL les **marteaux**) MASC NOUN
hammer

la **Martinique** FEM NOUN
Martinique

martyriser VERB [28]
to batter

masculin (FEM **masculine**) ADJECTIVE
1 men's
□ la mode masculine men's fashion
2 masculine
□ « Chat » est un nom masculin. 'Chat' is a
masculine noun. □ Elle a une allure assez
masculine. She looks rather masculine.

le **masque** MASC NOUN
1 mask (*disguise*)
2 face mask (*protective*)

le **massacre** MASC NOUN
massacre

massacrer VERB [28]
to massacre

le **massage** MASC NOUN
massage

la **masse** FEM NOUN
■ **une masse de** (*informal*) masses of □ J'ai
une masse de choses à faire. I've got masses of
things to do.
■ **produire en masse** to mass-produce □ des
meubles produits en masse mass-produced
furniture
■ **venir en masse** to come en masse □ Les
gens sont venus en masse pour accueillir le

président. People came en masse to welcome
the president.

masser VERB [28]
to massage
■ **se masser** to gather □ Les manifestants
se sont massés devant l'ambassade. The
demonstrators gathered in front of the embassy.

massif (FEM **massive**) ADJECTIVE
1 solid (*gold, silver, wood*)
□ un bracelet en or massif a solid gold bracelet
2 massive
□ une dose massive d'antibiotiques a massive
dose of antibiotics
3 mass
□ des départs massifs a mass exodus

mat (FEM **mate**) ADJECTIVE
matt
□ blanc mat matt white □ Je voudrais mes
photos en mat. I would like my photos matt.
■ **être mat** to be checkmate (*chess*)

le **match** MASC NOUN
match
□ un match de football a football match
■ **le match aller** the first leg
■ **le match retour** the second leg
■ **faire match nul** to draw

le **matelas** MASC NOUN
mattress
■ **un matelas pneumatique** an air bed

matelassé (FEM **matelassée**) ADJECTIVE
quilted
□ une veste matelassée a quilted jacket

le **matelot** MASC NOUN
sailor

les **matériaux** MASC PL NOUN
materials

le **matériel** MASC NOUN
1 equipment
□ du matériel de laboratoire laboratory
equipment
2 gear
□ Il a pris tout son matériel de pêche avec lui.
He took all his fishing gear with him.

maternel (FEM **maternelle**) ADJECTIVE
▷ *see also* **maternelle** NOUN
motherly
□ Elle est très maternelle. She's very
motherly.
■ **ma grand-mère maternelle** my mother's
mother
■ **mon oncle maternel** my mother's brother

la **maternelle** FEM NOUN
▷ *see also* **maternel** ADJECTIVE
nursery school

DID YOU KNOW...?
The **maternelle** is a state school for
2–6 year-olds.

la **maternité** FEM NOUN
- **le congé de maternité** maternity leave
- □ Notre professeur de musique est en congé de maternité. Our music teacher is on maternity leave.

les **mathématiques** FEM PL NOUN
mathematics

les **maths** FEM PL NOUN (*informal*)
maths

la **matière** FEM NOUN
subject
□ Le latin est une matière facultative. Latin is an optional subject.
- **sans matières grasses** fat-free
- **les matières premières** raw materials

le **matin** MASC NOUN
morning
□ à trois heures du matin at 3 o'clock in the morning □ du matin au soir from morning till night
- **Je suis du matin.** I'm at my best in the morning.
- **de bon matin** early in the morning

matinal (FEM **matinale**, MASC PL **matinaux**)
ADJECTIVE
morning
□ Je fais ma gymnastique matinale avant de déjeuner. I do my morning exercises before breakfast.
- **être matinal** to be up early □ Tu es bien matinal aujourd'hui ! You're up early today!

la **matinée** FEM NOUN
morning
□ Je t'appellerai demain dans la matinée. I'll call you sometime tomorrow morning. □ en début de matinée early in the morning

le **matou** MASC NOUN
tomcat

maudire VERB [46]
to curse

maudit (FEM **maudite**) ADJECTIVE (*informal*)
blasted
□ Où est passé ce maudit parapluie ? Where's that blasted umbrella got to?

maussade (FEM **maussade**) ADJECTIVE
sullen

mauvais (FEM **mauvaise**) ADJECTIVE, ADVERB
1 bad
□ une mauvaise note a bad mark □ Tu arrives au mauvais moment. You've come at a bad time.
- **Il fait mauvais.** The weather's bad.
- **être mauvais en** to be bad at □ Je suis mauvais en allemand. I'm bad at German.
2 poor
□ J'ai trouvé que le film était mauvais. I thought the film was poor. □ Il est en mauvaise santé. His health is poor.

- **Tu as mauvaise mine.** You don't look well.
3 wrong
□ Vous avez fait le mauvais numéro. You've dialled the wrong number.
- **des mauvaises herbes** weeds
- **sentir mauvais** to smell

les **maux** MASC PL NOUN ▷ *see* **mal** NOUN
- **des maux de ventre** stomachache
- **des maux de tête** headache

maximal (FEM **maximale**, MASC PL **maximaux**)
ADJECTIVE
maximum

le **maximum** MASC NOUN
maximum
- **au maximum 1** as much as one can
□ Remplis le seau au maximum. Fill the bucket as full as you can. **2** at the very most □ Ça va vous coûter deux cents euros au maximum. It'll cost you 200 euros at the very most.

la **mayonnaise** FEM NOUN
mayonnaise

le **mazout** MASC NOUN
fuel oil

me PRONOUN

> **me** changes to **m'** before a vowel and most words beginning with 'h'.

1 me
□ Elle me téléphone tous les jours. She phones me every day. □ Il m'attend depuis une heure. He's been waiting for me for an hour.
2 to me
□ Il me parle en allemand. He talks to me in German. □ Elle m'a expliqué la situation. She explained the situation to me.
3 myself
□ Je vais me préparer quelque chose à manger. I'm going to make myself something to eat.

> With reflexive verbs, **me** is often not translated.

□ Je me lève à sept heures tous les matins. I get up at 7 every morning.

le **mec** MASC NOUN (*informal*)
guy

le **mécanicien** MASC NOUN
mechanic

la **mécanique** FEM NOUN
1 mechanics
2 mechanism (*of watch, clock*)

le **mécanisme** MASC NOUN
mechanism

méchamment ADVERB
nastily
□ Il lui a répondu méchamment. He answered him nastily.

m

la **méchanceté** FEM NOUN
nastiness

méchant (FEM **méchante**) ADJECTIVE
nasty
□ C'est un homme méchant. He's a nasty man.
□ Ne sois pas méchant avec ton petit frère.
Don't be nasty to your little brother.
■ « Attention, chien méchant » 'Beware of
the dog'

la **mèche** FEM NOUN
lock (of hair)

mécontent (FEM **mécontente**) ADJECTIVE
■ mécontent de unhappy with □ Elle est
mécontente de sa coupe de cheveux. She's
unhappy with her haircut.

le **mécontentement** MASC NOUN
displeasure
□ Il a exprimé son mécontentement. He
expressed his displeasure.

la **médaille** FEM NOUN
medal

le **médecin** MASC NOUN
doctor
□ aller chez le médecin to go to the doctor

la **médecine** FEM NOUN
medicine (subject)
□ Il fait médecine. He's studying medicine.

les **médias** MASC PL NOUN
media sing
■ étude des médias media studies

médical (FEM **médicale**, MASC PL **médicaux**)
ADJECTIVE
medical
□ la recherche médicale medical research
■ passer une visite médicale to have a
medical

le **médicament** MASC NOUN
medicine (drug)

médiéval (FEM **médiévale**, MASC PL
médiévaux) ADJECTIVE
medieval

médiocre (FEM **médiocre**) ADJECTIVE
poor
□ des notes médiocres poor marks

la **Méditerranée** FEM NOUN
Mediterranean

méditerranéen (FEM **méditerranéenne**)
ADJECTIVE
Mediterranean

la **méduse** FEM NOUN
jellyfish

la **méfiance** FEM NOUN
mistrust

méfiant (FEM **méfiante**) ADJECTIVE
mistrustful

se **méfier** VERB [19]
■ se méfier de quelqu'un to distrust
somebody □ Si j'étais toi, je me méfierais de lui.
If I were you, I wouldn't trust him.

le **mégaoctet** MASC NOUN
megabyte

la **mégarde** FEM NOUN
■ par mégarde by mistake □ J'ai emporté son
livre par mégarde. I took his book by mistake.

le **mégot** MASC NOUN
cigarette end

meilleur (FEM **meilleure**) ADJECTIVE, ADVERB,
NOUN
better
□ Ce serait meilleur avec du fromage râpé. It
would be better with grated cheese. □ Il paraît
que le film est meilleur que le livre. They say that
the film is better than the book.
■ le meilleur the best □ le meilleur joueur de
l'équipe the best player in the team □ Je préfère
garder le meilleur pour la fin. I like to keep the
best for last. □ C'est elle qui est la meilleure en
sport. She's the best at sport.
■ le meilleur des deux the better of the two
■ meilleur marché cheaper □ La bière est
meilleur marché en France. Beer's cheaper
in France.

le **mél** MASC NOUN
email

mélancolique (FEM **mélancolique**)
ADJECTIVE
melancholy

le **mélange** MASC NOUN
mixture

mélanger VERB [45]
1 to mix
□ Mélangez le tout. Mix everything together.
2 to muddle up
□ Tu mélanges tout ! You're muddling
everything up!

la **mêlée** FEM NOUN
scrum

mêler VERB [28]
■ se mêler to mix □ Il ne cherche pas à se mêler
aux autres. He doesn't try to mix with the others.
■ Mêle-toi de ce qui te regarde ! (informal)
Mind your own business!

la **mélodie** FEM NOUN
melody

le **melon** MASC NOUN
melon

le **membre** MASC NOUN
1 limb
2 member
□ un membre de la famille a member of
the family □ les pays membres de l'Union

m

européenne the member countries of the European Union

le **mème** MASC NOUN
meme

même (FEM **même**) ADJECTIVE, ADVERB, PRONOUN
1 same
□ J'ai le même manteau. I've got the same coat.
□ Tiens, c'est curieux, j'ai le même ! That's strange, I've got the same one!
■ **en même temps** at the same time
■ **moi-même** myself □ Je l'ai fait moi-même. I did it myself.
■ **toi-même** yourself □ Est-ce que tu vas faire les travaux toi-même ? Are you going to do the work yourself?
■ **eux-mêmes** themselves
2 even
□ Il n'a même pas pleuré. He didn't even cry.
■ **même si** even if □ Je ne ferais jamais ça, même si tu me le demandais. I'd never do that, even if you asked me. □ Même si j'aime les maths, je trouve ça difficile. Although I like maths, I find it difficult.

la **mémé** FEM NOUN (*informal*)
granny

la **mémoire** FEM NOUN
memory

la **menace** FEM NOUN
threat

menacer VERB [12]
to threaten
■ **menacer de faire quelque chose** to threaten to do something □ Les hackers ont menacé de publier les données. The hackers threatened to publish the data.

le **ménage** MASC NOUN
housework
□ faire le ménage to do the housework
■ **une femme de ménage** a cleaning woman

ménager (FEM **ménagère**) ADJECTIVE
■ **les travaux ménagers** housework
■ **les arts ménagers** food technology

la **ménagère** FEM NOUN
housewife

le **mendiant** MASC NOUN
beggar

la **mendiante** FEM NOUN
beggar

mendier VERB [19]
to beg

mener VERB [43]
to lead
□ Cette rue mène directement à la gare. This street leads straight to the station.
■ **Cela ne vous mènera à rien !** That will get you nowhere!

la **méningite** FEM NOUN
meningitis

les **menottes** FEM PL NOUN
handcuffs

le **mensonge** MASC NOUN
lie

la **mensualité** FEM NOUN
monthly payment
□ en dix mensualités in ten monthly payments

mensuel (FEM **mensuelle**) ADJECTIVE
monthly

les **mensurations** FEM PL NOUN
measurements

mental (FEM **mentale**) ADJECTIVE
mental
□ le bien-être mental mental wellbeing

la **mentalité** FEM NOUN
mentality

le **menteur** MASC NOUN
liar

la **menteuse** FEM NOUN
liar

la **menthe** FEM NOUN
mint

la **mention** FEM NOUN
grade
□ Il a été reçu avec mention bien. He got a grade B pass.

mentionner VERB [28]
to mention

mentir VERB [77]
to lie
□ Tu mens ! You're lying!

le **menton** MASC NOUN
chin

menu (FEM **menue**) ADJECTIVE, ADVERB
▷ see also **menu** NOUN
1 slim
□ Elle est menue. She's slim. □ Elle est petite et menue. She's petite.
2 very fine
□ Les oignons doivent être coupés menu. The onions have to be cut up very fine.

le **menu** MASC NOUN
▷ see also **menu** ADJECTIVE, ADVERB
menu
□ le menu du jour today's menu □ le menu touristique the tourist menu □ le menu d'aide (*on a computer*) the help menu

la **menuiserie** FEM NOUN
woodwork

le **menuisier** MASC NOUN
joiner

le **mépris** MASC NOUN
contempt
□ Il nous a traités avec mépris. He treated us with contempt.

m

méprisant - mesurer

méprisant (FEM **méprisante**) ADJECTIVE
contemptuous

mépriser VERB [28]
to despise

la mer FEM NOUN

1 sea
□ en mer at sea
■ au bord de la mer at the seaside
■ la mer du Nord the North Sea

2 tide
□ La mer est basse. The tide is out. □ La mer sera haute à sept heures. It'll be high tide at 7 o'clock.

la mercerie FEM NOUN

1 haberdashery
2 haberdasher's shop

merci EXCLAMATION
thank you
□ Merci de m'avoir raccompagné. Thank you for taking me home.
■ merci beaucoup thank you very much

le mercredi MASC NOUN

1 Wednesday
□ Aujourd'hui, nous sommes mercredi. It's Wednesday today.

2 on Wednesday
□ Nous comptons partir mercredi. We plan to leave on Wednesday.
■ le mercredi on Wednesdays □ Le musée est fermé le mercredi. The museum is shut on Wednesdays.
■ tous les mercredis every Wednesday
■ mercredi dernier last Wednesday
■ mercredi prochain next Wednesday
■ À mercredi ! See you on Wednesday!

la mère FEM NOUN
mother

la merguez FEM NOUN
spicy sausage

méridional (FEM **méridionale**, MASC PL **méridionaux**) ADJECTIVE
southern
□ Il a un accent méridional. He's got a southern accent.

la meringue FEM NOUN
meringue

mériter VERB [28]
to deserve
■ mériter de to deserve to □ Elle mérite de réussir. She deserves to succeed.
■ se mériter to be earned □ La confiance, ça se mérite. Trust must be earned.

le merlan MASC NOUN
whiting

le merle MASC NOUN
blackbird

la merveille FEM NOUN
■ Cet ordinateur est une vraie merveille ! This computer's really wonderful!
■ à merveille wonderfully □ Elle se porte à merveille depuis son opération. She's been wonderfully well since the operation.

merveilleux (FEM **merveilleuse**) ADJECTIVE
marvellous

mes PL ADJECTIVE
my
□ mes parents my parents

Mesdames FEM PL NOUN
ladies
□ Bonjour, Mesdames. Good morning, ladies.

Mesdemoiselles FEM PL NOUN
ladies
□ Bonjour, Mesdemoiselles. Good morning, ladies.

mesquin (FEM **mesquine**) ADJECTIVE
mean

le message MASC NOUN
message
■ un message SMS a text message

la messagerie FEM NOUN
■ une messagerie vocale voice mail
■ la messagerie électronique email

la messe FEM NOUN
mass
□ aller à la messe to go to mass □ la messe de minuit midnight mass

messieurs MASC PL NOUN
gentlemen
□ Que puis-je faire pour vous, Messieurs ? What can I do for you, gentlemen?
■ Messieurs, ... (in letter) Dear Sirs, ...

la mesure FEM NOUN

1 measurement
□ J'ai pris les mesures de la fenêtre. I took the measurements of the window.
■ sur mesure tailor-made □ un costume sur mesure a tailor-made suit

2 measure
□ L'établissement a pris des mesures pour lutter contre le vandalisme. The school has taken measures to combat vandalism.
■ au fur et à mesure as one goes along
□ Quand je cuisine, je préfère faire la vaisselle au fur et à mesure. When I'm cooking, I prefer to wash up as I go along.
■ être en mesure de faire quelque chose to be in a position to do something □ Nous ne sommes pas en mesure de vous renseigner. We are not in a position to give you any information.

mesurer VERB [28]
to measure
□ Mesurez la longueur et la largeur. Measure the length and the width.

Numbers in brackets refer to verb tables on pages 650 to 658

- Il mesure un mètre quatre-vingts. He's 1 m 80 tall.

met VERB ▷ see **mettre**

le **métal** (PL les **métaux**) MASC NOUN
metal

métallique (FEM **métallique**) ADJECTIVE
metallic

la **météo** FEM NOUN
weather forecast
□ Que dit la météo pour cet après-midi ? What's the weather forecast for this afternoon?

la **méthode** FEM NOUN
1 method
□ des méthodes d'enseignement modernes modern teaching methods
2 tutor
□ une méthode de guitare a guitar tutor

le **métier** MASC NOUN
job
□ Tu aimerais faire quel métier plus tard ? What job would you like to do when you're older?

le **mètre** MASC NOUN
metre
- un mètre ruban a tape measure

le **métro** MASC NOUN
underground
□ prendre le métro to go by underground

mets VERB ▷ see **mettre**

le **metteur en scène** (PL les **metteurs en scène**) MASC NOUN
director (of film or play)

mettre VERB [47]

PRESENT TENSE

je mets	nous mettons
tu mets	vous mettez
il/elle met	ils/elles mettent

PAST PARTICIPLE
mis

1 to put
□ Où est-ce que tu as mis les clés ? Where have you put the keys?
2 to put on
□ Je mets mon manteau et j'arrive. I'll put on my coat and then I'll be ready. □ Il fait froid, je vais mettre le chauffage. It's cold, I'm going to put the heating on.
3 to wear
□ Elle ne met pas souvent de jupe. She doesn't often wear a skirt. □ Je n'ai rien à me mettre ! I've got nothing to wear!
4 to take
□ Combien de temps as-tu mis pour aller à Lille ? How long did it take you to get to Lille? □ Elle met des heures à se préparer. She takes hours getting ready.
- mettre en marche to start □ Comment met-on la machine à laver en marche ? How do you start the washing machine?

- Vous pouvez vous mettre là. You can sit there.
- se mettre au lit to get into bed
- se mettre en maillot de bain to put on one's swimsuit
- se mettre à to start □ Il s'est mis à la peinture à cinquante ans. He started painting when he was 50. □ Il est temps de se mettre au travail. It's time to start work. □ Elle s'est mise à pleurer. She started crying.

le **meuble** MASC NOUN
piece of furniture
□ Je me suis cogné contre un meuble. I bumped into a piece of furniture. □ de beaux meubles nice furniture

le **meublé** MASC NOUN
1 furnished flat
2 furnished room

meubler VERB [28]
to furnish

le **meurtre** MASC NOUN
murder

le **meurtrier** MASC NOUN
murderer

la **meurtrière** FEM NOUN
murderess

Mexico NOUN
Mexico City

le **Mexique** MASC NOUN
Mexico

le **mi** MASC NOUN
1 E
□ mi bémol E flat
2 mi
□ do, ré, mi ... do, re, mi ...

mi- PREFIX
1 half-
□ mi-clos half-shut
2 mid-
□ à la mi-janvier in mid-January

miauler VERB [28]
to mew

la **miche** FEM NOUN
loaf

mi-chemin
- à mi-chemin ADVERB halfway

le **micro** MASC NOUN
microphone

le **microbe** MASC NOUN
germ

le **micro-ondes** MASC NOUN
microwave oven

le **micro-ordinateur** MASC NOUN
microcomputer

le **microscope** MASC NOUN
microscope

le **midi** MASC NOUN

1 midday
□ à midi at midday
■ **midi et demi** half past twelve

2 lunchtime
□ On a bien mangé à midi. We had a good meal at lunchtime.
■ **le Midi** the South of France

la **mie** FEM NOUN
breadcrumbs

le **miel** MASC NOUN
honey

mien MASC PRONOUN
■ **le mien** mine □ Ce vélo-là, c'est le mien. That bike's mine.

mienne FEM PRONOUN
■ **la mienne** mine □ Cette valise-là, c'est la mienne. That case is mine.

miennes FEM PL PRONOUN
■ **les miennes** mine □ Tu as tes clés ? J'ai oublié les miennes. Have you got your keys? I forgot mine.

miens MASC PL PRONOUN
■ **les miens** mine □ Ces CD-là, ce sont les miens. Those CDs are mine.

la **miette** FEM NOUN
crumb (of bread, cake)

mieux (FEM+PL mieux) ADVERB, ADJECTIVE, NOUN
better
□ Je la connais mieux que son frère. I know her better than her brother. □ Elle va mieux. She's better. □ Les cheveux courts lui vont mieux. She looks better with short hair.
■ **Il vaut mieux que tu appelles ta mère.** You'd better phone your mother.
■ **le mieux** the best □ C'est la région que je connais le mieux. It's the region I know best.
■ **faire de son mieux** to do one's best □ Essaie de faire de ton mieux. Try to do your best.
■ **de mieux en mieux** better and better
■ **au mieux** at best

mignon (FEM mignonne) ADJECTIVE
sweet
□ Qu'est-ce qu'il est mignon ! Isn't he sweet!

la **migraine** FEM NOUN
migraine
□ J'ai la migraine. I've got a migraine.

mijoter VERB [28]
to simmer

le **milieu** (PL les milieux) MASC NOUN

1 middle
■ **au milieu de** in the middle of □ Place le vase au milieu de la table. Put the vase in the middle of the table.
■ **au beau milieu de** in the middle of □ Il est arrivé au beau milieu de la nuit. He arrived in the middle of the night.

2 background
□ le milieu familial the family background □ Il vient d'un milieu modeste. He comes from a modest background.

3 environment
□ le milieu marin the marine environment

militaire (FEM militaire) ADJECTIVE
▷ see also **militaire** NOUN
military
□ faire son service militaire to do one's military service

le **militaire** MASC NOUN
▷ see also **militaire** ADJECTIVE
serviceman
□ Son père est militaire. His father is a serviceman.
■ **un militaire de carrière** a professional soldier

mille NUMBER
a thousand
□ mille euros a thousand euros □ deux mille personnes two thousand people

le **millefeuille** MASC NOUN
vanilla slice

le **millénaire** MASC NOUN
millennium
□ le troisième millénaire the third millennium

le **milliard** MASC NOUN
billion
□ cinq milliards d'euros five billion euros

le/la **milliardaire** MASC/FEM NOUN
billionaire

le **millier** MASC NOUN
thousand
□ des milliers de personnes thousands of people
■ **par milliers** by the thousand

le **milligramme** MASC NOUN
milligram

le **millimètre** MASC NOUN
millimetre

le **million** MASC NOUN
million
□ deux millions de personnes two million people

le/la **millionnaire** MASC/FEM NOUN
millionaire

mi-long (FEM mi-longue) ADJECTIVE
medium-length

le/la **mime** MASC/FEM NOUN
mime artist

mimer VERB [28]
to mimic

minable (FEM minable) ADJECTIVE

1 shabby
□ un imperméable minable a shabby raincoat

2 pathetic

m

Numbers in brackets refer to verb tables on pages 650 to 658

mince (FEM **mince**) ADJECTIVE
1 thin
□ une mince tranche de jambon a thin slice of ham
2 slim
□ Il est grand et mince. He's tall and slim.
■ **Mince alors !** (informal) Oh bother!

la **minceur** FEM NOUN
1 thinness
□ la minceur des murs the thinness of the walls
2 slimness
□ Elle enviait la minceur de sa sœur. She envied her sister's slimness.

la **mine** FEM NOUN
1 expression
2 look
□ Tu as bonne mine. You look well. □ Il a mauvaise mine. He doesn't look well. □ Elle avait une mine fatiguée. She was looking tired.
3 appearance
□ Il ne faut pas juger les gens d'après leur mine. You shouldn't judge people by their appearance.
4 lead (of pencil)
5 mine
□ une mine de charbon a coal mine
■ **faire mine de faire quelque chose** to pretend to do something □ Elle a fait mine de le croire. She pretended to believe him.

minéral (FEM **minérale**, MASC PL **minéraux**)
ADJECTIVE
mineral
□ l'eau minérale mineral water

minéralogique (FEM **minéralogique**)
ADJECTIVE
■ **une plaque minéralogique** a number plate

mineur (FEM **mineure**) ADJECTIVE
▷ see also **mineur** NOUN, **mineure** NOUN
minor

le **mineur** MASC NOUN
▷ see also **mineur** ADJECTIVE
1 boy under 18
■ **les mineurs** the under-18s
2 miner
□ Mon grand-père était mineur. My grandfather was a miner.

la **mineure** FEM NOUN
▷ see also **mineur** ADJECTIVE
girl under 18

la **minijupe** FEM NOUN
miniskirt

minimal (FEM **minimale**, MASC PL **minimaux**)
ADJECTIVE
minimum

le **minimum** MASC NOUN
minimum
□ Il en fait le minimum. He does the absolute minimum.

■ **au minimum** at the very least

le **ministère** MASC NOUN
ministry
□ le ministère des Affaires étrangères the Foreign Office

le/la **ministre** MASC/FEM NOUN
minister
□ le ministre des Affaires étrangères the Foreign Secretary

la **minorité** FEM NOUN
minority

Minorque FEM NOUN
Minorca

le **minuit** MASC NOUN
midnight
□ à minuit et quart at a quarter past midnight

minuscule (FEM **minuscule**) ADJECTIVE
▷ see also **minuscule** NOUN
tiny

la **minuscule** FEM NOUN
▷ see also **minuscule** ADJECTIVE
small letter

la **minute** FEM NOUN
minute

minutieux (FEM **minutieuse**) ADJECTIVE
meticulous
■ **C'est un travail minutieux.** It's a fiddly job.

la **mirabelle** FEM NOUN
small yellow plum

le **miracle** MASC NOUN
miracle

le **miroir** MASC NOUN
mirror

mis (FEM **mise**) ADJECTIVE
■ **bien mis** well turned out □ Elle est toujours bien mise. She's always well turned out.

mis VERB ▷ see **mettre**

miser VERB [28] (informal)
to bank on
□ On ne peut pas miser là-dessus. We can't bank on it.

misérable (FEM **misérable**) ADJECTIVE
shabby-looking
□ une femme d'aspect misérable a shabby-looking woman

la **misère** FEM NOUN
extreme poverty
■ **un salaire de misère** starvation wages

le/la **missionnaire** MASC/FEM NOUN
missionary

mit VERB ▷ see **mettre**

la **mi-temps** FEM NOUN
1 half (of match)
□ la première mi-temps the first half □ la deuxième mi-temps the second half

m

2 half-time
□ Je lui parlerai à la mi-temps. I'll speak to him at half-time.
■ **travailler à mi-temps** to work part-time

la **mitraillette** FEM NOUN
submachine gun

le **mi-trimestre** MASC NOUN
half-term

mixte (FEM **mixte**) ADJECTIVE
■ **une école mixte** a mixed school

la **MJC** FEM NOUN (= *maison des jeunes et de la culture*)
youth club and arts centre

Mlle (PL **Mlles**) ABBREVIATION (= *Mademoiselle*)
Miss
□ Mlle Renoir Miss Renoir

Mme (PL **Mmes**) ABBREVIATION (= *Madame*)
Mrs
□ Mme Leroy Mrs Leroy

le **mobile** MASC NOUN
1 motive
□ Quel était le mobile du crime ? What was the motive for the crime?
2 mobile phone
□ Tu me donnes ton numéro de mobile ? Can you give me your mobile number?

le **mobilier** MASC NOUN
furniture

la **mobylette**® FEM NOUN
moped

moche (FEM **moche**) ADJECTIVE (*informal*)
1 awful
□ Cette couleur est vraiment moche. That colour's really awful. □ Je me trouve moche ! I think I look awful!
2 rotten
□ Il a la grippe, c'est moche pour lui. He's got flu, that's rotten for him.

la **mode** FEM NOUN
▷ *see also* **mode** NOUN
fashion
□ être à la mode to be fashionable

le **mode** MASC NOUN
▷ *see also* **mode** NOUN
■ **le mode d'emploi** directions for use
■ **le mode de vie** the way of life

le **modèle** MASC NOUN
1 model
□ Le nouveau modèle sort en septembre. The new model is coming out in September.
2 style (*of clothes*)
□ Est-ce que vous avez le même modèle en plus grand ? Have you got the same style in a bigger size?

modéré (FEM **modérée**) ADJECTIVE
moderate

moderne (FEM **moderne**) ADJECTIVE
modern

moderniser VERB [28]
to modernize

modeste (FEM **modeste**) ADJECTIVE
modest
□ Ne sois pas si modeste ! Don't be so modest!

la **modestie** FEM NOUN
modesty

moelleux (FEM **moelleuse**) ADJECTIVE
soft
□ un coussin moelleux a soft cushion

les **mœurs** FEM PL NOUN
social attitudes
■ **l'évolution des mœurs** changing attitudes

moi PRONOUN
me
□ Coucou, c'est moi ! Hello, it's me!
■ **Moi, je pense que tu as tort.** I personally think you're wrong.
■ **à moi** mine □ Ce livre n'est pas à moi. This book isn't mine. □ un ami à moi a friend of mine

moi-même PRONOUN
myself
□ J'ai tricoté ce pull moi-même. I knitted this jumper myself.

moindre (FEM **moindre**) ADJECTIVE
■ **le moindre** the slightest □ Il ne fait pas le moindre effort. He doesn't make the slightest effort. □ Je n'en ai pas la moindre idée. I haven't the slightest idea.

le **moine** MASC NOUN
monk

le **moineau** (PL les **moineaux**) MASC NOUN
sparrow

moins ADVERB, PREPOSITION
1 less
□ Il fait moins chaud aujourd'hui. It is less warm today.
■ **Il est cinq heures moins dix.** It's 10 to 5.
2 minus
□ quatre moins trois 4 minus 3 □ Il a fait moins cinq la nuit dernière. It was minus five last night.
■ **moins de 1** less (than) □ moins d'eau less water □ moins de deux ans less than two years **2** fewer (than) □ moins de gens fewer people □ Il y a moins de 10 élèves dans la classe. There are fewer than 10 pupils in the class.
■ **moins ... que** less ... than □ Il est moins sûr que moi. He is less confident than me.
■ **le moins** the least □ C'est le modèle le moins cher. It's the least expensive model. □ Ce sont les plages qui sont les moins polluées. These are the least polluted beaches. □ C'est l'album que j'aime le moins. This is the album I like the least.
■ **de moins en moins** less and less □ Il vient nous voir de moins en moins. He comes to see us less and less often.

■ **Il a trois ans de moins que moi.** He's three years younger than me.

■ **au moins** at least □ Ne te plains pas : au moins il ne pleut pas ! Don't complain: at least it's not raining!

■ **à moins que** unless

> à moins que is followed by a verb in the subjunctive.

□ Je te retrouverai à dix heures à moins que le train n'ait du retard. I'll meet you at 10 o'clock unless the train's late.

le **mois** MASC NOUN
month

le **moisi** MASC NOUN
■ **Ça sent le moisi.** It smells musty.

moisir VERB [38]
to go mouldy
□ Le pain a moisi. The bread's gone mouldy.

la **moisson** FEM NOUN
harvest

moite (FEM moite) ADJECTIVE
sweaty
□ J'ai toujours les mains moites. My hands are always sweaty.

la **moitié** FEM NOUN
half
□ Il a mangé la moitié du gâteau. He ate half the cake.

■ **la moitié du temps** half the time

■ **à la moitié de** halfway through □ Elle est partie à la moitié du film. She left halfway through the film.

■ **à moitié** half □ Ton verre est encore à moitié plein. Your glass is still half-full. □ Ce sac était à moitié prix. This bag was half-price.

■ **partager moitié moitié** to go halves □ On partage moitié moitié, d'accord ? We'll go halves, OK?

la **molaire** FEM NOUN
back tooth

la **Moldavie** FEM NOUN
Moldova

molle FEM ADJECTIVE ▷ see mou

le **mollet** MASC NOUN
▷ see also mollet ADJECTIVE
calf (of leg)

mollet ADJECTIVE
▷ see also mollet NOUN
■ **un œuf mollet** a soft-boiled egg

le/la **môme** MASC/FEM NOUN (informal)
kid

le **moment** MASC NOUN
moment
■ **en ce moment** at the moment □ Nous avons beaucoup de travail en ce moment. We have a lot of work at the moment.

■ **pour le moment** for the moment □ Nous ne pensons pas déménager pour le moment. We're not thinking of moving for the moment.

■ **au moment où** just as □ Il est arrivé au moment où j'allais partir. He turned up just as I was leaving.

■ **à ce moment-là** **1** at that point □ À ce moment-là, on a vu arriver la police. At that point, we saw the police coming. **2** in that case □ À ce moment-là, je devrai partir plus tôt. In that case I'll have to leave earlier.

■ **à tout moment** **1** at any moment □ Elle peut arriver à tout moment. She could arrive at any moment. **2** constantly □ Il nous dérange à tout moment pour des riens. He's constantly bothering us about silly little things.

■ **sur le moment** at the time □ Sur le moment je n'ai rien dit. At the time I didn't say anything.

■ **par moments** at times □ Elle se sent seule par moments. She feels lonely at times.

momentané (FEM momentanée) ADJECTIVE
momentary

la **momie** FEM NOUN
mummy (Egyptian)

mon (FEM ma, PL mes) ADJECTIVE
my
□ mon frère my brother □ mon ami my friend

la **monarchie** FEM NOUN
monarchy

le **monastère** MASC NOUN
monastery

le **monde** MASC NOUN
world
□ faire le tour du monde to go round the world

■ **Il y a du monde.** There are a lot of people.

■ **beaucoup de monde** a lot of people □ Il y avait beaucoup de monde au concert. There were a lot of people at the concert.

■ **peu de monde** not many people

mondial (FEM mondiale, MASC PL mondiaux)
ADJECTIVE
1 world
□ la population mondiale the world population
2 world-wide
□ une crise mondiale a world-wide crisis

le **moniteur** MASC NOUN
1 instructor
□ un moniteur de voile a sailing instructor
2 monitor
□ le moniteur de mon ordinateur my computer monitor

la **monitrice** FEM NOUN
instructor
□ une monitrice de ski a ski instructor

la **monnaie** FEM NOUN
■ **une pièce de monnaie** a coin
■ **avoir de la monnaie** to have change □ Est-ce que tu as de la monnaie ? Have you got any

m

change? □ Est-ce que vous avez la monnaie de dix euros ? Do you have change for 10 euros?

■ **rendre la monnaie à quelqu'un** to give somebody their change

BE CAREFUL!
monnaie does not mean **money**.

monoparental (FEM **monoparentale**, MASC PL **monoparentaux**) ADJECTIVE
■ **une famille monoparentale** a one-parent family

monotone (FEM **monotone**) ADJECTIVE
monotonous

Monsieur (PL **Messieurs**) MASC NOUN
1 Mr
□ Monsieur Dupont Mr Dupont
2 man
□ Il y a un monsieur qui veut te voir. There's a man to see you.
3 Sir
□ Monsieur, ... Dear Sir, ... (in letter) □ Monsieur ! Vous avez oublié votre parapluie ! Excuse me! You've forgotten your umbrella!

le **monstre** MASC NOUN
▷ see also **monstre** ADJECTIVE
monster

monstre (FEM **monstre**) ADJECTIVE
▷ see also **monstre** NOUN
■ **Nous avons un travail monstre.** We've got a terrific amount of work.

le **mont** MASC NOUN
mount
■ **le mont Everest** Mount Everest
■ **le mont Blanc** Mont Blanc

la **montagne** FEM NOUN
mountain
□ de hautes montagnes high mountains
□ des vacances à la montagne holidays in the mountains
■ **les montagnes russes** roller coaster

montagneux (FEM **montagneuse**) ADJECTIVE
mountainous
□ une région montagneuse a mountainous area

montant (FEM **montante**) ADJECTIVE
1 rising
□ la marée montante the rising tide
2 high
□ un pull à col montant a high-necked jumper

monter VERB [48, aux avoir or être]
1 to go up
□ Elle a du mal à monter les escaliers. She has difficulty going upstairs. □ Les prix ont encore monté. Prices have gone up again.
2 to assemble
□ Est-ce que ces étagères sont difficiles à monter ? Are these shelves difficult to assemble?

■ **monter dans** to get on □ Il est temps de monter dans l'avion. It's time to get on the plane.
■ **monter sur** to stand on □ Monte sur la chaise : tu verras mieux. Stand on the chair: you'll see better.
■ **monter à** to climb (up) □ Léa monte à un arbre. Léa is climbing a tree.
■ **monter à cheval** to ride

The verb **monter** uses **être** in the perfect tense when you talk about moving upwards. It uses **avoir** in the perfect tense when talking about a person or thing moving up something (for example, up the stairs), describing an increase of something, or talking about putting something together.

la **montre** FEM NOUN
watch

montrer VERB [28]
to show
□ Montre-moi ton nouveau manteau. Show me your new coat.

la **monture** FEM NOUN
frames (of glasses)

le **monument** MASC NOUN
monument

se **moquer** VERB [28]
■ **se moquer de 1** to make fun of □ Ils se sont moqués de mes chaussures jaunes. They made fun of my yellow shoes. **2** (informal) not to care about □ Il se moque complètement de la mode. He couldn't care less about fashion.

la **moquette** FEM NOUN
fitted carpet

moqueur (FEM **moqueuse**) ADJECTIVE
mocking

le **moral** MASC NOUN
■ **Elle a le moral.** She's in good spirits.
■ **J'ai le moral à zéro.** I'm feeling really down.

moral (FEM **morale**) ADJECTIVE
moral
□ une question morale a moral issue

la **morale** FEM NOUN
moral
□ La morale de cette histoire est ... The moral of the story is ...
■ **faire la morale à quelqu'un** to lecture somebody

le **morceau** (PL les **morceaux**) MASC NOUN
piece
□ un morceau de pain a piece of bread

mordre VERB [49]
to bite

mordu (FEM **mordue**) ADJECTIVE
■ **Il est mordu de jazz.** (informal) He's crazy about jazz.

m

la **morgue** FEM NOUN
mortuary

le **morse** MASC NOUN
walrus

la **morsure** FEM NOUN
bite

mort (FEM **morte**) ADJECTIVE
▷ *see also* **mort** VERB, NOUN
dead
□ Nous avons trouvé un oiseau mort. We found a dead bird.
■ **Il était mort de peur.** He was scared to death.
■ **Je suis morte de fatigue.** I'm dead tired.

mort VERB ▷ *see* **mourir**
▷ *see also* **mort** ADJECTIVE, NOUN
■ **Napoléon est mort en 1821.** Napoleon died in 1821.

la **mort** FEM NOUN
▷ *see also* **mort** ADJECTIVE, VERB
death

mortel (FEM **mortelle**) ADJECTIVE
1 deadly
□ un poison mortel a deadly poison □ Ces réunions de famille sont mortelles ! (*informal*) These family gatherings are deadly!
2 fatal
□ une chute mortelle a fatal fall

la **morue** FEM NOUN
cod

Moscou NOUN
Moscow

la **mosquée** FEM NOUN
mosque

le **mot** MASC NOUN
1 word
□ mot à mot word for word
■ **des mots croisés** a crossword
■ **un mot de passe** a password
■ **un gros mot** a swearword
2 note
□ Je vais lui écrire un mot pour lui dire qu'on arrive. I'll write her a note to say we're coming.

le **motard** MASC NOUN
1 biker
2 motorcycle cop (*informal*)
□ Il s'est fait arrêter par un motard. He was stopped by a motorcycle cop.

le **moteur** MASC NOUN
engine
■ **un bateau à moteur** a motor boat
■ **un moteur de recherche** a search engine

le **motif** MASC NOUN
pattern
□ des rideaux avec un motif d'oiseaux curtains with a bird pattern
■ **sans motif** for no reason □ Il s'est fâché sans motif. He got angry for no reason.

motivé (FEM **motivée**) ADJECTIVE
motivated

la **moto** FEM NOUN
motorbike

le/la **motocycliste** MASC/FEM NOUN
motorcyclist

mou (FEM **molle**) ADJECTIVE
1 soft
□ Mon matelas est trop mou. My mattress is too soft.
2 lethargic
□ Je le trouve un peu mou. I find him a bit lethargic.

la **mouche** FEM NOUN
fly
■ **prendre la mouche** to take the huff

se **moucher** VERB [28]
to blow one's nose

le **moucheron** MASC NOUN
midge

le **mouchoir** MASC NOUN
handkerchief
■ **un mouchoir en papier** a tissue

moudre VERB [50]
to grind

la **moue** FEM NOUN
pout
■ **faire la moue** to pout

la **mouette** FEM NOUN
seagull

la **moufle** FEM NOUN
mitt

mouillé (FEM **mouillée**) ADJECTIVE
wet

mouiller VERB [28]
to get wet
□ J'ai mouillé les manches de mon pull. I got the sleeves of my jumper wet.
■ **se mouiller** to get wet □ Attention, tu vas te mouiller ! Careful, you'll get wet!

moulant (FEM **moulante**) ADJECTIVE
figure-hugging
□ une robe moulante a figure-hugging dress

la **moule** FEM NOUN
▷ *see also* **moule** NOUN
mussel

le **moule** MASC NOUN
▷ *see also* **moule** NOUN
■ **un moule à gâteaux** a cake tin

le **moulin** MASC NOUN
mill

moulu VERB ▷ *see* **moudre**

mourir VERB [51], *aux* être
to die
■ **mourir de faim** to starve to death □ Des centaines de personnes sont mortes de faim.

m

Hundreds of people starved to death.
- **Je meurs de faim !** I'm starving!
- **mourir de froid** to die of exposure
- **Je meurs de froid !** I'm freezing!
- **mourir d'envie de faire quelque chose** to be dying to do something □ Je meurs d'envie d'aller me baigner. I'm dying to go for a swim.

la **mousse** FEM NOUN
1 moss
  □ un rocher recouvert de mousse a rock covered with moss
2 froth (on beer)
3 lather (of soap, shampoo)
4 mousse
  □ une mousse au chocolat a chocolate mousse
  □ une mousse de poisson a fish mousse
  - **la mousse à raser** shaving foam

mousseux (FEM **mousseuse**) ADJECTIVE
  - **un vin mousseux** a sparkling wine

la **moustache** FEM NOUN
  moustache
  - **les moustaches** (of a cat) whiskers

le **moustique** MASC NOUN
  mosquito

la **moutarde** FEM NOUN
  mustard

le **mouton** MASC NOUN
1 sheep
  □ une peau de mouton a sheepskin
2 mutton
  □ un gigot de mouton a leg of mutton

le **mouvement** MASC NOUN
  movement

mouvementé (FEM **mouvementée**)
  ADJECTIVE
  eventful
  □ des vacances mouvementées eventful holidays

moyen (FEM **moyenne**) ADJECTIVE
  ▷ see also **moyen** NOUN, **moyenne** NOUN
1 average
  □ Je suis plutôt moyenne en langues. I'm just average at languages.
2 medium
  □ Elle est de taille moyenne. She's of medium height.
  - **le Moyen Âge** the Middle Ages

le **moyen** MASC NOUN
  ▷ see also **moyen** ADJECTIVE
  way
  □ Quel est le meilleur moyen de le convaincre ? What's the best way of convincing him?
  - **Je n'en ai pas les moyens.** I can't afford it.
  - **Ils n'ont pas les moyens de s'acheter une voiture.** They can't afford to buy a car.
  - **un moyen de transport** a means of transport
  - **par tous les moyens** by every possible means

la **moyenne** FEM NOUN
  ▷ see also **moyen** ADJECTIVE
  - **avoir la moyenne** to get a pass mark
  □ J'espère avoir la moyenne en maths. I hope to get a pass mark in maths.
  - **en moyenne** on average
  - **la moyenne d'âge** the average age

le **Moyen-Orient** MASC NOUN
  Middle East

muet (FEM **muette**) ADJECTIVE
  with a speech impairment (not speaking)
  - **un film muet** a silent film

le **muguet** MASC NOUN
  lily of the valley

multiple (FEM **multiple**) ADJECTIVE
  numerous
  □ en de multiples occasions on numerous occasions

multiplier VERB [19]
  to multiply

multitâche ADJECTIVE
  multitasking (also for computer)

municipal (FEM **municipale**, MASC PL
  municipaux) ADJECTIVE
  - **la bibliothèque municipale** the public library

la **municipalité** FEM NOUN
  town council

munir VERB [38]
  - **munir quelqu'un de** to equip someone with
  - **se munir de** to equip oneself with

les **munitions** FEM PL NOUN
  ammunition sing

le **mur** MASC NOUN
  wall

mûr (FEM **mûre**) ADJECTIVE
  ▷ see also **mûre** NOUN
1 ripe (fruit)
2 mature (person)

la **mûre** FEM NOUN
  ▷ see also **mûr** ADJECTIVE
  bramble

mûrir VERB [38]
1 to ripen
  □ Les fraises ont mis du temps à mûrir. The strawberries took a while to ripen.
2 to make mature
  □ Cette expérience l'a beaucoup mûrie. That experience has made her much more mature.

murmurer VERB [28]
  to whisper
  □ Il m'a murmuré à l'oreille qu'il allait partir. He whispered in my ear that he was going to go.

la **muscade** FEM NOUN
  nutmeg

le **muscat** MASC NOUN
1 muscat grape
2 muscatel (*wine*)
□ un verre de muscat a glass of muscatel

le **muscle** MASC NOUN
muscle

musclé (FEM **musclée**) ADJECTIVE
muscular

la **musculation** FEM NOUN
weight training

le **museau** (PL les **museaux**) MASC NOUN
muzzle

le **musée** MASC NOUN
museum

musical (FEM **musicale**, MASC PL **musicaux**)
ADJECTIVE
musical
■ avoir l'oreille musicale to be musical

le **music-hall** MASC NOUN
variety
□ une chanteuse de music-hall a variety singer

le **musicien** MASC NOUN
musician

la **musicienne** FEM NOUN
musician

la **musique** FEM NOUN
music

musulman (FEM **musulmane**) ADJECTIVE,
NOUN
Muslim
■ un musulman a Muslim (*man*)
■ une musulmane a Muslim (*woman*)

la **mutation** FEM NOUN
transfer
□ Il a demandé sa mutation à Paris. He asked for
a transfer to Paris.

la **mutuelle** FEM NOUN
private health insurance

myope (FEM **myope**) ADJECTIVE
short-sighted

le **mystère** MASC NOUN
mystery

mystérieux (FEM **mystérieuse**) ADJECTIVE
mysterious

le **mythe** MASC NOUN
myth

m

Nn

n' PRONOUN ▷ *see* **ne**

la **nage** FEM NOUN
- **traverser une rivière à la nage** to swim across a river
- **être en nage** to be sweating profusely

la **nageoire** FEM NOUN
fin

nager VERB [45]
to swim

le **nageur** MASC NOUN
swimmer

la **nageuse** FEM NOUN
swimmer

naïf (FEM **naïve**) ADJECTIVE
naïve

la **naissance** FEM NOUN
birth
- **votre date de naissance** your date of birth

naître VERB [52, *aux* **être**]
to be born
- **Il est né en 2001.** He was born in 2001.

naïve FEM ADJECTIVE ▷ *see* **naïf**

la **nana** FEM NOUN (*informal*)
girl

la **nappe** FEM NOUN
tablecloth

la **narine** FEM NOUN
nostril

natal (FEM **natale**) ADJECTIVE
native
- mon pays natal my native country

la **natation** FEM NOUN
swimming
- La natation est mon sport favori. Swimming's my favourite sport.
- **faire de la natation** to go swimming

la **nation** FEM NOUN
nation
- les Nations Unies the United Nations

national (FEM **nationale**, MASC PL **nationaux**) ADJECTIVE
▷ *see also* **nationale** NOUN
national
- **la fête nationale espagnole** the national day of Spain

la **nationale** FEM NOUN
▷ *see also* **national** ADJECTIVE
main road
- En vélo, il vaut mieux éviter les nationales. When on a bike it's better to avoid main roads.

la **nationalité** FEM NOUN
nationality

la **natte** FEM NOUN
plait
- Cécile avait des nattes. Cécile had plaits.

la **nature** FEM NOUN
▷ *see also* **nature** ADJECTIVE
nature

nature (FEM **nature**) ADJECTIVE
▷ *see also* **nature** NOUN
plain
- un yaourt nature a plain yoghurt

naturel (FEM **naturelle**) ADJECTIVE
natural

naturellement ADVERB
of course
- Vous viendrez à notre fête ? — Naturellement ! Are you coming to our party? — Of course!
- Naturellement, il est encore en retard. Of course, he's late again.

le **naufrage** MASC NOUN
shipwreck

nautique (FEM **nautique**) ADJECTIVE
water
- **les sports nautiques** water sports
- **le ski nautique** water-skiing

le **navet** MASC NOUN
turnip

la **navette** FEM NOUN
shuttle
- la navette entre la gare et l'aéroport the shuttle between the station and the airport
- **faire la navette** to commute □ Je fais la navette entre Paris et Ivry. I commute between Paris and Ivry.

le **navigateur** MASC NOUN
browser (*on computer*)

la **navigation** FEM NOUN
- **La navigation est interdite ici.** Boats are not allowed here.

naviguer VERB [28]
   to sail

le **navire** MASC NOUN
   ship

ne ADVERB

> ne can be combined with other words to
> form negative phrases:
>
> | | |
> |---|---|
> | ne ... **pas** not | ne ... **personne** no one |
> | ne ... **que** only | ne ... **jamais** never |
> | ne ... **rien** nothing | ne ... **plus** no longer |
> | ne ... **ni** neither | ne ... **aucun(e)** none |

□ Je ne peux pas venir. I can't come. □ Ils ne
vont jamais en boîte. They never go to discos.
□ Je ne connais personne ici. I don't know
anyone here. □ Il ne veut ni manger ni dormir.
He neither wants to eat nor sleep.

> ne changes to n' before a vowel and most
> words beginning with 'h'.

□ Je n'ai pas d'argent. I haven't got any money.
□ Il n'habite plus à Paris. He doesn't live in Paris
any more.

> ne is sometimes not translated.

□ C'est plus loin que je ne le croyais. It's further
than I thought.

né VERB ▷ *see* **naître**
   born
   □ Elle est née en 2005. She was born in 2005.

néanmoins ADVERB
   nevertheless

nécessaire (FEM **nécessaire**) ADJECTIVE
   necessary
   □ Il est nécessaire de réserver. It's necessary
   to book.

la **nécessité** FEM NOUN
1 necessity
   □ par nécessité out of necessity
2 need
   □ la nécessité de mesures radicales the need for
   drastic measures

le **nectar** MASC NOUN
   ■ le nectar d'abricot apricot drink

néerlandais (FEM **néerlandaise**) ADJECTIVE,
   NOUN
   Dutch
   □ Manon parle néerlandais. Manon speaks
   Dutch.
   ■ un Néerlandais a Dutchman
   ■ une Néerlandaise a Dutchwoman
   ■ les Néerlandais the Dutch

négatif (FEM **négative**) ADJECTIVE
   ▷ *see also* **négatif** NOUN
   negative

le **négatif** MASC NOUN
   ▷ *see also* **négatif** ADJECTIVE
   negative (*of photo*)

négligé (FEM **négligée**) ADJECTIVE
   scruffy
   □ une tenue négligée scruffy clothes

négliger VERB [45]
   to neglect
   □ Ces derniers temps il a négligé son travail.
   He's been neglecting his work recently.

négocier VERB [19]
   to negotiate

la **neige** FEM NOUN
   snow
   ■ un bonhomme de neige a snowman

neiger VERB [45]
   to snow
   ■ Il neige. It's snowing.

le **nénuphar** MASC NOUN
   water lily

le **néon** MASC NOUN
   neon
   □ une lampe au néon a neon light □ La cuisine
   est éclairée au néon. The kitchen has a neon
   light.

néo-zélandais (FEM **néo-zélandaise**)
   ADJECTIVE, NOUN
   New Zealand
   □ Le champion néo-zélandais a gagné la
   course. The New Zealand champion won the
   race.
   ■ un Néo-Zélandais a New Zealander (*man*)
   ■ une Néo-Zélandaise a New Zealander
   (*woman*)

le **nerf** MASC NOUN
   nerve
   ■ taper sur les nerfs de quelqu'un to get on
   somebody's nerves □ Il me tape sur les nerfs.
   He's getting on my nerves.

nerveux (FEM **nerveuse**) ADJECTIVE
   nervous

la **nervosité** FEM NOUN
   nervousness

n'est-ce pas ADVERB

> n'est-ce pas is used to check that something
> is true.

□ Nous sommes le douze aujourd'hui, n'est-ce
pas ? It's the 12th today, isn't it? □ Ils sont
venus l'an dernier, n'est-ce pas ? They came
last year, didn't they? □ Elle aura dix-huit ans en
octobre, n'est-ce pas ? She'll be 18 in October,
won't she?

le **Net** MASC NOUN
   the Net

net (FEM **nette**) ADJECTIVE, ADVERB
1 clear
   □ L'image n'est pas nette. The picture isn't very
   clear.
2 net
   □ Poids net : 500 g. Net weight: 500 g.

n

3 flatly

☐ Il a refusé net de nous aider. He flatly refused to help us.

■ **s'arrêter net** to stop dead

nettement ADVERB

much

☐ Ce magasin est nettement plus cher. This shop is much more expensive.

le **nettoyage** MASC NOUN

cleaning

■ **le nettoyage à sec** dry cleaning

nettoyer VERB [53]

to clean

neuf (FEM **neuve**) ADJECTIVE

▷ see also **neuf** NUMBER

new

☐ des chaussures neuves new shoes

neuf NUMBER

▷ see also **neuf** ADJECTIVE

nine

☐ Claire a neuf ans. Claire is nine. ☐ Il est neuf heures du matin. It's nine in the morning.

■ **le neuf février** the ninth of February

neurodivergent (FEM **neurodivergente**) ADJECTIVE

neurodivergent

neutre (FEM **neutre**) ADJECTIVE

neutral

neuve FEM ADJECTIVE ▷ see **neuf**

neuvième (FEM **neuvième**) ADJECTIVE

ninth

☐ au neuvième étage on the ninth floor

le **neveu** (PL les **neveux**) MASC NOUN

nephew

le **nez** MASC NOUN

nose

■ **se trouver nez à nez avec quelqu'un** to come face to face with somebody

ni CONJUNCTION

■ **(ne ...) ni ... ni ...** neither ... nor ... ☐ Je n'aime ni les lentilles ni les épinards. I like neither lentils nor spinach. ☐ ni l'un ni l'autre neither of them

la **niche** FEM NOUN

kennel

le **nid** MASC NOUN

nest

la **nièce** FEM NOUN

niece

nier VERB [19]

to deny

n'importe ADVERB

■ **n'importe quel** any old ☐ N'importe quel stylo fera l'affaire. Any old pen will do.

■ **n'importe qui** anybody ☐ N'ouvre pas la porte à n'importe qui. Don't open the door to just anybody.

■ **n'importe quoi** anything ☐ Je ferais n'importe quoi pour elle. I'd do anything for her.

■ **Tu dis n'importe quoi.** You're talking rubbish.

■ **n'importe où** anywhere ☐ On trouve ces fleurs n'importe où. You can find these flowers anywhere.

■ **Ne laisse pas tes affaires n'importe où.** Don't leave your things lying everywhere.

■ **n'importe quand** any time ☐ Tu peux venir n'importe quand. You can come any time.

■ **n'importe comment** any old how ☐ Ces livres sont rangés n'importe comment. These books have been put away any old how.

le **niveau** (PL les **niveaux**) MASC NOUN

1 level

☐ le niveau de l'eau the water level ■ **Ces deux enfants n'ont pas le même niveau.** These two children aren't at the same level.

2 standard

■ **le niveau de vie** the standard of living

■ **Le niveau est très élevé.** The standard is very high.

noble (FEM **noble**) ADJECTIVE

noble

la **noblesse** FEM NOUN

nobility

la **noce** FEM NOUN

wedding

■ **un repas de noces** a wedding reception

■ **leurs noces d'or** their golden wedding anniversary

nocif (FEM **nocive**) ADJECTIVE

harmful

☐ une substance nocive a harmful substance

nocturne (FEM **nocturne**) ADJECTIVE

▷ see also **nocturne** NOUN

1 nocturnal

☐ un oiseau nocturne a nocturnal bird

2 by night

☐ Découvrez le Paris nocturne ! Discover Paris by night!

la **nocturne** FEM NOUN

▷ see also **nocturne** ADJECTIVE

late-night opening

☐ Nocturne le vendredi jusqu'à vingt-trois heures. Late-night opening until 11 p.m. on Fridays.

le **Noël** MASC NOUN

Christmas

☐ Qu'est-ce que tu as eu pour Noël ? What did you get for Christmas?

■ **Joyeux Noël !** Merry Christmas!

le **nœud** MASC NOUN

1 knot

☐ Il a fait un nœud à la corde. He tied a knot in the rope.

2 bow

□ Janet avait un nœud dans les cheveux. **Janet had a bow in her hair.**

■ **un nœud papillon** a bow tie

noir (FEM **noire**) ADJECTIVE

▷ *see also* **noir** NOUN

1 black

□ Elle porte une robe noire. **She's wearing a black dress.**

2 Black

□ Elle est noire. **She is Black.**

3 dark

□ Il fait noir dehors. **It's dark outside.**

le noir MASC NOUN

▷ *see also* **noir** ADJECTIVE

dark

□ J'ai peur du noir. **I'm afraid of the dark.**

■ **le travail au noir** moonlighting

la noisette FEM NOUN

hazelnut

la noix (PL **les noix**) FEM NOUN

walnut

■ **une noix de coco** a coconut

■ **les noix de cajou** cashew nuts

■ **une noix de beurre** a knob of butter

le nom MASC NOUN

1 name

□ votre nom **your name**

■ **mon nom de famille** my surname

■ **son nom de jeune fille** her maiden name

■ **mon nom d'utilisateur** my username

2 noun (*in grammar*)

□ un nom commun **a common noun** □ un nom propre **a proper noun**

le nombre MASC NOUN

number

□ Treize est un nombre impair. **Thirteen is an odd number.** □ un grand nombre d'amis **a large number of friends**

nombreux (FEM **nombreuse**) ADJECTIVE

1 many

□ Il a gagné de nombreux matchs. **He's won many matches.**

2 large

□ une famille nombreuse **a large family**

■ **peu nombreux** few □ Nous étions peu nombreux à la réunion. **There were few of us at the meeting.**

le nombril MASC NOUN

navel

nommer VERB [28]

1 to name

□ Il n'a voulu nommer personne. **He didn't want to name anybody.**

2 to appoint

□ Il a été nommé directeur. **He was appointed director.**

non ADVERB

no

□ Tu as vu Amandine ? — Non. **Have you seen Amandine? — No.**

■ **non seulement** not only □ Il est non seulement intelligent, mais aussi très gentil. **Not only is he intelligent, he's also very nice.**

■ **Moi non plus.** Neither do I. □ Je n'aime pas les hamburgers. — Moi non plus. **I don't like hamburgers. — Neither do I.** □ Il n'y est pas allé et moi non plus. **He didn't go and neither did I.**

non alcoolisé (FEM **non alcoolisée**)

ADJECTIVE

non-alcoholic

□ les boissons non alcoolisées **non-alcoholic drinks**

non-binaire ADJECTIVE

non-binary

□ les personnes non-binaires **non-binary people**

le non-fumeur MASC NOUN

non-smoker

□ Sébastien est un non-fumeur. **Sébastien's a non-smoker.**

le nord MASC NOUN

▷ *see also* **nord** ADJECTIVE

north

□ Ils vivent dans le nord de l'île. **They live in the north of the island.**

■ **vers le nord** northwards

■ **au nord de Paris** north of Paris

■ **l'Afrique du Nord** North Africa

■ **le vent du nord** the north wind

nord (FEM+PL **nord**) ADJECTIVE

▷ *see also* **nord** NOUN

1 north

□ la face nord du Mont-Blanc **the north face of Mont-Blanc**

■ **le pôle Nord** the North Pole

2 northern

□ Nous avons visité la partie nord de l'île. **We visited the northern part of the island.**

le nord-est MASC NOUN

north-east

□ les régions du nord-est **north-eastern regions**

le nord-ouest MASC NOUN

north-west

□ l'Europe du nord-ouest **north-west Europe**

normal (FEM **normale**, MASC PL **normaux**)

ADJECTIVE

1 normal

□ un bébé normal **a normal baby**

2 natural

□ C'est tout à fait normal. **It's perfectly natural.**

■ **Vous trouvez que c'est normal ?** Does that seem right to you?

normalement - nouvel

normalement ADVERB

normally
□ Les aéroports fonctionnent tous normalement. The airports are all working normally.
■ **Normalement, elle doit arriver à huit heures.** She's supposed to arrive at 8 o'clock.
■ **Tu es libre ce week-end ? — Oui, normalement.** Are you free this weekend? — Yes, I should be.

normand (FEM **normande**) ADJECTIVE
■ **un village normand** a village in Normandy
■ **la côte normande** the coast of Normandy

la **Normandie** FEM NOUN
Normandy

la **Norvège** FEM NOUN
Norway

norvégien (FEM **norvégienne**) ADJECTIVE, NOUN
Norwegian
□ Elle parle norvégien. She speaks Norwegian.
■ **un Norvégien** a Norwegian (*man*)
■ **une Norvégienne** a Norwegian (*woman*)

nos PL ADJECTIVE
our
□ Où sont nos affaires ? Where are our things?

le **notaire** MASC NOUN
solicitor
□ Son père est notaire. His father's a solicitor.

notamment ADVERB
in particular

la **note** FEM NOUN
1 note
□ J'ai pris des notes pendant la conférence. I took notes at the lecture. □ Il a joué quelques notes au piano. He played a few notes on the piano.
2 mark
□ Vincent a de bonnes notes en maths. Vincent's got good marks in maths.
3 bill
□ Il n'a pas payé sa note. He didn't pay his bill.

noter VERB [28]
to make a note of
□ Tu as noté leur adresse ? Did you make a note of their address?

les **notions** FEM PL NOUN
basics
□ Il faut avoir des notions d'anglais. You have to have some basic English. □ Elle a des notions de comptabilité. She knows the basics of accounting.

notre (FEM **notre**, PL **nos**) ADJECTIVE
our
□ Voici notre maison. Here's our house.

nôtre PRONOUN
■ **le nôtre** ours □ À qui est ce chien ? — C'est le nôtre. Whose dog is it? — It's ours.

■ **la nôtre** ours □ Leur voiture est rouge, la nôtre est bleue. Their car is red, ours is blue.

nôtres PL PRONOUN
■ **les nôtres** ours □ Ces places-là sont les nôtres. Those seats are ours.

nouer VERB [28]
to tie

les **nouilles** FEM PL NOUN
noodles

le **nounours** MASC NOUN
teddy bear

nourrir VERB [38]
to feed

la **nourriture** FEM NOUN
food

nous PL PRONOUN
1 we
□ Nous avons deux enfants. We have two children.
2 us
□ Viens avec nous. Come with us.
3 ourselves
□ Nous nous sommes bien amusés. We really enjoyed ourselves.

> With reflexive verbs, **nous** is often not translated.

□ Nous nous sommes levés très tard. We got up very late.
■ **nous-mêmes** ourselves
■ **à nous** ours □ Ces manteaux sont à nous. These coats are ours.

nouveau (FEM **nouvelle**, MASC PL **nouveaux**) ADJECTIVE
▷ *see also* **nouveau** NOUN
new
□ Il me faut un nouveau pantalon. I need some new trousers. □ Elle a une nouvelle voiture. She's got a new car.

> The masculine singular form **nouveau** changes to **nouvel** before a vowel and most words beginning with 'h'.

□ le nouvel élève dans ma classe the new boy in my class
■ **le nouvel an** New Year

le **nouveau** (PL les **nouveaux**) MASC NOUN
▷ *see also* **nouveau** ADJECTIVE
new pupil
□ Il y a plusieurs nouveaux dans la classe. There are several new pupils in the class.
■ **de nouveau** again □ Il pleut de nouveau. It's raining again.

le **nouveau-né** MASC NOUN
newborn child

la **nouveauté** FEM NOUN
novelty

nouvel, nouvelle ADJECTIVE ▷ *see* **nouveau**

Numbers in brackets refer to verb tables on pages 650 to 658

la **nouvelle** FEM NOUN
> ▷ *see also* **nouveau** ADJECTIVE
1 news
  □ Tu connais la nouvelle ? Teresa a gagné au loto.
  Have you heard the news? Teresa won the lottery.
  □ C'est une bonne nouvelle. That's good news.
2 short story
  □ une nouvelle de Balzac a short story by Balzac
  ■ **les nouvelles** the news □ J'ai écouté les
  nouvelles à la radio. I listened to the news on
  the radio.
  ■ **avoir des nouvelles de quelqu'un** to hear
  from somebody □ Je n'ai pas eu de nouvelles de
  lui. I haven't heard from him.

la **Nouvelle-Zélande** FEM NOUN
  New Zealand

novembre MASC NOUN
  November
  ■ **en novembre** in November

le **noyau** (PL les **noyaux**) MASC NOUN
  stone (*of fruit*)
  □ un noyau d'abricot an apricot stone

le **noyer** MASC NOUN
  > ▷ *see also* **noyer** VERB
  walnut tree

se **noyer** VERB [53]
  > ▷ *see also* **noyer** NOUN
  to drown
  □ Il s'est noyé dans la rivière. He drowned in
  the river.

nu (FEM **nue**) ADJECTIVE
1 naked
  □ Ils se sont baignés nus. They went for a swim
  naked. □ tout nus stark naked
2 bare
  □ Elle avait les bras nus. Her arms were bare.
  □ Les murs étaient nus. The walls were bare.

le **nuage** MASC NOUN
  cloud
  ■ **un nuage de lait** a drop of milk

nuageux (FEM **nuageuse**) ADJECTIVE
  cloudy

nucléaire (FEM **nucléaire**) ADJECTIVE
  nuclear
  □ l'énergie nucléaire nuclear power

le/la **nudiste** MASC/FEM NOUN
  nudist

la **nuit** FEM NOUN
  night
  □ Ils ont fait du bruit toute la nuit. They were
  noisy all night.
  ■ **Il fait nuit.** It's dark.
  ■ **cette nuit** tonight □ Il va rentrer cette nuit.
  He'll be back tonight.
  ■ **Bonne nuit !** Good night!
  ■ **de nuit** by night

nul (FEM **nulle**) ADJECTIVE
  rubbish
  □ Ce film est nul. (*informal*) This film's rubbish.
  ■ **être nul** to be no good □ Je suis nul en maths.
  I'm no good at maths.
  ■ **un match nul** a draw (*in sport*) □ Ils ont fait
  match nul. It was a draw.
  ■ **nulle part** nowhere □ Je ne le vois nulle part.
  I can't see it anywhere.

numérique (FEM **numérique**) ADJECTIVE
  digital
  □ un appareil photo numérique a digital camera

le **numéro** MASC NOUN
  number
  □ J'habite au numéro trois. I live at
  number 3.
  ■ **mon numéro de téléphone** my phone
  number
  ■ **le numéro de compte** the account number

nu-pieds (FEM+PL **nu-pieds**) ADJECTIVE, ADVERB
  barefoot
  □ Il se promenait nu-pieds. He was walking
  barefoot.

la **nuque** FEM NOUN
  nape of the neck

le **nylon** MASC NOUN
  nylon

n

Oo

obéir VERB [38]

to obey

■ **obéir à quelqu'un** to obey somebody □ Elle refuse d'obéir à ses parents. She refuses to obey her parents.

obéissant (FEM **obéissante**) ADJECTIVE

obedient

l'objectif MASC NOUN

aim

□ Notre objectif est de mettre fin au harcèlement dans notre collège. Our aim is to put an end to bullying in our school.

l'objet MASC NOUN

object

■ **les objets de valeur** valuables

■ **les objets trouvés** the lost property office

obligatoire (FEM **obligatoire**) ADJECTIVE

compulsory

obliger VERB [45]

■ **obliger quelqu'un à faire quelque chose** to force somebody to do something

■ **Je suis bien obligé d'accepter.** I can't really refuse.

obscur (FEM **obscure**) ADJECTIVE

dark

l'obscurité FEM NOUN

darkness

□ dans l'obscurité in the dark

l'obsédé MASC NOUN

sex maniac

■ **un obsédé sexuel** a sex maniac

obséder VERB [34]

to obsess

□ Il est obsédé par le travail. He's obsessed by work.

l'observation FEM NOUN

comment

□ J'ai une ou deux observations à faire. I've got one or two comments to make.

observer VERB [28]

1 to watch

□ Il observait les canards sur le lac. He watched the ducks on the lake.

2 to observe

□ Ils observent le règlement. They observe the rules.

l'obstacle MASC NOUN

1 obstacle

□ surmonter un obstacle to overcome an obstacle

2 fence (in show jumping)

■ **une course d'obstacles** an obstacle race

obstiné (FEM **obstinée**) ADJECTIVE

stubborn

obtenir VERB [83]

1 to get

□ Ils ont obtenu cinquante pour cent des voix. They got 50% of the votes.

2 to achieve

□ Nous avons obtenu de bons résultats. We achieved good results.

l'occasion FEM NOUN

1 opportunity

□ C'est une occasion à ne pas manquer. It's an opportunity not to be missed.

2 occasion

□ à l'occasion de son anniversaire on the occasion of his birthday □ à plusieurs occasions on several occasions

3 bargain

□ Cet ordinateur est une bonne occasion. This computer's a real bargain.

■ **d'occasion** second-hand □ une voiture d'occasion a second-hand car

l'Occident MASC NOUN

West

□ en Occident in the West

occidental (FEM **occidentale**, MASC PL **occidentaux**) ADJECTIVE

western

■ **les pays occidentaux** the West

l'occupation FEM NOUN

occupation

□ la France sous l'Occupation France during the Occupation

occupé (FEM **occupée**) ADJECTIVE

1 busy

□ Le directeur est très occupé. The director's very busy.

2 taken

□ Est-ce que cette place est occupée ? Is this seat taken?

o

3 engaged

□ Les toilettes sont occupées. The toilet's engaged. □ La ligne est occupée. The line's engaged.

occuper VERB [28]

to occupy

□ Les enfants ne sont pas faciles à occuper quand il pleut. Children aren't easy to keep occupied when it rains.

■ **s'occuper de quelque chose 1** to be in charge of something □ Elle s'occupe d'un club de sport. She's in charge of a sports club. **2** to deal with something □ Je vais m'occuper de ce dossier. I'm going to deal with this file.

■ **s'occuper de quelqu'un** to take care of someone □ Ils se sont très bien occupés de nous. They took very good care of us.

■ **On s'occupe de vous ?** (*in a shop*) Are you being attended to?

l'océan MASC NOUN

ocean

□ l'océan Indien the Indian Ocean

octobre MASC NOUN

October

■ **en octobre** in October

l'odeur FEM NOUN

smell

□ Il y a une drôle d'odeur ici. There's a funny smell round here.

odieux (FEM **odieuse**) ADJECTIVE

horrible

□ Elle a été odieuse avec nous. She was horrible to us.

l'œil (PL les **yeux**) MASC NOUN

eye

□ J'ai quelque chose dans l'œil. I've got something in my eye.

■ **à l'œil** (*informal*) for free □ Il est entré à l'œil. He got in for free.

l'œillet MASC NOUN

carnation

l'œuf MASC NOUN

egg

■ **un œuf à la coque** a soft-boiled egg

■ **un œuf dur** a hard-boiled egg

■ **un œuf au plat** a fried egg

■ **les œufs brouillés** scrambled eggs

■ **un œuf de Pâques** an Easter egg

l'œuvre FEM NOUN

work

□ J'étudie une œuvre de Molière. I'm studying one of Molière's works.

■ **une œuvre d'art** a work of art

offert VERB ▷ *see* **offrir**

l'office MASC NOUN

■ **un office du tourisme** a tourist office

officiel (FEM **officielle**) ADJECTIVE

official

l'officier MASC NOUN

officer

□ Il est officier de marine. He's a naval officer.

l'offre FEM NOUN

offer

□ une offre spéciale a special offer

■ **« offres d'emploi »** 'situations vacant'

offrir VERB [54]

■ **offrir quelque chose à quelqu'un 1** to offer something to someone □ On lui a offert un poste de secrétaire. They offered her a secretarial post. □ Elle lui a offert à boire. She offered him a drink. **2** to give something to someone □ Il lui a offert des roses. He gave her roses.

■ **s'offrir quelque chose** to treat oneself to something □ Je me suis offert un nouveau sac. I treated myself to a new bag.

l'oie FEM NOUN

goose

l'oignon MASC NOUN

onion

■ **Ce ne sont pas mes oignons !** (*informal*) It's none of my business!

l'oiseau (PL les **oiseaux**) MASC NOUN

bird

l'olive FEM NOUN

olive

□ l'huile d'olive olive oil

olympique (FEM **olympique**) ADJECTIVE

■ **les Jeux olympiques** the Olympic Games®

l'ombre FEM NOUN

1 shade

□ Je vais me mettre à l'ombre. I'm going to sit in the shade.

2 shadow

■ **l'ombre à paupières** eye shadow

l'omelette FEM NOUN

omelette

l'omnibus MASC NOUN

local train

on PRONOUN

1 we

□ On va à la plage demain. We're going to the beach tomorrow. □ On a pensé que ça te ferait plaisir. We thought you'd be pleased.

2 someone

□ On m'a volé mon sac. Someone has stolen my bag.

■ **On m'a dit d'attendre.** I was told to wait.

■ **On vous demande au téléphone.** There's a phone call for you.

3 you

□ On peut visiter le château en été. You can visit the castle in the summer. □ D'ici on peut voir la côte française. From here you can see the French coast.

o

l'**oncle** MASC NOUN
uncle

l'**onde** FEM NOUN
wave (*on radio*)
□ sur les grandes ondes on long wave

l'**ongle** MASC NOUN
nail
■ **se couper les ongles** to cut one's nails □ Elle s'est coupé les ongles. She cut her nails.

ont VERB ▷ *see* **avoir**
■ **Ils ont beaucoup d'argent.** They've got lots of money.
■ **Elles ont passé de bonnes vacances.** They had a good holiday.

l'**ONU** FEM NOUN (= *Organisation des Nations Unies*)
UN (= *United Nations*)

onze NUMBER
eleven
□ Elle a onze ans. She's eleven. □ à onze heures at eleven o'clock
■ **le onze février** the eleventh of February

onzième (FEM **onzième**) ADJECTIVE
eleventh
□ au onzième étage on the eleventh floor

l'**opéra** MASC NOUN
opera

l'**opération** FEM NOUN
operation

opérer VERB [34]
to operate on
□ Elle a été opérée de l'appendicite. She was operated on for appendicitis.
■ **se faire opérer** to have an operation □ Elle s'est fait opérer. She's had an operation.

l'**opinion** FEM NOUN
opinion

opposé (FEM **opposée**) ADJECTIVE
▷ *see also* **opposé** NOUN
opposite
□ Elle est partie dans la direction opposée. She went off in the opposite direction.
■ **être opposé à quelque chose** to be opposed to something

l'**opposé** MASC NOUN
▷ *see also* **opposé** ADJECTIVE
the opposite

opposer VERB [28]
■ **opposer quelqu'un à quelqu'un** to pit somebody against somebody □ Ce match oppose les Français aux Allemands. This match pits the French against the Germans.
■ **s'opposer** to conflict □ Ces deux points de vue s'opposent. These two points of view conflict.
■ **s'opposer à quelque chose** to oppose something □ Son père s'oppose à son mariage. Her father's against her marriage.

l'**opposition** FEM NOUN
opposition
■ **par opposition à** as opposed to □ la littérature contemporaine par opposition à la littérature classique modern literature, as opposed to classics
■ **faire opposition à un chèque** to stop a cheque

l'**opticien** MASC NOUN
optician
□ Il est opticien. He's an optician.

l'**opticienne** FEM NOUN
optician
□ Elle est opticienne. She's an optician.

optimiste (FEM **optimiste**) ADJECTIVE
optimistic

l'**option** FEM NOUN
option
■ **une matière à option** an optional subject

l'**or** MASC NOUN
▷ *see also* **or** CONJUNCTION
gold
□ un bracelet en or a gold bracelet

or CONJUNCTION
▷ *see also* **or** NOUN
and yet
□ Il était sûr de gagner, or il a perdu. He was sure he would win, and yet he lost.

l'**orage** MASC NOUN
thunderstorm

orageux (FEM **orageuse**) ADJECTIVE
stormy

oral (FEM **orale**, MASC PL **oraux**) ADJECTIVE
▷ *see also* **oral** NOUN
■ **une épreuve orale** an oral exam
■ **à prendre par voie orale** to be taken orally

l'**oral** (PL les **oraux**) MASC NOUN
▷ *see also* **oral** ADJECTIVE
oral (*exam*)
□ un oral de français a French oral

l'**orange** FEM NOUN
▷ *see also* **orange** ADJECTIVE
orange (*fruit*)

orange (FEM+PL **orange**) ADJECTIVE
▷ *see also* **orange** NOUN
orange (*in colour*)
□ des fleurs orange orange flowers

l'**orchestre** MASC NOUN
1 orchestra
□ un orchestre symphonique a symphony orchestra
2 band
□ un orchestre de jazz a jazz band

l'**ordi** MASC NOUN (*informal*)
computer

ordinaire (FEM **ordinaire**) ADJECTIVE
▷ *see also* **ordinaire** NOUN

1 ordinary
  □ des gens ordinaires ordinary people
2 standard
  □ un format ordinaire a standard size
l'**ordinaire** MASC NOUN
  ▷ see also **ordinaire** ADJECTIVE
  two-star (petrol)
  ■ **sortir de l'ordinaire** to be out of the ordinary
l'**ordinateur** MASC NOUN
  computer
  ■ **un ordinateur de bureau** a desktop computer
  ■ **un ordinateur portable** a laptop computer
l'**ordonnance** FEM NOUN
  prescription
ordonné (FEM **ordonnée**) ADJECTIVE
  tidy
ordonner VERB [28]
  ■ **ordonner à quelqu'un de faire quelque chose** to order somebody to do something
l'**ordre** MASC NOUN
  order
  □ par ordre alphabétique in alphabetical order
  ■ **dans l'ordre** in order □ dans le bon ordre in the right order
  ■ **mettre en ordre** to tidy up
  ■ **jusqu'à nouvel ordre** until further notice
les **ordures** FEM PL NOUN
  rubbish sing
  ■ **jeter quelque chose aux ordures** to throw something in the bin
l'**oreille** FEM NOUN
  ear
l'**oreiller** MASC NOUN
  pillow
les **oreillons** MASC PL NOUN
  mumps
l'**organe** MASC NOUN
  organ (in body)
l'**organisateur** MASC NOUN
  organizer
l'**organisation** FEM NOUN
  organization
l'**organisatrice** FEM NOUN
  organizer
organiser VERB [28]
  to organize
  ■ **s'organiser** to get organized □ Il ne sait pas s'organiser. He can't get himself organized.
l'**organisme** MASC NOUN
  body (organization)
l'**orgue** MASC NOUN
  organ
  □ Paul joue de l'orgue. Paul plays the organ.
orgueilleux (FEM **orgueilleuse**) ADJECTIVE
  proud

l'**Orient** MASC NOUN
  East
  □ en Orient in the East
oriental (FEM **orientale**, MASC PL **orientaux**) ADJECTIVE
1 Oriental
  □ un palais oriental an Oriental palace
2 eastern
  □ la frontière orientale de la Pologne Poland's eastern border
l'**orientation** FEM NOUN
  orientation
  ■ **avoir le sens de l'orientation** to have a good sense of direction
  ■ **l'orientation professionnelle** careers advice
originaire (FEM **originaire**) ADJECTIVE
  ■ **Elle est originaire de Paris.** She's from Paris.
original (FEM **originale**, MASC PL **originaux**) ADJECTIVE
  ▷ see also **original** NOUN
  original
  □ un film en version originale a film in the original language
l'**original** (PL les **originaux**) MASC NOUN
  ▷ see also **original** ADJECTIVE
  original
  □ L'original est au Louvre. The original is in the Louvre.
  ■ **un vieil original** an old eccentric
l'**origine** FEM NOUN
  origin
  ■ **à l'origine** originally
l'**orphelin** MASC NOUN
  orphan
l'**orpheline** FEM NOUN
  orphan
l'**orteil** MASC NOUN
  toe
l'**orthographe** FEM NOUN
  spelling
l'**os** MASC NOUN
  bone
  ■ **tomber sur un os** (informal) to hit a snag
oser VERB [28]
  to dare
  ■ **oser faire quelque chose** to dare to do something
l'**otage** MASC NOUN
  hostage
ôter VERB [28]
1 to take off
  □ Elle a ôté son manteau. She took off her coat.
2 to take away
ou CONJUNCTION
  or
  ■ **ou ... ou ...** either ... or ...
  ■ **ou bien** or else □ On pourrait aller au cinéma

o

ou bien rentrer directement. We could go to the cinema or else go straight home.

où PRONOUN, ADVERB

1 where
□ Où est Nick ? Where's Nick? □ Où allez-vous ? Where are you going? □ Je sais où il est. I know where he is. □ la maison où je suis né the house where I was born □ la ville d'où je viens the town I come from

2 that
□ Le jour où il est parti, tout le monde a pleuré. The day that he left, everyone cried.
■ **Par où allons-nous passer ?** Which way are we going to go?

ouais EXCLAMATION (*informal*)
yeah

l'**ouate** FEM NOUN
cotton wool

oublier VERB [19]

1 to forget
■ **oublier de faire quelque chose** to forget to do something □ N'oublie pas de fermer la porte. Don't forget to shut the door.

2 to leave
□ J'ai oublié mon sac chez Sabine. I left my bag at Sabine's.

l'**ouest** MASC NOUN
▷ *see also* **ouest** ADJECTIVE
west
□ Elle vit dans l'ouest de l'Angleterre. She lives in the West of England.
■ **à l'ouest de Paris** west of Paris
■ **vers l'ouest** westwards
■ **l'Europe de l'Ouest** Western Europe
■ **le vent d'ouest** the west wind

ouest (FEM+PL **ouest**) ADJECTIVE
▷ *see also* **ouest** NOUN

1 west
□ la côte ouest de l'Écosse the west coast of Scotland

2 western
□ la partie ouest du pays the western part of the country

ouf EXCLAMATION
phew!

oui ADVERB
yes

l'**ouragan** MASC NOUN
hurricane

l'**ourlet** MASC NOUN
seam

l'**ours** MASC NOUN
bear
■ **un ours en peluche** a teddy bear

l'**outil** MASC NOUN
tool

outré (FEM **outrée**) ADJECTIVE
outraged
□ Il a été outré de son insolence. He was outraged at her cheek.

ouvert (FEM **ouverte**) ADJECTIVE

1 open
□ Le magasin est ouvert. The shop's open.

2 on
□ Il a laissé le robinet ouvert. He left the tap on.
■ **avoir l'esprit ouvert** to be open-minded

ouvert VERB ▷ *see* **ouvrir**

l'**ouverture** FEM NOUN
opening
□ les heures d'ouverture opening hours

l'**ouvre-boîte** MASC NOUN
tin opener

l'**ouvre-bouteille** MASC NOUN
bottle-opener

l'**ouvreuse** FEM NOUN
usherette

l'**ouvrier** MASC NOUN
worker
□ Son père est ouvrier dans une usine. His father's a factory worker.

l'**ouvrière** FEM NOUN
worker

ouvrir VERB [55]
to open
□ Ouvrez ! Open up! □ Elle a ouvert la porte. She opened the door.
■ **s'ouvrir** to open □ La porte s'est ouverte. The door opened.

ovale (FEM **ovale**) ADJECTIVE
oval

l'**ovni** MASC NOUN (= *objet volant non identifié*)
UFO

l'**oxygène** MASC NOUN
oxygen

l'**ozone** MASC NOUN
ozone

o

Pp

le **Pacifique** MASC NOUN
Pacific
□ l'océan Pacifique the Pacific Ocean

le/la **pacifiste** MASC/FEM NOUN
pacifist

PACS MASC NOUN (= *pacte civil de solidarité*)
civil partnership

se **pacser** VERB [28]
to become civil partners
□ Ils se sont pacsés au lieu de se marier. They
became civil partners instead of getting
married.

la **pagaille** FEM NOUN
mess *sing*
□ Quelle pagaille ! What a mess!

la **page** FEM NOUN
page
□ Tournez la page. Turn the page.
■ **la page d'accueil** (*on internet*) the home
page

la **paie** FEM NOUN
wages

le **paiement** MASC NOUN
payment

le **paillasson** MASC NOUN
doormat

la **paille** FEM NOUN
straw

le **pain** MASC NOUN
1 bread
□ un morceau de pain a piece of bread □ une
tranche de pain a slice of bread
2 loaf
□ J'ai acheté un pain. I bought a loaf of bread.
■ **le pain complet** wholemeal bread
■ **le pain d'épice** gingerbread
■ **le pain de mie** sandwich loaf
■ **le pain grillé** toast

> **DID YOU KNOW...?**
> Bread is always served with a meal in French
> restaurants, at no extra cost.

pair (FEM **paire**) ADJECTIVE
▷ *see also* **paire** NOUN
even
□ un nombre pair an even number
■ **une jeune fille au pair** an au pair

la **paire** FEM NOUN
▷ *see also* **pair** ADJECTIVE
pair
□ une paire de chaussures a pair of shoes

paisible (FEM **paisible**) ADJECTIVE
peaceful
□ un village paisible a peaceful village

la **paix** FEM NOUN
peace
■ **faire la paix** 1 to make peace □ Les deux
pays ont fait la paix. The two countries have
made peace with each other. 2 to make it up
□ Laure a fait la paix avec son frère. Laure made
it up with her brother.
■ **avoir la paix** to have peace and quiet
□ J'aimerais bien avoir la paix. I'd like to have a
bit of peace and quiet.
■ **Fiche-moi la paix !** (*informal*) Leave me
alone!

le **palais** MASC NOUN
1 palace
□ le palais de Buckingham Buckingham Palace
2 palate (*in mouth*)

pâle (FEM **pâle**) ADJECTIVE
pale
□ bleu pâle pale blue

la **Palestine** FEM NOUN
Palestine

la **pâleur** FEM NOUN
paleness

le **palier** MASC NOUN
landing
□ Il m'attendait sur le palier. He was waiting for
me on the landing.

pâlir VERB [38]
to go pale

la **palme** FEM NOUN
flipper (*for swimming*)

palmé (FEM **palmée**) ADJECTIVE
webbed
□ Les canards ont les pieds palmés. Ducks have
webbed feet.

le **palmier** MASC NOUN
palm tree

palpitant (FEM **palpitante**) ADJECTIVE
thrilling
□ un roman palpitant a thrilling novel

le **pamplemousse** MASC NOUN
grapefruit

le **panaché** MASC NOUN
shandy

la **pancarte** FEM NOUN
sign
□ Il y a une pancarte dans la vitrine. There's a sign in the window.

la **pandémie** FEM NOUN
pandemic
□ une pandémie de grippe a flu pandemic

pané (FEM **panée**) ADJECTIVE
fried in breadcrumbs
□ du poisson pané fish in breadcrumbs

le **panier** MASC NOUN
basket

la **panique** FEM NOUN
panic

paniquer VERB [28]
to panic

la **panne** FEM NOUN
breakdown
■ **être en panne** to have broken down □ L'ascenseur est en panne. The lift's not working.
■ **tomber en panne** to break down □ Nous sommes tombés en panne sur l'autoroute. We broke down on the motorway.
■ **Nous sommes tombés en panne d'essence.** We've run out of petrol.
■ **une panne de courant** a power cut

le **panneau** (PL les **panneaux**) MASC NOUN
sign
□ Ce panneau dit que la maison est à vendre. This sign says that the house is for sale.
■ **panneau d'affichage 1** advertising hoarding **2** (in station) arrivals and departures board **3** (on internet) bulletin board

le **panorama** MASC NOUN
panorama

le **pansement** MASC NOUN
1 dressing (bandage)
2 sticking plaster

le **pantalon** MASC NOUN
trousers pl
□ Son pantalon est trop court. His trousers are too short.
■ **un pantalon de ski** a pair of ski pants

la **panthère** FEM NOUN
panther

la **pantoufle** FEM NOUN
slipper

la **PAO** ABBREVIATION (= publication assistée par ordinateur)
DTP (= desktop publishing)

le **paon** MASC NOUN
peacock

le **papa** MASC NOUN
dad

le **pape** MASC NOUN
pope

la **papeterie** FEM NOUN
stationer's

le **papi** MASC NOUN (informal)
granddad

le **papier** MASC NOUN
paper
□ une feuille de papier a sheet of paper
■ **Vos papiers, s'il vous plaît.** Your identity papers, please.
■ **les papiers d'identité** identity papers
■ **le papier à lettres** writing paper
■ **le papier hygiénique** toilet paper
■ **le papier peint** wallpaper

le **papillon** MASC NOUN
butterfly

le **paquebot** MASC NOUN
liner

la **pâquerette** FEM NOUN
daisy

Pâques MASC NOUN
Easter
□ Je viendrai te voir à Pâques. I'll come and see you at Easter.
■ **les œufs de Pâques** Easter eggs

DID YOU KNOW...?
In France, Easter eggs are said to be brought by the Easter bells or **cloches de Pâques** which fly from Rome and drop them in people's gardens.

le **paquet** MASC NOUN
1 packet
□ Je voudrais un paquet de chewing-gums. I'd like a packet of chewing-gum.
2 parcel
□ Sa mère lui a envoyé un paquet. His mother sent him a parcel.

le **paquet-cadeau** (PL les **paquets-cadeaux**) MASC NOUN
gift-wrapped parcel
□ La vendeuse m'a fait un paquet-cadeau. The shop assistant gift-wrapped it for me.

par PREPOSITION
1 by
□ L'Amérique a été découverte par Christophe Colomb. America was discovered by Christopher Columbus.
■ **deux par deux** two by two □ Les élèves sont entrés deux par deux. The pupils went in two by two.
2 with
□ Son nom commence par un H. His name begins with H.
3 out of
□ Elle regardait par la fenêtre. She was looking out of the window. □ par habitude out of habit

4 via
□ Nous sommes passés par Lyon pour aller à Grenoble. **We went via Lyon to Grenoble.**

5 through
□ Il faut passer par la douane avant de prendre l'avion. **You have to go through customs before boarding the plane.**

6 per
□ Prenez trois cachets par jour. **Take three tablets per day.** □ Le voyage coûte deux mille euros par personne. **The trip costs two thousand euros per person.**

■ **par ici 1** this way □ Il faut passer par ici pour y arriver. **You have to go this way to get there.**
2 round here □ Il y a beaucoup de touristes par ici. **There are lots of tourists round here.**

■ **par-ci, par-là** here and there

le **parachute** MASC NOUN
parachute

le/la **parachutiste** MASC/FEM NOUN
parachutist

le **paradis** MASC NOUN
heaven

les **parages** MASC PL NOUN
■ **dans les parages** in the area □ Il n'y a pas d'hôtel dans les parages. **There are no hotels in the area.**

le **paragraphe** MASC NOUN
paragraph

paraître VERB [56]
1 to seem
□ Ça paraît incroyable. **It seems unbelievable.**
2 to look
□ Elle paraît plus jeune que son frère. **She looks younger than her brother.**
■ **il paraît que** it seems that □ Il paraît que c'est la faute de la direction. **It seems that it's the management's fault.**

le **parallèle** MASC NOUN
▷ see also **parallèle** NOUN
parallel
□ Il a fait un parallèle entre ces deux événements. **He drew a parallel between the two events.**

la **parallèle** FEM NOUN
▷ see also **parallèle** NOUN
parallel line

paralympique ADJECTIVE
Paralympic

paralysé (FEM **paralysée**) ADJECTIVE
paralysed

le **parapluie** MASC NOUN
umbrella

le **parasol** MASC NOUN
parasol

le **parc** MASC NOUN
1 park
□ Le dimanche, Emma va se promener au parc.

On Sundays Emma goes for a walk in the park.
■ **un parc d'attractions** an amusement park
■ **un parc éolien** a wind farm
2 grounds
□ Le château est situé au milieu d'un grand parc. **The castle is surrounded by extensive grounds.**

parce que CONJUNCTION
because
□ Il n'est pas venu parce qu'il n'avait pas de voiture. **He didn't come because he didn't have a car.**

le **parcmètre** MASC NOUN
parking meter

parcourir VERB [16]
1 to cover
□ Gavin a parcouru cinquante kilomètres à vélo. **Gavin covered 50 kilometres on his bike.**
2 to glance through
□ J'ai parcouru le journal d'aujourd'hui. **I glanced through today's newspaper.**

le **parcours** MASC NOUN
journey

par-dessous ADVERB
underneath
□ Il portait un pull et une chemise par-dessous. **He was wearing a jumper with a shirt underneath.**

le **pardessus** MASC NOUN
overcoat

par-dessus ADVERB, PREPOSITION
1 on top
□ Elle porte un chemisier et un pull rouge par-dessus. **She's wearing a blouse with a red jumper on top.**
2 over
□ Elle a sauté par-dessus le mur. **She jumped over the wall.**
■ **en avoir par-dessus la tête** to have had enough □ J'en ai par-dessus la tête de tous ces problèmes. **I've had enough of all these problems.**

le **pardon** MASC NOUN
▷ see also **pardon** EXCLAMATION
forgiveness

pardon EXCLAMATION
▷ see also **pardon** NOUN
1 sorry!
□ Oh, pardon ! J'espère que je ne vous ai pas fait mal. **Oh, sorry! I hope I didn't hurt you.**
■ **demander pardon à quelqu'un** to apologize to somebody □ Il leur a demandé pardon. **He apologized to them.**
■ **Je vous demande pardon.** I'm sorry.
2 excuse me!
□ Pardon, madame ! Pouvez-vous me dire où se trouve la poste ? **Excuse me! Could you tell me where the post office is?**

P

pardonner - parrainer

3 pardon?
□ Pardon ? Je n'ai pas compris ce que vous avez dit. **Pardon? I didn't understand what you said.**

pardonner VERB [28]
to forgive
□ Nous lui avons pardonné de nous avoir menti. **We forgave him for lying to us.**

le **pare-brise** (PL les **pare-brise**) MASC NOUN
windscreen

le **pare-chocs** MASC NOUN
bumper

pareil (FEM **pareille**) ADJECTIVE
1 the same
□ Ces deux maisons ne sont pas pareilles. **These two houses aren't the same.**
2 like that
□ J'aime bien sa voiture. J'en voudrais une pareille. **I like his car. I'd like one like that.**
3 such
□ Je refuse d'écouter des bêtises pareilles. **I won't listen to such nonsense.**
■ **sans pareil** unequalled □ un talent sans pareil **an unequalled talent**

la **parenthèse** FEM NOUN
bracket
□ entre parenthèses **in brackets**

les **parents** MASC PL NOUN
1 parents
2 relatives
□ parents et amis **friends and relatives**

la **paresse** FEM NOUN
laziness

paresseux (FEM **paresseuse**) ADJECTIVE
lazy

parfait (FEM **parfaite**) ADJECTIVE
perfect

parfaitement ADVERB
perfectly
□ Il parle parfaitement l'arabe. **He speaks perfect Arabic.**

parfois ADVERB
sometimes

le **parfum** MASC NOUN
1 perfume
2 flavour
□ Je voudrais une glace. — Quel parfum veux-tu ? **I'd like an ice cream. — What flavour would you like?**

parfumé (FEM **parfumée**) ADJECTIVE
1 fragrant
□ une rose très parfumée **a very fragrant rose**
2 flavoured
□ des biscuits parfumés au café **coffee-flavoured biscuits**

la **parfumerie** FEM NOUN
perfume shop

le **pari** MASC NOUN
bet

parier VERB [19]
to bet

Paris NOUN
Paris
■ **à Paris 1** in Paris **2** to Paris

parisien (FEM **parisienne**) ADJECTIVE, NOUN
1 Parisian
□ un célèbre couturier parisien **a famous Parisian designer**
2 Paris
□ le métro parisien **the Paris metro**
■ **un Parisien** a Parisian (man)
■ **une Parisienne** a Parisian (woman)

le **parking** MASC NOUN
car park

BE CAREFUL!
The French word **parking** does not mean **parking**.

le **parlement** MASC NOUN
parliament

parler VERB [28]
1 to speak
□ Vous parlez français ? **Do you speak French?**
2 to talk
□ Nous étions en train de parler quand le directeur est entré. **We were talking when the headmaster came in.**
■ **parler de quelque chose à quelqu'un** to tell somebody about something □ Il m'a parlé de sa nouvelle voiture. **He told me about his new car.**

parmi PREPOSITION
among
□ Ils étaient parmi les meilleurs de la classe. **They were among the best pupils in the class.**

la **paroi** FEM NOUN
wall

la **paroisse** FEM NOUN
parish

la **parole** FEM NOUN
1 speech
□ l'usage de la parole **the power of speech**
2 word
□ Il m'a donné sa parole. **He gave me his word.**
□ Elle a tenu parole. **She kept her word.**
■ **les paroles** lyrics □ J'aime les paroles de cette chanson. **I like the lyrics of this song.**

le **parquet** MASC NOUN
floor (wooden)

le **parrain** MASC NOUN
godfather

parrainer VERB [28]
to sponsor
□ Cette entreprise parraine notre équipe de rugby. **This firm is sponsoring our rugby team.**

pars VERB ▷ *see* partir

la **part** FEM NOUN
1 share
□ Vous n'avez pas eu votre part. **You haven't had your share.**
2 piece
□ une part de gâteau **a piece of cake**
■ **prendre part à quelque chose** to take part in something □ Il va prendre part à la réunion. **He's going to take part in the meeting.**
■ **de la part de** 1 on behalf of □ Je dois vous remercier de la part de mon frère. **I must thank you on behalf of my brother.** 2 from □ C'est un cadeau pour toi, de la part de Clémence. **It's a present for you, from Clémence.**
■ **à part** apart from □ Ils sont tous venus, à part Romain. **They all came, apart from Romain.**

partager VERB [45]
1 to share
□ Ils partagent un appartement. **They share a flat.**
2 to divide
□ Lucie a partagé le gâteau en quatre. **Lucie divided the cake into four.**

le/la **partenaire** MASC/FEM NOUN
partner

le **parti** MASC NOUN
party
□ le Parti socialiste **the Socialist Party**

le **participant** MASC NOUN
participant

la **participante** FEM NOUN
participant

la **participation** FEM NOUN
participation

le **participe** MASC NOUN
participle
■ **le participe passé** the past participle
■ **le participe présent** the present participle

participer VERB [28]
■ **participer à quelque chose** 1 to take part in something □ Hugo va participer à la course. **Hugo is going to take part in the race.** 2 to contribute to something □ Je voudrais participer aux frais. **I would like to contribute to the cost.**

la **particularité** FEM NOUN
characteristic

la **particule** FEM NOUN
particle
■ **particules fines** fine particulate matter

particulier (FEM **particulière**) ADJECTIVE
1 private
□ une maison particulière **a private house**
2 distinctive
□ Ce vin a un arôme particulier. **This wine has a distinctive flavour.**

3 particular
□ Dans ce cas particulier, je ne peux rien faire. **In this particular case, I can't do anything.**
■ **en particulier** 1 particularly □ J'aime les fruits, en particulier les fraises. **I like fruit, particularly strawberries.** 2 in private □ Est-ce que je peux vous parler en particulier ? **Can I speak to you in private?**

particulièrement ADVERB
particularly

la **partie** FEM NOUN
1 part
□ Une partie du groupe partira en Italie. **Part of the group will go to Italy.**
2 game
□ Nous avons fait une partie de tennis. **We played a game of tennis.** □ une partie de cartes **a game of cards**
■ **en partie** partly □ Cela explique en partie le problème. **That partly explains the problem.**
■ **en grande partie** largely □ Son histoire est en grande partie vraie. **His story is largely true.**
■ **faire partie de** to be part of □ Ce tableau fait partie d'une très belle collection. **This picture is part of a very beautiful collection.**

partiel (FEM **partielle**) ADJECTIVE
partial

partir VERB [57, *aux* être]
to go
□ Je lui ai téléphoné mais il était déjà parti. **I phoned him but he'd already gone.**
■ **partir en vacances** to go on holiday
■ **partir de** to leave □ Il est parti de Nice à sept heures. **He left Nice at 7.**
■ **à partir de** from □ Je serai chez moi à partir de huit heures. **I'll be at home from eight o'clock onwards.**

la **partition** FEM NOUN
score (*in music*)
□ une partition de piano **a piano score**

partout ADVERB
everywhere

paru VERB ▷ *see* paraître

la **parution** FEM NOUN
publication
□ Ce roman a eu beaucoup de succès dès sa parution. **This novel was very successful from the moment it came out.**

parvenir VERB [89, *aux* être]
■ **parvenir à faire quelque chose** to manage to do something □ Elle est finalement parvenue à ouvrir la porte. **She finally managed to open the door.**
■ **faire parvenir quelque chose à quelqu'un** to send something to somebody □ Je vous ferai parvenir le colis avant lundi. **I'll send you the parcel before Monday.**

P

pas ADVERB
▷ see also **pas** NOUN
- **ne ... pas** not □ Il ne pleut pas. It's not raining. □ Elle n'est pas venue. She didn't come.
- **ne ... pas de** not (any) □ Ils n'ont pas de voiture. They haven't got a car. □ Je n'ai pas d'argent. I haven't got any money.
- **Vous viendrez à notre soirée, n'est-ce pas ?** You're coming to our party, aren't you?
- **C'est Harry qui a gagné, n'est-ce pas ?** Harry won, didn't he?
- **pas moi** not me □ Elle veut aller au cinéma, pas moi. She wants to go to the cinema, but I don't.
- **pas de** no □ pas de problème no problem
- **pas du tout** not at all □ Je n'aime pas du tout ça. I don't like that at all.
- **pas mal** not bad □ Ce n'est pas mal pour un début. That's not bad for a first attempt. □ Comment allez-vous ? — Pas mal. How are you? — Not bad.
- **pas mal de** quite a lot of □ Il y avait pas mal de monde au concert. There were quite a lot of people at the concert.

le **pas** MASC NOUN
▷ see also **pas** ADVERB
1 pace
□ Il marchait d'un pas rapide. He walked at a fast pace.
2 step
□ Faites trois pas en avant. Take three steps forward. □ un pas en arrière a step backwards
3 footstep
□ J'entends des pas dans l'escalier. I can hear footsteps on the stairs.
- **au pas** at walking pace □ Le cheval est parti au pas. The horse set off at walking pace.
- **faire les cent pas** to pace up and down □ Il faisait les cent pas dans le couloir. He was pacing up and down the corridor.

le **passage** MASC NOUN
passage
□ J'ai traduit un passage de ce livre. I translated a passage from this book.
- **Il a été éclaboussé au passage de la voiture.** He was soaked by a passing car.
- **de passage** passing through □ Nous sommes de passage à Toulouse. We're just passing through Toulouse.
- **un passage à niveau** a level crossing
- **un passage clouté** a pedestrian crossing
- **un passage protégé** a pedestrian crossing
- **un passage souterrain** a subway

passager (FEM **passagère**) ADJECTIVE
▷ see also **passager** NOUN, **passagère** NOUN
temporary

le **passager** MASC NOUN
▷ see also **passager** ADJECTIVE
passenger
- **un passager clandestin** a stowaway

la **passagère** FEM NOUN
▷ see also **passager** ADJECTIVE
passenger

le **passant** MASC NOUN
passer-by

la **passante** FEM NOUN
passer-by

passé (FEM **passée**) ADJECTIVE
▷ see also **passé** NOUN
1 last
□ Je l'ai vu la semaine passée. I saw him last week.
2 past
□ Il est minuit passé. It's past midnight.

le **passé** MASC NOUN
▷ see also **passé** ADJECTIVE
1 past
□ dans le passé in the past
2 past tense
□ Mettez ce verbe au passé. Put this verb into the past tense.
- **le passé composé** the perfect tense
- **le passé simple** the past historic

le **passeport** MASC NOUN
passport

passer VERB [58, aux **avoir** or **être**]
1 to cross
□ Nous avons passé la frontière belge. We crossed the Belgian border.
2 to go through
□ Il faut passer la douane en sortant. You have to go through customs on the way out.
3 to spend
□ Elle a passé la journée à ne rien faire. She spent the day doing nothing. □ Ils passent toujours leurs vacances au Danemark. They always spend their holidays in Denmark.
4 to take
□ Mathieu a passé ses examens la semaine dernière. Mathieu took his exams last week.

> **BE CAREFUL!**
> **passer un examen** does not mean **to pass an exam**.

5 to pass
□ Passe-moi le sel, s'il te plaît. Pass me the salt, please.
6 to show
□ On passe « Le Kid » au cinéma cette semaine. They're showing 'The Kid' at the cinema this week.
7 to call in
□ Je passerai chez vous ce soir. I'll call in this evening.
- **passer à la radio** to be on the radio □ Mon père passe à la radio demain soir. My father's on the radio tomorrow night.
- **passer à la télévision** to be on the television □ « Titanic » passe à la télé ce soir. 'Titanic' is on TV tonight.

■ **Ne quittez pas, je vous passe Madame Chevalier.** Hold on please, I'm putting you through to Mrs Chevalier.

■ **passer par** to go through □ Ils sont passés par Paris pour aller à Tours. They went through Paris to get to Tours.

■ **en passant** in passing □ Je lui ai dit en passant que j'allais me marier. I told him in passing that I was getting married.

■ **laisser passer** to let through □ Il m'a laissé passer. He let me through.

■ **se passer** **1** to take place □ Cette histoire se passe au Moyen Âge. This story takes place in the Middle Ages. **2** to go □ Comment se sont passés tes examens ? How did your exams go? **3** to happen □ Que s'est-il passé ? Un accident ? What happened? Was there an accident?

■ **Qu'est-ce qui se passe ? Pourquoi est-ce qu'elle pleure ?** What's the matter? Why is she crying?

■ **se passer de** to do without □ Je me passerai de café ce matin. I'll do without coffee this morning.

> The verb **passer** uses **avoir** in the perfect tense when it describes crossing something, going through something, spending time somewhere, taking a test, or passing something to someone else. It uses **être** in the perfect tense when it describes passing through a place, visiting somewhere, showing a film, or being on the TV or radio.

la **passerelle** FEM NOUN
1 footbridge (*over river*)
2 gangway (*onto plane, boat*)

le **passe-temps** MASC NOUN
pastime

passif (FEM **passive**) ADJECTIVE
▷ *see also* **passif** NOUN
passive

le **passif** MASC NOUN
▷ *see also* **passif** ADJECTIVE
passive
□ Mettez ce verbe au passif. Put this verb into the passive.

la **passion** FEM NOUN
passion

passionnant (FEM **passionnante**) ADJECTIVE
fascinating

passionné (FEM **passionnée**) ADJECTIVE
keen
□ Lucas est un lecteur passionné. Lucas is a keen reader.

■ **Il est passionné de voile.** He's a sailing fanatic.

passionner VERB [28]
■ **Son travail le passionne.** He's passionate about his work.

■ **se passionner pour quelque chose** to have a passion for something □ Alexis se passionne pour les perroquets. Alexis has a passion for parrots.

la **passoire** FEM NOUN
sieve

la **pastèque** FEM NOUN
watermelon

le **pasteur** MASC NOUN
minister (*priest*)

la **pastille** FEM NOUN
cough sweet

la **patate** FEM NOUN (*informal*)
potato
■ **une patate douce** a sweet potato

la **pâte** FEM NOUN
1 pastry
2 dough
3 cake mixture
■ **la pâte à crêpes** pancake batter
■ **la pâte à modeler** Plasticine®
■ **la pâte d'amandes** marzipan

le **pâté** MASC NOUN
pâté
□ Nous avons mangé du pâté en entrée. We had pâté as a starter.
■ **un pâté de maisons** a block (*of houses*)

paternel (FEM **paternelle**) ADJECTIVE
■ **ma grand-mère paternelle** my father's mother
■ **mon oncle paternel** my father's brother

les **pâtes** FEM PL NOUN
pasta *sing*

la **patience** FEM NOUN
patience

patient (FEM **patiente**) ADJECTIVE
▷ *see also* **patient** NOUN, **patiente** NOUN
patient

le **patient** MASC NOUN
▷ *see also* **patient** ADJECTIVE
patient

la **patiente** FEM NOUN
▷ *see also* **patient** ADJECTIVE
patient

patienter VERB [28]
to wait
□ Veuillez patienter un instant, s'il vous plaît. Please wait a moment.

le **patin** MASC NOUN
1 skate
□ Nic a enfilé ses patins. Nic put her skates on.
2 skating
□ Ils font du patin tous les mercredis. They go skating every Wednesday.
■ **les patins à glace** ice skates
■ **les patins en ligne** Rollerblades®
■ **les patins à roulettes** roller skates

P

le **patinage** MASC NOUN
skating
■ **le patinage artistique** figure skating

patiner VERB [28]
to skate

le **patineur** MASC NOUN
skater

la **patineuse** FEM NOUN
skater

la **patinoire** FEM NOUN
ice rink

la **pâtisserie** FEM NOUN
cake shop
■ **faire de la pâtisserie** to bake □ J'adore faire
de la pâtisserie. I love baking.
■ **les pâtisseries** cakes

le **pâtissier** MASC NOUN
confectioner

la **pâtissière** FEM NOUN
confectioner

la **patrie** FEM NOUN
homeland

le **patron** MASC NOUN
1 boss
2 pattern (*for dressmaking*)

la **patronne** FEM NOUN
boss
■ **Elle est patronne de café.** She runs a café.

patronner VERB [28]
to sponsor
□ Le festival est patronné par des entreprises
locales. The festival is sponsored by local
businesses.

la **patrouille** FEM NOUN
patrol

la **patte** FEM NOUN
1 paw (*of dog, cat*)
2 leg (*of bird, animal*)

paumer VERB [28] (*informal*)
to lose
□ J'ai paumé mes clés. I've lost my keys.

la **paupière** FEM NOUN
eyelid

la **pause** FEM NOUN
1 break
□ Ils font une pause. They're having a break.
□ une pause de midi a lunch break
2 pause
□ Il y a eu une pause dans la conversation. There
was a pause in the conversation.

pauvre (FEM **pauvre**) ADJECTIVE
poor
□ Sa famille est pauvre. His family is poor.
□ Pauvre Vincent ! Il n'a pas eu de chance ! Poor
Vincent! He was unlucky!

la **pauvreté** FEM NOUN
poverty

pavé (FEM **pavée**) ADJECTIVE
cobbled
□ Les rues étaient pavées. The streets were
cobbled.

le **pavillon** MASC NOUN
house
□ Ils habitent un pavillon de banlieue. They've
got a house in the suburbs.

payant (FEM **payante**) ADJECTIVE
paying
□ Ce sont des hôtes payants. They're paying
guests.
■ **C'est payant.** You have to pay. □ L'entrée de
la boîte est payante. You have to pay to get into
the nightclub.

la **paye** FEM NOUN
wages

payé (FEM **payée**) ADJECTIVE
■ **être mal payé** to be badly paid
■ **un travail bien payé** a well-paid job

payer VERB [59]
1 to pay for
□ Combien as-tu payé ta voiture ? How much
did you pay for your car?
■ **J'ai payé ce T-shirt vingt euros.** I paid 20
euros for this T-shirt.
2 to pay
□ Elle a été payée aujourd'hui. She got paid
today. □ Son métier paye bien. His job pays good
money. □ Elle est mal payée. She is badly paid.
■ **faire payer quelque chose à quelqu'un** to
charge somebody for something □ Il me l'a fait
payer dix euros. He charged me 10 euros for it.
■ **payer quelque chose à quelqu'un** to buy
somebody something □ Allez, je vous paye un
verre. Come on, I'll buy you a drink.

le **pays** MASC NOUN
country
■ **du pays** local □ le vin du pays the local wine

le **paysage** MASC NOUN
landscape

le **paysan** MASC NOUN
farmer

la **paysanne** FEM NOUN
farmer

les **Pays-Bas** MASC PL NOUN
Netherlands
■ **aux Pays-Bas** 1 in the Netherlands 2 to the
Netherlands

le **pays de Galles** MASC NOUN
Wales
■ **au pays de Galles** 1 in Wales □ Daphné
habite au pays de Galles. Daphné lives in Wales.
2 to Wales □ Elle part au pays de Galles la
semaine prochaine. She is going to Wales
next week.

P

Numbers in brackets refer to verb tables on pages 650 to 658

le **PC** MASC NOUN
▷ *see also* **PC** ABBREVIATION
PC (= *personal computer*)
□ Il a tapé le rapport sur son PC. **He typed the report on his PC.**

PC ABBREVIATION
▷ *see also* **PC** NOUN
(= *Parti communiste*)
Communist Party

le **PDG** MASC NOUN (= *président-directeur général*)
MD (= *managing director*)

le **péage** MASC NOUN
1 toll
□ Nous avons payé vingt euros de péage. **We paid a toll of 20 euros.**
2 tollbooth
□ Sabine s'est arrêtée au péage de l'autoroute. **Sabine stopped at the motorway tollbooth.**

> **DID YOU KNOW...?**
> French motorways charge a toll.

la **peau** (PL les **peaux**) FEM NOUN
skin
□ Elle a la peau douce. **She's got soft skin.**

la **pêche** FEM NOUN
1 peach
2 fishing
■ aller à la pêche to go fishing
■ la pêche à la ligne angling

le **péché** MASC NOUN
sin

pêcher VERB [28]
1 to fish for
□ Ils sont partis pêcher la truite. **They've gone fishing for trout.**
2 to catch
□ Léo a pêché deux saumons. **Léo caught two salmon.**

le **pêcheur** MASC NOUN
fisherman
□ Son père est pêcheur. **His father's a fisherman.**
■ un pêcheur à la ligne an angler

pédagogique (FEM **pédagogique**) ADJECTIVE
educational

la **pédale** FEM NOUN
pedal

le **pédalo** MASC NOUN
pedalo

pédestre (FEM **pédestre**) ADJECTIVE
■ une randonnée pédestre a ramble

le **peigne** MASC NOUN
comb

peigner VERB [28]
to comb
□ Elle peigne sa poupée. **She's combing her doll's hair.**
■ se peigner to comb one's hair □ Il faut que je me peigne. **I must comb my hair.**

le **peignoir** MASC NOUN
dressing gown
■ un peignoir de bain a bathrobe

peindre VERB [60]
to paint

la **peine** FEM NOUN
trouble
■ avoir de la peine à faire quelque chose to have trouble doing something □ J'ai eu beaucoup de peine à la convaincre. **I had a lot of trouble convincing her.**
■ se donner de la peine to make a real effort
□ Il s'est donné beaucoup de peine pour obtenir ces renseignements. **He made a real effort to get this information.**
■ prendre la peine de faire quelque chose to go to the trouble of doing something □ Il a pris la peine de me rapporter ma valise. **He went to the trouble of returning my case to me.**
■ faire de la peine à quelqu'un to upset somebody □ Ça me fait de la peine de la voir pleurer. **It upsets me to see her crying.**
■ ce n'est pas la peine there's no point □ Ce n'est pas la peine de téléphoner. **There's no point in phoning.**
■ à peine 1 hardly □ J'ai à peine eu le temps de me changer. **I hardly had time to get changed.** 2 only just □ Elle vient à peine de se lever. **She's only just got up.**

le/la **peintre** MASC/FEM NOUN
painter

la **peinture** FEM NOUN
1 painting
□ On expose des peintures d'Aurélie au musée. **There's an exhibition of Aurélie's paintings at the museum.**
2 paint
□ J'ai acheté de la peinture verte. **I bought some green paint.**
■ « peinture fraîche » 'wet paint'

pêle-mêle ADVERB
higgledy-piggledy

peler VERB [43]
to peel

la **pelle** FEM NOUN
1 shovel
2 spade

la **pellicule** FEM NOUN
film
□ une pellicule couleur a colour film

les **pellicules** FEM PL NOUN
dandruff *sing*

la **pelote** FEM NOUN
ball
□ une pelote de laine a ball of wool

la **pelouse** FEM NOUN
lawn

P

la **peluche** FEM NOUN
- **un animal en peluche** a soft toy

le **penchant** MASC NOUN
- **avoir un penchant pour quelque chose** to have a liking for something

pencher VERB [28]
to tilt
□ Ce tableau penche vers la droite. The picture's tilting to the right.
- **se pencher 1** to lean over □ Émilie s'est penchée sur son cahier. Émilie leant over her exercise book. **2** to bend down □ Il s'est penché pour ramasser sa casquette. He bent down to pick his cap up. **3** to lean out □ Annick s'est penchée par la fenêtre. Annick leant out of the window.

pendant PREPOSITION
during
□ Ça s'est passé pendant l'été. It happened during the summer.
- **pendant que** while □ Julien a téléphoné pendant que Louise prenait son bain. Julien phoned while Louise was having a bath.

le **pendentif** MASC NOUN
pendant

la **penderie** FEM NOUN
wardrobe (*for hanging clothes*)

pendre VERB [88]
to hang
□ Il a pendu sa veste dans l'armoire. He hung his jacket in the wardrobe.
- **pendre quelqu'un** to hang somebody □ L'assassin a été pendu. The murderer was hanged.

la **pendule** FEM NOUN
clock

pénétrer VERB [34]
1 to enter
□ Ils ont pénétré dans la maison en passant par le jardin. They entered the house through the garden.
2 to penetrate
□ L'armée a pénétré sur le territoire ennemi. The army penetrated enemy territory.

pénible (FEM **pénible**) ADJECTIVE
hard
□ Travailler sur un chantier est pénible. Working on a building site is hard.
- **Il est vraiment pénible.** He's a real nuisance.

péniblement ADVERB
with difficulty

la **péniche** FEM NOUN
barge

le **pénis** MASC NOUN
penis

la **pénombre** FEM NOUN
half-light

la **pensée** FEM NOUN
thought
□ Il était perdu dans ses pensées. He was lost in thought.

penser VERB [28]
to think
□ Je pense que Yann a eu raison de partir. I think Yann was right to leave.
- **penser à quelque chose** to think about something □ Je pense à mes vacances. I'm thinking about my holidays. □ Pensez-y. Think about it.
- **penser à faire quelque chose** to remember to do something □ Tu as pensé à prendre ton passeport ? Did you remember to take your passport?
- **faire penser à quelqu'un à quelque chose** to remind someone of something □ Cette photo me fait penser à la Grèce. This photo reminds me of Greece.
- **faire penser à quelqu'un à faire quelque chose** to remind someone to do something □ Fais-moi penser à téléphoner à Claire. Remind me to phone Claire.
- **penser faire quelque chose** to be planning to do something □ Ils pensent partir en Espagne en juillet. They're planning to go to Spain in July.

la **pension** FEM NOUN
1 boarding school
□ Leur fille est en pension. Their daughter is at boarding school.
2 pension
□ Ma grand-mère reçoit sa pension tous les mois. My grandma gets her pension every month.
3 boarding house
- **la pension complète** full board

le/la **pensionnaire** MASC/FEM NOUN
boarder

le **pensionnat** MASC NOUN
boarding school

la **pente** FEM NOUN
slope
□ une pente raide a steep slope
- **en pente** sloping □ Le toit de cette maison est en pente. This house has a sloping roof.

la **Pentecôte** FEM NOUN
Whitsun

le **pépin** MASC NOUN
1 pip
□ Cette orange est pleine de pépins. This orange is full of pips.
2 problem
□ avoir un pépin (*informal*) to have a slight problem

perçant (FEM **perçante**) ADJECTIVE
1 sharp
□ Il a une vue perçante. He has very sharp eyes.

P

Numbers in brackets refer to verb tables on pages 650 to 658

2 piercing

□ un cri perçant a piercing cry

percer VERB [12]

to pierce

□ Elle s'est fait percer les oreilles. She's had her ears pierced.

percuter VERB [28]

to smash into

le **perdant** MASC NOUN

loser

la **perdante** FEM NOUN

loser

perdre VERB [61]

to lose

□ Cécile a perdu ses clés. Cécile's lost her keys.

■ **J'ai perdu mon chemin.** I've lost my way.

■ **perdre un match** to lose a match

■ **perdre du temps** to waste time □ J'ai perdu beaucoup de temps ce matin. I've wasted a lot of time this morning. □ Nous avons perdu notre temps à cette réunion. That meeting was a waste of time.

■ **se perdre** to get lost □ Je me suis perdu en route. I got lost on the way here.

perdu VERB ▷ see **perdre**

le **père** MASC NOUN

father

■ **le père Noël** Father Christmas

perfectionné (FEM **perfectionnée**) ADJECTIVE

sophisticated

perfectionner VERB [28]

to improve

□ Elle a besoin de perfectionner son anglais. She needs to improve her English.

périmé (FEM **périmée**) ADJECTIVE

out-of-date

□ Mon passeport est périmé. My passport's out of date.

■ **Ces yaourts sont périmés.** These yoghurts are past their use-by date.

la **période** FEM NOUN

period

périodique (FEM **périodique**) ADJECTIVE

periodic

périphérique (FEM **périphérique**)

ADJECTIVE

▷ see also **périphérique** NOUN

outlying

□ un quartier périphérique an outlying district

le **périphérique** MASC NOUN

▷ see also **périphérique** ADJECTIVE

ring road

la **perle** FEM NOUN

pearl

la **permanence** FEM NOUN

■ **assurer une permanence** to operate a basic service □ Ma banque assure une permanence le

samedi matin. My bank operates a basic service on Saturday mornings.

■ **être de permanence** to be on duty □ Sophie ne peut pas venir, elle est de permanence ce soir. Sophie can't come, she's on duty tonight.

■ **en permanence** permanently □ Elle se plaint en permanence. She's always complaining.

permanent (FEM **permanente**) ADJECTIVE

▷ see also **permanente** NOUN

1 permanent

□ Il a un poste permanent. He has a permanent job.

2 continuous

□ J'en ai assez de tes critiques permanentes. I've had enough of your constant criticism.

la **permanente** FEM NOUN

▷ see also **permanent** ADJECTIVE

perm

permettre VERB [47]

to allow

■ **permettre à quelqu'un de faire quelque chose** to allow somebody to do something

□ Sa mère lui permet de sortir le soir. His mother allows him to go out at night.

le **permis** MASC NOUN

permit

□ Il vous faut un permis pour camper ici. You need a permit to camp here.

■ **le permis de conduire** driving licence

■ **un permis de séjour** a residence permit

■ **un permis de travail** a work permit

permis VERB ▷ see **permettre**

la **permission** FEM NOUN

permission

□ Qui t'a donné la permission d'entrer ? Who gave you permission to come in?

■ **avoir la permission de faire quelque chose** to have permission to do something □ J'ai la permission d'utiliser son ordinateur. I've got his permission to use his computer.

■ **être en permission** to be on leave (from the army)

le **Pérou** MASC NOUN

Peru

perpétuel (FEM **perpétuelle**) ADJECTIVE

perpetual

perplexe (FEM **perplexe**) ADJECTIVE

puzzled

□ Ma question l'a laissée perplexe. She was puzzled by my question.

le **perroquet** MASC NOUN

parrot

la **perruche** FEM NOUN

budgie

la **perruque** FEM NOUN

wig

P

le **persil** MASC NOUN
parsley
□ un bouquet de persil a bunch of parsley

le **personnage** MASC NOUN

1 figure
□ les grands personnages de l'histoire de France
the important figures in French history

2 character
□ le personnage principal du film the main
character in the film

la **personnalité** FEM NOUN

1 personality
□ Ophélie a une forte personnalité. Ophélie has
a strong personality.

2 prominent figure
□ Il y avait beaucoup de personnalités politiques
à ce dîner. There were lots of prominent political
figures at the dinner.

la **personne** FEM NOUN
▷ see also **personne** PRONOUN
person
□ Il y avait une trentaine de personnes dans la
pièce. There were about 30 people in the room.
□ une personne âgée an elderly person
■ **en personne** in person

personne PRONOUN
▷ see also **personne** NOUN

1 nobody
□ Il n'y a personne à la maison. There's nobody
at home. □ Personne n'est venu le chercher.
Nobody came to fetch him.

2 anybody
□ Elle ne veut voir personne. She doesn't want
to see anybody.

personnel (FEM **personnelle**) ADJECTIVE
▷ see also **personnel** NOUN
personal

le **personnel** MASC NOUN
▷ see also **personnel** ADJECTIVE
staff
□ Il nous faut plus de personnel. We need more
staff.
■ **le service du personnel** the personnel
department

personnellement ADVERB
personally
□ Personnellement, je ne suis pas d'accord.
Personally, I don't agree.

la **perspective** FEM NOUN
prospect
□ Les perspectives sont bonnes. The prospects
are good.
■ **perspectives d'avenir** prospects □ Il y a des
perspectives d'avenir dans ce métier. This job
has good prospects.
■ **en perspective** **1** in prospect □ Il y a des
changements en perspective. Changes are in
prospect. **2** in perspective □ Il a dessiné la

maison en perspective. He drew the house in
perspective.

persuader VERB [28]
to persuade
■ **persuader quelqu'un de faire quelque
chose** to persuade somebody to do something
□ Elle m'a persuadé de l'accompagner au
cinéma. She persuaded me to go to the cinema
with her.

la **perte** FEM NOUN

1 loss
□ des pertes d'emploi job losses

2 waste
□ Cette réunion a été une perte de temps.
The meeting was a waste of time.

perturber VERB [28]
to disrupt
□ Les manifestations perturbaient la circulation.
The demonstrations disrupted the traffic.

le **pèse-personne** MASC NOUN
bathroom scales pl

peser VERB [43]
to weigh
□ Elle pèse cent kilos. She weighs 100 kilos.

pessimiste (FEM **pessimiste**) ADJECTIVE
pessimistic

le **pétale** MASC NOUN
petal

la **pétanque** FEM NOUN

> **DID YOU KNOW...?**
> **pétanque** is a type of bowls played in France,
> especially in the south.

le **pétard** MASC NOUN
firecracker

péter VERB [34] (rude)
to fart

pétillant (FEM **pétillante**) ADJECTIVE
sparkling

petit (FEM **petite**) ADJECTIVE

1 small
□ Sonia habite une petite ville. Sonia lives in a
small town.

2 little
□ Elle a une petite maison à la campagne. She
has a little house in the country.
■ **petit à petit** bit by bit
■ **un petit ami** a boyfriend
■ **une petite amie** a girlfriend
■ **un petit pain** a bread roll
■ **les petites annonces** the small ads
■ **des petits pois** garden peas
■ **les petits** young (of animal) □ la lionne et ses
petits the lioness and her young

le **petit-déjeuner** (PL les **petits-déjeuners**)
MASC NOUN
breakfast
■ **prendre le petit-déjeuner** to have breakfast

la **petite-fille** (PL les **petites-filles**) FEM NOUN
granddaughter

le **petit-fils** (PL les **petits-fils**) MASC NOUN
grandson

les **petits-enfants** MASC PL NOUN
grandchildren

le **pétrole** MASC NOUN
oil
□ une lampe à pétrole an oil lamp

> **BE CAREFUL!**
> **pétrole** does not mean **petrol**.

peu ADVERB, NOUN
not much
□ J'ai peu mangé à midi. I didn't eat much
for lunch. □ Il voyage peu. He doesn't travel
much.
■ **un peu** a bit □ Elle est un peu timide. She's a
bit shy. □ un peu de gâteau a bit of cake
■ **un petit peu** a little bit □ un petit peu de
crème a little bit of cream
■ **un peu de** a little □ Il a un peu d'argent.
He has a little money.
■ **peu de** **1** not many □ Il y a peu de bons
films au cinéma. There aren't very many good
films on at the cinema. □ Elle a peu d'amis. She
hasn't got many friends. **2** not much □ Il a peu
d'espoir de réussir. He doesn't have much hope
of succeeding. □ Il lui reste peu d'argent. He
hasn't got much money left.
■ **à peu près** **1** more or less □ J'ai à peu près
fini. I've more or less finished. **2** about □ Le
voyage prend à peu près deux heures. The
journey takes about two hours.
■ **peu à peu** little by little
■ **peu avant** shortly before
■ **peu après** shortly afterwards
■ **de peu** only just □ Imane a manqué son train
de peu. Imane only just missed her train.

le **peuple** MASC NOUN
people
□ le peuple français the French people

la **peur** FEM NOUN
fear
■ **avoir peur de** to be afraid of □ Il a peur du
noir. He's afraid of the dark.
■ **avoir peur de faire quelque chose** to be
frightened of doing something □ Elle a peur d'y
aller toute seule. She's frightened of going on
her own.
■ **faire peur à quelqu'un** to frighten
somebody □ Cet homme-là me fait peur. That
man frightens me.

peureux (FEM **peureuse**) ADJECTIVE
fearful

peut VERB ▷ *see* pouvoir
■ **Il ne peut pas venir.** He can't come.

peut-être ADVERB
perhaps

□ Je l'ai peut-être oublié à la maison. Perhaps
I've left it at home.
■ **peut-être que** perhaps □ Peut-être qu'elles
n'ont pas pu téléphoner. Perhaps they weren't
able to phone.

peuvent, peux VERB ▷ *see* pouvoir
■ **Je ne peux pas le faire.** I can't do it.

p. ex. ABBREVIATION (= *par exemple*)
e.g.

le **phare** MASC NOUN
1 lighthouse
□ On voit le phare depuis le pont du bateau. You
can see the lighthouse from the ship's deck.
2 headlight
□ Elle a laissé ses phares allumés. She left her
headlights on.

la **pharmacie** FEM NOUN
chemist's

> **DID YOU KNOW...?**
> Chemists' shops in France are identified by a
> special green cross outside the shop.

le **pharmacien** MASC NOUN
pharmacist

la **pharmacienne** FEM NOUN
pharmacist

le **phasme** MASC NOUN
stick insect

le **phénomène** MASC NOUN
phenomenon

la **philosophie** FEM NOUN
philosophy

le **phoque** MASC NOUN
seal (*animal*)

la **photo** FEM NOUN
photograph
■ **en photo** in photographs □ Je n'ai vu
Venise qu'en photo. I've only seen Venice in
photographs.
■ **prendre quelqu'un en photo** to take a
photo of somebody □ Claire nous a pris en
photo. Claire took a photo of us.
■ **une photo d'identité** a passport
photograph

la **photocopie** FEM NOUN
photocopy

photocopier VERB [19]
to photocopy

la **photocopieuse** FEM NOUN
photocopier

le/la **photographe** MASC/FEM NOUN
photographer

la **photographie** FEM NOUN
1 photography
2 photograph

photographier VERB [19]
to photograph

P

photoshoper VERB [28]
to Photoshop

la **phrase** FEM NOUN
sentence

physique (FEM **physique**) ADJECTIVE
▷ see also **physique** NOUN
physical

le **physique** MASC NOUN
▷ see also **physique** NOUN, ADJECTIVE
■ **Il a un physique agréable.** He's quite good-looking.

la **physique** FEM NOUN
▷ see also **physique** NOUN, ADJECTIVE
physics
□ Il est professeur de physique. He's a physics teacher.

le/la **pianiste** MASC/FEM NOUN
pianist
□ Elle est pianiste. She's a pianist.

le **piano** MASC NOUN
piano

le **pic** MASC NOUN
peak
□ les pics enneigés des Alpes the snowy peaks of the Alps
■ **à pic 1** vertically □ La falaise tombe à pic dans la mer. The cliff drops vertically into the sea. **2** just at the right time □ Tu es arrivé à pic. You arrived just at the right time.

la **pièce** FEM NOUN
1 room
□ Mon lit est au centre de la pièce. My bed is in the middle of the room.
■ **un cinq-pièces** a five-roomed flat
2 play
□ On joue une pièce de Shakespeare au théâtre. There's a play by Shakespeare on at the theatre.
3 part
□ Il faut changer une pièce du moteur. There's an engine part which needs changing.
4 coin
□ des pièces d'un euro some one-euro coins
■ **cinquante euros pièce** 50 euros each □ J'ai acheté ces T-shirts dix euros pièce. I bought these T-shirts for ten euros each.
■ **un maillot une pièce** a one-piece swimsuit
■ **un maillot deux-pièces** a bikini
■ **Avez-vous une pièce d'identité ?** Have you got any identification?
■ **une pièce jointe** an email attachment

le **pied** MASC NOUN
foot
□ J'ai mal aux pieds. My feet are hurting.
■ **à pied** on foot
■ **avoir pied** to be able to touch the bottom
□ Justine n'aime pas nager là où elle n'a pas pied. Justine doesn't like swimming where she can't touch the bottom.

le **pied-noir** (PL les **pieds-noirs**) MASC NOUN

DID YOU KNOW...?
A **pied-noir** is a French person born in Algeria; most of them moved to France during the Algerian war in the 1950s.

□ Sa grand-mère est pied-noir. His grandmother was born in Algeria.

le **piège** MASC NOUN
trap
■ **prendre quelqu'un au piège** to trap somebody

piéger VERB [66]
to trap
■ **un colis piégé** a parcel bomb
■ **une voiture piégée** a car bomb

la **pierre** FEM NOUN
stone
■ **une pierre précieuse** a precious stone

le **piéton** MASC NOUN
pedestrian

la **piétonne** FEM NOUN
pedestrian

piétonnier (FEM **piétonnière**) ADJECTIVE
■ **une rue piétonnière** a pedestrianized street
■ **un quartier piétonnier** a pedestrianized area

la **pieuvre** FEM NOUN
octopus

le **pigeon** MASC NOUN
pigeon

piger VERB [45] (informal)
to understand

la **pile** FEM NOUN
▷ see also **pile** ADVERB
1 pile
□ Il y a une pile de disques sur la table. There's a pile of records on the table.
2 battery
□ La pile de ma montre est usée. The battery in my watch has run out.

pile ADVERB
▷ see also **pile** NOUN
■ **à deux heures pile** at two on the dot
■ **jouer à pile ou face** to toss up
■ **Pile ou face ?** Heads or tails?

le **pilote** MASC NOUN
pilot
■ **un pilote de course** a racing driver
■ **un pilote de ligne** an airline pilot

piloter VERB [28]
to fly (a plane)

la **pilule** FEM NOUN
pill
■ **prendre la pilule** to be on the pill

le **piment** MASC NOUN
chilli

le **pin** MASC NOUN
pine

le **pinard** MASC NOUN (*informal*)
wine

la **pince** FEM NOUN
1 pliers *pl* (*tool*)
2 pincer (*of crab*)
  ■ une pince à épiler tweezers
  ■ une pince à linge a clothes peg

le **pinceau** (PL les **pinceaux**) MASC NOUN
paintbrush

la **pincée** FEM NOUN
  ■ une pincée de sel a pinch of salt

pincer VERB [12]
to pinch
  □ Elle m'a pincé le bras. She pinched my arm.

le **pingouin** MASC NOUN
penguin

le **ping-pong** MASC NOUN
table tennis
  □ jouer au ping-pong to play table tennis

la **pintade** FEM NOUN
guinea fowl

le **pion** MASC NOUN
1 pawn (*in chess*)
2 piece (*in draughts*)
3 supervisor (*man*)

DID YOU KNOW...?
In French secondary schools, the teachers are not responsible for supervising the pupils outside class. This job is done by people called **pions** or **surveillants**.

---

la **pionne** FEM NOUN
supervisor (*woman*)

la **pipe** FEM NOUN
pipe
  □ Mon grand-père fume la pipe. My granddad smokes a pipe.

piquant (FEM **piquante**) ADJECTIVE
1 prickly
2 spicy

le **pique** MASC NOUN
  ▷ *see also* **pique** NOUN
spades *pl*
  □ l'as de pique the ace of spades

la **pique** FEM NOUN
  ▷ *see also* **pique** NOUN
cutting remark
  □ envoyer des piques à quelqu'un to make cutting remarks to somebody

le **pique-nique** MASC NOUN
picnic

piquer VERB [28]
1 to bite
  □ Nous avons été piqués par les moustiques. We were bitten by mosquitoes.

2 to burn
  □ Cette sauce me pique la langue. This sauce is burning my tongue.

3 to steal
  □ On m'a piqué mon porte-monnaie. (*informal*) I've had my purse stolen.
  ■ se piquer to prick oneself □ Il s'est piqué avec une aiguille. He pricked himself with a needle.

le **piquet** MASC NOUN
1 post
  □ Le chien est attaché à un piquet. The dog is tied to a post.

2 peg
  □ Il nous manque un des piquets de la tente. One of our tent pegs is missing.

la **piqûre** FEM NOUN
1 injection
  □ Le médecin lui a fait une piqûre. The doctor gave him an injection.

2 bite
  □ une piqûre de moustique a mosquito bite

3 sting
  □ une piqûre d'abeille a bee sting

le **pirate** MASC NOUN
pirate
  ■ un pirate informatique a hacker

pire (FEM **pire**) ADJECTIVE, NOUN
worse
  □ C'est encore pire qu'avant. It's even worse than before.
  ■ le pire the worst □ C'est la pire journée que j'aie jamais passée. That's the worst day I've ever had. □ Ce gamin est le pire de la bande. That boy is the worst in the group.
  ■ le pire de the worst of □ Le pire de tout, c'est qu'on s'ennuie tout le temps. The worst of it is that we're always bored.

la **piscine** FEM NOUN
swimming pool

pisser VERB [28] (*informal*)
to have a pee

la **pistache** FEM NOUN
pistachio
  □ une glace à la pistache a pistachio ice cream

la **piste** FEM NOUN
1 lead
  □ La police est sur une piste. The police are following a lead.

2 runway
  □ L'avion s'est posé sur la piste. The plane landed on the runway.

3 ski run
  □ Le skieur a descendu la piste. The skier came down the ski run.
  ■ une piste artificielle a dry ski slope
  ■ la piste de danse the dance floor
  ■ une piste cyclable a cycle lane

P

le **pistolet** MASC NOUN

pistol

pistonner VERB [28]

■ **Il a été pistonné pour avoir ce travail.** They pulled some strings to get him this job.

la **pitié** FEM NOUN

pity

■ **Il me fait pitié.** I feel sorry for him.

■ **avoir pitié de quelqu'un** to feel sorry for somebody

pittoresque (FEM **pittoresque**) ADJECTIVE

picturesque

la **pizza** FEM NOUN

pizza

le **placard** MASC NOUN

cupboard

la **place** FEM NOUN

1 place

□ Vincent a eu la troisième place au concours. Vincent got third place in the competition.

2 square

□ la place du village the village square

3 space

□ Il ne reste plus de place pour se garer. There's no more space to park. □ Ça prend de la place. It takes up a lot of room.

4 seat

□ Toutes les places ont été vendues. All the seats have been sold. □ Il y a vingt places assises. There are 20 seats.

■ **remettre quelque chose en place** to put something back in its place

■ **sur place** on the spot

■ **à la place** instead □ Il ne reste plus de tarte ; désirez-vous quelque chose d'autre à la place ? There's no pie left; would you like something else instead?

■ **à la place de** instead of

placer VERB [12]

1 to seat

□ Nous étions placés à côté du directeur. We were seated next to the manager.

2 to invest

□ Il a placé ses économies en Bourse. He invested his money on the Stock Exchange.

■ **se placer** □ Je vais me placer au premier rang. I'll sit in the front row.

le **plafond** MASC NOUN

ceiling

■ **se placer** □ Je vais me placer au premier rang. I'll sit in the front row.

la **plage** FEM NOUN

beach

la **plaie** FEM NOUN

wound

plaindre VERB [17]

■ **plaindre quelqu'un** to feel sorry for somebody □ Je te plains. I feel sorry for you.

■ **se plaindre** to complain □ Il n'arrête pas de se plaindre. He never stops complaining.

■ **se plaindre à quelqu'un** to complain to somebody □ Ils se sont plaints au directeur. They complained to the manager.

■ **se plaindre de quelque chose** to complain about something □ Elle s'est plainte du bruit. She complained about the noise.

la **plaine** FEM NOUN

plain (*level area*)

plaint VERB ▷ *see* **plaindre**

la **plainte** FEM NOUN

complaint

■ **porter plainte** to lodge a complaint

plaire VERB [62]

■ **Ce cadeau me plaît beaucoup.** I like this present a lot.

■ **Ce film plaît beaucoup aux jeunes.** The film is very popular with young people.

■ **Ça t'a plu d'aller en Italie ?** Did you enjoy going to Italy?

■ **Elle lui plaît.** He fancies her.

■ **s'il te plaît** please

■ **s'il vous plaît** please

plaisanter VERB [28]

to joke

la **plaisanterie** FEM NOUN

joke

le **plaisir** MASC NOUN

pleasure

■ **faire plaisir à quelqu'un** to please somebody □ J'y suis allé pour lui faire plaisir. I went there to please him. □ Ce cadeau me fait très plaisir. I'm very pleased with this present.

plaît VERB ▷ *see* **plaire**

le **plan** MASC NOUN

plan

■ **un plan de la ville** a street map

■ **au premier plan** in the foreground

la **planche** FEM NOUN

plank

■ **une planche à repasser** an ironing board

■ **une planche à roulettes** a skateboard

■ **une planche à voile** a sailboard

■ **une planche de surf** a surfboard

le **plancher** MASC NOUN

floor

planer VERB [28]

1 to glide

□ L'avion planait dans le ciel. The plane was gliding in the sky.

2 to have one's head in the clouds

■ **Ce garçon plane complètement.** (*informal*) He's not with us at all.

la **planète** FEM NOUN

planet

la **plante** FEM NOUN

plant

Numbers in brackets refer to verb tables on pages 650 to 658

planter VERB [28]

1 to plant
□ Daphné a planté des tomates. **Daphné planted some tomatoes.**

2 to hammer in
□ Karim a planté un clou dans le mur. **Karim hammered a nail into the wall.**

3 to pitch
□ Nathan a planté sa tente au bord du lac. **Nathan pitched his tent next to the lake.**
■ **Ne reste pas planté là ! Don't just stand there!**
■ **se planter** (*informal*) to fail □ Je me suis planté en maths. **I failed maths.**

la **plaque** FEM NOUN
(metal) plate
■ **une plaque de verglas** a patch of ice
■ **une plaque de chocolat** a bar of chocolate

plaqué (FEM **plaquée**) ADJECTIVE
■ **plaqué** or gold-plated
■ **plaqué argent** silver-plated

plaquer VERB [28] (*informal*)

1 to ditch
□ Elle a plaqué son copain. **She ditched her boyfriend.**

2 to pack in
□ Il a plaqué son boulot. **He packed in his job.**

la **plaquette** FEM NOUN
■ **une plaquette de chocolat** a bar of chocolate
■ **une plaquette de beurre** a pack of butter

le **plastique** MASC NOUN
plastic

plat (FEM **plate**) ADJECTIVE
▷ *see also* **plat** NOUN
flat
■ **être à plat ventre** to be lying face down
■ **l'eau plate** still water

le **plat** MASC NOUN
▷ *see also* **plat** ADJECTIVE

1 dish

2 course
□ le plat principal **the main course**
■ **un plat cuisiné** a pre-cooked meal
■ **le plat de résistance** the main course
■ **le plat du jour** the dish of the day

le **platane** MASC NOUN
plane tree

le **plateau** (PL les **plateaux**) MASC NOUN

1 tray
■ **un plateau de fromages** a selection of cheeses

2 plateau

le **platine** MASC NOUN
▷ *see also* **platine** NOUN
platinum

la **platine** FEM NOUN
▷ *see also* **platine** NOUN
turntable (*of record player*)
■ **une platine laser** a CD player

le **plâtre** MASC NOUN
plaster
□ une statue en plâtre **a statue made of plaster**
□ avoir un bras dans le plâtre **to have an arm in plaster**

plein (FEM **pleine**) ADJECTIVE
▷ *see also* **plein** NOUN
full
■ **à plein temps** full-time □ Elle travaille à plein temps. **She works full-time.**
■ **plein de** (*informal*) lots of □ un gâteau avec plein de crème **a cake with lots of cream**
■ **Il y a plein de gens dans la rue. The street is full of people.**
■ **en plein air** in the open air
■ **en pleine nuit** in the middle of the night
■ **en plein jour** in broad daylight

le **plein** MASC NOUN
▷ *see also* **plein** ADJECTIVE
■ **faire le plein** to fill up (*petrol tank*) □ Faites le plein, s'il vous plaît. **Fill it up, please.**

pleurer VERB [28]
to cry

pleut VERB ▷ *see* **pleuvoir**

pleuvoir VERB [63]
to rain
■ **Il pleut. It's raining.**

le **pli** MASC NOUN

1 fold

2 pleat
□ Elle a repassé les plis de sa jupe. **She ironed the pleats of her skirt.**

3 crease
□ Il y a un pli sur la manche de ta chemise. **There's a crease in the sleeve of your shirt.**

pliant (FEM **pliante**) ADJECTIVE
folding
□ un lit pliant **a folding bed**

plier VERB [19]

1 to fold
□ Elle a plié sa serviette. **She folded her towel.**

2 to bend
□ Elle a plié le bras. **She bent her arm.**

le **plomb** MASC NOUN

1 lead
□ Ces jouets sont en plomb. **These toys are made of lead.**

2 fuse
□ Les plombs ont sauté. **The fuses have blown.**
■ **l'essence sans plomb** unleaded petrol

le **plombier** MASC NOUN
plumber
■ **Il est plombier. He's a plumber.**

la **plongée** FEM NOUN
diving
□ faire de la plongée **to go diving**

le **plongeoir** MASC NOUN
diving board

le **plongeon** MASC NOUN
dive

plonger VERB [45]
to dive
□ Jean a plongé dans la piscine. Jean dived into the swimming pool.
■ **J'ai plongé ma main dans l'eau.** I plunged my hand into the water.
■ **être plongé dans son travail** to be absorbed in your work
■ **se plonger dans un livre** to get absorbed in a book

plu VERB ▷ see **plaire**, **pleuvoir**

la **pluie** FEM NOUN
rain
□ sous la pluie in the rain

la **plume** FEM NOUN
feather
□ une plume d'oiseau a bird's feather
■ **un stylo à plume** a fountain pen

plupart FEM NOUN
■ **la plupart** most (of them) □ La plupart ont moins de quinze ans. Most of them are under 15.
■ **la plupart de** most (of) □ La plupart des gens ont vu ce film. Most people have seen this film.
□ la plupart du temps most of the time

le **pluriel** MASC NOUN
plural
■ **au pluriel** in the plural

plus ADVERB, PREPOSITION
■ **ne ... plus** 1 not ... any more □ Je ne veux plus le voir. I don't want to see him any more.
2 no longer □ Il ne travaille plus ici. He's no longer working here.
■ **Je n'ai plus de pain.** I've got no bread left.
■ **plus ... que** more ... than □ Il est plus intelligent que son frère. He's more intelligent than his brother. □ Il travaille plus que moi. He works more than me. □ Elle est plus grande que moi. She's bigger than me.
■ **C'est le plus grand de la famille.** He's the tallest in his family.
■ **plus ... plus ...** the more ... the more ... □ Plus il gagne d'argent, plus il en veut. The more money he earns, the more he wants.
■ **plus de** 1 more □ Il nous faut plus de pain. We need more bread. 2 more than □ Il y avait plus de dix personnes. There were more than 10 people.
■ **de plus** more □ Il nous faut un joueur de plus. We need one more player. □ Le voyage a pris trois heures de plus que prévu. The journey took 3 hours more than planned.
■ **en plus** more □ J'ai apporté quelques gâteaux en plus. I brought a few more cakes.

■ **de plus en plus** more and more □ Il y a de plus en plus de touristes par ici. There are more and more tourists round here. □ Il fait de plus en plus chaud. It's getting hotter and hotter.
■ **un peu plus difficile** a bit more difficult □ Il fait un peu plus froid qu'hier. It's a bit colder than yesterday.
■ **plus ou moins** more or less
■ **Quatre plus deux égalent six.** 4 plus 2 is 6.

plusieurs PL PRONOUN
several
□ Elle a acheté plusieurs chemises. She bought several shirts. □ Il y en a plusieurs. There are several of them.

le **plus-que-parfait** MASC NOUN
pluperfect

plutôt ADVERB
1 quite
□ Elle est plutôt jolie. She's quite pretty.
2 rather
□ L'eau est plutôt froide. The water's rather cold.
3 instead
□ Demande-leur plutôt de venir avec toi. Ask them to come with you instead.
■ **plutôt que** rather than □ Invite Marie plutôt que Juliette. Invite Marie rather than Juliette.

pluvieux (FEM **pluvieuse**) ADJECTIVE
rainy

le **pneu** MASC NOUN
tyre

la **pneumonie** FEM NOUN
pneumonia

la **poche** FEM NOUN
pocket
■ **l'argent de poche** pocket money
■ **un livre de poche** a paperback

le **podcast** MASC NOUN
podcast
□ télécharger un podcast to download a podcast

podcaster VERB [28]
to podcast

la **poêle** FEM NOUN
frying pan
■ **une poêle à frire** a frying pan

le **poème** MASC NOUN
poem

la **poésie** FEM NOUN
1 poetry
2 poem

le **poète** MASC NOUN
poet

la **poétesse** FEM NOUN
poet

le **poids** MASC NOUN
weight
□ vendre quelque chose au poids to sell something by weight

■ **prendre du poids** to put on weight □ Il a pris du poids. He's put on weight.
■ **perdre du poids** to lose weight □ Elle a perdu du poids. She's lost weight.
■ **un poids lourd** a lorry

la **poignée** FEM NOUN
1 handful
□ une poignée de sel a handful of salt
2 handle
□ la poignée de la porte the door handle
■ **une poignée de main** a handshake

le **poignet** MASC NOUN
1 wrist
□ Je me suis fait mal au poignet. I've hurt my wrist.
2 cuff (of shirt)

le **poil** MASC NOUN
1 hair
□ Il y a des poils de chat partout sur la moquette. There are cat hairs all over the carpet.
2 fur
□ Ton chien a un beau poil. Your dog's got lovely fur.
■ **à poil** (informal) stark naked

poilu (FEM poilue) ADJECTIVE
hairy

poinçonner VERB [28]
to punch
□ Le contrôleur a poinçonné les billets. The conductor punched the tickets.

le **poing** MASC NOUN
fist
■ **un coup de poing** a punch

le **point** MASC NOUN
1 point
□ Je ne suis pas d'accord sur ce point. I don't agree with this point. □ Son point faible, c'est qu'elle est trop gentille. Her weak point is she's too nice.
■ **point de vue** point of view
2 full stop
■ **être sur le point de faire quelque chose** to be just about to do something □ J'étais sur le point de te téléphoner. I was just about to phone you.
■ **mettre au point** to finalize
■ **Ce n'est pas encore au point.** It's not finalized yet.
■ **à point** medium □ Comment voulez-vous votre steak ? — À point. How would you like your steak? — Medium.
■ **un point d'exclamation** an exclamation mark
■ **un point d'interrogation** a question mark
■ **un point noir** a blackhead

la **pointe** FEM NOUN
point
□ la pointe d'un couteau the point of a knife

■ **être à la pointe du progrès** to be in the forefront of progress
■ **sur la pointe des pieds** on tiptoe
■ **les heures de pointe** peak hours

le **pointillé** MASC NOUN
dotted line

pointu (FEM pointue) ADJECTIVE
pointed
□ un chapeau pointu a pointed hat

la **pointure** FEM NOUN
size (of shoes)
□ Quelle est votre pointure ? What size shoes do you take?

le **point-virgule** (PL points-virgules) MASC NOUN
semicolon

la **poire** FEM NOUN
pear

le **poireau** (PL les poireaux) MASC NOUN
leek
□ la soupe aux poireaux leek soup

le **pois** MASC NOUN
pea
■ **les petits pois** peas
■ **les pois chiches** chickpeas
■ **à pois** spotted □ une robe à pois a spotted dress

le **poison** MASC NOUN
poison

le **poisson** MASC NOUN
fish
□ Je n'aime pas le poisson. I don't like fish. □ Léo a pêché deux poissons. Léo caught two fish.
■ **les Poissons** Pisces □ Justine est Poissons. Justine is Pisces.
■ **Poisson d'avril !** April fool!

DID YOU KNOW...?
Pinning a paper fish to somebody's back is a traditional April fool joke in France.

■ **un poisson rouge** a goldfish

la **poissonnerie** FEM NOUN
fish shop

le **poissonnier** MASC NOUN
fishmonger

la **poitrine** FEM NOUN
1 chest
□ J'ai mal à la poitrine. My chest hurts.
2 bust
□ Quel est votre tour de poitrine ? What's your bust size?

le **poivre** MASC NOUN
pepper (spice)

le **poivron** MASC NOUN
pepper (vegetable)

le **polar** MASC NOUN
thriller

P

le **pôle** MASC NOUN

pole
- **le pôle Nord** the North Pole
- **le pôle Sud** the South Pole

poli (FEM **polie**) ADJECTIVE

polite

la **police** FEM NOUN

police
□ La police recherche le voleur. **The police are looking for the thief.**
- **police secours** emergency services □ Ils ont appelé police secours. **They phoned the emergency services.**
- **une police d'assurance** an insurance policy

policier (FEM **policière**) ADJECTIVE
▷ *see also* **policier** NOUN
- **un roman policier** a detective novel

le **policier** MASC NOUN
▷ *see also* **policier** ADJECTIVE
police officer
□ Il est policier. **He's a police officer.**

la **policière** FEM NOUN
police officer
□ Elle est policière. **She's a police officer.**

la **politesse** FEM NOUN
politeness

la **politique** FEM NOUN
politics
□ La politique ne l'intéresse pas du tout. **He's not at all interested in politics.**

pollué (FEM **polluée**) ADJECTIVE
polluted

polluer VERB [28]
to pollute

la **pollution** FEM NOUN
pollution

le **polo** MASC NOUN
polo shirt

la **Pologne** FEM NOUN
Poland

polonais (FEM **polonaise**) ADJECTIVE, NOUN
Polish
□ Elle parle polonais. **She speaks Polish.**
- **un Polonais** a Pole (*man*)
- **une Polonaise** a Pole (*woman*)
- **les Polonais** the Poles

la **Polynésie** FEM NOUN
Polynesia

la **pommade** FEM NOUN
ointment

la **pomme** FEM NOUN
apple
- **les pommes de terre** potatoes
- **les pommes frites** chips
- **les pommes vapeur** boiled potatoes
- **tomber dans les pommes** (*informal*) to faint

la **pompe** FEM NOUN
pump
- **une pompe à essence** a petrol pump
- **les pompes funèbres** undertakers

le **pompier** MASC NOUN
firefighter

le/la **pompiste** MASC/FEM NOUN
petrol pump attendant

ponctuel (FEM **ponctuelle**) ADJECTIVE
1 punctual
□ Elle est toujours très ponctuelle. **She's always very punctual.**
2 occasional
- **On a rencontré quelques problèmes ponctuels. We've had the occasional problem.**

pondre VERB [69]
to lay (*eggs*)

le **poney** MASC NOUN
pony

le **pont** MASC NOUN
1 bridge
2 deck (*of ship*)
- **faire le pont** to take a long weekend □ Nous faisons le pont pour la Pentecôte. **We're taking a long weekend for Whitsun.**

populaire (FEM **populaire**) ADJECTIVE
1 popular
□ Ce chanteur est très populaire en France. **This singer's very popular in France.**
2 working-class
□ un quartier populaire de la ville a working-class area of town

la **population** FEM NOUN
population

le **porc** MASC NOUN
1 pig
□ Ils élèvent des porcs. **They breed pigs.**
2 pork
□ du rôti de porc roast pork

la **porcelaine** FEM NOUN
china
□ une tasse en porcelaine a china cup

le **port** MASC NOUN
1 harbour
2 port

portable (FEM **portable**) ADJECTIVE
▷ *see also* **portable** NOUN
mobile (*telephone*)
- **un ordinateur portable** a laptop

le **portable** MASC NOUN
▷ *see also* **portable** ADJECTIVE
1 mobile phone
□ Je vais appeler Marie sur mon portable. **I'll phone Marie on my mobile.**
2 laptop
□ Je vais te montrer sur mon portable. **I'll show you on my laptop.**

le **portail** MASC NOUN
gate

portatif (FEM **portative**) ADJECTIVE
portable

la **porte** FEM NOUN

1 door
□ Ferme la porte, s'il te plaît. Close the door, please.
■ **la porte d'entrée** the front door

2 gate
□ Vol 432 à destination de Paris : porte numéro trois. Flight 432 to Paris: gate 3.
■ **mettre quelqu'un à la porte** to sack somebody

le **porte-bagages** MASC NOUN
luggage rack

le **porte-clés** MASC NOUN
key ring

la **portée** FEM NOUN
■ **à portée de main** within arm's reach
■ **hors de portée** out of reach

le **portefeuille** MASC NOUN
wallet

le **portemanteau** (PL les **portemanteaux**)
MASC NOUN

1 coat hanger
2 coat rack

le **porte-monnaie** (PL les **porte-monnaies**)
MASC NOUN
purse

le **porte-parole** (PL les **porte-parole**) MASC
NOUN
spokesperson

porter VERB [28]

1 to carry
□ Il portait une valise. He was carrying a suitcase.

2 to wear
□ Elle porte une robe bleue. She's wearing a blue dress.
■ **se porter bien** to be well
■ **se porter mal** to be unwell

le **porteur** MASC NOUN
porter

la **portière** FEM NOUN
door (of car)

la **portion** FEM NOUN
portion

le **porto** MASC NOUN
port (wine)

le **portrait** MASC NOUN
portrait

portugais (FEM **portugaise**) ADJECTIVE, NOUN
Portuguese
□ Il parle portugais. He speaks Portuguese.
■ **un Portugais** a Portuguese (man)
■ **une Portugaise** a Portuguese (woman)
■ **les Portugais** the Portuguese

le **Portugal** MASC NOUN
Portugal
■ **au Portugal 1** in Portugal **2** to Portugal

poser VERB [28]

1 to put down
□ J'ai posé la cafetière sur la table. I put the coffee pot down on the table.

2 to pose
□ Cela pose un problème. That poses a problem.
■ **poser une question à quelqu'un** to ask somebody a question
■ **se poser** to land □ L'avion s'est posé à huit heures. The plane landed at 8 o'clock.

positif (FEM **positive**) ADJECTIVE
positive

la **position** FEM NOUN
position

posséder VERB [34]
to own
□ Ils possèdent une jolie maison. They own a lovely house.

la **possibilité** FEM NOUN
possibility

possible (FEM **possible**) ADJECTIVE
possible
□ Samuel leur a dit que ce n'était pas possible. Samuel told them it wasn't possible.
■ **le plus de gens possible** as many people as possible
■ **le plus tôt possible** as early as possible
■ **le moins d'argent possible** as little money as possible
■ **Il travaille le moins possible.** He works as little as possible.
■ **dès que possible** as soon as possible
■ **faire son possible** to do all one can □ Je ferai tout mon possible. I'll do all I can.

la **poste** FEM NOUN
▷ see also **poste** NOUN

1 post
□ Je vais l'envoyer par la poste. I'm going to send it by post.

2 post office
□ Je vais à la poste pour acheter des timbres. I'm going to the post office to buy some stamps.
■ **mettre une lettre à la poste** to post a letter

le **poste** MASC NOUN
▷ see also **poste** NOUN

1 post
□ Bastien a trouvé un poste de professeur. Bastien has found a teaching post.

2 extension (phone)
□ Pouvez-vous me passer le poste de M. Salzedo ? Can you put me through to Mr Salzedo's extension?

3 set
□ un poste de radio a radio set
■ **un poste de police** a police station

P

poster – pourboire

poster VERB [28]
▷ *see also* **poster** NOUN
to post
□ Je vais poster ce colis. I'm going to post this parcel.

le **poster** MASC NOUN
▷ *see also* **poster** VERB
poster
□ un poster de la Grèce a poster of Greece

postérieur (FEM **postérieure**) ADJECTIVE
1 later
□ Ce document est postérieur à 1314. This document is from later than 1314.
2 back
□ la partie postérieure de ma jambe the back of my leg

le **pot** MASC NOUN
jar
□ J'ai fait trois pots de confiture. I've made three jars of jam.
■ **prendre un pot** (*informal*) to have a drink
□ On va prendre un pot ce soir. We're going for a drink tonight.
■ **un pot de fleurs** a plant pot

potable (FEM **potable**) ADJECTIVE
■ **eau potable** drinking water
■ **« eau non potable »** 'not drinking water'

le **potage** MASC NOUN
soup

le **potager** MASC NOUN
vegetable garden

le **pot-au-feu** (PL les **pots-au-feu**, les **pot-au-feu**) MASC NOUN
beef stew

le **pot-de-vin** (PL les **pots-de-vin**) MASC NOUN
bribe

le **pote** MASC NOUN (*informal*)
mate
□ Je sors avec mes potes ce soir. I'm going out with my mates tonight.

le **poteau** (PL les **poteaux**) MASC NOUN
post
□ Il s'est appuyé contre un poteau. He leant against a post.
■ **un poteau indicateur** a signpost

potentiel (FEM **potentielle**) ADJECTIVE
potential

la **poterie** FEM NOUN
1 pottery
□ Elle fait de la poterie à l'école. She does pottery at school.
2 piece of pottery
□ J'ai acheté deux poteries. I bought two pieces of pottery.

le **potier** MASC NOUN
potter

le **pou** (PL les **poux**) MASC NOUN
louse

la **poubelle** FEM NOUN
dustbin

le **pouce** MASC NOUN
1 thumb
□ Je me suis coincé le pouce dans la porte. I trapped my thumb in the door.
2 inch
□ Un pouce fait à peu près deux virgule cinq centimètres. 1 inch equals roughly 2.5 centimetres.
■ **manger sur le pouce** to have a quick snack

la **poudre** FEM NOUN
1 powder
2 face powder
■ **la poudre à laver** washing powder
■ **le lait en poudre** powdered milk
■ **le café en poudre** instant coffee

le **poulain** MASC NOUN
foal

la **poule** FEM NOUN
hen
■ **quand les poules auront des dents** (*informal*) pigs might fly

le **poulet** MASC NOUN
1 chicken
□ J'adore le poulet. I love chicken. □ un poulet rôti a roast chicken
2 cop
□ Il s'est fait attraper par les poulets. (*informal*) He got caught by the cops.

le **pouls** MASC NOUN
pulse
□ Il m'a pris le pouls. He took my pulse.

le **poumon** MASC NOUN
lung

la **poupée** FEM NOUN
doll

pour PREPOSITION
for
□ C'est un cadeau pour toi. It's a present for you. □ Qu'est-ce que tu veux pour ton petit déjeuner ? What would you like for breakfast?
■ **pour faire quelque chose** to do something
□ Je lui ai téléphoné pour l'inviter. I phoned him to invite him.
■ **Pour aller à Strasbourg, s'il vous plaît ?** Which way is it to Strasbourg, please?
■ **pour que** so that

pour que is followed by a verb in the subjunctive.

□ Je lui ai prêté mon pull pour qu'elle n'ait pas froid. I lent her my jumper so that she wouldn't be cold.
■ **pour cent** per cent

le **pourboire** MASC NOUN
tip
□ Il a donné un pourboire au garçon. He gave the waiter a tip.

P

le **pourcentage** MASC NOUN
percentage

pourquoi ADVERB, CONJUNCTION
why
□ Pourquoi est-ce qu'il ne vient pas avec nous ? Why isn't he coming with us? □ Elle ne m'a pas dit pourquoi. She didn't tell me why.

pourra, pourras, pourrai, pourrez VERB ▷ see **pouvoir**

pourri (FEM **pourrie**) ADJECTIVE
rotten

le **pourriel** MASC NOUN
spam (email)

pourrir VERB [38]
to go bad
□ Ces poires ont pourri. These pears have gone bad.

pourrons, pourront VERB ▷ see **pouvoir**

la **poursuite** FEM NOUN
chase
■ **se lancer à la poursuite de quelqu'un** to chase after somebody

poursuivre VERB [81]
to carry on with
□ Ils ont poursuivi leur travail. They carried on with their work.
■ **se poursuivre** to go on □ Le concert s'est poursuivi très tard. The concert went on very late.

pourtant ADVERB
yet
□ Il a raté son examen. Pourtant, il n'est pas bête. He failed his exam, yet he's not stupid.
■ **C'est pourtant facile !** But it's easy!

pourvu (FEM **pourvue**) ADJECTIVE
■ **pourvu que ...** let's hope that ...

pourvu que is followed by a verb in the subjunctive.

□ Pourvu qu'il ne pleuve pas ! Let's hope it doesn't rain!

pousser VERB [28]
1 to push
□ Ils ont dû pousser la voiture. They had to push the car.
2 to grow
□ Mes cheveux poussent vite. My hair grows quickly.
■ **pousser un cri** to give a cry
■ **se pousser** to move over □ Pousse-toi, je ne vois rien. Move over, I can't see a thing.

la **poussette** FEM NOUN
pushchair

la **poussière** FEM NOUN
1 dust
□ La table est couverte de poussière. The table's covered in dust.

2 speck of dust
□ J'ai une poussière dans l'œil. I've got a speck of dust in my eye.

poussiéreux (FEM **poussiéreuse**) ADJECTIVE
dusty

le **poussin** MASC NOUN
chick

pouvez VERB ▷ see **pouvoir**

pouvoir VERB [64]

PRESENT TENSE	
je peux	nous pouvons
tu peux	vous pouvez
il/elle peut	ils/elles peuvent
PAST PARTICIPLE	
pu	

▷ see also **pouvoir** NOUN
can
□ Je peux lui téléphoner si tu veux. I can phone her if you want. □ Puis-je venir vous voir samedi ? May I come and see you on Saturday? □ Je ne pourrai pas venir samedi. I can't come on Saturday. □ J'ai fait tout ce que j'ai pu. I did all I could.
■ **Je n'en peux plus.** I'm exhausted.
■ **Il se peut que ...** It's possible that ...

il se peut que is followed by a verb in the subjunctive.

□ Il se peut qu'elle ait déménagé. It's possible that she's moved house. □ Il se peut que j'y aille. I might go.

le **pouvoir** MASC NOUN
▷ see also **pouvoir** VERB
power
□ Le Premier ministre a beaucoup de pouvoir. The Prime Minister has a lot of power.

pouvons VERB ▷ see **pouvoir**

la **prairie** FEM NOUN
meadow

la **pratique** FEM NOUN
▷ see also **pratique** ADJECTIVE
practice
□ Je manque de pratique. I'm out of practice.

pratique (FEM **pratique**) ADJECTIVE
▷ see also **pratique** NOUN
practical
□ Ce sac est très pratique. This bag's very practical.

pratiquement ADVERB
virtually
□ J'ai pratiquement fini. I've virtually finished.

pratiquer VERB [28]
to practise
□ Je dois pratiquer mon espagnol. I need to practise my Spanish.
■ **Pratiquez-vous un sport ?** Do you do any sport?

P

French-English

le **pré** MASC NOUN
meadow

la **précarité** FEM NOUN
precariousness (of a situation)
■ **la précarité (de l'emploi)** job insecurity, lack
of job security (in economics)

la **précaution** FEM NOUN
precaution
□ prendre ses précautions to take precautions
■ **par précaution** as a precaution □ Il a pris une
assurance par précaution. He took out insurance
as a precaution.
■ **avec précaution** cautiously
■ **« à manipuler avec précaution »** 'handle
with care'

précédemment ADVERB
previously

précédent (FEM **précédente**) ADJECTIVE
previous

précieux (FEM **précieuse**) ADJECTIVE
precious
■ **une pierre précieuse** a precious stone
■ **de précieux conseils** invaluable advice

le **précipice** MASC NOUN
ravine
□ Leur voiture est tombée dans un précipice.
Their car fell into a ravine.

précipitamment ADVERB
hurriedly
□ Camille est partie précipitamment. Camille
left hurriedly.

la **précipitation** FEM NOUN
haste
□ Il a agi avec précipitation. He acted hastily.

se **précipiter** VERB [28]
to rush

précis (FEM **précise**) ADJECTIVE
precise
■ **à huit heures précises** at exactly eight
o'clock

précisément ADVERB
precisely

préciser VERB [28]
1 to be more specific about
□ Pouvez-vous préciser ce que vous voulez dire ?
Can you be more specific about what you want
to say?
2 to specify
□ Pouvez-vous préciser les raisons de ce
changement ? Can you specify the reasons for
this change?

la **précision** FEM NOUN
1 precision
2 detail
□ Je vais vous donner quelques précisions.
I'm going to give you some details.

la **préfecture** FEM NOUN

> **DID YOU KNOW...?**
> A **préfecture** is the headquarters of a
> **département**, one of the 96 administrative
> areas of France.

■ **la préfecture de police** the police
headquarters

préférable (FEM **préférable**) ADJECTIVE
preferable

préféré (FEM **préférée**) ADJECTIVE
favourite

la **préférence** FEM NOUN
preference
□ Je n'ai pas de préférence. I've no preference.
■ **de préférence** preferably

préférer VERB [34]
to prefer
□ Je préfère la cuisine de Teresa. I prefer Teresa's
cooking. □ Je préfère manger à la cantine.
I prefer to eat in the canteen.
■ **Je préférerais du thé.** I'd rather have tea.
■ **préférer quelqu'un à quelqu'un** to prefer
somebody to somebody □ Je le préfère à son
frère. I prefer him to his brother.

préhistorique (FEM **préhistorique**) ADJECTIVE
prehistoric

le **préjugé** MASC NOUN
prejudice
□ avoir des préjugés contre quelqu'un to be
prejudiced against somebody

premier (FEM **première**) ADJECTIVE
▷ see also **première**
first
□ au premier étage on the first floor □ C'est
notre premier jour de vacances. It's the first
day of our holiday. □ C'est la première fois que
je viens ici. It's the first time I've been here.
□ le premier mai the first of May □ Il est arrivé
premier. He came first.
■ **le Premier ministre** the Prime Minister

la **première** FEM NOUN
▷ see also **premier** ADJECTIVE
1 first class
□ Nous avons voyagé en première. We travelled
first class.
2 first gear
□ Passe en première pour prendre ce virage.
Change into first to go round this bend.
3 lower sixth form
□ Ma sœur est en première. My sister's in the
lower sixth.

> **DID YOU KNOW...?**
> In French secondary schools, years are
> counted from the **sixième** (youngest) to
> **première** and **terminale** (oldest).

premièrement ADVERB
firstly

prendre VERB [65]

to take

□ Prends tes affaires et viens avec moi. **Take your things and come with me.**

■ **prendre quelque chose à quelqu'un** to take something from somebody □ Il m'a pris mon stylo ! **He's taken my pen!**

■ **Nous avons pris le train de huit heures. We took the eight o'clock train.**

■ **Je prends toujours le train pour aller à Paris. I always go to Paris by train.**

■ **passer prendre** to pick up □ Je dois passer prendre Thomas. **I have to pick up Thomas.**

■ **prendre à gauche** to turn left □ Prenez à gauche en arrivant au rond-point. **Turn left at the roundabout.**

■ **Il se prend pour Napoléon. He thinks he's Napoléon.**

■ **s'en prendre à quelqu'un** to lay into somebody (*verbally*) □ Il s'en est pris à moi. **He laid into me.**

■ **s'y prendre** to set about it □ Tu t'y prends mal ! **You're setting about it the wrong way!**

le **prénom** MASC NOUN

first name

□ Quel est votre prénom ? **What's your first name?**

préoccupé (FEM **préoccupée**) ADJECTIVE

worried

la **préparation** FEM NOUN

preparation

préparer VERB [28]

1 to prepare

□ Elle prépare le dîner. **She's preparing dinner.**

2 to make

□ Je vais préparer le café. **I'm going to make the coffee.**

3 to prepare for

□ Laure prépare son examen d'économie. **Laure's preparing for her economics exam.**

■ **se préparer** to get ready □ Ils se préparent à partir. **They're getting ready to go.**

la **préposition** FEM NOUN

preposition

près ADVERB

■ **tout près** nearby □ J'habite tout près. **I live nearby.**

■ **près de 1** near (to) □ Est-ce que c'est près d'ici ? **Is it near here? 2** next to □ Assieds-toi près de moi. **Sit down next to me. 3** nearly □ Il y avait près de cinq cents spectateurs. **There were nearly 500 spectators.**

■ **de près** closely □ Il a regardé la photo de près. **He looked closely at the photo.**

■ **à peu de chose près** more or less

la **présence** FEM NOUN

1 presence

□ Sa présence est rassurante. **His presence is reassuring.**

2 attendance

□ La présence aux cours est obligatoire. **Attendance at lessons is compulsory.**

présent (FEM **présente**) ADJECTIVE

▷ see also **présent** NOUN

present

le **présent** MASC NOUN

▷ see also **présent** ADJECTIVE

1 present

■ **à présent** now

2 present tense

la **présentation** FEM NOUN

presentation

■ **faire les présentations** to do the introductions

présenter VERB [28]

to present

□ Il présentait le spectacle. **He presented the show.**

■ **présenter quelqu'un à quelqu'un** to introduce somebody to somebody □ Il m'a présenté à sa sœur. **He introduced me to his sister.**

■ **Marc, je te présente Anaïs. Marc, this is Anaïs.**

■ **se présenter 1** to introduce oneself □ Elle s'est présentée à ses collègues. **She introduced herself to her colleagues. 2** to arise □ Si l'occasion se présente, nous irons en Écosse. **If the chance arises, we'll go to Scotland. 3** to stand □ Monsieur Legros se présente encore aux élections. **Mr Legros is standing for election again.**

le **préservatif** MASC NOUN

condom

préserver VERB [28]

to protect

■ **préserver du froid** to protect from the cold

le **président** MASC NOUN

1 president

□ le président des États-Unis **the president of the United States**

2 chairperson

□ le président du conseil d'administration **the chairperson of the board of directors**

■ **le président-directeur général** the chairperson and managing director

présider VERB [28]

1 to chair

□ Martin a présidé la réunion. **Martin chaired the meeting.**

2 to be the guest of honour

□ Il présidait à table. **He was the guest of honour at the table.**

presque ADVERB

nearly

□ Il est presque six heures. **It's nearly 6 o'clock.**

□ Nous sommes presque arrivés. **We're nearly there.**

P

■ **presque rien** hardly anything □ Elle n'a presque rien mangé. She's hardly eaten anything.

■ **presque pas** hardly at all □ Il ne dort presque pas. He hardly sleeps at all.

■ **presque pas de** hardly any □ Il n'y a presque pas de place. There's hardly any space.

la **presqu'île** FEM NOUN
peninsula

la **presse** FEM NOUN
press
□ les représentants de la presse representatives of the press

pressé (FEM **pressée**) ADJECTIVE
1 in a hurry
□ Je ne peux pas rester, je suis pressé. I can't stay, I'm in a hurry.
2 urgent
□ Ce n'est pas très pressé. It's not very urgent.
■ **une orange pressée** a freshly squeezed orange juice

presser VERB [28]
1 to squeeze
□ Tu peux me presser un citron ? Can you squeeze me a lemon?
2 to be urgent
□ Est-ce que ça presse ? Is it urgent?
■ **se presser** to hurry up □ Allez, presse-toi, on va être en retard ! Come on, hurry up, we're going to be late!
■ **Rien ne presse.** There's no hurry.

le **pressing** MASC NOUN
dry-cleaner's

la **pression** FEM NOUN
1 pressure
■ **faire pression sur quelqu'un** to put pressure on somebody
2 draught beer (*informal*)

prêt (FEM **prête**) ADJECTIVE
▷ *see also* **prêt** NOUN
ready
□ Le déjeuner est prêt. Lunch is ready. □ Tu es prête ? Are you ready?

le **prêt** MASC NOUN
▷ *see also* **prêt** ADJECTIVE
loan

le **prêt-à-porter** MASC NOUN
ready-to-wear clothes *pl*

prétendre VERB [88]
■ **prétendre que** to claim that □ Il prétend qu'il ne la connaît pas. He claims he doesn't know her.

BE CAREFUL!
prétendre does not mean **to pretend**.

prétendu (FEM **prétendue**) ADJECTIVE
so-called
□ un prétendu expert a so-called expert

prétentieux (FEM **prétentieuse**) ADJECTIVE
pretentious

prêter VERB [28]
■ **prêter quelque chose à quelqu'un** to lend something to someone □ Il m'a prêté sa voiture. He lent me his car.
■ **prêter attention à quelque chose** to pay attention to something

le **prétexte** MASC NOUN
excuse
□ Il avait un prétexte pour ne pas venir. He had an excuse for not coming.
■ **sous aucun prétexte** on no account □ Ne le dérangez sous aucun prétexte. On no account must you disturb him.

prétexter VERB [28]
to give as an excuse
□ Elle a prétexté une réunion. She gave a meeting as her excuse. □ Il a prétexté qu'il avait un rendez-vous. He gave the excuse that he had an appointment.

le **prêtre** MASC NOUN
priest

la **preuve** FEM NOUN
1 evidence
□ Il y a des preuves contre lui. There's evidence against him.
2 proof
□ Vous n'avez aucune preuve. You haven't got any proof.
■ **faire preuve de courage** to show courage
■ **faire ses preuves** to prove oneself □ Pour être embauché ici, il faut faire ses preuves. To be employed here, you need to prove yourself.

prévenir VERB [89]
■ **prévenir quelqu'un** to warn somebody □ Je te préviens, il est de mauvaise humeur. I'm warning you, he's in a bad mood.

la **prévention** FEM NOUN
prevention
■ **des mesures de prévention** preventative measures
■ **la prévention routière** road safety

la **prévision** FEM NOUN
■ **les prévisions météorologiques** the weather forecast
■ **en prévision de quelque chose** in anticipation of something

prévoir VERB [92]
1 to plan
□ Nous prévoyons un pique-nique pour dimanche. We're planning to have a picnic on Sunday.
■ **Le départ est prévu pour dix heures.** The departure's scheduled for 10 o'clock.
2 to allow
□ J'ai prévu assez à manger pour quatre. I allowed enough food for four.

3 to foresee
□ J'avais prévu qu'il serait en retard. I'd foreseen that he'd be late.
■ **Je prévois qu'il me faudra une heure de plus.** I reckon on it taking me another hour.

prier VERB [19]
to pray to
□ Les Grecs priaient Dionysos. The Greeks prayed to Dionysos.
■ **prier quelqu'un de faire quelque chose** to ask somebody to do something □ Elle l'a prié de sortir. She asked him to leave.
■ **je vous en prie 1** please do □ Je peux m'asseoir ? — Je vous en prie. May I sit down? — Please do. **2** please □ Je vous en prie, ne me laissez pas seule. Please, don't leave me alone. **3** don't mention it □ Merci pour votre aide. — Je vous en prie. Thanks for your help. — Don't mention it.

la prière FEM NOUN
prayer
□ faire ses prières to say one's prayers
■ « **prière de ne pas fumer** » 'no smoking please'

le primaire MASC NOUN
primary education
□ Ses enfants sont encore en primaire. His children are still in primary education.
■ **l'école primaire** primary school

la prime FEM NOUN
1 bonus
□ Il a eu une prime en récompense de son travail. He received a bonus for his work.
2 free gift
□ J'ai eu ce stylo en prime avec l'agenda. I got this pen as a free gift with the diary.
3 premium
□ une prime d'assurance an insurance premium

la primevère FEM NOUN
primrose

le prince MASC NOUN
prince
□ le prince Charles Prince Charles

la princesse FEM NOUN
princess
□ la princesse Diana Princess Diana

principal (FEM **principale**, MASC PL **principaux**) ADJECTIVE
▷ see also **principal** NOUN
main
□ le rôle principal the main role

le principal (PL les **principaux**) MASC NOUN
▷ see also **principal** ADJECTIVE
1 head teacher
□ le principal du collège the head teacher of the school
2 main thing
□ Personne n'a été blessé ; c'est le principal. Nobody was injured; that's the main thing.

le principe MASC NOUN
principle
■ **pour le principe** on principle
■ **en principe 1** as a rule □ Il déjeune en principe à midi et demi. As a rule he has lunch at 12.30. **2** in theory □ En principe Anne doit arriver lundi. In theory, Anne should arrive on Monday.

le printemps MASC NOUN
spring
■ **au printemps** in spring

la priorité FEM NOUN
1 priority
□ C'est à faire en priorité. It needs to be done as a priority.
2 right of way
□ Tu n'as pas la priorité. You haven't got right of way.

pris (FEM **prise**) ADJECTIVE
▷ see also **prise** NOUN
1 taken
□ Est-ce que cette place est prise ? Is this seat taken?
2 busy
□ Je serai très pris la semaine prochaine. I'll be very busy next week.
■ **avoir le nez pris** to have a stuffy nose
■ **être pris de panique** to be panic-stricken

pris VERB ▷ see **prendre**

la prise FEM NOUN
▷ see also **pris** ADJECTIVE
1 plug
2 socket
■ **une prise de courant** a power point
■ **une prise multiple** an adaptor
■ **une prise de sang** a blood test

la prison FEM NOUN
prison
□ aller en prison to go to prison □ être en prison to be in prison

prisonnier (FEM **prisonnière**) ADJECTIVE
▷ see also **prisonnier** NOUN, **prisonnière** NOUN
captive

le prisonnier MASC NOUN
▷ see also **prisonnier** ADJECTIVE
prisoner

la prisonnière FEM NOUN
▷ see also **prisonnier** ADJECTIVE
prisoner

prit VERB ▷ see **prendre**

privé (FEM **privée**) ADJECTIVE
private
□ la propriété privée private property □ ma vie privée my private life
■ **en privé** in private

P

priver VERB [28]

■ **priver quelqu'un de quelque chose** to deprive somebody of something □ Le prisonnier a été privé de nourriture. The prisoner was deprived of food.

■ **Tu seras privé de dessert !** You won't get any pudding!

le **prix** MASC NOUN

1 price

□ Je n'arrive pas à lire le prix de ce livre. I can't see the price of this book.

2 prize

□ Cécile a eu le prix de la meilleure actrice. Cécile got the prize for best actress.

■ **hors de prix** exorbitantly priced □ Les repas sont hors de prix ici ! The price of meals here is exorbitant!

■ **à aucun prix** not at any price □ Je n'irai là-bas à aucun prix. I'm not going there, not at any price.

■ **à tout prix** at all costs □ Je veux à tout prix voir ce film. I want to see this film at all costs.

probable (FEM probable) ADJECTIVE

likely

□ Il est probable qu'elle viendra. It's likely she'll come.

■ **C'est peu probable.** That's unlikely.

probablement ADVERB

probably

le **problème** MASC NOUN

problem

le **procédé** MASC NOUN

process

le **procès** MASC NOUN

trial

□ Le procès du meurtrier commence mardi. The murder trial starts on Tuesday.

■ **Il est en procès avec son employeur.** He's involved in a lawsuit with his employer.

prochain (FEM prochaine) ADJECTIVE

next

□ Nous descendons au prochain arrêt. We're getting off at the next stop.

■ **la prochaine fois** next time

■ **la semaine prochaine** next week

■ **À la prochaine !** See you!

prochainement ADVERB

soon

proche (FEM proche) ADJECTIVE

1 near

□ Les magasins les plus proches étaient à trois kilomètres. The nearest shops were 3 kilometres away. □ dans un proche avenir in the near future

2 close

□ un ami proche a close friend

■ **proche de** near to □ La cathédrale est proche du château. The cathedral is near the castle.

■ **le Proche-Orient** the Middle East

les **proches** MASC PL NOUN

close relatives

proclamer VERB [28]

to proclaim

la **procréation** FEM NOUN

procreation

■ **procréation médicalement assistée, assistance médicale à la procréation** assisted reproduction

procurer VERB [28]

■ **procurer quelque chose à quelqu'un** to get something for somebody □ C'est lui qui m'a procuré ce travail. He got me this job.

■ **se procurer quelque chose** to get something □ Je me suis procuré leur dernier catalogue. I got their latest catalogue.

le **producteur** MASC NOUN

producer

la **production** FEM NOUN

production

la **productrice** FEM NOUN

producer

produire VERB [23]

to produce

■ **se produire** to take place □ Ces changements se sont produits l'an dernier. The changes took place last year.

le **produit** MASC NOUN

product

□ les produits de beauté beauty products

le/la **prof** MASC/FEM NOUN (informal)

teacher

□ Elle est prof de maths. She's a maths teacher.

le **professeur** MASC NOUN

1 teacher

□ Guillaume est professeur d'histoire. Guillaume's a history teacher.

2 professor

□ le professeur Dupont Professor Dupont

■ **un professeur de faculté** a university lecturer

la **profession** FEM NOUN

profession

□ Quelle est votre profession ? What's your profession?

■ **« sans profession »** 'unemployed'

professionnel (FEM professionnelle) ADJECTIVE

professional

le **profil** MASC NOUN

1 profile (of person)

□ de profil in profile

2 contours (of object)

le **profit** MASC NOUN

profit

□ La société a fait des profits importants. The company made significant profits.

■ **tirer profit de quelque chose** to profit from something

■ **au profit de** in aid of □ un spectacle au profit de l'UNICEF a show in aid of UNICEF

profiter VERB [28]

■ **profiter de quelque chose** to take advantage of something □ Profitez du beau temps pour aller faire du vélo. Take advantage of the good weather and go cycling.

■ **Profitez-en bien !** Make the most of it!

profond (FEM **profonde**) ADJECTIVE

deep

■ **peu profond** shallow

la **profondeur** FEM NOUN

depth

le **programme** MASC NOUN

1 programme
□ le programme du festival the festival programme

2 syllabus
□ le programme de maths the maths syllabus

3 program
□ un programme informatique a computer program

programmer VERB [28]

1 to show
□ Ce film est programmé dimanche soir. The film is showing on Sunday evening.

2 to program
□ Mon ordinateur n'est pas programmé pour ça. My computer isn't programmed to do that.

le **programmeur** MASC NOUN

programmer
□ Lucas est programmeur. Lucas is a programmer.

la **programmeuse** FEM NOUN

programmer
□ Elle est programmeuse. She's a programmer.

le **progrès** MASC NOUN

progress
□ faire des progrès to make progress

progresser VERB [28]

to progress

progressif (FEM **progressive**) ADJECTIVE

progressive

le **projecteur** MASC NOUN

1 projector
□ Le projecteur est en panne. The projector is broken.

2 spotlight
□ sous les projecteurs under the spotlight

le **projet** MASC NOUN

1 plan
□ des projets de vacances holiday plans

2 draft
□ le projet de construction d'un musée the draft for the construction of a museum

■ **un projet de loi** a bill (in parliament)

projeter VERB [41]

1 to plan
□ Ils projettent d'acheter une maison. They're planning to buy a house.

2 to cast
□ une ombre projetée sur le mur a shadow cast onto the wall

■ **Elle a été projetée hors de la voiture.** She was thrown out of the car.

prolonger VERB [45]

1 to prolong
□ Je vais prolonger mes vacances en Espagne. I'm going to prolong my holidays in Spain.

2 to extend
□ Je vais prolonger mon abonnement. I'm going to extend my subscription.

■ **se prolonger** to go on □ La réunion s'est prolongée tard. The meeting went on late.

la **promenade** FEM NOUN

walk
□ Il y a de belles promenades par ici. There are some nice walks round here.

■ **faire une promenade** to go for a walk

■ **faire une promenade en voiture** to go for a drive

■ **faire une promenade à vélo** to go for a bike ride

promener VERB [43]

to take for a walk
□ Cordelia promène son chien tous les jours. Cordelia takes her dog for a walk every day.

■ **se promener** to go for a walk □ Léa est partie se promener. Léa has gone for a walk.

la **promesse** FEM NOUN

promise
□ faire une promesse to make a promise □ tenir sa promesse to keep one's promise

promettre VERB [47]

to promise
□ On m'a promis une augmentation. They promised me a pay rise.

■ **promettre à quelqu'un de faire quelque chose** to promise someone to do something
□ Elle m'a promis de me téléphoner. She promised to phone me.

la **promotion** FEM NOUN

promotion
□ Il espère avoir bientôt une promotion. He's hoping to get a promotion soon.

■ **être en promotion** to be on special offer
□ Les côtes de porc sont en promotion. Pork chops are on special offer.

le **pronom** MASC NOUN

pronoun

prononcer VERB [12]

1 to pronounce
□ Le russe est difficile à prononcer. Russian is difficult to pronounce.

P

prononciation - proverbe

2 to deliver
□ prononcer un discours to deliver a speech
■ **se prononcer** to be pronounced □ Le « e » final ne se prononce pas. The final 'e' isn't pronounced.

la **prononciation** FEM NOUN
pronunciation

la **propagande** FEM NOUN
propaganda

se **propager** VERB [45]
to spread
□ Le feu s'est propagé rapidement. The fire spread quickly.

la **proportion** FEM NOUN
proportion

le **propos** MASC NOUN
■ **à propos** by the way □ À propos, quand est-ce que tu viens ? By the way, when are you coming?
■ **à propos de quelque chose** about something □ C'est à propos de la soirée de vendredi. It's about the party on Friday.

proposer VERB [28]
■ **proposer quelque chose à quelqu'un**
1 to suggest something to somebody □ Nous lui avons proposé une promenade en bateau. We suggested going on a boat ride to him.
2 to offer somebody something □ Ils m'ont proposé des chocolats. They offered me some chocolates.
■ **proposer de faire** to suggest doing □ Éric a proposé d'organiser une soirée. Eric suggested organising a party.

la **proposition** FEM NOUN
offer
□ J'accepte ta proposition avec plaisir. I'll be pleased to accept your offer.

propre (FEM **propre**) ADJECTIVE
▷ see also **propre** NOUN
1 clean
□ Ce mouchoir n'est pas propre. This handkerchief isn't clean.
2 own
□ Valentin l'a fabriqué de ses propres mains. Valentin made it with his own hands.
■ **propre à** characteristic of □ C'est une coutume propre au Berry. It's a custom you find in the Berry region.

BE CAREFUL!
The French word **propre** does not mean **proper**.

le **propre** MASC NOUN
▷ see also **propre** ADJECTIVE
■ **recopier quelque chose au propre** to make a fair copy of something

proprement ADVERB
properly
□ Mange proprement ! Eat properly!

■ **le village proprement dit** the village itself
■ **à proprement parler** strictly speaking

la **propreté** FEM NOUN
cleanliness

le **propriétaire** MASC NOUN
▷ see also **propriétaire** NOUN
1 owner
2 landlord

la **propriétaire** FEM NOUN
▷ see also **propriétaire** NOUN
1 owner
2 landlady

la **propriété** FEM NOUN
property
□ la propriété privée private property

le **prospectus** MASC NOUN
leaflet

prospère (FEM **prospère**) ADJECTIVE
prosperous

la **prostituée** FEM NOUN
prostitute

protecteur (FEM **protectrice**) ADJECTIVE
1 protective
□ un vernis protecteur a protective varnish
2 patronizing
□ un ton protecteur a patronizing tone

la **protection** FEM NOUN
protection

protéger VERB [66]
to protect

la **protéine** FEM NOUN
protein

protestant (FEM **protestante**) ADJECTIVE
Protestant
□ une église protestante a Protestant church
■ **Il est protestant.** He's a Protestant.

la **protestation** FEM NOUN
protest

protester VERB [28]
to protest
□ Ils protestent contre leurs conditions de travail. They're protesting about their working conditions.

prouver VERB [28]
to prove

la **provenance** FEM NOUN
origin
■ **un avion en provenance de Berlin** a plane arriving from Berlin

provenir VERB [89, aux être]
■ **provenir de 1** to come from □ Ces tomates proviennent d'Espagne. These tomatoes come from Spain. **2** to be the result of □ Cela provient d'un manque d'organisation. This is the result of a lack of organization.

le **proverbe** MASC NOUN
proverb

la **province** FEM NOUN
province
■ **en province** in the provinces □ Ils habitent en province. They live in the provinces.

le **proviseur** MASC NOUN
headteacher (of state secondary school)
□ Elle est proviseur. She's a headteacher.

la **provision** FEM NOUN
supply
□ une provision de pommes de terre a supply of potatoes

les **provisions** FEM PL NOUN
food
□ Nous n'avons plus beaucoup de provisions. We haven't got much food left.

provisoire (FEM provisoire) ADJECTIVE
temporary
□ un emploi provisoire a temporary job

provoquer VERB [28]
1 to provoke
□ Il l'a provoquée en la traitant d'imbécile. He provoked her by calling her stupid.
2 to cause
□ Cet accident a provoqué la mort de quarante personnes. The accident caused the death of 40 people.

la **proximité** FEM NOUN
proximity
■ **à proximité** nearby □ Sabine habite à proximité. Sabine lives nearby.

prudemment ADVERB
1 carefully
□ Conduisez prudemment ! Drive carefully!
2 wisely
□ Prudemment, il a fait des économies. Wisely, he saved some money.
3 cautiously
□ Le gouvernement a réagi prudemment. The government reacted cautiously.

la **prudence** FEM NOUN
caution
■ **avec prudence** carefully □ Ils ont conduit avec prudence. They drove carefully.

prudent (FEM prudente) ADJECTIVE
1 careful
□ Soyez prudents ! Be careful!
2 wise
□ Laisse ton passeport à la maison, c'est plus prudent. It would be wiser to leave your passport at home.

la **prune** FEM NOUN
plum

le **pruneau** (PL les pruneaux) MASC NOUN
prune

le/la **psychiatre** MASC/FEM NOUN
psychiatrist

la **psychologie** FEM NOUN
psychology

psychologique (FEM psychologique) ADJECTIVE
psychological

le/la **psychologue** MASC/FEM NOUN
psychologist

pu VERB ▷ see pouvoir
■ **Je n'ai pas pu venir.** I couldn't come.

la **pub** FEM NOUN (informal)
1 advertising
□ Il y a trop de pub à la télé. There's too much advertising on TV.
2 adverts
□ Le film a été coupé par la pub. The film was interrupted by adverts.

public (FEM publique) ADJECTIVE
▷ see also **public** NOUN
public
□ un jardin public a public park
■ **une école publique** a state school

le **public** MASC NOUN
▷ see also **public** ADJECTIVE
1 public
□ Ce parc est ouvert au public. The park's open to the public.
2 audience
□ Le public a applaudi le chanteur. The audience applauded the singer.
■ **en public** in public □ Je déteste parler en public. I hate speaking in public.

publicitaire (FEM publicitaire) ADJECTIVE
■ **une agence publicitaire** an advertising agency
■ **un film publicitaire** a publicity film

la **publicité** FEM NOUN
1 advertising
□ Marine travaille dans la publicité. Marine works in advertising.
2 advert
□ Il y a trop de publicités dans ce journal. There are too many adverts in this newspaper.
■ **faire de la publicité pour quelque chose** to publicize something

publier VERB [19]
to publish
□ Cédric vient de publier son nouveau roman. Cédric has just published his new novel.

publique FEM ADJECTIVE ▷ see public

la **puce** FEM NOUN
1 flea
□ Ce chien a des puces. This dog has fleas.
2 chip
□ une puce électronique a microchip
■ **une carte à puce** a smart card

les **puces** FEM PL NOUN
flea market sing

puer VERB [28]
to stink
□ Ça pue le tabac ici ! It stinks of tobacco round here!

puéril (FEM **puérile**) ADJECTIVE
childish

puis VERB ▷ see **pouvoir**
▷ see also **puis** ADVERB
■ Puis-je venir vous voir samedi ? May I come and see you on Saturday?

puis ADVERB
▷ see also **puis** VERB
then
□ Faites dorer le poulet, puis ajoutez le vin blanc. Fry the chicken till golden, then add white wine.

puisque CONJUNCTION
since
□ Puisque c'est si cher, nous irons manger ailleurs. Since it's so expensive, we'll eat elsewhere.

la **puissance** FEM NOUN
power

puissant (FEM **puissante**) ADJECTIVE
powerful

le **puits** MASC NOUN
well
□ Il a un puits dans son jardin. He's got a well in his garden.

le **pull** MASC NOUN
jumper

le **pull-over** MASC NOUN
jumper

le **pulvérisateur** MASC NOUN
spray
□ un pulvérisateur de parfum a perfume spray

pulvériser VERB [28]
1 to pulverize

□ L'explosion a pulvérisé le bâtiment. The explosion pulverized the building.
2 to spray
□ Il a pulvérisé de l'insecticide sur ses plantes. He sprayed insecticide on his plants.

la **punaise** FEM NOUN
drawing pin

punir VERB [38]
to punish
□ Il a été puni pour avoir menti. He was punished for lying.

la **punition** FEM NOUN
punishment

le **pupitre** MASC NOUN
desk (for pupil)

pur (FEM **pure**) ADJECTIVE
1 pure
□ L'eau de cette source est très pure. The water from this spring is very pure.
2 neat (undiluted)
□ du whisky pur neat whisky □ de l'eau de Javel pure concentrated bleach
■ C'est de la folie pure. It's sheer madness.

la **purée** FEM NOUN
mashed potatoes
■ la purée de marrons chestnut purée

le **puzzle** MASC NOUN
jigsaw puzzle

le **P.-V.** MASC NOUN (= procès-verbal)
parking ticket

le **pyjama** MASC NOUN
pyjamas pl

la **pyramide** FEM NOUN
pyramid

les **Pyrénées** FEM PL NOUN
Pyrenees
■ dans les Pyrénées in the Pyrenees

P

Qq

le **QI** MASC NOUN (= *quotient intellectuel*)
IQ

qu' CONJUNCTION, PRONOUN, ADVERB ▷ *see* **que**

le **quai** MASC NOUN

1 quay
□ être à quai to be alongside the quay

2 platform
□ Le train partira du quai numéro quatre. The train will leave from platform 4.

qualifié (FEM **qualifiée**) ADJECTIVE
qualified

qualifier VERB [19]
■ **se qualifier** to qualify □ Maxime s'est qualifié pour la demi-finale. Maxime has qualified for the semifinal.

la **qualité** FEM NOUN
quality
□ Ces outils sont de très bonne qualité. These are very good quality tools.

quand CONJUNCTION, ADVERB
when
□ Quand est-ce que tu pars en vacances ? When are you going on holiday? □ Quand je serai riche, j'achèterai une belle maison. When I'm rich, I'll buy a nice house.
■ **quand même** all the same □ Je ne voulais pas de dessert, mais j'en ai mangé quand même. I didn't want any dessert, but I had some all the same.

quant à PREPOSITION
regarding
□ Quant au problème de chauffage ... Regarding the problem with the heating ... □ Quant à moi, je n'arriverai qu'à dix heures. As for me, I won't be arriving till 10 o'clock.

la **quantité** FEM NOUN
amount
■ **des quantités de** a great deal of

la **quarantaine** FEM NOUN
about forty
□ une quarantaine de personnes about forty people
■ **Elle a la quarantaine.** She's in her forties.

quarante NUMBER
forty
□ Elle a quarante ans. She's forty.
■ **quarante et un** forty-one
■ **quarante-deux** forty-two

le **quart** MASC NOUN
quarter
■ **le quart de** a quarter of □ Elle a mangé le quart du gâteau. She ate a quarter of the cake.
■ **trois quarts** three quarters
■ **un quart d'heure** a quarter of an hour
■ **deux heures et quart** a quarter past two
■ **dix heures moins le quart** a quarter to ten
■ **Un quart d'eau minérale, s'il vous plaît.** A small bottle of mineral water, please.

le **quartier** MASC NOUN

1 area (*of town*)
□ un quartier tranquille a quiet area
■ **un cinéma de quartier** a local cinema

2 piece
□ un quartier d'orange a piece of orange

le **quartz** MASC NOUN
■ **une montre à quartz** a quartz watch

quasi ADVERB
nearly
□ La quasi-totalité des récoltes a été détruite. Nearly all of the crop was destroyed.

quasiment ADVERB
nearly
□ Le film est quasiment fini. The film's nearly finished.
■ **quasiment jamais** hardly ever □ Ils ne vont quasiment jamais en boîte. They hardly ever go clubbing.

quatorze NUMBER
fourteen
□ Mon frère a quatorze ans. My brother's fourteen. □ à quatorze heures at 2 p.m.
■ **le quatorze février** the fourteenth of February

quatre NUMBER
four
□ Il est quatre heures du matin. It's four in the morning. □ Il a quatre ans. He's four.
■ **le quatre février** the fourth of February
■ **faire les quatre cents coups** to be a bit wild
□ Todd a fait les quatre cents coups dans sa jeunesse. Todd was a bit wild in his youth.

quatre-vingts NUMBER
eighty

quatre-vingts is spelt with an **-s** when it is followed by a noun, but not when it is followed by another number.

q

□ quatre-vingts euros eighty euros □ Elle a quatre-vingt-deux ans. She's eighty-two.
■ **quatre-vingt-dix** ninety
■ **quatre-vingt-onze** ninety-one
■ **quatre-vingt-quinze** ninety-five
■ **quatre-vingt-dix-huit** ninety-eight

quatrième (FEM **quatrième**) ADJECTIVE
▷ see also **quatrième** NOUN
fourth
□ au quatrième étage on the fourth floor

la **quatrième** FEM NOUN
▷ see also **quatrième** ADJECTIVE
year 9
□ Mon frère est en quatrième. My brother's in year 9.

DID YOU KNOW...?
In French secondary schools, years are counted from the **sixième** (youngest) to **première** and **terminale** (oldest).

que CONJUNCTION, PRONOUN, ADVERB
1 that
□ Il sait que tu es là. He knows that you're here. □ la dame que j'ai rencontrée hier the lady that I met yesterday □ Le gâteau qu'elle a fait est délicieux. The cake she's made is delicious.
■ **Je veux que tu viennes.** I want you to come.
2 what
□ Que fais-tu ? What are you doing? □ Que vas-tu lui dire ? What are you going to tell him?
■ **Qu'est-ce que ...?** What ...? □ Qu'est-ce que tu fais ? What are you doing? □ Qu'est-ce que c'est ? What's that?
■ **plus ... que** more ... than □ C'est plus difficile que je ne le pensais. It's more difficult than I thought. □ Il est plus grand que moi. He's bigger than me.
■ **aussi ... que** as ... as □ Elle est aussi jolie que sa sœur. She's as pretty as her sister. □ Le train est aussi cher que l'avion. The train is as expensive as the plane.
■ **ne ... que** only □ Il ne boit que de l'eau. He only drinks water. □ Je ne l'ai vu qu'une fois. I've only seen him once.
■ **Qu'il est bête !** He's so silly!

le **Québec** MASC NOUN
Quebec (province)

québécois (FEM **québécoise**) ADJECTIVE, NOUN
from Quebec
■ **un Québécois** a Quebecois man
■ **une Québécoise** a Quebecois woman

queer (FEM **queer**) ADJECTIVE
queer
□ Il se définit comme queer. He identifies as queer.

quel (FEM **quelle**) ADJECTIVE
1 who
□ Quel est ton chanteur préféré ? Who's your favourite singer?
2 what

□ Quelle est ta couleur préférée ? What's your favourite colour? □ Quelle heure est-il ? What time is it? □ Quelle bonne surprise ! What a nice surprise! □ Quel dommage ! What a pity!
3 which
□ Quel groupe préfères-tu ? Which band do you like best?
■ **quel que soit 1** whoever □ quel que soit le coupable whoever is guilty **2** whatever □ quel que soit votre avis whatever your opinion

quelle FEM ADJECTIVE ▷ see **quel**

quelque (FEM **quelque**) ADJECTIVE, ADVERB
1 some
□ Il a quelques amis à Paris. He has some friends in Paris. □ J'ai acheté quelques disques. I bought some records.
2 a few
□ Il reste quelques bouteilles. There are a few bottles left.
3 few
□ Ils ont fini les quelques bouteilles qui restaient. They finished the few bottles that were left.
■ **quelque chose 1** something □ J'ai quelque chose pour toi. I've got something for you. □ Je voudrais quelque chose de moins cher. I'd like something cheaper. **2** anything □ Avez-vous quelque chose à déclarer ? Have you got anything to declare? □ Tu as pensé à quelque chose d'autre ? Did you think of anything else?
■ **quelque part 1** somewhere □ J'ai oublié mon sac quelque part. I've left my bag somewhere. **2** anywhere □ Vous allez quelque part ce week-end ? Are you going anywhere this weekend?

quelquefois ADVERB
sometimes

quelques-uns (FEM **quelques-unes**) PL PRONOUN
some
□ As-tu vu ses films ? J'en ai vu quelques-uns. Have you seen his films? I've seen some of them.

quelqu'un PRONOUN
1 somebody
□ Quelqu'un t'a appelé. Somebody phoned you. □ Il y a quelqu'un à la porte. There's somebody at the door.
2 anybody
□ Est-ce que quelqu'un a vu mon parapluie ? Has anybody seen my umbrella? □ Il y a quelqu'un ? Is there anybody there?

la **querelle** FEM NOUN
quarrel

qu'est-ce que ▷ see **que**

qu'est-ce qui ▷ see **qui**

la **question** FEM NOUN
1 question
□ Je t'ai posé une question. I asked you a question.

2 matter
□ Ils se sont disputés pour des questions d'argent. They argued over money matters.
■ **Il n'en est pas question.** There's no question of it. □ Il n'est pas question que je paye. There's no question of me paying.
■ **De quoi est-il question ?** What's it about? □ Il est question de l'organisation du concert. It's about the organization of the concert.
■ **hors de question** out of the question □ Il est hors de question que nous restions ici. It's out of the question that we stay here.

le **questionnaire** MASC NOUN
questionnaire

questionner VERB [28]
to question

la **queue** FEM NOUN
1 tail
□ Le chien a agité la queue. The dog wagged its tail.
■ **faire la queue** to queue
■ **une queue de cheval** a ponytail
2 rear
□ en queue du train at the rear of the train
3 bottom
□ en queue de liste at the bottom of the list
4 stalk (*of fruit, leaf*)
□ la queue d'une cerise a cherry stalk

qui PRONOUN
1 who
□ Qui a téléphoné ? Who phoned? □ Einstein, qui était un génie ... Einstein, who was a genius ...
2 whom
■ **C'est la personne à qui j'ai parlé hier.** It's the person who I spoke to yesterday.
3 that
□ Donne-moi la veste qui est sur la chaise. Give me the jacket that's on the chair.
■ **Qui est-ce qui ...?** Who ...? □ Qui est-ce qui t'emmène au spectacle ? Who's taking you to the show?
■ **Qui est-ce que ...?** Who ...? □ Qui est-ce que tu as vu à cette soirée ? Who did you see at the party?
■ **Qu'est-ce qui ...?** What ...? □ Qu'est-ce qui est sur la table ? What's on the table? □ Qu'est-ce qui te prend ? What's the matter with you?
■ **À qui est ce sac ?** Whose bag is this?
■ **À qui parlais-tu ?** Who were you talking to?

la **quille** FEM NOUN
■ **un jeu de quilles** skittles

la **quincaillerie** FEM NOUN
ironmonger's (shop)

le **quinquennat** MASC NOUN

DID YOU KNOW...?
le quinquennat is the five-year term of office of the French President.

la **quinzaine** FEM NOUN
about fifteen
□ Il y avait une quinzaine de personnes. There were about fifteen people there.
■ **une quinzaine de jours** a fortnight

quinze NUMBER
fifteen
□ Anaïs a quinze ans. Anaïs is fifteen. □ à quinze heures at 3 p.m.
■ **le quinze février** the fifteenth of February
■ **dans quinze jours** in a fortnight's time

la **quittance** FEM NOUN
1 receipt
2 bill

quitter VERB [28]
to leave
□ J'ai quitté la maison à huit heures. I left the house at 8 o'clock.
■ **se quitter** to part □ Les deux amis se sont quittés devant le café. The two friends parted in front of the café.
■ **Ne quittez pas.** (*on telephone*) Hold the line.
□ Ne quittez pas, je vous passe Monsieur Divan. Hold the line, I'll put you through to Monsieur Divan.

quoi PRONOUN
what
□ À quoi penses-tu ? What are you thinking about? □ C'est quoi, ce truc ? What's this thing?
■ **Quoi de neuf ?** What's new?
■ **As-tu de quoi écrire ?** Have you got anything to write with?
■ **Je n'ai pas de quoi acheter une voiture.** I can't afford to buy a car.
■ **Quoi qu'il arrive.** Whatever happens.
■ **Il n'y a pas de quoi.** Don't mention it.
■ **Il n'y a pas de quoi s'énerver.** There's no reason for getting worked up.
■ **En quoi puis-je vous aider ?** How may I help you?

quoique CONJUNCTION
even though

quoique is followed by a verb in the subjunctive.

□ Il va l'acheter quoique ce soit cher. He's going to buy it even though it's expensive.

quotidien (FEM **quotidienne**) ADJECTIVE
▷ *see also* **quotidien** NOUN
daily
□ Il est parti faire sa promenade quotidienne. He's gone for his daily walk.
■ **la vie quotidienne** everyday life

le **quotidien** MASC NOUN
▷ *see also* **quotidien** ADJECTIVE
daily paper
□ Le Monde est un quotidien. Le Monde is a daily paper.

q

Rr

le **rab** MASC NOUN (*informal*)
seconds (*of meal*)
□ Il y a du rab ? Are there any seconds?

le **rabais** MASC NOUN
reduction (*in price*)
■ au rabais at a discount

la **racaille** FEM NOUN
riff-raff

raccompagner VERB [28]
to take home
□ Tu peux me raccompagner ? Can you take me home?

le **raccourci** MASC NOUN
shortcut

raccrocher VERB [28]
to hang up (*telephone*)

la **race** FEM NOUN
1 race
□ la race humaine the human race
2 breed
□ De quelle race est ton chat ? What breed is your cat?
■ de race pedigree □ un chien de race a pedigree dog

racheter VERB [1]
1 to buy another
□ J'ai racheté un portefeuille. I've bought another wallet. □ racheter du lait to buy more milk
2 to buy
□ Il m'a racheté ma moto. He bought my bike from me.

la **racine** FEM NOUN
root

le **racisme** MASC NOUN
racism

raciste (FEM **raciste**) ADJECTIVE
racist

raconter VERB [28]
■ raconter quelque chose à quelqu'un to tell somebody about something □ Raconte-moi ce qui s'est passé. Tell me what happened.
□ Raconte-moi une histoire. Tell me a story.
■ Qu'est-ce que tu racontes ? What are you talking about?

le **radar** MASC NOUN
radar

le **radiateur** MASC NOUN
radiator
■ un radiateur électrique an electric heater

radin (FEM **radine**) ADJECTIVE (*informal*)
stingy

la **radio** FEM NOUN
1 radio
□ à la radio on the radio
■ une radio numérique a digital radio
2 X-ray
■ passer une radio to have an X-ray □ Elle a passé une radio des poumons. She had a chest X-ray.

le **radio-réveil** (PL les **radios-réveils**) MASC NOUN
clock radio

le **radis** MASC NOUN
radish

raffoler VERB [28]
■ raffoler de to be crazy about □ Elle raffole de la tarte aux pommes. She really loves apple tart.

rafraîchir VERB [38]
to cool down
■ se rafraîchir 1 to get cooler □ Le temps se rafraîchit. The weather's getting cooler. 2 to freshen up □ Il a pris une douche pour se rafraîchir. He had a shower to freshen up.

rafraîchissant (FEM **rafraîchissante**) ADJECTIVE
refreshing

la **rage** FEM NOUN
rabies
■ une rage de dents raging toothache

le **ragoût** MASC NOUN
stew

raide (FEM **raide**) ADJECTIVE
1 steep
□ Cette pente est raide. This is a steep slope.
2 straight
□ Laure a les cheveux raides. Laure has straight hair.
3 stiff
□ Son bras est encore raide. His arm's still stiff.
4 flat broke
□ Je suis raide ce mois-ci. (*informal*) I'm flat broke this month.

la **raie** FEM NOUN
1 skate (*fish*)
2 parting (*in hair*)

le **rail** MASC NOUN
rail
□ par rail by rail

le **raisin** MASC NOUN
grapes
□ le raisin blanc green grapes
■ des raisins secs raisins

la **raison** FEM NOUN
reason
□ sans raison for no reason □ Raison de plus pour y aller. All the more reason for going.
■ Ce n'est pas une raison. That's no excuse.
■ avoir raison to be right □ Tu as raison. You're right.
■ en raison de because of □ en raison d'une grève because of a strike

raisonnable (FEM **raisonnable**) ADJECTIVE
sensible
□ Elle est très raisonnable pour son âge. She's very sensible for her age.

le **raisonnement** MASC NOUN
reasoning
□ J'ai du mal à suivre son raisonnement. I have difficulty following his reasoning.

rajouter VERB [28]
to add

ralentir VERB [38]
to slow down

râler VERB [28] (*informal*)
to moan

le **ramassage** MASC NOUN
■ le ramassage scolaire the school bus service

ramasser VERB [28]
1 to pick up
□ Il a ramassé son crayon. He picked up his pencil.
2 to take in
□ Il a ramassé les copies. He took in the exam papers.

la **rame** FEM NOUN
1 oar (*of boat*)
2 train (*on the underground*)

le **rameau** (PL les **rameaux**) MASC NOUN
branch
■ le dimanche des Rameaux Palm Sunday

ramener VERB [43]
1 to bring back
□ J'ai ramené mes copains à la maison pour regarder le match. I brought my friends back to my place to watch the match.
2 to take home
□ Tu me ramènes ? Will you take me home?

ramer VERB [28]
to row

□ C'est Sébastien qui ramait. Sébastien was rowing.

la **rampe** FEM NOUN
banister

la **rancune** FEM NOUN
■ garder rancune à quelqu'un to bear somebody a grudge
■ Sans rancune ! No hard feelings!

rancunier (FEM **rancunière**) ADJECTIVE
vindictive

la **randonnée** FEM NOUN
■ une randonnée à vélo a bike ride
■ une randonnée pédestre a ramble
■ faire de la randonnée to go hiking

le **randonneur** MASC NOUN
hiker

la **randonneuse** FEM NOUN
hiker

le **rang** MASC NOUN
row (*line*)
□ au premier rang in the front row □ se mettre en rangs to get into rows

la **rangée** FEM NOUN
row (*line*)
□ une rangée de chaises a row of chairs

ranger VERB [45]
1 to put away
□ J'ai rangé tes affaires. I've put your things away.
2 to tidy up
□ Va ranger ta chambre. Go and tidy up your room.

le **rap** MASC NOUN
rap
□ C'est un chanteur de rap très connu. He's a well-known rapper.

râper VERB [28]
to grate
□ le fromage râpé grated cheese

rapide (FEM **rapide**) ADJECTIVE
1 fast
□ Cette voiture est très rapide. This is a very fast car.
2 quick
□ J'ai jeté un coup d'œil rapide sur ton travail. I had a quick glance at your work.

rapidement ADVERB
quickly

le **rappel** MASC NOUN
1 booster (*vaccination*)
2 curtain call

rappeler VERB [4]
to call back
□ Je te rappelle dans cinq minutes. I'll call you back in 5 minutes.
■ rappeler quelque chose à quelqu'un to remind somebody of something □ Cette odeur

me rappelle mon enfance. This smell reminds me of my childhood.

■ **rappeler à quelqu'un de faire quelque chose** to remind somebody to do something □ Rappelle-moi d'acheter des billets. Remind me to get tickets.

■ **se rappeler** to remember □ Il s'est rappelé qu'il avait une course à faire. He remembered he had some shopping to do.

le **rapport** MASC NOUN
▷ see also **rapports**

1 report
□ Il a écrit un rapport. He wrote a report.

2 connection
□ Je ne vois pas le rapport. I can't see the connection.

■ **par rapport** à in comparison with

rapporter VERB [28]
to bring back
□ Je leur ai rapporté un cadeau. I brought them back a present.

le **rapporteur** MASC NOUN
telltale

la **rapporteuse** FEM NOUN
telltale

les **rapports** MASC PL NOUN
▷ see also **rapport** NOUN
relations
□ Leurs rapports avec leurs voisins se sont améliorés. Their relations with their neighbours have improved.

■ **les rapports sexuels** sexual intercourse

rapprocher VERB [28]

1 to bring together
□ Cet accident a rapproché les deux frères. The accident brought the two brothers together.

2 to bring closer
□ Il a rapproché le fauteuil de la télé. He brought the armchair closer to the TV.

■ **se rapprocher** to come closer □ Rapproche-toi, tu verras mieux. Come closer, you'll see better.

la **raquette** FEM NOUN

1 racket (tennis)

2 bat (table tennis)

rare (FEM **rare**) ADJECTIVE
rare
□ une plante rare a rare plant

rarement ADVERB
rarely

ras (FEM **rase**) ADJECTIVE, ADVERB
short
□ un chien à poil ras a short-haired dog
■ **à ras bords** to the brim □ Il a rempli son verre à ras bords. He filled his glass to the brim.
■ **en avoir ras le bol de quelque chose** (informal) to be fed up with something
■ **un pull ras du cou** a crew-neck jumper

raser VERB [28]
to shave off
□ Anthony a rasé sa barbe. Anthony has shaved off his beard.
■ **se raser** to shave

le **rasoir** MASC NOUN
▷ see also **rasoir** ADJECTIVE
razor

rasoir (FEM+PL **rasoir**) ADJECTIVE (informal)
▷ see also **rasoir** NOUN
dead boring

rassembler VERB [28]
to assemble
□ Il a rassemblé les enfants dans la cour. He assembled the children in the playground.
■ **se rassembler** to gather together □ Les passagers se sont rassemblés près du car. The passengers gathered near the coach.

rassurer VERB [28]
to reassure
■ **Je suis rassuré.** I don't need to worry any more.
■ **se rassurer** to be reassured
■ **Rassure-toi !** Don't worry!

le **rat** MASC NOUN
rat

raté (FEM **ratée**) ADJECTIVE
failed
□ une tentative ratée a failed attempt

le **râteau** (PL les **râteaux**) MASC NOUN
rake

rater VERB [28]

1 to miss
□ Marion a raté son train. Marion missed her train.

2 to fail
□ J'ai raté mon examen de maths. I failed my maths exam.
■ **Elle a raté sa pizza.** Her pizza didn't turn out right.

la **RATP** FEM NOUN
Paris transport authority

rattacher VERB [28]
to tie up again
□ rattacher ses lacets to retie one's laces

rattraper VERB [28]

1 to recapture
□ La police a rattrapé le voleur. The police recaptured the thief.

2 to catch up with
□ Je vais rattraper Cécile. I'll catch up with Cécile.

3 to make up for
□ Il faut rattraper le temps perdu. We must make up for lost time.
■ **se rattraper** to make up for it □ Quand il ne mange pas à midi il se rattrape au dîner. When he doesn't have lunch he makes up for it at dinnertime.

la **rature** FEM NOUN
correction
▫ un texte sans ratures a text with no corrections

ravi (FEM **ravie**) ADJECTIVE
■ **être ravi** to be delighted ▫ Ils étaient ravis de nous voir. They were delighted to see us. ▫ Je suis ravi que vous puissiez venir. I'm delighted that you can come.

se **raviser** VERB [28]
to change your mind
▫ Il allait accepter, mais il s'est ravisé. He was going to accept, but he changed his mind.

ravissant (FEM **ravissante**) ADJECTIVE
lovely

rayé (FEM **rayée**) ADJECTIVE
striped
▫ une chemise rayée a striped shirt

rayer VERB [59]
1 to scratch
▫ Il a rayé la peinture de sa voiture. He scratched the paintwork of his car.
2 to cross off
▫ Son nom a été rayé de la liste. His name has been crossed off the list.

le **rayon** MASC NOUN
1 ray
▫ un rayon de soleil a ray of sunshine
2 radius
▫ le rayon d'un cercle the radius of a circle
3 shelf
▫ les rayons d'une bibliothèque the shelves of a bookcase
4 department
▫ le rayon hi-fi vidéo the hi-fi and video department
■ **les rayons X** X-rays

la **rayure** FEM NOUN
stripe

le **ré** MASC NOUN
1 D
▫ en ré majeur in D major
2 re
▫ do, ré, mi ... do, re, mi ...

la **réaction** FEM NOUN
reaction

réagir VERB [38]
to react

le **réalisateur** MASC NOUN
director (of film)
▫ Spielberg est réalisateur. Spielberg is a film director.

la **réalisatrice** FEM NOUN
director (of film)
▫ Elle est réalisatrice. She's a film director.

réaliser VERB [28]
1 to carry out

▫ Ils ont réalisé leur projet. They carried out their plan.
2 to fulfil
▫ Il a réalisé son rêve. He has fulfilled his dream.
3 to realize
▫ Tu réalises ce que tu dis ? Do you realize what you're saying?
4 to make
▫ réaliser un film to make a film
■ **se réaliser** to come true ▫ Mon rêve s'est réalisé. My dream has come true.

réaliste (FEM **réaliste**) ADJECTIVE
realistic

la **réalité** FEM NOUN
reality
■ **en réalité** in fact
■ **dans la réalité** in reality
■ **réalité augmentée** augmented reality

le **rebelle** MASC NOUN
rebel

rebondir VERB [38]
to bounce

le **rebord** MASC NOUN
edge
▫ le rebord du lavabo the edge of the washbasin
■ **le rebord de la fenêtre** the window ledge

recaler VERB [28] (informal)
■ **J'ai été recalé en maths.** I failed maths.

récemment ADVERB
recently

récent (FEM **récente**) ADJECTIVE
recent

le **récepteur** MASC NOUN
receiver

la **réception** FEM NOUN
reception desk

le/la **réceptionniste** MASC/FEM NOUN
receptionist
▫ Elle est réceptionniste. She's a receptionist.

la **recette** FEM NOUN
recipe

recevoir VERB [67]
1 to receive
▫ J'ai reçu une lettre. I received a letter.
2 to see
▫ Il a déjà reçu trois clients. He has already seen three clients.
3 to have round
▫ Je reçois des amis à dîner. I'm having friends round for dinner.
■ **être reçu à un examen** to pass an exam

le **rechange** MASC NOUN
■ **de rechange** spare (battery, bulb)
■ **des vêtements de rechange** a change of clothes

la **recharge** FEM NOUN
refill

recharger VERB [45]
to charge
□ Est-ce que je peux recharger mon téléphone ? Can I charge my phone?

le **réchaud** MASC NOUN
stove

le **réchauffement** MASC NOUN
warming
■ le **réchauffement climatique** global warming

réchauffer VERB [28]
1 to reheat
□ Je vais réchauffer les légumes. I'll reheat the vegetables.
2 to warm up
□ Un bon café va te réchauffer. A nice cup of coffee will warm you up.
■ **se réchauffer** to warm oneself □ Je vais me réchauffer près du feu. I'll go and warm myself by the fire.

la **recherche** FEM NOUN
research
□ Je voudrais faire de la recherche. I'd like to do some research.
■ **être à la recherche de quelque chose** to be looking for something □ Je suis à la recherche d'un emploi. I'm looking for a job.
■ **les recherches** search □ La police a interrompu les recherches. The police called off the search.

recherché (FEM **recherchée**) ADJECTIVE
much sought-after

rechercher VERB [28]
to look for
□ La police recherche l'assassin. The police are looking for the killer.

la **rechute** FEM NOUN
relapse

le **récipient** MASC NOUN
container

le **récit** MASC NOUN
story

réciter VERB [28]
to recite

la **réclamation** FEM NOUN
complaint
□ J'ai une réclamation à faire. I want to make a complaint.
■ **les réclamations** the complaints department

la **réclame** FEM NOUN
advert
□ une réclame de lessive an advert for washing powder
■ **en réclame** on special offer □ Le saumon était en réclame au supermarché. Salmon was on special offer at the supermarket.

réclamer VERB [28]
1 to demand
□ Nous réclamons la semaine de trente heures. We demand a 30-hour week.
2 to complain
□ Elles sont toujours en train de réclamer. They're always complaining about something.

reçois, reçoit VERB ▷ see **recevoir**

la **récolte** FEM NOUN
harvest

récolter VERB [28]
1 to harvest
□ Ils ont récolté le blé. They harvested the wheat.
2 to collect
□ Ils ont récolté deux cents euros. They collected 200 euros.
3 to get
□ Il a récolté une amende. (informal) He got a fine.

le **recommandé** MASC NOUN
registered mail
■ **en recommandé** by registered mail
■ **Je voudrais envoyer ce paquet en recommandé.** I'd like to send this parcel registered.

recommander VERB [28]
to recommend
□ Je vous recommande ce restaurant. I recommend this restaurant.

recommencer VERB [12]
1 to start again
□ Il a recommencé à pleuvoir. It's started raining again.
2 to do again
□ S'il n'est pas puni, il va recommencer. If he's not punished he'll do it again.

la **récompense** FEM NOUN
reward

récompenser VERB [28]
to reward
□ Il m'a récompensée de mes efforts. He rewarded me for my efforts.

réconcilier VERB [19]
■ **se réconcilier avec quelqu'un** to make it up with somebody □ Il s'est réconcilié avec sa sœur. He has made it up with his sister.

reconnaissant (FEM **reconnaissante**) ADJECTIVE
grateful

reconnaître VERB [14]
1 to recognize
□ Je ne l'ai pas reconnu. I didn't recognize him.
2 to admit
□ Je reconnais que j'ai eu tort. I admit I was wrong.

reconstruire VERB [23]
to rebuild

le **record** MASC NOUN
record
□ battre un record **to break a record**

recouvrir VERB [55]
to cover
□ La neige recouvre le sol. **The ground is covered in snow.**

la **récré** FEM NOUN (*informal*)
break (time)
□ La récré est dans dix minutes. **Break time is in ten minutes.**

la **récréation** FEM NOUN
break
□ Les élèves sont en récréation. **The pupils are having their break.**
■ **la cour de récréation** the playground (*of school*)

le **rectangle** MASC NOUN
rectangle

rectangulaire (FEM **rectangulaire**) ADJECTIVE
rectangular

rectifier VERB [19]
to correct

le **reçu** MASC NOUN
▷ *see also* **reçu** VERB
receipt

reçu VERB ▷ *see* **recevoir**
▷ *see also* **reçu** NOUN
■ **J'ai reçu un colis ce matin.** I received a parcel this morning.
■ **être reçu à un examen** to pass an exam

reculer VERB [28]
1 to step back
□ Il a reculé pour la laisser entrer. **He stepped back to let her in.**
2 to reverse
□ J'ai reculé pour laisser passer le camion. **I reversed to let the lorry past.**
3 to postpone
□ Ils ont reculé la date du spectacle. **They postponed the show.**

reculons
■ **à reculons** ADVERB backwards □ Elle est entrée à reculons. **She came in backwards.**

récupérer VERB [34]
1 to get back
□ Je vais récupérer ma voiture au garage. **I'm going to get my car back from the garage.**
2 to make up
□ J'ai des heures à récupérer. **I've got time to make up.**
3 to recover
□ J'ai besoin de récupérer. **I need to recover.**

recyclage MASC NOUN
recycling
■ **un centre de recyclage** a recycling centre
■ **faire le recyclage** to recycle

recycler VERB [28]
to recycle
■ **se recycler** to retrain □ Il a décidé de se recycler en informatique. **He decided to retrain in IT.**

la **rédaction** FEM NOUN
essay

redemander VERB [28]
1 to ask again for
□ Je vais lui redemander son adresse. **I'll ask him for his address again.**
2 to ask for more
□ Je vais redemander des carottes. **I'm going to ask for more carrots.**

redescendre VERB [24, *aux* avoir *or* être]
to go back down
□ Il est redescendu au premier étage. **He went back down to the first floor.** □ Elle a redescendu l'escalier. **She went back down the stairs.**

> The verb **redescendre** uses **être** in the perfect tense when talking about moving downwards. It uses **avoir** in the perfect tense when talking about a person or thing moving down something (for example, down the stairs).

rédiger VERB [45]
to write (*an essay*)

redoubler VERB [28]
to repeat a year
□ Il a raté son examen et doit redoubler. **He's failed his exam and will have to repeat the year.**

la **réduction** FEM NOUN
1 reduction
□ une réduction du nombre des touristes **a reduction in the number of tourists**
2 discount
□ une réduction de vingt euros **a 20 euro discount**

réduire VERB [23]
to cut
□ Ils ont réduit leurs prix. **They've cut their prices.** □ Il a réduit de moitié ses dépenses. **He has cut his spending by half.**

réel (FEM **réelle**) ADJECTIVE
real

réellement ADVERB
really

refaire VERB [36]
1 to do again
□ Je dois refaire ce rapport. **I've got to do this report again.**
2 to take up again
□ Je voudrais refaire de la gym. **I'd like to take up gymnastics again.**

le **réfectoire** MASC NOUN
refectory

r

la **référence** FEM NOUN
reference
■ **faire référence à quelque chose** to refer to something
■ **Ce n'est pas une référence !** That's no recommendation!

réfléchi (FEM **réfléchie**) ADJECTIVE
reflexive (*verb*)
■ **C'est tout réfléchi.** My mind's made up.

réfléchir VERB [38]
to think
□ Il est en train de réfléchir. He's thinking.
■ **réfléchir à quelque chose** to think about something □ Je vais réfléchir à ta proposition. I'll think about your suggestion.

le **reflet** MASC NOUN
reflection
□ les reflets du soleil sur la mer the reflection of the sun on the sea

refléter VERB [34]
to reflect

le **réflexe** MASC NOUN
reflex
□ avoir de bons réflexes to have good reflexes

la **réflexion** FEM NOUN
1 thought
□ Elle est en pleine réflexion. She's deep in thought.
2 remark
□ faire des réflexions désagréables to make nasty remarks
■ **réflexion faite** on reflection

le **refrain** MASC NOUN
chorus (*of song*)

le **réfrigérateur** MASC NOUN
refrigerator

refroidir VERB [38]
to cool
□ Laissez le gâteau refroidir. Leave the cake to cool.
■ **se refroidir** to get colder □ Le temps se refroidit. It's getting colder.

se **réfugier** VERB [19]
to take shelter
□ Je me suis réfugié sous un arbre. I took shelter under a tree.

le **refus** MASC NOUN
refusal
■ **Ce n'est pas de refus.** I wouldn't say no.
□ Voulez-vous une bière ? — Ce n'est pas de refus. Would you like a beer? — I wouldn't say no.

refuser VERB [28]
to refuse
□ On lui a refusé une augmentation. He was refused a pay rise.
■ **refuser de faire** to refuse to do □ Il a refusé de payer sa part. He refused to pay his share.

■ **Je refuse qu'on me parle ainsi !** I won't let anybody talk to me like that!

se **régaler** VERB [28]
■ **Merci beaucoup : je me suis régalé !** Thank you very much: it was absolutely delicious!

le **regard** MASC NOUN
look
□ Il lui a jeté un regard méfiant. He gave him a mistrustful look. □ On voyait à son regard qu'elle était contrariée. You could tell from the look in her eyes that she was upset.
■ **Tous les regards se sont tournés vers lui.** All eyes turned towards him.

regarder VERB [28]
1 to look at
□ Il regardait ses photos de vacances. He was looking at his holiday photos. □ Regarde ! J'ai presque fini. Look! I've nearly finished.
2 to watch
□ Je regarde la télévision. I'm watching television. □ Regarde où tu mets les pieds ! Watch where you put your feet!
3 to concern
□ Ça ne nous regarde pas. It doesn't concern us.
■ **ne pas regarder à la dépense** to spare no expense

le **régime** MASC NOUN
1 régime (*of a country*)
2 diet
□ un régime sans sel a salt-free diet □ se mettre au régime to go on a diet □ suivre un régime to be on a diet
■ **un régime de bananes** a bunch of bananas

la **région** FEM NOUN
region

régional (FEM **régionale**, MASC PL **régionaux**) ADJECTIVE
regional

le **registre** MASC NOUN
register

la **règle** FEM NOUN
1 ruler
□ Il a souligné son nom avec une règle. He underlined his name with a ruler.
2 rule
□ C'est la règle. That's the rule. □ en règle générale as a general rule
■ **être en règle** to be in order □ Mes papiers sont en règle. My papers are in order.
■ **les règles** period (*menstruation*)

le **règlement** MASC NOUN
rules
□ Le règlement est affiché à l'entrée. The rules are up on the wall by the entrance.

régler VERB [34]
1 to adjust
□ Il faut que je règle mon rétroviseur. I'll have to adjust my rear-view mirror.

2 to tune
□ J'ai réglé ma radio sur 476 FM. I tuned my radio to 476 FM.

3 to set
□ J'ai réglé le thermostat à vingt degrés. I've set the thermostat to 20 degrees.

4 to solve
□ Le problème est réglé. The problem's solved.

5 to settle
□ Elle a réglé sa facture. She's settled her bill.
□ J'ai réglé Justin pour l'essence. I've settled up with Justin for the petrol.

la **réglisse** FEM NOUN
liquorice

le **règne** MASC NOUN
reign
□ sous le règne d'Henri IV in the reign of Henry IV

régner VERB [34]
to reign

le **regret** MASC NOUN
regret
■ **à regret** reluctantly

regretter VERB [28]
1 to regret
□ Elle regrette ce qu'elle a dit. She regrets saying what she did.
■ **Je regrette.** I'm sorry. □ Je regrette, je ne peux pas vous aider. I'm sorry, I can't help you.
2 to miss
□ Je regrette mon ancien travail. I miss my old job.

regrouper VERB [28]
to group together
□ Nous avons regroupé les enfants suivant leur âge. We grouped the children together according to age.
■ **se regrouper** to gather together □ Les agriculteurs se sont regroupés pour constituer un syndicat. The farmers joined together to form a union.

régulier (FEM **régulière**) ADJECTIVE
1 regular
□ des livraisons régulières regular deliveries
□ des bus réguliers a regular bus service
2 steady
□ à un rythme régulier at a steady rate
3 scheduled
□ des vols réguliers pour Marseille scheduled flights to Marseille

régulièrement ADVERB
regularly

le **rein** MASC NOUN
kidney
■ **les reins** back (of body) □ J'ai mal aux reins. My back hurts.

la **reine** FEM NOUN
queen

rejoindre VERB [42]
to go back to
□ J'ai rejoint mes amis. I went back to my friends.
■ **Je te rejoins au café.** I'll see you at the café.
■ **se rejoindre** to meet up □ Elles se sont rejointes une heure après. They met up an hour later.

relâcher VERB [28]
to release (prisoner, animal)
■ **se relâcher** to get slack □ Il se relâche dans son travail. He is slacking in his work.

le **relais** MASC NOUN
relay race
□ le relais quatre fois cent mètres the 4 x 100 metre relay
■ **prendre le relais** to take over

la **relation** FEM NOUN
relationship
■ **les relations franco-britanniques** Anglo-French relations

relativement ADVERB
relatively

se **relaxer** VERB [28]
to relax

se **relayer** VERB [59]
■ **se relayer pour faire quelque chose** to take it in turns to do something

le **relevé** MASC NOUN
■ **un relevé de compte** a bank statement

relever VERB [43]
1 to collect
□ Je relève les copies dans cinq minutes. I'll collect the papers in five minutes.
2 to react to
□ Je n'ai pas relevé sa réflexion. I didn't react to his remark.
■ **relever la tête** to look up
■ **se relever** to get up □ Il est tombé mais s'est relevé aussitôt. He fell, but got up immediately.

la **religieuse** FEM NOUN
1 nun
2 choux cream bun
□ des religieuses au chocolat choux buns with chocolate cream and icing

religieux (FEM **religieuse**) ADJECTIVE
religious

la **religion** FEM NOUN
religion

relire VERB [44]
1 to read over
□ Il a relu sa copie avant de la rendre. He read his exam paper over before handing it in.
2 to read again
□ Je voudrais relire ce roman. I'd like to read this novel again.

remarquable (FEM **remarquable**) ADJECTIVE
remarkable

la **remarque** FEM NOUN

1 remark

□ Il a fait une remarque désagréable. **He made a nasty remark.**

2 comment

□ Avez-vous des remarques à faire ? **Have you any comments to make?**

remarquer VERB [28]

to notice

□ J'ai remarqué qu'elle avait l'air triste. **I noticed she was looking sad.**

■ **faire remarquer quelque chose à quelqu'un** to point something out to somebody □ Je lui ai fait remarquer que c'était un peu cher. **I pointed out to him that it was rather expensive.**

■ **Remarquez, il n'est pas si bête que ça.** **Mind you, he's not as stupid as all that.**

■ **se remarquer** to be noticeable □ David ne s'est pas rasé ce matin. Ça se remarque. **It's obvious David didn't shave this morning.**

■ **se faire remarquer** to call attention to oneself

le **remboursement** MASC NOUN
refund

rembourser VERB [28]

to pay back

□ Il m'a remboursé l'argent qu'il me devait. **He paid me back the money he owed me.**

■ **se faire rembourser** to get your money back

■ **« satisfait ou remboursé »** 'satisfaction or your money back'

le **remède** MASC NOUN

1 medicine

2 cure

remercier VERB [19]

to thank

□ Je te remercie pour ton cadeau. **Thank you for your present.**

■ **remercier quelqu'un d'avoir fait quelque chose** to thank somebody for doing something □ Je vous remercie de m'avoir invité. **Thank you for inviting me.**

remettre VERB [47]

1 to put back on

□ Il a remis son pull. **He put his sweater back on.**

2 to put back

□ Il a remis sa veste dans l'armoire. **He put his jacket back in the wardrobe.**

3 to put off

□ J'ai dû remettre mon rendez-vous. **I've had to put my appointment off.**

■ **se remettre** to recover (from illness) □ Mélusine s'est bien remise de son opération. **Mélusine has fully recovered from her operation.**

le **remonte-pente** MASC NOUN
ski-lift

remonter VERB [48, aux avoir or être]

1 to go back up

□ Il est remonté au premier étage. **He has gone back up to the first floor.**

2 to go up

□ Ils ont remonté la pente. **They went up the hill.**

3 to buck up

□ Cette nouvelle m'a un peu remontée. **The news bucked me up a bit.**

■ **remonter le moral à quelqu'un** to cheer somebody up

> The verb **remonter** uses être in the perfect tense when talking about moving upwards. It uses avoir in the perfect tense when talking about a person or thing moving up something (for example, up the hill), or when talking about cheering someone up.

le **remords** MASC NOUN

■ **avoir des remords** to feel remorse

la **remorque** FEM NOUN
trailer (of car)

les **remparts** MASC PL NOUN
city walls

le **remplaçant** MASC NOUN
supply teacher

la **remplaçante** FEM NOUN
supply teacher

remplacer VERB [12]

to replace

□ Il faut remplacer cette ampoule. **We need to replace this bulb.** □ Il remplace le prof de maths. **He's replacing the maths teacher.**

■ **remplacer par** to replace with

rempli (FEM **remplie**) ADJECTIVE

busy

□ une journée bien remplie **a very busy day**

■ **rempli de** full of □ La salle était remplie de monde. **The room was full of people.**

remplir VERB [38]

1 to fill up

□ Elle a rempli son verre de vin. **She filled up her glass with wine.**

2 to fill in

□ Tu as rempli ton formulaire ? **Have you filled in your form?**

■ **se remplir** to fill up □ La salle s'est remplie de monde. **The room filled up with people.**

remporter VERB [28]

to win (a competition, a prize)

remuer VERB [28]

1 to move

□ Elle a remué le bras. **She moved her arm.**

2 to stir

□ Remuez la sauce pendant deux minutes. **Stir the sauce for two minutes.**

■ **se remuer** (*informal*) to get a move on □ Rien n'est prêt et les invités arrivent dans une heure, il faut se remuer ! Nothing is ready and the guests arrive in an hour, we'd better get a move on!

le **renard** MASC NOUN
fox

la **rencontre** FEM NOUN
■ **faire la rencontre de quelqu'un** to meet somebody □ J'ai fait la rencontre de personnes intéressantes ce soir. I met some interesting people this evening.
■ **aller à la rencontre de quelqu'un** to go and meet somebody □ Je viendrai à ta rencontre. I'll come and meet you.

rencontrer VERB [28]
to meet
■ **se rencontrer** to meet □ Ils se sont rencontrés il y a deux ans. They met two years ago.

le **rendez-vous** MASC NOUN
1 appointment
□ J'ai rendez-vous chez le coiffeur. I've got an appointment at the hairdresser's. □ prendre rendez-vous avec quelqu'un to make an appointment with somebody
2 date
□ Tu sors ce soir ? — Oui, j'ai un rendez-vous. Are you going out tonight? — Yes, I've got a date.
■ **donner rendez-vous à quelqu'un** to arrange to meet somebody

rendre VERB [7]
1 to give back
□ J'ai rendu ses CD à Lucie. I've given Lucie her CDs back.
2 to take back
□ J'ai rendu mes livres à la bibliothèque. I've taken my books back to the library.
■ **rendre quelqu'un célèbre** to make somebody famous
■ **se rendre** **1** to go □ Elle se rend à Nantes. She is going to Nantes. **2** to give oneself up □ Le meurtrier s'est rendu à la police. The murderer gave himself up to the police.
■ **se rendre compte de quelque chose** to realize something

le **renfermé** MASC NOUN
■ **sentir le renfermé** to smell stuffy

renifler VERB [28]
to sniff

le **renne** MASC NOUN
reindeer

renommé (FEM **renommée**) ADJECTIVE
renowned
□ La Bretagne est renommée pour ses plages. Brittany is renowned for its beaches.

renoncer VERB [12]
■ **renoncer à** to give up □ Ils ont renoncé à leur projet. They've given up their plan.
■ **renoncer à faire quelque chose** to give up the idea of doing something

renouvelable (FEM **renouvelable**) ADJECTIVE
renewable
□ une énergie renouvelable a renewable energy source

renouveler VERB [4]
to renew (*passport, contract*)
■ **se renouveler** to happen again □ J'espère que ça ne se renouvellera pas. I hope that won't happen again.

le **renseignement** MASC NOUN
piece of information
□ Il me manque un renseignement. There's one piece of information I still need.
■ **les renseignements** **1** information □ Il m'a donné des renseignements. He gave me some information. **2** information desk
3 directory enquiries

renseigner VERB [28]
■ **renseigner quelqu'un sur quelque chose** to give somebody information about something
■ **Est-ce que je peux vous renseigner ?** Can I help you?
■ **se renseigner** to find out □ Je vais me renseigner pour voir s'il n'y a pas un vol direct. I'm going to find out if there's a direct flight.

rentable (FEM **rentable**) ADJECTIVE
profitable

la **rentrée** FEM NOUN
■ **la rentrée (des classes)** the start of the new school year

rentrer VERB [68, *aux* **avoir** *or* **être**]
1 to come in
□ Rentre, tu vas prendre froid. Come in, you'll catch cold.
2 to go in
□ Elle est rentrée dans le magasin. She went into the shop.
3 to get home
□ Je suis rentré à sept heures hier soir. I got home at 7 o'clock last night.
4 to put away
□ Tu as rentré la voiture ? Have you put the car away?
■ **rentrer dans** to crash into □ Sa voiture est rentrée dans un arbre. He crashed into a tree.
■ **rentrer dans l'ordre** to get back to normal

> The verb **rentrer** uses **être** in the perfect tense when talking about returning somewhere. It uses **avoir** in the perfect tense when when talking about putting an object away.

la **renverse** FEM NOUN
■ **tomber à la renverse** to fall backwards

renverser VERB [28]

1 to knock over

□ J'ai renversé mon verre. I knocked my glass over.

2 to knock down

□ Elle a été renversée par une voiture. She was knocked down by a car.

3 to spill

□ Il a renversé de l'eau partout. He has spilt water everywhere.

■ **se renverser** (*glass*, *vase*) to fall over

renvoyer VERB [33]

1 to send back

□ Je t'ai renvoyé ton courrier. I've sent your mail back to you.

2 to dismiss

□ On a renvoyé deux employés. Two employees have been dismissed.

répandu (FEM **répandue**) ADJECTIVE

common

□ C'est un préjugé très répandu. It's a very common prejudice.

■ **du vin répandu sur la table** wine spilt on the table

■ **des papiers répandus sur le sol** papers scattered over the floor

le **réparateur** MASC NOUN

repairman

la **réparation** FEM NOUN

repair

réparer VERB [28]

to repair

repartir VERB [57, *aux* être]

to set off again

□ Il s'est arrêté pour déjeuner avant de repartir. He stopped for lunch before setting off again.

□ Il était là tout à l'heure, mais il est reparti. He was here a moment ago, but he's gone again.

■ **repartir à zéro** to start again from scratch

le **repas** MASC NOUN

meal

■ **le repas de midi** lunch

■ **le repas du soir** dinner

le **repassage** MASC NOUN

ironing

□ Je déteste le repassage. I hate ironing.

repasser VERB [28, *aux* avoir or être]

1 to come back

□ Je repasserai demain. I'll come back tomorrow.

2 to go back

□ Je dois repasser au magasin. I've got to go back to the shop.

3 to iron

□ J'ai repassé ma chemise. I've ironed my shirt.

4 to resit

□ Elle doit repasser son examen. She's got to resit her exam.

The verb **repasser** uses **être** in the perfect tense when talking about going back somewhere. It uses **avoir** in the perfect tense when talking about tasks like doing ironing or taking a resit.

repérer VERB [34]

to spot

□ J'ai repéré deux fautes. I spotted two mistakes.

■ **se repérer** to find one's way around □ J'ai du mal à me repérer de nuit. I have difficulty finding my way around when it's dark.

le **répertoire** MASC NOUN

directory

répéter VERB [34]

1 to repeat

□ Elle répète toujours la même chose. She keeps repeating the same thing.

2 to rehearse

□ Les acteurs répètent une scène. The actors are rehearsing a scene.

■ **se répéter** to happen again □ J'espère que cela ne se répétera pas ! I hope this won't happen again!

la **répétition** FEM NOUN

1 repetition

□ Il y a beaucoup de répétitions dans ce texte. There's a lot of repetition in this text.

■ **des grèves à répétition** repeated strikes

2 rehearsal

□ Ils ont une répétition cet après-midi. They've got a rehearsal this afternoon.

■ **la répétition générale** the dress rehearsal

le **répondeur** MASC NOUN

answering machine

répondre VERB [69]

to answer

■ **répondre à quelqu'un** to reply to someone

la **réponse** FEM NOUN

answer

□ C'est la bonne réponse. That's the right answer.

le **reportage** MASC NOUN

1 report

□ J'ai vu ce reportage aux informations. I saw that report on the news.

2 story

□ J'ai lu ce reportage dans « La Gazette ». I read that story in 'La Gazette'.

le **reporter** MASC NOUN

reporter

□ Mathis est reporter. Mathis is a reporter.

le **repos** MASC NOUN

rest

reposer VERB [28]

to put back down

□ Elle a reposé son verre sur la table. She put her glass back down on the table.

■ **se reposer** to have a rest □ Tu pourras te reposer demain. You'll be able to have a rest tomorrow.

■ **se reposer sur quelqu'un** to rely on somebody

repousser VERB [28]

1 to grow again
□ Ses cheveux ont repoussé. Her hair has grown again.

2 to postpone
□ Le voyage est repoussé. The trip's been postponed.

reprendre VERB [65]

1 to take back
□ Il a repris son livre. He's taken his book back.

2 to go back to
□ Elle a repris le travail. She went back to work.

3 to start again
□ La réunion reprendra à deux heures. The meeting will start again at 2 o'clock.

■ **reprendre du pain** to take more bread
■ **reprendre la route** to set off again
■ **reprendre son souffle** to get one's breath back

le **représentant** MASC NOUN
rep
□ Il est représentant chez HarperCollins. He's a rep for HarperCollins.

la **représentante** FEM NOUN
rep
□ Elle est représentante. She's a sales rep.

la **représentation** FEM NOUN
performance
□ la dernière représentation d'une pièce the final performance of a play

représenter VERB [28]
to show
□ Le tableau représente un enfant et un chat. The picture shows a child with a cat.

■ **se représenter** to arise again □ Cette occasion ne se représentera pas. This opportunity won't arise again.

le **reproche** MASC NOUN
■ **faire des reproches à quelqu'un** to reproach somebody

reprocher VERB [28]
■ **reprocher quelque chose à quelqu'un** to reproach somebody for something □ Il m'a reproché mon retard. He reproached me for being late.

■ **Qu'est-ce que tu lui reproches ?** What have you got against him?

la **reproduction** FEM NOUN
reproduction

reproduire VERB [23]
to reproduce
■ **se reproduire** to happen again □ Je te promets que ça ne se reproduira pas ! I promise it won't happen again!

républicain (FEM **républicaine**) ADJECTIVE
republican

la **république** FEM NOUN
republic
□ la République française the French Republic

répugnant (FEM **répugnante**) ADJECTIVE
repulsive

la **réputation** FEM NOUN
reputation

le **requin** MASC NOUN
shark

le **RER** MASC NOUN
Greater Paris high-speed train service

le **réseau** (PL les **réseaux**) MASC NOUN
network
■ **les réseaux sociaux** social media

le **réseautage** MASC NOUN
networking
□ un site de réseautage a social networking site

la **réservation** FEM NOUN
reservation

la **réserve** FEM NOUN
stock
□ avoir quelque chose en réserve to have a stock of something
■ **mettre quelque chose en réserve** to put something aside

réservé (FEM **réservée**) ADJECTIVE

1 reserved
□ Cette table est réservée. This table's reserved.

2 shy
□ Mon frère est réservé. My brother is shy.

réserver VERB [28]

1 to reserve
□ Je voudrais réserver une table. I'd like to reserve a table.

2 to book
□ Nous avons réservé une chambre. We've booked a room.

3 to save
□ Je t'ai réservé une part de gâteau. I've saved you a piece of cake.

le **réservoir** MASC NOUN
petrol tank

la **résidence** FEM NOUN
block of flats
■ **une résidence secondaire** a second home

résistant (FEM **résistante**) ADJECTIVE

1 hard-wearing
□ Ce tissu est résistant. This fabric is hard-wearing.

2 robust
□ Il est très résistant. He's very robust.

résister VERB [28]
to resist

résolu (FEM **résolue**) ADJECTIVE
■ **Le problème est résolu.** The problem's solved.

r

résoudre - retirer

résoudre VERB [70]
to solve

le respect MASC NOUN
respect

respecter VERB [28]
to respect

la respiration FEM NOUN
breathing

respirer VERB [28]
to breathe

la responsabilité FEM NOUN
responsibility

responsable (FEM **responsable**) ADJECTIVE
▷ see also **responsable** NOUN
responsible
□ être responsable de quelque chose to be responsible for something

le/la responsable MASC/FEM NOUN
▷ see also **responsable** ADJECTIVE
1 person in charge
□ Je voudrais parler au responsable. I'd like to speak to the person in charge.
2 person responsible
□ Il faut punir les responsables. The people responsible must be punished.

ressembler VERB [28]
■ **ressembler à 1** to look like □ Elle ne ressemble pas à sa sœur. She doesn't look like her sister. **2** to be like □ Ça ressemble à un conte de fées. It's like a fairy tale.
■ **se ressembler 1** to look alike □ Les deux frères ne se ressemblent pas. The two brothers don't look alike. **2** to be alike □ Ces deux pays ne se ressemblent pas. These two countries aren't alike.

le ressort MASC NOUN
spring (*metal*)
□ Le ressort est cassé. The spring is broken.

ressortir VERB [79, *aux* être]
to go out again

les ressources FEM PL NOUN
resources
□ les ressources en énergie energy resources

le restaurant MASC NOUN
restaurant

le reste MASC NOUN
rest
■ **un reste de poulet** some left-over chicken
■ **les restes** the left-overs

rester VERB [71, *aux* être]
1 to stay
□ Je reste à la maison ce week-end. I'm staying at home this weekend.
2 to be left
□ Il reste du pain. There's some bread left.
□ Il me reste assez de temps. I still have enough time.

■ **Il ne me reste plus qu'à ...** I've just got to ...
□ Il ne me reste plus qu'à ranger mes affaires. I've just got to put my things away.
■ **Restons-en là.** Let's leave it at that.

le résultat MASC NOUN
result
□ le résultat des examens the exam results

le résumé MASC NOUN
summary

résumer VERB [28]
to summarize

BE CAREFUL!
résumer does not mean **to resume**.

se rétablir VERB [38]
to get well

le retard MASC NOUN
delay
□ un retard de livraison a delay in delivery
■ **avoir du retard** to be late
■ **être en retard** to be late □ On est en retard de deux heures. We are two hours late.
■ **prendre du retard** to be delayed

retarder VERB [28]
1 to be slow
□ Ma montre retarde. My watch is slow.
2 to put back
□ Je dois retarder la pendule d'une heure. I've got to put the clock back an hour.
■ **être retardé** to be delayed □ J'ai été retardé par un coup de téléphone. I was held up by a phone call.

retenir VERB [83]
1 to remember
□ Tu as retenu leur adresse ? Do you remember their address?
2 to book
□ J'ai retenu une chambre à l'hôtel. I've booked a room at the hotel.
■ **retenir son souffle** to hold one's breath

retenu (FEM **retenue**) ADJECTIVE
▷ see also **retenue** NOUN
1 reserved
□ Cette place est retenue. This seat is reserved.
2 held up
□ J'ai été retenu par un coup de téléphone. I was held up by a phone call.

la retenue FEM NOUN
▷ see also **retenu** ADJECTIVE
detention
□ Léa est en retenue. Léa's in detention.

retirer VERB [28]
1 to withdraw
□ Elle a retiré de l'argent. She withdrew some money.
2 to take off
□ Il a retiré son pull. He took off his sweater.

Numbers in brackets refer to verb tables on pages 650 to 658

r

le retour MASC NOUN
return
- **être de retour** to be back □ Je serai de retour la semaine prochaine. I'll be back next week.

retourner VERB [72, *aux* avoir *or* être]
1 to go back
  □ Est-ce que tu es retourné à Londres ? Have you been back to London?
2 to turn over
  □ Elle a retourné la crêpe. She turned the pancake over. □ Il a retourné la poubelle. He turned the bin upside down.
- **se retourner 1** to turn round □ Jade s'est retournée. Jade turned round. **2** to turn over □ La voiture s'est retournée. The car turned over.

> The verb **retourner** uses **être** in the perfect tense when talking about going back somewhere. It uses **avoir** in the perfect tense when talking about turning an object over.

la retraite FEM NOUN
- **être à la retraite** to be retired
- **prendre sa retraite** to retire

retraité (FEM **retraitée**) ADJECTIVE
▷ *see also* **retraité** NOUN, **retraitée** NOUN
retired
  □ Mon père est retraité. My dad's retired.

le retraité MASC NOUN
▷ *see also* **retraité** ADJECTIVE
pensioner

la retraitée FEM NOUN
▷ *see also* **retraité** ADJECTIVE
pensioner

rétrécir VERB [38]
to shrink
  □ Son pull a rétréci au lavage. Her sweater shrank in the wash.
- **se rétrécir** to get narrower □ La rue se rétrécit. The street gets narrower.

retrouver VERB [28]
1 to find
  □ J'ai retrouvé mon sac. I've found my bag
2 to meet up with
  □ Je te retrouve au café à trois heures. I'll meet you at the café at 3 o'clock.
- **se retrouver 1** to meet up □ Ils se sont retrouvés devant le cinéma. They met up in front of the cinema. **2** to find one's way around □ Je n'arrive pas à me retrouver. I can't find my way around.

le rétroviseur MASC NOUN
rear-view mirror

le retweet MASC NOUN
retweet

retweeter VERB [28]
to retweet

la réunion FEM NOUN
meeting
- **la Réunion** Réunion (Island)

se réunir VERB [38]
to meet
  □ Ils se sont réunis à cinq heures. They met at 5 o'clock.

réussi (FEM **réussie**) ADJECTIVE
successful
  □ une soirée très réussie a very successful party
- **être réussi** to be a success □ Le repas était très réussi. The meal was a success.

réussir VERB [38]
to be successful
  □ Tous ses enfants ont très bien réussi. All her children are very successful.
- **réussir à faire quelque chose** to succeed in doing something
- **réussir à un examen** to pass an exam

la réussite FEM NOUN
success

réutilisable (FEM **réutilisable**) ADJECTIVE
reusable

réutiliser VERB [28]
to reuse

la revanche FEM NOUN
return match
- **prendre sa revanche** to get one's own back □ Il a pris sa revanche en refusant de lui prêter son vélo. He got his own back by refusing to lend him his bike.
- **en revanche** on the other hand □ C'est cher mais en revanche c'est de la bonne qualité. It is expensive but on the other hand it's good quality.

le rêve MASC NOUN
dream
- **de rêve** fantastic □ des vacances de rêve fantastic holidays

le réveil MASC NOUN
alarm clock
- **mettre le réveil à huit heures** to set the alarm for eight o'clock

le réveille-matin (PL les **réveille-matins**, les **réveille-matin**) MASC NOUN
alarm clock

réveiller VERB [28]
to wake up
  □ réveiller quelqu'un to wake somebody up
- **se réveiller** to wake up

le réveillon MASC NOUN
- **le réveillon du Premier de l'an** New Year's Eve celebrations
- **le réveillon de Noël** Christmas Eve celebrations

réveillonner VERB [28]
1 to celebrate New Year's Eve
2 to celebrate Christmas Eve

revenir - rigoler

revenir VERB [73, *aux* **être**]

to come back

□ Reviens vite ! Come back soon! □ Son nom m'est revenu cinq minutes après. His name came back to me five minutes later.

■ **Ça revient au même.** It comes to the same thing.

■ **Ça revient cher.** It costs a lot.

■ **Je n'en reviens pas !** I can't get over it!

■ **revenir sur ses pas** to retrace one's steps

le **revenu** MASC NOUN

income

rêver VERB [28]

to dream

■ **rêver de quelque chose** to dream of something □ J'ai rêvé de mes vacances cette nuit. I dreamt about my holidays last night.

le **réverbère** MASC NOUN

street lamp

le **revers** MASC NOUN

1 backhand

□ Murray a un excellent revers. Murray has an excellent backhand.

2 lapel (*of jacket*)

■ **le revers de la médaille** the other side of the coin

revient VERB ▷ see **revenir**

réviser VERB [28]

1 to revise

□ Je dois réviser mon anglais. I've got to revise my English.

2 to service

□ Je dois faire réviser ma voiture. I must get my car serviced.

la **révision** FEM NOUN

revision

revoir VERB [92]

1 to see again

□ J'ai revu Sophie hier soir. I saw Sophie again last night.

2 to revise

□ Il est en train de revoir sa géographie. He's revising his geography.

■ **au revoir** goodbye

la **révolution** FEM NOUN

revolution

□ la Révolution française the French Revolution

le **revolver** MASC NOUN

revolver

la **revue** FEM NOUN

magazine

le **rez-de-chaussée** MASC NOUN

ground floor

□ au rez-de-chaussée on the ground floor

le **Rhin** MASC NOUN

Rhine

le **rhinocéros** MASC NOUN

rhinoceros

le **Rhône** MASC NOUN

Rhone

la **rhubarbe** FEM NOUN

rhubarb

le **rhum** MASC NOUN

rum

le **rhume** MASC NOUN

cold

□ J'ai attrapé un rhume. I've caught a cold.

■ **un rhume de cerveau** a head cold

■ **le rhume des foins** hay fever

ri VERB ▷ see **rire**

■ **Nous avons bien ri.** We had a good laugh.

riche (FEM **riche**) ADJECTIVE

1 well-off

□ Sa famille est très riche. His family's very well-off.

2 rich

□ riche en vitamines rich in vitamins

la **richesse** FEM NOUN

wealth

le **rideau** (PL les **rideaux**) MASC NOUN

curtain

□ tirer les rideaux to draw the curtains

ridicule (FEM **ridicule**) ADJECTIVE

ridiculous

□ Je trouve ça complètement ridicule. I think that's absolutely ridiculous.

rien PRONOUN

▷ *see also* **rien** NOUN

1 nothing

□ Qu'est-ce que tu as acheté ? — Rien. What have you bought? — Nothing. □ Ça n'a rien à voir. It has nothing to do with it.

■ **rien d'intéressant** nothing interesting

■ **rien d'autre** nothing else

■ **rien du tout** nothing at all

■ **rien ne ...** nothing ... □ Rien n'a été fait. Nothing has been done.

2 anything

□ Il n'a rien dit. He didn't say anything.

■ **rien que 1** just □ rien que pour lui faire plaisir just to please him □ Rien que la voiture coûte un million. The car alone costs a million. **2** nothing but □ rien que la vérité nothing but the truth

■ **De rien !** Not at all! □ Merci beaucoup ! — De rien ! Thank you very much! — Not at all!

le **rien** MASC NOUN

▷ *see also* **rien** PRONOUN

■ **Il se met en colère pour un rien.** He loses his temper over the slightest thing.

■ **en un rien de temps** in no time at all

rigoler VERB [28] (*informal*)

1 to laugh

□ Elle a rigolé en le voyant tomber. She laughed when she saw him fall.

2 to have fun
□ On a bien rigolé hier soir. We had good fun last night.
3 to be joking
□ Ne te fâche pas, je rigolais. Don't get upset, I was only joking.
■ **pour rigoler** for a laugh

rigolo (FEM **rigolote**) ADJECTIVE (*informal*)
funny

rincer VERB [12]
to rinse

rire VERB [74]
▷ *see also* **rire** NOUN
to laugh
□ Ce film m'a vraiment fait rire. That film really made me laugh. □ Nous avons bien ri. We had a good laugh.
■ **pour rire** for a laugh

le **rire** MASC NOUN
▷ *see also* **rire** VERB
laughter
□ Il a un rire bruyant. He has a loud laugh.

ris VERB ▷ *see* **rire**

le **risque** MASC NOUN
1 risk
□ prendre des risques to take risks □ à tes risques et périls at your own risk
2 danger
□ Il n'y a pas de risque qu'il l'apprenne. There's no danger of him finding out.

risqué (FEM **risquée**) ADJECTIVE
risky

risquer VERB [28]
to risk
■ **Ça ne risque rien.** It's quite safe.
■ **risquer de** □ Il risque de se tuer. He could get himself killed. □ C'est ce qui risque de se passer. That's what might well happen.

rit VERB ▷ *see* **rire**

le **rivage** MASC NOUN
shore

la **rivière** FEM NOUN
river

le **riz** MASC NOUN
rice

la **RN** FEM NOUN (= *route nationale*)
A road

la **robe** FEM NOUN
dress
■ **une robe de soirée** an evening dress
■ **une robe de mariée** a wedding dress
■ **une robe de chambre** a dressing gown

le **robinet** MASC NOUN
tap

le **robot** MASC NOUN
robot

la **roche** FEM NOUN
rock (*stone*)

le **rocher** MASC NOUN
rock

le **rock** MASC NOUN
rock (*music*)
□ un chanteur de rock a rock singer

rôder VERB [28]
to loiter
□ Il y a un homme louche qui rôde autour du parking. There's a suspicious man loitering around the car park.

les **rognons** MASC PL NOUN
kidneys (*in cooking*)

le **roi** MASC NOUN
king
■ **le jour des Rois** Twelfth Night

le **rôle** MASC NOUN
role

les **rollers** MASC PL NOUN
Rollerblades®

romain (FEM **romaine**) ADJECTIVE
Roman
□ des ruines romaines Roman remains

le **roman** MASC NOUN
novel
■ **un roman policier** a detective story
■ **un roman d'espionnage** a spy story

le **romancier** MASC NOUN
novelist

la **romancière** FEM NOUN
novelist

romantique (FEM **romantique**) ADJECTIVE
romantic

rompre VERB [75]
1 to split up
□ Paul et Justine ont rompu. Paul and Justine have split up.
2 to break off
□ Ils ont rompu leurs fiançailles. They've broken off their engagement.

les **ronces** FEM PL NOUN
brambles

ronchonner VERB [28] (*informal*)
to grouse

rond (FEM **ronde**) ADJECTIVE
▷ *see also* **rond** NOUN
1 round
□ La Terre est ronde. The earth is round.
■ **ouvrir des yeux ronds** to stare in amazement
2 chubby
□ Il a les joues rondes. He has chubby cheeks.
3 drunk
□ Il est complètement rond. (*informal*) He's completely drunk.

r

le **rond** MASC NOUN
▷ *see also* **rond** ADJECTIVE
circle
□ Elle a dessiné un rond sur le sable. She drew a circle in the sand.
■ **en rond** in a circle □ Ils se sont assis en rond. They sat down in a circle.
■ **tourner en rond** to go round in circles
■ **Je n'ai plus un rond.** (*informal*) I haven't a penny left.

la **rondelle** FEM NOUN
slice
□ une rondelle de citron a slice of lemon

le **rond-point** (PL les **ronds-points**) MASC NOUN
roundabout
□ La voiture s'est arrêtée au rond-point. The car stopped at the roundabout.

ronfler VERB [28]
to snore

le **rosbif** MASC NOUN
roast beef

la **rose** FEM NOUN
▷ *see also* **rose** ADJECTIVE
rose

rose (FEM **rose**) ADJECTIVE
▷ *see also* **rose** NOUN
pink

le **rosé** MASC NOUN
rosé (wine)
□ Je prendrai un verre de rosé. I'll have a glass of rosé.

le **rosier** MASC NOUN
rosebush

le **rôti** MASC NOUN
roast meat
■ **un rôti de bœuf** a joint of beef

rôtir VERB [38]
to roast
□ faire rôtir quelque chose to roast something

la **roue** FEM NOUN
wheel
□ une roue de secours a spare wheel

rouge (FEM **rouge**) ADJECTIVE
▷ *see also* **rouge** NOUN
red

le **rouge** MASC NOUN
▷ *see also* **rouge** ADJECTIVE
1 red
□ Le rouge est ma couleur préférée. Red is my favourite colour.
2 red wine
□ un verre de rouge a glass of red wine
■ **passer au rouge 1** to change to red □ Le feu est passé au rouge. The light changed to red.
2 to go through a red light □ Pierre est passé au rouge. Pierre went through a red light.
■ **un rouge à lèvres** a lipstick

la **rougeole** FEM NOUN
measles

rougir VERB [38]
1 to blush
□ Il a rougi en me voyant. He blushed when he saw me.
2 to flush
□ Il a rougi de colère. He flushed with anger.

la **rouille** FEM NOUN
rust

rouillé (FEM **rouillée**) ADJECTIVE
rusty

rouiller VERB [28]
to go rusty

roulant (FEM **roulante**) ADJECTIVE
■ **un fauteuil roulant** a wheelchair
■ **une table roulante** a trolley

le **rouleau** (PL les **rouleaux**) MASC NOUN
roll
□ un rouleau de papier peint a roll of wallpaper
■ **un rouleau à pâtisserie** a rolling pin

rouler VERB [28]
1 to go
□ Le train roulait à 250 km/h. The train was going at 250 km an hour.
2 to drive
□ Il a roulé sans s'arrêter. He drove without stopping.
3 to roll
□ Pauline a roulé une cigarette. Pauline rolled a cigarette.
4 to roll up
□ Il a roulé le tapis. He rolled the carpet up.
5 to con
□ Ils se sont fait rouler. (*informal*) They were conned.
■ **Alors, ça roule ?** (*informal*) How's it going?

la **Roumanie** FEM NOUN
Romania

le **rouquin** MASC NOUN (*informal*)
redhead

la **rouquine** FEM NOUN (*informal*)
redhead

rousse FEM ADJECTIVE ▷ *see* **roux**

la **rousse** FEM NOUN
▷ *see also* **rousse** ADJECTIVE
redhead

la **route** FEM NOUN
1 road
□ au bord de la route at the roadside
■ **une route nationale** an A road
2 way
□ Je ne connais pas la route. I don't know the way.
■ **Il y a trois heures de route.** It's a 3-hour journey.
■ **en route** on the way □ Ils se sont arrêtés en route. They stopped on the way.

Numbers in brackets refer to verb tables on pages 650 to 658

■ **mettre en route** to start up □ Il a mis le moteur en route. He started the engine up.
■ **se mettre en route** to set off □ Il s'est mis en route à cinq heures. He set off at 5 o'clock.

le **routier** MASC NOUN

1 lorry driver
□ Son père est routier. His father's a lorry driver.

2 transport café
□ Nous avons mangé dans un routier. We ate in a transport café.

la **routine** FEM NOUN
routine

roux (FEM **rousse**) ADJECTIVE
▷ see also **roux** NOUN

1 red
□ Harry a les cheveux roux. Harry has red hair.

2 red-haired
□ Gaëlle est rousse. Gaëlle's red-haired.

le **roux** MASC NOUN
▷ see also **roux** ADJECTIVE
redhead

royal (FEM **royale**, MASC PL **royaux**) ADJECTIVE
royal

le **royaume** MASC NOUN
kingdom
■ **le Royaume-Uni** the United Kingdom

le **RSA** MASC NOUN
Income Support
□ Il touche le RSA. He's on Income Support.

le **ruban** MASC NOUN
ribbon
■ **le ruban adhésif** adhesive tape

la **rubéole** FEM NOUN
German measles

la **ruche** FEM NOUN
hive

rudement ADVERB (informal)
terribly
□ C'était rudement bon. It was terribly good.

la **rue** FEM NOUN
street

la **ruelle** FEM NOUN
alley

le **rugby** MASC NOUN
rugby
□ Yann joue au rugby. Yann plays rugby.

rugueux (FEM **rugueuse**) ADJECTIVE
rough

la **ruine** FEM NOUN
ruin
□ les ruines de la cathédrale the ruins of the cathedral

ruiner VERB [28]
to ruin

le **ruisseau** (PL les **ruisseaux**) MASC NOUN
stream

la **rumeur** FEM NOUN
rumour

la **rupture** FEM NOUN
break-up

la **ruse** FEM NOUN
trickery
■ **une ruse** a trick

rusé (FEM **rusée**) ADJECTIVE
cunning

russe (FEM **russe**) ADJECTIVE, NOUN
Russian
□ Il parle russe. He speaks Russian.
■ **un Russe** a Russian (man)
■ **une Russe** a Russian (woman)
■ **les Russes** the Russians

la **Russie** FEM NOUN
Russia

le **rythme** MASC NOUN

1 rhythm
■ **J'aime le rythme de cette musique.** I like the beat of this music.

2 pace
□ Il marche à un bon rythme. He walks at a good pace.

r

Ss

s' PRONOUN ▷ see **se**

sa FEM ADJECTIVE
1 his
  □ Paul est allé voir sa grand-mère. Paul's gone to see his grandmother.
2 her
  □ Elle a embrassé sa mère. She kissed her mother.

sabbatique (FEM **sabbatique**) ADJECTIVE
  sabbatical
  ■ **une année sabbatique** a gap year

le sable MASC NOUN
  sand
  ■ **des sables mouvants** quicksand

le sablé MASC NOUN
  shortbread biscuit

le sabot MASC NOUN
1 clog
2 hoof (of horse)

le sac MASC NOUN
  bag
  ■ **un sac de voyage** a travel bag
  ■ **un sac de couchage** a sleeping bag
  ■ **un sac à main** a handbag
  ■ **un sac en plastique** a plastic bag
  ■ **voyager sac au dos** to go backpacking

le sachet MASC NOUN
  sachet (of sugar, coffee)
  ■ **du potage en sachet** packet soup
  ■ **un sachet de thé** a tea bag

la sacoche FEM NOUN
  bag
  ■ **une sacoche de bicyclette** a saddlebag

sacré (FEM **sacrée**) ADJECTIVE
  sacred

sage (FEM **sage**) ADJECTIVE
1 good (well-behaved)
  □ Sois sage. Be good.
2 wise (sensible)
  □ Il serait plus sage d'attendre. It would be wiser to wait.

la sagesse FEM NOUN
  wisdom
  □ Il a eu la sagesse de ne pas y aller. He wisely didn't go.
  ■ **une dent de sagesse** a wisdom tooth

le Sagittaire MASC NOUN
  Sagittarius
  □ Il est Sagittaire. He is Sagittarius.

saignant (FEM **saignante**) ADJECTIVE
  rare (meat)

saigner VERB [28]
  to bleed
  ■ **saigner du nez** to have a nosebleed

sain (FEM **saine**) ADJECTIVE
  healthy
  ■ **sain et sauf** safe and sound

saint (FEM **sainte**) ADJECTIVE
  ▷ see also **saint** NOUN, **sainte** NOUN
  holy
  □ la semaine sainte Holy Week □ le Saint-Esprit the Holy Spirit
  ■ **la Sainte Vierge** the Blessed Virgin
  ■ **le vendredi saint** Good Friday
  ■ **la Saint-Sylvestre** New Year's Eve
  ■ **la Saint-Valentin** Valentine's day

le saint MASC NOUN
  ▷ see also **saint** ADJECTIVE
  saint

la sainte FEM NOUN
  ▷ see also **saint** ADJECTIVE
  saint

sais VERB ▷ see **savoir**
  ■ **Je ne sais pas.** I don't know.

saisir VERB [38]
  to take hold of
  ■ **saisir l'occasion de faire quelque chose** to seize the opportunity to do something

la saison FEM NOUN
  season
  □ Ce n'est pas la saison des fraises. Strawberries are out of season. □ un temps de saison seasonable weather
  ■ **la saison des vendanges** harvest time

sait VERB ▷ see **savoir**
  ■ **Il sait que ...** He knows that ...
  ■ **On ne sait jamais !** You never know!

la salade FEM NOUN
1 lettuce
2 salad
  □ une salade composée a mixed salad □ une salade de fruits a fruit salad

le **saladier** MASC NOUN
salad bowl

le **salaire** MASC NOUN
salary

le **salami** MASC NOUN
salami

le **salarié** MASC NOUN
salaried employee

la **salariée** FEM NOUN
salaried employee

sale (FEM **sale**) ADJECTIVE
dirty

salé (FEM **salée**) ADJECTIVE

1 salty
□ La soupe est trop salée. The soup's too salty.

2 salted
□ du beurre salé salted butter

3 savoury
□ des biscuits salés savoury biscuits

saler VERB [28]
to put salt in
□ J'ai oublié de saler la soupe. I forgot to put salt in the soup.

la **saleté** FEM NOUN
dirt
□ J'ai horreur de la saleté. I hate dirt. □ Il y a une saleté sur ta chemise. There's some dirt on your shirt.
■ **faire des saletés** to make a mess

salir VERB [38]
■ **salir quelque chose** to get something dirty
■ **se salir** to get oneself dirty □ Mets un tablier, sinon tu vas te salir. Put on an apron or you'll get yourself dirty.

la **salle** FEM NOUN

1 room

2 audience
□ Toute la salle l'a applaudi. The whole audience applauded him.

3 ward (in hospital)
□ Il est à la salle douze. He's in Ward 12.
■ **la salle à manger** the dining room
■ **la salle de séjour** the living room
■ **la salle de bains** the bathroom
■ **la salle d'attente** the waiting room
■ **une salle de classe** a classroom
■ **la salle des professeurs** the staffroom
■ **la salle informatique** the computer room
■ **une salle de concert** a concert hall
■ **la salle d'embarquement** the departure lounge

le **salon** MASC NOUN
lounge
■ **un salon de thé** a tearoom
■ **un salon de coiffure** a hair salon
■ **un salon de beauté** a beauty salon
■ **un salon de discussion** a chatroom

la **salopette** FEM NOUN

1 dungarees

2 overalls

saluer VERB [28]
■ **saluer quelqu'un** 1 to say hello to somebody □ Je l'ai croisé dans la rue et il m'a salué. I met him in the street and he said hello.
2 to say goodbye to somebody □ Il nous a salués et il est parti. He said goodbye and left.

salut EXCLAMATION (informal)
hi!

la **salutation** FEM NOUN
greeting

le **samedi** MASC NOUN

1 Saturday
□ Aujourd'hui, nous sommes samedi. It's Saturday today.

2 on Saturday
□ Nous sommes allés au cinéma samedi. We went to the cinema on Saturday.
■ **le samedi** on Saturdays □ Le magasin ferme à dix-huit heures le samedi. The shop closes at 6 p.m. on Saturdays.
■ **tous les samedis** every Saturday
■ **samedi dernier** last Saturday
■ **samedi prochain** next Saturday
■ **À samedi !** See you on Saturday!

le **SAMU** MASC NOUN
ambulance service

la **sandale** FEM NOUN
sandal

le **sandwich** MASC NOUN
sandwich

le **sang** MASC NOUN
blood
■ **en sang** covered in blood

le **sang-froid** MASC NOUN
■ **garder son sang-froid** to keep calm
■ **perdre son sang-froid** to lose one's cool
■ **faire quelque chose de sang-froid** to do something in cold blood

le **sanglier** MASC NOUN
wild boar

le **sanglot** MASC NOUN
■ **éclater en sanglots** to burst into tears

sans PREPOSITION
without
□ Elle est venue sans son frère. She came without her brother.
■ **un pull sans manches** a sleeveless sweater

le/la **sans-abri** (PL les **sans-abris**, les **sans-abri**) MASC/FEM NOUN
homeless person
□ les sans-abri(s) the homeless

sans-gêne (FEM **sans-gêne**) ADJECTIVE
inconsiderate

la **santé** FEM NOUN

health

□ en bonne santé in good health □ la santé mentale mental health

■ Santé ! Cheers!

saoudien (FEM **saoudienne**) ADJECTIVE, NOUN

Saudi Arabian

■ un Saoudien a Saudi Arabian (*man*)

■ une Saoudienne a Saudi Arabian (*woman*)

le **sapeur-pompier** (PL les **sapeurs-pompiers**) MASC NOUN

firefighter

■ les sapeurs-pompiers the fire brigade

le **sapin** MASC NOUN

fir tree

■ un sapin de Noël a Christmas tree

la **Sardaigne** FEM NOUN

Sardinia

la **sardine** FEM NOUN

sardine

le **satellite** MASC NOUN

satellite

□ la télévision par satellite satellite TV

satisfaire VERB [36]

to satisfy

satisfaisant (FEM **satisfaisante**) ADJECTIVE

satisfactory

satisfait (FEM **satisfaite**) ADJECTIVE

satisfied

□ être satisfait de quelque chose to be satisfied with something

la **sauce** FEM NOUN

1 sauce

2 gravy

la **saucisse** FEM NOUN

sausage

le **saucisson** MASC NOUN

salami

sauf PREPOSITION

except

□ Tout le monde est venu sauf lui. Everyone came except him.

■ sauf si unless □ On ira se promener, sauf s'il fait mauvais. We'll go for a walk, unless the weather's bad.

■ sauf que except that □ Tout s'est bien passé, sauf que nous sommes arrivés en retard. Everything went OK, except that we arrived late.

le **saumon** MASC NOUN

salmon

saur MASC ADJECTIVE

■ un hareng saur a kipper

le **saut** MASC NOUN

jump

■ le saut en longueur the long jump

■ le saut en hauteur the high jump

■ le saut à la perche the pole vault

■ le saut à l'élastique bungee jumping

■ un saut périlleux a somersault

sauter VERB [28]

to jump

□ Nous avons sauté par-dessus la barrière. We jumped over the gate.

■ sauter à la corde to skip (*with a rope*)

■ faire sauter quelque chose to blow something up □ Ils ont fait sauter le pont. They blew up the bridge.

la **sauterelle** FEM NOUN

grasshopper

sauvage (FEM **sauvage**) ADJECTIVE

1 wild

□ les animaux sauvages wild animals □ faire du camping sauvage to camp in the wild

■ une région sauvage an unspoiled area

2 shy

□ Il est sauvage. He's shy.

sauvegarder VERB [28]

to save (*file on computer*)

sauver VERB [28]

to save

■ se sauver 1 to run away □ Il s'est sauvé à toutes jambes. He ran away as fast as he could. 2 (*informal*) to be off □ Allez, je me sauve ! Right, I'm off.

le **sauvetage** MASC NOUN

rescue

le **sauveur** MASC NOUN

saviour

savais, savait VERB ▷ *see* savoir

■ Je ne savais pas qu'il devait venir. I didn't know he was going to come.

le **savant** MASC NOUN

scientist

la **savante** FEM NOUN

scientist

savent VERB ▷ *see* savoir

■ Ils ne savent pas ce qu'ils veulent. They don't know what they want.

la **saveur** FEM NOUN

flavour

savez VERB ▷ *see* savoir

■ Est-ce que vous savez où elle habite ? Do you know where she lives?

savoir VERB [76]

to know

□ Je ne sais pas où il est allé. I don't know where he's gone. □ Nous ne savons pas s'il est bien arrivé. We don't know if he's arrived safely. □ Tu savais que Canberra était la capitale de l'Australie ? Did you know that Canberra was the capital of Australia? □ Il ne sait pas ce qu'il va faire ce week-end. He doesn't know what he's going to do this weekend.

■ Tu sais nager ? Can you swim?

le **savon** MASC NOUN
soap

la **savonnette** FEM NOUN
bar of soap

savons VERB ▷ *see* savoir

savoureux (FEM **savoureuse**) ADJECTIVE
tasty

le **saxo** MASC NOUN (*informal*)
sax

le **scandale** MASC NOUN
scandal
■ **faire scandale** to cause a scandal □ Ce film a fait scandale. The film caused a scandal.

scandaleux (FEM **scandaleuse**) ADJECTIVE
outrageous

le/la **Scandinave** MASC/FEM NOUN
Scandinavian

scandinave (FEM **scandinave**) ADJECTIVE
Scandinavian

la **Scandinavie** FEM NOUN
Scandinavia

le **scarabée** MASC NOUN
beetle

la **scène** FEM NOUN
scene
□ une scène d'amour a love scene □ la scène du crime the scene of the crime □ Il m'a fait une scène. He made a scene.
■ **une scène de ménage** a domestic row

sceptique (FEM **sceptique**) ADJECTIVE
sceptical

le **schéma** MASC NOUN
diagram

schématique (FEM **schématique**) ADJECTIVE
■ **l'explication schématique d'une théorie** the broad outline of a theory
■ **Cette interprétation est un peu trop schématique.** This interpretation is a bit oversimplified.

la **scie** FEM NOUN
saw
■ **une scie à métaux** a hacksaw

la **science** FEM NOUN
science
■ **Elle est forte en sciences.** She is good at science.
■ **les sciences physiques** physics
■ **les sciences naturelles** biology
■ **les sciences économiques** economics
■ **sciences po** (*informal*) politics □ Mon frère fait sciences po à Paris. My brother is studying politics in Paris.

la **science-fiction** FEM NOUN
science fiction

scientifique (FEM **scientifique**) ADJECTIVE
▷ *see also* **scientifique** NOUN
scientific

le/la **scientifique** MASC/FEM NOUN
▷ *see also* **scientifique** ADJECTIVE
1 scientist
2 science student

scier VERB [19]
to saw

scolaire (FEM **scolaire**) ADJECTIVE
school
□ l'année scolaire the school year □ les vacances scolaires the school holidays □ mon livret scolaire my school report

le **Scorpion** MASC NOUN
Scorpio
□ Océane est Scorpion. Océane is Scorpio.

le **Scotch**® MASC NOUN
adhesive tape

scotché (FEM **scotchée**) ADJECTIVE (*informal*)
□ Il reste des heures scotché devant la télévision. He spends hours glued to the television.
■ **je suis resté scotché** I was flabbergasted (*astounded*)

le **scrupule** MASC NOUN
scruple

sculpter VERB [28]
to sculpt

le **sculpteur** MASC NOUN
sculptor

la **sculpture** FEM NOUN
sculpture

le/la **SDF** MASC/FEM NOUN (= *sans domicile fixe*)
homeless person
■ **les SDF** the homeless

se PRONOUN

> se changes to **s'** before a vowel and most words beginning with 'h'.

1 himself
□ Il se regarde dans la glace. He's looking at himself in the mirror.
2 herself
□ Elle se regarde dans la glace. She's looking at herself in the mirror.
3 itself
□ Le chien s'est fait mal. The dog hurt itself.
4 oneself
□ se regarder dans une glace to look at oneself in a mirror
5 themselves
□ Ils se sont regardés dans la glace. They looked at themselves in the mirror.
6 each other
□ Ils s'aiment. They love each other.

> With reflexive verbs, se is often not translated.

□ Il s'est cassé le bras. He broke his arm.

séance FEM NOUN
1 session
□ une séance de rééducation a physiotherapy session
2 showing (*at the cinema*)
□ La prochaine séance est à dix-neuf heures. The next showing is at 7 p.m.

le **seau** (PL les **seaux**) MASC NOUN
bucket

sec (FEM **sèche**) ADJECTIVE
1 dry
□ Mon jean n'est pas encore sec. My jeans aren't dry yet.
2 dried
□ des figues sèches dried figs

sèche FEM ADJECTIVE ▷ *see* **sec**

le **sèche-cheveux** (PL les **sèche-cheveux**) MASC NOUN
hair dryer

le **sèche-linge** (PL les **sèche-linges**, PL les **sèche-linge**) MASC NOUN
tumble dryer

sécher VERB [34]
1 to dry
2 to be stumped
□ J'ai complètement séché à l'interrogation de maths. (*informal*) I was completely stumped in the maths test.
■ **se sécher** to dry oneself □ Sèche-toi avec cette serviette. Dry yourself with this towel.

la **sécheresse** FEM NOUN
drought
□ une terrible sécheresse a terrible drought

le **séchoir** MASC NOUN
dryer

second (FEM **seconde**) ADJECTIVE
▷ *see also* **second** NOUN
second
□ Il est arrivé second. He came second.

le **second** MASC NOUN
▷ *see also* **second** ADJECTIVE
second floor
□ Elle habite au second. She lives on the second floor.

secondaire (FEM **secondaire**) ADJECTIVE
secondary
□ l'enseignement secondaire secondary education
■ **des effets secondaires** side effects

la **seconde** FEM NOUN
▷ *see also* **second** ADJECTIVE
1 second
□ Attends une seconde ! Wait a second!
2 year 11
□ Ma sœur est en seconde. My sister's in year 11.

> **DID YOU KNOW...?**
> In French secondary schools, years are counted from the **sixième** (youngest) to **première** and **terminale** (oldest).

3 second class
□ voyager en seconde to travel second-class

secouer VERB [28]
to shake
□ secouer la tête to shake one's head

secourir VERB [16]
to rescue

le **secourisme** MASC NOUN
first aid
□ J'ai un brevet de secourisme. I've got a first aid qualification.

le **secours** MASC NOUN
help
□ Il est allé chercher du secours. He went to get help. □ Au secours ! Help!
■ **les premiers secours** first aid
■ **une sortie de secours** an emergency exit
■ **la roue de secours** the spare wheel

secret (FEM **secrète**) ADJECTIVE
▷ *see also* **secret** NOUN
secret

le **secret** MASC NOUN
▷ *see also* **secret** ADJECTIVE
secret

le **secrétaire** MASC NOUN
▷ *see also* **secrétaire** NOUN
1 secretary
2 writing desk

la **secrétaire** FEM NOUN
▷ *see also* **secrétaire** NOUN
secretary

le **secrétariat** MASC NOUN
secretary's office

le **secteur** MASC NOUN
sector
□ le secteur public the public sector □ le secteur privé the private sector

la **section** FEM NOUN
department (*of school*)

la **sécu** FEM NOUN (*informal*)
Social Security

la **sécurité** FEM NOUN
1 safety
■ **être en sécurité** to be safe □ On ne se sent pas en sécurité dans ce quartier. You don't feel safe in this neighbourhood.
■ **la sécurité routière** road safety
■ **une ceinture de sécurité** a seatbelt
2 security
□ par mesure de sécurité as a security measure
■ **la sécurité sociale** Social Security
■ **la sécurité de l'emploi** job security

séduisant (FEM **séduisante**) ADJECTIVE
attractive

le **seigle** MASC NOUN
rye
□ un pain de seigle a loaf of rye bread

S

le **seigneur** MASC NOUN
lord
■ **le Seigneur** the Lord

le **sein** MASC NOUN
breast
■ **au sein de** within □ Chaque pays est autonome au sein de l'Europe. Each country is independent within Europe.

seize NUMBER
sixteen
□ Elle a seize ans. She's sixteen. □ à seize heures at 4 p.m.
■ **le seize février** the sixteenth of February

seizième (FEM **seizième**) ADJECTIVE
sixteenth

le **séjour** MASC NOUN
stay
□ J'ai fait un séjour d'une semaine en Italie. I stayed in Italy for a week.

le **sel** MASC NOUN
salt

sélectionner VERB [28]
to select

le **self** MASC NOUN (informal)
self-service restaurant

selfie MASC NOUN
selfie
■ **une perche à selfie** a selfie stick

le **self-service** MASC NOUN
self-service restaurant

la **selle** FEM NOUN
saddle

selon PREPOSITION
according to
□ selon lui according to him □ selon mon humeur according to what mood I'm in □ Ils sont répartis selon leur âge. They're divided up according to age.

la **semaine** FEM NOUN
week
□ la semaine prochaine next week
■ **en semaine** on weekdays

semblable (FEM **semblable**) ADJECTIVE
similar

le **semblant** MASC NOUN
■ **faire semblant de faire quelque chose** to pretend to do something □ Il fait semblant de dormir. He's pretending to be asleep.

sembler VERB [28]
to seem
□ Le temps semble s'améliorer. The weather seems to be improving. □ Il me semble inutile de s'en inquiéter. It seems pointless to me to worry about it.

la **semelle** FEM NOUN
1 sole
2 insole

la **semoule** FEM NOUN
semolina

le **Sénégal** MASC NOUN
Senegal

le **sens** MASC NOUN
1 sense
□ avoir le sens de l'humour to have a sense of humour □ Je n'ai pas le sens de l'orientation. I've got no sense of direction. □ avoir le sens du rythme to have a sense of rhythm □ Ça n'a pas de sens. It doesn't make sense.
■ **le bon sens** common sense
2 direction
□ Tu tournes la poignée dans le mauvais sens. You're turning the handle in the wrong direction.
■ **sens dessus dessous** upside down
■ **un sens interdit** a one-way street □ J'ai failli prendre un sens interdit. I nearly went the wrong way down a one-way street.
■ **un sens unique** a one-way street

la **sensation** FEM NOUN
feeling

sensationnel (FEM **sensationnelle**) ADJECTIVE
sensational

sensé (FEM **sensée**) ADJECTIVE
sensible

sensible (FEM **sensible**) ADJECTIVE
1 sensitive
□ Elle est très sensible. She's very sensitive.
■ **Ce film est déconseillé aux personnes sensibles.** This film contains scenes which some viewers may find disturbing.
2 visible
□ une amélioration sensible a visible improvement

> **BE CAREFUL!**
> The French word **sensible** does not mean **sensible**.

sensiblement ADVERB
1 visibly
□ Elle a sensiblement progressé. She's made visible progress.
2 approximately
□ Elles sont sensiblement de la même taille. They are approximately the same height.

la **sentence** FEM NOUN
sentence (judgement)

le **sentier** MASC NOUN
path

le **sentiment** MASC NOUN
feeling

sentimental (FEM **sentimentale**, MASC PL **sentimentaux**) ADJECTIVE
sentimental

sentir VERB [77]

1 to smell
- □ Ça sent bon. That smells good. □ Ça sent mauvais. It smells bad.

2 to smell of
- □ Ça sent les frites ici. It smells of chips in here.

3 to taste
- □ Tu sens l'ail dans le rôti ? Can you taste the garlic in the roast?

4 to feel
- □ Ça t'a fait mal ? — Non, je n'ai rien senti. Did it hurt? — No, I didn't feel a thing.
- ■ **se sentir** to feel □ Je ne me sens pas bien. I don't feel well.
- ■ **Il ne peut pas la sentir.** (*informal*) He can't stand her.

séparé (FEM séparée) ADJECTIVE

separated
- □ Mes parents sont séparés. My parents are separated.

séparément ADVERB

separately

séparer VERB [28]

to separate
- □ Séparez le blanc du jaune. Separate the yolk from the white.
- ■ **se séparer** to separate □ Mes parents se sont séparés l'année dernière. My parents separated last year.

sept NUMBER

seven
- □ Il est arrivé à sept heures. He arrived at seven o'clock. □ Elle a sept ans. She's seven.
- ■ **le sept février** the seventh of February

septembre MASC NOUN

September
- ■ **en septembre** in September

septième (FEM septième) ADJECTIVE

seventh
- □ au septième étage on the seventh floor

sera, serai, serais, serait, seras, serez VERB ▷ see être

- ■ **Je serai de retour à dix heures.** I'll be back at 10 o'clock.

la série FEM NOUN

series

sérieusement ADVERB

seriously

sérieux (FEM sérieuse) ADJECTIVE

▷ see also **sérieux** NOUN

1 serious
- □ Il plaisantait ? — Non, il était sérieux. Was he joking? — No, he was serious.

2 responsible
- □ C'est un employé très sérieux. He's a very responsible employee.

le sérieux MASC NOUN

▷ see also **sérieux** ADJECTIVE
- ■ **garder son sérieux** to keep a straight face
- □ J'ai eu du mal à garder mon sérieux. I had trouble keeping a straight face.
- ■ **prendre quelque chose au sérieux** to take something seriously
- ■ **prendre quelqu'un au sérieux** to take somebody seriously
- ■ **Il manque un peu de sérieux.** He's not very responsible.

la seringue FEM NOUN

syringe

séronégatif (FEM séronégative) ADJECTIVE

HIV-negative

serons, seront VERB ▷ see être

séropositif (FEM séropositive) ADJECTIVE

HIV-positive

le serpent MASC NOUN

snake

la serre FEM NOUN

greenhouse
- ■ **l'effet de serre** the greenhouse effect

serré (FEM serrée) ADJECTIVE

1 tight
- □ Mon pantalon est trop serré. My trousers are too tight.

2 close-fought
- □ Ça a été un match serré. It was a close-fought game.

serrer VERB [28]

- ■ **Ce pantalon me serre trop.** These trousers are too tight for me.
- ■ **serrer la main à quelqu'un** to shake hands with somebody
- ■ **se serrer** to squeeze up □ Serrez-vous un peu pour que je puisse m'asseoir. Squeeze up a bit so I can sit down.
- ■ **serrer quelqu'un dans ses bras** to hug somebody
- ■ **« Serrer à droite »** 'Keep right'

la serrure FEM NOUN

lock

sers, sert VERB ▷ see servir

le serveur MASC NOUN

1 waiter (*in café*)
2 server (*computer*)

la serveuse FEM NOUN

waitress

serviable (FEM serviable) ADJECTIVE

helpful

le service MASC NOUN

1 service (*in restaurant*)
- □ Le service est compris. Service is included.
- ■ **être de service** to be on duty
- ■ **hors service** out of order
- ■ **faire le service** to serve (*at table*) □ Tu peux

faire le service s'il te plaît ? Could you serve please?

2 favour
□ rendre service à quelqu'un to do somebody a favour □ Est-ce que je peux te demander un service ? Can I ask you a favour?

3 serve (*sport*)
□ Il a un bon service. He's got a good serve.
■ **le service militaire** military service
■ **les services sociaux** the social services
■ **les services secrets** the secret service

la **serviette** FEM NOUN

1 towel
□ une serviette de bain a bath towel
■ **une serviette hygiénique** a sanitary towel

2 serviette (*napkin*)

3 briefcase

servir VERB [78]

to serve
□ On vous sert ? Are you being served?
■ **À toi de servir.** (*tennis*) It's your serve.
■ **se servir** to help oneself □ Servez-vous. Help yourself.
■ **se servir de** to use □ Tu te sers souvent de ton vélo ? Do you use your bike a lot?
■ **servir à quelqu'un** to be of use to somebody □ Ça m'a beaucoup servi. I found it very useful.
■ **À quoi ça sert ?** What's it for?
■ **Ça ne sert à rien.** It's no use. □ Ça ne sert à rien d'insister. It's no use insisting.

ses PL ADJECTIVE

1 his
□ Il est parti voir ses grands-parents. He's gone to see his grandparents.

2 her
□ Delphine a oublié ses baskets. Delphine's forgotten her trainers.

3 its
□ la ville et ses alentours the town and its surroundings

le **set** MASC NOUN

1 tablemat (*on table*)

2 set (*in tennis*)

le **seuil** MASC NOUN
doorstep

seul (FEM **seule**) ADJECTIVE, ADVERB

1 alone
□ vivre seul to live alone

2 by oneself
□ Elle est venue seule. She came by herself.
■ **faire quelque chose tout seul** to do something by oneself □ Elle a fait ça toute seule ? Did she do it by herself?
■ **se sentir seul** to feel lonely
■ **un seul livre** one book only □ Vous avez droit à un seul livre. You're entitled to one book only.
■ **Il reste une seule nectarine.** There's only one nectarine left.

■ **le seul livre que ...** the only book that ...
□ C'est le seul Agatha Christie que je n'aie pas lu. That's the only Agatha Christie I haven't read.
■ **le seul** the only one □ C'est la seule que je ne connaisse pas. She's the only one I don't know.

seulement ADVERB

only
■ **non seulement ... mais** not only ... but
□ Non seulement il a plu, mais en plus il a fait froid. Not only did it rain, but it was cold as well.

sévère (FEM **sévère**) ADJECTIVE

strict
□ Mon prof de maths est très sévère. My maths teacher is very strict.

le **sexe** MASC NOUN
sex

le **sexisme** MASC NOUN
sexism

sexuel (FEM **sexuelle**) ADJECTIVE
sexual
□ l'éducation sexuelle sex education

le **shampooing** MASC NOUN
shampoo
■ **se faire un shampooing** to wash one's hair

le **shopping** MASC NOUN
shopping
■ **faire du shopping** to go shopping

le **short** MASC NOUN
shorts
□ Il était en short. He was wearing shorts.

si CONJUNCTION, ADVERB
▷ *see also* **si** NOUN

1 if
□ si tu veux if you like □ Je me demande si elle va venir. I wonder if she'll come. □ si seulement if only

2 so
□ Elle est si gentille. She's so kind. □ Tout s'est passé si vite. Everything happened so fast.

3 yes
□ Tu n'es pas allé à l'école habillé comme ça ?
— Si. You didn't go to school dressed like that?
— Yes I did.

le **si** MASC NOUN
▷ *see also* **si** CONJUNCTION, ADVERB

1 B
□ en si bémol in B flat

2 ti
□ la, si, do la, ti, do

la **Sicile** FEM NOUN
Sicily

le **sida** MASC NOUN
AIDS
□ Il a le sida. He's got AIDS.

le **siècle** MASC NOUN
century
□ le vingtième siècle the twentieth century

S

le **siège** MASC NOUN
1 seat (in vehicle)
2 head office

sien MASC PRONOUN
■ **le sien** 1 his □ C'est le vélo de Paul ? — Oui, c'est le sien. Is this Paul's bike? — Yes, it's his. 2 hers □ C'est le vélo d'Isabelle ? — Oui, c'est le sien. Is this Isabelle's bike? — Yes, it's hers.

sienne FEM PRONOUN
■ **la sienne** 1 his □ C'est la montre de Paul ? — Oui, c'est la sienne. Is this Paul's watch? — Yes, it's his. 2 hers □ C'est la montre d'Isabelle ? — Oui, c'est la sienne. Is this Isabelle's watch? — Yes, it's hers.

siennes FEM PL PRONOUN
■ **les siennes** 1 his □ Ce sont les chaussures de Julien ? — Oui, ce sont les siennes. Are these Julien's shoes? — Yes, they're his. 2 hers □ Ce sont les lunettes de Marine ? — Oui, ce sont les siennes. Are these Marine's glasses? — Yes, they're hers.

siens MASC PL PRONOUN
■ **les siens** 1 his □ Ce sont les sandwichs de Pierre ? — Oui, ce sont les siens. Are these Pierre's sandwiches? — Yes, they're his. 2 hers □ Ce sont les sandwichs de Justine ? — Oui, ce sont les siens. Are these Justine's sandwiches? — Yes, they're hers.

la **sieste** FEM NOUN
nap
□ faire la sieste to have a nap

siffler VERB [28]
to whistle

le **sifflet** MASC NOUN
whistle

le **sigle** MASC NOUN
acronym

le **signal** (PL les **signaux**) MASC NOUN
signal

la **signature** FEM NOUN
signature

le **signe** MASC NOUN
sign
■ **faire un signe de la main** to wave
■ **faire signe à quelqu'un d'entrer** to beckon to somebody to come in
■ **les signes du zodiaque** the signs of the zodiac

signer VERB [28]
to sign

le **signet** MASC NOUN
bookmark

la **signification** FEM NOUN
meaning

signifier VERB [19]
to mean
□ Que signifie ce mot ? What does this word mean?

le **silence** MASC NOUN
silence
■ **Silence !** Be quiet!

silencieux (FEM **silencieuse**) ADJECTIVE
1 silent
□ Elle est restée silencieuse. She remained silent.
2 quiet
□ C'est très silencieux ici. It's very quiet here.

la **silhouette** FEM NOUN
figure
□ J'ai vu une silhouette dans le brouillard. I saw a figure in the mist.

similaire (FEM **similaire**) ADJECTIVE
similar

le **simple** MASC NOUN
▷ see also **simple** ADJECTIVE
singles (tennis)
□ le simple messieurs the men's singles □ le simple dames the women's singles

simple (FEM **simple**) ADJECTIVE
▷ see also **simple** NOUN
simple

simplement ADVERB
simply
□ C'est tout simplement inadmissible. It's quite simply unacceptable.

simuler VERB [28]
to simulate

simultané (FEM **simultanée**) ADJECTIVE
simultaneous

sincère (FEM **sincère**) ADJECTIVE
sincere

sincèrement ADVERB
sincerely

la **sincérité** FEM NOUN
sincerity

le **singe** MASC NOUN
monkey

le **singulier** MASC NOUN
singular
□ au féminin singulier in the feminine singular

sinistre (FEM **sinistre**) ADJECTIVE
sinister

sinon CONJUNCTION
otherwise
□ Dépêche-toi, sinon je pars sans toi. Hurry up, otherwise I'll leave without you.

la **sinusite** FEM NOUN
sinusitis
□ avoir de la sinusite to have sinusitis

la **sirène** FEM NOUN
mermaid
■ **la sirène d'alarme** the fire alarm

le **sirop** MASC NOUN
syrup
■ **le sirop contre la toux** cough mixture

le site MASC NOUN
setting
□ un site très sauvage a totally unspoiled setting
- **un site pittoresque** a beauty spot
- **un site touristique** a tourist attraction
- **un site archéologique** an archaeological site
- **un site web** a website

sitôt ADVERB
- **sitôt dit, sitôt fait** no sooner said than done
- **pas de sitôt** not for a long time □ On ne le reverra pas de sitôt. We won't see him again for a long time.

la situation FEM NOUN
1 situation
- **la situation de famille** marital status
2 job
□ Il a une belle situation. He's got a good job.

se situer VERB [28]
to be situated
□ Versailles se situe à l'ouest de Paris. Versailles is situated to the west of Paris.
- **bien situé** well situated

six NUMBER
six
□ Il est rentré à six heures. He got back at six o'clock. □ Il a six ans. He's six.
- **le six février** the sixth of February

sixième (FEM **sixième**) ADJECTIVE
▷ see also **sixième** NOUN
sixth
□ au sixième étage on the sixth floor

la sixième FEM NOUN
▷ see also **sixième** ADJECTIVE
year 7
□ Mon frère est en sixième. My brother's in year 7.

DID YOU KNOW...?
In French secondary schools, years are counted from the **sixième** (youngest) to **première** and **terminale** (oldest).

le skate MASC NOUN
skateboarding
- **faire du skate** to skateboard

le ski MASC NOUN
1 ski
□ J'ai loué des skis. I hired skis.
2 skiing
□ J'adore le ski. I love skiing. □ faire du ski to go skiing
- **le ski de fond** cross-country skiing
- **le ski nautique** water-skiing
- **le ski de piste** downhill skiing
- **le ski de randonnée** cross-country skiing

skier VERB [19]
to ski

le skieur MASC NOUN
skier

la skieuse FEM NOUN
skier

skyper VERB [28]
to Skype
□ Pour skyper, il faut une webcam et un micro. To Skype, you need a webcam and a microphone.

le slip MASC NOUN
pants
- **un slip de bain** swimming trunks

la Slovaquie FEM NOUN
Slovakia

la Slovénie FEM NOUN
Slovenia

le SMIC MASC NOUN
guaranteed minimum wage
□ Il touche le SMIC. He's on the legal minimum wage.

le smoking MASC NOUN
dinner suit

le SMS MASC NOUN
text message

la SNCF FEM NOUN (= *Société nationale des chemins de fer français*)
French railways

snob (FEM **snob**) ADJECTIVE
snobbish

sobre (FEM **sobre**) ADJECTIVE
1 sober
2 plain
□ C'est une veste très sobre. It's a very plain jacket.

social (FEM **sociale**, MASC PL **sociaux**) ADJECTIVE
social

le/la socialiste MASC/FEM NOUN
socialist

la société FEM NOUN
1 society
2 company
□ une société financière a finance company

la sociologie FEM NOUN
sociology

la socquette FEM NOUN
ankle sock

la sœur FEM NOUN
sister
- **une bonne sœur** (*informal*) a nun

soi PRONOUN
oneself
□ avoir confiance en soi to have confidence in oneself
- **rester chez soi** to stay at home
- **Ça va de soi.** It goes without saying.

soi-disant (FEM **soi-disante**) ADVERB, ADJECTIVE
supposedly

soie – solution

□ Il était soi-disant parti à Paris. He had supposedly left for Paris.

■ un soi-disant poète a so-called poet

la **soie** FEM NOUN
silk

la **soif** FEM NOUN
thirst

■ avoir soif to be thirsty

soigner VERB [28]
to look after (ill person, animal)

□ Soigne-toi bien ce week-end ! Take good care of yourself this weekend!

soigneux (FEM **soigneuse**) ADJECTIVE
careful

□ Tu devrais être plus soigneux avec tes livres. You should be more careful with your books.

soi-même PRONOUN
oneself

□ Il vaut mieux le faire soi-même. It's better to do it oneself.

le **soin** MASC NOUN
care

■ prendre soin de quelque chose to take care of something □ Prends bien soin de ce livre. Take good care of this book.

les **soins** MASC PL NOUN
treatment *sing*

■ les premiers soins first aid

■ « aux bons soins de Madame Martin » (on letter) 'c/o Mrs Martin'

le **soir** MASC NOUN
evening

□ ce soir this evening

■ à sept heures du soir at 7 p.m.

■ demain soir tomorrow night

■ hier soir last night

la **soirée** FEM NOUN
evening

□ en tenue de soirée in evening dress

sois VERB ▷ see être

■ Sois tranquille ! Don't worry!

soit CONJUNCTION

■ soit ... , soit ... either ... or ... □ soit lundi, soit mardi either Monday or Tuesday

la **soixantaine** FEM NOUN
about sixty

□ une soixantaine de personnes about sixty people

■ Elle a la soixantaine. She's in her sixties.

soixante NUMBER
sixty

□ Il a soixante ans. He's sixty. □ soixante et un sixty-one □ soixante-deux sixty-two

■ soixante et onze seventy-one

■ soixante-dix seventy

■ soixante-quinze seventy-five

le **soja** MASC NOUN
soya

■ des germes de soja beansprouts

le **sol** MASC NOUN

1 floor

□ un sol carrelé a tiled floor

■ à même le sol on the floor

2 soil

□ sur le sol français on French soil

3 G

□ sol dièse G sharp

4 so

□ do, ré, mi, fa, sol ... do, re, mi, fa, so ...

solaire (FEM **solaire**) ADJECTIVE
solar

□ le système solaire the solar system

■ la crème solaire sun cream

le **soldat** MASC NOUN
soldier

le **solde** MASC NOUN

■ être en solde to be reduced □ Les chemisiers sont en solde. The blouses are reduced.

■ les soldes the sales □ faire les soldes to go round the sales □ les soldes de janvier the January sales

soldé (FEM **soldée**) ADJECTIVE

■ être soldé to be reduced □ un article soldé à dix euros an item reduced to 10 euros

la **sole** FEM NOUN
sole (fish)

le **soleil** MASC NOUN
sun

□ au soleil in the sun

■ Il y a du soleil. It's sunny.

le **solfège** MASC NOUN
musical theory

□ un cours de solfège a music theory lesson

■ Il joue du violon sans connaître le solfège. He plays the violin but he can't read music.

solidaire (FEM **solidaire**) ADJECTIVE

■ être solidaire de quelqu'un to back somebody up

solide (FEM **solide**) ADJECTIVE

1 strong (person)

2 solid (object)

solitaire (FEM **solitaire**) ADJECTIVE
▷ see also solitaire NOUN
solitary

le/la **solitaire** MASC/FEM NOUN
▷ see also solitaire ADJECTIVE
loner

la **solitude** FEM NOUN
loneliness

la **solution** FEM NOUN
solution

■ une solution de facilité an easy way out

S

sombre (FEM **sombre**) ADJECTIVE
dark

le **sommaire** MASC NOUN
summary

la **somme** FEM NOUN
▷ *see also* **somme** NOUN
sum

le **somme** MASC NOUN
▷ *see also* **somme** NOUN
nap
□ faire un somme to take a nap

le **sommeil** MASC NOUN
sleep
■ avoir sommeil to be sleepy

sommes VERB ▷ *see* être
■ **Nous sommes en vacances.** We're on holiday.

le **sommet** MASC NOUN
summit

le **somnifère** MASC NOUN
sleeping pill

somptueux (FEM **somptueuse**) ADJECTIVE
sumptuous

son (FEM **sa**, PL **ses**) ADJECTIVE
▷ *see also* **son** NOUN
1 his
□ son père his father □ Il a perdu son portefeuille. He's lost his wallet.
2 her
□ son père her father □ Elle a perdu son sac. She's lost her bag.

le **son** MASC NOUN
▷ *see also* **son** ADJECTIVE
1 sound
□ Le son n'est pas très bon. The sound's not very good. □ baisser le son to turn the sound down
2 bran
■ le pain de son brown bread

le **sondage** MASC NOUN
survey
■ un sondage d'opinion an opinion poll

sonner VERB [28]
to ring
□ On a sonné. Somebody rang the doorbell.
□ Le téléphone a sonné. The phone rang.

la **sonnerie** FEM NOUN
1 bell (*electric*)
■ La sonnerie du téléphone l'a réveillé. He was woken by the phone ringing.
2 ringtone (*on mobile phone*)
□ J'ai téléchargé une nouvelle sonnerie sur mon portable. I've downloaded a new ringtone onto my mobile.

la **sonnette** FEM NOUN
bell
□ la sonnette d'alarme the alarm bell

la **sono** FEM NOUN (*informal*)
PA system

sont VERB ▷ *see* être
■ **Ils sont en vacances.** They're on holiday.

sophistiqué (FEM **sophistiquée**) ADJECTIVE
sophisticated

le **sorcier** MASC NOUN
wizard

la **sorcière** FEM NOUN
witch

le **sort** MASC NOUN
1 spell
□ jeter un sort à quelqu'un to cast a spell on somebody
■ un mauvais sort a curse
2 fate
□ abandonner quelqu'un à son triste sort to leave somebody to their fate
■ tirer au sort to draw lots

la **sorte** FEM NOUN
sort
□ C'est une sorte de gâteau. It's a sort of cake.
□ toutes sortes de choses all sorts of things

la **sortie** FEM NOUN
way out
□ Où est la sortie ? Where's the way out?
■ la sortie de secours the emergency exit
■ Attends-moi à la sortie de l'école. Meet me after school.

sortir VERB [79, *aux* avoir *or* être]
1 to go out
□ Il est sorti sans rien dire. He went out without saying a word. □ Il est sorti acheter un journal. He's gone out to buy a newspaper. □ J'aime sortir. I like going out.
2 to come out
□ Elle sort de l'hôpital demain. She's coming out of hospital tomorrow. □ Je l'ai rencontré en sortant de la pharmacie. I met him coming out of the chemist's. □ Ce modèle vient juste de sortir. This model has just come out.
3 to take out
□ Elle a sorti son porte-monnaie de son sac. She took her purse out of her handbag. □ Je vais sortir la voiture du garage. I'll get the car out of the garage.
■ sortir avec quelqu'un to be going out with somebody □ Tu sors avec lui ? Are you going out with him?
■ s'en sortir to manage □ Ne t'en fais pas, tu t'en sortiras. Don't worry, you'll manage OK.

> The verb **sortir** uses être in the perfect tense when talking about going out somewhere. It uses **avoir** when talking about taking an object out of something.

la **sottise** FEM NOUN
■ **Ne fais pas de sottises.** Don't do anything silly.
■ **Ne dis pas de sottises.** Don't talk nonsense.

le **sou** MASC NOUN
- **une machine à sous** a fruit machine
- **Je n'ai pas un sou sur moi.** I haven't got a penny on me.
- **être près de ses sous** (*informal*) to be tight-fisted

le **souci** MASC NOUN

worry
- **se faire du souci** to worry
- **pas de souci** (*informal*) no worries

soucieux (FEM **soucieuse**) ADJECTIVE

worried
- □ Tu as l'air soucieux. You look worried.

la **soucoupe** FEM NOUN

saucer
- **une soucoupe volante** a flying saucer

soudain (FEM **soudaine**) ADJECTIVE, ADVERB
1 sudden
- □ une douleur soudaine a sudden pain
2 suddenly
- □ Soudain, il s'est fâché. Suddenly, he got angry.

le **souffle** MASC NOUN

breath
- **à bout de souffle** out of breath

le **soufflé** MASC NOUN

soufflé
- □ un soufflé au fromage a cheese soufflé

souffler VERB [28]
1 to blow
- □ Le vent soufflait fort. The wind was blowing hard.
2 to blow out
- □ Souffle les bougies ! Blow out the candles!

la **souffrance** FEM NOUN

suffering

souffrant (FEM **souffrante**) ADJECTIVE

unwell

souffrir VERB [54]

to be in pain
- □ Il souffre beaucoup. He's in a lot of pain.

le **souhait** MASC NOUN

wish
- □ faire un souhait to make a wish □ Tous nos souhaits de réussite. All our best wishes for your success. □ les souhaits de bonne année New Year's wishes
- **Atchoum ! — À tes souhaits !** Atchoo! — Bless you!

souhaiter VERB [28]

to wish
- □ Il souhaite aller à l'université. He wishes to go to university. □ Nous vous souhaitons une bonne année. We wish you a happy New Year.

soûl (FEM **soûle**) ADJECTIVE (*informal*)

drunk

soulager VERB [45]

to relieve

soulever VERB [43]
1 to lift
- □ Je n'arrive pas à soulever cette valise. I can't lift this suitcase.
2 to raise
- □ Il faudra soulever la question lors de la réunion. We'll have to raise the matter at the meeting.

le **soulier** MASC NOUN

shoe

souligner VERB [28]

to underline

le **soupçon** MASC NOUN

suspicion
- **un soupçon de** a dash of □ Ajoutez un soupçon de rhum. Add a dash of rum.

soupçonner VERB [28]

to suspect

la **soupe** FEM NOUN

soup

souper VERB [28]

to have supper

le **soupir** MASC NOUN

sigh

soupirer VERB [28]

to sigh

souple (FEM **souple**) ADJECTIVE
1 supple (*person*)
2 flexible (*system*)

la **source** FEM NOUN

spring
- □ l'eau de source spring water

le **sourcil** MASC NOUN

eyebrow

sourd (FEM **sourde**) ADJECTIVE

deaf

souri VERB ▷ *see* **sourire**

souriant (FEM **souriante**) ADJECTIVE

cheerful

le **sourire** MASC NOUN
▷ *see also* **sourire** VERB

smile

sourire VERB [74]
▷ *see also* **sourire** NOUN

to smile
- □ sourire à quelqu'un to smile at somebody

la **souris** FEM NOUN
▷ *see also* **souris** VERB

mouse

souris, sourit VERB ▷ *see* **sourire**
▷ *see also* **souris** NOUN

sournois (FEM **sournoise**) ADJECTIVE

sly

sous PREPOSITION

under

Numbers in brackets refer to verb tables on pages 650 to 658

- **sous terre** underground
- **sous la pluie** in the rain

sous-entendu (FEM **sous-entendue**)
ADJECTIVE
▷ *see also* **sous-entendu** NOUN
implied

le **sous-entendu** MASC NOUN
▷ *see also* **sous-entendu** ADJECTIVE
insinuation

sous-marin (FEM **sous-marine**) ADJECTIVE
▷ *see also* **sous-marin** NOUN
underwater

le **sous-marin** MASC NOUN
▷ *see also* **sous-marin** ADJECTIVE
submarine

le **sous-sol** MASC NOUN
basement

le **sous-titre** MASC NOUN
subtitle

sous-titré (FEM **sous-titrée**) ADJECTIVE
with subtitles

la **soustraction** FEM NOUN
subtraction

les **sous-vêtements** MASC PL NOUN
underwear *sing*

soutenir VERB [83]
to support
□ Il m'a toujours soutenu contre elle. He's always supported me against her.
- **soutenir que** to maintain that □ Elle soutenait que c'était impossible. She maintained that it was impossible.
- **soutenir l'allure** to keep up □ Il marchait trop vite et je n'arrivais pas à soutenir l'allure. He was walking too fast and I couldn't keep up.

souterrain (FEM **souterraine**) ADJECTIVE
▷ *see also* **souterrain** NOUN
underground

le **souterrain** MASC NOUN
▷ *see also* **souterrain** ADJECTIVE
underground passage

le **soutien** MASC NOUN
support

le **soutien-gorge** (PL les **soutiens-gorge**)
MASC NOUN
bra

le **souvenir** MASC NOUN
▷ *see also* **souvenir** VERB
1 memory
□ garder un bon souvenir de quelque chose to have happy memories of something
2 souvenir
- **Garde ce livre en souvenir de moi.** Keep the book: it'll remind you of me.

se **souvenir** VERB [83]
▷ *see also* **souvenir** NOUN
- **se souvenir de quelque chose** to remember

something □ Je ne me souviens pas de son adresse. I can't remember his address.
- **se souvenir que** □ Je me souviens qu'il neigeait. I remember it was snowing.

souvent ADVERB
often

soyez, soyons VERB ▷ *see* être
- **Soyons clairs !** Let's be clear about this!
- **Soyez prudent.** Be careful.

la **SPA** FEM NOUN (= *Société protectrice des animaux*)
RSPCA

spacieux (FEM **spacieuse**) ADJECTIVE
spacious

les **spaghettis** MASC PL NOUN
spaghetti *sing*

le **sparadrap** MASC NOUN
sticking plaster

le **speaker** MASC NOUN
announcer

la **speakerine** FEM NOUN
announcer

spécial (FEM **spéciale**, MASC PL **spéciaux**)
ADJECTIVE
1 special
□ Qu'est-ce que tu fais ce week-end ? — Rien de spécial. What are you doing this weekend? — Nothing special.
- **les effets spéciaux** special effects
2 peculiar
□ Elle a des goûts un peu spéciaux. She has rather peculiar tastes.

spécialement ADVERB
1 specially
□ Il est venu spécialement pour te parler. He came specially to speak to you.
2 particularly
□ Ce n'est pas spécialement difficile. It's not particularly difficult.

se **spécialiser** VERB [28]
- **se spécialiser dans quelque chose** to specialize in something □ Je me suis spécialisé en histoire contemporaine. I specialized in modern history.

le/la **spécialiste** MASC/FEM NOUN
specialist

la **spécialité** FEM NOUN
speciality

spécifier VERB [19]
to specify

le **spectacle** MASC NOUN
show

spectaculaire (FEM **spectaculaire**) ADJECTIVE
spectacular

le **spectateur** MASC NOUN
1 member of the audience
2 spectator

S

la **spectatrice** FEM NOUN
1 member of the audience
2 spectator

la **spéléologie** FEM NOUN
potholing

spirituel (FEM **spirituelle**) ADJECTIVE
1 spiritual
2 witty

splendide (FEM **splendide**) ADJECTIVE
magnificent

spontané (FEM **spontanée**) ADJECTIVE
spontaneous

le **sport** MASC NOUN
▷ see also **sport** ADJECTIVE
sport
□ faire du sport to do sport
■ les sports d'hiver winter sports

sport (FEM+PL **sport**) ADJECTIVE
▷ see also **sport** NOUN
casual
□ une veste sport a casual jacket

sportif (FEM **sportive**) ADJECTIVE
▷ see also **sportif** NOUN
1 sporty
□ Elle est très sportive. She's very sporty.
2 sports
□ un club sportif a sports club

le **sportif** MASC NOUN
▷ see also **sportif** ADJECTIVE
sportsman

la **sportive** FEM NOUN
sportswoman

le **spot** MASC NOUN
spotlight
■ un spot publicitaire a commercial break

le **square** MASC NOUN
public gardens

le **squelette** MASC NOUN
skeleton

stable (FEM **stable**) ADJECTIVE
stable
■ un emploi stable a steady job

le **stade** MASC NOUN
stadium

le **stage** MASC NOUN
1 training course
□ faire un stage de formation professionnelle
to go on a vocational training course
2 work experience
□ Caroline a fait un stage chez Collins. Caroline
did work experience at Collins.
■ faire un stage en entreprise to do a work
placement

BE CAREFUL!
The French word **stage** does not mean
stage.

le/la **stagiaire** MASC/FEM NOUN
▷ see also **stagiaire** ADJECTIVE
trainee

stagiaire (FEM **stagiaire**) ADJECTIVE
▷ see also **stagiaire** ADJECTIVE
trainee
□ un professeur stagiaire a trainee teacher

le **stand** MASC NOUN
1 stand (at exhibition)
2 stall (at fair)

le/la **standardiste** MASC/FEM NOUN
operator

la **star** FEM NOUN
star
□ une star du football a football star

la **station** FEM NOUN
■ une station de métro an underground station
■ une station de taxis a taxi rank
■ une station de ski a ski resort

le **stationnement** MASC NOUN
parking
■ « stationnement interdit » 'no parking'

stationner VERB [28]
to park

la **station-service** (PL les **stations-service**)
FEM NOUN
service station

la **statistique** FEM NOUN
statistic

le **statut** MASC NOUN
status

le **steak** MASC NOUN
steak
■ un steak frites steak and chips
■ un steak haché a hamburger

la **sténo** FEM NOUN
shorthand
□ un cours de sténo a shorthand course

la **sténodactylo** FEM NOUN
shorthand typist

stérile (FEM **stérile**) ADJECTIVE
sterile

stimulant (FEM **stimulante**) ADJECTIVE
stimulating

stimuler VERB [28]
to stimulate

le **stop** MASC NOUN
stop sign
■ faire du stop to hitchhike

stopper VERB [28]
to stop

le **store** MASC NOUN
1 blind (on window)
2 awning

BE CAREFUL!
The French word **store** does not mean **store**.

la **stratégie** FEM NOUN
strategy

stratégique (FEM **stratégique**) ADJECTIVE
strategic

le **streaming** MASC NOUN
■ **écouter en streaming** to stream (*audio*)
■ **regarder en streaming** to stream (*video*)

stressant (FEM **stressante**) ADJECTIVE
stressful

stressé (FEM **stressée**) ADJECTIVE
stressed out

strict (FEM **stricte**) ADJECTIVE
1 strict (*person*)
□ Ma prof de français est très stricte. My French teacher's very strict.
2 severe (*clothes*)
□ une tenue très stricte a very severe outfit
■ **le strict minimum** the bare minimum

la **strophe** FEM NOUN
stanza

studieux (FEM **studieuse**) ADJECTIVE
studious

le **studio** MASC NOUN
1 studio flat
2 studio
□ un studio de télévision a television studio

stupéfait (FEM **stupéfaite**) ADJECTIVE
astonished

les **stupéfiants** MASC PL NOUN
narcotics

stupéfier VERB [19]
to astonish
□ Sa réponse m'a stupéfié. I was astonished by his answer.

stupide (FEM **stupide**) ADJECTIVE
stupid

le **style** MASC NOUN
style

le/la **styliste** MASC/FEM NOUN
designer

le **stylo** MASC NOUN
pen
■ **un stylo plume** a fountain pen
■ **un stylo bille** a ballpoint pen
■ **un stylo-feutre** a felt-tip pen

su VERB ▷ see **savoir**
■ **Si j'avais su ...** If I'd known ...

subir VERB [38]
to suffer (*defeat*)
■ **subir une opération** to have an operation

subit (FEM **subite**) ADJECTIVE
sudden

subitement ADVERB
suddenly

subjectif (FEM **subjective**) ADJECTIVE
subjective

le **subjonctif** MASC NOUN
subjunctive

substituer VERB [28]
to substitute
□ substituer un mot à un autre to substitute one word for another

subtil (FEM **subtile**) ADJECTIVE
subtle

la **subvention** FEM NOUN
subsidy

subventionner VERB [28]
to subsidize

le **succès** MASC NOUN
success
■ **avoir du succès** to be successful

le **successeur** MASC NOUN
successor

la **succursale** FEM NOUN
branch (*of company*)

sucer VERB [12]
to suck

la **sucette** FEM NOUN
lollipop

le **sucre** MASC NOUN
sugar
■ **un sucre** a sugar lump □ Je prends deux sucres dans mon café. I take two lumps of sugar in my coffee.
■ **du sucre en morceaux** lump sugar
■ **un sucre d'orge** a barley sugar
■ **du sucre en poudre** caster sugar
■ **du sucre glace** icing sugar

sucré (FEM **sucrée**) ADJECTIVE
1 sweet
□ Ce gâteau est un peu trop sucré. This cake is a bit too sweet.
2 sweetened
□ du lait concentré sucré sweetened condensed milk

les **sucreries** FEM PL NOUN
sweet things

le **sucrier** MASC NOUN
sugar bowl

le **sud** MASC NOUN
▷ see also **sud** ADJECTIVE
south
□ Ils vivent dans le sud de la France. They live in the South of France.
■ **vers le sud** southwards
■ **au sud de Paris** south of Paris
■ **l'Amérique du Sud** South America
■ **le vent du sud** the south wind

sud (FEM+PL **sud**) ADJECTIVE
▷ see also **sud** NOUN
1 south
□ la côte sud de l'Espagne the south coast of Spain
■ **le pôle Sud** the South Pole

2 southern

□ Nous avons visité la partie sud du pays. We visited the southern part of the country.

sud-africain (FEM **sud-africaine**)

ADJECTIVE

South African

sud-américain (FEM **sud-américaine**)

ADJECTIVE

South American

le **sud-est** MASC NOUN

south-east

□ au sud-est in the south-east

le **sud-ouest** MASC NOUN

south-west

□ au sud-ouest in the south-west

la **Suède** FEM NOUN

Sweden

suédois (FEM **suédoise**) ADJECTIVE, NOUN

Swedish

□ Ils parlent suédois. They speak Swedish.

■ **un Suédois** a Swede (*man*)
■ **une Suédoise** a Swede (*woman*)
■ **les Suédois** the Swedes

suer VERB [28]

to sweat

la **sueur** FEM NOUN

sweat

■ **en sueur** sweating

suffire VERB [80]

to be enough

□ Tiens, voilà dix euros. Ça te suffit ? Here's 10 euros. Is that enough for you?

■ **Ça suffit !** That's enough!

suffisamment ADVERB

enough

□ Ça n'est pas suffisamment grand. It's not big enough. □ Il n'y a pas suffisamment de chaises. There aren't enough chairs.

suffisant (FEM **suffisante**) ADJECTIVE

1 sufficient

□ Ça n'est pas une raison suffisante. That's not sufficient reason.

2 smug

□ Il est un peu trop suffisant. He's rather smug.

suffoquer VERB [28]

to suffocate

suggérer VERB [34]

to suggest

se **suicider** VERB [28]

to commit suicide

suis VERB ▷ *see* **être**, **suivre**

■ **Je suis écossais.** I'm Scottish.
■ **Suis-moi.** Follow me.

la **Suisse** FEM NOUN

▷ *see also* **suisse** ADJECTIVE, NOUN

Switzerland

□ la Suisse allemande German-speaking

Switzerland □ la Suisse romande French-speaking Switzerland

suisse (FEM **suisse**) ADJECTIVE, NOUN

▷ *see also* **Suisse** NOUN

Swiss

□ le franc suisse the Swiss franc

■ **un Suisse** a Swiss man
■ **une Suisse** a Swiss woman
■ **les Suisses** the Swiss

suit VERB ▷ *see* **suivre**

la **suite** FEM NOUN

1 rest

□ Je vous raconterai la suite de l'histoire demain. I'll tell you the rest of the story tomorrow.

2 sequel (*to book, film*)

■ **tout de suite** straightaway □ J'y vais tout de suite. I'll go straightaway.

■ **de suite** in succession □ Il a commis la même erreur trois fois de suite. He made the same mistake three times in succession.

■ **par la suite** subsequently □ Il s'est avéré par la suite qu'il était coupable. He subsequently turned out to be guilty.

suivant (FEM **suivante**) ADJECTIVE

following

□ le jour suivant the following day □ l'exercice suivant the following exercise

■ **Au suivant !** Next!

suivi VERB ▷ *see* **suivre**

suivre VERB [81]

1 to follow

□ Il m'a suivie jusque chez moi. He followed me home. □ Vous me suivez ou est-ce que je parle trop vite ? Are you following me or am I speaking too fast?

2 to do

□ Je suis un cours d'anglais à la fac. I'm doing an English course at college.

3 to keep up

□ Il n'arrive pas à suivre en maths. He can't keep up in maths. □ J'aime suivre l'actualité. I like to keep up with the news.

■ **« à suivre »** 'to be continued'
■ **suivre un régime** to be on a diet

le **sujet** MASC NOUN

▷ *see also* **sujet** ADJECTIVE

subject

■ **au sujet de** about □ C'est à quel sujet ? — C'est au sujet de l'annonce parue dans « Le Monde » d'aujourd'hui. What's it about? — It's about the advertisement in today's 'Le Monde'.

■ **un sujet de conversation** a topic of conversation

■ **un sujet d'examen** an examination question

■ **un sujet de plaisanterie** something to joke about

sujet (FEM **sujette**) ADJECTIVE

▷ *see also* **sujet** NOUN

■ **être sujet à** to be prone to □ Il est sujet à des crises de panique. He is prone to panic attacks.

super (FEM+PL **super**) ADJECTIVE
▷ *see also* **super** NOUN
great

le **super** MASC NOUN
▷ *see also* **super** ADJECTIVE
super (*petrol*)

superficiel (FEM **superficielle**) ADJECTIVE
superficial

superflu (FEM **superflue**) ADJECTIVE
superfluous

supérieur (FEM **supérieure**) ADJECTIVE
▷ *see also* **supérieur** NOUN

1 upper
□ la lèvre supérieure the upper lip

2 superior
□ qualité supérieure superior quality □ Il a toujours l'air tellement supérieur ! He always looks so superior!
■ **supérieur à** greater than □ Choisissez un nombre supérieur à cent. Choose a number greater than 100.

le **supérieur** MASC NOUN
▷ *see also* **supérieur** ADJECTIVE
superior
□ mon supérieur hiérarchique my immediate superior

la **supérieure** FEM NOUN
▷ *see also* **supérieur** ADJECTIVE
superior

le **supermarché** MASC NOUN
supermarket

superposé (FEM **superposée**) ADJECTIVE
■ **des lits superposés** bunk beds

superstitieux (FEM **superstitieuse**)
ADJECTIVE
superstitious

le **supplément** MASC NOUN
■ **payer un supplément** to pay an additional charge
■ **Le vin est en supplément.** Wine is extra.
■ **un supplément de travail** extra work

supplémentaire (FEM **supplémentaire**)
ADJECTIVE
additional
□ Voici quelques exercices supplémentaires. Here are some additional exercises.
■ **faire des heures supplémentaires** to do overtime

le **supplice** MASC NOUN
torture
□ C'était un supplice. It was torture.

supplier VERB [19]
■ **supplier quelqu'un de faire quelque chose** to beg somebody to do something □ Je t'en supplie ! I'm begging you!

supportable (FEM **supportable**) ADJECTIVE
bearable

supporter VERB [28]
to stand (*tolerate*)
□ Je ne supporte pas l'hypocrisie. I can't stand hypocrisy. □ Elle ne supporte pas qu'on la critique. She can't stand being criticized. □ Je ne peux pas la supporter. I can't stand her. □ Je supporte mal la chaleur. I can't stand hot weather.

> **BE CAREFUL!**
> **supporter** does not mean **to support**.

supposer VERB [28]
to suppose

supprimer VERB [28]

1 to cut
□ Deux mille emplois ont été supprimés. Two thousand jobs have been cut.

2 to cancel
□ Le train de Londres a été supprimé. The train to London has been cancelled.

3 to get rid of
□ Ils ont supprimé les témoins gênants. They got rid of the awkward witnesses.

sur PREPOSITION

1 on
□ Pose-le sur la table. Put it down on the table. □ Vous verrez l'hôpital sur votre droite. You'll see the hospital on your right. □ une conférence sur Balzac a lecture on Balzac

2 in
□ une personne sur dix 1 person in 10

3 out of
□ J'ai eu onze sur vingt en maths. I got 11 out of 20 in maths.

4 by
□ quatre mètres sur deux 4 metres by 2

sûr (FEM **sûre**) ADJECTIVE

1 sure
□ Tu es sûr ? Are you sure?
■ **sûr et certain** absolutely certain

2 reliable
□ C'est quelqu'un de très sûr. He's a very reliable person.

3 safe
□ Ce quartier n'est pas très sûr la nuit. This neighbourhood isn't very safe at night.
■ **sûr de soi** self-confident □ Elle est très sûre d'elle. She's very self-confident.

sûrement ADVERB
certainly
□ Sûrement pas ! Certainly not! □ Il est sûrement déjà parti. He'll certainly already have left.

la **sûreté** FEM NOUN
■ **mettre quelque chose en sûreté** to put something in a safe place

S

le **surf** MASC NOUN
surfing

la **surface** FEM NOUN
surface
■ **les grandes surfaces** the supermarkets

surfer VERB [28]
to go surfing
■ **surfer sur le Net** to surf the Net

surgelé (FEM **surgelée**) ADJECTIVE
frozen
□ des frites surgelées frozen chips

les **surgelés** MASC PL NOUN
frozen food *sing*

surhumain (FEM **surhumaine**) ADJECTIVE
superhuman

sur-le-champ ADVERB
immediately

le **surlendemain** MASC NOUN
■ **le surlendemain de son arrivée** two days
after he arrived
■ **le surlendemain dans la matinée** two days
later, in the morning

se **surmener** VERB [43]
to work too hard
□ Ne te surmène pas trop pendant le week-end.
Don't work too hard over the weekend.

surmonter VERB [48]
to overcome
□ Il nous reste de nombreux obstacles à
surmonter. We still have many obstacles to
overcome.

surnaturel (FEM **surnaturelle**) ADJECTIVE
supernatural

le **surnom** MASC NOUN
nickname

surnommer VERB [28]
to nickname
□ On l'a surnommé « Kiki ». We nicknamed
him 'Kiki'.

surpeuplé (FEM **surpeuplée**) ADJECTIVE
overpopulated

surprenant (FEM **surprenante**) ADJECTIVE
surprising

surprendre VERB [65]
to surprise
□ Ça me surprendrait beaucoup qu'il arrive à
l'heure. I'd be very surprised if he arrived on
time.
■ **surprendre quelqu'un en train de faire
quelque chose** to catch somebody doing
something □ Je l'ai surpris en train de fouiller
dans mon placard. I caught him rummaging in
my cupboard.

surpris (FEM **surprise**) ADJECTIVE
▷ *see also* **surprise** NOUN
surprised

□ Il était surpris de me voir. He was surprised
to see me.

la **surprise** FEM NOUN
▷ *see also* **surpris** ADJECTIVE
surprise
□ faire une surprise à quelqu'un to give
somebody a surprise

sursauter VERB [28]
to jump
□ J'ai sursauté en entendant mon nom. I jumped
when I heard my name.

surtout ADVERB
1 especially
□ Il est assez timide, surtout avec les filles. He's
rather shy, especially with girls.
2 crucially
□ Ce canapé est joli et surtout, il n'est pas
salissant. This sofa is pretty and, crucially, it
doesn't show the dirt.
■ **Surtout, ne répète pas ce que je t'ai dit !**
Whatever you do, don't repeat what I told you!

le **surveillant** MASC NOUN
supervisor (*man*)

> **DID YOU KNOW...?**
> In French secondary schools, the teachers
> are not responsible for supervising the pupils
> outside class. This job is done by people
> called **surveillants** or **pions**.

la **surveillante** FEM NOUN
supervisor (*woman*)

surveiller VERB [28]
1 to keep an eye on
□ Tu peux surveiller mes bagages ? Can you keep
an eye on my luggage?
2 to keep a watch on
■ **La police a surveillé la maison pendant
une semaine.** The police kept the house under
surveillance for a week.
3 to supervise
□ Nous sommes toujours surveillés pendant
la récréation. We're always supervised during
break.
■ **surveiller un examen** to invigilate an exam
■ **surveiller sa ligne** to watch one's figure

le **survêtement** MASC NOUN
tracksuit
□ un haut de survêtement a tracksuit top □ un
pantalon de survêtement tracksuit bottoms

la **survie** FEM NOUN
survival

le **survivant** MASC NOUN
survivor

la **survivante** FEM NOUN
survivor

survivre VERB [91]
to survive
□ survivre à un accident to survive an accident

survoler VERB [28]
to fly over

sus ADVERB
- **en sus** in addition

susceptible (FEM **susceptible**) ADJECTIVE
touchy

suspect (FEM **suspecte**) ADJECTIVE
suspicious
□ dans des circonstances suspectes under suspicious circumstances

suspecter VERB [28]
to suspect

le **suspense** MASC NOUN
suspense
- **un film à suspense** a thriller

la **suture** FEM NOUN
- **un point de suture** a stitch

svelte (FEM **svelte**) ADJECTIVE
slender

SVP ABBREVIATION (= *s'il vous plaît*)
please

le **sweat** MASC NOUN
sweatshirt

la **syllabe** FEM NOUN
syllable

le **symbole** MASC NOUN
symbol

symbolique (FEM **symbolique**) ADJECTIVE
symbolic

symboliser VERB [28]
to symbolize

symétrique (FEM **symétrique**) ADJECTIVE
symmetrical

sympa (FEM+PL **sympa**) ADJECTIVE (*informal*)
nice
□ Elle est très sympa. She's a really nice person.

la **sympathie** FEM NOUN
- **J'ai beaucoup de sympathie pour lui.** I like him a lot.

sympathique (FEM **sympathique**) ADJECTIVE
nice
□ Ce sont des gens très sympathiques. They're very nice people.

> **BE CAREFUL!**
> **sympathique** does not mean **sympathetic**.

sympathiser VERB [28]
to get on well
□ Nous avons immédiatement sympathisé avec nos voisins. We got on well with our neighbours straight away.

le **symptôme** MASC NOUN
symptom

la **synagogue** FEM NOUN
synagogue

le **syndicat** MASC NOUN
trade union
- **le syndicat d'initiative** the tourist information office

synonyme (FEM **synonyme**) ADJECTIVE
▷ see also **synonyme** NOUN
synonymous
□ être synonyme de to be synonymous with

le **synonyme** MASC NOUN
▷ see also **synonyme** ADJECTIVE
synonym

synthétique (FEM **synthétique**) ADJECTIVE
synthetic

la **Syrie** FEM NOUN
Syria

syrien (FEM **syrienne**) ADJECTIVE, NOUN
Syrian

systématique (FEM **systématique**)
ADJECTIVE
systematic

le **système** MASC NOUN
system

S

Tt

t' PRONOUN ▷ *see* **te**

ta FEM ADJECTIVE
your
□ J'ai vu ta sœur hier. I saw your sister yesterday.

le tabac MASC NOUN
1 tobacco
□ le tabac blond light tobacco □ le tabac brun dark tobacco
2 smoking
□ Le tabac est mauvais pour la santé. Smoking is bad for you.

la table FEM NOUN
table
■ **mettre la table** to lay the table
■ **se mettre à table** to sit down to eat
■ **À table !** Dinner's ready!
■ **une table de nuit** a bedside table
■ **« table des matières »** 'contents'

le tableau (PL les **tableaux**) MASC NOUN
painting
□ un tableau de Monet a painting by Monet
■ **le tableau d'affichage** the notice board
■ **le tableau noir** the blackboard

la tablette FEM NOUN
tablet (*computer*)
■ **une tablette de chocolat** a bar of chocolate

le tableur MASC NOUN
spreadsheet

le tablier MASC NOUN
apron

le tabouret MASC NOUN
stool

la tache FEM NOUN
mark (*stain*)
■ **des taches de rousseur** freckles

la tâche FEM NOUN
task

tacher VERB [28]
to leave a stain

tâcher VERB [28]
■ **tâcher de faire quelque chose** to try to do something □ Tâche d'être à l'heure ! Try to be on time!

le tact MASC NOUN
tact
■ **avoir du tact** to be tactful

tactile ADJECTIVE
■ **un écran tactile** a touchscreen

la tactique FEM NOUN
tactics
■ **changer de tactique** to try something different

la taie FEM NOUN
■ **une taie d'oreiller** a pillowcase

la taille FEM NOUN
1 waist
□ Elle a la taille fine. She has a slim waist.
2 height
□ un homme de taille moyenne a man of average height
3 size
□ Avez-vous ma taille ? Have you got my size?

le taille-crayon MASC NOUN
pencil sharpener

le tailleur MASC NOUN
1 tailor
2 suit (*lady's*)
■ **Il est assis en tailleur.** He's sitting cross-legged.

se taire VERB [82]
to stop talking
■ **Taisez-vous !** Be quiet!

le talon MASC NOUN
heel

le tambour MASC NOUN
drum

la Tamise FEM NOUN
Thames

le tampon MASC NOUN
pad
□ un tampon à récurer a scouring pad
■ **un tampon hygiénique** a tampon

tamponneuse FEM ADJECTIVE
■ **les autos tamponneuses** dodgems

tandis que CONJUNCTION
while
□ Il a toujours de bonnes notes, tandis que les miennes sont mauvaises. He always gets good marks, while mine are poor.

tant ADVERB
so much
□ Je l'aime tant ! I love him so much!

■ **tant de 1** so much □ tant de nourriture so much food **2** so many □ tant de livres so many books

■ **tant que 1** until □ Tu ne sortiras pas tant que tu n'auras pas fini tes devoirs. You're not going out until you've finished your homework. **2** while □ Profites-en tant que tu peux. Make the most of it while you can.

■ **tant mieux** so much the better

■ **tant pis** never mind

la **tante** FEM NOUN
aunt

tantôt ADVERB
sometimes
□ Nous venons tantôt à pied, tantôt en bus. Sometimes we walk, sometimes we come by bus.

le **tapage** MASC NOUN
1 racket
□ Ils ont fait du tapage toute la nuit. They made a racket all night long.
2 fuss
□ On a fait beaucoup de tapage autour de cette affaire. There was a lot of fuss about that business.

taper VERB [28]
to beat down
□ Le soleil tape. The sun's really beating down.
■ **taper quelqu'un** to hit somebody □ Maman, il m'a tapé ! Mum, he hit me!
■ **taper sur quelque chose** to bang on something
■ **taper des pieds** to stamp one's feet
■ **taper des mains** to clap one's hands
■ **taper à l'ordinateur** to type □ Tu sais taper à l'ordinateur ? Can you type? □ Je vais taper cette lettre. I'm going to type this letter.

le **tapis** MASC NOUN
carpet
■ **le tapis roulant 1** (for people) the Travelator® **2** (in factory) the conveyor belt **3** (at baggage reclaim) the carousel

tapisser VERB [28]
to paper

la **tapisserie** FEM NOUN
1 wallpaper
□ Tu aimes la tapisserie de ma chambre ? Do you like the wallpaper in my bedroom?
2 tapestry

taquiner VERB [28]
to tease

tard ADVERB
late
□ Il est tard. It's late.
■ **plus tard** later on
■ **au plus tard** at the latest

tardif (FEM **tardive**) ADJECTIVE
late
□ un petit déjeuner tardif a late breakfast

le **tarif** MASC NOUN
■ **le tarif des consommations** (in café) the price list
■ **une communication à tarif réduit** an off-peak phone call
■ **un billet de train à tarif réduit** a concessionary train ticket
■ **un billet de train à plein tarif** a full-price train ticket
■ **Est-ce que vous faites un tarif de groupe ?** Is there a reduction for groups?

la **tarte** FEM NOUN
tart

la **tartine** FEM NOUN
slice of bread
□ une tartine de confiture a slice of bread and jam

tartiner VERB [28]
to spread
■ **le fromage à tartiner** cheese spread

le **tas** MASC NOUN
heap
□ un tas de charbon a heap of coal
■ **un tas de** (informal) loads of □ J'ai lu un tas de livres pendant les vacances. I read loads of books in the holidays.

la **tasse** FEM NOUN
cup

le **tatouage** MASC NOUN
tattoo

le **taureau** (PL les **taureaux**) MASC NOUN
bull
■ **le Taureau** Taurus □ Ils sont tous les deux Taureau. They're both Taurus.

le **taux** MASC NOUN
rate
□ le taux de change the exchange rate

la **taxe** FEM NOUN
tax
■ **la boutique hors taxes** the duty-free shop

le **taxi** MASC NOUN
taxi

tchater, tchatter VERB [28]
to chat (on the internet)
to talk online

tchèque (FEM **tchèque**) ADJECTIVE, NOUN
Czech
■ **la République tchèque** the Czech Republic
■ **un Tchèque** a Czech (man)
■ **une Tchèque** a Czech (woman)
■ **les Tchèques** the Czechs

le **TDAH** MASC NOUN (= trouble du déficit de l'attention avec hyperactivité)
ADHD

t

te PRONOUN

> te changes to t' before a vowel and most words beginning with 'h'.

1 you
□ Je te vois. I can see you. □ Il t'a vu ? Did he see you?

2 to you
□ Est-ce qu'il te parle en français ? Does he talk to you in French? □ Elle t'a parlé ? Did she speak to you?

3 yourself
□ Tu vas te rendre malade. You'll make yourself sick.

> With reflexive verbs, te is often not translated.

□ Comment tu t'appelles ? What's your name?

le **technicien** MASC NOUN
technician

la **technicienne** FEM NOUN
technician

technique (FEM **technique**) ADJECTIVE
▷ see also **technique** NOUN
technical

la **technique** FEM NOUN
▷ see also **technique** ADJECTIVE
technique

la **techno** FEM NOUN
techno music

la **technologie** FEM NOUN
technology

le **teint** MASC NOUN
complexion
□ Elle a le teint clair. She's got a fair complexion.

la **teinte** FEM NOUN
shade (colour)

le **teinturier** MASC NOUN
dry cleaner's
□ Je vais porter ce manteau chez le teinturier. I'm going to take this coat to the dry cleaner's.

tel (FEM **telle**) ADJECTIVE
■ Il a un tel enthousiasme ! He's got such enthusiasm!
■ rien de tel nothing like □ Il n'y a rien de tel qu'une bonne nuit de sommeil. There's nothing like a good night's sleep.
■ J'ai tout laissé tel quel. I left everything as it was.
■ tel que such as

la **télé** FEM NOUN
telly
□ à la télé on telly

le **téléchargement** MASC NOUN
download

télécharger VERB [45]
1 to download (receive)
2 to upload (send)

la **télécommande** FEM NOUN
remote control

la **téléconférence** FEM NOUN
video conference

la **télécopie** FEM NOUN
fax

le **télégramme** MASC NOUN
telegram

le **télépéage** MASC NOUN
motorway toll payment system

> **DID YOU KNOW...?**
> Certain lanes at motorway tolls are reserved for drivers who have a sensor inside their car which allows them to pay monthly rather than on the spot. These lanes are marked with a yellow T and should be avoided by tourists.

le **téléphérique** MASC NOUN
cable car

le **téléphone** MASC NOUN
telephone
□ Elle est au téléphone. She's on the phone.
■ un téléphone portable a mobile phone

téléphoner VERB [28]
to phone
□ Je vais téléphoner à Claire. I'll phone Claire.
□ Je peux téléphoner ? Can I make a phone call?

la **téléréalité** FEM NOUN
reality TV

le **télésiège** MASC NOUN
chairlift

le **téléski** MASC NOUN
ski-tow

le **téléspectateur** MASC NOUN
viewer (TV)

la **téléspectatrice** FEM NOUN
viewer (TV)

le **télétravail** MASC NOUN
remote working

le **téléviseur** MASC NOUN
television set

la **télévision** FEM NOUN
television
□ à la télévision on television
■ la télévision numérique digital TV

telle FEM ADJECTIVE
▷ see also **tel**
■ Je n'ai jamais eu une telle peur. I've never had such a fright.
■ telle que such as

tellement ADVERB
1 so
□ Benjamin est tellement gentil. Benjamin's so nice. □ Il travaille tellement. He works so hard.
2 so much
□ Il a tellement mangé que ... He ate so much that ...

3 so many

□ Il y avait tellement de monde. **There were so many people.**

telles FEM PL ADJECTIVE

such

□ Je n'ai jamais entendu de telles bêtises ! **I've never heard such nonsense!**

tels MASC PL ADJECTIVE

such

□ Nous n'avons pas de tels orages chez nous. **We don't have such storms back home.**

le **témoignage** MASC NOUN

testimony

témoigner VERB [28]

to testify

le **témoin** MASC NOUN

witness

la **température** FEM NOUN

temperature

□ avoir de la température **to have a temperature**

la **tempête** FEM NOUN

storm

le **temple** MASC NOUN

1 church (*Protestant*)

2 temple (*Hindu, Sikh, Buddhist*)

temporaire (FEM **temporaire**) ADJECTIVE

temporary

le **temps** MASC NOUN

1 weather

□ Quel temps fait-il ? **What's the weather like?**

2 time

□ Je n'ai pas le temps. **I haven't got time.**
□ Prends ton temps. **Take your time.** □ Il est temps de partir. **It's time to go.**

- **juste à temps** just in time
- **de temps en temps** from time to time
- **en même temps** at the same time
- **à temps** in time □ Il est arrivé à temps pour le match. **He arrived in time for the match.**
- **à plein temps** full time □ Elle travaille à plein temps. **She works full time.**
- **à temps complet** full time
- **à temps partiel** part time □ le travail à temps partiel part-time work
- **dans le temps** at one time □ Dans le temps, on pouvait circuler en vélo sans danger. **At one time, it was safe to go around by bike.**

3 tense (*of verb*)

tenais, tenait VERB ▷ *see* tenir

la **tendance** FEM NOUN

- **avoir tendance à faire quelque chose** to tend to do something □ Il a tendance à exagérer. **He tends to exaggerate.**

tendre (FEM **tendre**) ADJECTIVE

▷ *see also* **tendre** VERB

tender

tendre VERB [88]

▷ *see also* **tendre** ADJECTIVE

to stretch out

□ Ils ont tendu une corde entre deux arbres. **They stretched out a rope between two trees.**

- **tendre quelque chose à quelqu'un** to hold something out to somebody □ Il lui a tendu les clés. **He held out the keys to her.**
- **tendre la main** to hold out one's hand
- **tendre le bras** to reach out
- **tendre un piège à quelqu'un** to set a trap for someone

tendrement ADVERB

tenderly

la **tendresse** FEM NOUN

tenderness

tendu (FEM **tendue**) ADJECTIVE

tense

□ Il était très tendu aujourd'hui. **He was very tense today.**

tenir VERB [83]

to hold

□ Tu peux tenir la lampe, s'il te plaît ? **Can you hold the torch, please?** □ Il tenait un enfant par la main. **He was holding a child by the hand.**

- **Tenez votre chien en laisse.** Keep your dog on the lead.
- **tenir à quelqu'un** to be attached to somebody □ Il tient beaucoup à elle. **He's very attached to her.**
- **tenir à faire quelque chose** to be determined to do something □ Elle tient à y aller. **She's determined to go.**
- **tenir de quelqu'un** to take after somebody □ Il tient de son père. **He takes after his father.**
- **Tiens, voilà un stylo.** Here's a pen.
- **Tiens, c'est Corentin là-bas !** Look, that's Corentin over there!
- **Tiens ?** Really?
- **se tenir 1** to stand □ Il se tenait près de la porte. **He was standing by the door. 2** to be held □ La foire va se tenir place du marché. **The fair will be held in the market place.**
- **se tenir droit 1** to stand up straight □ Tiens-toi droit ! **Stand up straight! 2** to sit up straight □ Arrête de manger le nez dans ton assiette, tiens-toi droit. **Don't slouch while you're eating, sit up straight.**
- **Tiens-toi bien !** Behave yourself!

le **tennis** MASC NOUN

1 tennis

□ Elle joue au tennis. **She plays tennis.**

- **le tennis de table** table tennis

2 tennis court

□ Il est au tennis. **He's at the tennis court.**

- **les tennis** trainers

tentant (FEM **tentante**) ADJECTIVE

tempting

t

la **tentation** FEM NOUN
temptation

la **tentative** FEM NOUN
attempt

la **tente** FEM NOUN
tent

tenter VERB [28]
to tempt
□ J'ai été tenté de tout abandonner. I was tempted to give up. □ Ça ne me tente vraiment pas d'aller à la piscine. I really don't fancy going to the swimming pool.
■ **tenter de faire quelque chose** to try to do something □ Il a tenté plusieurs fois de s'évader. He tried several times to escape.

tenu VERB ▷ see tenir

la **tenue** FEM NOUN
clothes
■ **en tenue de soirée** in evening dress

le **terme** MASC NOUN
■ **à court terme** short-term
■ **à long terme** long-term

la **terminale** FEM NOUN
upper sixth
□ Je suis en terminale. I'm in the upper sixth.

> **DID YOU KNOW...?**
> In French secondary schools, years are counted from the **sixième** (youngest) to **première** and **terminale** (oldest).

terminer VERB [28]
to finish
■ **terminer de faire** to finish doing □ Je dois terminer d'écrire ma dissertation. I have to finish writing my essay.
■ **se terminer** to end □ Les vacances se terminent demain. The holidays end tomorrow.

le **terminus** MASC NOUN
terminus

le **terrain** MASC NOUN
land
□ Il veut acheter un terrain en Normandie. He wants to buy some land in Normandy.
■ **un terrain de camping** a campsite
■ **un terrain de football** a football pitch
■ **un terrain de golf** a golf course
■ **un terrain de jeu** a playground
■ **un terrain de sport** a sports ground
■ **un terrain vague** a piece of waste ground

la **terrasse** FEM NOUN
terrace
■ **Si on s'asseyait en terrasse ?** (at café) Shall we sit outside?

la **terre** FEM NOUN
earth
■ **la Terre** the Earth
■ **Elle s'est assise par terre.** She sat on the floor.
■ **Il est tombé par terre.** He fell down.
■ **la terre cuite** terracotta □ un pot en terre cuite a terracotta pot
■ **la terre glaise** clay

terrible (FEM **terrible**) ADJECTIVE
terrible
□ Quelque chose de terrible est arrivé. Something terrible has happened.
■ **pas terrible** (informal) nothing special □ Ce film n'est pas terrible. The film's nothing special.

la **terrine** FEM NOUN
pâté

le **territoire** MASC NOUN
territory

terrorisé (FEM **terrorisée**) ADJECTIVE
terrified

le **terrorisme** MASC NOUN
terrorism

le/la **terroriste** MASC/FEM NOUN
terrorist

tes PL ADJECTIVE
your
□ J'aime bien tes baskets. I like your trainers.

le **test** MASC NOUN
test

le **testament** MASC NOUN
will
□ Il est mort sans testament. He died without leaving a will.

tester VERB [28]
to test

le **tétanos** MASC NOUN
tetanus

le **têtard** MASC NOUN
tadpole

la **tête** FEM NOUN
head
□ de la tête aux pieds from head to foot
■ **se laver la tête** to wash one's hair
■ **la tête la première** headfirst
■ **tenir tête à quelqu'un** to stand up to somebody
■ **faire la tête** to sulk
■ **en avoir par-dessus la tête** to be fed up

têtu (FEM **têtue**) ADJECTIVE
stubborn

le **texte** MASC NOUN
text (written work)

le **Texto**® MASC NOUN
text message

le **TGV** MASC NOUN (= train à grande vitesse)
high-speed train

le **thé** MASC NOUN
tea
□ Je vous offre un thé ? Would you like a cup of tea? □ un thé au lait a white tea

le **théâtre** MASC NOUN
theatre
■ **faire du théâtre** to act □ Est-ce que tu as déjà fait du théâtre ? Have you ever acted?

la **théière** FEM NOUN
teapot

le **thème** MASC NOUN
1 subject
□ Quel est le thème de l'émission ? What's the programme about?
2 prose (*translation into the foreign language*)

la **théorie** FEM NOUN
theory

le **thermomètre** MASC NOUN
thermometer

le **thon** MASC NOUN
tuna

la **thune** FEM NOUN (*informal*)
dosh

le **tibia** MASC NOUN
1 shinbone
□ une fracture du tibia a broken shinbone
2 shin
□ Il m'a donné un coup de pied dans le tibia. He kicked me in the shin.

les **TIC** FEM PL NOUN (= *technologies de l'information et de la communication*)
ICT *sing*

le **tic** MASC NOUN
nervous twitch

le **ticket** MASC NOUN
ticket
□ un ticket de métro an underground ticket
■ **le ticket de caisse** the till receipt

tiède (FEM **tiède**) ADJECTIVE
1 warm (*water, air*)
2 lukewarm (*food, drink*)

tien MASC PRONOUN
■ **le tien** yours □ J'ai oublié mon stylo. Tu peux me prêter le tien ? I've forgotten my pen. Can you lend me yours?

tienne FEM PRONOUN
■ **la tienne** yours □ Ce n'est pas ma raquette, c'est la tienne. It's not my racket, it's yours.
■ **À la tienne !** Cheers!

tiennes FEM PL PRONOUN
■ **les tiennes** yours □ J'ai pris mes baskets, mais j'ai oublié les tiennes. I've brought my trainers, but I've forgotten yours.

tiens MASC PL PRONOUN
■ **les tiens** yours □ Je ne trouve pas mes feutres. Je peux utiliser les tiens ? I can't find my felt pens. Can I use yours?

tiens, tient VERB ▷ *see* tenir

le **tiers** MASC NOUN
third

□ Un tiers de la classe était pour. A third of the class were in favour.
■ **le tiers-monde** the Third World

la **tige** FEM NOUN
stem

le **tigre** MASC NOUN
tiger

le **tilleul** MASC NOUN
lime tea

le **timbre** MASC NOUN
stamp

le **timbre-poste** MASC NOUN
postage stamp

timide (FEM **timide**) ADJECTIVE
shy

timidement ADVERB
shyly

la **timidité** FEM NOUN
shyness

le **tir** MASC NOUN
shooting
■ **le tir à l'arc** archery

le **tirage** MASC NOUN
■ **par tirage au sort** by drawing lots □ Les prix seront attribués par tirage au sort. The prizes will be awarded by drawing lots.

le **tire-bouchon** MASC NOUN
corkscrew

la **tirelire** FEM NOUN
money box

tirer VERB [28]
1 to pull
□ Elle a tiré un mouchoir de son sac. She pulled a handkerchief out of her bag. □ Il m'a tiré les cheveux. He pulled my hair. □ « Tirer » 'Pull'
2 to draw
□ tirer les rideaux to draw the curtains □ tirer un trait to draw a line □ tirer des conclusions to draw conclusions
■ **tirer au sort** to draw lots
3 to fire
□ Il a tiré plusieurs coups de feu. He fired several shots. □ Il a tiré sur les policiers. He fired at the police.
■ **Tu t'en tires bien.** You're doing well.

le **tiret** MASC NOUN
dash (*hyphen*)
■ **tiret du 8** underscore
■ **tiret du 6** dash

le **tiroir** MASC NOUN
drawer

la **tisane** FEM NOUN
herbal tea

tisser VERB [28]
to weave

t

le **tissu** MASC NOUN
material
■ **un sac en tissu** a cloth bag

le **titre** MASC NOUN
title
■ **les gros titres** the headlines
■ **un titre de transport** a travel ticket

tituber VERB [28]
to stagger

la **TNT** FEM NOUN (= *télévision numérique terrestre*)
digital television

le **toast** MASC NOUN
1 piece of toast
2 toast
  □ porter un toast à quelqu'un to drink a toast to somebody

le **toboggan** MASC NOUN
slide

toi PRONOUN
you
  □ Ça va ? — Oui, et toi ? How are you? — Fine, and you? □ J'ai faim, pas toi ? I'm hungry, aren't you?
■ **Assieds-toi.** Sit down.
■ **à toi** yours □ Est-ce que ce stylo est à toi ? Is this pen yours?
■ **C'est à toi de jouer.** It's your turn to play.

la **toile** FEM NOUN
■ **un pantalon de toile** cotton trousers
■ **un sac de toile** a canvas bag
■ **une toile cirée** an oilcloth
■ **une toile d'araignée** a cobweb
■ **la Toile** the internet

la **toilette** FEM NOUN
1 wash
  □ faire sa toilette to have a wash
2 outfit
  □ une toilette élégante an elegant outfit

les **toilettes** FEM PL NOUN
toilet *sing*

toi-même PRONOUN
yourself
  □ Tu as fait ça toi-même ? Did you do it yourself?

le **toit** MASC NOUN
roof
■ **un toit ouvrant** a sunroof

tolérant (FEM **tolérante**) ADJECTIVE
tolerant

tolérer VERB [34]
to tolerate

la **tomate** FEM NOUN
tomato

la **tombe** FEM NOUN
grave

le **tombeau** (PL les **tombeaux**) MASC NOUN
tomb

la **tombée** FEM NOUN
■ **à la tombée de la nuit** at nightfall

tomber VERB [84, *aux* être]
to fall
  □ Attention, tu vas tomber ! Be careful, you'll fall!
■ **laisser tomber 1** to drop □ Elle a laissé tomber son stylo. She dropped her pen. **2** to give up □ Il a laissé tomber le piano. He gave up the piano. **3** to let down □ Il ne laisse jamais tomber ses amis. He never lets his friends down.
■ **tomber amoureux de quelqu'un** to fall in love with somebody
■ **tomber sur quelqu'un** to bump into somebody □ Je suis tombé sur lui en sortant de chez Pierre. I bumped into him coming out of Pierre's place.
■ **Ça tombe bien.** That's lucky.
■ **Il tombe de sommeil.** He's asleep on his feet.

ton (FEM **ta**, PL **tes**) ADJECTIVE
  ▷ *see also* **ton** NOUN
your
  □ C'est ton stylo ? Is this your pen?

le **ton** MASC NOUN
  ▷ *see also* **ton** ADJECTIVE
1 tone of voice
  □ Ne me parle pas sur ce ton. Don't speak to me in that tone of voice.
2 colour
  □ J'adore les tons pastel. I love pastel colours.

la **tonalité** FEM NOUN
dialling tone

la **tondeuse** FEM NOUN
lawnmower

tondre VERB [69]
to mow

tonique (FEM **tonique**) ADJECTIVE
fortifying

la **tonne** FEM NOUN
tonne

le **tonneau** (PL les **tonneaux**) MASC NOUN
barrel

le **tonnerre** MASC NOUN
thunder

le **tonus** MASC NOUN
■ **avoir du tonus** to be energetic

le **torchon** MASC NOUN
tea towel

tordre VERB [49]
■ **se tordre la cheville** to twist one's ankle

tordu (FEM **tordue**) ADJECTIVE
1 bent
  □ Ce clou est un peu tordu. This nail's a bit bent.
2 crazy
  □ une histoire complètement tordue a crazy story

le **torrent** MASC NOUN
mountain stream

le **torse** MASC NOUN
chest
□ Il était torse nu. He was bare-chested.

le **tort** MASC NOUN
■ **avoir tort** to be wrong
■ **donner tort à quelqu'un** to lay the blame on somebody

le **torticolis** MASC NOUN
stiff neck
□ J'ai un torticolis. I've got a stiff neck.

la **tortue** FEM NOUN
tortoise

la **torture** FEM NOUN
torture

torturer VERB [28]
to torture

tôt ADVERB
early
■ **au plus tôt** at the earliest
■ **tôt ou tard** sooner or later

total (FEM **totale**, MASC PL **totaux**) ADJECTIVE
▷ see also **total** NOUN
total

le **total** (PL les **totaux**) MASC NOUN
▷ see also **total** ADJECTIVE
total
□ faire le total to work out the total
■ **au total** in total

totalement ADVERB
totally

la **totalité** FEM NOUN
■ **la totalité des profs** all the teachers
■ **la totalité du personnel** the entire staff

touchant (FEM **touchante**) ADJECTIVE
touching

la **touche** FEM NOUN
key (keyboard, phone)

toucher VERB [28]
1 to touch
□ Ne touche pas à mes livres ! Don't touch my books!
■ **Nos deux jardins se touchent.** Our gardens are next to each other.
2 to feel
□ Ce pull a l'air doux. Je peux toucher ? That sweater looks soft. Can I feel it?
3 to hit
□ La balle l'a touché en pleine poitrine. The bullet hit him right in the chest.
4 to affect
□ Ces nouvelles réformes ne nous touchent pas. The new reforms don't affect us.
5 to receive
□ Il a touché une grosse somme d'argent. He received a large sum of money.

toujours ADVERB
1 always
□ Il est toujours très gentil. He's always very nice.
■ **pour toujours** forever
2 still
□ Quand on est revenus, Pierre était toujours là. When we got back Pierre was still there.

le **toupet** MASC NOUN (informal)
■ **avoir du toupet** to have a nerve

la **tour** FEM NOUN
▷ see also **tour** NOUN
1 tower
■ **la Tour Eiffel** the Eiffel Tower
2 tower block
□ Il y a beaucoup de tours dans ce quartier. There are a lot of tower blocks in this area.

le **tour** MASC NOUN
▷ see also **tour** NOUN
turn
□ C'est ton tour de jouer. It's your turn to play.
■ **faire un tour** to go for a walk □ Allons faire un tour dans le parc. Let's go for a walk in the park.
■ **faire un tour en voiture** to go for a drive
■ **faire un tour à vélo** to go for a ride □ Tu veux aller faire un tour à vélo ? Do you want to go for a bike ride?
■ **faire le tour du monde** to travel round the world
■ **le Tour de France** the Tour de France

> **DID YOU KNOW...?**
> **Le Tour de France** is an annual cycle race, and is one of the biggest sporting events in the world. The route is always different, taking riders around France (and occasionally through neighbouring countries), but it always finishes on the Champs-Élysées in Paris.

■ **à tour de rôle** alternately

le **tourbillon** MASC NOUN
whirlpool

le **tourisme** MASC NOUN
tourism

le/la **touriste** MASC/FEM NOUN
tourist

touristique (FEM **touristique**) ADJECTIVE
tourist

se **tourmenter** VERB [28]
to fret
□ Ne te tourmente pas, ça s'arrangera. Don't fret about it, it'll be all right.

le **tournant** MASC NOUN
1 bend
□ Il y a beaucoup de tournants dangereux sur cette route. There are a lot of dangerous bends on this road.
2 turning point
□ Ça a été un tournant dans sa vie. It was a turning point in his life.

la **tournée** FEM NOUN

1 round

□ Le facteur commence sa tournée à sept heures du matin. The postman starts his round at 7 o'clock in the morning. □ Allez, qu'est-ce que vous voulez boire ? C'est ma tournée. Right, what are you drinking? It's my round.

2 tour

□ Il est en tournée aux États-Unis. He's on tour in the United States.

tourner VERB [28]

1 to turn

□ Tournez à droite au prochain feu. Turn right at the lights. □ Tourne-toi un peu plus vers moi, et souris ! Turn towards me a bit more, and smile!

2 to go sour

□ Le lait a tourné. The milk's gone sour.

■ **mal tourner** to go wrong □ Ça a mal tourné. It all went wrong.

■ **tourner le dos à quelqu'un** to have one's back to somebody

■ **tourner un film** to make a film

le **tournesol** MASC NOUN

sunflower

le **tournevis** MASC NOUN

screwdriver

le **tournoi** MASC NOUN

tournament

la **tourte** FEM NOUN

pie

□ une tourte aux poireaux a leek pie

tous PL ADJECTIVE, PL PRONOUN ▷ see tout

la **Toussaint** FEM NOUN

All Saints' Day

tousser VERB [28]

to cough

tout (FEM **toute**, MASC PL **tous**) ADJECTIVE, ADVERB, PRONOUN

1 all

□ tout le lait all the milk □ toute la nuit all night □ tous les livres all the books □ toutes les filles all the girls □ toute la journée all day □ tout le temps all the time □ C'est tout. That's all. □ Je les connais tous. I know them all. □ Nous y sommes toutes allées. We all went. □ Ça fait combien en tout ? How much is that all together?

■ **Il est tout seul.** He's all alone.

■ **pas du tout** not at all

■ **tout de même** all the same

2 every

□ tous les jours every day □ tous les deux jours every two days

■ **tout le monde** everybody

■ **tous les deux** both □ Nous y sommes allés tous les deux. We both went.

■ **tous les trois** all three □ Je les ai invités tous les trois. I invited all three of them.

3 everything

□ Il a tout organisé. He organized everything.

4 very

□ Elle habite tout près. She lives very close.

■ **tout en haut** right at the top

■ **tout droit** straight ahead

■ **tout d'abord** first of all

■ **tout à coup** suddenly

■ **tout à fait** absolutely

■ **tout à l'heure** **1** just now □ Je l'ai vu tout à l'heure. I saw him just now. **2** in a moment □ Je finirai ça tout à l'heure. I'll finish it in a moment.

■ **À tout à l'heure !** See you later!

■ **tout de suite** straight away

■ **Il a fait son travail tout en chantant.** He sang as he worked.

toutefois ADVERB

however

toutes FEM PL ADJECTIVE, FEM PL PRONOUN ▷ see tout

la **toux** FEM NOUN

cough

le/la **toxicomane** MASC/FEM NOUN

drug addict

la **toxicomanie** FEM NOUN

drug addiction

le **TP** MASC NOUN (= travaux pratiques)

practical class

■ **J'ai un TP de biologie à deux heures.** I've got a biology practical at two o'clock.

le **trac** MASC NOUN

■ **avoir le trac** to be feeling nervous

tracasser VERB [28]

to worry

□ La santé de mon père me tracasse. My dad's health worries me.

■ **se tracasser** to worry □ Arrête de te tracasser pour rien ! Stop worrying about nothing!

la **trace** FEM NOUN

1 trace

□ Le voleur n'a pas laissé de traces. The thief left no traces.

2 mark

□ des traces de doigts finger marks

■ **des traces de pas** footprints

tracer VERB [12]

to draw

□ tracer un trait to draw a line

le **tracteur** MASC NOUN

tractor

la **tradition** FEM NOUN

tradition

traditionnel (FEM **traditionnelle**) ADJECTIVE

traditional

le **traducteur** MASC NOUN

translator

la **traduction** FEM NOUN
translation

la **traductrice** FEM NOUN
translator

traduire VERB [23]
to translate

le **trafic** MASC NOUN
traffic
■ **le trafic de drogue** drug trafficking

le **trafiquant** MASC NOUN
■ **un trafiquant de drogue** a drug trafficker

la **tragédie** FEM NOUN
tragedy

tragique (FEM **tragique**) ADJECTIVE
tragic

trahir VERB [38]
to betray

la **trahison** FEM NOUN
betrayal

le **train** MASC NOUN
train
■ **un train électrique** a train set
■ **être en train de faire quelque chose** to be doing something □ Il est en train de manger. He's eating.

le **traîneau** (PL les **traîneaux**) MASC NOUN
sledge

traîner VERB [28]
1 to wander around
□ Ils traînaient en ville. They were wandering around town.
2 to hang about
□ Dépêche-toi, ne traîne pas ! Hurry up, don't hang about!
3 to drag on
□ La réunion a traîné jusqu'à midi. The meeting dragged on till 12 o'clock.
■ **traîner des pieds** to drag one's feet
■ **laisser traîner quelque chose** to leave something lying around □ Ne laisse pas traîner tes affaires. Don't leave your things lying around.

le **train-train** MASC NOUN
humdrum routine

traire VERB [85]
to milk

le **trait** MASC NOUN
1 line
□ Tracez un trait. Draw a line.
2 feature
□ Elle a les traits fins. She has delicate features.
■ **boire quelque chose d'un trait** to drink something down in one gulp
■ **un trait d'union** a hyphen

le **traitement** MASC NOUN
treatment

traiter VERB [28]
to treat
□ Elle le traite comme un chien. She treats him like a dog.
■ **Il m'a traité d'imbécile.** He called me an idiot.
■ **traiter de** to be about □ Cet article traite des sans-abri. This article is about the homeless.

le **traiteur** MASC NOUN
caterer

le **trajet** MASC NOUN
1 journey
□ Il n'a pas arrêté de parler pendant tout le trajet. He talked for the whole journey. □ J'ai une heure de trajet pour aller au travail. My journey to work takes an hour.
2 route
□ C'est le trajet le plus court. It's the shortest route.

le **tramway** MASC NOUN
tram

tranchant (FEM **tranchante**) ADJECTIVE
sharp (knife)

la **tranche** FEM NOUN
slice

tranquille (FEM **tranquille**) ADJECTIVE
quiet
□ Cette rue est très tranquille. This is a very quiet street.
■ **Sois tranquille, il ne va rien lui arriver.** Don't worry, nothing will happen to him.
■ **Tiens-toi tranquille !** Be quiet!
■ **Laisse-moi tranquille.** Leave me alone.
■ **Laisse ça tranquille.** Leave it alone.

tranquillement ADVERB
quietly
□ Nous étions tranquillement installés dans le salon. We were just sitting quietly in the living room.
■ **Je peux travailler tranquillement cinq minutes ?** Can I have five minutes to myself to work in peace?

la **tranquillité** FEM NOUN
peace and quiet

trans (FEM **trans**) ADJECTIVE (informal)
trans

transférer VERB [34]
to transfer

transformer VERB [28]
1 to transform
□ Son séjour en France l'a transformé. His stay in France has transformed him.
2 to convert
□ Ils ont transformé la grange en garage. They've converted the barn into a garage.
■ **se transformer en** to turn into □ La chenille se transforme en papillon. The caterpillar turns into a butterfly.

t

la **transfusion** FEM NOUN
- **une transfusion sanguine** a blood transfusion

transgenre (FEM **transgenre**) ADJECTIVE
transgender

transiger VERB [45]
to compromise

transmettre VERB [47]
- **transmettre quelque chose à quelqu'un** to pass something on to somebody

transpercer VERB [12]
to go through
□ La pluie a transpercé mes vêtements. The rain went through my clothes.

la **transpiration** FEM NOUN
perspiration

transpirer VERB [28]
to perspire

le **transport** MASC NOUN
transport
- **les transports en commun** public transport

transporter VERB [28]
1 to carry
□ Le train transportait des marchandises. The train was carrying freight.
2 to move
□ Je ne sais pas comment je vais transporter mes affaires. I don't know how I'm going to move my stuff.

traumatiser VERB [28]
to traumatize

le **travail** (PL les **travaux**) MASC NOUN
1 work
□ J'ai beaucoup de travail. I've got a lot of work.
2 job
□ Il a un travail intéressant. He's got an interesting job.
- **Il est sans travail depuis un an.** He has been out of work for a year.
- **le travail au noir** moonlighting

travailler VERB [28]
to work

travailleur (FEM **travailleuse**) ADJECTIVE
▷ see also **travailleur** NOUN, **travailleuse** NOUN
hard-working

le **travailleur** MASC NOUN
▷ see also **travailleur** ADJECTIVE
worker

la **travailleuse** FEM NOUN
▷ see also **travailleur** ADJECTIVE
worker

les **travaillistes** MASC PL NOUN
the Labour Party *sing*

les **travaux** MASC PL NOUN
1 work *sing*
□ des travaux de construction building work
2 roadworks
□ Il y a beaucoup de bruit à cause des travaux dans la rue. There's a lot of noise from the roadworks.
- **être en travaux** to be undergoing alterations
- **les travaux dirigés** supervised practical work
- **les travaux manuels** handicrafts
- **les travaux ménagers** housework
- **les travaux pratiques** practical work

le **travers** MASC NOUN
- **en travers de** across □ Il y avait un arbre en travers de la route. There was a tree lying across the road.
- **de travers** crooked □ Son chapeau était de travers. His hat was crooked.
- **comprendre de travers** to misunderstand
- **Elle comprend toujours tout de travers.** She always gets the wrong idea.
- **J'ai avalé de travers.** Something went down the wrong way.
- **à travers** through □ Cette vitre est tellement sale qu'on ne voit rien à travers. This window is so dirty you can't see anything through it.

la **traversée** FEM NOUN
crossing

traverser VERB [28]
1 to cross
□ Traversez la rue. Cross the street.
2 to go through
□ Nous avons traversé la France pour aller en Espagne. We went through France on the way to Spain. □ La pluie a traversé mon manteau. The rain went through my coat.

le **traversin** MASC NOUN
bolster

trébucher VERB [28]
to trip up

le **trèfle** MASC NOUN
1 clover
2 clubs (*at cards*)
□ le roi de trèfle the king of clubs

treize NUMBER
thirteen
□ Il a treize ans. He's thirteen. □ à treize heures at 1 p.m.
- **le treize février** the thirteenth of February

treizième (FEM **treizième**) ADJECTIVE
thirteenth

le **tréma** MASC NOUN
diaeresis

le **tremblement de terre** MASC NOUN
earthquake

trembler VERB [28]
to shake
□ trembler de peur to shake with fear
- **trembler de froid** to shiver

trempé (FEM **trempée**) ADJECTIVE
soaking wet
■ **trempé jusqu'aux os** soaked to the skin

tremper VERB [28]
to soak
■ **tremper sa main dans l'eau** to dip one's hand in the water

le **tremplin** MASC NOUN
springboard

la **trentaine** FEM NOUN
about thirty
□ une trentaine de personnes about thirty people
■ **Il a la trentaine.** He's in his thirties.

trente NUMBER
thirty
□ Elle a trente ans. She's thirty.
■ **le trente janvier** the thirtieth of January
■ **trente et un** thirty-one
■ **trente-deux** thirty-two

trentième (FEM **trentième**) ADJECTIVE
thirtieth

très ADVERB
very
□ J'ai très faim. I'm very hungry.

le **trésor** MASC NOUN
treasure

la **tresse** FEM NOUN
plait

le **triangle** MASC NOUN
triangle

la **tribu** FEM NOUN
tribe

le **tribunal** (PL les **tribunaux**) MASC NOUN
court

tricher VERB [28]
to cheat

tricolore (FEM **tricolore**) ADJECTIVE
three-coloured
■ **le drapeau tricolore** the French flag

DID YOU KNOW...?
le drapeau tricolore is the French flag which is blue, white and red.

le **tricot** MASC NOUN
1 knitting
□ On fait du tricot à l'école. We do knitting at school.
2 sweater
□ Mets un tricot, il fait froid. Put a sweater on, it's cold.

tricoter VERB [28]
to knit

trier VERB [19]
to sort out
□ Je vais trier mes papiers avant les vacances. I'm going to sort out my papers before the holidays.

le **trimestre** MASC NOUN
term

trinquer VERB [28]
to clink glasses

le **triomphe** MASC NOUN
triumph

triompher VERB [28]
to triumph

les **tripes** FEM PL NOUN
tripe

le **triple** MASC NOUN
■ **Ça m'a coûté le triple.** It cost me three times as much.
■ **Il gagne le triple de mon salaire.** He earns three times my salary.

tripler VERB [28]
to treble

les **triplés** MASC PL NOUN
triplets

triste (FEM **triste**) ADJECTIVE
sad

la **tristesse** FEM NOUN
sadness

le **trognon** MASC NOUN
core
□ un trognon de pomme an apple core

trois NUMBER
three
□ à trois heures du matin at three in the morning □ Elle a trois ans. She's three. □ trois fois three times
■ **le trois février** the third of February

troisième (FEM **troisième**) ADJECTIVE
▷ see also **troisième** NOUN
third
□ au troisième étage on the third floor

la **troisième** FEM NOUN
▷ see also **troisième** ADJECTIVE
year 10
□ Mon frère est en troisième. My brother's in year 10.

DID YOU KNOW...?
In French secondary schools, years are counted from the **sixième** (youngest) to **première** and **terminale** (oldest).

les **trois-quarts** MASC PL NOUN
three-quarters
□ les trois-quarts de la classe three-quarters of the class

le **troll** MASC NOUN
troll (online)

troller VERB [28]
to troll

le **trombone** MASC NOUN
1 trombone
□ Il joue du trombone. He plays the trombone.
2 paper clip

la **trompe** FEM NOUN
trunk
□ la trompe d'un éléphant an elephant's trunk

tromper VERB [28]
to deceive
■ **se tromper** to make a mistake □ Tout le monde peut se tromper. Anyone can make a mistake.
■ **se tromper de jour** to get the wrong day
■ **Vous vous êtes trompé de numéro.** You've got the wrong number.

la **trompette** FEM NOUN
trumpet
□ Il joue de la trompette. He plays the trumpet.
■ **Il a le nez en trompette.** He's got a turned-up nose.

le **tronc** MASC NOUN
trunk
□ un tronc d'arbre a tree trunk

trop ADVERB
1 too
□ Il conduit trop vite. He drives too fast.
2 too much
□ J'ai trop mangé. I've eaten too much.
■ **trop de** 1 too much □ J'ai acheté trop de pain. I bought too much bread. □ trois euros de trop 3 euros too much 2 too many □ J'ai apporté trop de vêtements. I've brought too many clothes.
■ **trois personnes de trop** 3 people too many

le **tropique** MASC NOUN
tropic

le **trottoir** MASC NOUN
pavement

le **trou** MASC NOUN
hole
■ **J'ai eu un trou de mémoire.** My mind went blank.

trouble (FEM **trouble**) ADJECTIVE, ADVERB
cloudy
□ L'eau est trouble. The water's cloudy.
■ **Sans mes lunettes je vois trouble.** Without my glasses I can't see properly.

les **troubles** MASC PL NOUN
■ **une période de troubles politiques** a period of political instability

trouer VERB [28]
to make a hole in
□ Il a troué la moquette avec sa cigarette. He made a hole in the carpet with his cigarette.

la **trouille** FEM NOUN
■ **avoir la trouille** (informal) to be scared to death

la **troupe** FEM NOUN
troop
■ **une troupe de théâtre** a theatre company

le **troupeau** (PL les **troupeaux**) MASC NOUN
■ **un troupeau de moutons** a flock of sheep
■ **un troupeau de vaches** a herd of cows

la **trousse** FEM NOUN
pencil case
■ **une trousse de secours** a first-aid kit
■ **une trousse de toilette** a toilet bag

trouver VERB [28]
1 to find
□ Je ne trouve pas mes lunettes. I can't find my glasses.
2 to think
□ Je trouve que c'est bête. I think it's stupid.
■ **se trouver** to be □ Où se trouve la poste ? Where is the post office? □ Nice se trouve dans le sud de la France. Nice is in the South of France.
■ **se trouver mal** to pass out

le **truc** MASC NOUN (informal)
1 thing
□ un truc en plastique a plastic thing □ J'ai plein de trucs à faire ce week-end. I've got loads of things to do this weekend.
2 trick
□ Je vais te montrer un truc qui réussit à tous les coups. I'll show you a trick that never fails.

la **truite** FEM NOUN
trout

le **T-shirt** MASC NOUN
T-shirt

TSVP ABBREVIATION (= tournez s'il vous plaît)
PTO (= please turn over)

tu PRONOUN
▷ see also **tu** VERB

tu is used when speaking to one person your own age or younger.

you
□ Est-ce que tu as un animal familier ? Have you got a pet?

tu VERB ▷ see se taire
▷ see also **tu** PRONOUN
■ **Nous nous sommes tus.** We stopped talking.

le **tuba** MASC NOUN
1 tuba
□ Je joue du tuba. I play the tuba.
2 snorkel

le **tube** MASC NOUN
1 tube
□ un tube de dentifrice a tube of toothpaste
■ **un tube de rouge à lèvres** a lipstick
2 hit
□ Ça va être le tube de l'été. It's going to be this summer's hit.

tuer VERB [28]
  to kill
  ■ **se tuer** to get killed □ Il s'est tué dans un accident de voiture. He got killed in a car accident.

tue-tête
  ■ **à tue-tête** ADVERB at the top of one's voice
  □ crier à tue-tête to shout at the top of one's voice □ Il chantait à tue-tête. He was singing at the top of his voice.

la **tuile** FEM NOUN
  tile
  □ un toit en tuiles a tiled roof

la **tunique** FEM NOUN
  tunic

la **Tunisie** FEM NOUN
  Tunisia

tunisien (FEM **tunisienne**) ADJECTIVE, NOUN
  Tunisian

le **tunnel** MASC NOUN
  tunnel
  ■ **le tunnel sous la Manche** the Channel Tunnel

turbulent (FEM **turbulente**) ADJECTIVE
  boisterous

turc (FEM **turque**) ADJECTIVE, NOUN
  Turkish
  □ Il parle turc. He speaks Turkish.
  ■ **un Turc** a Turk (*man*)
  ■ **une Turque** a Turk (*woman*)

la **Turquie** FEM NOUN
  Turkey

tutoyer VERB [53]
  ■ **tutoyer quelqu'un** to address somebody as 'tu'

■ **On se tutoie ?** Shall we use 'tu' with each other?

DID YOU KNOW...?

tutoyer quelqu'un means to use **tu** when speaking to someone, rather than **vous**. Use **tu** only when speaking to one person you know well or who is your own age or younger; use **vous** to everyone else. If in doubt use **vous**.

---

le **tuyau** (PL les **tuyaux**) MASC NOUN
1 pipe
  ■ **un tuyau d'arrosage** a hosepipe
2 tip
  □ Il m'a donné un bon tuyau. (*informal*) He gave me a handy tip.

la **TVA** FEM NOUN (= *taxe sur la valeur ajoutée*)
  VAT

le **tweet** MASC NOUN
  tweet

tweeter VERB [28]
  to tweet

le **tympan** MASC NOUN
  eardrum

le **type** MASC NOUN (*informal*)
  guy
  □ C'est un type formidable. He's a great guy.

typique (FEM **typique**) ADJECTIVE
  typical

le **tyran** MASC NOUN
  tyrant
  □ C'est un vrai tyran. He's a real tyrant.

le/la **tzigane** MASC/FEM NOUN
  Gipsy

t

Uu

l'UE FEM NOUN (= *Union européenne*)
the EU (= *European Union*)

l'Ukraine FEM NOUN
Ukraine

un (FEM **une**) ARTICLE, MASC PRONOUN, MASC ADJECTIVE

1 a
□ un garçon a boy

2 an
□ un œuf an egg

3 one
□ l'un des meilleurs one of the best □ un citron et deux oranges one lemon and two oranges □ Combien de timbres ? — Un. How many stamps? — One. □ Elle a un an. She's one year old.
■ **l'un ..., l'autre ...** one ..., the other ... □ L'un est grand, l'autre est petit. One is tall, the other is short.
■ **les uns ..., les autres ...** some ..., others ... □ Les uns marchaient, les autres couraient. Some were walking, others were running.
■ **l'un ou l'autre** either of them □ Prends l'un ou l'autre, ça m'est égal. Take either of them, I don't mind.
■ **un par un** one by one □ Ils entraient un par un. They went in one by one.

unanime (FEM **unanime**) ADJECTIVE
unanimous

l'unanimité FEM NOUN
■ **à l'unanimité** unanimously

une ARTICLE, FEM PRONOUN, FEM ADJECTIVE

1 a
□ une fille a girl

2 an
□ une pomme an apple

3 one
□ une pomme et deux bananes one apple and two bananas □ Combien de cartes postales ? — Une. How many postcards? — One. □ à une heure du matin at one in the morning □ l'une des meilleures one of the best
■ **l'une ..., l'autre ...** one ..., the other ... □ L'une est grande, l'autre est petite. One is tall, the other is short.
■ **les unes..., les autres...** some ..., others ... □ Les unes marchaient, les autres couraient.

Some were walking, others were running.
■ **l'une ou l'autre** either of them □ Prends l'une ou l'autre, ça m'est égal. Take either of them, I don't mind.
■ **une par une** one by one □ Elles entraient une par une. They went in one by one.

uni (FEM **unie**) ADJECTIVE

1 plain
□ un tissu uni a plain fabric

2 close-knit
□ une famille unie a close-knit family

l'uniforme MASC NOUN
uniform

l'union FEM NOUN
union
■ **l'Union européenne** the European Union

unique (FEM **unique**) ADJECTIVE
unique
□ Tout individu a des empreintes uniques. Everyone's fingerprints are unique. □ C'est une occasion unique. It's a unique opportunity.
■ **Il est fils unique.** He's an only child.
■ **Elle est fille unique.** She's an only child.

uniquement ADVERB
only

l'unité FEM NOUN

1 unity
□ l'unité européenne European unity

2 unit
□ une unité de mesure a unit of measurement

unir VERB [38]
to unite
■ **unir ses forces** to join forces

l'univers MASC NOUN
universe

universitaire (FEM **universitaire**) ADJECTIVE
university
□ un diplôme universitaire a university degree
■ **faire des études universitaires** to study at university

l'université FEM NOUN
university
□ aller à l'université to go to university

l'urgence FEM NOUN
emergency
□ l'urgence climatique climate emergency

Numbers in brackets refer to verb tables on pages 650 to 658

■ **C'est une urgence.** It's urgent.

■ **Il n'y a pas urgence.** It's not urgent.

■ **le service des urgences** the accident and emergency department

■ **Il a été transporté d'urgence à l'hôpital.** He was rushed to hospital.

■ **Téléphonez d'urgence.** Phone as soon as possible.

urgent (FEM **urgente**) ADJECTIVE
urgent

l'**urine** FEM NOUN
urine

les **USA** MASC PL NOUN
USA
■ **aux USA 1** in the USA **2** to the USA

l'**usage** MASC NOUN
use
□ à usage interne for internal use □ à usage externe for external use only
■ **hors d'usage** out of action □ Cet appareil est hors d'usage. That machine's out of action.

usagé (FEM **usagée**) ADJECTIVE
1 old
□ un manteau usagé an old coat
2 used
□ une seringue usagée a used syringe

l'**usager** MASC NOUN
user
□ les usagers de la route road users

usé (FEM **usée**) ADJECTIVE
worn
□ Mon jean est un peu usé. My jeans are a bit worn.

s'**user** VERB [28]
to wear out
□ Mes baskets se sont usées en quinze jours. My trainers wore out in two weeks.

l'**usine** FEM NOUN
factory
□ une usine de sardines a sardine factory

l'**ustensile** MASC NOUN
■ **un ustensile de cuisine** a kitchen utensil

usuel (FEM **usuelle**) ADJECTIVE
everyday
□ la langue usuelle everyday language

utile (FEM **utile**) ADJECTIVE
useful

l'**utilisation** FEM NOUN
use
□ L'utilisation des calculatrices est interdite. It is forbidden to use calculators.

utiliser VERB [28]
to use

l'**utilité** FEM NOUN
use
□ Cet objet n'est pas d'une grande utilité. This object isn't much use.

u

va VERB ▷ *see* **aller**

les **vacances** FEM PL NOUN
holidays
□ aller en vacances to go on holiday □ être en vacances to be on holiday
■ **les vacances de Noël** the Christmas holidays
■ **les vacances de Pâques** the Easter holidays
■ **les grandes vacances** the summer holidays

le **vacancier** MASC NOUN
holiday-maker

la **vacancière** FEM NOUN
holiday-maker

le **vacarme** MASC NOUN
racket
□ Qu'est-ce que c'est que ce vacarme ? What's all this racket?

le **vaccin** MASC NOUN
vaccine

la **vaccination** FEM NOUN
vaccination
□ La vaccination est obligatoire. Vaccination is compulsory.

vacciner VERB [28]
to vaccinate
□ se faire vacciner contre la rubéole to be vaccinated against German measles

la **vache** FEM NOUN
▷ *see also* **vache** ADJECTIVE
cow

vache (FEM **vache**) ADJECTIVE (*informal*)
▷ *see also* **vache** NOUN
mean
□ C'est vraiment vache, ce qu'il a dit. What he said was really mean. □ Il est vache. He's a mean sod.

vachement ADVERB (*informal*)
really
□ Viens te baigner, l'eau est vachement chaude. Come in the water, it's really warm.

le **vagabond** MASC NOUN
tramp

le **vagin** MASC NOUN
vagina

la **vague** FEM NOUN
▷ *see also* **vague** ADJECTIVE
wave (*in sea*)

■ **une vague de chaleur** a heat wave

vague (FEM **vague**) ADJECTIVE
▷ *see also* **vague** NOUN
vague
□ J'ai un vague souvenir de lui. I vaguely remember him.

vain (FEM **vaine**) ADJECTIVE
■ **en vain** in vain

vaincre VERB [86]
1 to defeat
□ L'armée a été vaincue. The army was defeated.
2 to overcome
□ Il a réussi à vaincre sa timidité. He managed to overcome his shyness.

le **vainqueur** MASC NOUN
winner

vais VERB ▷ *see* **aller**
■ **Je vais écrire à mes cousins.** I'm going to write to my cousins.

le **vaisseau** (PL les **vaisseaux**) MASC NOUN
■ **un vaisseau spatial** a spaceship
■ **un vaisseau sanguin** a blood vessel

la **vaisselle** FEM NOUN
1 washing-up (*of dishes*)
□ Je vais faire la vaisselle. I'll do the washing-up.
2 dishes
□ Tu peux ranger la vaisselle s'il te plaît ? Can you put the dishes away please?

valable (FEM **valable**) ADJECTIVE
valid
□ Ce billet d'avion est valable un an. This plane ticket is valid for one year.

le **valet** MASC NOUN
jack (*in card games*)
□ le valet de carreau the jack of diamonds

la **valeur** FEM NOUN
value
□ sans valeur of no value
■ **des objets de valeur** valuables □ Ne laissez pas d'objets de valeur dans votre chambre. Don't leave any valuables in your room.

valider VERB [28]
to stamp
□ Vous devez faire valider votre billet avant votre départ. You must get your ticket stamped before you leave.

Numbers in brackets refer to verb tables on pages 650 to 658

la **valise** FEM NOUN
suitcase
■ **faire sa valise** to pack

la **vallée** FEM NOUN
valley

valoir VERB [87]
to be worth
□ Ça vaut combien ? How much is it worth?
□ Cette voiture vaut très cher. This car's worth
a lot of money.
■ **valoir mieux** □ Il vaut mieux ne rien dire.
It would be better to say nothing.
■ **valoir la peine de faire** to be worth doing
□ Ça vaudrait la peine d'essayer. It would be
worth a try.

le **vampire** MASC NOUN
vampire

le **vandalisme** MASC NOUN
vandalism

la **vanille** FEM NOUN
vanilla
□ une glace à la vanille a vanilla ice cream

la **vanité** FEM NOUN
vanity

vaniteux (FEM **vaniteuse**) ADJECTIVE
conceited

se **vanter** VERB [28]
to boast

la **vapeur** FEM NOUN
steam
□ des légumes cuits à la vapeur steamed
vegetables

le **vapotage** MASC NOUN
vaping

vapoter VERB [28]
to vape

la **varappe** FEM NOUN
rock climbing
□ faire de la varappe to go rock climbing

variable (FEM **variable**) ADJECTIVE
changeable (weather)

la **varicelle** FEM NOUN
chickenpox
□ Elle a la varicelle. She's got chickenpox.

varié (FEM **variée**) ADJECTIVE
varied
□ Son travail est très varié. His job is very varied.

varier VERB [19]
to vary
■ **Le menu varie tous les jours.** The menu
changes every day.

la **variété** FEM NOUN
variety
□ Il n'y a pas beaucoup de variété. There isn't
much variety.

vas VERB ▷ see **aller**

le **vase** MASC NOUN
▷ see also **vase** NOUN
vase

la **vase** FEM NOUN
▷ see also **vase** NOUN
mud

vaste (FEM **vaste**) ADJECTIVE
vast

vaudrait, vaut VERB ▷ see **valoir**

le **vautour** MASC NOUN
vulture

le **veau** (PL les **veaux**) MASC NOUN
1 calf (animal)
2 veal (meat)

vécu VERB ▷ see **vivre**
■ **Il a vécu à Paris.** He lived in Paris.

la **vedette** FEM NOUN
1 star
□ une vedette de cinéma a film star
2 motor boat

végane (FEM **végane**) ADJECTIVE
vegan (diet and lifestyle)
□ des produits véganes vegan products

végétal (FEM **végétale**, MASC PL **végétaux**)
ADJECTIVE
vegetable
□ l'huile végétale vegetable oil
■ **des protéines d'origine végétale** plant-
based proteins

végétalien (FEM **végétalienne**) ADJÈCTIVE
vegan (dietary)
□ Je suis végétalien. I'm a vegan.

végétarien (FEM **végétarienne**) ADJECTIVE
vegetarian
□ Je suis végétarien. I'm a vegetarian.

la **végétation** FEM NOUN
vegetation

le **véhicule** MASC NOUN
vehicle

la **veille** FEM NOUN
the day before
□ la veille de son départ the day before he left
□ la veille au soir the previous evening
■ **la veille de Noël** Christmas Eve
■ **la veille du jour de l'An** New Year's Eve

veiller VERB [28]
to stay up
■ **veiller sur quelqu'un** to watch over
somebody

le **veinard** MASC NOUN (informal)
lucky devil

la **veinarde** FEM NOUN (informal)
lucky devil

la **veine** FEM NOUN
vein
■ **avoir de la veine** (informal) to be lucky

véliplanchiste - vernir

le/la **véliplanchiste** MASC/FEM NOUN
windsurfer

le **vélo** MASC NOUN
bike
□ faire du vélo to go cycling
■ un vélo tout-terrain a mountain bike

le **vélomoteur** MASC NOUN
moped

le **velours** MASC NOUN
velvet
□ une robe en velours a velvet dress
■ le velours côtelé corduroy □ un pantalon en velours côtelé corduroy trousers

les **vendanges** FEM PL NOUN
grape harvest *sing*
□ On fait les vendanges en septembre. The grape harvest is in September.

le **vendeur** MASC NOUN
shop assistant

la **vendeuse** FEM NOUN
shop assistant

vendre VERB [88]
to sell
■ vendre quelque chose à quelqu'un to sell somebody something □ Il m'a vendu son vélo. He sold me his bike.
■ « à vendre » 'for sale'

le **vendredi** MASC NOUN
1 Friday
□ Aujourd'hui, nous sommes vendredi. It's Friday today.
2 on Friday
□ Il est venu vendredi. He came on Friday.
■ le vendredi on Fridays □ Je joue au foot le vendredi. I play football on Fridays.
■ tous les vendredis every Friday
■ vendredi dernier last Friday
■ vendredi prochain next Friday
■ À vendredi ! See you on Friday!
■ le Vendredi saint Good Friday

vénéneux (FEM **vénéneuse**) ADJECTIVE
poisonous (*plant*)
□ un champignon vénéneux a poisonous mushroom

la **vengeance** FEM NOUN
revenge

se **venger** VERB [45]
to get revenge

venimeux (FEM **venimeuse**) ADJECTIVE
poisonous (*animal*)
□ un serpent venimeux a poisonous snake

le **venin** MASC NOUN
poison

venir VERB [89, *aux* être]
to come
□ Il viendra demain. He'll come tomorrow.
□ Il est venu nous voir. He came to see us.

■ **venir de** to have just □ Je viens de le voir. I've just seen him. □ Je viens de lui téléphoner. I've just phoned him.
■ **faire venir quelqu'un** to call somebody out □ faire venir le médecin to call the doctor out

le **vent** MASC NOUN
wind
□ Il y a du vent. It's windy.

la **vente** FEM NOUN
sale
■ **en vente** on sale □ Ce modèle est en vente dans les grands magasins. This model is on sale in the department stores.
■ la vente par téléphone telesales
■ une vente aux enchères an auction

le **ventilateur** MASC NOUN
fan (*for cooling*)

le **ventre** MASC NOUN
stomach
□ avoir mal au ventre to have stomachache

venu VERB ▷ *see* venir

le **ver** MASC NOUN
worm
■ un ver de terre an earthworm

le **verbe** MASC NOUN
verb

le **verdict** MASC NOUN
verdict

le **verger** MASC NOUN
orchard

verglacé (FEM **verglacée**) ADJECTIVE
icy
□ La route était verglacée. The road was icy.

le **verglas** MASC NOUN
black ice

véridique (FEM **véridique**) ADJECTIVE
truthful

la **vérification** FEM NOUN
check
□ une vérification d'identité an identity check

vérifier VERB [19]
to check

véritable (FEM **véritable**) ADJECTIVE
real
□ C'était un véritable cauchemar. It was a real nightmare.
■ en cuir véritable made of real leather

la **vérité** FEM NOUN
truth
□ dire la vérité to tell the truth

verni (FEM **vernie**) ADJECTIVE
varnished
■ des chaussures vernies patent leather shoes

vernir VERB [38]
to varnish

le **vernis** MASC NOUN
varnish
□ le vernis à ongles nail varnish

verra, verrai, verras VERB ▷ *see* **voir**
■ **on verra** ... we'll see ...

le **verre** MASC NOUN
1 glass
□ une table en verre a glass table □ un verre d'eau a glass of water
■ **boire un verre** to have a drink
2 lens (*of spectacles*)
□ des verres de contact contact lenses

verrez, verrons, verront VERB ▷ *see* **voir**

le **verrou** MASC NOUN
bolt (*on door*)

verrouiller VERB [28]
to bolt
□ N'oublie pas de verrouiller la porte du garage. Don't forget to bolt the garage door.

la **verrue** FEM NOUN
wart

le **vers** MASC NOUN
▷ *see also* **vers** PREPOSITION
line (*of poetry*)
□ au troisième vers in the third line

vers PREPOSITION
▷ *see also* **vers** NOUN
1 towards
□ Il allait vers la gare. He was going towards the station.
2 at about
□ Il est rentré chez lui vers cinq heures. He went home at about 5 o'clock.

verse
■ **à verse** ADVERB □ Il pleut à verse. It's pouring with rain.

le **Verseau** MASC NOUN
Aquarius
□ Georges est Verseau. Georges is Aquarius.

le **versement** MASC NOUN
instalment
□ en cinq versements in 5 instalments

verser VERB [28]
to pour
□ Est-ce que tu peux me verser un verre d'eau ? Could you pour me a glass of water?

la **version** FEM NOUN
1 version
2 translation (*from the foreign language*)
■ **un film en version originale** a film in the original language

le **verso** MASC NOUN
back (*of sheet of paper*)
■ **voir au verso** see overleaf

vert (FEM **verte**) ADJECTIVE
▷ *see also* **vert** NOUN
1 green

2 green (*ecological*)

le **vert** MASC NOUN
▷ *see also* **vert** ADJECTIVE
green
■ **les Verts** the Greens (*in politics*)

la **vertèbre** FEM NOUN
vertebra

vertical (FEM **verticale**, MASC PL **verticaux**) ADJECTIVE
vertical

le **vertige** MASC NOUN
vertigo
□ avoir le vertige to have vertigo

la **verveine** FEM NOUN
verbena tea

la **vessie** FEM NOUN
bladder

la **veste** FEM NOUN
jacket

le **vestiaire** MASC NOUN
1 cloakroom (*in theatre, museum*)
2 changing room (*at sports ground*)

le **vestibule** MASC NOUN
hall

le **vêtement** MASC NOUN
garment
■ **les vêtements** clothes

le/la **vétérinaire** MASC/FEM NOUN
vet
□ Elle est vétérinaire. She's a vet.

le **veuf** MASC NOUN
widower
□ Il est veuf. He's a widower.

veuille, veuillez, veuillons, veulent, veut VERB ▷ *see* **vouloir**
■ **Veuillez fermer la porte en sortant.** Please shut the door when you go out.

la **veuve** FEM NOUN
widow
□ Elle est veuve. She's a widow.

veux VERB ▷ *see* **vouloir**

vexer VERB [28]
■ **vexer quelqu'un** to hurt somebody's feelings
■ **se vexer** to be offended

la **viande** FEM NOUN
meat
■ **la viande hachée** mince

vibrer VERB [28]
to vibrate

le **vice** MASC NOUN
vice

vicieux (FEM **vicieuse**) ADJECTIVE
lecherous
■ **Il est un peu vicieux.** He's a bit of a lecher.

la **victime** FEM NOUN
victim

la **victoire** FEM NOUN
victory

vide (FEM **vide**) ADJECTIVE
▷ *see also* **vide** NOUN
empty

le **vide** MASC NOUN
▷ *see also* **vide** ADJECTIVE
vacuum
□ emballé sous vide vacuum-packed
■ **avoir peur du vide** to be afraid of heights

la **vidéo** FEM NOUN
▷ *see also* **vidéo** ADJECTIVE
video

vidéo (FEM+PL **vidéo**) ADJECTIVE
▷ *see also* **vidéo** NOUN
video
□ un jeu vidéo a video game □ une caméra vidéo a video camera
■ **un blog vidéo** a vlog

le **vidéoclip** MASC NOUN
music video

la **vidéosurveillance** FEM NOUN
CCTV

vider VERB [28]
to empty

la **vie** FEM NOUN
life
■ **être en vie** to be alive

vieil MASC ADJECTIVE

> **vieil** is used in place of **vieux** when the noun begins with a vowel sound.

old
□ un vieil arbre an old tree □ un vieil homme an old man

le **vieillard** MASC NOUN
old man

vieille FEM ADJECTIVE ▷ *see* **vieux**

la **vieille** FEM NOUN
▷ *see also* **vieux** ADJECTIVE
old woman
■ **Eh bien, ma vieille …** (*informal*) Well, my dear …

la **vieillesse** FEM NOUN
old age

vieillir VERB [38]
to age
□ Il a beaucoup vieilli. He's aged a lot.

viendrai, vienne, viens VERB ▷ *see* **venir**
■ **Je viendrai dès que possible.** I'll come as soon as possible.
■ **Je voudrais que tu viennes.** I'd like you to come.
■ **Viens ici !** Come here!

la **Vierge** FEM NOUN
▷ *see also* **vierge** ADJECTIVE
Virgo

□ Axel est Vierge. Axel is Virgo.
■ **la Vierge** the Virgin Mary

vierge (FEM **vierge**) ADJECTIVE
▷ *see also* **Vierge** NOUN
1 virgin
□ Il est vierge. He's a virgin.
2 blank
□ un CD vierge a blank CD

le **Viêt-Nam** MASC NOUN
Vietnam

vietnamien (FEM **vietnamienne**) ADJECTIVE, NOUN
Vietnamese
■ **un Vietnamien** a Vietnamese (*man*)
■ **une Vietnamienne** a Vietnamese (*woman*)
■ **les Vietnamiens** the Vietnamese

vieux (FEM **vieille**) ADJECTIVE
▷ *see also* **vieux** NOUN

> The masculine singular form **vieux** changes to **vieil** before a vowel or most words beginning with 'h'.

old
□ Il fait plus vieux que son âge. He looks older than he is. □ une vieille dame an old lady

le **vieux** MASC NOUN
▷ *see also* **vieux** ADJECTIVE
old man
■ **Eh bien, mon vieux …** (*informal*) Well, my old mate …
■ **les vieux** old people

vieux jeu (FEM+PL **vieux jeu**) ADJECTIVE
old-fashioned
□ Il est un peu vieux jeu. He's a bit old-fashioned.

vif (FEM **vive**) ADJECTIVE
1 sharp (*mentally*)
□ Il est très vif. He's very sharp.
■ **avoir l'esprit vif** to be quick-witted
2 crisp
□ L'air est plus vif à la campagne qu'en ville. The air is crisper in the country than in the town.
3 bright (*colour*)
□ un bleu vif a bright blue
■ **à vive allure** at a brisk pace
■ **de vive voix** in person
■ **Je te le dirai de vive voix.** I'll tell you about it when I see you.

la **vigne** FEM NOUN
vine
■ **des champs de vigne** vineyards

le **vigneron** MASC NOUN
wine grower

le **vignoble** MASC NOUN
vineyard

vilain (FEM **vilaine**) ADJECTIVE
1 naughty

□ C'est très vilain de dire des mensonges. It's very naughty to tell lies.

2 ugly

□ Il n'est pas vilain. He's not bad-looking.

la **villa** FEM NOUN

villa

□ une villa en multipropriété a time-share villa

le **village** MASC NOUN

village

le **villageois** MASC NOUN

villager

la **villageoise** FEM NOUN

villager

la **ville** FEM NOUN

town

□ Je vais en ville. I'm going into town.

■ **une grande ville** a city

le **vin** MASC NOUN

wine

□ le vin blanc white wine □ le vin rouge red wine □ le vin de pays the local wine □ le vin ordinaire table wine

le **vinaigre** MASC NOUN

vinegar

la **vinaigrette** FEM NOUN

French dressing

vingt NUMBER

twenty

□ Elle a vingt ans. She's twenty. □ à vingt heures at 8 p.m.

■ **le vingt février** the twentieth of February

■ **vingt et un** twenty-one

■ **vingt-deux** twenty-two

la **vingtaine** FEM NOUN

about twenty

□ une vingtaine de personnes about twenty people

■ **Il a une vingtaine d'années.** He's about twenty.

vingtième (FEM **vingtième**) ADJECTIVE

twentieth

le **viol** MASC NOUN

rape

violemment ADVERB

violently

la **violence** FEM NOUN

violence

■ **violence conjugale** domestic violence

violent (FEM **violente**) ADJECTIVE

violent

violer VERB [28]

to rape

violet (FEM **violette**) ADJECTIVE

purple

la **violette** FEM NOUN

violet (*flower*)

le **violon** MASC NOUN

violin

□ Je joue du violon. I play the violin.

le **violoncelle** MASC NOUN

cello

□ Elle joue du violoncelle. She plays the cello.

le/la **violoniste** MASC/FEM NOUN

violinist

la **vipère** FEM NOUN

viper

le **virage** MASC NOUN

bend

□ une route pleine de virages dangereux a road full of dangerous bends

viral (FEM **virale**, MASC PL **viraux**) MASC ADJECTIVE

viral

■ **une vidéo virale** a viral video

la **virgule** FEM NOUN

1 comma

2 decimal point

□ trois virgule cinq three point five

virtuel (FEM **virtuelle**) ADJECTIVE

virtual

□ la réalité virtuelle virtual reality

le **virus** MASC NOUN

virus

vis VERB ▷ *see* vivre

▷ *see also* **vis** NOUN

■ **Je vis en Écosse.** I live in Scotland.

la **vis** FEM NOUN

▷ *see also* **vis** VERB

screw

le **visa** MASC NOUN

visa

le **visage** MASC NOUN

face

□ Elle a le visage rond. She's got a round face.

vis-à-vis de PREPOSITION

with regard to

□ Ce n'est pas très juste vis-à-vis de lui. It's not very fair to him.

viser VERB [28]

to aim at

□ Il faut viser la cible. You have to aim at the target.

la **visibilité** FEM NOUN

visibility

visible (FEM **visible**) ADJECTIVE

visible

la **visière** FEM NOUN

peak (*of cap*)

la **visite** FEM NOUN

visit

■ **rendre visite à quelqu'un** to visit somebody

□ Je vais rendre visite à mon grand-père. I'm going to visit my grandfather.

■ **avoir de la visite** to have visitors □ Nous avons de la visite aujourd'hui. We've got visitors today.
■ **une visite guidée** a guided tour
■ **une visite médicale** a medical examination

visiter VERB [28]
to visit

le **visiteur** MASC NOUN
visitor

la **visiteuse** FEM NOUN
visitor

le **vison** MASC NOUN
mink (*fur*)
□ un manteau en vison a mink coat

vit VERB ▷ *see* vivre

vital (FEM **vitale**, MASC PL **vitaux**) ADJECTIVE
vital
□ C'est une question vitale. It's of vital importance.

la **vitamine** FEM NOUN
vitamin

vite ADVERB
1 quick
□ Vite, ils arrivent ! Quick, they're coming ! □ Je peux aller dire au revoir à Claire ? — Oui, mais fais vite ! Can I go and say goodbye to Claire? — Yes, but be quick! □ Prenons la voiture, ça ira plus vite. Let's take the car, it'll be quicker.
■ **Le temps passe vite.** Time flies.
2 fast
□ Il roule trop vite. He drives too fast.
3 soon
□ Il va vite oublier. He'll soon forget.
■ **Il a vite compris.** He understood immediately.

la **vitesse** FEM NOUN
1 speed
□ à toute vitesse at top speed □ Nous sommes rentrés à toute vitesse. We rushed back home.
2 gear

le **viticulteur** MASC NOUN
wine grower
□ Mon oncle est viticulteur. My uncle is a wine grower.

le **vitrail** (PL les **vitraux**) MASC NOUN
stained-glass window

la **vitre** FEM NOUN
window
□ Il a cassé une vitre. He broke a window.

la **vitrine** FEM NOUN
shop window

vivant (FEM **vivante**) ADJECTIVE
1 living
□ les êtres vivants living creatures
■ **les expériences sur les animaux vivants** experiments on live animals
2 lively
□ Elle est très vivante. She's very lively.

vive FEM ADJECTIVE ▷ *see* vif
▷ *see also* **vive** EXCLAMATION

vive EXCLAMATION
▷ *see also* **vive** FEM ADJECTIVE
■ **Vive le roi !** Long live the king!

vivement EXCLAMATION
■ **Vivement les vacances !** Roll on the holidays!

vivre VERB [91]
to live
□ J'aimerais vivre à l'étranger. I'd like to live abroad. □ Et ton grand-père ? Il vit encore ? What about your grandfather? Is he still alive?

vlan EXCLAMATION
wham!

la **VO** FEM NOUN
■ **un film en VO** a film in the original language

le **vocabulaire** MASC NOUN
vocabulary

la **vocation** FEM NOUN
vocation

le **vœu** (PL les **vœux**) MASC NOUN
wish
□ faire un vœu to make a wish □ Meilleurs vœux de bonne année ! Best wishes for the New Year!

la **vogue** FEM NOUN
fashion
■ **C'est très en vogue en ce moment.** It's very fashionable at the moment.

voici PREPOSITION
1 this is
□ Voici mon frère et voilà ma sœur. This is my brother and that's my sister.
2 here is
□ Tu as perdu ton stylo ? Tiens, en voici un autre. Have you lost your pen? Here's another one.
■ **Le voici !** Here he is! □ Tu veux tes clés ? Tiens, les voici ! You want your keys? Here you are!

la **voie** FEM NOUN
lane
□ une route à trois voies a 3-lane road
■ **par voie orale** orally □ à prendre par voie orale to be taken orally
■ **la voie ferrée** the railway track

voilà PREPOSITION
1 there is
□ Tiens ! Voilà Paul. Look! There's Paul. □ Tu as perdu ton stylo ? Tiens, en voilà un autre. Have you lost your pen? There's another one.
■ **Les voilà !** There they are!
2 that is
□ Voilà ma sœur. That's my sister.

la **voile** FEM NOUN
▷ *see also* **voile** NOUN
1 sail
2 sailing
□ faire de la voile to go sailing
■ **un bateau à voiles** a sailing boat

le **voile** MASC NOUN
▷ see also **voile** NOUN
veil
▢ un voile de mariée a wedding veil

le **voilier** MASC NOUN
sailing boat

voir VERB [92]

PRESENT TENSE	
je vois	nous voyons
tu vois	vous voyez
il/elle voit	ils/elles voient

PAST PARTICIPLE
vu

to see
▢ Venez me voir quand vous serez à Paris.
Come and see me when you're in Paris. ▢ Je ne
vois pas pourquoi il a fait ça. I can't see why he
did that.
■ **faire voir quelque chose à quelqu'un** to
show somebody something ▢ Il m'a fait voir sa
maison. He showed me his house.
■ **se voir** to be obvious ▢ Ça fait des années
qu'elle n'a pas joué au tennis — Oui, ça se voit !
She hasn't played tennis for years — Yes, that's
obvious! ▢ Est-ce que cette tache se voit ? Does
that stain show?
■ **avoir quelque chose à voir avec** to have
something to do with ▢ Ça n'a rien à voir avec
lui, c'est entre toi et moi. It's nothing to do with
him, it's between you and me.
■ **Je ne peux vraiment pas la voir.** (informal) I
really can't stand her.

vois VERB ▷ see **voir**

le **voisin** MASC NOUN
neighbour

le **voisinage** MASC NOUN
■ **dans le voisinage** in the vicinity

la **voisine** FEM NOUN
neighbour

voit VERB ▷ see **voir**

la **voiture** FEM NOUN
car
▢ une voiture de sport a sports car

la **voix** (PL les **voix**) FEM NOUN
1 voice
▢ à voix basse in a low voice
■ **à haute voix** aloud
2 vote
▢ Il a obtenu cinquante pour cent des voix.
He got 50% of the votes.

le **vol** MASC NOUN
1 flight
■ **à vol d'oiseau** as the crow flies
■ **le vol à voile** gliding
2 theft
▢ un vol à main armée an armed robbery

la **volaille** FEM NOUN
poultry

le **volant** MASC NOUN
1 steering wheel
2 shuttlecock

le **volcan** MASC NOUN
volcano

la **volée** FEM NOUN
volley (in tennis)
■ **rattraper une balle à la volée** to catch a ball
in mid-air

voler VERB [28]
1 to fly
▢ J'aimerais savoir voler. I'd like to be able to fly.
2 to steal
▢ On a volé mon appareil photo. My camera's
been stolen.
■ **voler quelque chose à quelqu'un** to steal
something from somebody ▢ Ça n'est pas son
stylo, il me l'a volé. That's not his pen, he stole
it from me.
■ **voler quelqu'un** to rob somebody

le **volet** MASC NOUN
shutter

le **voleur** MASC NOUN
thief
■ **Au voleur !** Stop thief!

la **voleuse** FEM NOUN
thief

le **volley** MASC NOUN
volleyball
▢ jouer au volley to play volleyball

le/la **volontaire** MASC/FEM NOUN
volunteer

la **volonté** FEM NOUN
willpower
▢ Il a beaucoup de volonté. He's got a lot of
willpower.
■ **la bonne volonté** goodwill
■ **la mauvaise volonté** lack of goodwill

volontiers ADVERB
1 gladly
▢ Je l'aiderais volontiers s'il me le demandait.
I'd gladly help him if he asked me.
2 please
▢ Voulez-vous boire quelque chose ? —
Volontiers ! Would you like something to drink?
— Yes, please!

le **volume** MASC NOUN
volume
▢ un dictionnaire en deux volumes a two-
volume dictionary

volumineux (FEM **volumineuse**) ADJECTIVE
bulky

vomir VERB [38]
to vomit
▢ Il a vomi toute la nuit. He was vomiting all
night.

vont VERB ▷ see **aller**

vos - vrac

vos PL ADJECTIVE

your
□ Rangez vos jouets, les enfants ! Children, put your toys away! □ Merci pour vos fleurs, M. Durand. Thanks for your flowers, Mr Durand.

le **vote** MASC NOUN

vote

voter VERB [28]

to vote

votre (FEM **votre**, PL **vos**) ADJECTIVE

your
□ C'est votre manteau ? Is this your coat?

vôtre PRONOUN

■ **le vôtre** yours □ J'aime bien notre prof de maths, mais le vôtre est plus patient. I like our maths teacher, but yours is more patient. □ À qui est cette écharpe ? C'est la vôtre ? Whose is this scarf? Is it yours?
■ **À la vôtre !** Cheers!

vôtres PL PRONOUN

■ **les vôtres** yours □ J'ai oublié mes lunettes de soleil. Vous avez les vôtres ? I've forgotten my sunglasses. Have you got yours?

voudra, voudrai, voudrais, voudrait, voudras, voudrez, voudrons, voudront, voulez VERB
▷ see **vouloir**

■ **Je voudrais ...** I'd like ... □ Je voudrais deux litres de lait, s'il vous plaît. I'd like two litres of milk, please. □ Je voudrais aller au concert. I'd like to go to the concert.

vouloir VERB [93]

PRESENT TENSE	
je veux	nous voulons
tu veux	vous voulez
il/elle veut	ils/elles veulent

PAST PARTICIPLE
voulu

to want
□ Elle veut un vélo pour Noël. She wants a bike for Christmas. □ Je ne veux pas de dessert. I don't want any pudding. □ Il ne veut pas venir. He doesn't want to come. □ On va au cinéma ? — Si tu veux. Shall we go to the cinema? — If you want.
■ **Je veux bien.** I'll be happy to. □ Je veux bien le faire à ta place si ça t'arrange. I'd be happy to do it for you if you prefer.
■ **Voulez-vous une tasse de thé ? — Je veux bien.** Would you like a cup of tea? — Yes, please.
■ **sans le vouloir** without meaning to □ Je l'ai vexé sans le vouloir. I upset him without meaning to.
■ **en vouloir à quelqu'un** to be angry with somebody □ Il m'en veut de ne pas l'avoir invité. He's angry with me for not inviting him.
■ **vouloir dire** to mean □ Qu'est-ce que ça veut dire ? What does that mean?

voulons, voulu VERB ▷ see **vouloir**

vous SING, PL PRONOUN

vous is used when speaking to several people, or to one person you don't know well.

1 you
□ Vous aimez la pizza ? Do you like pizza?
2 to you
□ Je vous écrirai bientôt. I'll write to you soon.
3 yourself
□ Vous vous êtes fait mal ? Have you hurt yourself?

With reflexive verbs, **vous** is often not translated.

□ Est-ce que vous vous intéressez à la politique ? Are you interested in politics?
■ **vous-même** yourself □ Vous l'avez fait vous-mêmes ? Did you do it yourselves?
■ **à vous** yours □ Lesquels sont à vous ? Which of these are yours?

vouvoyer VERB [53]

■ **vouvoyer quelqu'un** to address somebody as 'vous' □ Est-ce que je dois vouvoyer ta sœur ? Should I use 'vous' with your sister?

DID YOU KNOW...?

vouvoyer quelqu'un means to use **vous** when speaking to someone, rather than **tu**. Use **tu** only when speaking to one person you know well or who is your own age or younger; use **vous** to everyone else. If in doubt use **vous**.

le **voyage** MASC NOUN

journey
□ Avez-vous fait bon voyage ? Did you have a good journey?
■ **Bon voyage !** Have a good trip!

voyager VERB [45]

to travel

le **voyageur** MASC NOUN

passenger

la **voyageuse** FEM NOUN

passenger

voyaient, voyais, voyait VERB ▷ see **voir**

la **voyelle** FEM NOUN

vowel

voyez, voyiez, voyions VERB ▷ see **voir**

voyons VERB ▷ see **voir**

1 let's see
□ Voyons ce qu'on peut faire. Let's see what we can do.
2 come on
□ Voyons, sois raisonnable ! Come on, be reasonable!

le **voyou** MASC NOUN

hooligan

vrac

■ **en vrac** ADVERB loose □ du thé en vrac loose tea

vrai (FEM **vraie**) ADJECTIVE

true

□ une histoire vraie a true story □ C'est vrai ? Is that true?

■ **à vrai dire** to tell the truth

vraiment ADVERB

really

vraisemblable (FEM **vraisemblable**) ADJECTIVE

likely

□ C'est peu vraisemblable. That's not very likely.

■ **une excuse vraisemblable** a convincing excuse

le **VTT** MASC NOUN (= *vélo tout-terrain*)

mountain bike

vu VERB ▷ *see* **voir**

□ J'ai vu ce film au cinéma. I saw this film at the cinema.

■ **être bien vu** (*person*) to be popular □ Est-ce qu'il est bien vu à l'école ? Is he popular at school?

■ **C'est mal vu de fumer ici.** They don't like people smoking here.

la **vue** FEM NOUN

1 eyesight

□ J'ai une mauvaise vue. I've got bad eyesight.

2 view

□ Il y a une belle vue d'ici. There's a lovely view from here.

■ **à vue d'œil** visibly □ Elle grandit à vue d'œil. Every time you see her, she's got taller.

vulgaire (FEM **vulgaire**) ADJECTIVE

vulgar

□ Ne dis pas ça, c'est très vulgaire. Don't say that, it's very vulgar.

v

Ww

le **wagon** MASC NOUN
railway carriage

le **wagon-lit** (PL les **wagons-lits**) MASC NOUN
sleeper (*on train*)

le **wagon-restaurant** (PL les **wagons-restaurants**) MASC NOUN
restaurant car

wallon (FEM **wallonne**) ADJECTIVE, NOUN
Walloon (*French-speaking Belgian*)
■ **les Wallons** the French-speaking Belgians

la **Wallonie** FEM NOUN
French-speaking Belgium

les **W.-C.** MASC PL NOUN
toilet *sing*

le **Web** MASC NOUN
Web

la **webcam** FEM NOUN
webcam

le **webmaster** MASC NOUN
webmaster

le **webzine** MASC NOUN
webzine

le **week-end** MASC NOUN
weekend

le **western** MASC NOUN
western (*film*)

le **whisky** (PL les **whiskies**) MASC NOUN
whisky

le **wifi** MASC NOUN
Wi-Fi

xénophobe (FEM **xénophobe**) ADJECTIVE
prejudiced against foreigners

la **xénophobie** FEM NOUN
prejudice against foreigners

le **xylophone** MASC NOUN
xylophone
□ Elle joue du xylophone. She plays the xylophone.

x

Yy

y PRONOUN

there

□ Nous y sommes allés l'été dernier. We went there last summer. □ Regarde dans le tiroir : je pense que les clés y sont. Look in the drawer: I think the keys are in there.

> **y** replaces phrases with **à** in constructions like the ones below:

■ **Je pensais à l'examen. — Mais arrête d'y penser !** I was thinking about the exam. — Well, stop thinking about it!

■ **Je ne m'attendais pas à ça. — Moi, je m'y attendais.** I wasn't expecting that. — I was expecting it.

le **yaourt** MASC NOUN

yoghurt

□ un yaourt nature a plain yoghurt □ un yaourt aux fruits a fruit yoghurt

les **yeux** (SING **œil**) MASC PL NOUN

eyes

□ Elle a les yeux bleus. She's got blue eyes.

le **yoga** MASC NOUN

yoga

le **yoghourt** MASC NOUN

yoghurt

la **Yougoslavie** FEM NOUN

Yugoslavia

■ **l'ex-Yougoslavie** the former Yugoslavia

youpi EXCLAMATION

yippee!

le **yoyo** MASC NOUN

yo-yo

Zz

zapper VERB [28]
  to channel hop
le **zèbre** MASC NOUN
  zebra
le **zéro** MASC NOUN
  zero
  ■ **Ils ont gagné trois à zéro.** They won three-nil.
zézayer VERB [59]
  to lisp
  ■ **Il zézaie.** He's got a lisp.
le **zigzag** MASC NOUN
  ■ **faire des zigzags** to zigzag

la **zone** FEM NOUN
  zone
  ■ **une zone industrielle** an industrial
  estate
  ■ **une zone piétonne** a pedestrian precinct
le **zoo** MASC NOUN
  zoo
zoologique (FEM **zoologique**) ADJECTIVE
  zoological
  □ **un jardin zoologique** zoological gardens
zut EXCLAMATION
  oh heck!

French in Action

At home

Où habites-tu ?	Where do you live?
J'habite ...	I live ...
dans un village	in a village
dans une petite ville	in a small town
dans le centre-ville	in the town centre
dans la banlieue de Londres	in the suburbs of London
à la campagne	in the countryside
au bord de la mer	at the seaside
à 15 km de Manchester	15 km from Manchester
au nord de Glasgow	north of Glasgow
dans une maison individuelle	in a detached house
dans une maison jumelée	in a semi-detached house
dans une maison à deux étages	in a two-storey house
dans un immeuble	in a block of flats
dans un lotissement	on a housing estate
J'habite dans un appartement ...	**I live in a flat ...**
au rez-de-chaussée	on the ground floor
au premier étage	on the first floor
au deuxième étage	on the second floor
au dernier étage	on the top floor
J'habite ...	**I live ...**
dans une maison moderne	in a modern house
dans une maison neuve	in a new house
dans une vieille maison	in an old house

À la maison	At home
Au rez-de-chaussée, il y a ...	**On the ground floor there is ...**
la cuisine	the kitchen
la salle de séjour	the living room
la salle à manger	the dining room
le salon	the lounge
À l'étage, il y a ...	**Upstairs there is ...**
ma chambre	my bedroom
la chambre de mon frère	my brother's bedroom
la chambre de mes parents	my parents' room
la chambre d'amis	the spare bedroom
la salle de bains	the bathroom
un bureau	a study
un jardin	a garden
un court de tennis	a tennis court
un voisin	a neighbour
les voisins d'à côté	the next-door neighbours

De la maison au collège

From home to school

Le collège est assez loin de chez moi.	School is quite a long way from my house.
J'habite à cinq minutes à pied du collège.	I live five minutes' walk from school.
Mon père m'emmène au collège en voiture.	My dad drives me to school.
Je vais au collège en bus.	I go to school by bus.

Phrases utiles

Useful phrases

Chez moi, c'est tout petit.	My house is very small.
Ma chambre est bien rangée.	My room is tidy.
Je partage ma chambre avec mon frère.	I share my bedroom with my brother.
Mon meilleur copain habite dans la même rue que moi.	My best friend lives in the same street as me.
Il y a un court de tennis à côté de chez moi.	There's a tennis court next to my house.
Chez moi, il n'y a pas de salle à manger.	Our house doesn't have a dining room.
Nous déménageons le mois prochain.	We're moving next month.
Nous habitons ici depuis 5 ans.	We've been living here for 5 years.
Je n'aime pas mon quartier.	I don't like the area where I live.
C'est un quartier très calme.	It's a very quiet area.
Les transports en commun dans la ville sont excellents.	The public transport in the town is excellent.
Il n'y a pas grand-chose à faire dans mon quartier.	There's not much to do in my area.
Mon nouveau quartier est beaucoup plus agréable que l'ancien.	The new area I live in is much better than the old one.
Notre parc est le plus grand de la ville.	Our park is the biggest in town.

Quelques endroits importants — Some important places

Quelques endroits importants	Some important places
un cinéma	a cinema
un théâtre	a theatre
un musée	a museum
un parc	a park
un restaurant	a restaurant
un café	a café
un distributeur de billets	a cash machine
l'office de tourisme	the tourist office
une cathédrale	a cathedral
une église	a church
une mosquée	a mosque
une synagogue	a synagogue
l'hôpital	the hospital
le commissariat	the police station
les magasins	the shops
un centre commercial	a shopping centre
la mairie	the town hall
le marché	the market
une banque	a bank
la poste	the post office
la piscine	the swimming pool
le centre sportif	the sports centre
le stade de foot	the football stadium
la patinoire	the ice rink
le skate-parc	the skate park
le parc d'attractions	the amusement park
la bibliothèque	the library

Les choses à voir et à faire — Things to see and do

Les choses à voir et à faire	Things to see and do
visiter un musée	go to a museum
visiter la cathédrale	visit the cathedral
visiter la vieille ville	do a tour of the old town
se promener le long du fleuve	walk along the river
monter en haut de la tour	go up the tower
aller au théâtre	go to the theatre
faire du tourisme	go sightseeing
Visiter la ville	**Visiting the town**
Les endroits les plus importants à visiter sont dans le centre.	The most important sights are in the centre.
C'est intéressant de visiter le musée.	It's interesting to visit the museum.
N'oubliez pas de visiter la vieille ville.	Don't forget to go to the old town.

Les moyens de transport — Means of transport

Les moyens de transport	Means of transport
un bus	a bus
un car	a coach
le métro	the underground
le tramway	the tram
le train	the train
la gare	the station
la gare routière	the bus station
une ligne de métro	an underground line
changer de ligne	to change lines

Les directions — Directions

Les directions	Directions
en face de	opposite
à côté de	next to
près de	near
entre ... et ...	between ... and ...
derrière	behind
devant	in front of
Où se trouve la gare routière ?	Where's the bus station?
Je cherche l'office de tourisme.	I'm looking for the tourist office.
Allez jusqu'au bout de la rue.	Go right to the end of the street.
Tournez à droite.	Turn right.
Traversez le pont.	Cross the bridge.
Prenez la première rue à gauche.	Take the first street on the left.
C'est sur votre droite.	It's on your right.
C'est en face du cinéma.	It's opposite the cinema.
C'est à côté de la poste.	It's next to the post office.
L'arrêt de bus est près de l'école.	The bus stop is near the school.

Ville ou campagne ? — Town or country?

Ville ou campagne ?	Town or country?
La ville c'est bien parce qu'il y a beaucoup de magasins.	Cities are good because there are lots of shops.
Ce qui est bien à la campagne, c'est le calme.	The good thing about the countryside is that it's quiet.
Je n'aime pas habiter en ville, il y a trop de pollution.	I don't like living in town, there's too much pollution.
Il n'y a rien à faire à la campagne.	There's nothing to do in the country.

Describing someone

La personnalité	Personality
Il/Elle est ...	He/She is ...
drôle	funny
sympa	nice
gentil/gentille	nice, friendly
froid/froide	unfriendly
timide	shy
réservé/réservée	quiet
énervant/énervante	annoying
généreux/généreuse	generous
bavard/bavarde	talkative
intelligent/intelligente	intelligent
doué/douée	clever
bête	stupid, silly
radin/radine	stingy
bizarre	strange
sportif/sportive	sporty
mûr/mûre	mature
responsable	responsible
ordonné/ordonnée	tidy
désordonné/désordonnée	untidy

Les caractéristiques	Characteristics
Il/Elle est ...	He/She is ...
grand/grande	tall
petit/petite	small
mince	slim
gros/grosse	fat
beau/belle	good-looking
jeune	young
vieux/vieille	old
Il a une trentaine d'années.	He's about thirty.
Elle est grande, mince et blonde.	She's tall, slim and blonde.
Elle est plus vieille que moi.	She is older than me.
L'un de ses frères est grand, mais l'autre est petit.	One of his brothers is tall but the other one is short.
Elle ressemble à sa sœur.	She looks like her sister.

C'est quoi, un bon ami ? / What makes a good friend

Il/Elle me comprend. — He/She understands me.
Il/Elle me soutient. — He/She supports me.
Il/Elle m'aide. — He/She helps me.
Il/Elle me respecte. — He/She respects me.
Il/Elle ne me met pas la pression. — He/She doesn't put pressure on me.
Il/Elle ne me ment pas. — He/She doesn't lie to me.
Il/Elle ne me critique pas. — He/She doesn't criticize me.

Andrea est ma meilleure amie parce qu'elle est toujours là pour m'aider. — Andrea is my best friend because she is always there to help me.
Mes amis me soutiennent toujours quand j'ai des problèmes. — My friends have always supported me in difficult times.
Je m'entends bien avec mes parents parce qu'en général, ils respectent mes décisions. — I get on with my parents as generally they respect my decisions.
Ma sœur aînée m'aide à faire mes devoirs si je ne les comprends pas. — My big sister helps me with homework if I don't understand it.
Rafa est mon ami parce qu'avant tout, il me fait rire. — Rafa is my friend because, above all, he makes me laugh.
Ma grand-mère m'écoute quand j'ai des problèmes. — My grandmother listens to me when I have problems.
Un bon ami ne ment jamais. — A good friend never lies.

Les couleurs — Colours

Les couleurs	Colours
jaune (*pl* jaunes)	yellow
orange (*masc, fem, pl*)	orange
rouge (*pl* rouges)	red
rose (*pl* roses)	pink
violet/violette (*pl* violets/violettes)	purple
bleu/bleue (*pl* bleus/bleues)	blue
vert/verte (*pl* verts/vertes)	green
marron (*masc, fem, pl*)	brown
gris/grise (*pl* gris/grises)	grey
noir/noire (*pl* noirs/noires)	black
blanc/blanche (*pl* blancs/blanches)	white
bordeaux (*masc, fem, pl*)	maroon
bleu marine (*masc, fem, pl*)	navy (blue)
turquoise (*masc, fem, pl*)	turquoise
beige (*pl* beiges)	beige
crème (*masc, fem, pl*)	cream
pour les yeux :	**for eyes:**
noisette (*masc, fem, pl*)	hazel
pour les cheveux :	**for hair:**
blond/blonde (*pl* blonds/blondes)	blonde
châtain (*pl* châtains)	brown
châtain clair (*masc, fem, pl*)	light brown
brun/brune (*pl* bruns/brunes)	dark brown
roux/rousse (*pl* roux/rousses)	red

Les vêtements — Clothes

Les vêtements	Clothes
un pull	a jumper
un pantalon	trousers
un chemisier	a blouse
un T-shirt	a T-shirt
un manteau	a coat
un blouson	a jacket
un gilet	a cardigan
un jean	jeans
un sweat à capuche	a hoodie
une robe	a dress
une jupe	a skirt
une cravate	a tie
une veste	a jacket
une chemise	a shirt
des leggings	leggings
des chaussures	shoes
des baskets	trainers
des bottes	boots
des tongs	flip-flops
une tenue habillée	formal clothes
une tenue décontractée	casual clothes
une tenue élégante	smart clothes
des vêtements de sport	sports clothes
des vêtements confortables	comfortable clothes

Quand j'étais ... — When I was ...

Quand j'étais ...	When I was ...
Quand elle était petite, elle était très sympa.	When she was a child she was very friendly.
Quand j'étais petit, j'avais les cheveux longs.	When I was a child I had long hair.
À l'âge de 20 ans, mon père avait une moustache.	When my father was 20 he had a moustache.
Il était très timide quand il avait 15 ans. Maintenant, il est plus extraverti.	He was very shy at 15. Now he is more outgoing.
Avant, j'étais assez petit, mais j'ai grandi.	I used to be quite small but I have grown now.

Phrases utiles — Useful phrases

Phrases utiles	Useful phrases
J'ai les yeux noisette.	I've got hazel eyes.
Il a les cheveux châtain et courts.	He's got short brown hair.
Elle est rousse.	She's got red hair.
Il est chauve.	He's bald.
Elle a les cheveux blonds, longs et frisés.	She's got long curly blonde hair.
Il a une moustache/Il est barbu.	He's got a moustache/a beard.
Il porte des lunettes.	He wears glasses.
Ils portent toujours des couleurs vives.	They always wear bright colours.
Ces baskets sont très cool.	These trainers are really cool.
Elle porte un T-shirt bleu clair.	She's wearing a light blue T-shirt.
Il porte un costume gris foncé.	He's wearing a dark grey suit.
Je déteste les tenues formelles.	I hate formal clothes.
Je préfère les leggings parce qu'ils sont confortables.	I prefer leggings because they're comfortable.
À l'école, il faut porter un blazer.	At school, you have to wear a blazer.

School and my plans for the future

Les matières	Subjects
les langues vivantes	modern languages
l'anglais	English
la physique	physics
la chimie	chemistry
les maths	maths
la biologie	biology
le théâtre	drama
la danse	dance
la musique	music
les arts plastiques	art
la technologie	design and technology
l'informatique	computing
la géographie	geography
l'histoire	history
l'EPS (= éducation physique et sportive)	PE

C'est ...	It's ...
Je trouve ça ...	I find it ...
difficile	difficult
facile	easy
ennuyeux	boring
intéressant	interesting
pratique	practical
utile	useful

L'informatique est pratique et le français est utile, mais je trouve la chimie difficile.	Computing is practical and French is useful, but I find chemistry difficult.
Ma matière préférée, ce sont les maths parce que cela ne m'ennuie pas du tout.	My favourite subject is maths because it is not boring at all.
Bien que je déteste les maths, je trouve les statistiques très intéressantes.	Even though I hate maths, I find statistics interesting.
Je ne supporte pas le cours d'anglais parce que le professeur est très strict et me donne de mauvaises notes.	I can't stand going to English classes because the teacher is very strict and gives me bad marks.

Mon collège/ lycée	My (secondary) school
Mon collège/lycée a ...	My school has ...
des salles de classe	classrooms
des toilettes	toilets
une cantine	a dinner hall/canteen
une cour de récréation	a playground
une bibliothèque	a library
un gymnase	a gym (hall)
un laboratoire	a lab
une salle où se réunissent les élèves le matin	an assembly hall
un théâtre	a theatre
une salle de musique	a music room
une salle d'informatique	an IT room
une salle des professeurs	a staffroom
un bureau d'accueil	a reception
un bureau	an office

La journée au collège/lycée	The school day
le matin	in the morning
l'après-midi	in the afternoon
après la récréation	after break
Le mardi, j'ai cours de maths, d'informatique et aussi de français.	On Tuesdays I have maths, computing and also French.
Le lundi, mon premier cours est la biologie.	I have biology first period on a Monday.
Le vendredi, je fais deux heures d'EPS.	On Fridays I do two hours of PE.
Quelle est ta journée préférée ?	What's your favourite day?

Physical Education

Spanish

Maths

MUSIC

Biology

Design and Technology

Geography

Chemistry

HISTORY

School and my plans for the future

Les instruments de musique — Musical instruments

Je joue ...	I play the ...
du violon	violin
du piano	piano
de la guitare	guitar
de la flûte	flute
Je sais jouer du piano.	I can play the piano.
Je joue du violon depuis l'âge de huit ans.	I've been playing the violin since I was eight.
Je joue dans l'orchestre du collège.	I play in the school orchestra.
Je voudrais apprendre à jouer de la guitare.	I'd like to learn to play the guitar.

Les choses à faire — Things to do

faire ses devoirs	do homework
passer un examen	sit an exam
avoir de bonnes/ mauvaises notes	get good/bad marks
faire une activité	do an activity
résoudre un problème de maths	do/solve a maths problem
faire un exposé sur ...	do a project about ...
prendre des notes	take notes
répondre aux questions	answer the questions
faire des exercices	do exercises

Mes projets — My plans

Je voudrais faire des études ...	I'd like to study ...
de médecine	medicine
d'ingénieur	engineering
de droit	law
de sociologie	sociology
de psychologie	psychology
de langues	languages
d'architecture	architecture
d'informatique	computer science
Je voudrais ...	I'd like to ...
gagner beaucoup d'argent	earn lots of money
travailler dans un magasin	work in a shop
travailler comme médecin	work as a doctor
travailler avec des enfants	work with children
travailler dans le tourisme	work in tourism
avoir un diplôme	get a qualification

Les examens — Exams

un examen	an exam
un examen blanc	a mock exam
les résultats	the results
Cette année, je prépare le GCSE.	I'm doing my GCSEs this year.
Je vais passer mon premier examen blanc lundi prochain.	I'm doing my first mock exam next Monday.
J'espère réussir à mes examens.	I hope I'll pass my exams.
Je crois que j'ai raté mon examen de maths.	I think I've failed my maths exam.
J'aurai les résultats au mois d'août.	I'll get the results in August.
J'ai bien réussi à mes examens.	I've done well in my exams.
Il faut que je révise mes maths.	I need to revise my maths.
Je dois repasser mon GCSE d'anglais.	I need to resit my English GCSE.

Mes ambitions — My ambitions

J'ai l'intention d'aller à l'université.	I'm planning to go to university.
Après, j'aimerais bien aller à l'étranger.	Afterwards I'd like to go abroad.
Je voudrais voyager avant d'aller à l'université.	I'd like to go travelling before university.
Je ne sais pas encore ce que je veux faire.	I don't know yet what I want to do.
Je ferai peut-être des études de maths.	Maybe I'll study maths.
J'aimerais prendre une année de césure.	I'd like to take a gap year.

Jobs and hobbies

Les professions — Professions

Les professions	Professions
Je voudrais être ...	I'd like to be ...
avocat/avocate	a solicitor
prof	a teacher
dentiste	a dentist
chanteur/chanteuse	a singer
coiffeur/coiffeuse	a hairdresser
journaliste	a journalist
acteur/actrice	an actor
footballeur/footballeuse	a footballer
influenceur/influenceuse	an influencer
homme/femme politique	a politician
Je pense que c'est ...	**I think it's ...**
bien payé	well paid
mal payé	badly paid
intéressant	interesting
gratifiant	rewarding
stimulant	challenging

Les sports — Sports

Les sports	Sports
Je joue ...	I play ...
au foot	football
au basket	basketball
au netball	netball
au rugby	rugby
au tennis	tennis
au ping-pong	table tennis
Je fais ...	**I ...**
de la danse	dance/do dancing
de la gymnastique	do gymnastics
de la natation	swim
du cyclisme	cycle/go cycling
de l'équitation	go horse riding
de l'athlétisme	do athletics
de la randonnée	go hiking
Cet été, je vais faire un stage de foot.	I'm going to do a football course this summer.
Je n'ai jamais fait de ski.	I've never been skiing.
Je m'entraîne au foot deux fois par semaine.	I do football training twice a week.
J'ai participé à une compétition d'athlétisme.	I took part in an athletics competition.
Je fais partie de l'équipe de rugby.	I'm in the rugby team.

Le travail — Work

Le travail	Work
un CV	a CV
une demande d'emploi	a job application
poser sa candidature à un poste	to apply for a job
un entretien	an interview
le stage professionnel	work experience
un emploi à plein temps/à temps partiel	a full-/part-time job
un emploi en CDD/ en CDI	a temporary/ permanent job
les heures de travail	working hours
un emploi	a job
un poste	a job/position
le patron/la patronne	the boss
l'employé/l'employée	the employee
l'apprenti/l'apprentie	the apprentice
le/la stagiaire	the trainee/intern
la formation	training
l'expérience	experience
le salaire	salary
travailler	to work
être sans emploi	to be unemployed
être à la retraite	to be retired
faire un apprentissage	to do an apprenticeship
faire un stage	to do work experience
être payé/payée	to get paid
Je travaille ...	**I work ...**
au supermarché le samedi	at the supermarket on Saturdays
dans un magasin de vêtements	in a clothes shop
comme serveur/ serveuse	as a waiter/waitress
Je fais du baby-sitting.	I do baby-sitting.
Je distribue les journaux.	I deliver papers.
Je gagne 10 euros de l'heure.	I earn 10 euros an hour.
C'est fatigant comme travail.	It's a tiring job.
Je n'ai jamais travaillé.	I've never had a job.
Je vais chercher un boulot pour cet été.	I'm going to look for a job for this summer.
Mes parents ne me donnent pas d'argent de poche.	My parents don't give me pocket money.
Je suis stagiaire au sein d'une agence marketing.	I'm an intern at a marketing agency.

Mes hobbys — My hobbies

Mes hobbys	My hobbies
J'aime la lecture.	I like reading.
J'adore écouter de la musique.	I love listening to music.
J'aime bien aller en ville avec mes copines.	I love going into town with my friends.
Je suis passionné/passionnée de sport.	I'm mad about sports.
Faire du skate, c'est très cool.	Skateboarding is really cool.
Je déteste les activités en plein air.	I hate outdoor activities.
Je passe beaucoup de temps sur ma console.	I spend a lot of time on my games console.
Je préfère sortir avec mes copains.	I'd rather go out with my friends.
Je ne sais pas cuisiner.	I can't cook.

Les repas — Meals

le petit déjeuner	breakfast
le déjeuner	lunch
le goûter	afternoon snack
le dîner	dinner

J'adore ... — **I love ...**

le chocolat	chocolate
la salade	salad
les fraises	strawberries

J'aime ... — **I like ...**

le poisson	fish
la viande	meat
le fromage	cheese
les œufs	eggs
les bonbons	sweets
les légumes	vegetables

Je n'aime pas ... — **I don't like ...**

le jus d'orange	orange juice
l'eau gazeuse	sparkling water
l'eau plate	still water
les bananes	bananas

Je déteste ... — **I hate ...**

les épinards	spinach
Les légumes sont très bons pour la santé.	Vegetables are very good for you.
Je ne mange pas de porc.	I don't eat pork.
Je mange beaucoup de fruits.	I eat a lot of fruit.
J'évite les boissons gazeuses.	I avoid fizzy drinks.
Je suis végétarien/ végétarienne.	I'm (a) vegetarian.
Je suis végane.	I'm (a) vegan.
Je suis allergique aux cacahuètes.	I'm allergic to peanuts.
Bon appétit.	Enjoy your meal.
C'est très bon.	It's very tasty.
C'est délicieux.	It's delicious.

Des conseils — Some advice

Si tu veux améliorer ton mode de vie,	If you want to improve your lifestyle,
tu devrais ...	you should ...
tu dois ...	you have to ...
il est recommandé de ...	it's advisable to ...
faire de l'exercice deux fois par semaine	exercise twice a week
manger beaucoup de fruits	have lots of fruit
boire moins de café	drink less coffee
éviter le fast-food	avoid fast food

Comment je me sens — How I'm feeling

J'ai mal au ... — **I have a sore ...**

ventre	stomach
dos	back
genou	knee
pied	foot
cou	neck

J'ai mal à la ... — **I have a sore ...**

tête	head
gorge	throat
jambe	leg
J'ai mal aux dents.	I've got toothache.
J'ai mal aux oreilles.	I've got earache.
J'ai mal aux yeux.	My eyes are hurting.
J'ai la grippe.	I've got flu.
J'ai envie de vomir.	I feel sick.
Je suis enrhumé/ enrhumée.	I've got a cold.
Je suis fatigué/ fatiguée.	I'm tired.
Je suis malade.	I'm ill.
Je me suis cassé la jambe.	I broke my leg.
Il s'est coupé le doigt.	He cut his finger.

J'ai ... — **I'm ...**

froid	cold
chaud	hot
peur	scared
soif	thirsty
faim	hungry

Une vie saine — Staying healthy

Qu'est-ce que tu fais pour rester en forme ?	What do you do to keep fit?
Je fais du sport.	I do/play sports.
Je ne fume pas.	I don't smoke.
Je me couche de bonne heure.	I go to bed early.
Je vais au collège à pied.	I walk to school.
Vous devez manger des produits frais tous les jours.	You should eat fresh food every day.
Je dois boire plus d'eau.	I should drink more water.
Je n'en bois pas assez.	I don't drink enough.
C'est bon pour la santé.	It's good for your health.
L'alcool est mauvais pour la santé.	Alcohol is bad for your health.
Il mène une vie saine.	He has a healthy lifestyle.
Je ne bois pas d'alcool.	I don't drink (alcohol).

Relationships and feelings

Les relations — Relationships

Les relations	Relationships
Je m'entends très/assez bien avec ma sœur.	I get on very/quite well with my sister.
Je ne m'entends pas du tout avec mon frère.	I don't get on at all with my brother.
Je ne la supporte pas.	I can't stand her.
Mon meilleur copain s'appelle Tamir.	My best friend is called Tamir.
J'ai trois meilleures copines.	I've got three best friends.
Nous sommes inséparables.	We're always together.
Je me suis disputée avec Rachida.	I've had a quarrel with Rachida.
On ne se parle plus avec Nathan.	I'm not talking to Nathan any more.

Les émotions — Emotions

être ...	to be ...
triste	sad
content/contente	pleased
heureux/heureuse	happy
fâché/fâchée	angry
amoureux/amoureuse	in love
vexé/vexée	hurt
déprimé/déprimée	depressed
agité/agitée	nervous
de bonne/mauvaise humeur	in a good/bad mood

Je suis amoureuse de Fabien.	I'm in love with Fabien.
Bruno et moi, on s'est séparés.	Bruno and I have split up.
Je suis contente que tu viennes.	I'm pleased you're coming.
Je suis triste de partir.	I'm sad to be leaving.
Je m'ennuie, on s'en va ?	I'm bored, shall we go?
J'espère que tu n'es pas trop fâché.	I hope you're not too angry.
Elle était vexée de ne pas avoir été invitée.	She was hurt that she wasn't invited.

Les membres de la famille — Members of the family

Les membres de la famille	Members of the family
mon père	my father, my dad
ma mère	my mother, my mum
mes parents	my parents
mon beau-père	my stepfather
ma belle-mère	my stepmother
mon frère	my brother
ma sœur	my sister
mon demi-frère	my half-brother/stepbrother
ma demi-sœur	my half-sister/stepsister
mon beau-frère	my brother-in-law
ma belle-sœur	my sister-in-law
mon oncle	my uncle
ma tante	my aunt
mon cousin	my cousin (male)
ma cousine	my cousin (female)
mon grand-père	my grandfather
ma grand-mère	my grandmother
mes grands-parents	my grandparents
mon arrière-grand-père	my great-grandfather
mon arrière-grand-mère	my great-grandmother
mon grand frère	my big brother
ma petite sœur	my little sister

Phrases utiles — Useful phrases

Phrases utiles	Useful phrases
Voici ma sœur Sandrine.	This is my sister, Sandrine.
Elle va se marier l'été prochain.	She's getting married next summer.
J'ai une sœur jumelle.	I have a twin sister.
J'ai un demi-frère.	I have a half-brother.
Je suis fils unique.	I'm an only child. (boy)
Je suis fille unique.	I'm an only child. (girl)
Mes parents sont séparés/divorcés.	My parents are separated/divorced.
Mon grand-père est mort l'année dernière.	My grandfather died last year.
Ma mère s'est remariée.	My mother has got married again.
Elle est mère célibataire.	She's a single mother.
Il est père célibataire.	He's a single father.
Ils ne sont pas mariés.	They are not married.
Ils vivent en concubinage.	They are living together.
Ils sont pacsés.	They are in a civil partnership.
Il/Elle a un nouveau compagnon/une nouvelle compagne.	He/She has a new partner.

Greetings, meeting people and expressing opinions

Salutations et présentations	Greetings and introductions
Bonjour.	Hello/Good morning/Good afternoon.
Bonsoir.	Good evening
Bonne nuit.	Good night.
À plus tard.	See you later.
À bientôt.	See you soon.
À demain.	See you tomorrow.
À lundi/à la semaine prochaine.	See you on Monday/next week.
Au revoir !	Goodbye/Bye!
Passez une bonne journée !	Have a good day!
Je vous présente ma mère.	Let me introduce you to my mother.
Tu connais Sara ?	Have you met Sara?
Je vous présente Alberto.	This is Alberto.
Enchanté/enchantée.	Nice to meet you.
Ravi/ravie de faire votre connaissance.	Pleased to meet you.

Les opinions	Opinions
Génial !	Great!
C'est affreux !	That's dreadful!
Quelle horreur !	That's terrible!
C'est super !	That's great!
Cool !	Cool!
Comme c'est effrayant !	How scary!
Que c'est ennuyeux !	How boring!
Dommage !	What a shame!
Comme c'est gênant !	How embarrassing!
Je pense que ...	I think that ...
Je crois que ...	I think/I believe that ...
Il me semble que ...	I think that ...
Je pense que c'est une bonne idée.	I think it's a good idea.
À mon avis ...	In my opinion/view ...
Pour moi ...	For me ...
Je suis tout à fait d'accord avec ...	I totally agree with ...
Je suis complètement contre ...	I am completely against ...

Pour rencontrer quelqu'un / Arranging to meet someone

Aimerais-tu ... / **Would you like to ...**
Tu veux ... / **Do you want to ...**
aller au cinéma ? / go to the cinema?
faire du patin à glace ? / go skating?
jouer au foot ? / play football?
venir chez moi ? / come to my house?

Désolé/désolée, je dois ... / **I'm sorry, I have to ...**
faire mes devoirs. / do my homework.
faire le ménage. / do housework.
ranger ma chambre. / tidy my room.
aider mes parents. / help my parents.
aller promener le chien. / take the dog for a walk.

Je ne peux pas parce que ... / **I can't because ...**
je suis chez mes grands-parents. / I'm visiting my grandparents.
je suis absent/absente ce week-end. / I'm away this weekend.
je n'ai pas le droit de sortir. / I'm grounded.
je n'ai pas d'argent. / I don't have any money.

Si on se retrouvait ... / **Shall we meet ...**
en face du cinéma ? / opposite the cinema?
à l'arrêt de bus ? / at the bus stop?
C'est OK pour moi/c'est d'accord. / It's OK for me.
C'est bien. / That's fine.
D'accord. / Alright.
Ça me semble bien. / Sounds good to me.

Phrases utiles / Useful phrases

Qu'est-ce qu'on fait ce week-end ? / What shall we do this weekend?
Je ne peux pas venir samedi, mais dimanche après-midi, ça me va. / I can't come on Saturday but Sunday afternoon is OK for me.
Nous allons au cinéma ce soir. Tu veux venir avec nous ? / We are going to the cinema this evening. Would you like to come with us?
Je préfère rester à la maison aujourd'hui. / I'd rather not go out today.
Tu veux venir chez moi cet après-midi ? / Why don't you come round to mine this afternoon?
C'est dommage. J'ai des choses à faire. / What a shame! I've got things to do.
Pas question ! Je déteste le sport. / No way! I hate sports.

Communications: on the phone and online

Au téléphone	On the phone
le téléphone	telephone
le portable	mobile
le fixe	landline
l'indicatif régional	area code
le faux numéro	wrong number
un texto/SMS	a text
composer le numéro	to dial the number
répondre au téléphone	to answer the phone
appuyer sur la touche	to press the key
raccrocher	to hang up
connecter	to connect
un message vocal	a voice mail
la messagerie vocale	voice mail
envoyer un SMS	to send a text
transférer un message	to forward a message

En ligne	Online
une appli	an app
un post	a post
un mème	a meme
le nom d'utilisateur	username
le mot de passe	password
le wifi	Wi-Fi
le signal	signal
la connexion	connection
les données	data
les médias sociaux	social media
les réseaux sociaux	social networks
un blog	a blog
un blog vidéo/vlog	a vlog
en ligne	online
tweeter	to tweet
passer un appel vidéo	to make a video call
télécharger	to download
chatter	to chat

Avantages et inconvénients	Advantages and disadvantages
L'internet est ...	**The internet is ...**
utile	useful
pratique	handy/practical
rapide	fast
mais d'un autre côté, cela ...	**but on the other hand it is ...**
entraîne une dépendance	addictive
Les nouvelles technologies sont ...	**New technology is ...**
faciles	easy
populaires	popular
nécessaires	necessary
mais elles peuvent aussi être ...	**but it can also be ...**
dangereuses	dangerous

Le soir, je chatte avec mes copains.	I chat to my friends in the evenings.
Tu es sur TikTok®/ WhatsApp® ?	Are you on TikTok®/ WhatsApp®?
Tu peux télécharger une appli pour ça.	You can download an app for that.
Tu as le wifi ?	Do you have Wi-Fi?
J'ai cherché son nom sur Google®.	I googled his/ her name.

Phrases utiles / Useful phrases

Allô ! J'aimerais parler à ...	Hello! Could I speak to ...?
Un instant.	One moment please.
Je vais le/la chercher.	I'll get him/her for you.
Je suis désolé, j'ai fait un faux numéro.	I'm sorry, I dialled the wrong number.
Pourriez-vous lui demander de me rappeler ?	Would you ask him/her to call me back?
Pourriez-vous rappeler plus tard ?	Could you call back later?
Je rappellerai dans une demi-heure.	I'll call back in half an hour.
Il n'y a pas de réseau ici.	There's no signal here.
La batterie est à plat.	The battery has run out.
La ligne est très mauvaise.	It's a very bad line.
Je ne te capte plus !	You're breaking up!
Envoie-moi ton adresse par texto.	Text me your address.
J'ai mis mes photos sur Instagram®.	I put my photos on Instagram®.
Je partage des vidéos avec mes amis.	I share videos with my friends.
Il vient de poster une nouvelle vidéo.	He's just posted a new video.
On n'a pas droit au portable au collège.	We're not allowed phones in school.
Mets ton portable en silencieux.	Put your phone on silent.
Il faut éteindre les portables.	You have to switch your phones off.
Embrasse ... pour moi.	Give my love to ...
Samuel vous adresse ses amitiés.	Samuel sends his best wishes.
Amicalement	Best wishes
J'espère avoir bientôt de tes nouvelles.	Looking forward to hearing from you.

Les jours de la semaine	Days of the week
lundi	Monday
mardi	Tuesday
mercredi	Wednesday
jeudi	Thursday
vendredi	Friday
samedi	Saturday
dimanche	Sunday
lundi	on Monday
le lundi	on Mondays
tous les lundis	every Monday
mardi dernier	last Tuesday
vendredi prochain	next Friday
samedi dans une semaine	a week on Saturday

Les mois de l'an	Months of the year
janvier	January
février	February
mars	March
avril	April
mai	May
juin	June
juillet	July
août	August
septembre	September
octobre	October
novembre	November
décembre	December
Quelle est la date aujourd'hui ?	What date is it today?
Nous sommes le 16 juin.	It's the 16th of June.
Quelle est la date de ton anniversaire ?	What date is your birthday?
C'est le 22 mai.	It's the 22nd of May.

Les fêtes	Festivals
Noël (*masc*)	Christmas
le jour de Noël	Christmas Day
la veille de Noël	Christmas Eve
le réveillon de Noël	Christmas Eve
le lendemain de Noël	Boxing Day
la Saint-Sylvestre	New Year's Eve
le Nouvel An	New Year's Day
le Nouvel An chinois	Chinese New Year
la Saint-Valentin	Valentine's Day
mardi gras	Pancake Day
le premier avril	April Fools' Day
Pâques (*fem pl*)	Easter
la fête des Mères	Mother's Day
la fête des Pères	Father's Day
la Toussaint	All Saints' Day
le 11 novembre	Remembrance Day
l'Aïd	Eid
Hanoukka (*fem*)	Hanukkah
Joyeux Noël !	Happy Christmas!
Bonne année !	Happy New Year!
Poisson d'avril !	April fool!
fêter le Nouvel An	to celebrate New Year
Qu'est-ce que tu fais pour le réveillon ?	What are you doing on New Year's Eve?

Les vacances	Holidays
les grandes vacances	the summer holidays
les vacances de la Toussaint	the autumn half-term
les vacances de Noël	the Christmas holidays
les vacances de février	the spring half-term
les vacances de Pâques	the Easter holidays
la mer	the seaside
la montagne	the mountains
Qu'est-ce que tu vas faire pendant les vacances ?	What are you going to do in the holidays?
Cet été, nous partons une semaine en Italie.	We're going to Italy for a week this summer.
Nous ne partons pas en vacances cette année.	We're not going on holiday this year.
J'aimerais bien aller aux sports d'hiver cette année.	I'd like to go skiing this year.
L'été prochain, nous allons louer un gîte en Bretagne.	Next summer we're going to rent a house in Brittany.
Je déteste le camping.	I hate camping.

Our world: weather and climate

Our world

Le temps	The weather
Il fait froid.	It's cold.
Il fait chaud.	It's hot.
Il fait beau.	It's a nice day.
Il y a du vent.	It's windy.
Il y a du soleil.	It's sunny.
Il pleut/il neige.	It's raining/snowing.
Il fait 30 degrés.	It's 30 degrees.
Il gèle.	It's frosty.
Il y a du brouillard.	It's foggy.
Il fait beau/il ne fait pas beau aujourd'hui.	The weather is nice/ awful today.
Quelle est la météo pour aujourd'hui/ demain ?	What's the weather forecast for today/ tomorrow?

Le transport	Transport
une voiture électrique	an electric car
un véhicule à émission nulle	a zero emission vehicle
une borne de recharge	a charging point
On doit/Nous devons ...	**One/We should...**
marcher davantage/ faire davantage de bicyclette.	walk/cycle more.
prendre les transports en commun.	use public transport.
diminuer nos émissions.	reduce emissions.
acheter une voiture électrique.	buy an electric car.

Le climat et l'environnement / Climate and the environment

le changement climatique	climate change
l'éco-anxiété	climate anxiety
la crise/l'urgence climatique	climate crisis/emergency
les sciences du climat	climate science
une grève pour le climat	a climate strike
le réchauffement climatique	global warming
le gaz à effet de serre	greenhouse gas
la déforestation	deforestation
la désertification	desertification
les inondations	drought
la sécheresse	floods
les incendies	fires
les espèces en voie de disparition	endangered species
la pollution	pollution
la pollution plastique	plastic pollution
les énergies renouvelables	renewable energies
les énergies fossiles	fossil fuels
Nous devons ...	**We have to...**
protéger l'environnement.	protect the environment.
recycler le verre/les boîtes de conserve/ le papier/le métal.	recycle glass/tins/paper/metal.
éviter l'utilisation du plastique.	avoid using plastic.
éteindre les lumières/les appareils la nuit.	switch off the lights/devices at night.
ne pas gaspiller l'énergie.	not waste energy.
utiliser des énergies renouvelables.	use renewable energy.
utiliser moins souvent la voiture.	use the car less.
réduire notre empreinte carbone.	reduce our carbon footprint.
être neutre en carbone.	be carbon neutral.
planter plus d'arbres.	plant more trees.
manger moins de viande.	eat less meat.
économiser l'eau.	save water.

Phrases utiles	Useful phrases
À mon avis, la question majeure est la pollution plastique.	In my view, the main issue is plastic pollution.
Notre génération s'inquiète vraiment des effets du changement climatique.	Our generation is really worried about the effects of climate change.
Il est essentiel d'agir maintenant.	It is essential that we take action now.
À mon sens, la pollution de l'eau est le problème majeur.	In my view, water pollution is the main problem.
Il est important d'opter pour un mode de vie durable.	It is important to have a sustainable lifestyle.
Le nombre d'inondations/de feux de forêt augmente chaque année.	The number of floods/wild fires is increasing every year.

Les problèmes mondiaux	World problems
la pauvreté	poverty
les catastrophes naturelles	natural disasters
la famine	famine
la maladie	disease
le chômage	unemployment
le sans-abrisme	homelessness
la violence	violence
les guerres	wars
la migration	migration
le travail des enfants	child labour
la traite des personnes	people trafficking
l'inégalité	inequality
la discrimination	discrimination
le racisme	racism

Campagnes et bonnes causes

Qu'est-ce qu'on peut faire ?

On peut ...

se mobiliser.

respecter les autres.

être gentil/gentille.

acheter des produits issus du commerce équitable.

devenir travailleur/travailleuse humanitaire.

devenir bénévole.

faire du bénévolat.

apporter son aide dans un refuge.

donner de l'argent à des associations caritatives.

collaborer avec une ONG.

collecter des fonds.

lancer une pétition.

manifester/faire campagne contre ...

Campaigns and good causes

What can we do?

You can...

take action.

respect other people.

be kind.

buy Fairtrade products.

become an aid worker.

become a volunteer.

do voluntary work.

help at a refuge.

donate to charity.

collaborate with an NGO.

do some fundraising.

start a petition.

demonstrate/campaign against ...

Phrases utiles

L'inégalité est l'une des questions majeures du monde d'aujourd'hui.

Dans ma ville, il y a beaucoup de chômage.

Nous allons organiser une tombola afin de collecter des fonds pour un organisme caritatif pour enfants.

J'aime bien acheter mes vêtements dans les friperies.

Useful phrases

Inequality is one of the biggest issues in today's world.

In my town there is a lot of unemployment.

We are going to organize a raffle to raise funds for a children's charity.

I like to buy my clothes from second-hand shops.

Building phrases

Comparaisons	Comparisons
assez	quite
trop	too/too much
plus (que)	more (than)
plus grand/grande ou petit/petite (que)	bigger or smaller (than)
la majorité	the majority
mieux (que)	better (than)
moins (que)	less (than)
moins grand/grande ou petit/petite (que)	not as big or small (as)
comme	like
pareil/pareille (que)	the same (as)
semblable (à)	similar (to)
pire (que)	worse (than)
peu	little/few
un peu	a little/a few
aussi ... que ...	as ... as ...
autant ... que ...	as much/many ... as ...

Conjonctions	Conjunctions
malgré	despite
donc	so/therefore
même (si)	even (if)
bien que	although
parce que/puisque	as/because/since
à cause de	because of
quand	when
tandis que	whereas
ou	or
mais	but
c'est pour ça que ...	that's why ...
bon/eh bien, ...	well, ...
si	if
cependant	however
peut-être	perhaps/maybe
aussi	also
et	and

Prépositions	Prepositions
à	at/to
avec	with
de	from/of
dans/sur	in/on
vers	towards
jusqu'à	until/up to
pour	for/to/in order to
par	for/by
selon	according to
sans	without

Questions	Questions
où ?	where?
comment ?	how?
quel/quelle/quels/quelles ?	which?
quand ?	when?
combien ?	how much/many?
d'où ?	where ... from?
pourquoi ?	why?
quel jour/quelle date/quelle heure ?	which (day/date/time)?
qui ?	who?

Mots de liaison	Connectives
aussi	also
à part/sauf	apart from
manifestement	clearly
étant donné que	given that
c'est-à-dire	so/that is to say
d'un côté, ... d'un autre côté, ...	on the one hand ... on the other ...
sans aucun doute	without doubt
quand	when
où	where
que/qui	that/which/who

Négations	Negatives
ne ... pas	not
ne ... que	only
ne ... jamais	never
ni ... ni ...	neither ... nor ...
ne ... rien	nothing
ne ... personne	nobody/no one
aucun	none
sauf	except
non plus	neither
ne ... plus	no longer

Some examples in context

Ma ville est petite. → La ville **où** j'habite depuis 12 ans est petite, **et en plus**, elle **n**'est **pas** vivante **parce qu'**il n'y a pas d'activités pour les jeunes. **C'est pénible !**

Je m'entends bien avec ma mère. → Je m'entends très bien avec ma mère **parce que**, **bien que** nous soyons **assez** différentes, elle me soutient toujours.

Il est important de ne pas gaspiller l'énergie. → **À mon avis, pour** protéger l'environnement **autant que possible**, il est important de recycler et de **ne rien** gaspiller.

Aa

a ARTICLE

> Use **un** for masculine nouns, **une** for feminine nouns.

un *masc*
□ **a book** un livre □ **a year ago** il y a un an
une *fem*
□ **an apple** une pomme

> You do not translate 'a' when you want to describe somebody's job in French.

□ **He's a butcher.** Il est boucher. □ **She's a doctor.** Elle est médecin.
■ **once a week** une fois par semaine
■ **10 km an hour** dix kilomètres à l'heure
■ **£4 a kilo** quatre livres le kilo
■ **a hundred pounds** cent livres

AA NOUN (= *Automobile Association*)
la société de dépannage *fem*

aback ADVERB
■ **I was taken aback by his reaction.** Sa réaction m'a décontenancé.

to **abandon** VERB
abandonner [28]

abbey NOUN
l'abbaye *fem*

abbreviation NOUN
l'abréviation *fem*

ability NOUN
■ **to have the ability to do something** être [35] capable de faire quelque chose

able ADJECTIVE
■ **to be able to do something** être [35] capable de faire quelque chose

to **abolish** VERB
abolir [38]

abortion NOUN
l'avortement *masc*
■ **She had an abortion.** Elle s'est fait avorter.

about PREPOSITION, ADVERB
1 à propos de (*concerning*)
□ **He emailed me about the exams.** Il m'a envoyé un e-mail à propos des examens.
2 environ (*approximately*)
□ **It takes about 10 hours.** Ça prend dix heures environ.
■ **about a hundred pounds** une centaine de livres
■ **at about 11 o'clock** vers onze heures

3 dans (*around*)
□ **to walk about the town** se promener dans la ville
4 sur
□ **a book about London** un livre sur Londres
■ **to be about to do something** être [35] sur le point de faire quelque chose □ **I was about to go out.** J'étais sur le point de sortir.
■ **to talk about something** parler [28] de quelque chose
■ **What's it about?** De quoi s'agit-il ?
■ **How about going to the cinema?** Et si nous allions au cinéma ?

above PREPOSITION, ADVERB
1 au-dessus de (*higher than*)
□ **He put his hands above his head.** Il a mis ses mains au-dessus de sa tête.
■ **the flat above** l'appartement du dessus
■ **mentioned above** mentionné ci-dessus
■ **above all** par-dessus tout
2 plus de (*more than*)
□ **above 40 degrees** plus de quarante degrés

abroad ADVERB
à l'étranger
□ **to go abroad** partir à l'étranger

abrupt ADJECTIVE
brusque (FEM brusque)
□ **He was a bit abrupt with me.** Il s'est montré un peu brusque avec moi.

abruptly ADVERB
brusquement
□ **He got up abruptly.** Il s'est levé brusquement.

absence NOUN
l'absence *fem*

absent ADJECTIVE
absent (FEM absente)

absent-minded ADJECTIVE
distrait (FEM distraite)
□ **She's a bit absent-minded.** Elle est un peu distraite.

absolutely ADVERB
1 tout à fait (*completely*)
□ **Jia's absolutely right.** Jia a tout à fait raison.
2 absolument
□ **Do you think it's a good idea? — Absolutely!** Tu trouves que c'est une bonne idée ? — Absolument !

absorbed - accountable

absorbed ADJECTIVE
- **to be absorbed in something** être [35] absorbé par quelque chose
- **to be absorbed in a book** être [35] plongé dans un livre

absurd ADJECTIVE
absurde (FEM absurde)
□ That's absurd! C'est absurde !

abuse NOUN
▷ *see also* **abuse** VERB
l'abus *masc* (*misuse*)
- **to shout abuse at somebody** insulter [28] quelqu'un
- **the issue of child abuse** la question des enfants maltraités
- **the problem of drug abuse** le problème de la drogue

to **abuse** VERB
▷ *see also* **abuse** NOUN
1 maltraiter [28]
□ abused children les enfants maltraités *masc pl*
- **to be abused** être [35] maltraité (*person, animal*)
2 injurier [19] (*insult*)
- **to abuse drugs** se droguer [28]

abusive ADJECTIVE
insultant (FEM insultante) (*insulting*)
□ abusive behaviour un comportement insultant
- **When I refused, he became abusive.** Quand j'ai refusé, il s'est mis à m'injurier.
- **children with abusive parents** les enfants maltraités par leurs parents

academic ADJECTIVE
universitaire (FEM universitaire)
□ the academic year l'année universitaire *fem*

academy NOUN
le collège *masc*
□ a military academy un collège militaire

to **accelerate** VERB
accélérer [34]

accelerator NOUN
l'accélérateur *masc*

accent NOUN
l'accent *masc*
□ He's got a French accent. Il a l'accent français.

to **accept** VERB
accepter [28]

acceptable ADJECTIVE
acceptable (FEM acceptable)

access NOUN
1 l'accès *masc*
□ He has access to my phone. Il a accès à mon téléphone.
2 le droit de visite *masc*
□ Her ex-husband has access to the children. Son ex-mari a le droit de visite.

accessible ADJECTIVE
accessible (FEM accessible)

accessory NOUN
l'accessoire *masc*
□ fashion accessories les accessoires de mode

accident NOUN
l'accident *masc*
□ to have an accident avoir un accident
- **by accident** **1** (*by mistake*) accidentellement
□ I broke the glass by accident. J'ai cassé le verre accidentellement. **2** (*by chance*) par hasard
□ She met him by accident. Elle l'a rencontré par hasard.

accidental ADJECTIVE
accidentel (FEM accidentelle)

to **accommodate** VERB
accueillir [22]
□ The sports hall can accommodate 150 people. Le gymnase peut accueillir cent cinquante personnes.

accommodation NOUN
le logement *masc*

to **accompany** VERB
accompagner [28]

accord NOUN
- **of his own accord** de son plein gré □ He left of his own accord. Il est parti de son plein gré.

accordingly ADVERB
en conséquence

according to PREPOSITION
selon
□ According to him, everyone had gone. Selon lui, tout le monde était parti.

accordion NOUN
l'accordéon *masc*

account NOUN
1 le compte *masc*
□ a bank account un compte en banque
- **to do the accounts** tenir [83] la comptabilité
2 le compte rendu *masc* (PL les comptes rendus) (*report*)
□ He gave a detailed account of what happened. Il a donné un compte rendu détaillé des événements.
- **to take something into account** tenir [83] compte de quelque chose
- **on account of** à cause de □ We couldn't go out on account of the bad weather. Nous n'avons pas pu sortir à cause du mauvais temps.

to **account for** VERB
expliquer [28]
□ She had to account for her absence. Elle a dû expliquer son absence.

accountable ADJECTIVE
- **to be accountable to someone for something** être [35] responsable de quelque chose devant quelqu'un

accountancy NOUN
la comptabilité *fem*

accountant NOUN
le/la comptable *masc/fem*
□ She's an accountant. Elle est comptable.

accuracy NOUN
l'exactitude *fem*

accurate ADJECTIVE
précis (FEM précise)
□ accurate information les renseignements
précis *masc pl*

accurately ADVERB
avec précision

accusation NOUN
l'accusation *fem*

to **accuse** VERB
■ **to accuse somebody of something** accuser
[28] quelqu'un de quelque chose □ The police
are accusing her of murder. La police l'accuse
de meurtre.

ace NOUN
l'as *masc*
□ the ace of hearts l'as de cœur

ache NOUN
▷ see also **ache** VERB
la douleur *fem*

to **ache** VERB
▷ see also **ache** NOUN
■ **My leg's aching.** J'ai mal à la jambe.

to **achieve** VERB
1 atteindre [60] (*an aim*)
2 remporter [28] (*victory*)

achievement NOUN
l'exploit *masc*
□ That was quite an achievement. C'était un
véritable exploit.

acid NOUN
l'acide *masc*

acid rain NOUN
les pluies acides *fem pl*

acne NOUN
l'acné *fem*

acre NOUN
le demi-hectare *masc*

> **DID YOU KNOW...?**
> In France, land is measured in hectares. One
> acre is about 0.4 hectares.

acrobat NOUN
l'acrobate *masc/fem*
□ He's an acrobat. Il est acrobate.

across PREPOSITION, ADVERB
de l'autre côté de
□ the shop across the road la boutique de l'autre
côté de la rue
■ **to walk across the road** traverser [28]
la rue

■ **to run across the road** traverser [28] la rue
en courant
■ **across from** (*opposite*) en face de □ He sat
down across from her. Il s'est assis en face
d'elle.

to **act** VERB
▷ see also **act** NOUN
1 jouer [28] (*in play, film*)
□ He acts really well. Il joue vraiment bien.
□ She's acting the part of Juliet. Elle joue le rôle
de Juliette.
2 agir [38] (*take action*)
□ The police acted quickly. La police a agi
rapidement.
■ **She acts as his interpreter.** Elle lui sert
d'interprète.

act NOUN
▷ see also **act** VERB
l'acte *masc* (*in play*)
□ in the first act au premier acte

action NOUN
l'action *fem*
□ The film was full of action. Il y avait beaucoup
d'action dans le film.
■ **to take firm action against** prendre [65] des
mesures énergiques contre

active ADJECTIVE
actif (FEM active)
□ He's a very active person. Il est très actif.
■ **an active volcano** un volcan en activité

activity NOUN
l'activité *fem*
□ outdoor activities les activités de plein air

actor NOUN
l'acteur *masc*
□ Brad Pitt is a well-known actor. Brad Pitt est
un acteur connu.

actress NOUN
l'actrice *fem*
□ Jennifer Lawrence is a well-known actress.
Jennifer Lawrence est une actrice connue.

actual ADJECTIVE
réel (FEM réelle)
□ The film is based on actual events. Le film
repose sur des faits réels.
■ **What's the actual amount?** Quel est le
montant exact ?

> **BE CAREFUL!**
> Do not translate **actual** by the French word
> **actuel**.

actually ADVERB
1 vraiment (*really*)
□ Did it actually happen? Est-ce que c'est
vraiment arrivé ?
2 en fait (*in fact*)
□ Actually, I don't know him at all. En fait,

je ne le connais pas du tout.

> **BE CAREFUL!**
> Do not translate **actually** by the French word
> actuellement.

acupuncture NOUN
l'acuponcture *fem*

AD ABBREVIATION
ap. J.-C. (= *après Jésus-Christ*)
□ in 800 AD en huit cents après Jésus-Christ

ad NOUN
1 l'annonce *fem* (*in paper*)
2 la pub *fem* (*on TV, radio*)

to adapt VERB
adapter [28]
□ His novel was adapted for television. Son
roman a été adapté pour la télévision.
■ **to adapt to something** (*get used to*) s'adapter
[28] à quelque chose □ He adapted to his new
school very quickly. Il s'est adapté très vite à sa
nouvelle école.

adaptor NOUN
l'adaptateur *masc*

to add VERB
ajouter [28]
□ Add two eggs to the mixture. Ajoutez deux
œufs au mélange.

to add up VERB
additionner [28]
□ Add the figures up. Additionnez les chiffres.

addict NOUN
le drogué *masc*
la droguée *fem* (*drug addict*)
■ **Jean-Pierre's a football addict.** Jean-Pierre
est un mordu de football.

addicted ADJECTIVE
■ **to be addicted to** être [35] dépendant
de □ She's addicted to heroin. Elle est
héroïnomane.
■ **She's addicted to YouTube.** Elle est fan de
YouTube.

addition NOUN
■ **in addition** en plus □ He's broken his leg and,
in addition, he's caught a cold. Il s'est cassé la
jambe et en plus, il a attrapé un rhume.
■ **in addition to** en plus de □ There's a
swimming pool in addition to the gym. Il y a une
piscine en plus de la salle de gym.

address NOUN
l'adresse *fem*
□ What's your address? Quelle est votre
adresse ?

ADHD NOUN (= *attention deficit hyperactivity
disorder*)
le TDAH *masc* (= *trouble du déficit de l'attention
avec hyperactivité*)

adjective NOUN
l'adjectif *masc*

to adjust VERB
régler [34]
□ You can adjust the height of the chair. Tu peux
régler la hauteur de la chaise.
■ **to adjust to something** (*get used to*)
s'adapter [28] à quelque chose □ He adjusted to
his new school very quickly. Il s'est adapté très
vite à sa nouvelle école.

adjustable ADJECTIVE
réglable (FEM réglable)

administration NOUN
l'administration *fem*

admiral NOUN
l'amiral *masc*

to admire VERB
admirer [28]

admission NOUN
l'entrée *fem*
■ **'admission free'** « entrée gratuite »

to admit VERB
1 admettre [47] (*agree*)
□ I must admit that ... Je dois admettre que ...
2 reconnaître [14] (*confess*)
□ He admitted that he'd done it. Il a reconnu
qu'il l'avait fait.

admittance NOUN
■ **'no admittance'** « accès interdit »

adolescence NOUN
l'adolescence *fem*

adolescent NOUN
l'adolescent *masc*
l'adolescente *fem*

to adopt VERB
adopter [28]
□ Taylor was adopted. Taylor a été adopté.

adopted ADJECTIVE
adoptif (FEM adoptive)
□ an adopted son un fils adoptif

adoption NOUN
l'adoption *fem*

to adore VERB
adorer [28]

Adriatic Sea NOUN
la mer Adriatique *fem*

adult NOUN
l'adulte *masc/fem*
■ **adult education** l'enseignement pour
adultes *masc*

to advance VERB
▷ *see also* **advance** NOUN
1 avancer [12] (*move forward*)
□ The enemy is advancing. L'ennemi avance.
2 progresser [28] (*progress*)
□ Technology has advanced a lot. La technologie
a beaucoup progressé.

advance NOUN
▷ *see also* **advance** VERB
■ **in advance** à l'avance □ They bought the tickets in advance. Ils ont acheté les billets à l'avance.

advance booking NOUN
■ **Advance booking is essential.** Il est indispensable de réserver.

advanced ADJECTIVE
avancé (FEM avancée)

advantage NOUN
l'avantage *masc*
□ Going to university has many advantages. Aller à l'université présente de nombreux avantages.
■ **to take advantage of something** profiter [28] de quelque chose □ He took advantage of the good weather to go for a walk. Il a profité du beau temps pour faire une promenade.
■ **to take advantage of somebody** exploiter [28] quelqu'un □ She takes advantage of her younger brother. Elle exploite son frère cadet.

adventure NOUN
l'aventure *fem*

adverb NOUN
l'adverbe *masc*

advert, advertisement NOUN
1 la publicité *fem* (*on TV*)
2 l'annonce *fem* (*in newspaper*)

to advertise VERB
faire [36] de la publicité pour
□ They're advertising their new smartphone. Ils font de la publicité pour leur nouveau smartphone.
■ **Jobs are advertised on the website.** Le site Internet publie des offres d'emploi.

advertising NOUN
la publicité *fem*

advice NOUN
les conseils *masc pl*
□ to give somebody advice donner des conseils à quelqu'un
■ **a piece of advice** un conseil □ He gave me a good piece of advice. Il m'a donné un bon conseil.

to advise VERB
conseiller [28]
□ He advised me to wait. Il m'a conseillé d'attendre. □ He advised me not to go there. Il m'a conseillé de ne pas y aller.

aerial NOUN
l'antenne *fem*

aerobics NOUN
l'aérobic *fem*
□ I'm going to aerobics tonight. Je vais au cours d'aérobic ce soir.

aeroplane NOUN
l'avion *masc*

aerosol NOUN
la bombe *fem*

affair NOUN
1 l'aventure *fem* (*romantic*)
□ to have an affair with somebody avoir une aventure avec quelqu'un
2 l'affaire *fem* (*event*)
□ the contaminated blood affair l'affaire du sang contaminé

to affect VERB
affecter [28]

affectionate ADJECTIVE
affectueux (FEM affectueuse)

to afford VERB
avoir [8] les moyens de
□ I can't afford to buy a new pair of jeans. Je n'ai pas les moyens d'acheter un nouveau jean.
□ We can't afford to go on holiday. Nous n'avons pas les moyens de partir en vacances.

afraid ADJECTIVE
■ **to be afraid of something** avoir [8] peur de quelque chose □ I'm afraid of spiders. J'ai peur des araignées.
■ **I'm afraid I can't come.** Je crains de ne pouvoir venir.
■ **I'm afraid so.** Hélas oui.
■ **I'm afraid not.** Hélas non.

Africa NOUN
l'Afrique *fem*
■ **in Africa** en Afrique

African NOUN
▷ *see also* **African** ADJECTIVE
l'Africain *masc*
l'Africaine *fem*

African ADJECTIVE
▷ *see also* **African** NOUN
africain (FEM africaine)

after PREPOSITION, ADVERB, CONJUNCTION
après
□ after dinner après le dîner □ He ran after me. Il a couru après moi. □ soon after peu après
■ **after I'd had a rest** après m'être reposé
■ **after having asked** après avoir demandé
■ **after all** après tout □ After all, nobody can make us go. Après tout, personne ne peut nous obliger à y aller.

afternoon NOUN
l'après-midi *masc/fem*
□ 3 o'clock in the afternoon trois heures de l'après-midi □ this afternoon cet après-midi
□ on Saturday afternoon samedi après-midi

afters NOUN
le dessert *masc*

aftershave NOUN
l'après-rasage *masc*

afterwards ADVERB

après

□ She left not long afterwards. Elle est partie peu de temps après.

again ADVERB

1 de nouveau (once more)

□ They're friends again. Ils sont de nouveau amis.

2 encore une fois (one more time)

□ Can you tell me again? Tu peux me le dire encore une fois ?

■ **not … again** ne … plus □ I won't go there again. Je n'y retournerai plus.

■ **Do it again!** Refais-le !

■ **again and again** à plusieurs reprises

against PREPOSITION

contre

□ He leant against the wall. Il s'est appuyé contre le mur. □ I'm against drugs. Je suis contre les drogues.

age NOUN

l'âge masc

□ at the age of 16 à l'âge de seize ans □ an age limit une limite d'âge

■ **I haven't been to the cinema for ages.** Ça fait une éternité que je ne suis pas allé au cinéma.

aged ADJECTIVE

■ **aged 10** âgé de dix ans

agenda NOUN

l'ordre du jour masc

□ on the agenda à l'ordre du jour □ the agenda for today's activities l'ordre du jour des activités organisées aujourd'hui

BE CAREFUL!

Do not translate **agenda** by the French word **agenda**.

agent NOUN

l'agent masc

□ an estate agent un agent immobilier □ a travel agent un agent de voyage

aggressive ADJECTIVE

agressif (FEM agressive)

ago ADVERB

■ **two days ago** il y a deux jours

■ **two years ago** il y a deux ans

■ **not long ago** il n'y a pas longtemps

■ **How long ago did it happen?** Il y a combien de temps que c'est arrivé ?

agony NOUN

■ **to be in agony** souffrir [54] le martyre □ He was in agony. Il souffrait le martyre.

to agree VERB

■ **to agree with** être [35] d'accord avec □ I agree with Erin. Je suis d'accord avec Erin.

■ **to agree to do something** accepter [28] de faire quelque chose □ He agreed to go and pick

her up. Il a accepté d'aller la chercher.

■ **to agree that …** admettre [47] que … □ I agree that it's difficult. J'admets que c'est difficile.

■ **Garlic doesn't agree with me.** Je ne supporte pas l'ail.

agreed ADJECTIVE

convenu (FEM convenue)

□ at the agreed time au moment convenu

agreement NOUN

l'accord masc

■ **to be in agreement** être [35] d'accord □ Everybody was in agreement with Tomasz. Tout le monde était d'accord avec Tomasz.

agricultural ADJECTIVE

agricole (FEM agricole)

agriculture NOUN

l'agriculture fem

ahead ADVERB

devant

□ She looked straight ahead. Elle regardait droit devant elle.

■ **ahead of time** en avance

■ **to plan ahead** organiser [28] à l'avance

■ **The French are 5 points ahead.** Les Français ont cinq points d'avance.

■ **Go ahead!** Allez-y !

AI NOUN (= artificial intelligence)

l'IA fem (= intelligence artificielle)

aid NOUN

■ **in aid of charity** au profit d'associations caritatives

AIDS NOUN

le sida masc

to aim VERB

▷ see also **aim** NOUN

■ **to aim at** braquer [28] sur □ He aimed his gun at the target. Il a braqué son revolver sur la cible.

■ **The film is aimed at children.** Le film est destiné aux enfants.

■ **to aim to do something** avoir [8] l'intention de faire quelque chose □ Sami aimed to leave at 5 o'clock. Sami avait l'intention de partir à cinq heures.

aim NOUN

▷ see also **aim** VERB

l'objectif masc

□ The aim of the festival is to raise money. L'objectif du festival est de collecter des fonds.

air NOUN

l'air masc

□ to get some fresh air prendre l'air

■ **by air** en avion □ I prefer to travel by air. Je préfère voyager en avion.

air-conditioned ADJECTIVE

climatisé (FEM climatisée)

air conditioning NOUN
la climatisation *fem*

Air Force NOUN
l'armée de l'air *fem*

air hostess NOUN
l'hôtesse de l'air *fem*
□ She's an air hostess. Elle est hôtesse de l'air.

airline NOUN
la compagnie aérienne *fem*

airmail NOUN
■ **by airmail** par avion

airplane NOUN (US)
l'avion *masc*

airport NOUN
l'aéroport *masc*

aisle NOUN
l'allée centrale *fem*

alarm NOUN
l'alarme *fem* (*warning*)
■ **a fire alarm** une alarme à incendie

alarm clock NOUN
le réveil *masc*

album NOUN
l'album *masc*

alcohol NOUN
l'alcool *masc*

alcoholic NOUN
▷ *see also* **alcoholic** ADJECTIVE
l'alcoolique *masc/fem*
□ He's an alcoholic. C'est un alcoolique.

alcoholic ADJECTIVE
▷ *see also* **alcoholic** NOUN
alcoolisé (FEM alcoolisée)
□ alcoholic drinks des boissons alcoolisées

alert ADJECTIVE
1 vif (FEM vive) (*bright*)
□ a very alert baby un bébé très vif
2 vigilant (FEM vigilante) (*paying attention*)
□ We must stay alert. Nous devons rester vigilants.

A levels PL NOUN
le baccalauréat *masc sing*

DID YOU KNOW...?
The **baccalauréat** (or **bac** for short) is taken at the age of 17 or 18. Students have to sit a few compulsory classes, but are otherwise free to choose any combination of subjects they want. If you pass you have the right to a place at university.

Algeria NOUN
l'Algérie *fem*
■ **in Algeria** en Algérie

alien NOUN
l'extra-terrestre *masc/fem* (*from outer space*)

alike ADVERB
■ **to look alike** se ressembler [28] □ The two sisters look alike. Les deux sœurs se ressemblent.

alive ADJECTIVE
vivant (FEM vivante)

all ADJECTIVE, PRONOUN, ADVERB
tout (FEM toute, MASC PL tous)
□ all the time tout le temps □ I ate all of it. J'ai tout mangé. □ all day toute la journée □ all the books tous les livres □ all the girls toutes les filles
■ **All of us went.** Nous y sommes tous allés.
■ **after all** après tout □ After all, nobody can make us go. Après tout, personne ne peut nous obliger à y aller.
■ **all alone** tout seul □ She's all alone. Elle est toute seule.
■ **not at all** pas du tout □ I'm not tired at all. Je ne suis pas du tout fatigué.
■ **The score is 5 all.** Le score est de cinq partout.

allergic ADJECTIVE
allergique (FEM allergique)
■ **to be allergic to something** être [35] allergique à quelque chose □ I'm allergic to cat hair. Je suis allergique aux poils de chat.

allergy NOUN
le allergie *fem*

alley NOUN
la ruelle *fem*

to **allow** VERB
■ **to be allowed to do something** être [35] autorisé à faire quelque chose □ He's not allowed to go out at night. Il n'est pas autorisé à sortir le soir.
■ **to allow somebody to do something** permettre [47] à quelqu'un de faire quelque chose □ His mum allowed him to go bowling. Sa mère lui a permis d'aller au bowling.

all right ADVERB
1 bien (*okay*)
□ Everything turned out all right. Tout s'est bien terminé.
■ **Are you all right?** Ça va ?
2 pas mal (*not bad*)
□ The film was all right. Le film n'était pas mal.
3 d'accord (*when agreeing*)
□ We'll talk about it later. — All right. On en reparlera plus tard. — D'accord.
■ **Is that all right with you?** Tu es d'accord ?

all-round ADJECTIVE
général (FEM générale)
■ **a good all-round performance** de bons résultats à tous les niveaux

almond NOUN
l'amande *fem*

English-French

a

almost ADVERB
presque
□ I've almost finished. J'ai presque fini.

alone ADJECTIVE, ADVERB
seul (FEM seule)
□ She lives alone. Elle habite seule.
■ **to leave somebody alone** laisser [28] quelqu'un tranquille □ Leave her alone! Laisse-la tranquille !
■ **to leave something alone** ne pas toucher [28] à quelque chose □ Leave my things alone! Ne touche pas à mes affaires !

along PREPOSITION, ADVERB
le long de
□ Adam was walking along the beach. Adam se promenait le long de la plage.
■ **all along** depuis le début □ He was lying to me all along. Il m'a menti depuis le début.

aloud ADVERB
à haute voix
□ He read the poem aloud. Il a lu le poème à haute voix.

alphabet NOUN
l'alphabet masc

Alps PL NOUN
les Alpes fem pl

already ADVERB
déjà
□ Olivia had already gone. Olivia était déjà partie.

also ADVERB
aussi

altar NOUN
l'autel masc

to **alter** VERB
changer [45]

alternate ADJECTIVE
■ **on alternate days** tous les deux jours

alternative NOUN
▷ see also **alternative** ADJECTIVE
le choix masc
□ You have no alternative. Tu n'as pas le choix.
■ **Fruit is a healthy alternative to chocolate.** Les fruits sont plus sains que le chocolat.
■ **There are several alternatives.** Il y a plusieurs possibilités.

alternative ADJECTIVE
▷ see also **alternative** NOUN
autre (FEM autre)
□ They made alternative plans. Ils ont pris d'autres dispositions.
■ **an alternative solution** une solution de rechange
■ **alternative medicine** la médecine douce

alternatively ADVERB
■ **Alternatively, we could just stay at home.** On pourrait aussi rester à la maison.

although CONJUNCTION
bien que

bien que has to be followed by a verb in the subjunctive.

□ Although she is tired, she's going out tonight. Bien qu'elle soit fatiguée, elle sort ce soir.

altogether ADVERB
1 en tout (in total)
□ You owe me £20 altogether. Tu me dois vingt livres en tout.
2 tout à fait (completely)
□ I'm not altogether happy with your work. Je ne suis pas tout à fait satisfait de votre travail.

aluminium (US **aluminum**) NOUN
l'aluminium masc

always ADVERB
toujours
□ He's always moaning. Il est toujours en train de ronchonner.

am VERB ▷ see be

a.m. ABBREVIATION
du matin
□ at 4 a.m. à quatre heures du matin

amateur NOUN
l'amateur masc
l'amatrice fem

to **amaze** VERB
■ **to be amazed** être [35] stupéfait □ I was amazed that I managed to do it. J'étais stupéfait d'avoir réussi.

amazed ADJECTIVE
stupéfait (FEM stupéfaite)

amazing ADJECTIVE
1 stupéfiant (FEM stupéfiante) (surprising)
□ That's amazing news! C'est une nouvelle stupéfiante !
2 exceptionnel (FEM exceptionnelle) (excellent)
□ Emily's an amazing cook. Emily est une cuisinière exceptionnelle.

ambassador NOUN
l'ambassadeur masc
l'ambassadrice fem

amber ADJECTIVE
■ **an amber light** un feu orange

ambition NOUN
l'ambition fem

ambitious ADJECTIVE
ambitieux (FEM ambitieuse)
□ She's very ambitious. Elle est très ambitieuse.

ambulance NOUN
l'ambulance fem

amenities PL NOUN
les aménagements masc pl
■ **The hotel has very good amenities.** L'hôtel est très bien aménagé.

America NOUN

l'Amérique *fem*

■ **in America** en Amérique

■ **to America** en Amérique

American NOUN

▷ see also **American** ADJECTIVE

l'Américain *masc*

l'Américaine *fem*

■ **the Americans** les Américains

American ADJECTIVE

▷ see also **American** NOUN

américain (FEM américaine)

□ He's American. Il est américain. □ She's American. Elle est américaine.

among, amongst PREPOSITION

parmi

□ There were six children among them. Il y avait six enfants parmi eux.

■ **We were among friends.** Nous étions entre amis.

■ **among other things** entre autres

amount NOUN

1 la somme *fem*

□ a large amount of money une grosse somme d'argent

2 la quantité *fem*

□ a huge amount of rice une énorme quantité de riz

amp NOUN

1 l'ampère *masc* (*of electricity*)

2 l'ampli *masc* (*for hi-fi*)

amplifier NOUN

l'amplificateur *masc* (*for hi-fi*)

to **amuse** VERB

amuser [28]

□ He was very amused by the story. L'histoire l'a beaucoup amusé.

amusement arcade NOUN

la salle de jeux électroniques *fem*

an ARTICLE ▷ *see* **a**

to **analyse** VERB

analyser [28]

analysis NOUN

l'analyse *fem*

to **analyze** VERB (US)

analyser [28]

ancestor NOUN

l'ancêtre *masc/fem*

anchor NOUN

l'ancre *fem*

ancient ADJECTIVE

1 antique (FEM antique) (*civilization*)

□ ancient Greece la Grèce antique

2 ancien (FEM ancienne) (*custom, building*)

□ an ancient monument un monument ancien

and CONJUNCTION

et

□ you and me toi et moi □ 2 and 2 are 4 deux et deux font quatre

■ **Please try and come!** Essaie de venir !

■ **He talked and talked.** Il n'a pas arrêté de parler.

■ **better and better** de mieux en mieux

angel NOUN

l'ange *masc*

anger NOUN

la colère *fem*

angle NOUN

l'angle *masc*

angler NOUN

le pêcheur à la ligne *masc*

la pêcheuse à la ligne *fem*

angling NOUN

la pêche à la ligne *fem*

angry ADJECTIVE

en colère

□ Dad looks very angry. Papa a l'air très en colère.

■ **to be angry with somebody** être [35] furieux contre quelqu'un □ Mum's really angry with you. Maman est vraiment furieuse contre toi.

■ **to get angry** se fâcher [28]

animal NOUN

l'animal *masc* (PL les animaux)

ankle NOUN

la cheville *fem*

anniversary NOUN

l'anniversaire *masc*

□ a wedding anniversary un anniversaire de mariage

to **announce** VERB

annoncer [12]

announcement NOUN

l'annonce *fem*

to **annoy** VERB

agacer [12]

□ He's really annoying me. Il m'agace vraiment.

■ **to get annoyed** se fâcher [28] □ Don't get so annoyed! Ne vous fâchez pas !

annoying ADJECTIVE

agaçant (FEM agaçante)

□ It's really annoying. C'est vraiment agaçant.

annual ADJECTIVE

annuel (FEM annuelle)

□ an annual music festival un festival de musique annuel

anorak NOUN

l'anorak *masc*

anorexic ADJECTIVE

anorexique (FEM anorexique)

another ADJECTIVE

un autre (FEM une autre)

□ Would you like another piece of cake?
Tu veux un autre morceau de gâteau ?
□ Have you got another skirt? Tu as une autre jupe ?

a

to **answer** VERB
  ▷ see also **answer** NOUN
  répondre [69] à
  □ Can you answer my question? Peux-tu
  répondre à ma question ? □ to answer the phone
  répondre au téléphone
  ■ **to answer the door** aller [3'] ouvrir □ Can
  you answer the door please? Tu peux aller ouvrir
  s'il te plaît ?

answer NOUN
  ▷ see also **answer** VERB
  1 la réponse fem (to question)
  2 la solution fem (to problem)

answering machine NOUN
  le répondeur masc

ant NOUN
  la fourmi fem

Antarctic NOUN
  l'Antarctique fem

anthem NOUN
  ■ **the national anthem** l'hymne national masc

antibiotic NOUN
  l'antibiotique masc

antidepressant NOUN
  l'antidépresseur masc

antique NOUN
  le meuble ancien masc (furniture)

antique shop NOUN
  le magasin d'antiquités masc

antiseptic NOUN
  l'antiseptique masc

any ADJECTIVE, PRONOUN, ADVERB

> Use **du**, **de la** or **des** to translate 'any'
> according to the gender of the French noun
> that follows it. **du** and **de la** become **de l'**
> before a vowel and most words beginning
> with 'h'.

  1 du
    □ Have you got any bread? Avez-vous du pain ?
    de la
    □ Have you got any lemonade? Avez-vous de la
    limonade ?
    de l'
    □ Have you got any water? Avez-vous de l'eau ?
    des
    □ Have you got any crisps? Avez-vous des chips ?

> If you want to say you haven't got any of
> something, use **de** whatever the gender of
> the following noun is. **de** becomes **d'** before a
> vowel and most words beginning with 'h'.

  2 de
    □ I haven't got any books. Je n'ai pas de livres.
    d'
    □ I haven't got any money. Je n'ai pas d'argent.

  3 en

> Use **en** where there is no noun after 'any'.

    □ Sorry, I haven't got any. Désolé, je n'en
    ai pas.
    ■ **any more** 1 (additional) encore de □ Would
    you like any more coffee? Est-ce que tu veux
    encore du café ? 2 (no longer) ne ... plus
    □ I don't love him any more. Je ne l'aime plus.

anybody PRONOUN
  1 quelqu'un (in question)
    □ Has anybody got a pen? Est-ce que quelqu'un
    a un stylo ?
  2 n'importe qui (no matter who)
    □ Anybody can learn to swim. N'importe qui
    peut apprendre à nager.
  3 ne ... personne

> Use **ne ... personne** in a negative sentence.
> **ne** comes before the verb, **personne** after it.

    □ I can't see anybody. Je ne vois personne.

anyhow ADVERB
  de toute façon
  □ He doesn't want to go out and anyhow he's
  not allowed. Il ne veut pas sortir et de toute
  façon il n'y est pas autorisé.

anyone PRONOUN
  1 quelqu'un (in question)
    □ Has anyone got a pen? Est-ce que quelqu'un
    a un stylo ?
  2 n'importe qui (no matter who)
    □ Anyone can learn to swim. N'importe qui peut
    apprendre à nager.
  3 ne ... personne

> Use **ne ... personne** in a negative sentence.
> **ne** comes before the verb, **personne** after it.

    □ I can't see anyone. Je ne vois personne.

anything PRONOUN
  1 quelque chose (in question)
    □ Do you have anything to drink? Tu as quelque
    chose à boire ?
  2 n'importe quoi (no matter what)
    □ Anything could happen. Il pourrait arriver
    n'importe quoi.
  3 ne ... rien

> Use **ne ... rien** in a negative sentence. **ne**
> comes before the verb, **rien** after it.

    □ I can't hear anything. Je n'entends rien.

anyway ADVERB
  de toute façon
  □ He doesn't want to go out and anyway he's
  not allowed. Il ne veut pas sortir et de toute
  façon il n'y est pas autorisé.

anywhere ADVERB
  1 quelque part (in question)
    □ Have you seen my coat anywhere? Est-ce que
    tu as vu mon manteau quelque part ?

2 n'importe où (*no matter where*)
□ You can buy stamps almost anywhere. On peut acheter des timbres presque n'importe où.

3 ne … nulle part

> Use **ne … nulle part** in a negative sentence. **ne** comes before the verb, **nulle part** after it.

□ I can't find it anywhere. Je ne le trouve nulle part.

apart ADVERB
■ **The two towns are 10 kilometres apart.** Les deux villes sont à dix kilomètres l'une de l'autre.
■ **apart from** à part □ Apart from that, everything's fine. À part ça, tout va bien.

apartment NOUN
l'appartement *masc*

to **apologize** VERB
s'excuser [28]
□ He apologized for being late. Il s'est excusé de son retard.
■ **I apologize!** Je vous prie de m'excuser.

apology NOUN
les excuses *fem pl*

apostrophe NOUN
l'apostrophe *fem*

app NOUN (= *application*)
l'appli *fem*
□ a mobile app une appli pour portable

apparatus NOUN
1 le matériel *masc* (*in lab*)
2 les agrès *masc pl* (*in gym*)

apparent ADJECTIVE
apparent (FEM apparente)

apparently ADVERB
apparemment

to **appeal** VERB
▷ *see also* **appeal** NOUN
lancer [12] un appel
□ They appealed for help. Ils ont lancé un appel au secours.
■ **Greece doesn't appeal to me.** Ça ne me tente pas d'aller en Grèce.
■ **Does that appeal to you?** Ça te tente ?

appeal NOUN
▷ *see also* **appeal** VERB
l'appel *masc*
□ They have launched an appeal. Ils ont lancé un appel.

to **appear** VERB
1 apparaître [56¹] (*come into view*)
□ The bus appeared around the corner. Le bus est apparu au coin de la rue.
■ **to appear on TV** passer [58¹] à la télé
2 paraître [56] (*seem*)
□ She appeared to be asleep. Elle paraissait dormir.

appearance NOUN
l'apparence *fem* (*looks*)
□ She takes great care over her appearance. Elle prend grand soin de son apparence.

appendicitis NOUN
l'appendicite *fem*

appetite NOUN
l'appétit *masc*

to **applaud** VERB
applaudir [38]

applause NOUN
les applaudissements *masc pl*

apple NOUN
la pomme *fem*
■ **an apple tree** un pommier

applicant NOUN
le candidat *masc*
la candidate *fem*
□ There were a hundred applicants for the job. Il y avait cent candidats pour le poste.

application NOUN
■ **a job application** une candidature

application form NOUN
1 le dossier de candidature *masc* (*for job*)
2 le dossier d'inscription *masc* (*for university*)

to **apply** VERB
■ **to apply for a job** poser [28] sa candidature à un poste
■ **to apply to** (*be relevant*) s'appliquer [28] à
□ This rule doesn't apply to us. Ce règlement ne s'applique pas à nous.

appointment NOUN
le rendez-vous *masc*
□ I've got a dental appointment. J'ai rendez-vous chez le dentiste.

to **appreciate** VERB
être [35] reconnaissant de
□ I really appreciate your help. Je vous suis extrêmement reconnaissant de votre aide.

apprentice NOUN
l'apprenti *masc*
l'apprentie *fem*

to **approach** VERB
1 s'approcher [28] de (*get nearer to*)
□ He approached the house. Il s'est approché de la maison.
2 aborder [28] (*tackle*)
□ to approach a problem aborder un problème

appropriate ADJECTIVE
approprié (FEM appropriée)
□ Those shoes aren't very appropriate for school. Ces chaussures ne sont pas très appropriées pour aller à l'école.

approval NOUN
l'approbation *fem*

a

to **approve** VERB
- **to approve of** approuver [28] □ I don't approve of his choice. Je n'approuve pas son choix.
- **They didn't approve of his girlfriend.** Sa copine ne leur a pas plu.

approximate ADJECTIVE
approximatif (FEM approximative)

apricot NOUN
l'abricot *masc*

April NOUN
avril *masc*
- **in April** en avril
- **April Fools' Day** le premier avril

> **DID YOU KNOW...?**
> Pinning a paper fish to somebody's back is a traditional April Fool joke in France.

apron NOUN
le tablier *masc*

Aquarius NOUN
le Verseau *masc*
□ I'm Aquarius. Je suis Verseau.

Arab NOUN
▷ *see also* **Arab** ADJECTIVE
l'Arabe *masc/fem*

Arab ADJECTIVE
▷ *see also* **Arab** NOUN
arabe (FEM arabe)
□ the Arab countries les pays arabes

Arabic NOUN
l'arabe *masc*

arch NOUN
l'arc *masc*

archaeologist NOUN
l'archéologue *masc/fem*
□ He's an archaeologist. Il est archéologue.

archaeology NOUN
l'archéologie *fem*

archbishop NOUN
l'archevêque *masc/fem*

archeologist NOUN (US)
l'archéologue *masc/fem*
□ He's an archeologist. Il est archéologue.

archeology NOUN (US)
l'archéologie *fem*

architect NOUN
l'architecte *masc/fem*
□ She's an architect. Elle est architecte.

architecture NOUN
l'architecture *fem*

Arctic NOUN
l'Arctique *masc*

are VERB ▷ *see* be

area NOUN
1 la région *fem*
□ She lives in the Paris area. Elle habite dans la région parisienne.

2 le quartier *masc*
□ My favourite area of Paris is Montmartre. Montmartre est le quartier de Paris que je préfère.

3 la superficie *fem*
□ The field has an area of 1500m². Le champ a une superficie de mille cinq cents mètres carrés.

Argentina NOUN
l'Argentine *fem*
- **in Argentina** en Argentine

Argentinian ADJECTIVE
argentin (FEM argentine)

to **argue** VERB
se disputer [28]
□ They never stop arguing. Ils n'arrêtent pas de se disputer.

argument NOUN
- **to have an argument** se disputer [28]
□ They had an argument. Ils se sont disputés.

Aries NOUN
le Bélier *masc*
□ I'm Aries. Je suis Bélier.

arm NOUN
le bras *masc*

armchair NOUN
le fauteuil *masc*

armour (US **armor**) NOUN
l'armure *fem*

army NOUN
l'armée *fem*

around PREPOSITION, ADVERB
1 autour de
□ She wore a scarf around her neck. Elle portait une écharpe autour du cou.
2 environ (*approximately*)
□ It costs around £100. Cela coûte environ cent livres.
3 vers (*date, time*)
□ Let's meet at around 8 p.m. Retrouvons-nous vers vingt heures.
- **around here 1** (*nearby*) près d'ici □ Is there a chemist's around here? Est-ce qu'il y a une pharmacie près d'ici ? **2** (*in this area*) dans les parages □ He lives around here. Il habite dans les parages.

to **arrange** VERB
- **to arrange to do something** prévoir [92] de faire quelque chose □ They arranged to go out together on Friday. Ils ont prévu de sortir ensemble vendredi.
- **to arrange a meeting** convenir [89] d'un rendez-vous □ Can we arrange a meeting? Pouvons-nous convenir d'un rendez-vous ?
- **to arrange a party** organiser [28] une fête

arrangement NOUN
l'arrangement *masc* (*plan*)
- **They made arrangements to go out**

on Friday night. Ils ont organisé une sortie vendredi soir.

to arrest VERB
▷ see also **arrest** NOUN
arrêter [28]
□ The police have arrested 5 people. La police a arrêté cinq personnes.

arrest NOUN
▷ see also **arrest** VERB
l'arrestation *fem*
■ **to be under arrest** être [35] en état d'arrestation □ You're under arrest! Vous êtes en état d'arrestation !

arrival NOUN
l'arrivée *fem*

to arrive VERB
arriver [5⁹]
□ I arrived at 5 o'clock. Je suis arrivé à cinq heures.

arrow NOUN
la flèche *fem*

art NOUN
l'art *masc*

artery NOUN
l'artère *fem*

art gallery NOUN
la galerie d'art *fem*

article NOUN
l'article *masc*
□ a newspaper article un article de journal

artificial ADJECTIVE
artificiel (FEM artificielle)

artist NOUN
l'artiste *masc/fem*
□ She's an artist. C'est une artiste.

artistic ADJECTIVE
artistique (FEM artistique)

as CONJUNCTION, ADVERB
1 au moment où *(while)*
□ He came in as I was leaving. Il est arrivé au moment où je partais.
2 puisque *(since)*
□ As it's Sunday, you can have a lie-in. Tu peux faire la grasse matinée, puisque c'est dimanche.
■ **as ... as** aussi ... que □ Pierre's as tall as Michel. Pierre est aussi grand que Michel.
■ **twice as ... as** deux fois plus ... que □ Her coat cost twice as much as mine. Son manteau a coûté deux fois plus cher que le mien.
■ **as much ... as** autant ... que □ I haven't got as much money as you. Je n'ai pas autant d'argent que toi.
■ **as soon as possible** dès que possible □ I'll do it as soon as possible. Je le ferai dès que possible.
■ **as from tomorrow** à partir de demain □ As from tomorrow, the shop will be closed on

Sundays. À partir de demain, le magasin sera fermé le dimanche.
■ **as though** comme si □ She acted as though she hadn't seen me. Elle a fait comme si elle ne m'avait pas vu.
■ **as if** comme si
■ **He works as a waiter in the holidays.** Il travaille comme serveur pendant les vacances.

asap ABBREVIATION (= *as soon as possible*)
dès que possible

ashamed ADJECTIVE
■ **to be ashamed** avoir [8] honte □ You should be ashamed of yourself! Tu devrais avoir honte !

ashtray NOUN
le cendrier *masc*

Asia NOUN
l'Asie *fem*
■ **in Asia** en Asie

Asian NOUN
▷ see also **Asian** ADJECTIVE
l'Asiatique *masc/fem*

Asian ADJECTIVE
▷ see also **Asian** NOUN
asiatique (FEM asiatique)
■ **He's Asian.** C'est un Asiatique.
■ **She's Asian.** C'est une Asiatique.

to ask VERB
1 demander [28] *(inquire, request)*
□ 'Have you finished?' she asked. « Tu as fini ? » a-t-elle demandé.
■ **to ask somebody something** demander [28] quelque chose à quelqu'un □ He asked her how old she was. Il lui a demandé quel âge elle avait.
■ **to ask for something** demander [28] quelque chose □ He asked for a cup of tea. Il a demandé une tasse de thé.
■ **to ask somebody to do something** demander [28] à quelqu'un de faire quelque chose □ She asked him to do the shopping. Elle lui a demandé de faire les courses.
■ **to ask about something** se renseigner [28] sur quelque chose □ I asked about train times to Leeds. Je me suis renseigné sur les horaires des trains pour Leeds.
■ **to ask somebody a question** poser [28] une question à quelqu'un
2 inviter [28]
□ Have you asked Omar to the party? Est-ce que tu as invité Omar à la fête ?
■ **He asked her out.** *(on a date)* Il lui a demandé de sortir avec lui.

asleep ADJECTIVE
■ **to be asleep** dormir [29] □ He's asleep. Il dort.
■ **to fall asleep** s'endormir [29] □ I fell asleep in front of the TV. Je me suis endormi devant la télé.

asparagus NOUN
les asperges *fem pl*

aspect – attempt

aspect NOUN
l'aspect *masc*

aspirin NOUN
l'aspirine *fem*

assembly NOUN

> **DID YOU KNOW...?**
> There is no assembly in French schools.

asset NOUN
l'atout *masc*
□ Her knowledge of maths will be an asset in the exam. Ses connaissances en maths seront un atout à l'examen.

assignment NOUN
le devoir *masc* (*in school*)

assistance NOUN
l'aide *fem*

assistant NOUN
1 le vendeur *masc*
la vendeuse *fem* (*in shop*)
2 l'assistant *masc*
l'assistante *fem* (*helper*)

association NOUN
l'association *fem*

assortment NOUN
l'assortiment *masc*

to **assume** VERB
supposer [28]
□ I assume she won't be coming. Je suppose qu'elle ne viendra pas.

to **assure** VERB
assurer [28]
□ He assured me he was coming. Il m'a assuré qu'il viendrait.

asthma NOUN
l'asthme *masc*
□ I've got asthma. J'ai de l'asthme.

to **astonish** VERB
étonner [28]

astonished ADJECTIVE
étonné (FEM étonnée)

astonishing ADJECTIVE
étonnant (FEM étonnante)

astrology NOUN
l'astrologie *fem*

astronaut NOUN
l'astronaute *masc/fem*

astronomy NOUN
l'astronomie *fem*

asylum seeker NOUN
le demandeur d'asile *masc*
la demandeuse d'asile *fem*

at PREPOSITION
▷ *see also* **at** NOUN

> à + **le** becomes **au**, à + **les** becomes **aux**.

à

□ at 4 o'clock à quatre heures □ at Christmas à Noël □ at 50 km/h à cinquante km/h □ at home à la maison □ two at a time deux à la fois □ at school à l'école

au
□ at the office au bureau

aux
□ at the toilet aux toilettes
■ **at night** la nuit
■ **What are you doing at the weekend?**
Qu'est-ce que tu fais ce week-end ?

at NOUN
▷ *see also* **at** PREPOSITION
l'arobase *fem* (@ *symbol*)

ate VERB ▷ *see* **eat**

Athens NOUN
Athènes
■ **in Athens** à Athènes

athlete NOUN
l'athlète *masc/fem*

athletic ADJECTIVE
athlétique (FEM athlétique)

athletics NOUN
l'athlétisme *masc*
□ I love athletics. J'adore l'athlétisme.

Atlantic NOUN
l'océan Atlantique *masc*

atlas NOUN
l'atlas *masc*

atmosphere NOUN
l'atmosphère *fem*

atom NOUN
l'atome *masc*

atomic ADJECTIVE
atomique (FEM atomique)

to **attach** VERB
fixer [28]
□ He attached a rope to the car. Il a fixé une corde à la voiture.
■ **Please find attached ...** Veuillez trouver ci-joint ...

attached ADJECTIVE
■ **to be attached to** être [35] attaché à □ He's very attached to his family. Il est très attaché à sa famille.

attachment NOUN
la pièce jointe *fem* (*email*)

to **attack** VERB
▷ *see also* **attack** NOUN
attaquer [28]
□ The dog attacked her. Le chien l'a attaquée.

attack NOUN
▷ *see also* **attack** VERB
l'attaque *fem*

attempt NOUN
▷ *see also* **attempt** VERB
la tentative *fem*

Numbers in brackets refer to verb tables on pages 650 to 658

□ She gave up after several attempts. Elle y a renoncé après plusieurs tentatives.

to **attempt** VERB
▷ *see also* **attempt** NOUN
■ **to attempt to do something** essayer [59] de faire quelque chose □ I attempted to write a song. J'ai essayé d'écrire une chanson.

to **attend** VERB
assister [28] à
□ to attend a match assister à un match

BE CAREFUL!
Do not translate **to attend** by the French word **attendre**.

attention NOUN
■ **to pay attention to** faire [36] attention à
□ He didn't pay attention to what I was saying. Il ne faisait pas attention à ce que je disais.

attic NOUN
le grenier *masc*

attitude NOUN
l'attitude *fem* (*way of thinking*)
□ I really don't like your attitude! Je n'aime pas du tout ton attitude !

attorney NOUN (US)
l'avocat *masc*
l'avocate *fem*

to **attract** VERB
attirer [28]
□ Disneyland attracts lots of tourists. Disneyland attire de nombreux touristes.

attraction NOUN
l'attraction *fem*
□ a tourist attraction une attraction touristique

attractive ADJECTIVE
séduisant (FEM séduisante)
□ She's very attractive. Elle est très séduisante.

aubergine NOUN
l'aubergine *fem*

auction NOUN
la vente aux enchères *fem*

audience NOUN
les spectateurs *masc pl* (*in theatre*)

audition NOUN
l'audition *fem*

August NOUN
août *masc*
■ **in August** en août

aunt, aunty NOUN
la tante *fem*
□ my aunt ma tante

au pair NOUN
la jeune fille au pair *fem*
□ She's an au pair. Elle est jeune fille au pair.

Australia NOUN
l'Australie *fem*

■ **in Australia** en Australie
■ **to Australia** en Australie

Australian NOUN
▷ *see also* **Australian** ADJECTIVE
l'Australien *masc*
l'Australienne *fem*
■ **the Australians** les Australiens

Australian ADJECTIVE
▷ *see also* **Australian** NOUN
australien (FEM australienne)
□ He's Australian. Il est australien.

Austria NOUN
l'Autriche *fem*
■ **in Austria** en Autriche

Austrian NOUN
▷ *see also* **Austrian** ADJECTIVE
l'Autrichien *masc*
l'Autrichienne *fem*
■ **the Austrians** les Autrichiens

Austrian ADJECTIVE
▷ *see also* **Austrian** NOUN
autrichien (FEM autrichienne)
□ She's Austrian. Elle est autrichienne.

author NOUN
l'auteur *masc*
□ She's a famous author. C'est un auteur connu.

autism NOUN
l'autisme *masc*

autistic ADJECTIVE
autiste (FEM autiste)

autobiography NOUN
l'autobiographie *fem*

autograph NOUN
l'autographe *masc*

automatic ADJECTIVE
automatique (FEM automatique)
□ an automatic door une porte automatique

automatically ADVERB
automatiquement

autumn NOUN
l'automne *masc*
■ **in autumn** en automne

availability NOUN
la disponibilité *fem*

available ADJECTIVE
disponible (FEM disponible)
□ The album is available on the internet. L'album est disponible sur Internet. □ Is Mr Cooke available today? Est-ce que Monsieur Cooke est disponible aujourd'hui ?

avalanche NOUN
l'avalanche *fem*

avatar NOUN
l'avatar *masc*

avenue NOUN
l'avenue *fem*

average NOUN
▷ see also **average** ADJECTIVE
la moyenne *fem*
□ on average en moyenne

average ADJECTIVE
▷ see also **average** NOUN
moyen (FEM moyenne)
□ the average price le prix moyen

avocado NOUN
l'avocat *masc*

to **avoid** VERB
éviter [28]
□ He avoids her when she's in a bad mood.
Il l'évite lorsqu'elle est de mauvaise humeur.
■ **to avoid doing something** éviter [28] de
faire quelque chose □ Avoid going out on your
own at night. Évite de sortir seul le soir.

awake ADJECTIVE
■ **to be awake** être [35] réveillé □ Is she
awake? Elle est réveillée ?
■ **He was still awake.** Il ne dormait pas encore.

award NOUN
le prix *masc*
□ He's won an award. Il a remporté un prix.
□ the award for the best actor le prix du meilleur
acteur

aware ADJECTIVE
■ **to be aware of something** être [35]
conscient de quelque chose

away ADJECTIVE, ADVERB
absent (FEM absente) (*not here*)

□ André's away today. André est absent
aujourd'hui.
■ **He's away for a week.** Il est parti pour une
semaine.
■ **The town's 2 kilometres away.** La ville est à
deux kilomètres d'ici.
■ **The coast is 2 hours away by car.** La côte
est à deux heures de route.
■ **Go away!** Va-t'en !
■ **to put something away** ranger [45] quelque
chose □ He put this sports kit away in the
cupboard. Il a rangé ses affaires de sport dans
le placard.

away match NOUN
le match à l'extérieur *masc*

awful ADJECTIVE
affreux (FEM affreuse)
□ That's awful! C'est affreux !
■ **an awful lot of ...** énormément de ...

awfully ADVERB
■ **I'm awfully sorry.** Je suis vraiment désolé.

awkward ADJECTIVE
1 délicat (FEM délicate) (*difficult to deal with*)
□ an awkward situation une situation délicate
2 gênant (FEM gênante) (*embarrassing*)
□ an awkward question une question gênante
■ **It's a bit awkward for me to come and see
you.** Ce n'est pas très pratique pour moi de venir
vous voir.

axe NOUN
la hache *fem*

Bb

BA NOUN
la licence *fem*
■ **a BA in French** une licence de français

baby NOUN
le bébé *masc*

baby carriage NOUN (US)
le landau *masc*

to **babysit** VERB
faire [36] du baby-sitting

babysitter NOUN
le/la baby-sitter *masc/fem*

babysitting NOUN
le baby-sitting *masc*

bachelor NOUN
le célibataire *masc*
□ He's a bachelor. Il est célibataire.

back NOUN
▷ see also **back** ADJECTIVE, ADVERB, VERB
1 le dos *masc* (*of person, horse, book*)
2 l'arrière *masc* (*of car, house*)
□ in the back à l'arrière
3 le verso *masc* (*of page*)
□ on the back au verso
4 le fond *masc* (*of room, garden*)
□ at the back au fond

back ADJECTIVE, ADVERB
▷ see also **back** NOUN, VERB
arrière (FEM+PL arrière)
□ the back seat le siège arrière □ the back wheel of my bike la roue arrière de mon vélo
■ **the back door** la porte de derrière
■ **to get back** rentrer [68'] □ What time did you get back? À quelle heure est-ce que tu es rentré ?
■ **We went there by bus and walked back.** Nous y sommes allés en bus et nous sommes rentrés à pied.
■ **He's not back yet.** Il n'est pas encore rentré.
■ **to call somebody back** rappeler [4] quelqu'un □ I'll call back later. Je rappellerai plus tard.

to **back** VERB
▷ see also **back** NOUN, ADJECTIVE, ADVERB
soutenir [83] (*support*)
□ We're backing our school team. Nous soutenons l'équipe de notre école.

to **back out** VERB
se désister [28]
□ They backed out at the last minute. Ils se sont désistés au dernier moment.

to **back up** VERB
■ **to back somebody up** soutenir [83] quelqu'un

backache NOUN
le mal au dos *masc*
□ to have backache avoir mal au dos

backbone NOUN
la colonne vertébrale *fem*

to **backfire** VERB
échouer [28] (*go wrong*)

background NOUN
1 l'arrière-plan *masc* (*of picture*)
□ a house in the background une maison à l'arrière-plan
■ **background noise** les bruits de fond *masc pl*
2 le milieu *masc* (PL les milieux)
□ his family background son milieu familial

backhand NOUN
le revers *masc*

backing NOUN
le soutien *masc* (*support*)

backpack NOUN
le sac à dos *masc*

backpacker NOUN
1 le routard *masc*
la routarde *fem* (*globe-trotter*)
2 le randonneur *masc*
la randonneuse *fem* (*hill-walker*)

backpacking NOUN
■ **to go backpacking** voyager [45] sac au dos

back pain NOUN
le mal au dos *masc*
□ to have back pain avoir mal au dos

backside NOUN
le derrière *masc*

backstroke NOUN
le dos crawlé *masc*

backup NOUN
le soutien *masc* (*support*)
■ **a backup file** une sauvegarde

backwards ADVERB
en arrière

□ to take a step backwards faire un pas en arrière

■ **to fall backwards** tomber [84¹] à la renverse

back yard NOUN
la cour *fem*

bacon NOUN
1 le lard *masc* (*French type*)
2 le bacon *masc* (*British type*)
□ bacon and eggs des œufs au bacon

bad ADJECTIVE
1 mauvais (FEM mauvaise)
□ a bad film un mauvais film □ the bad weather le mauvais temps □ to be in a bad mood être de mauvaise humeur

---
WORD POWER

You can use a number of other words instead of **bad** to mean 'terrible':
awful affreux
□ an awful day une journée affreuse
dreadful terrible
□ a dreadful mistake une terrible erreur
rubbish nul
□ a rubbish team une équipe nulle
terrible épouvantable
□ a terrible book un livre épouvantable

■ **to be bad at something** être [35] mauvais en quelque chose □ I'm really bad at maths. Je suis vraiment mauvais en maths.
2 grave (FEM grave) (*serious*)
□ a bad accident un accident grave
3 vilain (FEM vilaine) (*naughty*)
□ You bad boy! Vilain !
■ **to go bad** (*food*) se gâter [28]
■ **I feel bad about it.** Ça m'ennuie.
■ **not bad** pas mal □ That's not bad at all. Ce n'est pas mal du tout.

badge NOUN
le badge *masc*

badly ADVERB
mal
□ badly paid mal payé
■ **badly wounded** grièvement blessé
■ **He badly needs a rest.** Il a sérieusement besoin de se reposer.

badminton NOUN
le badminton *masc*
□ to play badminton jouer au badminton

bad-tempered ADJECTIVE
■ **to be bad-tempered** **1** (*by nature*) avoir [8] mauvais caractère □ He's a really bad-tempered person. Il a vraiment mauvais caractère.
2 (*temporarily*) être [35] de mauvaise humeur
□ He was really bad-tempered yesterday. Il était vraiment de mauvaise humeur hier.

baffled ADJECTIVE
déconcerté (FEM déconcertée)

bag NOUN
le sac *masc*

baggage NOUN
les bagages *masc pl*

baggage reclaim NOUN
la livraison des bagages *fem*

baggy ADJECTIVE
ample (FEM ample)

bagpipes PL NOUN
la cornemuse *fem sing*
□ Ed plays the bagpipes. Ed joue de la cornemuse.

to **bake** VERB
■ **to bake a cake** faire [36] un gâteau

baked ADJECTIVE
cuit au four (FEM cuite au four)
□ baked potatoes les pommes de terre cuites au four *fem pl*
■ **baked beans** les haricots blancs en sauce *masc pl*

baker NOUN
le boulanger *masc*
la boulangère *fem*
□ He's a baker. Il est boulanger.

bakery NOUN
la boulangerie *fem*

baking ADJECTIVE
■ **It's baking in here!** Il fait une chaleur torride ici !

balance NOUN
l'équilibre *masc*
□ to lose one's balance perdre l'équilibre

balanced ADJECTIVE
équilibré (FEM équilibrée)

balcony NOUN
le balcon *masc*

bald ADJECTIVE
chauve (FEM chauve)

ball NOUN
1 la balle *fem* (*tennis, golf, cricket*)
2 le ballon *masc* (*football, rugby*)

ballet NOUN
le ballet *masc*
□ We went to a ballet. Nous sommes allés voir un ballet.
■ **ballet lessons** les cours de ballet *masc pl*

ballet dancer NOUN
le danseur classique *masc*
la danseuse classique *fem*

ballet shoes PL NOUN
les chaussons de ballet *masc pl*

balloon NOUN
le ballon *masc* (*for parties*)
■ **a hot-air balloon** une montgolfière

ballpoint pen NOUN
le stylo à bille *masc*

ballroom dancing NOUN
la danse de salon *fem*

ban NOUN
▷ *see also* **ban** VERB
l'interdiction *fem*

to **ban** VERB
▷ *see also* **ban** NOUN
interdire [27]

banana NOUN
la banane *fem*
□ a banana skin une peau de banane

band NOUN
1 le groupe *masc* (*rock band*)
2 la fanfare *fem* (*brass band*)

bandage NOUN
▷ *see also* **bandage** VERB
le bandage *masc*

to **bandage** VERB
▷ *see also* **bandage** NOUN
mettre [47] un bandage à
□ The nurse bandaged his arm. L'infirmière lui a mis un bandage au bras.

Band-Aid® NOUN (US)
le pansement adhésif *masc*

bandit NOUN
le bandit *masc*

bang NOUN
▷ *see also* **bang** VERB
1 la détonation *fem*
□ I heard a loud bang. J'ai entendu une forte détonation.
2 le coup *masc*
□ a bang on the head un coup sur la tête
■ **Bang!** Pan !

to **bang** VERB
▷ *see also* **bang** NOUN
se cogner [28] (*part of body*)
□ I banged my head. Je me suis cogné la tête.
■ **to bang the door** claquer [28] la porte
■ **to bang on the door** cogner [28] à la porte

banger NOUN
1 le tacot *masc* (*old car*)
□ His car's an old banger. Sa voiture est un vieux tacot.
2 la saucisse *fem* (*sausage*)
□ bangers and mash les saucisses à la purée

Bangladesh NOUN
le Bangladesh *masc*
■ **from Bangladesh** du Bangladesh

bank NOUN
1 la banque *fem* (*financial*)
2 le bord *masc* (*of river, lake*)

bank account NOUN
le compte en banque *masc*

banker NOUN
le banquier *masc*

bank holiday NOUN
le jour férié *masc*

banknote NOUN
le billet de banque *masc*

banned ADJECTIVE
interdit (FEM interdite)

bar NOUN
1 le bar *masc* (*pub*)
2 le comptoir *masc* (*counter*)
■ **a bar of chocolate** une tablette de chocolat
■ **a bar of soap** une savonnette

barbaric ADJECTIVE
barbare (FEM barbare)

barbecue NOUN
le barbecue *masc*

barber NOUN
le coiffeur pour hommes *masc*

bare ADJECTIVE
nu (FEM nue)

barefoot ADJECTIVE, ADVERB
nu-pieds (FEM+PL nu-pieds)
□ The children go around barefoot. Les enfants se promènent nu-pieds.
■ **to be barefoot** avoir [8] les pieds nus □ She was barefoot. Elle avait les pieds nus.

barely ADVERB
à peine
□ I could barely hear what she was saying. J'entendais à peine ce qu'elle disait.

bargain NOUN
l'affaire *fem*
□ It was a bargain! C'était une affaire !

barge NOUN
la péniche *fem*

to **bark** VERB
aboyer [53]

barmaid NOUN
la barmaid *fem*
□ She's a barmaid. Elle est barmaid.

barman NOUN
le barman *masc*
□ He's a barman. Il est barman.

barn NOUN
la grange *fem*

barrel NOUN
le tonneau *masc* (PL les tonneaux)

barrier NOUN
la barrière *fem*

bartender NOUN (US)
le barman *masc*
□ He's a bartender. Il est barman.

base NOUN
la base *fem*

baseball NOUN
le base-ball *masc*
■ **a baseball cap** une casquette de base-ball

based ADJECTIVE
- **based on** fondé sur

basement NOUN
le sous-sol *masc*

to **bash** VERB
▷ *see also* **bash** NOUN
- **to bash something** taper [28] sur quelque chose

bash NOUN
▷ *see also* **bash** VERB
- **I'll have a bash.** Je vais essayer.

basic ADJECTIVE
1 de base
  □ It's a basic model. C'est un modèle de base.
2 rudimentaire (FEM rudimentaire)
  □ The youth hostel is pretty basic. L'auberge de jeunesse est plutôt rudimentaire.

basically ADVERB
tout simplement
  □ Basically, I just don't like him. Tout simplement, je ne l'aime pas.

basics PL NOUN
les rudiments *masc pl*

basil NOUN
le basilic *masc*

basin NOUN
le lavabo *masc* (*washbasin*)

basis NOUN
- **on a daily basis** quotidiennement
- **on a regular basis** régulièrement

basket NOUN
le panier *masc*

BE CAREFUL!
Do not translate **basket** by the French word **basket**.

basketball NOUN
le basket *masc*

bass NOUN
1 la basse *fem* (*guitar, singer*)
  □ He plays the bass. Il joue de la basse. □ He's a bass. Il est basse.
  - **a bass guitar** une guitare basse
  - **a double bass** une contrebasse
2 les graves *masc pl* (*on hi-fi*)

bass drum NOUN
la grosse caisse *fem*

bassoon NOUN
le basson *masc*
  □ I play the bassoon. Je joue du basson.

bat NOUN
1 la batte *fem* (*for cricket, rounders*)
2 la raquette *fem* (*for table tennis*)
3 la chauve-souris *fem* (PL les chauves-souris) (*animal*)

bath NOUN
1 le bain *masc*
  □ to have a bath prendre un bain
  - **a hot bath** un bain chaud
2 la baignoire *fem* (*bathtub*)
  □ There's a spider in the bath. Il y a une araignée dans la baignoire.

to **bathe** VERB
se baigner [28]

bathing suit NOUN (US)
le maillot de bain *masc*

bathroom NOUN
la salle de bains *fem*

baths PL NOUN
la piscine *fem sing*

bath towel NOUN
la serviette de bain *fem*

batter NOUN
la pâte à frire *fem*

battery NOUN
1 la pile *fem* (*for torch, toy*)
2 la batterie *fem* (*of car*)

battle NOUN
la bataille *fem*
  □ the Battle of Hastings la bataille de Hastings
  - **It was a battle, but we managed in the end.** Il a fallu se battre, mais on a fini par y arriver.

battleship NOUN
le cuirassé *masc*

bay NOUN
la baie *fem*

BC ABBREVIATION (= *before Christ*)
av. J.-C. (= *avant Jésus-Christ*)
  □ in 200 BC en deux cents avant Jésus-Christ

to **be** VERB
être [35]
  □ I'm tired. Je suis fatigué. □ You're late. Tu es en retard. □ She's English. Elle est anglaise. □ Edinburgh is in Scotland. Édimbourg est en Écosse. □ It's 4 o'clock. Il est quatre heures. □ We are all happy. Nous sommes tous heureux. □ They are in Paris at the moment. Ils sont à Paris en ce moment. □ I've been ill. J'ai été malade.
  - **It's the 28th of October today.** Nous sommes le vingt-huit octobre.
  - **Have you been to Greece before?** Est-ce que tu es déjà allé en Grèce ?
  - **I've never been to Paris.** Je ne suis jamais allé à Paris.
  - **to be killed** être [35] tué

When you are saying what somebody's occupation is in French, you do not translate 'a'.

□ She's a doctor. Elle est médecin. □ He's a student. Il est étudiant.

> With certain adjectives, such as 'cold', 'hot', 'hungry' and 'thirsty', use **avoir** instead of **être**.

■ **I'm cold.** J'ai froid.
■ **I'm hungry.** J'ai faim.

> When saying how old somebody is, use **avoir** not **être**.

■ **I'm fourteen.** J'ai quatorze ans.
■ **How old are you?** Quel âge as-tu ?

> When referring to the weather, use **faire**.

■ **It's cold.** Il fait froid.
■ **It's a nice day.** Il fait beau.
■ **It's too hot.** Il fait trop chaud.

beach NOUN
la plage *fem*

bead NOUN
la perle *fem*

beak NOUN
le bec *masc*

beam NOUN
le rayon *masc*

beans NOUN
1 les haricots *masc pl*
2 les haricots blancs à la sauce tomate *masc pl* (*baked beans*)
■ **broad beans** les fèves *fem pl*
■ **green beans** les haricots verts *masc pl*
■ **kidney beans** les haricots rouges *masc pl*

bear NOUN
▷ *see also* **bear** VERB
l'ours *masc*

to **bear** VERB
▷ *see also* **bear** NOUN
■ **I can't bear it!** C'est insupportable !

beard NOUN
la barbe *fem*
■ **He's got a beard.** Il est barbu.
■ **a man with a beard** un barbu

bearded ADJECTIVE
barbu (*fem* barbue)

beat NOUN
▷ *see also* **beat** VERB
le rythme *masc*

to **beat** VERB
▷ *see also* **beat** NOUN
battre [9]
□ We beat them 3-0. On les a battus trois à zéro.
■ **Beat it!** Fiche le camp ! (*informal*)
■ **to beat somebody up** (*informal*) tabasser [28] quelqu'un

beautiful ADJECTIVE
beau (*fem* belle, *masc* *pl* beaux)

> **beau** changes to **bel** before a vowel and most words beginning with 'h'.

beautifully ADVERB
admirablement

beauty NOUN
la beauté *fem*

beauty spot NOUN
le site pittoresque *masc*

became VERB ▷ *see* **become**

because CONJUNCTION
parce que
□ I did it because … Je l'ai fait parce que …
■ **because of** à cause de □ because of the weather à cause du temps

to **become** VERB
devenir [25ᶠ]
□ He became a famous writer. Il est devenu un grand écrivain.

bed NOUN
le lit *masc*
□ in bed au lit
■ **to go to bed** aller [3ᶠ] se coucher
■ **to go to bed with somebody** coucher [28] avec quelqu'un

bed and breakfast NOUN
la chambre d'hôte *fem*
□ We stayed in a bed and breakfast. Nous avons logé dans une chambre d'hôte.
■ **How much is it for bed and breakfast?** C'est combien pour la chambre et le petit déjeuner ?

bedclothes PL NOUN
les draps et les couvertures *masc pl*

bedding NOUN
la literie *fem*

bedroom NOUN
la chambre *fem*

bedsit NOUN
la chambre meublée *fem*

bedspread NOUN
le dessus-de-lit *masc* (PL les dessus-de-lit)

bedtime NOUN
■ **Ten o'clock is my usual bedtime.** Je me couche généralement à dix heures.
■ **Bedtime!** Au lit !

bee NOUN
l'abeille *fem*

beef NOUN
le bœuf *masc*
■ **roast beef** le rosbif

beefburger NOUN
le hamburger *masc*

been VERB ▷ *see* **be**

beer NOUN
la bière *fem*

beetle NOUN
le scarabée *masc*

b

beetroot - beltway

beetroot NOUN
la betterave rouge *fem*

before PREPOSITION, CONJUNCTION, ADVERB
1 avant
  □ before Tuesday avant mardi
2 avant de
  □ before going avant de partir □ Before opening the packet, read the instructions. Avant d'ouvrir le paquet, lisez le mode d'emploi. □ I'll phone before I leave. J'appellerai avant de partir.
3 déjà (*already*)
  □ I've seen this film before. J'ai déjà vu ce film. □ Have you been rock climbing before? Vous avez déjà fait de la varappe ?
  ■ **the day before** la veille
  ■ **the week before** la semaine précédente

beforehand ADVERB
à l'avance

to **beg** VERB
1 mendier [19] (*for money*)
2 supplier [19]
  □ He begged me to stop. Il m'a supplié d'arrêter.

began VERB ▷ *see* **begin**

beggar NOUN
le mendiant *masc*
la mendiante *fem*

to **begin** VERB
commencer [12]
  ■ **to begin doing something** commencer [12] à faire quelque chose

beginner NOUN
le débutant *masc*
la débutante *fem*
  □ I'm just a beginner. Je ne suis qu'un débutant.

beginning NOUN
le début *masc*
  ■ **at the beginning** au début

begun VERB ▷ *see* **begin**

behalf NOUN
  ■ **on behalf of somebody** pour quelqu'un

to **behave** VERB
se comporter [28]
  □ He behaved like an idiot. Il s'est comporté comme un idiot. □ She behaved very badly. Elle s'est très mal comportée.
  ■ **to behave oneself** être [35] sage □ Did the children behave themselves? Est-ce que les enfants ont été sages ?
  ■ **Behave!** Sois sage !

behaviour (US **behavior**) NOUN
le comportement *masc*

behind PREPOSITION, ADVERB
  ▷ *see also* **behind** NOUN
derrière
  □ behind the television derrière la télévision
  ■ **to be behind** (*late*) avoir [8] du retard

□ I'm behind with my revision. J'ai du retard dans mes révisions.

behind NOUN
  ▷ *see also* **behind** PREPOSITION, ADVERB
le derrière *masc*

beige ADJECTIVE
beige (FEM beige)

Belgian NOUN
  ▷ *see also* **Belgian** ADJECTIVE
le/la Belge *masc/fem*
  ■ **the Belgians** les Belges

Belgian ADJECTIVE
  ▷ *see also* **Belgian** NOUN
belge (FEM belge)
  □ Belgian chocolate le chocolat belge □ She's Belgian. Elle est belge.

Belgium NOUN
la Belgique *fem*
  ■ **in Belgium** en Belgique

to **believe** VERB
croire [20]
  □ I don't believe you. Je ne te crois pas.
  ■ **to believe in something** croire [20] à quelque chose □ Do you believe in ghosts? Tu crois aux fantômes ?
  ■ **to believe in God** croire [20] en Dieu

bell NOUN
1 la sonnette *fem* (*doorbell*)
  ■ **to ring the bell** sonner [28] à la porte
2 la cloche *fem* (*in church*)
3 la sonnerie *fem* (*in school*)
4 la clochette *fem*
  □ Our cat has a bell on its collar. Notre chat a une clochette sur son collier.

belly NOUN
le ventre *masc*

to **belong** VERB
  ■ **to belong to somebody** être [35] à quelqu'un □ Who does it belong to? C'est à qui ? □ That belongs to me. C'est à moi.
  ■ **Do you belong to any clubs?** Est-ce que tu es membre d'un club ?
  ■ **Where does this belong?** Où est-ce que ça va ?

belongings PL NOUN
les affaires *fem pl*

below PREPOSITION, ADVERB
1 au-dessous de
  □ below the castle au-dessous du château
2 en dessous
  □ on the floor below à l'étage en dessous
  ■ **10 degrees below freezing** moins dix

belt NOUN
la ceinture *fem*

beltway NOUN (US)
le périphérique *masc*

Numbers in brackets refer to verb tables on pages 650 to 658

bench NOUN
1 le banc *masc* (*seat*)
2 l'établi *masc* (*for woodwork*)

benchmark NOUN
l'référence *fem*

bend NOUN
▷ *see also* **bend** VERB
1 le virage *masc* (*in road*)
2 le coude *masc* (*in river*)

to **bend** VERB
▷ *see also* **bend** NOUN
1 courber [28] (*back*)
2 plier [19] (*leg, arm*)
□ I can't bend my arm. Je n'arrive pas à plier le bras.
■ **'do not bend'** « ne pas plier »
3 tordre [49] (*object*)
□ You've bent it. Tu l'as tordu.
4 se tordre [49]
□ It bends easily. Ça se tord facilement.

to **bend down** VERB
se baisser [28]

to **bend over** VERB
se pencher [28]

beneath PREPOSITION
sous

benefit NOUN
▷ *see also* **benefit** VERB
l'avantage *masc* (*advantage*)
■ **She's on benefits.** Elle touche les allocations chômage.

to **benefit** VERB
▷ *see also* **benefit** NOUN
■ **He'll benefit from the change.** Le changement lui fera du bien.

bent VERB ▷ *see* **bend**

bent ADJECTIVE
tordu (FEM tordue)
□ a bent fork une fourchette tordue

beret NOUN
le béret *masc*

berserk ADJECTIVE
■ **to go berserk** devenir [25!] fou furieux □ She went berserk. Elle est devenue folle furieuse.

berth NOUN
la couchette *fem*

beside PREPOSITION
à côté de
□ beside the television à côté de la télévision
■ **He was beside himself.** Il était hors de lui.
■ **That's beside the point.** Cela n'a rien à voir.

besides ADVERB
en plus
□ Besides, it's too expensive. En plus, c'est trop cher.

best ADJECTIVE, ADVERB
1 meilleur (FEM meilleure)
□ He's the best player in the team. Il est le meilleur joueur de l'équipe. □ Layla's the best at maths. Layla est la meilleure en maths.
2 le mieux
□ Emma sings best. C'est Emma qui chante le mieux. □ That's the best I can do. Je ne peux pas faire mieux.
■ **to do one's best** faire [36] de son mieux
□ It's not perfect, but I did my best. Ça n'est pas parfait, mais j'ai fait de mon mieux.
■ **to make the best of it** s'en contenter [28]
□ We'll have to make the best of it. Il va falloir nous en contenter.

best man NOUN
le garçon d'honneur *masc*

bet NOUN
▷ *see also* **bet** VERB
le pari *masc*
□ to make a bet faire un pari

to **bet** VERB
▷ *see also* **bet** NOUN
parier [19]
□ I bet you he won't come. Je te parie qu'il ne viendra pas. □ I bet he forgot. Je parie qu'il a oublié.

to **betray** VERB
trahir [38]

better ADJECTIVE, ADVERB
1 meilleur (FEM meilleure)
□ This one's better than that one. Celui-ci est meilleur que celui-là. □ a better way to do it une meilleure façon de le faire
2 mieux
□ That's better! C'est mieux comme ça.
■ **better still** encore mieux □ Go and see her tomorrow, or better still, go today. Va la voir demain, ou encore mieux, vas-y aujourd'hui.
■ **the sooner the better** le plus tôt sera le mieux □ Phone her, the sooner the better. Appelle-la, le plus tôt sera le mieux.
■ **to get better** 1 (*improve*) s'améliorer [28]
□ I hope the weather gets better soon. J'espère que le temps va s'améliorer bientôt.
□ My French is getting better. Mon français s'améliore. 2 (*from illness*) se remettre [47]
□ I hope you get better soon. J'espère que tu vas vite te remettre.
■ **to feel better** se sentir [77] mieux □ Are you feeling better now? Tu te sens mieux maintenant ?
■ **You'd better do it straight away.** Vous feriez mieux de le faire immédiatement.
■ **I'd better go home.** Je ferais mieux de rentrer.

betting shop NOUN
le bureau de paris *masc*

between PREPOSITION
entre

b

□ Stroud is between Oxford and Bristol. Stroud est entre Oxford et Bristol. □ between 15 and 20 minutes entre quinze et vingt minutes

bewildered ADJECTIVE
■ **He looked bewildered.** Il avait l'air perplexe.

beyond PREPOSITION
au-delà de
□ There was a lake beyond the mountain. Il y avait un lac au-delà de la montagne.
■ **beyond belief** incroyable
■ **beyond repair** irréparable

biased ADJECTIVE
partial (FEM partiale)

Bible NOUN
la Bible fem

bicycle NOUN
le vélo masc

big ADJECTIVE
1 grand (FEM grande)
□ a big house une grande maison □ my big brother mon grand frère □ her big sister sa grande sœur

> **WORD POWER**
> You can use a number of other words instead of **big** to mean 'large':
> **enormous** énorme
> □ an enormous cake un gâteau énorme
> **gigantic** gigantesque
> □ a gigantic house une maison gigantesque
> **huge** immense
> □ a huge garden un jardin immense
> **massive** énorme
> □ a massive TV une télé énorme

■ **He's a big guy.** C'est un grand gaillard.
2 gros (FEM grosse) (car, animal, book, parcel)
□ a big car une grosse voiture

bigheaded ADJECTIVE
■ **to be bigheaded** avoir [8] la grosse tête

bike NOUN
le vélo masc
□ by bike en vélo

bikini NOUN
le bikini masc

bilingual ADJECTIVE
bilingue (FEM bilingue)

bill NOUN
1 l'addition fem (in restaurant)
□ Can we have the bill, please? L'addition, s'il vous plaît.
2 la facture fem (for gas, electricity)
3 le billet masc (US)
□ a five-dollar bill un billet de cinq dollars

billion NOUN
le milliard masc

bin NOUN
la poubelle fem

bingo NOUN
le bingo masc

binoculars PL NOUN
les jumelles fem pl
■ **a pair of binoculars** des jumelles

biochemistry NOUN
la biochimie fem

biofuel NOUN
le biocarburant masc

biography NOUN
la biographie fem

biology NOUN
la biologie fem

bird NOUN
l'oiseau masc (PL les oiseaux)

birdwatching NOUN
■ **My hobby's birdwatching.** Mon passe-temps favori est d'observer les oiseaux.
■ **to go birdwatching** aller [3ᵗ] observer les oiseaux

Biro® NOUN
le bic® masc

birth NOUN
la naissance fem
□ date of birth la date de naissance

birth certificate NOUN
l'acte de naissance masc

birth control NOUN
la contraception fem

birthday NOUN
l'anniversaire masc
□ When's your birthday? Quelle est la date de ton anniversaire ?
■ **a birthday cake** un gâteau d'anniversaire
■ **a birthday card** une carte d'anniversaire
■ **I'm going to have a birthday party.** Je vais faire une fête pour mon anniversaire.

biscuit NOUN
le gâteau sec masc (PL les gâteaux secs)

bisexual ADJECTIVE
bisexuel (FEM bisexuelle)

bishop NOUN
l'évêque masc/fem

bit VERB ▷ see **bite**

bit NOUN
le morceau masc (PL les morceaux)
□ Would you like another bit? Est-ce que tu en veux un autre morceau ?
■ **a bit of 1** (piece of) un morceau de □ a bit of cake un morceau de gâteau **2** (a little) un peu de □ a bit of music un peu de musique
■ **It's a bit of a nuisance.** C'est ennuyeux.
■ **a bit** un peu □ He's a bit mad. Il est un peu fou. □ a bit too hot un peu trop chaud □ Wait a bit! Attends un peu ! □ Do you play football? — A bit. Tu joues au football ? — Un peu.

■ **to fall to bits** se désintégrer [34]
■ **to take something to bits** démonter [28] quelque chose
■ **bit by bit** petit à petit

bitch NOUN
la chienne *fem* (*female dog*)

to **bite** VERB
▷ *see also* **bite** NOUN
1 mordre [49] (*person, dog*)
2 piquer [28] (*insect*)
□ I got bitten by mosquitoes. Je me suis fait piquer par des moustiques.
■ **to bite one's nails** se ronger [45] les ongles

bite NOUN
▷ *see also* **bite** VERB
1 la piqûre *fem* (*insect bite*)
2 la morsure *fem* (*animal bite*)
■ **to have a bite to eat** manger [45] un morceau

bitten VERB ▷ *see* **bite**

bitter ADJECTIVE
▷ *see also* **bitter** NOUN
1 amer (FEM amère)
2 glacial (FEM glaciale, MASC PL glaciaux) (*weather, wind*)
□ It's bitter today. Il fait un froid glacial aujourd'hui.

bitter NOUN
▷ *see also* **bitter** ADJECTIVE
la bière brune *fem*

Black ADJECTIVE
noir (FEM noire)
□ Black students les étudiants noirs

black ADJECTIVE
noir (FEM noire)
□ a black jacket une veste noire

blackberry NOUN
la mûre *fem*

blackbird NOUN
le merle *masc*

blackboard NOUN
le tableau noir *masc* (PL les tableaux noirs)

black coffee NOUN
le café *masc*

blackcurrant NOUN
le cassis *masc*

blackmail NOUN
▷ *see also* **blackmail** VERB
le chantage *masc*
□ That's blackmail! C'est du chantage !

to **blackmail** VERB
▷ *see also* **blackmail** NOUN
■ **to blackmail somebody** faire [36] chanter quelqu'un □ He blackmailed her. Il l'a fait chanter.

blackout NOUN
la panne d'électricité *fem* (*power cut*)

■ **to have a blackout** (*faint*) s'évanouir [38]

black pudding NOUN
le boudin *masc*

blade NOUN
la lame *fem*

to **blame** VERB
■ **Don't blame me!** Ça n'est pas ma faute !
■ **I blame the police.** À mon avis, c'est la faute de la police.
■ **He blamed it on my sister.** Il a dit que c'était la faute de ma sœur.

blank ADJECTIVE
▷ *see also* **blank** NOUN
1 blanc (FEM blanche) (*paper*)
2 vierge (FEM vierge) (*form*)
■ **My mind went blank.** J'ai eu un trou.

blank NOUN
▷ *see also* **blank** ADJECTIVE
le blanc *masc*
□ Fill in the blanks. Remplissez les blancs.

blank cheque NOUN
le chèque en blanc *masc*

blanket NOUN
la couverture *fem*

blast NOUN
■ **a bomb blast** une explosion

blatant ADJECTIVE
flagrant (FEM flagrante)

blaze NOUN
l'incendie *masc*

blazer NOUN
le blazer *masc*

bleach NOUN
l'eau de Javel *fem*

bleached ADJECTIVE
décoloré (FEM décolorée)
□ bleached hair les cheveux décolorés

bleak ADJECTIVE
désolé (FEM désolée) (*place*)
■ **The future looks bleak.** L'avenir semble peu prometteur.

to **bleed** VERB
saigner [28]
□ My nose is bleeding. Je saigne du nez.

bleeper NOUN
le bip *masc*

blender NOUN
le mixer *masc*

to **bless** VERB
bénir [38] (*religiously*)
■ **Bless you!** (*after sneezing*) À tes souhaits !

BE CAREFUL!
Do not translate **to bless** by the French word **blesser**.

blew VERB ▷ *see* **blow**

blind – board

blind ADJECTIVE
  ▷ see also **blind** NOUN
  aveugle (FEM aveugle)

blind NOUN
  ▷ see also **blind** ADJECTIVE
  le store *masc* (*for window*)

blindfold NOUN
  ▷ see also **blindfold** VERB
  le bandeau *masc* (PL les bandeaux)

to **blindfold** VERB
  ▷ see also **blindfold** NOUN
  ■ **to blindfold somebody** bander [28] les yeux
  à quelqu'un

to **blink** VERB
  cligner [28] des yeux

bliss NOUN
  ■ **It was bliss!** C'était merveilleux !

blister NOUN
  l'ampoule *fem*

blizzard NOUN
  la tempête de neige *fem*

blob NOUN
  la goutte *fem*
  □ a blob of glue une goutte de colle

block NOUN
  ▷ see also **block** VERB
  l'immeuble *masc*
  □ He lives in our block. Il habite dans notre
  immeuble.
  ■ **a block of flats** un immeuble

to **block** VERB
  ▷ see also **block** NOUN
  bloquer [28]

blockage NOUN
  l'obstruction *fem*

blog NOUN
  ▷ see also **blog** VERB
  le blog *masc*
  □ She has her own blog. Elle a son blog.

to **blog** VERB
  ▷ see also **blog** NOUN
  bloguer [28]
  ■ **He has been blogging about his school.**
  Il parle de son école sur son blog.

blogger NOUN
  le bloggeur *masc*
  la bloggeuse *fem*

blogpost NOUN
  le post de blog *masc*

bloke NOUN
  le mec *masc* (*informal*)

blonde ADJECTIVE
  blond (FEM blonde)
  □ She's got blonde hair. Elle a les cheveux
  blonds.

blood NOUN
  le sang *masc*

blood pressure NOUN
  ■ **to have high blood pressure** faire [36] de
  la tension

blood sports NOUN
  les sports sanguinaires *masc pl*

blood test NOUN
  la prise de sang *fem*

blouse NOUN
  le chemisier *masc*

blow NOUN
  ▷ see also **blow** VERB
  le coup *masc*

to **blow** VERB
  ▷ see also **blow** NOUN
  souffler [28] (*wind, person*)
  ■ **to blow one's nose** se moucher [28]
  ■ **to blow a whistle** siffler [28]
  ■ **to blow out a candle** éteindre [60] une
  bougie

to **blow up** VERB
1 faire [36] sauter
  □ The police station was blown up yesterday.
  On a fait sauter le commissariat hier.
2 gonfler [28]
  □ to blow up a balloon gonfler un ballon
  ■ **The house blew up.** La maison a sauté.

blow-dry NOUN
  le brushing *masc*
  ■ **A cut and blow-dry, please.** Une coupe
  brushing, s'il vous plaît.

blown VERB ▷ see **blow**

blue ADJECTIVE
  bleu (FEM bleue)
  □ a blue dress une robe bleue
  ■ **It came out of the blue.** C'était
  complètement inattendu.

blues PL NOUN
  le blues *masc sing*

to **bluff** VERB
  ▷ see also **bluff** NOUN
  bluffer [28]

bluff NOUN
  ▷ see also **bluff** VERB
  le bluff *masc*
  □ It's just a bluff. C'est du bluff.

blunder NOUN
  la gaffe *fem*

blunt ADJECTIVE
1 brusque (FEM brusque) (*person*)
2 émoussé (FEM émoussée) (*knife*)

to **blush** VERB
  rougir [38]

board NOUN
1 la planche *fem* (*wooden*)

Numbers in brackets refer to verb tables on pages 650 to 658

2 le tableau *masc* (PL les tableaux) (*blackboard*)
  □ on the board au tableau
3 le panneau *masc* (PL les panneaux)
  (*noticeboard*)
4 le jeu *masc* (PL les jeux) (*for board games*)
5 l'échiquier *masc* (*for chess*)
  ■ **on board** à bord
  ■ **full board** pension complète

boarder NOUN
  l'interne *masc/fem*

board game NOUN
  le jeu de société *masc* (PL les jeux de société)

boarding card NOUN
  la carte d'embarquement *fem*

boarding school NOUN
  le pensionnat *masc*
  ■ **I go to boarding school.** Je suis interne.

to **boast** VERB
  se vanter [28]
  □ Stop boasting! Arrête de te vanter !
  ■ **to boast about something** se vanter [28] de
  quelque chose

boat NOUN
  le bateau *masc* (PL les bateaux)

body NOUN
  le corps *masc*

bodybuilding NOUN
  le culturisme *masc*

bodyguard NOUN
  le garde du corps *masc*

bog NOUN
  la tourbière *fem* (*marsh*)

boil NOUN
  ▷ *see also* **boil** VERB
  le furoncle *masc*

to **boil** VERB
  ▷ *see also* **boil** NOUN
1 faire [36] bouillir
  □ to boil some water faire bouillir de l'eau
  ■ **to boil an egg** faire [36] cuire un œuf
2 bouillir [11]
  □ The water's boiling. L'eau bout. □ The water's
  boiled. L'eau a bouilli.

to **boil over** VERB
  déborder [28]

boiled ADJECTIVE
  à l'eau
  □ boiled potatoes des pommes de terre à l'eau
  ■ **a boiled egg** un œuf à la coque

boiling ADJECTIVE
  ■ **It's boiling in here!** Il fait une chaleur torride
  ici !
  ■ **boiling hot** torride □ a boiling hot day une
  journée torride

bolt NOUN
1 le verrou *masc* (*on door*)
2 le boulon *masc* (*with nut*)

bomb NOUN
  ▷ *see also* **bomb** VERB
  la bombe *fem*

to **bomb** VERB
  ▷ *see also* **bomb** NOUN
  bombarder [28]

bomber NOUN
  le bombardier *masc*

bombing NOUN
  l'attentat à la bombe *masc*

bond NOUN
  le lien *masc*

bone NOUN
1 l'os *masc* (*of human, animal*)
2 l'arête *fem* (*of fish*)

bone dry ADJECTIVE
  complètement sec (FEM complètement sèche)

bonfire NOUN
  le feu *masc* (PL les feux)

> **DID YOU KNOW...?**
> The French do not celebrate Bonfire Night,
> though they have fireworks on the 14th July,
> which is Bastille Day.

bonnet NOUN
  le capot *masc* (*of car*)

bonus NOUN
1 la prime *fem* (*extra payment*)
2 le plus *masc* (*added advantage*)

book NOUN
  ▷ *see also* **book** VERB
  le livre *masc*

to **book** VERB
  ▷ *see also* **book** NOUN
  réserver [28]
  □ We haven't booked. Nous n'avons pas
  réservé.

bookcase NOUN
  la bibliothèque *fem*

booklet NOUN
  la brochure *fem*

bookmark NOUN
  le signet *masc* (*computing*)

bookshelf NOUN
  l'étagère à livres *fem*

bookshop NOUN
  la librairie *fem*

to **boost** VERB
  stimuler [28]
  □ to boost the economy stimuler l'économie
  ■ **The win boosted the team's morale.** La
  victoire a remonté le moral de l'équipe.

boot NOUN
1 le coffre *masc* (*of car*)
2 la botte *fem* (*fashion boot*)
3 la chaussure de marche *fem* (*for hiking*)
  ■ **football boots** des chaussures de foot

booze NOUN
l'alcool *masc*

border NOUN
la frontière *fem*

bore VERB ▷ *see* **bear**

bored ADJECTIVE
■ **to be bored** s'ennuyer [53] □ I was bored.
Je m'ennuyais.
■ **to get bored** s'ennuyer [53]

boredom NOUN
l'ennui *masc*

boring ADJECTIVE
ennuyeux (FEM ennuyeuse)

born ADJECTIVE
■ **to be born** naître [52¹] □ I was born in 2000.
Je suis né en deux mille.

to **borrow** VERB
emprunter [28]
□ Can I borrow your tablet? Je peux emprunter
ta tablette ?
■ **to borrow something from somebody**
emprunter [28] quelque chose à quelqu'un
□ I borrowed some money from a friend. J'ai
emprunté de l'argent à un ami.

Bosnia NOUN
la Bosnie *fem*

Bosnian ADJECTIVE
bosniaque (FEM bosniaque)

boss NOUN
le patron *masc*
la patronne *fem*

to **boss around** VERB
■ **to boss somebody around** donner [28] des
ordres à quelqu'un

bossy ADJECTIVE
autoritaire (FEM autoritaire)

both ADJECTIVE, PRONOUN
tous les deux *masc pl*
toutes les deux *fem pl*
□ We both went. Nous y sommes allés tous les
deux. □ Emma and Zahara both went. Emma
et Zahara y sont allées toutes les deux. □ Both
of your answers are wrong. Vos réponses sont
toutes les deux mauvaises. □ Both of them
have left. Ils sont partis tous les deux. □ Both
of us went. Nous y sommes allés tous les deux.
□ Both Ava and Harry are against it. Ava et Harry
sont tous les deux contre.
■ **He speaks both German and Italian.**
Il parle allemand et italien.

to **bother** VERB
1 tracasser [28] (*worry*)
□ What's bothering you? Qu'est-ce qui te
tracasse ?
2 déranger [45] (*disturb*)
□ I'm sorry to bother you. Je suis désolé de
vous déranger.

■ **no bother** aucun problème
■ **Don't bother!** Ça n'est pas la peine !
■ **to bother to do something** prendre [65] la
peine de faire quelque chose □ He didn't bother
to tell me about it. Il n'a pas pris la peine de m'en
parler.

bottle NOUN
la bouteille *fem*

bottle bank NOUN
le conteneur à verre *masc*

bottle-opener NOUN
l'ouvre-bouteille *masc*

bottom NOUN
▷ *see also* **bottom** ADJECTIVE
1 le fond *masc* (*of container, bag, sea*)
2 le derrière *masc* (*buttocks*)
3 le bas *masc* (*of page, list*)

bottom ADJECTIVE
▷ *see also* **bottom** NOUN
inférieur (FEM inférieure)
□ the bottom shelf l'étagère inférieure
■ **the bottom sheet** le drap de dessous

bought VERB ▷ *see* **buy**

to **bounce** VERB
rebondir [38]

bouncer NOUN
le videur *masc*

bound ADJECTIVE
■ **He's bound to fail.** Il va sûrement échouer.

boundary NOUN
la frontière *fem*

bow NOUN
▷ *see also* **bow** VERB
1 le nœud *masc* (*knot*)
□ to tie a bow faire un nœud
2 l'arc *masc*
□ a bow and arrows un arc et des flèches

to **bow** VERB
▷ *see also* **bow** NOUN
faire [36] une révérence

bowels PL NOUN
les intestins *masc pl*

bowl NOUN
▷ *see also* **bowl** VERB
le bol *masc* (*for soup, cereal*)

to **bowl** VERB
▷ *see also* **bowl** NOUN
lancer [12] la balle (*in cricket*)

bowler NOUN
le lanceur *masc* (*in cricket*)

bowling NOUN
le bowling *masc*
■ **to go bowling** jouer [28] au bowling
■ **a bowling alley** un bowling

bowls NOUN
les boules *fem pl*
□ to play bowls jouer aux boules

bow tie NOUN
le nœud papillon *masc*

box NOUN
la boîte *fem*
□ a box of matches une boîte d'allumettes
■ **a cardboard box** un carton

boxer NOUN
le boxeur *masc*

boxer shorts PL NOUN
le caleçon *masc sing*

boxing NOUN
la boxe *fem*

Boxing Day NOUN
le lendemain de Noël *masc*
□ on Boxing Day le lendemain de Noël

boy NOUN
le garçon *masc*

boyfriend NOUN
le copain *masc*
□ Have you got a boyfriend? Est-ce que tu as
un copain ?

bra NOUN
le soutien-gorge *masc* (PL les soutiens-gorge)

brace NOUN
l'appareil *masc* (on teeth)
□ She wears a brace. Elle a un appareil.

bracelet NOUN
le bracelet *masc*

braces PL NOUN
l'appareil *masc sing* (on teeth)
□ She wears braces. Elle a un appareil.

brackets PL NOUN
■ **in brackets** entre parenthèses

brain NOUN
le cerveau *masc* (PL les cerveaux)

brainy ADJECTIVE
intelligent (FEM intelligente)

brake NOUN
▷ *see also* **brake** VERB
le frein *masc*

to **brake** VERB
▷ *see also* **brake** NOUN
freiner [28]

branch NOUN
1 la branche *fem* (of tree)
2 l'agence *fem* (of bank)

brand NOUN
la marque *fem*
□ a well-known brand of trainers une marque d
e baskets bien connue

brand name NOUN
la marque *fem*

brand-new ADJECTIVE
tout neuf (FEM toute neuve)

brandy NOUN
le cognac *masc*

brass NOUN
le cuivre *masc*
■ **the brass section** les cuivres

brass band NOUN
la fanfare *fem*

brat NOUN
■ **He's a spoiled brat.** C'est un enfant gâté.

brave ADJECTIVE
courageux (FEM courageuse)

Brazil NOUN
le Brésil *masc*
■ **in Brazil** au Brésil

bread NOUN
le pain *masc*
□ brown bread le pain complet □ white bread
le pain blanc
■ **bread and butter** les tartines de pain
beurrées *fem pl*

break NOUN
▷ *see also* **break** VERB
1 la pause *fem* (rest)
□ to take a break faire une pause
2 la récréation *fem* (at school)
□ during morning break pendant la récréation
du matin
■ **the Christmas break** les vacances de Noël
■ **Give me a break!** Laisse-moi tranquille !

to **break** VERB
▷ *see also* **break** NOUN
1 casser [28]
□ Careful, you'll break something! Attention, tu
vas casser quelque chose !
2 se casser [28] (get broken)
□ Careful, it'll break! Attention, ça va se casser !
■ **to break one's leg** se casser [28] la jambe
□ I broke my leg. Je me suis cassé la jambe.
■ **to break a promise** rompre [75] une
promesse
■ **to break a record** battre [9] un record
■ **to break the law** violer [28] la loi

to **break down** VERB
tomber [84ᵉ] en panne
□ The car broke down. La voiture est tombée
en panne.

to **break in** VERB
entrer [32ᵉ] par effraction

to **break off** VERB
1 casser [28]
□ He broke off a piece of chocolate. Il a cassé un
bout de chocolat.
2 se casser [28]
□ The branch broke off in the storm. La branche
s'est cassée pendant l'orage.

to **break open** VERB
forcer [12] (door, cupboard)

to **break out** VERB
1 se déclarer [28] (fire)

2 éclater [28] (*war*)

3 s'évader [28] (*prisoner*)
  ■ **to break out in a rash** être [35] couvert de boutons

to **break up** VERB

1 se disperser [28] (*crowd*)

2 se terminer [28] (*meeting, party*)

3 se séparer [28] (*couple*)
  ■ **to break up a fight** mettre [47] fin à une bagarre
  ■ **We break up next Wednesday.** Nos vacances commencent mercredi.

breakdown NOUN

1 la panne *fem* (*in vehicle*)
  □ to have a breakdown tomber en panne

2 la dépression *fem* (*mental*)
  □ to have a breakdown faire une dépression

breakdown van NOUN
  la dépanneuse *fem*

breakfast NOUN
  le petit déjeuner *masc*
  □ What would you like for breakfast? Qu'est-ce que vous voulez pour le petit déjeuner ?

break-in NOUN
  le cambriolage *masc*

breast NOUN
  le sein *masc* (*of woman*)
  ■ **chicken breast** le blanc de poulet

to **breast-feed** VERB
  allaiter [28]

breaststroke NOUN
  la brasse *fem*

breath NOUN
  l'haleine *fem*
  □ to have bad breath avoir mauvaise haleine
  ■ **to be out of breath** être [35] essoufflé
  ■ **to get one's breath back** reprendre [65] son souffle

to **breathe** VERB
  respirer [28]

to **breathe in** VERB
  inspirer [28]

to **breathe out** VERB
  expirer [28]

to **breed** VERB
  ▷ see also **breed** NOUN
  se reproduire [23] (*reproduce*)
  ■ **to breed dogs** faire [36] de l'élevage de chiens

breed NOUN
  ▷ see also **breed** VERB
  la race *fem*

breeze NOUN
  la brise *fem*

brewery NOUN
  la brasserie *fem*

to **bribe** VERB
  soudoyer [53]

brick NOUN
  la brique *fem*
  □ a brick wall un mur en brique

bricklayer NOUN
  le maçon *masc*

bride NOUN
  la mariée *fem*

bridegroom NOUN
  le marié *masc*

bridesmaid NOUN
  la demoiselle d'honneur *fem*

bridge NOUN

1 le pont *masc*
  □ a suspension bridge un pont suspendu

2 le bridge *masc*
  □ to play bridge jouer au bridge

brief ADJECTIVE
  bref (FEM brève)

briefcase NOUN
  la serviette *fem*

briefly ADVERB
  brièvement

briefs PL NOUN
  le slip *masc sing*
  ■ **a pair of briefs** un slip

bright ADJECTIVE

1 vif (FEM vive) (*colour, light*)
  □ a bright colour une couleur vive
  ■ **bright blue** bleu vif □ a bright blue car une voiture bleu vif

2 intelligent (FEM intelligente)
  □ He's not very bright. Il n'est pas très intelligent.

brilliant ADJECTIVE

1 génial (FEM géniale, MASC PL géniaux) (*wonderful*)
  □ Brilliant! Génial !

2 brillant (FEM brillante) (*clever*)
  □ a brilliant scientist un savant brillant

to **bring** VERB

1 apporter [28]
  □ I always bring my lunch with me. J'apporte toujours mon déjeuner. □ You never bring me a present. Tu ne m'apportes jamais de cadeau. □ She brought me some beautiful flowers. Elle m'a apporté de jolies fleurs. □ Bring warm clothes. Apportez des vêtements chauds. □ Could you bring me my trainers? Tu peux m'apporter mes baskets ?

2 amener [43] (*person*)
  □ Can I bring a friend? Est-ce que je peux amener un ami ?

to **bring back** VERB
  rapporter [28]

to **bring forward** VERB
  avancer [12]

□ The rugby match was brought forward. On a avancé le match de rugby.

to **bring up** VERB
élever [43]
□ She brought up 5 children on her own. Elle a élevé cinq enfants toute seule.

Britain NOUN
la Grande-Bretagne *fem*
■ **in Britain** en Grande-Bretagne
■ **to Britain** en Grande-Bretagne
■ **I'm from Britain.** Je suis britannique.
■ **Great Britain** la Grande-Bretagne

British ADJECTIVE
britannique (FEM britannique)
■ **the British** les Britanniques *masc pl*
■ **the British Isles** les îles Britanniques *fem pl*

Brittany NOUN
la Bretagne *fem*
■ **in Brittany** en Bretagne
■ **to Brittany** en Bretagne
■ **She's from Brittany.** Elle est bretonne.

broad ADJECTIVE
large (FEM large) (*wide*)
■ **in broad daylight** en plein jour
■ **broad beans** les fèves *fem pl*

broadband NOUN
l'ADSL *masc*
□ Do you have fast broadband? Tu as une connexion haut débit ?

broadcast NOUN
▷ *see also* **broadcast** VERB
l'émission *fem*

to **broadcast** VERB
▷ *see also* **broadcast** NOUN
diffuser [28]
□ The concert was broadcast yesterday. Le concert a été diffusé hier.
■ **to broadcast live** retransmettre [47] en direct

broad-minded ADJECTIVE
large d'esprit (FEM large d'esprit)

broccoli NOUN
les brocolis *masc pl*

brochure NOUN
la brochure *fem*

to **broil** VERB (US)
■ **to broil something** faire [36] griller quelque chose

broke VERB ▷ *see* **break**

broke ADJECTIVE
■ **to be broke** (*without money*) être [35] fauché

broken ADJECTIVE
cassé (FEM cassée)
□ It's broken. C'est cassé. □ a broken leg une jambe cassée □ He's got a broken arm. Il a le bras cassé.

bronchitis NOUN
la bronchite *fem*

bronze NOUN
le bronze *masc*
□ the bronze medal la médaille de bronze

brooch NOUN
la broche *fem*

broom NOUN
le balai *masc*

brother NOUN
le frère *masc*
□ my brother mon frère □ my big brother mon grand frère

brother-in-law NOUN
le beau-frère *masc* (PL les beaux-frères)

brought VERB ▷ *see* **bring**

brown ADJECTIVE
1 marron (FEM+PL marron) (*clothes*)
2 brun (FEM brune) (*hair*)
3 bronzé (FEM bronzée) (*tanned*)
■ **brown bread** le pain complet

Brownie NOUN
la jeannette *fem*

to **browse** VERB
parcourir [16] le Net (*on internet*)

browser NOUN
le navigateur *masc* (*for internet*)

bruise NOUN
le bleu *masc*

brush NOUN
▷ *see also* **brush** VERB
1 la brosse *fem*
2 le pinceau *masc* (PL les pinceaux) (*paintbrush*)

to **brush** VERB
▷ *see also* **brush** NOUN
brosser [28]
■ **to brush one's hair** se brosser [28] les cheveux □ I brushed my hair. Je me suis brossé les cheveux.
■ **to brush one's teeth** se brosser [28] les dents □ I brush my teeth every night. Je me brosse les dents tous les soirs.

Brussels NOUN
Bruxelles
■ **in Brussels** à Bruxelles
■ **to Brussels** à Bruxelles

Brussels sprouts PL NOUN
les choux de Bruxelles *masc pl*

brutal ADJECTIVE
brutal (FEM brutale, MASC PL brutaux)

BSc NOUN (= *Bachelor of Science*)
la licence *fem*
■ **a BSc in Mathematics** une licence de mathématiques

bubble NOUN
la bulle *fem*

bubble bath – burglarize

bubble bath NOUN
le bain moussant *masc*

bubble gum NOUN
le chewing-gum *masc*

bucket NOUN
le seau *masc* (PL les seaux)

buckle NOUN
la boucle *fem* (*on belt, watch, shoe*)

Buddhism NOUN
le bouddhisme *masc*

Buddhist ADJECTIVE
bouddhiste (FEM bouddhiste)

buddy NOUN (US)
le copain *masc*
la copine *fem*

budget NOUN
le budget *masc*

budgie NOUN
la perruche *fem*

buffet NOUN
le buffet *masc*

buffet car NOUN
la voiture-bar *fem*

bug NOUN
1 l'insecte *masc* (*insect*)
2 le microbe *masc* (*infection*)
□ There's a bug going round. Il y a un microbe qui traîne.
■ **a stomach bug** une gastroentérite
3 le bug *masc* (*in computer*)

bugged ADJECTIVE
sur écoute
□ The room was bugged. La pièce était sur écoute.

to **build** VERB
construire [23]
□ He's building a garage. Il construit un garage.

to **build up** VERB
s'accumuler [28] (*increase*)

builder NOUN
1 l'entrepreneur *masc* (*owner of firm*)
2 le maçon *masc* (*worker*)

building NOUN
le bâtiment *masc*
■ **a building site** un chantier

built VERB ▷ *see* build

bulb NOUN
l'ampoule *fem* (*electric*)

Bulgaria NOUN
la Bulgarie *fem*

bull NOUN
le taureau *masc* (PL les taureaux)

bullet NOUN
la balle *fem*

bulletin board NOUN
la messagerie électronique *fem* (*computer*)

bullfighting NOUN
la tauromachie *fem*

bully NOUN
▷ *see also* **bully** VERB
la brute *fem*
□ He's a big bully. C'est une brute.

to **bully** VERB
▷ *see also* **bully** NOUN
tyranniser [28]

bum NOUN
le derrière *masc* (*bottom*)

bum bag NOUN
la banane *fem*

bump NOUN
▷ *see also* **bump into** VERB
1 la bosse *fem* (*lump*)
2 l'accrochage *masc* (*minor accident*)
□ We had a bump. Nous avons eu un accrochage.

to **bump into** VERB
▷ *see also* **bump** NOUN
■ **to bump into something** rentrer [68†] dans quelque chose □ I bumped into the table in the dark. Je suis rentrée dans la table dans le noir.
■ **to bump into somebody** 1 (*literally*) rentrer [68†] dans quelqu'un □ He stopped suddenly and I bumped into him. Il s'est arrêté subitement et je lui suis rentré dedans.
2 (*meet by chance*) rencontrer [28] par hasard □ I bumped into Nadiya in the supermarket. J'ai rencontré Nadiya par hasard au supermarché.

bumper NOUN
le pare-chocs *masc* (PL les pare-chocs)

bumpy ADJECTIVE
cahoteux (FEM cahoteuse)

bun NOUN
le petit pain au lait *masc*

bunch NOUN
■ **a bunch of flowers** un bouquet de fleurs
■ **a bunch of grapes** une grappe de raisin
■ **a bunch of keys** un trousseau de clés

bunches PL NOUN
les couettes *fem pl*
□ She has her hair in bunches. Elle a des couettes.

bungalow NOUN
le bungalow *masc*

bunk NOUN
la couchette *fem*
■ **bunk beds** les lits superposés *masc pl*

burger NOUN
le hamburger *masc*

burglar NOUN
le cambrioleur *masc*
la cambrioleuse *fem*

to **burglarize** VERB (US)
cambrioler [28]

burglary NOUN
le cambriolage *masc*

to **burgle** VERB
cambrioler [28]
□ Her house was burgled. Sa maison a été cambriolée.

burn NOUN
▷ *see also* **burn** VERB
la brûlure *fem*

to **burn** VERB
▷ *see also* **burn** NOUN
1 brûler [28] (*rubbish, documents*)
2 faire [36] brûler (*food*)
□ I burned the cake. J'ai fait brûler le gâteau.
3 graver [28] (*CD, DVD*)
■ **to burn oneself** se brûler [28] □ I burned myself on the oven door. Je me suis brûlé sur la porte du four.
■ **I've burned my hand.** Je me suis brûlé la main.

to **burn down** VERB
brûler [28]
□ The factory burned down. L'usine a brûlé.

to **burst** VERB
éclater [28]
□ The balloon burst. Le ballon a éclaté.
■ **to burst a balloon** faire [36] éclater un ballon
■ **to burst out laughing** éclater [28] de rire
■ **to burst into flames** prendre [65] feu
■ **to burst into tears** fondre [69] en larmes

to **bury** VERB
enterrer [28]

bus NOUN
l'autobus *masc*
□ the bus driver le conducteur d'autobus
□ a bus stop un arrêt d'autobus
■ **the school bus** le car scolaire
■ **a bus pass** une carte d'abonnement pour le bus
■ **a bus station** une gare routière
■ **a bus ticket** un ticket de bus

bush NOUN
le buisson *masc*

business NOUN
1 l'entreprise *fem* (*firm*)
□ He's got his own business. Il a sa propre entreprise.
2 les affaires *fem pl* (*commerce*)
□ He's away on business. Il est en voyage d'affaires.
■ **a business trip** un voyage d'affaires
■ **It's none of my business.** Ça ne me regarde pas.

businessman NOUN
l'homme d'affaires *masc*

businesswoman NOUN
la femme d'affaires *fem*

busker NOUN
le musicien de rue *masc*
la musicienne de rue *fem*

bust NOUN
la poitrine *fem* (*chest*)

busy ADJECTIVE
1 occupé (FEM occupée) (*person, phone line*)
2 chargé (FEM chargée) (*day, schedule*)
3 très fréquenté (FEM très fréquentée) (*shop, street*)

busy signal NOUN (US)
la tonalité « occupé » *fem*

but CONJUNCTION
mais
□ I'd like to come, but I'm busy. J'aimerais venir mais je suis occupé.

butcher NOUN
le boucher *masc*
□ He's a butcher. Il est boucher.

butcher's NOUN
la boucherie *fem*

butter NOUN
le beurre *masc*

butterfly NOUN
le papillon *masc*

buttocks PL NOUN
les fesses *fem pl*

button NOUN
le bouton *masc*

to **buy** VERB
▷ *see also* **buy** NOUN
acheter [1]
□ I bought him an ice cream. Je lui ai acheté une glace.
■ **to buy something from somebody** acheter [1] quelque chose à quelqu'un □ I bought a watch from him. Je lui ai acheté une montre.

buy NOUN
▷ *see also* **buy** VERB
■ **It was a good buy.** C'était une bonne affaire.

by PREPOSITION
1 par
□ The thieves were caught by the police. Les voleurs ont été arrêtés par la police.
2 de
□ a painting by Picasso un tableau de Picasso
□ a book by Philip Pullman un livre de Philip Pullman
3 en
□ by car en voiture □ by train en train □ by bus en autobus
4 à côté de (*close to*)
□ Where's the bank? — It's by the post office. Où est la banque ? — Elle est à côté de la poste.
5 avant (*not later than*)
□ We have to be there by 4 o'clock. Nous devons y être avant quatre heures.
■ **by the time ...** quand ... □ By the time I got

bye – bypass

there it was too late. Quand je suis arrivé il était déjà trop tard. □ It'll be ready by the time you get back. Ça sera prêt quand vous reviendrez.

■ **That's fine by me.** Ça me va.
■ **all by himself** tout seul
■ **all by herself** toute seule

■ **I did it all by myself.** Je l'ai fait tout seul.
■ **by the way** au fait

bye EXCLAMATION
salut !

bypass NOUN
la route de contournement *fem*

Cc

cab NOUN
le taxi *masc*

cabbage NOUN
le chou *masc* (PL les choux)

cabin NOUN
la cabine *fem* (*on ship*)

cabinet NOUN
■ **a bathroom cabinet** une armoire de salle de bain

cable NOUN
le câble *masc*

cable car NOUN
le téléphérique *masc*

cable television NOUN
la télévision par câble *fem*

cactus NOUN
le cactus *masc*

cadet NOUN
■ **a police cadet** un élève policier
■ **a cadet officer** un élève officier

café NOUN
le café *masc*

> **DID YOU KNOW...?**
> Cafés in France sell both alcoholic and non-alcoholic drinks.

cafeteria NOUN
la cafétéria *fem*

cage NOUN
la cage *fem*

cagoule NOUN
le K-way® *masc*

cake NOUN
le gâteau *masc* (PL les gâteaux)

to **calculate** VERB
calculer [28]

calculation NOUN
le calcul *masc*

calculator NOUN
la machine à calculer *fem*

calendar NOUN
le calendrier *masc*

calf NOUN
1 le veau *masc* (PL les veaux) (*of cow*)
2 le mollet *masc* (*of leg*)

call NOUN
▷ *see also* **call** VERB
l'appel *masc* (*by phone*)
□ Thanks for your call. Merci de votre appel.
■ **a phone call** un coup de téléphone
■ **to be on call** (*doctor*) être [35] de permanence
□ He's on call this evening. Il est de permanence ce soir.

to **call** VERB
▷ *see also* **call** NOUN
appeler [4]
□ I'll tell him you called. Je lui dirai que vous avez appelé. □ This is the number to call. C'est le numéro à appeler. □ We called the police. Nous avons appelé la police. □ Everyone calls him Jimmy. Tout le monde l'appelle Jimmy.
■ **to be called** s'appeler [4] □ He's called Fluffy. Il s'appelle Fluffy. □ What's she called? Elle s'appelle comment ?
■ **to call somebody names** insulter [28] quelqu'un
■ **He called me an idiot.** Il m'a traité d'idiot.

to **call back** VERB
rappeler [4] (*phone again*)
□ I'll call back at 6 o'clock. Je rappellerai à six heures.

to **call for** VERB
passer [58ᵉ] prendre
□ I'll call for you at 2.30. Je passerai te prendre à deux heures et demie.

to **call off** VERB
annuler [28]
□ The match was called off. Le match a été annulé.

call box NOUN
la cabine téléphonique *fem*

call centre NOUN
le centre d'appels *masc*

calm ADJECTIVE
calme (FEM calme)

to **calm down** VERB
se calmer [28]
□ Calm down! Calme-toi !

Calor gas® NOUN
le butane *masc*

calorie NOUN
la calorie *fem*

calves – canned

calves PL NOUN ▷ *see* **calf**

Cambodia NOUN
le Cambodge *masc*
- **in Cambodia** au Cambodge

camcorder NOUN
le caméscope *masc*

came VERB ▷ *see* **come**

camel NOUN
le chameau *masc* (PL les chameaux)

camera NOUN
1 l'appareil photo *masc* (PL les appareils photo) (*for photos*)
2 la caméra *fem* (*for filming, TV*)

cameraman NOUN
le caméraman *masc*

camera phone NOUN
le téléphone appareil photo *masc*

to **camp** VERB
▷ *see also* **camp** NOUN
camper [28]

camp NOUN
▷ *see also* **camp** VERB
le camp *masc*
- **a camp bed** un lit de camp

campaign NOUN
la campagne *fem*

camper NOUN
1 le campeur *masc*
la campeuse *fem* (*person*)
2 le camping-car *masc* (*van*)

camping NOUN
le camping *masc*
- **to go camping** faire [36] du camping □ We went camping in Cornwall. Nous avons fait du camping en Cornouailles.

camping gas NOUN
le butane *masc*

campsite NOUN
le camping *masc*

campus NOUN
le campus *masc*

can VERB
▷ *see also* **can** NOUN
1 pouvoir [64] (*be able to, to be allowed to*)
□ I can call her. Je peux l'appeler. □ You can come with me. Vous pouvez venir avec moi. □ He can help you. Il peut t'aider. □ I can't come. Je ne peux pas venir. □ Can I help you? Est-ce que je peux vous aider ? □ Can I use your phone? Est-ce que je peux me servir de votre téléphone ? □ You could hire a bike. Tu pourrais louer un vélo. □ I couldn't sleep because of the noise. Je ne pouvais pas dormir à cause du bruit.

'can' is sometimes not translated.

□ I can't hear you. Je ne t'entends pas. □ I can't

remember. Je ne m'en souviens pas. □ Can you speak French? Parlez-vous français ?
2 savoir [76] (*have learnt how to*)
□ I can swim. Je sais nager. □ He can't drive. Il ne sait pas conduire.
- **That can't be true!** Ce n'est pas possible !
- **You could be right.** Vous avez peut-être raison.

can NOUN
▷ *see also* **can** VERB
1 la boîte *fem* (*tin*)
□ a can of sweetcorn une boîte de maïs
- **a can of beer** une cannette de bière
2 le bidon *masc* (*container*)
□ a can of petrol un bidon d'essence

Canada NOUN
le Canada *masc*
- **in Canada** au Canada
- **to Canada** au Canada

Canadian NOUN
▷ *see also* **Canadian** ADJECTIVE
le Canadien *masc*
la Canadienne *fem*

Canadian ADJECTIVE
▷ *see also* **Canadian** NOUN
canadien (FEM canadienne)

canal NOUN
le canal *masc* (PL les canaux)

Canaries PL NOUN
- **the Canaries** les îles Canaries *fem pl*

canary NOUN
le canari *masc*

to **cancel** VERB
annuler [28]
□ The match was cancelled. Le match a été annulé.

cancellation NOUN
l'annulation *fem*

cancer NOUN
1 le cancer *masc*
□ He's got cancer. Il a le cancer.
2 le Cancer *masc*
□ I'm Cancer. Je suis Cancer.

candidate NOUN
le candidat *masc*
la candidate *fem*

candle NOUN
la bougie *fem*

candy NOUN (US)
les bonbons *masc pl*
- **a candy** un bonbon

candyfloss NOUN
la barbe à papa *fem*

cannabis NOUN
le cannabis *masc*

canned ADJECTIVE
en conserve (*food*)

Numbers in brackets refer to verb tables on pages 650 to 658

cannot VERB ▷ *see* **can**

canoe NOUN
le canoë *masc*

canoeing NOUN
■ **to go canoeing** faire [36] du canoë □ We went canoeing. Nous avons fait du canoë.

can-opener NOUN
l'ouvre-boîte *masc*

can't VERB ▷ *see* **can**

canteen NOUN
la cantine *fem*

to **canter** VERB
aller [3⁵] au petit galop

canvas NOUN
la toile *fem*

cap NOUN
1 la casquette *fem* (*hat*)
2 le bouchon *masc* (*of bottle, tube*)

capable ADJECTIVE
capable (FEM capable)

capacity NOUN
la capacité *fem*

capital NOUN
1 la capitale *fem*
□ Cardiff is the capital of Wales. Cardiff est la capitale du pays de Galles.
2 la majuscule *fem* (*letter*)
□ Write your address in capitals. Écris ton adresse en majuscules.

capitalism NOUN
le capitalisme *masc*

capital punishment NOUN
la peine capitale *fem*

Capricorn NOUN
le Capricorne *masc*
□ I'm Capricorn. Je suis Capricorne.

to **capsize** VERB
chavirer [28]

captain NOUN
le capitaine *masc*
□ She's captain of the hockey team. Elle est capitaine de l'équipe de hockey.

caption NOUN
la légende *fem*

to **capture** VERB
capturer [28]

car NOUN
la voiture *fem*
■ **to go by car** aller [3⁵] en voiture □ We went by car. Nous y sommes allés en voiture.
■ **a car crash** un accident de voiture

caramel NOUN
le caramel *masc*

caravan NOUN
la caravane *fem*
□ a caravan site un camping pour caravanes

carbohydrate NOUN
le glucide *masc*

carbon footprint NOUN
l'empreinte carbone *fem*
□ We need to reduce our carbon footprint. Nous devons réduire notre empreinte carbone.

card NOUN
la carte *fem*
■ **a card game** un jeu de cartes

cardboard NOUN
le carton *masc*
■ **a cardboard box** un carton

cardigan NOUN
le cardigan *masc*

care NOUN
▷ *see also* **care** VERB
le soin *masc*
□ with care avec soin
■ **to take care of** s'occuper [28] de □ I take care of the children on Saturdays. Le samedi, je m'occupe des enfants.
■ **Take care!** 1 (*Be careful!*) Fais attention !
2 (*Look after yourself!*) Prends bien soin de toi !

to **care** VERB
▷ *see also* **care** NOUN
■ **to care about** se soucier [19] de □ They don't really care about global warming. Ils ne se soucient pas trop du réchauffement climatique.
■ **I don't care!** Ça m'est égal ! □ She doesn't care. Ça lui est égal.
■ **to care for somebody** (*patients, old people*) s'occuper [28] de quelqu'un

career NOUN
la carrière *fem*
■ **a careers adviser** un conseiller d'orientation

careful ADJECTIVE
■ **Be careful!** Fais attention !

carefully ADVERB
1 soigneusement
□ She carefully avoided talking about it. Elle évitait soigneusement d'en parler.
2 prudemment (*safely*)
□ Drive carefully! Conduisez prudemment !
■ **Think carefully!** Réfléchis bien !

careless ADJECTIVE
1 peu soigné (FEM peu soignée) (*work*)
■ **a careless mistake** une faute d'inattention
2 peu soigneux (FEM peu soigneuse) (*person*)
□ She's very careless. Elle est bien peu soigneuse.
3 imprudent (FEM imprudente)
□ a careless driver un conducteur imprudent

carer NOUN
l'aidant *masc*
l'aidante *fem*

English-French

caretaker NOUN
le gardien *masc*
la gardienne *fem*

car-ferry NOUN
le ferry *masc*

cargo NOUN
la cargaison *fem*

car hire NOUN
la location de voitures *fem*

Caribbean NOUN
▷ *see also* **Caribbean** ADJECTIVE
1 les Caraïbes *fem pl* (*islands*)
   □ We're going to the Caribbean. Nous allons aux Caraïbes.
   ■ **He's from the Caribbean.** Il est antillais.
2 la mer des Caraïbes *fem* (*sea*)

Caribbean ADJECTIVE
▷ *see also* **Caribbean** NOUN
antillais (FEM antillaise)
   □ Caribbean food la cuisine antillaise

caring ADJECTIVE
   ■ **She's a very caring teacher.** C'est un professeur qui se préoccupe du bien-être de ses élèves.
   ■ **She has very caring parents.** Ses parents sont très affectueux.

carnation NOUN
l'œillet *masc*

carnival NOUN
le carnaval *masc*

carol NOUN
   ■ **a Christmas carol** un chant de Noël

car park NOUN
le parking *masc*

carpenter NOUN
le charpentier *masc*
   □ He's a carpenter. Il est charpentier.

carpentry NOUN
la menuiserie *fem*

carpet NOUN
1 le tapis *masc*
   □ a Persian carpet un tapis persan
2 la moquette *fem* (*fitted*)

car phone NOUN
le téléphone de voiture *masc*

car rental NOUN (US)
la location de voitures *fem*

carriage NOUN
la voiture *fem*

carrier bag NOUN
le sac en plastique *masc*

carrot NOUN
la carotte *fem*

to **carry** VERB
1 porter [28]
   □ I'll carry your bag. Je vais porter ton sac.

2 transporter [28]
   □ a plane carrying 100 passengers un avion transportant cent passagers

to **carry on** VERB
continuer [28]
   □ Carry on! Continue ! □ She carried on talking. Elle a continué à parler.

to **carry out** VERB
exécuter [28] (*orders*)

cart NOUN
la charrette *fem*

carton NOUN
la brique *fem* (*of milk, juice*)

cartoon NOUN
1 le dessin animé *masc* (*film*)
2 le dessin humoristique *masc* (*in newspaper*)
   ■ **a strip cartoon** une bande dessinée

cartridge NOUN
la cartouche *fem*

to **carve** VERB
découper [28] (*meat*)

case NOUN
1 la valise *fem*
   □ I've packed my case. J'ai fait ma valise.
2 le cas *masc* (PL les cas)
   □ in some cases dans certains cas
   ■ **in that case** dans ce cas □ I don't want it. — In that case, I'll take it. Je n'en veux pas. — Dans ce cas, je le prends.
   ■ **in case** au cas où □ in case it rains au cas où il pleuvrait
   ■ **just in case** à tout hasard □ Take some money, just in case. Prends de l'argent à tout hasard.

cash NOUN
l'argent *masc*
   □ I'm a bit short of cash. Je suis un peu à court d'argent.
   ■ **in cash** en liquide □ £2000 in cash deux mille livres en liquide
   ■ **to pay cash** payer [59] comptant
   ■ **a cash card** une carte de retrait
   ■ **the cash desk** la caisse
   ■ **a cash machine** un distributeur de billets
   ■ **a cash register** une caisse

cashew NOUN
la noix de cajou *fem* (PL les noix de cajou)

cashier NOUN
le caissier *masc*
la caissière *fem*

cashmere NOUN
le cachemire *masc*
   □ a cashmere sweater un pull en cachemire

casino NOUN
le casino *masc*

casserole NOUN
le ragoût *masc*

Numbers in brackets refer to verb tables on pages 650 to 658

□ I'm going to make a casserole. Je vais faire un ragoût.

■ **a casserole dish** une cocotte

cast NOUN
les acteurs *masc pl*
□ the cast of Star Wars les acteurs de la série La Guerre des étoiles.

castle NOUN
le château *masc* (PL les châteaux)

casual ADJECTIVE
1 décontracté (FEM décontractée)
□ casual clothes les vêtements décontractés
2 désinvolte (FEM désinvolte)
□ a casual attitude une attitude désinvolte
3 en passant
□ It was just a casual remark. C'était juste une remarque en passant.

casually ADVERB
■ **to dress casually** s'habiller [28] de façon décontractée

casualty NOUN
les urgences *fem pl* (*in hospital*)

cat NOUN
le chat *masc*
la chatte *fem*
□ Have you got a cat? Est-ce que tu as un chat ?

catalogue NOUN
le catalogue *masc*

catalytic converter NOUN
le catalyseur *masc*

catarrh NOUN
le rhume chronique *masc*

catastrophe NOUN
la catastrophe *fem*

to **catch** VERB
1 attraper [28]
□ to catch a thief attraper un voleur □ My cat catches birds. Mon chat attrape des oiseaux.
■ **to catch a cold** attraper [28] un rhume
2 surprendre [65]
■ **to catch somebody doing something** surprendre [65] quelqu'un en train de faire quelque chose
□ She caught him playing computer games in class. Elle l'a surpris en train de jouer à des jeux vidéo en classe.
3 saisir [38] (*hear*)
□ I didn't catch his name. Je n'ai pas saisi son nom.
4 prendre [65] (*bus, train*)
□ We caught the last bus. On a pris le dernier bus.

to **catch up** VERB
rattraper [28] son retard
□ I was off yesterday so I've got to catch up. J'étais absent hier, donc je dois rattraper mon retard.

catching ADJECTIVE
contagieux (FEM contagieuse)
□ It's not catching. Ce n'est pas contagieux.

catering NOUN
la restauration *fem*

cathedral NOUN
la cathédrale *fem*

Catholic ADJECTIVE
▷ *see also* **Catholic** NOUN
catholique (FEM catholique)

Catholic NOUN
▷ *see also* **Catholic** ADJECTIVE
le/la catholique *masc/fem*
□ I'm a Catholic. Je suis catholique.

cattle PL NOUN
le bétail *masc sing*

caught VERB ▷ *see* **catch**

cauliflower NOUN
le chou-fleur *masc* (PL les choux-fleurs)

cause NOUN
▷ *see also* **cause** VERB
la cause *fem*

to **cause** VERB
▷ *see also* **cause** NOUN
provoquer [28]
□ to cause an accident provoquer un accident

cautious ADJECTIVE
prudent (FEM prudente)

cautiously ADVERB
avec précaution
□ She cautiously opened the door. Elle a ouvert la porte avec précaution.

cave NOUN
la grotte *fem*

CCTV NOUN (= *closed-circuit television*)
la vidéosurveillance *fem*

CCTV camera NOUN
la caméra de vidéosurveillance *fem*

CD NOUN
le CD *masc* (PL les CD)

CD burner NOUN
le graveur de CD *masc*

CD player NOUN
la platine laser *fem*

CD-ROM NOUN
le CD-ROM *masc* (PL les CD-ROM)

ceasefire NOUN
le cessez-le-feu *masc* (PL les cessez-le-feu)

ceiling NOUN
le plafond *masc*

to **celebrate** VERB
fêter [28] (*birthday*)

celebrity NOUN
la célébrité *fem*

celery NOUN
le céleri *masc*

C

cell – chance

cell NOUN
la cellule *fem*

cellar NOUN
la cave *fem*
□ a wine cellar une cave à vins

cello NOUN
le violoncelle *masc*
□ I play the cello. Je joue du violoncelle.

cell phone NOUN (US)
le téléphone portable *masc*

cement NOUN
le ciment *masc*

cemetery NOUN
le cimetière *masc*

cent NOUN
le cent *masc*
□ twenty cents vingt cents

centenary NOUN
le centenaire *masc*

center NOUN (US)
le centre *masc*

centigrade ADJECTIVE
centigrade (FEM centigrade)
□ 20 degrees centigrade vingt degrés centigrade

centimetre (US **centimeter**) NOUN
le centimètre *masc*

central ADJECTIVE
central (FEM centrale, MASC PL centraux)

central heating NOUN
le chauffage central *masc*

centre NOUN
le centre *masc*
□ a sports centre un centre sportif

century NOUN
le siècle *masc*
□ the 20th century le vingtième siècle □ the 21st century le vingt et unième siècle

cereal NOUN
les céréales *fem pl*
□ I have cereal for breakfast. Je prends des céréales au petit déjeuner.

ceremony NOUN
la cérémonie *fem*

certain ADJECTIVE
certain (FEM certaine)
□ a certain person une certaine personne □ I'm absolutely certain it was him. Je suis absolument certain que c'était lui.
■ **I don't know for certain.** Je n'en suis pas certain.
■ **to make certain** s'assurer [28] □ I made certain the door was locked. Je me suis assuré que la porte était fermée à clé.

certainly ADVERB
vraiment

□ I certainly expected something better. Je m'attendais vraiment à quelque chose de mieux.
■ **Certainly not!** Certainement pas !
■ **So it was a surprise? — It certainly was!** C'était donc une surprise ? — Ça oui alors !

certificate NOUN
le certificat *masc*

CFCs PL NOUN
les CFC *masc pl*

chain NOUN
la chaîne *fem*

chair NOUN
1 la chaise *fem* (*wooden, metal*)
2 le fauteuil *masc* (*armchair*)

chairlift NOUN
le télésiège *masc*

chairman NOUN
le président *masc*

chairperson NOUN
le président *masc*
la présidente *fem*

chairwoman NOUN
la présidente *fem*

chalet NOUN
le chalet *masc*

chalk NOUN
la craie *fem*

challenge NOUN
▷ *see also* **challenge** VERB
le défi *masc*

to **challenge** VERB
▷ *see also* **challenge** NOUN
■ **She challenged me to a race.** Elle m'a proposé de faire la course avec elle.

challenging ADJECTIVE
stimulant (FEM stimulante) (*exam, job*)

champagne NOUN
le champagne *masc*

champion NOUN
le champion *masc*
la championne *fem*

championship NOUN
le championnat *masc*

chance NOUN
1 la chance *fem*
□ Do you think I've got any chance? Tu crois que j'ai une chance ? □ Their chances of winning are very good. Ils ont de fortes chances de gagner.
■ **No chance!** Pas question !
2 l'occasion *fem*
□ I'd like to have a chance to travel. J'aimerais avoir l'occasion de voyager.
■ **I'll text you when I get the chance.** Je t'enverrai un SMS quand j'aurai un moment.
■ **by chance** par hasard □ We met by chance. Nous nous sommes rencontrés par hasard.
■ **to take a chance** prendre [65] un risque

□ I'm taking no chances! Je ne veux prendre aucun risque !

Chancellor of the Exchequer NOUN
le chancelier de l'Échiquier masc

to change VERB
▷ see also **change** NOUN

1 changer [45]
□ The town has changed a lot. La ville a beaucoup changé. □ I'd like to change £50. Je voudrais changer cinquante livres.

2 changer [45] de

> Use **changer de** when you change one thing for another.

□ You have to change trains in Paris. Il faut changer de train à Paris. □ I'm going to change my shoes. Je vais changer de chaussures. □ He wants to change his job. Il veut changer d'emploi.
■ **to change one's mind** changer [45] d'avis □ I've changed my mind. J'ai changé d'avis.
■ **to change gear** changer [45] de vitesse

3 se changer [45]
□ She changed to go to the party. Elle s'est changée pour aller à la fête.
■ **to get changed** se changer [45] □ I'm going to get changed. Je vais me changer.

4 échanger [45] (swap)
□ Can I change this jumper? It's too small. Est-ce que je peux échanger ce pull ? Il est trop petit.

change NOUN
▷ see also **change** VERB

1 le changement masc
□ There's been a change of plan. Il y a eu un changement de programme.

2 la monnaie fem (money)
□ I haven't got any change. Je n'ai pas de monnaie.
■ **a change of clothes** des vêtements de rechange
■ **for a change** pour changer □ Let's go ice skating for a change. Si on faisait du patin à glace pour changer ?

changeable ADJECTIVE
variable (FEM variable)

changing room NOUN
1 la cabine d'essayage fem (in shop)
2 le vestiaire masc (for sport)

channel NOUN
la chaîne fem (TV)
□ There's football on the other channel. Il y a du football sur l'autre chaîne.
■ **the Channel** la Manche
■ **the Channel Islands** les îles Anglo-Normandes fem pl
■ **the Channel Tunnel** le tunnel sous la Manche

chaos NOUN
le chaos masc

chapel NOUN
la chapelle fem (part of church)

chapter NOUN
le chapitre masc

character NOUN
1 le caractère masc
■ **She's quite a character.** C'est un drôle de numéro.
2 le personnage masc (in play, film)
□ the main character in the book le personnage principal du livre

characteristic NOUN
la caractéristique fem

charcoal NOUN
le charbon de bois masc

charge NOUN
▷ see also **charge** VERB
les frais masc pl
□ Is there a charge for delivery? Est-ce qu'il y a des frais de livraison ?
■ **an extra charge** un supplément
■ **free of charge** gratuit
■ **to be in charge** être [35] responsable
□ Anne was in charge of the group. Anne était responsable du groupe.

to charge VERB
▷ see also **charge** NOUN
1 prendre [65] (money)
□ How much did he charge you? Combien est-ce qu'il vous a pris ? □ They charge £10 an hour. Ils prennent dix livres de l'heure.
2 inculper [28] (with crime)
□ The police have charged him with murder. La police l'a inculpé de meurtre.
3 charger [28] (battery, phone)

charger NOUN
le chargeur masc (phone, computer)

charity NOUN
l'association caritative fem
□ He gave the money to charity. Il a donné l'argent à une association caritative.

charm NOUN
le charme masc
□ He's got a lot of charm. Il a beaucoup de charme.

charming ADJECTIVE
charmant (FEM charmante)

chart NOUN
le tableau masc (PL les tableaux)
□ The chart shows the rise in the number of students taking A-levels. Le tableau indique la progression du nombre de lycéens qui passent le bac.
■ **the charts** le hit-parade □ This album is number one in the charts. Cet album est numéro un au hit-parade.

to **chase** VERB
▷ *see also* **chase** NOUN
pourchasser [28]

chase NOUN
▷ *see also* **chase** VERB
la poursuite *fem*
□ a car chase une poursuite en voiture

chat NOUN
▷ *see also* **chat** VERB
■ **to have a chat** bavarder [28]

to **chat** VERB
▷ *see also* **chat** NOUN
bavarder [28]
■ **to chat somebody up** draguer [28]
quelqu'un (*informal*) □ He likes to chat up the
girls. Il aime bien draguer les filles.
■ **She likes chatting online.** Elle aime chatter
sur Internet.

chatroom NOUN
le forum de discussion *masc*

chat show NOUN
le talk-show *masc*

cheap ADJECTIVE
pas cher (FEM pas chère)
□ a cheap T-shirt un T-shirt pas cher

cheaper ADJECTIVE
moins cher (FEM moins chère)
□ It's cheaper by bus. C'est moins cher en bus.

to **cheat** VERB
▷ *see also* **cheat** NOUN
tricher [28]
□ You're cheating! Tu triches !

cheat NOUN
▷ *see also* **cheat** VERB
le tricheur *masc*
la tricheuse *fem*

check NOUN
▷ *see also* **check** VERB
1 le contrôle *masc*
□ a security check un contrôle de sécurité
2 le chèque *masc* (US)
□ to write a check faire un chèque
3 l'addition *fem* (US)
□ Can we have the check, please? L'addition, s'il
vous plaît.

to **check** VERB
▷ *see also* **check** NOUN
vérifier [19]
□ I'll check the time of the train. Je vais vérifier
l'heure du train. □ Check that you haven't made
any mistakes. Vérifiez que vous n'avez pas fait
de fautes.

to **check in** VERB
1 se présenter [28] à l'enregistrement
(*at airport*)
□ Where do we check in? Où est-ce qu'on doit se
présenter à l'enregistrement ?

■ **They checked in online.** Ils se sont
enregistré sur Internet.
2 se présenter [28] à la réception (*in hotel*)
■ **I'd like to check in.** Je voudrais prendre ma
chambre.

to **check out** VERB
régler [34] la note (*from hotel*)
□ Can I check out, please? Je peux régler la note,
s'il vous plaît ?

checked ADJECTIVE
à carreaux (*fabric*)

check-in NOUN
l'enregistrement *masc*

checking account NOUN (US)
le compte courant *masc* (PL les comptes
courants)

checkout NOUN
la caisse *fem*

check-up NOUN
l'examen de routine *masc*

cheek NOUN
1 la joue *fem*
□ He kissed her on the cheek. Il l'a embrassée
sur la joue.
2 le culot *masc*
□ What a cheek! Quel culot !

cheeky ADJECTIVE
effronté (FEM effrontée)
□ Don't be cheeky! Ne sois pas effronté !
■ **a cheeky smile** un sourire malicieux

cheer NOUN
▷ *see also* **cheer** VERB
les hourras *masc pl*
■ **to give a cheer** pousser [28] des hourras
■ **Cheers!** 1 (*good health*) À la vôtre !
2 (*thanks*) Merci !

to **cheer** VERB
▷ *see also* **cheer** NOUN
applaudir [38]
■ **to cheer somebody up** remonter [48] le
moral à quelqu'un □ I was trying to cheer him
up. J'essayais de lui remonter le moral.
■ **Cheer up!** Ne te laisse pas abattre !

cheerful ADJECTIVE
gai (FEM gaie)

cheerio EXCLAMATION
salut !

cheese NOUN
le fromage *masc*

chef NOUN
le chef *masc*

chemical NOUN
le produit chimique *masc*

chemist NOUN
1 le pharmacien *masc*
la pharmacienne *fem* (*dispenser*)

Numbers in brackets refer to verb tables on pages 650 to 658

2 la pharmacie *fem* (*shop*)
□ You get it from the chemist. C'est vendu en pharmacie.

> **DID YOU KNOW...?**
> Chemists' shops in France are identified by a special green cross outside the shop.

3 le/la chimiste *masc/fem* (*scientist*)

chemistry NOUN
la chimie *fem*
□ the chemistry lab le laboratoire de chimie

cheque NOUN
le chèque *masc*
□ to write a cheque faire un chèque □ to pay by cheque payer par chèque

chequebook NOUN
le carnet de chèques *masc*

cherry NOUN
la cerise *fem*

chess NOUN
les échecs *masc pl*
□ to play chess jouer aux échecs

chessboard NOUN
l'échiquier *masc*

chest NOUN
la poitrine *fem* (*of person*)
□ his chest measurement son tour de poitrine
■ a chest of drawers une commode

chestnut NOUN
le marron *masc*
□ We have turkey with chestnuts. Nous mangeons de la dinde aux marrons.

to **chew** VERB
mâcher [28]

chewing gum NOUN
le chewing-gum *masc*

chick NOUN
le poussin *masc*
□ a hen and her chicks une poule et ses poussins

chicken NOUN
le poulet *masc*

chickenpox NOUN
la varicelle *fem*

chickpeas PL NOUN
les pois chiches *masc pl*

chief NOUN
▷ *see also* **chief** ADJECTIVE
le chef *masc*
□ the chief of security le chef de la sécurité

chief ADJECTIVE
▷ *see also* **chief** NOUN
principal (FEM principale)
□ My chief problem was that I didn't understand the question. Mon problème principal, c'était que je n'avais pas compris la question.

child NOUN
l'enfant *masc/fem*
□ all the children tous les enfants

childish ADJECTIVE
puéril (FEM puérile)

child minder NOUN
la nourrice *fem*

children PL NOUN ▷ *see* **child**

Chile NOUN
le Chili *masc*
■ in Chile au Chili

to **chill** VERB
mettre [47] au frais
□ Put the juice in the fridge to chill. Mets le jus de fruits au frais dans le réfrigérateur.

chilli NOUN
le piment *masc*

chilly ADJECTIVE
froid (FEM froide)

chimney NOUN
la cheminée *fem*

chin NOUN
le menton *masc*

China NOUN
la Chine *fem*
■ in China en Chine

china NOUN
la porcelaine *fem*
□ a china plate une assiette en porcelaine

Chinese NOUN
▷ *see also* **Chinese** ADJECTIVE
le chinois *masc* (*language*)
■ the Chinese les Chinois

Chinese ADJECTIVE
▷ *see also* **Chinese** NOUN
chinois (FEM chinoise)
□ a Chinese restaurant un restaurant chinois
■ a Chinese man un Chinois
■ a Chinese woman une Chinoise

chip NOUN
1 la frite *fem* (*food*)
□ We bought some chips. Nous avons acheté des frites.
2 la puce *fem* (*in computer*)

chiropodist NOUN
le/la pédicure *masc/fem*
□ He's a chiropodist. Il est pédicure.

chives PL NOUN
la ciboulette *fem sing*

chocolate NOUN
le chocolat *masc*
□ a chocolate cake un gâteau au chocolat
■ hot chocolate le chocolat chaud

choice NOUN
le choix *masc*
□ I had no choice. Je n'avais pas le choix.

C

choir NOUN
la chorale *fem*
□ I sing in the school choir. Je chante dans la chorale de l'école.

to **choke** VERB
s'étrangler [28]
□ He choked on a fishbone. Il s'est étranglé avec une arête de poisson.

to **choose** VERB
choisir [38]
□ It's difficult to choose. C'est difficile de choisir.

to **chop** VERB
▷ see also **chop** NOUN
émincer [12]
□ Chop the onions. Émincez les oignons.

chop NOUN
▷ see also **chop** VERB
la côte *fem*
□ a pork chop une côte de porc

chopsticks PL NOUN
les baguettes *fem pl*

chose, chosen VERB ▷ see **choose**

Christ NOUN
le Christ *masc*
□ the birth of Christ la naissance du Christ

christening NOUN
le baptême *masc*

Christian NOUN
▷ see also **Christian** ADJECTIVE
le chrétien *masc*
la chrétienne *fem*

Christian ADJECTIVE
▷ see also **Christian** NOUN
chrétien (FEM chrétienne)

Christian name NOUN
le prénom *masc*

Christmas NOUN
Noël *masc*
□ Happy Christmas! Joyeux Noël !
■ **Christmas Day** le jour de Noël
■ **Christmas Eve** la veille de Noël
■ **a Christmas tree** un arbre de Noël
■ **a Christmas card** une carte de Noël

DID YOU KNOW...?
The French more often send greetings cards (**une carte de vœux**) with best wishes for the New Year rather than for Christmas.

■ **Christmas dinner** le repas de Noël

DID YOU KNOW...?
Most French people have their Christmas meal (**réveillon de Noël**) on the evening of Christmas Eve, though some have a **repas de Noël** on Christmas Day. The French usually have a Yule log (**une bûche de Noël**) for pudding at the Christmas meal.
---

chubby ADJECTIVE
potelé (FEM potelée)
□ a chubby baby un bébé potelé

chunk NOUN
le gros morceau *masc* (PL les gros morceaux)
□ Cut the meat into chunks. Coupez la viande en gros morceaux.

church NOUN
l'église *fem*
□ I don't go to church every Sunday. Je ne vais pas à l'église tous les dimanches.
■ **the Church of England** l'Église anglicane

cider NOUN
le cidre *masc*

cigar NOUN
le cigare *masc*

cigarette NOUN
la cigarette *fem*

cigarette lighter NOUN
le briquet *masc*

cinema NOUN
le cinéma *masc*
□ I'm going to the cinema this evening. Je vais au cinéma ce soir.

cinnamon NOUN
la cannelle *fem*

circle NOUN
le cercle *masc*

circular ADJECTIVE
circulaire (FEM circulaire)

circulation NOUN
1 la circulation *fem* (of blood)
2 le tirage *masc* (of newspaper)

circumflex NOUN
l'accent circonflexe *masc*

circumstances PL NOUN
les circonstances *fem pl*

circus NOUN
le cirque *masc*

citizen NOUN
le citoyen *masc*
la citoyenne *fem*
□ a French citizen un citoyen français

citizenship NOUN
la citoyenneté *fem*

city NOUN
la ville *fem*
■ **the city centre** le centre-ville □ It's in the city centre. C'est au centre-ville.

city technology college NOUN
le collège technique *masc*

civilization NOUN
la civilisation *fem*

civil servant NOUN
le/la fonctionnaire *masc/fem*

civil war NOUN
la guerre civile *fem*

to claim VERB
1 prétendre [88]
□ He claims to have found the money. Il prétend avoir trouvé l'argent.
2 percevoir [28] (*receive*)
□ She's claiming housing benefit. Elle perçoit des allocations logement.
■ **She can't claim housing benefit.** Elle n'a pas droit à l'allocation logement.

to clap VERB
applaudir [38] (*applaud*)
■ **to clap one's hands** frapper [28] dans ses mains □ My dog sits when I clap my hands. Mon chien s'assoit quand je frappe dans mes mains.

clarinet NOUN
la clarinette *fem*
□ I play the clarinet. Je joue de la clarinette.

to clash VERB
1 jurer [28] (*colours*)
□ These two colours clash. Ces deux couleurs jurent.
2 tomber [84⁵] en même temps (*events*)
□ The concert clashes with Ella's party. Le concert tombe en même temps que la soirée d'Ella.

clasp NOUN
le fermoir *masc* (*of necklace*)

class NOUN
1 la classe *fem* (*group*)
□ We're in the same class. Nous sommes dans la même classe.
2 le cours *masc* (*lesson*)
□ I go to dancing classes. Je vais à des cours de danse.

classic ADJECTIVE
▷ *see also* **classic** NOUN
classique (FEM classique)
□ a classic example un cas classique

classic NOUN
▷ *see also* **classic** ADJECTIVE
le classique *masc* (*book, film*)

classical ADJECTIVE
classique (FEM classique)
□ I like classical music. J'aime la musique classique.

classmate NOUN
le/la camarade de classe *masc/fem*

classroom NOUN
la classe *fem*

classroom assistant NOUN
l'aide-éducateur *masc*
l'aide-éducatrice *fem*

claw NOUN
1 la griffe *fem* (*of cat, dog*)

2 la serre *fem* (*of bird*)
3 la pince *fem* (*of crab, lobster*)

clean ADJECTIVE
▷ *see also* **clean** VERB
propre (FEM propre)
□ a clean shirt une chemise propre

to clean VERB
▷ *see also* **clean** ADJECTIVE
nettoyer [53]

cleaner NOUN
la femme de ménage *fem*
l'agent d'entretien *masc* (*woman, man*)

cleaner's NOUN
la teinturerie *fem*

cleaning lady NOUN
la femme de ménage *fem*

cleansing lotion NOUN
la lotion démaquillante *fem*

clear ADJECTIVE
▷ *see also* **clear** VERB
1 clair (FEM claire)
□ a clear explanation une explication claire □ It's clear you don't believe me. Il est clair que tu ne me crois pas.
2 libre (FEM libre) (*road, way*)
□ The road's clear now. La route est libre maintenant.

to clear VERB
▷ *see also* **clear** ADJECTIVE
1 dégager [45]
□ The police are clearing the road after the accident. La police dégage la route après l'accident.
2 se dissiper [28] (*fog, mist*)
□ The mist cleared. La brume s'est dissipée.
■ **to be cleared of a crime** être [35] reconnu non coupable d'un crime □ She was cleared of murder. Elle a été reconnue non coupable du meurtre.
■ **to clear the table** débarrasser [28] la table
□ I'll clear the table. Je vais débarrasser la table.

to clear up VERB
ranger [45]
□ Who's going to clear all this up? Qui va ranger tout ça ?
■ **I think it's going to clear up.** (*weather*) Je pense que le temps va se lever.

clearly ADVERB
1 clairement
□ She explained it very clearly. Elle l'a expliqué très clairement.
2 nettement
□ You could clearly make out the French coast. On distinguait nettement la côte française.
3 distinctement
□ to speak clearly parler distinctement

clementine NOUN
la clémentine *fem*

clever - clothes

clever ADJECTIVE
1 intelligent (FEM intelligente)
□ She's very clever. Elle est très intelligente.
2 astucieux (FEM astucieuse) (*ingenious*)
□ a clever system un système astucieux
■ **What a clever idea!** Quelle bonne idée !

click NOUN
▷ *see also* **click** VERB
1 le petit bruit *masc* (*of door, camera*)
2 le clic *masc* (*with mouse*)

to click VERB
▷ *see also* **click** NOUN
cliquer [28] (*with mouse*)
□ to click on an icon cliquer sur une icône

client NOUN
le client *masc*
la cliente *fem*

cliff NOUN
la falaise *fem*

climate NOUN
le climat *masc*
■ **climate crisis** la crise climatique

climate change NOUN
le changement climatique *masc*
□ We need to combat climate change. Nous devons lutter contre le changement climatique.

to climb VERB
1 escalader [28]
□ We're going to climb Snowdon. Nous allons escalader le Snowdon.
2 monter [48] (*stairs*)

climber NOUN
le grimpeur *masc*
la grimpeuse *fem*

climbing NOUN
l'escalade *fem*
■ **to go climbing** faire [36] de l'escalade
□ We're going climbing in Scotland. Nous allons faire de l'escalade en Écosse.

Clingfilm® NOUN
le film alimentaire *masc*

clinic NOUN
le centre médical *masc* (PL les centres médicaux)

clip NOUN
1 la barrette *fem* (*for hair*)
2 le court extrait *masc* (*film*)
□ some clips from Disney's latest film quelques courts extraits du dernier film Disney

clippers PL NOUN
■ **nail clippers** le coupe-ongle *sing*

cloakroom NOUN
1 le vestiaire *masc* (*for coats*)
2 les toilettes *fem pl* (*toilet*)

clock NOUN
1 l'horloge *fem*
□ the church clock l'horloge de l'église
2 la pendule *fem* (*smaller*)
■ **an alarm clock** un réveil
■ **a clock-radio** un radio-réveil

clockwork NOUN
■ **Everything went like clockwork.** Tout a marché comme sur des roulettes.

clog NOUN
le sabot *masc*

clone NOUN
▷ *see also* **clone** VERB
le clone *masc* (*animal, plant*)

to clone VERB
▷ *see also* **clone** NOUN
cloner [28]
□ a cloned sheep un mouton cloné

close ADJECTIVE, ADVERB
▷ *see also* **close** VERB
1 près (FEM+PL près) (*near*)
□ The shops are very close. Les magasins sont tout près.
■ **close to** près de □ The youth hostel is close to the station. L'auberge de jeunesse est près de la gare.
■ **Come closer.** Rapproche-toi.
2 proche (FEM proche) (*in relationship*)
□ We're just inviting close relations. Nous n'invitons que les parents proches. □ She's a close friend of mine. C'est une proche amie. □ I'm very close to my sister. Je suis très proche de ma sœur.
3 très serré (FEM très serrée) (*contest*)
□ It's going to be very close. Ça va être très très serré.
4 lourd (FEM lourde) (*weather*)
□ It's close this afternoon. Il fait lourd cet après-midi.

to close VERB
▷ *see also* **close** ADJECTIVE, ADVERB
1 fermer [28]
□ What time does the pool close? La piscine ferme à quelle heure ? □ The shops close at 5.30. Les magasins ferment à cinq heures et demie. □ Please close the door. Fermez la porte, s'il vous plaît.
2 se fermer [28]
□ The doors close automatically. Les portes se ferment automatiquement.

closed ADJECTIVE
fermé (FEM fermée)
□ The bank's closed. La banque est fermée.

closely ADVERB
de près (*look, examine*)

cloth NOUN
le tissu *masc* (*material*)
■ **a cloth** un chiffon □ Wipe it with a damp cloth. Nettoyez-le avec un chiffon humide.

clothes PL NOUN
les vêtements *masc pl*

□ new clothes des vêtements neufs
■ **a clothes line** un fil à linge
■ **a clothes peg** une pince à linge

cloud NOUN
▷ see also **cloud** ADJECTIVE
1 le nuage masc
2 le cloud masc
□ My photos are stored in the cloud. Mes photos sont stockées dans le cloud.

cloud ADJECTIVE
▷ see also **cloud** NOUN
■ **cloud computing** l'informatique dans le cloud
■ **cloud applications** les applications dans le cloud

cloudy ADJECTIVE
nuageux (FEM nuageuse)

clove NOUN
■ **a clove of garlic** une gousse d'ail

clown NOUN
le clown masc

club NOUN
le club masc
□ a golf club un club de golf
■ **the youth club** la maison des jeunes
■ **clubs** (in cards) le trèfle sing □ the ace of clubs l'as de trèfle

to **club together** VERB
se cotiser [28]
□ We clubbed together to buy her a present. Nous nous sommes cotisés pour lui acheter un cadeau.

clubbing NOUN
■ **to go clubbing** sortir [79†] en boîte

clue NOUN
l'indice masc
□ an important clue un indice important
■ **I haven't got a clue.** Je n'en ai pas la moindre idée.

clumsy ADJECTIVE
maladroit (FEM maladroite)

clutch NOUN
la pédale d'embrayage fem (of car)

clutter NOUN
le désordre masc
□ There's too much clutter in here. Il y a trop de désordre ici.

coach NOUN
1 le car masc
□ We went there by coach. Nous y sommes allés en car.
■ **the coach station** la gare routière
■ **a coach trip** une excursion en car
2 l'entraîneur masc (trainer)
□ the French coach l'entraîneur de l'équipe de France

coal NOUN
le charbon masc
■ **a coal mine** une mine de charbon
■ **a coal miner** un mineur

coarse ADJECTIVE
1 rugueux (FEM rugueuse) (surface, fabric)
□ The bag was made of coarse cloth. Le sac était fait d'un tissu rugueux.
2 grossier (FEM grossière) (vulgar)
□ coarse language un langage grossier

coast NOUN
la côte fem
□ It's on the west coast of Scotland. C'est sur la côte ouest de l'Écosse.

coastguard NOUN
le garde-côte masc (PL les garde-côtes)

coat NOUN
le manteau masc (PL les manteaux)
□ a warm coat un manteau chaud
■ **a coat of paint** une couche de peinture

coat hanger NOUN
le cintre masc

cobweb NOUN
la toile d'araignée fem

cock NOUN
le coq masc (cockerel)

cockerel NOUN
le coq masc

cockney NOUN
le cockney masc
□ I'm a cockney. Je suis cockney.

cocoa NOUN
le cacao masc
□ a cup of cocoa une tasse de cacao

coconut NOUN
la noix de coco fem

cod NOUN
le cabillaud masc

code NOUN
▷ see also **code** VERB
le code masc

to **code** VERB
▷ see also **code** NOUN
coder [28]

coffee NOUN
le café masc
■ **a white coffee** un café au lait
■ **A cup of coffee, please.** Un café, s'il vous plaît.

coffeepot NOUN
la cafetière fem

coffee table NOUN
la table basse fem

coffin NOUN
le cercueil masc

coin - combine

coin NOUN
la pièce de monnaie *fem*
- **a 2 euro coin** une pièce de deux euros

BE CAREFUL!
Do not translate **coin** by the French word
coin.

coincidence NOUN
la coïncidence *fem*

Coke® NOUN
le coca *masc*
□ a can of Coke® une cannette de coca

colander NOUN
la passoire *fem*

cold ADJECTIVE
▷ *see also* **cold** NOUN
froid (FEM froide)
□ The water's cold. L'eau est froide.
- **It's cold today.** Il fait froid aujourd'hui.
- **to be cold** (*person*) avoir [8] froid □ I'm cold.
J'ai froid. □ Are you cold? Est-ce que tu as froid ?

cold NOUN
▷ *see also* **cold** ADJECTIVE
1 le froid *masc*
□ I can't stand the cold. Je ne supporte pas le
froid.
2 le rhume *masc*
□ to catch a cold attraper un rhume
- **to have a cold** avoir [8] un rhume □ I've got a
bad cold. J'ai un gros rhume.
- **a cold sore** un bouton de fièvre

coleslaw NOUN
la salade de chou cru à la mayonnaise *fem*

to **collapse** VERB
s'effondrer [28]
□ He collapsed. Il s'est effondré.

collar NOUN
1 le col *masc* (*of coat, shirt*)
2 le collier *masc* (*for animal*)

collarbone NOUN
la clavicule *fem*
□ I broke my collarbone. Je me suis cassé la
clavicule.

colleague NOUN
le/la collègue *masc/fem*

to **collect** VERB
1 ramasser [28]
□ The teacher collected the exercise books. Le
professeur a ramassé les cahiers. □ They collect
the rubbish on Fridays. Ils ramassent les ordures
le vendredi.
2 collectionner [28]
□ I collect comics. Je collectionne les BD.
3 aller [3f] chercher
□ Their dad collects them from school. Leur père
va les chercher à l'école.

4 faire [36] une collecte
□ They're collecting for charity. Ils font une
collecte pour une association caritative.

collect call NOUN (US)
la communication en PCV *fem*

collection NOUN
1 la collection *fem*
□ my jewellery collection ma collection de bijoux
2 la collecte *fem*
□ a collection for charity une collecte pour une
association caritative
3 la levée *fem* (*of mail*)
□ Next collection: 5p.m. Prochaine levée :
17 heures

collector NOUN
le collectionneur *masc*
la collectionneuse *fem*

college NOUN
le collège *masc*
□ a technical college un collège d'enseignement
technique

to **collide** VERB
entrer [32f] en collision

colliery NOUN
la houillère *fem*

collision NOUN
la collision *fem*

colon NOUN
les deux-points *masc pl* (*punctuation mark*)

colonel NOUN
le colonel *masc*

colour (US **color**) NOUN
la couleur *fem*
□ What colour is it? C'est de quelle couleur ?
- **a colour film** (*for camera*) une pellicule en
couleur

colourful (US **colorful**) ADJECTIVE
coloré (FEM colorée)

colouring (US **coloring**) NOUN
le colorant *masc* (*for food*)

comb NOUN
▷ *see also* **comb** VERB
le peigne *masc*

to **comb** VERB
▷ *see also* **comb** NOUN
- **to comb one's hair** se peigner [28] □ You
haven't combed your hair. Tu ne t'es pas peigné.

combination NOUN
la combinaison *fem*

to **combine** VERB
1 allier [19]
□ The film combines humour with suspense.
Le film allie l'humour au suspense.
2 concilier [19]
□ It's difficult to combine playing sport with
studying for exams. Il est difficile de concilier la
pratique du sport et la révision des examens.

to **come** VERB

1 venir [89^t]

□ I come when I can. Je viens quand je peux.
□ You never come with us. Tu ne viens jamais avec nous. □ He always comes to see us. Il vient toujours nous voir. □ Can I come too? Est-ce que je peux venir aussi ? □ Some friends came to see us. Quelques amis sont venus nous voir. □ I'll come with you. Je viens avec toi.

2 arriver [5^t] (*arrive*)

□ I'm coming! J'arrive ! □ They came late. Ils sont arrivés en retard. □ The letter came this morning. La lettre est arrivée ce matin.

■ **Where do you come from?** Tu viens d'où ?

■ **Come on!** Allez !

to **come back** VERB

revenir [73^t]

□ Come back! Reviens !

to **come down** VERB

1 descendre [24^t] (*person, lift*)
2 baisser [28] (*prices*)

to **come in** VERB

entrer [32^t]

□ Come in! Entrez !

to **come out** VERB

sortir [79^t]

□ I tripped as we came out of the cinema. J'ai trébuché quand nous sommes sortis du cinéma. □ The film has just come out in the UK. Le film vient de sortir au Royaume-Uni.

■ **None of my photos came out.** Mes photos n'ont rien donné.

to **come round** VERB

reprendre [65] connaissance (*after faint, operation*)

to **come up** VERB

monter [48^t]

□ Come up here! Monte !

■ **to come up to somebody 1** s'approcher [28] de quelqu'un □ She came up to me and kissed me. Elle s'est approchée de moi et m'a embrassé. **2** (*to speak to them*) aborder [28] quelqu'un □ A man came up to me and said ... Un homme m'a abordé et m'a dit ...

comedian NOUN

le comique *masc*

comedy NOUN

la comédie *fem*

comfortable ADJECTIVE

1 confortable (FEM confortable) (*bed, chair*)
2 à l'aise (*person*)

□ I'm very comfortable, thanks. Je suis parfaitement à l'aise, merci.

comic NOUN

l'illustré *masc* (*magazine*)

comic strip NOUN

la bande dessinée *fem*

coming ADJECTIVE

prochain (FEM prochaine)

□ in the coming months au cours des prochains mois

comma NOUN

la virgule *fem*

command NOUN

l'ordre *masc*

comment NOUN

▷ *see also* **comment** VERB

le commentaire *masc*

□ He made no comment. Il n'a fait aucun commentaire.

■ **No comment!** Je n'ai rien à dire !

to **comment** VERB

▷ *see also* **comment** NOUN

■ **to comment on something** faire [36] des commentaires sur quelque chose

commentary NOUN

le reportage en direct *masc* (*on TV, radio*)

commentator NOUN

le commentateur sportif *masc*
la commentatrice sportive *fem*

commercial NOUN

le spot publicitaire *masc*

to **commit** VERB

■ **to commit a crime** commettre [47] un crime
■ **to commit oneself** s'engager [45] □ I don't want to commit myself. Je ne veux pas m'engager.
■ **to commit suicide** se suicider [28] □ He committed suicide. Il s'est suicidé.

committee NOUN

le comité *masc*

common ADJECTIVE

▷ *see also* **common** NOUN

courant (FEM courante)

□ 'Smith' is a very common surname. « Smith » est un nom de famille très courant.

■ **in common** en commun □ We've got a lot in common. Nous avons beaucoup de choses en commun.

common NOUN

▷ *see also* **common** ADJECTIVE

le terrain communal *masc*

□ The boys play football on the common. Les garçons jouent au football sur le terrain communal.

Commons PL NOUN

■ **the House of Commons** la Chambre des communes

common sense NOUN

le bon sens *masc*

□ Use your common sense! Sers-toi de ton bon sens !

to **communicate** VERB

communiquer [28]

communication – compliment

communication NOUN
la communication *fem*

communion NOUN
la communion *fem*
□ my First Communion ma première communion

communism NOUN
le communisme *masc*

communist NOUN
▷ *see also* **communist** ADJECTIVE
le/la communiste *masc/fem*

communist ADJECTIVE
▷ *see also* **communist** NOUN
communiste (FEM communiste)
■ **the Communist Party** le Parti communiste

community NOUN
la communauté *fem*

to **commute** VERB
faire [36] la navette
□ She commutes between Brighton and London. Elle fait la navette entre Brighton et Londres.

compact disc NOUN
le disque compact *masc*
■ **a compact disc player** une platine laser

companion NOUN
le compagnon *masc*
la compagne *fem*

company NOUN
1 la société *fem*
□ He works for a big company. Il travaille pour une grosse société.
2 la compagnie *fem*
□ an insurance company une compagnie d'assurance □ a theatre company une compagnie théâtrale
■ **to keep somebody company** tenir [83] compagnie à quelqu'un □ I'll keep you company. Je vais te tenir compagnie.

comparatively ADVERB
relativement

to **compare** VERB
comparer [28]
□ People always compare him with his brother. On le compare toujours à son frère.
■ **compared with** en comparaison de
□ Oxford is small compared with London. Oxford est une petite ville en comparaison de Londres.

comparison NOUN
la comparaison *fem*

compartment NOUN
le compartiment *masc*

compass NOUN
la boussole *fem*

compensation NOUN
l'indemnité *fem*

□ They got £2000 compensation. Ils ont reçu une indemnité de deux mille livres.

compere NOUN
l'animateur *masc*
l'animatrice *fem*

to **compete** VERB
participer [28]
□ I'm competing in the marathon. Je participe au marathon.
■ **to compete for something** se disputer [28] quelque chose □ There are 50 students competing for 6 places. Ils sont cinquante étudiants à se disputer six places.

competent ADJECTIVE
compétent (FEM compétente)

competition NOUN
le concours *masc*
□ a singing competition un concours de chant

competitive ADJECTIVE
compétitif (FEM compétitive)
□ a very competitive price un prix très compétitif
■ **to be competitive** (*person*) avoir [8] l'esprit de compétition □ He's a very competitive person. Il a vraiment l'esprit de compétition.

competitor NOUN
le concurrent *masc*
la concurrente *fem*

to **complain** VERB
se plaindre [17]
□ I'm going to complain to the manager. Je vais me plaindre au directeur. □ We complained about the noise. Nous nous sommes plaints du bruit.

complaint NOUN
la plainte *fem*
□ There were lots of complaints about the food. Il y a eu beaucoup de plaintes à propos de la nourriture.
■ **to make a complaint** faire [36] une réclamation □ I'd like to make a complaint. J'ai une réclamation à faire.

complete ADJECTIVE
complet (FEM complète)

completely ADVERB
complètement

complexion NOUN
le teint *masc*

complicated ADJECTIVE
compliqué (FEM compliquée)

compliment NOUN
▷ *see also* **compliment** VERB
le compliment *masc*

to **compliment** VERB
▷ *see also* **compliment** NOUN
complimenter [28]
□ They complimented me on my French. Ils m'ont complimenté sur mon français.

Numbers in brackets refer to verb tables on pages 650 to 658

complimentary ADJECTIVE
1 élogieux (FEM élogieuse) (*flattering*)
  □ He was very complimentary about my haircut.
  Il a été très élogieux à propos de ma coupe de cheveux.
2 gratuit (FEM gratuite) (*free*)
  □ I've got two complimentary tickets for tonight.
  J'ai deux places gratuites pour ce soir.

composer NOUN
  le compositeur *masc*
  la compositrice *fem*

comprehension NOUN
1 la compréhension *fem* (*understanding*)
2 l'exercice de compréhension *masc* (*school exercise*)

comprehensive ADJECTIVE
  complet (FEM complète)
  □ a comprehensive guide un guide complet

> **BE CAREFUL!**
> Do not translate **comprehensive** by the French word **compréhensif**.

comprehensive school NOUN
1 le collège *masc*
2 le lycée *masc*

> **DID YOU KNOW...?**
> In France, pupils go to a **collège** between the ages of 11 and 15, and then to a **lycée** until the age of 18.

compromise NOUN
  ▷ see also **compromise** VERB
  le compromis *masc*
  □ We reached a compromise. Nous sommes parvenus à un compromis.

to **compromise** VERB
  ▷ see also **compromise** NOUN
  ■ Let's compromise. Essayons de trouver un compromis.

compulsory ADJECTIVE
  obligatoire (FEM obligatoire)

computer NOUN
  l'ordinateur *masc*

computer game NOUN
  le jeu vidéo *masc* (PL les jeux vidéo)

computer programmer NOUN
  le programmeur *masc*
  la programmeuse *fem*
  □ She's a computer programmer. Elle est programmeuse.

computer room NOUN
  la salle informatique *fem*

computer science NOUN
  l'informatique *fem*

computing NOUN
  l'informatique *fem*

to **concentrate** VERB
  se concentrer [28]
  □ I couldn't concentrate. Je n'arrivais pas à me concentrer.

concentration NOUN
  la concentration *fem*

concern NOUN
  l'inquiétude *fem* (*preoccupation*)
  □ They expressed concern about her health.
  Ils ont exprimé leur inquiétude concernant sa santé.

concerned ADJECTIVE
  ■ to be concerned s'inquiéter [34] □ His mother is concerned about him. Sa mère s'inquiète à son sujet.
  ■ as far as I'm concerned en ce qui me concerne

concerning PREPOSITION
  concernant
  □ Your teacher will give you information concerning the new timetable. Votre professeur vous donnera les informations concernant le nouvel emploi du temps.

concert NOUN
  le concert *masc*

concrete NOUN
  le béton *masc*

to **condemn** VERB
  condamner [28]
  □ The university has condemned the decision.
  L'université a condamné la décision.

condition NOUN
1 la condition *fem*
  □ I'll do it, on one condition. Je veux bien le faire, à une condition.
2 l'état *masc*
  □ in bad condition en mauvais état □ in good condition en bon état

conditional NOUN
  le conditionnel *masc*

conditioner NOUN
  le baume démêlant *masc* (*for hair*)

condom NOUN
  le préservatif *masc*

to **conduct** VERB
  diriger [45] (*orchestra*)

conductor NOUN
  le chef d'orchestre *masc*

> **BE CAREFUL!**
> Do not translate **conductor** by the French word **conducteur**.

cone NOUN
  le cornet *masc*
  □ an ice-cream cone un cornet de glace

conference NOUN
  la conférence *fem*

to **confess** VERB
  avouer [28]

□ He finally confessed. Il a fini par avouer.
□ He confessed to the murder. Il a avoué avoir commis le meurtre.

confession NOUN
la confession *fem*

confetti NOUN
les confettis *masc pl*

confidence NOUN
1 la confiance *fem*
□ I've got confidence in you. J'ai confiance en toi.
2 l'assurance *fem*
□ She lacks confidence. Elle manque d'assurance.

confident ADJECTIVE
sûr (FEM sûre)
□ I'm confident everything will be okay. Je suis sûr que tout ira bien.
■ **She's seems quite confident.** Elle a l'air sûre d'elle.

confidential ADJECTIVE
confidentiel (FEM confidentielle)

to **confirm** VERB
confirmer [28] (*booking*)

confirmation NOUN
la confirmation *fem*

conflict NOUN
le conflit *masc*

to **confuse** VERB
■ **to confuse somebody** embrouiller [28] les idées de quelqu'un □ Don't confuse me! Ne m'embrouille pas les idées !

confused ADJECTIVE
désorienté (FEM désorientée)

confusing ADJECTIVE
■ **The road signs are confusing.** Les panneaux de signalisation ne sont pas clairs.

confusion NOUN
la confusion *fem*

to **congratulate** VERB
féliciter [28]
□ My aunt congratulated me on my results. Ma tante m'a félicité pour mes résultats.

congratulations PL NOUN
les félicitations *fem pl*
□ Congratulations on winning the match! Félicitations pour votre victoire lors du match !

conjunction NOUN
la conjonction *fem*

conjurer NOUN
le prestidigitateur *masc*

connection NOUN
1 le rapport *masc*
□ There's no connection between the two events. Il n'y a aucun rapport entre les deux événements.
2 le contact *masc* (*electrical*)
□ There's a loose connection. Il y a un mauvais contact.

3 la correspondance *fem* (*of trains, planes*)
□ We missed our connection. Nous avons raté la correspondance.

to **conquer** VERB
conquérir [2]

conscience NOUN
la conscience *fem*

conscious ADJECTIVE
conscient (FEM consciente)

consciousness NOUN
la connaissance *fem*
■ **to lose consciousness** perdre [61] connaissance □ I lost consciousness. J'ai perdu connaissance.

consequence NOUN
la conséquence *fem*
□ What are the consequences for the environment? Quelles sont les conséquences pour l'environnement ?
■ **as a consequence** en conséquence

consequently ADVERB
par conséquent

conservation NOUN
la protection *fem*

Conservative NOUN
le conservateur *masc*
la conservatrice *fem*
■ **to vote Conservative** voter [28] conservateur
■ **the Conservatives** les conservateurs

conservative ADJECTIVE
conservateur (FEM conservatrice)
■ **the Conservative Party** le parti conservateur

conservatory NOUN
le jardin d'hiver *masc*

to **consider** VERB
1 considérer [34]
□ He considers it a waste of time. Il considère que c'est une perte de temps.
2 envisager [45]
□ We considered cancelling our holiday. Nous avons envisagé d'annuler nos vacances.
■ **I'm considering the idea.** J'y songe.

considerate ADJECTIVE
délicat (FEM délicate)

considering PREPOSITION
1 étant donné
□ Considering we were there for a month ... Étant donné que nous étions là pour un mois ...
2 tout compte fait
□ I got a good mark, considering. J'ai eu une bonne note, tout compte fait.

to **consist** VERB
■ **to consist of** être [35] composé de □ The band consists of a singer and a guitarist. Le groupe est composé d'un chanteur et d'un guitariste.

consonant NOUN
la consonne *fem*

constant ADJECTIVE
constant (FEM constante)

constantly ADVERB
constamment

constipated ADJECTIVE
constipé (FEM constipée)

to **construct** VERB
construire [23]

construction NOUN
la construction *fem*

to **consult** VERB
consulter [28]

consumer NOUN
le consommateur *masc*
la consommatrice *fem*

contact NOUN
▷ *see also* **contact** VERB
le contact *masc*
□ I'm in contact with her. Je suis en contact avec elle.
■ **your contact details** vos coordonnées
■ **a contact number** un numéro de téléphone

to **contact** VERB
▷ *see also* **contact** NOUN
joindre [42]
□ Where can we contact you? Où pouvons-nous vous joindre ?

contact lenses PL NOUN
les verres de contact *masc pl*

contactless ADJECTIVE
sans contact

to **contain** VERB
contenir [83]

container NOUN
le récipient *masc*

contempt NOUN
le mépris *masc*

contents PL NOUN
1 le contenu *masc sing* (*of container*)
2 la table des matières *fem sing* (*of book*)

contest NOUN
le concours *masc*

contestant NOUN
le concurrent *masc*
la concurrente *fem*

context NOUN
le contexte *masc*

continent NOUN
le continent *masc*
□ How many continents are there? Combien y a-t-il de continents ?

continental breakfast NOUN
le petit déjeuner à la française *masc*

to **continue** VERB
1 continuer [28]

□ She continued talking to her friend. Elle a continué à parler à son amie.
2 reprendre [65] (*after interruption*)
□ We continued working after lunch. Nous avons repris le travail après le déjeuner.

continuous ADJECTIVE
continu (FEM continue)
■ **continuous assessment** le contrôle continu

contraceptive NOUN
le contraceptif *masc*

contract NOUN
le contrat *masc*

to **contradict** VERB
contredire [27]

contrary NOUN
le contraire *masc*
■ **on the contrary** au contraire

contrast NOUN
le contraste *masc*

to **contribute** VERB
1 contribuer [28] (*to success, achievement*)
□ The treaty will contribute to world peace. Le traité va contribuer à la paix dans le monde.
2 participer [28] (*share in*)
□ He didn't contribute to the discussion. Il n'a pas participé à la discussion.
3 donner [28] (*give*)
□ She contributed £10. Elle a donné dix livres.

contribution NOUN
1 la contribution *fem*
2 la cotisation *fem* (*to pension, national insurance*)

control NOUN
▷ *see also* **control** VERB
le contrôle *masc*
■ **to lose control** (*of vehicle*) perdre [61] le contrôle □ He lost control of the car. Il a perdu le contrôle de son véhicule.
■ **the controls** les commandes *fem pl* (*of machine*)
■ **to be in control** être [35] maître de la situation
■ **to keep control** (*of people*) se faire [36] obéir
□ He can't keep control of the class. Il ne se fait pas obéir de la classe.
■ **out of control** (*child, class*) déchaîné

to **control** VERB
▷ *see also* **control** NOUN
1 diriger [45] (*country, organization*)
2 se faire [36] obéir de
□ He can't control the class. Il ne se fait pas obéir de la classe.
3 maîtriser [28]
□ I couldn't control the horse. Je ne suis pas arrivé à maîtriser le cheval.
■ **to control oneself** se contrôler [28]

controversial ADJECTIVE
controversé (FEM controversée)
□ a controversial book un livre controversé

convenient ADJECTIVE
bien situé (FEM bien située) (place)
□ Our house is convenient for the school.
Notre maison est bien située par rapport à
l'école.
■ **It's not a convenient time for me.** C'est
une heure qui ne m'arrange pas.
■ **Would Monday be convenient for you?**
Est-ce que lundi vous conviendrait ?

conventional ADJECTIVE
conventionnel (FEM conventionnelle)

convent school NOUN
le couvent masc
□ She goes to convent school. Elle va au
couvent.

conversation NOUN
la conversation fem
□ a French conversation class un cours de
conversation française

to **convert** VERB
transformer [28]
□ We've converted the loft into a spare room.
Nous avons transformé le grenier en chambre
d'amis.

to **convict** VERB
reconnaître [14] coupable
□ He was convicted of the murder. Il a été
reconnu coupable du meurtre.

to **convince** VERB
persuader [28]
□ I'm not convinced. Je n'en suis pas persuadé.

to **cook** VERB
▷ see also **cook** NOUN
1 faire [36] la cuisine
□ I can't cook. Je ne sais pas faire la cuisine.
2 préparer [28]
□ She's cooking lunch. Elle est en train de
préparer le déjeuner.
3 faire [36] cuire
□ Cook the pasta for 10 minutes. Faites cuire les
pâtes pendant dix minutes.
■ **to be cooked** être [35] cuit □ When the
potatoes are cooked ... Lorsque les pommes de
terre sont cuites ...

cook NOUN
▷ see also **cook** VERB
le cuisinier masc
la cuisinière fem
□ Matthew's an excellent cook. Matthew est un
excellent cuisinier.

cookbook NOUN
le livre de cuisine masc

cooker NOUN
la cuisinière fem
□ a gas cooker une cuisinière à gaz

cookery NOUN
la cuisine fem

cookie NOUN (US)
le gâteau sec masc (PL les gâteaux secs)

cooking NOUN
la cuisine fem
□ I like cooking. J'aime bien faire la cuisine.

cool ADJECTIVE
1 frais (FEM fraîche)
□ a cool place un endroit frais
2 cool (FEM+PL cool) (great)
□ That's really cool! C'est vraiment cool !

cooperation NOUN
la coopération fem

cop NOUN
le flic masc (informal)

co-parent VERB
élever [43] en coparentalité

to **cope** VERB
se débrouiller [28]
□ It was hard, but we coped. C'était dur, mais
nous nous sommes débrouillés.
■ **to cope with** faire [36] face à □ She's got a lot
of problems to cope with. Elle doit faire face à de
nombreux problèmes.

copper NOUN
1 le cuivre masc
□ a copper bracelet un bracelet en cuivre
2 le flic masc (informal: police officer)

copy NOUN
▷ see also **copy** VERB
1 la copie fem (of letter, document)
2 l'exemplaire masc (of book)

to **copy** VERB
▷ see also **copy** NOUN
copier [19]
□ The teacher accused him of copying. Le
professeur l'a accusé d'avoir copié.
■ **to copy and paste** copier-coller [28]

core NOUN
le trognon masc (of fruit)
□ an apple core un trognon de pomme

cork NOUN
1 le bouchon masc (of bottle)
2 le liège masc (material)
□ a cork notice board un panneau d'affichage
en liège

corkscrew NOUN
le tire-bouchon masc

corn NOUN
1 le blé masc (wheat)
2 le maïs masc (sweetcorn)
■ **corn on the cob** l'épi de maïs masc

corner NOUN
1 le coin masc
□ in a corner of the room dans un coin de la
pièce
■ **the shop on the corner** la boutique au coin
de la rue

■ **He lives just round the corner.** Il habite tout près d'ici.
2 le corner *masc* (*in football*)

cornet NOUN
1 le cornet à pistons *masc*
□ He plays the cornet. Il joue du cornet à pistons.
2 le cornet *masc* (*ice cream*)

cornflakes PL NOUN
les corn-flakes *masc pl*

cornstarch NOUN (US)
la farine de maïs *fem*

Cornwall NOUN
la Cornouailles *fem*
■ **in Cornwall** en Cornouailles

coronavirus NOUN
le coronavirus *masc*

corporal NOUN
le caporal *masc*

corporal punishment NOUN
le châtiment corporel *masc*

corpse NOUN
le cadavre *masc*

correct ADJECTIVE
▷ *see also* **correct** VERB
exact (FEM exacte)
□ That's correct. C'est exact.
■ **the correct choice** le bon choix
■ **the correct answer** la bonne réponse

to **correct** VERB
▷ *see also* **correct** ADJECTIVE
corriger [45]

correction NOUN
la correction *fem*

correctly ADVERB
correctement

correspondent NOUN
le correspondant *masc*
la correspondante *fem*
□ our foreign correspondent notre correspondant à l'étranger

corridor NOUN
le couloir *masc*

corruption NOUN
la corruption *fem*

Corsica NOUN
la Corse *fem*
■ **in Corsica** en Corse

cosmetics PL NOUN
les produits de beauté *masc pl*

cosmetic surgery NOUN
la chirurgie esthétique *fem*

to **cost** VERB
▷ *see also* **cost** NOUN
coûter [28]
□ His sweatshirt cost £50. Son sweat-shirt

a coûté 50 livres. □ How much does it cost? Combien est-ce que ça coûte ? □ It costs too much. Ça coûte trop cher.

cost NOUN
▷ *see also* **cost** VERB
le coût *masc*
■ **the cost of living** le coût de la vie
■ **at all costs** à tout prix

costume NOUN
le costume *masc*

cosy ADJECTIVE
douillet (FEM douillette)

cot NOUN
le lit d'enfant *masc*

cottage NOUN
le cottage *masc*

cotton NOUN
le coton *masc*
□ a cotton shirt une chemise en coton
■ **cotton wool** le coton hydrophile

couch NOUN
le canapé *masc*

couchette NOUN
la couchette *fem*

to **cough** VERB
▷ *see also* **cough** NOUN
tousser [28]

cough NOUN
▷ *see also* **cough** VERB
la toux *fem*
□ a bad cough une mauvaise toux
■ **I've got a cough.** Je tousse.
■ **a cough sweet** une pastille

could VERB ▷ *see* **can**

council NOUN
le conseil *masc*

DID YOU KNOW...?
The nearest French equivalent of a local council would be a **conseil municipal**, which administers a **commune**.

■ **He's on the council.** Il fait partie du conseil municipal.
■ **a council estate** une cité HLM
■ **a council house** une HLM

DID YOU KNOW...?
HLM stands for **habitation à loyer modéré** which means 'low-rent home'.

councillor NOUN
■ **She's a local councillor.** Elle fait partie du conseil municipal.

to **count** VERB
compter [28]

to **count on** VERB
compter [28] sur
□ You can count on me. Tu peux compter sur moi.

counter NOUN
1 le comptoir masc (in shop)
2 le guichet masc (in post office, bank)
3 le jeton masc (in game)

country NOUN
1 le pays masc
□ the border between the two countries la frontière entre les deux pays
2 la campagne fem
□ I live in the country. J'habite à la campagne.
■ **country dancing** la danse folklorique

countryside NOUN
la campagne fem

county NOUN
le comté masc

> **DID YOU KNOW...?**
> The nearest French equivalent of a county would be a **département**.

■ **the county council**

> **DID YOU KNOW...?**
> The nearest French equivalent of a county council would be a **conseil général**, which administers a **département**.

couple NOUN
le couple masc
□ the couple who live next door le couple qui habite à côté
■ **a couple** deux □ a couple of hours deux heures
■ **Could you wait a couple of minutes?** Pourriez-vous attendre quelques minutes ?

courage NOUN
le courage masc

courgette NOUN
la courgette fem

courier NOUN
1 l'accompagnateur masc
l'accompagnatrice fem (for tourists)
2 le coursier masc (delivery service)
□ They sent it by courier. Ils l'ont envoyé par coursier.

> **BE CAREFUL!**
> Do not translate **courier** by the French word **courrier**.

course NOUN
1 le cours masc
□ a French course un cours de français □ to go on a course suivre un cours
2 le plat masc
□ the main course le plat principal
■ **the first course** l'entrée fem
3 le terrain masc
□ a golf course un terrain de golf
■ **of course** bien sûr □ Do you love me? — Of course I do! Tu m'aimes ? — Bien sûr que oui !

court NOUN
1 le tribunal masc (PL les tribunaux) (of law)
□ He was in court yesterday. Il est passé devant le tribunal hier.
2 le court masc (tennis)
□ There are tennis and squash courts. Il y a des courts de tennis et de squash.

courtyard NOUN
la cour fem

cousin NOUN
le cousin masc
la cousine fem

cover NOUN
▷ see also **cover** VERB
1 la couverture fem (of book)
2 la housse fem (of duvet)

to **cover** VERB
▷ see also **cover** NOUN
couvrir [55]
□ My face was covered with mosquito bites. J'avais le visage couvert de piqûres de moustique.
■ **to cover up a scandal** étouffer [28] un scandale

COVID NOUN
le COVID masc

cow NOUN
la vache fem

coward NOUN
le lâche masc
□ She's a coward. Elle est lâche.

cowardly ADJECTIVE
lâche (FEM lâche)

crab NOUN
le crabe masc

crack NOUN
▷ see also **crack** VERB
1 la fissure fem (in wall)
2 la fêlure fem (in cup, window)
■ **I'll have a crack at it.** Je vais tenter le coup.

to **crack** VERB
▷ see also **crack** NOUN
casser [28] (nut, egg)
■ **to crack a joke** sortir [79] une blague

to **crack down** VERB
être [35] ferme
□ The police are cracking down on drink-drivers. La police va être ferme avec les automobilistes en état d'ébriété.

cracked ADJECTIVE
fêlé (FEM fêlée) (cup, window)

cracker NOUN
1 le cracker masc (biscuit)
2 la papillote fem (Christmas cracker)

cradle NOUN
le berceau *masc* (PL les berceaux)

craft NOUN
les travaux manuels *masc pl*
□ We do craft at school. Nous avons des cours de travaux manuels à l'école.
■ **a craft centre** un centre artisanal

craftsman NOUN
l'artisan *masc*

to **cram** VERB
1 entasser [28]
□ We crammed our stuff into the boot. Nous avons entassé nos affaires dans le coffre.
2 bachoter [28] (*for exams*)

crammed ADJECTIVE
■ **crammed with** bourré de □ Her bag was crammed with books. Son sac était bourré de livres.

crane NOUN
la grue *fem* (*machine*)

to **crash** VERB
▷ *see also* **crash** NOUN
avoir [8] un accident
□ He's crashed his car. Il a eu un accident de voiture.
■ **The plane crashed.** L'avion s'est écrasé.

crash NOUN
▷ *see also* **crash** VERB
1 la collision *fem* (*of car*)
2 l'accident *masc* (*of plane*)
■ **a crash helmet** un casque
■ **a crash course** un cours intensif

to **crawl** VERB
▷ *see also* **crawl** NOUN
marcher [28] à quatre pattes (*baby*)

crawl NOUN
▷ *see also* **crawl** VERB
le crawl *masc*
□ to do the crawl nager le crawl

crazy ADJECTIVE
fou (FEM folle)

fou changes to **fol** before a vowel and most words beginning with 'h'.

cream ADJECTIVE
▷ *see also* **cream** NOUN
crème (FEM+PL crème) (*colour*)

cream NOUN
▷ *see also* **cream** ADJECTIVE
la crème *fem*
□ strawberries and cream les fraises à la crème
■ **a cream cake** un gâteau à la crème

■ **cream cheese** le fromage à la crème
■ **sun cream** la crème solaire

crease NOUN
le pli *masc*

creased ADJECTIVE
froissé (FEM froissée)

to **create** VERB
créer [18]

creation NOUN
la création *fem*

creative ADJECTIVE
créatif (FEM créative)

creature NOUN
la créature *fem*

crèche NOUN
la crèche *fem*

credit NOUN
le crédit *masc*
□ on credit à crédit
■ **I've no credit left on my phone.** Je n'ai plus de crédit sur mon portable.

credit card NOUN
la carte de crédit *fem*

creeps PL NOUN
■ **It gives me the creeps.** Ça me donne la chair de poule.

to **creep up** VERB
■ **to creep up on somebody** s'approcher [28] de quelqu'un à pas de loup

crept VERB ▷ *see* **creep up**

cress NOUN
le cresson *masc*

crew NOUN
1 l'équipage *masc* (*of ship, plane*)
2 l'équipe *fem*
□ a film crew une équipe de tournage

crew cut NOUN
les cheveux en brosse *masc pl*

cricket NOUN
1 le cricket *masc*
□ I play cricket. Je joue au cricket.
■ **a cricket bat** une batte de cricket
2 le grillon *masc* (*insect*)

crime NOUN
1 le délit *masc*
□ Murder is a crime. Le meurtre est un délit.
2 la criminalité *fem* (*lawlessness*)
□ Crime is rising. La criminalité augmente.

criminal NOUN
▷ *see also* **criminal** ADJECTIVE
le criminel *masc*
la criminelle *fem*

criminal ADJECTIVE
▷ *see also* **criminal** NOUN
criminel (FEM criminelle)
□ It's criminal! C'est criminel !

■ **It's a criminal offence.** C'est un crime puni par la loi.

■ **to have a criminal record** avoir [8] un casier judiciaire

crisis NOUN
la crise *fem*

crisp ADJECTIVE
croquant (FEM croquante) (*food*)

crisps PL NOUN
les chips *fem pl*
□ a packet of crisps un paquet de chips

criterion NOUN
le critère *masc*

critic NOUN
le critique *masc*

critical ADJECTIVE
critique (FEM critique)
■ **a critical remark** une critique

criticism NOUN
la critique *fem*

to **criticize** VERB
critiquer [28]

Croatia NOUN
la Croatie *fem*
■ **in Croatia** en Croatie

to **crochet** VERB
crocheter [1]

crocodile NOUN
le crocodile *masc*

crook NOUN
l'escroc *masc* (*criminal*)

crop NOUN
la récolte *fem*
□ a good crop of apples une bonne récolte de pommes

cross NOUN
▷ *see also* **cross** ADJECTIVE, VERB
la croix *fem*

cross ADJECTIVE
▷ *see also* **cross** NOUN, VERB
fâché (FEM fâchée)
□ to be cross about something être fâché à propos de quelque chose

to **cross** VERB
▷ *see also* **cross** ADJECTIVE, NOUN
traverser [28] (*street*, *bridge*)

to **cross out** VERB
barrer [28]

to **cross over** VERB
traverser [28]

cross-country NOUN
le cross *masc* (*race*)
■ **cross-country skiing** le ski de fond

crossing NOUN
1 la traversée *fem* (*by boat*)
□ the crossing from Dover to Calais la traversée de Douvres à Calais
2 le passage clouté *masc* (*for pedestrians*)

crossroads NOUN
le carrefour *masc*

crossword NOUN
les mots croisés *masc pl*
□ I like doing crosswords. J'aime faire les mots croisés.

to **crouch down** VERB
s'accroupir [38]

crow NOUN
le corbeau *masc* (PL les corbeaux)

crowd NOUN
la foule *fem*
■ **the crowd** (*at sports match*) les spectateurs

crowded ADJECTIVE
bondé (FEM bondée)

crowdfunding NOUN
la crowdfunding *masc*

crown NOUN
la couronne *fem*

crucifix NOUN
le crucifix *masc*

crude ADJECTIVE
grossier (FEM grossière) (*vulgar*)

cruel ADJECTIVE
cruel (FEM cruelle)

cruise NOUN
la croisière *fem*
□ to go on a cruise faire une croisière

crumb NOUN
la miette *fem*

to **crush** VERB
écraser [28]

crutch NOUN
la béquille *fem*

cry NOUN
▷ *see also* **cry** VERB
le cri *masc*
□ He gave a cry of surprise. Il a poussé un cri de surprise.
■ **Go on, have a good cry!** Vas-y, pleure un bon coup !

to **cry** VERB
▷ *see also* **cry** NOUN
pleurer [28]
□ The baby's crying. Le bébé pleure.

crystal NOUN
le cristal *masc* (PL les cristaux)

CTC NOUN (= *city technology college*)
le collège technique *masc*

cub NOUN
1 le petit *masc* (*animal*)
2 le louveteau *masc* (PL les louveteaux) (*scout*)

cube NOUN
le cube *masc*

cubic ADJECTIVE
■ **a cubic metre** un mètre cube

cucumber NOUN
le concombre *masc*

cuddle NOUN
▷ *see also* **cuddle** VERB
le câlin *masc*
□ Come and give me a cuddle. Viens me faire un câlin.

cuddle VERB
▷ *see also* **cuddle** NOUN
■ **to cuddle something** faire [36] un câlin à quelque chose □ Emma cuddled her teddy bear. Emma a fait un câlin à son nounours.

cue NOUN
la queue de billard *fem* (*for snooker, pool*)

culottes PL NOUN
la jupe-culotte *fem sing*

cultural ADJECTIVE
culturale (FEM culturelle)

culture NOUN
la culture *fem*

cunning ADJECTIVE
1 rusé (FEM rusée) (*person*)
2 astucieux (FEM astucieuse) (*plan, idea*)

cup NOUN
1 la tasse *fem*
□ a china cup une tasse en porcelaine
■ **a cup of coffee** un café
2 la coupe *fem* (*trophy*)

cupboard NOUN
le placard *masc*

to **cure** VERB
▷ *see also* **cure** NOUN
guérir [38]

cure NOUN
▷ *see also* **cure** VERB
le remède *masc*

curious ADJECTIVE
curieux (FEM curieuse)

curl NOUN
la boucle *fem* (*in hair*)

curly ADJECTIVE
1 bouclé (FEM bouclée) (*loosely curled*)
2 frisé (FEM frisée) (*tightly curled*)

currant NOUN
le raisin sec *masc* (*dried fruit*)

currency NOUN
la devise *fem*
□ foreign currency les devises étrangères

current NOUN
▷ *see also* **current** ADJECTIVE
le courant *masc*
□ The current is very strong. Le courant est très fort.

current ADJECTIVE
▷ *see also* **current** NOUN

actuel (FEM actuelle)
□ the current situation la situation actuelle

current account NOUN
le compte courant *masc*

current affairs PL NOUN
l'actualité *fem*

curriculum NOUN
le programme *masc*

curriculum vitae NOUN
le curriculum vitae *masc*

curry NOUN
le curry *masc*

curse NOUN
la malédiction *fem* (*spell*)

curtain NOUN
le rideau *masc* (PL les rideaux)
□ to draw the curtains tirer les rideaux

cushion NOUN
le coussin *masc*

custard NOUN
la crème anglaise *fem* (*for pouring*)

custody NOUN
la garde *fem* (*of child*)

custom NOUN
la coutume *fem, masc*
□ It's an old custom. C'est une ancienne coutume.

customer NOUN
le client *masc*
la cliente *fem*

customs PL NOUN
la douane *fem sing*

customs officer NOUN
le douanier *masc*
la douanière *fem*

cut NOUN
▷ *see also* **cut** VERB
1 la coupure *fem*
□ He's got a cut on his forehead. Il a une coupure au front.
2 la coupe *fem*
□ a cut and blow-dry une coupe brushing
3 la réduction *fem* (*in price, spending*)

to **cut** VERB
▷ *see also* **cut** NOUN
1 couper [28]
□ I'll cut some bread. Je vais couper du pain.
■ **to cut oneself** se couper [28] □ I cut my foot on a piece of glass. Je me suis coupé au pied avec un morceau de verre.
2 réduire [23] (*price, spending*)

to **cut down** VERB
abattre [9] (*tree*)

to **cut off** VERB
couper [28]
□ The electricity was cut off. L'électricité a été coupée.

to **cut up** VERB
hacher [28] (*vegetables, meat*)

cutback NOUN
la réduction *fem*
▢ staff cutbacks des réductions de personnel

cute ADJECTIVE
mignon (FEM mignonne)

cutlery NOUN
les couverts *masc pl*

cutting NOUN
la coupure de presse *fem* (*from newspaper*)

CV NOUN
le C.V. *masc*

cyberbully NOUN
le personne *fem* coupable de cyberharcèlement

cyberbullying NOUN
le cyberharcèlement *masc*

cybercafé NOUN
le cybercafé *masc*

to **cycle** VERB
▷ *see also* **cycle** NOUN
faire [36] de la bicyclette
■ **I cycle to school.** Je vais à l'école à bicyclette.

cycle NOUN
▷ *see also* **cycle** VERB
la bicyclette *fem*
■ **a cycle ride** une promenade à bicyclette
■ **a cycle lane** une piste cyclable

cycling NOUN
le cyclisme *masc*

cyclist NOUN
le/la cycliste *masc/fem*

cylinder NOUN
le cylindre *masc*

Cyprus NOUN
Chypre
■ **in Cyprus** à Chypre
■ **to Cyprus** à Chypre

Czech NOUN
▷ *see also* **Czech** ADJECTIVE
1 le/la Tchèque *masc/fem* (*person*)
2 le tchèque *masc* (*language*)

Czech ADJECTIVE
▷ *see also* **Czech** NOUN
tchèque (FEM tchèque)
■ **the Czech Republic** la République tchèque

Dd

dad NOUN
1 le **père** *masc*
  □ my dad mon père □ her dad son père
2 le **papa** *masc*

> Use **papa** only when you are talking to your father or using it as his name; otherwise use **père**.

  ■ **Dad!** Papa ! □ I'll ask Dad. Je vais demander à papa.

daddy NOUN
  le **papa** *masc*
  □ Say hello to your daddy! Dis bonjour à ton papa ! □ Hello Daddy! Bonjour Papa !

daffodil NOUN
  la **jonquille** *fem*

daft ADJECTIVE
  idiot (FEM idiote)

daily ADJECTIVE, ADVERB
1 **quotidien** (FEM quotidienne)
  □ It's part of my daily routine. Ça fait partie de mes occupations quotidiennes.
2 **tous les jours**
  □ The pool is open daily. La piscine est ouverte tous les jours.

dairy NOUN
  la **crémerie** *fem* (*shop*)

dairy products PL NOUN
  les **produits laitiers** *masc pl*

daisy NOUN
  la **pâquerette** *fem*

dam NOUN
  le **barrage** *masc*

damage NOUN
  ▷ *see also* **damage** VERB
  les **dégâts** *masc pl*
  □ The storm did a lot of damage. La tempête a fait beaucoup de dégâts.

to damage VERB
  ▷ *see also* **damage** NOUN
  endommager [45]

damp ADJECTIVE
  humide (FEM humide)

dance NOUN
  ▷ *see also* **dance** VERB
1 la **danse** *fem*

□ The last dance was a waltz. La dernière danse était une valse.
2 le **bal** *masc*
  □ Are you going to the dance tonight? Tu vas au bal ce soir ?

to dance VERB
  ▷ *see also* **dance** NOUN
  danser [28]
  ■ **to go dancing** aller [3] danser □ Let's go dancing! Si on allait danser ?

dancer NOUN
  le **danseur** *masc*
  la **danseuse** *fem*

dandruff NOUN
  les **pellicules** *fem pl*

Dane NOUN
  le **Danois** *masc*
  la **Danoise** *fem*

danger NOUN
  le **danger** *masc*
  ■ **in danger** en danger □ His life is in danger. Sa vie est en danger.
  ■ **to be in danger of** risquer [28] de □ We were in danger of missing the plane. Nous risquions de rater l'avion.

dangerous ADJECTIVE
  dangereux (FEM dangereuse)

Danish ADJECTIVE
  ▷ *see also* **Danish** NOUN
  danois (FEM danoise)

Danish NOUN
  ▷ *see also* **Danish** ADJECTIVE
  le **danois** *masc* (*language*)

to dare VERB
  oser [28]
  ■ **to dare to do something** oser [28] faire quelque chose □ I didn't dare to tell my parents. Je n'ai pas osé le dire à mes parents.
  ■ **I dare say it'll be okay.** Je suppose que ça va aller.

daring ADJECTIVE
  audacieux (FEM audacieuse)

dark ADJECTIVE
  ▷ *see also* **dark** NOUN
1 **sombre** (FEM sombre) (*room*)
  □ It's dark. (*inside*) Il fait sombre.

d

- **It's dark outside.** Il fait nuit dehors.
- **It's getting dark.** La nuit tombe.
2 foncé (FEM foncée) (colour)
  - □ She's got dark hair. Elle a les cheveux foncés.
  - □ a dark green sweater un pull vert foncé

dark NOUN
▷ see also **dark** ADJECTIVE
le noir masc
□ I'm afraid of the dark. J'ai peur du noir.
- **after dark** après la tombée de la nuit

darkness NOUN
l'obscurité fem
□ The room was in darkness. La chambre était dans l'obscurité.

darling NOUN
le chéri masc
la chérie fem
□ Thank you, darling! Merci, chéri !

dart NOUN
la fléchette fem
□ to play darts jouer aux fléchettes

to **dash** VERB
▷ see also **dash** NOUN
se précipiter [28]
□ Everyone dashed to the window. Tout le monde s'est précipité vers la fenêtre.
- **I must dash!** Il faut que je me sauve !

dash NOUN
▷ see also **dash** VERB
le tiret masc (punctuation mark)

data PL NOUN
les données fem pl

database NOUN
la base de données fem (on computer)

date NOUN
1 la date fem
  □ my date of birth ma date de naissance
  - **What's the date today?** Quel jour sommes-nous ?
  - **to have a date with somebody** sortir [79⁶] avec quelqu'un □ She's got a date with Ethan tonight. Elle sort avec Ethan ce soir.
  - **out of date** 1 (passport) périmé
  2 (technology) dépassé 3 (clothes) démodé
2 la datte fem (fruit)

daughter NOUN
la fille fem

daughter-in-law NOUN
la belle-fille fem (PL les belles-filles)

dawn NOUN
l'aube fem
□ at dawn à l'aube

day NOUN

Use **jour** to refer to the whole 24-hour period. **journée** only refers to the time when you are awake.

1 le jour masc
  □ We stayed in Nice for three days. Nous sommes restés trois jours à Nice.
  - **every day** tous les jours
2 la journée fem
  □ during the day dans la journée □ I stayed at home all day. Je suis resté à la maison toute la journée.
  - **the day before** la veille □ the day before my birthday la veille de mon anniversaire
  - **the day after** le lendemain
  - **the day after tomorrow** après-demain □ We're leaving the day after tomorrow. Nous partons après-demain.
  - **the day before yesterday** avant-hier □ He arrived the day before yesterday. Il est arrivé avant-hier.

dead ADJECTIVE, ADVERB
1 mort (FEM morte)
  □ He was already dead when the doctor came. Il était déjà mort quand le docteur est arrivé.
  - **He was shot dead.** Il a été abattu.
2 absolument (totally)
  □ You're dead right! Tu as absolument raison !
  - **dead on time** à l'heure pile □ The train arrived dead on time. Le train est arrivé à l'heure pile.

dead end NOUN
l'impasse fem

deadline NOUN
la date limite fem
□ The deadline for entries is May 2nd. La date limite d'inscription est le deux mai.

deaf ADJECTIVE
sourd (FEM sourde)

deafening ADJECTIVE
assourdissant (FEM assourdissante)

deal NOUN
▷ see also **deal** VERB
le marché masc
- **It's a deal!** Marché conclu !
- **a great deal** beaucoup □ a great deal of money beaucoup d'argent

to **deal** VERB
▷ see also **deal** NOUN
donner [28] (cards)
□ It's your turn to deal. C'est à toi de donner.
- **to deal with something** s'occuper [28] de quelque chose □ He promised to deal with it immediately. Il a promis de s'en occuper immédiatement.

dealer NOUN
1 le marchand masc
  la marchande fem
2 le dealer masc (of drugs)

dealt VERB ▷ see **deal**

dear ADJECTIVE
1 cher (FEM chère)

□ Dear Mrs Duval Chère Madame Duval
■ **Dear Sir/Madam** (*in a letter*) Madame,
Monsieur
2 coûteux (FEM coûteuse) (*expensive*)

death NOUN
la mort *fem*
□ after his death après sa mort
■ **I was bored to death.** Je me suis ennuyé à
mourir.

debate NOUN
▷ *see also* **debate** VERB
le débat *masc*

to **debate** VERB
▷ *see also* **debate** NOUN
débattre [9]

debt NOUN
la dette *fem*
□ He's got a lot of debts. Il a beaucoup de
dettes.
■ **to be in debt** avoir [8] des dettes

decade NOUN
la décennie *fem*

decaffeinated ADJECTIVE
décaféiné (FEM décaféinée)

to **decay** VERB
se délabrer [28] (*building*)
□ a decaying mansion un manoir qui se délabre

to **deceive** VERB
tromper [28]

> **BE CAREFUL!**
> Do not translate **to deceive** by the French
> word **décevoir**.

December NOUN
décembre *masc*
■ **in December** en décembre

decent ADJECTIVE
convenable (FEM convenable)
□ a decent education une éducation convenable

to **decide** VERB
1 décider [28]
□ I decided to write to her. J'ai décidé de lui
écrire. □ I decided not to go. J'ai décidé de ne
pas y aller.
2 se décider [28]
□ I can't decide. Je n'arrive pas à me décider.
□ Haven't you decided yet? Tu ne t'es pas encore
décidé ?
■ **to decide on something** se mettre [47]
d'accord sur quelque chose □ They haven't
decided on a name yet. Ils ne se sont pas encore
mis d'accord sur un nom.

decimal ADJECTIVE
décimal (FEM décimale)
□ the decimal system le système décimal

decision NOUN
la décision *fem*

■ **to make a decision** prendre [65] une décision

decisive ADJECTIVE
décidé (FEM décidée) (*person*)

deck NOUN
1 le pont *masc* (*of ship*)
■ **on deck** sur le pont
2 le jeu *masc* (PL les jeux) (*of cards*)

deckchair NOUN
la chaise longue *fem*

to **declare** VERB
déclarer [28]

to **decorate** VERB
1 décorer [28]
□ I decorated the cake with pink icing. J'ai
décoré le gâteau avec un glaçage rose.
2 peindre [60] (*paint*)
3 tapisser [28] (*wallpaper*)

decrease NOUN
▷ *see also* **decrease** VERB
la diminution *fem*
□ a decrease in the number of unemployed une
diminution du nombre de chômeurs

to **decrease** VERB
▷ *see also* **decrease** NOUN
diminuer [28]

dedicated ADJECTIVE
dévoué (FEM dévouée)
□ a very dedicated teacher un professeur très
dévoué
■ **dedicated to** 1 consacré à □ a museum
dedicated to Napoleon un musée consacré à
Napoléon 2 dédicacé à □ The book is dedicated
to Emma. Le livre est dédicacé à Emma.

dedication NOUN
1 le dévouement *masc* (*commitment*)
2 la dédicace *fem* (*in book, on radio*)

to **deduct** VERB
déduire [23]

deep ADJECTIVE
1 profond (FEM profonde) (*water, hole, cut*)
□ Is it deep? Est-ce que c'est profond ?
■ **How deep is the lake?** Quelle est la
profondeur du lac ?
■ **a hole 4 metres deep** un trou de quatre
mètres de profondeur
2 épais (FEM épaisse) (*layer*)
□ a deep layer of snow une épaisse couche de
neige □ The snow was really deep. Il y avait une
épaisse couche de neige.
■ **He's got a deep voice.** Il a la voix grave.
■ **to take a deep breath** respirer [28] à fond

deeply ADVERB
profondément (*depressed*)

deer NOUN
1 le cerf *masc* (*red deer*)
2 le daim *masc* (*fallow deer*)
3 le chevreuil *masc* (*roe deer*)

defeat - demanding

defeat NOUN

▷ see also **defeat** VERB

la défaite *fem*

to **defeat** VERB

▷ see also **defeat** NOUN

battre [9]

defect NOUN

le défaut *masc*

defence NOUN

la défense *fem*

to **defend** VERB

défendre [88]

defender NOUN

le défenseur *masc*

to **define** VERB

définir [38]

definite ADJECTIVE

1 précis (FEM précise)
□ I haven't got any definite plans. Je n'ai pas de projets précis.

2 net (FEM nette)
□ It's a definite improvement. Cela constitue une nette amélioration.

3 sûr (FEM sûre)
□ We might go to Spain, but it's not definite. Nous irons peut-être en Espagne, mais ce n'est pas sûr.
■ **He was definite about it.** Il a été catégorique.

definitely ADVERB

vraiment
□ He's definitely the best player. C'est vraiment lui le meilleur joueur.
■ **He's the best player. — Definitely!** C'est le meilleur joueur. — C'est sûr !
■ **I definitely think he'll come.** Je suis sûr qu'il va venir.

definition NOUN

la définition *fem*

defriend VERB

supprimer [28] de sa liste d'amis
□ Her brother has defriended her on Facebook. Son frère l'a supprimée de sa liste d'amis sur Facebook.

degree NOUN

1 le degré *masc*
□ a temperature of 30 degrees une température de trente degrés

2 la licence *fem*
□ a degree in English une licence d'anglais

to **delay** VERB

▷ see also **delay** NOUN

1 retarder [28]
□ We decided to delay our departure. Nous avons décidé de retarder notre départ.

2 tarder [28]
□ Don't delay! Ne tarde pas !

■ **to be delayed** être [35] retardé □ Our flight was delayed. Notre vol a été retardé.

delay NOUN

▷ see also **delay** VERB

le retard *masc*
□ There will be delays to trains on the London-Brighton line. Il y aura des retards sur la ligne Londres-Brighton.

> **BE CAREFUL!**
> Do not translate **delay** by the French word **délai**.

to **delete** VERB

effacer [12] (*on computer, tape*)

deliberate ADJECTIVE

délibéré (FEM délibérée)

deliberately ADVERB

exprès
□ She did it deliberately. Elle l'a fait exprès.

delicate ADJECTIVE

délicat (FEM délicate)

delicatessen NOUN

l'épicerie fine *fem*

delicious ADJECTIVE

délicieux (FEM délicieuse)

delight NOUN

■ **to her delight** à sa plus grande joie

delighted ADJECTIVE

ravi (FEM ravie)
□ He'll be delighted to see you. Il sera ravi de vous voir.

delightful ADJECTIVE

délicieux (FEM délicieuse) (*meal, evening*)

to **deliver** VERB

1 livrer [28]
□ I deliver newspapers. Je livre les journaux.

2 distribuer [28] (*mail*)

delivery NOUN

la livraison *fem*

to **demand** VERB

▷ see also **demand** NOUN

exiger [45]

> **BE CAREFUL!**
> Do not translate **to demand** by the French word **demander**.

demand NOUN

▷ see also **demand** VERB

la demande *fem* (*for product*)

demanding ADJECTIVE

1 astreignant (FEM astreignante)
□ It's a very demanding job. C'est un travail très astreignant.

2 exigeant (FEM exigeante)
□ a very demanding child un enfant très exigeant.

demo NOUN
la manif fem (protest)

democracy NOUN
la démocratie fem

democratic ADJECTIVE
démocratique (FEM démocratique)

to **demolish** VERB
démolir [38]

to **demonstrate** VERB
1 faire [36] une démonstration de (show)
□ She demonstrated the technique. Elle a fait une démonstration de la technique.
2 manifester [28] (protest)
□ to demonstrate against something manifester contre quelque chose

demonstration NOUN
1 la démonstration fem (of method, technique)
2 la manifestation fem (protest)

demonstrator NOUN
le manifestant masc
la manifestante fem (protester)

denim NOUN
le jean masc
□ a denim jacket une veste en jean

denims PL NOUN
le jean masc sing (jeans)

Denmark NOUN
le Danemark masc
■ **in Denmark** au Danemark
■ **to Denmark** au Danemark

dense ADJECTIVE
1 dense (FEM dense) (crowd, fog)
2 épais (FEM épaisse) (smoke)
■ **He's so dense!** Il est vraiment bouché !

dent NOUN
▷ see also **dent** VERB
la bosse fem

to **dent** VERB
▷ see also **dent** NOUN
cabosser [28]

dental ADJECTIVE
dentaire (FEM dentaire)
■ **dental floss** le fil dentaire

dentist NOUN
le/la dentiste masc/fem
□ Catherine is a dentist. Catherine est dentiste.

to **deny** VERB
nier [19]
□ She denied everything. Elle a tout nié.

deodorant NOUN
le déodorant masc

to **depart** VERB
partir [57⁵]

department NOUN
1 le rayon masc (in shop)
□ the shoe department le rayon chaussures
2 le département masc (in university, school)
□ the English department le département d'anglais

department store NOUN
le grand magasin masc

departure NOUN
le départ masc

departure lounge NOUN
le hall des départs masc

to **depend** VERB
■ **to depend on** dépendre [88] de □ The price depends on which model it is. Le prix dépend du modèle.
■ **depending on the weather** selon le temps
■ **It depends.** Ça dépend.

to **deport** VERB
expulser [28]

deposit NOUN
1 les arrhes fem pl (part payment)
□ You have to pay a deposit when you book. Il faut verser des arrhes lors de la réservation.
2 la caution fem (when hiring something)
□ You get the deposit back when you return the bike. On vous remboursera la caution quand vous ramènerez le vélo.
3 la consigne fem (on bottle)

depressed ADJECTIVE
déprimé (FEM déprimée)
□ I'm feeling depressed. Je suis déprimé.

depressing ADJECTIVE
déprimant (FEM déprimante)

depth NOUN
la profondeur fem

deputy head NOUN
le directeur adjoint masc
la directrice adjointe fem

to **descend** VERB
descendre [24⁵]

to **describe** VERB
décrire [30]

description NOUN
la description fem

desert NOUN
le désert masc

desert island NOUN
l'île déserte fem

to **deserve** VERB
mériter [28]

design NOUN
▷ see also **design** VERB
1 la conception fem
□ It's a completely new design. C'est une conception entièrement nouvelle.
2 le motif masc
□ a geometric design un motif géométrique
■ **fashion design** le stylisme

to **design** VERB
▷ see also **design** NOUN
dessiner [28] (clothes, furniture)

designer NOUN
le/la styliste masc/fem (of clothes)
■ **designer clothes** les vêtements griffés

desire NOUN
▷ see also **desire** VERB
le désir masc

to **desire** VERB
▷ see also **desire** NOUN
désirer [28]

desk NOUN
1 le bureau masc (PL les bureaux) (in office)
2 le pupitre masc (for pupil)
3 la réception fem (in hotel)
4 le comptoir masc (at airport)

desktop NOUN
l'ordinateur de bureau masc (PL les ordinateurs de bureau) (computer)

despair NOUN
le désespoir masc
■ **I was in despair.** J'étais désespéré.

desperate ADJECTIVE
désespéré (FEM désespérée)
□ a desperate situation une situation désespérée
■ **to get desperate** désespérer [34] □ I was getting desperate. Je commençais à désespérer.

desperately ADVERB
1 terriblement
□ We're desperately worried. Nous sommes terriblement inquiets.
2 désespérément
□ He was desperately trying to persuade her. Il essayait désespérément de la persuader.

to **despise** VERB
mépriser [28]

despite PREPOSITION
malgré

dessert NOUN
le dessert masc
□ for dessert comme dessert

destination NOUN
la destination fem

to **destroy** VERB
détruire [23]

destruction NOUN
la destruction fem

detached house NOUN
la maison individuelle fem

detail NOUN
le détail masc
□ in detail en détail

detailed ADJECTIVE
détaillé (FEM détaillée)

detective NOUN
l'inspecteur de police masc
■ **a private detective** un détective privé
■ **a detective story** un roman policier

detention NOUN
■ **to get a detention** être [35] consigné

detergent NOUN
1 le détergent masc
2 la lessive fem (US)

determined ADJECTIVE
déterminé (FEM déterminée)
■ **to be determined to do something** être [35] déterminé à faire quelque chose □ She's determined to succeed. Elle est déterminée à réussir.

detour NOUN
le détour masc

devaluation NOUN
la dévaluation fem

devastated ADJECTIVE
anéanti (FEM anéantie)
□ I was devastated. J'étais anéanti.

devastating ADJECTIVE
1 accablant (FEM accablante) (upsetting)
2 dévastateur (FEM dévastatrice) (flood, storm)

to **develop** VERB
1 développer [28]
□ The teacher helped them develop their writing skills. L'enseignant les a aidés à développer leur aptitude à l'écriture.
2 se développer [28]
□ Girls often develop faster. Les filles souvent se développent plus vite.
■ **to develop into** se transformer [28] en □ The argument developed into a fight. La dispute s'est transformée en bagarre.
■ **a developing country** un pays en voie de développement

development NOUN
le développement masc
□ the latest developments les derniers développements

device NOUN
l'appareil masc

devil NOUN
le diable masc
□ Poor devil! Pauvre diable !

to **devise** VERB
concevoir [67]

devoted ADJECTIVE
dévoué (FEM dévouée)
□ He's completely devoted to her. Il lui est très dévoué.

diabetes NOUN
le diabète masc

diabetic NOUN
le/la diabétique *masc/fem*
□ I'm a diabetic. Je suis diabétique.

diagonal ADJECTIVE
diagonal (FEM diagonale, MASC PL diagonaux)

diagram NOUN
le diagramme *masc*

to **dial** VERB
composer [28] (*number*)

dialling tone NOUN
la tonalité *fem*

dialogue NOUN
le dialogue *masc*

diamond NOUN
le diamant *masc*
□ a diamond ring une bague en diamant
■ **diamonds** (*in cards*) le carreau *sing* □ the ace of diamonds l'as de carreau

diaper NOUN (US)
la couche *fem*

diarrhoea NOUN
la diarrhée *fem*
□ I've got diarrhoea. J'ai la diarrhée.

diary NOUN
1 l'agenda *masc*
□ She put the date of the school concert in her diary. Elle a noté la date du concert de l'école dans son agenda.
2 le journal *masc* (PL les journaux)
□ I keep a diary. Je tiens un journal.

dice NOUN
le dé *masc*

dictation NOUN
la dictée *fem*

dictionary NOUN
le dictionnaire *masc*

did VERB ▷ *see* **do**

to **die** VERB
mourir [51]
□ He died last year. Il est mort l'année dernière.
■ **to be dying to do something** mourir [51] d'envie de faire quelque chose □ I'm dying to see you. Je meurs d'envie de te voir.

diesel NOUN
1 le gazole *masc* (*fuel*)
□ 30 litres of diesel trente litres de gazole
2 la voiture diesel *fem* (*car*)
□ My car's a diesel. J'ai une voiture diesel.

diet NOUN
▷ *see also* **diet** VERB
1 l'alimentation *fem*
□ a healthy diet une alimentation saine
2 le régime *masc* (*for slimming*)
□ I'm on a diet. Je suis au régime.

to **diet** VERB
▷ *see also* **diet** NOUN
faire [36] un régime
□ I've been dieting for two months. Je fais un régime depuis deux mois.

difference NOUN
la différence *fem*
□ There's not much difference in age between us. Il n'y a pas une grande différence d'âge entre nous.
■ **It makes no difference.** Ça revient au même.

different ADJECTIVE
différent (FEM différente)
□ We are very different. Nous sommes très différents. □ Paris is different from London. Paris est différent de Londres.

difficult ADJECTIVE
difficile (FEM difficile)
□ It's difficult to choose. C'est difficile de choisir.

difficulty NOUN
la difficulté *fem*
□ without difficulty sans difficulté
■ **to have difficulty doing something** avoir [8] du mal à faire quelque chose

to **dig** VERB
1 creuser [28] (*hole*)
2 bêcher [28] (*garden*)
■ **to dig something up** déterrer [28] quelque chose

digestion NOUN
la digestion *fem*

digger NOUN
la pelleteuse *fem* (*machine*)

digital television NOUN
la télévision numérique *fem*

dim ADJECTIVE
1 faible (FEM faible) (*light*)
2 limité (FEM limitée) (*stupid*)

dimension NOUN
la dimension *fem*

to **diminish** VERB
diminuer [28]

din NOUN
le vacarme *masc*

diner NOUN (US)
le snack *masc*

dinghy NOUN
■ **a rubber dinghy** un canot pneumatique
■ **a sailing dinghy** un dériveur

dining car NOUN
le wagon-restaurant *masc* (PL les wagons-restaurants)

dining room NOUN
la salle à manger *fem*

dinner NOUN
1 le déjeuner *masc* (*at midday*)
2 le dîner *masc* (*in the evening*)

dinner jacket - discuss

dinner jacket NOUN
le smoking *masc*

dinner lady NOUN
la dame de service *fem*

dinner party NOUN
le dîner *masc*

dinner time NOUN
1 l'heure du déjeuner *fem* (*midday*)
2 l'heure du dîner *fem* (*in the evening*)

dinosaur NOUN
le dinosaure *masc*

dip NOUN
▷ *see also* **dip** VERB
■ **to go for a dip** aller [3¹] se baigner

to **dip** VERB
▷ *see also* **dip** NOUN
tremper [28]
□ He dipped a biscuit into his tea. Il a trempé un biscuit dans son thé.

diploma NOUN
le diplôme *masc*
□ a diploma in social work un diplôme d'assistante sociale

diplomat NOUN
le/la diplomate *masc/fem*

diplomatic ADJECTIVE
diplomatique (FEM diplomatique)

direct ADJECTIVE, ADVERB
▷ *see also* **direct** VERB
direct (FEM directe)
□ the most direct route le chemin le plus direct
□ You can't fly to Nice direct from Cork. Il n'y a pas de vols directs de Cork à Nice.

to **direct** VERB
▷ *see also* **direct** ADJECTIVE, ADVERB
1 réaliser [28] (*film, programme*)
2 mettre [47] en scène (*play, show*)

direction NOUN
la direction *fem*
□ We're going in the wrong direction. Nous allons dans la mauvaise direction.
■ **to ask somebody for directions** demander [28] son chemin à quelqu'un

director NOUN
1 le directeur *masc*
la directrice *fem* (*of company*)
2 le metteur en scène *masc* (*of play*)
3 le réalisateur *masc*
la réalisatrice *fem* (*of film, programme*)

directory NOUN
1 l'annuaire *masc* (*phone book*)
2 le répertoire *masc* (*computing*)

dirt NOUN
la saleté *fem*

dirty ADJECTIVE
sale (FEM sale)
■ **to get dirty** se salir [38]

■ **to get something dirty** salir [38] quelque chose

disabled ADJECTIVE
handicapé (FEM handicapée)
■ **the disabled** les handicapés

disadvantage NOUN
le désavantage *masc*

to **disagree** VERB
■ We always disagree. Nous ne sommes jamais d'accord.
■ I disagree! Je ne suis pas d'accord !
■ He disagrees with me. Il n'est pas d'accord avec moi.

disagreement NOUN
le désaccord *masc*

to **disappear** VERB
disparaître [56]

disappearance NOUN
la disparition *fem*

disappointed ADJECTIVE
déçu (FEM déçue)

disappointing ADJECTIVE
décevant (FEM décevante)

disappointment NOUN
la déception *fem*

disaster NOUN
le désastre *masc*

disastrous ADJECTIVE
désastreux (FEM désastreuse)

disc NOUN
le disque *masc*

discipline NOUN
la discipline *fem*

disco NOUN
la soirée disco *fem*
□ There's a disco at the school tonight. Il y a une soirée disco à l'école ce soir.

to **disconnect** VERB
1 débrancher [28] (*electrical equipment*)
2 couper [28] (*telephone, water supply*)

discount NOUN
la réduction *fem*
□ a discount for students une réduction pour les étudiants

to **discourage** VERB
décourager [45]
■ **to get discouraged** se décourager [45]
□ Don't get discouraged! Ne te décourage pas !

to **discover** VERB
découvrir [55]

discrimination NOUN
la discrimination *fem*
□ racial discrimination la discrimination raciale

to **discuss** VERB
1 discuter [28] de

Numbers in brackets refer to verb tables on pages 650 to 658

□ I'll discuss it with my parents. Je vais en discuter avec mes parents.

2 discuter [28] sur (*topic*)

□ We discussed the problem of pollution. Nous avons discuté sur le problème de la pollution.

discussion NOUN
la discussion *fem*

disease NOUN
la maladie *fem*

disgraceful ADJECTIVE
scandaleux (FEM scandaleuse)

to **disguise** VERB
déguiser [28]

□ He was disguised as a police officer. Il était déguisé en policier.

disgusted ADJECTIVE
dégoûté (FEM dégoûtée)

□ I was absolutely disgusted. J'étais complètement dégoûté.

disgusting ADJECTIVE

1 dégoûtant (FEM dégoûtante) (*food, smell*)

□ It looks disgusting. Ça a l'air dégoûtant.

2 honteux (FEM honteuse) (*disgraceful*)

□ That's disgusting! C'est honteux !

dish NOUN
le plat *masc*

□ a china dish un plat en porcelaine □ a vegetarian dish un plat végétarien

■ **to do the dishes** faire [36] la vaisselle

□ He never does the dishes. Il ne fait jamais la vaisselle.

dishonest ADJECTIVE
malhonnête (FEM malhonnête)

dish soap NOUN (US)
le produit à vaisselle *masc*

dish towel NOUN (US)
le torchon *masc*

dishwasher NOUN
le lave-vaisselle *masc* (PL les lave-vaisselle)

disinfectant NOUN
le désinfectant *masc*

disk NOUN
le disque *masc*

■ **the hard disk** le disque dur

diskette NOUN
la disquette *fem*

to **dislike** VERB

▷ *see also* **dislike** NOUN

ne pas aimer [28]

□ I really dislike cabbage. Je n'aime vraiment pas le chou.

dislike NOUN

▷ *see also* **dislike** VERB

■ **my likes and dislikes** ce que j'aime et ce que je n'aime pas

dismal ADJECTIVE
lugubre (FEM lugubre)

to **dismiss** VERB
renvoyer [33] (*employee*)

disobedient ADJECTIVE
désobéissant (FEM désobéissante)

display NOUN

▷ *see also* **display** VERB

l'étalage *masc*

□ There was a lovely display of fruit in the window. Il y avait un superbe étalage de fruits en vitrine.

■ **to be on display** être [35] exposé □ Her best paintings were on display. Ses meilleurs tableaux étaient exposés.

■ **a firework display** un feu d'artifice

to **display** VERB

▷ *see also* **display** NOUN

1 montrer [28]

□ She proudly displayed her medal. Elle a montré sa médaille avec fierté.

2 exposer [28] (*in shop window*)

disposable ADJECTIVE
jetable (FEM jetable)

to **disqualify** VERB
disqualifier [19]

■ **to be disqualified** être [35] disqualifié □ He was disqualified. Il a été disqualifié.

to **disrupt** VERB
perturber [28]

□ Protesters disrupted the meeting. Des manifestants ont perturbé la réunion. □ Train services are being disrupted by the strike. Les horaires de train sont perturbés par la grève.

dissatisfied ADJECTIVE

■ **We were dissatisfied with the service.** Nous n'étions pas satisfaits du service.

to **dissolve** VERB
dissoudre [70]

distance NOUN
la distance *fem*

□ a distance of 40 kilometres une distance de quarante kilomètres

■ **It's within walking distance.** On peut y aller à pied.

■ **in the distance** au loin

distant ADJECTIVE
lointain (FEM lointaine)

□ in the distant future dans un avenir lointain

distillery NOUN
la distillerie *fem*

□ a whisky distillery une distillerie de whisky

distinction NOUN

1 la distinction *fem*

□ to make a distinction between ... faire la distinction entre ...

d

English-French

2 la mention très bien *fem*
□ I got a distinction in my piano exam. J'ai eu la mention très bien à mon examen de piano.

distinctive ADJECTIVE
distinctif (FEM distinctive)

to **distract** VERB
distraire [85]

to **distribute** VERB
distribuer [28]

district NOUN
1 le quartier *masc* (*of town*)
2 la région *fem* (*of country*)

to **disturb** VERB
déranger [45]
□ I'm sorry to disturb you. Je suis désolé de vous déranger.

ditch NOUN
▷ see also **ditch** VERB
le fossé *masc*

to **ditch** VERB
▷ see also **ditch** NOUN
plaquer [28] (*informal*)
□ She's just ditched her boyfriend. Elle vient de plaquer son copain.

dive NOUN
▷ see also **dive** VERB
le plongeon *masc*

to **dive** VERB
▷ see also **dive** NOUN
plonger [45]

diver NOUN
le plongeur *masc*
la plongeuse *fem*

diverse ADJECTIVE
divers (FEM diverse)
□ people from diverse cultures des gens de cultures diverses

diversion NOUN
la déviation *fem* (*for traffic*)

diversity NOUN
la diversité *fem*
□ cultural diversity la diversité culturelle

to **divide** VERB
1 diviser [28]
□ Divide the cake in half. Divisez le gâteau en deux. □ 12 divided by 3 is 4. Douze divisé par trois égale quatre.

2 se diviser [28]
□ We divided into two groups. Nous nous sommes divisés en deux groupes.

diving NOUN
la plongée *fem*
■ **a diving board** un plongeoir

division NOUN
la division *fem*

divorce NOUN
le divorce *masc*

divorced ADJECTIVE
divorcé (FEM divorcée)
□ My parents are divorced. Mes parents sont divorcés.

DIY NOUN
le bricolage *masc*
□ to do DIY faire du bricolage □ a DIY shop un magasin de bricolage

dizzy ADJECTIVE
■ **to feel dizzy** avoir [8] la tête qui tourne
□ I feel dizzy. J'ai la tête qui tourne.

DJ NOUN
le disc-jockey *masc*

to **do** VERB
1 faire [36]
□ What are you doing this evening? Qu'est-ce que tu fais ce soir ? □ I do a lot of cycling. Je fais beaucoup de vélo. □ I haven't done my homework. Je n'ai pas fait mes devoirs. □ She did it by herself. Elle l'a fait toute seule. □ I'll do my best. Je ferai de mon mieux.
■ **to do well** marcher [28] bien □ She's doing well at school. Ses études marchent bien.

2 aller [3ᵗ] (*be enough*)
□ It's not very good, but it'll do. Ce n'est pas très bon, mais ça ira.
■ **That'll do, thanks.** Ça ira, merci.

> In English 'do' is used to make questions. In French questions are made either with **est-ce que** or by reversing the order of verb and subject.

□ Do you like French food? Est-ce que vous aimez la cuisine française ? □ Where does he live? Où est-ce qu'il habite ? □ Do you speak English? Parlez-vous anglais ? □ What do you do in your free time? Qu'est-ce que vous faites pendant vos loisirs ? □ Where did you go for your holidays? Où es-tu allé pendant tes vacances ?

> Use **ne ... pas** in negative sentences for 'don't'.

□ I don't understand. Je ne comprends pas.
□ Why didn't you come? Pourquoi n'êtes-vous pas venus ?

> 'do' is not translated when it is used in place of another verb.

□ I hate maths. — So do I. Je déteste les maths. — Moi aussi. □ I didn't like the film. — Neither did I. Je n'ai pas aimé le film. — Moi non plus. □ Do you like horses? — No I don't. Est-ce que tu aimes les chevaux ? — Non.

> Use **n'est-ce pas** to check information.

□ You go swimming on Fridays, don't you? Tu fais de la natation le vendredi, n'est-ce pas ?
□ The bus stops at the youth hostel, doesn't it? Le bus s'arrête à l'auberge de jeunesse, n'est-ce pas ?
■ **How do you do?** Enchanté !

d

to **do up** VERB
1 lacer [12] (*shoes*)
□ Do up your shoes! Lace tes chaussures !
2 retaper [28] (*renovate*)
□ They're doing up my grandparents' house.
Ils retapent la maison de mes grands-parents.
3 boutonner [28] (*shirt, cardigan*)
■ **Do up your zip!** (*on trousers*) Ferme ta
braguette !

to **do without** VERB
se passer [58] de
□ I couldn't do without my computer. Je ne
pourrais pas me passer de mon ordinateur.

dock NOUN
le dock *masc* (*for ships*)

doctor NOUN
le médecin *masc*
□ She's a doctor. Elle est médecin. □ I'd like to
be a doctor. Je voudrais être médecin.

document NOUN
le document *masc*

documentary NOUN
le documentaire *masc*

to **dodge** VERB
échapper [28] à (*attacker*)

dodgems PL NOUN
les autos tamponneuses *fem pl*
□ to go on the dodgems aller faire un tour
d'autos tamponneuses

does VERB ▷ *see* **do**

doesn't = **does not**

dog NOUN
le chien *masc*
la chienne *fem*
□ Have you got a dog? Est-ce que tu as un chien ?

do-it-yourself NOUN
le bricolage *masc*

dole NOUN
les allocations chômage *fem pl*
■ **to be on the dole** toucher [28] le chômage
□ A lot of people are on the dole. Beaucoup de
gens touchent le chômage.
■ **to go on the dole** s'inscrire [30] au chômage

doll NOUN
la poupée *fem*

dollar NOUN
le dollar *masc*

dolphin NOUN
le dauphin *masc*

domestic ADJECTIVE
■ **a domestic flight** un vol intérieur

dominoes PL NOUN
■ **to have a game of dominoes** faire [36] une
partie de dominos

to **donate** VERB
donner [28]

done VERB ▷ *see* **do**

dongle NOUN
le dongle *masc*

donkey NOUN
l'âne *masc*

donor NOUN
1 le donateur *masc*
la donatrice *fem* (*to charity*)
2 le donneur *masc*
la donneuse *fem* (*of blood, organ for transplant*)

don't = **do not**

door NOUN
1 la porte *fem*
□ the first door on the right la première porte
à droite
2 la portière *fem* (*of car, train*)

doorbell NOUN
la sonnette *fem*
■ **to ring the doorbell** sonner [28]
■ **Suddenly the doorbell rang.** Soudain, on
a sonné.

doorman NOUN
le portier *masc*

doorstep NOUN
le pas de la porte *masc*

dormitory NOUN
le dortoir *masc*

dose NOUN
la dose *fem*

dosh NOUN
le fric *masc* (*informal: money*)

dot NOUN
le point *masc* (*on letter 'i', in email address*)
■ **on the dot** à l'heure pile □ He arrived at
9 o'clock on the dot. Il est arrivé à neuf heures
pile.

double ADJECTIVE, ADVERB
▷ *see also* **double** VERB
double (FEM double)
□ a double helping une double portion
■ **to cost double** coûter [28] le double □ First-
class tickets cost double. Les billets de première
classe coûtent le double.
■ **a double bed** un grand lit
■ **a double room** une chambre pour deux
personnes
■ **a double-decker bus** un autobus à impériale

to **double** VERB
▷ *see also* **double** ADJECTIVE, ADVERB
doubler [28]
□ The number of attacks has doubled. Le
nombre d'agressions a doublé.

double bass NOUN
la contrebasse *fem*
□ I play the double bass. Je joue de la
contrebasse.

to **double-click** VERB
double-cliquer [28]

d

□ to double-click on an icon double-cliquer sur une icône

double glazing NOUN
le double vitrage *masc*

doubles PL NOUN
le double *masc* (*in tennis*)
□ to play mixed doubles jouer en double mixte

doubt NOUN
▷ *see also* **doubt** VERB
le doute *masc*
□ I have my doubts. J'ai des doutes.

to **doubt** VERB
▷ *see also* **doubt** NOUN
douter [28] de
■ **I doubt it.** J'en doute.
■ **to doubt that** douter [28] que

> douter que has to be followed by a verb in the subjunctive.

□ I doubt he'll agree. Je doute qu'il soit d'accord.

doubtful ADJECTIVE
■ **to be doubtful about doing something** hésiter [28] à faire quelque chose □ I'm doubtful about going by myself. J'hésite à y aller tout seul.
■ **It's doubtful.** Ce n'est pas sûr.
■ **You sound doubtful.** Tu n'as pas l'air sûr.

dough NOUN
la pâte *fem*

doughnut NOUN
le beignet *masc*
□ a jam doughnut un beignet à la confiture

Dover NOUN
Douvres
□ We went from Dover to Boulogne. Nous sommes allés de Douvres à Boulogne.
■ **in Dover** à Douvres

down ADVERB, ADJECTIVE, PREPOSITION
1 en bas (*below*)
□ His office is down on the first floor. Son bureau est en bas, au premier étage. □ It's down there. C'est là-bas.
2 à terre (*to the ground*)
□ He threw down his racket. Il a jeté sa raquette à terre.
■ **They live just down the road.** Ils habitent tout à côté.
■ **to come down** descendre [24¹] □ Come down here! Descends !
■ **to go down** descendre [24¹] □ The rabbit went down the hole. Le lapin est descendu dans le terrier.
■ **to sit down** s'asseoir [6] □ Sit down! Asseyez-vous !
■ **to feel down** avoir [8] le cafard □ I'm feeling a bit down. J'ai un peu le cafard.
■ **The computer's down.** L'ordinateur est en panne.

to **download** VERB
▷ *see also* **download** NOUN
télécharger [45]
□ to download a file télécharger un fichier

download NOUN
▷ *see also* **download** VERB
le téléchargement *masc*
□ a free download un téléchargement gratuit

downpour NOUN
la pluie torrentielle *fem*
□ a sudden downpour une pluie soudaine et torrentielle

downstairs ADVERB, ADJECTIVE
1 au rez-de-chaussée
□ The bathroom's downstairs. La salle de bain est au rez-de-chaussée.
2 du rez-de-chaussée
□ the downstairs bathroom la salle de bain du rez-de-chaussée
■ **the people downstairs** les voisins du dessous

downtown ADJECTIVE (US)
dans le centre

to **doze** VERB
sommeiller [28]

to **doze off** VERB
s'assoupir [38]

dozen NOUN
la douzaine *fem*
□ two dozen deux douzaines □ a dozen eggs une douzaine d'œufs
■ **I've told you that dozens of times.** Je t'ai dit ça des centaines de fois.

drab ADJECTIVE
terne (FEM terne) (*clothes*)

draft NOUN (US)
le courant d'air *masc*

to **drag** VERB
▷ *see also* **drag** NOUN
traîner [28] (*thing, person*)
■ **'drag and drop'** « glisser déposer »

drag NOUN
▷ *see also* **drag** VERB
■ **It's a real drag!** (*informal*) C'est la barbe !
■ **in drag** travesti □ He was in drag. Il était travesti.

dragon NOUN
le dragon *masc*

drain NOUN
▷ *see also* **drain** VERB
l'égout *masc*
□ The drains are blocked. Les égouts sont bouchés.

to **drain** VERB
▷ *see also* **drain** NOUN
égoutter [28] (*vegetables, pasta*)

d

draining board NOUN
l'égouttoir *masc*

drainpipe NOUN
le tuyau d'écoulement *masc*

drama NOUN
l'art dramatique *masc*
□ Drama is my favourite subject. L'art dramatique est ma matière préférée.
■ **drama school** l'école d'art dramatique □ I'd like to go to drama school. J'aimerais entrer dans une école d'art dramatique.
■ **Greek drama** le théâtre grec

dramatic ADJECTIVE
spectaculaire (FEM spectaculaire)
□ It was really dramatic! C'était vraiment spectaculaire ! □ a dramatic improvement une amélioration spectaculaire
■ **dramatic news** une nouvelle extraordinaire

drank VERB ▷ *see* drink

drapes PL NOUN (US)
les rideaux *masc pl*

drastic ADJECTIVE
radical (FEM radicale, MASC PL radicaux) (*change*)
■ **to take drastic action** prendre [65] des mesures énergiques

draught NOUN
le courant d'air *masc*

draughts NOUN
les dames *fem pl*
□ to play draughts jouer aux dames

to draw VERB
▷ *see also* draw NOUN
1 dessiner [28]
□ He's good at drawing. Il dessine bien.
■ **to draw a picture** faire [36] un dessin
■ **to draw a picture of somebody** faire [36] le portrait de quelqu'un
■ **to draw a line** tirer [28] un trait
2 faire [36] match nul (*sport*)
□ We drew 2-2. Nous avons fait match nul deux à deux.
■ **to draw the curtains** tirer [28] les rideaux
■ **to draw lots** tirer [28] au sort

draw NOUN
▷ *see also* draw VERB
1 le match nul *masc* (*sport*)
□ The game ended in a draw. La partie s'est soldée par un match nul.
2 le tirage au sort *masc* (*in lottery*)
□ The draw takes place on Saturday. Le tirage au sort a lieu samedi.

drawback NOUN
l'inconvénient *masc*

drawer NOUN
le tiroir *masc*

drawing NOUN
le dessin *masc*

drawing pin NOUN
la punaise *fem*

drawn VERB ▷ *see* draw

dreadful ADJECTIVE
1 terrible (FEM terrible)
□ a dreadful mistake une terrible erreur
2 affreux (FEM affreuse)
□ The weather was dreadful. Il a fait un temps affreux.
■ **I feel dreadful.** Je ne me sens vraiment pas bien.
■ **You look dreadful.** (*ill*) Tu as une mine affreuse.

to dream VERB
▷ *see also* dream NOUN
rêver [28]
□ I dreamed I was playing basketball. J'ai rêvé que je jouais au basket.

dream NOUN
▷ *see also* dream VERB
le rêve *masc*
□ It was just a dream. Ce n'était qu'un rêve.
■ **a bad dream** un cauchemar

to drench VERB
■ **to get drenched** se faire [36] tremper □ We got drenched. Nous nous sommes fait tremper.

dress NOUN
▷ *see also* dress VERB
la robe *fem*

to dress VERB
▷ *see also* dress NOUN
s'habiller [28]
□ I got up, dressed, and went downstairs. Je me suis levé, je me suis habillé et je suis descendu.
■ **to dress somebody** habiller [28] quelqu'un
□ She dressed the children. Elle a habillé les enfants.
■ **to get dressed** s'habiller [28] □ I got dressed quickly. Je me suis habillé rapidement.

to dress up VERB
se déguiser [28]
□ I dressed up as a ghost. Je me suis déguisé en fantôme.

dressed ADJECTIVE
habillé (FEM habillée)
□ I'm not dressed yet. Je ne suis pas encore habillé. □ How was she dressed? Comment est-ce qu'elle était habillée ?
■ **She was dressed in a green jumper and jeans.** Elle portait un pull vert et un jean.

dresser NOUN
le vaisselier *masc* (*furniture*)

dressing gown NOUN
la robe de chambre *fem*

dressing table NOUN
la coiffeuse *fem*

drew VERB ▷ *see* draw

dried VERB ▷ *see* dry

drier NOUN
le séchoir *masc*

drift NOUN
▷ *see also* **drift** VERB
■ **a snow drift** une congère

to **drift** VERB
▷ *see also* **drift** NOUN
1 aller [3⁴] à la dérive (*boat*)
2 s'amonceler [4] (*snow*)

drill NOUN
▷ *see also* **drill** VERB
la perceuse *fem*

to **drill** VERB
▷ *see also* **drill** NOUN
percer [12]

to **drink** VERB
▷ *see also* **drink** NOUN
boire [10]
□ What would you like to drink? Qu'est-ce que vous voulez boire ? □ She drank three cups of tea. Elle a bu trois tasses de thé. □ He'd been drinking. Il avait bu.
■ **I don't drink.** Je ne bois pas d'alcool.

drink NOUN
▷ *see also* **drink** VERB
la boisson *fem*
□ a cold drink une boisson fraîche □ a hot drink une boisson chaude
■ **They've gone out for a drink.** Ils sont allés prendre un verre.
■ **to have a drink** prendre [65] un verre

drinking water NOUN
l'eau potable *fem*

drive NOUN
▷ *see also* **drive** VERB
1 le tour en voiture *masc*
■ **to go for a drive** aller [3⁴] faire un tour en voiture □ We went for a drive in the country. Nous sommes allés faire un tour à la campagne.
■ **We've got a long drive tomorrow.** Nous avons une longue route à faire demain.
2 l'allée *fem* (*of house*)
□ He parked his car in the drive. Il a garé sa voiture dans l'allée.

to **drive** VERB
▷ *see also* **drive** NOUN
1 conduire [23] (*a car*)
□ She's learning to drive. Elle apprend à conduire. □ Can you drive? Tu sais conduire ?
2 aller [3⁴] en voiture (*go by car*)
□ I'd rather drive than take the train. Je préfère conduire que de prendre le train.
3 emmener [43] en voiture
□ My mother drives me to school. Ma mère m'emmène à l'école en voiture.
■ **to drive somebody home** raccompagner [28] quelqu'un □ He offered to drive me home. Il m'a proposé de me raccompagner.

■ **to drive somebody mad** rendre [7] quelqu'un fou □ He drives her mad. Il la rend folle.

driver NOUN
1 le conducteur *masc*
la conductrice *fem*
□ She's an excellent driver. C'est une excellente conductrice.
2 le chauffeur *masc* (*of taxi, bus*)
□ He's a bus driver. Il est chauffeur d'autobus.

driver's license NOUN (US)
le permis de conduire *masc*

driving instructor NOUN
le moniteur d'auto-école *masc*
□ He's a driving instructor. Il est moniteur d'auto-école.

driving lesson NOUN
la leçon de conduite *fem*

driving licence NOUN
le permis de conduire *masc*

driving test NOUN
■ **to take one's driving test** passer [58] son permis de conduire □ He's taking his driving test tomorrow. Il passe son permis de conduire demain.
■ **She's just passed her driving test.** Elle vient d'avoir son permis.

drizzle NOUN
la bruine *fem*

drop NOUN
▷ *see also* **drop** VERB
la goutte *fem*
□ a drop of water une goutte d'eau

to **drop** VERB
▷ *see also* **drop** NOUN
1 laisser [28] tomber
□ I dropped the glass and it broke. J'ai laissé tomber le verre et il s'est cassé. □ I'm going to drop chemistry. Je vais laisser tomber la chimie.
2 déposer [28]
□ Could you drop me at the station? Pouvez-vous me déposer à la gare ?

drought NOUN
la sécheresse *fem*

drove VERB ▷ *see* **drive**

to **drown** VERB
se noyer [53]
□ A boy drowned here yesterday. Un jeune garçon s'est noyé ici hier.

drug NOUN
1 le médicament *masc* (*medicine*)
□ They need food and drugs. Ils ont besoin de nourriture et de médicaments.
2 la drogue *fem* (*illegal*)
□ hard drugs les drogues dures □ soft drugs les drogues douces
■ **to take drugs** se droguer [28]

■ **a drug addict** un drogué □ She's a drug addict. C'est une droguée.

■ **a drug dealer** un dealer

■ **a drug smuggler** un trafiquant de drogue

■ **the drugs squad** la brigade antidrogue

■ **the problem of drug abuse** le problème de la drogue

drugstore NOUN (US)
le drugstore *masc*

drum NOUN
le tambour *masc*
□ an African drum un tambour africain

■ **a drum kit** une batterie

■ **drums** la batterie *sing* □ I play drums. Je joue de la batterie.

drummer NOUN
le batteur *masc*
la batteuse *fem* (*in rock group*)

drunk ADJECTIVE
▷ *see also* **drunk** NOUN
ivre (FEM ivre)
□ He was drunk. Il était ivre.

drunk NOUN
▷ *see also* **drunk** ADJECTIVE
l'ivrogne *masc/fem*
□ The streets were full of drunks. Les rues étaient pleines d'ivrognes.

dry ADJECTIVE
▷ *see also* **dry** VERB
1 sec (FEM sèche)
□ The paint isn't dry yet. La peinture n'est pas encore sèche.
2 sans pluie (*weather*)
□ a long dry period une longue période sans pluie

to **dry** VERB
▷ *see also* **dry** ADJECTIVE
1 sécher [34]
□ The washing will dry quickly in the sun. Le linge va sécher vite au soleil. □ some dried flowers des fleurs séchées

■ **to dry one's hair** se sécher [34] les cheveux □ I haven't dried my hair yet. Je ne me suis pas encore séché les cheveux.
2 faire [36] sécher (*clothes*)
□ There's nowhere to dry clothes here. Il n'y a pas d'endroit où faire sécher les vêtements ici.

■ **to dry the dishes** essuyer [53] la vaisselle

dry-cleaner's NOUN
la teinturerie *fem*

dryer NOUN
le séchoir *masc* (*for clothes*)

■ **a tumble dryer** un séchoir à linge

■ **a hair dryer** un sèche-cheveux

DTP NOUN (= *desktop publishing*)
la PAO *fem* (= *publication assistée par ordinateur*)

dubbed ADJECTIVE
doublé (FEM doublée)

□ The film was dubbed into French. Le film était doublé en français.

dubious ADJECTIVE
réticent (FEM réticente)
□ My parents were a bit dubious about it. Mes parents étaient un peu réticents à ce sujet.

duck NOUN
le canard *masc*

due ADJECTIVE, ADVERB
■ **to be due to do something** devoir [26] faire quelque chose □ He's due to arrive tomorrow. Il doit arriver demain.

■ **The plane's due in half an hour.** L'avion doit arriver dans une demi-heure.

■ **When's the baby due?** Le bébé est prévu pour quand ?

■ **due to** à cause de □ The trip was cancelled due to bad weather. Le voyage a été annulé à cause du mauvais temps.

dug VERB ▷ *see* **dig**

dull ADJECTIVE
1 ennuyeux (FEM ennuyeuse)
□ He's nice, but a bit dull. Il est sympathique, mais un peu ennuyeux.
2 maussade (FEM maussade) (*weather, day*)
□ It was dull this morning. Le temps était maussade ce matin.

dumb ADJECTIVE
bête (FEM bête)
□ That was a really dumb thing I did! C'était vraiment bête de ma part !

dummy NOUN
la tétine *fem* (*for baby*)

dump NOUN
▷ *see also* **dump** VERB
■ **It's a real dump!** C'est un endroit minable !

■ **a rubbish dump** une décharge

to **dump** VERB
▷ *see also* **dump** NOUN
1 déposer [28] (*waste*)
□ 'no dumping' « défense de déposer des ordures »
2 plaquer [28] (*informal*)
□ He's just dumped his girlfriend. Il vient de plaquer sa copine.

dungarees PL NOUN
la salopette *fem sing*

dungeon NOUN
le cachot *masc*

duration NOUN
la durée *fem*

during PREPOSITION
pendant
□ during the day pendant la journée

dusk NOUN
le crépuscule *masc*
□ at dusk au crépuscule

dust – dyspraxic

dust NOUN
▷ *see also* **dust** VERB
la poussière *fem*

to **dust** VERB
▷ *see also* **dust** NOUN
épousseter [41]
□ I dusted the shelves. J'ai épousseté les étagères.
■ **I hate dusting!** Je déteste faire les poussières !

dustbin NOUN
la poubelle *fem*

dustman NOUN
l'éboueur *masc*
□ He's a dustman. Il est éboueur.

dusty ADJECTIVE
poussiéreux (FEM poussiéreuse)

Dutch NOUN
▷ *see also* **Dutch** ADJECTIVE
le hollandais *masc* (*language*)
■ **the Dutch** les Hollandais

Dutch ADJECTIVE
▷ *see also* **Dutch** NOUN
hollandais (FEM hollandaise)
□ She's Dutch. Elle est hollandaise.

Dutchman NOUN
le Hollandais *masc*

Dutchwoman NOUN
la Hollandaise *fem*

duty NOUN
le devoir *masc*
□ It was his duty to tell the police. C'était son devoir de prévenir la police.
■ **to be on duty 1** (*police officer*) être [35] de service **2** (*doctor, nurse*) être [35] de garde

duty-free ADJECTIVE
hors taxes
■ **the duty-free shop** la boutique hors taxes

duvet NOUN
la couette *fem*

DVD NOUN
le DVD *masc* (PL les DVD)
□ I've got that film on DVD. J'ai ce film en DVD.

DVD player NOUN
le lecteur de DVD *masc*

dying VERB ▷ *see* **die**

dynamic ADJECTIVE
dynamique (FEM dynamique)

dyslexia NOUN
la dyslexie *fem*

dyslexic ADJECTIVE
dyslexique (FEM dyslexique)

dyspraxia NOUN
le dyspraxie *fem*

dyspraxic ADJECTIVE
dyspraxique (FEM dyspraxique)

Numbers in brackets refer to verb tables on pages 650 to 658

Ee

each ADJECTIVE, PRONOUN

1 chaque (FEM chaque)
□ each day chaque jour □ Each house in our street has its own garden. Chaque maison dans notre rue a son propre jardin.

2 chacun (FEM chacune)
□ The girls each have their own bedroom. Les filles ont chacune leur chambre. □ They have 10 points each. Ils ont dix points chacun. □ The postcards cost £1 each. Les cartes postales coûtent une livre chacune. □ He gave each of us £10. Il nous a donné dix livres à chacun.

> Use a reflexive verb to translate 'each other'.

■ **They hate each other.** Ils se détestent.
■ **We wrote to each other.** Nous nous sommes écrit.
■ **They don't know each other.** Ils ne se connaissent pas.

eager ADJECTIVE
■ **to be eager to do something** être [35] impatient de faire quelque chose

ear NOUN
l'oreille fem

earache NOUN
■ **to have earache** avoir [8] mal aux oreilles

earlier ADVERB

1 tout à l'heure
□ I saw him earlier. Je l'ai vu tout à l'heure.

2 plus tôt (in the morning)
□ I ought to get up earlier. Je devrais me lever plus tôt.

early ADVERB, ADJECTIVE

1 tôt (early in the day)
□ I have to get up early. Je dois me lever tôt.
■ **to have an early night** se coucher [28] tôt

2 en avance (ahead of time)
□ I came early to get a good seat. Je suis venu en avance pour avoir une bonne place.

to **earn** VERB
gagner [28]
□ She earns £10 an hour. Elle gagne dix livres de l'heure.

earnings PL NOUN
le salaire masc sing

earphones PL NOUN
les écouteurs pl noun

earring NOUN
la boucle d'oreille fem

earth NOUN
la terre fem

earthquake NOUN
le tremblement de terre masc

easily ADVERB
facilement

east ADJECTIVE, ADVERB
▷ see also **east** NOUN

1 est (FEM+PL est)
□ the east coast la côte est
■ **an east wind** un vent d'est
■ **east of** à l'est de □ It's east of London. C'est à l'est de Londres.

2 vers l'est
□ We were travelling east. Nous allions vers l'est.

east NOUN
▷ see also **east** ADJECTIVE, ADVERB
l'est masc
□ in the east dans l'est

eastbound ADJECTIVE
■ **The car was eastbound on the M25.** Le voiture se trouvait sur la M25 en direction de l'est.
■ **Eastbound traffic is moving very slowly.** La circulation vers l'est avance très lentement.

Easter NOUN
Pâques fem
□ at Easter à Pâques □ We went to my grandparents' for Easter. Nous sommes allés chez mes grands-parents à Pâques.

Easter egg NOUN
l'œuf de Pâques masc

> **DID YOU KNOW…?**
> In France, Easter eggs are said to be brought by the Easter bells or **cloches de Pâques** which fly from Rome and drop them in people's gardens.

eastern ADJECTIVE
■ **the eastern part of the island** la partie est de l'île
■ **Eastern Europe** l'Europe de l'Est

easy ADJECTIVE
facile (FEM facile)

easy chair NOUN
le fauteuil *masc*

easy-going ADJECTIVE
facile à vivre (FEM facile à vivre)
□ She's very easy-going. Elle est très facile à vivre.

to **eat** VERB
manger [45]
■ **Would you like something to eat?** Est-ce que tu veux manger quelque chose ?

e-book NOUN
le livre numérique *masc*

EC NOUN (= *European Community*)
la CE *fem* (= *Communauté européenne*)

e-card NOUN
la carte de vœux électronique *fem*

eccentric ADJECTIVE
excentrique (FEM excentrique)

echo NOUN
l'écho *masc*

eco-friendly ADJECTIVE
respectueux de l'environnement (FEM respectueuse de l'environnement)

ecological ADJECTIVE
écologique (FEM écologique)

ecology NOUN
l'écologie *fem*

e-commerce NOUN
le commerce électronique *masc*

economic ADJECTIVE
rentable (FEM rentable) (*profitable*)

economical ADJECTIVE
1 économe (FEM économe) (*person*)
2 économique (FEM économique) (*method, car*)

economics NOUN
l'économie *fem*
□ He's studying economics. Il étudie les sciences économiques.

to **economize** VERB
faire [36] des économies
□ to economize on something faire des économies sur quelque chose

economy NOUN
l'économie *fem*

ecstasy NOUN
l'ecstasy *fem* (*drug*)
■ **to be in ecstasy** s'extasier [19]

eczema NOUN
l'eczéma *masc*

edge NOUN
le bord *masc*

edgy ADJECTIVE
tendu (FEM tendue)

Edinburgh NOUN
Édimbourg

editor NOUN
le rédacteur en chef *masc*
la rédactrice en chef *fem* (*of newspaper*)

educated ADJECTIVE
cultivé (FEM cultivée)

education NOUN
1 l'éducation *fem*
□ There should be more investment in education. On devrait investir plus dans l'éducation.
2 l'enseignement *masc* (*teaching*)
□ She works in education. Elle travaille dans l'enseignement.

educational ADJECTIVE
éducatif (FEM éducative) (*experience, toy*)
□ It was very educational. C'était très éducatif.

effect NOUN
l'effet *masc*
□ special effects les effets spéciaux

effective ADJECTIVE
efficace (FEM efficace)

effectively ADVERB
efficacement

BE CAREFUL!
Do not translate **effectively** by the French word **effectivement**.

efficient ADJECTIVE
efficace (FEM efficace)

effort NOUN
l'effort *masc*

e.g. ABBREVIATION
p. ex. (= *par exemple*)

egg NOUN
l'œuf *masc*
□ a hard-boiled egg un œuf dur □ a soft-boiled egg un œuf à la coque □ a fried egg un œuf sur le plat
■ **scrambled eggs** les œufs brouillés

egg cup NOUN
le coquetier *masc*

eggplant NOUN (US)
l'aubergine *fem*

Egypt NOUN
l'Égypte *fem*
■ **in Egypt** en Égypte

Eid NOUN
l'Aïd *masc*

Eiffel Tower NOUN
la tour Eiffel *fem*

eight NUMBER
huit
□ She's eight. Elle a huit ans.

eighteen NUMBER
dix-huit
□ She's eighteen. Elle a dix-huit ans.

Numbers in brackets refer to verb tables on pages 650 to 658

eighteenth ADJECTIVE

dix-huitième (FEM dix-huitième)

□ her eighteenth birthday son dix-huitième anniversaire □ the eighteenth floor le dix-huitième étage

■ **the eighteenth of August** le dix-huit août

eighth ADJECTIVE

huitième (FEM huitième)

□ the eighth floor le huitième étage

■ **the eighth of August** le huit août

eighty NUMBER

quatre-vingts

Eire NOUN

la République d'Irlande *fem*

■ **in Eire** en République d'Irlande

either ADVERB, CONJUNCTION, PRONOUN

non plus

□ I don't like milk, and I don't like eggs either. Je n'aime pas le lait, et je n'aime pas les œufs non plus. □ I've never been to Spain. — I haven't either. Je ne suis jamais allé en Espagne. — Moi non plus.

■ **either ... or ...** soit ... soit ... □ You can have either ice cream or yoghurt. Tu peux prendre soit une glace soit un yaourt.

■ **either of them** l'un ou l'autre □ Take either of them. Prends l'un ou l'autre.

■ **I don't like either of them.** Je n'aime ni l'un ni l'autre.

elastic NOUN

l'élastique *masc*

elastic band NOUN

l'élastique *masc*

elbow NOUN

le coude *masc*

elder ADJECTIVE

aîné (FEM aînée)

□ my elder sister ma sœur aînée

elderly ADJECTIVE

âgé (FEM âgée)

eldest ADJECTIVE

aîné (FEM aînée)

□ my eldest sister ma sœur aînée □ He's the eldest. C'est l'aîné.

to **elect** VERB

élire [44]

election NOUN

l'élection *fem*

electric ADJECTIVE

électrique (FEM électrique)

□ an electric fire un radiateur électrique □ an electric guitar une guitare électrique

■ **an electric blanket** une couverture chauffante

■ **an electric shock** une décharge

electrical ADJECTIVE

électrique (FEM électrique)

■ **an electrical engineer** un ingénieur électricien

electrician NOUN

l'électricien *masc*

□ He's an electrician. Il est électricien.

electricity NOUN

l'électricité *fem*

electronic ADJECTIVE

électronique (FEM électronique)

electronics NOUN

l'électronique *fem*

□ My hobby is electronics. Ma passion, c'est l'électronique.

elegant ADJECTIVE

élégant (FEM élégante)

elementary school NOUN (US)

l'école primaire *fem*

elephant NOUN

l'éléphant *masc*

elevator NOUN (US)

l'ascenseur *masc*

eleven NUMBER

onze

□ She's eleven. Elle a onze ans.

eleventh ADJECTIVE

onzième (FEM onzième)

□ the eleventh floor le onzième étage □ the eleventh of August le onze août

else ADVERB

d'autre

□ somebody else quelqu'un d'autre □ nobody else personne d'autre □ nothing else rien d'autre

■ **something else** autre chose

■ **anything else** autre chose □ Would you like anything else? Désirez-vous autre chose ?

■ **I don't want anything else.** Je ne veux rien d'autre.

■ **somewhere else** ailleurs

■ **anywhere else** autre part

email NOUN

▷ see also **email** VERB

l'e-mail *masc*

le mail *masc*

■ **email address** adresse e-mail *fem* □ My email address is: ... Mon adresse e-mail, c'est : ...

to **email** VERB

▷ see also **email** NOUN

■ **to email somebody** envoyer [33] un mail à quelqu'un

□ Email me your essay. Envoyez-moi par mail votre rédaction d'anglais.

embankment NOUN

le talus *masc*

embarrassed ADJECTIVE

gêné (FEM gênée)

□ I was really embarrassed. J'étais vraiment gêné.

embarrassing ADJECTIVE
gênant (FEM gênante)
□ It was so embarrassing. C'était tellement gênant.

embassy NOUN
l'ambassade fem
□ the British Embassy l'ambassade de Grande-Bretagne □ the French Embassy l'ambassade de France

to **embroider** VERB
broder [28]

embroidery NOUN
la broderie fem
□ I do embroidery. Je fais de la broderie.

emergency NOUN
l'urgence fem
□ This is an emergency! C'est une urgence !
■ **in an emergency** en cas d'urgence
■ **an emergency exit** une sortie de secours
■ **an emergency landing** un atterrissage forcé
■ **the emergency services** les services d'urgence masc pl

to **emigrate** VERB
émigrer [28]

emoji NOUN
l'emoji masc

emotion NOUN
l'émotion fem

emotional ADJECTIVE
émotif (FEM émotive) (person)

emperor NOUN
l'empereur masc

to **emphasize** VERB
■ **to emphasize something** insister [28] sur quelque chose
■ **to emphasize that ...** souligner [28] que ...

empire NOUN
l'empire masc

to **employ** VERB
employer [53]
□ The factory employs 600 people. L'usine emploie six cents personnes.

employee NOUN
l'employé masc
l'employée fem

employer NOUN
l'employeur masc

employment NOUN
l'emploi masc

empty ADJECTIVE
▷ see also **empty** VERB
vide (FEM vide)

to **empty** VERB
▷ see also **empty** ADJECTIVE
vider [28]
■ **to empty something out** vider [28] quelque chose

to **encourage** VERB
encourager [45]
■ **to encourage somebody to do something** encourager [45] quelqu'un à faire quelque chose

encouragement NOUN
l'encouragement masc

encyclopedia NOUN
l'encyclopédie fem

end NOUN
▷ see also **end** VERB
1 la fin fem
□ the end of the film la fin du film □ the end of the holidays la fin des vacances
■ **in the end** en fin de compte □ In the end I decided to stay at home. En fin de compte j'ai décidé de rester à la maison.
■ **It turned out all right in the end.** Ça s'est bien terminé.
2 le bout masc
□ at the end of the street au bout de la rue □ at the other end of the table à l'autre bout de la table
■ **for hours on end** des heures entières

to **end** VERB
▷ see also **end** NOUN
finir [38]
□ What time does the film end? À quelle heure est-ce que le film finit ?
■ **to end up doing something** finir [38] par faire quelque chose □ I ended up walking home. J'ai fini par rentrer chez moi à pied.

ending NOUN
la fin fem
□ It was an exciting film, especially the ending. C'était un film passionnant, surtout la fin.

endless ADJECTIVE
interminable (FEM interminable)
□ The journey seemed endless. Le voyage a paru interminable.

enemy NOUN
l'ennemi masc
l'ennemie fem

energetic ADJECTIVE
énergique (FEM énergique) (person)

energy NOUN
l'énergie fem

engaged ADJECTIVE
1 occupé (FEM occupée) (busy, in use)
□ I phoned, but it was engaged. J'ai téléphoné, mais c'était occupé.
2 fiancé (FEM fiancée) (to be married)
□ She's engaged to Jacob. Elle est fiancée à Jacob.
■ **to get engaged** se fiancer [12]

engaged tone NOUN
la tonalité « occupé » fem

engagement NOUN
les fiançailles *fem pl*
□ an engagement ring une bague de fiançailles

engine NOUN
le moteur *masc*

> **BE CAREFUL!**
> Do not translate **engine** by the French word **engin**.

engineer NOUN
l'ingénieur *masc*
□ He's an engineer. Il est ingénieur.

engineering NOUN
l'ingénierie *fem*

England NOUN
l'Angleterre *fem*
■ **in England** en Angleterre
■ **to England** en Angleterre
■ **I'm from England.** Je suis anglais.

English NOUN
▷ see also **English** ADJECTIVE
l'anglais *masc* (*language*)
□ Do you speak English? Est-ce que vous parlez anglais ?
■ **the English** les Anglais

English ADJECTIVE
▷ see also **English** NOUN
anglais (FEM anglaise)
□ I'm English. Je suis anglais.
■ **English people** les Anglais

Englishman NOUN
l'Anglais *masc*

Englishwoman NOUN
l'Anglaise *fem*

to **enjoy** VERB
aimer [28]
□ Did you enjoy the film? Est-ce que vous avez aimé le film ?
■ **to enjoy oneself** s'amuser [28] □ I really enjoyed myself. Je me suis vraiment bien amusé.
□ Did you enjoy yourselves at the party? Est-ce vous vous êtes bien amusés à la fête ?

enjoyable ADJECTIVE
agréable (FEM agréable)

enlargement NOUN
l'agrandissement *masc* (*of photo*)

enormous ADJECTIVE
énorme (FEM énorme)

enough PRONOUN, ADJECTIVE
assez de
□ enough time assez de temps □ I didn't have enough money. Je n'avais pas assez d'argent.
□ Have you got enough? Tu en as assez ? □ I've had enough! J'en ai assez !
■ **big enough** suffisamment grand
■ **warm enough** suffisamment chaud
■ **That's enough.** Ça suffit.

to **enquire** VERB
■ **to enquire about something** se renseigner [28] sur quelque chose □ I am going to enquire about train times. Je vais me renseigner sur les horaires de trains.

enquiry NOUN
■ **to make enquiries (about something)** se renseigner [28] (sur quelque chose)
□ 'enquiries' « renseignements »

to **enter** VERB
entrer [32ᶠ]
■ **to enter a room** entrer [32ᶠ] dans une pièce
■ **to enter a competition** s'inscrire [30] à une compétition

to **entertain** VERB
recevoir [67] (*guests*)

entertainer NOUN
l'artiste de variétés *masc/fem*

entertaining ADJECTIVE
amusant (FEM amusante)

enthusiasm NOUN
l'enthousiasme *masc*

enthusiast NOUN
■ **a maths enthusiast** un passionné de maths
■ **She's a DIY enthusiast.** C'est une passionnée de bricolage.

enthusiastic ADJECTIVE
enthousiaste (FEM enthousiaste)

entire ADJECTIVE
entier (FEM entière)
□ the entire world le monde entier

entirely ADVERB
entièrement

entrance NOUN
l'entrée *fem*
■ **an entrance exam** un concours d'entrée
■ **entrance fee** le prix d'entrée

entry NOUN
l'entrée *fem*
■ **'no entry'** **1** (*on door*) « défense d'entrer »
2 (*on road sign*) « sens interdit »
■ **an entry form** une feuille d'inscription

entry phone NOUN
l'interphone *masc*

envelope NOUN
l'enveloppe *fem*

envious ADJECTIVE
envieux (FEM envieuse)

environment NOUN
l'environnement *masc*

environmental ADJECTIVE
écologique (FEM écologique)

environmentally-friendly ADJECTIVE
écologique (FEM écologique)

envy NOUN
▷ see also **envy** VERB
l'envie *fem*

e

to **envy** VERB
▷ *see also* **envy** NOUN
envier [19]
□ I don't envy you! Je ne t'envie pas !

epileptic ADJECTIVE
épileptique (FEM épileptique)

episode NOUN
l'épisode *masc* (*of TV programme, story*)

equal ADJECTIVE
▷ *see also* **equal** VERB
égal (FEM égale, MASC PL égaux)

to **equal** VERB
▷ *see also* **equal** ADJECTIVE
égaler [28]

equality NOUN
l'égalité *fem*

to **equalize** VERB
égaliser [28] (*in sport*)

equator NOUN
l'équateur *masc*

equipment NOUN
l'équipement *masc*
□ fishing equipment l'équipement de pêche
□ skiing equipment l'équipement de ski

equipped ADJECTIVE
■ **equipped with** équipé de
■ **to be well equipped** être [35] bien équipé

equivalent NOUN
l'équivalent *masc*
■ **equivalent to** équivalent à

e-reader NOUN
liseuse *fem*

error NOUN
l'erreur *fem*

escalator NOUN
l'escalier roulant *masc*

escape NOUN
▷ *see also* **escape** VERB
l'évasion *fem* (*from prison*)

to **escape** VERB
▷ *see also* **escape** NOUN
s'échapper [28]
□ A lion has escaped. Un lion s'est échappé.
■ **to escape from prison** s'évader [28] de prison

escort NOUN
l'escorte *fem*
□ a police escort une escorte de police

especially ADVERB
surtout
□ It's very hot there, especially in the summer. Il fait très chaud là-bas, surtout en été.

essay NOUN
la dissertation *fem*
□ a history essay une dissertation d'histoire

essential ADJECTIVE
essentiel (FEM essentielle)
□ It's essential to bring warm clothes. Il est essentiel d'apporter des vêtements chauds.

estate NOUN
la cité *fem* (*housing estate*)
□ I live on an estate. J'habite dans une cité.

estate agent NOUN
l'agent immobilier *masc*

estate car NOUN
le break *masc*

to **estimate** VERB
estimer [28]
□ They estimated it would take three weeks. Ils ont estimé que cela prendrait trois semaines.

etc ABBREVIATION (= *et cetera*)
etc.

Ethiopia NOUN
l'Éthiopie *fem*
■ **in Ethiopia** en Éthiopie

ethnic ADJECTIVE
1 ethnique (FEM ethnique) (*background*)
□ an ethnic minority une minorité ethnique
2 folklorique (FEM folklorique) (*clothes, music*)

e-ticket NOUN
le billet électronique *masc*

EU NOUN (= *European Union*)
l'Union européenne *fem*

euro NOUN
l'euro *masc*
□ 50 euros 50 euros

Europe NOUN
l'Europe *fem*
■ **in Europe** en Europe
■ **to Europe** en Europe

European NOUN
▷ *see also* **European** ADJECTIVE
l'Européen *masc*
l'Européenne *fem* (*person*)

European ADJECTIVE
▷ *see also* **European** NOUN
européen (FEM européenne)

to **evacuate** VERB
évacuer [28]

eve NOUN
■ **Christmas Eve** la veille de Noël
■ **New Year's Eve** la Saint-Sylvestre

even ADVERB
▷ *see also* **even** ADJECTIVE
même
□ I like all animals, even snakes. J'aime tous les animaux, même les serpents.
■ **even if** même si □ I'd never do that, even if you asked me. Je ne ferais jamais ça, même si tu me le demandais.
■ **not even** même pas □ He never stops working, not even at the weekend. Il n'arrête

Numbers in brackets refer to verb tables on pages 650 to 658

jamais de travailler, même pas le week-end.
■ **even though** bien que

> bien que has to be followed by a verb in the subjunctive.

□ He wants to go out, even though it's raining. Il veut sortir bien qu'il pleuve.
■ **even more** encore plus □ I liked Boulogne even more than Paris. J'ai encore plus aimé Boulogne que Paris.

even ADJECTIVE
▷ see also **even** ADVERB
régulier (FEM régulière)
□ an even layer of snow une couche régulière de neige
■ **an even number** un nombre pair
■ **to get even with somebody** prendre [65] sa revanche sur quelqu'un □ He wanted to get even with her. Il voulait prendre sa revanche sur elle.

evening NOUN
le soir masc
□ in the evening le soir □ yesterday evening hier soir □ tomorrow evening demain soir
■ **all evening** toute la soirée
■ **Good evening!** Bonsoir !

evening class NOUN
le cours du soir masc (PL les cours du soir)

event NOUN
l'événement masc
■ **a sporting event** une épreuve sportive

eventful ADJECTIVE
mouvementé (FEM mouvementée)

eventual ADJECTIVE
final (FEM finale)

> BE CAREFUL!
> Do not translate **eventual** by the French word **éventuel**.

eventually ADVERB
finalement

> BE CAREFUL!
> Do not translate **eventually** by the French word **éventuellement**.

ever ADVERB
■ **Have you ever been to Germany?** Est-ce que tu es déjà allé en Allemagne ?
■ **Have you ever seen her?** Vous l'avez déjà vue ?
■ **I haven't ever done that.** Je ne l'ai jamais fait.
■ **the best I've ever seen** le meilleur que j'aie jamais vu
■ **for the first time ever** pour la première fois
■ **ever since** depuis que □ ever since I met him depuis que je l'ai rencontré
■ **ever since then** depuis ce moment-là

every ADJECTIVE
chaque (FEM chaque)
□ every pupil chaque élève
■ **every time** chaque fois □ Every time I see him he's depressed. Chaque fois que je le vois il est déprimé.
■ **every day** tous les jours
■ **every week** toutes les semaines
■ **every now and then** de temps en temps

everybody PRONOUN
tout le monde
□ Everybody had a good time. Tout le monde s'est bien amusé. □ Everybody makes mistakes. Tout le monde peut se tromper.

everyone PRONOUN
tout le monde
□ Everyone opened their presents. Tout le monde a ouvert ses cadeaux. □ Everyone should have a hobby. Tout le monde devrait avoir un passe-temps.

everything PRONOUN
tout
□ You've thought of everything! Tu as pensé à tout !
■ **Have you remembered everything?** Est-ce que tu n'as rien oublié ?
■ **Money isn't everything.** L'argent ne fait pas le bonheur.

everywhere ADVERB
partout
□ I looked everywhere, but I couldn't find it. J'ai regardé partout, mais je n'ai pas pu le trouver.
□ There were police officers everywhere. Il y avait des policiers partout.

evil ADJECTIVE
mauvais (FEM mauvaise)

ex- PREFIX
ex-
□ his ex-wife son ex-femme

exact ADJECTIVE
exact (FEM exacte)

exactly ADVERB
exactement
□ exactly the same exactement le même □ Not exactly. Pas exactement.
■ **It's exactly 10 o'clock.** Il est dix heures précises.

to **exaggerate** VERB
exagérer [34]

exaggeration NOUN
l'exagération fem

exam NOUN
l'examen masc
□ a French exam un examen de français
□ the exam results les résultats des examens masc pl

examination NOUN
l'examen *masc*

to **examine** VERB
examiner [28]
□ He examined her passport. Il a examiné son passeport. □ The doctor examined him. Le docteur l'a examiné.

examiner NOUN
l'examinateur *masc*
l'examinatrice *fem*

example NOUN
l'exemple *masc*
■ **for example** par exemple

excellent ADJECTIVE
excellent (FEM excellente)
□ Her results were excellent. Elle a eu d'excellents résultats.
■ **It was excellent fun.** C'était vraiment super.

except PREPOSITION
sauf
□ everyone except me tout le monde sauf moi
■ **except for** sauf
■ **except that** sauf que □ The holiday was great, except that it rained. Les vacances étaient super, sauf qu'il a plu.

exception NOUN
l'exception *fem*
■ **to make an exception** faire [36] une exception

exceptional ADJECTIVE
exceptionnel (FEM exceptionnelle)

excess baggage NOUN
l'excédent de bagages *masc*

to **exchange** VERB
échanger [45]
□ I exchanged the book for a game. J'ai échangé le livre contre un jeu.

exchange rate NOUN
le taux de change *masc*

excited ADJECTIVE
excité (FEM excitée)

exciting ADJECTIVE
passionnant (FEM passionnante)

exclamation mark NOUN
le point d'exclamation *masc*

excuse NOUN
▷ *see also* **excuse** VERB
l'excuse *fem*

to **excuse** VERB
▷ *see also* **excuse** NOUN
■ **Excuse me!** Pardon !

to **execute** VERB
exécuter [28]

execution NOUN
l'exécution *fem*

executive NOUN
le cadre *masc* (*in business*)
□ He's an executive. Il est cadre.

exercise NOUN
l'exercice *masc*
■ **an exercise bike** un vélo d'appartement
■ **an exercise book** un cahier

exhausted ADJECTIVE
épuisé (FEM épuisée)

exhaust fumes PL NOUN
les gaz d'échappement *masc pl*

exhaust pipe NOUN
le tuyau d'échappement *masc*

exhibition NOUN
l'exposition *fem*

ex-husband NOUN
l'ex-mari *masc*

to **exist** VERB
exister [28]

exit NOUN
la sortie *fem*

exotic ADJECTIVE
exotique (FEM exotique)

to **expect** VERB
1 attendre [7]
□ I'm expecting him for dinner. Je l'attends pour dîner. □ She's expecting a baby. Elle attend un enfant.
2 s'attendre [7] à
□ I was expecting the worst. Je m'attendais au pire.
3 supposer [28]
□ I expect it's a mistake. Je suppose qu'il s'agit d'une erreur.

expedition NOUN
l'expédition *fem*

to **expel** VERB
■ **to get expelled** (*from school*) se faire [36] renvoyer

expenses PL NOUN
les frais *masc pl*

expensive ADJECTIVE
cher (FEM chère)

experience NOUN
l'expérience *fem*

experienced ADJECTIVE
expérimenté (FEM expérimentée)

experiment NOUN
l'expérience *fem*

expert NOUN
le/la spécialiste *masc/fem*
□ He's a computer expert. C'est un spécialiste en informatique.
■ **He's an expert cook.** Il cuisine très bien.

to **expire** VERB
expirer [28]

to explain VERB
expliquer [28]

explanation NOUN
l'explication *fem*

to explode VERB
exploser [28]

to exploit VERB
exploiter [28]

exploitation NOUN
l'exploitation *fem*

to explore VERB
explorer [28] (*place*)

explorer NOUN
l'explorateur *masc*
l'exploratrice *fem*

explosion NOUN
l'explosion *fem*

explosive ADJECTIVE
▷ *see also* **explosive** NOUN
explosif (FEM explosive)

explosive NOUN
▷ *see also* **explosive** ADJECTIVE
l'explosif *masc*

to express VERB
exprimer [28]
■ **to express oneself** s'exprimer [28] □ It's
hard to express oneself in French. C'est dur de
s'exprimer en français.

expression NOUN
l'expression *fem*
□ It's an English expression. C'est une
expression anglaise.

expressway NOUN (US)
l'autoroute urbaine *fem*

extension NOUN
1 l'annexe *fem* (*of building*)
2 le poste *masc* (*telephone*)
■ **Extension 3137, please.** Poste trente et un
trente-sept, s'il vous plaît.

In France, phone numbers are broken into
groups of two digits where possible.

extensive ADJECTIVE
1 vaste (FEM vaste) (*knowledge, range*)
□ The castle is set in extensive grounds. Le
château est situé au cœur d'un vaste domaine.
2 considérable (FEM considérable) (*damage,
alterations*)
□ The earthquake caused extensive damage. Le
tremblement de terre a causé des dommages
considérables.

extensively ADVERB
■ **He has travelled extensively in Europe.**

Il a beaucoup voyagé en Europe.
■ **The building was extensively renovated
last year.** Le bâtiment a eu d'importantes
rénovations l'année dernière.

extent NOUN
■ **to some extent** dans une certaine mesure

exterior ADJECTIVE
extérieur (FEM extérieure)

extinct ADJECTIVE
■ **to become extinct** disparaître [56]
■ **to be extinct** avoir [8] disparu □ The species
is almost extinct. Cette espèce a presque
disparu.

extinguisher NOUN
l'extincteur *masc* (*fire extinguisher*)

extortionate ADJECTIVE
exorbitant (FEM exorbitante)

extra ADJECTIVE, ADVERB
supplémentaire (FEM supplémentaire)
□ an extra blanket une couverture
supplémentaire
■ **to pay extra** payer [59] un supplément
■ **Breakfast is extra.** Il y a un supplément pour
le petit déjeuner.
■ **It costs extra.** Il y a un supplément.

extraordinary ADJECTIVE
extraordinaire (FEM extraordinaire)

extravagant ADJECTIVE
dépensier (FEM dépensière) (*person*)

extreme ADJECTIVE
extrême (FEM extrême)

extremely ADVERB
extrêmement

extremist NOUN
l'extrémiste *masc/fem*

eye NOUN
l'œil *masc* (PL les yeux)
□ I've got green eyes. J'ai les yeux verts.
■ **to keep an eye on something** surveiller [28]
quelque chose

eyebrow NOUN
le sourcil *masc*

eyelash NOUN
le cil *masc*

eyelid NOUN
la paupière *fem*

eyeliner NOUN
l'eye-liner *masc*

eye shadow NOUN
l'ombre à paupières *fem*

eyesight NOUN
la vue *fem*

Ff

fabric NOUN
le tissu *masc*

fabulous ADJECTIVE
fabuleux (FEM fabuleuse)
□ The show was fabulous. Le spectacle était fabuleux.

face NOUN
▷ *see also* **face** VERB
1 le visage *masc* (*of person*)
2 le cadran *masc* (*of clock*)
3 la paroi *fem* (*of cliff*)
■ **on the face of it** à première vue
■ **in the face of these difficulties** face à ces difficultés
■ **face to face** face à face

to **face** VERB
▷ *see also* **face** NOUN
faire [36] face à (*place, problem*)
■ **to face up to something** faire [36] face à quelque chose □ You must face up to your responsibilities. Vous devez faire face à vos responsabilités.

Facebook® NOUN
Facebook® *masc*

to **facebook** VERB
facebooker [28]

face cloth NOUN
le gant de toilette *masc*

DID YOU KNOW...?
The French traditionally wash with a towelling glove rather than a flannel.

face mask NOUN
le masque *masc* (*protective*)

facilities PL NOUN
l'équipement *masc sing*
□ This school has excellent facilities. Cette école dispose d'un excellent équipement.
■ **toilet facilities** les toilettes *fem pl*
■ **cooking facilities** la cuisine équipée *sing*

fact NOUN
le fait *masc*
■ **in fact** en fait

factory NOUN
l'usine *fem*

to **fade** VERB
1 passer [58] (*colour*)

□ The colour has faded in the sun. La couleur a passé au soleil.
■ **My jeans have faded.** Mon jean est délavé.
2 baisser [28]
□ The light was fading fast. La lumière baissait rapidement.
3 diminuer [28]
□ The noise gradually faded. Le bruit a diminué peu à peu.

fag NOUN
la clope *fem* (*cigarette*)

to **fail** VERB
▷ *see also* **fail** NOUN
1 rater [28]
□ I failed the history exam. J'ai raté l'examen d'histoire.
2 échouer [28]
□ In our class, no one failed. Dans notre classe, personne n'a échoué.
3 lâcher [28]
□ My brakes failed. Mes freins ont lâché.
■ **to fail to do something** ne pas faire [36] quelque chose □ She failed to return her library books. Elle n'a pas rendu ses livres à la bibliothèque.

fail NOUN
▷ *see also* **fail** VERB
■ **without fail** sans faute

failure NOUN
1 l'échec *masc*
□ feelings of failure un sentiment d'échec *sing*
2 le raté *masc*
la ratée *fem*
□ He's a failure. C'est un raté.
3 la défaillance *fem*
□ a mechanical failure une défaillance mécanique

faint ADJECTIVE
▷ *see also* **faint** VERB
faible (FEM faible)
□ a very faint voice une voix très faible
■ **to feel faint** se trouver [28] mal

to **faint** VERB
▷ *see also* **faint** ADJECTIVE
s'évanouir [38]
□ All of a sudden she fainted. Tout à coup elle s'est évanouie.

fair ADJECTIVE
▷ *see also* **fair** NOUN
1 juste (FEM juste)
□ That's not fair. Ce n'est pas juste.
2 blond (FEM blonde) (*hair*)
□ He's got fair hair. Il a les cheveux blonds.
3 clair (FEM claire) (*skin*)
□ people with fair skin les gens qui ont la peau claire
4 beau (FEM belle) (*weather*)
□ The weather was fair. Il faisait beau.
5 assez bon (FEM assez bonne) (*good enough*)
□ I have a fair chance of winning. J'ai d'assez bonnes chances de gagner.
6 considérable (FEM considérable) (*sizeable*)
□ That's a fair distance. Ça représente une distance considérable.

fair NOUN
▷ *see also* **fair** ADJECTIVE
la foire *fem*
□ They went to the fair. Ils sont allés à la foire.
■ **a trade fair** une foire commerciale

fairground NOUN
le champ de foire *masc*

fair-haired ADJECTIVE
■ **My mother is fair-haired.** Ma mère a les cheveux blonds.

fairly ADVERB
1 équitablement
□ The cake was divided fairly. Le gâteau a été partagé équitablement.
2 assez (*quite*)
□ That's fairly good. C'est assez bien.

fairness NOUN
la justice *fem*

fairy NOUN
la fée *fem*

fairy tale NOUN
le conte de fées *masc*

faith NOUN
1 la foi *fem*
□ the Catholic faith la foi catholique
2 la confiance *fem*
□ People have lost faith in the government. Les gens ont perdu confiance dans le gouvernement.

faithful ADJECTIVE
fidèle (FEM fidèle)

faithfully ADVERB
■ **Yours faithfully …** (*in letter*) Veuillez agréer mes salutations distinguées …

fake NOUN
▷ *see also* **fake** ADJECTIVE
le faux *masc*
□ The painting was a fake. Le tableau était un faux.

fake ADJECTIVE
▷ *see also* **fake** NOUN
faux (FEM fausse)
□ She wore fake fur. Elle portait une fausse fourrure.

fall NOUN
▷ *see also* **fall** VERB
1 la chute *fem*
□ a fall of snow une chute de neige □ She had a nasty fall. Elle a fait une mauvaise chute.
■ **Niagara Falls** les chutes du Niagara
2 l'automne *masc* (US: *autumn*)

to **fall** VERB
▷ *see also* **fall** NOUN
1 tomber [84f]
□ He tripped and fell. Il a trébuché et il est tombé.
2 baisser [28]
□ Prices are falling. Les prix baissent.

to **fall down** VERB
1 tomber [84f] (*person*)
□ She's fallen down. Elle est tombée.
2 s'écrouler [28] (*building*)
□ The house is slowly falling down. La maison est en train de s'écrouler.

to **fall for** VERB
1 se laisser [28] prendre à
□ They fell for it. Ils s'y sont laissé prendre.
2 tomber [84f] amoureux de
□ She's falling for him. Elle est en train de tomber amoureuse de lui.

to **fall off** VERB
tomber [84f] de
□ The book fell off the shelf. Le livre est tombé de l'étagère.

to **fall out** VERB
■ **to fall out with somebody** se fâcher [28] avec quelqu'un □ Sarah's fallen out with her boyfriend. Sarah s'est fâchée avec son copain.

to **fall through** VERB
tomber [84f] à l'eau
□ Our plans have fallen through. Nos projets sont tombés à l'eau.

fallen VERB ▷ *see* **fall**

false ADJECTIVE
faux (FEM fausse)
■ **a false alarm** une fausse alerte
■ **false teeth** les fausses dents

fame NOUN
la renommée *fem*

familiar ADJECTIVE
familier (FEM familière)
□ a familiar face un visage familier
■ **to be familiar with something** bien connaître [14] quelque chose □ I'm familiar with his work. Je connais bien ses œuvres.

f

family - fatal

family NOUN
la famille *fem*
- **the Cooke family** la famille Cooke

famine NOUN
la famine *fem*

famous ADJECTIVE
célèbre (FEM célèbre)

fan NOUN
1 l'éventail *masc* (*hand-held*)
2 le ventilateur *masc* (*electric*)
3 le/la fan *masc/fem* (*of person, band*)
  □ I'm a fan of Ed Sheeran. Je suis une fan d'Ed Sheeran.
4 le/la supporter *masc/fem* (*of sport*)
  □ football fans les supporters de football

fanatic NOUN
le/la fanatique *masc/fem*

to **fancy** VERB
- **to fancy something** avoir [8] envie de quelque chose □ I fancy an ice cream. J'ai envie d'une glace.
- **to fancy doing something** avoir [8] envie de faire quelque chose
- **He fancies her.** Elle lui plaît.

fancy dress NOUN
le déguisement *masc*
  □ He was wearing fancy dress. Il portait un déguisement.
- **a fancy-dress ball** un bal costumé

fantastic ADJECTIVE
fantastique (FEM fantastique)

far ADJECTIVE, ADVERB
loin
  □ Is it far? Est-ce que c'est loin ?
- **far from** loin de □ It's not far from Manchester. Ce n'est pas loin de Manchester. □ It's far from easy. C'est loin d'être facile.
- **How far is it?** C'est à quelle distance ?
- **How far is it to Geneva?** Combien y a-t-il jusqu'à Genève ?
- **How far have you got?** (*with a task*) Où en êtes-vous ?
- **at the far end** à l'autre bout □ at the far end of the room à l'autre bout de la pièce
- **far better** beaucoup mieux
- **as far as I know** pour autant que je sache

fare NOUN
1 le prix du billet *masc* (*on trains, buses*)
2 le prix de la course *masc* (*in taxi*)
- **half fare** le demi-tarif
- **full fare** le plein tarif

Far East NOUN
l'Extrême-Orient *masc*
- **in the Far East** en Extrême-Orient

farm NOUN
la ferme *fem*

farmer NOUN
l'agriculteur *masc*

l'agricultrice *fem*
  □ He's a farmer. Il est agriculteur.
- **a farmers' market** un marché fermier

farmhouse NOUN
la ferme *fem*

farming NOUN
l'agriculture *fem*
- **dairy farming** l'industrie laitière

fascinating ADJECTIVE
fascinant (FEM fascinante)

fashion NOUN
la mode *fem*
  □ a fashion show un défilé de mode
- **in fashion** à la mode

fashionable ADJECTIVE
à la mode
  □ Aisha wears very fashionable clothes. Aisha porte des vêtements très à la mode. □ a fashionable restaurant un restaurant à la mode

fast ADJECTIVE, ADVERB
1 vite
  □ He can run fast. Il sait courir vite.
2 rapide (FEM rapide)
  □ a fast car une voiture rapide
- **That clock's fast.** Cette pendule avance.
- **He's fast asleep.** Il est profondément endormi.

fast food NOUN
le fast-food *masc*

fat ADJECTIVE
▷ see also **fat** NOUN
gros (FEM grosse)

> **WORD POWER**
> You can use a number of other words instead of **fat**:
> **chubby** potelé
> □ a chubby baby un bébé potelé
> **overweight** trop gros
> □ an overweight child un enfant trop gros
> **plump** dodu
> □ a plump woman une femme dodue

fat NOUN
▷ see also **fat** ADJECTIVE
1 le gras *masc* (*on meat, in food*)
  □ It's very high in fat. C'est très gras.
2 les matières grasses *fem pl* (*for cooking*)
  □ Don't use too much fat when you cook. En cuisinant, n'utilisez pas trop de matières grasses.

fatal ADJECTIVE
1 mortel (FEM mortelle) (*causing death*)
  □ a fatal accident un accident mortel
2 fatal (FEM fatale) (*disastrous*)
  □ He made a fatal mistake. Il a fait une erreur fatale.

father NOUN
le père *masc*
□ my father mon père

father-in-law NOUN
le beau-père *masc* (PL les beaux-pères)

faucet NOUN (US)
le robinet *masc*

fault NOUN
1 la faute *fem* (*mistake*)
□ It's my fault. C'est de ma faute.
2 le défaut *masc* (*defect*)
□ There's a fault in this material. Ce tissu a un défaut.
■ **a mechanical fault** une défaillance mécanique

faulty ADJECTIVE
défectueux (FEM défectueuse)
□ This machine is faulty. Cette machine est défectueuse.

favour (US **favor**) NOUN
le service *masc*
■ **to do somebody a favour** rendre [7] service à quelqu'un □ Could you do me a favour? Tu peux me rendre service ?
■ **to be in favour of something** être [35] pour quelque chose □ I'm in favour of recycling. Je suis pour le recyclage.

favourite (US **favorite**) ADJECTIVE
▷ *see also* **favourite** NOUN
favori (FEM favorite)
□ Blue's my favourite colour. Le bleu est ma couleur favorite.

favourite (US **favorite**) NOUN
▷ *see also* **favourite** ADJECTIVE
le favori *masc*
la favorite *fem*
□ Liverpool are favourites to win the Cup. L'équipe de Liverpool est favorite pour la coupe.

fear NOUN
▷ *see also* **fear** VERB
la peur *fem*

to **fear** VERB
▷ *see also* **fear** NOUN
craindre [17]
□ You have nothing to fear. Vous n'avez rien à craindre.

feather NOUN
la plume *fem*

feature NOUN
la caractéristique *fem* (*of person, object*)
□ an important feature une caractéristique essentielle

February NOUN
février *masc*
■ **in February** en février

fed VERB ▷ *see* **feed**

fed up ADJECTIVE
■ **to be fed up with something** en avoir [8] marre de quelque chose □ I'm fed up with waiting for him. J'en ai marre de l'attendre.

to **feed** VERB
donner [28] à manger à
□ Have you fed the cat? Est-ce que tu as donné à manger au chat ?
■ **He worked hard to feed his family.** Il travaillait dur pour nourrir sa famille.

to **feel** VERB
1 se sentir [77]
□ I don't feel well. Je ne me sens pas bien.
□ I feel a bit lonely. Je me sens un peu seul.
2 sentir [77]
□ I didn't feel much pain. Je n'ai presque rien senti.
3 toucher [28]
□ The doctor felt his forehead. Le docteur lui a touché le front.
■ **I was feeling hungry.** J'avais faim.
■ **I was feeling cold, so I went inside.** J'avais froid, alors je suis rentré.
■ **I feel like ...** (*want*) J'ai envie de ... □ Do you feel like an ice cream? Tu as envie d'une glace ?

feeling NOUN
1 la sensation *fem* (*physical*)
□ a burning feeling une sensation de brûlure
2 le sentiment *masc* (*emotional*)
□ a feeling of satisfaction un sentiment de satisfaction

feet PL NOUN ▷ *see* **foot**

fell VERB ▷ *see* **fall**

felt VERB ▷ *see* **feel**

felt-tip pen NOUN
le stylo-feutre *masc*

female ADJECTIVE
▷ *see also* **female** NOUN
1 femelle (FEM femelle)
□ a female animal un animal femelle
2 féminin (FEM féminine)
□ the female sex le sexe féminin

female NOUN
▷ *see also* **female** ADJECTIVE
la femelle *fem* (*animal*)

feminine ADJECTIVE
féminin (FEM féminine)

feminist NOUN
le/la féministe *masc/fem*

fence NOUN
la barrière *fem*

fern NOUN
la fougère *fem*

ferret NOUN
le furet *masc*

ferry NOUN
le ferry *masc*

f

■ **the ferry crossing** la traversée en ferry
■ **the ferry terminal** le terminal pour ferries

fertile ADJECTIVE
fertile (FEM fertile)

fertilizer NOUN
l'engrais *masc*

festival NOUN
le festival *masc*
□ a rock festival un festival de rock

to **fetch** VERB
1 aller [3¹] chercher
□ Fetch the bucket. Va chercher le seau.
2 se vendre [88] (*sell for*)
□ His painting fetched £5000. Son tableau s'est vendu cinq mille livres.

fever NOUN
la fièvre *fem* (*temperature*)

few ADJECTIVE, PRONOUN
peu de (*not many*)
□ few books peu de livres
■ **a few 1** quelques □ a few hours quelques heures **2** quelques-uns □ How many apples do you want? — A few. Tu veux combien de pommes ? — Quelques-unes.
■ **quite a few people** pas mal de monde

fewer ADJECTIVE
moins de
□ There are fewer people than there were yesterday. Il y a moins de monde qu'hier.
□ There are fewer pupils in this class. Il y a moins d'élèves dans cette classe.

fiancé NOUN
le fiancé *masc*
□ He's my fiancé. C'est mon fiancé.

fiancée NOUN
la fiancée *fem*
□ She's my fiancée. C'est ma fiancée.

fiction NOUN
les romans *masc pl* (*novels*)

field NOUN
1 le champ *masc* (*in countryside*)
□ a field of wheat un champ de blé
2 le terrain *masc* (*for sport*)
□ a football field un terrain de football
3 le domaine *masc* (*subject*)
□ He's an expert in his field. C'est un expert dans son domaine.

fierce ADJECTIVE
1 féroce (FEM féroce)
□ The dog looked very fierce. Le chien avait l'air très féroce.
2 violent (FEM violente)
□ The wind was very fierce. Le vent était très violent. □ a fierce attack une attaque violente

fifteen NUMBER
quinze
□ I'm fifteen. J'ai quinze ans.

fifteenth ADJECTIVE
quinzième (FEM quinzième)
□ the fifteenth floor le quinzième étage
■ **the fifteenth of August** le quinze août

fifth ADJECTIVE
cinquième (FEM cinquième)
□ the fifth floor le cinquième étage
■ **the fifth of August** le cinq août

fifty NUMBER
cinquante
□ He's fifty. Il a cinquante ans.

fifty-fifty ADJECTIVE, ADVERB
moitié-moitié
□ They split the prize money fifty-fifty. Ils ont partagé l'argent du prix moitié-moitié.
■ **a fifty-fifty chance** une chance sur deux

fight NOUN
▷ see also **fight** VERB
1 la bagarre *fem*
□ There was a fight in the playground. Il y a eu une bagarre dans la cour de récréation.
2 la lutte *fem*
□ the fight against cancer la lutte contre le cancer

to **fight** VERB
▷ see also **fight** NOUN
1 se battre [9]
□ They were fighting. Ils se battaient. □ Women are fighting for equal rights. Les femmes se battent pour obtenir l'égalité des droits.
2 lutter [28] contre
□ This organization fights against racism. Cette organisation lutte contre le racisme.

fighting NOUN
les bagarres *fem pl*
□ Fighting broke out on the football pitch. Des bagarres ont éclaté sur le terrain de foot.

figure NOUN
1 le chiffre *masc* (*number*)
□ Can you give me the exact figures? Pouvez-vous me donner les chiffres exacts ?
2 la silhouette *fem* (*outline of person*)
□ Yasmin saw the figure of a man on the bridge. Yasmin a vu la silhouette d'un homme sur le pont.
■ **She's got a good figure.** Elle est bien faite.
■ **I have to watch my figure.** Je dois faire attention à ma ligne.
3 le personnage *masc* (*personality*)
□ She's an important political figure. C'est un personnage politique important.

to **figure out** VERB
1 calculer [28]
□ I'll try to figure out how much it'll cost. Je vais essayer de calculer combien ça va coûter.
2 voir [92]
□ I couldn't figure out what it meant. Je n'arrivais pas à voir ce que ça voulait dire.

3 cerner [28]
□ I can't figure him out at all. Je n'arrive pas du tout à le cerner.

file NOUN
▷ see also **file** VERB
1 le dossier *masc* (*document*)
□ Have we got a file on the suspect? Est-ce que nous avons un dossier sur le suspect ?
2 la chemise *fem* (*folder*)
□ She keeps all her notes in a cardboard file. Elle garde toutes ses notes dans une chemise en carton.
3 le classeur *masc* (*ring binder*)
4 le fichier *masc* (*on computer*)
5 la lime *fem* (*for nails, metal*)

to file VERB
▷ see also **file** NOUN
1 classer [28] (*papers*)
2 limer [28] (*nails, metal*)
□ to file one's nails se limer les ongles

to fill VERB
remplir [38]
□ She filled the glass with water. Elle a rempli le verre d'eau.

to fill in VERB
1 remplir [38]
□ Can you fill this form in please? Est-ce que vous pouvez remplir ce formulaire s'il vous plaît ?
2 boucher [28]
□ He filled the hole in with soil. Il a bouché le trou avec de la terre.

to fill up VERB
remplir [38]
□ He filled the cup up to the brim. Il a rempli la tasse à ras bords.

film NOUN
1 le film *masc* (*movie*)
2 la pellicule *fem* (*for camera*)

film star NOUN
la vedette de cinéma *fem*
□ He's a film star. C'est une vedette de cinéma.

filthy ADJECTIVE
dégoûtant (FEM dégoûtante)

final ADJECTIVE
▷ see also **final** NOUN
1 dernier (FEM dernière) (*last*)
□ our final farewells nos derniers adieux
2 définitif (FEM définitive) (*definite*)
□ a final decision une décision définitive
■ **I'm not going and that's final.** Je n'y vais pas, un point c'est tout.

final NOUN
▷ see also **final** ADJECTIVE
la finale *fem*
□ Andy Murray is in the final. Andy Murray va disputer la finale.

finally ADVERB
1 enfin (*lastly*)
□ Finally, I would like to say ... Enfin, je voudrais dire ...
2 finalement (*eventually*)
□ She finally chose the red shoes. Elle a finalement choisi les chaussures rouges.

to find VERB
1 trouver [28]
□ I can't find the exit. Je ne trouve pas la sortie.
2 retrouver [28] (*something lost*)
□ Did you find your pen? Est-ce que tu as retrouvé ton crayon ?

to find out VERB
découvrir [55]
□ I'm determined to find out the truth. Je suis décidé à découvrir la vérité.
■ **to find out about 1** (*make enquiries*) se renseigner [28] sur □ Try to find out about the exam. Essaye de te renseigner sur l'examen.
2 (*by chance*) apprendre [65] □ I found out about what he said. J'ai appris ce qu'il avait dit.

fine ADJECTIVE, ADVERB
▷ see also **fine** NOUN
1 excellent (FEM excellente) (*very good*)
□ He's a fine musician. C'est un excellent musicien.
■ **to be fine** aller [3] bien □ How are you? — I'm fine. Comment ça va ? — Ça va bien.
■ **I feel fine.** Je me sens bien.
■ **The weather is fine today.** Il fait beau aujourd'hui.
2 fin (FEM fine) (*not coarse*)
□ She's got very fine hair. Elle a les cheveux très fins.

fine NOUN
▷ see also **fine** ADJECTIVE, ADVERB
1 l'amende *fem*
□ She got a £50 fine. Elle a eu une amende de cinquante livres.
2 la contravention *fem* (*for traffic offence*)
□ My dad got a fine for speeding. Mon père a eu une contravention pour excès de vitesse.

finger NOUN
le doigt *masc*
■ **my little finger** mon petit doigt

fingernail NOUN
l'ongle *masc*

finish NOUN
▷ see also **finish** VERB
l'arrivée *fem* (*of race*)
□ We saw the finish of the London Marathon. Nous avons vu l'arrivée du marathon de Londres.

to finish VERB
▷ see also **finish** NOUN
1 finir [38]
□ I've finished! J'ai fini !

■ **to finish doing something** finir [38] de faire
quelque chose
2 terminer [28]
□ I've finished the book. J'ai terminé ce livre.
□ The film has finished. Le film est terminé.

Finland NOUN
la Finlande *fem*
■ **in Finland** en Finlande
■ **to Finland** en Finlande

Finn NOUN
le Finlandais *masc*
la Finlandaise *fem*

Finnish NOUN
▷ *see also* **Finnish** ADJECTIVE
le finnois *masc* (*language*)

Finnish ADJECTIVE
▷ *see also* **Finnish** NOUN
finlandais (*FEM* finlandaise)

fire NOUN
▷ *see also* **fire** VERB
1 le feu *masc* (PL les feux)
□ He made a fire in the woods. Il a fait du feu
dans les bois.
■ **to be on fire** être [35] en feu
2 l'incendie *masc* (*accidental*)
□ The house was destroyed by fire. La maison a
été détruite par un incendie.
3 le radiateur *masc* (*heater*)
□ Turn the fire on. Allume le radiateur.
■ **the fire brigade** les pompiers *masc pl*
■ **a fire alarm** une alarme à incendie
■ **a fire engine** une voiture de pompiers
■ **a fire escape** un escalier de secours
■ **a fire extinguisher** un extincteur
■ **a fire station** une caserne de pompiers

to **fire** VERB
▷ *see also* **fire** NOUN
tirer [28] (*shoot*)
□ She fired twice. Elle a tiré deux fois.
■ **to fire at somebody** tirer [28] sur quelqu'un
■ **to fire a gun** tirer [28] un coup de feu
■ **to fire somebody** mettre [47] quelqu'un à
la porte □ He was fired from his job. Il a été mis
à la porte.

fire exit NOUN
la sortie de secours *fem*

firefighter NOUN
le pompier *masc*
□ She's a firefighter. Elle est pompier.

fireplace NOUN
la cheminée *fem*

fireworks PL NOUN
le feu d'artifice *masc sing*
□ Are you going to see the fireworks? Est-ce que
tu vas voir le feu d'artifice ?

firm ADJECTIVE
▷ *see also* **firm** NOUN
ferme (*FEM* ferme)

□ to be firm with somebody se montrer ferme
avec quelqu'un

firm NOUN
▷ *see also* **firm** ADJECTIVE
l'entreprise *fem*
□ He works for a large firm in Newcastle.
Il travaille pour une grande entreprise à
Newcastle.

first ADJECTIVE, ADVERB
▷ *see also* **first** NOUN
1 premier (*FEM* première)
□ the first of September le premier septembre
□ the first time la première fois
■ **to come first** (*in exam, race*) arriver [5ᵗ]
premier □ Rachel came first. Rachel est arrivée
première.
2 d'abord
□ I want to get a job, but first I have to graduate.
Je veux trouver du travail, mais d'abord je dois
finir mes études.
■ **first of all** tout d'abord

first NOUN
▷ *see also* **first** ADJECTIVE, ADVERB
le premier *masc*
la première *fem*
□ She was the first to arrive. Elle est arrivée la
première.
■ **at first** au début

first aid NOUN
les premiers secours *masc pl*
■ **a first aid kit** une trousse de secours

first-class ADJECTIVE, ADVERB
1 de première classe
□ She has booked a first-class ticket. Elle a
réservé un billet de première classe.
■ **to travel first class** voyager [45] en première
2 excellent (*FEM* excellente)
□ a first-class meal un excellent repas
■ **a first-class stamp**

DID YOU KNOW...?
In France, there is no first-class or second-
class postage. However you can buy a
lettre verte stamp for your letters: this
method of delivery avoids airmail, making it
a more eco-friendly way to send mail.

firstly ADVERB
premièrement
□ Firstly, let's see what the book is about.
Premièrement, voyons de quoi parle ce livre.

fir tree NOUN
le sapin *masc*

fish NOUN
▷ *see also* **fish** VERB
le poisson *masc*
□ I caught three fish. J'ai pêché trois poissons.
□ I don't like fish. Je n'aime pas le poisson.
■ **a fish tank** un aquarium

to **fish** VERB
▷ see also **fish** NOUN
pêcher [28]
■ **to go fishing** aller [3ᵗ] à la pêche □ We went fishing in the River Dee. Nous sommes allés à la pêche sur la Dee.

fisherman NOUN
le pêcheur *masc*
□ He's a fisherman. Il est pêcheur.

fish fingers PL NOUN
les bâtonnets de poisson *masc pl*

fishing NOUN
la pêche *fem*
□ My hobby is fishing. La pêche est mon passe-temps favori.

fishing boat NOUN
le bateau de pêche *masc*

fishing rod NOUN
la canne à pêche *fem*

fishing tackle NOUN
le matériel de pêche *masc*

fish sticks PL NOUN (US)
les bâtonnets de poisson *masc pl*

fist NOUN
le poing *masc*

fit ADJECTIVE
▷ see also **fit** VERB, NOUN
en forme (*in condition*)
□ He likes to stay fit. Il aime se maintenir en forme.
■ **to keep fit** se maintenir [83] en forme □ She does zumba to keep fit. Elle fait de la zumba pour se maintenir en forme.

fit NOUN
▷ see also **fit** ADJECTIVE, VERB
■ **to have a fit** **1** (*medical*) avoir [8] une crise **2** (*be angry*) piquer [28] une crise de nerfs □ My mum will have a fit when she sees the carpet! Ma mère va piquer une crise de nerfs quand elle va voir la moquette !

to **fit** VERB
▷ see also **fit** ADJECTIVE, NOUN
1 être [35] la bonne taille (*be the right size*)
□ Does it fit? Est-ce que c'est la bonne taille ?

In French you usually specify whether something is too big, small, tight etc.

■ **These trousers don't fit me.** **1** (*too big*) Ce pantalon est trop grand pour moi. **2** (*too small*) Ce pantalon est trop petit pour moi.
■ **My clothes won't all fit in my backpack.** Mes vêtements ne rentreront pas tous dans mon sac à dos.
2 installer [28] (*fix up*)
□ He fitted an alarm in his car. Il a installé une alarme dans sa voiture.
3 poser [28] (*attach*)
□ She fitted a lock on her bedroom door. Elle a posé un cadenas sur la porte de sa chambre.

to **fit in** VERB
s'intégrer [28] (*person*)
□ She fitted in well at her new school. Elle s'est bien intégrée dans sa nouvelle école.
■ **We fitted in a visit to the Eiffel Tower.** On a trouvé le temps de visiter la tour Eiffel.

fitness NOUN
la forme physique *fem*

fitting room NOUN
la cabine d'essayage *fem*

five NUMBER
cinq
□ He's five. Il a cinq ans.

to **fix** VERB
1 réparer [28] (*mend*)
□ Can you fix my bike? Est-ce que tu peux réparer mon vélo ?
2 fixer [28] (*decide*)
□ Let's fix a date for the party. Fixons une date pour la soirée. □ They fixed a price for the laptop. Ils ont fixé un prix pour l'ordinateur portable.
3 préparer [28]
□ Dylan's dad fixed some food for us. Le père de Dylan nous a préparé à manger.

fixed ADJECTIVE
fixe (FEM fixe)
□ at a fixed time à une heure fixe □ at a fixed price à un prix fixe □ a fixed-price menu un menu à prix fixe
■ **My parents have very fixed ideas.** Mes parents ont des idées très arrêtées.

fizzy ADJECTIVE
gazeux (FEM gazeuse)
□ I don't like fizzy drinks. Je n'aime pas les boissons gazeuses.

flabby ADJECTIVE
flasque (FEM flasque)

flag NOUN
le drapeau *masc* (PL les drapeaux)

flame NOUN
la flamme *fem*

flamingo NOUN
le flamant rose *masc*

flan NOUN
1 la quiche *fem* (*savoury*)
□ a cheese and onion flan une quiche au fromage et aux oignons
2 la tarte *fem* (*sweet*)
□ a raspberry flan une tarte aux framboises

flannel NOUN
le gant de toilette *masc* (*for face*)

DID YOU KNOW...?
The French traditionally wash with a towelling glove rather than a flannel.

to **flap** VERB
battre [9] de

flash - flow

□ The bird flapped its wings. L'oiseau battait des ailes.

flash NOUN

▷ *see also* **flash** VERB

le flash *masc* (PL les flashes)

□ Did the flash go off? Le flash s'est déclenché ?

■ **a flash of lightning** un éclair

■ **in a flash** en un clin d'œil

to **flash** VERB

▷ *see also* **flash** NOUN

1 clignoter [28]

□ The light on the police car was flashing. Le gyrophare de la voiture de police clignotait.

2 projeter [41]

□ They flashed a torch in his face. Ils lui ont projeté la lumière d'une torche en plein visage.

■ **She flashed her headlights.** Elle a fait un appel de phares.

flask NOUN

le thermos *masc* (*vacuum flask*)

flat ADJECTIVE

▷ *see also* **flat** NOUN

1 plat (FEM plate)

□ a flat roof un toit plat □ flat shoes des chaussures plates

2 crevé (FEM crevée) (*tyre*)

□ I've got a flat tyre. J'ai un pneu crevé.

flat NOUN

▷ *see also* **flat** ADJECTIVE

l'appartement *masc*

□ She lives in a flat. Elle habite un appartement.

to **flatter** VERB

flatter [28]

flattered ADJECTIVE

flatté (FEM flattée)

flavour (US **flavor**) NOUN

1 le goût *masc* (*taste*)

□ It has a very strong flavour. Ça a un goût très fort.

2 le parfum *masc* (*variety*)

□ Which flavour of ice cream would you like? Quel parfum de glace est-ce que tu veux ?

flavouring (US **flavoring**) NOUN

le parfum *masc*

flew VERB ▷ *see* **fly**

flexible ADJECTIVE

flexible (FEM flexible)

□ flexible working hours les horaires flexibles

to **flick** VERB

appuyer [53] sur

□ She flicked the switch to turn the light on. Elle a appuyé sur le bouton pour allumer la lumière.

■ **to flick through a book** feuilleter [41] un livre

to **flicker** VERB

trembloter [28]

□ The light flickered. La lumière a trembloté.

flight NOUN

le vol *masc*

□ What time is the flight to Paris? À quelle heure est le vol pour Paris ?

■ **a flight of stairs** un escalier

flight attendant NOUN

1 l'hôtesse de l'air *fem* (*woman*)

2 le steward *masc* (*man*)

to **fling** VERB

jeter [41]

□ He flung the book onto the floor. Il a jeté le livre par terre.

flippers NOUN

les palmes *fem pl*

to **float** VERB

flotter [28]

□ A leaf was floating on the water. Une feuille flottait sur l'eau.

flock NOUN

■ **a flock of sheep** un troupeau de moutons

■ **a flock of birds** un vol d'oiseaux

flood NOUN

▷ *see also* **flood** VERB

1 l'inondation *fem*

□ We had a flood in the kitchen. On a eu une inondation dans la cuisine.

2 le flot *masc*

□ He received a flood of emails. Il a reçu un flot de mails.

to **flood** VERB

▷ *see also* **flood** NOUN

inonder [28]

□ The river has flooded the village. La rivière a inondé le village.

flooding NOUN

les inondations *fem pl*

floor NOUN

1 le sol *masc*

□ a tiled floor un sol carrelé

■ **on the floor** par terre

2 l'étage *masc* (*storey*)

□ the first floor le premier étage

■ **the ground floor** le rez-de-chaussée

■ **on the third floor** au troisième étage

flop NOUN

le fiasco *masc*

□ The film was a flop. Le film a été un fiasco.

florist NOUN

le/la fleuriste *masc/fem*

flour NOUN

la farine *fem*

to **flow** VERB

1 couler [28] (*river*)

2 s'écouler [28] (*flow out*)

□ Water was flowing from the pipe. De l'eau s'écoulait du tuyau.

flower NOUN
▷ *see also* **flower** VERB
la fleur *fem*

to **flower** VERB
▷ *see also* **flower** NOUN
fleurir [38]

flown VERB ▷ *see* **fly**

flu NOUN
la grippe *fem*
□ She's got flu. Elle a la grippe.

fluent ADJECTIVE
■ **He speaks fluent French.** Il parle couramment le français.

flung VERB ▷ *see* **fling**

flush NOUN
▷ *see also* **flush** VERB
la chasse d'eau *fem* (*of toilet*)

to **flush** VERB
▷ *see also* **flush** NOUN
■ **to flush the toilet** tirer [28] la chasse

flute NOUN
la flûte *fem*
□ I play the flute. Je joue de la flûte.

fly NOUN
▷ *see also* **fly** VERB
la mouche *fem* (*insect*)

to **fly** VERB
▷ *see also* **fly** NOUN
1 voler [28]
□ The plane flew through the night. L'avion a volé toute la nuit.
2 aller [3⁹] en avion (*passenger*)
□ He flew from Paris to New York. Il est allé de Paris à New York en avion.

to **fly away** VERB
s'envoler [28]
□ The bird flew away. L'oiseau s'est envolé.

foal NOUN
le poulain *masc*

focus NOUN
▷ *see also* **focus** VERB
■ **to be out of focus** être [35] flou □ The house is out of focus in this photo. La maison est floue sur cette photo.

to **focus** VERB
▷ *see also* **focus** NOUN
mettre [47] au point
□ Try to focus the binoculars. Essaye de mettre les jumelles au point.
■ **to focus on something 1** (*with camera, telescope*) régler [34] la mise au point sur quelque chose □ The cameraman focused on the bird. Le caméraman a réglé la mise au point sur l'oiseau. **2** (*concentrate*) se concentrer [28] sur quelque chose □ Let's focus on the plot of the play. Concentrons-nous sur l'intrigue de la pièce.

fog NOUN
le brouillard *masc*

foggy ADJECTIVE
■ **It's foggy.** Il y a du brouillard.
■ **a foggy day** un jour de brouillard

foil NOUN
le papier d'aluminium *masc* (*kitchen foil*)
□ She wrapped the meat in foil. Elle a enveloppé la viande dans du papier d'aluminium.

fold NOUN
▷ *see also* **fold** VERB
le pli *masc*

to **fold** VERB
▷ *see also* **fold** NOUN
plier [19]
□ He folded the newspaper in half. Il a plié le journal en deux.
■ **to fold something up** plier [19] quelque chose
■ **to fold one's arms** croiser [28] ses bras
□ She folded her arms. Elle a croisé les bras.

folder NOUN
1 la chemise *fem*
□ She kept all her notes in a folder. Elle gardait toutes ses notes dans une chemise.
2 le classeur *masc* (*ring binder*)

folding ADJECTIVE
■ **a folding chair** une chaise pliante
■ **a folding bed** un lit pliant

to **follow** VERB
suivre [81]
□ She followed him. Elle l'a suivi. □ You go first and I'll follow. Va devant, je te suis.
■ **to follow somebody** (*social media*) suivre [81] quelqu'un □ I follow Taylor Swift on Instagram. Je suis Taylor Swift sur Instagram.

follower NOUN
le follower *masc* (*on social media*)
□ How do I get more followers? Comment puis-je avoir plus de followers ?

following ADJECTIVE
suivant (FEM suivante)
□ the following day le jour suivant

fond ADJECTIVE
■ **to be fond of somebody** aimer [28] beaucoup quelqu'un □ I'm very fond of her. Je l'aime beaucoup.

food NOUN
la nourriture *fem*
■ **We need to buy some food.** Nous devons acheter à manger.
■ **cat/dog food** la nourriture pour chat/chien

food processor NOUN
le robot *masc*

fool NOUN
l'idiot *masc*
l'idiote *fem*

f

foot NOUN

1 le pied *masc* (*of person*)
  □ My feet are aching. J'ai mal aux pieds.
  ■ **on foot** à pied

2 la patte *fem* (*of animal*)
  □ The rabbit's foot was injured. Le lapin était blessé à la patte.

3 le pied *masc* (*12 inches*)

> **DID YOU KNOW…?**
> In France, measurements are in metres and centimetres rather than feet and inches. A foot is about 30 centimetres.

  ■ **Hassan is 6 foot tall.** Hassan mesure un mètre quatre-vingts.
  ■ **That mountain is 5000 feet high.** Cette montagne fait mille six cents mètres de haut.

football NOUN

1 le football *masc* (*game*)
  □ I like playing football. J'aime jouer au football.

2 le ballon *masc* (*ball*)
  □ Paul threw the football over the fence. Paul a envoyé le ballon par dessus la clôture.

footballer NOUN

le footballeur *masc*
la footballeuse *fem*

football player NOUN

le joueur de football *masc*
la joueuse de football *fem*
  □ He's a famous football player. C'est un joueur de football célèbre.

footie NOUN

le foot *masc* (*informal*)

footpath NOUN

le sentier *masc*
  □ Chloe followed the footpath through the forest. Chloe a suivi le sentier à travers la forêt.

footprint NOUN

la trace de pas *fem*
  □ He saw some footprints in the sand. Il a vu des traces de pas sur le sable.

footstep NOUN

le pas *masc*
  □ I can hear footsteps on the stairs. J'entends des pas dans l'escalier.

for PREPOSITION

> There are several ways of translating 'for'. Scan the examples to find one that is similar to what you want to say.

1 pour
  □ a present for me un cadeau pour moi
  □ the train for York le train pour York □ He works for the government. Il travaille pour le gouvernement. □ I'll do it for you. Je vais le faire pour toi. □ Can you do it for tomorrow? Est-ce que vous pouvez le faire pour demain ? □ Are you for or against the idea? Êtes-vous pour ou contre cette idée ? □ Oxford is famous for its university.

Oxford est célèbre pour son université.

> When referring to periods of time, use **pendant** for the future and completed actions in the past, and **depuis** (with the French verb in the present tense) for something that started in the past and is still going on.

2 pendant
  □ He worked in France for two years. Il a travaillé en France pendant deux ans. □ She will be away for a month. Elle sera absente pendant un mois. □ There are roadworks for three kilometres. Il y a des travaux pendant trois kilomètres.

3 depuis
  □ He's been learning French for two years. Il apprend le français depuis deux ans. □ She's been away for a month. Elle est absente depuis un mois.

> When talking about amounts of money, you do not translate 'for'.

  □ I sold it for £5. Je l'ai vendu cinq livres. □ He paid fifty pence for his ticket. Il a payé son billet cinquante pence.
  ■ **What's the French for 'house'?** Comment dit-on « house » en français ?
  ■ **It's time for lunch.** C'est l'heure du déjeuner.
  ■ **What for?** Pour quoi faire ? □ Give me some money! — What for? Donne-moi de l'argent ! — Pour quoi faire ?
  ■ **What's it for?** Ça sert à quoi ?
  ■ **for sale** à vendre
  ■ **The factory's for sale.** L'usine est en vente.

to forbid VERB

défendre [88]
  ■ **to forbid somebody to do something** défendre [88] à quelqu'un de faire quelque chose □ I forbid you to go out tonight! Je te défends de sortir ce soir.

forbidden ADJECTIVE

défendu (FEM défendue)
  □ Smoking is strictly forbidden. Il est strictement défendu de fumer.

force NOUN

  ▷ *see also* **force** VERB
la force *fem*
  □ the force of the explosion la force de l'explosion
  ■ **in force** en vigueur □ No-smoking rules are now in force. Un règlement qui interdit de fumer est maintenant en vigueur.

to force VERB

  ▷ *see also* **force** NOUN
forcer [12]
  □ They forced him to open the safe. Ils l'ont forcé à ouvrir le coffre-fort.

forecast NOUN

  ■ **the weather forecast** la météo

foreground NOUN

le premier plan *masc*

□ in the foreground au premier plan

forehead NOUN

le front *masc*

foreign ADJECTIVE

étranger (FEM étrangère)

foreigner NOUN

l'étranger *masc*

l'étrangère *fem*

to **foresee** VERB

prévoir [92]

□ He had foreseen the problem. Il avait prévu ce problème.

forest NOUN

la forêt *fem*

forever ADVERB

1 pour toujours

□ He's gone forever. Il est parti pour toujours.

2 toujours (*always*)

□ She's forever complaining. Elle est toujours en train de se plaindre.

forgave VERB ▷ *see* **forgive**

to **forge** VERB

contrefaire [36]

□ She tried to forge his signature. Elle a essayé de contrefaire sa signature.

forged ADJECTIVE

faux (FEM fausse)

□ forged banknotes des faux billets

to **forget** VERB

oublier [19]

□ I've forgotten his name. J'ai oublié son nom.

□ I'm sorry, I completely forgot! Je suis désolé, j'ai complètement oublié !

to **forgive** VERB

■ **to forgive somebody** pardonner [28] à quelqu'un □ I forgive you. Je te pardonne.

■ **to forgive somebody for doing something** pardonner [28] à quelqu'un d'avoir fait quelque chose □ She forgave him for forgetting her birthday. Elle lui a pardonné d'avoir oublié son anniversaire.

forgot, forgotten VERB ▷ *see* **forget**

fork NOUN

1 la fourchette *fem* (*for eating*)

2 la fourche *fem* (*for gardening*)

3 la bifurcation *fem* (*in road*)

form NOUN

1 le formulaire *masc* (*paper*)

□ to fill in a form remplir un formulaire

2 la forme *fem* (*type*)

□ I'm against hunting in any form. Je suis contre la chasse sous toutes ses formes.

■ **in top form** en pleine forme

formal ADJECTIVE

1 officiel (FEM officielle) (*occasion*)

□ a formal dinner un dîner officiel

2 guindé (FEM guindée) (*person*)

3 soutenu (FEM soutenue) (*language*)

□ In English, 'residence' is a formal term. En anglais, « residence » est un terme soutenu.

■ **formal clothes** une tenue habillée

■ **He's got no formal education.** Il n'a pas fait beaucoup d'études.

former ADJECTIVE

ancien (FEM ancienne)

□ a former pupil un ancien élève □ the former Prime Minister l'ancien Premier ministre

formerly ADVERB

autrefois

fort NOUN

le fort *masc*

forth ADVERB

■ **to go back and forth** aller [3f] et venir [89f]

■ **and so forth** et ainsi de suite

fortnight NOUN

■ **a fortnight** quinze jours □ I'm going on holiday for a fortnight. Je pars en vacances pendant quinze jours.

fortunate ADJECTIVE

■ **to be fortunate** avoir [8] de la chance □ He was extremely fortunate to survive. Il a eu énormément de chance de survivre.

■ **It's fortunate that I remembered the map.** C'est une chance que j'aie pris la carte.

fortunately ADVERB

heureusement

□ Fortunately, it didn't rain. Heureusement, il n'a pas plu.

fortune NOUN

la fortune *fem*

□ Kate earns a fortune! Kate gagne une fortune !

■ **to tell somebody's fortune** dire [27] la bonne aventure à quelqu'un

forty NUMBER

quarante

□ He's forty. Il a quarante ans.

forward ADVERB

▷ *see also* **forward** VERB

■ **to move forward** avancer [12]

to **forward** VERB

▷ *see also* **forward** ADVERB

faire [36] suivre

□ Can you forward the email she sent you? Est-ce que tu peux me faire suivre le mail qu'elle t'a envoyé ?

forward slash NOUN

la barre oblique *fem*

to **foster** VERB

■ **She has fostered more than fifteen children.** Plus de quinze enfants ont été placés chez elle.

foster child NOUN
l'enfant adoptif *masc*
l'enfant adoptive *fem*

fought VERB ▷ *see* **fight**

foul ADJECTIVE
▷ *see also* **foul** NOUN
infect (FEM infecte)
□ The weather was foul. Le temps était infect.
□ What a foul smell! Quelle odeur infecte !

foul NOUN
▷ *see also* **foul** ADJECTIVE
la faute *fem*
□ Ferguson committed a foul. Ferguson a fait une faute.

found VERB ▷ *see* **find**

to **found** VERB
fonder [28]
□ Baden Powell founded the Scout Movement. Baden Powell a fondé le mouvement scout.

foundations PL NOUN
les fondations *fem pl*

fountain NOUN
la fontaine *fem*

fountain pen NOUN
le stylo à encre *masc*

four NUMBER
quatre
□ She's four. Elle a quatre ans.

fourteen NUMBER
quatorze
□ I'm fourteen. J'ai quatorze ans.

fourteenth ADJECTIVE
quatorzième (FEM quatorzième)
□ the fourteenth floor le quatorzième étage
■ **the fourteenth of August** le quatorze août

fourth ADJECTIVE
quatrième (FEM quatrième)
□ the fourth floor le quatrième étage
■ **the fourth of July** le quatre juillet

fox NOUN
le renard *masc*

fragile ADJECTIVE
fragile (FEM fragile)

frame NOUN
le cadre *masc* (*for picture*)

France NOUN
la France *fem*
■ **in France** en France
■ **to France** en France
■ **He's from France.** Il est français.

frantic ADJECTIVE
■ **I was going frantic.** J'étais dans tous mes états.
■ **to be frantic with worry** être [35] fou d'inquiétude

fraud NOUN
1 la fraude *fem* (*crime*)
□ He was jailed for fraud. On l'a mis en prison pour fraude.
2 l'imposteur *masc* (*person*)
□ He's not a real doctor, he's a fraud. Ce n'est pas un vrai médecin, c'est un imposteur.

freckles PL NOUN
les taches de rousseur *fem pl*

free ADJECTIVE
▷ *see also* **free** VERB
1 gratuit (FEM gratuite) (*free of charge*)
□ a free brochure une brochure gratuite
2 libre (FEM libre) (*not busy, not taken*)
□ Is this seat free? Est-ce que cette place est libre ? □ Are you free after school? Tu es libre après l'école ?

to **free** VERB
▷ *see also* **free** ADJECTIVE
libérer [34]

freedom NOUN
la liberté *fem*

freeway NOUN (US)
l'autoroute *fem*

to **freeze** VERB
1 geler [43]
□ The water had frozen. L'eau avait gelé.
2 congeler [43] (*food*)
□ She froze the rest of the raspberries. Elle a congelé le reste des framboises.

freezer NOUN
le congélateur *masc*

freezing ADJECTIVE
■ **It's freezing!** Il fait un froid de canard ! (*informal*)
■ **I'm freezing!** Je suis gelé ! (*informal*)
■ **3 degrees below freezing** moins trois

freight NOUN
la cargaison *fem* (*goods*)
■ **a freight train** un train de marchandises

French NOUN
▷ *see also* **French** ADJECTIVE
le français *masc* (*language*)
□ Do you speak French? Est-ce que tu parles français ?
■ **the French** (*people*) les Français

French ADJECTIVE
▷ *see also* **French** NOUN
français (FEM française)
□ He's French. Il est français. □ She's French. Elle est française.

French beans PL NOUN
les haricots verts *masc pl*

French fries PL NOUN
les frites *fem pl*

French horn NOUN
le cor (d'harmonie) *masc*
□ I play the French horn. Je joue du cor.

Numbers in brackets refer to verb tables on pages 650 to 658

French kiss NOUN
le baiser profond *masc*

French loaf NOUN
la baguette *fem*

Frenchman NOUN
le Français *masc*

French windows PL NOUN
la porte-fenêtre *fem sing* (PL les portes-fenêtres)

Frenchwoman NOUN
la Française *fem*

frequent ADJECTIVE
fréquent (FEM fréquente)
□ frequent showers des averses fréquentes
■ **There are frequent buses to the town centre.** Il y a beaucoup de bus pour le centre ville.

fresh ADJECTIVE
frais (FEM fraîche)
■ **I need some fresh air.** J'ai besoin de prendre l'air.

to **freshen up** VERB
faire [36] un brin de toilette
□ I'd like to go and freshen up. Je voudrais faire un brin de toilette.

to **fret** VERB
se tracasser [28]
□ Theo was fretting about his exams. Theo se tracassait au sujet de ses examens.

Friday NOUN
le vendredi *masc*
□ on Friday vendredi □ on Fridays le vendredi □ every Friday tous les vendredis □ last Friday vendredi dernier □ next Friday vendredi prochain

fridge NOUN
le frigo *masc*
■ **a fridge magnet** un aimant pour frigo

fried ADJECTIVE
frit (FEM frite)
□ fried vegetables des légumes frits
■ **a fried egg** un œuf sur le plat

friend NOUN
▷ *see also* **friend** VERB
l'ami *masc*
l'amie *fem*

to **friend** VERB
▷ *see also* **friend** NOUN
ajouter [28] comme ami
□ I've friended her on Facebook. Je l'ai ajoutée comme amie sur Facebook.

friendly ADJECTIVE
1 gentil (FEM gentille)
□ She's really friendly. Elle est vraiment gentille.
2 accueillant (FEM accueillante)
□ Liverpool is a very friendly city. Liverpool est une ville très accueillante.

friendship NOUN
l'amitié *fem*

fright NOUN
la peur *fem*
□ I got a terrible fright! Ça m'a fait une peur terrible !

to **frighten** VERB
faire [36] peur à
□ Horror films frighten him. Les films d'horreur lui font peur.

frightened ADJECTIVE
■ **to be frightened** avoir [8] peur □ I'm frightened! J'ai peur !
■ **to be frightened of something** avoir [8] peur de quelque chose □ Anna's frightened of spiders. Anna a peur des araignées.

frightening ADJECTIVE
effrayant (FEM effrayante)

fringe NOUN
la frange *fem* (*of hair*)
□ She's got a fringe. Elle a une frange.

Frisbee® NOUN
le Frisbee® *masc*
□ to play Frisbee jouer au Frisbee

fro ADVERB
■ **to go to and fro** aller [3ᵉ] et venir [89ᵉ]

frog NOUN
la grenouille *fem*
■ **frogs' legs** les cuisses de grenouille

from PREPOSITION
de
□ Where do you come from? D'où venez-vous ?
□ I come from Perth. Je viens de Perth. □ a letter from my sister une lettre de ma sœur □ The hotel is one kilometre from the beach. L'hôtel est à un kilomètre de la plage.
■ **from ... to ...** de ... à ... □ He flew from Birmingham to Paris. Il a pris l'avion de Birmingham à Paris. □ from 1 o'clock to 2 d'une heure à deux heures □ The price was reduced from £10 to £5. Ils ont réduit le prix de dix livres à cinq.
■ **from ... onwards** à partir de ... □ We'll be at home from 7 o'clock onwards. Nous serons chez nous à partir de sept heures.

front NOUN
▷ *see also* **front** ADJECTIVE
le devant *masc*
□ the front of the house le devant de la maison
■ **in front** devant □ a house with a car in front une maison avec une voiture devant □ the car in front la voiture de devant
■ **in front of** devant □ in front of the house devant la maison □ the car in front of us la voiture devant nous
■ **in the front** (*of car*) à l'avant □ I was sitting in the front. J'étais assis à l'avant.
■ **at the front of the train** à l'avant du train

front ADJECTIVE
▷ *see also* **front** NOUN

f

1 de devant
□ the front row la rangée de devant
2 avant
□ the front seats of the car les sièges avant de la voiture
■ **the front door** la porte d'entrée

frontier NOUN
la frontière *fem*

frost NOUN
le gel *masc*

frosting NOUN (US)
le glaçage *masc* (*on cake*)

frosty ADJECTIVE
■ **It's frosty today.** Il gèle aujourd'hui.

to **frown** VERB
froncer [12] les sourcils
□ He frowned. Il a froncé les sourcils.

froze, frozen VERB ▷ *see* **freeze**

frozen ADJECTIVE
surgelé (FEM surgelée) (*food*)
□ frozen chips des frites surgelées

fruit NOUN
le fruit *masc*
■ **fruit juice** le jus de fruits
■ **a fruit salad** une salade de fruits

fruit machine NOUN
la machine à sous *fem*

frustrated ADJECTIVE
frustré (FEM frustrée)

to **fry** VERB
faire [36] frire
□ Fry the onions for 5 minutes. Faites frire les oignons pendant cinq minutes.

frying pan NOUN
la poêle *fem*

fuel NOUN
le carburant *masc* (*for car, aeroplane*)
□ to run out of fuel avoir une panne de carburant

to **fulfil** VERB
réaliser [28]
□ Josh fulfilled his dream to visit China. Josh a réalisé son rêve de visiter la Chine.

full ADJECTIVE, ADVERB
1 plein (FEM pleine)
□ The tank's full. Le réservoir est plein.
2 complet (FEM complète)
□ He asked for full details about the job. Il a demandé des renseignements complets sur le poste.
■ **your full name** vos nom et prénoms □ My full name is Oliver Luke Marr. Mes noms et prénoms sont Oliver Luke Marr.
■ **I'm full.** (*after meal*) J'ai bien mangé.
■ **at full speed** à toute vitesse □ He drove at full speed. Il conduisait à toute vitesse.
■ **There was a full moon.** C'était la pleine lune.

full stop NOUN
le point *masc*

full-time ADJECTIVE, ADVERB
à plein temps
□ She's got a full-time job. Elle a un travail à plein temps. □ She works full-time. Elle travaille à plein temps.

fully ADVERB
complètement
□ He hasn't fully recovered from his illness. Il n'est pas complètement remis de sa maladie.

fumes PL NOUN
les fumées *fem pl*
□ There was a smell of fumes from the factory. On sentait les fumées s'échappant de l'usine.
■ **exhaust fumes** les gaz d'échappement *masc pl*

fun ADJECTIVE
▷ *see also* **fun** NOUN
marrant (FEM marrante)
□ She's a fun person. Elle est marrante.

fun NOUN
▷ *see also* **fun** ADJECTIVE
■ **to have fun** s'amuser [28] □ We had great fun playing in the snow. Nous nous sommes bien amusés à jouer dans la neige.
■ **for fun** pour rire □ He entered the competition just for fun. Il a participé à la compétition juste pour rire.
■ **to make fun of somebody** se moquer [28] de quelqu'un □ They made fun of him. Ils se sont moqués de lui.
■ **It's fun!** C'est chouette !
■ **Have fun!** Amuse-toi bien !

funds PL NOUN
les fonds *masc pl*
□ to raise funds collecter des fonds

funeral NOUN
l'enterrement *masc*

funfair NOUN
la fête foraine *fem*

funny ADJECTIVE
1 drôle (FEM drôle) (*amusing*)
□ It was really funny. C'était vraiment drôle.
2 bizarre (FEM bizarre) (*strange*)
□ There's something funny about him. Il est un peu bizarre.

fur NOUN
1 la fourrure *fem*
□ a fur coat un manteau de fourrure
2 le poil *masc*
□ the dog's fur le poil du chien

furious ADJECTIVE
furieux (FEM furieuse)
□ Dad was furious with me. Papa était furieux contre moi.

furniture NOUN

les meubles *masc pl*

□ a piece of furniture un meuble

further ADVERB, ADJECTIVE

plus loin

□ London is further from Manchester than Leeds is. Londres est plus loin de Manchester que Leeds.

■ **How much further is it?** C'est encore loin ?

further education NOUN

l'enseignement postscolaire *masc*

fuse NOUN

le fusible *masc*

□ The fuse has blown. Le fusible a sauté.

fuss NOUN

l'agitation *fem*

□ What's all the fuss about? Qu'est-ce que c'est que toute cette agitation ?

■ **to make a fuss** faire [36] des histoires

□ He's always making a fuss about nothing. Il fait toujours des histoires pour rien.

fussy ADJECTIVE

difficile (FEM difficile)

□ She is very fussy about her food. Elle est très difficile sur la nourriture.

future NOUN

1 l'avenir *masc*

□ What are your plans for the future? Quels sont vos projets pour l'avenir ?

■ **in future** à l'avenir □ Be more careful in future. Sois plus prudent à l'avenir.

2 le futur *masc* (*in grammar*)

□ Put this sentence into the future. Mettez cette phrase au futur.

f

Gg

to **gain** VERB
- **to gain weight** prendre [65] du poids
- **to gain speed** prendre [65] de la vitesse

gallery NOUN
le musée *masc*
□ an art gallery un musée d'art

to **gamble** VERB
jouer [28]
□ He gambled £100 on the horse race. Il a joué cent livres à la course de chevaux.

gambler NOUN
le joueur *masc*

gambling NOUN
le jeu *masc*
□ He likes gambling. Il aime le jeu.

game NOUN
1 le jeu *masc* (PL les jeux)
□ The children were playing a game. Les enfants jouaient à un jeu.
2 le match *masc* (sport)
□ a game of football un match de football
- **a game of cards** une partie de cartes

to **game** VERB
jouer [28] aux jeux vidéo

gamer NOUN
le gameur *masc*
la gameuse *fem*

games console NOUN
la console de jeux *fem*

gaming NOUN
les jeux (*video games*)

gang NOUN
la bande *fem*

gangster NOUN
le gangster *masc*

gap NOUN
1 le trou *masc*
□ There's a gap in the hedge. Il y a un trou dans la haie.
2 l'intervalle *masc*
□ a gap of four years un intervalle de quatre ans

gap year NOUN
l'année de césure
□ My sister's in Australia on her gap year. Ma sœur prend une année de césure en Australie.

garage NOUN
le garage *masc*

garbage NOUN
les ordures *fem pl*

garden NOUN
le jardin *masc*

gardener NOUN
le jardinier *masc*
□ He's a gardener. Il est jardinier.

gardening NOUN
le jardinage *masc*
□ My gran loves gardening. Ma grand-mère aime le jardinage.

gardens PL NOUN
le jardin public *masc sing*

garlic NOUN
l'ail *masc*

garment NOUN
le vêtement *masc*

gas NOUN
1 le gaz *masc*
- **a gas cooker** une cuisinière à gaz
- **a gas cylinder** une bouteille de gaz
- **a gas fire** un radiateur à gaz
- **a gas leak** une fuite de gaz
2 l'essence *fem* (US: *petrol*)

gasoline NOUN (US)
l'essence *fem*

gate NOUN
1 le portail *masc* (of garden)
2 la barrière *fem* (of field)
3 la porte *fem* (at airport)

gateau NOUN
le gâteau à la crème *masc*

to **gather** VERB
se rassembler [28] (*assemble*)
□ People gathered in front of Buckingham Palace. Les gens se sont rassemblés devant Buckingham Palace.
- **to gather speed** prendre [65] de la vitesse
□ The train gathered speed. Le train a pris de la vitesse.

gave VERB ▷ see **give**

gay ADJECTIVE
homosexuel (FEM homosexuelle)

Numbers in brackets refer to verb tables on pages 650 to 658

to **gaze** VERB
■ **to gaze at something** fixer [28] quelque chose du regard □ He gazed at her. Il l'a fixée du regard.

GCSE NOUN
le brevet des collèges *masc*

> **DID YOU KNOW...?**
> Exams in France are different from exams in Britain. **le brevet des collèges** is an exam you take at the end of fourth year in secondary school.

gear NOUN
1 la vitesse *fem* (*in car*)
□ in first gear en première vitesse □ to change gear changer de vitesse
2 le matériel *masc*
□ camping gear le matériel de camping
■ **your sports gear** (*clothes*) tes affaires de sport

gear lever NOUN
le levier de vitesse *masc*

gearshift NOUN (US)
le levier de vitesse *masc*

geese PL NOUN ▷ see **goose**

gel NOUN
le gel *masc*
■ **hair gel** le gel pour les cheveux

gem NOUN
la pierre précieuse *fem*

Gemini NOUN
les Gémeaux *masc pl*
□ I'm Gemini. Je suis Gémeaux.

gender NOUN
1 le sexe *masc* (*of person*)
2 le genre *masc* (*of noun*)

gene NOUN
le gène *masc*

general NOUN
▷ see also **general** ADJECTIVE
le général *masc* (PL les généraux)

general ADJECTIVE
▷ see also **general** NOUN
général (FEM générale, MASC PL généraux)
■ **in general** en général

general election NOUN
les élections législatives *fem pl*

general knowledge NOUN
les connaissances générales *fem pl*

generally ADVERB
généralement
□ I generally go shopping on Saturday. Généralement, je fais mes courses le samedi.

generation NOUN
la génération *fem*
□ the younger generation la nouvelle génération

generator NOUN
le générateur *masc*

generous ADJECTIVE
généreux (FEM généreuse)
□ That's very generous of you. C'est très généreux de votre part.

genetic ADJECTIVE
génétique (FEM génétique)

genetically-modified ADJECTIVE
génétiquement modifié (FEM génétiquement modifiée)

genetics NOUN
la génétique *fem*

Geneva NOUN
Genève
■ **in Geneva** à Genève
■ **to Geneva** à Genève
■ **Lake Geneva** le lac Léman

genius NOUN
le génie *masc*
□ She's a genius! C'est un génie !

gentle ADJECTIVE
doux (FEM douce)

> **BE CAREFUL!**
> Do not translate **gentle** by the French word **gentil**.

gentleman NOUN
le monsieur *masc* (PL les messieurs)
□ Good morning, gentlemen. Bonjour messieurs.

gently ADVERB
doucement

gents NOUN
les toilettes pour hommes *fem pl*
□ Can you tell me where the gents is, please? Pouvez-vous me dire où sont les toilettes, s'il vous plaît ?
■ **'gents'** (*on sign*) « messieurs »

genuine ADJECTIVE
1 véritable (FEM véritable) (*real*)
□ These are genuine diamonds. Ce sont de véritables diamants.
2 sincère (FEM sincère) (*sincere*)
□ She's a very genuine person. C'est quelqu'un de très sincère.

geography NOUN
la géographie *fem*

gerbil NOUN
la gerbille *fem*

germ NOUN
le microbe *masc*

German NOUN
▷ see also **German** ADJECTIVE
1 l'Allemand *masc*
l'Allemande *fem* (*person*)
2 l'allemand (*language*)
□ Do you speak German? Parlez-vous allemand ?

g

German ADJECTIVE
▷ *see also* **German** NOUN
allemand (FEM allemande)

German measles NOUN
la rubéole *fem*

Germany NOUN
l'Allemagne *fem*
- **in Germany** en Allemagne
- **to Germany** en Allemagne

gesture NOUN
le geste *masc*

to **get** VERB

> There are several ways of translating 'get'. Scan the examples to find one that is similar to what you want to say.

1 avoir [8] (*have, receive*)
□ I got lots of presents. J'ai eu beaucoup de cadeaux. □ He got first prize. Il a eu le premier prix. □ He got good exam results. Il a eu de bons résultats aux examens. □ How many have you got? Combien en avez-vous ?

2 aller [3ᵗ] chercher (*fetch*)
□ Quick, get help! Allez vite chercher de l'aide !

3 attraper [28] (*catch*)
□ They've got the thief. Ils ont attrapé le voleur.

4 prendre [65] (*train, bus*)
□ I'm getting the bus into town. Je prends le bus pour aller en ville.

5 comprendre [65] (*understand*)
□ I don't get it. Je ne comprends pas.

6 aller [3ᵗ] (*go*)
□ How do you get to the castle? Comment est-ce qu'on va au château ?

7 arriver [5ᵗ] (*arrive*)
□ He should get here soon. Il devrait arriver bientôt.

8 devenir [25ᵗ] (*become*)
□ to get old devenir vieux
- **to get something done** faire [36] faire quelque chose □ to get one's hair cut se faire couper les cheveux
- **to get something for somebody** trouver [28] quelque chose pour quelqu'un □ The librarian got the book for me. Le bibliothécaire m'a trouvé le livre.

to **get away** VERB
s'échapper [28]
□ One of the burglars got away. L'un des cambrioleurs s'est échappé.

to **get back** VERB

1 rentrer [68ᵗ]
□ What time did you get back? Tu es rentré à quelle heure ?

2 récupérer [34]
□ He got his money back. Il a récupéré son argent.

to **get in** VERB
rentrer [68ᵗ]
□ What time did you get in last night? Tu es rentré à quelle heure hier soir ?

to **get into** VERB
monter [48ᵗ] dans
□ Marek got into the car. Marek est monté dans la voiture.

to **get off** VERB
descendre [24ᵗ] de (*vehicle, bike*)
□ Ella got off the train. Ella est descendue du train.

to **get on** VERB

1 monter [48ᵗ] dans (*vehicle*)
□ Mohammed got on the bus. Mohammed est monté dans le bus.

2 enfourcher [28] (*bike*)
□ Jessica got on her bike. Jessica a enfourché son vélo.
- **to get on with somebody** s'entendre [88] avec quelqu'un □ He doesn't get on with his parents. Il ne s'entend pas avec ses parents. □ We got on really well. Nous nous sommes très bien entendus.

to **get out** VERB
sortir [79ᵗ]
□ Brodie got out of the car. Brodie est sorti de la voiture. □ Get out! Sortez !
- **to get something out** sortir [79] quelque chose □ She got the map out. Elle a sorti la carte.

to **get over** VERB
se remettre [47]
□ She never got over his death. Elle ne s'est jamais remise de sa mort.

to **get together** VERB
se retrouver [28]
□ Could we get together this evening? Pourrait-on se retrouver ce soir ?

to **get up** VERB
se lever [43]
□ What time do you get up? Tu te lèves à quelle heure ?

ghost NOUN
le fantôme *masc*

giant ADJECTIVE
▷ *see also* **giant** NOUN
énorme (FEM énorme)
□ They ate a giant meal. Ils ont mangé un énorme repas.

giant NOUN
▷ *see also* **giant** ADJECTIVE
le géant *masc*
la géante *fem*

gift NOUN

1 le cadeau *masc* (PL les cadeaux) (*present*)

2 le don *masc* (*talent*)
- **to have a gift for something** être [35]

Numbers in brackets refer to verb tables on pages 650 to 658

doué pour quelque chose □ Lucas has a gift for painting. Lucas est doué pour la peinture.

gifted ADJECTIVE
doué (FEM douée)
□ Maryam is a gifted dancer. Maryam est douée pour la danse.

gift shop NOUN
la boutique de cadeaux *fem*

gig NOUN
1 le show *masc* (*performance*)
2 le giga *masc* (*gigabyte*)

gigantic ADJECTIVE
gigantesque (FEM gigantesque)

gin NOUN
le gin *masc*

ginger NOUN
▷ *see also* **ginger** ADJECTIVE
le gingembre *masc*
□ Add a teaspoon of ginger. Ajoutez une cuillère à café de gingembre.

ginger ADJECTIVE
▷ *see also* **ginger** NOUN
roux (FEM rousse)
□ Robbie has ginger hair. Robbie a les cheveux roux.

giraffe NOUN
la girafe *fem*

girl NOUN
1 la fille *fem*
□ They've got a girl and two boys. Ils ont une fille et deux garçons.
2 la petite fille *fem* (*young*)
□ a five-year-old girl une petite fille de cinq ans
3 la jeune fille *fem* (*older*)
□ a sixteen-year-old girl une jeune fille de seize ans □ an English girl une jeune Anglaise

girlfriend NOUN
1 la copine *fem* (*lover*)
□ Jake's girlfriend is called Erin. La copine de Jake s'appelle Erin.
2 l'amie *fem* (*friend*)
□ She often went out with her girlfriends. Elle sortait souvent avec ses amies.

to give VERB
donner [28]
□ I give you what I can. Je te donne ce que je peux. □ You give good advice. Tu donnes de bons conseils. □ He gives me money when I need it. Il me donne de l'argent quand j'en ai besoin.
■ **to give something to somebody** donner [28] quelque chose à quelqu'un □ He gave me £10. Il m'a donné dix livres.
■ **to give something back to somebody** rendre [7] quelque chose à quelqu'un □ I gave the book back to him. Je lui ai rendu le livre.
■ **to give way** céder [34] la priorité (*in traffic*)

to give in VERB
céder [34]
□ His mum gave in and let him go out. Sa mère a cédé et l'a laissé sortir.

to give out VERB
distribuer [28]
□ He gave out the exam papers. Il a distribué les sujets d'examen.

to give up VERB
laisser [28] tomber
□ I couldn't do it, so I gave up. Je n'arrivais pas à le faire, alors j'ai laissé tomber.
■ **to give up doing something** arrêter [28] de faire quelque chose □ He gave up smoking. Il a arrêté de fumer.
■ **to give oneself up** se rendre [7] □ The thief gave himself up. Le voleur s'est rendu.

glad ADJECTIVE
content (FEM contente)
□ She's glad she's done it. Elle est contente de l'avoir fait.

glamorous ADJECTIVE
1 glamour (FEM+PL glamour) (*person*)
□ She's very glamorous. Elle est très glamour.
2 prestigieux (FEM prestigieuse) (*job*)
■ **to have a glamorous lifestyle** vivre [91] comme une star

to glance VERB
▷ *see also* **glance** NOUN
■ **to glance at something** jeter [41] un coup d'œil à quelque chose □ Aaron glanced at his watch. Aaron a jeté un coup d'œil à sa montre.

glance NOUN
▷ *see also* **glance** VERB
le coup d'œil *masc*
□ at first glance au premier coup d'œil

to glare VERB
■ **to glare at somebody** lancer [12] un regard furieux à quelqu'un □ He glared at me. Il m'a lancé un regard furieux.

glaring ADJECTIVE
■ **a glaring mistake** une erreur qui saute aux yeux

glass NOUN
le verre *masc*
□ a glass of milk un verre de lait

glasses PL NOUN
les lunettes *fem pl*
□ Jean-Pierre wears glasses. Jean-Pierre porte des lunettes.

glider NOUN
le planeur *masc*

gliding NOUN
le vol à voile *masc*
□ My hobby is gliding. Je fais du vol à voile.

global ADJECTIVE
mondial (FEM mondiale, MASC PL mondiaux)
■ **on a global scale** à l'échelle mondiale

global warming NOUN
le réchauffement climatique *masc*

globe NOUN
le globe *masc*

gloomy ADJECTIVE
1 morose (FEM morose)
□ She looked gloomy when she heard the news. Elle avait l'air morose quand elle a entendu les nouvelles.
2 lugubre (FEM lugubre)
□ He lives in a small gloomy flat. Il habite un petit appartement lugubre.

glorious ADJECTIVE
magnifique (FEM magnifique)

glove NOUN
le gant *masc*

glove compartment NOUN
la boîte à gants *fem*

glue NOUN
▷ *see also* **glue** VERB
la colle *fem*

to **glue** VERB
▷ *see also* **glue** NOUN
coller [28]

gluten NOUN
le gluten *masc*
■ **gluten-free** sans gluten □ a gluten-free diet un régime sans gluten

GM ADJECTIVE (= *genetically modified*)
génétiquement modifié (FEM génétiquement modifiée)
□ GM foods les aliments génétiquement modifiés *masc pl*
■ **GM-free** sans OGM

GMO ABBREVIATION (= *genetically-modified organism*)
l'OGM *masc* (= *l'organisme génétiquement modifié*)

go NOUN
▷ *see also* **go** VERB
■ **to have a go at doing something** essayer [59] de faire quelque chose □ He had a go at making a cake. Il a essayé de faire un gâteau.
■ **Whose go is it?** À qui le tour ?

to **go** VERB
▷ *see also* **go** NOUN
1 aller [3ᵗ]
□ I'm going to the cinema tonight. Je vais au cinéma ce soir.
2 partir [57ᵗ] (*leave*)
□ Where's Jin? — He's gone. Où est Jin ? — Il est parti.
3 s'en aller [3] (*go away*)
□ I'm going now. Je m'en vais.

4 marcher [28] (*vehicle*)
□ My car won't go. Ma voiture ne marche pas.
■ **to go home** rentrer [68ᵗ] à la maison □ I go home at about 4 o'clock. Je rentre à la maison vers quatre heures.
■ **to go for a walk** aller [3ᵗ] se promener □ Shall we go for a walk? Si on allait se promener ?
■ **How did it go?** Comment est-ce que ça s'est passé ?
■ **I'm going to do it tomorrow.** Je vais le faire demain.
■ **It's going to be difficult.** Ça va être difficile.

to **go after** VERB
suivre [81]
□ Quick, go after them! Vite, suivez-les !

to **go ahead** VERB
■ **The meeting with your parents will go ahead as planned.** La réunion avec vos parents aura bien lieu comme prévu.
■ **We'll go ahead with your plan.** Nous allons mettre votre projet à exécution.
■ **Go ahead!** Vas-y !

to **go away** VERB
s'en aller [3]
□ Go away! Allez-vous-en !

to **go back** VERB

> Use **retourner** in most cases, unless you are entering a building (usually your home) when you would use **rentrer**.

1 retourner [72ᵗ]
□ We went back to the same place. Nous sommes retournés au même endroit.
2 rentrer [68ᵗ]
□ After the film he went back home. Il est rentré chez lui après le film.

to **go by** VERB
passer [58ᵗ]
□ A group of tourists went by. Un groupe de touristes est passé.

to **go down** VERB
1 descendre [24ᵗ] (*person*)
□ to go down the stairs descendre l'escalier

> The verb **descendre** uses **avoir** in the perfect tense instead of **être** when talking about a person or thing moving down something (for example, down the stairs).

2 baisser [28] (*decrease*)
□ The price of computers has gone down. Le prix des ordinateurs a baissé.
3 se dégonfler [28] (*deflate*)
□ My airbed kept going down. Mon matelas pneumatique se dégonflait constamment.
■ **My brother's gone down with flu.** Mon frère a attrapé la grippe.

to **go for** VERB
attaquer [28] (*attack*)

go in - gold-plated

□ Suddenly the dog went for me. Soudain, le chien m'a attaqué.

■ **Go for it!** (*go on!*) Vas-y, fonce !

to **go in** VERB
entrer [32ᵗ]

□ He knocked on the door and went in. Il a frappé à la porte et il est entré.

to **go off** VERB
1 exploser [28] (*bomb*)
□ The bomb went off. La bombe a explosé.

2 se déclencher [28] (*alarm, gun*)
□ The fire alarm went off. L'alarme à incendie s'est déclenchée.

3 sonner [28] (*alarm clock*)
□ My alarm clock goes off at seven every morning. Mon réveil sonne à sept heures tous les matins.

4 tourner [28] (*food*)
□ The milk's gone off. Le lait a tourné.

5 partir [57ᵗ] (*go away*)
□ He went off in a huff. Il est parti de mauvaise humeur.

to **go on** VERB
1 se passer [58] (*happen*)
□ What's going on? Qu'est-ce qui se passe ?

2 continuer [28] (*carry on*)
□ The concert went on until 11 o'clock at night. Le concert a continué jusqu'à onze heures du soir.

■ **to go on doing something** continuer [28] à faire quelque chose □ He went on reading. Il a continué à lire.

■ **to go on at somebody** être [35] sur le dos de quelqu'un □ My parents always go on at me. Mes parents sont toujours sur mon dos.

■ **Go on!** Allez ! □ Go on, tell me what the problem is! Allez, dis-moi quel est le problème !

to **go out** VERB
1 sortir [79ᵗ] (*person*)
□ Are you going out tonight? Tu sors ce soir ?

■ **to go out with somebody** sortir [79ᵗ] avec quelqu'un □ Are you going out with him? Est-ce que tu sors avec lui ?

2 s'éteindre [60] (*light, fire, candle*)
□ Suddenly the lights went out. Soudain, les lumières se sont éteintes.

to **go past** VERB
■ **to go past something** passer [58ᵗ] devant quelque chose □ He went past the shop. Il est passé devant la boutique.

to **go round** VERB
■ **to go round a corner** prendre [65] un tournant

■ **to go round to somebody's house** aller [3ᵗ] chez quelqu'un

■ **to go round a museum** visiter [28] un musée

■ **to go round the shops** faire [36] les boutiques

■ **There's a bug going round.** Il y a un microbe qui circule.

to **go through** VERB
traverser [28]
□ We went through Paris to get to Rennes. Nous avons traversé Paris pour aller à Rennes.

to **go up** VERB
1 monter [48ᵗ] (*person*)
□ to go up the stairs monter l'escalier

> The verb **monter** uses **avoir** in the perfect tense instead of **être** when talking about a person or thing moving up something (for example, up the stairs).

2 augmenter [28] (*increase*)
□ The price has gone up. Le prix a augmenté.

■ **to go up in flames** s'embraser [28] □ The whole factory went up in flames. L'usine toute entière s'est embrasée.

to **go with** VERB
aller [3ᵗ] avec
□ Does this T-shirt go with this skirt? Est-ce que ce tee-shirt va avec cette jupe ?

goal NOUN
le but *masc*
□ to score a goal marquer un but □ His goal is to become the world champion. Son but est de devenir champion du monde.

goalkeeper NOUN
le gardien de but *masc*

goat NOUN
la chèvre *fem*
■ **goat's cheese** le fromage de chèvre

god NOUN
le dieu *masc* (PL les dieux)
□ I believe in God. Je crois en Dieu.

goddaughter NOUN
la filleule *fem*

godfather NOUN
le parrain *masc*

godmother NOUN
la marraine *fem*

godson NOUN
le filleul *masc*

goggles PL NOUN
1 les lunettes de protection *fem pl* (*of welder, mechanic etc*)
2 les lunettes de plongée *fem pl* (*of swimmer*)

gold NOUN
l'or *masc*
□ They found some gold. Ils ont trouvé de l'or.
□ a gold necklace un collier en or

goldfish NOUN
le poisson rouge *masc*
□ I've got five goldfish. J'ai cinq poissons rouges.

gold-plated ADJECTIVE
plaqué or (FEM plaquée or)

golf NOUN

le golf *masc*

□ My dad plays golf. Mon père joue au golf.

■ **a golf club** un club de golf

golf course NOUN

le terrain de golf *masc*

gone VERB ▷ *see* **go**

good ADJECTIVE

1 bon (FEM bonne)

□ It's a very good film. C'est un très bon film.
□ Vegetables are good for you. Les légumes sont bons pour la santé.

■ **to be good at something** être [35] bon en quelque chose □ Samir's very good at maths. Samir est très bon en maths.

> **WORD POWER**
>
> You can use a number of other words instead of **good** to mean 'great':
>
> **excellent** excellent
> □ an excellent book un livre excellent
> **fantastic** fantastique
> □ fantastic weather un temps fantastique
> **great** génial
> □ a great film un film génial
> **super** formidable
> □ a super idea une idée formidable

2 gentil (FEM gentille) (*kind*)

□ They were very good to me. Ils ont été très gentils avec moi. □ That's very good of you. C'est très gentil de votre part.

3 sage (FEM sage) (*not naughty*)

□ Be good! Sois sage !

■ **for good** pour de bon □ One day he left for good. Un jour il est parti pour de bon.

■ **Good morning!** Bonjour !

■ **Good afternoon!** Bonjour !

■ **Good evening!** Bonsoir !

■ **Good night!** Bonne nuit !

■ **It's no good complaining.** Cela ne sert à rien de se plaindre.

goodbye EXCLAMATION

au revoir !

Good Friday NOUN

le Vendredi saint *masc*

good-looking ADJECTIVE

beau (FEM belle, MASC PL beaux)

□ He's very good-looking. Il est très beau.

> **beau** changes to **bel** before a vowel and most words beginning with 'h'.

□ a good-looking man un bel homme

good-natured ADJECTIVE

facile à vivre (FEM facile à vivre) (*person*)

goods PL NOUN

les marchandises *fem pl* (*in shop*)

■ **a goods train** un train de marchandises

to **google** VERB

googler [28]

goose NOUN

l'oie *fem*

gooseberry NOUN

la groseille à maquereau *fem*

gorgeous ADJECTIVE

1 superbe (FEM superbe)

□ She's gorgeous! Elle est superbe !

2 splendide (FEM splendide)

□ The weather was gorgeous. Il a fait un temps splendide.

gorilla NOUN

le gorille *masc*

gospel NOUN

le gospel *masc* (*music*)

gossip NOUN

▷ *see also* **gossip** VERB

1 les cancans *masc pl* (*rumours*)

□ Tell me the gossip! Raconte-moi les cancans !

2 la commère *fem* (*woman*)

□ She's such a gossip! C'est une vraie commère !

3 le bavard *masc* (*man*)

□ What a gossip! Quel bavard !

to **gossip** VERB

▷ *see also* **gossip** NOUN

1 bavarder [28] (*chat*)

□ They were always gossiping. Elles étaient tout le temps en train de bavarder.

2 faire [36] des commérages (*about somebody*)

□ They gossiped about her. Elles faisaient des commérages à son sujet.

got VERB ▷ *see* **get**

gotten VERB (US) ▷ *see* **get**

government NOUN

le gouvernement *masc*

GP NOUN

le médecin généraliste *masc*

GPS NOUN

le GPS *masc*

to **grab** VERB

saisir [38]

graceful ADJECTIVE

élégant (FEM élégante)

grade NOUN

la note *fem* (*at school*)

□ He got good grades in his exams. Il a eu de bonnes notes à ses examens.

grade school NOUN (US)

l'école primaire *fem*

gradual ADJECTIVE

progressif (FEM progressive)

gradually ADVERB

peu à peu

□ We gradually got used to it. Nous nous y sommes habitués peu à peu.

graduate NOUN
1 le diplômé *masc*
la diplômée *fem* (*from university*)
2 le bachelier *masc*
la bachelière *fem* (*from US high school*)

graffiti PL NOUN
les graffiti *masc pl*

grain NOUN
le grain *masc*

gram NOUN
le gramme *masc*

grammar NOUN
la grammaire *fem*

grammar school NOUN
1 le collège *masc*
2 le lycée *masc*

> **DID YOU KNOW…?**
> In France, pupils go to a **collège** between the ages of 11 and 15, and then to a **lycée** until the age of 18. French schools are mostly non-selective.

grammatical ADJECTIVE
grammatical (FEM grammaticale, MASC PL grammaticaux)

gramme NOUN
le gramme *masc*
□ 500 grammes of cheese cinq cents grammes de fromage

grand ADJECTIVE
somptueux (FEM somptueuse)
□ Samantha lives in a very grand house. Samantha habite une maison somptueuse.

grandchild NOUN
le petit-fils *masc*
la petite-fille *fem*
■ **my grandchildren** mes petits-enfants *masc pl*

granddad NOUN
le papi *masc*
□ my granddad mon papi

granddaughter NOUN
la petite-fille *fem* (PL les petites-filles)

grandfather NOUN
le grand-père *masc* (PL les grands-pères)
□ my grandfather mon grand-père

grandma NOUN
la mamie *fem*
□ my grandma ma mamie

grandmother NOUN
la grand-mère *fem* (PL les grands-mères)
□ my grandmother ma grand-mère

grandpa NOUN
le papi *masc*

□ my grandpa mon papi

grandparents PL NOUN
les grands-parents *masc pl*
□ my grandparents mes grands-parents

grandson NOUN
le petit-fils *masc* (PL les petits-fils)

granny NOUN
la mamie *fem*
□ my granny ma mamie

grant NOUN
la bourse *fem*

grape NOUN
le raisin *masc*

grapefruit NOUN
le pamplemousse *masc*

graph NOUN
le graphique *masc*

graphics PL NOUN
1 les images de synthèse *fem pl* (*computer generated*)
2 le graphisme *masc pl* (*graphic design*)
□ I designed the graphics, she wrote the text. J'ai fait le graphisme, elle a écrit le texte.
■ **He wants to study computer graphics.** Il veut faire des études d'infographie.

to **grasp** VERB
saisir [38]

grass NOUN
l'herbe *fem*
□ The grass is long. L'herbe est haute.
■ **to cut the grass** tondre [69] le gazon

grasshopper NOUN
la sauterelle *fem*

to **grate** VERB
râper [28]
□ to grate some cheese râper du fromage

grateful ADJECTIVE
reconnaissant (FEM reconnaissante)

grave NOUN
la tombe *fem*

gravel NOUN
le gravier *masc*

graveyard NOUN
le cimetière *masc*

gravy NOUN
la sauce au jus de viande *fem*

grease NOUN
le lubrifiant *masc*

greasy ADJECTIVE
gras (FEM grasse)
□ He has greasy hair. Il a les cheveux gras. □ The food was very greasy. La nourriture était très grasse.

great ADJECTIVE
1 génial (FEM géniale, MASC PL géniaux)

g

□ That's great! C'est génial !

> **WORD POWER**
>
> You can use a number of other words instead
> of **great** to mean 'good':
>
> **amazing** extraordinaire
> □ an amazing view une vue extraordinaire
> **fabulous** formidable
> □ a fabulous idea une idée formidable
> **terrific** super
> □ a terrific party une super fête
> **wonderful** formidable
> □ a wonderful opportunity une occasion
> formidable

2 grand (FEM grande)
□ a great mansion un grand manoir

Great Britain NOUN
la Grande-Bretagne *fem*
■ **in Great Britain** en Grande-Bretagne
■ **to Great Britain** en Grande-Bretagne
■ **I'm from Great Britain.** Je suis britannique.

great-grandfather NOUN
l'arrière-grand-père *masc* (PL les arrière-grands-
pères)

great-grandmother NOUN
l'arrière-grand-mère *fem* (PL les arrière-grands-
mères)

Greece NOUN
la Grèce *fem*
■ **in Greece** en Grèce
■ **to Greece** en Grèce

greedy ADJECTIVE
1 gourmand (FEM gourmande) *(for food)*
□ I want some more cake. — Don't be so greedy! Je
veux encore du gâteau. — Ne sois pas si gourmand !
2 avide (FEM avide) *(for money)*

Greek NOUN
▷ *see also* **Greek** ADJECTIVE
1 le Grec *masc*
la Grecque *fem* *(person)*
2 le grec *masc* *(language)*

Greek ADJECTIVE
▷ *see also* **Greek** NOUN
grec (FEM grecque)
□ Dionysis is Greek. Dionysis est grec. □ She's
Greek. Elle est grecque.

green ADJECTIVE
▷ *see also* **green** NOUN
1 vert (FEM verte)
□ a green car une voiture verte □ a green light
un feu vert □ a green salad une salade verte
2 écologiste (FEM écologiste) *(movement,
candidate)*
□ the Green Party le parti écologiste
■ **green beans** les haricots verts *masc pl*

green NOUN
▷ *see also* **green** ADJECTIVE
le vert *masc*

□ a dark green un vert foncé
■ **greens** *(vegetables)* les légumes verts *masc pl*
■ **the Greens** *(party)* les Verts *masc pl*

greengrocer's NOUN
le marchand de fruits et légumes *masc*

greenhouse NOUN
la serre *fem*
■ **the greenhouse effect** l'effet de serre *masc*
■ **greenhouse gases** les gaz à effet de serre
masc pl

Greenland NOUN
le Groenland *masc*

to greet VERB
accueillir [22]
□ He greeted me with a kiss. Il m'a accueillie en
me faisant la bise.

greeting NOUN
■ **Greetings from Bangor!** Bonjour de Bangor !
■ **'Season's greetings'** « Meilleurs vœux pour
les fêtes de fin d'année »

greetings card NOUN
la carte de vœux *fem*

grew VERB ▷ *see* **grow**

grey ADJECTIVE
gris (FEM grise)
□ She's got grey hair. Elle a les cheveux gris.
■ **He's going grey.** Il grisonne.

grey-haired ADJECTIVE
grisonnant (FEM grisonnante)

grid NOUN
1 la grille *fem* *(in road)*
2 le réseau *masc* (PL les réseaux) *(of electricity)*

grief NOUN
le chagrin *masc*

grill NOUN
▷ *see also* **grill** VERB
le gril *masc* *(of cooker)*

to grill VERB
▷ *see also* **grill** NOUN
■ **to grill something** faire [36] griller quelque
chose

grim ADJECTIVE
sinistre (FEM sinistre)

to grin VERB
▷ *see also* **grin** NOUN
sourire [74]
□ Aziz grinned at me. Aziz m'a souri.

grin NOUN
▷ *see also* **grin** VERB
le large sourire *masc*

to grind VERB
moudre [50] *(coffee, pepper)*

to grip VERB
saisir [38]

gripping ADJECTIVE
palpitant (FEM palpitante) *(exciting)*

g

grit NOUN
le gravillon *masc*

to groan VERB
▷ *see also* **groan** NOUN
gémir [38]
□ He groaned with pain. Il a gémi sous l'effet de la douleur.

groan NOUN
▷ *see also* **groan** VERB
le gémissement *masc* (*of pain*)

grocer NOUN
l'épicier *masc*
□ He's a grocer. Il est épicier.

groceries PL NOUN
les provisions *fem pl*

grocer's NOUN
l'épicerie *fem*

grocer's shop NOUN
l'épicerie *fem*

grocery store NOUN (US)
l'épicerie *fem*

groom NOUN
le marié *masc* (*bridegroom*)
□ the groom and his best man le marié et son témoin

to grope VERB
■ **to grope for something** chercher [28] quelque chose à tâtons □ He groped for the light switch. Il a cherché à tâtons l'interrupteur.

gross ADJECTIVE
dégoûtant (FEM dégoûtante) (*revolting*)
□ It was really gross! C'était vraiment dégoûtant !

grossly ADVERB
largement
□ We're grossly underpaid. Nous sommes largement sous-payés.

ground VERB ▷ *see* **grind**

ground NOUN
▷ *see also* **ground** ADJECTIVE
1 le sol *masc* (*earth*)
□ The ground's wet. Le sol est mouillé.
2 le terrain *masc* (*for sport*)
□ a football ground un terrain de football
3 la raison *fem* (*reason*)
□ We've got grounds for complaint. Nous avons des raisons de nous plaindre.
■ **on the ground** par terre □ We sat on the ground. Nous nous sommes assis par terre.

ground ADJECTIVE
▷ *see also* **ground** NOUN
■ **ground coffee** le café moulu

ground floor NOUN
le rez-de-chaussée *masc*
■ **on the ground floor** au rez-de-chaussée

group NOUN
le groupe *masc*

to grow VERB
1 pousser [28] (*plant*)
□ Grass grows quickly. L'herbe pousse vite.
2 grandir [38] (*person, animal*)
□ Haven't you grown! Comme tu as grandi !
3 augmenter [28] (*increase*)
□ The number of pupils who go to university has grown. Le nombre d'élèves qui accèdent à l'université a augmenté.
4 faire [36] pousser (*cultivate*)
□ My dad grows potatoes. Mon père fait pousser des pommes de terre.
■ **to grow a beard** se laisser [28] pousser la barbe
■ **He's grown out of his jacket.** Sa veste est devenue trop petite pour lui.

to grow up VERB
grandir [38]
■ **Oh, grow up!** Ne fais pas l'enfant !

to growl VERB
grogner [28]

grown VERB ▷ *see* **grow**

growth NOUN
la croissance *fem*
□ economic growth la croissance économique

grub NOUN
la bouffe *fem* (*informal*)

grudge NOUN
la rancune *fem*
■ **to bear a grudge against somebody** garder [28] rancune à quelqu'un

gruesome ADJECTIVE
horrible (FEM horrible)

guarantee NOUN
▷ *see also* **guarantee** VERB
la garantie *fem*
■ **a five-year guarantee** une garantie de cinq ans

to guarantee VERB
▷ *see also* **guarantee** NOUN
garantir [38]
□ I can't guarantee he'll come. Je ne peux pas garantir qu'il viendra.

to guard VERB
▷ *see also* **guard** NOUN
garder [28]
□ They guarded the palace. Ils gardaient le palais.
■ **to guard against something** protéger [66] contre quelque chose

guard NOUN
▷ *see also* **guard** VERB
le chef de train *masc* (*of train*)
■ **a security guard** un vigile
■ **a guard dog** un chien de garde

to guess VERB
▷ *see also* **guess** NOUN
deviner [28]

□ Guess what this is! Devine ce que c'est !
■ **to guess wrong** se tromper [28] □ Daniel guessed wrong. Daniel s'est trompé.

guess NOUN
▷ see also **guess** VERB
la supposition *fem*
□ It's just a guess. C'est une simple supposition.
■ **Have a guess!** Devine !

guest NOUN
1 l'invité *masc*
l'invitée *fem*
□ We have guests staying with us. Nous avons des invités.
2 le client *masc*
la cliente *fem* (*of hotel*)

guesthouse NOUN
le petit hôtel *masc*

guide NOUN
1 le guide *masc* (*book, person*)
□ We bought a guide to Paris. Nous avons acheté un guide sur Paris. □ The guide showed us round the castle. Le guide nous a fait visiter le château.
2 l'éclaireuse *fem* (*girl guide*)
■ **the Guides** les Éclaireuses

guidebook NOUN
le guide *masc*

guide dog NOUN
le chien d'aveugle *masc*

guilty ADJECTIVE
coupable (FEM coupable)
□ to feel guilty se sentir coupable □ She was found guilty. Elle a été reconnue coupable.

guinea pig NOUN
le cobaye *masc*

guitar NOUN
la guitare *fem*
□ I play the guitar. Je joue de la guitare.

gum NOUN
le chewing-gum *masc* (*sweet*)
■ **gums** (*in mouth*) les gencives *fem pl*

gun NOUN
1 le revolver *masc* (*small*)
2 le fusil *masc* (*rifle*)

gunpoint NOUN
■ **at gunpoint** sous la menace d'une arme

gust NOUN
■ **a gust of wind** une rafale de vent

guy NOUN
le type *masc*
□ Who's that guy? C'est qui ce type ? □ He's a nice guy. C'est un type sympa.

gym NOUN
la gym *fem*
□ I go to the gym every day. Je vais tous les jours à la gym.

gymnast NOUN
le/la gymnaste *masc/fem*
□ She's a gymnast. Elle est gymnaste.

gymnastics NOUN
la gymnastique *fem*
□ to do gymnastics faire de la gymnastique

Gypsy NOUN
le Tzigane *masc*
la Tzigane *fem*

Hh

habit NOUN
l'habitude *fem*
□ a bad habit une mauvaise habitude

to **hack** VERB
■ **to hack into a system** s'introduire [23] dans un système

hacker NOUN
le/la pirate informatique *masc/fem*

had VERB ▷ *see* **have**

haddock NOUN
l'églefin *masc*

hadn't = had not

hail NOUN
▷ *see also* **hail** VERB
la grêle *fem*

to **hail** VERB
▷ *see also* **hail** NOUN
grêler [28]
□ It's hailing. Il grêle.

hair NOUN
1 les cheveux *masc pl*
□ She's got long hair. Elle a les cheveux longs.
□ He's got black hair. Il a les cheveux noirs.
□ He's losing his hair. Il perd ses cheveux.
■ **to brush one's hair** se brosser [28] les cheveux □ I'm brushing my hair. Je me brosse les cheveux.
■ **to wash one's hair** se laver [28] les cheveux □ I need to wash my hair. Il faut que je me lave les cheveux.
■ **to have one's hair cut** se faire [36] couper les cheveux □ I've just had my hair cut. Je viens de me faire couper les cheveux.
■ **a hair** 1 (*from head*) un cheveu 2 (*from body*) un poil
2 le pelage *masc* (*fur of animal*)

hairbrush NOUN
la brosse à cheveux *fem*

haircut NOUN
la coupe *fem*
■ **to have a haircut** se faire [36] couper les cheveux □ I've just had a haircut. Je viens de me faire couper les cheveux.

hairdresser NOUN
le coiffeur *masc*
la coiffeuse *fem*
□ He's a hairdresser. Il est coiffeur.

hairdresser's NOUN
le coiffeur *masc*
□ at the hairdresser's chez le coiffeur

hair dryer NOUN
le sèche-cheveux *masc* (PL les sèche-cheveux)

hair gel NOUN
le gel pour les cheveux *masc*

hairgrip NOUN
la pince à cheveux *fem*

hair spray NOUN
la laque *fem*

hair straighteners PL NOUN
le lisseur *masc*

hairstyle NOUN
la coiffure *fem*

hairy ADJECTIVE
poilu (FEM poilue)
□ He's got hairy legs. Il a les jambes poilues.

half NOUN
▷ *see also* **half** ADJECTIVE, ADVERB
1 la moitié *fem*
□ half of the cake la moitié du gâteau
2 le billet demi-tarif *masc* (*ticket*)
□ A half to York, please. Un billet demi-tarif pour York, s'il vous plaît.
■ **two and a half** deux et demi
■ **half an hour** une demi-heure
■ **half past ten** dix heures et demie
■ **half a kilo** cinq cents grammes
■ **to cut something in half** couper [28] quelque chose en deux

half ADJECTIVE, ADVERB
▷ *see also* **half** NOUN
1 demi (FEM demie)
□ a half chicken un demi-poulet
2 à moitié
□ He was half asleep. Il était à moitié endormi.

half-brother NOUN
le demi-frère *masc* (PL les demi-frères)

half-hour NOUN
la demi-heure *fem*

half-price ADJECTIVE, ADVERB
■ **at half-price** à moitié prix

half-sister NOUN
la demi-sœur *fem* (PL les demi-sœurs)

h

half-term - handy

half-term NOUN
les petites vacances *fem pl*

> **DID YOU KNOW...?**
> There are two half-term holidays in France:
> **les vacances de la Toussaint** (in October/
> November) and **les vacances de février**
> (in February).

half-time NOUN
la mi-temps *fem*

halfway ADVERB
1 à mi-chemin
□ halfway between Oxford and Swindon
à mi-chemin entre Oxford et Swindon
2 à la moitié
□ halfway through the chapter à la moitié du
chapitre

hall NOUN
1 l'entrée *fem* (*in house*)
2 la salle *fem*
□ the village hall la salle des fêtes

Hallowe'en NOUN
la veille de la Toussaint *fem*

> **DID YOU KNOW...?**
> The French do not traditionally celebrate
> Hallowe'en (although it is starting to become
> more popular). The next day, All Saints' Day
> (November 1st), is a public holiday, and is the
> day when people often visit family graves.

hallway NOUN
le vestibule *masc*

halt NOUN
■ **to come to a halt** s'arrêter [28] □ The train
came to a halt at the station. Le train s'est arrêté
dans la gare.

ham NOUN
le jambon *masc*
□ a ham sandwich un sandwich au jambon

hamburger NOUN
le hamburger *masc*

hammer NOUN
le marteau *masc* (PL les marteaux)

hamster NOUN
le hamster *masc*

hand NOUN
▷ *see also* **hand** VERB
1 la main *fem* (*of person*)
■ **to give somebody a hand** donner [28] un
coup de main à quelqu'un □ Can you give me a
hand? Tu peux me donner un coup de main ?
■ **on the one hand ..., on the other hand ...**
d'une part ..., d'autre part ...
2 l'aiguille *fem* (*of clock*)

to **hand** VERB
▷ *see also* **hand** NOUN
passer [58]
□ He handed me the book. Il m'a passé le livre.

■ **to hand something in** rendre [7] quelque
chose □ He handed his exam paper in. Il a rendu
sa copie d'examen.
■ **to hand something out** distribuer [28]
quelque chose □ The teacher handed out the
books. Le professeur a distribué les livres.
■ **to hand something over** remettre [47]
quelque chose □ She handed the keys over to
me. Elle m'a remis les clés.

handbag NOUN
le sac à main *masc*

handball NOUN
le handball *masc* (*game*)
■ **to play handball** jouer [28] au handball

handbook NOUN
le manuel *masc*

handcuffs PL NOUN
les menottes *fem pl*

handkerchief NOUN
le mouchoir *masc*

handle NOUN
▷ *see also* **handle** VERB
1 la poignée *fem* (*of door*)
2 l'anse *fem* (*of cup*)
3 le manche *masc* (*of knife*)
4 la queue *fem* (*of saucepan*)

to **handle** VERB
▷ *see also* **handle** NOUN
■ **He handled it well.** Il s'en est bien tiré.
■ **Phoebe's mum handled the travel
arrangements.** La mère de Phoebe s'est
occupée de l'organisation du voyage.
■ **She's good at handling children.** Elle sait
bien s'y prendre avec les enfants.

handlebars PL NOUN
le guidon *masc sing*

handmade ADJECTIVE
fait à la main (FEM faite à la main)

hand sanitizer NOUN
le désinfectant pour les mains *masc*

hands-free kit NOUN
le kit mains libres *masc* (*for phone*)

handsome ADJECTIVE
beau (FEM belle, MASC PL beaux)
□ He's handsome. Il est beau.

> **beau** changes to **bel** after a vowel and most
> words beginning with 'h'.

□ a handsome man un bel homme

handwriting NOUN
l'écriture *fem*

handy ADJECTIVE
1 pratique (FEM pratique)
□ This knife's very handy. Ce couteau est très
pratique.
2 sous la main
□ Have you got a pen handy? Est-ce que tu as un
stylo sous la main ?

Numbers in brackets refer to verb tables on pages 650 to 658

to hang VERB

1 accrocher [28]
   □ Riley hung the painting on the wall. Riley a accroché le tableau au mur.
2 pendre [88]
   □ They hanged the criminal. Ils ont pendu le criminel.

to hang around VERB

traîner [28]
   □ On Saturdays we hang around in the park. Le samedi nous traînons dans le parc.

to hang on VERB

patienter [28]
   □ Hang on a minute please. Patientez une minute s'il vous plaît.

to hang up VERB

1 accrocher [28] (clothes)
   □ Hang your jacket up on the hook. Accrochez votre veste au portemanteau.
2 raccrocher [28] (phone)
   □ Don't hang up! Ne raccroche pas !
   ■ **to hang up on someone** raccrocher [28] au nez de quelqu'un □ He always hangs up on me. Il me raccroche toujours au nez.

hanger NOUN

le cintre masc (coat hanger)

hang-gliding NOUN

le deltaplane masc
   ■ **to go hang-gliding** faire [36] du deltaplane

hangover NOUN

la gueule de bois fem
   □ He's got a terrible hangover. Il a une gueule de bois terrible.

Hanukkah NOUN

Hanoukka fem

to happen VERB

se passer [58]
   □ What's happened? Qu'est-ce qui s'est passé ?
   ■ **as it happens** justement □ As it happens, I don't want to go. Justement, je ne veux pas y aller.

happily ADVERB

1 joyeusement
   □ 'I passed!' he said happily. « Je suis reçu ! » dit-il joyeusement.
2 heureusement (fortunately)
   □ Happily, everything went well. Heureusement, tout s'est bien passé.

happiness NOUN

le bonheur masc

happy ADJECTIVE

heureux (FEM heureuse)
   □ Rafi looks happy. Rafi a l'air heureux.
   ■ **I'm very happy with your work.** Je suis très satisfait de ton travail.
   ■ **Happy birthday!** Bon anniversaire !

WORD POWER

You can use a number of other words instead of **happy** to mean 'glad':
cheerful gai
   □ a cheerful song une chanson gaie
delighted ravi
   □ a delighted smile un sourire ravi
glad content
   □ to be glad être content
satisfied satisfait
   □ a satisfied customer un client satisfait

---

harassment NOUN

le harcèlement masc
   □ police harassment le harcèlement policier

harbour (US **harbor**) NOUN

le port masc

hard ADJECTIVE, ADVERB

1 dur (FEM dure)
   □ This cheese is very hard. Ce fromage est très dur. □ He's worked very hard. Il a travaillé très dur.
2 difficile (FEM difficile)
   □ This question's too hard for me. Cette question est trop difficile pour moi.

hard disk NOUN

le disque dur masc (of computer)

hardly ADVERB

   ■ **I've hardly got any money.** Je n'ai presque pas d'argent.
   ■ **I hardly know you.** Je te connais à peine.
   ■ **hardly ever** presque jamais

hard up ADJECTIVE

fauché (FEM fauchée)

hardware NOUN

le hardware masc (computing)

hare NOUN

le lièvre masc

to harm VERB

   ■ **to harm somebody** faire [36] du mal à quelqu'un □ I didn't mean to harm you. Je ne voulais pas te faire de mal.
   ■ **to harm something** nuire [23] à quelque chose □ Chemicals harm the environment. Les produits chimiques nuisent à l'environnement.

harmful ADJECTIVE

nocif (FEM nocive)
   □ harmful chemicals des produits chimiques nocifs

harmless ADJECTIVE

inoffensif (FEM inoffensive)
   □ Most spiders are harmless. La plupart des araignées sont inoffensives.

harsh ADJECTIVE

dur (FEM dure)

has VERB ▷ see **have**

h

hashtag NOUN
le hashtag *masc*

hasn't = has not

hat NOUN
le chapeau *masc* (PL les chapeaux)

to **hate** VERB
détester [28]
□ I hate maths. Je déteste les maths.

hatred NOUN
la haine *fem*

haunted ADJECTIVE
hanté (FEM hantée)
□ a haunted house une maison hantée

to **have** VERB
1 avoir [8]
□ I have a cold. J'ai un rhume. □ You have a beautiful smile. Tu as un beau sourire. □ She has two brothers. Elle a deux frères. □ Have you got a sister? Tu as une sœur ? □ He's got blue eyes. Il a les yeux bleus. □ He's done it, hasn't he? Il l'a fait, non ? □ Have you got any money? — No, I haven't! Est-ce que tu as de l'argent ? — Non, je n'en ai pas !
2 être [35]

> The perfect tense of some verbs is formed with **être**.

□ They have arrived. Ils sont arrivés. □ Has he gone? Est-ce qu'il est parti ?
3 prendre [65]
□ He had his breakfast. Il a pris son petit déjeuner. □ to have a shower prendre une douche
■ **to have got to do something** devoir [26] faire quelque chose □ She's got to do it. Elle doit le faire.
■ **to have a party** faire [36] une fête
■ **to have one's hair cut** se faire [36] couper les cheveux

haven't = have not

hay NOUN
le foin *masc*

hay fever NOUN
le rhume des foins *masc*
□ Do you get hay fever? Est-ce que vous êtes sujet au rhume des foins ?

hazelnut NOUN
la noisette *fem*

he PRONOUN
il
□ He loves dogs. Il aime les chiens.

head NOUN
▷ *see also* **head** VERB
1 la tête *fem* (*of person*)
□ I have a sore head. J'ai mal à la tête.
2 le directeur *masc*
la directrice *fem* (*of private or primary school*)
3 le proviseur *masc* (*of state secondary school*)

4 le chef *masc* (*leader*)
□ a head of state un chef d'État
■ **Heads or tails? — Heads.** Pile ou face ? — Face.

to **head** VERB
▷ *see also* **head** NOUN
■ **to head for something** se diriger [45] vers quelque chose □ They headed for the church. Ils se sont dirigés vers l'église.

headache NOUN
■ **I've got a headache.** J'ai mal à la tête.

headlight NOUN
le phare *masc*

headline NOUN
le titre *masc*

headmaster NOUN
1 le directeur *masc* (*of private or primary school*)
2 le proviseur *masc* (*of state secondary school*)

headmistress NOUN
1 la directrice *fem* (*of private or primary school*)
2 le proviseur *masc* (*of state secondary school*)

headphones PL NOUN
les écouteurs *masc pl*

headquarters PL NOUN
le siège *masc sing* (*of organization*)

headteacher NOUN
1 le directeur *masc*
la directrice *fem* (*of private or primary school*)
2 le proviseur *masc* (*of state secondary school*)
□ She's a headteacher. Elle est proviseur.

to **heal** VERB
cicatriser [28]
□ The wound soon healed. La blessure a vite cicatrisé.

health NOUN
la santé *fem*
□ mental health la santé mentale

healthy ADJECTIVE
1 en bonne santé (*person*)
□ My grandparents are still very healthy. Mes grands-parents sont toujours en très bonne santé.
2 sain (FEM saine) (*climate, food*)
□ a healthy diet une alimentation saine

heap NOUN
le tas *masc*
□ a rubbish heap un tas d'ordures

to **hear** VERB
1 entendre [88]
□ He heard the dog bark. Il a entendu le chien aboyer. □ She can't hear very well. Elle entend mal. □ I heard that she was ill. J'ai entendu dire qu'elle était malade.
■ **to hear about something** entendre [88] parler de quelque chose
2 apprendre [65] (*news*)
□ Did you hear the good news? Est-ce que tu as appris la bonne nouvelle ?

h

■ **to hear from somebody** avoir [8] des nouvelles de quelqu'un □ I haven't heard from him recently. Je n'ai pas eu de ses nouvelles récemment.

heart NOUN
le cœur *masc*
□ My heart's beating very fast. J'ai le cœur qui bat très fort.
■ **to learn something by heart** apprendre [65] quelque chose par cœur
■ **hearts** (*in cards*) le cœur *sing* □ the ace of hearts l'as de cœur

heart attack NOUN
la crise cardiaque *fem*

heartbroken ADJECTIVE
■ **to be heartbroken** avoir [8] le cœur brisé

heat NOUN
▷ *see also* **heat** VERB
la chaleur *fem*

to **heat** VERB
▷ *see also* **heat** NOUN
faire [36] chauffer
□ Heat gently for 5 minutes. Faire chauffer à feu doux pendant cinq minutes.

to **heat up** VERB
1 faire [36] réchauffer (*cooked food*)
□ He heated the soup up. Il a fait réchauffer la soupe.
2 chauffer [28] (*water, oven*)
□ The water is heating up. L'eau chauffe.

heater NOUN
le radiateur *masc*
□ an electric heater un radiateur électrique

heather NOUN
la bruyère *fem*

heating NOUN
le chauffage *masc*

heaven NOUN
le paradis *masc*

heavily ADVERB
lourdement
□ The car was heavily loaded. La voiture était lourdement chargée.
■ **He drinks heavily.** C'est un gros buveur.

heavy ADJECTIVE
1 lourd (FEM lourde)
□ This bag's very heavy. Ce sac est très lourd.
■ **heavy rain** une grosse averse
2 chargé (FEM chargée) (*busy*)
□ I've got a very heavy week ahead. Je vais avoir une semaine très chargée.
■ **to be a heavy drinker** être [35] un gros buveur

he'd = he would, he had

hedge NOUN
la haie *fem*

hedgehog NOUN
le hérisson *masc*

heel NOUN
le talon *masc*

height NOUN
1 la taille *fem* (*of person*)
2 la hauteur *fem* (*of object*)
3 l'altitude *fem* (*of mountain*)

heir NOUN
l'héritier *masc*

heiress NOUN
l'héritière *fem*

held VERB ▷ *see* **hold**

helicopter NOUN
l'hélicoptère *masc*

hell NOUN
l'enfer *masc*

he'll = he will, he shall

hello EXCLAMATION
bonjour !

helmet NOUN
le casque *masc*

to **help** VERB
▷ *see also* **help** NOUN
aider [28]
□ Can you help me? Est-ce que vous pouvez m'aider ?
■ **Help!** Au secours !
■ **Help yourself!** Servez-vous !
■ **He can't help it.** Il n'y peut rien.

help NOUN
▷ *see also* **help** VERB
l'aide *fem*
□ Do you need any help? Vous avez besoin d'aide ?

help desk NOUN
le service d'assistance *masc*
■ **an IT help desk** un service d'assistance informatique

helpful ADJECTIVE
serviable (FEM serviable)
□ He was very helpful. Il a été très serviable.

helpline NOUN
le service d'assistance téléphonique *masc*
■ **a customer helpline** un service clients
□ Why don't you call the customer helpline? Pourquoi n'appelles-tu pas le service clients ?

hen NOUN
la poule *fem*

her ADJECTIVE
▷ *see also* **her** PRONOUN
son *masc*
□ her father son père
sa *fem*
□ her mother sa mère
ses *pl*
□ her parents ses parents

sa becomes **son** before a vowel sound.

h

her - high

■ **her friend** **1** (*male*) son ami **2** (*female*) son amie

> Do not use **son/sa/ses** with parts of the body.

□ She's going to wash her hair. Elle va se laver les cheveux. □ She's cleaning her teeth. Elle se brosse les dents. □ She's hurt her foot. Elle s'est fait mal au pied.

her PRONOUN

▷ *see also* **her** ADJECTIVE

1 la

□ I can see her. Je la vois. □ Look at her! Regarde-la !

l'

> **la** becomes **l'** before a vowel sound.

□ I saw her. Je l'ai vue.

2 lui

> Use **lui** when 'her' means 'to her'.

□ I gave her a book. Je lui ai donné un livre. □ I told her the truth. Je lui ai dit la vérité.

3 elle

> Use **elle** after prepositions.

□ I'm going with her. Je vais avec elle. □ He sat next to her. Il s'est assis à côté d'elle.

> **elle** is also used in comparisons.

□ I'm older than her. Je suis plus âgé qu'elle.

herb NOUN

l'herbe *fem*

■ **herbs** les fines herbes *fem pl* □ What herbs do you use in this sauce? Quelles fines herbes utilise-t-on pour cette sauce ?

here ADVERB

ici

□ I live here. J'habite ici.

■ **here is ...** voici ... □ Here's Elise. Voici Elise. □ Here he is! Le voici !

■ **here are ...** voici ... □ Here are the books. Voici les livres.

heritage NOUN

le patrimoine *masc*

hero NOUN

le héros *masc*

□ He's a real hero! C'est un véritable héros !

heroin NOUN

l'héroïne *fem*

□ Heroin is a hard drug. L'héroïne est une drogue dure.

■ **a heroin addict** un héroïnomane □ She's a heroin addict. C'est une héroïnomane.

heroine NOUN

l'héroïne *fem*

□ the heroine of the novel l'héroïne du roman

hers PRONOUN

le sien + *masc noun*

□ Is this her coat? — No, hers is black. C'est son manteau ? — Non, le sien est noir.

la sienne + *fem noun*

□ Is this her car? — No, hers is white. C'est sa voiture ? — Non, la sienne est blanche.

les siens + *masc pl noun*

□ my parents and hers mes parents et les siens

les siennes + *fem pl noun*

□ my shoes and hers mes chaussures et les siennes

■ **Is this hers?** C'est à elle ?

■ **This book is hers.** Ce livre est à elle.

■ **Whose is this? — It's hers.** C'est à qui ? — À elle.

herself PRONOUN

1 se

□ She's hurt herself. Elle s'est blessée.

2 elle (*after preposition*)

□ She talked mainly about herself. Elle a surtout parlé d'elle.

3 elle-même

□ She did it herself. Elle l'a fait elle-même.

■ **by herself** toute seule □ She doesn't like travelling by herself. Elle n'aime pas voyager toute seule.

he's = **he is, he has**

to **hesitate** VERB

hésiter [28]

heterosexual ADJECTIVE

hétérosexuel (FEM hétérosexuelle)

hi EXCLAMATION

salut !

hiccups PL NOUN

■ **to have hiccups** avoir [8] le hoquet

to **hide** VERB

se cacher [28]

□ He hid behind a bush. Il s'est caché derrière un buisson.

■ **to hide something** cacher [28] quelque chose □ Lucy hid the present. Lucy a caché le cadeau.

hide-and-seek NOUN

■ **to play hide-and-seek** jouer [28] à cache-cache

hideous ADJECTIVE

hideux (FEM hideuse)

hi-fi NOUN

la chaîne hi-fi *fem* (PL les chaînes hi-fi)

high ADJECTIVE, ADVERB

1 haut (FEM haute)

□ It's too high. C'est trop haut.

■ **How high is the wall?** Quelle est la hauteur du mur ?

■ **The wall's 2 metres high.** Le mur fait deux mètres de haut.

2 élevé (FEM élevée)

□ a high price un prix élevé □ a high temperature une température élevée

■ **at high speed** à grande vitesse

■ **It's very high in fat.** C'est très gras.

■ **She's got a very high voice.** Elle a la voix très aiguë.

higher education NOUN
l'enseignement supérieur *masc*

high-heeled ADJECTIVE
à hauts talons
□ high-heeled shoes des chaussures à hauts talons

high jump NOUN
le saut en hauteur *masc* (*sport*)

highlight NOUN
▷ *see also* **highlight** VERB
le clou *masc*
□ the highlight of the evening le clou de la soirée

to **highlight** VERB
▷ *see also* **highlight** NOUN
1 souligner [28] (*underline*)
2 surligner [28] (*with highlighter pen*)

highlighter NOUN
le surligneur *masc*

high-rise NOUN
la tour *fem*
□ I live in a high-rise. J'habite dans une tour.

high school NOUN
1 le collège *masc*
2 le lycée *masc*

> **DID YOU KNOW...?**
> In France, pupils go to a **collège** between the ages of 11 and 15, then to a **lycée** until the age of 18.

to **hijack** VERB
détourner [28]

hijacker NOUN
le pirate de l'air *masc*

hike NOUN
la randonnée *fem*

hiking NOUN
■ **to go hiking** faire [36] une randonnée

hilarious ADJECTIVE
hilarant (FEM hilarante)
□ It was hilarious! C'était hilarant !

hill NOUN
la colline *fem*
□ She walked up the hill. Elle a gravi la colline.

hill-walking NOUN
la randonnée de basse montagne *fem*
□ to go hill-walking faire de la randonnée de basse montagne

him PRONOUN
1 le
□ I can see him. Je le vois. □ Look at him! Regarde-le !
l'
> **le** becomes **l'** before a vowel sound.

□ I saw him. Je l'ai vu.
2 lui
> Use **lui** when 'him' means 'to him', and after prepositions.

□ I gave him a book. Je lui ai donné un livre. □ I told him the truth. Je lui ai dit la vérité. □ I'm going with him. Je vais avec lui. □ She sat next to him. Elle s'est assise à côté de lui.
> **lui** is also used in comparisons.

□ I'm older than him. Je suis plus âgé que lui.

himself PRONOUN
1 se
□ He's hurt himself. Il s'est blessé.
2 lui
□ He talked mainly about himself. Il a surtout parlé de lui.
3 lui-même
□ He did it himself. Il l'a fait lui-même.
■ **by himself** tout seul □ He was travelling by himself. Il voyageait tout seul.

Hindu ADJECTIVE
hindou (FEM hindoue)
□ a Hindu temple un temple hindou

hint NOUN
▷ *see also* **hint** VERB
l'allusion *fem*
■ **to drop a hint** faire [36] une allusion

to **hint** VERB
▷ *see also* **hint** NOUN
laisser [28] entendre
□ He hinted that something was going on. Il a laissé entendre qu'il se passait quelque chose.
■ **What are you hinting at?** Qu'est-ce que vous voulez dire par là ?

hip NOUN
la hanche *fem*

hippie NOUN
le/la hippie *masc/fem*

hippo NOUN
l'hippopotame *masc*

to **hire** VERB
▷ *see also* **hire** NOUN
1 louer [28]
□ to hire a car louer une voiture
2 engager [45] (*person*)
□ They hired a cleaner. Ils ont engagé une femme de ménage.

hire NOUN
▷ *see also* **hire** VERB
la location *fem*
■ **car hire** location de voitures
■ **for hire** à louer

hire car NOUN
la voiture de location *fem*

his ADJECTIVE

▷ see also **his** PRONOUN

son *masc*

□ his father son père

sa *fem*

□ his mother sa mère

ses *pl*

□ his parents ses parents

> **sa** becomes **son** before a vowel sound.

■ **his friend** **1** (*male*) son ami **2** (*female*) son amie

> Do not use **son/sa/ses** with parts of the body.

□ He's going to wash his hair. Il va se laver les cheveux. □ He's cleaning his teeth. Il se brosse les dents. □ He's hurt his foot. Il s'est fait mal au pied.

his PRONOUN

▷ see also **his** ADJECTIVE

le sien *masc*

□ Is this his coat? — No, his is black. C'est son manteau ? — Non, le sien est noir.

la sienne *fem*

□ Is this his car? — No, his is white. C'est sa voiture ? — Non, la sienne est blanche.

les siens *masc pl*

□ my parents and his mes parents et les siens

les siennes *fem pl*

□ my shoes and his mes chaussures et les siennes

■ **Is this his?** C'est à lui ?

■ **This book is his.** Ce livre est à lui.

■ **Whose is this? — It's his.** C'est à qui ? — À lui.

history NOUN

l'histoire *fem*

to hit VERB

▷ see also **hit** NOUN

1 frapper [28]

□ Andrew hit him. Andrew l'a frappé.

2 renverser [28]

□ He was hit by a car. Il a été renversé par une voiture.

3 toucher [28]

□ The arrow hit the target. La flèche a touché la cible.

hit NOUN

▷ see also **hit** VERB

1 le tube *masc* (*song*)

□ Beyoncé's latest hit le dernier tube de Beyoncé

2 le succès *masc* (*success*)

□ The film was a massive hit. Le film a eu un immense succès.

hitch NOUN

le contretemps *masc*

□ There's been a slight hitch. Il y a eu un léger contretemps.

to hitchhike VERB

faire [36] de l'auto-stop

hitchhiker NOUN

l'auto-stoppeur *masc*

l'auto-stoppeuse *fem*

hitchhiking NOUN

l'auto-stop *masc*

□ Hitchhiking can be dangerous. Il peut être dangereux de faire de l'auto-stop.

hit man NOUN

le tueur à gages *masc*

HIV-negative ADJECTIVE

séronégatif (FEM séronégative)

HIV-positive ADJECTIVE

séropositif (FEM séropositive)

hobby NOUN

le passe-temps favori *masc*

□ What are your hobbies? Quels sont tes passe-temps favoris ?

hockey NOUN

le hockey *masc*

□ I play hockey. Je joue au hockey.

to hold VERB

1 tenir [83] (*hold on to*)

□ She held the baby. Elle tenait le bébé.

2 contenir [83] (*contain*)

□ This bottle holds one litre. Cette bouteille contient un litre.

■ **to hold a meeting** avoir [8] une réunion

■ **Hold it!** (*wait*) Attends !

■ **to get hold of something** (*obtain*) trouver [28] quelque chose □ I couldn't get hold of it. Je n'ai pas réussi à en trouver.

to hold on VERB

1 tenir [83] bon (*keep hold*)

□ Hold on! I'll help you get down. Tiens bon ! Je vais t'aider à descendre.

■ **to hold on to something** se cramponner [28] à quelque chose □ He held on to the chair. Il se cramponnait à la chaise.

2 attendre [7] (*wait*)

□ Hold on, I'm coming! Attends, je viens !

■ **Hold on!** (*on telephone*) Ne quittez pas !

to hold up VERB

■ **to hold up one's hand** lever [43] la main

□ Pierre held up his hand. Pierre a levé la main.

■ **to hold somebody up** (*delay*) retenir [83] quelqu'un □ I was held up at the office. J'ai été retenu au bureau.

■ **to hold up a bank** (*rob*) braquer [28] une banque (*informal*)

hold-up NOUN

1 le hold-up *masc* (*at bank*)

2 le retard *masc* (*delay*)

3 le bouchon *masc* (*traffic jam*)

hole NOUN

le trou *masc*

holiday NOUN
1 les vacances *fem pl*
  □ Did you have a good holiday? Tu as passé de bonnes vacances ? □ our holidays in Italy nos vacances en Italie
  ■ **on holiday** en vacances □ to go on holiday partir en vacances □ We are on holiday. Nous sommes en vacances.
  ■ **the school holidays** les vacances scolaires
2 le jour férié *masc* (*public holiday*)
  □ Next Wednesday is a holiday. Mercredi prochain est un jour férié.
3 le jour de congé *masc* (*day off*)
  □ He took a day's holiday. Il a pris un jour de congé.
  ■ **a holiday camp** un camp de vacances

holiday home NOUN
la maison de vacances *fem*

Holland NOUN
la Hollande *fem*
  ■ **in Holland** en Hollande
  ■ **to Holland** en Hollande

hollow ADJECTIVE
creux (FEM creuse)

holly NOUN
le houx *masc*
  □ a sprig of holly un brin de houx

holy ADJECTIVE
saint (FEM sainte)

home NOUN
  ▷ see also **home** ADVERB
la maison *fem*
  ■ **at home** à la maison
  ■ **Make yourself at home.** Faites comme chez vous.
  ■ **My aunt's at home from 5 p.m.** Ma tante est chez elle à partir de cinq heures.

home ADVERB
  ▷ see also **home** NOUN
à la maison
  □ I'll be home at 5 o'clock. Je serai à la maison à cinq heures.
  ■ **to get home** rentrer [68'] □ What time did he get home? Il est rentré à quelle heure ?

home address NOUN
l'adresse *fem*
  □ What's your home address? Quelle est votre adresse ?

homeland NOUN
la patrie *fem*

homeless ADJECTIVE
sans abri
  ■ **the homeless** les sans-abri

home match NOUN
le match à domicile *masc*

homeopathy NOUN
l'homéopathie *fem*

home page NOUN
la page d'accueil *fem*

homesick ADJECTIVE
  ■ **to be homesick** avoir [8] le mal du pays

homework NOUN
les devoirs *masc pl*
  □ Have you done your homework? Est-ce que tu as fait tes devoirs ? □ my geography homework mes devoirs de géographie

homosexual ADJECTIVE
  ▷ see also **homosexual** NOUN
homosexuel (FEM homosexuelle)

homosexual NOUN
  ▷ see also **homosexual** ADJECTIVE
l'homosexuel *masc*
l'homosexuelle *fem*

honest ADJECTIVE
1 honnête (FEM honnête) (*trustworthy*)
  □ She's a very honest person. Elle est très honnête.
2 franc (FEM franche) (*sincere*)
  □ He was very honest with her. Il a été très franc avec elle.

honestly ADVERB
franchement
  □ I honestly don't know. Franchement, je n'en sais rien.

honesty NOUN
l'honnêteté *fem*

honey NOUN
le miel *masc*

honeymoon NOUN
la lune de miel *fem*

honour (US **honor**) NOUN
l'honneur *masc*

hood NOUN
1 la capuche *fem* (*on coat*)
2 le capot *masc* (US: *of car*)

hook NOUN
le crochet *masc*
  □ He hung the painting on the hook. Il a suspendu le tableau au crochet.
  ■ **to take the phone off the hook** décrocher [28] le téléphone
  ■ **a fish hook** un hameçon

hooligan NOUN
le voyou *masc* (PL les voyoux)

hooray EXCLAMATION
hourra !

Hoover® NOUN
l'aspirateur *masc*

to **hoover** VERB
passer [58] l'aspirateur
  □ to hoover the lounge passer l'aspirateur dans le salon

h

to **hope** VERB

▷ *see also* **hope** NOUN

espérer [34]

□ I hope he comes. J'espère qu'il va venir. □ I'm hoping for good marks in the exam. J'espère avoir de bonnes notes à l'examen.

■ **I hope so.** Je l'espère.

■ **I hope not.** J'espère que non.

hope NOUN

▷ *see also* **hope** VERB

l'espoir *masc*

■ **to give up hope** perdre [61] espoir □ Don't give up hope! Ne perds pas espoir !

hopeful ADJECTIVE

1 plein d'espoir (FEM pleine d'espoir)

□ I'm hopeful. Je suis plein d'espoir.

■ **He's hopeful of winning.** Il a bon espoir de gagner.

2 prometteur (FEM prometteuse) (*situation*)

□ The future looks hopeful. L'avenir semble prometteur.

hopefully ADVERB

avec un peu de chance

□ Hopefully he'll make it in time. Avec un peu de chance, il arrivera à temps.

hopeless ADJECTIVE

nul (FEM nulle)

□ I'm hopeless at maths. Je suis nul en maths.

horizon NOUN

l'horizon *masc*

horizontal ADJECTIVE

horizontal (FEM horizontale, MASC PL horizontaux)

horn NOUN

1 le klaxon *masc*

□ He sounded his horn. Il a klaxonné.

2 le cor *masc*

□ I play the horn. Je joue du cor.

horoscope NOUN

l'horoscope *masc*

horrible ADJECTIVE

horrible (FEM horrible)

□ What a horrible dress! Quelle robe horrible !

horrifying ADJECTIVE

effrayant (FEM effrayante)

horror NOUN

l'horreur *fem*

horror film NOUN

le film d'horreur *masc*

horse NOUN

le cheval *masc* (PL les chevaux)

horse-racing NOUN

les courses de chevaux *fem pl*

horseshoe NOUN

le fer à cheval *masc*

hose NOUN

le tuyau *masc* (PL les tuyaux)

□ a garden hose un tuyau d'arrosage

hosepipe NOUN

le tuyau d'arrosage *masc*

hospital NOUN

l'hôpital *masc* (PL les hôpitaux)

□ Take me to the hospital! Emmenez-moi à l'hôpital ! □ in hospital à l'hôpital

hospitality NOUN

l'hospitalité *fem*

host NOUN

l'hôte *masc*

l'hôtesse *fem*

□ Don't forget to thank your hosts. N'oublie pas de remercier tes hôtes.

hostage NOUN

l'otage *masc*

■ **to take somebody hostage** prendre [65] quelqu'un en otage

hostel NOUN

le foyer *masc* (*for refugees, homeless people*)

■ **a youth hostel** une auberge de jeunesse

hostile ADJECTIVE

hostile (FEM hostile)

hot ADJECTIVE

1 chaud (FEM chaude) (*warm*)

□ a hot bath un bain chaud □ a hot country un pays chaud

> When you are talking about a person being hot, you use **avoir chaud**.

□ I'm hot. J'ai chaud. □ I'm too hot. J'ai trop chaud.

> When you mean that the weather is hot, you use **faire chaud**.

□ It's hot. Il fait chaud. □ It's very hot today. Il fait très chaud aujourd'hui.

2 épicé (FEM épicée) (*spicy*)

□ a very hot curry un curry très épicé

hot dog NOUN

le hot-dog *masc*

hotel NOUN

l'hôtel *masc*

□ We stayed in a hotel. Nous avons logé à l'hôtel.

hour NOUN

l'heure *fem*

□ She always takes hours to get ready. Elle passe toujours des heures à se préparer.

■ **a quarter of an hour** un quart d'heure

■ **half an hour** une demi-heure

■ **two and a half hours** deux heures et demie

hourly ADJECTIVE, ADVERB

toutes les heures

□ There are hourly buses. Il y a des bus toutes les heures.

■ **to be paid hourly** être [35] payé à l'heure

house NOUN
la maison *fem*
□ Our house is at the end of the road. Notre maison est au bout de la rue.
- **at his house** chez lui
- **We stayed at their house.** Nous avons séjourné chez eux.

housewife NOUN
la femme au foyer *fem*
□ She's a housewife. Elle est femme au foyer.

housework NOUN
le ménage *masc*
- **to do the housework** faire [36] le ménage

hovercraft NOUN
l'aéroglisseur *masc*

how ADVERB
comment
□ How are you? Comment allez-vous ?
- **How many?** Combien ?
- **How many ...?** Combien de ... ? □ How many pupils are there in the class? Combien d'élèves y a-t-il dans la classe ?
- **How much?** Combien ?
- **How much ...?** Combien de ... ? □ How much sugar do you want? Combien de sucres voulez-vous ?
- **How old are you?** Quel âge as-tu ?
- **How far is it to Edinburgh?** Combien y a-t-il de kilomètres d'ici à Édimbourg ?
- **How long have you been here?** Depuis combien de temps êtes-vous là ?
- **How do you say 'apple' in French?** Comment dit-on « apple » en français ?

however CONJUNCTION
pourtant
□ This, however, isn't true. Pourtant, ce n'est pas vrai.

to **howl** VERB
hurler [28]

HTML NOUN
le langage HTML *masc*
□ an HTML document un document en langage HTML

to **hug** VERB
▷ see also **hug** NOUN
serrer [28] dans ses bras
□ He hugged her. Il l'a serrée dans ses bras.

hug NOUN
▷ see also **hug** VERB
- **to give somebody a hug** serrer [28] quelqu'un dans ses bras □ She gave them a hug. Elle les a serrés dans ses bras.

huge ADJECTIVE
immense (FEM immense)

to **hum** VERB
fredonner [28]

human ADJECTIVE
humain (FEM humaine)
□ the human body le corps humain

human being NOUN
l'être humain *masc*

humble ADJECTIVE
humble (FEM humble)

humour (US **humor**) NOUN
l'humour *masc*
- **to have a sense of humour** avoir [8] le sens de l'humour

hundred NUMBER
- **a hundred** cent □ a hundred euros cent euros
- **five hundred** cinq cents
- **five hundred and one** cinq cent un
- **hundreds of people** des centaines de personnes

hung VERB ▷ see **hang**

Hungarian NOUN
▷ see also **Hungarian** ADJECTIVE
1 le Hongrois *masc*
la Hongroise *fem* (*person*)
2 le hongrois *masc* (*language*)

Hungarian ADJECTIVE
▷ see also **Hungarian** NOUN
hongrois (FEM hongroise)
□ She's Hungarian. Elle est hongroise.

Hungary NOUN
la Hongrie *fem*
- **in Hungary** en Hongrie
- **to Hungary** en Hongrie

hunger NOUN
la faim *fem*

hungry ADJECTIVE
- **to be hungry** avoir [8] faim □ I'm hungry. J'ai faim.

to **hunt** VERB
1 chasser [28] (*animal*)
□ It's illegal to hunt foxes. Il est interdit de chasser le renard.
- **to go hunting** aller [3f] à la chasse
2 pourchasser [28] (*criminal*)
□ The police are hunting the killer. La police pourchasse le criminel.
- **to hunt for something** (*search*) chercher [28] quelque chose partout □ I hunted everywhere for that book. J'ai cherché ce livre partout.

hunting NOUN
la chasse *fem*
□ I'm against hunting. Je suis contre la chasse.
- **fox-hunting** la chasse au renard

hurdle NOUN
l'obstacle *masc*

hurricane NOUN
l'ouragan *masc*

hurry - hyphen

to **hurry** VERB

▷ *see also* **hurry** NOUN

se dépêcher [28]

□ Amber hurried back home. Amber s'est dépêchée de rentrer chez elle.

■ **Hurry up!** Dépêche-toi !

hurry NOUN

▷ *see also* **hurry** VERB

■ **to be in a hurry** être [35] pressé

■ **to do something in a hurry** faire [36] quelque chose en vitesse

■ **There's no hurry.** Rien ne presse.

to **hurt** VERB

▷ *see also* **hurt** ADJECTIVE

■ **to hurt somebody** **1** (*physically*) faire [36] mal à quelqu'un □ You're hurting me! Tu me fais mal ! **2** (*emotionally*) blesser [28] quelqu'un □ His remarks really hurt me. Ses remarques m'ont vraiment blessé.

■ **to hurt oneself** se faire [36] mal □ I fell over and hurt myself. Je me suis fait mal en tombant.

■ **That hurts.** Ça fait mal. □ It hurts to have a tooth out. Ça fait mal de se faire arracher une dent.

■ **My leg hurts.** J'ai mal à la jambe.

hurt ADJECTIVE

▷ *see also* **hurt** VERB

blessé (FEM blessée)

□ Is he badly hurt? Est-ce qu'il est grièvement blessé ? □ He was hurt in the leg. Il a été blessé à la jambe. □ I was hurt by what he said. J'ai été blessé par ce qu'il a dit.

■ **Luckily, nobody got hurt.** Heureusement, il n'y a pas eu de blessés.

husband NOUN

le mari *masc*

hut NOUN

la hutte *fem*

hybrid ADJECTIVE

hybride (FEM hybride)

□ a hybrid car une voiture hybride □ hybrid learning l'enseignement hybride □ hybrid working le travail hybride

hymn NOUN

le cantique *masc*

hypermarket NOUN

l'hypermarché *masc*

hyphen NOUN

le trait d'union *masc*

I PRONOUN

1 je

□ I speak French. Je parle français.

> **je** changes to **j'** before a vowel and most words beginning with 'h'.

j'

□ I love cats. J'aime les chats.

2 moi

□ Lily and I Lily et moi

ice NOUN

1 la glace *fem*

□ There was ice on the lake. Il y avait de la glace sur le lac.

2 le verglas *masc* (*on road*)

iceberg NOUN

l'iceberg *masc*

icebox NOUN (US)

le frigo *masc*

ice cream NOUN

la glace *fem*

□ vanilla ice cream la glace à la vanille

ice cube NOUN

le glaçon *masc*

ice hockey NOUN

le hockey sur glace *masc*

Iceland NOUN

l'Islande *fem*

■ **in Iceland** en Islande

■ **to Iceland** en Islande

ice lolly NOUN

la glace à l'eau *fem*

ice rink NOUN

la patinoire *fem*

ice-skating NOUN

le patinage sur glace *masc*

■ **to go ice-skating** faire [36] du patin à glace

icing NOUN

le glaçage *masc* (*on cake*)

■ **icing sugar** le sucre glace

icon NOUN

l'icône *fem*

ICT NOUN (= *information and communications technology*)

l'informatique *fem*

icy ADJECTIVE

glacial (FEM glaciale, MASC PL glaciaux)

□ There was an icy wind. Il y avait un vent glacial.

■ **The roads are icy.** Il y a du verglas sur les routes.

I'd = **I had**, **I would**

idea NOUN

l'idée *fem*

□ Good idea! Bonne idée !

ideal ADJECTIVE

idéal (FEM idéale, MASC PL idéaux)

identical ADJECTIVE

identique (FEM identique)

identification NOUN

l'identification *fem*

to identify VERB

identifier [19]

identity card NOUN

la carte d'identité *fem*

idiot NOUN

l'idiot *masc*

l'idiote *fem*

idiotic ADJECTIVE

stupide (FEM stupide)

idle ADJECTIVE

fainéant (FEM fainéante) (*lazy*)

i.e. ABBREVIATION

c.-à-d. (= *c'est-à-dire*)

if CONJUNCTION

si

□ You can have it if you like. Tu peux le prendre si tu veux.

s'

> **si** changes to **s'** before **il** and **ils**.

□ Do you know if he's there? Savez-vous s'il est là ?

■ **if only** si seulement □ If only I had more money! Si seulement j'avais plus d'argent !

■ **if not** sinon □ Are you coming? If not, I'll go with Zhu. Est-ce que tu viens ? Sinon, j'irai avec Zhu.

ignorant ADJECTIVE

ignorant (FEM ignorante)

to ignore VERB

■ **to ignore something** ne tenir [83] aucun compte de quelque chose □ She ignored my advice. Elle n'a tenu aucun compte de mes conseils.

■ **to ignore somebody** ignorer [28] quelqu'un □ She saw me, but she ignored me. Elle m'a vu, mais elle m'a ignoré.

■ **Just ignore him!** Ne fais pas attention à lui !

ill ADJECTIVE

malade (FEM malade) (*sick*)

■ **to be taken ill** tomber [84£] malade □ She was taken ill while on holiday. Elle est tombée malade pendant qu'elle était en vacances.

I'll = I will

illegal ADJECTIVE

illégal (FEM illégale, MASC PL illégaux)

illegible ADJECTIVE

illisible (FEM illisible)

illness NOUN

la maladie *fem*

to **ill-treat** VERB

maltraiter [28]

illusion NOUN

l'illusion *fem*

illustration NOUN

l'illustration *fem*

image NOUN

l'image *fem*

□ She wants to change her image. Elle veut changer son image.

imagination NOUN

l'imagination *fem*

to **imagine** VERB

imaginer [28]

□ You can imagine how I felt! Tu peux imaginer ce que j'ai ressenti ! □ Is he angry? — I imagine so. Est-ce qu'il est en colère ? — J'imagine que oui.

to **imitate** VERB

imiter [28]

imitation NOUN

l'imitation *fem*

immediate ADJECTIVE

immédiat (FEM immédiate)

immediately ADVERB

immédiatement

□ I'll do it immediately. Je vais le faire immédiatement.

immigrant NOUN

l'immigré *masc*

l'immigrée *fem*

immigration NOUN

l'immigration *fem*

immoral ADJECTIVE

immoral (FEM immorale, MASC PL immoraux)

impartial ADJECTIVE

impartial (FEM impartiale, MASC PL impartiaux)

impatience NOUN

l'impatience *fem*

impatient ADJECTIVE

impatient (FEM impatiente)

■ **to get impatient** s'impatienter [28] □ People are getting impatient. Les gens commencent à s'impatienter.

impatiently ADVERB

avec impatience

□ We waited impatiently. Nous avons attendu avec impatience.

impersonal ADJECTIVE

impersonnel (FEM impersonnelle)

importance NOUN

l'importance *fem*

important ADJECTIVE

important (FEM importante)

impossible ADJECTIVE

impossible (FEM impossible)

to **impress** VERB

impressionner [28]

□ She's trying to impress you. Elle essaie de t'impressionner.

impressed ADJECTIVE

impressionné (FEM impressionnée)

□ I'm very impressed! Je suis très impressionné !

impression NOUN

l'impression *fem*

□ I was under the impression that ... J'avais l'impression que ...

impressive ADJECTIVE

impressionnant (FEM impressionnante)

to **improve** VERB

1 améliorer [28] (*make better*)

□ They have improved the sports facilities. Ils ont amélioré les installations sportives.

2 s'améliorer [28] (*get better*)

□ The weather is improving. Le temps s'améliore. □ My French has improved. Mon français s'est amélioré.

improvement NOUN

1 l'amélioration *fem* (*of condition*)

□ It's a great improvement. C'est une nette amélioration.

2 le progrès *masc* (*of learner*)

□ There's been an improvement in his physics. Il a fait des progrès en physique.

in PREPOSITION, ADVERB

There are several ways of translating 'in'. Scan the examples to find one that is similar to what you want to say. For other expressions with 'in', see the verbs 'go', 'come', 'get', 'give' etc.

1 dans

□ in the house dans la maison □ in my bag

dans mon sac □ in the sixties dans les années
soixante □ I'll see you in three weeks. Je te verrai
dans trois semaines.

2 à
□ in the country à la campagne □ in school à
l'école □ in hospital à l'hôpital □ in Cardiff à
Cardiff □ in spring au printemps □ in the sun au
soleil □ in the shade à l'ombre □ in a loud voice
à voix haute □ the boy in the blue shirt le garçon
à la chemise bleue □ It was written in pencil.
C'était écrit au crayon.

3 en
□ in French en français □ in summer en été □ in
May en mai □ in 2019 en deux mille dix-neuf
□ I did it in three hours. Je l'ai fait en trois
heures. □ in town en ville □ in prison en prison
□ in tears en larmes □ in good condition en
bon état

> When 'in' refers to a country which is
> feminine, use **en**; when the country is
> masculine, use **au**; when the country is
> plural, use **aux**.

□ in France en France □ in Portugal au Portugal
□ in the United States aux États-Unis

4 de
□ the best pupil in the class le meilleur élève
de la classe □ the best team in the world la
meilleure équipe du monde □ the tallest person
in the family le plus grand de la famille □ at
4 o'clock in the afternoon à quatre heures de
l'après-midi □ at 6 in the morning à six heures
du matin
■ **in the afternoon** l'après-midi
■ **You look good in that dress.** Tu es jolie avec
cette robe.
■ **in time** à temps □ We arrived in time for
dinner. Nous sommes arrivés à temps pour le
dîner.
■ **in here** ici □ It's hot in here. Il fait chaud ici.
■ **in the rain** sous la pluie
■ **one person in ten** une personne sur dix
■ **to be in** (at home, work) être [35] là □ He
wasn't in. Il n'était pas là.
■ **to ask somebody in** inviter [28] quelqu'un
à entrer

inaccurate ADJECTIVE
inexact (FEM inexacte)

inadequate ADJECTIVE
inadéquat (FEM inadéquate) (measures, resources)
■ **I felt completely inadequate.** Je ne me
sentais absolument pas à la hauteur.

inbox NOUN
la boîte de réception fem

incentive NOUN
■ **There is no incentive to work.** Il n'y a rien
qui incite à travailler.

inch NOUN
le pouce masc

> **DID YOU KNOW...?**
> In France, measurements are in metres and
> centimetres rather than feet and inches. An
> inch is about 2.5 centimetres.

■ **6 inches** quinze centimètres

incident NOUN
l'incident masc

inclined ADJECTIVE
■ **to be inclined to do something** avoir [8]
tendance à faire quelque chose □ He's inclined
to be lazy. Il a tendance à être paresseux. □ I'm
inclined to agree. J'aurais tendance à être
d'accord.

to **include** VERB
comprendre [65]
□ Service is not included. Le service n'est pas
compris.

including PREPOSITION
compris
□ It will be 200 euros, including tax. Ça coûtera
deux cents euros, toutes taxes comprises.

inclusive ADJECTIVE
inclus (FEM incluse)
□ from Monday to Thursday inclusive de lundi à
jeudi inclus
■ **inclusive of tax** taxes comprises

income NOUN
le revenu masc

income tax NOUN
l'impôt sur le revenu masc

incompetent ADJECTIVE
incompétent (FEM incompétente)

incomplete ADJECTIVE
incomplet (FEM incomplète)

inconsistent ADJECTIVE
incohérent (FEM incohérente)

inconvenience NOUN
■ **I don't want to cause any inconvenience.**
Je ne veux pas vous déranger.

inconvenient ADJECTIVE
■ **That's very inconvenient for me.** Ça ne
m'arrange pas du tout.

incorrect ADJECTIVE
incorrect (FEM incorrecte)

increase NOUN
▷ see also **increase** VERB
l'augmentation fem
□ an increase in road accidents une
augmentation des accidents de la route

to **increase** VERB
▷ see also **increase** NOUN
augmenter [28]

incredible ADJECTIVE
incroyable (FEM incroyable)

indecisive ADJECTIVE
indécis (FEM indécise) (person)

indeed - informal

indeed ADVERB
vraiment
□ It's very hard indeed. C'est vraiment très difficile.
■ **Know what I mean? — Indeed I do.** Tu vois ce que je veux dire ? — Oui, tout à fait.
■ **Thank you very much indeed!** Merci beaucoup !

independence NOUN
l'indépendance *fem*

independent ADJECTIVE
indépendant (FEM indépendante)
■ **an independent school** une école privée

index NOUN
l'index *masc* (*in book*)

index finger NOUN
l'index *masc*

India NOUN
l'Inde *fem*
■ **in India** en Inde
■ **to India** en Inde

Indian NOUN
▷ see also **Indian** ADJECTIVE
l'Indien *masc*
l'Indienne *fem* (*person*)
■ **an American Indian** un Indien d'Amérique

Indian ADJECTIVE
▷ see also **Indian** NOUN
indien (FEM indienne)

to **indicate** VERB
indiquer [28]

indicator NOUN
le clignotant *masc* (*on car*)
□ Put your indicator on. Mets ton clignotant.

indigestion NOUN
l'indigestion *fem*
■ **I've got indigestion.** J'ai une indigestion.

individual ADJECTIVE
individuel (FEM individuelle)

indoor ADJECTIVE
■ **an indoor swimming pool** une piscine couverte

indoors ADVERB
à l'intérieur
□ They're indoors. Ils sont à l'intérieur.
■ **to go indoors** rentrer [68'] □ We'd better go indoors. Nous ferions mieux de rentrer.

industrial ADJECTIVE
industriel (FEM industrielle)

industrial estate NOUN
la zone industrielle *fem*

industry NOUN
l'industrie *fem*
□ the tourist industry l'industrie du tourisme
□ the oil industry l'industrie pétrolière

inefficient ADJECTIVE
inefficace (FEM inefficace)

inevitable ADJECTIVE
inévitable (FEM inévitable)

inexpensive ADJECTIVE
bon marché (FEM+PL bon marché)
□ an inexpensive hotel un hôtel bon marché
□ inexpensive holidays des vacances bon marché

inexperienced ADJECTIVE
inexpérimenté (FEM inexpérimentée)

infant school NOUN
■ **He's just started at infant school.** Il vient d'entrer au cours préparatoire.

> **DID YOU KNOW...?**
> **CP (cours préparatoire)** is the equivalent of first-year infants, and **CE1 (cours élémentaire première année)** the equivalent of second-year infants.

infection NOUN
l'infection *fem*
□ an ear infection une infection de l'oreille
■ **a throat infection** une angine

infectious ADJECTIVE
contagieux (FEM contagieuse)
□ It's not infectious. Ce n'est pas contagieux.

infinitive NOUN
l'infinitif *masc*

infirmary NOUN
l'hôpital *masc* (PL les hôpitaux)

inflatable ADJECTIVE
gonflable (FEM gonflable) (*mattress, dinghy*)

inflation NOUN
l'inflation *fem*

influence NOUN
▷ see also **influence** VERB
l'influence *fem*
□ He's a bad influence on her. Il a mauvaise influence sur elle.

to **influence** VERB
▷ see also **influence** NOUN
influencer [12]

influencer NOUN
l'influenceur *masc*
l'influenceuse *fem* (*social media*)

influenza NOUN
la grippe *fem*

to **inform** VERB
informer [28]
■ **to inform somebody of something** informer [28] quelqu'un de quelque chose
□ Nobody informed me that the class had been cancelled. Personne ne m'a informé de l'annulation du cours.

informal ADJECTIVE
1 décontracté (FEM décontractée) (*person, party*)
2 familier (FEM familière) (*colloquial*)

□ informal language le langage familier
■ **an informal visit** une visite non officielle

information NOUN
les renseignements *masc pl*
□ important information les renseignements importants
■ **a piece of information** un renseignement
■ **Could you give me some information about trains to Paris?** Pourriez-vous me renseigner sur les trains pour Paris ?

information office NOUN
le bureau des renseignements *masc* (PL les bureaux des renseignements)

information technology NOUN
l'informatique *fem*

infuriating ADJECTIVE
exaspérant (FEM exaspérante)

ingenious ADJECTIVE
ingénieux (FEM ingénieuse)

ingredient NOUN
l'ingrédient *masc*

inhabitant NOUN
l'habitant *masc*
l'habitante *fem*

inhaler NOUN
l'inhalateur
□ I mustn't forget my inhaler. Il ne faut pas que j'oublie mon inhalateur.

to **inherit** VERB
hériter [28] de
□ She inherited her father's house. Elle a hérité de la maison de son père.

initials PL NOUN
les initiales *fem pl*
□ Her initials are CDT. Ses initiales sont CDT.

initiative NOUN
l'initiative *fem*

to **inject** VERB
injecter [28] (*drug*)

injection NOUN
la piqûre *fem*

to **injure** VERB
blesser [28]

injured ADJECTIVE
blessé (FEM blessée)

injury NOUN
la blessure *fem*

> **BE CAREFUL!**
> Do not translate **injury** by the French word **injure**.

injury time NOUN
les arrêts de jeu *masc pl*

injustice NOUN
l'injustice *fem*

ink NOUN
l'encre *fem*

in-laws PL NOUN
les beaux-parents *masc pl*

inn NOUN
l'auberge *fem*

inner ADJECTIVE
intérieur (FEM intérieure)
■ **the inner city** les quartiers déshérités du centre ville

inner tube NOUN
la chambre à air *fem*

innocent ADJECTIVE
innocent (FEM innocente)

inquest NOUN
l'enquête *fem*

to **inquire** VERB
■ **to inquire about something** se renseigner [28] sur quelque chose □ I'm going to inquire about train times. Je vais me renseigner sur les horaires des trains.

inquiries office NOUN
le bureau des renseignements *masc* (PL les bureaux des renseignements)

inquiry NOUN
■ **to make inquiries about something** faire [36] des demandes de renseignement
□ 'inquiries' « renseignements »

inquisitive ADJECTIVE
curieux (FEM curieuse)

insane ADJECTIVE
fou (FEM folle)

> **fou** changes to **fol** before a vowel and most words beginning with 'h'.

inscription NOUN
l'inscription *fem*

insect NOUN
l'insecte *masc*

insect repellent NOUN
l'insectifuge *masc*

insensitive ADJECTIVE
indélicat (FEM indélicate)
□ That was a bit insensitive of you. C'était un peu indélicat de ta part.

inside NOUN
▷ *see also* **inside** ADVERB, PREPOSITION
l'intérieur *masc*

inside ADVERB, PREPOSITION
▷ *see also* **inside** NOUN
à l'intérieur
□ They're inside. Ils sont à l'intérieur. □ inside the house à l'intérieur de la maison
■ **to go inside** rentrer [68¹]
■ **Come inside!** Rentrez !

insincere ADJECTIVE
peu sincère (FEM peu sincère)

to **insist** VERB
insister [28]

i

□ I didn't want to, but he insisted. Je ne voulais pas, mais il a insisté.

■ **to insist on doing something** insister [28] pour faire quelque chose □ She insisted on paying. Elle a insisté pour payer.

■ **He insisted he was innocent.** Il affirmait qu'il était innocent.

inspector NOUN

l'inspecteur *masc* (*police*)

□ Inspector Jill Brown l'inspecteur Jill Brown

■ **ticket inspector** le contrôleur (*on trains*)

instalment NOUN

1 le versement *masc* (*payment*)

□ to pay in instalments payer en plusieurs versements

2 l'épisode *masc* (*episode*)

instance NOUN

■ **for instance** par exemple

instant ADJECTIVE

immédiat (FEM immédiate)

□ It was an instant success. Ça a été un succès immédiat.

■ **instant coffee** le café instantané

instantly ADVERB

tout de suite

instead ADVERB

■ **instead of 1** (*followed by noun*) à la place de □ He went instead of Finn. Il y est allé à la place de Finn. **2** (*followed by verb*) au lieu de □ We played tennis instead of going swimming. Nous avons joué au tennis au lieu d'aller nager.

■ **The pool was closed, so we played tennis instead.** La piscine était fermée, alors nous avons joué au tennis.

instinct NOUN

l'instinct *masc*

institute NOUN

l'institut *masc*

institution NOUN

l'institution *fem*

to **instruct** VERB

■ **to instruct somebody to do something** donner [28] l'ordre à quelqu'un de faire quelque chose □ She instructed us to wait outside. Elle nous a donné l'ordre d'attendre dehors.

instructions PL NOUN

1 les instructions *fem pl*

□ Follow the instructions carefully. Suivez soigneusement les instructions.

2 le mode d'emploi *masc sing* (*booklet*)

□ Where are the instructions? Où est le mode d'emploi ?

instructor NOUN

le moniteur *masc*

la monitrice *fem*

□ a skiing instructor un moniteur de ski □ a driving instructor un moniteur d'auto-école

instrument NOUN

l'instrument *masc*

□ Do you play an instrument? Est-ce que tu joues d'un instrument ?

insufficient ADJECTIVE

insuffisant (FEM insuffisante)

insulin NOUN

l'insuline *fem*

insult NOUN

▷ see also **insult** VERB

l'insulte *fem*

to **insult** VERB

▷ see also **insult** NOUN

insulter [28]

insurance NOUN

l'assurance *fem*

□ his car insurance son assurance automobile

■ **an insurance policy** une police d'assurance

intelligent ADJECTIVE

intelligent (FEM intelligente)

to **intend** VERB

■ **to intend to do something** avoir [8] l'intention de faire quelque chose □ I intend to do geography at university. J'ai l'intention d'étudier la géographie à l'université.

intense ADJECTIVE

intense (FEM intense)

intensive ADJECTIVE

intensif (FEM intensive)

intention NOUN

l'intention *fem*

intercom NOUN

l'interphone *masc*

interest NOUN

▷ see also **interest** VERB

l'intérêt *masc*

□ to show an interest in something manifester de l'intérêt pour quelque chose

■ **What interests do you have?** Quels sont tes centres d'intérêt ?

■ **My main interest is music.** Ce qui m'intéresse le plus c'est la musique.

to **interest** VERB

▷ see also **interest** NOUN

intéresser [28]

□ It doesn't interest me. Ça ne m'intéresse pas.

■ **to be interested in something** s'intéresser [28] à quelque chose □ I'm not interested in politics. Je ne m'intéresse pas à la politique.

interesting ADJECTIVE

intéressant (FEM intéressante)

interior NOUN

l'intérieur *masc*

interior designer NOUN

l'architecte d'intérieur *masc/fem*

intermediate ADJECTIVE

moyen (FEM moyenne) (*course, level*)

internal ADJECTIVE
interne (FEM interne)

international ADJECTIVE
international (FEM internationale, MASC PL internationaux)

internet NOUN
l'Internet *masc*
□ on the internet sur Internet

internet user NOUN
l'internaute *masc/fem*

to **interpret** VERB
faire [36] l'interprète
□ Jack interpreted into English for his friend. Jack a fait l'interprète en anglais pour son ami.

interpreter NOUN
l'interprète *masc/fem*

to **interrupt** VERB
interrompre [75]

interruption NOUN
l'interruption *fem*

interval NOUN
l'entracte *masc* (*in play, concert*)

interview NOUN
▷ *see also* **interview** VERB
1 l'interview *fem* (*on TV, radio*)
2 l'entretien *masc* (*for job*)

to **interview** VERB
▷ *see also* **interview** NOUN
interviewer [28] (*on TV, radio*)
□ I was interviewed on the radio. J'ai été interviewé à la radio.

interviewer NOUN
l'interviewer *masc* (*on TV, radio*)

intimate ADJECTIVE
intime (FEM intime)

into PREPOSITION
1 dans
□ He got into the car. Il est monté dans la voiture.
2 en
□ I'm going into town. Je vais en ville.
□ Translate it into French. Traduisez ça en français. □ Divide into two groups. Répartissez-vous en deux groupes.

to **introduce** VERB
présenter [28]
□ I'd like to introduce Michelle Davies. Je vous présente Michelle Davies. □ He introduced me to his parents. Il m'a présenté à ses parents.

introduction NOUN
l'introduction *fem* (*in book*)

intruder NOUN
l'intrus *masc*
l'intruse *fem*

intuition NOUN
l'intuition *fem*

to **invade** VERB
envahir [38]

invalid NOUN
le/la malade *masc/fem*

to **invent** VERB
inventer [28]

invention NOUN
l'invention *fem*

inventor NOUN
l'inventeur *masc*
l'inventrice *fem*

investigation NOUN
l'enquête *fem* (*police*)

investment NOUN
l'investissement *masc*
□ They bought the house as an investment. Ils ont acheté la maison comme investissement.

invigilator NOUN
le surveillant *masc*
la surveillante *fem*

invisible ADJECTIVE
invisible (FEM invisible)

invitation NOUN
l'invitation *fem*

to **invite** VERB
inviter [28]
□ He's not invited. Il n'est pas invité. □ To invite somebody to a party. Inviter quelqu'un à une fête.

to **involve** VERB
nécessiter [28]
□ His job involves a lot of travelling. Son travail nécessite de nombreux déplacements.
■ **to be involved in something** (*crime*) être [35] impliqué dans quelque chose
■ **to be involved with somebody** (*in relationship*) avoir [8] une relation avec quelqu'un

iPad® NOUN
l'iPad® *masc*

iPhone® NOUN
l'iPhone® *masc*

iPod® NOUN
l'iPod® *masc*

IQ NOUN (= *intelligence quotient*)
le Q.I. *masc* (= *quotient intellectuel*)

Iran NOUN
l'Iran *masc*
■ **in Iran** en Iran

Iranian NOUN
▷ *see also* **Iranian** ADJECTIVE
l'Iranien *masc*
l'Iranienne *fem*
■ **the Iranians** les Iraniens

Iranian ADJECTIVE
▷ *see also* **Iranian** NOUN
iranien (FEM iranienne)

i

Iraq – it

Iraq NOUN
l'Irak *masc*
■ **in Iraq** en Irak

Iraqi NOUN
▷ *see also* **Iraqi** ADJECTIVE
l'Irakien *masc*
l'Irakienne *fem*

Iraqi ADJECTIVE
▷ *see also* **Iraqi** NOUN
irakien (FEM irakienne)

Ireland NOUN
l'Irlande *fem*
■ **in Ireland** en Irlande
■ **to Ireland** en Irlande
■ **I'm from Ireland.** Je suis irlandais.

Irish NOUN
▷ *see also* **Irish** ADJECTIVE
l'irlandais *masc* (*language*)
■ **the Irish** (*people*) les Irlandais

Irish ADJECTIVE
▷ *see also* **Irish** NOUN
irlandais (FEM irlandaise)
□ Irish music la musique irlandaise

Irishman NOUN
l'Irlandais *masc*

Irishwoman NOUN
l'Irlandaise *fem*

iron NOUN
▷ *see also* **iron** VERB
1 le fer *masc* (*metal*)
2 le fer à repasser *masc* (*for clothes*)

to iron VERB
▷ *see also* **iron** NOUN
repasser [28]

ironic ADJECTIVE
ironique (FEM ironique)

ironing NOUN
le repassage *masc*
□ to do the ironing faire le repassage

ironing board NOUN
la planche à repasser *fem*

ironmonger's NOUN
la quincaillerie *fem*

ironmonger's shop NOUN
la quincaillerie *fem*

irrelevant ADJECTIVE
hors de propos
□ That's irrelevant. C'est hors de propos.

irresponsible ADJECTIVE
irresponsable (FEM irresponsable)
□ That was irresponsible of him. C'était irresponsable de sa part.

irritating ADJECTIVE
irritant (FEM irritante)

is VERB ▷ *see* **be**

Islam NOUN
l'Islam *masc*

Islamic ADJECTIVE
islamique (FEM islamique)
□ Islamic law la loi islamique
■ **Islamic fundamentalists** les intégristes musulmans

island NOUN
l'île *fem*

isle NOUN
■ **the Isle of Man** l'île de Man *fem*
■ **the Isle of Wight** l'île de Wight *fem*

isolated ADJECTIVE
isolé (FEM isolée)

ISP NOUN (= *internet service provider*)
le fournisseur d'accès à Internet *masc*

Israel NOUN
Israël *masc*
■ **in Israel** en Israël

Israeli ADJECTIVE
▷ *see also* **Israeli** NOUN
israélien (FEM israélienne)

Israeli NOUN
▷ *see also* **Israeli** ADJECTIVE
l'Israélien *masc*
l'Israélienne *fem*

issue NOUN
▷ *see also* **issue** VERB
1 la question *fem* (*matter*)
□ a controversial issue une question controversée
2 le numéro *masc* (*of magazine*)

to issue VERB
▷ *see also* **issue** NOUN
distribuer [28] (*equipment, supplies*)

it PRONOUN

> Remember to check if 'it' stands for a masculine or feminine noun.

1 il
□ Where's my book? — It's on the table. Où est mon livre ? — Il est sur la table.
elle
□ When does the library close? — It closes at 8. La bibliothèque ferme à quelle heure ? — Elle ferme à vingt heures.

> Use **le** or **la** when 'it' is the object of the sentence. **le** and **la** change to **l'** before a vowel and most words beginning with 'h'.

2 le
□ There's a croissant left. Do you want it? Il reste un croissant. Tu le veux ?
la
□ I don't want this apple. Take it. Je ne veux pas de cette pomme. Prends-la.

l'

□ It's a good film. Did you see it? C'est un bon film. L'as-tu vu ? □ He's got a new car. — Yes, I saw it. Il a une nouvelle voiture. — Oui, je l'ai vue.

■ **It's raining.** Il pleut.

■ **It's 6 o'clock.** Il est six heures.

■ **It's Friday tomorrow.** Demain c'est vendredi.

■ **Who is it? — It's me.** Qui est-ce ? — C'est moi.

■ **It's expensive.** C'est cher.

Italian NOUN

▷ see also **Italian** ADJECTIVE

1 l'Italien *masc*
l'Italienne *fem* (*person*)

2 l'italien *masc* (*language*)

Italian ADJECTIVE

▷ see also **Italian** NOUN

italien (FEM italienne)

Italy NOUN

l'Italie *fem*

■ **in Italy** en Italie

■ **to Italy** en Italie

to **itch** VERB

■ **It itches.** Ça me démange.

■ **My head's itching.** J'ai des démangeaisons à la tête.

itchy ADJECTIVE

■ **My arm is itchy.** J'ai des fourmis dans le bras.

it'd = **it had**, **it would**

item NOUN

l'article *masc* (*object*)

itinerary NOUN

l'itinéraire *masc*

it'll = **it will**

its ADJECTIVE

Remember to check if 'its' refers to a masculine, feminine or plural noun.

son *masc*

□ What's its name? Quel est son nom ?

sa *fem*

□ Every thing in its place. Chaque chose à sa place.

ses *pl*

□ The dog is losing its hair. Le chien perd ses poils.

it's = **it is**, **it has**

itself PRONOUN

se

se changes to **s'** before a vowel and most words beginning with 'h'.

s'

□ The heating switches itself off. Le chauffage s'arrête automatiquement.

I've = **I have**

Jj

jab NOUN
la piqûre *fem* (*injection*)

jack NOUN
1 le cric *masc* (*for car*)
2 le valet *masc* (*playing card*)

jacket NOUN
la veste *fem*
■ **jacket potatoes** les pommes de terre en robe des champs

jackpot NOUN
le gros lot *masc*
□ to win the jackpot gagner le gros lot

jail NOUN
▷ *see also* **jail** VERB
la prison *fem*
■ **to go to jail** aller [3] en prison

to **jail** VERB
▷ *see also* **jail** NOUN
emprisonner [28]

jam NOUN
la confiture *fem*
□ strawberry jam la confiture de fraises
■ **a traffic jam** un embouteillage

jam jar NOUN
le pot à confiture *masc*

jammed ADJECTIVE
coincé (FEM coincée)
□ The window's jammed. La fenêtre est coincée.

jam-packed ADJECTIVE
bondé (FEM bondée)
□ The shopping centre was jam-packed. Le centre commercial était bondé.

janitor NOUN
le/la concierge *masc/fem*
□ He's a janitor. Il est concierge.

January NOUN
janvier *masc*
■ **in January** en janvier

Japan NOUN
le Japon *masc*
■ **in Japan** au Japon
■ **from Japan** du Japon

Japanese NOUN
▷ *see also* **Japanese** ADJECTIVE
1 le Japonais *masc*
la Japonaise *fem* (*person*)

■ **the Japanese** les Japonais
2 le japonais *masc* (*language*)

Japanese ADJECTIVE
▷ *see also* **Japanese** NOUN
japonais (FEM japonaise)

jar NOUN
le bocal *masc* (PL les bocaux)
□ an empty jar un bocal vide
■ **a jar of honey** un pot de miel

jaundice NOUN
la jaunisse *fem*

javelin NOUN
le javelot *masc*

jaw NOUN
la mâchoire *fem*

jazz NOUN
le jazz *masc*

jealous ADJECTIVE
jaloux (FEM jalouse)

jeans PL NOUN
le jean *masc sing*

Jehovah's Witness NOUN
le témoin de Jéhovah *masc*
□ She's a Jehovah's Witness. Elle est témoin de Jéhovah.

Jello® NOUN (US)
la gelée *fem*

jelly NOUN
la gelée *fem*

jellyfish NOUN
la méduse *fem*

jersey NOUN
le pull-over *masc* (*pullover*)

Jesus NOUN
Jésus *masc*

jet NOUN
le jet *masc* (*plane*)

jetlag NOUN
■ **to be suffering from jetlag** être [35] sous le coup du décalage horaire

jetty NOUN
la jetée *fem*

Jew NOUN
le Juif *masc*
la Juive *fem*

jewel NOUN
le bijou *masc* (PL les bijoux)

jeweller (US **jeweler**) NOUN
le bijoutier *masc*
la bijoutière *fem*
□ He's a jeweller. Il est bijoutier.

jeweller's shop (US **jeweler's shop**) NOUN
la bijouterie *fem*

jewellery (US **jewelry**) NOUN
les bijoux *masc pl*

Jewish ADJECTIVE
juif (FEM juive)

jigsaw NOUN
le puzzle *masc*

job NOUN
1 l'emploi *masc*
□ He's lost his job. Il a perdu son emploi.
■ **I've got a Saturday job.** Je travaille le samedi.
2 le travail *masc* (PL les travaux) (*chore, task*)
□ That was a difficult job. C'était un travail difficile.

job centre NOUN
l'agence pour l'emploi *fem*

jobless ADJECTIVE
sans emploi

jockey NOUN
le jockey *masc*

to **jog** VERB
faire [36] du jogging

jogging NOUN
le jogging *masc*
■ **to go jogging** faire [36] du jogging

john NOUN (US)
les toilettes *fem pl*

to **join** VERB
1 s'inscrire [30] à (*become member of*)
□ I'm going to join the ski club. Je vais m'inscrire au club de ski.
2 se joindre [42] à
□ Do you mind if I join you? Puis-je me joindre à vous ?

joiner NOUN
le menuisier *masc*
□ He's a joiner. Il est menuisier.

joint NOUN
1 l'articulation *fem* (*in body*)
2 le rôti *masc* (*of meat*)

joke NOUN
▷ *see also* **joke** VERB
la plaisanterie *fem*
□ to tell a joke raconter une plaisanterie

to **joke** VERB
▷ *see also* **joke** NOUN
plaisanter [28]
□ I'm only joking. Je plaisante.

jolly ADJECTIVE
jovial (FEM joviale, MASC PL joviaux)

Jordan NOUN
la Jordanie *fem* (*country*)
■ **in Jordan** en Jordanie

to **jot down** VERB
noter [28]

jotter NOUN
le bloc-notes *masc* (PL les blocs-notes) (*pad*)

journalism NOUN
le journalisme *masc*

journalist NOUN
le/la journaliste *masc/fem*
□ She's a journalist. Elle est journaliste.

journey NOUN
1 le voyage *masc*
□ I don't like long journeys. Je n'aime pas les longs voyages.
■ **to go on a journey** faire [36] un voyage
2 le trajet *masc* (*to school, work*)
□ The journey to school takes about half an hour. Il y a une demi-heure de trajet pour aller à l'école.
■ **a bus journey** un trajet en autobus

joy NOUN
la joie *fem*

joystick NOUN
la manette de jeu *fem* (*for computer game*)

judge NOUN
▷ *see also* **judge** VERB
le juge *masc*
□ She's a judge. Elle est juge.

to **judge** VERB
▷ *see also* **judge** NOUN
juger [45]

judo NOUN
le judo *masc*
□ My hobby is judo. Je fais du judo.

jug NOUN
le pot *masc*

juggler NOUN
le jongleur *masc*
la jongleuse *fem*

juice NOUN
le jus *masc*
□ orange juice le jus d'orange

July NOUN
juillet *masc*
■ **in July** en juillet

> **DID YOU KNOW...?**
> The fourteenth of July (**la fête nationale**) is the French national holiday. There's a firework display and military parade in Paris.

jumble sale NOUN
la vente de charité *fem*

j

to **jump** VERB

sauter [28]

□ to jump over something sauter par-dessus quelque chose □ to jump out of the window sauter par la fenêtre □ to jump off the roof sauter du toit

jumper NOUN

le pull-over *masc* (*pullover*)

junction NOUN

le carrefour *masc* (*of roads*)

June NOUN

juin *masc*

■ **in June** en juin

jungle NOUN

la jungle *fem*

junior NOUN

■ **the juniors** (*in school*) les élèves des petites classes

junior school NOUN

l'école primaire *fem*

junk NOUN

le bric-à-brac *masc* (*old things*)

□ The attic's full of junk. Le grenier est rempli de bric-à-brac.

■ **You eat too much junk food.** Tu manges trop de cochonneries.

■ **a junk shop** un magasin de brocante

jury NOUN

le jury *masc*

just ADVERB

juste

□ just after Christmas juste après Noël □ We had just enough money. Nous avions juste assez d'argent. □ just in time juste à temps

■ **just here** ici

■ **I'm rather busy just now.** Je suis assez occupé en ce moment.

■ **I did it just now.** Je viens de le faire.

■ **He's just arrived.** Il vient d'arriver.

■ **I'm just coming!** J'arrive !

■ **It's just a suggestion.** Ce n'est qu'une suggestion.

justice NOUN

la justice *fem*

to **justify** VERB

justifier [19]

Kk

kangaroo NOUN
le kangourou *masc*

karaoke NOUN
le karaoké *masc*

karate NOUN
le karaté *masc*

kebab NOUN
1 la brochette *fem* (*shish kebab*)
2 le doner kebab *masc* (*doner kebab*)

keen ADJECTIVE
enthousiaste (FEM enthousiaste)
□ He doesn't seem very keen. Il n'a pas l'air très enthousiaste.
■ **She's a keen student.** C'est une étudiante assidue.
■ **to be keen on something** aimer [28] quelque chose □ I'm keen on maths. J'aime les maths. □ I'm not very keen on maths. Je n'aime pas trop les maths.
■ **to be keen on somebody** (*fancy them*) être [35] très attiré par quelqu'un □ He's keen on her. Il est très attiré par elle.
■ **to be keen on doing something** avoir [8] très envie de faire quelque chose □ I'm not very keen on going. Je n'ai pas très envie d'y aller.

to **keep** VERB
1 garder [28] (*retain*)
□ You can keep it. Tu peux le garder.
2 rester [71⁵] (*remain*)
□ Keep still! Reste tranquille !
■ **Keep quiet!** Tais-toi !
■ **I keep forgetting my keys.** J'oublie tout le temps mes clés.

to **keep on** VERB
■ **to keep on doing something** 1 (*continue*) continuer [28] à faire quelque chose □ He kept on reading. Il a continué à lire.
2 (*repeatedly*) ne pas arrêter [28] de faire quelque chose □ The car keeps on breaking down. La voiture n'arrête pas de tomber en panne.

to **keep out** VERB
■ **'keep out'** « défense d'entrer »

to **keep up** VERB
se maintenir [83] à la hauteur de quelqu'un
□ Matthew walks so fast I can't keep up. Matthew marche tellement vite que je n'arrive pas à me maintenir à sa hauteur.

■ **I can't keep up with the rest of the class.** Je n'arrive pas à suivre le reste de la classe.

keep-fit NOUN
la gymnastique d'entretien *fem*
■ **I go to keep-fit classes.** Je vais à des cours de gymnastique.

kennel NOUN
la niche *fem*

kept VERB ▷ *see* **keep**

kerosene NOUN (US)
le pétrole *masc*

kettle NOUN
la bouilloire *fem*

key NOUN
la clé *fem*

keyboard NOUN
le clavier *masc*
□ ... with Matt Bellamy on keyboards ... avec Matt Bellamy aux claviers

keyring NOUN
le porte-clés *masc* (PL les porte-clés)

kick NOUN
▷ *see also* **kick** VERB
le coup de pied *masc*

to **kick** VERB
▷ *see also* **kick** NOUN
■ **to kick somebody** donner [28] un coup de pied à quelqu'un □ He kicked me. Il m'a donné un coup de pied. □ He kicked the ball hard. Il a donné un bon coup de pied dans le ballon.

to **kick off** VERB
donner [28] le coup d'envoi (*in football*)

kick-off NOUN
le coup d'envoi *masc*
□ Kick-off is at 10 o'clock. Le coup d'envoi sera donné à dix heures.

kid NOUN
▷ *see also* **kid** VERB
le/la gosse *masc/fem* (*child*)

to **kid** VERB
▷ *see also* **kid** NOUN
plaisanter [28]
□ I'm just kidding. Je plaisante.

to **kidnap** VERB
kidnapper [28]

k

kidney - knickers

kidney NOUN
1 le rein *masc* (*human*)
□ He's got kidney trouble. Il a des problèmes de reins.
2 le rognon *masc* (*to eat*)
□ I don't like kidneys. Je n'aime pas les rognons.
■ **kidney beans** les haricots rouges *masc pl*

to **kill** VERB
tuer [28]
□ He was killed in a car accident. Il a été tué dans un accident de voiture.
■ **Luckily, nobody was killed.** Il n'y a heureusement pas eu de victimes.
■ **Six people were killed in the accident.** L'accident a fait six morts.
■ **to kill oneself** se suicider [28] □ He killed himself. Il s'est suicidé.

killer NOUN
1 le meurtrier *masc*
la meurtrière *fem* (*murderer*)
□ The police are searching for the killer. La police recherche le meurtrier.
2 le tueur *masc*
la tueuse *fem* (*assassin*)
□ a hired killer un tueur à gages
■ **Meningitis can be a killer.** La méningite peut être mortelle.

kilo NOUN
le kilo *masc*
□ 10 euros a kilo dix euros le kilo

kilometre (US **kilometer**) NOUN
le kilomètre *masc*

kilt NOUN
le kilt *masc*

kind ADJECTIVE
▷ *see also* **kind** NOUN
gentil (FEM gentille)
■ **to be kind to somebody** être [35] gentil avec quelqu'un
■ **Thank you for being so kind.** Merci pour votre gentillesse.

kind NOUN
▷ *see also* **kind** ADJECTIVE
la sorte *fem*
□ It's a kind of sausage. C'est une sorte de saucisse.

kindergarten NOUN
l'école maternelle *fem*

kindly ADVERB
gentiment
□ 'Don't worry,' she said kindly. « Ne t'en fais pas », m'a-t-elle dit gentiment.

kindness NOUN
la gentillesse *fem*

king NOUN
le roi *masc*

kingdom NOUN
le royaume *masc*

kiosk NOUN
la cabine téléphonique *fem* (*phone box*)

kipper NOUN
le hareng fumé *masc*

kiss NOUN
▷ *see also* **kiss** VERB
le baiser *masc*
□ a passionate kiss un baiser passionné

DID YOU KNOW...?
Between friends and family members, the normal French way of saying hello and goodbye is with two kisses, usually one on each cheek, but sometimes three or even four depending on the region. Boys shake hands with their friends or kiss them on the cheek when they arrive at school in the morning.

---

to **kiss** VERB
▷ *see also* **kiss** NOUN
1 embrasser [28]
□ He kissed her passionately. Il l'a embrassée passionnément.
2 s'embrasser [28]
□ They kissed. Ils se sont embrassés.

kit NOUN
1 les affaires *fem pl* (*clothes for sport*)
□ I've forgotten my gym kit. J'ai oublié mes affaires de gym.
2 la trousse *fem*
□ a tool kit une trousse à outils □ a first aid kit une trousse de secours □ a puncture repair kit une trousse de réparations
■ **a drum kit** une batterie
■ **a sewing kit** un nécessaire à couture

kitchen NOUN
la cuisine *fem*
□ a fitted kitchen une cuisine aménagée
■ **the kitchen units** les éléments de cuisine
■ **a kitchen knife** un couteau de cuisine

kite NOUN
le cerf-volant *masc* (PL les cerfs-volants)

kitten NOUN
le chaton *masc*

knee NOUN
le genou *masc* (PL les genoux)
□ He was on his knees. Il était à genoux.

to **kneel** VERB
s'agenouiller [28]

to **kneel down** VERB
s'agenouiller [28]

knew VERB ▷ *see* **know**

knickers PL NOUN
la culotte *fem sing*
■ **a pair of knickers** une culotte

Numbers in brackets refer to verb tables on pages 650 to 658

knife NOUN
le couteau *masc* (PL les couteaux)
- **a kitchen knife** un couteau de cuisine
- **a penknife** un canif

to **knit** VERB
tricoter [28]

knitting NOUN
le tricot *masc*
□ I like knitting. J'aime faire du tricot.

knives PL NOUN ▷ *see* **knife**

knob NOUN
le bouton *masc* (*on door, radio, TV, radiator*)

to **knock** VERB
▷ *see also* **knock** NOUN
frapper [28]
□ Someone's knocking at the door. Quelqu'un frappe à la porte.

knock NOUN
▷ *see also* **knock** VERB
le coup *masc*

to **knock down** VERB
renverser [28]
□ She was knocked down by a car. Elle a été renversée par une voiture.

to **knock out** VERB
1 éliminer [28] (*defeat*)
□ They were knocked out early in the tournament. Ils ont été éliminés au début du tournoi.
2 assommer [28] (*stun*)
□ They knocked out the security guard. Ils ont assommé le vigile.

knot NOUN
le nœud *masc*
- **to tie a knot in something** faire [36] un nœud à quelque chose

to **know** VERB

> Use **savoir** for knowing facts, **connaître** for knowing people and places.

1 savoir [76]
□ It's a long way. — Yes, I know. C'est loin. — Oui, je sais. □ You know what you have to do. Tu sais ce que tu dois faire. □ She knows where we live. Elle sait où nous habitons. □ I don't know. Je ne sais pas. □ I don't know what to do. Je ne sais

pas quoi faire. □ I don't know how to do it. Je ne sais pas comment faire.
2 connaître [14]
□ I know her. Je la connais. □ I know Bordeaux well. Je connais bien Bordeaux.
- **I don't know any German.** Je ne parle pas du tout allemand.
- **to know that ...** savoir [76] que ... □ I know that you like chocolate. Je sais que tu aimes le chocolat. □ I didn't know that your dad was a police officer. Je ne savais pas que ton père était policier.
- **to know about something** 1 (*be aware of*) être [35] au courant de quelque chose □ Do you know about the training session this afternoon? Tu es au courant de la séance d'entraînement cet après-midi ? 2 (*be knowledgeable about*) s'y connaître [14] en quelque chose □ He knows a lot about cars. Il s'y connaît en voitures. □ I don't know much about computers. Je ne m'y connais pas bien en informatique.
- **to get to know somebody** apprendre [65] à connaître quelqu'un
- **How should I know?** (*I don't know!*) Comment veux-tu que je le sache ?
- **You never know!** On ne sait jamais !

know-all NOUN
le/la je-sais-tout *masc/fem*
□ He's such a know-all! C'est Monsieur je-sais-tout !

know-how NOUN
le savoir-faire *masc*

knowledge NOUN
la connaissance *fem*

knowledgeable ADJECTIVE
- **to be knowledgeable about something** s'y connaître [14] en quelque chose □ She's very knowledgeable about martial arts. Elle s'y connaît bien en arts martiaux.

known VERB ▷ *see* **know**

Koran NOUN
le Coran *masc*

Korea NOUN
la Corée *fem*
- **in Korea** en Corée

kosher ADJECTIVE
kascher (FEM+PL kascher)

k

lab NOUN (= *laboratory*)
le labo *masc*
- **a lab technician** un laborantin

label NOUN
l'étiquette *fem*

labor NOUN (US)
- **to be in labor** être [35] en train d'accoucher
- **the labor market** le marché du travail
- **a labor union** un syndicat

laboratory NOUN
le laboratoire *masc*

Labour NOUN
les travaillistes *masc pl*
☐ My parents vote Labour. Mes parents votent pour les travaillistes.
- **the Labour Party** le parti travailliste

labour NOUN
- **to be in labour** être [35] en train d'accoucher
- **the labour market** le marché du travail

labourer NOUN
le manœuvre *masc*
- **a farm labourer** un ouvrier agricole

lace NOUN
1 le lacet *masc* (*of shoe*)
2 la dentelle *fem*
☐ a lace collar un col en dentelle

lack NOUN
le manque *masc*
☐ He got the job despite his lack of experience. Il a obtenu le poste en dépit de son manque d'expérience.
- **There was no lack of volunteers.** Les volontaires ne manquaient pas.

lacquer NOUN
la laque *fem*

lad NOUN
le gars *masc*

ladder NOUN
l'échelle *fem*

lady NOUN
la dame *fem*
- **a young lady** une jeune fille
- **Ladies and gentlemen ...** Mesdames, Messieurs ...
- **the ladies** les toilettes pour dames *fem pl*

ladybird NOUN
la coccinelle *fem*

to **lag behind** VERB
rester [71⁵] en arrière

lager NOUN
la bière blonde *fem*

laid VERB ▷ *see* **lay**

laid-back ADJECTIVE
relaxe (FEM relaxe)

lain VERB ▷ *see* **lie**

lake NOUN
le lac *masc*
- **Lake Geneva** le lac Léman

lamb NOUN
l'agneau *masc* (PL les agneaux)
- **a lamb chop** une côtelette d'agneau

lame ADJECTIVE
boiteux (FEM boiteuse)
☐ My pony is lame. Mon poney boite.

lamp NOUN
la lampe *fem*

lamppost NOUN
le réverbère *masc*

lampshade NOUN
l'abat-jour *masc* (PL les abat-jour)

land NOUN
▷ *see also* **land** VERB
la terre *fem*
- **a piece of land** un terrain

to **land** VERB
▷ *see also* **land** NOUN
atterrir [38] (*plane, passenger*)

landing NOUN
1 l'atterrissage *masc* (*of plane*)
2 le palier *masc* (*of staircase*)

landlady NOUN
la propriétaire *fem*

landline NOUN
la ligne fixe *fem*
☐ Shall I call you on the landline? Je t'appelle sur ta ligne fixe ?

landlord NOUN
le propriétaire *masc*

landmark NOUN
le point de repère *masc* (*for finding your way*)
- **Big Ben is one of London's most famous**

landmarks. Big Ben est l'un des sites les plus célèbres du paysage londonien.

landowner NOUN
le propriétaire terrien *masc*

landscape NOUN
le paysage *masc*

lane NOUN
1 le chemin *masc* (*in country*)
2 la voie *fem* (*on motorway*)

language NOUN
la langue *fem*
□ French isn't a difficult language. Le français n'est pas une langue difficile.
■ **to use bad language** dire [27] des grossièretés

language laboratory NOUN
le laboratoire de langues *masc*

lanky ADJECTIVE
dégingandé (FEM dégingandée)
□ a lanky boy un garçon dégingandé

lap NOUN
le tour de piste *masc* (*sport*)
□ I ran ten laps. J'ai fait dix tours de piste en courant.
■ **on my lap** sur mes genoux

laptop NOUN
le portable *masc* (*computer*)

larder NOUN
le garde-manger *masc* (PL les garde-manger)

large ADJECTIVE
1 grand (FEM grande)
□ a large house une grande maison
2 gros (FEM grosse) (*person, animal*)
□ a large dog un gros chien

> **BE CAREFUL!**
> Do not translate **large** by the French word **large**.

largely ADVERB
en grande partie
□ It's largely your own fault. C'est en grande partie de ta faute.

laser NOUN
le laser *masc*

lass NOUN
la jeune fille *fem*

last ADJECTIVE, ADVERB
▷ *see also* **last** VERB
1 dernier (FEM dernière)
□ last Friday vendredi dernier □ last week la semaine dernière □ last summer l'été dernier
2 en dernier
□ He arrived last. Il est arrivé en dernier.
3 pour la dernière fois
□ I've lost my bag. — When did you see it last? J'ai perdu mon sac. — Quand est-ce que tu l'as vu pour la dernière fois ? □ When I last saw him,

he was wearing a blue shirt. La dernière fois que je l'ai vu, il portait une chemise bleue.
■ **the last time** la dernière fois □ the last time I saw her la dernière fois que je l'ai vue □ That's the last time I take your advice! C'est la dernière fois que je suis tes conseils !
■ **last night 1** (*evening*) hier soir □ I got home at midnight last night. Je suis rentré à minuit hier soir. **2** (*sleeping hours*) la nuit dernière □ I couldn't sleep last night. J'ai eu du mal à dormir la nuit dernière.
■ **at last** enfin

to **last** VERB
▷ *see also* **last** ADJECTIVE, ADVERB
durer [28]
□ The concert lasts two hours. Le concert dure deux heures.

lastly ADVERB
finalement
□ Lastly, what time do you arrive? Finalement, à quelle heure arrives-tu ?

late ADJECTIVE, ADVERB
1 en retard
□ Hurry up or you'll be late! Dépêche-toi, sinon tu vas être en retard ! □ I'm often late for school. J'arrive souvent en retard à l'école.
■ **to arrive late** arriver [5ʲ] en retard □ She arrived late. Elle est arrivée en retard.
2 tard
□ I went to bed late. Je me suis couché tard.
■ **in the late afternoon** en fin d'après-midi
■ **in late May** fin mai

lately ADVERB
ces derniers temps
□ I haven't seen him lately. Je ne l'ai pas vu ces derniers temps.

later ADVERB
plus tard
□ I'll do it later. Je ferai ça plus tard.
■ **See you later!** À tout à l'heure !

latest ADJECTIVE
dernier (FEM dernière)
□ their latest album leur dernier album
■ **at the latest** au plus tard □ by 10 o'clock at the latest à dix heures au plus tard

Latin NOUN
le latin *masc*
□ I do Latin. Je fais du latin.

Latin America NOUN
l'Amérique latine *fem*
■ **in Latin America** en Amérique latine

Latin American ADJECTIVE
latino-américain (FEM latino-américaine)

latter NOUN
le second *masc*
la seconde *fem*
■ **the former ..., the latter ...** le premier ..., le second ... □ The former lives in the US, the latter

in Australia. Le premier habite aux États-Unis, le second en Australie.

■ **The latter is the more expensive of the two games consoles.** Cette dernière console de jeu est la plus coûteuse des deux.

laugh NOUN

▷ see also **laugh** VERB

le rire *masc*

■ **It was a good laugh.** (*it was fun*) On s'est bien amusés.

to **laugh** VERB

▷ see also **laugh** NOUN

rire [74]

■ **to laugh at something** se moquer [28] de quelque chose □ They laughed at her. Ils se sont moqués d'elle.

to **launch** VERB

lancer [12] (*product, rocket, boat*)

□ They're going to launch a new model. Ils vont lancer un nouveau modèle.

Launderette® NOUN

la laverie *fem*

Laundromat® NOUN (US)

la laverie *fem*

laundry NOUN

le linge *masc* (*clothes*)

lavatory NOUN

les toilettes *fem pl*

lavender NOUN

la lavande *fem*

law NOUN

1 la loi *fem*

□ The laws are very strict. Les lois sont très sévères.

■ **It's against the law.** C'est illégal.

2 le droit *masc* (*subject*)

□ My sister's studying law. Ma sœur fait des études de droit.

lawn NOUN

la pelouse *fem*

lawnmower NOUN

la tondeuse à gazon *fem*

law school NOUN (US)

la faculté de droit *fem*

lawyer NOUN

l'avocat *masc*

l'avocate *fem*

□ My mother's a lawyer. Ma mère est avocate.

to **lay** VERB

'lay' is also a form of the verb 'lie'.

mettre [47]

□ She laid the baby in her cot. Elle a mis le bébé dans son lit. □ He laid the table. Il a mis la table.

■ **to lay something on 1** (*provide*) organiser [28] quelque chose □ They laid on extra buses. Ils ont organisé un service de bus supplémentaire. **2** (*prepare*) préparer [28]

quelque chose □ They laid on a special meal. Ils ont préparé un repas soigné.

to **lay off** VERB

licencier [19]

□ My father's been laid off. Mon père a été licencié.

lay-by NOUN

l'aire de stationnement *fem*

layer NOUN

la couche *fem*

□ the ozone layer la couche d'ozone

layout NOUN

la disposition *fem* (*of house, buildings*)

□ No one likes the new layout of the classroom. Personne n'aime la nouvelle disposition de la salle de classe.

lazy ADJECTIVE

paresseux (FEM paresseuse)

lead NOUN

▷ see also **lead** VERB

This word has two pronunciations. Make sure you choose the right translation.

1 le fil *masc* (*cable*)

2 la laisse *fem* (*for dog*)

■ **to be in the lead** être [35] en tête □ Our team is in the lead. Notre équipe est en tête.

3 le plomb *masc* (*metal*)

to **lead** VERB

▷ see also **lead** NOUN

mener [43]

□ the road that leads to the airport la route qui mène à l'aéroport

■ **to lead the way** montrer [28] le chemin

■ **to lead somebody away** emmener [43] quelqu'un □ The police led the man away. La police a emmené l'homme.

leader NOUN

1 le chef *masc* (*of expedition, gang*)

2 le dirigeant *masc*

la dirigeante *fem* (*of political party*)

lead singer NOUN

le chanteur principal *masc*

la chanteuse principale *fem*

leaf NOUN

la feuille *fem*

leaflet NOUN

la brochure *fem*

league NOUN

le championnat *masc*

□ They are at the top of the league. Ils sont en tête du championnat.

■ **the Premier League** la première division

leak NOUN

▷ see also **leak** VERB

la fuite *fem*

□ a gas leak une fuite de gaz

to **leak** VERB
▷ *see also* **leak** NOUN
fuir [39] (*pipe, water, gas*)

to **lean** VERB
se pencher [28]
■ **to be leaning against something** être [35] appuyé contre quelque chose □ The ladder was leaning against the wall. L'échelle était appuyée contre le mur.
■ **to lean something against a wall** appuyer [53] quelque chose contre un mur □ He leant his bike against the wall. Il a appuyé son vélo contre le mur.

to **lean forward** VERB
se pencher [28] en avant

to **lean on** VERB
■ **to lean on something** s'appuyer [53] contre quelque chose □ He leant on the wall. Il s'est appuyé contre le mur.

to **lean out** VERB
se pencher [28] au dehors
■ **She leant out of the window.** Elle s'est penchée par la fenêtre.

to **lean over** VERB
se pencher [28]
□ Don't lean over too far. Ne te penche pas trop loin.

to **leap** VERB
sauter [28]
□ They leapt over the stream. Ils ont sauté pour traverser la rivière.
■ **He leapt out of his chair when his team scored.** Il s'est levé d'un bond lorsque son équipe a marqué.

leap year NOUN
l'année bissextile *fem*

to **learn** VERB
apprendre [65]
□ I'm learning to ski. J'apprends à skier.

learner NOUN
■ **She's a quick learner.** Elle apprend vite.
■ **French learners** (*people learning French*) ceux qui apprennent le français

learner driver NOUN
le conducteur débutant *masc*
la conductrice débutante *fem*

learnt VERB ▷ *see* **learn**

least ADVERB, ADJECTIVE, PRONOUN
■ **the least** 1 (*followed by noun*) le moins de □ It takes the least time. C'est ce qui prend le moins de temps. 2 (*after a verb*) le moins □ Maths is the subject I like the least. Les maths sont la matière que j'aime le moins.

When 'least' is followed by an adjective, the translation depends on whether the noun referred to is masculine, feminine or plural.

■ **the least ...** 1 le moins ... □ the least expensive hotel l'hôtel le moins cher 2 la moins ... □ the least expensive seat la place la moins chère 3 les moins ... □ the least expensive hotels les hôtels les moins chers □ the least expensive seats les places les moins chères
■ **It's the least I can do.** C'est le moins que je puisse faire.
■ **at least** 1 au moins □ It'll cost at least £200. Ça va coûter au moins deux cents livres. 2 du moins □ ... but at least nobody was hurt. ... mais du moins personne n'a été blessé. □ It's totally unfair – at least, that's my opinion. C'est vraiment injuste – du moins c'est ce que je pense.

leather NOUN
le cuir *masc*
□ a black leather jacket un blouson en cuir noir

leave NOUN
▷ *see also* **leave** VERB
1 le congé *masc* (*from job*)
2 la permission *fem* (*from army*)
□ My brother is on leave for a week. Mon frère est en permission pendant une semaine.

to **leave** VERB
▷ *see also* **leave** NOUN
1 laisser [28] (*deliberately*)
□ Don't leave your camera in the car. Ne laisse pas ton appareil photo dans la voiture.
2 oublier [19] (*by mistake*)
□ I've left my book at home. J'ai oublié mon livre à la maison. □ Make sure you haven't left anything behind. Vérifiez bien que vous n'avez rien oublié.
3 partir [57⁹] (*go*)
□ The bus leaves at 8. Le car part à huit heures. □ She's just left. Elle vient de partir.
4 quitter [28] (*go away from*)
□ We leave Cambridge at six o'clock. Nous quittons Cambridge à six heures. □ My sister left home last year. Ma sœur a quitté la maison l'an dernier.
■ **to leave somebody alone** laisser [28] quelqu'un tranquille □ Leave me alone! Laisse-moi tranquille !

to **leave out** VERB
mettre [47] à l'écart
□ As the new girl, I felt really left out. En tant que nouvelle, je me suis vraiment sentie à l'écart.

leaves PL NOUN ▷ *see* **leaf**

Lebanon NOUN
le Liban *masc*
■ **in Lebanon** au Liban

lecture NOUN
▷ *see also* **lecture** VERB
1 la conférence *fem* (*public*)

When 'least' is followed by an adjective, the translation depends on whether the noun referred to is masculine, feminine or plural.

lecture – lesson

2 le cours magistral *masc* (PL les cours magistraux) (*at university*)

> **BE CAREFUL!**
> Do not translate **lecture** by the French word **lecture**.

to **lecture** VERB

> ▷ *see also* **lecture** NOUN

1 enseigner [28]
□ She lectures at the university. Elle enseigne à l'université.

2 faire [36] la morale
□ He's always lecturing us. Il n'arrête pas de nous faire la morale.

lecturer NOUN

le professeur d'université *masc*
□ She's a lecturer. Elle est professeur d'université.

led VERB ▷ *see* **lead**

leek NOUN

le poireau *masc* (PL les poireaux)

left VERB ▷ *see* **leave**

left ADJECTIVE, ADVERB

> ▷ *see also* **left** NOUN

1 gauche (FEM gauche) (*not right*)
□ my left hand ma main gauche □ on the left side of the road sur le côté gauche de la route

2 à gauche
□ Turn left at the traffic lights. Tournez à gauche aux prochains feux.
■ **I haven't got any money left.** Il ne me reste plus d'argent.

left NOUN

> ▷ *see also* **left** ADJECTIVE, ADVERB

la gauche *fem*
■ **on the left** à gauche □ Remember to drive on the left. N'oubliez pas de conduire à gauche.

left-hand ADJECTIVE

■ **the left-hand side** la gauche □ It's on the left-hand side. C'est à gauche.

left-handed ADJECTIVE

gaucher (FEM gauchère)

left-luggage locker NOUN

la consigne automatique *fem*

left-luggage office NOUN

la consigne *fem*

leg NOUN

la jambe *fem*
□ She's broken her leg. Elle s'est cassé la jambe.
■ **a chicken leg** une cuisse de poulet
■ **a leg of lamb** un gigot d'agneau

legal ADJECTIVE

légal (FEM légale, MASC PL légaux)

leggings PL NOUN

les leggings *masc pl*

leisure NOUN

les loisirs *masc pl*

□ What do you do in your leisure time? Qu'est-ce que tu fais pendant tes loisirs ?

leisure centre NOUN

le centre de loisirs *masc*

lemon NOUN

le citron *masc*

lemonade NOUN

la limonade *fem*

to **lend** VERB

prêter [28]
□ I can lend you some money. Je peux te prêter de l'argent.

length NOUN

la longueur *fem*
■ **It's about a metre in length.** Ça fait environ un mètre de long.

lens NOUN

1 la lentille *fem* (*contact lens*)
2 le verre *masc* (*of spectacles*)
3 l'objectif *masc* (*of camera*)

Lent NOUN

le carême *masc*

lent VERB ▷ *see* **lend**

lentil NOUN

la lentille *fem*

Leo NOUN

le Lion *masc*
□ I'm Leo. Je suis Lion.

leotard NOUN

le justaucorps *masc*

lesbian NOUN

la lesbienne *fem*

less PRONOUN, ADVERB, ADJECTIVE

1 moins
□ He's less intelligent than her. Il est moins intelligent qu'elle. □ A bit less, please. Un peu moins, s'il vous plaît.

2 moins de
□ I've got less time for hobbies now. J'ai moins de temps pour les loisirs maintenant.
■ **less than** **1** (*with amounts*) moins de □ It's less than a kilometre from here. C'est à moins d'un kilomètre d'ici. □ It costs less than 100 euros. Ça coûte moins de cent euros. □ less than half moins de la moitié **2** (*in comparisons*) moins que □ He spent less than me. Il a dépensé moins que moi. □ I've got less than you. J'en ai moins que toi. □ It cost less than we thought. Ça a coûté moins cher que nous ne le pensions.

lesson NOUN

1 la leçon *fem*
□ a history lesson une leçon d'histoire □ 'Lesson Sixteen' (*in textbook*) « Leçon seize »

2 le cours *masc* (*class*)
□ The lessons last forty minutes each. Chaque cours dure quarante minutes.

to let VERB

1 laisser [28] (*allow*)

■ **to let somebody do something** laisser [28] quelqu'un faire quelque chose □ Let me have a look. Laisse-moi voir. □ My parents won't let me stay out that late. Mes parents ne me laissent pas sortir aussi tard.

■ **to let somebody know** faire [36] savoir à quelqu'un □ I'll let you know as soon as possible. Je vous le ferai savoir dès que possible.

■ **to let somebody go** lâcher [28] quelqu'un □ Let me go! Lâche-moi !

To make suggestions using 'let's', you can ask questions beginning with **si on**.

□ Let's go to the cinema! Si on allait au cinéma ?

■ **Let's go!** Allons-y !

2 louer [28] (*hire out*)

■ **'to let'** « à louer »

to let down VERB

décevoir [67]

□ I won't let you down. Je ne vous décevrai pas.

to let in VERB

laisser [28] entrer

□ They wouldn't let me in because I was under 18. Ils ne m'ont pas laissé entrer parce que j'avais moins de dix-huit ans.

letter NOUN

la lettre *fem*

letterbox NOUN

la boîte à lettres *fem*

lettuce NOUN

la salade *fem*

leukaemia NOUN

la leucémie *fem*

level ADJECTIVE

▷ *see also* **level** NOUN

plan (FEM plane)

□ A snooker table must be perfectly level. Un billard doit être parfaitement plan.

level NOUN

▷ *see also* **level** ADJECTIVE

le niveau *masc* (PL les niveaux)

□ The level of the river is rising. Le niveau de la rivière monte.

■ **A levels** le baccalauréat

DID YOU KNOW...?

The French **baccalauréat** (or **bac** for short) is taken at the age of 17 or 18. Students have to sit a few compulsory classes, but are otherwise free to choose any combination of subjects they want. If you pass you have the right to a place at university.

level crossing NOUN

le passage à niveau *masc*

lever NOUN

le levier *masc*

LGBTQ ADJECTIVE (= *lesbian, gay, bisexual, transgender, queer/ questioning*)

LGBTQ (FEM LGBTQ)

□ LGBTQ groups des groupes LGBTQ

liable ADJECTIVE

■ **He's liable to lose his temper.** Il se met facilement en colère.

liar NOUN

le menteur *masc*

la menteuse *fem*

liberal ADJECTIVE

libéral (FEM libérale, MASC PL libéraux) (*opinions*)

■ **the Liberal Democrats** le parti libéral-démocrate

liberation NOUN

la libération *fem*

Libra NOUN

la Balance *fem*

□ I'm Libra. Je suis Balance.

librarian NOUN

le/la bibliothécaire *masc/fem*

library NOUN

la bibliothèque *fem*

BE CAREFUL!

Do not translate **library** by the French word **librairie**.

Libya NOUN

la Libye *fem*

■ **in Libya** en Libye

licence (US **license**) NOUN

le permis *masc*

■ **a driving licence** un permis de conduire

to lick VERB

lécher [34]

lid NOUN

le couvercle *masc*

to lie VERB

▷ *see also* **lie** NOUN

mentir [77] (*not tell the truth*)

□ I know she's lying. Je sais qu'elle ment.

■ **to lie down** s'allonger [45]

■ **to be lying down** être [35] allongé □ He was lying down on the sofa. Il était allongé sur le canapé.

■ **to lie on the beach** être [35] allongé sur la plage

lie NOUN

▷ *see also* **lie** VERB

le mensonge *masc*

■ **to tell a lie** mentir [77]

■ **That's a lie!** Ce n'est pas vrai !

lie-in NOUN

■ **to have a lie-in** faire [36] la grasse matinée □ I have a lie-in on Sundays. Je fais la grasse matinée le dimanche.

lieutenant NOUN
le lieutenant *masc*

life NOUN
la vie *fem*

lifebelt NOUN
la bouée de sauvetage *fem*

lifeboat NOUN
le canot de sauvetage *masc*

lifeguard NOUN
le maître nageur *masc*

life jacket NOUN
le gilet de sauvetage *masc*

life-saving NOUN
le sauvetage *masc*
□ I've done a course in life-saving. J'ai pris des cours de sauvetage.

lifestyle NOUN
le style de vie *masc*

to lift VERB
▷ *see also* **lift** NOUN
soulever [43]
□ It's too heavy, I can't lift it. C'est trop lourd, je ne peux pas le soulever.

lift NOUN
▷ *see also* **lift** VERB
l'ascenseur *masc*
□ The lift isn't working. L'ascenseur est en panne.
■ **He gave me a lift to the cinema.** Il m'a emmené au cinéma en voiture.
■ **Would you like a lift?** Est-ce que je peux vous déposer quelque part ?

light ADJECTIVE
▷ *see also* **light** NOUN, VERB
1 léger (FEM légère) (*not heavy*)
□ a light jacket une veste légère □ a light meal un repas léger
2 clair (FEM claire) (*colour*)
□ a light blue coat un manteau bleu clair

light NOUN
▷ *see also* **light** ADJECTIVE, VERB
1 la lumière *fem*
□ to switch on the light allumer la lumière □ to switch off the light éteindre la lumière
2 la lampe *fem*
□ There's a light by my bed. Il y a une lampe près de mon lit.
■ **the traffic lights** les feux *masc pl*

to light VERB
▷ *see also* **light** ADJECTIVE, NOUN
allumer [28] (*candle, cigarette, fire*)

light bulb NOUN
l'ampoule *fem*

lighthouse NOUN
le phare *masc*

lightning NOUN
les éclairs *masc pl*

■ **a flash of lightning** un éclair

to like VERB
▷ *see also* **like** PREPOSITION
1 aimer [28]
□ I don't like mustard. Je n'aime pas la moutarde. □ I like riding. J'aime monter à cheval.

> Note that **aimer** also means to love, so make sure you use **aimer bien** for just liking somebody.

2 aimer [28] bien
□ I like Kieran, but I don't want to go out with him. J'aime bien Kieran, mais je ne veux pas sortir avec lui.
■ **I'd like ...** Je voudrais ... □ I'd like an orange juice, please. Je voudrais un jus d'orange, s'il vous plaît. □ Would you like some coffee? Voulez-vous du café ?
■ **I'd like to ...** J'aimerais ... □ I'd like to go to Russia one day. J'aimerais aller en Russie un jour. □ I'd like to wash my hands. J'aimerais me laver les mains.
■ **Would you like to go for a walk?** Tu veux aller faire une promenade ?
■ **... if you like** ... si tu veux

like PREPOSITION
▷ *see also* **like** VERB
comme
□ It's fine like that. C'est bien comme ça. □ Do it like this. Fais-le comme ça. □ a city like Chicago une ville comme Chicago □ It's a bit like salmon. C'est un peu comme du saumon.
■ **What's the weather like?** Quel temps fait-il ?
■ **to look like somebody** ressembler [28] à quelqu'un □ You look like my brother. Tu ressembles à mon frère.

likely ADJECTIVE
probable (FEM probable)
□ That's not very likely. C'est peu probable.
■ **She's likely to come.** Elle viendra probablement.
■ **She's not likely to come.** Elle ne viendra probablement pas.

Lilo® NOUN
le matelas pneumatique *masc*

lily of the valley NOUN
le muguet *masc*

> **DID YOU KNOW...?**
> On May 1st French people celebrate May Day by giving each other small bunches of lily of the valley.

lime NOUN
le citron vert *masc* (*fruit*)

limit NOUN
la limite *fem*
□ The speed limit is 70 mph. La vitesse est limitée à cent dix kilomètres à l'heure.

limousine NOUN
la limousine *fem*

to **limp** VERB
boiter [28]

line NOUN
1 la ligne *fem*
□ a straight line une ligne droite
2 le trait *masc* (*to divide, cancel*)
□ Draw a line under each answer. Tirez un trait après chaque réponse.
3 la voie *fem* (*railway track*)
■ **It's a very bad line.** La ligne est très mauvaise.

linen NOUN
le lin *masc*
□ a linen jacket une veste en lin

liner NOUN
le paquebot *masc* (*ship*)

linguist NOUN
■ **to be a good linguist** être [35] doué pour les langues □ She's a good linguist. Elle est douée pour les langues.

lining NOUN
la doublure *fem* (*of jacket, skirt etc*)

link NOUN
▷ *see also* **link** VERB
1 le rapport *masc*
□ the link between smoking and cancer le rapport entre le tabagisme et le cancer
2 le lien *masc* (*computing*)

to **link** VERB
▷ *see also* **link** NOUN
relier [19]

lino NOUN
le linoléum *masc*

lion NOUN
le lion *masc*

lioness NOUN
la lionne *fem*

lip NOUN
la lèvre *fem*

to **lip-read** VERB
lire [44] sur les lèvres

lip salve NOUN
la pommade pour les lèvres *fem*

lipstick NOUN
le rouge à lèvres *masc*

liqueur NOUN
la liqueur *fem*

liquid NOUN
le liquide *masc*

liquidizer NOUN
le mixer *masc*

list NOUN
▷ *see also* **list** VERB
la liste *fem*

to **list** VERB
▷ *see also* **list** NOUN
faire [36] une liste de
□ List your hobbies and say which is your favourite. Fais une liste de tes hobbies et dis quel est ton préféré.

to **listen** VERB
écouter [28]
□ Listen to this! Écoutez ceci ! □ Listen to me! Écoutez-moi !

listener NOUN
l'auditeur *masc*
l'auditrice *fem*

lit VERB ▷ *see* **light**

liter NOUN (US)
le litre *masc*

literally ADVERB
vraiment (*completely*)
□ It was literally impossible to find a seat. Il était vraiment impossible de trouver une place.
■ **to translate literally** faire [36] une traduction littérale

literature NOUN
la littérature *fem*
□ I'm studying English Literature. J'étudie la littérature anglaise.

litre NOUN
le litre *masc*

litter NOUN
les ordures *fem pl*

litter bin NOUN
la poubelle *fem*

little ADJECTIVE
petit (FEM petite)
□ a little girl une petite fille

WORD POWER

You can use a number of other words instead of **little** to mean 'small':
miniature miniature
□ a miniature version une version miniature
minute infime
□ a minute chance une chance infime
tiny minuscule
□ a tiny garden un jardin minuscule

■ **a little** un peu □ How much would you like? — Just a little. Combien en voulez-vous ? — Juste un peu.
■ **very little** très peu □ We've got very little time. Nous avons très peu de temps.
■ **little by little** petit à petit

live ADJECTIVE
▷ *see also* **live** VERB
1 vivant (FEM vivante) (*animal*)
2 en direct (*broadcast*)
■ **There's live music on Fridays.** Il y a des musiciens qui jouent le vendredi.

to **live** VERB
▷ *see also* **live** ADJECTIVE

l

1 vivre [91]
□ I live with my grandmother. Je vis avec ma grand-mère.

2 habiter [28] (*reside*)
□ Where do you live? Où est-ce que tu habites ?
□ I live in Edinburgh. J'habite à Édimbourg.

to **live together** VERB

1 partager [45] un appartement (*as flatmates*)
□ She and her sister are living together in London. Elle partage un appartement à Londres avec sa sœur.

2 vivre [91] ensemble
□ My parents aren't living together any more. Mes parents ne vivent plus ensemble.
■ **They're not married, they're living together.** Ils ne sont pas mariés, ils vivent en concubinage.

lively ADJECTIVE

animé (FEM animée)
□ It was a lively party. C'était une soirée animée.
■ **She's got a lively personality.** Elle est pleine de vitalité.

liver NOUN

le foie *masc*

lives PL NOUN ▷ *see* **life**

livestream NOUN

▷ *see also* **livestream** VERB
la diffusion en direct sur Internet *fem*

to **livestream** VERB

▷ *see also* **livestream** NOUN
diffuser [28] en direct sur Internet

living NOUN

■ **to make a living** gagner [28] sa vie
■ **What does she do for a living?** Qu'est-ce qu'elle fait dans la vie ?

living room NOUN

la salle de séjour *fem*

lizard NOUN

le lézard *masc*

load NOUN

▷ *see also* **load** VERB
■ **loads of** un tas de □ loads of people un tas de gens □ loads of money un tas d'argent
■ **You're talking a load of rubbish!** Tu ne dis que des bêtises !

to **load** VERB

▷ *see also* **load** NOUN
charger [45]
□ a trolley loaded with luggage un chariot chargé de bagages

loaf NOUN

le pain *masc*
■ **a loaf of bread** un pain

loan NOUN

▷ *see also* **loan** VERB
le prêt *masc*

to **loan** VERB

▷ *see also* **loan** NOUN
prêter [28]

to **loathe** VERB

détester [28]
□ I loathe her. Je la déteste.

loaves PL NOUN ▷ *see* **loaf**

lobster NOUN

le homard *masc*

local ADJECTIVE

local (FEM locale, MASC PL locaux)
□ the local paper le journal local

location NOUN

l'endroit *masc*
□ a beautiful location un endroit magnifique

> **BE CAREFUL!**
> Do not translate **location** by the French word **location**.

loch NOUN

le loch *masc*

lock NOUN

▷ *see also* **lock** VERB
la serrure *fem*
□ The lock is broken. La serrure est cassée.

to **lock** VERB

▷ *see also* **lock** NOUN
fermer [28] à clé
□ Make sure you lock your door. N'oubliez pas de fermer votre porte à clé.

to **lock out** VERB

■ **The door slammed and I was locked out.** La porte a claqué et je me suis retrouvé à la porte.

lockdown NOUN

le confinement *masc*
■ **to go into lockdown** (*place*) entrer [32E] en confinement

locker NOUN

le casier *masc*
■ **the locker room** le vestiaire
■ **the left-luggage lockers** la consigne automatique *sing*

locket NOUN

le médaillon *masc*

lodger NOUN

le/la locataire *masc/fem*

loft NOUN

le grenier *masc*

log NOUN

la bûche *fem* (*of wood*)

to **log in** VERB

se connecter [28]

to **log off** VERB

se déconnecter [28]

to **log on** VERB

se connecter [28]

to **log out** VERB
se déconnecter [28]

logical ADJECTIVE
logique (FEM logique)

lollipop NOUN
la sucette *fem*

lolly NOUN
la glace à l'eau *fem* (*ice lolly*)

London NOUN
Londres
■ **in London** à Londres
■ **to London** à Londres
■ **I'm from London.** Je suis de Londres.

Londoner NOUN
le Londonien *masc*
la Londonienne *fem*

loneliness NOUN
la solitude *fem*

lonely ADJECTIVE
seul (FEM seule)
■ **to feel lonely** se sentir [77] seul □ She feels a bit lonely. Elle se sent un peu seule.

long ADJECTIVE, ADVERB
▷ *see also* **long** VERB
long (FEM longue)
□ She's got long hair. Elle a les cheveux longs.
■ **The room is 6 metres long.** La pièce fait six mètres de long.
■ **how long?** (*time*) combien de temps ? □ How long did you stay there? Combien de temps êtes-vous resté là-bas ? □ How long have you been here? Depuis combien de temps êtes-vous ici ? □ How long is the flight? Combien de temps dure le vol ?
■ **I've been waiting a long time.** J'attends depuis longtemps.
■ **It takes a long time.** Ça prend du temps.
■ **as long as** si □ I'll come as long as it's not too expensive. Je viendrai si ce n'est pas trop cher.

to **long** VERB
▷ *see also* **long** ADJECTIVE, ADVERB
■ **to long to do something** attendre [7] avec impatience de faire quelque chose □ I'm longing to see my boyfriend again. J'attends avec impatience de revoir mon copain.

long-distance ADJECTIVE
■ **a long-distance call** une communication interurbaine

longer ADVERB
▷ *see also* **long** ADJECTIVE, ADVERB
■ **They're no longer going out together.** Ils ne sortent plus ensemble.
■ **I can't stand it any longer.** Je ne peux plus le supporter.

long jump NOUN
le saut en longueur *masc*

loo NOUN
les toilettes *fem pl*

□ Where's the loo? Où sont les toilettes ?

look NOUN
▷ *see also* **look** VERB
■ **to have a look** regarder [28] □ Have a look at this! Regardez ceci !
■ **I don't like the look of it.** Ça ne me dit rien.

to **look** VERB
▷ *see also* **look** NOUN
1 regarder [28]
□ Look! Regardez !
■ **to look at something** regarder [28] quelque chose □ Look at the picture. Regardez cette image.
2 avoir [8] l'air (*seem*)
□ She looks surprised. Elle a l'air surprise. □ That cake looks nice. Ce gâteau a l'air bon. □ It looks fine. Ça a l'air bien.
■ **to look like somebody** ressembler [28] à quelqu'un □ He looks like his brother. Il ressemble à son frère.
■ **What does she look like?** Comment est-elle physiquement ?
■ **to look forward to something** attendre [7] quelque chose avec impatience □ I'm looking forward to the holidays. J'attends les vacances avec impatience.
■ **Looking forward to hearing from you ...** J'espère avoir bientôt de tes nouvelles ... (*at the end of email, letter*)
■ **Look out!** Attention !

to **look after** VERB
s'occuper [28] de
□ I look after my little sister. Je m'occupe de ma petite sœur.

to **look for** VERB
chercher [28]
□ I'm looking for my passport. Je cherche mon passeport.

to **look round** VERB
1 se retourner [72] (*look behind*)
□ I shouted and he looked round. J'ai crié et il s'est retourné.
2 jeter [41] un coup d'œil (*have a look*)
□ I'm just looking round. Je jette simplement un coup d'œil.
■ **to look round a museum** visiter [28] un musée
■ **I like looking round the shops.** J'aime faire les boutiques.

to **look up** VERB
chercher [28] (*word, name*)
□ Look the word up in the dictionary. Cherchez le mot dans le dictionnaire.

loose ADJECTIVE
ample (FEM ample) (*clothes*)
■ **loose change** la petite monnaie

lord NOUN
le seigneur *masc* (*feudal*)
■ **the House of Lords** la Chambre des lords

lorry NOUN
le camion *masc*

lorry driver NOUN
le routier *masc*
□ He's a lorry driver. Il est routier.

to **lose** VERB
perdre [61]
□ I've lost my purse. J'ai perdu mon porte-monnaie.
■ **to get lost** se perdre [61] □ I was afraid of getting lost. J'avais peur de me perdre.

loser NOUN
1 le perdant *masc*
la perdante *fem*
■ **to be a bad loser** être [35] mauvais perdant
2 le loser *masc* (*pathetic person*)
□ He's such a loser! C'est un vrai loser !

loss NOUN
la perte *fem*

lost VERB ▷ see lose

lost ADJECTIVE
perdu (FEM perdue)

lost-and-found NOUN (US)
les objets trouvés *masc pl*

lost property office NOUN
les objets trouvés *masc pl*

lot NOUN
■ **a lot** beaucoup
■ **a lot of** beaucoup de □ We saw a lot of interesting things. Nous avons vu beaucoup de choses intéressantes.
■ **lots of** un tas de □ She's got lots of money. Elle a un tas d'argent. □ He's got lots of friends. Il a un tas d'amis.
■ **What did you do at the weekend? — Not a lot.** Qu'as-tu fait ce week-end ? — Pas grand-chose.
■ **Do you like football? — Not a lot.** Tu aimes le football ? — Pas tellement.
■ **That's the lot.** C'est tout.

lottery NOUN
la loterie *fem*
□ to win the lottery gagner à la loterie

loud ADJECTIVE
fort (FEM forte)
□ The television is too loud. La télévision est trop forte.

loudly ADVERB
fort

loudspeaker NOUN
le haut-parleur *masc*

lounge NOUN
le salon *masc*

lousy ADJECTIVE
infect (FEM infecte)
□ The food in the canteen is lousy. La nourriture de la cantine est infecte.

■ **I feel lousy.** Je suis mal fichu. (*informal*)

love NOUN
▷ see also **love** VERB
l'amour *masc*
■ **to be in love** être [35] amoureux □ She's in love with Ryan. Elle est amoureuse de Ryan.
■ **Give your brother my love.** Embrasse ton frère pour moi.
■ **Love, Mum.** Bisous, Maman.

to **love** VERB
▷ see also **love** NOUN
1 aimer [28] (*be in love with*)
□ I love you. Je t'aime.
2 aimer [28] beaucoup (*like a lot*)
□ Everybody loves her. Tout le monde l'aime beaucoup. □ I'd love to come. J'aimerais beaucoup venir.
3 adorer [28] (*things*)
□ I love chocolate. J'adore le chocolat. □ I love skiing. J'adore le ski.

lovely ADJECTIVE
charmant (FEM charmante)
□ What a lovely surprise! Quelle charmante surprise ! □ She's a lovely person. Elle est charmante.
■ **It's a lovely day.** Il fait très beau aujourd'hui.
■ **Is your meal OK? — Yes, it's lovely.** Est-ce que c'est bon ? — Oui, c'est délicieux.
■ **They've got a lovely house.** Ils ont une très belle maison.
■ **Have a lovely time!** Amusez-vous bien !

lover NOUN
1 l'amant *masc*
la maîtresse *fem* (*in relationship*)
2 l'amateur *masc* (*fan*)
□ a music lover un amateur de musique

low ADJECTIVE, ADVERB
bas (FEM basse) (*price, level*)
□ That plane is flying very low. Cet avion vole très bas.
■ **the low season** la basse saison □ in the low season en basse saison

lower ADJECTIVE
▷ see also **lower** VERB
inférieur (FEM inférieure)
□ on the lower floor a l'étage inférieur

to **lower** VERB
▷ see also **lower** ADJECTIVE
baisser [28]

low-fat ADJECTIVE
allégé (FEM allégée)
□ a low-fat yoghurt un yaourt allégé

loyalty NOUN
la fidélité *fem*

loyalty card NOUN
la carte de fidélité *fem*

L-plates PL NOUN
les plaques de conducteur débutant *fem pl*

luck NOUN
la chance *fem*
□ She hasn't had much luck. Elle n'a pas eu beaucoup de chance.
■ **Good luck!** Bonne chance !
■ **Bad luck!** Pas de chance !

luckily ADVERB
heureusement

lucky ADJECTIVE
■ **to be lucky** **1** (*be fortunate*) avoir [8] de la chance □ Lucky you! Tu as de la chance ! □ He's lucky, he's got a job. Il a de la chance, il a un emploi. □ He wasn't hurt. — That was lucky! Il n'a pas été blessé. — C'est une chance ! **2** (*bring luck*) porter [28] bonheur □ Black cats are lucky in Britain. Les chats noirs portent bonheur en Grande-Bretagne.
■ **a lucky horseshoe** un fer à cheval porte-bonheur

luggage NOUN
les bagages *masc pl*

lukewarm ADJECTIVE
tiède (FEM tiède) (*water, food*)
■ **The response was lukewarm.** La réponse a été peu enthousiaste.

lump NOUN
1 le morceau *masc* (PL les morceaux)
□ a lump of butter un morceau de beurre
2 la bosse *fem* (*swelling*)
□ He's got a lump on his forehead. Il a une bosse sur le front.

lunch NOUN
le déjeuner *masc*
■ **to have lunch** déjeuner [28] □ We have lunch at 12.30. Nous déjeunons à midi et demi.

luncheon voucher NOUN
le ticket-restaurant *masc*

lung NOUN
le poumon *masc*
□ lung cancer le cancer du poumon

luscious ADJECTIVE
délicieux (FEM délicieuse)

lush ADJECTIVE
luxuriant (FEM luxuriante)

lust NOUN
le désir *masc*

Luxembourg NOUN
1 le Luxembourg *masc* (*country*)
■ **in Luxembourg** au Luxembourg
■ **to Luxembourg** au Luxembourg
2 Luxembourg (*city*)
■ **in Luxembourg** à Luxembourg

luxurious ADJECTIVE
luxueux (FEM luxueuse)

luxury NOUN
le luxe *masc*
□ It was luxury! C'était le luxe !
■ **a luxury hotel** un hôtel de luxe

lying VERB ▷ *see* **lie**

lyrics PL NOUN
les paroles *fem pl* (*of song*)

l

Mm

mac NOUN
l'imper *masc*

macaroni NOUN
les macaronis *masc pl*

machine NOUN
la machine *fem*

machine gun NOUN
la mitrailleuse *fem*

machinery NOUN
les machines *fem pl*

mackerel NOUN
le maquereau *masc* (PL les maquereaux)

mad ADJECTIVE
1 fou (FEM folle) (*insane*)
□ You're mad! Tu es fou !

> **fou** changes to **fol** before a vowel and most words beginning with 'h'.

2 furieux (FEM furieuse) (*angry*)
□ She'll be mad when she finds out. Elle sera furieuse quand elle va s'en apercevoir.
■ **to be mad about** 1 (*sport, activity*) être [35] dingue de □ He's mad about basketball. Il est dingue de basket. 2 (*person, animal*) adorer [28] □ She's mad about horses. Elle adore les chevaux.

madam NOUN
madame *fem*
□ Would you like to order, Madam? Désirez-vous commander, Madame ?

made VERB ▷ see **make**

madly ADVERB
■ **They're madly in love.** Ils sont éperdument amoureux.

madman NOUN
le fou *masc*

madness NOUN
la folie *fem*
□ It's absolute madness. C'est de la pure folie.

magazine NOUN
le magazine *masc*

maggot NOUN
l'asticot *masc*

magic ADJECTIVE
▷ *see also* **magic** NOUN
1 magique (FEM magique) (*magical*)

□ a magic wand une baguette magique
2 super (FEM+PL super) (*brilliant*)
□ It was magic! C'était super !

magic NOUN
▷ *see also* **magic** ADJECTIVE
la magie *fem*
■ **a magic trick** un tour de magie
■ **My hobby is magic.** Je fais des tours de magie.

magician NOUN
le prestidigitateur *masc* (*conjurer*)

magnet NOUN
l'aimant *masc*

magnificent ADJECTIVE
1 magnifique (FEM magnifique) (*beautiful*)
□ a magnificent view une vue magnifique
2 superbe (FEM superbe) (*outstanding*)
□ It was a magnificent effort. Ils ont fait un superbe effort.

magnifying glass NOUN
la loupe *fem*

maid NOUN
la domestique *fem* (*servant*)

maiden name NOUN
le nom de jeune fille *masc*

mail NOUN
▷ *see also* **mail** VERB
1 le courrier *masc*
□ Here's your mail. Voici ton courrier.
2 les mails *masc pl* (*emails*)
□ Can I check my mail on your laptop? Je peux consulter mes mails sur ton ordinateur portable ?
■ **by mail** par la poste

to mail VERB
▷ *see also* **mail** NOUN
■ **to mail something** (*email*) envoyer [33] quelque chose par mail □ I'll mail you my address. Je t'enverrai mon adresse par mail.

mailbox NOUN (US)
la boîte à lettres *fem*

mailing list NOUN
la liste d'adresses *fem*

mailman NOUN (US)
le facteur *masc*

main ADJECTIVE
principal (FEM principale, MASC PL principaux)

□ the main problem le principal problème

■ **the main thing is to ...** l'essentiel est de ...

mainly ADVERB

principalement

main road NOUN

la grande route *fem*

□ I don't like cycling on main roads. Je n'aime pas faire du vélo sur les grandes routes.

to **maintain** VERB

entretenir [83] (*machine, building*)

maintenance NOUN

l'entretien *masc* (*of machine, building*)

maize NOUN

le maïs *masc*

majesty NOUN

la majesté *fem*

■ **Your Majesty** Votre Majesté

major ADJECTIVE

majeur (FEM majeure)

□ a major problem un problème majeur

■ **in C major** en do majeur

■ **a major operation** une opération d'envergure

Majorca NOUN

Majorque *fem*

□ We went to Majorca in August. Nous sommes allés à Majorque en août.

majority NOUN

la majorité *fem*

make NOUN

▷ *see also* **make** VERB

la marque *fem*

□ What make is that car? De quelle marque est cette voiture ?

to **make** VERB

▷ *see also* **make** NOUN

1 faire [36]

□ I'm going to make a cake. Je vais faire un gâteau. □ He made it himself. Il l'a fait lui-même. □ I make my bed every morning. Je fais mon lit tous les matins. □ 2 and 2 make 4. Deux et deux font quatre.

2 fabriquer [28] (*manufacture*)

□ made in France fabriqué en France

3 gagner [28] (*earn*)

□ He makes a lot of money. Il gagne beaucoup d'argent.

■ **to make somebody do something** obliger [45] quelqu'un à faire quelque chose □ My mother makes me do my homework. Ma mère m'oblige à faire mes devoirs.

■ **to make lunch** préparer [28] le repas

□ She's making lunch. Elle prépare le repas.

■ **to make a phone call** donner [28] un coup de téléphone □ I'd like to make a phone call. J'aimerais donner un coup de téléphone.

■ **to make fun of somebody** se moquer [28] de quelqu'un □ They made fun of him. Ils se sont moqués de lui.

■ **What time do you make it?** Quelle heure avez-vous ?

to **make out** VERB

1 déchiffrer [28] (*read*)

□ I can't make out the address on the label. Je n'arrive pas à déchiffrer l'adresse sur l'étiquette.

2 comprendre [65] (*understand*)

□ I can't make her out at all. Je n'arrive pas du tout à la comprendre.

3 prétendre [88] (*claim, pretend*)

□ They're making out it was my fault. Ils prétendent que c'était ma faute.

to **make up** VERB

1 inventer [28] (*invent*)

□ He made up the whole story. Il a inventé cette histoire de toutes pièces.

2 se réconcilier [19] (*after argument*)

□ They had a quarrel, but soon made up. Ils se sont disputés, mais se sont vite réconciliés.

makeover NOUN

le relookage *masc*

■ **She had a complete makeover.** Elle est relookée des pieds à la tête.

maker NOUN

1 le fabricant *masc*

□ Europe's biggest car maker le plus grand fabricant de voitures d'Europe

2 la machine *fem*

□ a bread maker une machine à pain □ a pasta maker une machine à pâtes

■ **an ice-cream maker** une sorbetière

■ **a film maker** un cinéaste

make-up NOUN

le maquillage *masc*

Malaysia NOUN

la Malaisie *fem*

■ **in Malaysia** en Malaisie

male ADJECTIVE

1 mâle (FEM mâle) (*animals, plants*)

□ a male kitten un chaton mâle

2 masculin (FEM masculine) (*person, on official forms*)

□ Sex: male. Sexe : masculin.

■ **Most of the players are male.** La plupart des joueurs sont des hommes.

■ **a male nurse** un infirmier

malicious ADJECTIVE

malveillant (FEM malveillante)

□ a malicious rumour une rumeur malveillante

BE CAREFUL!

Do not translate **malicious** by the French word **malicieux**.

m

mall NOUN
le centre commercial *masc*

Malta NOUN
Malte
- **in Malta** à Malte
- **to Malta** à Malte

mammoth NOUN
▷ *see also* **mammoth** ADJECTIVE
le mammouth *masc*

mammoth ADJECTIVE
▷ *see also* **mammoth** NOUN
monstre (FEM monstre)
□ a mammoth task un travail monstre

man NOUN
l'homme *masc*
□ an old man un vieil homme

to **manage** VERB
1 diriger [45] (*be in charge of*)
□ She manages a big store. Elle dirige un grand magasin. □ He manages our football team. Il dirige notre équipe de foot.
2 se débrouiller [28] (*get by*)
□ We haven't got much money, but we manage. Nous n'avons pas beaucoup d'argent, mais nous nous débrouillons. □ It's okay, I can manage. Ça va, je me débrouille.
- **Can you manage okay?** Tu y arrives ?
- **to manage to do something** réussir [38] à faire quelque chose □ Luckily I managed to pass the exam. J'ai heureusement réussi à avoir mon examen.
- **I can't manage all that.** (*food*) C'est trop pour moi.

manageable ADJECTIVE
faisable (FEM faisable) (*task*)

management NOUN
1 la gestion *fem* (*organization*)
□ He's responsible for the management of the sports centre. Il est responsable de la gestion du centre sportif.
2 la direction *fem* (*people in charge*)
- **'under new management'** « changement de direction »

manager NOUN
1 le directeur *masc*
la directrice *fem* (*of company*)
2 le gérant *masc*
la gérante *fem* (*of shop, restaurant*)
3 le manager *masc* (*of team, performer*)

manageress NOUN
la gérante *fem*

mandarin NOUN
la mandarine *fem* (*fruit*)

mango NOUN
la mangue *fem*

mania NOUN
la manie *fem*

maniac NOUN
le fou *masc*
la folle *fem*
□ He drives like a maniac. Il conduit comme un fou.

to **manipulate** VERB
manipuler [28]

mankind NOUN
l'humanité *fem*

man-made ADJECTIVE
synthétique (FEM synthétique) (*fibre*)

manner NOUN
la façon *fem*
□ She was behaving in an odd manner. Elle se comportait de façon étrange.
- **He has a confident manner.** Il a de l'assurance.

manners PL NOUN
les manières *fem pl*
□ good manners les bonnes manières □ Her manners are appalling. Elle a de très mauvaises manières.
- **It's bad manners to speak with your mouth full.** Ce n'est pas poli de parler la bouche pleine.

manpower NOUN
la main-d'œuvre *fem*

mansion NOUN
le manoir *masc*

mantelpiece NOUN
la cheminée *fem*

manual NOUN
le manuel *masc*

to **manufacture** VERB
fabriquer [28]

manufacturer NOUN
le fabricant *masc*
la fabricante *fem*

manure NOUN
le fumier *masc*

manuscript NOUN
le manuscrit *masc*

many ADJECTIVE, PRONOUN
beaucoup de
□ The country has many natural resources. Le pays a beaucoup de ressources naturelles. □ He hasn't got many friends. Il n'a pas beaucoup d'amis. □ Were there many people at the concert? Est-ce qu'il y avait beaucoup de gens au concert ?
- **very many** beaucoup de □ I haven't got very many summer clothes. Je n'ai pas beaucoup de vêtements d'été.
- **Not many.** Pas beaucoup.
- **How many?** Combien ? □ How many do you want? Combien en veux-tu ?
- **how many ...?** combien de ... ? □ How many euros do you get for £100? Combien

m

d'euros a-t-on pour cent livres ?

■ **too many** trop □ That's too many. C'est trop.

■ **too many** trop de ... □ She makes too many mistakes. Elle fait trop d'erreurs.

■ **so many** autant □ I didn't know there would be so many. Je ne pensais pas qu'il y en aurait autant.

■ **so many ...** autant de ... □ I've never seen so many police officers. Je n'ai jamais vu autant de policiers.

map NOUN

1 la carte *fem* (*of country, area*)

2 le plan *masc* (*of town*)

marathon NOUN

le marathon *masc*

□ the London marathon le marathon de Londres

marble NOUN

le marbre *masc*

□ a marble statue une statue en marbre

■ **to play marbles** jouer [28] aux billes

March NOUN

mars *masc*

■ **in March** en mars

march NOUN

▷ see also **march** VERB

la manifestation *fem* (*demonstration*)

to **march** VERB

▷ see also **march** NOUN

1 marcher [28] au pas (*soldiers*)

2 défiler [28] (*protesters*)

mare NOUN

la jument *fem*

margarine NOUN

la margarine *fem*

margin NOUN

la marge *fem*

□ Write notes in the margin. Écrivez vos notes dans la marge.

marijuana NOUN

la marijuana *fem*

marina NOUN

la marina *fem*

marital status NOUN

la situation de famille *fem*

mark NOUN

▷ see also **mark** VERB

1 la note *fem* (*in school*)

□ I get good marks for maths. J'ai de bonnes notes en maths.

2 la tache *fem* (*stain*)

□ You've got a mark on your skirt. Tu as une tache sur ta jupe.

to **mark** VERB

▷ see also **mark** NOUN

corriger [45]

□ The teacher hasn't marked my homework yet. Le professeur n'a pas encore corrigé mon devoir.

market NOUN

le marché *masc*

marketing NOUN

le marketing *masc*

marketplace NOUN

la place du marché *fem*

marmalade NOUN

la confiture d'oranges *fem*

maroon ADJECTIVE

bordeaux (FEM+PL bordeaux) (*colour*)

marriage NOUN

le mariage *masc*

married ADJECTIVE

marié (FEM mariée)

□ They are not married. Ils ne sont pas mariés.

□ They have been married for 15 years. Ils sont mariés depuis quinze ans. □ a married couple un couple marié

marrow NOUN

la courge *fem* (*vegetable*)

■ **bone marrow** la moelle

to **marry** VERB

épouser [28]

□ He wants to marry her. Il veut l'épouser.

■ **to get married** se marier [19] □ My sister's getting married in June. Ma sœur se marie en juin.

marvellous (US **marvelous**) ADJECTIVE

1 excellent (FEM excellente)

□ She's a marvellous cook. C'est une excellente cuisinière.

2 superbe (FEM superbe)

□ The weather was marvellous. Il a fait un temps superbe.

marzipan NOUN

la pâte d'amandes *fem*

mascara NOUN

le mascara *masc*

masculine ADJECTIVE

masculin (FEM masculine)

mashed potatoes PL NOUN

la purée *fem sing*

□ chicken with mashed potatoes du poulet avec de la purée

mask NOUN

le masque *masc*

masked ADJECTIVE

masqué (FEM masquée)

mass NOUN

1 la multitude *fem*

□ a mass of books and papers une multitude de livres et de papiers

2 la messe *fem* (*in church*)

□ We go to mass on Sunday. Nous allons à la messe le dimanche.

■ **the mass media** les médias

m

massage NOUN
le massage *masc*

massive ADJECTIVE
énorme (FEM énorme)

to **master** VERB
maîtriser [28]

masterpiece NOUN
le chef-d'œuvre *masc* (PL les chefs-d'œuvre)

mat NOUN
le paillasson *masc* (*doormat*)
■ **a table mat** un set de table
■ **a beach mat** un tapis de plage

match NOUN
▷ *see also* **match** VERB
1 l'allumette *fem*
□ a box of matches une boîte d'allumettes
2 le match *masc* (*sport*)
□ a football match un match de foot

to **match** VERB
▷ *see also* **match** NOUN
être [35] assorti à
□ The jacket matches the trousers. La veste est assortie au pantalon.
■ **These colours don't match.** Ces couleurs ne vont pas ensemble.

matching ADJECTIVE
assorti (FEM assortie)
□ My bedroom has matching wallpaper and curtains. Ma chambre a du papier peint et des rideaux assortis.

mate NOUN
le pote *masc* (*informal*)
□ On Friday night I go out with my mates. Vendredi soir, je sors avec mes potes.

material NOUN
1 le tissu *masc* (*cloth*)
2 la documentation *fem* (*information, data*)
□ I'm collecting material for my project. Je rassemble une documentation pour mon dossier.
■ **raw materials** les matières premières *fem pl*

mathematics NOUN
les mathématiques *fem pl*

maths NOUN
les maths *fem pl*

matron NOUN
l'infirmière-chef *fem* (PL les infirmières-chefs) (*in hospital*)

matter NOUN
▷ *see also* **matter** VERB
la question *fem*
□ It's a matter of life and death. C'est une question de vie ou de mort.
■ **What's the matter?** Qu'est-ce qui ne va pas ?
■ **as a matter of fact** en fait

to **matter** VERB
▷ *see also* **matter** NOUN

■ **it doesn't matter 1** (*I don't mind*) ça ne fait rien □ I can't give you the money today. — It doesn't matter. Je ne peux pas te donner l'argent aujourd'hui. — Ça ne fait rien. **2** (*it makes no difference*) ça n'a pas d'importance □ It doesn't matter if you're late. Ça n'a pas d'importance si tu es en retard.
■ **It matters a lot to me.** C'est très important pour moi.

mattress NOUN
le matelas *masc*

mature ADJECTIVE
mûr (FEM mûre)
□ She's quite mature for her age. Elle est très mûre pour son âge.

maximum NOUN
▷ *see also* **maximum** ADJECTIVE
le maximum *masc*

maximum ADJECTIVE
▷ *see also* **maximum** NOUN
maximum (FEM+PL maximum)
□ The maximum speed is 100 km/h. La vitesse maximum autorisée est de cent kilomètres à l'heure.
■ **the maximum amount** le maximum

May NOUN
mai *masc*
■ **in May** en mai
■ **May Day** le Premier Mai

may VERB
■ **He may come.** Il va peut-être venir. □ It may rain. Il va peut-être pleuvoir.
■ **May I sit down?** Est-ce que je peux m'asseoir ?

maybe ADVERB
peut-être
□ maybe not peut-être pas □ a bit boring, maybe peut-être un peu ennuyeux □ Maybe she's at home. Elle est peut-être chez elle.
□ Maybe he'll change his mind. Il va peut-être changer d'avis.

mayonnaise NOUN
la mayonnaise *fem*

mayor NOUN
le maire *masc*

maze NOUN
le labyrinthe *masc*

me PRONOUN
1 me
□ Could you lend me your ruler? Est-ce que tu peux me prêter ton ta règle ?
m'

me becomes **m'** before a vowel sound.

□ Can you tell me the way to the station? Est-ce que vous pouvez m'indiquer le chemin de la gare ? □ Can you help me? Est-ce que tu peux m'aider ? □ He heard me. Il m'a entendu.

2 moi

> moi is used in exclamations.

□ Me too! Moi aussi ! □ Excuse me! Excusez-moi ! □ Look at me! Regarde-moi ! □ Wait for me! Attends-moi ! □ Come with me! Suivez-moi !

> moi is also used after prepositions and in comparisons.

□ You're after me. Tu es après moi. □ Is it for me? C'est pour moi ? □ She's older than me. Elle est plus âgée que moi.

meal NOUN
le repas masc

mealtime NOUN
■ **at mealtimes** aux heures des repas

to mean VERB
▷ see also **mean** ADJECTIVE, **means** NOUN
vouloir [93] dire
□ What does 'complet' mean? Qu'est-ce que « complet » veut dire ? □ I don't know what it means. Je ne sais pas ce que ça veut dire. □ What do you mean? Qu'est que vous voulez dire ? □ That's not what I meant. Ce n'est pas ce que je voulais dire.
■ **Which one do you mean?** Duquel veux-tu parler ?
■ **Do you really mean it?** Tu es sérieux ?
■ **to mean to do something** avoir [8] l'intention de faire quelque chose □ I didn't mean to offend you. Je n'avais pas l'intention de vous blesser.

mean ADJECTIVE
▷ see also **mean** VERB, **means** NOUN
1 radin (FEM radine) (with money)
□ He's too mean to buy Christmas presents. Il est trop radin pour acheter des cadeaux de Noël.
2 méchant (FEM méchante) (unkind)
□ You're being mean to me. Tu es méchant avec moi.
■ **That's a really mean thing to say!** Ce n'est vraiment pas gentil de dire ça !

meaning NOUN
le sens masc

means NOUN
▷ see also **mean** VERB, ADJECTIVE
le moyen masc
□ He'll do it by any possible means. Il le fera par tous les moyens. □ a means of transport un moyen de transport
■ **by means of** au moyen de □ He got in by means of a stolen key. Il est entré au moyen d'une clé volée.
■ **by all means** bien sûr □ Can I come? — By all means! Est-ce que je peux venir ? — Bien sûr !

meant VERB ▷ see **mean**

meanwhile ADVERB
pendant ce temps

measles NOUN
la rougeole fem

to measure VERB
1 mesurer [28]
□ I measured the page. J'ai mesuré la page.
2 faire [36]
□ The room measures 3 metres by 4. La pièce fait trois mètres sur quatre.

measurements PL NOUN
1 les dimensions fem pl (of object)
□ What are the measurements of the room? Quelles sont les dimensions de la pièce ?
2 les mensurations fem pl (of body)
□ What are your measurements? Quelles sont tes mensurations ?
■ **my waist measurement** mon tour de taille
■ **What's your neck measurement?** Quel est votre tour de cou ?

meat NOUN
la viande fem
□ I don't eat meat. Je ne mange pas de viande.

Mecca NOUN
La Mecque

mechanic NOUN
le mécanicien masc
□ He's a mechanic. Il est mécanicien.

mechanical ADJECTIVE
mécanique (FEM mécanique)

medal NOUN
la médaille fem
■ **the gold medal** la médaille d'or

medallion NOUN
le médaillon masc

media PL NOUN
les médias masc pl

median strip NOUN (US)
le terre-plein central masc

medical ADJECTIVE
▷ see also **medical** NOUN
médical (FEM médicale, MASC PL médicaux)
□ medical treatment les soins médicaux
■ **medical insurance** l'assurance maladie
■ **to have medical problems** avoir [8] des problèmes de santé
■ **She's a medical student.** Elle est étudiante en médecine.

medical NOUN
▷ see also **medical** ADJECTIVE
■ **to have a medical** passer [58] une visite médicale

medicine NOUN
1 la médecine fem (subject)
□ I want to study medicine. Je veux faire médecine.
■ **alternative medicine** la médecine douce
2 le médicament masc (medication)
□ I need some medicine. J'ai besoin d'un médicament.

m

English-French

Mediterranean ADJECTIVE

méditerranéen (FEM méditerranéenne)
- **the Mediterranean** la Méditerranée

medium ADJECTIVE

moyen (FEM moyenne)
□ a man of medium height un homme de taille moyenne

medium-sized ADJECTIVE

de taille moyenne
□ a medium-sized town une ville de taille moyenne

to **meet** VERB

1 rencontrer [28] (by chance)
□ I met Ali in the street. J'ai rencontré Ali dans la rue. □ Have you met him before? Tu l'as déjà rencontré ?

2 se rencontrer [28]
□ We met by chance in the shopping centre. Nous nous sommes rencontrés par hasard dans le centre commercial.

3 retrouver [28] (by arrangement)
□ I'm going to meet my friends. Je vais retrouver mes amis.

4 se retrouver [28]
□ Let's meet in front of the tourist office. Retrouvons-nous devant l'office de tourisme.
- **I like meeting new people.** J'aime faire de nouvelles connaissances.

5 aller [3⁵] chercher (pick up)
□ I'll meet you at the station. J'irai te chercher à la gare.

to **meet up** VERB

se retrouver [28]
□ What time shall we meet up? On se retrouve à quelle heure ?

meeting NOUN

1 la réunion fem (for work)
□ a business meeting une réunion d'affaires

2 la rencontre fem (socially)
□ their first meeting leur première rencontre

meg NOUN (= megabyte)
le mégaoctet masc

mega ADJECTIVE
- **He's mega rich.** Il est hyper-riche. (informal)

melody NOUN
la mélodie fem

melon NOUN
le melon masc

to **melt** VERB

fondre [69]
□ The snow is melting. La neige est en train de fondre.

member NOUN
le/la membre masc/fem
- **a Member of Parliament** un député

membership NOUN
l'adhésion fem (of club)

□ to apply for membership faire une demande d'adhésion

membership card NOUN
la carte de membre fem

meme NOUN
le mème masc

memento NOUN
le souvenir masc

memorial NOUN
le monument masc
□ a war memorial un monument aux morts

to **memorize** VERB
apprendre [65] par cœur

memory NOUN

1 la mémoire fem (also for computer)
□ I haven't got a good memory. Je n'ai pas une bonne mémoire.

2 le souvenir masc (recollection)
□ That brings back memories. Cela me rappelle des souvenirs.

memory card NOUN
la carte mémoire fem

memory stick NOUN
la clé USB fem (for computer)

men PL NOUN ▷ see **man**

to **mend** VERB
réparer [28]

meningitis NOUN
la méningite fem

mental ADJECTIVE
mental (FEM mentale, MASC PL mentaux)
□ a mental illness une maladie mentale

mentality NOUN
la mentalité fem

to **mention** VERB
mentionner [28]
- **Thank you! — Don't mention it!** Merci ! — Il n'y a pas de quoi !

mentor NOUN
▷ see also **mentor** VERB
le mentor masc

mentor VERB
▷ see also **mentor** NOUN
servir [78] de mentor à

menu NOUN
le menu masc
□ Could I have the menu please? Est-ce que je pourrais avoir le menu s'il vous plaît ?

merchant NOUN
le marchand masc
la marchande fem
□ a wine merchant un marchand de vin

mercy NOUN
la pitié fem

mere ADJECTIVE
- **a mere five per cent** à peine cinq pour cent

m

■ **It's a mere formality.** C'est une simple formalité.

■ **the merest hint of criticism** la moindre petite critique

meringue NOUN
la meringue *fem*

merry ADJECTIVE
■ **Merry Christmas!** Joyeux Noël !

merry-go-round NOUN
le manège *masc*

mess NOUN
le fouillis *masc*
□ My bedroom's usually in a mess. Il y a généralement du fouillis dans ma chambre.

to **mess about** VERB
■ **to mess about with something** (*interfere with*) tripoter [28] quelque chose □ Stop messing about with my computer! Arrête de tripoter mon ordinateur !
■ **Don't mess about with my things!** Ne touche pas à mes affaires !

to **mess up** VERB
■ **to mess something up** mettre [47] la pagaille dans quelque chose □ My little brother has messed up my drawings. Mon petit frère a mis la pagaille dans mes dessins.

message NOUN
▷ *see also* **message** VERB
le message *masc*

to **message** VERB
▷ *see also* **message** NOUN
envoyer [33] un message
□ She messaged me on Facebook. Elle m'a envoyé un message sur Facebook.

messenger NOUN
le messager *masc*

messy ADJECTIVE
1 salissant (FEM salissante) (*dirty*)
□ a messy job un travail salissant
2 en désordre (*untidy*)
□ Your desk is really messy. Ton bureau est vraiment en désordre.
3 désordonné (FEM désordonnée) (*person*)
□ She's so messy! Elle est tellement désordonnée !
■ **My writing is terribly messy.** J'ai une écriture de cochon.

met VERB ▷ *see* **meet**

metal NOUN
le métal *masc* (PL les métaux)

meter NOUN
1 le compteur *masc* (*for gas, electricity, taxi*)
2 le parcmètre *masc* (*parking meter*)
3 le mètre *masc* (US: *unit of measurement*)

method NOUN
la méthode *fem*

metre NOUN
le mètre *masc*

metric ADJECTIVE
métrique (FEM métrique)

Mexico NOUN
le Mexique *masc*
■ **in Mexico** au Mexique
■ **to Mexico** au Mexique

to **miaow** VERB
miauler [28]

mice PL NOUN ▷ *see* **mouse**

microblog NOUN
le microblog *masc*

microblogging site NOUN
le site de microblogging *masc*

microchip NOUN
la puce *fem*

microphone NOUN
le microphone *masc*

microscope NOUN
le microscope *masc*

microwave oven NOUN
le four à micro-ondes *masc*

mid ADJECTIVE
■ **in mid May** à la mi-mai

midday NOUN
midi *masc*
■ **at midday** à midi

middle NOUN
le milieu *masc*
□ in the middle of the road au milieu de la route
□ in the middle of the night au milieu de la nuit
□ the middle seat la place du milieu

middle-aged ADJECTIVE
d'un certain âge
□ a middle-aged man un homme d'un certain âge
■ **to be middle-aged** avoir [8] la cinquantaine
■ **She's middle-aged.** Elle a la cinquantaine.

Middle Ages PL NOUN
■ **the Middle Ages** le Moyen Âge *sing*

middle-class ADJECTIVE
de la classe moyenne
□ a middle-class family une famille de la classe moyenne

Middle East NOUN
le Moyen-Orient *masc*
■ **in the Middle East** au Moyen-Orient

middle name NOUN
le deuxième nom *masc*

midge NOUN
le moucheron *masc*

midnight NOUN
minuit *masc*
■ **at midnight** à minuit

m

midwife NOUN
la sage-femme *fem* (PL les sages-femmes)
□ She's a midwife. Elle est sage-femme.

might VERB
□ He might come later. Il va peut-être venir plus tard. □ We might go to Spain next year. Nous irons peut-être en Espagne l'an prochain. □ She might not have understood. Elle n'a peut-être pas compris.

migraine NOUN
la migraine *fem*
□ I've got a migraine. J'ai la migraine.

mike NOUN
le micro *masc*

mild ADJECTIVE
doux (FEM douce)
□ The winters are quite mild. Les hivers sont assez doux.

mile NOUN
le mille *masc*
□ It's 5 miles from here. C'est à huit kilomètres d'ici.

> **DID YOU KNOW...?**
> In France, distances are expressed in kilometres. A mile is about 1.6 kilometres.

■ **We walked miles!** Nous avons fait des kilomètres à pied !

military ADJECTIVE
militaire (FEM militaire)

milk NOUN
▷ *see also* **milk** VERB
le lait *masc*
□ tea with milk du thé au lait

to milk VERB
▷ *see also* **milk** NOUN
traire [85]

milk chocolate NOUN
le chocolat au lait *masc*

milk shake NOUN
le milk-shake *masc*

mill NOUN
le moulin *masc* (for grain)

millennium NOUN
le millénaire *masc*
□ the third millennium le troisième millénaire

millimetre (US millimeter) NOUN
le millimètre *masc*

million NOUN
le million *masc*

millionaire NOUN
le/la millionnaire *masc/fem*

to mimic VERB
imiter [28]

mince NOUN
la viande hachée *fem*

mince pie NOUN
la tartelette de Noël *fem*

to mind VERB
▷ *see also* **mind** NOUN
1 garder [28]
□ Could you mind the baby this afternoon? Est-ce que tu pourrais garder le bébé cet après-midi ?
2 surveiller [28] (keep an eye on)
□ Could you mind my bags for a few minutes? Est-ce que vous pourriez surveiller mes bagages pendant quelques minutes ?
■ **Do you mind if I open the window?** Est-ce que je pourrais ouvrir la fenêtre ?
■ **I don't mind.** Ça ne me dérange pas. □ I don't mind the noise. Le bruit ne me dérange pas.
■ **Never mind!** Ça ne fait rien !
■ **Mind that bike!** Attention au vélo !
■ **Mind the step!** Attention à la marche !

mind NOUN
▷ *see also* **mind** VERB
■ **to make up one's mind** se décider [28]
□ I haven't made up my mind yet. Je ne me suis pas encore décidé.
■ **to change one's mind** changer [45] d'avis
□ He's changed his mind. Il a changé d'avis.
■ **Are you out of your mind?** Tu as perdu la tête ?

mindfulness NOUN
la pleine conscience *fem*

mine PRONOUN
▷ *see also* **mine** NOUN
le mien + *masc noun*
□ Is this your coat? — No, mine's black. C'est ton manteau ? — Non, le mien est noir.
la mienne + *fem noun*
□ Is this your car? — No, mine's green. C'est ta voiture ? — Non, la mienne est verte.
les miens + *masc pl noun*
□ her parents and mine ses parents et les miens
les miennes + *fem pl noun*
□ Your hands are dirty, mine are clean. Tes mains sont sales, les miennes sont propres.
■ **It's mine.** C'est à moi. □ This book is mine. Ce livre est à moi. □ Whose is this? — It's mine. C'est à qui ? — À moi.

mine NOUN
▷ *see also* **mine** PRONOUN
la mine *fem*
□ a coal mine une mine de charbon □ a land mine une mine terrestre

miner NOUN
le mineur *masc*

mineral water NOUN
l'eau minérale *fem*

miniature ADJECTIVE
▷ *see also* **miniature** NOUN
miniature (FEM miniature)
□ a miniature version une version miniature

Numbers in brackets refer to verb tables on pages 650 to 658

miniature NOUN
▷ *see also* **miniature** ADJECTIVE
la miniature *fem*

minibus NOUN
le minibus *masc*

minicab NOUN
le taxi *masc*

> **DID YOU KNOW...?**
> In France, the distinction between black taxis and minicabs does not exist.

minimum NOUN
▷ *see also* **minimum** ADJECTIVE
le minimum *masc*

minimum ADJECTIVE
▷ *see also* **minimum** NOUN
minimum (FEM+PL minimum)
□ The minimum age for driving is 17. L'âge minimum pour conduire est dix-sept ans.
■ **the minimum amount** le minimum

miniskirt NOUN
la mini-jupe *fem*

minister NOUN
1 le ministre *masc* (*in government*)
2 le pasteur *masc* (*of church*)

ministry NOUN
le ministère *masc* (*in government*)
□ The Ministry of Defence Le ministère de la Défense

minor ADJECTIVE
mineur (FEM mineure)
□ a minor problem un problème mineur
■ **in D minor** en ré mineur
■ **a minor operation** une opération bénigne

minority NOUN
la minorité *fem*

mint NOUN
1 la menthe *fem* (*plant*)
□ mint sauce la sauce à la menthe
2 le bonbon à la menthe *masc* (*sweet*)

minus PREPOSITION
moins
□ 16 minus 3 is 13. Seize moins trois égale treize. □ It's minus two degrees outside. Il fait moins deux dehors. □ I got a B minus. J'ai eu un B moins.

minute NOUN
▷ *see also* **minute** ADJECTIVE
la minute *fem*
□ Wait a minute! Attends une minute !

minute ADJECTIVE
▷ *see also* **minute** NOUN
minuscule (FEM minuscule)
□ Her flat is minute. Son appartement est minuscule.

miracle NOUN
le miracle *masc*

mirror NOUN
1 la glace *fem* (*on wall*)
2 le rétroviseur *masc* (*in car*)

to misbehave VERB
se conduire [23] mal

miscellaneous ADJECTIVE
divers (FEM diverse)

mischief NOUN
les bêtises *fem pl*
□ My little sister's always up to mischief. Ma petite sœur fait constamment des bêtises.

mischievous ADJECTIVE
coquin (FEM coquine)

miser NOUN
l'avare *masc/fem*

miserable ADJECTIVE
1 malheureux (FEM malheureuse) (*person*)
□ You're looking miserable. Tu as l'air malheureux.
2 épouvantable (FEM épouvantable) (*weather*)
□ The weather was miserable. Il faisait un temps épouvantable.
■ **to feel miserable** ne pas avoir [8] le moral
□ I'm feeling miserable. Je n'ai pas le moral.

misery NOUN
1 la tristesse *fem* (*unhappiness*)
□ All that money brought nothing but misery. Tout cet argent n'a apporté que de la tristesse.
2 le pleurnicheur *masc*
la pleurnicheuse *fem* (*unhappy person*)
□ She's a real misery. C'est une vraie pleurnicheuse.

misfortune NOUN
le malheur *masc*

mishap NOUN
la mésaventure *fem*

to misjudge VERB
mal juger [45] (*person*)
□ I've misjudged her. Je l'ai mal jugée.
■ **He misjudged the bend.** Il a mal pris le virage.

to mislay VERB
égarer [28]
□ I've mislaid my passport. J'ai égaré mon passeport.

misleading ADJECTIVE
trompeur (FEM trompeuse)

Miss NOUN
1 Mademoiselle (PL Mesdemoiselles)
2 Mlle (PL Mlles) (*in address*)

to miss VERB
1 rater [28]
□ Hurry or you'll miss the bus. Dépêche-toi ou tu vas rater le bus. □ He missed the target. Il a raté la cible.
2 manquer [28]
□ to miss an opportunity manquer une occasion

m

■ **I miss you.** Tu me manques. □ I'm missing my family. Ma famille me manque. □ I miss him. Il me manque. □ I miss them. Ils me manquent.

missing ADJECTIVE
manquant (FEM manquante)
□ the missing part la pièce manquante
■ **to be missing** avoir [8] disparu □ My rucksack is missing. Mon sac à dos a disparu. □ Two members of the group are missing. Deux membres du groupe ont disparu.

missionary NOUN
le/la missionnaire *masc/fem*

mist NOUN
la brume *fem*

mistake NOUN
▷ *see also* **mistake** VERB
1 la faute *fem* (*slip*)
□ a spelling mistake une faute d'orthographe
■ **to make a mistake 1** (*in writing, speaking*) faire [36] une faute **2** (*get mixed up*) se tromper [28] □ I'm sorry, I made a mistake. Je suis désolé, je me suis trompé.
2 l'erreur *fem* (*misjudgement*)
□ It was a mistake to come. J'ai fait une erreur en venant.
■ **by mistake** par erreur □ I took his bag by mistake. J'ai pris son sac par erreur.

to mistake VERB
▷ *see also* **mistake** NOUN
■ **He mistook me for my sister.** Il m'a prise pour ma sœur.

mistaken ADJECTIVE
■ **to be mistaken** se tromper [28] □ If you think I'm coming with you, you're mistaken. Si tu penses que je vais venir avec toi, tu te trompes.

mistakenly ADVERB
à tort

mistletoe NOUN
le gui *masc*

mistook VERB ▷ *see* **mistake**

misty ADJECTIVE
brumeux (FEM brumeuse)
□ a misty morning un matin brumeux

to misunderstand VERB
mal comprendre [65]
□ Sorry, I misunderstood you. Je suis désolé, je t'avais mal compris.

misunderstanding NOUN
le malentendu *masc*

misunderstood VERB ▷ *see* **misunderstand**

mix NOUN
▷ *see also* **mix** VERB
le mélange *masc*
□ It's a mix of science fiction and comedy. C'est un mélange de science-fiction et de comédie.
■ **a cake mix** une préparation pour gâteau

to mix VERB
▷ *see also* **mix** NOUN
1 mélanger [45]
□ Mix the flour with the sugar. Mélangez la farine au sucre.
2 combiner [28]
□ He's mixing business with pleasure. Il combine les affaires et le plaisir.
■ **to mix with somebody** (*associate*) fréquenter [28] quelqu'un
■ **He doesn't mix much.** Il se tient à l'écart.

to mix up VERB
confondre [69] (*people*)
□ He always mixes me up with my sister. Il me confond toujours avec ma sœur.
■ **The travel agent mixed up the bookings.** L'agence de voyage s'est embrouillée dans les réservations.
■ **I'm getting mixed up.** Je ne m'y retrouve plus.

mixed ADJECTIVE
■ **a mixed salad** une salade composée
■ **a mixed school** une école mixte
■ **a mixed grill** un assortiment de grillades

mixer NOUN
le mixeur *masc*
■ **She's a good mixer.** Elle est très sociable.

mixture NOUN
le mélange *masc*
□ a mixture of spices un mélange d'épices
■ **cough mixture** le sirop pour la toux

mix-up NOUN
la confusion *fem*

MMS NOUN (= *multimedia messaging service*)
le MMS *masc*

to moan VERB
râler [28]
□ She's always moaning. Elle est toujours en train de râler.

mobile NOUN
le portable *masc* (*phone*)

mobile banking NOUN
les services bancaires mobiles *masc pl*

mobile home NOUN
le mobile home *masc*

mobile phone NOUN
le portable *masc*
■ **a mobile-phone mast** une antenne-relais

to mock VERB
▷ *see also* **mock** ADJECTIVE
ridiculiser [28]

mock ADJECTIVE
▷ *see also* **mock** VERB
■ **a mock exam** un examen blanc

model NOUN
▷ *see also* **model** ADJECTIVE

1 le modèle *masc* (*type*)
□ His TV is the latest model. Sa télé est le tout dernier modèle.

2 la maquette *fem* (*mock-up*)
□ a model of the castle une maquette du château

3 le mannequin *masc* (*fashion*)
□ She's a famous model. C'est un mannequin célèbre.

model ADJECTIVE
▷ *see also* **model** NOUN
■ **a model plane** un modèle réduit d'avion
■ **a model railway** un modèle réduit de voie ferrée
■ **He's a model pupil.** C'est un élève modèle.

to model VERB
▷ *see also* **model** NOUN
■ **She was modelling a Victoria Beckham outfit.** Elle présentait une tenue de la collection Victoria Beckham.

modem NOUN
le modem *masc*

moderate ADJECTIVE
modéré (FEM modérée)
□ His views are quite moderate. Ses opinions sont assez modérées.
■ **a moderate amount of** un peu de
■ **a moderate price** un prix raisonnable

modern ADJECTIVE
moderne (FEM moderne)

to modernize VERB
moderniser [28]

modest ADJECTIVE
modeste (FEM modeste)

to modify VERB
modifier [19]

moist ADJECTIVE
humide (FEM humide) (*skin, soil*)
□ Make sure the soil is moist. Assurez-vous que la terre est humide.

moisture NOUN
l'humidité *fem*

moisturizer NOUN
1 la crème hydratante *fem* (*cream*)
2 le lait hydratant *masc* (*lotion*)

moldy ADJECTIVE (US)
moisi (FEM moisie)

mole NOUN
1 la taupe *fem* (*animal*)
2 le grain de beauté *masc* (*on skin*)

moment NOUN
l'instant *masc*
□ Could you wait a moment? Pouvez-vous attendre un instant ? □ in a moment dans un instant □ Just a moment! Un instant !
■ **at the moment** en ce moment

■ **any moment now** d'un moment à l'autre
□ They'll be arriving any moment now. Ils vont arriver d'un moment à l'autre.

momentous ADJECTIVE
capital (FEM capitale) (*event*)

Monaco NOUN
Monaco
■ **in Monaco** à Monaco

monarch NOUN
le monarque *masc*

monarchy NOUN
la monarchie *fem*

monastery NOUN
le monastère *masc*

Monday NOUN
le lundi *masc*
□ on Monday lundi □ on Mondays le lundi
□ every Monday tous les lundis □ last Monday lundi dernier □ next Monday lundi prochain

to monetize VERB
monétiser [28]

money NOUN
l'argent *masc*
□ I need to change some money. J'ai besoin de changer de l'argent.
■ **to make money** gagner [28] de l'argent

> **BE CAREFUL!**
> Do not translate **money** by the French word **monnaie**.

mongrel NOUN
le bâtard *masc*
□ My dog's a mongrel. Mon chien est un bâtard.

monitor NOUN
le moniteur *masc* (*of computer*)

monk NOUN
le moine *masc*

monkey NOUN
le singe *masc*

monotonous ADJECTIVE
monotone (FEM monotone)

monster NOUN
le monstre *masc*

month NOUN
le mois *masc*
□ this month ce mois-ci □ next month le mois prochain □ last month le mois dernier □ every month tous les mois □ at the end of the month à la fin du mois

monthly ADJECTIVE
mensuel (FEM mensuelle)

monument NOUN
le monument *masc*

mood NOUN
l'humeur *fem*
■ **to be in a bad mood** être [35] de mauvaise humeur

m

moody – most

■ **to be in a good mood** être [35] de bonne humeur

moody ADJECTIVE
1 lunatique (FEM lunatique) (*temperamental*)
2 maussade (FEM maussade) (*in a bad mood*)

moon NOUN
la lune *fem*
□ There's a full moon tonight. Il y a pleine lune ce soir.
■ **to be over the moon** (*happy*) être [35] aux anges

moor NOUN
▷ *see also* **moor** VERB
la lande *fem*

to **moor** VERB
▷ *see also* **moor** NOUN
amarrer [28] (*boat*)

mop NOUN
le balai laveur *masc* (*for floor*)

moped NOUN
le cyclomoteur *masc*

moral ADJECTIVE
▷ *see also* **moral** NOUN
moral (FEM morale, MASC PL moraux)

moral NOUN
▷ *see also* **moral** ADJECTIVE
la morale *fem*
□ the moral of the story la morale de l'histoire
■ **morals** la moralité

morale NOUN
le moral *masc*
□ Their morale is very low. Leur moral est très bas.

more ADJECTIVE, PRONOUN, ADVERB

> When comparing one amount with another, you usually use **plus**.

1 plus
□ The cost of living is more expensive in Britain. Le coût de la vie est plus élevé en Grande-Bretagne. □ Could you speak more slowly? Est-ce que vous pourriez parler plus lentement ? □ a bit more un peu plus □ There isn't any more. Il n'y en a plus.
■ **more … than** plus … que □ He's more intelligent than me. Il est plus intelligent que moi. □ She practises more than I do. Elle s'entraîne plus que moi. □ More girls than boys do French. Il y a plus de filles que de garçons qui font du français.
2 plus de (*followed by noun*)
□ There are more girls in the class. Il y a plus de filles dans la classe. □ I get more homework than you do. J'ai plus de devoirs que toi. □ I spent more than 500 euros. J'ai dépensé plus de cinq cents euros.

> When referring to an additional amount, more than there is already, you usually use **encore**.

3 encore
□ Is there any more? Est-ce qu'il y en a encore ?
□ Would you like some more? Vous en voulez encore ? □ It'll take a few more days. Ça prendra encore quelques jours.
4 encore de (*followed by noun*)
□ Could I have some more chips? Est-ce que je pourrais avoir encore des frites ? □ Do you want some more tea? Voulez-vous encore du thé ?
■ **more or less** plus ou moins
■ **more than ever** plus que jamais

moreover ADVERB
en outre

morning NOUN
le matin *masc*
□ this morning ce matin □ tomorrow morning demain matin □ every morning tous les matins
■ **in the morning** le matin □ at 7 o'clock in the morning à sept heures du matin

Morocco NOUN
le Maroc *masc*
■ **in Morocco** au Maroc

Moscow NOUN
Moscou
■ **in Moscow** à Moscou

mosque NOUN
la mosquée *fem*

mosquito NOUN
le moustique *masc*
■ **a mosquito bite** une piqûre de moustique

most ADVERB, ADJECTIVE, PRONOUN

> Use **la plupart de** when 'most (of)' is followed by a plural noun and **la majeure partie (de)** when 'most (of)' is followed by a singular noun.

1 la plupart de
□ most of my friends la plupart de mes amis
□ most people la plupart des gens □ Most cats are affectionate. La plupart des chats sont affectueux.
■ **most of them** la plupart d'entre eux
■ **most of the time** la plupart du temps
2 la majeure partie de
□ most of the work la majeure partie du travail
□ most of the class la majeure partie de la classe
□ most of the night la majeure partie de la nuit
■ **the most** le plus □ He's the one who talks the most. C'est lui qui parle le plus.

> When 'most' is followed by an adjective, the translation depends on whether the noun referred to is masculine, feminine or plural.

■ **the most …** 1 les plus … □ the most expensive restaurants les restaurants les plus chers □ the most expensive seats les places les plus chères 2 le plus … □ the most expensive restaurant le restaurant le plus cher 3 la plus … □ the most expensive seat la place la plus chère

■ **to make the most of something** profiter
[28] au maximum de quelque chose
■ **at the most** au maximum □ Two hours at the
most. Deux heures au maximum.

mostly ADVERB
■ **The teachers are mostly quite nice.** La
plupart des professeurs sont assez gentils.

MOT NOUN
le contrôle technique *masc*
□ Her car failed its MOT. Sa voiture n'a pas
obtenu le certificat du contrôle technique.

motel NOUN
le motel *masc*

moth NOUN
le papillon de nuit *masc*

mother NOUN
la mère *fem*
□ my mother ma mère
■ **mother tongue** la langue maternelle

mother-in-law NOUN
la belle-mère *fem* (PL les belles-mères)

Mother's Day NOUN
la fête des Mères *fem*

> **DID YOU KNOW...?**
> Mother's Day is usually on the last Sunday of
> May in France.

motionless ADJECTIVE
immobile (FEM immobile)

motivated ADJECTIVE
motivé (FEM motivée)
□ He is highly motivated. Il est très motivé.

motivation NOUN
la motivation *fem*

motive NOUN
le mobile *masc*
□ the motive for the killing le mobile du crime

motor NOUN
le moteur *masc*
□ The boat has a motor. Le bateau a un moteur.

motorbike NOUN
la moto *fem*

motorboat NOUN
le bateau à moteur *masc* (PL les bateaux à
moteur)

motorcycle NOUN
le vélomoteur *masc*

motorcyclist NOUN
le motard *masc*
la motarde *fem*

motorist NOUN
l'automobiliste *masc/fem*

motor mechanic NOUN
le mécanicien garagiste *masc*

motor racing NOUN
la course automobile *fem*

motorway NOUN
l'autoroute *fem*
□ on the motorway sur l'autoroute

mouldy ADJECTIVE
moisi (FEM moisie)

to mount VERB
1 monter [48]
□ They're mounting a publicity campaign.
Ils montent une campagne publicitaire.
2 augmenter [28]
□ Tension is mounting. La tension augmente.

to mount up VERB
1 s'accumuler [28]
□ The bills are mounting up. Les factures
s'accumulent.
2 augmenter [28]
□ My savings are mounting up gradually. Mes
économies augmentent progressivement.

mountain NOUN
la montagne *fem*
■ **a mountain bike** un VTT (= *vélo tout-terrain*)

mountaineer NOUN
l'alpiniste *masc/fem*

mountaineering NOUN
l'alpinisme *masc*
□ I go mountaineering. Je fais de l'alpinisme.

mountainous ADJECTIVE
montagneux (FEM montagneuse)

mouse NOUN
la souris *fem* (*also for computer*)

mouse mat NOUN
le tapis de souris *masc*

mousse NOUN
1 la mousse *fem* (*food*)
□ chocolate mousse la mousse au chocolat
2 la mousse coiffante *fem* (*for hair*)

moustache NOUN
la moustache *fem*
□ He's got a moustache. Il a une moustache.
■ **a man with a moustache** un moustachu

mouth NOUN
la bouche *fem*

mouthful NOUN
la bouchée *fem*

mouthwash NOUN
le bain de bouche *masc*

move NOUN
▷ see also **move** VERB
1 le tour *masc*
□ It's your move. C'est ton tour.
2 le déménagement *masc*
□ Our move from Oxford to Luton ... Notre
déménagement d'Oxford à Luton ...
■ **to get a move on** se remuer [28] □ Get a
move on! Remue-toi !

m

English-French

to **move** VERB

▷ *see also* **move** NOUN

1 bouger [45]

□ Don't move! Ne bouge pas ! □ Could you move your stuff please? Est-ce que tu peux bouger tes affaires s'il te plaît ?

2 avancer [12]

□ The taxi was moving very slowly. Le taxi avançait très lentement.

3 émouvoir [31]

□ I was very moved by the film. J'ai été très émue par ce film.

■ **to move house** déménager [45] □ We're moving house in July. Nous allons déménager en juillet.

to **move forward** VERB

avancer [12]

to **move in** VERB

emménager [45]

□ They're moving in next week. Ils emménagent la semaine prochaine.

to **move over** VERB

se pousser [28]

□ Could you move over a bit? Est-ce que vous pouvez vous pousser un peu ?

movement NOUN

le mouvement *masc*

movie NOUN

le film *masc*

■ **the movies** le cinéma □ Let's go to the movies! Si on allait au cinéma ?

moving ADJECTIVE

1 en marche (*not stationary*)

□ a moving bus un bus en marche

2 touchant (FEM touchante) (*touching*)

□ a moving story une histoire touchante

to **mow** VERB

tondre [69]

□ to mow the lawn tondre le gazon

mower NOUN

la tondeuse à gazon *fem*

mown VERB ▷ *see* **mow**

MP NOUN

le député *masc*

□ She's an MP. Elle est députée.

MP3 player NOUN

le baladeur numérique *masc*

□ I need a new MP3 player. Il me faut un nouveau baladeur numérique.

mph ABBREVIATION (= *miles per hour*)

km/h (= *kilomètres-heure*)

□ to drive at 50 mph rouler à 80 km/h

> **DID YOU KNOW...?**
> In France, speed is expressed in kilometres per hour. 50 mph is about 80 km/h.

Mr NOUN

1 Monsieur (PL Messieurs)

2 M. (PL MM.) (*in address*)

Mrs NOUN

1 Madame (PL Mesdames)

2 Mme (PL Mmes) (*in address*)

MS NOUN (= *multiple sclerosis*)

la sclérose en plaques *fem*

□ She's got MS. Elle a la sclérose en plaques.

Ms NOUN

1 Madame (PL Mesdames)

2 Mme (PL Mmes) (*in address*)

> **DID YOU KNOW...?**
> There isn't a direct equivalent of 'Ms' in French. If you are writing to somebody and don't know whether she is married, use **Madame**.

much ADJECTIVE, ADVERB, PRONOUN

1 beaucoup (*with verb*)

□ Do you go out much? Tu sors beaucoup ? □ I don't like sport much. Je n'aime pas beaucoup le sport. □ I feel much better now. Je me sens beaucoup mieux maintenant.

2 beaucoup de (*with noun*)

□ I haven't got much money. Je n'ai pas beaucoup d'argent. □ I don't want much rice. Je ne veux pas beaucoup de riz.

■ **very much** **1** (*with verb*) beaucoup □ I enjoyed the film very much. J'ai beaucoup apprécié le film. □ Thank you very much. Merci beaucoup. **2** (*followed by noun*) beaucoup de □ I haven't got very much money. Je n'ai pas beaucoup d'argent.

■ **not much** **1** pas beaucoup □ Have you got a lot of luggage? — No, not much. As-tu beaucoup de bagages ? — Non, pas beaucoup. **2** pas grand-chose □ What's on TV? — Not much. Qu'est-ce qu'il y a à la télé ? — Pas grand-chose. □ What did you think of it? — Not much. Qu'est-ce que tu en as pensé ? — Pas grand-chose.

■ **How much?** Combien ? □ How much do you want? Tu en veux combien ? □ How much time have you got? Tu as combien de temps ? □ How much is it? (*cost*) Combien est-ce que ça coûte ?

■ **too much** trop □ That's too much! C'est trop ! □ It costs too much. Ça coûte trop cher. □ They give us too much homework. Ils nous donnent trop de devoirs.

■ **so much** autant □ I didn't think it would cost so much. Je ne pensais pas que ça coûterait autant. □ I've never seen so much traffic. Je n'ai jamais vu autant de circulation.

mud NOUN

la boue *fem*

muddle NOUN

le désordre *masc*

□ The photos are in a muddle. Les photos sont en désordre.

to **muddle up** VERB
confondre [69] (*people*)
□ He muddles me up with my sister. Il me
confond avec ma sœur.
■ **to get muddled up** s'embrouiller [28]
□ I'm getting muddled up. Je m'embrouille.

muddy ADJECTIVE
boueux (FEM boueuse)

muesli NOUN
le muesli *masc*

muffler NOUN (US)
le silencieux *masc*

mug NOUN
▷ *see also* **mug** VERB
la grande tasse *fem*
□ Do you want a cup or a mug? Est-ce que vous
voulez une tasse normale ou une grande tasse ?

to **mug** VERB
▷ *see also* **mug** NOUN
agresser [28]
□ He was mugged in the city centre. Il s'est fait
agresser au centre-ville.

mugger NOUN
l'agresseur *masc*

mugging NOUN
l'agression *fem*

muggy ADJECTIVE
lourd (FEM lourde)
□ It's muggy today. Il fait lourd aujourd'hui.

multiple choice test NOUN
le QCM *masc* (= *le questionnaire à choix multiples*)

multiple sclerosis NOUN
la sclérose en plaques *fem*
□ She's got multiple sclerosis. Elle a la sclérose
en plaques.

multiplication NOUN
la multiplication *fem*

to **multiply** VERB
multiplier [19]
□ to multiply 6 by 3 multiplier six par trois

multi-storey car park NOUN
le parking à plusieurs étages *masc*

mum NOUN

> You use **mère** in most cases, except when
> you are talking to your mother or using it as
> her name, then you would use **maman**.

1 la mère *fem*
□ my mum ma mère □ her mum sa mère
2 la maman *fem*
□ Mum! Maman ! □ I'll ask Mum. Je vais
demander à maman.

mummy NOUN
1 la maman *fem* (*mum*)
□ Mummy says I can go. Maman dit que je peux
y aller.
2 la momie *fem* (*Egyptian*)

mumps NOUN
les oreillons *masc pl*

murder NOUN
▷ *see also* **murder** VERB
le meurtre *masc*

to **murder** VERB
▷ *see also* **murder** NOUN
assassiner [28]
□ He was murdered. Il a été assassiné.

murderer NOUN
l'assassin *masc*

muscle NOUN
le muscle *masc*

muscular ADJECTIVE
musclé (FEM musclée)

museum NOUN
le musée *masc*

mushroom NOUN
le champignon *masc*
□ a mushroom omelette une omelette aux
champignons

music NOUN
la musique *fem*

musical ADJECTIVE
▷ *see also* **musical** NOUN
doué pour la musique (FEM douée pour la
musique)
□ I'm not musical. Je ne suis pas doué pour la
musique.
■ **a musical instrument** un instrument de
musique

musical NOUN
▷ *see also* **musical** ADJECTIVE
la comédie musicale *fem*

music centre NOUN
la chaîne stéréo *fem* (PL les chaînes stéréo)

musician NOUN
le musicien *masc*
la musicienne *fem*

Muslim NOUN
le musulman *masc*
la musulmane *fem*
□ He's a Muslim. Il est musulman.

mussel NOUN
la moule *fem*

must VERB

> When 'must' means that you assume or
> suppose something, use **devoir**; when it
> means it's necessary to do something, eg 'I
> must buy some presents', use **il faut que** ...,
> which comes from the verb **falloir** and is
> followed by a verb in the subjunctive.

1 devoir [26] (*I suppose*)
□ You must be tired. Tu dois être fatigué. □ They
must have plenty of money. Ils doivent avoir

m

beaucoup d'argent. □ There must be some problem. Il doit y avoir un problème.

2 il faut que

□ I must buy some presents. Il faut que j'achète des cadeaux. □ I really must go now. Il faut que j'y aille.

■ **You mustn't forget to send her a card.** N'oublie surtout pas de lui envoyer une carte.

■ **You must come and see us.** (*invitation*) Venez donc nous voir.

mustard NOUN
la moutarde *fem*

mustn't VERB = **must not**

to **mutter** VERB
marmonner [28]

mutton NOUN
le mouton *masc*

my ADJECTIVE
mon *masc*
□ my father mon père
ma *fem*
□ my aunt ma tante
mes *pl*
□ my parents mes parents

ma becomes **mon** before a vowel sound.

■ **my friend** **1** (*male*) mon ami **2** (*female*) mon amie

Do not use **mon/ma/mes** with parts of the body.

□ I want to wash my hair. Je voudrais me laver les cheveux. □ I'm going to clean my teeth. Je vais me brosser les dents. □ I've hurt my foot. Je me suis fait mal au pied.

myself PRONOUN

1 me
□ I've hurt myself. Je me suis fait mal. □ I really enjoyed myself. Je me suis vraiment bien amusé. □ ... when I look at myself in the mirror. ... quand je me regarde dans la glace.

2 moi
□ I don't like talking about myself. Je n'aime pas parler de moi.

3 moi-même
□ I made it myself. Je l'ai fait moi-même.
■ **by myself** tout seul □ I don't like travelling by myself. Je n'aime pas voyager tout seul.

mysterious ADJECTIVE
mystérieux (FEM mystérieuse)

mystery NOUN
le mystère *masc*
■ **a murder mystery** (*novel*) un roman policier

myth NOUN

1 le mythe *masc* (*legend*)
□ a Greek myth un mythe grec

2 l'idée reçue *fem* (*untrue idea*)
□ That's a myth. C'est une idée reçue.

mythology NOUN
la mythologie *fem*

m

Nn

to nag VERB
harceler [43] (scold)
□ She's always nagging me. Elle me harcèle constamment.

nail NOUN
1 l'ongle masc (on finger, toe)
□ Don't bite your nails! Ne te ronge pas les ongles !
2 le clou masc (made of metal)

nailbrush NOUN
la brosse à ongles fem

nailfile NOUN
la lime à ongles fem

nail scissors PL NOUN
les ciseaux à ongles masc pl

nail varnish NOUN
le vernis à ongles masc
■ **nail varnish remover** le dissolvant

naked ADJECTIVE
nu (FEM nue)

name NOUN
le nom masc
■ **What's your name?** Comment vous appelez-vous ?

nanny NOUN
la garde d'enfants fem
□ She's a nanny. C'est une garde d'enfants.

nap NOUN
le petit somme masc
■ **to have a nap** faire [36] un petit somme

napkin NOUN
la serviette fem

nappy NOUN
la couche fem

narrow ADJECTIVE
étroit (FEM étroite)

narrow-minded ADJECTIVE
borné (FEM bornée)

nasty ADJECTIVE
1 mauvais (FEM mauvaise) (bad)
□ a nasty cold un mauvais rhume □ a nasty smell une mauvaise odeur
2 méchant (FEM méchante) (unfriendly)
□ He gave me a nasty look. Il m'a regardé d'un air méchant.

nation NOUN
la nation fem

national ADJECTIVE
national (FEM nationale, MASC PL nationaux)
□ He's the national champion. C'est le champion national.
■ **the national elections** les élections législatives

national anthem NOUN
l'hymne national masc

National Health Service NOUN
la Sécurité sociale fem

> **DID YOU KNOW...?**
> In France you have to pay for medical treatment when you receive it, and then claim it back from the **Sécurité sociale**.

nationalism NOUN
le nationalisme masc
□ Scottish nationalism le nationalisme écossais

nationalist NOUN
le/la nationaliste masc/fem

nationality NOUN
la nationalité fem

National Lottery NOUN
la Loterie nationale fem

national park NOUN
le parc national masc (PL les parcs nationaux)

native ADJECTIVE
natal (FEM natale)
□ my native country mon pays natal
■ **native language** la langue maternelle
□ English is not their native language. L'anglais n'est pas leur langue maternelle.

natural ADJECTIVE
naturel (FEM naturelle)

naturalist NOUN
le naturaliste masc

naturally ADVERB
naturellement
□ Naturally, we were very disappointed. Nous avons naturellement été très déçus.

nature NOUN
la nature fem

naughty ADJECTIVE
vilain (FEM vilaine)

□ Naughty girl! Vilaine ! □ Don't be naughty! Ne fais pas le vilain !

navy NOUN
la marine *fem*
□ He's in the navy. Il est dans la marine.

navy-blue ADJECTIVE
bleu marine (FEM+PL bleu marine)
□ a navy-blue skirt une jupe bleu marine

Nazi NOUN
le Nazi *masc*
la Nazie *fem*
□ the Nazis les Nazis

near ADJECTIVE
▷ *see also* **near** PREPOSITION, ADVERB
proche (FEM proche)
□ It's fairly near. C'est assez proche.
■ **It's near enough to walk.** On peut facilement y aller à pied.
■ **the nearest** le plus proche □ Where's the nearest service station? Où est la station-service la plus proche ? □ The nearest shops were three kilometres away. Les magasins les plus proches étaient à trois kilomètres.

near PREPOSITION, ADVERB
▷ *see also* **near** ADJECTIVE
près de
□ I live near Liverpool. J'habite près de Liverpool.
□ near my house près de chez moi
■ **near here** près d'ici □ Is there a bank near here? Est-ce qu'il y a une banque près d'ici ?
■ **near to** près de □ It's very near to the school. C'est tout près de l'école.

nearby ADVERB
▷ *see also* **nearby** ADJECTIVE
à proximité
□ There's a supermarket nearby. Il y a un supermarché à proximité.

nearby ADJECTIVE
▷ *see also* **nearby** ADVERB
1 proche (FEM proche) (*close*)
□ a nearby garage un garage proche
2 voisin (FEM voisine) (*neighbouring*)
□ We went to the nearby village of Torrance. Nous sommes allés à Torrance, le village voisin.

nearly ADVERB
presque
□ Dinner's nearly ready. Le dîner est presque prêt. □ I'm nearly 15. J'ai presque quinze ans.
■ **I nearly missed the train.** J'ai failli rater le train.

neat ADJECTIVE
soigné (FEM soignée)
□ She has very neat writing. Elle a une écriture très soignée.

neatly ADVERB
soigneusement

□ neatly folded soigneusement plié
■ **neatly dressed** impeccable

necessarily ADVERB
■ **not necessarily** pas forcément

necessary ADJECTIVE
nécessaire (FEM nécessaire)

necessity NOUN
la chose nécessaire *fem*
□ A car is a necessity, not a luxury. Une voiture est une chose nécessaire et non pas un luxe.

neck NOUN
1 le cou *masc* (*of body*)
■ **a stiff neck** un torticolis
2 l'encolure *fem* (*of garment*)
□ a V-neck sweater un pull avec une encolure en V

necklace NOUN
le collier *masc*

to **need** VERB
▷ *see also* **need** NOUN
avoir [8] besoin de
□ I need a bigger size. J'ai besoin d'une plus grande taille.
■ **to need to do something** avoir [8] besoin de faire quelque chose □ I need to change some money. J'ai besoin de changer de l'argent.

need NOUN
▷ *see also* **need** VERB
■ **There's no need to book.** Il n'est pas nécessaire de réserver.

needle NOUN
l'aiguille *fem*

negative NOUN
▷ *see also* **negative** ADJECTIVE
le négatif *masc* (*photo*)

negative ADJECTIVE
▷ *see also* **negative** NOUN
négatif (FEM négative)
□ He's got a very negative attitude. Il a une attitude très négative.

neglected ADJECTIVE
mal tenu (FEM mal tenue) (*untidy*)
□ The garden is neglected. Le jardin est mal tenu.

negligee NOUN
le déshabillé *masc*

to **negotiate** VERB
négocier [19]

negotiations PL NOUN
les négociations *fem pl*

neighbour (US **neighbor**) NOUN
le voisin *masc*
la voisine *fem*
□ the neighbours' garden le jardin des voisins

neighbourhood (US **neighborhood**) NOUN
le quartier *masc*

neither PRONOUN, CONJUNCTION, ADVERB
aucun des deux
□ Neither of them is coming. Aucun des deux
ne vient. □ Carrots or peas? — Neither, thanks.
Des carottes ou des petits pois ? — Aucun des
deux merci.
aucune des deux
□ neither team aucune des deux équipes
■ **neither … nor …** ni … ni … □ neither of them
ni l'un ni l'autre □ Neither Sarah nor Tamsin
is coming to the party. Ni Sarah ni Tamsin ne
viennent à la soirée.
■ **Neither do I.** Moi non plus. □ I don't like him.
— Neither do I! Je ne l'aime pas. — Moi non plus !
■ **Neither have I.** Moi non plus. □ I've never
been to Spain. — Neither have I. Je ne suis
jamais allé en Espagne. — Moi non plus.

neon NOUN
le néon *masc*
□ a neon light une lampe au néon

nephew NOUN
le neveu *masc* (PL les neveux)
□ my nephew mon neveu

nerve NOUN
1 le nerf *masc*
□ She sometimes gets on my nerves. Elle me
tape quelquefois sur les nerfs.
2 le toupet *masc* (*cheek*)
□ He's got a nerve! Il a du toupet !

nerve-racking ADJECTIVE
angoissant (FEM angoissante)

nervous ADJECTIVE
tendu (FEM tendue) (*tense*)
□ I bite my nails when I'm nervous. Je me ronge
les ongles quand je suis tendu.
■ **to be nervous about something**
appréhender [28] de faire quelque chose □ I'm a
bit nervous about flying to the States by myself.
J'appréhende un peu d'aller toute seule en avion
aux États-Unis.

nest NOUN
le nid *masc*

Net NOUN
le Net *masc*
□ to surf the Net surfer sur le Net

net NOUN
le filet *masc*
□ a fishing net un filet de pêche

netball NOUN
■ **Netball is a bit like basketball.** Le netball
ressemble un peu au basket.

Netherlands PL NOUN
les Pays-Bas *masc*
■ **in the Netherlands** aux Pays-Bas

network NOUN
1 le réseau *masc* (PL les réseaux)

2 l'opérateur *masc* (*for mobile phone*)
□ Which network are you on? Tu es avec quel
opérateur ?

neurodivergent ADJECTIVE
neurodivergent (FEM neurodivergente)

neurotic ADJECTIVE
névrosé (FEM névrosée)

never ADVERB
1 jamais
□ Have you ever been to Germany? — No, never.
Est-ce que tu es déjà allé en Allemagne ? — Non,
jamais. □ When are you going to phone him?
— Never! Quand est-ce que tu vas l'appeler ?
— Jamais !
2 ne … jamais
Add **ne** if the sentence contains a verb.
□ I never write letters. Je n'écris jamais. □ I have
never been camping. Je n'ai jamais fait de
camping. □ Never leave valuables in your locker.
Ne laissez jamais d'objets de valeur dans votre
casier.
■ **Never again!** Plus jamais !
■ **Never mind.** Ça ne fait rien.

new ADJECTIVE
1 nouveau (FEM nouvelle, MASC PL nouveaux)
□ her new boyfriend son nouveau copain
□ I need a new dress. J'ai besoin d'une nouvelle
robe.
nouveau changes to **nouvel** before a vowel
and most words beginning with 'h'.
□ the new hotel le nouvel hôtel
2 neuf (FEM neuve) (*brand new*)
□ They've got a new car. Ils ont une voiture
neuve.

newborn ADJECTIVE
■ **a newborn baby** un nouveau-né

newcomer NOUN
le nouveau venu *masc* (MASC PL les nouveaux
venus)
la nouvelle venue *fem*

news NOUN
1 les nouvelles *fem pl*
□ good news de bonnes nouvelles □ I've
had some bad news. J'ai reçu de mauvaises
nouvelles. □ It was nice to have your news.
J'ai été content d'avoir de tes nouvelles.
2 la nouvelle *fem* (*single piece of news*)
□ That's wonderful news! Quelle bonne
nouvelle !
3 le journal télévisé *masc* (*on TV*)
□ I watch the news every evening. Je regarde le
journal télévisé tous les soirs.
4 les informations *fem pl* (*on radio*)
□ I listen to the news every morning. J'écoute les
informations tous les matins.

n

newsagent NOUN
le marchand de journaux *masc*
la marchande de journaux *fem*

newspaper NOUN
le journal *masc* (PL les journaux)
□ I deliver newspapers. Je distribue des journaux.

newsreader NOUN
le présentateur *masc*
la présentatrice *fem*

New Year NOUN
le Nouvel An *masc*
□ to celebrate New Year fêter le Nouvel An
■ **Happy New Year!** Bonne Année !
■ **New Year's Day** le Premier de l'an
■ **New Year's Eve** la Saint-Sylvestre

New Zealand NOUN
la Nouvelle-Zélande *fem*
■ **in New Zealand** en Nouvelle-Zélande

New Zealander NOUN
le Néo-Zélandais *masc*
la Néo-Zélandaise *fem*

next ADJECTIVE, ADVERB, PREPOSITION
1 prochain (FEM prochaine) (*in time*)
□ next Saturday samedi prochain □ next year l'année prochaine □ next summer l'été prochain
2 suivant (FEM suivante) (*in sequence*)
□ the next train le train suivant □ Next please! Au suivant !
3 ensuite (*afterwards*)
□ What shall I do next? Qu'est-ce que je fais ensuite ? □ What happened next? Qu'est-ce qui s'est passé ensuite ?
■ **next to** à côté de □ next to the bank à côté de la banque
■ **the next day** le lendemain □ The next day we visited Versailles. Le lendemain nous avons visité Versailles.
■ **the next time** la prochaine fois □ the next time you see her la prochaine fois que tu la verras
■ **next door** à côté □ They live next door. Ils habitent à côté. □ the people next door les gens d'à côté
■ **the next room** la pièce d'à côté

NHS NOUN
la Sécurité sociale *fem*

DID YOU KNOW...?
In France, you have to pay for medical treatment when you receive it, and then claim it back from the **Sécurité sociale**.

nice ADJECTIVE
1 gentil (FEM gentille) (*kind*)
□ Your parents are very nice. Tes parents sont très gentils. □ It was nice of you to remember my birthday. C'était gentil de ta part de te souvenir de mon anniversaire.

■ **to be nice to somebody** être [35] gentil avec quelqu'un
2 joli (FEM jolie) (*pretty*)
□ That's a nice dress! Qu'est-ce qu'elle est jolie, cette robe ! □ Aix is a nice town. Aix est une jolie ville.

WORD POWER
You can use a number of other words instead of **nice** to mean 'pretty':
attractive séduisant
□ an attractive girl une fille séduisante
beautiful beau
□ a beautiful painting un beau tableau
lovely charmant
□ a lovely surprise une charmante surprise
pretty joli
□ a pretty dress une jolie robe

3 bon (FEM bonne) (*food*)
□ It's very nice. C'est très bon. □ a nice cup of coffee une bonne tasse de café
■ **Have a nice time!** Amuse-toi bien !
■ **nice weather** le beau temps
■ **It's a nice day.** Il fait beau.

nickname NOUN
le surnom *masc*

niece NOUN
la nièce *fem*
□ my niece ma nièce

Nigeria NOUN
le Nigéria *masc*
■ **in Nigeria** au Nigéria

night NOUN
1 la nuit *fem*
□ I want a single room for two nights. Je veux une chambre à un lit pour deux nuits.
■ **My mother works nights.** Ma mère travaille de nuit.
■ **at night** la nuit
■ **Goodnight!** Bonne nuit !
2 le soir *masc* (*evening*)
□ last night hier soir

night club NOUN
la boîte de nuit *fem*

nightdress NOUN
la chemise de nuit *fem*

nightie NOUN
la chemise de nuit *fem*

nightlife NOUN
■ **There's plenty of nightlife.** Il y a plein de choses à faire le soir.

nightmare NOUN
le cauchemar *masc*
□ It was a real nightmare! Ça a été un vrai cauchemar !
■ **to have a nightmare** faire [36] un cauchemar

nightshirt NOUN
la chemise de nuit *fem*

nil NOUN
le zéro *masc*
□ **We won one-nil.** Nous avons gagné un à zéro.

nine NUMBER
neuf
□ She's nine. Elle a neuf ans.

nineteen NUMBER
dix-neuf
□ She's nineteen. Elle a dix-neuf ans.

nineteenth ADJECTIVE
dix-neuvième (FEM dix-neuvième)
□ her nineteenth birthday son dix-neuvième anniversaire □ the nineteenth floor le dix-neuvième étage
■ **the nineteenth of August** le dix-neuf août

ninety NUMBER
quatre-vingt-dix

ninth ADJECTIVE
neuvième (FEM neuvième)
□ the ninth floor le neuvième étage
■ **the ninth of August** le neuf août

no ADVERB, ADJECTIVE
1 non
□ Are you coming? — No. Est-ce que vous venez ? — Non. □ Would you like some more? — No thank you. Vous en voulez encore ? — Non merci.
2 pas de (*not any*)
□ There's no hot water. Il n'y a pas d'eau chaude. □ There are no trains on Sundays. Il n'y a pas de trains le dimanche. □ No problem. Pas de problème.
■ **I've got no idea.** Je n'en ai aucune idée.
■ **No way!** Pas question !
■ **'no smoking'** « défense de fumer »

nobody PRONOUN
1 personne
□ Who's going with you? — Nobody. Qui t'accompagne ? — Personne.
2 ne ... personne

Add **ne** if the sentence contains a verb.

□ There was nobody in the office. Il n'y avait personne au bureau.
■ **Nobody likes him.** Personne ne l'aime.

to nod VERB
acquiescer [12] d'un signe de tête (*in agreement*)
■ **to nod at somebody** (*as greeting*) saluer [28] quelqu'un d'un signe de tête

noise NOUN
le bruit *masc*
□ Please make less noise. Faites moins de bruit s'il vous plaît.

noisy ADJECTIVE
bruyant (FEM bruyante)

to nominate VERB
1 nommer [28] (*appoint*)
□ She was nominated as director. Elle a été nommée directrice.
2 proposer [28] (*propose*)
□ I nominate Kyle Alexander as team captain. Je propose Kyle Alexander comme capitaine de l'équipe.
■ **He was nominated for an Oscar.** Il a été nominé pour un Oscar.

non-binary ADJECTIVE
non-binaire (FEM non-binaire)
□ non-binary people les personnes non-binaires

none PRONOUN
1 aucun
□ What sports do you do? — None. Qu'est-ce que tu fais comme sport ? — Je n'en fais aucun.
aucune
□ How many sisters have you got? — None. Tu as combien de sœurs ? — Aucune.
2 aucun ... ne

Add **ne** if the sentence contains a verb.

□ None of my friends wanted to come. Aucun de mes amis n'a voulu venir.
■ **There's none left.** Il n'y en a plus.
■ **There are none left.** Il n'y en a plus.

nonsense NOUN
les bêtises *fem pl*
□ She talks a lot of nonsense. Elle dit beaucoup de bêtises. □ Nonsense! Ne dis pas de bêtises !

non-smoker NOUN
le non-fumeur *masc*
□ He's a non-smoker. Il est non-fumeur.

non-stop ADJECTIVE, ADVERB
1 direct (FEM directe)
□ a non-stop flight un vol direct □ We flew non-stop. Nous avons pris un vol direct.
2 sans arrêt
□ He talks non-stop. Il parle sans arrêt.

noodles PL NOUN
les nouilles *fem pl*

noon NOUN
midi *masc*
□ at noon à midi □ before noon avant midi

no one PRONOUN
1 personne
□ Who's going with you? — No one. Qui t'accompagne ? — Personne.
2 ne ... personne

Add **ne** if the sentence contains a verb.

□ There was no one in the office. Il n'y avait personne au bureau.
■ **No one likes Harry.** Personne n'aime Harry.

nor CONJUNCTION
■ **neither ... nor** ni ... ni □ neither the cinema nor the swimming pool ni le cinéma, ni la piscine

n

normal - note down

■ **Nor do I.** Moi non plus. □ I didn't like the film. — Nor did I. Je n'ai pas aimé le film. — Moi non plus.

■ **Nor have I.** Moi non plus. □ I haven't seen him. — Nor have I. Je ne l'ai pas vu. — Moi non plus.

normal ADJECTIVE

1 habituel (FEM habituelle) (*usual*)
□ at the normal time à l'heure habituelle
2 normal (FEM normale, MASC PL normaux) (*standard*)
□ a normal car une voiture normale

normally ADVERB

1 généralement (*usually*)
□ I normally arrive at nine o'clock. J'arrive généralement à neuf heures.
2 normalement (*as normal*)
□ In spite of the strike, the airports are working normally. Malgré la grève, les aéroports fonctionnent normalement.

Normandy NOUN

la Normandie *fem*
■ **in Normandy** en Normandie
■ **to Normandy** en Normandie

north ADJECTIVE, ADVERB

▷ *see also* **north** NOUN
1 nord (FEM+PL nord)
□ the north coast la côte nord
■ **a north wind** un vent du nord
2 vers le nord
□ We were travelling north. Nous allions vers le nord.
■ **north of** au nord de □ It's north of London. C'est au nord de Londres.

north NOUN

▷ *see also* **north** ADJECTIVE, ADVERB
le nord *masc*
□ in the north dans le nord

North America NOUN

l'Amérique du Nord *fem*

northbound ADJECTIVE

■ **The truck was northbound on the M5.** Le camion se trouvait sur la M5 en direction du nord.
■ **Northbound traffic is moving very slowly.** La circulation vers le nord avance très lentement.

northeast NOUN

le nord-est *masc*
□ in the northeast au nord-est

northern ADJECTIVE

■ **the northern part of the island** la partie nord de l'île
■ **Northern Europe** l'Europe du Nord

Northern Ireland NOUN

l'Irlande du Nord *fem*
■ **in Northern Ireland** en Irlande du Nord

■ **to Northern Ireland** en Irlande du Nord
■ **I'm from Northern Ireland.** Je viens d'Irlande du Nord.

North Pole NOUN

le pôle Nord *masc*

North Sea NOUN

la mer du Nord *fem*

northwest NOUN

le nord-ouest *masc*
□ in the northwest au nord-ouest

Norway NOUN

la Norvège *fem*
■ **in Norway** en Norvège

Norwegian NOUN

▷ *see also* **Norwegian** ADJECTIVE
1 le Norvégien *masc*
la Norvégienne *fem* (*person*)
2 le norvégien *masc* (*language*)

Norwegian ADJECTIVE

▷ *see also* **Norwegian** NOUN
norvégien (FEM norvégienne)

nose NOUN

le nez *masc* (PL les nez)

nosebleed NOUN

■ **to have a nosebleed** saigner [28] du nez
□ I often get nosebleeds. Je saigne souvent du nez.

nosy ADJECTIVE

fouineur (FEM fouineuse)

not ADVERB

1 pas
□ Are you coming or not? Est-ce que tu viens ou pas ?
■ **not really** pas vraiment
■ **not at all** pas du tout
■ **not yet** pas encore □ Have you finished? — Not yet. As-tu fini ? — Pas encore.
2 ne ... pas

> Add **ne** if the sentence contains a verb.

□ I'm not sure. Je ne suis pas sûr. □ It's not raining. Il ne pleut pas. □ You shouldn't do that. Tu ne devrais pas faire ça. □ They haven't arrived yet. Ils ne sont pas encore arrivés.
3 non
□ I hope not. J'espère que non. □ Can you lend me £10? — I'm afraid not. Est-ce que tu peux me prêter dix livres ? — Non, désolé.

note NOUN

1 la note *fem*
□ to take notes prendre des notes
2 le mot *masc* (*letter*)
□ I'll write her a note. Je vais lui écrire un mot.
3 le billet *masc* (*banknote*)
□ a £5 note un billet de cinq livres

to note down VERB

noter [28]

Numbers in brackets refer to verb tables on pages 650 to 658

notebook NOUN
le carnet *masc*

notepad NOUN
le bloc-notes *masc* (PL les blocs-notes)

notepaper NOUN
le papier à lettres *masc*

nothing NOUN

1 rien
□ What's wrong? — Nothing. Qu'est-ce qui ne va pas ? — Rien. □ nothing special rien de particulier

2 ne ... rien

Add **ne** if the sentence contains a verb.

□ He does nothing. Il ne fait rien. □ He ate nothing for breakfast. Il n'a rien mangé au petit déjeuner.
■ **Nothing is open on Sundays.** Rien n'est ouvert le dimanche.

notice NOUN
▷ *see also* **notice** VERB
le panneau *masc* (PL les panneaux) (*sign*)
■ **to put up a notice** mettre [47] un panneau
■ **a warning notice** un avertissement
■ **Don't take any notice of him!** Ne fais pas attention à lui !

to **notice** VERB
▷ *see also* **notice** NOUN
remarquer [28]

notice board NOUN
le panneau d'affichage *masc* (PL les panneaux d'affichage)

nought NOUN
le zéro *masc*

noun NOUN
le nom *masc*

novel NOUN
le roman *masc*

novelist NOUN
le romancier *masc*
la romancière *fem*

November NOUN
novembre *masc*
■ **in November** en novembre

now ADVERB, CONJUNCTION
maintenant
□ What are you doing now? Qu'est-ce que tu fais maintenant ?
■ **just now** en ce moment □ I'm rather busy just now. Je suis très occupé en ce moment.
■ **I did it just now.** Je viens de le faire.
■ **He should be there by now.** Il doit être arrivé à l'heure qu'il est.
■ **It should be ready by now.** Ça devrait être déjà prêt.

■ **now and then** de temps en temps

nowhere ADVERB
nulle part
□ **nowhere else** nulle part ailleurs

nuclear ADJECTIVE
nucléaire (FEM nucléaire)
□ **nuclear power** l'énergie nucléaire □ **a nuclear power station** une centrale nucléaire

nude ADJECTIVE
▷ *see also* **nude** NOUN
nu (FEM nue)

nude NOUN
▷ *see also* **nude** ADJECTIVE
■ **in the nude** nu

nudist NOUN
le/la nudiste *masc/fem*

nuisance NOUN
■ **It's a nuisance.** C'est très embêtant.
■ **Sorry to be a nuisance.** Désolé de vous déranger.

numb ADJECTIVE
engourdi (FEM engourdie)
□ My leg's gone numb. J'ai la jambe engourdie.
■ **numb with cold** engourdi par le froid

number NOUN

1 le nombre *masc* (*total amount*)
□ **a large number of people** un grand nombre de gens

2 le numéro *masc* (*of house, telephone, bank account*)
□ They live at number 5. Ils habitent au numéro cinq. □ What's your phone number? Quel est votre numéro de téléphone ? □ You've got the wrong number. Vous vous êtes trompé de numéro.

3 le chiffre *masc* (*figure, digit*)
□ I can't read the second number. Je n'arrive pas à lire le deuxième chiffre.

number plate NOUN
la plaque d'immatriculation *fem*

nun NOUN
la religieuse *fem*
□ She's a nun. Elle est religieuse.

nurse NOUN
l'infirmier *masc*
l'infirmière *fem*
□ She's a nurse. Elle est infirmière.

nursery NOUN

1 la crèche *fem* (*for children*)

2 la pépinière *fem* (*for plants*)

nursery school NOUN
l'école maternelle *fem*

DID YOU KNOW...?
The **école maternelle** is a state school for 2-6 year-olds.

n

nursery slope - nylon

nursery slope NOUN
la piste pour débutants *fem*

nut NOUN
1 la cacahuète *fem* (*peanut*)
2 la noisette *fem* (*hazelnut*)
3 la noix *fem* (PL les noix) (*walnut*)
4 l'écrou *masc* (*made of metal*)

nutmeg NOUN
la noix de muscade *fem*

nutritious ADJECTIVE
nourrissant (FEM nourrissante)

nuts ADJECTIVE
■ **He's nuts.** Il est dingue.

nylon NOUN
le nylon *masc*

n

Numbers in brackets refer to verb tables on pages 650 to 658

Oo

oak NOUN
le chêne *masc*
□ an oak table une table en chêne

oar NOUN
l'aviron *masc*

oats NOUN
l'avoine *fem*

obedient ADJECTIVE
obéissant (FEM obéissante)

to **obey** VERB
■ **to obey the rules** respecter [28] le règlement

object NOUN
l'objet *masc*
□ a familiar object un objet familier

objection NOUN
l'objection *fem*

objective NOUN
l'objectif *masc*

oblong ADJECTIVE
rectangulaire (FEM rectangulaire)

oboe NOUN
le hautbois *masc*
□ I play the oboe. Je joue du hautbois.

obscene ADJECTIVE
obscène (FEM obscène)

observant ADJECTIVE
observateur (FEM observatrice)

to **observe** VERB
observer [28]

obsessed ADJECTIVE
obsédé (FEM obsédée)
□ He's obsessed with trains. Il est obsédé par
les trains.

obsession NOUN
l'obsession *fem*
□ It's getting to be an obsession with you. Ça
devient une obsession chez toi.
■ **Football's an obsession of mine.** Le football
est une de mes passions.

obsolete ADJECTIVE
dépassé (FEM dépassée)

obstacle NOUN
l'obstacle *masc*

obstinate ADJECTIVE
obstiné (FEM obstinée)

to **obstruct** VERB
bloquer [28]
□ A lorry was obstructing the traffic. Un camion
bloquait la circulation.

to **obtain** VERB
obtenir [83]

obvious ADJECTIVE
évident (FEM évidente)

obviously ADVERB
1 évidemment (*of course*)
□ Do you want to pass the exam? — Obviously!
Tu veux être reçu à l'examen ? — Évidemment !
■ **Obviously not!** Bien sûr que non !
2 manifestement (*visibly*)
□ She was obviously exhausted. Elle était
manifestement épuisée.

occasion NOUN
l'occasion *fem*
□ a special occasion une occasion spéciale
■ **on several occasions** à plusieurs reprises

occasionally ADVERB
de temps en temps

occupation NOUN
la profession *fem*

to **occupy** VERB
occuper [28]
□ That seat is occupied. Cette place est occupée.

to **occur** VERB
avoir [8] lieu (*happen*)
□ The accident occurred yesterday. L'accident a
eu lieu hier.
■ **It suddenly occurred to me that ...** Il m'est
soudain venu à l'esprit que ...

OCD NOUN (= *obsessive compulsive disorder*)
le TOC *masc* (= *trouble obsessionnel compulsif*)

ocean NOUN
l'océan *masc*

o'clock ADVERB
■ **at four o'clock** à quatre heures
■ **It's five o'clock.** Il est cinq heures.

October NOUN
octobre *masc*
■ **in October** en octobre

octopus NOUN
la pieuvre *fem*

o

odd – okay

odd ADJECTIVE
1 bizarre (FEM bizarre)
  □ That's odd! C'est bizarre !
2 impair (FEM impaire)
  □ an odd number un chiffre impair

of PREPOSITION
1 de
  □ some photos of my holiday des photos de mes vacances □ a boy of ten un garçon de dix ans

> **de** changes to **d'** before a vowel and most words beginning with 'h'.

d'
  □ a kilo of oranges un kilo d'oranges

> **de** + **le** changes to **du**, and **de** + **les** changes to **des**.

du
  □ the end of the film la fin du film
des
  □ the end of the holidays la fin des vacances
2 en (with quantity, amount)
  □ He's got four sisters. I've met two of them. Il a quatre sœurs. J'en ai rencontré deux. □ Can I have half of that? Je peux en avoir la moitié ?
  ■ **three of us** trois d'entre nous
  ■ **a friend of mine** un de mes amis
  ■ **the 14th of September** le quatorze septembre
  ■ **That's very kind of you.** C'est très gentil de votre part.
  ■ **It's made of wood.** C'est en bois.

off ADVERB, PREPOSITION, ADJECTIVE

> For other expressions with 'off', see the verbs 'get', 'take', 'turn' etc.

1 éteint (FEM éteinte) (heater, light, TV)
  □ All the lights are off. Toutes les lumières sont éteintes.
2 fermé (FEM fermée) (tap, gas)
  □ Are you sure the tap is off? Tu es sûr que le robinet est fermé ?
3 annulé (FEM annulée) (cancelled)
  □ The match is off. Le match est annulé.
  ■ **to be off sick** être [35] malade
  ■ **a day off** un jour de congé □ **to take a day off work** prendre un jour de congé
  ■ **She's off school today.** Elle n'est pas à l'école aujourd'hui.
  ■ **I must be off now.** Je dois m'en aller maintenant.
  ■ **I'm off.** Je m'en vais.

offence (US **offense**) NOUN
le délit masc (crime)

offensive ADJECTIVE
choquant (FEM choquante)

offer NOUN
▷ see also **offer** VERB
la proposition fem

□ a good offer une proposition intéressante
  ■ **'on special offer'** « en promotion »

to offer VERB
▷ see also **offer** NOUN
proposer [28]
  □ He offered to help me. Il m'a proposé de m'aider. □ I offered to go with them. Je leur ai proposé de les accompagner.

office NOUN
le bureau masc (PL les bureaux)
  □ She works in an office. Elle travaille dans un bureau.

officer NOUN
l'officier masc

official ADJECTIVE
officiel (FEM officielle)

off-licence NOUN
le marchand de vins et spiritueux masc

off-peak ADVERB
hors saison (off-season)
  □ It's cheaper to go on holiday off-peak. C'est moins cher de partir en vacances hors saison.
  ■ **an off-peak gym membership** un abonnement à une salle de sport en heures creuses

offside ADJECTIVE
hors jeu (in football)

often ADVERB
souvent
  □ It often rains. Il pleut souvent. □ How often do you go to the gym? Tu vas souvent à la gym ? □ I'd like to go skiing more often. J'aimerais aller skier plus souvent.

oil NOUN
▷ see also **oil** VERB
1 l'huile fem (for lubrication, cooking)
  ■ **an oil painting** une peinture à l'huile
2 le pétrole masc (crude oil)
  □ North Sea oil le pétrole de la mer du Nord

to oil VERB
▷ see also **oil** NOUN
graisser [28]

oil rig NOUN
la plateforme pétrolière fem
  □ He works on an oil rig. Il travaille sur une plateforme pétrolière.

oil slick NOUN
la marée noire fem

oil well NOUN
le puits de pétrole masc (PL les puits de pétrole)

ointment NOUN
la pommade fem

okay EXCLAMATION, ADJECTIVE
d'accord (agreed)
  □ Could you call back later? — Okay! Tu peux rappeler plus tard ? — D'accord ! □ I'll meet you

at six o'clock, okay? Je te retrouve à six heures, d'accord ? □ Is that okay? C'est d'accord ?
- **I'll do it tomorrow, if that's okay with you.** Je le ferai demain, si tu es d'accord.
- **Are you okay?** Ça va ?
- **How was your holiday? — It was okay.** C'était comment tes vacances ? — Pas mal.
- **What's your teacher like? — He's okay.** Il est comment ton prof ? — Il est sympa. (*informal*)

old ADJECTIVE
1 vieux (FEM vieille, MASC PL vieux)
□ an old dog un vieux chien □ an old house une vieille maison

> **vieux** changes to **vieil** before a vowel and most words beginning with 'h'.

vieil
□ an old man un vieil homme
âgé (FEM âgée)

> When talking about people it is more polite to use **âgé** instead of **vieux**.

□ old people les personnes âgées
2 ancien (FEM ancienne) (*former*)
□ my old English teacher mon ancien professeur d'anglais
- **How old are you?** Quel âge as-tu ?
- **He's ten years old.** Il a dix ans.
- **my older brother** mon frère aîné □ my older sister ma sœur aînée
- **She's two years older than me.** Elle a deux ans de plus que moi.
- **I'm the oldest in the family.** Je suis l'aîné de la famille.

old age pensioner NOUN
le retraité *masc*
la retraitée *fem*
□ She's an old age pensioner. Elle est retraitée.

old-fashioned ADJECTIVE
1 démodé (FEM démodée)
□ She wears old-fashioned clothes. Elle porte des vêtements démodés.
2 vieux jeu (FEM+PL vieux jeu) (*person*)
□ My parents are rather old-fashioned. Mes parents sont plutôt vieux jeu.

olive NOUN
l'olive *fem*

olive oil NOUN
l'huile d'olive *fem*

olive tree NOUN
l'olivier *masc*

Olympic® ADJECTIVE
olympique (FEM olympique)
- **the Olympics®** les Jeux olympiques *masc pl*

omelette NOUN
l'omelette *fem*

on PREPOSITION, ADVERB
▷ *see also* **on** ADJECTIVE

> There are several ways of translating 'on'. Scan the examples to find one that is similar to what you want to say. For other expressions with 'on', see the verbs 'go', 'put', 'turn' etc.

1 sur
□ on the table sur la table □ on an island sur une île
2 à
□ on the left à gauche □ on the 2nd floor au deuxième étage □ I go to school on my bike. Je vais à l'école à vélo.

> With days and dates 'on' is not translated.

□ on Friday vendredi □ on Fridays le vendredi □ on Christmas Day le jour de Noël □ on June 20th le vingt juin □ on my birthday le jour de mon anniversaire
- **on TV** à la télé □ What's on TV? Qu'est-ce qu'il y a à la télé ?
- **on the radio** à la radio □ I heard it on the radio. Je l'ai entendu à la radio.
- **on the bus** 1 (*by bus*) en bus □ I go into town on the bus. Je vais en ville en bus.
2 (*inside bus*) dans le bus □ There were no empty seats on the bus. Il n'y avait pas de places libres dans le bus.
- **on holiday** en vacances □ They're on holiday. Ils sont en vacances.
- **on strike** en grève

on ADJECTIVE
▷ *see also* **on** PREPOSITION, ADVERB
1 allumé (FEM allumée) (*heater, light, TV*)
□ I think I left the light on. Je crois que j'ai laissé la lumière allumée.
2 ouvert (FEM ouverte) (*tap, gas*)
□ Leave the tap on. Laisse le robinet ouvert.
3 en marche (*machine*)
□ Is the dishwasher on? Est-ce que le lave-vaisselle est en marche ?
- **What's on at the cinema?** Qu'est-ce qui passe au cinéma ?

once ADVERB
une fois
□ once a week une fois par semaine □ once more encore une fois □ I've been to France once before. J'ai déjà été une fois en France.
- **Once upon a time …** Il était une fois …
- **at once** tout de suite
- **once in a while** de temps en temps

one NUMBER, PRONOUN

> Use **un** for masculine nouns and **une** for feminine nouns.

1 un
□ one day un jour □ Do you need a pencil? — No thanks, I've got one. Est-ce que tu as besoin d'un crayon ? — Non merci, j'en ai un.
une
□ one minute une minute □ I've got one brother and one sister. J'ai un frère et une sœur.

oneself - opposite

2 on (*impersonal*)
□ One never knows. On ne sait jamais.
■ **this one** **1** celui-ci *masc* □ Which foot is hurting? — This one. Quel pied te fait mal ? — Celui-ci. **2** celle-ci *fem* □ Which is the best photo? — This one. Quelle est la meilleure photo ? — Celle-ci.
■ **that one** **1** celui-là *masc* □ Which bag is yours? — That one. Lequel est ton sac ? — Celui-là. **2** celle-là *fem* □ Which seat do you want? — That one. Quelle place voulez-vous ? — Celle-là.

oneself PRONOUN
1 se
□ to hurt oneself se faire mal
2 soi-même
□ It's quicker to do it oneself. C'est plus rapide de le faire soi-même.

one-way ADJECTIVE
■ **a one-way street** une impasse

onion NOUN
l'oignon *masc*
□ onion soup la soupe à l'oignon

online ADJECTIVE, ADVERB
en ligne
□ online banking les services bancaires en ligne
■ **to go online** se connecter [28] à Internet

only ADVERB, ADJECTIVE, CONJUNCTION
1 seul (FEM seule)
□ Monday is the only day I'm free. Le lundi est le seul jour où je suis libre. □ French is the only subject I like. Le français est la seule matière que j'aime.
2 seulement
□ How much was it? — Only 10 euros. Combien c'était ? — Seulement dix euros.
3 ne ... que
□ We only want to stay for one night. Nous ne voulons rester qu'une nuit. □ These are only 3 euros. Ceux-ci coûtent que trois euros.
4 mais
□ I'd like the same jumper, only in black. Je voudrais le même pull, mais en noir.
■ **an only child** un enfant unique

onwards ADVERB
à partir de
□ from July onwards à partir de juillet

open ADJECTIVE
▷ see also **open** VERB
ouvert (FEM ouverte)
□ The baker's is open on Sunday morning. La boulangerie est ouverte le dimanche matin.
■ **in the open air** en plein air

to **open** VERB
▷ see also **open** ADJECTIVE
1 ouvrir [55]
□ Can I open the window? Est-ce que je peux ouvrir la fenêtre ? □ What time do the shops open? Les magasins ouvrent à quelle heure ?
2 s'ouvrir [55]
□ The door opens automatically. La porte s'ouvre automatiquement. □ The door opened and in came the teacher. La porte s'est ouverte et le professeur est entré.

opening hours PL NOUN
les heures d'ouverture *fem pl*

opera NOUN
l'opéra *masc*

to **operate** VERB
1 fonctionner [28]
□ The lights operate on a timer. Les lumières fonctionnent avec une minuterie.
2 faire [36] fonctionner
□ How do you operate the remote control? Comment fait-on fonctionner la télécommande ?
3 opérer [34] (*perform surgery*)
■ **to operate on someone** opérer [34] quelqu'un

operation NOUN
l'opération *fem*
□ a major operation une grave opération
■ **to have an operation** se faire [36] opérer
□ I have never had an operation. Je ne me suis jamais fait opérer.

operator NOUN
le/la standardiste *masc/fem* (*on telephone*)

opinion NOUN
l'avis *masc*
□ in my opinion à mon avis □ He asked me my opinion. Il m'a demandé mon avis.
■ **What's your opinion?** Qu'est-ce que vous en pensez ?

opinion poll NOUN
le sondage *masc*

opponent NOUN
l'adversaire *masc/fem*

opportunity NOUN
l'occasion *fem*
■ **to have the opportunity to do something** avoir [8] l'occasion de faire quelque chose □ I've never had the opportunity to go abroad. Je n'ai jamais eu l'occasion d'aller à l'étranger.

opposed ADJECTIVE
■ **I've always been opposed to eating meat.** J'ai toujours été contre la consommation de viande.
■ **as opposed to** par opposition à

opposing ADJECTIVE
opposé (FEM opposée) (*team*)

opposite ADJECTIVE, ADVERB, PREPOSITION
1 opposé (FEM opposée)
□ It's in the opposite direction. C'est dans la direction opposée.
2 en face
□ They live opposite. Ils habitent en face.

3 en face de

□ the girl sitting opposite me la fille assise en face de moi

■ **the opposite sex** l'autre sexe

opposition NOUN

l'opposition *fem*

optician NOUN

l'opticien *masc*

l'opticienne *fem*

□ She's an optician. Elle est opticienne.

optimist NOUN

l'optimiste *masc/fem*

optimistic ADJECTIVE

optimiste (FEM optimiste)

option NOUN

1 le choix *masc* (*choice*)

□ I've got no option. Je n'ai pas le choix.

2 la matière à option *fem* (*optional subject*)

□ I'm doing geology as my option. La géologie est ma matière à option.

optional ADJECTIVE

facultatif (FEM facultative)

or CONJUNCTION

1 ou

□ Would you like tea or coffee? Est-ce que tu veux du thé ou du café ?

Use **ni ... ni** in negative sentences.

□ I don't eat meat or fish. Je ne mange ni viande, ni poisson.

2 sinon (*otherwise*)

□ Hurry up or you'll miss the bus. Dépêche-toi, sinon tu vas rater le bus.

■ **Give me the money, or else!** Donne-moi l'argent, sinon tu vas le regretter !

oral ADJECTIVE

▷ *see also* **oral** NOUN

oral (FEM orale, MASC PL oraux)

■ **an oral exam** un oral

oral NOUN

▷ *see also* **oral** ADJECTIVE

l'oral *masc* (PL les oraux)

□ I've got my French oral soon. Je vais bientôt passer mon oral de français.

orange NOUN

▷ *see also* **orange** ADJECTIVE

l'orange *fem*

■ **an orange juice** un jus d'orange

orange ADJECTIVE

▷ *see also* **orange** NOUN

orange (FEM+PL orange)

orchard NOUN

le verger *masc*

orchestra NOUN

l'orchestre *masc*

□ I play in the school orchestra. Je joue dans l'orchestre de l'école.

order NOUN

▷ *see also* **order** VERB

1 l'ordre *masc* (*sequence*)

□ in alphabetical order dans l'ordre alphabétique

2 la commande *fem* (*instruction*)

□ The waiter took our order. Le garçon a pris notre commande.

■ **in order to** pour □ He does it in order to earn money. Il le fait pour gagner de l'argent.

■ **'out of order'** « en panne »

to order VERB

▷ *see also* **order** NOUN

commander [28]

□ We ordered steak and chips. Nous avons commandé un steak frites. □ Are you ready to order? Vous êtes prêt à commander ?

■ **to order somebody about** donner [28] des ordres à quelqu'un □ She liked to order him about. Elle aimait lui donner des ordres.

ordinary ADJECTIVE

1 ordinaire (FEM ordinaire)

□ an ordinary day une journée ordinaire

2 comme les autres (*people*)

□ an ordinary family une famille comme les autres □ He's just an ordinary guy. C'est un type comme les autres.

organ NOUN

l'orgue *masc* (*instrument*)

□ I play the organ. Je joue de l'orgue.

organic ADJECTIVE

biologique (FEM biologique) (*vegetables, fruit*)

organization NOUN

l'organisation *fem*

to organize VERB

organiser [28]

origin NOUN

l'origine *fem*

original ADJECTIVE

original (FEM originale, MASC PL originaux)

□ It's a very original idea. C'est une idée très originale.

■ **Our original plan was to go camping.** À l'origine nous avions l'intention de faire du camping.

originally ADVERB

à l'origine

Orkney NOUN

les Orcades *fem pl*

■ **in Orkney** dans les Orcades

ornament NOUN

le bibelot *masc*

orphan NOUN

l'orphelin *masc*

l'orpheline *fem*

ostrich NOUN

l'autruche *fem*

o

other ADJECTIVE, PRONOUN

autre (FEM autre)

□ Have you got these jeans in other colours? Est-ce que vous avez ce jean dans d'autres couleurs ? □ on the other side of the street de l'autre côté de la rue □ the other day l'autre jour

■ **the other one** l'autre □ This one? — No, the other one. Celui-ci ? — Non, l'autre.

■ **the others** les autres □ The others are going but I'm not. Les autres y vont mais pas moi.

otherwise ADVERB, CONJUNCTION

1 sinon (*if not*)

□ Note down the number, otherwise you'll forget it. Note le numéro, sinon tu vas l'oublier. □ Put some sunscreen on, you'll burn otherwise. Mets de la crème solaire, sinon tu vas attraper des coups de soleil.

2 à part ça (*in other ways*)

□ I'm tired, but otherwise I'm fine. Je suis fatigué, mais à part ça, ça va.

ought VERB

To translate 'ought to' use the conditional tense of **devoir**.

□ I ought to phone my parents. Je devrais appeler mes parents. □ You ought not to do that. Tu ne devrais pas faire ça. □ He ought to win. Il devrait gagner.

ounce NOUN

l'once *fem*

DID YOU KNOW...?

In France, measurements are in grams and kilograms. One ounce is about 30 grams.

□ 8 ounces of cheese 250 grammes de fromage

our ADJECTIVE

notre (FEM notre, PL nos)

□ Our house is quite big. Notre maison est plutôt grande. □ Our neighbours are very nice. Nos voisins sont très gentils.

ours PRONOUN

le nôtre + *masc noun*

□ Your garden is very big, ours is much smaller. Votre jardin est très grand, le nôtre est beaucoup plus petit.

la nôtre + *fem noun*

□ Your school is very different from ours. Votre école est très différente de la nôtre.

les nôtres + *pl noun*

□ Our teachers are strict. — Ours are too. Nos professeurs sont sévères. — Les nôtres aussi.

■ **Is this ours?** C'est à nous ? □ This car is ours. Cette voiture est à nous. □ Whose is this? — It's ours. C'est à qui ? — À nous.

ourselves PRONOUN

1 nous

□ We really enjoyed ourselves. Nous nous sommes vraiment bien amusés.

2 nous-mêmes

□ We built our garage ourselves. Nous avons construit notre garage nous-mêmes.

out ADVERB, ADJECTIVE

There are several ways of translating 'out'. Scan the examples to find one that is similar to what you want to say. For other expressions with 'out', see the verbs 'go', 'put', 'turn' etc.

1 dehors (*outside*)

□ It's cold out. Il fait froid dehors.

2 éteint (FEM éteinte) (*light, fire*)

□ All the lights are out. Toutes les lumières sont éteintes.

■ **She's out.** Elle est sortie.

■ **She's out shopping.** Elle est sortie faire des courses.

■ **She's out for the afternoon.** Elle ne sera pas là de tout l'après-midi.

■ **out there** dehors □ It's cold out there. Il fait froid dehors.

■ **to go out** sortir [79⁵] □ I'm going out tonight. Je sors ce soir.

■ **to go out with somebody** sortir [79⁵] avec quelqu'un □ I've been going out with him for two months. Je sors avec lui depuis deux mois.

■ **out of** 1 dans □ to drink out of a glass boire dans un verre 2 sur □ in 9 cases out of 10 dans neuf cas sur dix 3 en dehors de □ He lives out of town. Il habite en dehors de la ville.

■ **3 km out of town** à trois kilomètres de la ville

■ **out of curiosity** par curiosité

■ **out of work** sans emploi

■ **That is out of the question.** C'est hors de question.

■ **You're out!** (*in game*) Tu es éliminé !

■ **'way out'** « sortie »

outbreak NOUN

1 l'épidémie *fem* (*of disease*)

□ a flu outbreak une épidémie de grippe

2 le début *masc*

□ the outbreak of war le début de la guerre

outcome NOUN

l'issue *fem*

□ What was the outcome of the negotiations? Quelle a été l'issue des négociations ?

outdoor ADJECTIVE

en plein air

□ an outdoor swimming pool une piscine en plein air

■ **outdoor activities** les activités de plein air

outdoors ADVERB

au grand air

outfit NOUN

la tenue *fem*

□ She bought a new outfit for the wedding. Elle a acheté une nouvelle tenue pour le mariage.

■ **a cowboy outfit** une panoplie de cowboy

o

outgoing ADJECTIVE
extraverti (FEM extravertie)
□ She's very outgoing. Elle est très extravertie.

outing NOUN
la sortie *fem*
□ to go on an outing faire une sortie

outline NOUN
1 les grandes lignes *fem pl* (*summary*)
□ This is an outline of the plan. Voici les grandes lignes du projet.
2 les contours *masc pl* (*shape*)
□ We could see the outline of the mountain in the mist. Nous distinguions les contours de la montagne dans la brume.

outlook NOUN
1 l'attitude *fem* (*attitude*)
□ my outlook on life mon attitude face à la vie
2 les perspectives *fem pl* (*prospects*)
□ the economic outlook les perspectives économiques
■ The outlook is poor. Les choses s'annoncent mal.

outrageous ADJECTIVE
1 scandaleux (FEM scandaleuse) (*behaviour*)
2 exorbitant (FEM exorbitante) (*price*)

outset NOUN
le début *masc*
□ at the outset dès le début

outside NOUN
▷ *see also* **outside** ADJECTIVE, ADVERB, PREPOSITION
l'extérieur *masc*

outside ADJECTIVE, ADVERB, PREPOSITION
▷ *see also* **outside** NOUN
1 extérieur (FEM extérieure)
□ the outside walls les murs extérieurs
2 dehors
□ It's very cold outside. Il fait très froid dehors.
3 en dehors de
□ outside the school en dehors de l'école
□ outside school hours en dehors des heures de cours

outskirts PL NOUN
la banlieue *fem*
□ on the outskirts of the town dans les banlieues de la ville

outstanding ADJECTIVE
remarquable (FEM remarquable)

oval ADJECTIVE
ovale (FEM ovale)

oven NOUN
le four *masc*

over PREPOSITION, ADVERB, ADJECTIVE

When there is movement over something, use **par-dessus**; when something is located above something, use **au-dessus de**.

1 par-dessus
□ The ball went over the wall. Le ballon est passé par-dessus le mur.

2 au-dessus de
□ There's a mirror over the washbasin. Il y a une glace au-dessus du lavabo.
3 plus de (*more than*)
□ It's over twenty kilos. Ça pèse plus de vingt kilos. □ The temperature was over thirty degrees. Il faisait une température de plus de trente degrés.
4 pendant (*during*)
□ over the holidays pendant les vacances □ over Christmas pendant les fêtes de Noël
5 terminé (FEM terminée) (*finished*)
□ I'll be happy when the exams are over. Je serai content quand les examens seront terminés.
■ over here ici
■ over there là-bas
■ all over Scotland dans toute l'Écosse
■ The baker's is over the road. La boulangerie est de l'autre côté de la rue.
■ I spilled orange juice over my shirt. J'ai renversé du jus d'orange sur ma chemise.

overall ADVERB
dans l'ensemble (*generally*)
□ My results were quite good overall. Mes résultats étaient assez bons dans l'ensemble.

overalls PL NOUN
les bleus de travail *masc pl*

overcast ADJECTIVE
couvert (FEM couverte)
□ The sky was overcast. Le ciel était couvert.

to **overcharge** VERB
■ He overcharged me. Il m'a fait payer trop cher.
■ They overcharged us for the meal. Ils nous ont fait payer de trop pour le repas.

overcoat NOUN
le pardessus *masc*

overdone ADJECTIVE
trop cuit (FEM trop cuite) (*food*)

overdraft NOUN
le découvert *masc*
■ to have an overdraft être [35] à découvert

to **overestimate** VERB
surestimer [28]

to **overlook** VERB
1 donner [28] sur (*have view of*)
□ The hotel overlooked the beach. L'hôtel donnait sur la plage.
2 négliger [45] (*forget about*)
□ He had overlooked one important problem. Il avait négligé un problème important.

overseas ADVERB
à l'étranger
□ I'd like to work overseas. J'aimerais travailler à l'étranger.

oversight NOUN
l'oubli *masc*

o

to **oversleep** VERB
se réveiller [28] en retard
□ I overslept this morning. Je me suis réveillé en retard ce matin.

to **overtake** VERB
dépasser [58]

overtime NOUN
les heures supplémentaires *fem pl*
□ to work overtime faire des heures supplémentaires

overtook VERB ▷ *see* **overtake**

overweight ADJECTIVE
trop gros (FEM trop grosse)

to **owe** VERB
devoir [26]
■ **to owe somebody something** devoir [26] quelque chose à quelqu'un □ I owe you 50 euros. Je te dois cinquante euros

owing to PREPOSITION
en raison de
□ owing to bad weather en raison du mauvais temps

owl NOUN
le hibou *masc* (PL les hiboux)

own ADJECTIVE
▷ *see also* **own** VERB
propre (FEM propre)
□ I've got my own bathroom. J'ai ma propre salle de bain.
■ **I'd like a room of my own.** J'aimerais avoir une chambre à moi.
■ **on his own** tout seul □ on her own toute seule □ on our own tout seuls

to **own** VERB
▷ *see also* **own** ADJECTIVE
posséder [34]

to **own up** VERB
avouer [28]
■ **to own up to something** admettre [47] quelque chose

owner NOUN
le/la propriétaire *masc/fem*

oxygen NOUN
l'oxygène *masc*

oyster NOUN
l'huître *fem*

ozone NOUN
l'ozone *fem*

ozone layer NOUN
la couche d'ozone *fem*

Pp

PA NOUN
le/la secrétaire de direction *masc/fem* (*personal assistant*)
□ She's a PA. Elle est secrétaire de direction.
■ **the PA system** (*public address*) la sono

pace NOUN
l'allure *fem* (*speed*)
□ He was walking at a brisk pace. Il marchait à vive allure.

Pacific NOUN
le Pacifique *masc*

pacifier NOUN (US)
la tétine *fem*

to **pack** VERB
▷ *see also* **pack** NOUN
faire [36] ses bagages
□ I'll help you pack. Je vais t'aider à faire tes bagages.
■ **I've already packed my case.** J'ai déjà fait ma valise.
■ **Pack it in!** (*stop it*) Laisse tomber !

pack NOUN
▷ *see also* **pack** VERB
1 le paquet *masc* (*packet*)
□ a pack of chewing gum un paquet de chewing-gum
2 le pack *masc* (*of yoghurts, cans*)
□ a six-pack un pack de six
■ **a pack of cards** un jeu de cartes

package NOUN
le paquet *masc*
■ **a package holiday** un voyage organisé

packed ADJECTIVE
bondé (FEM bondée)
□ The cinema was packed. Le cinéma était bondé.

packed lunch NOUN
le repas froid *masc*
□ I take a packed lunch to school. J'apporte un repas froid à l'école.

> **DID YOU KNOW...?**
> French schoolchildren do not take packed lunches to school. They either eat at the canteen or go home.

packet NOUN
le paquet *masc*
□ a packet of biscuits un paquet de biscuits

pad NOUN
le bloc-notes *masc* (PL les blocs-notes) (*notepad*)

to **paddle** VERB
▷ *see also* **paddle** NOUN
1 pagayer [59] (*canoe*)
2 faire [36] trempette (*in water*)

paddle NOUN
▷ *see also* **paddle** VERB
la pagaie *fem* (*for canoe*)
■ **to go for a paddle** faire [36] trempette

padlock NOUN
le cadenas *masc*

page NOUN
la page *fem* (*of book*)

pager NOUN
le récepteur d'appel *masc*

paid VERB ▷ *see* **pay**

paid ADJECTIVE
1 rémunéré (FEM rémunérée) (*work*)
2 payé (FEM payée)
□ 3 weeks' paid holiday trois semaines de congés payés

pail NOUN
le seau *masc* (PL les seaux)

pain NOUN
la douleur *fem*
□ a terrible pain une douleur insupportable
■ **I've got a pain in my stomach.** J'ai mal à l'estomac.
■ **to be in pain** souffrir [54] □ She's in a lot of pain. Elle souffre beaucoup.
■ **He's a real pain.** Il est vraiment pénible.

painful ADJECTIVE
douloureux (FEM douloureuse)
□ to suffer from painful periods souffrir de règles douloureuses
■ **Is it painful?** Ça te fait mal ?

painkiller NOUN
l'analgésique *masc*

paint NOUN
▷ *see also* **paint** VERB
la peinture *fem*

to **paint** VERB
▷ *see also* **paint** NOUN
peindre [60]

P

Core vocabulary is shaded.

□ to paint something green peindre quelque chose en vert

paintbrush NOUN
le pinceau *masc* (PL les pinceaux)

painter NOUN
le/la peintre *masc/fem*

painting NOUN
1 la peinture *fem*
□ My hobby is painting. Je fais de la peinture.
2 le tableau *masc* (PL les tableaux) (*picture*)
□ a painting by Picasso un tableau de Picasso

pair NOUN
la paire *fem*
□ a pair of shoes une paire de chaussures □ a pair of scissors une paire de ciseaux
■ **a pair of trousers** un pantalon
■ **a pair of jeans** un jean
■ **a pair of pants** 1 (*briefs*) un slip 2 (*boxer shorts*) un caleçon 3 (US: *trousers*) un pantalon
■ **in pairs** deux par deux □ We work in pairs. On travaille deux par deux.

pajamas PL NOUN (US)
le pyjama *masc sing*
□ my pajamas mon pyjama □ a pair of pajamas un pyjama
■ **a pajama top** un haut de pyjama

Pakistan NOUN
le Pakistan *masc*
■ **in Pakistan** au Pakistan
■ **to Pakistan** au Pakistan
■ **He's from Pakistan.** Il est pakistanais.

Pakistani NOUN
▷ *see also* **Pakistani** ADJECTIVE
le Pakistanais *masc*
la Pakistanaise *fem*

Pakistani ADJECTIVE
▷ *see also* **Pakistani** NOUN
pakistanais (FEM pakistanaise)

pal NOUN
le copain *masc*
la copine *fem*

palace NOUN
le palais *masc*

pale ADJECTIVE
pâle (FEM pâle)
□ a pale blue shirt une chemise bleu pâle

Palestine NOUN
la Palestine *fem*
■ **in Palestine** en Palestine

Palestinian NOUN
▷ *see also* **Palestinian** ADJECTIVE
le Palestinien *masc*
la Palestinienne *fem*

Palestinian ADJECTIVE
▷ *see also* **Palestinian** NOUN
palestinien (FEM palestinienne)

palm NOUN
la paume *fem* (*of hand*)
■ **a palm tree** un palmier

pamphlet NOUN
la brochure *fem*

pan NOUN
1 la casserole *fem* (*saucepan*)
2 la poêle *fem* (*frying pan*)

pancake NOUN
la crêpe *fem*
■ **Pancake Day** mardi gras

> DID YOU KNOW...?
> Pancake Day is celebrated in France as well. Children dress up and eat **crêpes**.

pandemic NOUN
la pandémie *fem*
□ a flu pandemic une pandémie de grippe

panic NOUN
▷ *see also* **panic** VERB
la panique *fem*

to **panic** VERB
▷ *see also* **panic** NOUN
s'affoler [28]
■ **Don't panic!** Pas de panique !

panther NOUN
la panthère *fem*

panties PL NOUN
le slip *masc sing*

pantomime NOUN
le spectacle de Noël pour enfants *masc*

> DID YOU KNOW...?
> Pantomimes don't exist in France.

pants PL NOUN
1 le slip *masc sing* (*briefs*)
□ a pair of pants un slip
2 le caleçon *masc sing* (*boxer shorts*)
□ a pair of pants un caleçon
3 le pantalon *masc sing* (*trousers*: US)
□ a pair of pants un pantalon

pantyhose PL NOUN (US)
le collant *masc sing*

paper NOUN
1 le papier *masc*
□ a piece of paper un morceau de papier
■ **a paper towel** une serviette en papier
■ **an exam paper** une épreuve écrite
2 le journal *masc* (PL les journaux) (*newspaper*)
□ I saw an advert in the paper. J'ai vu une annonce dans le journal.

paperback NOUN
le livre de poche *masc*

paper boy NOUN
le livreur de journaux *masc*

paper clip NOUN
le trombone *masc*

paper girl NOUN
la livreuse de journaux *fem*

paper round NOUN
la tournée de distribution de journaux *fem*

paperweight NOUN
le presse-papiers *masc*

paperwork NOUN
la paperasse *fem*
□ He had a lot of paperwork to do. Il avait beaucoup de paperasse à faire.

parachute NOUN
le parachute *masc*

parade NOUN
le défilé *masc*

paradise NOUN
le paradis *masc*

paragraph NOUN
le paragraphe *masc*

parallel ADJECTIVE
parallèle (FEM parallèle)

paralysed ADJECTIVE
paralysé (FEM paralysée)

paramedic NOUN
l'auxiliaire médical *masc*
l'auxiliaire médicale *fem*

parcel NOUN
le colis *masc*

pardon NOUN
■ **Pardon?** Pardon ?

parent NOUN
1 le père *masc* (*father*)
2 la mère *fem* (*mother*)
■ **my parents** mes parents *masc pl*

Paris NOUN
Paris *masc*
■ **in Paris** à Paris
■ **to Paris** à Paris
■ **She's from Paris.** Elle est parisienne.

Parisian NOUN
▷ *see also* **Parisian** ADJECTIVE
le Parisien *masc*
la Parisienne *fem*

Parisian ADJECTIVE
▷ *see also* **Parisian** NOUN
parisien (FEM parisienne)

park NOUN
▷ *see also* **park** VERB
le parc *masc*
■ **a national park** un parc national
■ **a theme park** un parc à thème
■ **a car park** un parking

to **park** VERB
▷ *see also* **park** NOUN
1 garer [28]
□ Where can I park my car? Où est-ce que je peux garer ma voiture ?

2 se garer [28]
□ We couldn't find anywhere to park. Nous avons eu du mal à nous garer.

parking NOUN
le stationnement *masc*
□ 'no parking' « stationnement interdit »

> **BE CAREFUL!**
> Do not translate **parking** by the French word **parking**.

parking lot NOUN (US)
le parking *masc*

parking meter NOUN
le parcmètre *masc*

parking ticket NOUN
le P.-V. *masc* (= *procès-verbal*)

parliament NOUN
le parlement *masc*

parrot NOUN
le perroquet *masc*

parsley NOUN
le persil *masc*

part NOUN
1 la partie *fem* (*section*)
□ The first part of the film was boring. La première partie du film était ennuyeuse.
2 la pièce *fem* (*component*)
□ spare parts les pièces de rechange
3 le rôle *masc* (*in play, film*)
■ **to take part in something** participer [28] à quelque chose □ A lot of people took part in the demonstration. Beaucoup de gens ont participé à la manifestation.

to **part with** VERB
■ **to part with something** se défaire [36] de quelque chose

particular ADJECTIVE
particulier (FEM particulière)
□ Are you looking for anything particular? Est-ce que vous voulez quelque chose de particulier ?
■ **nothing in particular** rien de particulier

particularly ADVERB
particulièrement

parting NOUN
la raie *fem* (*in hair*)

partly ADVERB
en partie

partner NOUN
1 le/la partenaire *masc/fem* (*in game*)
2 l'associé *masc*
l'associée *fem* (*in business*)
3 le cavalier *masc*
la cavalière *fem* (*in dance*)
4 le compagnon *masc*
la compagne *fem* (*in relationship*)

part-time ADJECTIVE, ADVERB
à temps partiel

P

□ a part-time job un travail à temps partiel
□ She works part-time. Elle travaille à temps partiel.

party NOUN
1 la fête *fem*
□ a birthday party une fête d'anniversaire □ a Christmas party une fête de Noël □ a New Year party une fête du Nouvel An
2 la soirée *fem* (*more formal*)
□ I'm going to a party on Saturday. Je vais à une soirée samedi.
3 le parti *masc* (*political*)
□ the Conservative Party le Parti conservateur
4 le groupe *masc* (*group*)
□ a party of tourists un groupe de touristes

pass NOUN
▷ *see also* **pass** VERB
1 le col *masc* (*in mountains*)
□ The pass was blocked with snow. Le col était enneigé.
2 la passe *fem* (*in football*)
■ **to get a pass** (*in exam*) être [35] reçu □ She got a pass in her piano exam. Elle a été reçue à son examen de piano. □ I got six passes. J'ai été reçu dans six matières.
■ **a bus pass** une carte de bus

to **pass** VERB
▷ *see also* **pass** NOUN
1 être [35] reçu (*exam*)
□ Did you pass? Tu as été reçu ?
■ **to pass an exam** être [35] reçu à un examen □ I hope I'll pass the exam. J'espère que je serai reçu à l'examen.

BE CAREFUL!
Do not translate **to pass an exam** by the French expression **passer un examen**.

2 passer [58]
□ Could you pass me the salt, please? Est-ce que vous pourriez me passer le sel, s'il vous plaît ?
□ The time has passed quickly. Le temps a passé rapidement.
3 passer [58] devant
□ I pass his house on my way to school. Je passe devant chez lui en allant à l'école.

to **pass out** VERB
s'évanouir [38] (*faint*)

passage NOUN
1 le passage *masc* (*piece of writing*)
□ Read the passage carefully. Lisez attentivement le passage.
2 le couloir *masc* (*corridor*)

passenger NOUN
le passager *masc*
la passagère *fem*

passion NOUN
la passion *fem*

passive ADJECTIVE
passif (FEM passive)
■ **passive smoking** le tabagisme passif

Passover NOUN
la Pâque juive *fem*
□ at Passover à la Pâque juive

passport NOUN
le passeport *masc*
□ passport control le contrôle des passeports

password NOUN
le mot de passe *masc*

past ADVERB, PREPOSITION
▷ *see also* **past** NOUN
après (*beyond*)
□ It's on the right, just past the station. C'est sur la droite, juste après la gare.
■ **to go past** 1 passer [58] □ The bus went past without stopping. Le bus est passé sans s'arrêter. 2 passer [58] devant □ The bus goes past our house. Le bus passe devant notre maison.
■ **It's half past ten.** Il est dix heures et demie.
■ **It's quarter past nine.** Il est neuf heures et quart.
■ **It's ten past eight.** Il est huit heures dix.
■ **It's past midnight.** Il est minuit passé.

past NOUN
▷ *see also* **past** ADVERB, PREPOSITION
le passé *masc*
□ She lives in the past. Elle vit dans le passé.
■ **in the past** (*previously*) autrefois □ This was common in the past. C'était courant autrefois.

pasta NOUN
les pâtes *fem pl*
□ Pasta is easy to cook. Les pâtes sont faciles à préparer.

paste NOUN
la colle *fem* (*glue*)

pasteurized ADJECTIVE
pasteurisé (FEM pasteurisée)

pastime NOUN
le passe-temps *masc* (PL les passe-temps)
□ Her favourite pastime is knitting. Son passe-temps favori est le tricot.

pastry NOUN
la pâte *fem*
■ **pastries** les pâtisseries *fem pl*

patch NOUN
1 la pièce *fem*
□ a patch of material une pièce de tissu
2 la rustine *fem* (*for flat tyre*)
■ **He's got a bald patch.** Il a le crâne dégarni.

patched ADJECTIVE
rapiécé (FEM rapiécée)
□ a pair of patched jeans un jean rapiécé

pâté NOUN
le pâté *masc*

path NOUN
1 le chemin *masc* (*footpath*)
2 l'allée *fem* (*in garden, park*)

pathetic ADJECTIVE
lamentable (FEM lamentable)
□ Our team was pathetic. Notre équipe a été lamentable.

patience NOUN
1 la patience *fem*
□ He hasn't got much patience. Il n'a pas beaucoup de patience.
2 la réussite *fem* (*card game*)
□ to play patience faire une réussite

patient NOUN
▷ *see also* **patient** ADJECTIVE
le patient *masc*
la patiente *fem*

patient ADJECTIVE
▷ *see also* **patient** NOUN
patient (FEM patiente)

patio NOUN
le patio *masc*

patriotic ADJECTIVE
patriote (FEM patriote)

patrol NOUN
la patrouille *fem*

patrol car NOUN
la voiture de police *fem*

pattern NOUN
le motif *masc*
□ a geometric pattern un motif géométrique
■ **a sewing pattern** un patron

pause NOUN
la pause *fem*

pavement NOUN
le trottoir *masc*

pavilion NOUN
le pavillon *masc*

paw NOUN
la patte *fem*

pay NOUN
▷ *see also* **pay** VERB
le salaire *masc*

to **pay** VERB
▷ *see also* **pay** NOUN
1 payer [59]
□ They pay me more on Sundays. Je suis payé davantage le dimanche.
2 régler [34]
□ to pay by cheque régler par chèque □ to pay by credit card régler par carte de crédit
■ **to pay for something** payer [59] quelque chose □ I paid for my ticket. J'ai payé mon billet. □ I paid 50 euros for it. Je l'ai payé cinquante euros.
■ **to pay extra for something** payer [59] un supplément pour quelque chose □ You have to pay extra for breakfast. Il faut payer un supplément pour le petit déjeuner.
■ **to pay attention** faire [36] attention □ Don't pay any attention to him! Ne fais pas attention à lui !
■ **to pay somebody a visit** rendre [7] visite à quelqu'un □ Meena paid us a visit last night. Meena nous a rendu visite hier soir.
■ **to pay somebody back** rembourser [28] quelqu'un □ I'll pay you back tomorrow. Je te rembourserai demain.

payment NOUN
le paiement *masc*

payphone NOUN
le téléphone public *masc*

PC NOUN (= *personal computer*)
le PC *masc*
□ She typed the report on her PC. Elle a tapé le rapport sur son PC.

PE NOUN (= *physical education*)
l'EPS *fem* (= *éducation physique et sportive*)
□ We do PE twice a week. Nous avons EPS deux fois par semaine.

pea NOUN
le petit pois *masc*

peace NOUN
1 la paix *fem* (*after war*)
2 le calme *masc* (*quietness*)

peaceful ADJECTIVE
1 paisible (FEM paisible) (*calm*)
□ a peaceful afternoon un après-midi paisible
2 pacifique (FEM pacifique) (*not violent*)
□ a peaceful protest une manifestation pacifique

peach NOUN
la pêche *fem*

peacock NOUN
le paon *masc*

peak NOUN
la cime *fem* (*of mountain*)
■ **in peak season** en haute saison
■ **It's more expensive during peak travel times.** C'est plus cher en haute saison.

peanut NOUN
la cacahuète *fem*
□ a packet of peanuts un paquet de cacahuètes

peanut butter NOUN
le beurre de cacahuètes *masc*
□ a peanut-butter sandwich un sandwich au beurre de cacahuètes

pear NOUN
la poire *fem*

pearl NOUN
la perle *fem*

pebble NOUN
le galet *masc*
□ a pebble beach une plage de galets

P

peckish - peppermill

peckish ADJECTIVE
- **to feel a bit peckish** avoir [8] un petit creux

peculiar ADJECTIVE
bizarre (FEM bizarre)
- □ He's a peculiar person. Il est bizarre.
- □ It tastes peculiar. Ça a un goût bizarre.

pedal NOUN
la pédale fem

pedestrian NOUN
le piéton masc
la piétonne fem

pedestrian crossing NOUN
le passage pour piétons masc

pedestrianized ADJECTIVE
- **a pedestrianized street** une rue piétonne

pedestrian precinct NOUN
la zone piétonnière fem

pedigree ADJECTIVE
de race (animal)
- □ a pedigree dog un chien de race □ a pedigree labrador un labrador de pure race

pee NOUN
- **to have a pee** faire [36] pipi

peek NOUN
- **to have a peek at something** jeter [41] un coup d'œil à quelque chose
- **No peeking!** On ne regarde pas !

peel NOUN
▷ see also **peel** VERB
l'écorce fem (of orange)

to **peel** VERB
▷ see also **peel** NOUN
1 éplucher [28]
- □ Shall I peel the potatoes? J'épluche les pommes de terre ?
2 peler [43]
- □ My nose is peeling. Mon nez pèle.

peg NOUN
1 le portemanteau masc (PL les portemanteaux) (for coats)
2 la pince à linge fem (clothes peg)
3 le piquet masc (tent peg)

Pekinese NOUN
le pékinois masc

pelican crossing NOUN
le passage pour piétons masc

pellet NOUN
le plomb masc (for gun)

pelvis NOUN
le bassin masc

pen NOUN
le stylo masc

to **penalize** VERB
pénaliser [28]

penalty NOUN
1 la peine fem (punishment)
- **the death penalty** la peine de mort

2 le penalty masc (in football)
3 la pénalité fem (in rugby)
- **a penalty shoot-out** les tirs au but

pence PL NOUN
les pence masc pl

pencil NOUN
le crayon masc
- **in pencil** au crayon

pencil case NOUN
la trousse fem

pencil sharpener NOUN
le taille-crayon masc (PL les taille-crayons)

pendant NOUN
le pendentif masc

penfriend NOUN
le correspondant masc
la correspondante fem

penguin NOUN
le pingouin masc

penicillin NOUN
la pénicilline fem

penis NOUN
le pénis masc

penitentiary NOUN (US)
la prison fem

penknife NOUN
le canif masc

penny NOUN
le penny masc (PL les pence)

pension NOUN
la retraite fem

pensioner NOUN
le retraité masc
la retraitée fem

pentathlon NOUN
le pentathlon masc

people PL NOUN
1 les gens masc pl
- □ The people were nice. Les gens étaient sympathiques. □ a lot of people beaucoup de gens
2 les personnes fem pl (individuals)
- □ six people six personnes □ several people plusieurs personnes
- **How many people are there in your family?** Vous êtes combien dans votre famille ?
- **French people** les Français
- **People say that …** On dit que …

pepper NOUN
1 le poivre masc (spice)
- □ Pass the pepper, please. Passez-moi le poivre, s'il vous plaît.
2 le poivron masc (vegetable)
- □ a green pepper un poivron vert

peppermill NOUN
le moulin à poivre masc

peppermint NOUN
la pastille de menthe *fem* (*sweet*)
■ **peppermint chewing gum** le chewing-gum à la menthe

per PREPOSITION
par
□ per day par jour □ per week par semaine
■ **30 miles per hour** trente miles à l'heure

per cent ADVERB
pour cent
□ fifty per cent cinquante pour cent

percentage NOUN
le pourcentage *masc*

percolator NOUN
la cafetière électrique *fem*

percussion NOUN
la percussion *fem*
□ I play percussion. Je joue des percussions.

perfect ADJECTIVE
parfait (FEM parfaite)
□ Chantal speaks perfect English. Chantal parle un anglais parfait.

perfectly ADVERB
parfaitement

to **perform** VERB
jouer [28] (*act, play*)

performance NOUN
1 le spectacle *masc* (*show*)
□ The performance lasts two hours. Le spectacle dure deux heures.
2 l'interprétation *fem* (*acting*)
□ his performance as Hamlet son interprétation d'Hamlet
3 la performance *fem* (*results*)
□ the team's poor performance la médiocre performance de l'équipe

perfume NOUN
le parfum *masc*

perhaps ADVERB
peut-être
□ a bit boring, perhaps peut-être un peu ennuyeux □ Perhaps he's ill. Il est peut-être malade.
■ **perhaps not** peut-être pas

period NOUN
1 la période *fem*
□ for a limited period pour une période limitée
2 l'époque *fem* (*in history*)
□ the Victorian period l'époque victorienne
3 les règles *fem pl* (*menstruation*)
□ I'm having my period. J'ai mes règles.
4 le cours *masc* (*lesson time*)
□ Each period lasts forty minutes. Chaque cours dure quarante minutes.

permanent ADJECTIVE
permanent (FEM permanente)

permission NOUN
la permission *fem*
□ Could I have permission to leave early? Pourrais-je avoir la permission de partir plus tôt ?

permit NOUN
le permis *masc*
□ a fishing permit un permis de pêche

to **persecute** VERB
persécuter [28]

Persian ADJECTIVE
■ **a Persian cat** un chat persan

persistent ADJECTIVE
tenace (FEM tenace) (*person*)

person NOUN
la personne *fem*
□ She's a very nice person. C'est une personne très sympathique.
■ **in person** en personne

personal ADJECTIVE
personnel (FEM personnelle)

personality NOUN
la personnalité *fem*

personally ADVERB
personnellement
□ I don't know him personally. Je ne le connais pas personnellement. □ Personally I don't agree. Personnellement, je ne suis pas d'accord.

personnel NOUN
le personnel *masc*

perspiration NOUN
la transpiration *fem*

to **persuade** VERB
persuader [28]
■ **to persuade somebody to do something** persuader [28] quelqu'un de faire quelque chose
□ She persuaded me to go with her. Elle m'a persuadé de l'accompagner.

pessimist NOUN
le/la pessimiste *masc/fem*
□ I'm a pessimist. Je suis un(e) pessimiste.

pessimistic ADJECTIVE
pessimiste (FEM pessimiste)

pest NOUN
le/la casse-pieds *masc/fem* (*person*)
□ He's a real pest! C'est un vrai casse-pieds !

to **pester** VERB
importuner [28]

pet NOUN
l'animal familier *masc*
□ Have you got a pet? Est-ce que tu as un animal familier ?
■ **She's the teacher's pet.** C'est la chouchoute de la maîtresse.

petition NOUN
la pétition *fem*

P

petrified ADJECTIVE
pétrifié (FEM pétrifiée)

petrol NOUN
l'essence *fem*
■ **unleaded petrol** l'essence sans plomb

> BE CAREFUL!
> Do not translate **petrol** by the French word
> **pétrole**.

petrol station NOUN
la station-service *fem* (PL les stations-service)

petrol tank NOUN
le réservoir d'essence *masc*

phantom NOUN
le fantôme *masc*

pharmacy NOUN
la pharmacie *fem*

> DID YOU KNOW...?
> Pharmacies in France are identified by a
> special green cross outside the shop.

pheasant NOUN
le faisan *masc*

philosophy NOUN
la philosophie *fem*

phobia NOUN
la phobie *fem*

phone NOUN
▷ *see also* **phone** VERB
le téléphone *masc*
□ Where's the phone? Où est le téléphone ? □ Is
there a phone here? Est-ce qu'il y a un téléphone
ici ?
■ **by phone** par téléphone
■ **to be on the phone** être [35] au téléphone
□ She's on the phone at the moment. Elle est au
téléphone en ce moment.
■ **Can I use your phone, please?** Est-ce que je
peux utiliser votre téléphone, s'il vous plaît ?

to phone VERB
▷ *see also* **phone** NOUN
appeler [4]
□ I'll phone the station. Je vais appeler la gare.

phone bill NOUN
la facture de téléphone *fem*

phone book NOUN
l'annuaire *masc*

phone box NOUN
la cabine téléphonique *fem*

phone call NOUN
l'appel *masc*
□ There's a phone call for you. Il y a un appel
pour vous.
■ **to make a phone call** téléphoner [28]
□ Can I make a phone call? Est-ce que peux
téléphoner ?

phonecard NOUN
la carte téléphonique *fem*

phone number NOUN
le numéro de téléphone *masc*

photo NOUN
la photo *fem*
■ **to take a photo** prendre [65] une photo
■ **to take a photo of somebody** prendre [65]
quelqu'un en photo

photocopier NOUN
la photocopieuse *fem*

photocopy NOUN
▷ *see also* **photocopy** VERB
la photocopie *fem*

to photocopy VERB
▷ *see also* **photocopy** NOUN
photocopier [19]

photograph NOUN
▷ *see also* **photograph** VERB
la photo *fem*
■ **to take a photograph** prendre [65] une
photo
■ **to take a photograph of somebody** prendre
[65] quelqu'un en photo

to photograph VERB
▷ *see also* **photograph** NOUN
photographier [19]

photographer NOUN
le/la photographe *masc/fem*
□ She's a photographer. Elle est photographe.

photography NOUN
la photo *fem*
□ My hobby is photography. Je fais de la photo.

Photoshop® NOUN
▷ *see also* **Photoshop** VERB
Photoshop® *masc*

to Photoshop VERB
▷ *see also* **Photoshop** NOUN
photoshoper [28]

phrase NOUN
l'expression *fem*

phrase book NOUN
le guide de conversation *masc*

physical ADJECTIVE
▷ *see also* **physical** NOUN
physique (FEM physique)

physical NOUN (US)
▷ *see also* **physical** ADJECTIVE
l'examen médical *masc*

physicist NOUN
le physicien *masc*
la physicienne *fem*
□ He's a physicist. Il est physicien.

physics NOUN
la physique *fem*
□ She teaches physics. Elle enseigne la
physique.

physiotherapist NOUN
le/la kinésithérapeute *masc/fem*

physiotherapy NOUN
la kinésithérapie *fem*

pianist NOUN
le/la pianiste *masc/fem*

piano NOUN
le piano *masc*
□ I play the piano. Je joue du piano. □ I have piano lessons. Je prends des leçons de piano.

pick NOUN
▷ *see also* **pick** VERB
■ **Take your pick!** Faites votre choix !

to **pick** VERB
▷ *see also* **pick** NOUN
1 choisir [38] (*choose*)
□ I picked the biggest piece. J'ai choisi le plus gros morceau.
2 sélectionner [28] (*for team*)
□ I've been picked for the team. J'ai été sélectionné pour faire partie de l'équipe.
3 cueillir [22] (*fruit, flowers*)

to **pick on** VERB
harceler [43]
□ She's always picking on me. Elle me harcèle constamment.

to **pick out** VERB
choisir [38]
□ I like them all — it's difficult to pick one out. Ils me plaisent tous — c'est difficile d'en choisir un.

to **pick up** VERB
1 venir [89] chercher (*collect*)
□ We'll come to the airport to pick you up. Nous viendrons vous chercher à l'aéroport.
2 ramasser [28] (*from floor*)
□ Could you help me pick up the toys? Tu peux m'aider à ramasser les jouets ?
3 apprendre [65] (*learn*)
□ I picked up some Spanish during my holiday. J'ai appris quelques mots d'espagnol pendant mes vacances.

pickpocket NOUN
le/la pickpocket *masc/fem*

picnic NOUN
le pique-nique *masc*
■ **to have a picnic** pique-niquer [28] □ We had a picnic on the beach. Nous avons pique-niqué sur la plage.

picture NOUN
1 l'illustration *fem*
□ Children's books have lots of pictures. Il y a beaucoup d'illustrations dans les livres pour enfants.
2 la photo *fem*
□ My picture was in the paper. Ma photo était dans le journal.
3 le tableau *masc* (PL les tableaux) (*painting*)
□ a famous picture un tableau célèbre

■ **to paint a picture of something** peindre [60] quelque chose
4 le dessin *masc* (*drawing*)
■ **to draw a picture of something** dessiner [28] quelque chose

picture messaging NOUN
l'envoi de photos par MMS *masc*

picturesque ADJECTIVE
pittoresque (FEM pittoresque)

pie NOUN
la tourte *fem*
□ an apple pie une tourte aux pommes

piece NOUN
le morceau *masc* (PL les morceaux)
□ A small piece, please. Un petit morceau, s'il vous plaît.
■ **a piece of furniture** un meuble
■ **a piece of advice** un conseil

pier NOUN
la jetée *fem*

to **pierce** VERB
percer [12]
□ She's going to have her ears pierced. Elle va se faire percer les oreilles.

pierced ADJECTIVE
percé (FEM percée)
□ I've got pierced ears. J'ai les oreilles percées.

piercing NOUN
le piercing *masc*
□ She has several piercings. Elle a plusieurs piercings.

pig NOUN
le cochon *masc*

pigeon NOUN
le pigeon *masc*

piggyback NOUN
■ **to give somebody a piggyback** porter [28] quelqu'un sur son dos □ I can't give you a piggyback, you're too heavy. Je ne peux pas te porter sur mon dos, tu es trop lourd.

piggy bank NOUN
la tirelire *fem*

pigtail NOUN
la natte *fem*

pile NOUN
1 le tas *masc* (*untidy heap*)
2 la pile *fem* (*tidy stack*)

pile-up NOUN
le carambolage *masc*

pill NOUN
la pilule *fem*
■ **to be on the pill** prendre [65] la pilule

pillar NOUN
le pilier *masc*

pillar box NOUN
la boîte aux lettres *fem*

P

pillow - plain

pillow NOUN
l'oreiller *masc*

pilot NOUN
le pilote *masc*
□ He's a pilot. Il est pilote.

pimple NOUN
le bouton *masc*

PIN NOUN (= *personal identification number*)
le code confidentiel *masc*
■ **chip and PIN** la CB

pin NOUN
l'épingle *fem*
■ **I've got pins and needles.** J'ai des fourmis dans les jambes.

pinafore NOUN
le tablier *masc*

pinball NOUN
le flipper *masc*
□ to play pinball jouer au flipper
■ **a pinball machine** un flipper

to **pinch** VERB
1 pincer [12]
□ He pinched me! Il m'a pincé !
2 piquer [28] (*informal: steal*)
□ Who's pinched my pen? Qui est-ce qui m'a piqué mon stylo ?

pine NOUN
le pin *masc*
□ a pine table une table en pin

pineapple NOUN
l'ananas *masc*

pink ADJECTIVE
rose (FEM rose)

pint NOUN
la pinte *fem*

> DID YOU KNOW...?
> In France, measurements are in litres and centilitres. A pint is about 0.6 litres.

■ **a pint of milk** un demi-litre de lait
■ **to have a pint** boire [10] une bière □ He's gone out for a pint. Il est parti boire une bière.

pipe NOUN
1 la conduite *fem* (*for water, gas*)
□ The pipes froze. Les conduites d'eau ont gelé.
2 la pipe *fem* (*for smoking*)
□ He smokes a pipe. Il fume la pipe.
■ **the pipes** (*bagpipes*) la cornemuse □ He plays the pipes. Il joue de la cornemuse.

pirate NOUN
le pirate *masc*

Pisces NOUN
les Poissons *masc*
□ I'm Pisces. Je suis Poissons.

pistol NOUN
le pistolet *masc*

pitch NOUN
▷ see also **pitch** VERB
le terrain *masc*
□ a football pitch un terrain de football

to **pitch** VERB
▷ see also **pitch** NOUN
dresser [28] (*tent*)
□ We pitched our tent near the beach. Nous avons dressé notre tente près de la plage.

pity NOUN
▷ see also **pity** VERB
la pitié *fem*
■ **What a pity!** Quel dommage !

to **pity** VERB
▷ see also **pity** NOUN
plaindre [17]

pizza NOUN
la pizza *fem*

place NOUN
▷ see also **place** VERB
1 l'endroit *masc* (*location*)
□ It's a quiet place. C'est un endroit tranquille.
□ There are a lot of interesting places to visit. Il y a beaucoup d'endroits intéressants à visiter.
2 la place *fem* (*space*)
□ a parking place une place de parking □ a university place une place à l'université
■ **to change places** changer [45] de place
□ Lara, change places with Delphine! Lara, change de place avec Delphine !
■ **to take place** avoir [8] lieu
■ **at your place** chez toi □ Shall we meet at your place? On se retrouve chez toi ?
■ **to my place** chez moi □ Do you want to come round to my place? Tu veux venir chez moi ?

to **place** VERB
▷ see also **place** NOUN
1 poser [28]
□ He placed his hand on hers. Il a posé la main sur la sienne.
2 classer [28] (*in competition, contest*)

placement NOUN
le stage *masc*
■ **to do a work placement** faire [36] un stage en entreprise

plaid ADJECTIVE
écossais (FEM écossaise)
□ a plaid shirt une chemise écossaise

plain NOUN
▷ see also **plain** ADJECTIVE, ADVERB
la plaine *fem*

plain ADJECTIVE, ADVERB
▷ see also **plain** NOUN
1 uni (FEM unie) (*not patterned*)
□ a plain carpet un tapis uni
2 simple (FEM simple) (*not fancy*)
□ a plain white blouse un chemisier blanc simple

P

plain chocolate NOUN
le chocolat à croquer *masc*

plait NOUN
la natte *fem*
□ She wears her hair in a plait. Elle a une natte.

plan NOUN
▷ *see also* **plan** VERB
1 le projet *masc*
□ What are your plans for the holidays? Quels sont tes projets pour les vacances ? □ to make plans faire des projets
■ **Everything went according to plan.** Tout s'est passé comme prévu.
2 le plan *masc* (*map*)
□ a plan of the campsite un plan du terrain de camping
■ **my essay plan** le plan de ma dissertation

to **plan** VERB
▷ *see also* **plan** NOUN
1 préparer [28] (*make plans for*)
□ We're planning a trip to Canada. Nous préparons un voyage au Canada.
2 planifier [19] (*make schedule for*)
□ Plan your revision carefully. Planifiez vos révisions avec soin.
■ **to plan to do something** avoir [8] l'intention de faire quelque chose □ I'm planning to get a job in the holidays. J'ai l'intention de trouver un job pour les vacances.

plane NOUN
l'avion *masc*
□ by plane en avion

planet NOUN
la planète *fem*

planning NOUN
la préparation *fem*
□ The trip needs careful planning. Le voyage nécessite une préparation méticuleuse.
■ **family planning** le planning familial

plant NOUN
▷ *see also* **plant** VERB
1 la plante *fem*
□ to water the plants arroser les plantes
2 l'usine *fem* (*factory*)

to **plant** VERB
▷ *see also* **plant** NOUN
planter [28]

plant-based ADJECTIVE
d'origine végétale
□ plant-based proteins des protéines d'origine végétale

plant pot NOUN
le pot de fleurs *masc*

plaque NOUN
la plaque *fem* (*on wall*)

plaster NOUN
1 le pansement adhésif *masc* (*sticking plaster*)

□ Have you got a plaster, by any chance? Vous n'auriez pas un pansement adhésif, par hasard ?
2 le plâtre *masc* (*for fracture*)
□ Her leg's in plaster. Elle a la jambe dans le plâtre.

plastic NOUN
▷ *see also* **plastic** ADJECTIVE
le plastique *masc*
□ It's made of plastic. C'est en plastique.

plastic ADJECTIVE
▷ *see also* **plastic** NOUN
en plastique
□ a plastic bag un sac en plastique

plate NOUN
l'assiette *fem* (*for food*)

platform NOUN
1 le quai *masc* (*at station*)
□ on platform 7 sur le quai numéro sept
2 l'estrade *fem* (*for performers*)

play NOUN
▷ *see also* **play** VERB
la pièce *fem*
□ a play by Shakespeare une pièce de Shakespeare
■ **to put on a play** monter [48] une pièce

to **play** VERB
▷ *see also* **play** NOUN
1 jouer [28]
□ He's playing with his friends. Il joue avec ses amis. □ What sort of music do they play? Quel genre de musique jouent-ils ?
2 jouer [28] contre (*against person, team*)
□ France will play Scotland next month. La France jouera contre l'Écosse le mois prochain.
3 jouer [28] à (*sport, game*)
□ I play hockey. Je joue au hockey. □ Can you play pool? Tu sais jouer au billard américain ?
4 jouer [28] de (*instrument*)
□ I play the guitar. Je joue de la guitare.
5 écouter [28] (*CD, music*)
□ She's always playing that song. Elle écoute tout le temps cette chanson.

to **play down** VERB
dédramatiser [28]
□ He tried to play down his illness. Il a essayé de dédramatiser sa maladie.

player NOUN
1 le joueur *masc*
la joueuse *fem* (*of sport*)
□ a football player un joueur de football
2 le musicien *masc*
la musicienne *fem* (*of instrument*)
■ **a piano player** un pianiste
■ **a saxophone player** un saxophoniste

playful ADJECTIVE
espiègle (FEM espiègle)

playground NOUN
1 la cour de récréation *fem* (*at school*)
2 l'aire de jeux *fem* (*in park*)

playgroup NOUN
la garderie *fem*

playing card NOUN
la carte à jouer *fem*

playing field NOUN
le terrain de sport *masc*

playtime NOUN
la récréation *fem*

playwright NOUN
le dramaturge *masc*

pleasant ADJECTIVE
agréable (FEM agréable)

please EXCLAMATION
1 s'il vous plaît (*polite form*)
□ Two coffees, please. Deux cafés, s'il vous plaît.
2 s'il te plaît (*familiar form*)
□ Please come with me. Viens avec moi, s'il te plaît.

pleased ADJECTIVE
content (FEM contente)
□ My mum's not going to be very pleased. Ma mère ne va pas être contente du tout. □ It's beautiful: she'll be pleased with it. C'est beau : elle va être contente.
■ **Pleased to meet you!** Enchanté !

pleasure NOUN
le plaisir *masc*
□ I read for pleasure. Je lis pour le plaisir.

plenty NOUN
largement assez
□ I've got plenty. J'en ai largement assez.
□ That's plenty, thanks. Ça suffit largement, merci.
■ **plenty of** 1 (*a lot*) beaucoup de □ I've got plenty of things to do. J'ai beaucoup de choses à faire. 2 (*enough*) largement assez de □ I've got plenty of money. J'ai largement assez d'argent. □ We've got plenty of time. Nous avons largement le temps.

pliers PL NOUN
la pince *fem sing*
■ **a pair of pliers** une pince

plot NOUN
▷ see also **plot** VERB
1 l'intrigue *fem* (*of story, play*)
2 la conspiration *fem* (*against somebody*)
□ a plot against the president une conspiration contre le président
3 le carré *masc* (*of land*)
□ a vegetable plot un carré de légumes

to plot VERB
▷ see also **plot** NOUN
comploter [28]

□ They were plotting to kill him. Ils complotaient son assassinat.

plough NOUN
▷ see also **plough** VERB
la charrue *fem*

to plough VERB
▷ see also **plough** NOUN
labourer [28]

plug NOUN
1 la prise de courant *fem* (*electrical*)
□ The plug is faulty. La prise est défectueuse.
2 le bouchon *masc* (*for sink*)

to plug in VERB
brancher [28]
□ Is it plugged in? Est-ce que c'est branché ?

plum NOUN
la prune *fem*
□ plum jam la confiture de prunes

plumber NOUN
le plombier *masc*
□ He's a plumber. Il est plombier.

plump ADJECTIVE
dodu (FEM dodue)

to plunge VERB
plonger [45]

plural NOUN
le pluriel *masc*

plus PREPOSITION, ADJECTIVE
plus
□ 4 plus 3 equals 7. Quatre plus trois égalent sept. □ three children plus a dog trois enfants plus un chien

p.m. ABBREVIATION
■ **at 8 p.m.** à huit heures du soir
■ **at 2 p.m.** à quatorze heures

DID YOU KNOW...?
In France, times are often given using the 24-hour clock.

pneumonia NOUN
la pneumonie *fem*

poached ADJECTIVE
■ **a poached egg** un œuf poché

pocket NOUN
la poche *fem*
■ **pocket money** l'argent de poche *masc*
□ £8 a week pocket money huit livres d'argent de poche par semaine

pocket calculator NOUN
la calculette *fem*

podcast NOUN
le podcast *masc*
■ **to download a podcast** télécharger [45] un podcast

poem NOUN
le poème *masc*

poet NOUN
le poète *masc*
la poétesse *fem*

poetry NOUN
la poésie *fem*

point NOUN
▷ *see also* **point** VERB
1 le point *masc* (*spot, score*)
  □ a point on the horizon un point à l'horizon
  □ They scored 5 points. Ils ont marqué cinq points.
2 la remarque *fem* (*comment*)
  □ He made some interesting points. Il a fait quelques remarques intéressantes.
3 la pointe *fem* (*tip*)
  □ a pencil with a sharp point un crayon à la pointe aiguisée
4 le moment *masc* (*in time*)
  □ At that point, we decided to leave. À ce moment-là, nous avons décidé de partir.
  ■ **a point of view** un point de vue
  ■ **to get the point** comprendre [65] □ Sorry, I don't get the point. Désolé, je ne comprends pas.
  ■ **That's a good point!** C'est vrai !
  ■ **There's no point.** Cela ne sert à rien.
  □ There's no point in waiting. Cela ne sert à rien d'attendre.
  ■ **What's the point?** À quoi bon ? □ What's the point of leaving so early? À quoi bon partir si tôt ?
  ■ **Physics isn't my strong point.** La physique n'est pas mon fort.
  ■ **two point five (2.5)** deux virgule cinq (2,5)

> **DID YOU KNOW...?**
> In decimal numbers, the French use a comma instead of a point.

to **point** VERB
▷ *see also* **point** NOUN
montrer [28] du doigt
  □ Don't point! Ne montre pas du doigt !
  ■ **to point at somebody** montrer [28] quelqu'un du doigt □ She pointed at Maryam. Elle a montré Maryam du doigt.
  ■ **to point a gun at somebody** braquer [28] un revolver sur quelqu'un

to **point out** VERB
1 montrer [28] (*show*)
  □ The guide pointed out Notre-Dame to us. Le guide nous a montré Notre-Dame.
2 signaler [28] (*mention*)
  □ I should point out that ... Je dois vous signaler que ...

pointless ADJECTIVE
inutile (FEM inutile)
  □ It's pointless to argue. Il est inutile de discuter.

poison NOUN
▷ *see also* **poison** VERB
le poison *masc*

to **poison** VERB
▷ *see also* **poison** NOUN
empoisonner [28]

poisonous ADJECTIVE
1 venimeux (FEM venimeuse) (*snake*)
2 vénéneux (FEM vénéneuse) (*plant, mushroom*)
3 toxique (FEM toxique) (*gas*)

to **poke** VERB
  ■ **He poked the ground with his stick.** Il tapotait le sol avec sa canne.
  ■ **She poked me in the ribs.** Elle m'a enfoncé le doigt dans les côtes.

poker NOUN
le poker *masc*
  □ I play poker. Je joue au poker.

Poland NOUN
la Pologne *fem*
  ■ **in Poland** en Pologne
  ■ **to Poland** en Pologne

polar bear NOUN
l'ours blanc *masc*

Pole NOUN
le Polonais *masc*
la Polonaise *fem*

pole NOUN
le poteau *masc* (PL les poteaux)
  □ a telegraph pole un poteau télégraphique
  ■ **a tent pole** un montant de tente
  ■ **a ski pole** un bâton de ski
  ■ **the North Pole** le pôle Nord
  ■ **the South Pole** le pôle Sud

pole vault NOUN
le saut à la perche *masc*

police PL NOUN
la police *fem*
  □ We called the police. Nous avons appelé la police.
  ■ **a police car** une voiture de police
  ■ **a police station** un commissariat de police

> **DID YOU KNOW...?**
> There are several different types of police force in France. The **police nationale** are in charge of national security and public order in general, while the **police municipale** mainly deal with traffic and minor crimes. The **gendarmerie nationale** look after rural policing and border patrols. The **CRS** are involved in crowd and riot control.

policeman NOUN
le policier *masc*
  □ He's a policeman. Il est policier.

police officer NOUN
le policier *masc*
la policière *fem*

policewoman NOUN
la policière *fem*
  □ She's a policewoman. Elle est policière.

P

polio NOUN
la polio *fem*

Polish NOUN
▷ *see also* **Polish** ADJECTIVE
le polonais *masc* (*language*)

Polish ADJECTIVE
▷ *see also* **Polish** NOUN
polonais (FEM polonaise)

polish NOUN
▷ *see also* **polish** VERB
1 le cirage *masc* (*for shoes*)
2 la cire *fem* (*for furniture*)

to **polish** VERB
▷ *see also* **polish** NOUN
1 cirer [28] (*shoes, furniture*)
2 faire [36] briller (*glass*)

polite ADJECTIVE
poli (FEM polie)

politely ADVERB
poliment

politeness NOUN
la politesse *fem*

political ADJECTIVE
politique (FEM politique)

politician NOUN
1 l'homme politique *masc*
2 la femme politique *fem*

politics PL NOUN
la politique *fem sing*
□ I'm not interested in politics. La politique ne m'intéresse pas.

poll NOUN
le sondage *masc*
□ A recent poll revealed that ... Un sondage récent a révélé que ...

pollen NOUN
le pollen *masc*

to **pollute** VERB
polluer [28]

polluted ADJECTIVE
pollué (FEM polluée)

pollution NOUN
la pollution *fem*

polo-necked sweater NOUN
le pull à col roulé *masc*

polo shirt NOUN
le polo *masc*

polythene bag NOUN
le sac en plastique *masc*

pond NOUN
1 l'étang *masc* (*big*)
2 la mare *fem* (*smaller*)
3 le bassin *masc* (*in garden*)
□ We've got a pond in our garden. Nous avons un bassin dans notre jardin.

pony NOUN
le poney *masc*

ponytail NOUN
la queue de cheval *fem*
□ He's got a ponytail. Il a une queue de cheval.

pony trekking NOUN
■ **to go pony trekking** faire [36] une randonnée à dos de poney

poodle NOUN
le caniche *masc*

pool NOUN
1 la flaque *fem* (*puddle*)
2 l'étang *masc* (*pond*)
3 la piscine *fem* (*for swimming*)
4 le billard américain *masc* (*game*)
□ Shall we have a game of pool? Si on jouait au billard américain ?

poor ADJECTIVE
1 pauvre (FEM pauvre)
□ a poor family une famille pauvre □ Poor David, he's very unlucky! Le pauvre David, il n'a vraiment pas de chance !
■ **the poor** les pauvres *masc*
2 médiocre (FEM médiocre) (*bad*)
□ a poor mark une note médiocre

poorly ADJECTIVE
souffrant (FEM souffrante)
□ She's poorly. Elle est souffrante.

pop ADJECTIVE
pop (FEM+PL pop)
□ pop music la musique pop □ a pop star une pop star □ a pop group un groupe pop □ a pop song une chanson pop

to **pop in** VERB
passer [58]
□ I just popped in to say hello. Je suis juste passé dire bonjour. □ I need to pop in to the supermarket for some milk. Je dois passer au supermarché pour chercher du lait.

to **pop out** VERB
sortir [79]
□ He's just popped out to the supermarket. Il vient de sortir pour aller au supermarché.

to **pop round** VERB
passer [58]
□ I'm just popping round to my aunt's. Je vais juste passer chez ma tante.

popcorn NOUN
le pop-corn *masc*

poppy NOUN
le coquelicot *masc*

Popsicle® NOUN (US)
la glace à l'eau *fem*

popular ADJECTIVE
populaire (FEM populaire)

□ She's a very popular girl. C'est une fille très populaire. □ This is a very popular style. C'est un style très populaire.

population NOUN
la population *fem*

porch NOUN
le porche *masc*

pork NOUN
le porc *masc*
□ a pork chop une côtelette de porc □ I don't eat pork. Je ne mange pas de porc.

pornography NOUN
la pornographie *fem*

porridge NOUN
le porridge *masc*

port NOUN
1 le port *masc* (*harbour*)
2 le porto *masc* (*wine*)
□ a glass of port un verre de porto

portable ADJECTIVE
portable (FEM portable)

porter NOUN
1 le portier *masc* (*in hotel*)
2 le porteur *masc* (*at station*)

portion NOUN
la portion *fem*
□ a large portion of chips une grosse portion de frites

portrait NOUN
le portrait *masc*

Portugal NOUN
le Portugal *masc*
■ **in Portugal** au Portugal
■ **We went to Portugal.** Nous sommes allés au Portugal.

Portuguese NOUN
▷ see also **Portuguese** ADJECTIVE
1 le Portugais *masc*
la Portugaise *fem* (*person*)
2 le portugais *masc* (*language*)

Portuguese ADJECTIVE
▷ see also **Portuguese** NOUN
portugais (FEM portugaise)

posh ADJECTIVE
chic (FEM+PL chic)
□ a posh hotel un hôtel chic

position NOUN
la position *fem*
□ an uncomfortable position une position inconfortable

positive ADJECTIVE
1 positif (FEM positive) (*good*)
□ a positive attitude une attitude positive
2 certain (FEM certaine) (*sure*)
□ I'm positive. J'en suis certain.

to **possess** VERB
posséder [34]

possession NOUN
■ **Have you got all your possessions?** Est-ce que tu as toutes tes affaires ?

possibility NOUN
■ **It's a possibility.** C'est possible.

possible ADJECTIVE
possible (FEM possible)
□ as soon as possible aussitôt que possible

possibly ADVERB
peut-être (*perhaps*)
□ Are you coming to the party? — Possibly. Est-ce que tu viens à la soirée ? — Peut-être.
■ **... if you possibly can.** ... si cela vous est possible.
■ **I can't possibly come.** Je ne peux vraiment pas venir.

post NOUN
▷ see also **post** VERB
1 le courrier *masc* (*letters*)
□ Is there any post for me? Est-ce qu'il y a du courrier pour moi ?
2 le poteau *masc* (PL les poteaux) (*pole*)
□ The ball hit the post. Le ballon a heurté le poteau.
3 le post *masc* (*on forum, blog*)

to **post** VERB
▷ see also **post** NOUN
poster [28] (*also online*)
□ I've got some cards to post. J'ai quelques cartes à poster. □ She posted it on my wall. Elle l'a posté sur mon mur.

postage NOUN
l'affranchissement *masc*

postbox NOUN
la boîte aux lettres *fem*

DID YOU KNOW...?
French postboxes are yellow.

postcard NOUN
la carte postale *fem*

postcode NOUN
le code postal *masc*

poster NOUN
1 le poster *masc*
□ I've got posters on my bedroom walls. J'ai des posters sur les murs de ma chambre.
2 l'affiche *fem* (*advertising*)
□ There are posters all over town. Il y a des affiches dans toute la ville.

postman NOUN
le facteur *masc*
□ He's a postman. Il est facteur.

postmark NOUN
le cachet de la poste *masc*

P

post office NOUN
la poste *fem*
□ Where's the post office, please? Où est la poste, s'il vous plaît ? □ She works for the post office. Elle travaille à la poste.

to postpone VERB
remettre [47] à plus tard
□ The match has been postponed. Le match a été remis à plus tard.

postwoman NOUN
la factrice *fem*
□ She's a postwoman. Elle est factrice.

pot NOUN
1 le pot *masc*
□ a pot of jam un pot de confiture
■ **the pots and pans** les casseroles
2 la théière *fem* (*teapot*)
3 la cafetière *fem* (*coffeepot*)

potato NOUN
la pomme de terre *fem*
□ potato salad la salade de pommes de terre
■ **mashed potatoes** la purée
■ **boiled potatoes** les pommes vapeur
■ **a baked potato** une pomme de terre en robe des champs

potential NOUN
▷ see also **potential** ADJECTIVE
■ **He has great potential.** Il a de l'avenir.

potential ADJECTIVE
▷ see also **potential** NOUN
possible (FEM possible)
□ a potential problem un problème possible

pothole NOUN
le nid de poule *masc* (*in road*)

pot plant NOUN
la plante en pot *fem*

pottery NOUN
la poterie *fem*

pound NOUN
▷ see also **pound** VERB
la livre *fem* (*weight, money*)
□ How many euros do you get to the pound? Combien d'euros a-t-on pour une livre ? □ a pound coin une pièce d'une livre

> **DID YOU KNOW...?**
> In France, measurements are in grams and kilograms. One pound is about 450 grams.

□ a pound of carrots un demi-kilo de carottes

to pound VERB
▷ see also **pound** NOUN
battre [9]
□ My heart was pounding. J'avais le cœur qui battait.

to pour VERB
1 verser [28] (*liquid*)
□ She poured some water into the pan. Elle a versé de l'eau dans la casserole.
■ **She poured him a drink.** Elle lui a servi à boire.
■ **Shall I pour you a cup of tea?** Je vous sers une tasse de thé ?
2 pleuvoir [63] à verse (*rain*)
□ It's pouring. Il pleut à verse.
■ **in the pouring rain** sous une pluie torrentielle

poverty NOUN
la pauvreté *fem*

powder NOUN
la poudre *fem*

power NOUN
1 le courant *masc* (*electricity*)
□ The power's off. Le courant est coupé.
■ **a power cut** une coupure de courant
■ **a power point** une prise de courant
■ **a power station** une centrale électrique
2 l'énergie *fem* (*energy*)
□ nuclear power l'énergie nucléaire □ solar power l'énergie solaire
3 le pouvoir *masc* (*authority*)
□ to be in power être au pouvoir

powerful ADJECTIVE
puissant (FEM puissante)

practical ADJECTIVE
pratique (FEM pratique)
□ a practical suggestion un conseil pratique
■ **She's very practical.** Elle a l'esprit pratique.

practically ADVERB
pratiquement
□ It's practically impossible. C'est pratiquement impossible.

practice NOUN
l'entraînement *masc* (*for sport*)
□ football practice l'entraînement de foot
■ **I've got to do my clarinet practice.** Je dois travailler ma clarinette.
■ **It's normal practice in our school.** C'est ce qui se fait dans notre école.
■ **in practice** en pratique
■ **a medical practice** un cabinet médical

to practise (US practice) VERB
1 s'exercer [12] (*music, hobby*)
□ I ought to practise more. Je devrais m'exercer davantage.
2 travailler [28] (*instrument*)
□ I practise the flute every evening. Je travaille ma flûte tous les soirs.
3 pratiquer [28] (*language*)
□ I practised my French when we were on holiday. J'ai pratiqué mon français pendant les vacances.
4 s'entraîner [28] (*sport*)
□ The team practises on Thursdays. L'équipe

s'entraîne le jeudi. □ **I don't practise enough.**
Je ne m'entraîne pas assez.

practising ADJECTIVE
pratiquant (FEM pratiquante)
□ **She's a practising Catholic.** Elle est catholique
pratiquante.

to **praise** VERB
faire [36] l'éloge de
□ **Everyone praises her cooking.** Tout le monde
fait l'éloge de sa cuisine. □ **The teachers praised
our work.** Les professeurs ont fait l'éloge de
notre travail.

pram NOUN
le landau *masc*

prawn NOUN
la crevette *fem*

prawn cocktail NOUN
le cocktail de crevettes *masc*

to **pray** VERB
prier [19]
□ **to pray for something** prier pour quelque
chose

prayer NOUN
la prière *fem*

precaution NOUN
la précaution *fem*
■ **to take precautions** prendre [65] ses
précautions

preceding ADJECTIVE
précédent (FEM précédente)

precinct NOUN
■ **a shopping precinct** un centre commercial
■ **a pedestrian precinct** une zone piétonnière

precious ADJECTIVE
précieux (FEM précieuse)

precise ADJECTIVE
précis (FEM précise)
□ **at that precise moment** à cet instant précis

precisely ADVERB
précisément
□ **Precisely!** Précisément !
■ **at 10 a.m. precisely** à dix heures précises

to **predict** VERB
prédire [27]

predictable ADJECTIVE
prévisible (FEM prévisible)

prefect NOUN

DID YOU KNOW...?
French schools do not have prefects. You
could explain what a prefect is using the
example given.

■ **My sister's a prefect.** Ma sœur est en
dernière année et est chargée de maintenir la
discipline.

to **prefer** VERB
préférer [34]

□ **Which would you prefer?** Lequel préfères-tu ?
□ **I prefer biology to chemistry.** Je préfère les SVT
à la chimie.

preference NOUN
la préférence *fem*

pregnant ADJECTIVE
enceinte
□ **She's six months pregnant.** Elle est enceinte
de six mois.

prehistoric ADJECTIVE
préhistorique (FEM préhistorique)

prejudice NOUN
1 le préjugé *masc*
□ **That's just a prejudice.** C'est un préjugé.
2 les préjugés *masc pl*
□ **There's a lot of racial prejudice.** Il y a beaucoup
de préjugés raciaux.

prejudiced ADJECTIVE
■ **to be prejudiced against somebody** avoir
[8] des préjugés contre quelqu'un

premature ADJECTIVE
prématuré (FEM prématurée)
■ **a premature baby** un prématuré

Premier League NOUN
la première division *fem*
□ **in the Premier League** en première division

premises PL NOUN
les locaux *masc pl*
□ **They're moving to new premises.** Ils vont
occuper de nouveaux locaux.

premonition NOUN
la prémonition *fem*

preoccupied ADJECTIVE
préoccupé (FEM préoccupée)

prep NOUN
les devoirs *masc pl* (*homework*)
□ **history prep** les devoirs d'histoire

preparation NOUN
la préparation *fem*

to **prepare** VERB
préparer [28]
□ **She has to prepare lessons in the evening.**
Elle doit préparer ses cours le soir.
■ **to prepare for something** se préparer [28]
pour quelque chose □ **We're preparing for our
skiing holiday.** Nous nous préparons pour nos
vacances à la neige.

prepared ADJECTIVE
■ **to be prepared to do something** être [35]
prêt à faire quelque chose □ **I'm prepared to
help you.** Je suis prêt à t'aider.

prep school NOUN
l'école primaire privée *fem*

Presbyterian NOUN
▷ *see also* **Presbyterian** ADJECTIVE
le presbytérien *masc*
la presbytérienne *fem*

P

Presbyterian - pretty

Presbyterian ADJECTIVE
▷ *see also* **Presbyterian** NOUN
presbytérien (FEM presbytérienne)

to **prescribe** VERB
prescrire [30]

prescription NOUN
l'ordonnance *fem*
□ You can't get it without a prescription. On ne peut pas se le procurer sans ordonnance.

presence NOUN
la présence *fem*
■ **presence of mind** présence d'esprit

present ADJECTIVE
▷ *see also* **present** NOUN, VERB
1 présent (FEM présente) (*in attendance*)
□ He wasn't present at the school assembly. Il n'était pas présent à l'assemblée de l'école.
2 actuel (FEM actuelle) (*current*)
□ the present situation la situation actuelle
■ **the present tense** le présent

present NOUN
▷ *see also* **present** ADJECTIVE, VERB
1 le cadeau *masc* (PL les cadeaux) (*gift*)
□ I'm going to buy presents. Je vais acheter des cadeaux.
■ **to give somebody a present** offrir [54] un cadeau à quelqu'un
2 le présent *masc* (*time*)
□ up to the present jusqu'à présent
■ **for the present** pour l'instant
■ **at present** en ce moment

to **present** VERB
▷ *see also* **present** ADJECTIVE, NOUN
■ **to present somebody with something** (*prize, medal*) remettre [47] quelque chose à quelqu'un

presenter NOUN
le présentateur *masc*
la présentatrice *fem* (*on TV*)

presently ADVERB
1 bientôt (*soon*)
□ You'll feel better presently. Tu vas bientôt te sentir mieux.
2 actuellement (*at present*)
□ They're presently on tour. Ils sont actuellement en tournée.

president NOUN
le président *masc*
la présidente *fem*

press NOUN
▷ *see also* **press** VERB
la presse *fem*
■ **a press conference** une conférence de presse

to **press** VERB
▷ *see also* **press** NOUN

1 appuyer [53]
□ Don't press too hard! N'appuie pas trop fort !
2 appuyer [53] sur
□ He pressed the start button. Il a appuyé sur le bouton de démarrage.

pressed ADJECTIVE
■ **We are pressed for time.** Le temps nous manque.

press-up NOUN
■ **to do press-ups** faire [36] des pompes □ I do twenty press-ups every morning. Je fais vingt pompes tous les matins.

pressure NOUN
▷ *see also* **pressure** VERB
la pression *fem*
□ He's under a lot of pressure at work. Il est sous pression au travail.
■ **a pressure group** un groupe de pression

to **pressure** VERB
▷ *see also* **pressure** NOUN
faire [36] pression sur
□ My parents are pressuring me. Mes parents font pression sur moi.

to **pressurize** VERB
■ **to pressurize somebody to do something** faire [36] pression sur quelqu'un pour qu'il fasse quelque chose □ My parents are pressurizing me to stay on at school. Mes parents font pression sur moi pour que je reste à l'école.

prestige NOUN
le prestige *masc*

prestigious ADJECTIVE
prestigieux (FEM prestigieuse)

presumably ADVERB
vraisemblablement

to **presume** VERB
supposer [28]
□ I presume so. Je suppose que oui.

to **pretend** VERB
■ **to pretend to do something** faire [36] semblant de faire quelque chose □ He pretended to be asleep. Il faisait semblant de dormir.

> **BE CAREFUL!**
> Do not translate **to pretend** by the French word **prétendre**.

pretty ADJECTIVE, ADVERB
1 joli (FEM jolie)
□ She's very pretty. Elle est très jolie.
2 plutôt (*rather*)
□ That film was pretty bad. Ce film était plutôt mauvais.
■ **The weather was pretty awful.** Il faisait un temps minable.
■ **It's pretty much the same.** C'est pratiquement la même chose.

to **prevent** VERB
empêcher [28]
■ **to prevent somebody from doing something** empêcher [28] quelqu'un de faire quelque chose □ They tried to prevent us from staying out late. Ils ont essayé de nous empêcher de rentrer tard.

previous ADJECTIVE
précédent (FEM précédente)

previously ADVERB
auparavant

prey NOUN
la proie fem
□ a bird of prey un oiseau de proie

price NOUN
le prix masc

price list NOUN
la liste des prix fem

to **prick** VERB
piquer [28]
□ I've pricked my finger. Je me suis piqué le doigt.

pride NOUN
la fierté fem

priest NOUN
le prêtre masc
□ He's a priest. Il est prêtre.

primarily ADVERB
principalement

primary ADJECTIVE
principal (FEM principale, MASC PL principaux)

primary school NOUN
l'école primaire fem
□ She's still at primary school. Elle est encore à l'école primaire.

> **DID YOU KNOW...?**
> In France, children start primary school at the age of six. The first year is **CP**, followed by **CE1** and **CE2**. The last two years are **CM1** and **CM2**.

prime minister NOUN
le Premier ministre masc

primitive ADJECTIVE
primitif (FEM primitive)

prince NOUN
le prince masc
□ the Prince of Wales le prince de Galles

princess NOUN
la princesse fem
□ Princess Anne la princesse Anne

principal ADJECTIVE
▷ see also **principal** NOUN
principal (FEM principale, MASC PL principaux)

principal NOUN
▷ see also **principal** ADJECTIVE
le principal masc (PL les principaux) (of college)

principle NOUN
le principe masc
■ **on principle** par principe

print NOUN
1 les caractères masc pl (letters)
□ in small print en petits caractères
2 l'empreinte digitale fem (fingerprint)
3 la gravure fem (picture)
□ a framed print une gravure encadrée

printer NOUN
l'imprimante fem (machine)

printout NOUN
le tirage masc

priority NOUN
la priorité fem

prison NOUN
la prison fem
■ **in prison** en prison

prisoner NOUN
le prisonnier masc
la prisonnière fem

prison officer NOUN
le gardien de prison masc
la gardienne de prison fem

privacy NOUN
l'intimité fem

private ADJECTIVE
privé (FEM privée)
□ a private school une école privée
■ **'private property'** « propriété privée »
■ **'private'** (on envelope) « personnel »
■ **a private bathroom** une salle de bain individuelle
■ **I have private lessons.** Je prends des cours particuliers.

to **privatize** VERB
privatiser [28]

privilege NOUN
le privilège masc

prize NOUN
le prix masc
□ to win a prize gagner un prix

prize-giving NOUN
la distribution des prix fem

prizewinner NOUN
le gagnant masc
la gagnante fem

pro NOUN
■ **the pros and cons** le pour et le contre □ We weighed up the pros and cons. Nous avons pesé le pour et le contre.

probability NOUN
la probabilité fem

probable ADJECTIVE
probable (FEM probable)

P

probably – promote

probably ADVERB
probablement
□ probably not probablement pas

problem NOUN
le problème *masc*
□ No problem! Pas de problème !

proceeds PL NOUN
la recette *fem sing*

process NOUN
le processus *masc*
□ the peace process le processus de paix
■ **to be in the process of doing something**
être [35] en train de faire quelque chose □ We're
in the process of painting the kitchen. Nous
sommes en train de peindre la cuisine.

procession NOUN
la procession *fem* (*religious*)

to **produce** VERB
1 produire [23] (*manufacture*)
2 monter [48] (*play, show*)

producer NOUN
le metteur en scène *masc* (*of play, show*)

product NOUN
le produit *masc*

production NOUN
1 la production *fem*
□ The latest smartphone has just gone into
production. On vient de lancer la production du
tout dernier smartphone.
2 la mise en scène *fem* (*play, show*)
□ a production of 'Hamlet' une mise en scène
de « Hamlet »

profession NOUN
la profession *fem*

professional NOUN
▷ *see also* **professional** ADJECTIVE
le professionnel *masc*
la professionnelle *fem*

professional ADJECTIVE
▷ *see also* **professional** NOUN
professionnel (FEM professionnelle) (*player*)
□ a professional musician un musicien
professionnel
■ **a very professional piece of work** un vrai
travail de professionnel

professionally ADVERB
■ **She sings professionally.** C'est une
chanteuse professionnelle.

professor NOUN
le professeur d'université *masc*
■ **He's the French professor.** Il est titulaire de
la chaire de français.

profit NOUN
le bénéfice *masc*

profitable ADJECTIVE
rentable (FEM rentable)

program NOUN
▷ *see also* **program** VERB
le programme *masc*
□ a computer program un programme
informatique
■ **a TV program** (US) une émission de
télévision

to **program** VERB
▷ *see also* **program** NOUN
programmer [28] (*computer*)

programme NOUN
1 l'émission *fem* (*on TV, radio*)
2 le programme *masc* (*of events*)

programmer NOUN
le programmeur *masc*
la programmeuse *fem*
□ She's a programmer. Elle est programmeuse.

programming NOUN
la programmation *fem*

progress NOUN
le progrès *masc*
□ You're making progress! Vous faites des
progrès !

to **prohibit** VERB
interdire [27]
□ Smoking is prohibited. Il est interdit de fumer.

project NOUN
1 le projet *masc* (*plan*)
□ a development project un projet de
développement
2 le dossier *masc* (*research*)
□ I'm doing a project on education in France. Je
prépare un dossier sur l'éducation en France.

projector NOUN
le projecteur *masc*

promenade NOUN
le front de mer *masc*

promise NOUN
▷ *see also* **promise** VERB
la promesse *fem*
□ He made me a promise. Il m'a fait une
promesse.
■ **That's a promise!** C'est promis !

to **promise** VERB
▷ *see also* **promise** NOUN
promettre [47]
□ She promised to write. Elle a promis d'écrire.
□ I'll text you, I promise! Je t'enverrai un SMS,
c'est promis !

promising ADJECTIVE
■ **a promising player** un joueur
prometteur

to **promote** VERB
■ **to be promoted** être [35] promu □ She was
promoted after six months. Elle a été promue au
bout de six mois.

P

promotion NOUN
la promotion *fem*

prompt ADJECTIVE, ADVERB
rapide (FEM rapide)
□ a prompt reply une réponse rapide
■ **at eight o'clock prompt** à huit heures précises

promptly ADVERB
■ **We left promptly at seven.** Nous sommes partis à sept heures précises.

pronoun NOUN
le pronom *masc*

to **pronounce** VERB
prononcer [12]
□ How do you pronounce that word? Comment est-ce qu'on prononce ce mot ?

pronunciation NOUN
la prononciation *fem*

proof NOUN
la preuve *fem*

proper ADJECTIVE
1 vrai (FEM vraie) (*genuine*)
□ proper French bread du vrai pain français
□ We didn't have a proper lunch, just sandwiches. Nous n'avons pas pris de vrai repas, juste des sandwichs.
■ **It's difficult to get a proper job.** Il est difficile de trouver un travail correct.
2 adéquat (FEM adéquate)
□ You have to have the proper equipment. Il faut avoir l'équipement adéquat. □ We need proper training. Il nous faut une formation adéquate.
■ **If you had come at the proper time ...** Si tu étais venu à l'heure dite ...

BE CAREFUL!
Do not translate **proper** by the French word **propre**.

properly ADVERB
1 comme il faut (*correctly*)
□ You're not doing it properly. Tu ne t'y prends pas comme il faut.
2 convenablement (*appropriately*)
□ Dress properly for your interview. Habille-toi convenablement pour ton entretien.

property NOUN
la propriété *fem*
■ **'private property'** « propriété privée »
■ **stolen property** les objets volés

proportional ADJECTIVE
proportionnel (FEM proportionnelle)
□ proportional representation la représentation proportionnelle

proposal NOUN
la proposition *fem* (*suggestion*)

to **propose** VERB
proposer [28]

□ I propose a new plan. Je propose un changement de programme.
■ **to propose to do something** avoir [8] l'intention de faire quelque chose □ What do you propose to do? Qu'est-ce que tu as l'intention de faire ?
■ **to propose to somebody** (*for marriage*) demander [28] quelqu'un en mariage □ He proposed to her at the restaurant. Il l'a demandée en mariage au restaurant.

to **prosecute** VERB
poursuivre [81] en justice
□ They were prosecuted for murder. Ils ont été poursuivis en justice pour meurtre.
■ **'Trespassers will be prosecuted'** « Défense d'entrer sous peine de poursuites »

prospect NOUN
la perspective *fem*
□ It'll improve my career prospects. Ça va améliorer mes perspectives d'avenir.

prospectus NOUN
le prospectus *masc*

to **protect** VERB
protéger [66]

protection NOUN
la protection *fem*

protein NOUN
la protéine *fem*

protest NOUN
▷ *see also* **protest** VERB
la protestation *fem*
□ He ignored their protests. Il a ignoré leurs protestations.
■ **a protest march** une manifestation

to **protest** VERB
▷ *see also* **protest** NOUN
protester [28]

Protestant NOUN
▷ *see also* **Protestant** ADJECTIVE
le protestant *masc*
la protestante *fem*
□ I'm a Protestant. Je suis protestant.

Protestant ADJECTIVE
▷ *see also* **Protestant** NOUN
protestant (FEM protestante)
□ a Protestant church une église protestante

protester NOUN
le manifestant *masc*
la manifestante *fem*

proud ADJECTIVE
fier (FEM fière)
□ Her parents are proud of her. Ses parents sont fiers d'elle.

to **prove** VERB
prouver [28]
□ The police couldn't prove it. La police n'a pas pu le prouver.

P

proverb NOUN
le proverbe *masc*

to provide VERB
fournir [38]
- **to provide somebody with something**
fournir [38] quelque chose à quelqu'un □ They provided us with maps. Ils nous ont fourni des cartes.

to provide for VERB
subvenir [89] aux besoins de
□ He can't provide for his family any more. Il ne peut plus subvenir aux besoins de sa famille.

provided CONJUNCTION
à condition que

> **à condition que** has to be followed by the subjunctive.

□ He'll play in the next match provided he's fit. Il jouera dans le prochain match, à condition qu'il soit en forme.

provisional ADJECTIVE
provisoire (FEM provisoire)

prowler NOUN
le rôdeur *masc*
la rôdeuse *fem*

prune NOUN
le pruneau *masc* (PL les pruneaux)

to pry VERB
- **He's always prying into other people's affairs.** Il met toujours son nez dans les affaires des autres.

pseudonym NOUN
le pseudonyme *masc*

psychiatrist NOUN
le/la psychiatre *masc/fem*
□ She's a psychiatrist. Elle est psychiatre.

psychoanalyst NOUN
le/la psychanalyste *masc/fem*

psychological ADJECTIVE
psychologique (FEM psychologique)

psychologist NOUN
le/la psychologue *masc/fem*
□ He's a psychologist. Il est psychologue.

psychology NOUN
la psychologie *fem*

PTO ABBREVIATION (= please turn over)
TSVP (= tournez, s'il vous plaît)

pub NOUN
le pub *masc*

public NOUN
▷ see also **public** ADJECTIVE
le public *masc*
□ open to the public ouvert au public
- **in public** en public

public ADJECTIVE
▷ see also **public** NOUN
public (FEM publique)

- **a public holiday** un jour férié
- **public opinion** l'opinion publique *fem*
- **the public address system** la sono *fem*

publican NOUN
le patron de pub *masc*
la patronne de pub *fem*
- **My uncle's a publican.** Mon oncle tient un pub.

publicity NOUN
la publicité *fem*

public school NOUN
l'école privée *fem*

public transport NOUN
les transports en commun *masc pl*

to publish VERB
publier [19]

publisher NOUN
l'éditeur *masc*

pudding NOUN
le dessert *masc*
□ What's for pudding? Qu'est-ce qu'il y a comme dessert ?
- **rice pudding** le riz au lait
- **black pudding** le boudin noir

puddle NOUN
la flaque *fem*

puff pastry NOUN
la pâte feuilletée *fem*

to pull VERB
tirer [28]
□ Pull! Tirez !
- **He pulled the trigger.** Il a appuyé sur la gâchette.
- **to pull a muscle** se froisser [28] un muscle
□ I pulled a muscle when I was training. Je me suis froissé un muscle à l'entraînement.
- **You're pulling my leg!** Tu me fais marcher !

to pull down VERB
démolir [38]

to pull out VERB
1 arracher [28] (*tooth, weed*)
2 déboîter [28] (*car*)
□ The car pulled out to overtake. La voiture a déboîté pour doubler.
3 se retirer [28] (*withdraw*)
□ She pulled out of the tournament. Elle s'est retirée du tournoi.

to pull through VERB
s'en sortir [79]
□ They think he'll pull through. Ils pensent qu'il va s'en sortir.

to pull up VERB
s'arrêter [28] (*car*)
□ A black car pulled up beside me. Une voiture noire s'est arrêtée à côté de moi.

pullover NOUN
le pull-over *masc*

pulse NOUN
le pouls *masc*
□ The nurse took his pulse. L'infirmière a pris son pouls.

pulses PL NOUN
les légumes secs *masc pl*

pump NOUN
▷ *see also* **pump** VERB
1 la pompe *fem*
□ a bicycle pump une pompe à vélo □ a petrol pump une pompe à essence
2 le chausson de gym *masc* (*shoe*)

to **pump** VERB
▷ *see also* **pump** NOUN
pomper [28]

to **pump up** VERB
gonfler [28] (*tyre*)

pumpkin NOUN
le potiron *masc*

punch NOUN
▷ *see also* **punch** VERB
1 le coup de poing *masc* (*blow*)
□ He gave me a punch. Il m'a donné un coup de poing.
2 le punch *masc* (*drink*)

to **punch** VERB
▷ *see also* **punch** NOUN
1 donner [28] un coup de poing à (*hit*)
□ He punched me! Il m'a donné un coup de poing !
2 composter [28] (*in ticket machine*)
□ Remember to punch your ticket. N'oublie pas de composter ton billet.
3 poinçonner [28] (*by hand*)
□ He forgot to punch my ticket. Il a oublié de poinçonner mon billet.

punch-up NOUN
la bagarre *fem* (*informal*)

punctual ADJECTIVE
ponctuel (FEM ponctuelle)

punctuation NOUN
la ponctuation *fem*

puncture NOUN
la crevaison *fem*
□ I had to mend a puncture. J'ai dû réparer une crevaison.
■ **to have a puncture** crever [43] □ I had a puncture on the motorway. J'ai crevé sur l'autoroute.

to **punish** VERB
punir [38]
■ **to punish somebody for something** punir [38] quelqu'un pour quelque chose
■ **to punish somebody for doing something** punir [38] quelqu'un d'avoir fait quelque chose

punishment NOUN
la punition *fem*

pupil NOUN
l'élève *masc/fem*

puppet NOUN
la marionnette *fem*

puppy NOUN
le chiot *masc*

to **purchase** VERB
acheter [1]

pure ADJECTIVE
pur (FEM pure)
□ pure orange juice du pur jus d'orange □ He's doing pure maths. Il fait des maths pures.

purple ADJECTIVE
violet (FEM violette)

purpose NOUN
le but *masc*
□ What is the purpose of these changes? Quel est le but de ces changements ? □ his purpose in life son but dans la vie
■ **on purpose** exprès □ He did it on purpose. Il l'a fait exprès.

to **purr** VERB
ronronner [28]

purse NOUN
1 le porte-monnaie *masc* (PL les porte-monnaie)
2 le sac à main *masc* (US: *handbag*)

to **pursue** VERB
poursuivre [81]

pursuit NOUN
l'activité *fem*
□ outdoor pursuits les activités de plein air

push NOUN
▷ *see also* **push** VERB
■ **to give somebody a push** pousser [28] quelqu'un □ He gave me a push. Il m'a poussé.

to **push** VERB
▷ *see also* **push** NOUN
1 pousser [28]
□ Don't push! Arrêtez de pousser !
2 appuyer [53] sur (*button*)
■ **to push somebody to do something** pousser [28] quelqu'un à faire quelque chose
□ My parents are pushing me to go to university. Mes parents me poussent à entrer à l'université.

to **push around** VERB
bousculer [28]
□ He likes pushing people around. Il aime bien bousculer les gens.

to **push through** VERB
se frayer [59] un passage
□ The paramedics pushed through the crowd. Les secouristes se sont frayé un passage dans la foule.

pushchair – puzzle

■ **I pushed my way through.** Je me suis frayé un passage.

pushchair NOUN
la poussette *fem*

push-up NOUN
■ **to do push-ups** faire [36] des pompes □ I do twenty push-ups every morning. Je fais vingt pompes tous les matins.

to **put** VERB
1 mettre [47] (*place*)
□ Where shall I put my things? Où est-ce que je peux mettre mes affaires ? □ She's putting the baby to bed. Elle met le bébé au lit.
2 écrire [30] (*write*)
□ Don't forget to put your name on the paper. N'oubliez pas d'écrire votre nom sur la feuille.

to **put aside** VERB
mettre [47] de côté
□ Can you put this aside for me till tomorrow? Est-ce que vous pouvez mettre ça de côté pour moi jusqu'à demain ?

to **put away** VERB
ranger [45]
□ Can you put away the dishes, please? Tu peux ranger la vaisselle, s'il te plaît ?

to **put back** VERB
remettre [47] en place (*replace*)
□ Put it back when you've finished with it. Remets-le en place une fois que tu auras fini.

to **put down** VERB
1 poser [28]
□ I'll put these bags down for a minute. Je vais poser ces sacs une minute.
2 noter [28] (*in writing*)
□ I've put down a few ideas. J'ai noté quelques idées.
■ **to have an animal put down** faire [36] piquer un animal □ We had to have our old dog put down. Nous avons dû faire piquer notre vieux chien.

to **put forward** VERB
1 avancer [12] (*clock*)
□ Don't forget to put the clocks forward. N'oubliez pas d'avancer les pendules d'une heure.
2 proposer [28] (*idea, argument*)
□ to put forward a suggestion proposer une suggestion

to **put in** VERB
installer [28] (*install*)
□ We're going to get central heating put in. Nous allons faire installer le chauffage central.
■ **He has put in a lot of work on this project.** Il a fourni beaucoup de travail pour ce projet.

to **put off** VERB
1 éteindre [60] (*switch off*)

□ Shall I put the light off? Est-ce que j'éteins la lumière ?
2 remettre [47] à plus tard (*postpone*)
□ I keep putting it off. Je n'arrête pas de remettre ça à plus tard.
3 déranger [45] (*distract*)
□ Stop putting me off! Arrête de me déranger !
4 décourager [45] (*discourage*)
□ He's not easily put off. Il ne se laisse pas facilement décourager.

to **put on** VERB
1 mettre [47] (*clothes, lipstick, album*)
□ I'll put my coat on. Je vais mettre mon manteau.
2 allumer [28] (*light, heater, TV*)
□ Shall I put the heater on? J'allume le chauffage ?
3 monter [48] (*play, show*)
□ We're putting on 'Bugsy Malone'. Nous sommes en train de monter « Bugsy Malone ».
4 mettre [47] à cuire
□ I'll put the potatoes on. Je vais mettre les pommes de terre à cuire.
■ **to put on weight** grossir [38] □ He's put on a lot of weight. Il a beaucoup grossi.

to **put out** VERB
éteindre [60] (*light, cigarette, fire*)
□ It took them five hours to put out the fire. Ils ont mis cinq heures à éteindre l'incendie.

to **put through** VERB
passer [58]
□ Can you put me through to the manager? Est-ce que vous pouvez me passer le directeur ?
■ **I'm putting you through.** Je vous passe la communication.

to **put up** VERB
1 mettre [47] (*pin up*)
□ I'll put the poster up on my wall. Je vais mettre le poster sur mon mur.
2 monter [48] (*tent*)
□ We put up our tent in a field. Nous avons monté la tente dans un champ.
3 augmenter [28] (*price*)
□ They've put up the price. Ils ont augmenté le prix.
4 héberger [45] (*accommodate*)
□ My friend will put me up for the night. Mon ami va m'héberger pour la nuit.
■ **to put one's hand up** lever [43] la main
□ If you have any questions, put up your hand. Si vous avez une question, levez la main.
■ **to put up with something** supporter [28] quelque chose □ I'm not going to put up with it any longer. Je ne vais pas supporter ça plus longtemps.

puzzle NOUN
le puzzle *masc* (*jigsaw*)

P

puzzled - Pyrenees

English-French

puzzled ADJECTIVE
perplexe (FEM perplexe)
□ You look puzzled! Tu as l'air perplexe !

puzzling ADJECTIVE
déconcertant (FEM déconcertante)

pyjamas PL NOUN
le pyjama *masc sing*
□ my pyjamas mon pyjama □ a pair of pyjamas
un pyjama

■ a pyjama top un haut de pyjama

pyramid NOUN
la pyramide *fem*

Pyrenees PL NOUN
les Pyrénées *fem pl*
■ in the Pyrenees dans les Pyrénées
■ We went to the Pyrenees.
Nous sommes allés dans les
Pyrénées.

Core vocabulary is shaded. 517

Qq

quaint ADJECTIVE
pittoresque (FEM pittoresque) (house, village)

qualification NOUN
le diplôme masc
□ to leave school without any qualifications
quitter l'école sans aucun diplôme
■ **vocational qualifications** des qualifications
professionnelles

qualified ADJECTIVE
1 qualifié (FEM qualifiée) (trained)
□ a qualified driving instructor un moniteur
d'auto-école qualifié
2 diplômé (FEM diplômée) (nurse, teacher)
□ a qualified nurse une infirmière diplômée

to **qualify** VERB
1 obtenir [83] son diplôme (for job)
□ She qualified as a teacher last year. Elle a
obtenu son diplôme de professeur l'année
dernière.
2 se qualifier [19] (in competition)
□ Our team didn't qualify. Notre équipe ne s'est
pas qualifiée.

quality NOUN
la qualité fem
□ a good quality of life une bonne qualité
de vie □ good-quality ingredients des
ingrédients de bonne qualité □ She's got
lots of good qualities. Elle a beaucoup de
qualités.

quantity NOUN
la quantité fem

quarrel NOUN
▷ see also **quarrel** VERB
la dispute fem

to **quarrel** VERB
▷ see also **quarrel** NOUN
se disputer [28]

quarry NOUN
la carrière fem (for stone)

quarter NOUN
le quart masc
■ **three quarters** trois quarts
■ **a quarter of an hour** un quart d'heure
□ three quarters of an hour trois quarts d'heure
■ **a quarter past ten** dix heures et quart
■ **a quarter to eleven** onze heures moins le
quart

quarter final NOUN
le quart de finale masc

quartet NOUN
le quatuor masc
□ a string quartet un quatuor à cordes

quay NOUN
le quai masc

queasy ADJECTIVE
■ **to feel queasy** avoir [8] mal au cœur
□ I'm feeling queasy. J'ai mal au cœur.

queen NOUN
1 la reine fem
□ Queen Elizabeth la reine Élisabeth
2 la dame fem (playing card)
□ the queen of hearts la dame de cœur
■ **the Queen Mother** la reine mère

queer ADJECTIVE
queer (FEM queer)
□ He identifies as queer. Il se définit comme
queer.

query NOUN
▷ see also **query** VERB
la question fem

to **query** VERB
▷ see also **query** NOUN
mettre [47] en question
□ No one queried my decision. Personne n'a mis
en question ma décision.

question NOUN
▷ see also **question** VERB
la question fem
□ Can I ask a question? Est-ce que je peux poser
une question ? □ That's a difficult question.
C'est une question difficile.
■ **It's out of the question.** C'est hors de
question.

to **question** VERB
▷ see also **question** NOUN
interroger [45]
□ He was questioned by the police. Il a été
interrogé par la police.

question mark NOUN
le point d'interrogation masc

questionnaire NOUN
le questionnaire masc

queue NOUN
▷ *see also* **queue** VERB
la queue *fem*

to **queue** VERB
▷ *see also* **queue** NOUN
faire [36] la queue
■ **to queue for something** faire [36] la queue pour avoir quelque chose □ We had to queue for tickets. Nous avons dû faire la queue pour avoir les billets.

quick ADJECTIVE, ADVERB
rapide (FEM rapide)
□ a quick lunch un déjeuner rapide □ It's quicker by train. C'est plus rapide en train.
■ **Be quick!** Dépêche-toi !
■ **She's a quick learner.** Elle apprend vite.
■ **Quick, phone the police!** Téléphonez vite à la police !

quickly ADVERB
vite
□ It was all over very quickly. Ça s'est passé très vite.

quiet ADJECTIVE
1 silencieux (FEM silencieuse) (*not talkative or noisy*)
□ You're very quiet today. Tu es bien silencieux aujourd'hui. □ The engine's very quiet. Le moteur est très silencieux.
2 tranquille (FEM tranquille) (*peaceful*)
□ a quiet little town une petite ville tranquille □ a quiet weekend un week-end tranquille
■ **Be quiet!** Tais-toi !
■ **Quiet!** Silence !

quietly ADVERB
1 doucement (*speak*)
□ 'She's dead,' he said quietly. « Elle est morte » dit-il doucement.
2 silencieusement (*move*)
■ **He quietly opened the door.** Il a ouvert la porte sans faire de bruit.

quilt NOUN
la couette *fem* (*duvet*)

to **quit** VERB
quitter [28] (*place, premises, job*)

□ She's decided to quit her job. Elle a décidé de quitter son emploi.
■ **I quit!** J'abandonne !

quite ADVERB
1 assez (*rather*)
□ It's quite warm today. Il fait assez bon aujourd'hui. □ I quite liked the play, but ... J'ai trouvé la pièce assez bonne, mais ...
2 tout à fait (*entirely*)
□ I'm not quite sure. Je n'en suis pas tout à fait sûr. □ It's not quite the same. Ce n'est pas tout à fait la même chose.
■ **quite good** pas mal
■ **I've been there quite a lot.** J'y suis allé pas mal de fois.
■ **quite a lot of money** pas mal d'argent
■ **It costs quite a lot to go abroad.** Ça coûte assez cher d'aller à l'étranger.
■ **It's quite a long way.** C'est assez loin.
■ **It was quite a shock.** Ça a été un sacré choc.
■ **There were quite a few people there.** Il y avait pas mal de gens.

quiz NOUN
le jeu-concours *masc*

quota NOUN
le quota *masc*

quotation NOUN
la citation *fem*
□ a quotation from Shakespeare une citation de Shakespeare

quote NOUN
▷ *see also* **quote** VERB
la citation *fem*
□ a Shakespeare quote une citation de Shakespeare
■ **quotes** (*quotation marks*) les guillemets *masc pl* □ in quotes entre guillemets

to **quote** VERB
▷ *see also* **quote** NOUN
citer [28]
□ He's always quoting Shakespeare. Il n'arrête pas de citer Shakespeare.

q

Rr

rabbi NOUN
le rabbin *masc*

rabbit NOUN
le lapin *masc*
■ **a rabbit hutch** un clapier

rabies NOUN
la rage *fem*
■ **a dog with rabies** un chien enragé

race NOUN
▷ *see also* **race** VERB
1 la course *fem* (*sport*)
□ a cycle race une course cycliste
2 la race *fem* (*species*)
□ the human race la race humaine
■ **race relations** les relations interraciales *fem pl*

to **race** VERB
▷ *see also* **race** NOUN
1 courir [16]
□ We raced to catch the bus. Nous avons couru pour attraper le bus.
2 faire [36] la course (*have a race*)
■ **I'll race you!** On fait la course !

racecourse NOUN
le champ de courses *masc*

racehorse NOUN
le cheval de course *masc* (PL les chevaux de course)

racer NOUN
le vélo de course *masc* (*bike*)

racetrack NOUN
la piste *fem*

racial ADJECTIVE
racial (FEM raciale, MASC PL raciaux)
□ racial discrimination la discrimination raciale

racing car NOUN
la voiture de course *fem*

racing driver NOUN
le pilote de course *masc*

racism NOUN
le racisme *masc*

racist ADJECTIVE
▷ *see also* **racist** NOUN
raciste (FEM raciste)

racist NOUN
▷ *see also* **racist** ADJECTIVE
le/la raciste *masc/fem*

rack NOUN
le porte-bagages *masc* (PL les porte-bagages) (*for luggage*)

racket NOUN
1 la raquette *fem* (*for sport*)
□ my tennis racket ma raquette de tennis
2 le boucan *masc* (*noise*)
□ They're making a terrible racket. Ils font un boucan de tous les diables. (*informal*)

racquet NOUN
la raquette *fem*

radar NOUN
le radar *masc*

radiation NOUN
la radiation *fem*

radiator NOUN
le radiateur *masc*

radio NOUN
la radio *fem*
■ **on the radio** à la radio
■ **a radio station** une station de radio

radioactive ADJECTIVE
radioactif (FEM radioactive)

radio-controlled ADJECTIVE
téléguidé (FEM téléguidée) (*model plane, car*)

radish NOUN
le radis *masc*

RAF NOUN (= Royal Air Force)
la R.A.F. *fem*
□ He's in the RAF. Il est dans la R.A.F.

raffle NOUN
la tombola *fem*
□ a raffle ticket un billet de tombola

raft NOUN
le radeau *masc* (PL les radeaux)

rag NOUN
le chiffon *masc*
□ a piece of rag un chiffon
■ **dressed in rags** en haillons

rage NOUN
la rage *fem*
□ mad with rage fou de rage

■ **to be in a rage** être [35] furieux □ She was in a rage. Elle était furieuse.

raid NOUN
▷ *see also* **raid** VERB
1 le hold-up *masc* (PL les hold-up) (*burglary*)
□ There was a bank raid near my house. Il y a eu un hold-up dans une banque près de chez moi.
2 la descente *fem*
□ a police raid une descente de police

to **raid** VERB
▷ *see also* **raid** NOUN
faire [36] une descente dans (*police*)
□ The police raided the club. La police a fait une descente dans le club.

rail NOUN
1 la rampe *fem* (*on stairs*)
2 la balustrade *fem* (*on bridge, balcony*)
□ Don't lean over the rail! Ne vous penchez pas sur la balustrade !
3 le rail *masc* (*on railway line*)
■ **by rail** en train

railcard NOUN
la carte de chemin de fer *fem*
□ a young person's railcard une carte de chemin de fer tarif jeune

railroad NOUN (US)
le chemin de fer *masc*
■ **a railroad line** une ligne de chemin de fer
■ **a railroad station** une gare

railway NOUN
le chemin de fer *masc*
□ the privatization of the railways la privatisation des chemins de fer
■ **a railway line** une ligne de chemin de fer
■ **a railway station** une gare

rain NOUN
▷ *see also* **rain** VERB
la pluie *fem*
□ in the rain sous la pluie

to **rain** VERB
▷ *see also* **rain** NOUN
pleuvoir [63]
□ It rains a lot here. Il pleut beaucoup par ici.
■ **It's raining.** Il pleut.

rainbow NOUN
l'arc-en-ciel *masc* (PL les arcs-en-ciel)

raincoat NOUN
l'imperméable *masc*

rainforest NOUN
la forêt tropicale humide *fem*

rainy ADJECTIVE
pluvieux (FEM pluvieuse)

to **raise** VERB
1 lever [43] (*lift*)
□ He raised his hand. Il a levé la main.

2 améliorer [28] (*improve*)
□ They want to raise standards in schools. Ils veulent améliorer le niveau dans les écoles.
■ **to raise money** collecter [28] des fonds
□ The school is raising money for a new gym. L'école collecte des fonds pour un nouveau gymnase.

raisin NOUN
le raisin sec *masc*

rake NOUN
le râteau *masc* (PL les râteaux)

rally NOUN
1 le rassemblement *masc* (*of people*)
2 le rallye *masc* (*sport*)
□ a rally driver un pilote de rallye
3 l'échange *masc* (*in tennis*)

ram NOUN
▷ *see also* **ram** VERB
le bélier *masc* (*sheep*)

to **ram** VERB
▷ *see also* **ram** NOUN
emboutir [2] (*vehicle*)
□ The thieves rammed a police car. Les voleurs ont embouti une voiture de police.

Ramadan NOUN
le ramadan *masc*

ramble NOUN
la randonnée *fem*
□ to go for a ramble faire une randonnée

rambler NOUN
le randonneur *masc*
la randonneuse *fem*

ramp NOUN
la rampe d'accès *fem* (*for wheelchairs*)

ran VERB ▷ *see* **run**

ranch NOUN
le ranch *masc*

random ADJECTIVE
■ **a random selection** une sélection effectuée au hasard
■ **at random** au hasard □ We picked the number at random. Nous avons pris le numéro au hasard.

rang VERB ▷ *see* **ring**

range NOUN
▷ *see also* **range** VERB
le choix *masc*
□ a wide range of colours un grand choix de coloris
■ **a range of subjects** diverses matières
□ We study a range of subjects. Nous étudions diverses matières.
■ **a mountain range** une chaîne de montagnes

to **range** VERB
▷ *see also* **range** NOUN

r

rank – reach

■ **to range from ... to** se situer [28] entre ... et
□ Temperatures in summer range from 20 to 35 degrees. Les températures estivales se situent entre vingt et trente-cinq degrés.
■ **Tickets range from £2 to £20.** Les billets coûtent entre deux et vingt livres.

rank NOUN
▷ see also **rank** VERB
■ **a taxi rank** une station de taxis

to **rank** VERB
▷ see also **rank** NOUN
■ **He's ranked third in the United States.** Il est classé troisième aux États-Unis.

ransom NOUN
la rançon fem

rap NOUN
le rap masc (music)

rape NOUN
▷ see also **rape** VERB
le viol masc

to **rape** VERB
▷ see also **rape** NOUN
violer [28]

rapids PL NOUN
les rapides masc pl

rapist NOUN
le violeur masc

rare ADJECTIVE
1 rare (FEM rare) (unusual)
□ a rare plant une plante rare
2 saignant (FEM saignante) (steak)

rash NOUN
l'éruption de boutons fem
□ I've got a rash on my chest. J'ai une éruption de boutons sur la poitrine.

rasher NOUN
la tranche fem
□ an egg and two rashers of bacon un œuf et deux tranches de bacon

raspberry NOUN
la framboise fem
□ raspberry jam la confiture de framboises

rat NOUN
le rat masc

rate NOUN
▷ see also **rate** VERB
1 le tarif masc (price)
□ There are reduced rates for students. Il y a des tarifs réduits pour les étudiants.
2 le taux masc (level)
□ the divorce rate le taux de divorce □ a high rate of interest un taux d'intérêt élevé

to **rate** VERB
▷ see also **rate** NOUN
considérer [34] comme
■ **He is rated the best.** Il est considéré comme le meilleur.

■ **How do you rate him?** Qu'est-ce que vous pensez de lui ?

rather ADVERB
plutôt
□ I was rather disappointed. J'étais plutôt déçu.
□ £20! That's rather a lot! Vingt livres ! C'est plutôt cher !
■ **rather a lot of** pas mal de □ I've got rather a lot of homework to do. J'ai pas mal de devoirs à faire.
■ **rather than** plutôt que □ We decided to camp, rather than stay at a hotel. Nous avons décidé de camper plutôt que d'aller à l'hôtel.
■ **I'd rather ...** J'aimerais mieux ... □ I'd rather stay in tonight. J'aimerais mieux rester à la maison ce soir. □ I'd rather have an apple than a banana. J'aimerais mieux une pomme qu'une banane.

rattle NOUN
le hochet masc (for baby)

rattlesnake NOUN
le serpent à sonnette masc

to **rave** VERB
s'extasier [19]
□ They raved about the film. Ils se sont extasiés sur le film.

raven NOUN
le corbeau masc (PL les corbeaux)

ravenous ADJECTIVE
■ **to be ravenous** avoir [8] une faim de loup
□ I'm ravenous! J'ai une faim de loup !

raving ADJECTIVE
■ **raving mad** fou à lier □ She's raving mad! Elle est folle à lier.

raw ADJECTIVE
cru (FEM crue) (food)
■ **raw materials** les matières premières fem pl

razor NOUN
le rasoir masc
□ some disposable razors des rasoirs jetables
■ **a razor blade** une lame de rasoir

RE NOUN
l'éducation religieuse fem

reach NOUN
▷ see also **reach** VERB
■ **out of reach** hors de portée □ The light switch was out of reach. L'interrupteur était hors de portée.
■ **within easy reach of** à proximité de □ The campsite is within easy reach of the bus station. Le camping se trouve à proximité de la gare routière.

to **reach** VERB
▷ see also **reach** NOUN
1 arriver [5⁴] à
□ We reached the hotel at 7 p.m. Nous sommes arrivés à l'hôtel à sept heures du soir.

■ **We hope to reach the final.** Nous espérons aller en finale.

2 parvenir [89¹] à (*decision*)
□ Eventually they reached a decision. Ils sont finalement parvenus à une décision.
■ **He reached for his phone.** Il a tendu la main pour prendre son téléphone.

to **react** VERB
réagir [38]

reaction NOUN
la réaction *fem*

reactor NOUN
le réacteur *masc*
□ a nuclear reactor un réacteur nucléaire

to **read** VERB
lire [44]
□ I don't read much. Je ne lis pas beaucoup.
□ Have you read 'The Hunger Games'? Est-ce que tu as lu « Hunger Games » ? □ Read the text out loud. Lis le texte à haute voix.

to **read out** VERB
lire [44]
□ He read out the article to me. Il m'a lu l'article.
■ **to read out the results** annoncer [12] les résultats

reader NOUN
le lecteur *masc*
la lectrice *fem* (*person*)

readily ADVERB
volontiers
□ She readily agreed. Elle a accepté volontiers.

reading NOUN
la lecture *fem*
□ Reading is one of my hobbies. La lecture est l'un de mes passe-temps.

ready ADJECTIVE
prêt (FEM prête)
□ She's nearly ready. Elle est presque prête.
□ He's always ready to help. Il est toujours prêt à rendre service.
■ **a ready meal** un plat cuisiné
■ **to get ready** se préparer [28] □ She's getting ready to go out. Elle est en train de se préparer pour sortir.
■ **to get something ready** préparer [28] quelque chose □ He's getting the dinner ready. Il est en train de préparer le dîner.

real ADJECTIVE
1 vrai (FEM vraie)
□ He wasn't a real police officer. Ce n'était pas un vrai policier. □ Her real name is Cordelia. Son vrai nom est Cordelia.
2 véritable (FEM véritable)
□ It's real leather. C'est du cuir véritable.
□ It was a real nightmare. C'était un véritable cauchemar.

■ **in real life** dans la réalité

realistic ADJECTIVE
réaliste (FEM réaliste)

reality NOUN
la réalité *fem*

reality TV NOUN
la téléréalité *fem*
□ a reality TV show une émission de téléréalité

to **realize** VERB
■ **to realize that ...** se rendre [7] compte que ...
□ We realized that something was wrong. Nous nous sommes rendu compte que quelque chose n'allait pas.

really ADVERB
vraiment
□ She's really nice. Elle est vraiment sympathique. □ Do you want to go? — Not really. Tu veux y aller ? — Pas vraiment.
■ **I'm learning German. — Really?** J'apprends l'allemand. — Ah bon ?
■ **Do you really think so?** Tu es sûr ?

realtor NOUN (US)
l'agent immobilier *masc*

rear ADJECTIVE
▷ *see also* **rear** NOUN
arrière (FEM+PL arrière)
□ a rear wheel une roue arrière

rear NOUN
▷ *see also* **rear** ADJECTIVE
l'arrière *masc*
□ at the rear of the train à l'arrière du train

reason NOUN
la raison *fem*
□ There's no reason to think that ... Il n'y a aucune raison de penser que ... □ for security reasons pour des raisons de sécurité
■ **That was the main reason I went.** C'est surtout pour ça que j'y suis allé.

reasonable ADJECTIVE
1 raisonnable (FEM raisonnable) (*sensible*)
□ Be reasonable! Sois raisonnable !
2 correct (FEM correcte) (*not bad*)
□ He wrote a reasonable essay. Sa dissertation était correcte.

reasonably ADVERB
raisonnablement
□ The team played reasonably well. L'équipe a joué raisonnablement bien.
■ **reasonably priced jeans** un jean à un prix raisonnable

to **reassure** VERB
rassurer [28]

reassuring ADJECTIVE
rassurant (FEM rassurante)

rebellious ADJECTIVE
rebelle (FEM rebelle)

r

English-French

receipt NOUN
le reçu *masc*

to **receive** VERB
recevoir [67]

receiver NOUN
le combiné *masc* (*of phone*)
■ **to pick up the receiver** décrocher [28]

recent ADJECTIVE
récent (FEM récente)

recently ADVERB
ces derniers temps
□ I've been doing a lot of training recently. Je me suis beaucoup entraîné ces derniers temps.

reception NOUN
la réception *fem*
□ Please leave your key at reception. Merci de laisser votre clé à la réception. □ The reception will be at a big hotel. La réception aura lieu dans un grand hôtel.

receptionist NOUN
le/la réceptionniste *masc/fem*

recession NOUN
la récession *fem*

recipe NOUN
la recette *fem*

to **reckon** VERB
penser [28]
□ What do you reckon? Qu'est-ce que tu en penses ?

reclining ADJECTIVE
■ **a reclining seat** un siège inclinable

recognizable ADJECTIVE
reconnaissable (FEM reconnaissable)

to **recognize** VERB
reconnaître [14]
□ You'll recognize me by my red hair. Vous me reconnaîtrez à mes cheveux roux.

to **recommend** VERB
conseiller [28]
□ What do you recommend? Qu'est-ce que vous me conseillez ?

to **reconsider** VERB
reconsidérer [34]

record NOUN
▷ see also **record** VERB
1 le record *masc* (*sport*)
□ the world record le record du monde
■ **in record time** en un temps record □ She finished the job in record time. Elle a terminé le travail en un temps record.
2 le disque *masc* (*recording*)
□ my favourite record mon disque préféré
■ **a criminal record** un casier judiciaire
□ He's got a criminal record. Il a un casier judiciaire.
■ **records** (*of police, hospital*) les archives *fem*

pl □ I'll check in the records. Je vais vérifier dans les archives.
■ **There is no record of your booking.** Il n'y a aucune trace de votre réservation.

to **record** VERB
▷ see also **record** NOUN
enregistrer [28] (*on film*)
□ They've just recorded their new album. Ils viennent d'enregistrer leur nouveau disque.

recorded delivery NOUN
■ **to send something recorded delivery** envoyer [33] quelque chose en recommandé

recorder NOUN
la flûte à bec *fem* (*instrument*)
□ She plays the recorder. Elle joue de la flûte à bec.

recording NOUN
l'enregistrement *masc*

record player NOUN
le tourne-disque *masc*

to **recover** VERB
se remettre [47]
□ He's recovering from a knee injury. Il se remet d'une blessure au genou.

recovery NOUN
le rétablissement *masc*
■ **Best wishes for a speedy recovery!** Meilleurs vœux de prompt rétablissement !

rectangle NOUN
le rectangle *masc*

rectangular ADJECTIVE
rectangulaire (FEM rectangulaire)

to **recycle** VERB
recycler [28]

recycling NOUN
le recyclage *masc*

red ADJECTIVE
1 rouge (FEM rouge)
□ a red rose une rose rouge □ red meat la viande rouge
■ **a red light** (*traffic light*) un feu rouge □ to go through a red light brûler un feu rouge
2 roux (FEM rousse) (*hair*)
□ Sam's got red hair. Sam a les cheveux roux.

Red Cross NOUN
la Croix-Rouge *fem*

redcurrant NOUN
la groseille *fem*

to **redecorate** VERB
1 retapisser [28] (*with wallpaper*)
2 refaire [36] les peintures (*with paint*)

red-haired ADJECTIVE
roux (FEM rousse)

red-handed ADJECTIVE
■ **to catch somebody red-handed** prendre [65] quelqu'un la main dans le sac □ He was

r

caught red-handed. Il a été pris la main dans le sac.

redhead NOUN
le roux *masc*
la rousse *fem*

to **redo** VERB
refaire [36]

to **reduce** VERB
réduire [23]
□ at a reduced price à prix réduit

reduction NOUN
la réduction *fem*
□ a 5% reduction une réduction de cinq pour cent

redundancy NOUN
le licenciement *masc*
□ There were fifty redundancies. Il y a eu cinquante licenciements.
■ **his redundancy payment** ses indemnités de licenciement

redundant ADJECTIVE
■ **to be made redundant** être [35] licencié
□ He was made redundant yesterday. Il a été licencié hier.

red wine NOUN
le vin rouge *masc*

reed NOUN
le roseau *masc* (PL les roseaux) (*plant*)

reel NOUN
la bobine *fem* (*of thread*)

to **refer** VERB
■ **to refer to** faire [36] allusion à □ What are you referring to? À quoi faites-vous allusion ?

referee NOUN
l'arbitre *masc*

reference NOUN
1 l'allusion *fem*
□ He made no reference to the murder. Il n'a fait aucune allusion au meurtre.
2 les références *fem pl* (*for job application*)
□ Would you please give me a reference? Pouvez-vous me fournir des références ?
■ **a reference book** un ouvrage de référence

to **refill** VERB
remplir [38] à nouveau
□ He refilled my glass. Il a rempli mon verre à nouveau.

refinery NOUN
la raffinerie *fem*

to **reflect** VERB
refléter [34] (*light, image*)

reflection NOUN
le reflet *masc* (*in mirror*)

reflex NOUN
le réflexe *masc*

reflexive ADJECTIVE
réfléchi (FEM réfléchie)
□ a reflexive verb un verbe réfléchi

refresher course NOUN
le cours de remise à niveau *masc*

refreshing ADJECTIVE
rafraîchissant (FEM rafraîchissante)

refreshments PL NOUN
les rafraîchissements *masc pl*

refrigerator NOUN
le réfrigérateur *masc*

to **refuel** VERB
se ravitailler [28] en carburant
□ The plane stops in Boston to refuel. L'avion s'arrête à Boston pour se ravitailler en carburant.

refuge NOUN
le refuge *masc*

refugee NOUN
le réfugié *masc*
la réfugiée *fem*

refund NOUN
▷ *see also* **refund** VERB
le remboursement *masc*

to **refund** VERB
▷ *see also* **refund** NOUN
rembourser [28]

refusal NOUN
le refus *masc*

to **refuse** VERB
▷ *see also* **refuse** NOUN
refuser [28]

refuse NOUN
▷ *see also* **refuse** VERB
les ordures *fem pl*
■ **refuse collection** le ramassage des ordures

to **regain** VERB
■ **to regain consciousness** reprendre [65] connaissance

regard NOUN
▷ *see also* **regard** VERB
■ **Give my regards to Alice.** Transmettez mon bon souvenir à Alice.
■ **Louis sends his regards.** Vous avez le bonjour de Louis.
■ **'kind regards'** « bien cordialement »

to **regard** VERB
▷ *see also* **regard** NOUN
■ **to regard something as** considérer [34] quelque chose comme
■ **as regards ...** concernant ...

regarding PREPOSITION
relatif à (FEM relative à)
□ the laws regarding the export of animals les lois relatives à l'exportation des animaux
■ **Regarding John, ...** Quant à John, ...

r

regardless ADVERB
- **regardless of the weather** peu importe le temps
- **regardless of the consequences** peu importent les conséquences

regiment NOUN
le régiment *masc*

region NOUN
la région *fem*

regional ADJECTIVE
régional (FEM régionale, MASC PL régionaux)

register NOUN
▷ *see also* **register** VERB
le registre d'absences *masc* (*in school*)

to **register** VERB
▷ *see also* **register** NOUN
s'inscrire [30] (*at school, college*)

registered ADJECTIVE
- **a registered letter** une lettre recommandée

registration NOUN
1 l'appel *masc* (*roll call*)
2 le numéro d'immatriculation *masc* (*of car*)

regret NOUN
▷ *see also* **regret** VERB
le regret *masc*
- **I've got no regrets.** Je ne regrette rien.

to **regret** VERB
▷ *see also* **regret** NOUN
regretter [28]
□ Give me the money or you'll regret it! Donne-moi l'argent, sinon tu vas le regretter !
- **to regret doing something** regretter [28] d'avoir fait quelque chose □ I regret saying that. Je regrette d'avoir dit ça.

regular ADJECTIVE
1 régulier (FEM régulière)
□ at regular intervals à intervalles réguliers
□ a regular verb un verbe régulier
- **to take regular exercise** faire [36] régulièrement de l'exercice
2 normal (FEM normale, MASC PL normaux) (*average*)
□ a regular portion of fries une portion de frites normale

regularly ADVERB
régulièrement

regulation NOUN
le règlement *masc*

rehearsal NOUN
la répétition *fem*

to **rehearse** VERB
répéter [34]

rein NOUN
la rêne *fem*
□ the reins les rênes

reindeer NOUN
le renne *masc*

to **reject** VERB
rejeter [41] (*idea, suggestion*)
□ We rejected that idea straight away. Nous avons immédiatement rejeté cette idée.
- **I applied but they rejected me.** J'ai posé ma candidature mais ils l'ont rejetée.

relapse NOUN
la rechute *fem*
□ to have a relapse faire une rechute

related ADJECTIVE
apparenté (FEM apparentée) (*people*)
□ We're related. Nous sommes apparentés.
- **The two events were not related.** Il n'y avait aucun rapport entre les deux événements.

relation NOUN
1 le parent *masc*
la parente *fem* (*person*)
□ He's a distant relation. C'est un parent éloigné. □ my close relations mes parents proches
- **my relations** ma famille
- **I've got relations in Spain.** J'ai de la famille en Espagne.
2 le rapport *masc* (*connection*)
□ It has no relation to reality. Cela n'a aucun rapport avec la réalité.
- **in relation to** par rapport à

relationship NOUN
les relations *fem pl*
□ We have a good relationship. Nous avons de bonnes relations.
- **I'm not in a relationship at the moment.** Je ne sors avec personne en ce moment.

relative NOUN
le parent *masc*
la parente *fem*
□ my close relatives mes proches parents
- **all her relatives** toute sa famille

relatively ADVERB
relativement

to **relax** VERB
se détendre [88]
□ I relax by listening to music. Je me détends en écoutant de la musique.
- **Relax! Everything's fine.** Ne t'en fais pas ! Tout va bien.

relaxation NOUN
la détente *fem*
□ I don't have much time for relaxation. Je n'ai pas beaucoup de moments de détente.

relaxed ADJECTIVE
détendu (FEM détendue)

relaxing ADJECTIVE
reposant (FEM reposante)

r

■ **I find cooking relaxing.** Cela me détend de faire la cuisine.

relay NOUN
■ **a relay race** une course de relais

to **release** VERB
▷ *see also* **release** NOUN
1 libérer [34] (*prisoner*)
2 divulguer [28] (*report, news*)
3 sortir [79] (*film, album*)

release NOUN
▷ *see also* **release** VERB
la libération *fem* (*from prison*)
□ the release of the prisoners la libération des prisonniers
■ **the band's latest release** le dernier disque du groupe

relegated ADJECTIVE
relégué (FEM reléguée) (*sport*)

relevant ADJECTIVE
approprié (FEM appropriée) (*documents*)
■ **That's not relevant.** Ça n'a aucun rapport.
■ **to be relevant to something** être [35] en rapport avec quelque chose □ Education should be relevant to real life. L'enseignement devrait être en rapport avec la réalité.

reliable ADJECTIVE
fiable (FEM fiable)
□ a reliable car une voiture fiable □ He's not very reliable. Il n'est pas très fiable.

relief NOUN
le soulagement *masc*
□ That's a relief! Quel soulagement !

to **relieve** VERB
soulager [45]
□ This injection will relieve the pain. Cette piqûre va soulager la douleur.

relieved ADJECTIVE
soulagé (FEM soulagée)
□ I was relieved to hear ... J'ai été soulagé d'apprendre ...

religion NOUN
la religion *fem*
□ What religion are you? Quelle est votre religion ?

religious ADJECTIVE
1 religieux (FEM religieuse)
□ my religious beliefs mes croyances religieuses
2 croyant (FEM croyante)
□ I'm not religious. Je ne suis pas croyant.

reluctant ADJECTIVE
réticent (FEM réticente)
■ **to be reluctant to do something** être [35] peu disposé à faire quelque chose □ They were reluctant to help us. Ils étaient peu disposés à nous aider.

reluctantly ADVERB
à contrecœur
□ She reluctantly accepted. Elle a accepté à contrecœur.

to **rely on** VERB
compter [28] sur
□ I'm relying on you. Je compte sur toi.

to **remain** VERB
rester [71ᵉ]
■ **to remain silent** garder [28] le silence

remaining ADJECTIVE
le reste de
□ the remaining ingredients le reste des ingrédients

remains PL NOUN
les restes *masc pl*
□ the remains of the picnic les restes du pique-nique □ human remains des restes humains
■ **Roman remains** les vestiges romains

remake NOUN
le remake *masc* (*of film*)

remark NOUN
la remarque *fem*

remarkable ADJECTIVE
remarquable (FEM remarquable)

remarkably ADVERB
remarquablement

to **remarry** VERB
se remarier [19]
□ She remarried three years ago. Elle s'est remariée il y a trois ans.

remedy NOUN
le remède *masc*
□ a good remedy for a sore throat un bon remède contre le mal de gorge

to **remember** VERB
se souvenir [83] de
□ I can't remember his name. Je ne me souviens pas de son nom. □ I don't remember. Je ne m'en souviens pas.

In French you often say 'don't forget' instead of 'remember'.

□ Remember your passport! N'oublie pas ton passeport ! □ Remember to write your name on the form. N'oubliez pas d'écrire votre nom sur le formulaire.

Remembrance Day NOUN
le jour de l'Armistice *masc*
□ on Remembrance Day le jour de l'Armistice

to **remind** VERB
rappeler [4]
□ It reminds me of Scotland. Cela me rappelle l'Écosse. □ I'll remind you tomorrow. Je te le rappellerai demain. □ Remind me to speak to Mariusz. Rappelle-moi de parler à Mariusz.

r

remorse NOUN
le remords *masc*
□ He showed no remorse. Il n'a manifesté aucun remords.

remote ADJECTIVE
isolé (FEM isolée)
□ a remote village un village isolé

remote control NOUN
la télécommande *fem*

remote learning NOUN
l'enseignement à distance *masc*

remotely ADVERB
■ **I'm not remotely interested.** Je ne suis absolument pas intéressé.
■ **Do you think it would be remotely possible?** Pensez-vous que cela serait éventuellement possible ?

removable ADJECTIVE
amovible (FEM amovible)

removal NOUN
le déménagement *masc* (*from house*)
■ **a removal van** un camion de déménagement

to **remove** VERB
1 enlever [43]
□ Can you remove your laptop from my seat? Est-ce que vous pouvez enlever votre ordinateur portable de mon siège ?
2 faire [36] partir (*stain*)
□ Did you remove the stain? Est-ce que tu as fait partir la tache ?

rendezvous NOUN
le rendez-vous *masc* (PL les rendez-vous)

to **renew** VERB
renouveler [4] (*passport, licence*)

renewable ADJECTIVE
renouvelable (FEM renouvelable) (*energy, resource*)

to **renovate** VERB
rénover [28]
□ The leisure centre has been renovated. Le centre de loisirs a été rénové.

renowned ADJECTIVE
renommé (FEM renommée)

rent NOUN
▷ *see also* **rent** VERB
le loyer *masc*

to **rent** VERB
▷ *see also* **rent** NOUN
louer [28]
□ We rented a car. Nous avons loué une voiture.

rental NOUN
la location *fem*
□ Car rental is included in the price. Le prix comprend la location d'une voiture.

rental car NOUN
la voiture de location *fem*

to **reorganize** VERB
réorganiser [28]

rep NOUN (= *representative*)
le représentant *masc*
la représentante *fem*

repaid VERB ▷ *see* **repay**

to **repair** VERB
▷ *see also* **repair** NOUN
réparer [28]
■ **to get something repaired** faire [36] réparer quelque chose □ I got the washing machine repaired. J'ai fait réparer la machine à laver.

repair NOUN
▷ *see also* **repair** VERB
la réparation *fem*

to **repay** VERB
rembourser [28] (*money*)

repayment NOUN
le remboursement *masc*

to **repeat** VERB
▷ *see also* **repeat** NOUN
répéter [34]

repeat NOUN
▷ *see also* **repeat** VERB
la rediffusion *fem*
□ There are too many repeats on TV. Il y a trop de rediffusions à la télé.

repeatedly ADVERB
à plusieurs reprises

repellent NOUN
■ **insect repellent** l'insectifuge *masc*

repetitive ADJECTIVE
répétitif (FEM répétitive) (*movement, work*)

to **replace** VERB
remplacer [12]

replay NOUN
▷ *see also* **replay** VERB
■ **There will be a replay on Friday.** Le match sera rejoué vendredi.

to **replay** VERB
▷ *see also* **replay** NOUN
rejouer [28] (*match*)

replica NOUN
la réplique *fem*

reply NOUN
▷ *see also* **reply** VERB
la réponse *fem*

to **reply** VERB
▷ *see also* **reply** NOUN
répondre [69]

report NOUN
▷ *see also* **report** VERB
1 le compte rendu *masc* (PL les comptes rendus) (*of event*)
2 le reportage *masc* (*news report*)
□ a report in the paper un reportage dans le journal

3 le bulletin scolaire *masc* (*at school*)
□ I got a good report this term. J'ai un bon bulletin scolaire ce trimestre.

to **report** VERB
▷ *see also* **report** NOUN

1 signaler [28]
□ I reported the theft to the police. J'ai signalé le vol au commissariat.

2 se présenter [28]
□ Report to the caretaker when you arrive. Présentez-vous chez le gardien à votre arrivée.

reporter NOUN
le reporter *masc*
□ I'd like to be a reporter. J'aimerais être reporter.

to **represent** VERB
représenter [28]

representative ADJECTIVE
représentatif (FEM représentative)

reproduction NOUN
la reproduction *fem*

reptile NOUN
le reptile *masc*

republic NOUN
la république *fem*

repulsive ADJECTIVE
repoussant (FEM repoussante)

reputable ADJECTIVE
de bonne réputation

reputation NOUN
la réputation *fem*

request NOUN
▷ *see also* **request** VERB
la demande *fem*

to **request** VERB
▷ *see also* **request** NOUN
demander [28]

to **require** VERB
exiger [45]
□ The job requires good IT skills. Cet emploi exige une bonne connaissance de l'informatique.
■ **What qualifications are required?** Quels sont les diplômes requis ?

requirement NOUN
la condition requise *fem*
□ What are the requirements for this apprenticeship? Quelles sont les conditions requises pour cet apprentissage ?
■ **entry requirements** (*for university*) les critères d'entrée

to **rescue** VERB
▷ *see also* **rescue** NOUN
sauver [28]

rescue NOUN
▷ *see also* **rescue** VERB

1 le sauvetage *masc*
□ a rescue operation une opération de sauvetage
■ **a mountain rescue team** une équipe de sauvetage en montagne

2 le secours *masc*
□ the rescue services les services de secours
■ **to come to somebody's rescue** venir [89ᵗ] au secours de quelqu'un □ He came to my rescue. Il est venu à mon secours.

research NOUN

1 la recherche *fem* (*experimental*)
□ He's doing research. Il fait de la recherche.

2 les recherches *fem pl* (*theoretical*)
□ She's doing some research in the library. Elle fait des recherches à la bibliothèque.

resemblance NOUN
la ressemblance *fem*

to **resent** VERB
être [35] contrarié par
□ I really resented your criticism. J'ai été vraiment contrarié par tes critiques.

resentful ADJECTIVE
plein de ressentiment (FEM pleine de ressentiment)
■ **to feel resentful towards somebody** en vouloir [93] à quelqu'un

reservation NOUN
la réservation *fem* (*booking*)
□ I've got a reservation for two nights. J'ai une réservation pour deux nuits. □ I'd like to make a reservation for this evening. J'aimerais faire une réservation pour ce soir.

reserve NOUN
▷ *see also* **reserve** VERB

1 la réserve *fem* (*place*)
□ a nature reserve une réserve naturelle

2 le remplaçant *masc*
la remplaçante *fem* (*person*)
□ I was reserve in the game last Saturday. J'étais remplaçant dans le match de samedi dernier.

to **reserve** VERB
▷ *see also* **reserve** NOUN
réserver [28]
□ I'd like to reserve a table for tomorrow evening. J'aimerais réserver une table pour demain soir.

reserved ADJECTIVE
réservé (FEM réservée)
□ a reserved seat une place réservée □ He's quite reserved. Il est assez réservé.

reservoir NOUN
le réservoir *masc*

resident NOUN
le résident *masc*
la résidente *fem*

r

residential ADJECTIVE

résidentiel (FEM résidentielle)

□ a residential area un quartier résidentiel

to resign VERB

donner [28] sa démission

to resit VERB

repasser [28]

□ I'm resitting the exam in December. Je vais repasser l'examen en décembre.

resolution NOUN

la résolution fem

■ Have you made any New Year's resolutions? Tu as pris de bonnes résolutions pour l'année nouvelle ?

resort NOUN

la station balnéaire fem (at seaside)

□ It's a resort on the Costa del Sol. C'est une station balnéaire sur la Costa del Sol.

■ a ski resort une station de ski

■ as a last resort en dernier recours

resource NOUN

la ressource fem

respect NOUN

▷ see also **respect** VERB

le respect masc

to respect VERB

▷ see also **respect** NOUN

respecter [28]

respectable ADJECTIVE

1 respectable (FEM respectable)

2 correct (FEM correcte) (standard, marks)

respectively ADVERB

respectivement

responsibility NOUN

la responsabilité fem

responsible ADJECTIVE

1 responsable (FEM responsable) (in charge)

■ to be responsible for something être [35] responsable de quelque chose □ He's responsible for booking the tickets. Il est responsable de la réservation des billets.

■ It's a responsible job. C'est un poste à responsabilités.

2 sérieux (FEM sérieuse) (mature)

□ You should be more responsible. Tu devrais être un peu plus sérieux.

rest NOUN

▷ see also **rest** VERB

1 le repos masc (relaxation)

□ five minutes' rest cinq minutes de repos

■ to have a rest se reposer [28] □ We stopped to have a rest. Nous nous sommes arrêtés pour nous reposer.

2 le reste masc (remainder)

□ I'll do the rest. Je ferai le reste. □ the rest of the money le reste de l'argent

■ the rest of them les autres □ The rest of them went swimming. Les autres sont allés nager.

to rest VERB

▷ see also **rest** NOUN

1 se reposer [28] (relax)

□ She's resting in her room. Elle se repose dans sa chambre.

2 ménager [45] (not overstrain)

□ He has to rest his knee. Il doit ménager son genou.

3 appuyer [53] (lean)

□ I rested my bike against the window. J'ai appuyé mon vélo contre la fenêtre.

restaurant NOUN

le restaurant masc

□ We don't often go to restaurants. Nous n'allons pas souvent au restaurant.

restful ADJECTIVE

reposant (FEM reposante)

restless ADJECTIVE

agité (FEM agitée)

restoration NOUN

la restauration fem

to restore VERB

restaurer [28] (building, picture)

to restrict VERB

limiter [28]

rest room NOUN (US)

les toilettes fem pl

result NOUN

▷ see also **result** VERB

le résultat masc

□ my exam results mes résultats d'examen

□ What was the result? — One-nil. Quel a été le résultat ? — Un à zéro.

to result VERB

▷ see also **result** NOUN

■ to result in occasionner [28] □ Many road accidents result in head injuries. De nombreux accidents de la route occasionnent des blessures à la tête.

to resume VERB

reprendre [65]

□ They've resumed work. Ils ont repris le travail.

> **BE CAREFUL!**
> Do not translate **to resume** by the French word **résumer**.

résumé NOUN (US)

le curriculum vitae masc

to retire VERB

prendre [65] sa retraite

□ He retired last year. Il a pris sa retraite l'an dernier.

retired ADJECTIVE
retraité (FEM retraitée)
  □ She's retired. Elle est retraitée.
  ■ **a retired teacher** un professeur à la retraite

retirement NOUN
la retraite *fem*

to **retrace** VERB
  ■ **to retrace one's steps** revenir [73ᶠ] sur ses
  pas □ I retraced my steps. Je suis revenu sur
  mes pas.

return NOUN
  ▷ *see also* **return** VERB
1 le retour *masc*
  □ after our return à notre retour
  ■ **the return journey** le voyage de retour
  ■ **a return match** un match retour
2 l'aller-retour *masc* (*ticket*)
  □ A return to Avignon, please. Un aller-retour
  pour Avignon, s'il vous plaît.
  ■ **in return** en échange □ ... and I help her in
  return ... et je l'aide en échange
  ■ **in return for** en échange de
  ■ **Many happy returns!** Bon anniversaire !

to **return** VERB
  ▷ *see also* **return** NOUN
1 revenir [73ᶠ] (*come back*)
  □ I've just returned from holiday. Je viens de
  revenir de vacances.
  ■ **to return home** rentrer [68ᶠ] à la maison
2 retourner [72ᶠ] (*go back*)
  □ He returned to China the following year. Il est
  retourné en Chine l'année suivante.
3 rendre [7] (*give back*)
  □ She borrows my things and doesn't return
  them. Elle m'emprunte mes affaires et ne me
  les rend pas.

retweet NOUN
  ▷ *see also* **retweet** VERB
le retweet *masc*

to **retweet** VERB
  ▷ *see also* **retweet** NOUN
retweeter [28]

reunion NOUN
la réunion *fem*

reusable ADJECTIVE
réutilisable (FEM réutilisable)

to **reuse** VERB
réutiliser [28]

to **reveal** VERB
révéler [34]

revenge NOUN
la vengeance *fem*
  □ in revenge par vengeance
  ■ **to take revenge** se venger [45]

to **reverse** VERB
  ▷ *see also* **reverse** ADJECTIVE
faire [36] marche arrière (*car*)

□ He reversed without looking. Il a fait marche
arrière sans regarder.

reverse ADJECTIVE
  ▷ *see also* **reverse** VERB
inverse (FEM inverse)
  □ in reverse order dans l'ordre inverse
  ■ **in reverse gear** en marche arrière

review NOUN
la critique *fem* (*of book, film, programme*)
  □ The book had good reviews. Ce livre a eu de
  bonnes critiques.

to **revise** VERB
réviser [28]
  □ I haven't started revising yet. Je n'ai pas
  encore commencé à réviser.
  ■ **I've revised my opinion.** J'ai changé
  d'opinion.

revision NOUN
les révisions *fem pl*
  □ Have you done a lot of revision? Est-ce que tu
  as fait beaucoup de révisions ?

to **revive** VERB
ranimer [28]
  □ The nurses tried to revive him. Les infirmières
  ont essayé de le ranimer.

revolting ADJECTIVE
dégoûtant (FEM dégoûtante)

revolution NOUN
la révolution *fem*
  ■ **the French Revolution** la Révolution
  française

revolutionary ADJECTIVE
révolutionnaire (FEM révolutionnaire)

revolver NOUN
le revolver *masc*

reward NOUN
la récompense *fem*

rewarding ADJECTIVE
gratifiant (FEM gratifiante)
  □ a rewarding job un travail gratifiant

rheumatism NOUN
le rhumatisme *masc*

Rhine NOUN
le Rhin *masc*

rhinoceros NOUN
le rhinocéros *masc*

Rhone NOUN
le Rhône *masc*

rhubarb NOUN
la rhubarbe *fem*
  □ a rhubarb tart une tarte à la rhubarbe

rhythm NOUN
le rythme *masc*

rib NOUN
la côte *fem*

ribbon – ring

ribbon NOUN
le ruban *masc*

rice NOUN
le riz *masc*
■ **rice pudding** le riz au lait

rich ADJECTIVE
riche (FEM riche)
■ **the rich** les riches *masc pl*

to **rid** VERB
■ **to get rid of** se débarrasser [28] de □ I want to get rid of some old clothes. Je veux me débarrasser de vieux vêtements.

ridden VERB ▷ *see* **ride**

ride NOUN
▷ *see also* **ride** VERB
■ **to go for a ride 1** (*on horse*) monter [48†] à cheval **2** (*on bike*) faire [36] un tour en vélo □ We went for a bike ride. Nous sommes allés faire un tour en vélo.
■ **It's a short bus ride to the town centre.** Ce n'est pas loin du centre-ville en bus.

to **ride** VERB
▷ *see also* **ride** NOUN
monter [48†] à cheval (*on horse*)
□ I'm learning to ride. J'apprends à monter à cheval.
■ **to ride a bike** faire [36] du vélo □ Can you ride a bike? Tu sais faire du vélo ?

rider NOUN
1 le cavalier *masc*
la cavalière *fem* (*on horse*)
□ She's a good rider. C'est une bonne cavalière.
2 le/la cycliste *masc/fem* (*on bike*)

ridiculous ADJECTIVE
ridicule (FEM ridicule)
□ Don't be ridiculous! Ne sois pas ridicule !

riding NOUN
l'équitation *fem*
■ **to go riding** faire [36] de l'équitation
■ **a riding school** une école d'équitation

rifle NOUN
le fusil *masc*

rig NOUN
■ **an oil rig** une plateforme pétrolière

right ADJECTIVE, ADVERB
▷ *see also* **right** NOUN

There are several ways of translating 'right'. Scan the examples to find one that is similar to what you want to say.

1 bon (FEM bonne) (*factually correct, suitable*)
□ the right answer la bonne réponse □ It isn't the right size. Ce n'est pas la bonne taille.
□ We're on the right train. Nous sommes dans le bon train.
■ **Is this the right road for Arles?** Est-ce que c'est bien la route pour aller à Arles ?

2 correctement (*correctly*)
□ Am I pronouncing it right? Est-ce que je prononce ça correctement ?
■ **to be right 1** (*person*) avoir [8] raison □ You were right! Tu avais raison !
2 (*statement, opinion*) être [35] vrai □ That's right! C'est vrai !

3 juste (FEM juste) (*accurate*)
□ Do you have the right time? Est-ce que vous avez l'heure juste ?

4 bien (*morally correct*)
□ It's not right to behave like that. Ce n'est pas bien d'agir comme ça.
■ **I think you did the right thing.** Je pense que tu as bien fait.

5 droit (FEM droite) (*not left*)
□ my right hand ma main droite

6 à droite (*turn, look*)
□ Turn right at the traffic lights. Tournez à droite aux prochains feux.
■ **Right! Let's get started.** Bon ! On commence.
■ **right away** tout de suite □ I'll do it right away. Je vais le faire tout de suite.

right NOUN
▷ *see also* **right** ADJECTIVE, ADVERB
1 le droit *masc*
■ **You've got no right to do that.** Vous n'avez pas le droit de faire ça.
2 la droite *fem* (*not left*)
■ **on the right** à droite □ Remember to drive on the right. N'oubliez pas de conduire à droite.
■ **right of way** la priorité □ It was our right of way. Nous avions la priorité.

right-hand ADJECTIVE
■ **the right-hand side** la droite □ It's on the right-hand side. C'est à droite.

right-handed ADJECTIVE
droitier (FEM droitière)

rightly ADVERB
avec raison
□ She rightly decided not to go. Elle a décidé, avec raison, de ne pas y aller.
■ **if I remember rightly** si je me souviens bien

rim NOUN
la monture *fem*
□ glasses with wire rims des lunettes avec une monture métallique

ring NOUN
▷ *see also* **ring** VERB
1 l'anneau *masc* (PL les anneaux)
□ a gold ring un anneau en or
2 la bague *fem* (*with stones*)
□ a diamond ring une bague de diamants
■ **a wedding ring** une alliance
3 le cercle *masc* (*circle*)
□ to stand in a ring se mettre en cercle

4 le coup de sonnette *masc (of bell)*
□ I was woken by a ring at the door. J'ai été réveillé par un coup de sonnette.
■ **to give somebody a ring** appeler [4] quelqu'un □ I'll give you a ring this evening. Je t'appellerai ce soir.

to ring VERB
▷ *see also* **ring** NOUN
1 téléphoner [28]
□ Your mother rang this morning. Ta mère a téléphoné ce matin.
■ **to ring somebody** appeler [4] quelqu'un □ I'll ring you tomorrow morning. Je t'appellerai demain matin.
2 sonner [28]
□ The phone's ringing. Le téléphone sonne.
■ **to ring the bell** *(doorbell)* sonner [28] à la porte □ I rang the bell three times. J'ai sonné trois fois à la porte.

to ring back VERB
rappeler [4]
□ I'll ring back later. Je rappellerai plus tard.

to ring up VERB
■ **to ring somebody up** donner [28] un coup de fil à quelqu'un

ring binder NOUN
le classeur *masc*

ring road NOUN
1 la rocade *fem (ordinary road)*
2 le périphérique *masc (motorway)*

ringtone NOUN
la sonnerie *fem*

rink NOUN
1 la patinoire *fem (for ice-skating)*
2 la piste *fem (for roller-skating)*

to rinse VERB
rincer [12]

riot NOUN
▷ *see also* **riot** VERB
l'émeute *fem*

to riot VERB
▷ *see also* **riot** NOUN
faire [36] une émeute

to rip VERB
1 déchirer [28]
□ I've ripped my jeans. J'ai déchiré mon jean.
2 se déchirer [28]
□ My skirt's ripped. Ma jupe s'est déchirée.

to rip off VERB
arnaquer [28]
□ The hotel ripped us off. L'hôtel nous a arnaqués.

to rip up VERB
déchirer [28]
□ He read the note and then ripped it up. Il a lu le mot, puis l'a déchiré.

ripe ADJECTIVE
mûr (FEM mûre)

rip-off NOUN
■ **It's a rip-off!** C'est de l'arnaque ! *(informal)*

rise NOUN
▷ *see also* **rise** VERB
1 la hausse *fem (in prices, temperature)*
□ a sudden rise in temperature une hausse subite de température
2 l'augmentation *fem (pay rise)*

to rise VERB
▷ *see also* **rise** NOUN
1 augmenter [28] *(increase)*
□ Prices are rising. Les prix augmentent.
2 se lever [43]
□ The sun rises early in June. Le soleil se lève tôt en juin.

riser NOUN
■ **to be an early riser** être [35] matinal

risk NOUN
▷ *see also* **risk** VERB
le risque *masc*
■ **to take risks** prendre [65] des risques
■ **It's at your own risk.** C'est à vos risques et périls.

to risk VERB
▷ *see also* **risk** NOUN
risquer [28]
□ You risk getting a fine. Vous risquez de recevoir une amende.
■ **I wouldn't risk it if I were you.** À votre place, je ne prendrais pas ce risque.

risky ADJECTIVE
risqué (FEM risquée)

rival NOUN
▷ *see also* **rival** ADJECTIVE
le rival *masc* (PL les rivaux)
la rivale *fem*

rival ADJECTIVE
▷ *see also* **rival** NOUN
1 rival (FEM rivale, MASC PL rivaux)
□ a rival gang une bande rivale
2 concurrent (FEM concurrente)
□ a rival company une société concurrente

rivalry NOUN
la rivalité *fem (between towns, schools)*

river NOUN
1 la rivière *fem*
□ The river runs alongside the canal. La rivière longe le canal.
2 le fleuve *masc (major)*
□ the rivers of France les fleuves de France
■ **the river Seine** la Seine

Riviera NOUN
■ **the French Riviera** la Côte d'Azur
■ **the Italian Riviera** la Riviera italienne

road NOUN
1 la route *fem*
□ There's a lot of traffic on the roads. Il y a beaucoup de circulation sur les routes.
2 la rue *fem* (*street*)
□ They live across the road. Ils habitent de l'autre côté de la rue.

road map NOUN
la carte routière *fem*

road rage NOUN
l'agressivité au volant *fem*

road sign NOUN
le panneau de signalisation *masc* (PL les panneaux de signalisation)

roadworks PL NOUN
les travaux *masc pl*

roast ADJECTIVE
rôti (FEM rôtie)
□ roast chicken le poulet rôti □ roast potatoes les pommes de terre rôties
■ **roast pork** le rôti de porc
■ **roast beef** le rôti de bœuf

to **rob** VERB
■ **to rob somebody** voler [28] quelqu'un □ I've been robbed. On m'a volé.
■ **to rob somebody of something** voler [28] quelque chose à quelqu'un □ He was robbed of his wallet. On lui a volé son portefeuille.
■ **to rob a bank** dévaliser [28] une banque

robber NOUN
le voleur *masc*
la voleuse *fem*
■ **a bank robber** un braqueur de banques

robbery NOUN
le vol *masc*
■ **a bank robbery** un hold-up
■ **armed robbery** le vol à main armée

robin NOUN
le rouge-gorge *masc*

robot NOUN
le robot *masc*

rock NOUN
▷ *see also* **rock** VERB
1 la roche *fem* (*substance*)
□ They tunnelled through the rock. Ils ont creusé un tunnel dans la roche.
2 le rocher *masc* (*boulder*)
□ I sat on a rock. Je me suis assis sur un rocher.
3 la pierre *fem* (*stone*)
□ The crowd started to throw rocks. La foule s'est mise à lancer des pierres.
4 le rock *masc* (*music*)
□ a rock concert un concert de rock □ He's a rock star. C'est une rock star.
■ **rock and roll** le rock'n'roll

to **rock** VERB
▷ *see also* **rock** NOUN
ébranler [28]
□ The explosion rocked the building. L'explosion a ébranlé le bâtiment.

rockery NOUN
la rocaille *fem*

rocket NOUN
la fusée *fem* (*firework, spacecraft*)

rocking chair NOUN
le rocking-chair *masc*

rocking horse NOUN
le cheval à bascule *masc* (PL les chevaux à bascule)

rod NOUN
la canne à pêche *fem* (*for fishing*)

rode VERB ▷ *see* **ride**

role NOUN
le rôle *masc*

role play NOUN
le jeu de rôle *masc* (PL les jeux de rôles)
□ to do a role play faire un jeu de rôle

roll NOUN
▷ *see also* **roll** VERB
1 le rouleau *masc* (PL les rouleaux)
□ a roll of tape un rouleau de ruban adhésif
□ a toilet roll un rouleau de papier hygiénique
2 le petit pain *masc* (*bread*)

to **roll** VERB
▷ *see also* **roll** NOUN
rouler [28]
■ **to roll out the pastry** abaisser [28] la pâte

roll call NOUN
l'appel *masc*

roller NOUN
le rouleau *masc* (PL les rouleaux)

Rollerblade® NOUN
le roller *masc*
□ a pair of Rollerblades une paire de rollers

rollercoaster NOUN
les montagnes russes *fem pl*

roller skates PL NOUN
les patins à roulettes *masc pl*

roller-skating NOUN
le patin à roulettes *masc*
■ **to go roller-skating** faire [36] du patin à roulettes

rolling pin NOUN
le rouleau à pâtisserie *masc*

Roman ADJECTIVE, NOUN
romain (FEM romaine) (*ancient*)
□ a Roman villa une villa romaine □ the Roman empire l'Empire romain
■ **the Romans** les Romains

Numbers in brackets refer to verb tables on pages 650 to 658

Roman Catholic NOUN

le/la catholique *masc/fem*

□ He's a Roman Catholic. Il est catholique.

romance NOUN

1 l'amour *masc* (*love*)

□ There's no romance between them. Il n'y a pas d'histoire d'amour entre eux.

2 le charme *masc* (*glamour*)

□ the romance of Paris le charme de Paris

■ **a holiday romance** une idylle de vacances

Romania NOUN

la Roumanie *fem*

■ **in Romania** en Roumanie

Romanian NOUN

▷ *see also* **Romanian** ADJECTIVE

1 le Roumain *masc*

la Roumaine *fem* (*person*)

2 le roumain *masc* (*language*)

Romanian ADJECTIVE

▷ *see also* **Romanian** NOUN

roumain (FEM roumaine)

romantic ADJECTIVE

romantique (FEM romantique)

roof NOUN

le toit *masc*

roof rack NOUN

la galerie *fem*

room NOUN

1 la pièce *fem*

□ the biggest room in the house la plus grande pièce de la maison

2 la chambre *fem* (*bedroom*)

□ She's in her room. Elle est dans sa chambre.

■ **a single room** une chambre pour une personne

■ **a double room** une chambre pour deux personnes

3 la salle *fem* (*in school*)

□ the music room la salle de musique

4 la place *fem* (*space*)

□ There's no room for that box. Il n'y a pas de place pour cette boîte.

roommate NOUN

le/la camarade de chambre *masc/fem*

root NOUN

la racine *fem*

to **root around** VERB

fouiller [28]

□ She started rooting around in her handbag. Elle a commencé à fouiller dans son sac à main.

rope NOUN

la corde *fem*

to **rope in** VERB

enrôler [28]

□ I was roped in to help with the school concert.

J'ai été enrôlé pour aider à l'organisation du concert de l'école.

rose VERB ▷ *see* **rise**

rose NOUN

la rose *fem* (*flower*)

to **rot** VERB

pourrir [38]

rotten ADJECTIVE

pourri (FEM pourrie) (*decayed*)

□ a rotten apple une pomme pourrie

■ **rotten weather** un temps pourri

■ **That's a rotten thing to do.** Ce n'est vraiment pas gentil.

■ **to feel rotten** être [35] mal fichu (*informal*)

rough ADJECTIVE

1 rêche (FEM rêche) (*surface*)

□ My hands are rough. J'ai les mains rêches.

2 violent (FEM violente) (*game*)

□ Rugby's a rough sport. Le rugby est un sport violent.

3 difficile (FEM difficile) (*place*)

□ It's a rough area. C'est un quartier difficile.

4 houleux (FEM houleuse) (*water*)

□ The sea was rough. La mer était houleuse.

5 approximatif (FEM approximative)

□ I've got a rough idea. J'en ai une idée approximative.

■ **to feel rough** ne pas être [35] dans son assiette □ I feel rough. Je ne suis pas dans mon assiette.

roughly ADVERB

à peu près

□ It weighs roughly 20 kilos. Ça pèse à peu près vingt kilos.

round ADJECTIVE, ADVERB, PREPOSITION

▷ *see also* **round** NOUN

1 rond (FEM ronde)

□ a round table une table ronde

2 autour de (*around*)

□ We were sitting round the table. Nous étions assis autour de la table. □ She wore a scarf round her neck. Elle portait une écharpe autour du cou.

■ **It's just round the corner.** (*very near*) C'est tout près.

■ **to go round to somebody's house** aller [3ᵉ] chez quelqu'un □ I went round to my friend's house. Je suis allé chez mon ami.

■ **to have a look round** faire [36] un tour □ We're going to have a look round. Nous allons faire un tour.

■ **to go round a museum** visiter [28] un musée

■ **round here** près d'ici □ Is there a bakery round here? Est-ce qu'il y a une boulangerie près d'ici ?

■ **He lives round here.** Il habite dans les parages.

r

■ **all year round** toute l'année
■ **round about** (*roughly*) environ □ It costs round about £100. Cela coûte environ cent livres. □ round about 8 o'clock à huit heures environ

round NOUN

▷ *see also* **round** ADJECTIVE, ADVERB, PREPOSITION

1 la manche *fem* (*of tournament*)
2 le round *masc* (*of boxing match*)
■ **a round of golf** une partie de golf
■ **a round of drinks** une tournée □ He bought a round of drinks. Il a offert une tournée.

to round off VERB

terminer [28]
□ They rounded off the holiday with a helicopter trip. Ils ont terminé leurs vacances par une excursion en hélicoptère.

to round up VERB

1 rassembler [28] (*sheep, cattle, suspects*)
2 arrondir [38] (*figure*)

roundabout NOUN

1 le rond-point *masc* (PL les ronds-points) (*at junction*)
2 le manège *masc* (*at funfair*)

rounders NOUN

■ **Rounders is a bit like baseball.** Le « rounders » ressemble un peu au base-ball.

> **DID YOU KNOW...?**
> Rounders is not played in France.

round trip NOUN (US)

l'aller-retour *masc*
■ **a round-trip ticket** un billet aller-retour

route NOUN

1 l'itinéraire *masc*
□ We're planning our route. Nous préparons notre itinéraire.
2 le parcours *masc* (*of bus*)

routine NOUN

■ **my daily routine** mes occupations quotidiennes

row NOUN

> This word has two pronunciations. Make sure you choose the right translation.

1 la rangée *fem*
□ a row of houses une rangée de maisons
2 le rang *masc* (*of seats*)
□ Our seats are in the front row. Nos places se trouvent au premier rang.
■ **five times in a row** cinq fois d'affilée
3 le vacarme *masc* (*noise*)
□ What's that terrible row? Qu'est-ce que c'est que ce vacarme ?
4 la dispute *fem* (*quarrel*)
■ **to have a row** se disputer [28] □ They've had a row. Ils se sont disputés.

to row VERB

1 ramer [28]
□ We took turns to row. Nous avons ramé à tour de rôle.
2 faire [36] de l'aviron (*as sport*)

rowboat NOUN (US)

le bateau à rames *masc*

rowing NOUN

l'aviron *masc* (*sport*)
□ My hobby is rowing. Je fais de l'aviron.
■ **a rowing boat** un bateau à rames

royal ADJECTIVE

royal (FEM royale, MASC PL royaux)
■ **the royal family** la famille royale

to rub VERB

1 frotter [28] (*stain*)
2 se frotter [28] (*part of body*)
□ Don't rub your eyes! Ne te frotte pas les yeux !
■ **to rub something out** effacer [12] quelque chose

rubber NOUN

1 le caoutchouc *masc*
□ rubber soles des semelles en caoutchouc
2 la gomme *fem* (*eraser*)
□ Can I borrow your rubber? Je peux emprunter ta gomme ?
■ **a rubber band** un élastique

rubbish NOUN

▷ *see also* **rubbish** ADJECTIVE

1 les ordures *fem pl* (*refuse*)
□ When do they collect the rubbish? Quand est-ce qu'ils ramassent les ordures ?
2 la camelote *fem* (*junk*)
□ They sell a lot of rubbish at the market. Ils vendent beaucoup de camelote au marché.
3 les bêtises *fem pl* (*nonsense*)
□ Don't talk rubbish! Ne dis pas de bêtises !
■ **That's a load of rubbish!** C'est vraiment n'importe quoi ! (*informal*)
■ **a rubbish bin** une poubelle
■ **a rubbish dump** une décharge

rubbish ADJECTIVE

▷ *see also* **rubbish** NOUN

nul (FEM nulle)
□ They're a rubbish team! Cette équipe est nulle !

rucksack NOUN

le sac à dos *masc*

rude ADJECTIVE

1 impoli (FEM impolie) (*impolite*)
□ It's rude to interrupt. C'est impoli de couper la parole aux gens.
2 grossier (FEM grossière) (*offensive*)
□ a rude joke une plaisanterie grossière □ He was very rude to me. Il a été très grossier avec moi.
■ **a rude word** un gros mot

rug NOUN
1 le tapis *masc*
  □ a Persian rug un tapis persan
2 la couverture *fem* (*blanket*)
  □ a tartan rug une couverture écossaise

rugby NOUN
  le rugby *masc*
  □ I play rugby. Je joue au rugby.

ruin NOUN
  ▷ *see also* **ruin** VERB
  la ruine *fem*
  □ the ruins of the castle les ruines du château
  ■ **in ruins** en ruine

to **ruin** VERB
  ▷ *see also* **ruin** NOUN
1 abîmer [28]
  □ You'll ruin your shoes. Tu vas abîmer tes chaussures.
2 gâcher [28]
  □ It ruined our holiday. Ça a gâché nos vacances.
3 ruiner [28] (*financially*)
  □ That one mistake ruined the business. Cette seule erreur a ruiné l'entreprise.

rule NOUN
1 la règle *fem*
  □ the rules of grammar les règles de grammaire
  ■ **as a rule** en règle générale
2 le règlement *masc* (*regulation*)
  □ It's against the rules. C'est contre le règlement.

to **rule out** VERB
  écarter [28] (*possibility*)
  □ I'm not ruling anything out. Je n'écarte aucune possibilité.

ruler NOUN
  la règle *fem*
  □ Can I borrow your ruler? Je peux emprunter ta règle ?

rum NOUN
  le rhum *masc*

rumour (US **rumor**) NOUN
  la rumeur *fem*
  □ It's just a rumour. Ce n'est qu'une rumeur.

rump steak NOUN
  le romsteak *masc*

run NOUN
  ▷ *see also* **run** VERB
  le point *masc* (*in cricket*)
  □ to score a run marquer un point
  ■ **to go for a run** courir [16] □ I go for a run every morning. Je cours tous les matins.
  ■ **I did a ten-kilometre run.** J'ai couru dix kilomètres.
  ■ **on the run** en fuite □ The criminals are still on the run. Les criminels sont toujours en fuite.
  ■ **in the long run** à long terme

to **run** VERB
  ▷ *see also* **run** NOUN
1 courir [16]
  □ I ran five kilometres. J'ai couru cinq kilomètres.
  ■ **to run a marathon** participer [28] à un marathon
2 diriger [45] (*manage*)
  □ He runs a large company. Il dirige une grosse société.
3 organiser [28] (*organize*)
  □ They run music courses in the holidays. Ils organisent des cours de musique pendant les vacances.
4 couler [28] (*water*)
  □ Don't leave the tap running. Ne laisse pas couler le robinet.
  ■ **to run a bath** faire [36] couler un bain
5 conduire [23] (*by car*)
  □ I can run you to the station. Je peux te conduire à la gare.

to **run away** VERB
  s'enfuir [39]
  □ They ran away before the police came. Ils se sont enfuis avant l'arrivée de la police.

to **run out** VERB
  ■ **Time is running out.** Il ne reste plus beaucoup de temps.
  ■ **to run out of something** se trouver [28] à court de quelque chose □ We ran out of money. Nous nous sommes trouvés à court d'argent.

to **run over** VERB
  ■ **to run somebody over** écraser [28] quelqu'un
  ■ **to get run over** se faire [36] écraser □ Be careful, or you'll get run over! Fais attention, sinon tu vas te faire écraser !

rung VERB ▷ *see* **ring**

runner NOUN
  le coureur *masc*
  la coureuse *fem*

runner beans PL NOUN
  les haricots verts *masc pl*

runner-up NOUN
  le second *masc*
  la seconde *fem*

running NOUN
  la course *fem*
  □ Running is my favourite sport. La course est mon sport préféré.

run-up NOUN
  ■ **in the run-up to Christmas** pendant la période de préparation de Noël

runway NOUN
  la piste *fem*

rural ADJECTIVE
  rural (FEM rurale, MASC PL ruraux)

English-French

rush NOUN
▷ *see also* **rush** VERB
la hâte *fem*
■ **in a rush** à la hâte

to **rush** VERB
▷ *see also* **rush** NOUN
1 se précipiter [28] (*run*)
□ Everyone rushed outside. Tout le monde s'est précipité dehors.
2 se dépêcher [28] (*hurry*)
□ There's no need to rush. Ce n'est pas la peine de se dépêcher.

rush hour NOUN
les heures de pointe *fem pl*
□ in the rush hour aux heures de pointe

rusk NOUN
la biscotte *fem*

Russia NOUN
la Russie *fem*
■ **in Russia** en Russie

■ **to Russia** en Russie

Russian NOUN
▷ *see also* **Russian** ADJECTIVE
1 le/la Russe *masc/fem* (*person*)
2 le russe *masc* (*language*)

Russian ADJECTIVE
▷ *see also* **Russian** NOUN
russe (FEM russe)

rust NOUN
la rouille *fem*

rusty ADJECTIVE
rouillé (FEM rouillée)
□ a rusty bike un vélo rouillé □ My French is very rusty. Mon français est très rouillé.

ruthless ADJECTIVE
sans pitié

rye NOUN
le seigle *masc*
■ **rye bread** le pain de seigle

r

Ss

English-French

Sabbath NOUN
1 le dimanche masc (*Christian*)
2 le sabbat masc (*Jewish*)

sack NOUN
▷ see also **sack** VERB
le sac masc
■ **to get the sack** être [35] mis à la porte

to **sack** VERB
▷ see also **sack** NOUN
■ **to sack somebody** mettre [47] quelqu'un
à la porte □ He was sacked. On l'a mis à la porte.

sacred ADJECTIVE
sacré (FEM sacrée)

sacrifice NOUN
le sacrifice masc

sad ADJECTIVE
triste (FEM triste)

saddle NOUN
la selle fem

saddlebag NOUN
la sacoche fem

sadly ADVERB
1 tristement
□ 'She's gone,' he said sadly. « Elle est partie, »
a-t-il dit tristement.
2 malheureusement (*unfortunately*)
□ Sadly, it was too late. Malheureusement, il
était trop tard.

safe NOUN
▷ see also **safe** ADJECTIVE
le coffre-fort masc (PL les coffres-forts)
□ She put the money in the safe. Elle a mis
l'argent dans le coffre-fort.

safe ADJECTIVE
▷ see also **safe** NOUN
1 sans danger
□ Don't worry, it's perfectly safe. Ne vous
inquiétez pas, c'est absolument sans danger.
■ **Is it safe?** Ça n'est pas dangereux ?
2 sûr (FEM sûre) (*machine, ladder*)
□ This car isn't safe. Cette voiture n'est pas sûre.
3 hors de danger (*out of danger*)
□ You're safe now. Vous êtes hors de danger
maintenant.
■ **to feel safe** se sentir [77] en sécurité
■ **safe sex** les rapports (sexuels) protégés

safety NOUN
la sécurité fem
■ **a safety belt** une ceinture de sécurité
■ **a safety pin** une épingle à nourrice

Sagittarius NOUN
le/la Sagittaire masc/fem
□ I'm Sagittarius. Je suis Sagittaire.

Sahara NOUN
■ **the Sahara Desert** le Sahara

said VERB ▷ see **say**

sail NOUN
▷ see also **sail** VERB
la voile fem

to **sail** VERB
▷ see also **sail** NOUN
1 naviguer [28] (*travel*)
2 prendre [65] la mer (*set off*)
□ The boat sails at eight o'clock. Le bateau prend
la mer à huit heures.

sailing NOUN
la voile fem
□ His hobby is sailing. Son passe-temps, c'est
la voile.
■ **to go sailing** faire [36] de la voile
■ **a sailing boat** un voilier
■ **a sailing ship** un grand voilier

sailor NOUN
le marin masc
□ He's a sailor. Il est marin.

saint NOUN
le saint masc
la sainte fem

sake NOUN
■ **for the sake of** dans l'intérêt de

salad NOUN
la salade fem
■ **salad cream** la mayonnaise
■ **salad dressing** la vinaigrette

salami NOUN
le salami masc

salary NOUN
le salaire masc

sale NOUN
les soldes masc pl (*reductions*)
□ There's a sale on at the department store.
Il y a des soldes dans le grand magasin.

S

Core vocabulary is shaded.

sales assistant - save

- **on sale** en vente
- **The factory's for sale.** L'usine est en vente.
- **'for sale'** « à vendre »

sales assistant NOUN
le vendeur *masc*
la vendeuse *fem*
□ She's a sales assistant. Elle est vendeuse.

salesman NOUN
1 le représentant *masc* (*sales rep*)
□ He's a salesman. Il est représentant.
- **a double-glazing salesman** un représentant en doubles vitrages
2 le vendeur *masc* (*sales assistant*)

sales rep NOUN
le représentant *masc*
la représentante *fem*

saleswoman NOUN
1 la représentante *fem* (*sales rep*)
□ She's a saleswoman. Elle est représentante.
2 la vendeuse *fem* (*sales assistant*)

salmon NOUN
le saumon *masc*

salon NOUN
le salon *masc*
□ a hair salon un salon de coiffure □ a beauty salon un salon de beauté

saloon car NOUN
la berline *fem*

salt NOUN
le sel *masc*

salty ADJECTIVE
salé (FEM salée)

to **salute** VERB
saluer [28]

Salvation Army NOUN
l'armée du Salut *fem*

same ADJECTIVE
même (FEM même)
□ the same primary school la même école primaire □ at the same time en même temps
- **They're exactly the same.** Ils sont exactement pareils.
- **It's not the same.** Ça n'est pas pareil.

same-sex ADJECTIVE
homosexuel (FEM homosexuelle) (*relationship*)
- **same-sex marriage** le mariage du même sexe

sample NOUN
l'échantillon *masc*

sand NOUN
le sable *masc*

sandal NOUN
la sandale *fem*
□ a pair of sandals une paire de sandales

sand castle NOUN
le château de sable *masc* (PL les châteaux de sable)

sandwich NOUN
le sandwich *masc*
□ a cheese sandwich un sandwich au fromage

sandwich course NOUN
le cours avec stage pratique *masc*

sang VERB ▷ *see* sing

sanitary towel NOUN
la serviette hygiénique *fem*

sank VERB ▷ *see* sink

Santa Claus NOUN
le père Noël *masc*

sarcastic ADJECTIVE
sarcastique (FEM sarcastique)

sardine NOUN
la sardine *fem*

sat VERB ▷ *see* sit

satchel NOUN
le cartable *masc*

satellite NOUN
le satellite *masc*
□ satellite television la télévision par satellite
- **a satellite dish** une antenne parabolique

satisfactory ADJECTIVE
satisfaisant (FEM satisfaisante)

satisfied ADJECTIVE
satisfait (FEM satisfaite)

sat nav NOUN
le GPS *masc*

Saturday NOUN
le samedi *masc*
□ on Saturday samedi □ on Saturdays le samedi
□ every Saturday tous les samedis □ last Saturday samedi dernier □ next Saturday samedi prochain
- **I've got a Saturday job.** Je travaille le samedi.

sauce NOUN
la sauce *fem*

saucepan NOUN
la casserole *fem*

saucer NOUN
la soucoupe *fem*

Saudi Arabia NOUN
l'Arabie Saoudite *fem*
- **in Saudi Arabia** en Arabie Saoudite

sauna NOUN
le sauna *masc*

sausage NOUN
1 la saucisse *fem*
2 le saucisson *masc* (*salami*)
- **a sausage roll** un friand à la saucisse

to **save** VERB
1 mettre [47] de côté (*save up money*)
□ I've saved £50 already. J'ai déjà mis cinquante livres de côté.

Numbers in brackets refer to verb tables on pages 650 to 658

2 économiser [28] (*spend less*)
□ I saved £20 by waiting for the sales. J'ai économisé vingt livres en attendant les soldes.
■ **to save time** gagner [28] du temps □ We took a taxi to save time. Nous avons pris un taxi pour gagner du temps. □ It saved us time. Ça nous a fait gagner du temps.
3 sauver [28] (*rescue*)
□ Luckily, all the passengers were saved. Heureusement, tous les passagers ont été sauvés.
4 sauvegarder [28] (*on computer*)
□ Don't forget to save your work regularly. N'oublie pas de sauvegarder ton travail régulièrement.

to **save up** VERB
mettre [47] de l'argent de côté
□ I'm saving up for a new bike. Je mets de l'argent de côté pour un nouveau vélo.

savings PL NOUN
les économies *fem pl*
□ She spent all her savings on a computer. Elle a dépensé toutes ses économies en achetant un ordinateur.

savoury ADJECTIVE
salé (FEM salée)
□ Is it sweet or savoury? C'est sucré ou salé ?

saw VERB ▷ see **see**

saw NOUN
la scie *fem*

sax NOUN
le saxo *masc* (*informal*)
□ I play the sax. Je joue du saxo.

saxophone NOUN
le saxophone *masc*
□ I play the saxophone. Je joue du saxophone.

to **say** VERB
dire [27]
□ I say what I think. Je dis ce que je pense.
□ You never say anything. Tu ne dis jamais rien.
□ He says he loves me. Il me dit qu'il m'aime.
□ What did he say? Qu'est-ce qu'il a dit ? □ Did you hear what she said? Tu as entendu ce qu'elle a dit ?
■ **Could you say that again?** Pourriez-vous répéter s'il vous plaît ?
■ **That goes without saying.** Cela va sans dire.

saying NOUN
le dicton *masc*
□ It's just a saying. C'est juste un dicton.

scale NOUN
1 l'échelle *fem* (*of map*)
□ a large-scale map une carte à grande échelle
2 l'ampleur *fem* (*size, extent*)
□ a disaster on a massive scale un désastre d'une ampleur incroyable
3 la gamme *fem* (*in music*)

scales PL NOUN
la balance *fem sing* (*in kitchen, shop*)
■ **bathroom scales** le pèse-personne *sing*

scampi PL NOUN
les scampi *masc pl*

scandal NOUN
1 le scandale *masc* (*outrage*)
□ It caused a scandal. Ça a fait scandale.
2 les ragots *masc pl* (*gossip*)
□ It's just scandal. Ce ne sont que des ragots.

Scandinavia NOUN
la Scandinavie *fem*
■ **in Scandinavia** en Scandinavie

Scandinavian ADJECTIVE
scandinave (FEM scandinave)

scar NOUN
la cicatrice *fem*

scarce ADJECTIVE
limité (FEM limitée)
□ scarce resources des ressources limitées
■ **Jobs are scarce these days.** Il y a peu de travail ces temps-ci.

scarcely ADVERB
à peine
□ I scarcely knew him. Je le connaissais à peine.

scare NOUN
▷ see also **scare** VERB
la panique *fem*
■ **a bomb scare** une alerte à la bombe

to **scare** VERB
▷ see also **scare** NOUN
■ **to scare somebody** faire [36] peur à quelqu'un □ He scares me. Il me fait peur.

scarecrow NOUN
l'épouvantail *masc*

scared ADJECTIVE
■ **to be scared** avoir [8] peur □ I was scared stiff. J'avais terriblement peur.
■ **to be scared of** avoir [8] peur de □ Are you scared of him? Est-ce que tu as peur de lui ?

scarf NOUN
1 l'écharpe *fem* (*long*)
2 le foulard *masc* (*square*)

scary ADJECTIVE
effrayant (FEM effrayante)
□ It was really scary. C'était vraiment effrayant.

scene NOUN
1 les lieux *masc pl* (*place*)
□ The police were soon on the scene. La police est vite arrivée sur les lieux. □ the scene of the crime les lieux du crime
2 le spectacle *masc* (*event, sight*)
□ It was an amazing scene. C'était un spectacle étonnant.
■ **to make a scene** faire [36] une scène

scenery NOUN
le paysage masc (landscape)

scent NOUN
le parfum masc (perfume)

schedule NOUN
le programme masc
□ a busy schedule un programme chargé
■ **on schedule** comme prévu
■ **to be behind schedule** avoir [8] du retard

scheduled flight NOUN
le vol régulier masc

scheme NOUN
1 le truc masc (idea)
□ a crazy scheme he dreamed up un truc farfelu
qu'il a inventé
2 le projet masc (project)
■ **a scheme to make extra pocket money**
un plan pour gagner plus d'argent de poche

scholarship NOUN
la bourse fem

school NOUN
l'école fem
■ **to go to school** aller [3ᶠ] à l'école

schoolbag NOUN
le cartable masc

schoolbook NOUN
le livre scolaire masc

schoolboy NOUN
l'écolier masc

schoolchildren NOUN
les écoliers masc pl

schoolgirl NOUN
l'écolière fem

school uniform NOUN
l'uniforme scolaire masc

science NOUN
la science fem

science fiction NOUN
la science-fiction fem

scientific ADJECTIVE
scientifique (FEM scientifique)

scientist NOUN
le chercheur masc
la chercheuse fem
■ **He trained as a scientist.** Il a une formation
scientifique.

scissors PL NOUN
les ciseaux masc pl
□ a pair of scissors une paire de ciseaux

to **scoff** VERB
bouffer [28] (informal: eat)
□ My brother scoffed all the sandwiches. Mon
frère a bouffé tous les sandwichs.

scone NOUN
le scone masc

scooter NOUN
1 le scooter masc
2 la trottinette fem (child's toy)

score NOUN
▷ see also **score** VERB
le score masc
□ The score was three-nil. Le score était de trois
à zéro.

to **score** VERB
▷ see also **score** NOUN
1 marquer [28] (goal, point)
□ to score a goal marquer un but □ Our team
didn't score. Notre équipe n'a pas marqué de
but.
■ **to score 6 out of 10** obtenir [83] un score de
six sur dix
2 compter [28] les points (keep score)
□ Who's going to score? Qui va compter les
points ?

Scorpio NOUN
le Scorpion masc
□ I'm Scorpio. Je suis Scorpion.

Scot NOUN
l'Écossais masc
l'Écossaise fem

Scotch tape® NOUN (US)
le scotch® masc

Scotland NOUN
l'Écosse fem
■ **in Scotland** en Écosse
■ **to Scotland** en Écosse
■ **I'm from Scotland.** Je suis écossais.

Scots ADJECTIVE
écossais (FEM écossaise)
□ a Scots accent un accent écossais

Scotsman NOUN
l'Écossais masc

Scotswoman NOUN
l'Écossaise fem

Scottish ADJECTIVE
écossais (FEM écossaise)
□ a Scottish accent un accent écossais

scout NOUN
le scout masc
□ I'm in the Scouts. Je suis scout.

scrambled eggs PL NOUN
les œufs brouillés masc pl

scrap NOUN
▷ see also **scrap** VERB
1 le bout masc
□ a scrap of paper un bout de papier
2 la bagarre fem (fight)
■ **scrap iron** la ferraille

to **scrap** VERB
▷ see also **scrap** NOUN
abandonner [28] (plan)

S

□ The idea was scrapped. L'idée a été abandonnée.

scrapbook NOUN
l'album *masc*

to **scratch** VERB
▷ *see also* **scratch** NOUN
se gratter [28]
□ Stop scratching! Arrête de te gratter !

scratch NOUN
▷ *see also* **scratch** VERB
l'égratignure *fem* (*on skin*)
■ **to start from scratch** partir [57ᵗ] de zéro

scream NOUN
▷ *see also* **scream** VERB
le hurlement *masc*

to **scream** VERB
▷ *see also* **scream** NOUN
hurler [28]

screen NOUN
l'écran *masc*

screw NOUN
la vis *fem*

screwdriver NOUN
le tournevis *masc*

to **scribble** VERB
griffonner [28]

to **scrub** VERB
récurer [28]
□ to scrub a pan récurer une casserole

sculpture NOUN
la sculpture *fem*

sea NOUN
la mer *fem*

seafood NOUN
les fruits de mer *masc pl*
□ I don't like seafood. Je n'aime pas les fruits de mer.

seagull NOUN
la mouette *fem*

seal NOUN
▷ *see also* **seal** VERB
1 le phoque *masc* (*animal*)
2 le cachet *masc* (*on letter*)

to **seal** VERB
▷ *see also* **seal** NOUN
1 sceller [28] (*document*)
2 coller [28] (*letter*)

seaman NOUN
le marin *masc*

to **search** VERB
▷ *see also* **search** NOUN
fouiller [28]
□ They searched the woods for her. Ils ont fouillé les bois pour la trouver.
■ **to search for something** chercher [28]

quelque chose □ He searched for evidence. Il cherchait des preuves.

search NOUN
▷ *see also* **search** VERB
la fouille *fem*

search engine NOUN
le moteur de recherche *masc*

search party NOUN
l'expédition de secours *fem*

seashore NOUN
le bord de la mer *masc*
□ on the seashore au bord de la mer

seasick ADJECTIVE
■ **to be seasick** avoir [8] le mal de mer

seaside NOUN
le bord de la mer *masc*
□ at the seaside au bord de la mer

season NOUN
la saison *fem*
□ What's your favourite season? Quelle est ta saison préférée ?
■ **out of season** hors saison □ It's cheaper to go there out of season. C'est moins cher d'y aller hors saison.
■ **during the holiday season** en période de vacances
■ **a season ticket** une carte d'abonnement

seat NOUN
le siège *masc*

seat belt NOUN
la ceinture de sécurité *fem*

sea water NOUN
l'eau de mer *fem*

seaweed NOUN
les algues *fem pl*

second ADJECTIVE
▷ *see also* **second** NOUN
deuxième (FEM deuxième)
□ on the second page à la deuxième page
■ **to come second** (*in race*) arriver [5ᵗ] deuxième
■ **the second of March** le deux mars

second NOUN
▷ *see also* **second** ADJECTIVE
la seconde *fem*
□ It'll only take a second. Ça va prendre juste une seconde.

secondary school NOUN
1 le collège *masc*
2 le lycée *masc*

> **DID YOU KNOW...?**
> In France, pupils go to a **collège** between the ages of 11 and 15, and then to a **lycée** until the age of 18.

second-class ADJECTIVE, ADVERB
1 de seconde classe (*ticket, compartment*)

S

■ **to travel second class** voyager [45] en seconde

2 à tarif réduit (*stamp*, *letter*)
□ **to send something second class** envoyer quelque chose à tarif réduit

secondhand ADJECTIVE
d'occasion
□ **a secondhand car** une voiture d'occasion

secondly ADVERB
deuxièmement
■ **firstly … secondly …** d'abord … ensuite …
□ Firstly, it's too expensive. Secondly, it wouldn't work anyway. D'abord, c'est trop cher. Ensuite, ça ne marcherait pas de toute façon.

secret ADJECTIVE
▷ *see also* **secret** NOUN
secret (FEM secrète)
□ **a secret mission** une mission secrète

secret NOUN
▷ *see also* **secret** ADJECTIVE
le secret *masc*
□ It's a secret. C'est un secret. □ Can you keep a secret? Tu sais garder un secret ?
■ **in secret** en secret

secretary NOUN
le/la secrétaire *masc/fem*
□ She's a secretary. Elle est secrétaire.

secretly NOUN
secrètement

section NOUN
la section *fem*

security NOUN
la sécurité *fem*
□ **a feeling of security** un sentiment de sécurité
□ **a campaign to improve airport security** une campagne visant à améliorer la sécurité dans les aéroports
■ **job security** la sécurité de l'emploi

security guard NOUN
1 l'agent de sécurité *masc* (*in building*, *shop*)
2 le garde chargé de la sécurité *masc* (*on guard*)
3 un convoyeur de fonds (*transporting money*)

sedan NOUN (US)
la berline *fem*

to see VERB
voir [92]
□ I see her every day. Je la vois tous les jours.
□ You see things clearly. Tu vois les choses clairement. □ He sees them at weekends. Il les voit le week-end. □ I can't see. Je n'y vois rien.
□ I saw him yesterday. Je l'ai vu hier. □ Have you seen him? Est-ce que tu l'as vu ?
■ **See you!** Salut !
■ **See you soon!** À bientôt !
■ **to see to something** s'occuper [28] de quelque chose □ Can you see to lunch, please? Tu peux t'occuper du déjeuner, s'il te plaît ?

seed NOUN
la graine *fem*
□ **sunflower seeds** des graines de tournesol

to seek VERB
chercher [28]
■ **to seek help** chercher [28] de l'aide

to seem VERB
avoir [8] l'air
□ She seems tired. Elle a l'air fatiguée. □ The shop seemed to be closed. Le magasin avait l'air d'être fermé.
■ **That seems like a good idea.** Ce n'est pas une mauvaise idée.
■ **It seems that …** Il paraît que … □ It seems she's getting married. Il paraît qu'elle va se marier.
■ **There seems to be a problem.** Il semble y avoir un problème.

seen VERB ▷ *see* **see**

seesaw NOUN
la balançoire à bascule *fem*

see-through ADJECTIVE
transparent (FEM transparente)

seldom ADVERB
rarement

to select VERB
sélectionner [28]

selection NOUN
la sélection *fem*

self-assured ADJECTIVE
sûr de soi (FEM sûre de soi)
□ He's very self-assured. Il est très sûr de lui.

self-catering ADJECTIVE
■ **a self-catering apartment** un appartement de vacances

self-centred (US **self-centered**) ADJECTIVE
égocentrique (FEM égocentrique)

self-confidence NOUN
la confiance en soi *fem*
□ He hasn't got much self-confidence. Il n'a pas très confiance en lui.

self-conscious ADJECTIVE
■ **to be self-conscious 1** (*embarrassed*) être [35] mal à l'aise □ She was really self-conscious at first. Elle était vraiment mal à l'aise au début.
2 (*shy*) manquer [28] d'assurance □ He's always been rather self-conscious. Il a toujours un peu manqué d'assurance.

self-contained ADJECTIVE
■ **a self-contained flat** un appartement indépendant

self-control NOUN
le sang-froid *masc*

self-defence (US **self-defense**) NOUN
l'autodéfense *fem*
□ **self-defence classes** les cours d'autodéfense

■ **She killed him in self-defence.** Elle l'a tué en légitime défense.

self-discipline NOUN
l'autodiscipline *fem*

self-employed ADJECTIVE
■ **to be self-employed** travailler [28] à son compte □ He's self-employed. Il travaille à son compte.
■ **the self-employed** les travailleurs indépendants

selfie NOUN
le selfie *masc*

selfie stick NOUN
la perche *fem* à selfie

selfish ADJECTIVE
égoïste (FEM égoïste)
□ Don't be so selfish. Ne sois pas si égoïste.

self-respect NOUN
l'amour-propre *masc*

self-service ADJECTIVE
■ **It's self-service.** (*café, shop*) C'est un self-service.
■ **a self-service restaurant** un restaurant self-service

to **sell** VERB
vendre [88]
□ He sold it to me. Il me l'a vendu.

to **sell off** VERB
liquider [28]

to **sell out** VERB
se vendre [88]
□ The tickets sold out in three hours. Les billets se sont tous vendus en trois heures. □ The show didn't quite sell out. Ce spectacle ne s'est pas très bien vendu.
■ **The tickets are all sold out.** Il ne reste plus de billets.

sell-by date NOUN
la date limite de vente *fem*

selling price NOUN
le prix de vente *masc*

Sellotape® NOUN
le ruban adhésif *masc*

semi NOUN
la maison jumelée *fem*
□ We live in a semi. Nous habitons dans une maison jumelée.

semicircle NOUN
le demi-cercle *masc*

semicolon NOUN
le point-virgule *masc*

semi-detached house NOUN
la maison jumelée *fem*
□ We live in a semi-detached house. Nous habitons dans une maison jumelée.

semi-final NOUN
la demi-finale *fem*

semi-skimmed milk NOUN
le lait demi-écrémé *masc*

to **send** VERB
envoyer [33]
□ She sent me a birthday card. Elle m'a envoyé une carte d'anniversaire.

to **send back** VERB
renvoyer [33]

to **send off** VERB
1 envoyer [33] (*goods, letter*)
2 renvoyer [33] du terrain (*in sports match*)
□ He was sent off. On l'a renvoyé du terrain.
■ **to send off for something 1** (*free*) se faire [36] envoyer quelque chose □ I've sent off for a catalogue. Je me suis fait envoyer un catalogue. **2** (*paid for*) commander [28] quelque chose par correspondance □ She sent off for a new passport. Elle a commandé un nouveau passeport.

to **send out** VERB
envoyer [33]
■ **to send out for** commander [28] par téléphone □ Shall we send out for a pizza? Et si on commandait une pizza par téléphone ?

sender NOUN
l'expéditeur *masc*
l'expéditrice *fem*

senior ADJECTIVE
haut placé (FEM haut placée)
■ **senior management** les cadres supérieurs
■ **senior school** le lycée
■ **senior pupils** les grandes classes

senior citizen NOUN
la personne du troisième âge *fem*

sensational ADJECTIVE
sensationnel (FEM sensationnelle)

sense NOUN
1 le bon sens *masc* (*wisdom*)
□ Use your common sense! Un peu de bon sens, voyons !
■ **It makes sense.** C'est logique.
■ **It doesn't make sense.** Ça n'a pas de sens.
2 le sens *masc* (*faculty*)
□ the five senses les cinq sens
■ **the sense of touch** le toucher
■ **the sense of smell** l'odorat *masc*
■ **the sixth sense** le sixième sens
■ **sense of humour** le sens de l'humour □ He's got no sense of humour. Il n'a aucun sens de l'humour.

senseless ADJECTIVE
insensé (FEM insensée)

sensible ADJECTIVE
raisonnable (FEM raisonnable)
□ Lara is a very sensible girl. Lara est une jeune fille très raisonnable.

S

■ **That wasn't a sensible idea.** Cela n'était pas une idée judicieuse

> **BE CAREFUL!**
> Do not translate **sensible** by the French word **sensible**.

sensitive ADJECTIVE
sensible (FEM sensible)
□ She's very sensitive. Elle est très sensible.

sensuous ADJECTIVE
sensuel (FEM sensuelle)

sent VERB ▷ see **send**

sentence NOUN
▷ see also **sentence** VERB
1 la phrase fem
□ What does this sentence mean? Que veut dire cette phrase ?
2 la peine fem (punishment)
□ the death sentence la peine de mort
■ **He got a life sentence.** Il a été condamné à la réclusion à perpétuité.

to **sentence** VERB
▷ see also **sentence** NOUN
condamner [28]
■ **to sentence somebody to life imprisonment** condamner [28] quelqu'un à la réclusion à perpétuité
■ **to sentence somebody to death** condamner [28] quelqu'un à mort

sentimental ADJECTIVE
sentimental (FEM sentimentale, MASC PL sentimentaux)

separate ADJECTIVE
▷ see also **separate** VERB
séparé (FEM séparée)
□ I wrote it on a separate sheet. Je l'ai écrit sur une feuille séparée.
■ **The children have separate rooms.** Les enfants ont chacun leur chambre.
■ **on separate occasions** à différentes reprises

to **separate** VERB
▷ see also **separate** ADJECTIVE
1 séparer [28]
2 se séparer [28] (married couple)
□ My parents are separated. Mes parents sont séparés.

separately ADVERB
séparément

separation NOUN
la séparation fem

September NOUN
septembre masc
■ **in September** en septembre

sequel NOUN
la suite fem (book, film)

sequence NOUN
1 l'ordre masc

■ **in sequence** par ordre
■ **a sequence of events** une succession d'événements
2 la séquence fem (in film)

sergeant NOUN
1 le sergent masc (army)
2 le brigadier masc (police)

serial NOUN
le feuilleton masc

series NOUN
1 la série fem
□ a TV series une série télévisée
2 la suite fem (of numbers)

serious ADJECTIVE
1 sérieux (FEM sérieuse)
□ You look very serious. Tu as l'air sérieux.
■ **Are you serious?** Sérieusement ?
2 grave (FEM grave) (illness, mistake)

seriously ADVERB
sérieusement
□ No, but seriously ... Non, mais sérieusement ...
■ **to take somebody seriously** prendre [65] quelqu'un au sérieux
■ **seriously injured** gravement blessé
■ **Seriously?** Sérieusement ?

sermon NOUN
le sermon masc

servant NOUN
le/la domestique masc/fem

to **serve** VERB
▷ see also **serve** NOUN
1 servir [78]
□ Dinner is served. Le dîner est servi. □ It's Murray's turn to serve. C'est à Murray de servir.
2 purger [45] (prison sentence)
■ **to serve time** être [35] en prison
■ **It serves you right.** C'est bien fait pour toi.

serve NOUN
▷ see also **serve** VERB
le service masc (tennis)
■ **It's your serve.** C'est à toi de servir.

server NOUN
le serveur masc (computing)

to **service** VERB
▷ see also **service** NOUN
réviser [28] (car, washing machine)

service NOUN
▷ see also **service** VERB
1 le service masc
□ Service is included. Le service est compris.
2 la révision fem (of car)
3 l'office masc (church service)
■ **the Fire Service** les sapeurs-pompiers
■ **the armed services** les forces armées

service area NOUN
l'aire de service *fem*

service charge NOUN
le service *masc*
□ There's no service charge. Le service est compris.

serviceman NOUN
le militaire *masc*
□ He's a serviceman. Il est militaire.

service station NOUN
la station-service *fem* (PL les stations-service)

servicewoman NOUN
la femme soldat *fem*
□ She's a servicewoman. Elle est femme soldat.

serviette NOUN
la serviette *fem*

session NOUN
la séance *fem*

set NOUN
▷ see also **set** VERB
1 le jeu *masc* (PL les jeux)
□ a set of keys un jeu de clés □ a chess set un jeu d'échecs
■ **a train set** un train électrique
2 le set *masc* (*in tennis*)

to **set** VERB
▷ see also **set** NOUN
1 mettre [47] à sonner (*alarm clock*)
□ I set the alarm for 7 o'clock. J'ai mis le réveil à sonner pour sept heures.
2 établir [38] (*record*)
□ The world record was set last year. Le record du monde a été établi l'année dernière.
3 se coucher [28] (*sun*)
□ The sun was setting. Le soleil se couchait.
■ **The film is set in Morocco.** L'action du film se déroule au Maroc.
■ **to set sail** prendre [65] la mer
■ **to set the table** mettre [47] le couvert

to **set off** VERB
partir [57ᵉ]
□ We set off for Newcastle at 9 o'clock. Nous sommes partis pour Newcastle à neuf heures.

to **set out** VERB
partir [57ᵉ]
□ We set out for Newcastle at 9 o'clock. Nous sommes partis pour Newcastle à neuf heures.

settee NOUN
le canapé *masc*

to **settle** VERB
1 résoudre [70] (*problem*)
2 régler [34] (*argument, account*)
■ **to settle on something** opter [28] pour quelque chose

to **settle down** VERB
se calmer [28] (*calm down*)

■ **Settle down!** Du calme !

to **settle in** VERB
s'installer [28]

seven NUMBER
sept
□ She's seven. Elle a sept ans.

seventeen NUMBER
dix-sept
□ He's seventeen. Il a dix-sept ans.

seventeenth ADJECTIVE
dix-septième (FEM dix-septième)
■ her seventeenth birthday son dix-septième anniversaire □ the seventeenth floor le dix-septième étage
■ **the seventeenth of August** le dix-sept août

seventh ADJECTIVE
septième (FEM septième)
□ the seventh floor le septième étage
■ **the seventh of August** le sept août

seventy NUMBER
soixante-dix

several ADJECTIVE, PRONOUN
plusieurs
□ several schools plusieurs écoles
■ **several of them** plusieurs □ I've seen several of them. J'en ai vu plusieurs.

to **sew** VERB
coudre [15]

to **sew up** VERB
recoudre [15] (*tear*)

sewing NOUN
la couture *fem*
□ I like sewing. J'aime faire de la couture.
■ **a sewing machine** une machine à coudre

sewn VERB ▷ see **sew**

sex NOUN
le sexe *masc*
■ **to have sex with somebody** coucher [28] avec quelqu'un
■ **sex education** l'éducation sexuelle *fem*

sexism NOUN
le sexisme *masc*

sexist ADJECTIVE
sexiste (FEM sexiste)

sexual ADJECTIVE
sexuel (FEM sexuelle)
□ sexual discrimination la discrimination sexuelle □ sexual harassment le harcèlement sexuel

sexuality NOUN
la sexualité *fem*

sexy ADJECTIVE
sexy (FEM+PL sexy)

shabby ADJECTIVE
miteux (FEM miteuse)

shade NOUN

1 l'ombre *fem*
■ **in the shade** à l'ombre □ It was 35 degrees in the shade. Il faisait trente-cinq à l'ombre.

2 la nuance *fem* (*colour*)
□ a shade of blue une nuance de bleu

shadow NOUN

l'ombre *fem*

to shake VERB

1 secouer [28]
□ She shook the rug. Elle a secoué le tapis.

2 trembler [28] (*tremble*)
□ He was shaking with cold. Il tremblait de froid.
■ **to shake one's head** (*in refusal*) faire [36] non de la tête
■ **to shake hands with somebody** serrer [28] la main à quelqu'un □ They shook hands. Ils se sont serré la main.

> **DID YOU KNOW...?**
> Boys shake hands with their friends or kiss them on the cheek when they arrive at school in the morning.

shaken ADJECTIVE

secoué (FEM secouée)
□ I was feeling a bit shaken. J'étais un peu secoué.

shaky ADJECTIVE

tremblant (FEM tremblante) (*hand, voice*)

shall VERB

■ **Shall I shut the window?** Vous voulez que je ferme la fenêtre ?
■ **Shall we ask him to come with us?** Si on lui demandait de venir avec nous ?

shallow ADJECTIVE

peu profond (FEM peu profonde) (*water, pool*)

shambles NOUN

la pagaille *fem*
□ It's a complete shambles. C'est la pagaille complète.

shame NOUN

la honte *fem*
□ The shame of it! Quelle honte !
■ **What a shame!** Quel dommage !
■ **It's a shame that ...** C'est dommage que ...

> **c'est dommage que** has to be followed by a verb in the subjunctive.

□ It's a shame he isn't here. C'est dommage qu'il ne soit pas ici.

shampoo NOUN

le shampooing *masc*
□ a bottle of shampoo une bouteille de shampooing

shandy NOUN

le panaché *masc*

shan't = shall not

shape NOUN

la forme *fem*

share NOUN

▷ *see also* **share** VERB

1 l'action *fem* (*in company*)
□ They've got shares in the company. Ils ont des actions dans la société.

2 la part *fem*
□ Everybody pays their share. Tout le monde paie sa part.

to share VERB

▷ *see also* **share** NOUN
partager [45]
□ to share a room with somebody partager une chambre avec quelqu'un

to share out VERB

distribuer [28]
□ They shared the sweets out among the children. Ils ont distribué les bonbons aux enfants.

shark NOUN

le requin *masc*

sharp ADJECTIVE

1 tranchant (FEM tranchante) (*razor, knife*)

2 pointu (FEM pointue) (*spike, point*)

3 intelligent (FEM intelligente) (*clever*)
□ She's very sharp. Elle est très intelligente.
■ **at two o'clock sharp** à deux heures pile

to shave VERB

se raser [28] (*have a shave*)
■ **to shave one's legs** se raser [28] les jambes

shaver NOUN

■ **an electric shaver** un rasoir électrique

shaving cream NOUN

la crème à raser *fem*

shaving foam NOUN

la mousse à raser *fem*

she PRONOUN

elle
□ She's very nice. Elle est très gentille.

shed NOUN

la remise *fem*

she'd = she had, she would

sheep NOUN

le mouton *masc*

sheepdog NOUN

le chien de berger *masc*

sheer ADJECTIVE

pur (FEM pure)
□ It's sheer greed. C'est de l'avidité pure.

sheet NOUN

le drap *masc* (*on bed*)
■ **a sheet of paper** une feuille de papier

shelf NOUN

1 l'étagère *fem* (*in house*)

2 le rayon *masc* (*in shop*)

Numbers in brackets refer to verb tables on pages 650 to 658

shell NOUN
1 le coquillage *masc* (*on beach*)
2 la coquille *fem* (*of egg, nut*)
3 l'obus *masc* (*explosive*)

she'll = she will

shellfish NOUN
les fruits de mer *masc pl*

shell suit NOUN
le survêtement *masc*

shelter NOUN
■ **to take shelter** se mettre [47] à l'abri
■ **a bus shelter** un arrêt d'autobus

shelves PL NOUN ▷ *see* **shelf**

shepherd NOUN
le berger *masc*

sheriff NOUN
le shérif *masc*

sherry NOUN
le xérès *masc*

she's = she is, she has

Shetland NOUN
les îles Shetland *fem pl*

shield NOUN
le bouclier *masc*

shift NOUN
▷ *see also* **shift** VERB
le service *masc*
□ His shift starts at 8 o'clock. Il prend son service à huit heures. □ the night shift le service de nuit
■ **to do shift work** faire [36] les trois-huit

to **shift** VERB
▷ *see also* **shift** NOUN
déplacer [12] (*move*)
□ I couldn't shift the wardrobe on my own. Je n'ai pas pu déplacer l'armoire tout seul.
■ **Shift yourself!** Pousse-toi de là ! (*informal*)

shifty ADJECTIVE
1 louche (FEM louche) (*person*)
□ He looked shifty. Il avait l'air louche.
2 fuyant (FEM fuyante) (*eyes*)

shin NOUN
le tibia *masc*

to **shine** VERB
briller [28]
□ The sun was shining. Le soleil brillait.

shiny ADJECTIVE
brillant (FEM brillante)

ship NOUN
1 le bateau *masc* (PL les bateaux)
2 le navire *masc* (*warship*)

shipbuilding NOUN
la construction navale *fem*

shipwreck NOUN
le naufrage *masc*

shipwrecked ADJECTIVE
■ **to be shipwrecked** faire [36] naufrage

shipyard NOUN
le chantier naval *masc*

shirt NOUN
1 la chemise *fem* (*man's*)
2 le chemisier *masc* (*woman's*)

to **shiver** VERB
frissonner [28]

shock NOUN
▷ *see also* **shock** VERB
le choc *masc*
■ **to get a shock** 1 (*surprise*) avoir [8] un choc
2 (*electric*) recevoir [67] une décharge
■ **an electric shock** une décharge

to **shock** VERB
▷ *see also* **shock** NOUN
1 bouleverser [28] (*upset*)
□ They were shocked by the tragedy. Ils ont été bouleversés par la tragédie.
2 choquer [28] (*scandalize*)
□ I was rather shocked by her attitude. J'ai été assez choqué par son attitude. □ He'll be shocked if you say that. Tu vas le choquer si tu dis ça.

shocking ADJECTIVE
choquant (FEM choquante)
□ It's shocking! C'est choquant !
■ **a shocking waste** un gaspillage épouvantable

shoe NOUN
la chaussure *fem*

shoelace NOUN
le lacet *masc*

shoe polish NOUN
le cirage *masc*

shoe shop NOUN
le magasin de chaussures *masc*

shone VERB ▷ *see* **shine**

shook VERB ▷ *see* **shake**

to **shoot** VERB
1 abattre [9] (*kill*)
□ He was shot by a police officer. Il a été abattu par un policier.
2 fusiller [28] (*execute*)
□ He was shot at dawn. Il a été fusillé à l'aube.
3 tirer [28] (*gun*)
□ Don't shoot! Ne tirez pas !
■ **to shoot at somebody** tirer [28] sur quelqu'un
■ **He shot himself with a revolver.** (*dead*) Il s'est suicidé d'un coup de revolver.
■ **He was shot in the leg.** (*wounded*) Il a reçu une balle dans la jambe.
■ **to shoot an arrow** envoyer [33] une flèche
4 tourner [28] (*film*)
□ The film was shot in Prague. Le film a été tourné à Prague.
5 shooter [28] (*in football*)

S

shooting – show

shooting NOUN
1 les coups de feu *masc pl*
   □ They heard shooting. Ils ont entendu des coups de feu.
   ■ **a shooting** une fusillade □ a drive-by shooting une fusillade au volant d'une voiture
2 la chasse *fem* (*hunting*)
   □ to go shooting aller à la chasse

shop NOUN
le magasin *masc*
   □ a sports shop un magasin de sports

shop assistant NOUN
le vendeur *masc*
la vendeuse *fem*
   □ She's a shop assistant. Elle est vendeuse.

shopkeeper NOUN
le commerçant *masc*
la commerçante *fem*
   □ He's a shopkeeper. Il est commerçant.

shoplifting NOUN
le vol à l'étalage *masc*

shopping NOUN
les courses *fem pl* (*purchases*)
   □ Can you get the shopping from the car? Tu peux aller chercher les courses dans la voiture ?
   ■ **I love shopping.** J'adore faire du shopping.
   ■ **to go shopping** 1 (*to buy food*) faire [36] des courses 2 (*for pleasure*) faire [36] du shopping
   ■ **a shopping bag** un sac à provisions
   ■ **a shopping centre** un centre commercial

shop window NOUN
la vitrine *fem*

shore NOUN
le rivage *masc*
   ■ **on shore** à terre

short ADJECTIVE
1 court (FEM courte)
   □ a short skirt une jupe courte □ short hair les cheveux courts
   ■ **too short** trop court □ It was a great holiday, but too short. C'étaient des vacances super, mais trop courtes.
2 petit (FEM petite) (*person, period of time*)
   □ She's quite short. Elle est assez petite. □ a short break une petite pause □ a short walk une petite promenade
   ■ **to be short of something** être [35] à court de quelque chose □ I'm short of money. Je suis à court d'argent.
   ■ **at short notice** au dernier moment
   ■ **In short, the answer's no.** Bref, la réponse est non.

shortage NOUN
la pénurie *fem*
   □ a water shortage une pénurie d'eau

short cut NOUN
le raccourci *masc*

□ I took a short cut. J'ai pris un raccourci.

shorthand NOUN
la sténo *fem*

shortly ADVERB
bientôt

shorts PL NOUN
le short *masc sing*
   ■ **a pair of shorts** un short

short-sighted ADJECTIVE
myope (FEM myope)

short story NOUN
la nouvelle *fem*

shot VERB ▷ *see* **shoot**

shot NOUN
1 le coup de feu *masc* (*gunshot*)
2 la photo *fem* (*photo*)
   □ a shot of Edinburgh Castle une photo du château d'Édimbourg
3 le vaccin *masc* (*vaccination*)

shotgun NOUN
le fusil de chasse *masc*

should VERB

When 'should' means 'ought to', use **devoir**.

devoir [26]
   □ You should take more exercise. Vous devriez faire plus d'exercice. □ He should be there by now. Il devrait être arrivé maintenant. □ That shouldn't be too hard. Ça ne devrait pas être trop difficile.
   ■ **should have** avoir dû □ I should have told you before. J'aurais dû te le dire avant.

When 'should' means 'would', use the conditional tense.

   □ I should go if I were you. Si j'étais vous, j'irais.
   □ I should be so lucky! Ça serait trop beau !

shoulder NOUN
l'épaule *fem*
   ■ **a shoulder bag** un sac à bandoulière

shouldn't = **should not**

to shout VERB
   ▷ *see also* **shout** NOUN
   crier [19]
   □ Don't shout! Ne criez pas ! □ 'Go away!' he shouted. « Allez-vous-en ! » a-t-il crié.

shout NOUN
   ▷ *see also* **shout** VERB
   le cri *masc*

shovel NOUN
la pelle *fem*

show NOUN
   ▷ *see also* **show** VERB
1 le spectacle *masc* (*performance*)
2 l'émission *fem* (*programme*)
3 le salon *masc* (*exhibition*)

Numbers in brackets refer to verb tables on pages 650 to 658

□ The cinema shut down last year. Le cinéma a fermé l'année dernière.

to shut up VERB
1 fermer [28] (*close*)
2 se taire [82] (*be quiet*)
□ Shut up! Tais-toi !

shutters NOUN
les volets *masc pl*

shuttle NOUN
la navette *fem*

shuttlecock NOUN
le volant *masc* (*badminton*)

shy ADJECTIVE
timide (FEM timide)

Sicily NOUN
la Sicile *fem*
■ **in Sicily** en Sicile
■ **to Sicily** en Sicile

sick ADJECTIVE
1 malade (FEM malade) (*ill*)
□ He was sick for four days. Il a été malade pendant quatre jours.
2 de mauvais goût (*joke, humour*)
□ That's really sick! C'est vraiment de mauvais goût !
■ **to be sick** (*vomit*) vomir [38]
■ **I feel sick.** J'ai envie de vomir.
■ **to be sick of something** en avoir [8] assez de quelque chose □ I'm sick of your jokes. J'en ai assez de tes plaisanteries.

sickening ADJECTIVE
écœurant (FEM écœurante)

sick leave NOUN
le congé maladie *masc*

sickness NOUN
la maladie *fem*

sick note NOUN
1 le mot d'absence *masc* (*from parents*)
2 le certificat médical *masc* (*from doctor*)

sick pay NOUN
l'indemnité de maladie *fem*

side NOUN
1 le côté *masc* (*of object, building, car*)
□ He was driving on the wrong side of the road. Il roulait du mauvais côté de la route.
2 le bord *masc* (*of pool, river, road*)
□ by the side of the lake au bord du lac
3 le flanc *masc* (*of hill*)
4 l'équipe *fem* (*team*)
■ **He's on my side.** 1 (*on my team*) Il est dans mon équipe. 2 (*supporting me*) Il est de mon côté.
■ **side by side** côte à côte
■ **the side entrance** l'entrée latérale
■ **to take sides** prendre [65] parti □ She always takes his side. Elle prend toujours son parti.

---

to show VERB
▷ *see also* **show** NOUN
1 montrer [28]
■ **to show somebody something** montrer [28] quelque chose à quelqu'un □ Have I shown you my new trainers? Je t'ai montré mes nouvelles baskets ?
2 faire [36] preuve de
□ She showed great courage. Elle a fait preuve de beaucoup de courage.
■ **It shows.** Ça se voit. □ I've never been riding before. — It shows. Je n'ai jamais fait de cheval. — Ça se voit.

to show off VERB
frimer [28] (*informal*)

to show up VERB
se pointer [28] (*turn up*)
□ He showed up late as usual. Il s'est pointé en retard comme d'habitude.

shower NOUN
1 la douche *fem*
■ **to have a shower** prendre [65] une douche
2 l'averse *fem* (*of rain*)

showerproof ADJECTIVE
imperméabilisé (FEM imperméabilisée)

showing NOUN
la projection *fem* (*of film*)

shown VERB ▷ *see* **show**

show-off NOUN
le frimeur *masc*
la frimeuse *fem*

shrank VERB ▷ *see* **shrink**

to shriek VERB
hurler [28]

shrimps PL NOUN
les crevettes *fem pl*

to shrink VERB
rétrécir [38] (*clothes, fabric*)

Shrove Tuesday NOUN
le mardi gras *masc*

to shrug VERB
■ **to shrug one's shoulders** hausser [28] les épaules

shrunk VERB ▷ *see* **shrink**

to shudder VERB
frissonner [28]

to shuffle VERB
■ **to shuffle the cards** battre [9] les cartes

to shut VERB
fermer [28]
□ What time do you shut? À quelle heure est-ce que vous fermez ? □ What time does the left-luggage office shut? À quelle heure est-ce que la consigne ferme ?

to shut down VERB
fermer [28]

S

sideboard - since

sideboard NOUN
le buffet *masc*

side-effect NOUN
l'effet secondaire *masc*

side street NOUN
la petite rue transversale *fem*

sidewalk NOUN (US)
le trottoir *masc*

sideways ADVERB
1 de côté (*look, be facing*)
2 de travers (*move*)
■ **sideways on** de profil

sieve NOUN
la passoire *fem*

sigh NOUN
▷ *see also* **sigh** VERB
le soupir *masc*

to sigh VERB
▷ *see also* **sigh** NOUN
soupirer [28]

sight NOUN
1 la vue *fem*
□ to have poor sight avoir une mauvaise vue
■ **to know somebody by sight** connaître [14]
quelqu'un de vue
2 le spectacle *masc*
□ It was an amazing sight. C'était un spectacle
étonnant.
■ **in sight** visible
■ **out of sight** hors de vue
■ **the sights** (*tourist spots*) les attractions
touristiques
■ **to see the sights of Rome** visiter [28] Rome

sightseeing NOUN
le tourisme *masc*
■ **to go sightseeing** faire [36] du tourisme

sign NOUN
▷ *see also* **sign** VERB
1 le panneau *masc* (PL les panneaux) (*notice*)
□ There was a big sign saying 'private'. Il y avait
un grand panneau indiquant « privé ».
■ **a road sign** un panneau
2 le signe *masc* (*gesture, indication*)
□ There's no sign of improvement. Il n'y a aucun
signe d'amélioration.
■ **What sign are you?** (*star sign*) Tu es de quel
signe ?

to sign VERB
▷ *see also* **sign** NOUN
signer [28]

to sign on VERB
s'inscrire [30] au chômage (*as unemployed*)

signal NOUN
▷ *see also* **signal** VERB
le signal *masc* (PL les signaux)

to signal VERB
▷ *see also* **signal** NOUN

■ **to signal to somebody** faire [36] un signe à
quelqu'un

signature NOUN
la signature *fem*

significance NOUN
l'importance *fem*

significant ADJECTIVE
important (FEM importante)

sign language NOUN
le langage des signes *masc*

signpost NOUN
le poteau indicateur *masc*

silence NOUN
le silence *masc*

silencer NOUN
le silencieux *masc*

silent ADJECTIVE
silencieux (FEM silencieuse)

silicon chip NOUN
la puce électronique *fem*

silk NOUN
▷ *see also* **silk** ADJECTIVE
la soie *fem*

silk ADJECTIVE
▷ *see also* **silk** NOUN
en soie
□ a silk scarf un foulard en soie

silky ADJECTIVE
soyeux (FEM soyeuse)

silly ADJECTIVE
bête (FEM bête)

silver NOUN
l'argent *masc*
□ a silver medal une médaille d'argent

similar ADJECTIVE
semblable (FEM semblable)
■ **similar to** semblable à

simple ADJECTIVE
simple (FEM simple)
□ It's very simple. C'est très simple.

simply ADVERB
simplement
□ It's simply not possible. Ça n'est tout
simplement pas possible.

simultaneous ADJECTIVE
simultané (FEM simultanée)

sin NOUN
▷ *see also* **sin** VERB
le péché *masc*

to sin VERB
▷ *see also* **sin** NOUN
pécher [28]

since PREPOSITION, ADVERB, CONJUNCTION
1 depuis
□ since Christmas depuis Noël □ since then

depuis ce moment-là □ I haven't seen him since. Je ne l'ai pas vu depuis.
■ **ever since** depuis ce moment-là

2 depuis que
□ I haven't seen her since she left. Je ne l'ai pas vue depuis qu'elle est partie.

3 puisque (*because*)
□ Since you're tired, let's stay at home. Puisque tu es fatigué, restons à la maison.

sincere ADJECTIVE
sincère (FEM sincère)

sincerely ADVERB
■ **Yours sincerely ...** **1** (*in business letter*) Veuillez agréer l'expression de mes sentiments les meilleurs ... **2** (*in personal letter*) Cordialement ...

to **sing** VERB
chanter [28]
□ He sang out of tune. Il chantait faux. □ Have you ever sung this tune before? Vous avez déjà chanté cet air-là ?

singer NOUN
le chanteur *masc*
la chanteuse *fem*

singing NOUN
le chant *masc*

single ADJECTIVE
▷ *see also* **single** NOUN
célibataire (FEM célibataire) (*unmarried*)
■ **a single room** une chambre pour une personne
■ **not a single thing** rien du tout

single NOUN
▷ *see also* **single** ADJECTIVE
l'aller simple *masc* (*ticket*)
□ A single to Toulouse, please. Un aller simple pour Toulouse, s'il vous plaît.

single parent NOUN
■ **She's a single parent.** Elle élève ses enfants toute seule.
■ **a single-parent family** une famille monoparentale

singles PL NOUN
le simple *masc sing* (*in tennis*)
□ the women's singles le simple dames

singular NOUN
le singulier *masc*
□ in the singular au singulier

sinister ADJECTIVE
sinistre (FEM sinistre)

sink NOUN
▷ *see also* **sink** VERB
l'évier *masc*

to **sink** VERB
▷ *see also* **sink** NOUN
couler [28]

sir NOUN
monsieur *masc*
■ **Yes sir.** Oui, Monsieur.

siren NOUN
la sirène *fem*

sister NOUN
1 la sœur *fem*
□ my little sister ma petite sœur
2 l'infirmière en chef *fem* (*nurse*)

sister-in-law NOUN
la belle-sœur *fem* (PL les belles-sœurs)

to **sit** VERB
s'asseoir [6]
■ **to sit on something** s'asseoir [6] sur quelque chose □ She sat on the chair. Elle s'est assise sur la chaise.
■ **to be sitting** être [35] assis
■ **to sit an exam** passer [58] un examen

to **sit down** VERB
s'asseoir [6]

sitcom NOUN
la comédie de situation *fem*

site NOUN
1 le site *masc*
□ an archaeological site un site archéologique
■ **the site of the accident** le lieu de l'accident
2 le camping *masc* (*campsite*)
■ **a building site** un chantier

sitting room NOUN
le salon *masc*

situated ADJECTIVE
■ **to be situated** être [35] situé □ The village is situated on a hill. Le village est situé sur une colline.

situation NOUN
la situation *fem*

six NUMBER
six
□ He's six. Il a six ans.

sixteen NUMBER
seize
□ He's sixteen. Il a seize ans.

sixteenth ADJECTIVE
seizième (FEM seizième)
□ the sixteenth floor le seizième étage
■ **the sixteenth of August** le seize août

sixth ADJECTIVE
sixième (FEM sixième)
□ the sixth floor le sixième étage
■ **the sixth of August** le six août

sixth form NOUN
le lycée *masc*

sixty NUMBER
soixante

size NOUN
1 la taille *fem* (*of object, clothing*)

S

□ What size do you take? Quelle taille est-ce que vous faites ?
■ **I'm a size ten.** Je fais du trente-huit.
2 la pointure *fem* (*of shoes*)
■ **I take size six.** Je fais du trente-neuf.

> **DID YOU KNOW...?**
> France uses the European system to show clothing and shoe sizes.

to **skate** VERB
1 faire [36] du patin à glace (*ice-skate*)
2 faire [36] du patin à roulettes (*roller-skate*)

skateboard NOUN
le skateboard *masc*

skateboarding NOUN
le skateboard *masc*
□ to go skateboarding faire du skateboard

skates NOUN
les patins *masc pl*

skating NOUN
le patin à glace *masc*
□ to go skating faire du patin à glace
■ **a skating rink** une patinoire

skeleton NOUN
le squelette *masc*

sketch NOUN
▷ *see also* **sketch** VERB
le croquis *masc* (*drawing*)

to **sketch** VERB
▷ *see also* **sketch** NOUN
■ **to sketch something** faire [36] un croquis de quelque chose

ski NOUN
▷ *see also* **ski** VERB
le ski *masc*
■ **ski boots** les chaussures de ski *fem pl*
■ **a ski lift** un remonte-pente
■ **ski pants** le fuseau *sing*
■ **a ski pole** un bâton de ski
■ **a ski slope** une piste de ski
■ **a ski suit** une combinaison de ski

to **ski** VERB
▷ *see also* **ski** NOUN
skier [19]
□ Can you ski? Tu sais skier ?

to **skid** VERB
déraper [28]

skier NOUN
le skieur *masc*
la skieuse *fem*

skiing NOUN
le ski *masc*
■ **to go skiing** faire [36] du ski
■ **to go on a skiing holiday** aller [3] aux sports d'hiver

skilful ADJECTIVE
adroit (FEM adroite)

skill NOUN
le talent *masc*
□ He played with great skill. Il a joué avec beaucoup de talent.

skilled ADJECTIVE
■ **a skilled worker** un ouvrier spécialisé

skimmed milk NOUN
le lait écrémé *masc*

skimpy ADJECTIVE
1 minuscule (FEM minuscule) (*clothes*)
2 maigre (FEM maigre) (*meal*)

skin NOUN
la peau *fem* (PL les peaux)
■ **skin cancer** le cancer de la peau

skinhead NOUN
le/la skinhead *masc/fem*

skinny ADJECTIVE
maigre (FEM maigre)

skin-tight ADJECTIVE
collant (FEM collante)

skip NOUN
▷ *see also* **skip** VERB
la benne *fem* (*container*)

to **skip** VERB
▷ *see also* **skip** NOUN
sauter [28]
□ to skip a meal sauter un repas
■ **to skip a lesson** sécher [34] un cours

skirt NOUN
la jupe *fem*

skittles NOUN
les quilles *fem pl*
□ to play skittles jouer aux quilles

to **skive** VERB
tirer [28] au flanc (*be lazy*)

to **skive off** VERB
sécher [34] (*informal*)
□ to skive off school sécher les cours

skull NOUN
le crâne *masc*

sky NOUN
le ciel *masc*

Skype® NOUN
▷ *see also* **Skype** VERB
Skype® *masc*

to **Skype** VERB
▷ *see also* **Skype** NOUN
skyper [28]

skyscraper NOUN
le gratte-ciel *masc* (PL les gratte-ciel)

slack ADJECTIVE
1 lâche (FEM lâche) (*rope*)
2 négligent (FEM négligente) (*person*)

to **slag off** VERB
■ **to slag somebody off** dire [27] du mal de quelqu'un

to **slam** VERB
claquer [28]
□ The door slammed. La porte a claqué. □ She slammed the door. Elle a claqué la porte.

slang NOUN
l'argot *masc*

slap NOUN
▷ *see also* **slap** VERB
la claque *fem*

to **slap** VERB
▷ *see also* **slap** NOUN
■ **to slap somebody** donner [28] une claque à quelqu'un

slate NOUN
l'ardoise *fem*

sledge NOUN
la luge *fem*

sledging NOUN
■ **to go sledging** faire [36] de la luge

sleep NOUN
▷ *see also* **sleep** VERB
le sommeil *masc*
■ **I need some sleep.** J'ai besoin de dormir.
■ **to go to sleep** s'endormir [29]

to **sleep** VERB
▷ *see also* **sleep** NOUN
dormir [29]
□ I couldn't sleep last night. J'ai mal dormi la nuit dernière.
■ **to sleep with somebody** coucher [28] avec quelqu'un

to **sleep in** VERB
1 ne pas se réveiller [28] (*accidentally*)
□ I'm sorry I'm late, I slept in. Désolé d'être en retard : je ne me suis pas réveillé.
2 faire [36] la grasse matinée (*on purpose*)

to **sleep together** VERB
coucher [28] ensemble

sleeping bag NOUN
le sac de couchage *masc*

sleeping car NOUN
le wagon-lit *masc* (PL les wagons-lits)

sleeping pill NOUN
le somnifère *masc*

sleepy ADJECTIVE
■ **to feel sleepy** avoir [8] sommeil □ I was feeling sleepy. J'avais sommeil.
■ **a sleepy little village** un petit village tranquille

sleet NOUN
▷ *see also* **sleet** VERB
la neige fondue *fem*

to **sleet** VERB
▷ *see also* **sleet** NOUN
■ **It's sleeting.** Il tombe de la neige fondue.

sleeve NOUN
la manche *fem*
□ long sleeves les manches longues □ short sleeves les manches courtes

sleigh NOUN
le traîneau *masc* (PL les traîneaux)

slept VERB ▷ *see* **sleep**

slice NOUN
▷ *see also* **slice** VERB
la tranche *fem*

to **slice** VERB
▷ *see also* **slice** NOUN
couper [28] en tranches

slick NOUN
■ **an oil slick** une marée noire

slide NOUN
▷ *see also* **slide** VERB
1 le toboggan *masc* (*in playground*)
2 la diapositive *fem* (*photo*)
3 la barrette *fem* (*hair slide*)

to **slide** VERB
▷ *see also* **slide** NOUN
glisser [28]

slight ADJECTIVE
léger (FEM légère)
□ a slight problem un léger problème □ a slight improvement une légère amélioration

slightly ADVERB
légèrement

slim ADJECTIVE
▷ *see also* **slim** VERB
mince (FEM mince)

to **slim** VERB
▷ *see also* **slim** ADJECTIVE
faire [36] un régime (*be on a diet*)
□ I'm slimming. Je fais un régime.

sling NOUN
l'écharpe *fem*
□ She had her arm in a sling. Elle avait le bras en écharpe.

slip NOUN
▷ *see also* **slip** VERB
1 l'erreur *fem* (*mistake*)
2 le jupon *masc* (*underskirt*)
3 la combinaison *fem* (*full-length underskirt*)
■ **a slip of paper** un bout de papier
■ **a slip of the tongue** un lapsus

to **slip** VERB
▷ *see also* **slip** NOUN
glisser [28]
□ He slipped on the ice. Il a glissé sur le verglas.

to **slip up** VERB
faire [36] une erreur (*make a mistake*)

slipper NOUN
le chausson *masc*
■ **a pair of slippers** des chaussons

S

slippery ADJECTIVE
glissant (FEM glissante)

slip-up NOUN
l'erreur fem

slope NOUN
la pente fem

sloppy ADJECTIVE
1 bâclé (FEM bâclée) (work)
2 négligé (FEM négligée) (person, appearance)

slot NOUN
la fente fem

slot machine NOUN
1 la machine à sous fem (for gambling)
2 le distributeur automatique masc (vending machine)

slow ADJECTIVE
lent (FEM lente)
  □ We are behind a very slow lorry. On est derrière un camion très lent.
  ■ **My watch is slow.** Ma montre retarde.

to **slow down** VERB
ralentir [38]

slowly ADVERB
lentement

slug NOUN
la limace fem

slum NOUN
1 le quartier insalubre masc (area)
2 le taudis masc (house)

slush NOUN
la neige fondue fem

sly ADJECTIVE
rusé (FEM rusée) (person)
  ■ **a sly smile** un sourire sournois

smack NOUN
  ▷ see also **smack** VERB
la tape fem

to **smack** VERB
  ▷ see also **smack** NOUN
  ■ **to smack somebody** donner [28] une tape à quelqu'un

small ADJECTIVE
petit (FEM petite)
  ■ **small change** la petite monnaie

WORD POWER
You can use a number of other words instead of **small** to mean 'little':
miniature miniature
  □ a miniature version une version miniature
minute infime
  □ a minute chance une chance infime
tiny minuscule
  □ a tiny garden un jardin minuscule

---

smart ADJECTIVE
1 chic (FEM+PL chic) (elegant)

2 intelligent (FEM intelligente) (clever)
  ■ **a smart idea** une idée astucieuse

smartphone NOUN
le smartphone masc

smash NOUN
  ▷ see also **smash** VERB
l'accident masc

to **smash** VERB
  ▷ see also **smash** NOUN
1 casser [28] (break)
  □ I've smashed my watch. J'ai cassé ma montre.
2 se briser [28] (get broken)
  □ The glass smashed into tiny pieces. Le verre s'est brisé en mille morceaux.

smell NOUN
  ▷ see also **smell** VERB
l'odeur fem
  ■ **the sense of smell** l'odorat masc

to **smell** VERB
  ▷ see also **smell** NOUN
1 sentir [77] mauvais
  □ That old dog really smells! Qu'est-ce qu'il sent mauvais, ce vieux chien !
  ■ **to smell of something** sentir [77] quelque chose □ It smells of petrol. Ça sent l'essence.
2 sentir [77] (detect)
  □ I can't smell anything. Je ne sens rien.

smelly ADJECTIVE
qui sent mauvais
  □ He's got smelly feet. Il a les pieds qui sentent mauvais.

smelt VERB ▷ see **smell**

smile NOUN
  ▷ see also **smile** VERB
le sourire masc

to **smile** VERB
  ▷ see also **smile** NOUN
sourire [74]

smiley NOUN
l'émoticon masc

smoke NOUN
  ▷ see also **smoke** VERB
la fumée fem

to **smoke** VERB
  ▷ see also **smoke** NOUN
fumer [28]
  □ I don't smoke. Je ne fume pas. □ He smokes cigars. Il fume le cigare.

smoker NOUN
le fumeur masc
la fumeuse fem

smoking NOUN
  ■ **to give up smoking** arrêter [28] de fumer
  ■ **Smoking is bad for you.** Le tabac est mauvais pour la santé.
  ■ **'no smoking'** « défense de fumer »

S

smooth ADJECTIVE
1 lisse (FEM lisse) (surface)
2 mielleux (FEM mielleuse) (person)

SMS NOUN
le SMS masc
▫ I'll send you an SMS. Je t'enverrai un SMS.

smudge NOUN
la bavure fem

smug ADJECTIVE
suffisant (FEM suffisante)

to smuggle VERB
passer [58] en fraude (goods)
▫ to smuggle drugs into a country faire passer de la drogue en fraude dans un pays
■ **They managed to smuggle him out of prison.** Ils ont réussi à le faire sortir de prison clandestinement.

smuggler NOUN
le contrebandier masc
la contrebandière fem

smuggling NOUN
la contrebande fem

snack NOUN
l'en-cas masc (PL les en-cas)
■ **to have a snack** prendre [65] un en-cas

snack bar NOUN
le snack-bar masc

snail NOUN
l'escargot masc

snake NOUN
le serpent masc

to snap VERB
casser [28] net (break)
▫ The branch snapped. La branche a cassé net.
■ **to snap one's fingers** faire [36] claquer ses doigts

snap fastener NOUN
le bouton-pression masc (PL les boutons-pression)

snapshot NOUN
la photo fem

to snarl VERB
gronder [28] (animal)

to snatch VERB
■ **to snatch something from somebody** arracher [28] quelque chose à quelqu'un ▫ He snatched the keys from my hand. Il m'a arraché les clés des mains.
■ **My bag was snatched.** On m'a arraché mon sac.

to sneak VERB
■ **to sneak in** entrer [32⁵] furtivement
■ **to sneak out** sortir [79⁵] furtivement
■ **to sneak up on somebody** s'approcher [28] de quelqu'un sans faire de bruit

to sneeze VERB
éternuer [28]

to sniff VERB
1 renifler [28]
▫ Stop sniffing! Arrête de renifler !
2 flairer [28]
▫ The dog sniffed my hand. Le chien m'a flairé la main.

snob NOUN
le/la snob masc/fem

snooker NOUN
le billard masc
▫ to play snooker jouer au billard

snooze NOUN
le petit somme masc
▫ to have a snooze faire un petit somme

to snore VERB
ronfler [28]

snow NOUN
▷ see also **snow** VERB
la neige fem

to snow VERB
▷ see also **snow** NOUN
neiger [45]
▫ It's snowing. Il neige.

snowball NOUN
la boule de neige fem

snowflake NOUN
le flocon de neige masc

snowman NOUN
le bonhomme de neige masc
▫ to build a snowman faire un bonhomme de neige

so CONJUNCTION, ADVERB
1 alors
▫ The shop was closed, so I went home. Le magasin était fermé, alors je suis rentré chez moi. ▫ So, have you always lived in Cambridge? Alors, vous avez toujours vécu à Cambridge ?
■ **So what?** Et alors ?
■ **It rained, so I got wet.** Il pleuvait, donc j'ai été mouillé.
2 tellement (very)
▫ It was so heavy! C'était tellement lourd ! ▫ He was talking so fast I couldn't understand. Il parlait tellement vite que je ne comprenais pas.
■ **It's not so heavy!** Ça n'est pas si lourd que ça !
■ **How's your father? — Not so good.** Comment va ton père ? — Pas très bien.
■ **so much** (a lot) tellement ▫ I love you so much. Je t'aime tellement.
■ **so much ...** tellement de ... ▫ I've got so much work. J'ai tellement de travail.
■ **so many ...** tellement de ... ▫ I've got so many things to do today. J'ai tellement de choses à faire aujourd'hui.

English-French

3 aussi (in comparisons)
□ He's like his sister but not so clever. Il est comme sa sœur mais pas aussi intelligent.
■ **so do I** moi aussi □ I love horses. — So do I. J'aime les chevaux. — Moi aussi.
■ **so have we** nous aussi □ I've been to Ireland twice. — So have we. Je suis allé en Irlande deux fois. — Nous aussi.
■ **I think so.** Je crois.
■ **I hope so.** J'espère bien.
■ **That's not so.** Ça n'est pas le cas.
■ **so far** jusqu'à présent □ It's been easy so far. Ça a été facile jusqu'à présent.
■ **so far so good** jusqu'ici ça va
■ **ten or so people** environ dix personnes
■ **at five o'clock or so** à environ cinq heures

to **soak** VERB
tremper [28]

soaked ADJECTIVE
trempé (FEM trempée)
□ By the time we got back we were soaked. Nous sommes rentrés trempés.

soaking ADJECTIVE
trempé (FEM trempée)
□ By the time we got back we were soaking. Nous sommes rentrés trempés.
■ **soaking wet** trempé □ Your shoes are soaking wet. Tes chaussures sont trempées.

soap NOUN
le savon masc

soap opera NOUN
le feuilleton à l'eau de rose masc

soap powder NOUN
la lessive fem

to **sob** VERB
sangloter [28]
□ She was sobbing. Elle sanglotait.

sober ADJECTIVE
sobre (FEM sobre)

to **sober up** VERB
dessoûler [28]

soccer NOUN
le football masc
□ to play soccer jouer au football
■ **a soccer player** un joueur de football

social ADJECTIVE
social (FEM sociale, MASC PL sociaux)
□ a social class une classe sociale
■ **I have a good social life.** Je vois beaucoup de monde.
■ **social media** les médias sociaux
■ **social distancing** la distanciation sociale

socialism NOUN
le socialisme masc

socialist ADJECTIVE
▷ see also **socialist** NOUN
socialiste (FEM socialiste)

socialist NOUN
▷ see also **socialist** ADJECTIVE
le/la socialiste masc/fem

social network NOUN
le réseau social masc

social security NOUN
1 l'aide sociale fem (money)
■ **to be on social security** recevoir [67] des aides sociales
2 la sécurité sociale fem (organization)

social worker NOUN
l'assistant social masc
l'assistante sociale fem
□ She's a social worker. Elle est assistante sociale.

society NOUN
1 la société fem
□ We live in a multi-cultural society. Nous vivons dans une société multiculturelle.
2 le club masc
□ a drama society un club de théâtre

sociology NOUN
la sociologie fem

sock NOUN
la chaussette fem

socket NOUN
la prise de courant fem

soda NOUN
le soda masc (soda water)

soda pop NOUN (US)
le soda masc

sofa NOUN
le canapé masc

soft ADJECTIVE
1 doux (FEM douce) (fabric, texture)
2 mou (FEM molle) (pillow, bed)
■ **soft cheeses** les fromages à pâte molle
3 fin (FEM fine) (hair)
■ **to be soft on somebody** (be kind to) être [35] indulgent avec quelqu'un
■ **a soft drink** une boisson non alcoolisée
■ **soft drugs** les drogues douces fem pl
■ **a soft option** une solution de facilité

software NOUN
le logiciel masc

soggy ADJECTIVE
1 trempé (FEM trempée) (soaked)
□ a soggy tissue un mouchoir trempé
2 mou (FEM molle) (not crisp)
□ soggy chips des frites molles

soil NOUN
la terre fem

solar ADJECTIVE
solaire (FEM solaire)
■ **a solar panel** un panneau solaire

solar power NOUN
l'énergie solaire *fem*

sold VERB ▷ *see* **sell**

soldier NOUN
le soldat *masc*
□ He's a soldier. Il est soldat.

solicitor NOUN
1 l'avocat *masc*
l'avocate *fem* (*for lawyers*)
□ He's a solicitor. Il est avocat.
2 le notaire *masc* (*for wills, property*)
□ She's a solicitor. Elle est notaire.

solid ADJECTIVE
1 massif (FEM massive) (*not hollow*)
□ solid gold l'or massif
2 solide (FEM solide)
□ a solid wall un mur solide
■ **for three hours solid** pendant trois heures entières

solo NOUN
le solo *masc*
□ a guitar solo un solo de guitare

solution NOUN
la solution *fem*

to **solve** VERB
résoudre [70]

some ADJECTIVE, PRONOUN

> When 'some' means 'a certain amount of', use **du**, **de la** or **des** according to the gender of the French noun that follows it. **du** and **de la** become **de l'** when they are followed by a noun starting with a vowel.

1 du
□ Would you like some bread? Voulez-vous du pain ?
de la
□ Would you like some lemonade? Voulez-vous de la limonade ?
de l'
□ Would you like some water? Voulez-vous de l'eau ?
des
□ I've got some crisps. J'ai des chips.
■ **Some people say that ...** Il y a des gens qui disent que ...
■ **some day** un de ces jours
■ **some day next week** un jour la semaine prochaine
2 certains (FEM certaines) (*some but not all*)
□ Are these mushrooms poisonous? — Only some. Est-ce que ces champignons sont vénéneux ? — Certains le sont.
■ **some of them** quelques-uns □ I only sold some of them. J'en ai seulement vendu quelques-uns.
■ **I only took some of it.** J'en ai seulement pris un peu.

■ **I'm going to buy some sweets. Do you want some too?** Je vais acheter des bonbons. Tu en veux aussi ?
■ **Would you like some coffee? — No thanks, I've got some.** Tu veux du café ? — Non merci, j'en ai déjà.

somebody PRONOUN
quelqu'un
□ Somebody stole my purse. Quelqu'un a volé mon porte-monnaie.

somehow ADVERB
■ **I'll do it somehow.** Je trouverai le moyen de le faire.
■ **Somehow I don't think he believed me.** Quelque chose me dit qu'il ne m'a pas cru.

someone PRONOUN
quelqu'un
□ Someone stole my purse. Quelqu'un a volé mon porte-monnaie.

someplace ADVERB (US)
quelque part

something PRONOUN
quelque chose
□ something special quelque chose de spécial
□ Wear something warm. Mets quelque chose de chaud. □ That's really something! C'est vraiment quelque chose ! □ It cost £100, or something like that. Ça a coûté cent livres, ou quelque chose comme ça. □ His name is Pierre or something. Il s'appelle Pierre, ou quelque chose comme ça.

sometime ADVERB
un de ces jours
□ You must come and see us sometime. Passez donc nous voir un de ces jours.
■ **sometime last month** dans le courant du mois dernier

sometimes ADVERB
quelquefois
□ Sometimes I think she hates me. Quelquefois j'ai l'impression qu'elle me déteste.

somewhere ADVERB
quelque part
□ I left my keys somewhere. J'ai laissé mes clés quelque part. □ I'd like to go on holiday somewhere sunny. J'aimerais aller en vacances, quelque part où il y a du soleil.

son NOUN
le fils *masc*

song NOUN
la chanson *fem*

son-in-law NOUN
le gendre *masc*

soon ADVERB
bientôt
□ very soon très bientôt

Core vocabulary is shaded.

S

559

■ **soon afterwards** peu après
■ **as soon as possible** aussitôt que possible

sooner ADVERB
plus tôt
□ Can't you come a bit sooner? Tu ne peux pas venir un peu plus tôt ?
■ **sooner or later** tôt ou tard

soot NOUN
la suie _fem_

soppy ADJECTIVE
sentimental (FEM sentimentale, MASC PL sentimentaux)

soprano NOUN
le/la soprano _masc/fem_ (_singer_)

sorcerer NOUN
le sorcier _masc_

sore ADJECTIVE
▷ _see also_ **sore** NOUN
■ **My feet are sore.** J'ai mal aux pieds.
■ **It's sore.** Ça fait mal.
■ **That's a sore point.** C'est un point sensible.

sore NOUN
▷ _see also_ **sore** ADJECTIVE
la plaie _fem_

sorry ADJECTIVE
désolé (FEM désolée)
□ I'm really sorry. Je suis vraiment désolé. □ I'm sorry, I haven't got any change. Je suis désolé, je n'ai pas de monnaie. □ I'm sorry I'm late. Je suis désolé d'être en retard.
■ **sorry!** pardon !
■ **sorry?** pardon ?
■ **I'm sorry about the noise.** Je m'excuse pour le bruit.
■ **You'll be sorry!** Tu le regretteras !
■ **to feel sorry for somebody** plaindre [17] quelqu'un

sort NOUN
la sorte _fem_
□ What sort of bike have you got? Quelle sorte de vélo as-tu ?

to sort out VERB
1 ranger [45] (_objects_)
2 résoudre [70] (_problems_)

so-so ADVERB
comme ci comme ça
□ How are you feeling? — So-so. Comment est-ce que tu te sens ? — Comme ci comme ça.

sought VERB ▷ _see_ **seek** VERB

soul NOUN
1 l'âme _fem_ (_spirit_)
2 la soul _fem_ (_music_)

sound NOUN
▷ _see also_ **sound** VERB, ADJECTIVE, ADVERB
1 le bruit _masc_ (_noise_)
□ Don't make a sound! Pas un bruit ! □ the sound of footsteps des bruits de pas

2 le son _masc_
□ Can I turn the sound down? Je peux baisser le son ?

to sound VERB
▷ _see also_ **sound** NOUN, ADJECTIVE, ADVERB
■ **That sounds interesting.** Ça a l'air intéressant.
■ **It sounds as if she's doing well at school.** Elle a l'air de bien travailler à l'école.
■ **That sounds like a good idea.** C'est une bonne idée.

sound ADJECTIVE, ADVERB
▷ _see also_ **sound** NOUN, VERB
bon (FEM bonne)
□ That's sound advice. C'est un bon conseil.
■ **sound asleep** profondément endormi

soundtrack NOUN
la bande sonore _fem_

soup NOUN
la soupe _fem_
□ vegetable soup la soupe aux légumes

sour ADJECTIVE
aigre (FEM aigre)

south ADJECTIVE, ADVERB
▷ _see also_ **south** NOUN
1 sud (FEM+PL sud)
□ the south coast la côte sud
2 vers le sud
□ We were travelling south. Nous allions vers le sud.
■ **south of** au sud de □ It's south of London. C'est au sud de Londres.

south NOUN
▷ _see also_ **south** ADJECTIVE, ADVERB
le sud _masc_
□ in the south dans le sud □ the South of France le sud de la France

South Africa NOUN
l'Afrique du Sud _fem_
■ **in South Africa** en Afrique du Sud
■ **to South Africa** en Afrique du Sud

South America NOUN
l'Amérique du Sud _fem_
■ **in South America** en Amérique du Sud
■ **to South America** en Amérique du Sud

South American NOUN
▷ _see also_ **South American** ADJECTIVE
le Sud-Américain _masc_
la Sud-Américaine _fem_

South American ADJECTIVE
▷ _see also_ **South American** NOUN
sud-américain (FEM sud-américaine)

southbound ADJECTIVE
■ **The southbound carriageway is blocked.** La route est bloquée en direction du sud.
■ **We were going southbound on the M1.** Nous étions sur la M1 en direction du sud.

southeast NOUN

le sud-est *masc*

◻ southeast England le sud-est de l'Angleterre

southern ADJECTIVE

■ **the southern part of the island** la partie sud de l'île

■ **Southern England** le sud de l'Angleterre

South Pole NOUN

le pôle Sud *masc*

South Wales NOUN

le sud du pays de Galles *masc*

southwest NOUN

le sud-ouest *masc*

◻ southwest France le sud-ouest de la France

souvenir NOUN

le souvenir *masc*

■ **a souvenir shop** une boutique de souvenirs

soya NOUN

le soja *masc*

soy sauce NOUN

la sauce de soja *fem*

space NOUN

1 la place *fem*

◻ There isn't enough space. Il n'y a pas suffisamment de place.

■ **a parking space** une place de parking

2 l'espace *masc* (*universe, gap*)

◻ to go into space aller dans l'espace ◻ Leave a space after your answer. Laissez un espace après votre réponse.

■ **a space shuttle** une navette spatiale

spacecraft NOUN

l'engin spatial *masc*

spade NOUN

la pelle *fem*

■ **spades** (*in cards*) le pique *sing* ◻ the ace of spades l'as de pique

Spain NOUN

l'Espagne *fem*

■ **in Spain** en Espagne

■ **to Spain** en Espagne

Spaniard NOUN

l'Espagnol *masc*

l'Espagnole *fem*

spaniel NOUN

l'épagneul *masc*

Spanish NOUN

▷ *see also* **Spanish** ADJECTIVE

l'espagnol *masc* (*language*)

■ **the Spanish** les Espagnols

Spanish ADJECTIVE

▷ *see also* **Spanish** NOUN

espagnol (FEM espagnole)

◻ She's Spanish. Elle est espagnole.

to spank VERB

■ **to spank somebody** donner [28] une fessée à quelqu'un

spanner NOUN

la clé anglaise *fem*

spare ADJECTIVE

▷ *see also* **spare** VERB, NOUN

de rechange

◻ spare batteries des piles de rechange ◻ a spare part une pièce de rechange

■ **a spare room** une chambre d'amis

■ **spare time** le temps libre ◻ What do you do in your spare time? Qu'est-ce que tu fais pendant ton temps libre ?

■ **spare wheel** une roue de secours

to spare VERB

▷ *see also* **spare** ADJECTIVE, NOUN

■ **Can you spare a moment?** Vous pouvez m'accorder un instant ?

■ **I can't spare the time.** Je n'ai pas le temps.

■ **There's no room to spare.** Il n'y a plus de place.

■ **We arrived with time to spare.** Nous sommes arrivés en avance.

spare NOUN

▷ *see also* **spare** ADJECTIVE, VERB

■ **a spare** un autre ◻ I've lost my key. — Have you got a spare? J'ai perdu ma clé. — Tu en as une autre ?

sparkling ADJECTIVE

pétillant (FEM pétillante) (*water*)

■ **sparkling wine** le mousseux

sparrow NOUN

le moineau *masc* (PL les moineaux)

spat VERB ▷ *see* spit

to speak VERB

parler [28]

◻ Do you speak English? Est-ce que vous parlez anglais ?

■ **to speak to somebody** parler [28] à quelqu'un ◻ Have you spoken to him? Tu lui as parlé ? ◻ She spoke to him about it. Elle lui en a parlé.

to speak up VERB

parler [28] plus fort

◻ Speak up, we can't hear you. Parle plus fort, nous ne t'entendons pas.

speaker NOUN

1 l'enceinte *fem* (*loudspeaker*)

2 l'intervenant *masc*

l'intervenante *fem* (*in debate*)

special ADJECTIVE

spécial (FEM spéciale, MASC PL spéciaux)

specialist NOUN

le/la spécialiste *masc/fem*

speciality NOUN

la spécialité *fem*

to specialize VERB

se spécialiser [28]

◻ We specialize in skiing equipment. Nous nous spécialisons dans les articles de ski.

S

specially ADVERB

spécialement

□ It's specially designed for teenagers. C'est spécialement conçu pour les adolescents.

■ **not specially** pas spécialement □ Do you like volleyball? — Not specially. Tu aimes le volley ? — Pas spécialement.

species NOUN

l'espèce *fem*

specific ADJECTIVE

1 particulier (FEM particulière) (*particular*)

□ certain specific issues certains problèmes particuliers

2 précis (FEM précise) (*precise*)

□ Could you be more specific? Est-ce que vous pourriez être plus précis ?

specifically ADVERB

1 spécialement

□ It's specifically designed for teenagers. C'est spécialement conçu pour les adolescents.

2 particulièrement

□ in Britain, or more specifically in England en Grande-Bretagne, ou plus particulièrement en Angleterre

■ **I specifically said that ...** J'ai clairement dit que ...

specs, spectacles PL NOUN

les lunettes *fem pl*

spectacular ADJECTIVE

spectaculaire (FEM spectaculaire)

spectator NOUN

le spectateur *masc*

la spectatrice *fem*

speech NOUN

le discours *masc*

□ to make a speech faire un discours

speechless ADJECTIVE

muet (FEM muette)

□ speechless with admiration muet d'admiration

■ **I was speechless.** Je suis resté sans voix.

speed NOUN

la vitesse *fem*

□ a ten-speed bike un vélo à dix vitesses □ at top speed à toute vitesse

to **speed up** VERB

accélérer [34]

speedboat NOUN

la vedette *fem*

speeding NOUN

l'excès de vitesse *masc*

□ He was fined for speeding. Il a reçu une contravention pour excès de vitesse.

speed limit NOUN

la limitation de vitesse *fem*

■ **to break the speed limit** faire [36] un excès de vitesse

speedometer NOUN

le compteur *masc*

to **spell** VERB

▷ see also **spell** NOUN

1 écrire [30] (*in writing*)

□ How do you spell that? Comment est-ce que ça s'écrit ?

2 épeler [4] (*out loud*)

□ Can you spell that please? Est-ce que vous pouvez épeler, s'il vous plaît ?

■ **I can't spell.** Je fais des fautes d'orthographe.

spell NOUN

▷ see also **spell** VERB

■ **to cast a spell on somebody** jeter [41] un sort à quelqu'un

■ **to be under somebody's spell** être [35] sous le charme de quelqu'un

spelling NOUN

l'orthographe *fem*

□ My spelling is terrible. Je fais beaucoup de fautes d'orthographe.

■ **a spelling mistake** une faute d'orthographe

spelt VERB ▷ see **spell**

to **spend** VERB

1 dépenser [28] (*money*)

2 passer [58] (*time*)

□ He spent a month in Germany. Il a passé un mois en Allemagne.

spice NOUN

l'épice *fem*

spicy ADJECTIVE

épicé (FEM épicée)

spider NOUN

l'araignée *fem*

to **spill** VERB

1 renverser [28] (*tip over*)

□ He spilled his coffee over his trousers. Il a renversé son café sur son pantalon.

2 se répandre [9] (*get spilt*)

□ The soup spilled all over the table. La soupe s'est répandue sur la table.

spinach NOUN

les épinards *masc pl*

spin drier NOUN

l'essoreuse *fem*

spine NOUN

la colonne vertébrale *fem*

spire NOUN

la flèche *fem*

spirit NOUN

1 le courage *masc* (*courage*)

■ **to be in good spirits** être [35] de bonne humeur

2 l'énergie *fem* (*energy*)

spirits PL NOUN
les alcools forts *masc pl*
□ I don't drink spirits. Je ne bois pas d'alcools forts.

spiritual ADJECTIVE
religieux (FEM religieuse)
□ the spiritual leader of Tibet le chef religieux du Tibet

spit NOUN
▷ *see also* **spit** VERB
la salive *fem*

to **spit** VERB
▷ *see also* **spit** NOUN
cracher [28]
■ **to spit something out** cracher [28] quelque chose

spite NOUN
▷ *see also* **spite** VERB
■ **in spite of** malgré
■ **out of spite** par méchanceté

to **spite** VERB
▷ *see also* **spite** NOUN
contrarier [19]
□ He just did it to spite me. Il a fait ça juste pour me contrarier.

spiteful ADJECTIVE
1 méchant (FEM méchante) (*action*)
2 rancunier (FEM rancunière) (*person*)

to **splash** VERB
▷ *see also* **splash** NOUN
éclabousser [28]
□ Careful! Don't splash me! Attention ! Ne m'éclabousse pas !

splash NOUN
▷ *see also* **splash** VERB
le plouf *masc*
□ I heard a splash. J'ai entendu un plouf.
■ **a splash of colour** une touche de couleur

splendid ADJECTIVE
splendide (FEM splendide)

splint NOUN
l'attelle *fem*

splinter NOUN
l'écharde *fem*

to **split** VERB
1 fendre [88] (*break apart*)
□ He split the wood with an axe. Il a fendu le bois avec une hache.
2 se fendre [88]
□ The ship hit a rock and split in two. Le bateau a percuté un rocher et s'est fendu en deux.
3 partager [45] (*divide up*)
□ They decided to split the profits. Ils ont décidé de partager les bénéfices.

to **split up** VERB
1 rompre [75] (*couple*)

□ My parents have split up. Mes parents ont rompu.
2 se disperser [28] (*group*)

to **spoil** VERB
1 abîmer [28] (*object*)
2 gâcher [28] (*occasion*)
3 gâter [28] (*child*)

spoiled ADJECTIVE
gâté (FEM gâtée)
□ a spoiled child un enfant gâté

spoilsport NOUN
le/la trouble-fête *masc/fem*

spoilt ADJECTIVE
gâté (FEM gâtée)
□ a spoilt child un enfant gâté

spoilt VERB ▷ *see* **spoil**

spoke VERB ▷ *see* **speak**

spoke NOUN
le rayon *masc* (*of wheel*)

spoken VERB ▷ *see* **speak**
■ **spoken French** le français parlé

spokesman NOUN
le porte-parole *masc* (PL les porte-parole)

spokesperson NOUN
le porte-parole *masc* (PL les porte-parole)

spokeswoman NOUN
le porte-parole *masc* (PL les porte-parole)

sponge NOUN
l'éponge *fem*
■ **a sponge cake** un biscuit de Savoie

sponsor NOUN
▷ *see also* **sponsor** VERB
1 le donateur *masc*
la donatrice *fem* (*charity donor*)
2 le sponsor *masc* (*of event, sports team*)

to **sponsor** VERB
▷ *see also* **sponsor** NOUN
parrainer [28]
□ The festival was sponsored by ... Le festival a été parrainé par ...

spontaneous ADJECTIVE
spontané (FEM spontanée)

spooky ADJECTIVE
1 sinistre (FEM sinistre) (*eerie*)
■ **a spooky story** une histoire qui fait froid dans le dos
2 étrange (FEM étrange) (*strange*)
□ a spooky coincidence une étrange coïncidence

spoon NOUN
la cuiller *fem*

spoonful NOUN
la cuillerée *fem*
□ two spoonfuls of sugar deux cuillerées de sucre

sport NOUN
le sport *masc*

S

□ What's your favourite sport? Quel est ton sport préféré ?

■ **a sports bag** un sac de sport

■ **a sports car** une voiture de sport

sportsman NOUN
le sportif *masc*

sportsperson NOUN
le sportif *masc*
la sportive *fem*

sportswear NOUN
les vêtements de sport *masc pl*

sportswoman NOUN
la sportive *fem*

sporty ADJECTIVE
sportif (FEM sportive)
□ I'm not very sporty. Je ne suis pas très sportif.

spot NOUN
▷ *see also* **spot** VERB

1 la tache *fem* (*mark*)
□ There's a spot on your shirt. Il y a une tache sur ta chemise.

2 le pois *masc* (*in pattern*)
□ a red dress with white spots une robe rouge à pois blancs

3 le bouton *masc* (*pimple*)
□ He's covered in spots. Il est couvert de boutons.

4 le coin *masc* (*place*)
□ It's a lovely spot for a picnic. C'est un coin agréable pour un pique-nique.

■ **on the spot** **1** (*immediately*) sur-le-champ
□ They gave her the job on the spot. Ils lui ont offert le poste sur-le-champ. **2** (*at the same place*) sur place □ Luckily they were able to repair the car on the spot. Heureusement ils ont pu réparer la voiture sur place.

to **spot** VERB
▷ *see also* **spot** NOUN
repérer [34]
□ I spotted a mistake. J'ai repéré une faute.

spotless ADJECTIVE
immaculé (FEM immaculée)

spotlight NOUN
le projecteur *masc*
□ The universities have been in the spotlight recently. Les universités ont été sous le feu des projecteurs ces derniers temps.

spotty ADJECTIVE
boutonneux (FEM boutonneuse) (*pimply*)

spouse NOUN
l'époux *masc*
l'épouse *fem*

to **sprain** VERB
▷ *see also* **sprain** NOUN
■ **to sprain one's ankle** se faire [36] une entorse à la cheville

sprain NOUN
▷ *see also* **sprain** VERB
l'entorse *fem*
□ It's just a sprain. C'est juste une entorse.

spray NOUN
▷ *see also* **spray** VERB
la bombe *fem* (*spray can*)

to **spray** VERB
▷ *see also* **spray** NOUN

1 vaporiser [28]
□ to spray perfume on one's wrist se vaporiser du parfum sur le poignet

2 traiter [28] (*crops*)

3 peindre [60] avec une bombe (*graffiti*)
□ Somebody had sprayed graffiti on the wall. Quelqu'un avait peint des graffiti avec une bombe sur le mur.

spread NOUN
▷ *see also* **spread** VERB
■ **cheese spread** le fromage à tartiner
■ **chocolate spread** le chocolat à tartiner

to **spread** VERB
▷ *see also* **spread** NOUN

1 étaler [28]
□ to spread butter on a slice of bread étaler du beurre sur une tranche de pain

2 se propager [45] (*disease, news*)
□ The news spread rapidly. La nouvelle s'est propagée rapidement.

to **spread out** VERB
se disperser [28] (*people*)
□ The soldiers spread out across the field. Les soldats se sont dispersés dans le champ.

spreadsheet NOUN
le tableur *masc* (*computer program*)

spring NOUN

1 le printemps *masc* (*season*)
■ **in spring** au printemps

2 le ressort *masc* (*metal coil*)

3 la source *fem* (*water hole*)

spring-cleaning NOUN
le grand nettoyage de printemps *masc*

springtime NOUN
le printemps *masc*
■ **in springtime** au printemps

sprinkler NOUN
l'arroseur *masc* (*for lawn*)

sprint NOUN
▷ *see also* **sprint** VERB
le sprint *masc*

to **sprint** VERB
▷ *see also* **sprint** NOUN
courir [16] à toute vitesse
□ She sprinted for the bus. Elle a couru à toute vitesse pour attraper le bus.

S

sprinter NOUN
le sprinteur *masc*
la sprinteuse *fem*

sprouts PL NOUN
■ **Brussels sprouts** les choux de Bruxelles *masc pl*

spy NOUN
▷ *see also* **spy** VERB
l'espion *masc*
l'espionne *fem*

to **spy** VERB
▷ *see also* **spy** NOUN
■ **to spy on somebody** espionner [28]
quelqu'un

spying NOUN
l'espionnage *masc*

to **squabble** VERB
se chamailler [28]
□ Stop squabbling! Arrêtez de vous chamailler !

square NOUN
▷ *see also* **square** ADJECTIVE
1 le carré *masc*
□ a square and a triangle un carré et un triangle
2 la place *fem*
□ the town square la place de l'hôtel de ville

square ADJECTIVE
▷ *see also* **square** NOUN
carré (FEM carrée)
□ two square metres deux mètres carrés
■ **It's two metres square.** Ça fait deux mètres
sur deux.

squash NOUN
▷ *see also* **squash** VERB
le squash *masc* (*sport*)
□ I play squash. Je joue au squash.
■ **a squash court** un court de squash
■ **a squash racket** une raquette de squash
■ **orange squash** l'orangeade *fem*
■ **lemon squash** la citronnade
■ **mint squash** le sirop de menthe

to **squash** VERB
▷ *see also* **squash** NOUN
écraser [28]
□ You're squashing me. Tu m'écrases.

to **squeak** VERB
1 pousser [28] un petit cri (*mouse, child*)
2 grincer [12] (*creak*)

to **squeeze** VERB
1 presser [28] (*fruit, toothpaste*)
2 serrer [28] (*hand, arm*)

to **squeeze in** VERB
1 trouver [28] une petite place
□ It was a tiny car, but we managed to squeeze
in. La voiture était toute petite, mais nous avons
réussi à trouver une petite place.
2 caser [28] (*for appointment*)
□ I can squeeze you in at two o'clock. Je peux
vous caser à deux heures.

to **squint** VERB
▷ *see also* **squint** NOUN
loucher [28]

squint NOUN
▷ *see also* **squint** VERB
■ **He has a squint.** Il louche.

squirrel NOUN
l'écureuil *masc*

to **stab** VERB
poignarder [28]

stable NOUN
▷ *see also* **stable** ADJECTIVE
l'écurie *fem*

stable ADJECTIVE
▷ *see also* **stable** NOUN
stable (FEM stable)
□ a stable relationship une relation stable

stack NOUN
la pile *fem*
□ a stack of books une pile de livres

stadium NOUN
le stade *masc*

staff NOUN
1 le personnel *masc* (*in company*)
2 les professeurs *masc pl* (*in school*)

staffroom NOUN
la salle des professeurs *fem*

stage NOUN
1 la scène *fem* (*in plays*)
2 l'estrade *fem* (*for speeches, lectures*)
■ **at this stage   1** à ce stade □ at this stage in
the negotiations à ce stade des négociations
2 pour l'instant □ At this stage, we can't be sure.
Pour l'instant, nous n'avons aucune certitude.
■ **to do something in stages** faire [36]
quelque chose étape par étape

BE CAREFUL!
Do not translate **stage** by the French word
stage.

to **stagger** VERB
chanceler [4]

stain NOUN
▷ *see also* **stain** VERB
la tache *fem*

to **stain** VERB
▷ *see also* **stain** NOUN
tacher [28]

stainless steel NOUN
l'inox *masc*

stain remover NOUN
le détachant *masc*

stair NOUN
la marche *fem* (*step*)

staircase NOUN
l'escalier *masc*

stairs PL NOUN
l'escalier *masc sing*

stale ADJECTIVE
rassis (FEM rassie) (*bread*)

stalemate NOUN
le pat *masc* (*in chess*)

stall NOUN
le stand *masc*
□ He's got a market stall. Il a un stand au marché.
■ **the stalls** (*in theatre*) l'orchestre *masc sing*

stamina NOUN
l'endurance *fem*

stammer NOUN
le bégaiement *masc*
■ **He's got a stammer.** Il bégaie.

to **stamp** VERB
▷ *see also* **stamp** NOUN
affranchir [38] (*letter*)
■ **to stamp one's foot** taper [28] du pied

stamp NOUN
▷ *see also* **stamp** VERB
1 le timbre *masc*
□ My grandad's hobby is stamp collecting. Mon grand-père collectionne les timbres.
■ **a stamp album** un album de timbres
■ **a stamp collection** une collection de timbres
2 le tampon *masc* (*rubber stamp*)

stamped ADJECTIVE
affranchi (FEM affranchie)
□ The letter wasn't stamped. La lettre n'était pas affranchie.
■ **Enclose a stamped addressed envelope.**
Joindre une enveloppe affranchie à vos nom et adresse.

to **stand** VERB
1 être [35] debout (*be standing*)
□ He was standing by the door. Il était debout à la porte.
2 se lever [43] (*stand up*)
3 supporter [28] (*tolerate, withstand*)
□ I can't stand all this noise. Je ne supporte pas tout ce bruit.

to **stand for** VERB
1 être [35] l'abréviation de (*be short for*)
□ 'DM' stands for 'direct message'. « DM » est l'abréviation de « direct message ».
2 supporter [28] (*tolerate*)
□ I won't stand for it! Je ne supporterai pas ça !
■ **to stand in for somebody** remplacer [12] quelqu'un

to **stand out** VERB
se distinguer [28]
□ None of the candidates really stood out. Aucun des candidats ne s'est vraiment distingué.
■ **She really stands out in that orange coat.**
Tout le monde la remarque avec ce manteau orange.

to **stand up** VERB
se lever [43] (*get up*)
■ **to stand up for** défendre [88] □ Stand up for your rights! Défendez vos droits !

standard ADJECTIVE
▷ *see also* **standard** NOUN
1 courant (FEM courante)
□ standard French le français courant
2 ordinaire (FEM ordinaire) (*equipment*)
■ **the standard procedure** la procédure normale

standard NOUN
▷ *see also* **standard** ADJECTIVE
le niveau *masc* (PL les niveaux)
□ The standard is very high. Le niveau est très haut.
■ **the standard of living** le niveau de vie
■ **She's got high standards.** Elle est très exigeante.

stand-by ticket NOUN
le billet stand-by *masc*

standpoint NOUN
le point de vue *masc*

stands PL NOUN
la tribune *fem sing* (*at sports ground*)

stank VERB ▷ *see* **stink**

staple NOUN
▷ *see also* **staple** VERB
l'agrafe *fem*

to **staple** VERB
▷ *see also* **staple** NOUN
agrafer [28]

stapler NOUN
l'agrafeuse *fem*

star NOUN
▷ *see also* **star** VERB
1 l'étoile *fem* (*in sky*)
2 la vedette *fem* (*celebrity*)
□ He's a TV star. C'est une vedette de la télé.
■ **the stars** (*horoscope*) l'horoscope *masc*

to **star** VERB
▷ *see also* **star** NOUN
être [35] la vedette
□ to star in a film être la vedette d'un film
■ **The film stars Kristen Stewart.** Le film a pour vedette Kristen Stewart.
■ **... starring Johnny Depp** ... avec Johnny Depp

to **stare** VERB
■ **to stare at something** fixer [28] quelque chose

stark ADVERB
■ **stark naked** complètement nu

start NOUN
▷ *see also* **start** VERB

1 le début *masc*
□ It's not much, but it's a start. Ce n'est pas grand-chose, mais c'est un début.
■ **Shall we make a start on the washing-up?**
On commence à faire la vaisselle ?
2 le départ *masc* (*of race*)

to **start** VERB
▷ *see also* **start** NOUN
1 commencer [12]
□ What time does it start? À quelle heure est-ce que ça commence ?
■ **to start doing something** commencer [12] à faire quelque chose □ I started learning Chinese three years ago. J'ai commencé à apprendre le chinois il y a trois ans.
2 créer [18] (*organization*)
□ He wants to start his own business. Il veut créer sa propre entreprise.
3 organiser [28] (*campaign*)
□ She started a campaign against drugs. Elle a organisé une campagne contre la drogue.
4 démarrer [28] (*car*)
□ He couldn't start the car. Il n'a pas réussi à démarrer la voiture. □ The car wouldn't start. La voiture ne voulait pas démarrer.

to **start off** VERB
commencer [12]
□ Things started off badly. Les choses ont mal commencé. □ Let's start off with a reminder of what we did last week. Commençons par un rappel de ce que nous avons fait la semaine dernière. □ She started off by thanking everyone. Elle a commencé par remercier tout le monde.

starter NOUN
l'entrée *fem* (*first course*)

to **starve** VERB
mourir [51] de faim
□ People were literally starving. Les gens mouraient littéralement de faim.
■ **I'm starving!** Je meurs de faim !

state NOUN
▷ *see also* **state** VERB
l'état *masc*
■ **He was in a real state.** Il était dans tous ses états.
■ **the state** (*government*) l'État
■ **the States** (*USA*) les États-Unis *masc pl*

to **state** VERB
▷ *see also* **state** NOUN
1 déclarer [28] (*say*)
□ The prime minister stated that... Le Premier ministre a déclaré que...
2 donner [28] (*give*)
□ Please state your name and address. Veuillez donner vos nom et adresse. □ He stated his opinion. Il a donné son avis.

stately home NOUN
le château *masc* (PL les châteaux)

statement NOUN
la déclaration *fem*

station NOUN
la gare *fem* (*railway*)
■ **the bus station** la gare routière
■ **a police station** un poste de police
■ **a radio station** une station de radio

stationer's NOUN
la papeterie *fem*

station wagon NOUN (US)
le break *masc*

statue NOUN
la statue *fem*

status NOUN
le statut *masc*
□ She's changed her status. Elle a changé son statut.

stay NOUN
▷ *see also* **stay** VERB
le séjour *masc*
□ my stay in Switzerland mon séjour en Suisse

to **stay** VERB
▷ *see also* **stay** NOUN
1 rester [71⁵] (*remain*)
□ Stay here! Reste ici !
2 loger [45] (*spend the night*)
□ to stay with friends loger chez des amis
□ Where are you staying? Où est-ce que vous logez ?
■ **to stay the night** passer [58] la nuit
■ **We stayed in Belgium for a few days.**
Nous avons passé quelques jours en Belgique.

to **stay in** VERB
rester [71⁵] à la maison (*not go out*)

to **stay up** VERB
rester [71⁵] debout
□ We stayed up till midnight. Nous sommes restés debout jusqu'à minuit.

steady ADJECTIVE
1 régulier (FEM régulière)
□ steady progress des progrès réguliers
2 stable (FEM stable)
□ a steady job un emploi stable
3 ferme (FEM ferme) (*voice, hand*)
4 calme (FEM calme) (*person*)
■ **a steady boyfriend** un copain
■ **a steady girlfriend** une copine

steak NOUN
le steak *masc* (*beef*)
□ steak and chips un steak frites

to **steal** VERB
voler [28]

steam NOUN
la vapeur *fem*
□ a steam engine une locomotive à vapeur

steel NOUN
l'acier *masc*
□ a steel door une porte en acier

steep ADJECTIVE
raide (FEM raide) (*slope*)

steeple NOUN
le clocher *masc*

steering wheel NOUN
le volant *masc*

step NOUN
▷ see also **step** VERB
1 le pas *masc* (*pace*)
□ He took a step forward. Il a fait un pas en avant.
2 la marche *fem* (*stair*)
□ She tripped over the step. Elle a trébuché sur la marche.

to **step** VERB
▷ see also **step** NOUN
■ to step aside faire [36] un pas de côté
■ to step back faire [36] un pas en arrière

stepbrother NOUN
le demi-frère *masc*

stepdaughter NOUN
la belle-fille *fem* (PL les belles-filles)

stepfather NOUN
le beau-père *masc* (PL les beaux-pères)

stepladder NOUN
l'escabeau *masc* (PL les escabeaux)

stepmother NOUN
la belle-mère *fem* (PL les belles-mères)

stepsister NOUN
la demi-sœur *fem*

stepson NOUN
le beau-fils *masc* (PL les beaux-fils)

stereo NOUN
la chaîne *fem* (PL les chaînes)

sterling ADJECTIVE
■ £500 sterling cinq cents livres sterling

stew NOUN
le ragoût *masc*

steward NOUN
le steward *masc*

stewardess NOUN
l'hôtesse de l'air *fem*

stick NOUN
▷ see also **stick** VERB
1 le bâton *masc*
2 la canne *fem* (*walking stick*)

to **stick** VERB
▷ see also **stick** NOUN
coller [28] (*with adhesive*)
□ Stick the stamps on the envelope. Collez les timbres sur l'enveloppe.

to **stick out** VERB
sortir [79] (*project*)
□ A pen was sticking out of his pocket. Un stylo sortait de sa poche.
■ **She stuck out her tongue.** Elle a tiré la langue.

sticker NOUN
l'autocollant *masc*

stick insect NOUN
le phasme *masc*

sticky ADJECTIVE
1 poisseux (FEM poisseuse)
□ to have sticky hands avoir les mains poisseuses
2 adhésif (FEM adhésive)
□ a sticky label une étiquette adhésive

stiff ADJECTIVE, ADVERB
rigide (FEM rigide) (*rigid*)
■ to have a stiff neck avoir [8] un torticolis
■ to feel stiff avoir [8] des courbatures
■ to be bored stiff s'ennuyer [53] à mourir
■ to be frozen stiff être [35] mort de froid
■ to be scared stiff être [35] mort de peur

still ADVERB
▷ see also **still** ADJECTIVE
1 encore
□ I still haven't finished. Je n'ai pas encore fini.
□ Are you still in bed? Tu es encore au lit ?
■ better still encore mieux
2 quand même (*even so*)
□ We lost, but it was still a good match. On a perdu, mais c'était quand même un bon match.
3 enfin (*after all*)
□ Still, it's the thought that counts. Enfin, c'est l'intention qui compte.

still ADJECTIVE
▷ see also **still** ADVERB
■ Keep still! Ne bouge pas !
■ Sit still! Reste tranquille !

sting NOUN
▷ see also **sting** VERB
la piqûre *fem*
□ a bee sting une piqûre d'abeille

to **sting** VERB
▷ see also **sting** NOUN
piquer [28]
□ I've been stung. J'ai été piqué.

stingy ADJECTIVE
pingre (FEM pingre)

to **stink** VERB
▷ see also **stink** NOUN
puer [28]
□ It stinks! Ça pue !

stink NOUN
▷ see also **stink** VERB
la puanteur *fem*

to stir VERB
remuer [28]

to stitch VERB
▷ *see also* **stitch** NOUN
coudre [15] (*cloth*)

stitch NOUN
▷ *see also* **stitch** VERB
1 le point *masc* (*in sewing*)
2 le point de suture *masc* (*in wound*)
□ I had five stitches. J'ai eu cinq points de suture.

stock NOUN
▷ *see also* **stock** VERB
1 la réserve *fem* (*supply*)
2 le stock *masc* (*in shop*)
□ in stock en stock
■ **out of stock** épuisé
3 le bouillon *masc*
□ chicken stock du bouillon de volaille

to stock VERB
▷ *see also* **stock** NOUN
avoir [8] (*have in stock*)
□ Do you stock board games? Vous avez des jeux de société ?

to stock up VERB
s'approvisionner [28]
□ to stock up with something s'approvisionner en quelque chose

stock cube NOUN
le cube de bouillon *masc*

stocking NOUN
le bas *masc*

stole, stolen VERB ▷ *see* **steal**

stomach NOUN
l'estomac *masc*
□ to have an upset stomach avoir l'estomac barbouillé

stomachache NOUN
■ **to have stomachache** avoir [8] mal au ventre

stone NOUN
1 la pierre *fem* (*rock*)
□ a stone wall un mur en pierre
2 le noyau *masc* (PL les noyaux) (*in fruit*)
□ a peach stone un noyau de pêche

> **DID YOU KNOW…?**
> In France, weight is expressed in kilos. A stone is about 6.3 kg.

■ **I weigh eight stone.** Je pèse cinquante kilos.

stood VERB ▷ *see* **stand**

stool NOUN
le tabouret *masc*

to stop VERB
▷ *see also* **stop** NOUN
1 arrêter [28]
□ a campaign to stop whaling une campagne pour arrêter la chasse à la baleine

2 s'arrêter [28]
□ The bus doesn't stop there. Le bus ne s'arrête pas là. □ I think the rain's going to stop. Je pense qu'il va s'arrêter de pleuvoir.
■ **to stop doing something** arrêter [28] de faire quelque chose □ to stop smoking arrêter de fumer
■ **to stop somebody doing something** empêcher [28] quelqu'un de faire quelque chose
■ **Stop!** Stop !

stop NOUN
▷ *see also* **stop** VERB
l'arrêt *masc*
□ a bus stop un arrêt de bus
■ **This is my stop.** Je descends ici.

stopwatch NOUN
le chronomètre *masc*

store NOUN
▷ *see also* **store** VERB
1 le magasin *masc* (*shop*)
□ a furniture store un magasin de meubles
2 la réserve *fem* (*stock, storeroom*)

> **BE CAREFUL!**
> Do not translate **store** by the French word **store**.

to store VERB
▷ *see also* **store** NOUN
1 garder [28]
□ They store potatoes in the cellar. Ils gardent des pommes de terre dans la cave.
2 enregistrer [28] (*information*)

storey NOUN
l'étage *masc*
□ a three-storey building un immeuble à trois étages

storm NOUN
1 la tempête *fem* (*gale*)
2 l'orage *masc* (*thunderstorm*)

stormy ADJECTIVE
orageux (FEM orageuse)

story NOUN
l'histoire *fem*

stove NOUN
1 la cuisinière *fem* (*in kitchen*)
2 le réchaud *masc* (*camping stove*)

straight ADJECTIVE
1 droit (FEM droite)
□ a straight line une ligne droite
2 raide (FEM raide)
□ straight hair les cheveux raides
3 hétéro (FEM hétéro) (*heterosexual*)
■ **straight away** tout de suite
■ **straight on** tout droit

straighteners PL NOUN
le fer à lisser *masc sing*
■ **a pair of straighteners** un fer à lisser

S

straightforward - string

straightforward ADJECTIVE
simple (FEM simple)

strain NOUN
▷ see also **strain** VERB
le stress *masc*
■ **It was a strain.** C'était éprouvant.

to **strain** VERB
▷ see also **strain** NOUN
se faire [36] mal à
□ I strained my back. Je me suis fait mal au dos.
■ **to strain a muscle** se froisser [28] un muscle

strained ADJECTIVE
froissé (FEM froissée) (*muscle*)

stranded ADJECTIVE
■ **We were stranded.** Nous étions coincés.

strange ADJECTIVE
bizarre (FEM bizarre)
□ That's strange! C'est bizarre !

stranger NOUN
l'inconnu *masc*
l'inconnue *fem*
□ Don't talk to strangers. Ne parle pas aux inconnus.
■ **I'm a stranger here.** Je ne suis pas d'ici.

to **strangle** VERB
étrangler [28]

strap NOUN
1 la courroie *fem* (*of bag, camera, suitcase*)
2 la bretelle *fem* (*of bra, dress*)
3 la lanière *fem* (*on shoe*)
4 le bracelet *masc* (*of watch*)

straw NOUN
la paille *fem*
■ **That's the last straw!** Ça, c'est le comble !

strawberry NOUN
la fraise *fem*
□ strawberry jam la confiture de fraises □ a strawberry ice cream une glace à la fraise

stray NOUN
■ **a stray cat** un chat perdu

stream NOUN
le ruisseau *masc* (PL les ruisseaux)

to **stream** VERB
1 ruisseler [43] (*water*)
2 regarder [28] en streaming (*film, TV*)
□ You can stream the series in full. Tu peux regarder la série entière en streaming.
3 écouter [28] en streaming (*audio*)
□ You can stream music and podcasts on the app. On peut écouter de la musique et des podcasts en streaming sur cette appli.

street NOUN
la rue *fem*
□ in the street dans la rue

streetcar NOUN (US)
le tramway *masc*

streetlamp NOUN
le réverbère *masc*

street plan NOUN
le plan de la ville *masc*

streetwise ADJECTIVE
dégourdi (FEM dégourdie)

strength NOUN
la force *fem*

to **stress** VERB
▷ see also **stress** NOUN
souligner [28] (*emphasize*)

stress NOUN
▷ see also **stress** VERB
le stress *masc*

to **stretch** VERB
1 s'étirer [28] (*person, animal*)
□ The dog woke up and stretched. Le chien s'est réveillé et s'est étiré.
2 se détendre [88] (*get bigger*)
□ My jumper stretched when I washed it. Mon pull s'est détendu au lavage.
3 tendre [88] (*stretch out*)
□ They stretched a rope between two trees. Ils ont tendu une corde entre deux arbres.
■ **to stretch out one's arms** tendre [88] les bras

stretcher NOUN
le brancard *masc*

stretchy ADJECTIVE
élastique (FEM élastique)

strict ADJECTIVE
strict (FEM stricte)

strike NOUN
▷ see also **strike** VERB
la grève *fem*
■ **to be on strike** être [35] en grève
■ **to go on strike** faire [36] grève

to **strike** VERB
▷ see also **strike** NOUN
1 sonner [28] (*clock*)
□ The clock struck three. L'horloge a sonné trois heures.
2 faire [36] grève (*go on strike*)
3 frapper [28] (*hit*)
■ **to strike a match** frotter [28] une allumette

striker NOUN
1 le/la gréviste *masc/fem* (*person on strike*)
2 le buteur *masc* (*footballer*)

striking ADJECTIVE
1 en grève (*on strike*)
□ striking journalists les journalistes en grève
2 frappant (FEM frappante) (*noticeable*)

string NOUN
1 la ficelle *fem*
□ a piece of string un bout de ficelle

2 la corde *fem* (*of violin, guitar*)

to **strip** VERB
▷ *see also* **strip** NOUN
se déshabiller [28] (*get undressed*)

strip NOUN
▷ *see also* **strip** VERB
la bande *fem*
■ **a strip cartoon** une bande dessinée

stripe NOUN
la rayure *fem*

striped ADJECTIVE
à rayures
□ a striped skirt une jupe à rayures

stripy ADJECTIVE
rayé (FEM rayée)
□ a stripy shirt une chemise rayée

to **stroke** VERB
▷ *see also* **stroke** NOUN
caresser [28]

stroke NOUN
▷ *see also* **stroke** VERB
l'attaque *fem*
□ to have a stroke avoir une attaque

stroll NOUN
■ **to go for a stroll** aller [3¹] faire une petite
promenade

stroller NOUN (US)
le poussette *fem*

strong ADJECTIVE
1 fort (FEM forte)
□ She's very strong. Elle est très forte.
2 résistant (FEM résistante) (*material*)

strongly ADVERB
fortement
□ We recommend strongly that … Nous
recommandons fortement que …
■ **He smelt strongly of garlic.** Il sentait fort
l'ail.
■ **strongly built** solidement bâti
■ **I don't feel strongly about it.** Ça m'est égal.

struck VERB ▷ *see* **strike**

to **struggle** VERB
▷ *see also* **struggle** NOUN
se débattre [9] (*physically*)
□ He struggled, but he couldn't escape. Il s'est
débattu, mais il n'a pas pu s'échapper.
■ **to struggle to do something 1** (*fight*)
se battre [9] pour faire quelque chose □ He
struggled to get custody of his daughter. Il s'est
battu pour obtenir la garde de sa fille.
2 (*have difficulty*) avoir [8] du mal à faire quelque
chose □ She struggled to get the door open. Elle
a eu du mal à ouvrir la porte.

struggle NOUN
▷ *see also* **struggle** VERB
la lutte *fem* (*for independence, equality*)
■ **It was a struggle.** Ça a été laborieux.

stub NOUN
le mégot *masc* (*of cigarette*)

to **stub out** VERB
écraser [28] (*cigarette*)

stubborn ADJECTIVE
têtu (FEM têtue)

stuck VERB ▷ *see* **stick**

stuck ADJECTIVE
coincé (FEM coincée) (*jammed*)
□ It's stuck. C'est coincé.
■ **to get stuck** rester [71¹] coincé □ We got
stuck in a traffic jam. Nous sommes restés
coincés dans un embouteillage.

stuck-up ADJECTIVE
coincé (FEM coincée) (*informal*)

stud NOUN
1 la boucle d'oreille *fem* (*earring*)
2 le crampon *masc* (*on football boots*)

student NOUN
l'étudiant *masc*
l'étudiante *fem*

studio NOUN
le studio *masc*
□ a TV studio un studio de télévision
■ **a studio flat** un studio

to **study** VERB
1 faire [36] des études (*at university*)
□ I plan to study biology. J'ai l'intention de faire
des études de biologie.
2 travailler [281] (*do homework*)
□ I've got to study tonight. Je dois travailler ce
soir.

stuff NOUN
1 le truc *masc* (*substance*)
□ I need some stuff for hay fever. J'ai besoin d'un
truc contre le rhume des foins.
2 les trucs *masc pl* (*things*)
□ There's some stuff on the table for you. Il y a
des trucs sur la table pour toi.
3 les affaires *fem pl* (*possessions*)
□ Have you got all your stuff? Est-ce que tu as
toutes tes affaires ?

stuffy ADJECTIVE
mal aéré (FEM mal aérée) (*room*)
■ **It's really stuffy in here.** On étouffe ici.

to **stumble** VERB
trébucher [28]

stung VERB ▷ *see* **sting**

stunk VERB ▷ *see* **stink**

stunned ADJECTIVE
sidéré (FEM sidérée) (*amazed*)
□ I was stunned. J'étais sidéré.

stunning ADJECTIVE
superbe (FEM superbe)

stunt NOUN
la cascade *fem* (*in film*)

S

stupid ADJECTIVE
stupide (FEM stupide)
□ a stupid joke une plaisanterie stupide
■ **Me, go running? Don't be stupid!** Moi, faire du jogging ? Ne dis pas de bêtises !

to stutter VERB
▷ *see also* **stutter** NOUN
bégayer [59]

stutter NOUN
▷ *see also* **stutter** VERB
■ **He's got a stutter.** Il bégaie.

style NOUN
le style *masc*
□ That's not his style. Ça n'est pas son style.

subject NOUN
1 le sujet *masc*
□ The subject of my presentation was social media. Le sujet de mon exposé, c'était les médias sociaux.
2 la matière *fem* (*at school*)
□ What's your favourite subject? Quelle est ta matière préférée ?

subjunctive NOUN
le subjonctif *masc*
□ in the subjunctive au subjonctif

submarine NOUN
le sous-marin *masc*

subscription NOUN
l'abonnement *masc* (*to paper, magazine*)
■ **to take out a subscription to something** s'abonner [28] à quelque chose

subsequently ADVERB
en conséquence

to subsidize VERB
subventionner [28]

subsidy NOUN
la subvention *fem*

substance NOUN
la substance *fem*

substitute NOUN
▷ *see also* **substitute** VERB
le remplaçant *masc*
la remplaçante *fem* (*person*)

to substitute VERB
▷ *see also* **substitute** NOUN
substituer [28]
□ to substitute A for B substituer A à B

subtitled ADJECTIVE
sous-titré (FEM sous-titrée)

subtitles PL NOUN
les sous-titres *masc pl*
□ a French film with English subtitles un film français avec des sous-titres en anglais

subtle ADJECTIVE
subtil (FEM subtile)

to subtract VERB
retrancher [28]
□ to subtract 3 from 5 retrancher trois de cinq

suburb NOUN
la banlieue *fem*
□ a suburb of Paris une banlieue de Paris
■ **the suburbs** la banlieue □ They live in the suburbs. Ils habitent en banlieue.

suburban ADJECTIVE
de banlieue
□ a suburban train un train de banlieue

subway NOUN
le passage souterrain *masc* (*underpass*)

to succeed VERB
réussir [38]
□ to succeed in doing something réussir à faire quelque chose

success NOUN
le succès *masc*
□ The play was a great success. La pièce a eu beaucoup de succès.

successful ADJECTIVE
réussi (FEM réussie)
□ a successful attempt une tentative réussie
■ **to be successful in doing something** réussir [38] à faire quelque chose
■ **She's a successful designer.** C'est une designer couronnée de succès.

successfully ADVERB
avec succès

successive ADJECTIVE
■ **on four successive occasions** quatre fois de suite

such ADJECTIVE, ADVERB
si
□ such nice people des gens si gentils □ such a long journey un voyage si long
■ **such a lot of** tellement de □ such a lot of work tellement de travail
■ **such as** (*like*) comme □ hot countries, such as India les pays chauds, comme l'Inde
■ **not as such** pas exactement □ He's not an expert as such, but … Ce n'est pas exactement un expert, mais …
■ **There's no such thing.** Ça n'existe pas.
□ There's no such thing as the yeti. Le yéti n'existe pas.

such-and-such ADJECTIVE
tel ou tel (FEM telle ou telle)
□ such-and-such a place tel ou tel endroit

to suck VERB
sucer [12]
□ to suck one's thumb sucer son pouce

sudden ADJECTIVE
soudain (FEM soudaine)
□ a sudden change un changement soudain

- **all of a sudden** tout à coup

suddenly ADVERB
1 brusquement (*stop, leave, change*)
2 subitement (*die*)
3 soudain (*at beginning of sentence*)
□ Suddenly, the door opened. Soudain, la porte s'est ouverte.

suede NOUN
le daim *masc*
□ a suede jacket une veste en daim

to **suffer** VERB
souffrir [54]
□ She was really suffering. Elle souffrait beaucoup.
- **to suffer from a disease** avoir [8] une maladie □ I suffer from hay fever. J'ai le rhume des foins.

to **suffocate** VERB
suffoquer [28]

sugar NOUN
le sucre *masc*
□ Do you take sugar? Est-ce que vous prenez du sucre ?

to **suggest** VERB
suggérer [34]
□ I suggested they set off early. Je leur ai suggéré de partir de bonne heure.

suggestion NOUN
la suggestion *fem*
□ to make a suggestion faire une suggestion

suicide NOUN
le suicide *masc*
- **to commit suicide** se suicider [28]

suicide bomber NOUN
le/la kamikaze *masc/fem*

suit NOUN
▷ *see also* **suit** VERB
1 le costume *masc* (*man's*)
2 le tailleur *masc* (*woman's*)

to **suit** VERB
▷ *see also* **suit** NOUN
1 convenir [89] à (*be convenient for*)
□ What time would suit you? Quelle heure vous conviendrait ?
- **That suits me fine.** Ça m'arrange.
- **Suit yourself!** Comme tu veux !
2 aller [3*] bien à (*look good on*)
□ That dress really suits you. Cette robe te va vraiment bien.

suitable ADJECTIVE
1 convenable (FEM convenable)
□ a suitable time une heure convenable
2 approprié (FEM appropriée) (*clothes*)
□ suitable clothing des vêtements appropriés

suitcase NOUN
la valise *fem*

suite NOUN
1 la suite *fem* (*in hotel*)
2 l'ensemble de meubles *masc*
□ a bathroom suite un ensemble de meubles de salle de bains

to **sulk** VERB
bouder [28]

sulky ADJECTIVE
boudeur (FEM boudeuse)

sultana NOUN
le raisin sec *masc* (PL les raisins secs)

sum NOUN
1 le calcul *masc* (*calculation*)
□ She's good at sums. Elle est bonne en calcul.
2 la somme *fem* (*amount*)
□ a sum of money une somme d'argent

to **sum up** VERB
résumer [28]

to **summarize** VERB
résumer [28]

summary NOUN
le résumé *masc*

summer NOUN
l'été *masc*
- **in summer** en été
- **summer clothes** les vêtements d'été
- **the summer holidays** les vacances d'été
- **a summer camp** (US) une colonie de vacances

summertime NOUN
l'été *masc*
- **in summertime** en été

summit NOUN
le sommet *masc*

sun NOUN
le soleil *masc*
□ in the sun au soleil

to **sunbathe** VERB
se bronzer [28]

sunblock NOUN
l'écran total *masc*

sunburn NOUN
le coup de soleil *masc*

sunburnt ADJECTIVE
- **I got sunburnt.** J'ai attrapé un coup de soleil.

Sunday NOUN
le dimanche *masc*
□ on Sunday dimanche □ on Sundays le dimanche □ every Sunday tous les dimanches □ last Sunday dimanche dernier □ next Sunday dimanche prochain

Sunday school NOUN
le catéchisme *masc*
□ to go to Sunday school aller au catéchisme

sunflower NOUN
le tournesol *masc*
□ sunflower seeds des graines de tournesol

sung VERB ▷ *see* **sing**

sunglasses PL NOUN
les lunettes de soleil *fem pl*

sunk VERB ▷ *see* **sink**

sunlight NOUN
le soleil *masc*

sunny ADJECTIVE
ensoleillé (FEM ensoleillée)
□ a sunny morning une matinée ensoleillée
■ **It's sunny.** Il y a du soleil.
■ **a sunny day** une journée ensoleillée

sunrise NOUN
le lever du soleil *masc*

sunroof NOUN
le toit ouvrant *masc*

sunscreen NOUN
la crème solaire *fem*

sunset NOUN
le coucher du soleil *masc*

sunshine NOUN
le soleil *masc*

sunstroke NOUN
l'insolation *fem*
□ to get sunstroke attraper une insolation

suntan NOUN
le bronzage *masc*
■ **suntan lotion** la crème solaire

super ADJECTIVE
formidable (FEM formidable)

superb ADJECTIVE
superbe (FEM superbe)

supermarket NOUN
le supermarché *masc*

supernatural ADJECTIVE
surnaturel (FEM surnaturelle)

superstitious ADJECTIVE
superstitieux (FEM superstitieuse)

to **supervise** VERB
surveiller [28]

supervisor NOUN
1 le surveillant *masc*
la surveillante *fem* (*in factory*)
2 le chef de rayon *masc* (*in department store*)

supper NOUN
le dîner *masc*

supplement NOUN
le supplément *masc*

supplies PL NOUN
les vivres *masc pl* (*food*)

to **supply** VERB
▷ *see also* **supply** NOUN
fournir [38] (*provide*)
■ **to supply somebody with something**
fournir [38] quelque chose à quelqu'un □ The

centre supplied us with all the equipment. Le
centre nous a fourni tout l'équipement.

supply NOUN
▷ *see also* **supply** VERB
la provision *fem*
□ a supply of paper une provision de papier
■ **the water supply** (*to town*)
l'approvisionnement en eau *masc*

supply teacher NOUN
le remplaçant *masc*
la remplaçante *fem*

to **support** VERB
▷ *see also* **support** NOUN
1 soutenir [83]
□ My mum has always supported me. Ma mère
m'a toujours soutenu.
2 être [35] supporter de
□ What team do you support? Tu es supporter
de quelle équipe ?
3 subvenir [89] aux besoins de (*financially*)
□ She had to support five children on her own.
Elle a dû subvenir toute seule aux besoins de
cinq enfants.

> **BE CAREFUL!**
> Do not translate **to support** by the French
> word **supporter**.

support NOUN
▷ *see also* **support** VERB
le soutien *masc* (*backing*)

supporter NOUN
1 le supporter *masc*
□ a Liverpool supporter un supporter de
Liverpool
2 le sympathisant *masc*
la sympathisante *fem*
□ a supporter of the Labour Party un
sympathisant du parti travailliste

to **suppose** VERB
imaginer [28]
□ I suppose he's late. J'imagine qu'il est en
retard. □ Suppose you won the lottery. Imaginez
que vous gagniez à la loterie.
■ **I suppose so.** J'imagine.
■ **to be supposed to do something** être [35]
censé faire quelque chose □ You're supposed to
show your passport. On est censé montrer son
passeport.

supposing CONJUNCTION
si
□ Supposing you won the lottery ... Si tu gagnais
à la loterie ...

surcharge NOUN
la surcharge *fem*

sure ADJECTIVE
sûr (FEM sûre)
□ Are you sure? Tu es sûr ?

Numbers in brackets refer to verb tables on pages 650 to 658

■ **Sure!** Bien sûr !
■ **to make sure that ...** vérifier [19] que ...
□ I'm going to make sure the door's locked. Je vais vérifier que la porte est fermée à clé.

surely ADVERB
■ **Surely you haven't forgotten?** Tu n'as sûrement pas oublié, n'est-ce pas ?
■ **She will get into university, surely?** J'imagine qu'elle ira à l'université, non ?

surf NOUN
▷ see also **surf** VERB
le ressac *masc*

to **surf** VERB
▷ see also **surf** NOUN
surfer [28]
■ **to go surfing** faire [36] du surf
■ **to surf the Net** surfer [28] sur le Net

surface NOUN
la surface *fem*

surfboard NOUN
la planche de surf *fem*

surfing NOUN
le surf *masc*
□ to go surfing faire du surf

surgeon NOUN
le chirurgien *masc*
□ She's a surgeon. Elle est chirurgien.

surgery NOUN
le cabinet médical *masc* (*doctor's surgery*)
■ **surgery hours** les heures de consultation *fem pl*

surname NOUN
le nom de famille *masc*

surprise NOUN
la surprise *fem*

surprised ADJECTIVE
surpris (FEM surprise)
□ I was surprised to see him. J'ai été surpris de le voir.

surprising ADJECTIVE
surprenant (FEM surprenante)

to **surrender** VERB
capituler [28]

surrogate mother NOUN
la mère porteuse *fem*

to **surround** VERB
encercler [28]
□ The police surrounded the house. La police a encerclé la maison.
■ **surrounded by** entouré de □ The house is surrounded by trees. La maison est entourée d'arbres.

surroundings PL NOUN
le cadre *masc sing*
□ a hotel in beautiful surroundings un hôtel situé dans un beau cadre

survey NOUN
l'enquête *fem* (*research*)

surveyor NOUN
1 l'expert en bâtiment *masc* (*of buildings*)
2 le/la géomètre *masc/fem* (*of land*)

survivor NOUN
le survivant *masc*
la survivante *fem*

to **suspect** VERB
▷ see also **suspect** NOUN
soupçonner [28]

suspect NOUN
▷ see also **suspect** VERB
le suspect *masc*
la suspecte *fem*

to **suspend** VERB
1 exclure [13] (*from school, team*)
□ He's been suspended. Il s'est fait exclure.
2 suspendre [88] (*from job*)

suspenders PL NOUN (US)
les bretelles *fem pl* (*braces*)

suspense NOUN
1 l'attente *fem* (*waiting*)
□ The suspense was terrible. L'attente a été terrible.
2 le suspense *masc* (*in story*)
□ a film with lots of suspense un film avec beaucoup de suspense

suspension NOUN
1 l'exclusion *fem* (*from school, team*)
2 la suspension *fem* (*from job*)

suspicious ADJECTIVE
1 méfiant (FEM méfiante)
□ He was suspicious at first Il était méfiant au début.
2 louche (FEM louche) (*suspiciou. ooking*)
□ a suspicious person un individu louche

sustainable ADJECTIVE
durable (FEM durable) (*development*)

to **swallow** VERB
avaler [28]

swam VERB ▷ see **swim**

swan NOUN
le cygne *masc*

to **swap** VERB
échanger [45]
□ Do you want to swap? Tu veux échanger ?
□ to swap A for B échanger A contre B

to **swat** VERB
écraser [28]

to **sway** VERB
osciller [28]

to **swear** VERB
jurer [28] (*make an oath, curse*)

swearword NOUN
le gros mot *masc*

sweat NOUN
▷ *see also* **sweat** VERB
la transpiration *fem*

to **sweat** VERB
▷ *see also* **sweat** NOUN
transpirer [28]

sweater NOUN
le pull *masc*

sweatshirt NOUN
le sweat *masc*

sweaty ADJECTIVE
1 en sueur (*person, face*)
□ I'm all sweaty. Je suis en sueur.
2 moite (FEM moite) (*hands*)

Swede NOUN
le Suédois *masc*
la Suédoise *fem* (*person*)

swede NOUN
le rutabaga *masc* (*vegetable*)

Sweden NOUN
la Suède *fem*
■ **in Sweden** en Suède
■ **to Sweden** en Suède

Swedish NOUN
▷ *see also* **Swedish** ADJECTIVE
le suédois *masc* (*language*)

Swedish ADJECTIVE
▷ *see also* **Swedish** NOUN
suédois (FEM suédoise)
□ She's Swedish. Elle est suédoise.

to **sweep** VERB
balayer [59]
■ **to sweep the floor** balayer [59]

sweet NOUN
▷ *see also* **sweet** ADJECTIVE
1 le bonbon *masc* (*candy*)
□ a bag of sweets un paquet de bonbons
2 le dessert *masc* (*pudding*)
□ What sweet did you have? Qu'est-ce que vous avez mangé comme dessert ?

sweet ADJECTIVE
▷ *see also* **sweet** NOUN
1 sucré (FEM sucrée) (*not savoury*)
2 gentil (FEM gentille) (*kind*)
□ That was really sweet of you. C'était vraiment gentil de ta part.
3 mignon (FEM mignonne) (*cute*)
□ Isn't she sweet? Comme elle est mignonne !
■ **sweet and sour chicken** le poulet à la sauce aigre-douce

sweetcorn NOUN
le maïs doux *masc*

sweltering ADJECTIVE
■ **It was sweltering.** Il faisait une chaleur étouffante.

swept VERB ▷ *see* **sweep**

to **swerve** VERB
faire [36] une embardée
□ He swerved to avoid the cyclist. Il a fait une embardée pour éviter le cycliste.

swim NOUN
▷ *see also* **swim** VERB
■ **to go for a swim** aller [3ᵗ] se baigner

to **swim** VERB
▷ *see also* **swim** NOUN
nager [45]
□ Can you swim? Tu sais nager ?
■ **She swam across the river.** Elle a traversé la rivière à la nage.

swimmer NOUN
le nageur *masc*
la nageuse *fem*
□ She's a good swimmer. C'est une bonne nageuse.

swimming NOUN
la natation *fem*
□ Do you like swimming? Tu aimes la natation ?
■ **to go swimming** (*in a pool*) aller [3ᵗ] à la piscine
■ **a swimming cap** un bonnet de bain
■ **a swimming costume** un maillot de bain
■ **a swimming pool** une piscine
■ **swimming trunks** le maillot de bain

swimsuit NOUN
le maillot de bain *masc*

swing NOUN
▷ *see also* **swing** VERB
la balançoire *fem* (*in playground, garden*)

to **swing** VERB
▷ *see also* **swing** NOUN
1 se balancer [12]
□ A bunch of keys swung from his belt. Un trousseau de clés se balançait à sa ceinture.
■ **Sam was swinging an umbrella as he walked.** Sam balançait son parapluie en marchant.
2 virer [28]
□ The canoe swung round sharply. Le canoë a viré brusquement.

Swiss NOUN
▷ *see also* **Swiss** ADJECTIVE
le/la Suisse *masc/fem* (*person*)
■ **the Swiss** les Suisses

Swiss ADJECTIVE
▷ *see also* **Swiss** NOUN
suisse (FEM suisse)
□ Sabine's Swiss. Sabine est suisse.

switch NOUN
▷ *see also* **switch** VERB
le bouton *masc* (*for light, radio etc*)

to **switch** VERB
▷ *see also* **switch** NOUN
changer [45] de

Numbers in brackets refer to verb tables on pages 650 to 658

□ We switched partners. Nous avons changé de partenaire.

to **switch off** VERB
1 éteindre [60] (*electrical appliance*)
2 arrêter [28] (*engine, machine*)

to **switch on** VERB
1 allumer [28] (*electrical appliance*)
2 mettre [47] en marche (*engine, machine*)

Switzerland NOUN
la Suisse *fem*
■ **in Switzerland** en Suisse

swollen ADJECTIVE
enflé (FEM enflée) (*arm, leg*)

to **swop** VERB
échanger [45]
□ Do you want to swop? Tu veux échanger ?
□ to swop A for B échanger A contre B

sword NOUN
l'épée *fem*

swore, sworn VERB ▷ *see* **swear**

swot NOUN
▷ *see also* **swot** VERB
le bûcheur *masc*
la bûcheuse *fem*

to **swot** VERB
▷ *see also* **swot** NOUN
bosser [28] dur

□ I'll have to swot for my maths exam.
Je vais devoir bosser dur pour mon examen de maths.

swum VERB ▷ *see* **swim**

swung VERB ▷ *see* **swing**

syllabus NOUN
le programme *masc*
□ on the syllabus au programme

symbol NOUN
le symbole *masc*

sympathetic ADJECTIVE
compréhensif (FEM compréhensive)

BE CAREFUL!
Do not translate **sympathetic** by the French word **sympathique**.

to **sympathize** VERB
■ **to sympathize with somebody** comprendre [65] quelqu'un

sympathy NOUN
la compassion *fem*

symptom NOUN
le symptôme *masc*

syringe NOUN
la seringue *fem*

system NOUN
le système *masc*

S

Tt

table NOUN
la table *fem*
□ to lay the table mettre la table

tablecloth NOUN
la nappe *fem*

tablespoon NOUN
la grande cuillère *fem*
■ **two tablespoons of sugar** deux cuillerées à soupe de sucre

tablet NOUN
1 le comprimé *masc* (*medicine*)
2 la tablette *fem* (*computer*)

table tennis NOUN
le ping-pong *masc*
□ to play table tennis jouer au ping-pong

tabloid NOUN
le tabloïd *masc*

tackle NOUN
▷ *see also* **tackle** VERB
1 le tacle *masc* (*in football*)
2 le plaquage *masc* (*in rugby*)
■ **fishing tackle** le matériel de pêche

to **tackle** VERB
▷ *see also* **tackle** NOUN
1 tacler [28] (*in football*)
2 plaquer [28] (*in rugby*)
■ **to tackle a problem** s'attaquer [28] à un problème

tact NOUN
le tact *masc*

tactful ADJECTIVE
plein de tact (FEM pleine de tact)

tactics PL NOUN
la tactique *fem sing*

tactless ADJECTIVE
■ **to be tactless** manquer [28] de tact □ a tactless remark une remarque qui manque de tact

tadpole NOUN
le têtard *masc*

tag NOUN
l'étiquette *fem* (*label*)

tail NOUN
la queue *fem*
■ **Heads or tails?** Pile ou face ?

tailor NOUN
le tailleur *masc*
la tailleuse *fem*

to **take** VERB
1 prendre [65]
□ Are you taking your new camera? Tu prends ton nouvel appareil photo ? □ He took a plate from the cupboard. Il a pris une assiette dans le placard. □ It takes about an hour. Ça prend environ une heure.
2 emmener [43] (*person*)
□ When will you take me to London? Quand est-ce que tu vas m'emmener à Londres ?
■ **to take something somewhere** emporter [28] quelque chose quelque part □ Do you take your exercise books home? Vous emportez vos cahiers chez vous ? □ Don't take anything valuable with you. N'emportez pas d'objets de valeur. □ I'm going to take my coat to the cleaner's. Je vais donner mon manteau à nettoyer.
3 demander [28] (*effort, skill*)
□ That takes a lot of courage. Cela demande beaucoup de courage.
■ **It takes a lot of money to do that.** Il faut beaucoup d'argent pour faire ça.
4 supporter [28] (*tolerate*)
□ He can't take being criticized. Il ne supporte pas d'être critiqué.
5 passer [58] (*exam, test*)
□ Have you taken your driving test yet? Est-ce que tu as déjà passé ton permis de conduire ?
6 faire [36] (*subject*)
□ I decided to take French instead of German. J'ai décidé de faire du français au lieu de l'allemand.

to **take after** VERB
ressembler [28] à
□ She takes after her mother. Elle ressemble à sa mère.

to **take apart** VERB
■ **to take something apart** démonter [28] quelque chose

to **take away** VERB
1 emporter [28] (*object*)
2 emmener [43] (*person*)
■ **to take something away** (*confiscate*)

Numbers in brackets refer to verb tables on pages 650 to 658

confisquer [28] quelque chose
■ **pizza to take away** pizzas à emporter

to **take back** VERB
rapporter [28]
□ I took it back to the shop. Je l'ai rapporté au magasin.
■ **I take it all back!** Je retire ce que j'ai dit !

to **take down** VERB
1 enlever [43] (poster, sign)
2 décrocher [28] (painting, curtains)
3 démonter [28] (tent, scaffolding)
4 prendre [65] en note (make a note of)
□ He took down the details in his notebook. Il a pris tous les détails en note dans son carnet.

to **take in** VERB
comprendre [65] (understand)
□ I didn't really take it in. Je n'ai pas bien compris.

to **take off** VERB
1 décoller [28] (plane)
□ The plane took off twenty minutes late. L'avion a décollé avec vingt minutes de retard.
2 enlever [43] (clothes)
□ Take your coat off. Enlevez votre manteau.

to **take out** VERB
sortir [79] (from container, pocket)
■ **He took her out to the theatre.** Il l'a emmenée au théâtre.

to **take over** VERB
prendre [65] la relève
□ I'll take over now. Je vais prendre la relève.
■ **to take over from somebody** remplacer [12] quelqu'un

takeaway NOUN
le plat à emporter masc (meal)
■ **a Chinese takeaway** un restaurant chinois qui vend des plats à emporter

taken VERB ▷ see take

takeoff NOUN
le décollage masc (of plane)

talcum powder NOUN
le talc masc

tale NOUN
le conte masc (story)

talent NOUN
le talent masc
□ She's got lots of talent. Elle a beaucoup de talent.
■ **to have a talent for something** être [35] doué pour quelque chose □ He's got a real talent for languages. Il est vraiment doué pour les langues.

talented ADJECTIVE
■ **She's a talented pianist.** C'est une pianiste de talent.

talk NOUN
▷ see also **talk** VERB

1 l'exposé masc (speech)
□ She gave a talk on rock climbing. Elle a fait un exposé sur la varappe.
2 la conversation fem (conversation)
□ I had a talk with my mum about it. J'ai eu une conversation avec ma mère à ce sujet.
3 les racontars masc pl (gossip)
□ It's just talk. Ce sont des racontars.

to **talk** VERB
▷ see also **talk** NOUN
parler [28]
□ to talk about something parler de quelque chose
■ **to talk something over with somebody** discuter [28] de quelque chose avec quelqu'un

talkative ADJECTIVE
bavard (FEM bavarde)

tall ADJECTIVE
1 grand (FEM grande) (person, tree)
■ **to be 2 metres tall** mesurer [28] deux mètres
2 haut (FEM haute) (building)

tame ADJECTIVE
apprivoisé (FEM apprivoisée) (animal)
□ They've got a tame hedgehog. Ils ont un hérisson apprivoisé.

tampon NOUN
le tampon masc

tan NOUN
le bronzage masc
□ She's got an amazing tan. Elle a un bronzage superbe.

tangerine NOUN
la mandarine fem

tangle NOUN
1 l'enchevêtrement masc (ropes, cables)
2 le nœud masc (hair)
■ **to be in a tangle 1** (ropes, cables) être [35] enchevêtré **2** (hair) être [35] emmêlé

tank NOUN
1 le réservoir masc (for water, petrol)
2 le char d'assaut masc (military)
■ **a fish tank** un aquarium

tanker NOUN
1 le pétrolier masc (ship)
■ **an oil tanker** un pétrolier
2 le camion-citerne masc (truck)
■ **a petrol tanker** un camion-citerne

tap NOUN
1 le robinet masc (water tap)
2 la petite tape fem (gentle blow)

tap-dancing NOUN
les claquettes fem pl
□ I do tap-dancing. Je fais des claquettes.

tape NOUN
le ruban adhésif masc (sticky tape)

tape measure NOUN
le mètre à ruban masc

t

target NOUN
la cible *fem*

tarmac NOUN
le macadam *masc* (*on road*)

tart NOUN
la tarte *fem*
□ an apple tart une tarte aux pommes

tartan ADJECTIVE
écossais (FEM écossaise)
□ a tartan scarf une écharpe écossaise

task NOUN
la tâche *fem*

taste NOUN
▷ *see also* **taste** VERB
le goût *masc*
□ It's got a really strange taste. Ça a un goût vraiment bizarre. □ a joke in bad taste une plaisanterie de mauvais goût
■ **Would you like a taste?** Tu veux goûter ?

to **taste** VERB
▷ *see also* **taste** NOUN
goûter [28]
□ Would you like to taste it? Vous voulez y goûter ?
■ **to taste of something** avoir [8] un goût de quelque chose □ It tastes of fish. Ça a un goût de poisson.
■ **You can taste the garlic in it.** Ça a bien le goût d'ail.

tasteful ADJECTIVE
de bon goût

tasteless ADJECTIVE
1 fade (FEM fade) (*food*)
2 de mauvais goût (*in bad taste*)
□ a tasteless remark une remarque de mauvais goût

tasty ADJECTIVE
savoureux (FEM savoureuse)

tattoo NOUN
le tatouage *masc*

taught VERB ▷ *see* **teach**

Taurus NOUN
le Taureau *masc*
□ I'm Taurus. Je suis Taureau.

tax NOUN
1 les impôts *masc pl* (*on income*)
2 la taxe *fem* (*on goods, alcohol*)

taxi NOUN
le taxi *masc*
■ **a taxi driver** un chauffeur de taxi

taxi rank NOUN
la station de taxis *fem*

TB NOUN
la tuberculose *fem*

tea NOUN
1 le thé *masc*

□ a cup of tea une tasse de thé
■ **a tea bag** un sachet de thé
2 le dîner *masc* (*evening meal*)
■ **We were having tea.** Nous étions en train de dîner.

> **DID YOU KNOW...?**
> In France, it is more common to have lemon with your tea.

to **teach** VERB
1 apprendre [65]
□ My sister taught me to swim. Ma sœur m'a appris à nager. □ That'll teach you! Ça t'apprendra !
2 enseigner [28] (*in school*)
□ She teaches physics. Elle enseigne la physique.

teacher NOUN
1 le professeur *masc* (*in secondary school*)
□ a maths teacher un professeur de maths
□ She's a teacher. Elle est professeur.
2 l'instituteur *masc*
l'institutrice *fem* (*in primary school*)
□ He's a primary school teacher. Il est instituteur.

teacher's pet NOUN
le chouchou *masc*
la chouchoute *fem*

teaching assistant NOUN
l'aide-éducateur *masc*
l'aide-éducatrice *fem*

tea cloth NOUN
le torchon *masc*

team NOUN
l'équipe *fem*
□ a football team une équipe de football □ She was in my team. Elle était dans mon équipe.

teapot NOUN
la théière *fem*

tear NOUN
la larme *fem*
□ She was in tears. Elle était en larmes.

to **tear** VERB
1 déchirer [28]
□ Be careful or you'll tear the page. Fais attention, tu vas déchirer la page.
2 se déchirer [28]
□ It won't tear, it's very strong. Ça ne se déchire pas, c'est très solide.

to **tear up** VERB
déchirer [28]
□ He tore up the letter. Il a déchiré la lettre.

tear gas NOUN
le gaz lacrymogène *masc*

to **tease** VERB
1 tourmenter [28] (*unkindly*)
□ Stop teasing that poor animal! Arrête de tourmenter cette pauvre bête !

2 taquiner [28] (*jokingly*)
  □ He's teasing you. Il te taquine.
  ■ **I was only teasing.** Je plaisantais.

teaspoon NOUN
  la petite cuillère *fem*
  ■ **two teaspoons of sugar** deux cuillerées à café de sucre

teatime NOUN
  l'heure du dîner *fem* (*in evening*)
  □ It was nearly teatime. C'était presque l'heure du dîner.

tea towel NOUN
  le torchon *masc*

technical ADJECTIVE
  technique (FEM technique)

technician NOUN
  le technicien *masc*
  la technicienne *fem*

technique NOUN
  la technique *fem*

techno NOUN
  la techno *fem* (*music*)

technological ADJECTIVE
  technologique (FEM technologique)

technology NOUN
  la technologie *fem*

teddy bear NOUN
  le nounours *masc*

teenage ADJECTIVE
  1 pour les jeunes
  □ a teenage magazine un magazine pour les jeunes
  2 adolescent (FEM adolescente) (*boys, girls*)
  □ She has two teenage daughters. Elle a deux filles adolescentes.

teenager NOUN
  l'adolescent *masc*
  l'adolescente *fem*

teens PL NOUN
  ■ **She's in her teens.** C'est une adolescente.

tee-shirt NOUN
  le tee-shirt *masc*

teeth PL NOUN
  les dents *fem pl*

to **teethe** VERB
  faire [36] ses dents

teetotal ADJECTIVE
  ■ **I'm teetotal.** Je ne bois jamais d'alcool.

telecommunications PL NOUN
  les télécommunications *fem pl*

telephone NOUN
  le téléphone *masc*
  □ on the telephone au téléphone
  ■ **a telephone box** une cabine téléphonique
  ■ **a telephone call** un coup de téléphone

  ■ **a telephone number** un numéro de téléphone

telesales PL NOUN
  la vente par téléphone *fem sing*
  ■ **She works in telesales.** Elle est télévendeuse.

telescope NOUN
  le télescope *masc*

television NOUN
  la télévision *fem*
  ■ **on television** à la télévision
  ■ **a television licence** une redevance de télévision
  ■ **a television programme** une émission de télévision

to **tell** VERB
  dire [27]
  ■ **to tell somebody something** dire [27] quelque chose à quelqu'un □ Did you tell your mother? Tu l'as dit à ta mère ? □ I told him that I was going on holiday. Je lui ai dit que je partais en vacances.
  ■ **to tell somebody to do something** dire [27] à quelqu'un de faire quelque chose □ He told me to wait a moment. Il m'a dit d'attendre un moment.
  ■ **to tell lies** dire [27] des mensonges
  ■ **to tell a story** raconter [28] une histoire
  ■ **I can't tell the difference between them.** Je n'arrive pas à les distinguer.

to **tell off** VERB
  gronder [28]

telly NOUN
  la télé *fem*
  □ to watch telly regarder la télé
  ■ **on telly** à la télé

temper NOUN
  le caractère *masc*
  □ He's got a terrible temper. Il a un sale caractère.
  ■ **to be in a temper** être [35] en colère
  ■ **to lose one's temper** se mettre [47] en colère □ I lost my temper. Je me suis mis en colère.

temperature NOUN
  la température *fem* (*of oven, water, person*)
  ■ **The temperature was 30 degrees.** Il faisait trente degrés.
  ■ **to have a temperature** avoir [8] de la fièvre

temple NOUN
  le temple *masc*

temporary ADJECTIVE
  temporaire (FEM temporaire)

to **tempt** VERB
  tenter [28]
  □ I'm very tempted! Je suis très tenté !
  ■ **to tempt somebody to do something** persuader [28] quelqu'un de faire quelque chose

temptation NOUN
la tentation *fem*

tempting ADJECTIVE
tentant (FEM tentante)

ten NUMBER
dix
□ She's ten. Elle a dix ans.

tenant NOUN
le locataire *masc*
la locataire *fem*

to **tend** VERB
■ **to tend to do something** avoir [8] tendance
à faire quelque chose □ He tends to arrive late.
Il a tendance à arriver en retard.

tender ADJECTIVE
1 tendre (FEM tendre) *(food)*
2 sensible (FEM sensible) *(part of body)*
□ My feet are really tender. J'ai les pieds très
sensibles.

tennis NOUN
le tennis *masc*
□ Do you play tennis? Vous jouez au tennis ?
■ **a tennis ball** une balle de tennis
■ **a tennis court** un court de tennis
■ **a tennis racket** une raquette de tennis

tennis player NOUN
le joueur de tennis *masc*
la joueuse de tennis *fem*
□ He's a tennis player. Il est joueur de
tennis.

tenor NOUN
le ténor *masc*

tenpin bowling NOUN
le bowling *masc*
□ to go tenpin bowling jouer au bowling

tense ADJECTIVE
▷ *see also* **tense** NOUN
tendu (FEM tendue)

tense NOUN
▷ *see also* **tense** ADJECTIVE
■ **the present tense** le présent
■ **the future tense** le futur

tension NOUN
la tension *fem*

tent NOUN
la tente *fem*
■ **a tent peg** un piquet de tente
■ **a tent pole** un montant de tente

tenth ADJECTIVE
dixième (FEM dixième)
□ the tenth floor le dixième étage
■ **the tenth of August** le dix août

term NOUN
1 le trimestre *masc* *(at school)*
2 le terme *masc*
□ a short-term solution une solution à
court terme

■ **to come to terms with something** accepter
[28] quelque chose

terminal ADJECTIVE
▷ *see also* **terminal** NOUN
incurable (FEM incurable) *(illness, patient)*

terminal NOUN
▷ *see also* **terminal** ADJECTIVE
un terminal *(of computer)*
■ **an oil terminal** un terminal pétrolier
■ **an air terminal** une aérogare

terminally ADVERB
■ **to be terminally ill** être [35] condamné

terrace NOUN
1 la terrasse *fem* *(patio)*
2 la rangée de maisons *fem* *(row of houses)*
■ **the terraces** *(at stadium)* les gradins *masc pl*

terraced ADJECTIVE
■ **a terraced house** une maison mitoyenne

terrible ADJECTIVE
épouvantable (FEM épouvantable)
□ My French is terrible. Mon français est
épouvantable.

terribly ADVERB
1 terriblement
□ He suffers terribly. Il souffre terriblement.
2 vraiment
□ I'm terribly sorry. Je suis vraiment désolé.

terrier NOUN
le terrier *masc*

terrific ADJECTIVE
super (FEM+PL super) *(wonderful)*
□ That's terrific! C'est super !
■ **You look terrific!** Tu es superbe !

terrified ADJECTIVE
terrifié (FEM terrifiée)
□ I was terrified! J'étais terrifié !

terrorism NOUN
le terrorisme *masc*

terrorist NOUN
le/la terroriste *masc/fem*
■ **a terrorist attack** un attentat terroriste

test NOUN
▷ *see also* **test** VERB
1 l'interrogation *fem* *(at school)*
□ I've got a test tomorrow. J'ai une interrogation
demain.
2 l'essai *masc* *(trial, check)*
□ nuclear tests les essais nucléaires
3 l'analyse *fem* *(medical)*
□ a blood test une analyse de sang □ They're
going to do some more tests. Ils vont faire
d'autres analyses.
■ **driving test** l'examen du permis de conduire
□ He's got his driving test tomorrow. Il passe son
permis de conduire demain.

to **test** VERB
▷ *see also* **test** NOUN

1 essayer [59]

□ to test something out essayer quelque chose

2 interroger [45] (*class*)

□ He tested us on the vocabulary. Il nous a interrogés sur le vocabulaire.

■ **She was tested for drugs.** On lui a fait subir un contrôle antidopage.

test match NOUN

le match international *masc*

test tube NOUN

l'éprouvette *fem*

tetanus NOUN

le tétanos *masc*

□ a tetanus injection un vaccin contre le tétanos

text NOUN

▷ *see also* **text** VERB

1 le texte *masc*

2 le SMS *masc* (*on mobile phone*)

to text VERB

▷ *see also* **text** NOUN

■ **to text someone** envoyer [33] un SMS à quelqu'un

textbook NOUN

le manuel *masc*

□ a French textbook un manuel de français

text message NOUN

le SMS *masc*

Thames NOUN

la Tamise *fem*

than CONJUNCTION

que

□ She's taller than me. Elle est plus grande que moi. □ I've got more books than him. J'ai plus de livres que lui.

■ **more than ten years** plus de dix ans

■ **more than once** plus d'une fois

to thank VERB

remercier [19]

□ Don't forget to thank them. N'oublie pas de les remercier.

■ **thank you** merci

■ **thank you very much** merci beaucoup

thanks EXCLAMATION

merci !

■ **thanks to** grâce à □ Thanks to him, everything went OK. Grâce à lui, tout s'est bien passé.

that ADJECTIVE, PRONOUN, CONJUNCTION

Use **ce** when 'that' is followed by a masculine noun, and **cette** when 'that' is followed by a feminine noun. **ce** changes to **cet** before a vowel and before most words beginning with 'h'.

1 ce

□ that book ce livre

cet

□ that man cet homme

cette

□ that woman cette femme □ that road cette route

■ **THAT road** cette route-là

■ **that one** **1** celui-là *masc* □ This man? — No, that one. Cet homme-ci ? — Non, celui-là. **2** celle-là *fem* □ Do you like this photo? — No, I prefer that one. Tu aimes cette photo ? — Non, je préfère celle-là.

2 ça

□ You see that? Tu vois ça ?

■ **What's that?** Qu'est-ce que c'est ?

■ **Who's that?** Qui est-ce ?

■ **Is that you?** C'est toi ?

■ **That's ...** C'est ... □ That's my teacher. C'est mon prof. □ That's what he said. C'est ce qu'il a dit.

In relative phrases use **qui** when 'that' refers to the subject of the sentence, and **que** when it refers to the object.

3 qui

□ the man that saw us l'homme qui nous a vus

□ the man that spoke to us l'homme qui nous a parlé

4 que

□ the man that we saw l'homme que nous avons vu □ the man that we spoke to l'homme à qui nous avons parlé

que changes to **qu'** before a vowel and before most words beginning with 'h'.

□ the dog that she bought le chien qu'elle a acheté □ He thought that Henri was ill. Il pensait qu'Henri était malade. □ I know that she likes chocolate. Je sais qu'elle aime le chocolat.

■ **It was that big.** Il était grand comme ça.

■ **It's about that high.** C'est à peu près haut comme ça.

■ **It's not that difficult.** Ça n'est pas si difficile que ça.

the ARTICLE

Use **le** with a masculine noun, and **la** with a feminine noun. Use **l'** before a vowel and most words beginning with 'h'. For plural nouns always use **les**.

le

□ the boy le garçon

l'

□ the man l'homme *masc* □ the air l'air *masc* □ the habit l'habitude *fem*

la

□ the girl la fille

les

□ the children les enfants

theatre (US **theater**) NOUN

le théâtre *masc*

theft NOUN

le vol *masc*

their ADJECTIVE

leur (PL leurs)

□ their house leur maison □ their parents leurs parents

theirs PRONOUN

le leur + *masc noun*

□ It's not our garage, it's theirs. Ce n'est pas notre garage, c'est le leur.

la leur + *fem noun*

□ It's not our car, it's theirs. Ce n'est pas notre voiture, c'est la leur.

les leurs + *pl noun*

□ They're not our ideas, they're theirs. Ce ne sont pas nos idées, ce sont les leurs.

■ **Is this theirs?** **1** (*masculine owners*) C'est à eux ? **2** (*feminine owners*) C'est à elles ? □ This car is theirs. Cette voiture est à eux. □ Whose is this? — It's theirs. C'est à qui ? — À eux.

them PRONOUN

1 les

□ I didn't see them. Je ne les ai pas vus.

> Use **leur** when 'them' means 'to them'.

2 leur

□ I gave them some brochures. Je leur ai donné des brochures. □ I told them the truth. Je leur ai dit la vérité.

> Use **eux** or **elles** after a preposition.

3 eux *masc pl*

□ It's for them. C'est pour eux.

elles *fem pl*

□ Layla and Sophie came — Louis was with them. Layla et Sophie sont venues — Louis était avec elles.

theme NOUN

le thème *masc*

theme park NOUN

le parc d'attractions *masc*

themselves PRONOUN

1 se

□ Did they hurt themselves? Est-ce qu'ils se sont fait mal ?

2 eux-mêmes *masc*

elles-mêmes *fem*

□ They did it themselves. Ils l'ont fait eux-mêmes.

then ADVERB, CONJUNCTION

1 ensuite (*next*)

□ I get dressed. Then I have breakfast. Je m'habille. Ensuite je prends mon petit déjeuner.

2 alors (*in that case*)

□ My pen's run out. — Use a pencil then! Il n'y a plus d'encre dans mon stylo. — Alors utilise un crayon !

3 à l'époque (*at that time*)

□ There was no electricity then. Il n'y avait pas l'électricité à l'époque.

■ **now and then** de temps en temps □ Do you play chess? — Now and then. Vous jouez aux échecs ? — De temps en temps.

■ **By then it was too late.** Il était déjà trop tard.

therapy NOUN

la thérapie *fem*

there ADVERB

1 là

□ Put it there, on the table. Mets-le là, sur la table.

■ **over there** là-bas

■ **in there** là

■ **on there** là

■ **up there** là-haut

■ **down there** là-bas

■ **There he is!** Le voilà !

2 y

□ He went there on Friday. Il y est allé vendredi. □ Brussels? I've never been there. Bruxelles ? Je n'y suis jamais allé.

■ **There is …** Il y a … □ There's a factory near my house. Il y a une usine près de chez moi.

■ **There are …** Il y a … □ There are five people in my family. Il y a cinq personnes dans ma famille.

■ **There has been an accident.** Il y a eu un accident.

■ **Will there be a buffet?** Est-ce qu'il y aura un buffet ?

therefore ADVERB

donc

there's = there is, there has

thermometer NOUN

le thermomètre *masc*

Thermos® NOUN

le thermos® *masc*

these ADJECTIVE, PRONOUN

1 ces

□ these shoes ces chaussures

■ **THESE shoes** ces chaussures-là

2 ceux-ci *masc*

□ I want these! Je veux ceux-ci !

celles-ci *fem*

□ I'm looking for some sandals. Can I try these? Je cherche des sandales. Je peux essayer celles-ci ?

they PRONOUN

> Check if 'they' stands for a masculine or feminine noun.

ils

□ Are there any tickets left? — No, they're sold out. Est-ce qu'il reste des billets ? — Non, ils sont tous vendus.

elles

□ Do you like those shoes? — No, they're horrible. Tu aimes ces chaussures ? — Non, elles sont affreuses.

- **They say that ...** On dit que ...

they'd = they had, they would

they'll = they will

they're = they are

they've = they have

thick ADJECTIVE
1 épais (FEM épaisse) (not thin)
- **The walls are one metre thick.** Les murs font un mètre d'épaisseur.
2 bête (FEM bête) (stupid)

thief NOUN
le voleur masc
la voleuse fem
- **Stop thief!** Au voleur !

thigh NOUN
la cuisse fem

thin ADJECTIVE
1 mince (FEM mince) (person, slice)
2 maigre (FEM maigre) (skinny)

> **WORD POWER**
> You can use a number of other words instead of **thin** to mean 'skinny':
> **lanky** dégingandé
> □ a lanky boy un garçon dégingandé
> **skinny** maigre
> □ a skinny dog un chien maigre
> **slim** mince
> □ a slim girl une fille mince

thing NOUN
1 la chose fem
- □ beautiful things de belles choses
2 le truc masc (thingy)
- □ What's that thing called? Comment s'appelle ce truc ?
- **my things** (belongings) mes affaires fem pl
- **You poor thing!** Mon pauvre !

to **think** VERB
1 penser [28] (believe)
- □ I think you're wrong. Je pense que vous avez tort. □ What do you think about the war? Que pensez-vous de la guerre ?
2 réfléchir [38] (spend time thinking)
- □ Think carefully before you reply. Réfléchis bien avant de répondre. □ I'll think about it. Je vais y réfléchir.
- **What are you thinking about?** À quoi tu penses ?
3 imaginer [28] (imagine)
- □ Just think — tomorrow we'll be on holiday! T'imagines : demain, on sera en vacances !
- **I think so.** Oui, je crois.
- **I don't think so.** Je ne crois pas.
- **I'll think it over.** Je vais y réfléchir.

third ADJECTIVE
▷ see also **third** NOUN
troisième (FEM troisième)

□ the third day le troisième jour □ the third time la troisième fois □ I came third. Je suis arrivé troisième.
- **the third of March** le trois mars

third NOUN
▷ see also **third** ADJECTIVE
le tiers masc
□ a third of the population un tiers de la population

thirdly ADVERB
troisièmement

Third World NOUN
le tiers-monde masc

thirst NOUN
la soif fem

thirsty ADJECTIVE
- **to be thirsty** avoir [8] soif

thirteen NUMBER
treize
□ I'm thirteen. J'ai treize ans.

thirteenth ADJECTIVE
treizième (FEM treizième)
□ her thirteenth birthday son treizième anniversaire □ the thirteenth floor le treizième étage
- **the thirteenth of August** le treize août

thirty NUMBER
trente

this ADJECTIVE, PRONOUN

> Use **ce** when 'this' is followed by a masculine noun, and **cette** when 'this' is followed by a feminine noun. **ce** changes to **cet** before a vowel and before most words beginning with 'h'.

1 ce
□ this book ce livre
cet
□ this man cet homme
cette
□ this woman cette femme □ this road cette route
- **THIS road** cette route-ci
- **this one** **1** celui-ci masc □ Pass me that pen. — This one? Passe-moi ce stylo. — Celui-ci ? **2** celle-ci fem □ Of the two photos, I prefer this one. Des deux photos, c'est celle-ci que je préfère.
2 ça
□ You see this? Tu vois ça ?
- **What's this?** Qu'est-ce que c'est ?
- **This is my mother.** (introduction) Je te présente ma mère.
- **This is Izzy speaking.** (on the phone) C'est Izzy à l'appareil.

thistle NOUN
le chardon masc

thorough ADJECTIVE
minutieux (FEM minutieuse)
□ She's very thorough. Elle est très minutieuse.

thoroughly ADVERB
à fond (examine)

those ADJECTIVE, PRONOUN
1 ces
□ those shoes ces chaussures
■ **THOSE shoes** ces chaussures-là
2 ceux-là masc
□ I want those! Je veux ceux-là !
celles-là fem
□ I'm looking for some sandals. Can I try those?
Je cherche des sandales. Je peux essayer celles-là ?

though CONJUNCTION, ADVERB
bien que
□ Though it's raining … Bien qu'il pleuve …

bien que has to be followed by a verb in the
subjunctive.

■ **He's a nice person, though he's not very
clever.** Il est sympa, mais pas très malin.

thought VERB ▷ see **think**

thought NOUN
l'idée fem (idea)
□ I've just had a thought. Je viens d'avoir une
idée.
■ **It was a nice thought, thank you.** C'est
gentil de ta part, merci.

thoughtful ADJECTIVE
1 pensif (FEM pensive) (deep in thought)
□ You look thoughtful. Tu as l'air pensif.
2 prévenant (FEM prévenante) (considerate)
□ She's very thoughtful. Elle est très prévenante.

thoughtless ADJECTIVE
■ **He's completely thoughtless.** Il ne pense
absolument pas aux autres.

thousand NUMBER
■ **a thousand** mille □ a thousand euros mille
euros
■ **£2000** deux mille livres
■ **thousands of people** des milliers de
personnes

thousandth ADJECTIVE, NOUN
le millième masc

thread NOUN
le fil masc

threat NOUN
la menace fem

to **threaten** VERB
menacer [12]
□ to threaten to do something menacer de faire
quelque chose

three NUMBER
trois
□ She's three. Elle a trois ans.

three-dimensional ADJECTIVE
à trois dimensions

threw VERB ▷ see **throw**

thrifty ADJECTIVE
économe (FEM économe)

thrill NOUN
l'émotion fem (excitement)

thrilled ADJECTIVE
■ **I was thrilled.** (pleased) J'étais absolument ravi.

thriller NOUN
le thriller masc

thrilling ADJECTIVE
palpitant (FEM palpitante)

throat NOUN
la gorge fem
□ to have a sore throat avoir mal à la gorge

to **throb** VERB
■ **a throbbing pain** un élancement
■ **My arm's throbbing.** J'ai des élancements
dans le bras.

throne NOUN
le trône masc

through PREPOSITION, ADJECTIVE, ADVERB
1 par
□ through the window par la fenêtre □ I know
her through my sister. Je la connais par ma
sœur. □ to go through Birmingham passer par
Birmingham
■ **to go through a tunnel** traverser [28] un
tunnel
2 à travers
□ through the mist à travers la brume □ through
the crowd à travers la foule
■ **a through train** un train direct
■ **'no through road'** « impasse »

throughout PREPOSITION
■ **throughout Britain** dans toute la Grande-
Bretagne
■ **throughout the year** pendant toute l'année

to **throw** VERB
lancer [12]
□ He threw the ball to me. Il m'a lancé le ballon.
■ **to throw a party** organiser [28] une soirée
■ **That really threw him.** Ça l'a déconcentré.

to **throw away** VERB
1 jeter [41] (rubbish)
2 perdre [61] (chance)

to **throw out** VERB
1 jeter [41] (throw away)
2 mettre [47] à la porte (person)
□ I threw him out. Je l'ai mis à la porte.

to **throw up** VERB
vomir [38]

thug NOUN
le voyou masc

thumb NOUN
le pouce masc

thumb tack NOUN (US)
la punaise *fem*

to **thump** VERB
■ **to thump somebody** donner [28] un coup de poing à quelqu'un

thunder NOUN
le tonnerre *masc*

thunderstorm NOUN
l'orage *masc*

thundery ADJECTIVE
orageux (FEM orageuse)

Thursday NOUN
le jeudi *masc*
□ on Thursday jeudi □ on Thursdays le jeudi
□ every Thursday tous les jeudis □ last Thursday jeudi dernier □ next Thursday jeudi prochain

thyme NOUN
le thym *masc*

tick NOUN
▷ *see also* **tick** VERB
1 la coche *fem* (*mark*)
2 le tic-tac *masc* (*of clock*)
■ **I'll be back in a tick.** J'en ai pour une seconde.

to **tick** VERB
▷ *see also* **tick** NOUN
1 cocher [28]
□ Tick the correct answer. Cochez la bonne réponse.
2 faire [36] tic-tac (*clock*)

to **tick off** VERB
1 cocher [28] (*check*)
□ He ticked off our names on the list. Il a coché nos noms sur la liste.
2 passer [58] un savon à (*tell off*)
□ She ticked me off for being late. Elle m'a passé un savon à cause de mon retard.

ticket NOUN

> **BE CAREFUL!**
> Be careful to choose correctly between **le ticket** and **le billet**.

1 le ticket *masc* (*for bus, tube, cinema, museum*)
□ an underground ticket un ticket de métro
2 le billet *masc* (*for plane, train, theatre, concert*)
■ **a parking ticket** un P.-V.

ticket inspector NOUN
le contrôleur *masc*
la contrôleuse *fem*

ticket office NOUN
le guichet *masc*

to **tickle** VERB
chatouiller [28]

ticklish ADJECTIVE
chatouilleux (FEM chatouilleuse)
□ Are you ticklish? Tu es chatouilleux ?

tide NOUN
la marée *fem*
■ **high tide** la marée haute
■ **low tide** la marée basse

tidy ADJECTIVE
▷ *see also* **tidy** VERB
1 bien rangé (FEM bien rangée) (*room*)
□ Your room's very tidy. Ta chambre est bien rangée.
2 ordonné (FEM ordonnée) (*person*)
□ She's very tidy. Elle est très ordonnée.

to **tidy** VERB
▷ *see also* **tidy** ADJECTIVE
ranger [45]
□ Go and tidy your room. Va ranger ta chambre.

to **tidy up** VERB
ranger [45]
□ Don't forget to tidy up afterwards. N'oubliez pas de ranger après.

tie NOUN
▷ *see also* **tie** VERB
la cravate *fem* (*necktie*)
■ **It was a tie.** (*in sport*) Ils ont fait match nul.

to **tie** VERB
▷ *see also* **tie** NOUN
1 nouer [28] (*ribbon, shoelaces*)
■ **to tie a knot in something** faire [36] un nœud à quelque chose
2 faire [36] match nul (*in sport*)
□ They tied three all. Ils ont fait match nul, trois à trois.

to **tie up** VERB
1 ficeler [4] (*parcel*)
2 attacher [28] (*dog, boat*)
3 ligoter [28] (*prisoner*)

tiger NOUN
le tigre *masc*

tight ADJECTIVE
1 moulant (FEM moulante) (*tight-fitting*)
□ tight clothes les vêtements moulants
2 juste (FEM juste) (*too tight*)
□ This dress is a bit tight. Cette robe est un peu juste.

to **tighten** VERB
1 tendre [88] (*rope*)
2 resserrer [28] (*screw*)

tightly ADVERB
fort (*hold*)

tights PL NOUN
le collant *masc sing*

tile NOUN
1 la tuile *fem* (*on roof*)
2 le carreau *masc* (PL les carreaux) (*on wall, floor*)

tiled ADJECTIVE
1 en tuiles (*roof*)
2 carrelé (FEM carrelée) (*wall, floor, room*)

till NOUN

▷ *see also* **till** PREPOSITION, CONJUNCTION

la caisse *fem*

till PREPOSITION, CONJUNCTION

▷ *see also* **till** NOUN

1 jusqu'à
  □ I waited till ten o'clock. J'ai attendu jusqu'à dix heures.
  ■ **till now** jusqu'à présent
  ■ **till then** jusque-là

2 avant

> Use **avant** if the sentence you want to translate contains a negative such as 'not' or 'never'.

  □ Till last year I'd never been to France. Avant l'année dernière, je n'étais jamais allé en France.
  □ It won't be ready till next week. Ça ne sera pas prêt avant la semaine prochaine.

time NOUN

1 l'heure *fem* (*on clock*)
  □ What time is it? Quelle heure est-il ? □ What time do you get up? À quelle heure tu te lèves ? □ It was two o'clock, French time. Il était deux heures, heure française.
  ■ **on time** à l'heure □ He never arrives on time. Il n'arrive jamais à l'heure.

2 le temps *masc* (*amount of time*)
  □ I'm sorry, I haven't got time. Je suis désolé, je n'ai pas le temps.
  ■ **from time to time** de temps en temps
  ■ **in time** à temps □ We arrived in time for lunch. Nous sommes arrivés à temps pour le déjeuner.
  ■ **just in time** juste à temps
  ■ **in no time** en un rien de temps □ It was ready in no time. Ça a été prêt en un rien de temps.
  ■ **It's time to go.** Il est temps de partir.
  ■ **a long time** longtemps □ Have you lived here for a long time? Vous habitez ici depuis longtemps ?

3 le moment *masc* (*moment*)
  □ This isn't a good time to ask him. Ce n'est pas le bon moment pour lui demander.
  ■ **for the time being** pour le moment

4 la fois *fem* (*occasion*)
  □ this time cette fois-ci □ next time la prochaine fois □ two at a time deux à la fois
  ■ **How many times?** Combien de fois ?
  ■ **at times** parfois
  ■ **in a week's time** dans une semaine □ I'll come back in a month's time. Je reviendrai dans un mois.
  ■ **Come and see us any time.** Venez nous voir quand vous voulez.
  ■ **to have a good time** bien s'amuser [28]
  □ Did you have a good time? Vous vous êtes bien amusés ?
  ■ **2 times 2 is 4** deux fois deux égalent quatre

time bomb NOUN

la bombe à retardement *fem*

time off NOUN

le temps libre *masc*

timer NOUN

le minuteur *masc*

time-share NOUN

l'appartement en multipropriété *masc*

timetable NOUN

1 l'horaire *masc* (*for train, bus*)
2 l'emploi du temps *masc* (*at school*)

time zone NOUN

le fuseau horaire *masc*

tin NOUN

1 la boîte *fem*
  □ a tin of soup une boîte de soupe □ a biscuit tin une boîte à biscuits
2 la boîte de conserve *fem*
  □ The bin was full of tins. La poubelle était pleine de boîtes de conserve.
3 l'étain *masc* (*type of metal*)

tinned ADJECTIVE

en boîte (*food*)
  □ tinned peaches des pêches en boîte

tin opener NOUN

l'ouvre-boîte *masc*

tinsel NOUN

les guirlandes de Noël *fem pl*

tinted ADJECTIVE

teinté (FEM teintée) (*spectacles, glass*)

tiny ADJECTIVE

minuscule (FEM minuscule)

tip NOUN

▷ *see also* **tip** VERB

1 le pourboire *masc* (*money*)
  □ Shall I give him a tip? Je lui donne un pourboire ?
2 le tuyau *masc* (PL les tuyaux) (*advice*)
  □ a useful tip un bon tuyau (*informal*)
3 le bout *masc* (*end*)
  □ It's on the tip of my tongue. Je l'ai sur le bout de la langue.
  ■ **a rubbish tip** une décharge
  ■ **This place is a complete tip!** Quel fouillis !

to **tip** VERB

▷ *see also* **tip** NOUN

donner [28] un pourboire à
  □ Don't forget to tip the taxi driver. N'oubliez pas de donner un pourboire au chauffeur de taxi.

tipsy ADJECTIVE

pompette (FEM pompette)

tiptoe NOUN

  ■ **on tiptoe** sur la pointe des pieds

tired ADJECTIVE

fatigué (FEM fatiguée)
  □ I'm tired. Je suis fatigué.

■ **to be tired of something** en avoir [8] assez
de quelque chose

tiring ADJECTIVE
fatigant (FEM fatigante)

tissue NOUN
le kleenex® *masc*
□ Have you got a tissue? Tu as un kleenex® ?

title NOUN
le titre *masc*

title role NOUN
le rôle principal *masc*

to PREPOSITION

> à + **le** changes to **au**. à + **les** changes to **aux**.

1 à
□ to go to Lyon aller à Lyon □ to go to school
aller à l'école □ a letter to his mother une lettre à
sa mère □ the answer to the question la réponse
à la question
au
□ to go to the theatre aller au théâtre
aux
□ We said goodbye to the neighbours. Nous
avons dit au revoir aux voisins.
■ **ready to go** prêt à partir
■ **ready to eat** prêt à manger
■ **It's easy to do.** C'est facile à faire.
■ **something to drink** quelque chose à boire
■ **I've got things to do.** J'ai des choses à faire.
■ **from ... to ...** de ... à ... □ from nine o'clock
to half past three de neuf heures à trois heures
et demie

2 de
□ the train to Carlisle le train de Carlisle □ the
road to Edinburgh la route d'Édimbourg □ the
key to the front door la clé de la porte d'entrée
■ **It's difficult to say.** C'est difficile à dire.
■ **It's easy to criticize.** C'est facile de critiquer.

> When referring to someone's house, shop or
> office, use **chez**.

3 chez
□ to go to the doctor's aller chez le docteur □ to
go to the butcher's aller chez le boucher □ Let's
go to Max's house. Si on allait chez Max ?

> When 'to' refers to a country which is
> feminine, use **en**; when the country is
> masculine, use **au**.

4 en
□ to go to France aller en France
au
□ to go to Portugal aller au Portugal

5 jusqu'à (*up to*)
□ to count to ten compter jusqu'à dix

6 pour (*in order to*)
□ I did it to help you. Je l'ai fait pour vous
aider. □ She's too young to go to school. Elle
est trop jeune pour aller à l'école.

toad NOUN
le crapaud *masc*

toadstool NOUN
le champignon vénéneux *masc*

toast NOUN
1 le pain grillé *masc*
□ a piece of toast une tranche de pain grillé
2 le toast *masc* (*speech*)
□ to drink a toast to somebody porter un toast
à quelqu'un

toaster NOUN
le grille-pain *masc* (PL les grille-pain)

toastie NOUN
le sandwich chaud *masc*
■ **a cheese and ham toastie** un croque-
monsieur

tobacco NOUN
le tabac *masc*

tobacconist's NOUN
le bureau de tabac *masc* (PL les bureaux de
tabac)

toboggan NOUN
la luge *fem*

tobogganing NOUN
■ **to go tobogganing** faire [36] de la luge

today ADVERB
aujourd'hui
□ What did you do today? Qu'est-ce que tu as
fait aujourd'hui ?

toddler NOUN
le bambin *masc*

toe NOUN
le doigt de pied *masc*

toffee NOUN
le caramel *masc*

together ADVERB
1 ensemble
□ Are they still together? Ils sont toujours
ensemble ?
2 en même temps (*at the same time*)
□ Don't all speak together! Ne parlez pas tous en
même temps !
■ **together with** (*with person*) avec

toilet NOUN
les toilettes *fem pl*

toilet paper NOUN
le papier hygiénique *masc*

toiletries PL NOUN
les articles de toilette *masc pl*

toilet roll NOUN
le rouleau de papier hygiénique *masc* (PL les
rouleaux de papier hygiénique)

token NOUN
■ **a gift token** un bon-cadeau

told VERB ▷ *see* **tell**

t

tolerant ADJECTIVE
tolérant (FEM tolérante)

toll NOUN
le péage masc (on bridge, motorway)

tomato NOUN
la tomate fem
□ tomato sauce la sauce tomate □ tomato soup la soupe à la tomate

tomboy NOUN
le garçon manqué masc
□ She's a real tomboy. C'est un vrai garçon manqué.

tomorrow ADVERB
demain
□ tomorrow morning demain matin
□ tomorrow night demain soir
■ **the day after tomorrow** après-demain

ton NOUN
la tonne fem
□ That old bike weighs a ton. Ce vieux vélo pèse une tonne.

> **DID YOU KNOW...?**
> In France, measurements are in metric tonnes rather than tons. A ton is slightly more than a **tonne**.

tongue NOUN
la langue fem
■ **to say something tongue in cheek** dire [27] quelque chose en plaisantant

tonic NOUN
le Schweppes® masc (tonic water)
■ **a gin and tonic** un gin tonic

tonight ADVERB
1 ce soir (this evening)
□ Are you going out tonight? Tu sors ce soir ?
2 cette nuit (during the night)
□ I'll sleep well tonight. Je dormirai bien cette nuit.

tonsillitis NOUN
l'angine fem

tonsils PL NOUN
les amygdales fem pl

too ADVERB
1 aussi (as well)
□ My sister came too. Ma sœur est venue aussi.
2 trop (excessively)
□ The water's too hot. L'eau est trop chaude.
□ We arrived too late. Nous sommes arrivés trop tard.
■ **too much 1** (with noun) trop de □ too much noise trop de bruit **2** (with verb) trop □ At Christmas we always eat too much. À Noël nous mangeons toujours trop. **3** (too expensive) trop cher □ Fifty euros? That's too much. Cinquante euros ? C'est trop cher.

■ **too many** trop de □ too many hamburgers trop de burgers
■ **Too bad!** Tant pis !

took VERB ▷ see take

tool NOUN
l'outil masc
■ **a tool box** une boîte à outils

tooth NOUN
la dent fem

toothache NOUN
le mal de dents masc
□ to have toothache avoir mal aux dents

toothbrush NOUN
la brosse à dents fem

toothpaste NOUN
le dentifrice masc

top NOUN
▷ see also **top** ADJECTIVE
1 le haut masc (of page, ladder, garment)
□ at the top of the page en haut de la page
□ She wore jeans and a top. Elle portait un jean et un haut.
■ **a bikini top** un haut de bikini
2 le sommet masc (of mountain)
3 le dessus masc (of table)
■ **on top of** (on) sur □ on top of the fridge sur le frigo
■ **You need to pay a tip on top of that.** Il faut payer un pourboire en plus.
■ **from top to bottom** de fond en comble
□ I searched the house from top to bottom. J'ai fouillé la maison de fond en comble.
4 le couvercle masc (of box, jar)
5 le bouchon masc (of bottle)

top ADJECTIVE
▷ see also **top** NOUN
grand (FEM grande) (first-class)
□ a top surgeon un grand chirurgien
■ **a top model** un top model
■ **He always gets top marks in chemistry.** Il a toujours d'excellentes notes en chimie.
■ **the top floor** le dernier étage □ on the top floor au dernier étage

topic NOUN
le sujet masc
□ The essay can be on any topic. Cette dissertation peut être sur n'importe quel sujet.

topical ADJECTIVE
d'actualité
□ a topical issue un sujet d'actualité

torch NOUN
la lampe de poche fem

tore, torn VERB ▷ see tear

tortoise NOUN
la tortue fem

torture NOUN
▷ *see also* **torture** VERB
la torture *fem*
□ It was pure torture. C'était une vraie torture.

to **torture** VERB
▷ *see also* **torture** NOUN
torturer [28]
□ Stop torturing that poor animal! Arrête de torturer cette pauvre bête !

Tory ADJECTIVE
▷ *see also* **Tory** NOUN
conservateur (FEM conservatrice)
□ the Tory government le gouvernement conservateur

Tory NOUN
▷ *see also* **Tory** ADJECTIVE
le conservateur *masc*
la conservatrice *fem*
■ **the Tories** les conservateurs

to **toss** VERB
■ **to toss pancakes** faire [36] sauter les crêpes
■ **Shall we toss for it?** On joue à pile ou face ?

total ADJECTIVE
▷ *see also* **total** NOUN
total (FEM totale, MASC PL totaux)
■ **the total amount** le total

total NOUN
▷ *see also* **total** ADJECTIVE
le total *masc* (PL les totaux)
■ **the grand total** le total

totally ADVERB
complètement
□ He's totally useless. Il est complètement nul.

touch NOUN
▷ *see also* **touch** VERB
■ **to get in touch with somebody** prendre [65] contact avec quelqu'un
■ **to keep in touch with somebody** rester [71ᵃ] en contact avec quelqu'un
■ **Keep in touch!** Donne-moi de tes nouvelles !
■ **to lose touch** se perdre [61] de vue
■ **to lose touch with somebody** perdre [61] quelqu'un de vue

to **touch** VERB
▷ *see also* **touch** NOUN
toucher [28]
■ **Don't touch that!** N'y touche pas !

touchdown NOUN
l'atterrissage *masc*

touched ADJECTIVE
touché (FEM touchée)
□ I was really touched. Ça m'a beaucoup touché.

touching ADJECTIVE
touchant (FEM touchante)

touchline NOUN
la ligne de touche *fem*

touchpad NOUN
le pavé tactile *masc*

touchy ADJECTIVE
susceptible (FEM susceptible)
□ She's a bit touchy. Elle est susceptible.

tough ADJECTIVE
1 dur (FEM dure)
□ It was tough, but I managed OK. C'était dur, mais je m'en suis tiré. □ It's a tough job. C'est dur.
■ **The meat's tough.** La viande est coriace.
2 solide (FEM solide) (*strong*)
□ tough leather gloves de solides gants en cuir
□ She's tough. She can take it. Elle est solide. Elle tiendra le coup.
3 dangereux (FEM dangereuse) (*rough, violent*)
■ **He thinks he's a tough guy.** Il se prend pour un gros dur.
■ **Tough luck!** C'est comme ça !

toupee NOUN
le postiche *masc*

tour NOUN
▷ *see also* **tour** VERB
1 la visite *fem* (*of town, museum*)
□ We went on a tour of the city. Nous avons visité la ville.
■ **a package tour** un voyage organisé
2 la tournée *fem* (*by singer, group*)
□ on tour en tournée
■ **to go on tour** faire [36] une tournée

to **tour** VERB
▷ *see also* **tour** NOUN
■ **Rihanna is touring Europe.** Rihanna est en tournée en Europe.

tour guide NOUN
le/la guide *masc/fem*

tourism NOUN
le tourisme *masc*

tourist NOUN
le/la touriste *masc/fem*
■ **tourist information office** l'office du tourisme *masc*

tournament NOUN
le tournoi *masc*

tour operator NOUN
le tour-opérateur *masc*

towards PREPOSITION
1 vers (*in the direction of*)
□ He came towards me. Il est venu vers moi.
2 envers (*of attitude*)
□ my feelings towards him mes sentiments envers lui

towel NOUN
la serviette *fem*

tower NOUN
la tour *fem*
■ **a tower block** une tour

t

town NOUN
la ville *fem*
□ a town plan un plan de ville
■ **the town centre** le centre-ville
■ **the town hall** la mairie

tow truck NOUN (US)
la dépanneuse *fem*

toy NOUN
le jouet *masc*
□ a toy shop un magasin de jouets
■ **a toy car** une petite voiture

trace NOUN
▷ *see also* **trace** VERB
la trace *fem*
□ There was no trace of the robbers. Il n'y avait pas de trace des voleurs.

to **trace** VERB
▷ *see also* **trace** NOUN
décalquer [28] (*draw*)

tracing paper NOUN
le papier calque *masc*

track NOUN
1 le chemin *masc* (*dirt road*)
2 la voie ferrée *fem* (*railway line*)
3 la piste *fem* (*in sport*)
□ two laps of the track deux tours de piste
4 la chanson *fem* (*song*)
□ This is my favourite track. C'est ma chanson préférée.
5 les traces *fem pl* (*trail*)
□ They followed the tracks for miles. Ils ont suivi les traces sur des kilomètres.

to **track down** VERB
■ **to track somebody down** retrouver [28] quelqu'un □ The police never tracked down the thief. La police n'a jamais retrouvé le voleur.

tracksuit NOUN
le jogging *masc*

tractor NOUN
le tracteur *masc*

trade NOUN
le métier *masc* (*skill*, *job*)
□ to learn a trade apprendre un métier

trade union NOUN
le syndicat *masc*

trade unionist NOUN
le/la syndicaliste *masc/fem*

tradition NOUN
la tradition *fem*

traditional ADJECTIVE
traditionnel (FEM traditionnelle)

traffic NOUN
la circulation *fem*
□ The traffic was terrible. Il y avait une circulation épouvantable.

traffic circle NOUN (US)
le rond-point *masc* (PL les ronds-points)

traffic jam NOUN
l'embouteillage *masc*

traffic lights PL NOUN
les feux *masc pl*

traffic warden NOUN
le contractuel *masc*
la contractuelle *fem*

tragedy NOUN
la tragédie *fem*

tragic ADJECTIVE
tragique (FEM tragique)

trailer NOUN
1 la remorque *fem* (*vehicle*)
2 la bande-annonce *fem* (*film advert*)

train NOUN
▷ *see also* **train** VERB
1 le train *masc*
■ **a train set** un train électrique
2 la rame *fem* (*on underground*)

to **train** VERB
▷ *see also* **train** NOUN
s'entraîner [28] (*sport*)
□ to train for a race s'entraîner pour une course
■ **to train as a teacher** suivre [81] une formation d'enseignant
■ **to train an animal to do something** dresser [28] un animal à faire quelque chose

trained ADJECTIVE
■ **She's a trained nurse.** Elle est infirmière diplômée.

trainee NOUN
1 le/la stagiaire *masc/fem* (*in profession*)
□ She's a trainee. Elle est stagiaire.
2 l'apprenti *masc*
l'apprentie *fem* (*apprentice*)
□ a trainee plumber un apprenti plombier

trainer NOUN
1 l'entraîneur *masc* (*sports coach*)
2 le dompteur *masc*
la dompteuse *fem* (*of animals*)

trainers PL NOUN
les baskets *fem pl*
□ a pair of trainers une paire de baskets

training NOUN
1 la formation *fem*
□ a training course un stage de formation
2 l'entraînement *masc* (*sport*)

tram NOUN
le tramway *masc*

tramp NOUN
le clochard *masc*
la clocharde *fem*

trampoline NOUN
le trampoline *masc*

Numbers in brackets refer to verb tables on pages 650 to 658

trans ADJECTIVE (*informal*)
trans (FEM trans)

transfer NOUN
▷ *see also* **transfer** VERB
le transfert *masc*

to **transfer** VERB
▷ *see also* **transfer** NOUN
transférer [34] (*object, patient*)
■ **to transfer money to somebody** faire [36] un virement à quelqu'un

transfusion NOUN
la transfusion *fem*

transgender ADJECTIVE
transgenre (FEM transgenre)

transit NOUN
le transit *masc*
□ in transit en transit

transit lounge NOUN
la salle de transit *fem*

to **translate** VERB
traduire [23]
□ to translate something into English traduire quelque chose en anglais

translation NOUN
la traduction *fem*

translator NOUN
le traducteur *masc*
la traductrice *fem*
□ Anita's a translator. Anita est traductrice.

transparent ADJECTIVE
transparent (FEM transparente)

transplant NOUN
la greffe *fem*
□ a heart transplant une greffe du cœur

transport NOUN
▷ *see also* **transport** VERB
le transport *masc*
□ public transport les transports en commun

to **transport** VERB
▷ *see also* **transport** NOUN
transporter [28]

trap NOUN
le piège *masc*

trash NOUN (US)
les ordures *fem pl*
■ **the trash can** la poubelle

trashy ADJECTIVE
nul (FEM nulle)

traumatic ADJECTIVE
traumatisant (FEM traumatisante)
□ It was a traumatic experience. Ça a été une expérience traumatisante.

travel NOUN
▷ *see also* **travel** VERB
les voyages *masc pl*

to **travel** VERB
▷ *see also* **travel** NOUN
voyager [45]
□ I prefer to travel by train. Je préfère voyager en train.
■ **I'd like to travel round the world.** J'aimerais faire le tour du monde.
■ **We travelled over 800 kilometres.** Nous avons fait plus de huit cents kilomètres.
■ **News travels fast!** Les nouvelles circulent vite !

travel agency NOUN
l'agence de voyages *fem*

travel agent NOUN
■ **She's a travel agent.** Elle travaille dans une agence de voyages.

traveller (US **traveler**) NOUN
1 le voyageur *masc*
la voyageuse *fem* (*on bus, train, plane*)
2 le/la nomade *masc/fem* (*Gypsy*)

travelling (US **traveling**) NOUN
■ **I love travelling.** J'adore les voyages.

travel sickness NOUN
le mal des transports *masc*

tray NOUN
le plateau *masc* (PL les plateaux)

to **tread** VERB
marcher [28]
□ to tread on something marcher sur quelque chose

treasure NOUN
le trésor *masc*

treat NOUN
▷ *see also* **treat** VERB
1 le petit cadeau *masc* (PL les petits cadeaux) (*present*)
2 la gâterie *fem* (*food*)
■ **to give somebody a treat** faire [36] plaisir à quelqu'un

to **treat** VERB
▷ *see also* **treat** NOUN
traiter [28] (*well, badly*)
■ **to treat somebody to something** offrir [54] quelque chose à quelqu'un □ He treated us to an ice cream. Il nous a offert une glace.

treatment NOUN
le traitement *masc*

to **treble** VERB
tripler [28]
□ The cost of living there has trebled. Le coût de la vie là-bas a triplé.

tree NOUN
l'arbre *masc*

to **tremble** VERB
trembler [28]

tremendous ADJECTIVE
énorme (FEM énorme)
□ a tremendous success un succès énorme

t

trend NOUN
1 la mode *fem* (*fashion*)
□ to set a trend lancer [12] une mode
2 la tendance *fem* (*tendency*)
□ a downward trend in exam results une tendance à la baisse dans les résultats aux examens.

trendy ADJECTIVE
branché (FEM branchée)

trial NOUN
le procès *masc* (*in court*)

triangle NOUN
le triangle *masc*

tribe NOUN
la tribu *fem*

trick NOUN
▷ *see also* **trick** VERB
1 le tour *masc*
□ to play a trick on somebody jouer un tour à quelqu'un
2 le truc *masc* (*knack*)
□ It's not easy: there's a trick to it. Ce n'est pas facile : il y a un truc.

to **trick** VERB
▷ *see also* **trick** NOUN
■ to trick somebody rouler [28] quelqu'un

tricky ADJECTIVE
délicat (FEM délicate)

tricycle NOUN
le tricycle *masc*

trifle NOUN
le diplomate *masc* (*dessert*)

to **trim** VERB
▷ *see also* **trim** NOUN
1 égaliser [28] (*hair*)
2 tondre [69] (*grass*)

trim NOUN
▷ *see also* **trim** VERB
la coupe d'entretien *fem* (*haircut*)
□ to have a trim se faire rafraîchir la coupe

trip NOUN
▷ *see also* **trip** VERB
le voyage *masc*
□ to go on a trip faire un voyage □ Have a good trip! Bon voyage !
■ a day trip une excursion d'une journée

to **trip** VERB
▷ *see also* **trip** NOUN
trébucher [28] (*stumble*)

triple ADJECTIVE
triple (FEM triple)

triplets PL NOUN
les triplés *masc pl*
les triplées *fem pl*

trivial ADJECTIVE
insignifiant (FEM insignifiante)

trod, trodden VERB ▷ *see* **tread**

troll NOUN
le troll *masc* (*online*)

to **troll** VERB
troller [28] (*online*)

trolley NOUN
le chariot *masc*

trombone NOUN
le trombone *masc*
□ I play the trombone. Je joue du trombone.

troops PL NOUN
les troupes *masc pl*
□ British troops les troupes britanniques

trophy NOUN
le trophée *masc*
□ to win a trophy gagner un trophée

tropical ADJECTIVE
tropical (FEM tropicale)
□ The weather was tropical. Il faisait une chaleur tropicale.

to **trot** VERB
trotter [28]

trouble NOUN
le problème *masc*
□ The trouble is, it's too expensive. Le problème, c'est que c'est trop cher.
■ to be in trouble avoir [8] des ennuis
■ What's the trouble? Qu'est-ce qui ne va pas ?
■ stomach trouble troubles gastriques
■ to take a lot of trouble over something se donner [28] beaucoup de mal pour quelque chose
■ Don't worry, it's no trouble. Mais non, ça ne me dérange pas du tout.

troublemaker NOUN
l'élément perturbateur *masc*

trousers PL NOUN
le pantalon *masc sing*
□ a pair of trousers un pantalon

trout NOUN
la truite *fem*

truant NOUN
■ to play truant faire [36] l'école buissonnière

truck NOUN
le camion *masc*

truck driver NOUN
le camionneur *masc*
la conductrice de camion *fem*
□ He's a truck driver. Il est camionneur.

true ADJECTIVE
vrai (FEM vraie)
■ That's true. C'est vrai.
■ to come true se réaliser [28] □ I hope my dream will come true. J'espère que mon rêve se réalisera.
■ true love le grand amour

truly ADVERB
vraiment

□ It was a truly remarkable victory. C'était vraiment une victoire remarquable.

trumpet NOUN
la trompette *fem*
□ She plays the trumpet. Elle joue de la trompette.

trunk NOUN
1 le tronc *masc* (*of tree*)
2 la trompe *fem* (*of elephant*)
3 la malle *fem* (*luggage*)
4 le coffre *masc* (*us: of car*)

trunks PL NOUN
■ **swimming trunks** le maillot de bain
■ **a pair of trunks** un maillot de bain

trust NOUN
▷ *see also* **trust** VERB
la confiance *fem*
□ to have trust in somebody avoir confiance en quelqu'un

to **trust** VERB
▷ *see also* **trust** NOUN
■ **to trust somebody** faire [36] confiance à quelqu'un □ Don't you trust me? Tu ne me fais pas confiance ? □ Trust me! Fais-moi confiance !

trusting ADJECTIVE
confiant (FEM confiante)

truth NOUN
la vérité *fem*

truthful ADJECTIVE
■ **She's a very truthful person.** Elle dit toujours la vérité.

try NOUN
▷ *see also* **try** VERB
l'essai *masc*
□ his third try son troisième essai
■ **to have a try** essayer [59]
■ **It's worth a try.** Ça vaut la peine d'essayer.
■ **to give something a try** essayer [59] quelque chose

to **try** VERB
▷ *see also* **try** NOUN
1 essayer [59] (*attempt*)
□ to try to do something essayer de faire quelque chose
■ **to try again** refaire [36] un essai
2 goûter [28] (*taste*)
□ Would you like to try some? Voulez-vous goûter ?

to **try on** VERB
essayer [59] (*clothes*)

to **try out** VERB
essayer [59]

T-shirt NOUN
le tee-shirt *masc*

tube NOUN
le tube *masc*
■ **the Tube** (*underground*) le métro

tuberculosis NOUN
la tuberculose *fem*

Tuesday NOUN
le mardi *masc*
□ on Tuesday mardi □ on Tuesdays le mardi
□ every Tuesday tous les mardis □ last Tuesday mardi dernier □ next Tuesday mardi prochain
■ **Shrove Tuesday** (*Pancake Tuesday*) le mardi gras

tug-of-war NOUN
la lutte à la corde *fem*

tuition NOUN
les cours *masc pl*
■ **private tuition** les cours particuliers

tulip NOUN
la tulipe *fem*

tumble dryer NOUN
le sèche-linge *masc* (PL les sèche-linge)

tummy NOUN
le ventre *masc*

tuna NOUN
le thon *masc*

tune NOUN
l'air *masc* (*melody*)
■ **to play in tune** jouer [28] juste
■ **to sing out of tune** chanter [28] faux

Tunisia NOUN
la Tunisie *fem*
■ **in Tunisia** en Tunisie

tunnel NOUN
le tunnel *masc*
■ **the Channel Tunnel** le tunnel sous la Manche

Turk NOUN
le Turc *masc*
la Turque *fem*

Turkey NOUN
la Turquie *fem*
■ **in Turkey** en Turquie
■ **to Turkey** en Turquie

turkey NOUN
1 la dinde *fem* (*meat*)
2 le dindon *masc* (*live bird*)

Turkish NOUN
▷ *see also* **Turkish** ADJECTIVE
le turc *masc* (*language*)

Turkish ADJECTIVE
▷ *see also* **Turkish** NOUN
turc (FEM turque)

turn NOUN
▷ *see also* **turn** VERB
1 le tournant *masc* (*bend in road*)
■ **'no left turn'** « défense de tourner à gauche »
2 le tour *masc* (*go*)
□ It's my turn! C'est mon tour !

to **turn** VERB
▷ *see also* **turn** NOUN
1 tourner [28]
□ Turn right at the lights. Tournez à droite aux feux.
2 devenir [25!] (*become*)
□ to turn red devenir rouge
■ **to turn into something** se transformer [28] en quelque chose □ The frog turned into a prince. La grenouille s'est transformée en prince.

to **turn back** VERB
faire [36] demi-tour
□ We turned back. Nous avons fait demi-tour.

to **turn down** VERB
1 refuser [28] (*offer*)
2 baisser [28] (*radio, TV, heating*)
□ Shall I turn the heating down? Je baisse le chauffage ?

to **turn off** VERB
1 éteindre [60] (*light, radio*)
2 fermer [28] (*tap*)
3 arrêter [28] (*engine*)

to **turn on** VERB
1 allumer [28] (*light, radio*)
2 ouvrir [55] (*tap*)
3 mettre [47] en marche (*engine*)

to **turn out** VERB
■ **It turned out to be a mistake.** Il s'est avéré que c'était une erreur.
■ **It turned out that she was right.** Il s'est avéré qu'elle avait raison.

to **turn round** VERB
1 faire [36] demi-tour (*car*)
2 se retourner [72] (*person*)

to **turn up** VERB
1 arriver [5!] (*arrive*)
2 monter [48] (*heater*)
■ **Could you turn up the radio?** Tu peux monter le son de la radio ?

turning NOUN
■ **It's the third turning on the left.** C'est la troisième à gauche.
■ **We took the wrong turning.** Nous n'avons pas tourné au bon endroit.

turnip NOUN
le navet *masc*

turquoise ADJECTIVE
turquoise (FEM+PL turquoise) (*colour*)

turtle NOUN
la tortue *fem*

tutor NOUN
le professeur particulier *masc* (*private teacher*)

tuxedo NOUN (US)
le smoking *masc*

TV NOUN
la télé *fem*

tweet NOUN
▷ *see also* **tweet** VERB
le tweet *masc* (*on Twitter*)

to **tweet** VERB
▷ *see also* **tweet** NOUN
tweeter [28] (*on Twitter*)

tweezers PL NOUN
la pince à épiler *fem sing*

twelfth ADJECTIVE
douzième (FEM douzième)
□ the twelfth floor le douzième étage
■ **the twelfth of August** le douze août

twelve NUMBER
douze
□ She's twelve. Elle a douze ans.
■ **twelve o'clock 1** (*midday*) midi
2 (*midnight*) minuit

twentieth ADJECTIVE
vingtième (FEM vingtième)
□ the twentieth time la vingtième fois
■ **the twentieth of May** le vingt mai

twenty NUMBER
vingt
□ He's twenty. Il a vingt ans.
■ **in twenty fourteen** en deux mille quatorze

twice ADVERB
deux fois
■ **twice as much** deux fois plus □ He gets twice as much pocket money as me. Il a deux fois plus d'argent de poche que moi.

twin NOUN
le jumeau *masc* (MASC PL les jumeaux)
la jumelle *fem*
■ **my twin brother** mon frère jumeau
■ **her twin sister** sa sœur jumelle
■ **identical twins** les vrais jumeaux
■ **a twin room** une chambre à deux lits

twinned ADJECTIVE
jumelé (FEM jumelée)
□ Stroud is twinned with Châteaubriant. Stroud est jumelée avec Châteaubriant.

to **twist** VERB
1 tordre [49] (*bend*)
2 déformer [281] (*distort*)
□ You're twisting my words. Tu déformes ce que j'ai dit.

twit NOUN
le crétin *masc*
la crétine *fem*

Twitter® NOUN
Twitter®

two NUMBER
deux
□ She's two. Elle a deux ans.

type NOUN
> ▷ see also **type** VERB
le type *masc*
□ What type of smartphone have you got?
Quel type de smartphone as-tu ?

to **type** VERB
> ▷ see also **type** NOUN
taper [28] à la machine

typewriter NOUN
la machine à écrire *fem*

typical ADJECTIVE
typique (FEM typique)
□ That's just typical! C'est typique !

tyre NOUN
le pneu *masc*

t

Uu

UFO NOUN
l'OVNI *masc* (= *objet volant non identifié*)

ugh EXCLAMATION
pouah !

ugly ADJECTIVE
laid (FEM laide)

UK NOUN (= *United Kingdom*)
le Royaume-Uni *masc*
- **from the UK** du Royaume-Uni
- **in the UK** au Royaume-Uni
- **to the UK** au Royaume-Uni

Ukraine NOUN
l'Ukraine *fem*
- **in Ukraine** en Ukraine
- **to Ukraine** en Ukraine

ulcer NOUN
l'ulcère *masc*
- **a mouth ulcer** un aphte

Ulster NOUN
l'Irlande du Nord *fem*
- **in Ulster** en Irlande du Nord

ultimate ADJECTIVE
suprême (FEM suprême)
□ the ultimate challenge le défi suprême
- **It was the ultimate adventure.** C'était la grande aventure.

ultimately ADVERB
au bout du compte
□ Ultimately, it's your decision. Au bout du compte, c'est votre décision.

umbrella NOUN
1 le parapluie *masc*
2 le parasol *masc* (*for sun*)

umpire NOUN
1 l'arbitre *masc* (*in cricket*)
2 le juge de chaise *masc* (*in tennis*)

UN NOUN (= *United Nations*)
l'ONU *fem* (= *Organisation des Nations Unies*)

unable ADJECTIVE
- **to be unable to do something** ne pas pouvoir [64] faire quelque chose □ I was unable to come. Je n'ai pas pu venir.

unacceptable ADJECTIVE
inacceptable (FEM inacceptable)

unanimous ADJECTIVE
unanime (FEM unanime)
□ a unanimous decision une décision unanime

unattended ADJECTIVE
- **to leave something unattended** laisser [28] quelque chose sans surveillance □ Never leave pets unattended in your car. Ne laissez jamais d'animaux domestiques sans surveillance dans votre voiture.

unavoidable ADJECTIVE
inévitable (FEM inévitable)

unaware ADJECTIVE
- **to be unaware** **1** (*not know about*) ignorer [28] □ I was unaware of the regulations. J'ignorais le règlement. **2** (*not notice*) ne pas se rendre [7] compte □ She was unaware that she was being filmed. Elle ne se rendait pas compte qu'on la filmait.

unbearable ADJECTIVE
insupportable (FEM insupportable)

unbeatable ADJECTIVE
imbattable (FEM imbattable)

unbelievable ADJECTIVE
incroyable (FEM incroyable)

unborn ADJECTIVE
- **the unborn child** le fœtus

unbreakable ADJECTIVE
incassable (FEM incassable)

uncanny ADJECTIVE
étrange (FEM étrange)
□ That's uncanny! C'est étrange !
- **an uncanny resemblance** une ressemblance troublante

uncertain ADJECTIVE
incertain (FEM incertaine)
□ The future is uncertain. L'avenir est incertain.
- **to be uncertain about something** ne pas être [35] sûr de quelque chose

uncivilized ADJECTIVE
barbare (FEM barbare)

uncle NOUN
l'oncle *masc*
□ my uncle mon oncle

uncomfortable ADJECTIVE
pas confortable (FEM pas confortable)
□ The seats are rather uncomfortable. Les sièges ne sont pas très confortables.

unconscious ADJECTIVE
sans connaissance

u

Numbers in brackets refer to verb tables on pages 650 to 658

uncontrollable ADJECTIVE
incontrôlable (FEM incontrôlable)

unconventional ADJECTIVE
peu conventionnel (FEM peu conventionnelle)

under PREPOSITION
1 sous
□ The cat's under the table. Le chat est sous la table. □ The tunnel goes under the Channel. Le tunnel passe sous la Manche.
■ **under there** là-dessous □ What's under there? Qu'est-ce qu'il y a là-dessous ?
2 moins de (*less than*)
□ under 20 people moins de vingt personnes □ children under 10 les enfants de moins de dix ans

underage ADJECTIVE
■ He's underage. Il n'a pas l'âge réglementaire.

undercover ADJECTIVE, ADVERB
secret (FEM secrète)
□ an undercover agent un agent secret
■ **She was working undercover.** Elle travaillait sous une fausse identité.

to **underestimate** VERB
sous-estimer [28]
□ I underestimated her. Je l'ai sous-estimée.

to **undergo** VERB
subir [38] (*operation, examination, change*)
■ **to be undergoing repairs** être [35] en réparation

underground ADJECTIVE, ADVERB
▷ *see also* **underground** NOUN
1 souterrain (FEM souterraine)
□ an underground car park un parking souterrain
2 sous terre
□ Moles live underground. Les taupes vivent sous terre.

underground NOUN
▷ *see also* **underground** ADJECTIVE, ADVERB
le métro *masc*
□ Is there an underground in Lille? Est-ce qu'il y a un métro à Lille ?

to **underline** VERB
souligner [28]

underneath PREPOSITION, ADVERB
1 sous
□ underneath the carpet sous la moquette
2 dessous
□ I got out of the car and looked underneath. Je suis descendu de la voiture et j'ai regardé dessous.

underpaid ADJECTIVE
sous-payé (FEM sous-payée)
□ I'm underpaid. Je suis sous-payé.

underpants PL NOUN
le slip *masc sing*

underpass NOUN
1 le passage souterrain *masc* (*for people*)
2 le passage inférieur *masc* (*for cars*)

undershirt NOUN (US)
le maillot de corps *masc*

to **understand** VERB
comprendre [65]
□ Do you understand? Vous comprenez ? □ I don't understand this word. Je ne comprends pas ce mot. □ Is that understood? C'est compris ?

understanding ADJECTIVE
compréhensif (FEM compréhensive)
□ She's very understanding. Elle est très compréhensive.

understood VERB ▷ *see* **understand**

undertaker NOUN
l'entrepreneur des pompes funèbres *masc*

underwater ADJECTIVE, ADVERB
sous l'eau
□ This sequence was filmed underwater. Cette séquence a été filmée sous l'eau.
■ **an underwater camera** un appareil photographique de plongée
■ **underwater photography** la photographie subaquatique

underwear NOUN
les sous-vêtements *masc pl*

underwent VERB ▷ *see* **undergo**

to **undo** VERB
1 défaire [36] (*buttons, knot*)
2 déballer [28] (*parcel*)

to **undress** VERB
se déshabiller [28] (*get undressed*)
□ The doctor told me to undress. Le médecin m'a dit de me déshabiller.

uneconomic ADJECTIVE
pas rentable (FEM pas rentable)

unemployed ADJECTIVE
au chômage
□ He's unemployed. Il est au chômage. □ He's been unemployed for a year. Ça fait un an qu'il est au chômage.
■ **the unemployed** les chômeurs *masc pl*

unemployment NOUN
le chômage *masc*

unexpected ADJECTIVE
inattendu (FEM inattendue)
□ an unexpected visitor un visiteur inattendu

unexpectedly ADVERB
à l'improviste
□ They arrived unexpectedly. Ils sont arrivés à l'improviste.

unfair ADJECTIVE
injuste (FEM injuste)
□ It's unfair to girls. C'est injuste pour les filles.

u

unfamiliar – unnatural

unfamiliar ADJECTIVE
■ **I heard an unfamiliar voice.** J'ai entendu une voix que je ne connaissais pas.

unfashionable ADJECTIVE
démodé (FEM démodée)

unfit ADJECTIVE
■ **I'm rather unfit.** Je ne suis pas en très bonne condition physique.

to **unfold** VERB
déplier [19]
□ She unfolded the map. Elle a déplié la carte.

unforgettable ADJECTIVE
inoubliable (FEM inoubliable)

unfortunately ADVERB
malheureusement
□ Unfortunately, I arrived late. Malheureusement, je suis arrivé en retard.

to **unfriend** VERB
supprimer [28] de sa liste d'amis
□ Her brother has unfriended her on Facebook. Son frère l'a supprimée de sa liste d'amis sur Facebook.

unfriendly ADJECTIVE
pas aimable (FEM pas aimable)
□ The waiters are a bit unfriendly. Les serveurs ne sont pas très aimables.

ungrateful ADJECTIVE
ingrat (FEM ingrate)

unhappy ADJECTIVE
malheureux (FEM malheureuse)
□ He was very unhappy as a child. Il était très malheureux quand il était petit.
■ **to look unhappy** avoir [8] l'air triste

unhealthy ADJECTIVE
1 maladif (FEM maladive) (*person*)
2 malsain (FEM malsaine) (*place, habit*)
3 pas sain (FEM pas saine) (*food*)

uni NOUN
la fac fem (*university*)
□ to go to uni aller à la fac

uniform NOUN
l'uniforme *masc*
□ school uniform l'uniforme scolaire

> **DID YOU KNOW...?**
> Most French children don't wear school uniform.

uninhabited ADJECTIVE
inhabité (FEM inhabitée)

union NOUN
le syndicat *masc* (*trade union*)

Union Jack NOUN
le drapeau du Royaume-Uni *masc*

unique ADJECTIVE
unique (FEM unique)

unit NOUN
1 l'unité *fem*

□ a unit of measurement une unité de mesure
2 l'élément *masc* (*piece of furniture*)
□ a kitchen unit un élément de cuisine

United Kingdom NOUN
le Royaume-Uni *masc*

United Nations NOUN
les Nations Unies *fem pl*

United States NOUN
les États-Unis *masc pl*
■ **in the United States** aux États-Unis
■ **to the United States** aux États-Unis

universe NOUN
l'univers *masc*

university NOUN
l'université *fem*
□ She's at university. Elle va à l'université. □ Do you want to go to university? Tu veux aller à l'université ? □ Lancaster University l'université de Lancaster

unleaded ADJECTIVE
■ **unleaded petrol** l'essence sans plomb *fem*

unleaded petrol NOUN
l'essence sans plomb *fem*

unless CONJUNCTION
■ **unless he leaves** à moins qu'il ne parte
□ I won't come unless you phone me. Je ne viendrai pas à moins que tu ne me téléphones.

unlike PREPOSITION
contrairement à
□ Unlike him, I really enjoy flying. Contrairement à lui, j'adore prendre l'avion.

unlikely ADJECTIVE
peu probable (FEM peu probable)
□ It's possible, but unlikely. C'est possible, mais peu probable.

to **unload** VERB
décharger [45]
□ We unloaded the car. Nous avons déchargé la voiture. □ The lorries go there to unload. Les camions y vont pour être déchargés.

to **unlock** VERB
ouvrir [55]
□ He unlocked the door of the car. Il a ouvert la portière de la voiture.

unlucky ADJECTIVE
■ **to be unlucky 1** (*number, object*) porter [28] malheur □ They say thirteen is an unlucky number. On dit que le nombre treize porte malheur. **2** (*person*) ne pas avoir [8] de chance □ Did you win? — No, I was unlucky. Vous avez gagné ? — Non, je n'ai pas eu de chance.

unmarried ADJECTIVE
célibataire (FEM célibataire) (*person*)
■ **an unmarried couple** un couple non marié

unnatural ADJECTIVE
pas naturel (FEM pas naturelle)

unnecessary ADJECTIVE
inutile (FEM inutile)

unofficial ADJECTIVE
1 non officiel (FEM non officielle) (*meeting, leader*)
2 sauvage (FEM sauvage) (*strike*)

to **unpack** VERB
1 défaire [36]
  □ I unpacked my suitcase. J'ai défait ma valise.
2 déballer [28] ses affaires
  □ I went to my room to unpack. Je suis allé dans ma chambre pour déballer mes affaires. □ I haven't unpacked my clothes yet. Je n'ai pas encore déballé mes affaires.

unpleasant ADJECTIVE
désagréable (FEM désagréable)

to **unplug** VERB
débrancher [28]

unpopular ADJECTIVE
impopulaire (FEM impopulaire)

unpredictable ADJECTIVE
imprévisible (FEM imprévisible)

unreal ADJECTIVE
incroyable (FEM incroyable) (*incredible*)
  □ It was unreal! C'était incroyable !

unrealistic ADJECTIVE
peu réaliste (FEM peu réaliste)

unreasonable ADJECTIVE
pas raisonnable (FEM pas raisonnable)
  □ Her attitude was completely unreasonable. Son attitude n'était pas du tout raisonnable.

unreliable ADJECTIVE
pas fiable (FEM pas fiable) (*car, machine*)
  □ It's a nice car, but a bit unreliable. C'est une belle voiture, mais elle n'est pas très fiable.
  ■ He's completely unreliable. On ne peut pas du tout compter sur lui.

to **unroll** VERB
dérouler [28]

unsatisfactory ADJECTIVE
insatisfaisant (FEM insatisfaisante)

to **unscrew** VERB
dévisser [28]
  □ She unscrewed the top of the bottle. Elle a dévissé le bouchon de la bouteille.

unshaven ADJECTIVE
mal rasé

unskilled ADJECTIVE
  ■ unskilled worker le manœuvre

unstable ADJECTIVE
instable (FEM instable)

unsteady ADJECTIVE
mal assuré (FEM mal assurée) (*walk, voice*)
  ■ He was unsteady on his feet. Il marchait d'un pas mal assuré.

unsuccessful ADJECTIVE
vain (FEM vaine) (*attempt*)

  ■ to be unsuccessful ne pas réussir [38] □ an unsuccessful artist un artiste qui n'a pas réussi

unsuitable ADJECTIVE
inapproprié (FEM inappropriée) (*clothes, equipment*)

untidy ADJECTIVE
1 en désordre
  □ My bedroom's always untidy. Ma chambre est toujours en désordre.
2 débraillé (FEM débraillée) (*appearance, person*)
  □ He's always untidy. Il est toujours débraillé.
3 désordonné (FEM désordonnée) (*in character*)
  □ He's a very untidy person. Il est très désordonné.

to **untie** VERB
1 défaire [36] (*knot, parcel*)
2 détacher [28] (*animal*)

until PREPOSITION, CONJUNCTION
1 jusqu'à
  □ I waited until ten o'clock. J'ai attendu jusqu'à dix heures.
  ■ until now jusqu'à présent □ It's never been a problem until now. Ça n'a jamais été un problème jusqu'à présent.
  ■ until then jusque-là □ Until then I'd never been to France. Jusque-là je n'étais jamais allé en France.
2 avant

> Use **avant** if the sentence you want to translate contains a negative, such as 'not' or 'never'

  □ It won't be ready until next week. Ça ne sera pas prêt avant la semaine prochaine. □ Until last year I'd never been to France. Avant l'année dernière, je n'étais jamais allé en France.

unusual ADJECTIVE
1 insolite (FEM insolite)
  □ an unusual shape une forme insolite
2 rare (FEM rare)
  □ It's unusual to get snow at this time of year. Il est rare qu'il neige à cette époque de l'année.

unwilling ADJECTIVE
  ■ to be unwilling to do something ne pas être [35] disposé à faire quelque chose □ He was unwilling to help me. Il n'était pas disposé à m'aider.

to **unwind** VERB
se détendre [88] (*relax*)

unwise ADJECTIVE
imprudent (FEM imprudente) (*person*)
  □ That was rather unwise of you. C'était plutôt imprudent de votre part.

unwound VERB ▷ *see* **unwind**

to **unwrap** VERB
déballer [28]
  □ After the meal we unwrapped the presents. Après le repas nous avons déballé les cadeaux.

u

up PREPOSITION, ADVERB

> For other expressions with 'up', see the verbs 'go', 'come', 'put', 'turn' etc.

en haut
□ up on the hill en haut de la colline
■ **up here** ici
■ **up there** là-haut
■ **up north** dans le nord
■ **to be up** (*out of bed*) être [35] levé □ We were up at 6. Nous étions levés à six heures. □ He's not up yet. Il n'est pas encore levé.
■ **What's up?** Qu'est-ce qu'il y a ? □ What's up with her? Qu'est-ce qu'elle a ?
■ **to get up** (*in the morning*) se lever [43]
□ What time do you get up? À quelle heure est-ce que tu te lèves ?
■ **to go up** monter [48f] □ The bus went up the hill. Le bus a monté la colline.

> The verb **monter** uses **avoir** in the perfect tense instead of **être** when talking about a person or thing moving up something (for example, up the hill).

■ **to go up to somebody** s'approcher [28] de quelqu'un □ She came up to me. Elle s'est approchée de moi.
■ **up to** (*as far as*) jusqu'à □ to count up to fifty compter jusqu'à cinquante □ up to three hours jusqu'à trois heures □ up to now jusqu'à présent
■ **It's up to you.** C'est à vous de décider.

upbringing NOUN
l'éducation *fem*

uphill ADVERB
■ **to go uphill** monter [48f]

to upload VERB
télécharger [45]

upper ADJECTIVE
supérieur (FEM supérieure)
□ on the upper floor à l'étage supérieur

upright ADJECTIVE
■ **to stand upright** se tenir [83] droit

upset NOUN
▷ *see also* **upset** ADJECTIVE, VERB
■ **a stomach upset** une indigestion

upset ADJECTIVE
▷ *see also* **upset** NOUN, VERB
contrarié (FEM contrariée)
□ She's still a bit upset. Elle est encore un peu contrariée.
■ **I had an upset stomach.** J'avais l'estomac dérangé.

to upset VERB
▷ *see also* **upset** NOUN, ADJECTIVE
■ **to upset somebody** contrarier [19] quelqu'un

upside down ADVERB
à l'envers

□ That painting is upside down. Ce tableau est à l'envers.

upstairs ADVERB
en haut
□ Where's your coat? — It's upstairs. Où est ton manteau ? — Il est en haut.
■ **to go upstairs** monter [48f]

uptight ADJECTIVE
tendu (FEM tendue)
□ She's really uptight. Elle est très tendue.

up-to-date ADJECTIVE
1 moderne (FEM moderne) (*car, stereo*)
2 à jour (*information*)
□ an up-to-date timetable un horaire à jour
■ **to bring something up to date** moderniser [28] quelque chose

upwards ADVERB
vers le haut
□ to look upwards regarder vers le haut

urgent ADJECTIVE
urgent (FEM urgente)
□ Is it urgent? C'est urgent ?

urine NOUN
l'urine *fem*

US NOUN (= *United States*)
les USA *masc pl*

us PRONOUN
nous
□ They helped us. Ils nous ont aidés. □ They gave us a map. Ils nous ont donné une carte.

USA NOUN
les USA *masc pl*

USB stick NOUN
la clé USB *fem*

use NOUN
▷ *see also* **use** VERB
■ **It's no use.** Ça ne sert à rien. □ It's no use shouting, she's deaf. Ça ne sert à rien de crier, elle est sourde.
■ **It's no use, I can't do it.** Il n'y a rien à faire, je n'y arrive pas.
■ **to make use of something** utiliser [28] quelque chose

to use VERB
▷ *see also* **use** NOUN
utiliser [28]
□ Can we use a dictionary in the exam? Est-ce qu'on peut utiliser un dictionnaire à l'examen ?
■ **Can I use your phone?** Je peux téléphoner ?
■ **to use the toilet** aller [3f] aux W.C.
■ **I used to live in London.** J'habitais à Londres autrefois.
■ **I didn't use to like maths, but now I do.** Avant, je n'aimais pas les maths, mais maintenant je les aime.
■ **to be used to something** avoir [8] l'habitude de quelque chose □ He wasn't used to getting

up early. Il n'avait pas l'habitude de se lever tôt. □ Don't worry, I'm used to it. Ne t'inquiète pas, j'ai l'habitude.
■ **a used car** une voiture d'occasion

to **use up** VERB
1 finir [38]
  □ We've used up all the paint. Nous avons fini la peinture.
2 dépenser [28] (*money*)

useful ADJECTIVE
utile (FEM utile)

useless ADJECTIVE
nul (FEM nulle)
  □ This app is just useless. Cette appli est vraiment nulle. □ You're useless! Tu es nul !
■ **It's useless!** Ça ne sert à rien !

user NOUN
l'utilisateur *masc*
l'utilisatrice *fem*

user-friendly ADJECTIVE
facile à utiliser (FEM facile à utiliser)

username NOUN
le nom d'utilisateur *masc*
■ **What's your username?** Quel est ton nom d'utilisateur ?

usual ADJECTIVE
habituel (FEM habituelle)
■ **as usual** comme d'habitude

usually ADVERB
1 en général (*generally*)
  □ I usually get to school at about half past eight. En général, j'arrive à l'école vers huit heures et demie.
2 d'habitude (*when making a contrast*)
  □ Usually I don't wear make-up, but today is a special occasion. D'habitude je ne me maquille pas, mais aujourd'hui c'est spécial.

utility room NOUN
la buanderie *fem*

U-turn NOUN
le demi-tour *masc*
  □ to do a U-turn faire demi-tour

u

Vv

vacancy NOUN
1 le poste vacant *masc* (*job*)
2 la chambre disponible *fem* (*room in hotel*)

vacant ADJECTIVE
libre (FEM libre)

vacation NOUN (US)
les vacances *fem pl*
□ to be on vacation être en vacances □ to take a vacation prendre des vacances

to **vaccinate** VERB
vacciner [28]

vaccination NOUN
la vaccination *fem*

vaccine NOUN
le vaccin *masc*

to **vacuum** VERB
passer [58] l'aspirateur
□ to vacuum the hall passer l'aspirateur dans le couloir

vacuum cleaner NOUN
l'aspirateur *masc*

vagina NOUN
le vagin *masc*

vague ADJECTIVE
vague (FEM vague)

vain ADJECTIVE
vaniteux (FEM vaniteuse)
□ He's so vain! Qu'est-ce qu'il est vaniteux !
■ in vain en vain

Valentine's Day NOUN
la Saint-Valentin *fem*

valid ADJECTIVE
valable (FEM valable)
□ This ticket is valid for three months. Ce billet est valable trois mois.

valley NOUN
la vallée *fem*

valuable ADJECTIVE
1 de valeur
□ a valuable picture un tableau de valeur
2 précieux (FEM précieuse)
□ valuable help une aide précieuse

valuables PL NOUN
les objets de valeur *masc pl*
□ Don't take any valuables with you.
N'emportez pas d'objets de valeur.

value NOUN
la valeur *fem*

van NOUN
la camionnette *fem*

vandal NOUN
le/la vandale *masc/fem*

vandalism NOUN
le vandalisme *masc*

to **vandalize** VERB
saccager [45]

vanilla NOUN
la vanille *fem*
□ vanilla ice cream la glace à la vanille

to **vanish** VERB
disparaître [56]

to **vape** VERB
vapoter [28]

vaping NOUN
le vapotage *masc*
le vape *fem*

variable ADJECTIVE
variable (FEM variable)

varied ADJECTIVE
varié (FEM variée)

variety NOUN
la variété *fem*

various ADJECTIVE
plusieurs
□ We visited various villages in the area. Nous avons visité plusieurs villages de la région.

to **vary** VERB
varier [19]

vase NOUN
le vase *masc*

VAT NOUN (= value added tax)
la TVA *fem* (= taxe sur la valeur ajoutée)

veal NOUN
le veau *masc*

vegan NOUN
1 le/la végane *masc/fem* (*diet and lifestyle*)
2 le végétalien *masc*
la végétalienne *fem* (*diet only*)
□ I'm a vegan. Je suis végétalien.

vegetable NOUN
le légume *masc*

□ vegetable soup la soupe aux légumes

vegetarian ADJECTIVE
▷ *see also* **vegetarian** NOUN
végétarien (FEM végétarienne)
□ I'm vegetarian. Je suis végétarien.
□ vegetarian lasagne les lasagnes végétariennes
fem pl

vegetarian NOUN
▷ *see also* **vegetarian** ADJECTIVE
le végétarien *masc*
la végétarienne *fem*
□ I'm a vegetarian. Je suis végétarien.

vehicle NOUN
le véhicule *masc*

vein NOUN
la veine *fem*

velvet NOUN
le velours *masc*

vending machine NOUN
le distributeur automatique *masc*

Venetian blind NOUN
le store vénitien *masc*

verb NOUN
le verbe *masc*

verdict NOUN
le verdict *masc*

vertical ADJECTIVE
vertical (FEM verticale, MASC PL verticaux)

vertigo NOUN
le vertige *masc*
□ I get vertigo. J'ai le vertige.

very ADVERB
très
□ very tall très grand □ not very interesting pas
très intéressant
■ **very much** beaucoup

vest NOUN
1 le maillot de corps *masc* (*underclothing*)
2 le gilet *masc* (US: *waistcoat*)

vet NOUN
le/la vétérinaire *masc/fem*
□ She's a vet. Elle est vétérinaire.

via PREPOSITION
en passant par
□ We went to Paris via Boulogne. Nous sommes
allés à Paris en passant par Boulogne.

vicar NOUN
le pasteur *masc*
□ He's a vicar. Il est pasteur.

vice NOUN
l'étau *masc* (*for holding things*)

vice versa ADVERB
vice versa

vicious ADJECTIVE
1 brutal (FEM brutale, MASC PL brutaux)
□ a vicious attack une agression brutale

2 méchant (FEM méchante) (*dog, person*)
■ **a vicious circle** un cercle vicieux

victim NOUN
la victime *fem*
□ He was the victim of a mugging. Il a été
victime d'une agression.

victory NOUN
la victoire *fem*

to **video** VERB
▷ *see also* **video** NOUN
filmer [28] (*with video camera*)

video NOUN
▷ *see also* **video** VERB
la vidéo *fem* (*film*)
□ to watch a video regarder une vidéo □ a video
of my family on holiday une vidéo de ma famille
en vacances
■ **a video call** un appel vidéo
■ **a video camera** une caméra vidéo
■ **a video game** un jeu vidéo □ He likes playing
video games. Il aime les jeux vidéo.

Vietnam NOUN
le Viêt-Nam *masc*
■ **in Vietnam** au Viêt-Nam

Vietnamese ADJECTIVE
vietnamien (FEM vietnamienne)

view NOUN
1 la vue *fem*
□ There's an amazing view. Il y a une vue
extraordinaire.
2 l'avis *masc* (*opinion*)
□ in my view à mon avis

viewer NOUN
le téléspectateur *masc*
la téléspectatrice *fem*

viewpoint NOUN
le point de vue *masc*

vile ADJECTIVE
dégoûtant (FEM dégoûtante) (*smell, food*)

villa NOUN
la villa *fem*

village NOUN
le village *masc*

villain NOUN
1 le malfrat *masc* (*criminal*)
2 le méchant *masc* (*in film*)

vine NOUN
la vigne *fem*

vinegar NOUN
le vinaigre *masc*

vineyard NOUN
le vignoble *masc*

viola NOUN
l'alto *masc*
□ I play the viola. Je joue de l'alto.

violence NOUN
la violence *fem*

violent ADJECTIVE
violent (FEM violente)

violin NOUN
le violon *masc*
▫ I play the violin. Je joue du violon.

violinist NOUN
le/la violoniste *masc/fem*

viral ADJECTIVE
viral (FEM virale, MASC PL viraux)
■ **a viral video** une vidéo virale

virgin NOUN
la vierge *fem*
▫ to be a virgin être vierge

Virgo NOUN
la Vierge *fem*
▫ I'm Virgo. Je suis Vierge.

virtual reality NOUN
la réalité virtuelle *fem*

virus NOUN
le virus *masc* (*also computing*)

visa NOUN
le visa *masc*

visible ADJECTIVE
visible (FEM visible)

visit NOUN
▷ *see also* **visit** VERB
1 la visite *fem* (*to museum*)
2 le séjour *masc* (*to country*)
▫ Did you enjoy your visit to France? Ton séjour en France s'est bien passé ?
■ **my last visit to my grandmother** la dernière fois que je suis allé voir ma grand-mère

to visit VERB
▷ *see also* **visit** NOUN
1 rendre [7] visite à (*person*)
▫ to visit somebody rendre visite à quelqu'un
2 visiter [28] (*place*)
▫ We'd like to visit the castle. Nous voudrions visiter le château.

visitor NOUN
1 le visiteur *masc*
la visiteuse *fem* (*tourist*)
2 l'invité *masc*
l'invitée *fem* (*guest*)
■ **to have a visitor** avoir [8] de la visite

visual ADJECTIVE
visuel (FEM visuelle)

to visualize VERB
imaginer [28]

vital ADJECTIVE
vital (FEM vitale, MASC PL vitaux)

vitamin NOUN
la vitamine *fem*

vivid ADJECTIVE
vif (FEM vive) (*colour*)
■ **to have a vivid imagination** avoir [8] une imagination débordante

vlog NOUN
le blog vidéo *masc* (PL les blogs vidéo)

vlogger NOUN
le vidéo-blogueur *masc*
la vidéo-blogueuse *fem*

vocabulary NOUN
le vocabulaire *masc*

vocational ADJECTIVE
professionnel (FEM professionnelle)
■ **a vocational course** un stage de formation professionnelle

vodka NOUN
la vodka *fem*

voice NOUN
la voix *fem* (PL les voix)

voice mail NOUN
la boîte vocale *fem*

volcano NOUN
le volcan *masc*

volleyball NOUN
le volley-ball *masc*
▫ to play volleyball jouer au volley-ball

volt NOUN
le volt *masc*

voltage NOUN
le voltage *masc*

voluntary ADJECTIVE
volontaire (FEM volontaire) (*contribution*)
■ **to do voluntary work** travailler [28] bénévolement

volunteer NOUN
▷ *see also* **volunteer** VERB
le/la volontaire *masc/fem*

to volunteer VERB
▷ *see also* **volunteer** NOUN
■ **to volunteer to do something** se proposer [28] pour faire quelque chose

to vomit VERB
vomir [38]

to vote VERB
voter [28]

voucher NOUN
le bon *masc*
▫ a gift voucher un bon d'achat

vowel NOUN
la voyelle *fem*

vulgar ADJECTIVE
vulgaire (FEM vulgaire)

Ww

wafer NOUN
la gaufrette *fem*

wage NOUN
le salaire *masc*
□ He collected his wages. Il a retiré son salaire.

waist NOUN
la taille *fem*

waistcoat NOUN
le gilet *masc*

to **wait** VERB
attendre [7]
■ **to wait for something** attendre [7] quelque chose
■ **to wait for somebody** attendre [7] quelqu'un □ I'll wait for you. Je t'attendrai.
■ **Wait for me!** Attends-moi !
■ **Wait a minute!** Attends !
■ **to keep somebody waiting** faire [36] attendre quelqu'un □ They kept us waiting for hours. Ils nous ont fait attendre pendant des heures.
■ **I can't wait for the holidays.** J'ai hâte d'être en vacances.
■ **I can't wait to see him again.** J'ai hâte de le revoir.

to **wait up** VERB
attendre [7] pour se coucher
□ My mum always waits up till I get in. Ma mère attend toujours que je rentre pour se coucher.

waiter NOUN
le serveur *masc*
■ **Waiter!** Excusez-moi !

waiting list NOUN
la liste d'attente *fem*

waiting room NOUN
la salle d'attente *fem*

waitress NOUN
la serveuse *fem*

to **wake up** VERB
se réveiller [28]
□ I woke up at six o'clock. Je me suis réveillé à six heures.
■ **to wake somebody up** réveiller [28] quelqu'un □ Please would you wake me up at seven o'clock? Pourriez-vous me réveiller à sept heures ?

Wales NOUN
le pays de Galles *masc*
■ **in Wales** au pays de Galles
■ **to Wales** au pays de Galles
■ **I'm from Wales.** Je suis gallois.
■ **the Prince of Wales** le prince de Galles

to **walk** VERB
▷ *see also* **walk** NOUN
1 marcher [28]
□ He walks fast. Il marche vite.
2 aller [3] à pied (*go on foot*)
□ Are you walking or going by bus? Tu y vas à pied ou en bus ? □ We walked 10 kilometres. Nous avons fait dix kilomètres à pied.
■ **to walk the dog** promener [43] le chien

walk NOUN
▷ *see also* **walk** VERB
la promenade *fem*
□ to go for a walk faire une promenade
■ **It's 10 minutes' walk from here.** C'est à dix minutes d'ici à pied.

walking NOUN
la randonnée *fem*
□ I did some walking in the Alps last summer. J'ai fait de la randonnée dans les Alpes l'été dernier.

walking stick NOUN
la canne *fem*

wall NOUN
le mur *masc*

wallet NOUN
le portefeuille *masc*

wallpaper NOUN
1 le papier peint *masc*
2 le fond d'écran *masc* (*for phone, PC*)

walnut NOUN
la noix *fem* (PL les noix)

to **wander** VERB
■ **to wander around** flâner [28] □ I just wandered around for a while. J'ai flâné un peu.

to **want** VERB
vouloir [93]
□ Do you want some cake? Tu veux du gâteau ?
■ **to want to do something** vouloir [93] faire quelque chose □ I want to go to the cinema. Je veux aller au cinéma. □ What do you want to do tomorrow? Qu'est-ce que tu veux faire demain ?

war NOUN
la guerre *fem*

ward NOUN
la salle *fem* (*room in hospital*)

warden NOUN
le directeur *masc*
la directrice *fem* (*of youth hostel*)

wardrobe NOUN
l'armoire *fem* (*piece of furniture*)

warehouse NOUN
l'entrepôt *masc*

warm ADJECTIVE
1 chaud (FEM chaude)
   □ warm water l'eau chaude
   ■ **It's warm in here.** Il fait chaud ici.
   ■ **to be warm** (*person*) avoir [8] chaud □ I'm too warm. J'ai trop chaud.
2 chaleureux (FEM chaleureuse)
   □ a warm welcome un accueil chaleureux

to **warm up** VERB
1 s'échauffer [28] (*for sport*)
2 réchauffer [28] (*food*)
   □ I'll warm up some pasta for you. Je vais te réchauffer des pâtes.

to **warn** VERB
prévenir [89]
   □ Well, I warned you! Je t'avais prévenu !
   ■ **to warn somebody to do something** conseiller [28] à quelqu'un de faire quelque chose

warning NOUN
l'avertissement *masc*

Warsaw NOUN
Varsovie

wart NOUN
la verrue *fem*

was VERB ▷ *see* be

wash NOUN
   ▷ *see also* **wash** VERB
   ■ **to have a wash** se laver [28] □ I had a wash. Je me suis lavé.
   ■ **to give something a wash** laver [28] quelque chose □ He gave the car a wash. Il a lavé la voiture.

to **wash** VERB
   ▷ *see also* **wash** NOUN
1 laver [28]
   □ to wash something laver quelque chose
2 se laver [28] (*have a wash*)
   □ Every morning I get up, wash and get dressed. Tous les matins je me lève, je me lave et je m'habille.
   ■ **to wash one's hands** se laver [28] les mains
   ■ **to wash one's hair** se laver [28] les cheveux

to **wash up** VERB
faire [36] la vaisselle

washbasin NOUN
le lavabo *masc*

washcloth NOUN (US)
le gant de toilette *masc*

> **DID YOU KNOW…?**
> The French traditionally wash with a towelling glove rather than a flannel.

washing NOUN
le linge *masc*
   □ dirty washing du linge sale
   ■ **Have you got any washing?** Tu as du linge à laver ?
   ■ **to do the washing** faire [36] la lessive

washing machine NOUN
la machine à laver *fem*

washing powder NOUN
la lessive *fem*

washing-up NOUN
   ■ **to do the washing-up** faire [36] la vaisselle

washing-up liquid NOUN
le produit à vaisselle *masc*

wasn't = was not

wasp NOUN
la guêpe *fem*

waste NOUN
   ▷ *see also* **waste** VERB
1 le gaspillage *masc*
   □ It's such a waste! C'est vraiment du gaspillage !
   ■ **It's a waste of time.** C'est une perte de temps.
2 les déchets *masc pl* (*rubbish*)
   □ nuclear waste les déchets nucléaires

to **waste** VERB
   ▷ *see also* **waste** NOUN
gaspiller [28]
   □ I don't like wasting money. Je n'aime pas gaspiller de l'argent.
   ■ **to waste time** perdre [61] du temps
   □ There's no time to waste. Il n'y a pas de temps à perdre.

wastepaper basket NOUN
la corbeille à papier *fem*

watch NOUN
   ▷ *see also* **watch** VERB
la montre *fem*

to **watch** VERB
   ▷ *see also* **watch** NOUN
1 regarder [28]
   □ to watch television regarder la télévision
   □ Watch me! Regarde-moi !
2 surveiller [28] (*keep a watch on*)
   □ The police were watching the house. La police surveillait la maison.

to **watch out** VERB
faire [36] attention
   ■ **Watch out!** Attention !

water NOUN
> ▷ see also **water** VERB
l'eau *fem*

to **water** VERB
> ▷ see also **water** NOUN
arroser [28]
□ He was watering his garden. Il arrosait son jardin.

waterfall NOUN
la cascade *fem*

watering can NOUN
l'arrosoir *masc*

watermelon NOUN
la pastèque *fem*

waterproof ADJECTIVE
imperméable (FEM imperméable)
□ Is this jacket waterproof? Ce blouson est-il imperméable ?
■ **a waterproof watch** une montre étanche

water-skiing NOUN
le ski nautique *masc*
□ to go water-skiing faire du ski nautique

wave NOUN
> ▷ see also **wave** VERB
1 la vague *fem* (*in water*)
2 le signe *masc* (*of hand*)
□ We gave him a wave. Nous lui avons fait signe.

to **wave** VERB
> ▷ see also **wave** NOUN
faire [36] un signe de la main
□ to wave at somebody faire un signe de la main à quelqu'un
■ **to wave goodbye** faire [36] au revoir de la main □ I waved her goodbye. Je lui ai fait au revoir de la main.

wavy ADJECTIVE
ondulé (FEM ondulée)
□ wavy hair les cheveux ondulés

wax NOUN
la cire *fem*

way NOUN
1 la façon *fem* (*manner*)
□ She looked at me in a strange way. Elle m'a regardé d'une façon étrange.
■ **This website tells you the right way to do it.** Ce site Internet explique comment il faut faire.
■ **You're doing it the wrong way.** Ce n'est pas comme ça qu'il faut faire.
■ **in a way ...** dans un sens ...
■ **a way of life** un mode de vie
2 le chemin *masc* (*route*)
□ I don't know the way. Je ne connais pas le chemin.
■ **on the way** en chemin □ We stopped on the way. Nous nous sommes arrêtés en chemin.
■ **It's a long way.** C'est loin. □ Sydney is a long

way from London. Sydney est loin de Londres.
■ **Which way is it?** C'est par où ?
■ **The supermarket is this way.** Le supermarché est par ici.
■ **Do you know the way to the station?** Vous savez comment aller à la gare ?
■ **He's on his way.** Il arrive.
■ **'way in'** « entrée »
■ **'way out'** « sortie »
■ **by the way ...** au fait ...

we PRONOUN
nous
□ We're staying here for a week. Nous restons une semaine ici.

weak ADJECTIVE
faible (FEM faible)

wealth NOUN
la richesse *fem*

wealthy ADJECTIVE
riche (FEM riche)

weapon NOUN
l'arme *fem*

to **wear** VERB
porter [28] (*clothes*)
□ She was wearing a sweatshirt and leggings. Elle portait un sweat-shirt et un legging.
■ **She was wearing black.** Elle était en noir.

weather NOUN
le temps *masc*
□ What was the weather like? Quel temps a-t-il fait ? □ The weather was lovely. Il a fait un temps magnifique.

weather forecast NOUN
la météo *fem*

web NOUN
1 la toile *fem* (*spider*)
2 le Web *masc* (*World Wide Web*)

web address NOUN
l'adresse web *fem*

web browser NOUN
le navigateur *masc*

webcam NOUN
la webcam *fem*

website NOUN
le site web *masc*

webzine NOUN
le webzine *masc*

we'd = we had, we would

wedding NOUN
le mariage *masc*
■ **wedding anniversary** l'anniversaire de mariage *masc*
■ **wedding dress** la robe de mariée

Wednesday NOUN
le mercredi *masc*
□ on Wednesday mercredi □ on Wednesdays le mercredi □ every Wednesday tous les mercredis

w

□ last Wednesday mercredi dernier □ next Wednesday mercredi prochain

weed NOUN
la mauvaise herbe *fem*
□ The garden's full of weeds. Le jardin est plein de mauvaises herbes.

week NOUN
la semaine *fem*
□ last week la semaine dernière □ every week toutes les semaines □ next week la semaine prochaine □ in a week's time dans une semaine
■ **a week on Friday** vendredi en huit

weekday NOUN
■ **on weekdays** en semaine

weekend NOUN
le week-end *masc*
□ at weekends le week-end □ last weekend le week-end dernier □ next weekend le week-end prochain

to **weep** VERB
pleurer [28]

to **weigh** VERB
peser [43]
□ How much do you weigh? Combien est-ce que tu pèses ? □ First, weigh the flour. Tout d'abord, pesez la farine.
■ **to weigh oneself** se peser [43]

weight NOUN
le poids *masc*
■ **to lose weight** maigrir [38]
■ **to put on weight** grossir [38]

weightlifter NOUN
l'haltérophile *masc/fem*

weightlifting NOUN
l'haltérophilie *fem*

weird ADJECTIVE
bizarre (FEM bizarre)

welcome NOUN
▷ *see also* **welcome** VERB
l'accueil *masc*
□ They gave her a warm welcome. Ils lui ont fait un accueil chaleureux.
■ **Welcome!** Bienvenue ! □ Welcome to France! Bienvenue en France !

to **welcome** VERB
▷ *see also* **welcome** NOUN
■ **to welcome somebody** accueillir [22] quelqu'un
■ **Thank you! — You're welcome!** Merci ! — De rien !

well ADJECTIVE, ADVERB
▷ *see also* **well** NOUN
1 bien
□ You did that really well. Tu as très bien fait ça.
■ **to do well** réussir [38] bien □ She's doing really well at school. Elle réussit vraiment bien à l'école.

■ **to be well** (*in good health*) aller [3ʰ] bien □ I'm not very well at the moment. Je ne vais pas très bien en ce moment.
■ **get well soon!** remets-toi vite !
■ **well done!** bravo !
2 enfin
□ It's enormous! Well, quite big anyway. C'est énorme ! Enfin, c'est assez grand.
■ **as well** aussi □ I decided to have dessert as well. J'ai décidé de prendre aussi un dessert.
□ We went to Chartres as well as Paris. Nous sommes allés à Paris et à Chartres aussi.

well NOUN
▷ *see also* **well** ADJECTIVE, ADVERB
le puits *masc* (PL les puits)

we'll = we will

well-behaved ADJECTIVE
sage (FEM sage)

well-dressed ADJECTIVE
bien habillé (FEM bien habillée)

wellingtons PL NOUN
les bottes en caoutchouc *fem pl*

well-known ADJECTIVE
célèbre (FEM célèbre)
□ a well-known film star une vedette de cinéma célèbre

well-off ADJECTIVE
aisé (FEM aisée)

Welsh NOUN
▷ *see also* **Welsh** ADJECTIVE
le gallois *masc* (*language*)

Welsh ADJECTIVE
▷ *see also* **Welsh** NOUN
gallois (FEM galloise)
□ She's Welsh. Elle est galloise.
■ **Welsh people** les Gallois *masc pl*

Welshman NOUN
le Gallois *masc*

Welshwoman NOUN
la Galloise *fem*

went VERB ▷ *see* go

wept VERB ▷ *see* weep

were VERB ▷ *see* be

we're = we are

weren't = were not

west NOUN
▷ *see also* **west** ADJECTIVE, ADVERB
l'ouest *masc*
□ in the west dans l'ouest

west ADJECTIVE, ADVERB
▷ *see also* **west** NOUN
1 ouest (FEM+PL ouest)
□ the west coast la côte ouest
■ **west of** à l'ouest de □ Stroud is west of Oxford. Stroud est à l'ouest d'Oxford.

2 vers l'ouest
□ We were travelling west. Nous allions vers l'ouest.
■ **the West Country** le sud-ouest de l'Angleterre

westbound ADJECTIVE
■ **The truck was westbound on the M5.** Le camion roulait sur la M5 en direction de l'ouest.
■ **Westbound traffic is moving very slowly.** La circulation en direction de l'ouest est très ralentie.

western NOUN
▷ *see also* **western** ADJECTIVE
le western *masc* (film)

western ADJECTIVE
▷ *see also* **western** NOUN
■ **the western part of the island** la partie ouest de l'île
■ **Western Europe** l'Europe de l'Ouest

West Indian NOUN
▷ *see also* **West Indian** ADJECTIVE
l'Antillais *masc*
l'Antillaise *fem* (person)

West Indian ADJECTIVE
▷ *see also* **West Indian** NOUN
antillais (FEM antillaise)
□ She's West Indian. Elle est antillaise.

West Indies PL NOUN
les Antilles *fem pl*
■ **in the West Indies** aux Antilles

wet ADJECTIVE
mouillé (FEM mouillée)
□ wet clothes les vêtements mouillés
■ **to get wet** se faire (36) mouiller
■ **dripping wet** trempé
■ **wet weather** le temps pluvieux
■ **It was wet all week.** Il a plu toute la semaine.

wetsuit NOUN
la combinaison de plongée *fem*

we've = we have

whale NOUN
la baleine *fem*

what ADJECTIVE, PRONOUN
1 quel (FEM quelle) (*which*)
□ What subjects are you studying? Quelles matières est-ce que tu fais ? □ What colour is it? C'est de quelle couleur ? □ What's the capital of Turkey? Quelle est la capitale de la Turquie ? □ What a mess! Quel fouillis !
2 qu'est-ce que
□ What are you doing? Qu'est-ce que vous faites ? □ What did you say? Qu'est-ce que vous avez dit ? □ What is it? Qu'est-ce que c'est ? □ What's the matter? Qu'est-ce qu'il y a ?
3 qu'est-ce qui
□ What happened? Qu'est-ce qui s'est passé ?

□ What's bothering you? Qu'est-ce qui te préoccupe ?

In relative phrases use **ce qui** or **ce que** depending on whether 'what' refers to the subject or the object of the sentence.

4 ce qui (*subject*)
□ I saw what happened. J'ai vu ce qui est arrivé.
□ I know what's bothering you. Je sais ce qui préoccupe.
ce que (*object*)
□ Tell me what you did. Dites-moi ce que vous avez fait. □ I heard what he said. J'ai entendu ce qu'il a dit.
■ **What?** (*what did you say*) Comment ?
■ **What!** (*shocked*) Quoi !

wheat NOUN
le blé *masc*

wheel NOUN
la roue *fem*
■ **the steering wheel** le volant

wheelchair NOUN
le fauteuil roulant *masc*

when ADVERB, CONJUNCTION
quand
□ When did he go? Quand est-ce qu'il est parti ?
□ She was reading when I came in. Elle lisait quand je suis entré.

where ADVERB, CONJUNCTION
où
□ Where's Emma today? Où est Emma aujourd'hui ? □ Where do you live? Où habites-tu ? □ Where are you going? Où vas-tu ? □ a shop where you can buy croissants un magasin où l'on peut acheter des croissants

whether CONJUNCTION
si
□ I don't know whether to go or not. Je ne sais pas si je dois y aller ou non.

which ADJECTIVE, PRONOUN
1 quel (FEM quelle)
□ Which flavour do you want? Quel parfum est-ce que tu veux ?

When asking 'which one' use **lequel** or **laquelle**, depending on whether the noun is masculine or feminine.

■ **I know his brother. — Which one?** Je connais son frère. — Lequel ?
■ **I know his sister. — Which one?** Je connais sa sœur. — Laquelle ?
■ **Which would you like?** Lequel est-ce que vous voulez ?
■ **Which of these are yours?** Lesquels sont à vous ?

In relative phrases use **qui** or **que** depending on whether 'which' refers to the subject or the object of the sentence.

2 qui (subject)
□ the film which is on TV now le film qui passe en ce moment à la télé
que (object)
□ the film which I saw yesterday le film que j'ai vu hier

while CONJUNCTION
▷ see also **while** NOUN

1 pendant que
□ You hold the torch while I look inside. Tiens la lampe électrique pendant que je regarde à l'intérieur.

2 alors que
□ Abby is very dynamic, while Kay is more laid-back. Abby est très dynamique, alors que Kay est plus relax.

while NOUN
▷ see also **while** CONJUNCTION
le moment masc
□ after a while au bout d'un moment
■ a while ago il y a un moment □ He was here a while ago. Il était là il y a un moment.
■ for a while pendant quelque temps □ I lived in London for a while. J'ai vécu à Londres pendant quelque temps.
■ quite a while longtemps □ quite a while ago il y a longtemps □ I haven't seen him for quite a while. Ça fait longtemps que je ne l'ai pas vu.

whip NOUN
▷ see also **whip** VERB
le fouet masc

to whip VERB
▷ see also **whip** NOUN
1 fouetter [28] (person, animal)
2 battre [9] (eggs)

whipped cream NOUN
la crème fouettée fem

whisk NOUN
le fouet masc

whiskers PL NOUN
les moustaches fem pl

whisky NOUN
le whisky masc (PL les whiskies)

to whisper VERB
chuchoter [28]

whistle NOUN
▷ see also **whistle** VERB
le sifflet masc
■ The referee blew his whistle. L'arbitre a sifflé.

to whistle VERB
▷ see also **whistle** NOUN
siffler [28]

White ADJECTIVE
blanc (FEM blanche)
□ She is White. Elle est blanche.

white ADJECTIVE
blanc (FEM blanche)

□ He's got white hair. Il a les cheveux blancs.
■ white wine le vin blanc
■ white bread le pain blanc
■ white coffee le café au lait

whiteboard NOUN
le tableau blanc masc
□ an interactive whiteboard un tableau blanc interactif

Whitsun NOUN
la Pentecôte fem

who PRONOUN
1 qui
□ Who said that? Qui a dit ça ? □ Who is Emmanuel Macron? Qui est Emmanuel Macron ?

> In relative phrases use **qui** or **que** depending on whether 'who' refers to the subject or the object of the verb.

2 qui (subject)
□ the man who saw us l'homme qui nous a vus
□ the man who spoke to us l'homme qui nous a parlé
que (object)
□ the man who we saw l'homme que nous avons vu □ the man who she married l'homme qu'elle a épousé

whole ADJECTIVE
▷ see also **whole** NOUN
tout (FEM toute)
□ the whole class toute la classe □ the whole afternoon tout l'après-midi
■ a whole box of chocolates toute une boîte de chocolats
■ the whole world le monde entier

whole NOUN
▷ see also **whole** ADJECTIVE
■ The whole of Wales was affected. Le pays de Galles tout entier a été touché.
■ on the whole dans l'ensemble

wholemeal ADJECTIVE
complet (FEM complète)
■ wholemeal bread le pain complet

wholewheat ADJECTIVE (US)
complet (FEM complète)

whom PRONOUN
qui
□ Whom did you see? Qui avez-vous vu ? □ the man to whom I spoke l'homme à qui j'ai parlé

whose PRONOUN, ADJECTIVE
1 à qui
□ Whose is this? À qui est-ce ? □ I know whose it is. Je sais à qui c'est. □ Whose necklace is this? À qui est ce collier ?

2 dont (after noun)
□ the girl whose picture was in the paper la jeune fille dont la photo était dans le journal

why ADVERB
pourquoi

□ Why did you do that? Pourquoi avez-vous fait ça ? □ That's why he did it. Voilà pourquoi il a fait ça. □ Tell me why. Dis-moi pourquoi.
- **Why not?** Je n'ai pas fait mes devoirs. — Pourquoi ?
- **All right, why not?** D'accord, pourquoi pas ?

wicked ADJECTIVE
1 méchant (FEM méchante) (*evil*)
2 génial (FEM géniale, MASC PL géniaux) (*really great*)

wicket NOUN
le guichet *masc* (*stumps*)

wide ADJECTIVE, ADVERB
large (FEM large)
□ a wide road une route large
- **wide open** grand ouvert □ The door was wide open. La porte était grande ouverte. □ The windows were wide open. Les fenêtres étaient grandes ouvertes.
- **wide awake** complètement réveillé

widow NOUN
la veuve *fem*
□ She's a widow. Elle est veuve.

widower NOUN
le veuf *masc*
□ He's a widower. Il est veuf.

width NOUN
la largeur *fem*

wife NOUN
la femme *fem*
□ She's his wife. C'est sa femme.

Wi-Fi NOUN
le wifi *masc*

wig NOUN
la perruque *fem*

wild ADJECTIVE
1 sauvage (FEM sauvage) (*not tame*)
□ a wild animal un animal sauvage
2 fou (FEM folle) (*crazy*)
□ She's a bit wild. Elle est un peu folle.

fou changes to fol before a vowel and most words beginning with 'h'.

wildlife NOUN
la nature *fem*
□ I'm interested in wildlife. Je m'intéresse à la nature.

will NOUN
▷ *see also* **will** VERB
le testament *masc*
□ He left me some money in his will. Il m'a laissé de l'argent dans son testament.

will VERB
▷ *see also* **will** NOUN
- **I'll show you your room.** Je vais te montrer ta chambre.

- **I'll give you a hand.** Je vais t'aider.

Use the French future tense when referring to the more distant future.

- **I will finish it tomorrow.** Je le finirai demain.
- **It won't take long.** Ça ne prendra pas longtemps.
- **Will you wash up? — No, I won't.** Est-ce que tu peux faire la vaisselle ? — Non.
- **Will you help me?** Est-ce que tu peux m'aider ?
- **Will you be quiet!** Voulez-vous bien vous taire !
- **That will be the postman.** Ça doit être le facteur.

willing ADJECTIVE
- **to be willing to do something** être [35] prêt à faire quelque chose

to win VERB
▷ *see also* **win** NOUN
gagner [28]
□ Did you win? Est-ce que tu as gagné ?
- **to win a prize** remporter [28] un prix

win NOUN
▷ *see also* **win** VERB
la victoire *fem*

to wind VERB
▷ *see also* **wind** NOUN
1 enrouler [28] (*rope, wool, wire*)
2 serpenter [28] (*river, path*)
□ The road winds through the valley. La route serpente à travers la vallée.

wind NOUN
▷ *see also* **wind** VERB
le vent *masc*
□ There was a strong wind. Il y avait beaucoup de vent.
- **a wind farm** un parc éolien
- **a wind instrument** un instrument à vent
- **wind power** l'énergie éolienne *fem*
- **a wind turbine** une éolienne

windmill NOUN
le moulin à vent *masc*

window NOUN
1 la fenêtre *fem* (*of building*)
2 la vitre *fem* (*in car, train*)
- **a shop window** une vitrine
3 le carreau *masc* (PL les carreaux) (*window pane*)
□ to break a window casser un carreau □ a broken window un carreau cassé

windscreen NOUN
le pare-brise *masc* (PL les pare-brise)

windscreen wiper NOUN
l'essuie-glace *masc* (PL les essuie-glace)

windshield NOUN (US)
le pare-brise *masc* (PL les pare-brise)

windshield wiper NOUN (US)
l'essuie-glace *masc* (PL les essuie-glace)

windy ADJECTIVE

venteux (FEM venteuse) (*place*)

- **It's windy.** Il y a du vent.

wine NOUN

le vin *masc*

□ **a bottle of wine** une bouteille de vin □ **a glass of wine** un verre de vin

- **white wine** le vin blanc
- **red wine** le vin rouge
- **a wine bar** un bar à vin
- **a wine glass** un verre à vin
- **the wine list** la carte des vins

wing NOUN

l'aile *fem*

to wink VERB

- **to wink at somebody** faire [36] un clin d'œil à quelqu'un □ **He winked at me.** Il m'a fait un clin d'œil.

winner NOUN

le gagnant *masc*
la gagnante *fem*

winning ADJECTIVE

- **the winning team** l'équipe gagnante
- **the winning goal** le but décisif

winter NOUN

l'hiver *masc*

- **in winter** en hiver

winter sports PL NOUN

les sports d'hiver *masc pl*

to wipe VERB

essuyer [53]

- **to wipe one's feet** s'essuyer [53] les pieds □ **Wipe your feet!** Essuie-toi les pieds !

to wipe up VERB

essuyer [53]

wire NOUN

le fil de fer *masc*

wireless ADJECTIVE

sans fil

□ **wireless technology** la technologie sans fil

wisdom tooth NOUN

la dent de sagesse *fem*

wise ADJECTIVE

sage (FEM sage)

to wish VERB

▷ *see also* **wish** NOUN

- **to wish for something** souhaiter [28] quelque chose □ **What more could you wish for?** Que pourrais-tu souhaiter de plus ?
- **to wish to do something** désirer [28] faire quelque chose □ **I wish to make a complaint.** Je désire porter plainte.
- **I wish you were here!** Si seulement tu étais ici !
- **I wish you'd told me!** Si seulement tu m'en avais parlé !

wish NOUN

▷ *see also* **wish** VERB

le vœu *masc* (PL les vœux)

□ **to make a wish** faire un vœu

- **'best wishes'** **1** (*on greetings card*) « meilleurs vœux » **2** (*at the end of email, letter*) « bien amicalement »

wit NOUN

l'esprit *masc* (*humour*)

with PREPOSITION

1 avec

□ **Come with me.** Venez avec moi. □ **He walks with a stick.** Il marche avec une canne.

- **a woman with blue eyes** une femme aux yeux bleus

2 chez (*at the home of*)

□ **We stayed with friends.** Nous avons logé chez des amis.

3 de

□ **green with envy** vert de jalousie □ **to shake with fear** trembler de peur □ **Fill the jug with water.** Remplis la carafe d'eau.

within PREPOSITION

- **The shops are within easy reach.** Les magasins sont à proximité.
- **within the week** avant la fin de la semaine

without PREPOSITION

sans

□ **without a coat** sans manteau □ **without speaking** sans parler

witness NOUN

le témoin *masc*

□ **There were no witnesses.** Il n'y avait pas de témoins.

witty ADJECTIVE

spirituel (FEM spirituelle)

wives PL NOUN ▷ *see* wife

woke up, woken up VERB

▷ *see* wake up

wolf NOUN

le loup *masc*

woman NOUN

la femme *fem*

won VERB ▷ *see* win

to wonder VERB

se demander [28]

□ **I wonder why she said that.** Je me demande pourquoi elle a dit ça. □ **I wonder what that means.** Je me demande ce que ça veut dire. □ **I wonder where Caroline is.** Je me demande où est Caroline.

wonderful ADJECTIVE

formidable (FEM formidable)

won't = will not

wood NOUN

le bois *masc* (*timber, forest*)

□ **It's made of wood.** C'est en bois. □ **We went**

for a walk in the wood. Nous sommes allés nous promener dans le bois.

wooden ADJECTIVE
en bois
□ a wooden chair une chaise en bois

woodwork NOUN
la menuiserie *fem*
□ My hobby is woodwork. Je fais de la menuiserie.

wool NOUN
la laine *fem*
□ It's made of wool. C'est en laine.

word NOUN
le mot *masc*
□ a difficult word un mot difficile
■ **What's the word for 'shop' in French?** Comment dit-on « shop » en français ?
■ **in other words** en d'autres termes
■ **to have a word with somebody** parler [28] avec quelqu'un
■ **the words** (*lyrics*) les paroles *fem pl* □ I really like the words of this song. J'adore les paroles de cette chanson.

word processing NOUN
le traitement de texte *masc*

word processor NOUN
le traitement de texte *masc*

wore VERB ▷ *see* wear

work NOUN
▷ *see also* **work** VERB
le travail *masc* (PL les travaux)
□ She's looking for work. Elle cherche du travail.
□ He's at work at the moment. Il est au travail en ce moment.
■ **It's hard work.** C'est dur.
■ **to be off work** (*sick*) être [35] malade □ He's been off work for a week. Il est malade depuis une semaine.
■ **He's out of work.** Il est sans emploi.

to work VERB
▷ *see also* **work** NOUN
1 travailler [28] (*person*)
□ She works in a shop. Elle travaille dans un magasin. □ to work hard travailler dur □ to work remotely travailler à distance
2 marcher [28] (*machine, plan*)
□ The heating isn't working. Le chauffage ne marche pas. □ My plan worked perfectly. Mon plan a marché impeccablement.

to work out VERB
1 faire [36] de l'exercice (*exercise*)
□ I work out twice a week. Je fais de l'exercice deux fois par semaine.
2 marcher [28] (*turn out*)
□ In the end it worked out really well. Au bout du compte, ça a très bien marché.
3 arriver [5¹] à comprendre (*figure out*)
□ I just couldn't work it out. Je n'arrivais pas du tout à comprendre.

■ **It works out at £10 each.** Ça fait dix livres chacun.

worker NOUN
l'ouvrier *masc*
l'ouvrière *fem* (*in factory*)
■ **He's a factory worker.** Il est ouvrier.
■ **She's a good worker.** Elle travaille bien.

work experience NOUN
le stage *masc*
□ I'm going to do work experience in an office. Je vais faire un stage dans un bureau.

working-class ADJECTIVE
ouvrier (FEM ouvrière)
□ a working-class family une famille ouvrière

workman NOUN
l'ouvrier *masc*

works NOUN
l'usine *fem* (*factory*)

worksheet NOUN
la feuille d'exercices *fem*

workshop NOUN
l'atelier *masc*
□ a drama workshop un atelier de théâtre

workspace NOUN
l'espace de travail *masc* (*computing*)

workstation NOUN
le poste de travail *masc*

world NOUN
le monde *masc*
■ **He's the world champion.** Il est champion du monde.

worm NOUN
le ver *masc*

worn VERB ▷ *see* wear

worn ADJECTIVE
usé (FEM usée)
□ The carpet is a bit worn. La moquette est un peu usée.
■ **worn out** (*tired*) épuisé (FEM épuisée)

worried ADJECTIVE
inquiet (FEM inquiète)
□ She's very worried. Elle est très inquiète.
■ **to be worried about something** s'inquiéter [34] pour quelque chose □ I'm worried about the exams. Je m'inquiète pour les examens.
■ **to look worried** avoir [8] l'air inquiet □ She looks a bit worried. Elle a l'air un peu inquiète.

to worry VERB
s'inquiéter [34]
■ **Don't worry!** Ne t'inquiète pas !

worse ADJECTIVE, ADVERB
1 pire (FEM pire)
□ It was even worse than that. C'était encore pire que ça. □ My results were bad, but his were even worse. Mes notes étaient mauvaises, mais les siennes étaient encore pires.

2 plus mal
- □ I'm feeling worse. Je me sens plus mal.

to **worship** VERB
vénérer [34] (God)
- ■ **He really worships her.** Il est en adoration devant elle.

worst ADJECTIVE
▷ see also **worst** NOUN
- ■ **the worst** le plus mauvais □ **the worst student in the class** le plus mauvais élève de la classe □ **He got the worst mark in the whole class.** Il a eu la plus mauvaise note de toute la classe.
- ■ **my worst enemy** mon pire ennemi
- ■ **Maths is my worst subject.** Je suis vraiment nul en maths.

worst NOUN
▷ see also **worst** ADJECTIVE
le pire masc
- □ **The worst of it is that ...** Le pire c'est que ...
- ■ **at worst** au pire
- ■ **if the worst comes to the worst** au pire

worth ADJECTIVE
- ■ **to be worth** valoir [87] □ It's worth a lot of money. Ça vaut très cher. □ **How much is it worth?** Ça vaut combien ?
- ■ **It's worth it.** Ça vaut la peine. □ **Is it worth it?** Est-ce que ça vaut la peine ? □ **It's not worth it.** Ça ne vaut pas la peine.

would VERB
- ■ **Would you like a biscuit?** Vous voulez un petit gâteau ?
- ■ **Would you like to go and see a film?** Est-ce que tu veux aller voir un film ?
- ■ **Would you close the door please?** Vous pouvez fermer la porte, s'il vous plaît ?
- ■ **I'd like ...** J'aimerais ... □ **I'd like to go to America.** J'aimerais aller en Amérique. □ **Shall we go and see a film? — Yes, I'd like that.** Si on allait voir un film ? — Oui, j'aimerais bien.
- ■ **I said I would do it.** J'ai dit que je le ferais.
- ■ **If you asked him he'd do it.** Si vous le lui demandiez, il le ferait.
- ■ **If you had asked him he would have done it.** Si vous le lui aviez demandé, il l'aurait fait.

wouldn't = would not

wound NOUN
▷ see also **wound** VERB
la blessure fem

to **wound** VERB
▷ see also **wound** NOUN
blesser [28]
- □ **He was wounded in the leg.** Il a été blessé à la jambe.

to **wrap** VERB
emballer [28]
- □ **She's wrapping her Christmas presents.** Elle est en train d'emballer ses cadeaux de Noël.
- ■ **Can you wrap it for me please?** (in shop) Vous pouvez me faire un papier cadeau, s'il vous plaît ?

to **wrap up** VERB
emballer [28]

wrapping paper NOUN
le papier cadeau masc

wreck NOUN
▷ see also **wreck** VERB
1 le tas de ferraille masc (vehicle, machine)
- □ **That car is a wreck!** Cette voiture est un tas de ferraille !
2 la loque fem (person)
- □ **After the exams I was a complete wreck.** Après les examens j'étais une véritable loque.

to **wreck** VERB
▷ see also **wreck** NOUN
1 démolir [38] (building, vehicle)
- □ **The explosion wrecked the whole house.** L'explosion a démoli toute la maison.
2 ruiner [28] (plan, holiday)
- □ **The trip was wrecked by bad weather.** Le voyage a été ruiné par le mauvais temps.

wreckage NOUN
1 les débris masc pl (of vehicle)
2 les décombres masc pl (of building)

wrestler NOUN
le lutteur masc
la lutteuse fem

wrestling NOUN
la lutte fem

wrinkled ADJECTIVE
ridé (FEM ridée)

wrist NOUN
le poignet masc

to **write** VERB
écrire [30]
- □ **to write a letter** écrire une lettre
- ■ **to write to somebody** écrire [30] à quelqu'un □ **I'm going to write her an email in French.** Je vais lui écrire un mail en français.

to **write down** VERB
noter [28]
- □ **I wrote down the address.** J'ai noté l'adresse.
- ■ **Can you write it down for me, please?** Vous pouvez me l'écrire, s'il vous plaît ?

writer NOUN
l'écrivain masc
- □ **She's a writer.** Elle est écrivain.

writing NOUN
l'écriture fem
- □ **I can't read your writing.** Je n'arrive pas à lire ton écriture.
- ■ **in writing** par écrit

written VERB ▷ see **write**

wrong ADJECTIVE, ADVERB
1 faux (FEM fausse) (incorrect)

□ The information they gave us was wrong. Les renseignements qu'ils nous ont donnés étaient faux.

■ **the wrong answer** la mauvaise réponse

■ **You've got the wrong number.** Vous vous êtes trompé de numéro.

2 mal (*morally bad*)

□ I think hunting is wrong. Je trouve que c'est mal de chasser.

■ **to be wrong** (*mistaken*) se tromper [28]

□ You're wrong about that. Tu te trompes.

■ **to do something wrong** se tromper [28]

□ You've done it wrong. Tu t'es trompé.

■ **to go wrong** (*plan*) mal tourner [28]

□ The robbery went wrong and they got caught. Le cambriolage a mal tourné et ils ont été pris.

■ **What's wrong?** Qu'est-ce qui ne va pas ?

■ **What's wrong with her?** Qu'est-ce qu'elle a ?

wrote VERB ▷ *see* **write**

WWW NOUN (= *World Wide Web*)

le Web *masc*

w

Xmas NOUN (= *Christmas*)
Noël

to **X-ray** VERB
▷ *see also* **X-ray** NOUN
■ **to X-ray something** faire [36] une radio
de quelque chose ▢ They X-rayed my arm.

Ils ont fait une radio de mon bras.

X-ray NOUN
▷ *see also* **X-ray** VERB
la radio *fem*
▢ to have an X-ray passer une
radio

Yy

yacht NOUN
1 le voilier *masc* (*sailing boat*)
2 le yacht *masc* (*luxury motorboat*)

yard NOUN
1 la cour *fem* (*of building*)
□ in the yard dans la cour
2 le mètre *masc*

> **DID YOU KNOW...?**
> In France, measurements are in metres rather than yards. A yard is slightly less than a metre.

to **yawn** VERB
bâiller [28]

year NOUN
l'an *masc*
□ last year l'an dernier □ next year l'an prochain
■ **to be 15 years old** avoir [8] quinze ans
■ **an eight-year-old child** un enfant de huit ans

> **DID YOU KNOW...?**
> In French secondary schools, years are counted from the **sixième** (youngest) to **première** and **terminale** (oldest).

□ year 7 la sixième □ year 8 la cinquième
□ year 9 la quatrième □ year 10 la troisième
□ year 11 la seconde
■ **She's in year 11.** Elle est en seconde.
■ **He's a first-year.** Il est en sixième.

to **yell** VERB
hurler [28]

yellow ADJECTIVE
jaune (FEM jaune)

yes ADVERB
1 oui
□ Do you like it? — Yes. Tu aimes ça ? — Oui.
■ **Would you like a cup of tea? — Yes please.**
Voulez-vous une tasse de thé ? — Je veux bien.
2 si

> Use si when answering negative questions.

□ Don't you like it? — Yes! Tu n'aimes pas ça ? — Si ! □ You're not Swiss, are you? — Yes I am! Tu n'es pas suisse, si ? — Si !

yesterday ADVERB
hier
□ yesterday morning hier matin □ yesterday

afternoon hier après-midi □ yesterday evening hier soir □ all day yesterday toute la journée d'hier

yet ADVERB
encore
■ **not yet** pas encore □ It's not finished yet. Ce n'est pas encore fini.
■ **not as yet** pas encore □ There's no news as yet. Nous n'avons pas encore de nouvelles.
■ **Have you finished yet?** Vous avez fini ?

to **yield** VERB (US)
céder [34] le passage (*on road sign*)

yob NOUN
le loubard *masc*

yoghurt NOUN
le yaourt *masc*

yolk NOUN
le jaune d'œuf *masc*

you PRONOUN

> Only use **tu** when speaking to one person you know well or who is your own age or younger. If in doubt use **vous**.

1 vous (*polite form or plural*)
□ Do you like football? Est-ce que vous aimez le football ? □ Can I help you? Est-ce que je peux vous aider ? □ It's for you. C'est pour vous.
2 tu (*familiar singular*)
□ Do you like athletics? Tu aimes l'athlétisme ?

> **vous** never changes, but **tu** has different forms. When 'you' is the object of the sentence use **te** not **tu**. **te** becomes **t'** before a vowel sound.

3 te
□ I know you. Je te connais. □ I gave it to you. Je te l'ai donné.
t'
□ I saw you. Je t'ai vu. □ I'll help you. Je vais t'aider.
4 toi

> **toi** is used instead of **tu** after a preposition and in comparisons.

□ It's for you. C'est pour toi. □ I'll come with you. Je viens avec toi. □ She's younger than you. Elle est plus jeune que toi.

young ADJECTIVE
jeune (FEM jeune)
■ **young people** les jeunes

y

Core vocabulary is shaded.

younger - youth hostel

younger ADJECTIVE

plus jeune (FEM plus jeune)

□ He's younger than me. Il est plus jeune que moi.

■ **my younger brother** mon frère cadet

■ **my younger sister** ma sœur cadette

youngest ADJECTIVE

plus jeune (FEM plus jeune)

□ my youngest brother mon plus jeune frère □ She's the youngest. C'est la plus jeune.

your ADJECTIVE

Only use **ton/ta/tes** when speaking to one person of your own age or younger. If in doubt use **votre/vos**.

1 votre (FEM votre) (polite form or plural)

□ your house votre maison

vos pl

□ your seats vos places

2 ton masc (familiar singular)

□ your brother ton frère

ta fem

□ your sister ta sœur

tes pl

□ your parents tes parents

ta becomes **ton** before a vowel sound

■ **your friend** 1 (male) ton ami 2 (female) ton amie

Do not use **votre/vos** or **ton/ta/tes** with parts of the body.

□ Would you like to wash your hands? Est-ce que vous voulez vous laver les mains ? □ Do you want to wash your hair? Tu veux te laver les cheveux ?

yours PRONOUN

Only use **le tien/la tienne/les tiens/les tiennes** when talking to one person of your own age or younger. If in doubt use **le vôtre/la vôtre/les vôtres**. The same applies to **à toi** and **à vous**.

1 le vôtre + masc noun

□ I've lost my pen. Can I use yours? J'ai perdu mon stylo. Je peux utiliser le vôtre ?

la vôtre + fem noun

□ I like that car. Is it yours? J'aime cette voiture-là. C'est la vôtre ?

les vôtres + pl noun

□ my parents and yours mes parents et les vôtres

■ **Is this yours?** C'est à vous ? □ This book is yours. Ce livre est à vous. □ Whose is this? — It's yours. C'est à qui ? — À vous.

■ **Yours sincerely ...** Veuillez agréer l'expression de mes sentiments les meilleurs ...

2 le tien + masc noun

□ I've lost my pen. Can I use yours? J'ai perdu mon stylo. Je peux utiliser le tien ?

la tienne + fem noun

□ I like that car. Is it yours? J'aime cette voiture-là. C'est la tienne ?

les tiens + masc pl noun

□ my parents and yours mes parents et les tiens

les tiennes + fem pl noun

□ My hands are dirty, yours are clean. Mes mains sont sales, les tiennes sont propres.

■ **Is this yours?** C'est à toi ? □ This book is yours. Ce livre est à toi. □ Whose is this? — It's yours. C'est à qui ? — À toi.

yourself PRONOUN

Only use **te** when talking to one person of your own age or younger; use **vous** to everyone else. If in doubt use **vous**.

1 vous (polite form)

□ Have you hurt yourself? Est-ce que vous vous êtes fait mal ? □ Tell me about yourself! Parlez-moi de vous !

2 te (familiar form)

□ Have you hurt yourself? Est-ce que tu t'es fait mal ?

3 toi (familiar form)

After a preposition, use **toi** instead of **te**.

□ Tell me about yourself! Parle-moi de toi !

4 toi-même

□ Do it yourself! Fais-le toi-même !

5 vous-même

□ Do it yourself! Faites-le vous-même !

yourselves PRONOUN

1 vous

□ Did you enjoy yourselves? Vous vous êtes bien amusés ?

2 vous-mêmes

□ Did you make it yourselves? Vous l'avez fait vous-mêmes ?

youth club NOUN

le centre de loisirs masc

youth hostel NOUN

l'auberge de jeunesse fem

y

Zz

zany ADJECTIVE
  loufoque (FEM loufoque)

zebra NOUN
  le zèbre *masc*

zebra crossing NOUN
  le passage clouté *masc*

zero NOUN
  le zéro *masc*

Zimbabwe NOUN
  le Zimbabwe *masc*
  ■ **in Zimbabwe** au Zimbabwe

Zimmer frame® NOUN
  le déambulateur *masc*

zip NOUN
  la fermeture éclair® *fem* (PL les fermetures éclair®)

zip code NOUN (US)
  le code postal *masc*

zipper NOUN (US)
  la fermeture éclair® *fem* (PL les fermetures éclair®)

zit NOUN
  le bouton *masc*

zodiac NOUN
  le zodiaque *masc*
  □ **the signs of the zodiac** les signes du zodiaque

zone NOUN
  la zone *fem*

zoo NOUN
  le zoo *masc*

zoom lens NOUN
  le zoom *masc*

zucchini NOUN (US)
  la courgette *fem*

Z

Contents

French verb tables

This section is designed to help you find all the verb forms you need in French. From pages 629–649 you will find 21 very common regular and irregular verbs shown in full, with example phrases.

From pages 650–658 you will see a list of 93 regular and irregular verbs with full conjugation of their main forms.

How to find the verb you need

Most of the French verbs on both sides of the dictionary, when they appear in the infinitive form (-er, -ir or -re), are followed by a number in square brackets. Each of these numbers corresponds to a verb in this section. For example:

> **regarder** VERB [28]
> **1** to look at

Here, the number [28] after the verb **regarder** means that **regarder** follows the same pattern as verb number 28 in the list at the end of this section, which is **donner**. This is one of the very common verbs shown in full at the start of this section. For other verbs, a summary of the main forms is given. For example:

> **avancer** VERB [12]
> **1** to move forward

Here, **avancer** follows the same pattern as verb number [12] in the list at the end of this section, which is **commencer**. On page 650 of this section, you can see that the main forms of **commencer** are given to show you how this verb (and others like it) works.

In the full verb tables, you will find examples of regular verbs: a regular -er verb (**donner**), a regular -ir verb (**finir**) and a regular -re verb (**vendre**). Regular verbs follow one of three set patterns. When you have learnt these patterns, you will be able to form any regular verb.

You will also find **avoir** (to have) and **être** (to be) in the full verb tables. These are very important verbs which must be learnt. You use them when you want to say 'I have' *etc* or 'I am' *etc*. The present tense of **avoir** or **être** is also used to form the **perfect tense**. In most cases, **avoir** is used to form the perfect, but reflexive verbs like **se taire** (to stop talking) and verbs of movement like **aller** (to go) and **venir** (to come) use **être** – for example, the French for both 'he's gone' and 'he went' is **il *est* allé**, not **il *a* allé**.

On the French side of the dictionary, where a verb uses **être** to form the **perfect tense**, this is shown after the verb number. For example:

tomber VERB [84, *aux* être]
to fall

On the English side, the symbol ^E after the verb number in the translation shows which verbs use **être** in the **perfect tense**. For example:

to **arrive** VERB
arriver [5^E]

Verb tenses

The present tense

The present tense is used to talk about what is true at the moment, what happens regularly and what is happening now, for example, 'I'm a student'; 'He works as a consultant'; 'I'm studying French'.

There is more than one way to express the present tense in English. For example, you can either say 'I give', 'I am giving' or occasionally 'I do give'. In French, you use the same form **je donne** for all these.

In English you can also use the present to talk about something that is going to happen in the near future. You can do the same in French.

J'emménage à la fin du mois.	**I'm moving in** at the end of the month.
On sort avec Aurélie ce soir.	**We're going out** with Aurélie tonight.

The future tense

The future tense is used to talk about something that will happen or will be true. There are several ways to express the future tense in English: you can use the future tense ('I'll ask him on Tuesday'), the present tense ('I'm not working tomorrow'), or 'going to' followed by an infinitive ('She's going to study in France for a year'). In French you can also use the future tense, the present tense, or the verb **aller** (to go) followed by an infinitive.

Elle ne rentrera pas avant minuit.	**She won't be back** before midnight.
Il arrive dans dix minutes.	**He's coming** in ten minutes.
Je vais me faire couper les cheveux.	**I'm going to** have my hair cut.

The imperfect tense

The imperfect tense is one of the tenses used to talk about the past, especially in descriptions, and to say what used to happen, for example 'I used to work in Manchester'; 'It was sunny yesterday'.

Je ne faisais rien de spécial.	**I wasn't doing anything** special.
C'était une super fête.	**It was** a great party.
Avant, **il était** professeur.	**He used to be** a teacher.

The perfect tense

The perfect tense is made up of two parts: the present tense of **avoir** or **être**, and the French past participle (like 'given', 'finished' and 'done' in English).

Most verbs form the perfect tense with **avoir**. There are two main groups of verbs which form their perfect tense with **être** instead of **avoir**: all reflexive verbs (see **s'asseoir** page 631 and **se taire** page 645) and a group of verbs that are mainly used to talk about movement or a change of some kind, including:

aller	to go
venir	to come
arriver	to arrive, to happen
partir	to leave, to go
descendre	to go down, to come down, to get off
monter	to go up, to come up
entrer	to go in, to come in
sortir	to go out, to come out
mourir	to die
naître	to be born
devenir	to become
rester	to stay
tomber	to fall

Richard **est parti** de bonne heure.	Richard **left** early.
Tu es sortie hier soir?	**Did you go out** last night?
On est resté trois jours à Toulouse.	**We stayed** in Toulouse for three days.

Some verbs can use either **avoir** or **être** in the perfect tense, depending on their meaning. These verbs are marked in the dictionary as '*aux* **avoir** *or* **être**' after the verb number, with an explanatory note about which to use and when.

The imperative

An imperative is a form of the verb used when giving orders and instructions, for example, 'Be quiet!', 'Don't forget your passport!', 'Please fill in this form'.

In French, there are several forms of the imperative that are used to give instructions or orders to someone. These correspond to **tu**, **vous** and **nous**. The **nous** form means the same as 'let's' in English. For regular verbs, the imperative is the same as the **tu**, **nous** and **vous** forms of the present tense, except that you do not say the pronouns **tu**, **nous** and **vous**. Also, in the **tu** form of -**er** verbs like **donner**, the final -**s** is dropped.

Arrête de me faire rire! **Stop** making me laugh!
Venez déjeuner chez nous. **Come** round to ours for lunch.
Allons voir ce qu'ils font. **Let's go** and see what they're up to.

The subjunctive

The subjunctive is a verb form that is used in certain circumstances to express
some sort of feeling, or to show there is doubt about whether something will
happen or something is true. It is used after certain structures in French,
for example, **il faut que** and **il faudrait que**.

Il faut que je rentre. **I have to** get back.
Il faudrait qu'on loue une voiture. **We should** hire a car.
Je veux que tu viennes avec moi. **I want** you to come with me.

The conditional

The conditional is a verb form used to talk about things that would happen or that
would be true under certain conditions, for instance, 'I would help you if I could'.
It is also used to say what you would like or need, for example, 'Could you give me
the bill?'.

Je voudrais deux billets. **I'd like** two tickets.
Si j'étais toi, **je téléphonerais**. **I'd call** if I were you.

aller (to go)

	PRESENT		**PRESENT SUBJUNCTIVE**
je	**vais**	j'	**aille**
tu	**vas**	tu	**ailles**
il/elle/on	**va**	il/elle/on	**aille**
nous	**allons**	nous	**allions**
vous	**allez**	vous	**alliez**
ils/elles	**vont**	ils/elles	**aillent**

	PERFECT		**IMPERFECT**
je	**suis allé(e)**	j'	**allais**
tu	**es allé(e)**	tu	**allais**
il/elle/on	**est allé(e)**	il/elle/on	**allait**
nous	**sommes allé(e)s**	nous	**allions**
vous	**êtes allé(e)(s)**	vous	**alliez**
ils/elles	**sont allé(e)s**	ils/elles	**allaient**

	FUTURE		**CONDITIONAL**
j'	**irai**	j'	**irais**
tu	**iras**	tu	**irais**
il/elle/on	**ira**	il/elle/on	**irait**
nous	**irons**	nous	**irions**
vous	**irez**	vous	**iriez**
ils/elles	**iront**	ils/elles	**iraient**

PRESENT PARTICIPLE	**PAST PARTICIPLE**
allant	allé

IMPERATIVE

va / allons / allez

....

EXAMPLE PHRASES

Vous **allez** au cinéma? Are you going to the cinema?
Je **suis allé** à Londres. I went to London.
Est-ce que tu **es** déjà **allé** en Allemagne? Have you ever been to Germany?

je/j' = I **tu** = you **il** = he/it **elle** = she/it **on** = we/one **nous** = we **vous** = you **ils/elles** = they

s'asseoir (to sit down)

PRESENT

je	m'assieds/m'assois
tu	t'assieds/t'assois
il/elle/on	s'assied/s'assoit
nous	nous asseyons/ nous assoyons
vous	vous asseyez/ vous assoyez
ils/elles	s'asseyent/s'assoient

PRESENT SUBJUNCTIVE

je	m'asseye
tu	t'asseyes
il/elle/on	s'asseye
nous	nous asseyions
vous	vous asseyiez
ils/elles	s'asseyent

PERFECT

je	me suis assis(e)
tu	t'es assis(e)
il/elle/on	s'est assis(e)
nous	nous sommes assis(es)
vous	vous êtes assis(e(s))
ils/elles	se sont assis(es)

IMPERFECT

je	m'asseyais
tu	t'asseyais
il/elle/on	s'asseyait
nous	nous asseyions
vous	vous asseyiez
ils/elles	s'asseyaient

FUTURE

je	m'assiérai
tu	t'assiéras
il/elle/on	s'assiéra
nous	nous assiérons
vous	vous assiérez
ils/elles	s'assiéront

CONDITIONAL

je	m'assiérais
tu	t'assiérais
il/elle/on	s'assiérait
nous	nous assiérions
vous	vous assiériez
ils/elles	s'assiéraient

PRESENT PARTICIPLE

s'asseyant

PAST PARTICIPLE

assis

IMPERATIVE

assieds-toi / asseyons-nous / asseyez-vous

EXAMPLE PHRASES

Assieds-toi, Nicole. Sit down, Nicole.
Asseyez-vous, les enfants. Sit down, children.
Je peux **m'asseoir**? May I sit down?
Je **me suis assise** sur un chewing-gum! I've sat on some chewing gum!

---

je/j' = I tu = you il = he/it elle = she/it on = we/one nous = we vous = you ils/elles = they

avoir (to have)

	PRESENT		**PRESENT SUBJUNCTIVE**
j'	**ai**	j'	**aie**
tu	**as**	tu	**aies**
il/elle/on	**a**	il/elle/on	**ait**
nous	**avons**	nous	**ayons**
vous	**avez**	vous	**ayez**
ils/elles	**ont**	ils/elles	**aient**

	PERFECT		**IMPERFECT**
j'	**ai eu**	j'	**avais**
tu	**as eu**	tu	**avais**
il/elle/on	**a eu**	il/elle/on	**avait**
nous	**avons eu**	nous	**avions**
vous	**avez eu**	vous	**aviez**
ils/elles	**ont eu**	ils/elles	**avaient**

	FUTURE		**CONDITIONAL**
j'	**aurai**	j'	**aurais**
tu	**auras**	tu	**aurais**
il/elle/on	**aura**	il/elle/on	**aurait**
nous	**aurons**	nous	**aurions**
vous	**aurez**	vous	**auriez**
ils/elles	**auront**	ils/elles	**auraient**

PRESENT PARTICIPLE

ayant

PAST PARTICIPLE

eu

IMPERATIVE

aie / ayons / ayez

....

EXAMPLE PHRASES

Il **a** les yeux bleus.   He's got blue eyes.
Quel âge **as**-tu?   How old are you?
Il **a eu** un accident.   He's had an accident.
J'**avais** faim.   I was hungry.
Il y **a** beaucoup de monde.   There are lots of people.

je/j' = I **tu** = you **il** = he/it **elle** = she/it **on** = we/one **nous** = we **vous** = you **ils/elles** = they

croire (to believe)

	PRESENT			**PRESENT SUBJUNCTIVE**
je	crois		je	croie
tu	crois		tu	croies
il/elle/on	croit		il/elle/on	croie
nous	croyons		nous	croyions
vous	croyez		vous	croyiez
ils/elles	croient		ils/elles	croient

	PERFECT			**IMPERFECT**
j'	ai cru		je	croyais
tu	as cru		tu	croyais
il/elle/on	a cru		il/elle/on	croyait
nous	avons cru		nous	croyions
vous	avez cru		vous	croyiez
ils/elles	ont cru		ils/elles	croyaient

	FUTURE			**CONDITIONAL**
je	croirai		je	croirais
tu	croiras		tu	croirais
il/elle/on	croira		il/elle/on	croirait
nous	croirons		nous	croirions
vous	croirez		vous	croiriez
ils/elles	croiront		ils/elles	croiraient

PRESENT PARTICIPLE

croyant

PAST PARTICIPLE

cru

IMPERATIVE

crois / croyons / croyez

EXAMPLE PHRASES

Je ne te **crois** pas. I don't believe you.

J'**ai cru** que tu n'allais pas venir. I thought you weren't going to come.

Elle **croyait** encore au père Noël. She still believed in Santa.

je/j' = I **tu** = you **il** = he/it **elle** = she/it **on** = we/one **nous** = we **vous** = you **ils/elles** = they

devoir (to have to; to owe)

	PRESENT		PRESENT SUBJUNCTIVE
je	dois	je	doive
tu	dois	tu	doives
il/elle/on	doit	il/elle/on	doive
nous	devons	nous	devions
vous	devez	vous	deviez
ils/elles	doivent	ils/elles	doivent

	PERFECT		IMPERFECT
j'	ai dû	je	devais
tu	as dû	tu	devais
il/elle/on	a dû	il/elle/on	devait
nous	avons dû	nous	devions
vous	avez dû	vous	deviez
ils/elles	ont dû	ils/elles	devaient

	FUTURE		CONDITIONAL
je	devrai	je	devrais
tu	devras	tu	devrais
il/elle/on	devra	il/elle/on	devrait
nous	devrons	nous	devrions
vous	devrez	vous	devriez
ils/elles	devront	ils/elles	devraient

PRESENT PARTICIPLE

devant

PAST PARTICIPLE

dû (*NB*: due, dus, dues)

IMPERATIVE

dois / devons / devez

EXAMPLE PHRASES

Je **dois** aller faire les courses ce matin.   I have to do the shopping this morning.
À quelle heure est-ce que tu **dois** partir?   What time do you have to leave?
Il **a dû** faire ses devoirs hier soir.   He had to do his homework last night.
Il **devait** prendre le train pour aller travailler.   He had to go to work by train.

je/j' = I tu = you il = he/it elle = she/it on = we/one nous = we vous = you ils/elles = they

dire (to say)

	PRESENT			PRESENT SUBJUNCTIVE
je	**dis**		je	**dise**
tu	**dis**		tu	**dises**
il/elle/on	**dit**		il/elle/on	**dise**
nous	**disons**		nous	**disions**
vous	**dites**		vous	**disiez**
ils/elles	**disent**		ils/elles	**disent**

	PERFECT			IMPERFECT
j'	**ai dit**		je	**disais**
tu	**as dit**		tu	**disais**
il/elle/on	**a dit**		il/elle/on	**disait**
nous	**avons dit**		nous	**disions**
vous	**avez dit**		vous	**disiez**
ils/elles	**ont dit**		ils/elles	**disaient**

	FUTURE			CONDITIONAL
je	**dirai**		je	**dirais**
tu	**diras**		tu	**dirais**
il/elle/on	**dira**		il/elle/on	**dirait**
nous	**dirons**		nous	**dirions**
vous	**direz**		vous	**diriez**
ils/elles	**diront**		ils/elles	**diraient**

PRESENT PARTICIPLE	PAST PARTICIPLE
disant	**dit**

IMPERATIVE
dis / disons / dites

EXAMPLE PHRASES

Qu'est-ce qu'elle **dit**?   What is she saying?
"Bonjour!", **a**-t-il **dit**.   "Hello!" he said.
Ils m'**ont dit** que le film était nul.   They told me that the film was rubbish.
Comment ça **se dit** en anglais?   How do you say that in English?

je/j' = I **tu** = you **il** = he/it **elle** = she/it **on** = we/one **nous** = we **vous** = you **ils/elles** = they

donner (to give)

	PRESENT		**PRESENT SUBJUNCTIVE**
je	donne	je	donne
tu	donnes	tu	donnes
il/elle/on	donne	il/elle/on	donne
nous	donnons	nous	donnions
vous	donnez	vous	donniez
ils/elles	donnent	ils/elles	donnent

	PERFECT		**IMPERFECT**
j'	ai donné	je	donnais
tu	as donné	tu	donnais
il/elle/on	a donné	il/elle/on	donnait
nous	avons donné	nous	donnions
vous	avez donné	vous	donniez
ils/elles	ont donné	ils/elles	donnaient

	FUTURE		**CONDITIONAL**
je	donnerai	je	donnerais
tu	donneras	tu	donnerais
il/elle/on	donnera	il/elle/on	donnerait
nous	donnerons	nous	donnerions
vous	donnerez	vous	donneriez
ils/elles	donneront	ils/elles	donneraient

PRESENT PARTICIPLE	**PAST PARTICIPLE**
donnant	donné

IMPERATIVE

donne / donnons / donnez

....

EXAMPLE PHRASES

Donne-moi la main.   Give me your hand.
Est-ce que je t'**ai donné** mon adresse?   Did I give you my address?
L'appartement **donne** sur la place.   The flat overlooks the square.

être (to be)

	PRESENT		PRESENT SUBJUNCTIVE
je	suis	je	sois
tu	es	tu	sois
il/elle/on	est	il/elle/on	soit
nous	sommes	nous	soyons
vous	êtes	vous	soyez
ils/elles	sont	ils/elles	soient

	PERFECT		IMPERFECT
j'	ai été	j'	étais
tu	as été	tu	étais
il/elle/on	a été	il/elle/on	était
nous	avons été	nous	étions
vous	avez été	vous	étiez
ils/elles	ont été	ils/elles	étaient

	FUTURE		CONDITIONAL
je	serai	je	serais
tu	seras	tu	serais
il/elle/on	sera	il/elle/on	serait
nous	serons	nous	serions
vous	serez	vous	seriez
ils/elles	seront	ils/elles	seraient

PRESENT PARTICIPLE

étant

PAST PARTICIPLE

été

IMPERATIVE

sois / soyons / soyez

EXAMPLE PHRASES

Mon père **est** professeur. My father's a teacher.

Quelle heure **est**-il? – Il **est** dix heures. What time is it? – It's 10 o'clock.

Ils ne **sont** pas encore arrivés. They haven't arrived yet.

je/j' = I tu = you il = he/it elle = she/it on = we/one nous = we vous = you ils/elles = they

faire (to do; to make)

	PRESENT		**PRESENT SUBJUNCTIVE**
je	**fais**	je	**fasse**
tu	**fais**	tu	**fasses**
il/elle/on	**fait**	il/elle/on	**fasse**
nous	**faisons**	nous	**fassions**
vous	**faites**	vous	**fassiez**
ils/elles	**font**	ils/elles	**fassent**

	PERFECT		**IMPERFECT**
j'	**ai fait**	je	**faisais**
tu	**as fait**	tu	**faisais**
il/elle/on	**a fait**	il/elle/on	**faisait**
nous	**avons fait**	nous	**faisions**
vous	**avez fait**	vous	**faisiez**
ils/elles	**ont fait**	ils/elles	**faisaient**

	FUTURE		**CONDITIONAL**
je	**ferai**	je	**ferais**
tu	**feras**	tu	**ferais**
il/elle/on	**fera**	il/elle/on	**ferait**
nous	**ferons**	nous	**ferions**
vous	**ferez**	vous	**feriez**
ils/elles	**feront**	ils/elles	**feraient**

PRESENT PARTICIPLE

faisant

PAST PARTICIPLE

fait

IMPERATIVE

fais / faisons / faites

EXAMPLE PHRASES

Qu'est-ce que tu **fais**?   What are you doing?
Qu'est-ce qu'il **a fait**?   What has he done? or What did he do?
J'**ai fait** un gâteau.   I've made a cake or I made a cake.
Il **s'est fait** couper les cheveux.   He's had his hair cut.

---

je/j' = I tu = you il = he/it elle = she/it on = we/one nous = we vous = you ils/elles = they

finir (to finish)

	PRESENT			PRESENT SUBJUNCTIVE
je	finis		je	finisse
tu	finis		tu	finisses
il/elle/on	finit		il/elle/on	finisse
nous	finissons		nous	finissions
vous	finissez		vous	finissiez
ils/elles	finissent		ils/elles	finissent

	PERFECT			IMPERFECT
j'	ai fini		je	finissais
tu	as fini		tu	finissais
il/elle/on	a fini		il/elle/on	finissait
nous	avons fini		nous	finissions
vous	avez fini		vous	finissiez
ils/elles	ont fini		ils/elles	finissaient

	FUTURE			CONDITIONAL
je	finirai		je	finirais
tu	finiras		tu	finirais
il/elle/on	finira		il/elle/on	finirait
nous	finirons		nous	finirions
vous	finirez		vous	finiriez
ils/elles	finiront		ils/elles	finiraient

PRESENT PARTICIPLE	PAST PARTICIPLE
finissant	fini

IMPERATIVE

finis / finissons / finissez

EXAMPLE PHRASES

Finis ta soupe!   Finish your soup!
J'ai **fini**!   I've finished!
Je **finirai** mes devoirs demain.   I'll finish my homework tomorrow.

je/j' = I tu = you il = he/it elle = she/it on = we/one nous = we vous = you ils/elles = they

mettre (to put)

PRESENT

je	**mets**
tu	**mets**
il/elle/on	**met**
nous	**mettons**
vous	**mettez**
ils/elles	**mettent**

PRESENT SUBJUNCTIVE

je	**mette**
tu	**mettes**
il/elle/on	**mette**
nous	**mettions**
vous	**mettiez**
ils/elles	**mettent**

PERFECT

j'	**ai mis**
tu	**as mis**
il/elle/on	**a mis**
nous	**avons mis**
vous	**avez mis**
ils/elles	**ont mis**

IMPERFECT

je	**mettais**
tu	**mettais**
il/elle/on	**mettait**
nous	**mettions**
vous	**mettiez**
ils/elles	**mettaient**

FUTURE

je	**mettrai**
tu	**mettras**
il/elle/on	**mettra**
nous	**mettrons**
vous	**mettrez**
ils/elles	**mettront**

CONDITIONAL

je	**mettrais**
tu	**mettrais**
il/elle/on	**mettrait**
nous	**mettrions**
vous	**mettriez**
ils/elles	**mettraient**

PRESENT PARTICIPLE

mettant

PAST PARTICIPLE

mis

IMPERATIVE

mets / mettons / mettez

EXAMPLE PHRASES

Mets ton manteau!   Put your coat on!
Où est-ce que tu **as mis** les clés?   Where have you put the keys?
J'**ai mis** le livre sur la table.   I put the book on the table.
Elle **s'est mise** à pleurer.   She started crying.

je/j' = I **tu** = you **il** = he/it **elle** = she/it **on** = we/one **nous** = we **vous** = you **ils/elles** = they

639

ouvrir (to open)

	PRESENT		**PRESENT SUBJUNCTIVE**
j'	ouvre	j'	ouvre
tu	ouvres	tu	ouvres
il/elle/on	ouvre	il/elle/on	ouvre
nous	ouvrons	nous	ouvrions
vous	ouvrez	vous	ouvriez
ils/elles	ouvrent	ils/elles	ouvrent

	PERFECT		**IMPERFECT**
j'	ai ouvert	j'	ouvrais
tu	as ouvert	tu	ouvrais
il/elle/on	a ouvert	il/elle/on	ouvrait
nous	avons ouvert	nous	ouvrions
vous	avez ouvert	vous	ouvriez
ils/elles	ont ouvert	ils/elles	ouvraient

	FUTURE		**CONDITIONAL**
j'	ouvrirai	j'	ouvrirais
tu	ouvriras	tu	ouvrirais
il/elle/on	ouvrira	il/elle/on	ouvrirait
nous	ouvrirons	nous	ouvririons
vous	ouvrirez	vous	ouvririez
ils/elles	ouvriront	ils/elles	ouvriraient

PRESENT PARTICIPLE	**PAST PARTICIPLE**
ouvrant	ouvert

IMPERATIVE

ouvre / ouvrons / ouvrez

EXAMPLE PHRASES

Elle **a ouvert** la porte.   She opened the door.
Est-ce que tu pourrais **ouvrir** la fenêtre?   Could you open the window?
Je me suis coupé en **ouvrant** une boîte de conserve.   I cut myself opening a tin.
La porte **s'est ouverte**.   The door opened.

partir (to leave)

PRESENT		PRESENT SUBJUNCTIVE	
je	pars	je	parte
tu	pars	tu	partes
il/elle	part	il/elle	parte
nous	partons	nous	partions
vous	partez	vous	partiez
ils/elles	partent	ils/elles	partent

PERFECT		IMPERFECT	
je	suis parti(e)	je	partais
tu	es parti(e)	tu	partais
il/elle	est parti(e)	il/elle	partait
nous	sommes parti(e)s	nous	partions
vous	êtes parti(e)s	vous	partiez
ils/elles	sont parti(e)s	ils/elles	partaient

FUTURE		CONDITIONAL	
je	partirai	je	partirais
tu	partiras	tu	partirais
il/elle	partira	il/elle	partirait
nous	partirons	nous	partirions
vous	partirez	vous	partiriez
ils/elles	partiront	ils/elles	partiraient

PRESENT PARTICIPLE
partant

PAST PARTICIPLE
parti

IMPERATIVE
pars / partons / partez

EXAMPLE PHRASES

On **part** en vacances le 15 août.   We're going on holiday on the 15th of August.
Elle **est partie** tôt ce matin.   She left early this morning.
Ne **partez** pas sans moi.   Don't leave without me!
Il faut qu'on **parte** de bonne heure.   We have to leave early.
Il **partait** à huit heures tous les matins.   He left at eight o'clock every morning.

je/j' = I tu = you il = he/it elle = she/it on = we/one nous = we vous = you ils/elles = they

pouvoir (to be able)

	PRESENT			**PRESENT SUBJUNCTIVE**
je	peux		je	puisse
tu	peux		tu	puisses
il/elle/on	peut		il/elle/on	puisse
nous	pouvons		nous	puissions
vous	pouvez		vous	puissiez
ils/elles	peuvent		ils/elles	puissent

	PERFECT			**IMPERFECT**
j'	ai pu		je	pouvais
tu	as pu		tu	pouvais
il/elle/on	a pu		il/elle/on	pouvait
nous	avons pu		nous	pouvions
vous	avez pu		vous	pouviez
ils/elles	ont pu		ils/elles	pouvaient

	FUTURE			**CONDITIONAL**
je	pourrai		je	pourrais
tu	pourras		tu	pourrais
il/elle/on	pourra		il/elle/on	pourrait
nous	pourrons		nous	pourrions
vous	pourrez		vous	pourriez
ils/elles	pourront		ils/elles	pourraient

PRESENT PARTICIPLE

pouvant

PAST PARTICIPLE

pu

IMPERATIVE

not used

EXAMPLE PHRASES

Je **peux** t'aider, si tu veux. I can help you if you like.
J'ai fait tout ce que j'**ai pu**. I did all I could.
Je ne **pourrai** pas venir samedi. I won't be able to come on Saturday.

je/j' = I tu = you il = he/it elle = she/it on = we/one nous = we vous = you ils/elles = they

prendre (to take)

	PRESENT		PRESENT SUBJUNCTIVE
je	prends	je	prenne
tu	prends	tu	prennes
il/elle	prend	il/elle	prenne
nous	prenons	nous	prenions
vous	prenez	vous	preniez
ils/elles	prennent	ils/elles	prennent

	PERFECT		IMPERFECT
j'	ai pris	je	prenais
tu	as pris	tu	prenais
il/elle	a pris	il/elle	prenait
nous	avons pris	nous	prenions
vous	avez pris	vous	preniez
ils/elles	ont pris	ils/elles	prenaient

	FUTURE		CONDITIONAL
je	prendrai	je	prendrais
tu	prendras	tu	prendrais
il/elle	prendra	il/elle	prendrait
nous	prendrons	nous	prendrions
vous	prendrez	vous	prendriez
ils/elles	prendront	ils/elles	prendraient

PRESENT PARTICIPLE

prenant

PAST PARTICIPLE

pris

IMPERATIVE

prends / prenons / prenez

....

EXAMPLE PHRASES

J'**ai pris** plein de photos. I took lots of pictures.
Prends ton appareil photo. Take your camera.
Il faut que je **prenne** mes affaires de gym. I have to take my gym kit.
Il **prendra** le train de 8h20. He'll take the 8.20 train.

je/j' = I **tu** = you **il** = he/it **elle** = she/it **on** = we/one **nous** = we **vous** = you **ils/elles** = they

savoir (to know)

	PRESENT		PRESENT SUBJUNCTIVE
je	sais	je	sache
tu	sais	tu	saches
il/elle/on	sait	il/elle/on	sache
nous	savons	nous	sachions
vous	savez	vous	sachiez
ils/elles	savent	ils/elles	sachent

	PERFECT		IMPERFECT
j'	ai su	je	savais
tu	as su	tu	savais
il/elle/on	a su	il/elle/on	savait
nous	avons su	nous	savions
vous	avez su	vous	saviez
ils/elles	ont su	ils/elles	savaient

	FUTURE		CONDITIONAL
je	saurai	je	saurais
tu	sauras	tu	saurais
il/elle/on	saura	il/elle/on	saurait
nous	saurons	nous	saurions
vous	saurez	vous	sauriez
ils/elles	sauront	ils/elles	sauraient

PRESENT PARTICIPLE

sachant

PAST PARTICIPLE

su

IMPERATIVE

sache / sachons / sachez

....

EXAMPLE PHRASES

Tu **sais** ce que tu vas faire l'année prochaine?   Do you know what you're doing next year?

Je ne **sais** pas.   I don't know.

Elle ne **sait** pas nager.   She can't swim.

Tu **savais** que son père était pakistanais?   Did you know her father was Pakistani?

je/j' = I **tu** = you **il** = he/it **elle** = she/it **on** = we/one **nous** = we **vous** = you **ils/elles** = they

se taire (to stop talking)

PRESENT

je	me tais
tu	te tais
il/elle/on	se tait
nous	nous taisons
vous	vous taisez
ils/elles	se taisent

PRESENT SUBJUNCTIVE

je	me taise
tu	te taises
il/elle/on	se taise
nous	nous taisions
vous	vous taisiez
ils/elles	se taisent

PERFECT

je	me suis tu(e)
tu	t'es tu(e)
il/elle/on	s'est tu(e)
nous	nous sommes tu(e)s
vous	vous êtes tu(e)(s)
ils/elles	se sont tu(e)s

IMPERFECT

je	me taisais
tu	te taisais
il/elle/on	se taisait
nous	nous taisions
vous	vous taisiez
ils/elles	se taisaient

FUTURE

je	me tairai
tu	te tairas
il/elle/on	se taira
nous	nous tairons
vous	vous tairez
ils/elles	se tairont

CONDITIONAL

je	me tairais
tu	te tairais
il/elle/on	se tairait
nous	nous tairions
vous	vous tairiez
ils/elles	se tairaient

PRESENT PARTICIPLE

se taisant

PAST PARTICIPLE

tu

IMPERATIVE

tais-toi / taisons-nous / taisez-vous

....

EXAMPLE PHRASES

Il **s'est tu**. He stopped talking.
Taisez-vous! Be quiet!
Sophie, **tais-toi**! Be quiet, Sophie!

je/j' = I **tu** = you **il** = he/it **elle** = she/it **on** = we/one **nous** = we **vous** = you **ils/elles** = they

vendre (to sell)

	PRESENT		**PRESENT SUBJUNCTIVE**
je	vends	je	vende
tu	vends	tu	vendes
il/elle/on	vend	il/elle/on	vende
nous	vendons	nous	vendions
vous	vendez	vous	vendiez
ils/elles	vendent	ils/elles	vendent

	PERFECT		**IMPERFECT**
j'	ai vendu	je	vendais
tu	as vendu	tu	vendais
il/elle/on	a vendu	il/elle/on	vendait
nous	avons vendu	nous	vendions
vous	avez vendu	vous	vendiez
ils/elles	ont vendu	ils/elles	vendaient

	FUTURE		**CONDITIONAL**
je	vendrai	je	vendrais
tu	vendras	tu	vendrais
il/elle/on	vendra	il/elle/on	vendrait
nous	vendrons	nous	vendrions
vous	vendrez	vous	vendriez
ils/elles	vendront	ils/elles	vendraient

PRESENT PARTICIPLE

vendant

PAST PARTICIPLE

vendu

IMPERATIVE

vends / vendons / vendez

EXAMPLE PHRASES

Il m'**a vendu** son vélo pour 50 euros.   He sold me his bike for 50 euros.
Est-ce que vous **vendez** des piles?   Do you sell batteries?
Elle voudrait **vendre** sa voiture.   She would like to sell her car.

je/j' = I **tu** = you **il** = he/it **elle** = she/it **on** = we/one **nous** = we **vous** = you **ils/elles** = they

venir (to come)

	PRESENT		**PRESENT SUBJUNCTIVE**
je	viens	je	vienne
tu	viens	tu	viennes
il/elle/on	vient	il/elle/on	vienne
nous	venons	nous	venions
vous	venez	vous	veniez
ils/elles	viennent	ils/elles	viennent

	PERFECT		**IMPERFECT**
je	suis venu(e)	je	venais
tu	es venu(e)	tu	venais
il/elle/on	est venu(e)	il/elle/on	venait
nous	sommes venu(e)s	nous	venions
vous	êtes venu(e)(s)	vous	veniez
ils/elles	sont venu(e)s	ils/elles	venaient

	FUTURE		**CONDITIONAL**
je	viendrai	je	viendrais
tu	viendras	tu	viendrais
il/elle/on	viendra	il/elle/on	viendrait
nous	viendrons	nous	viendrions
vous	viendrez	vous	viendriez
ils/elles	viendront	ils/elles	viendraient

PRESENT PARTICIPLE	**PAST PARTICIPLE**
venant	venu

IMPERATIVE

viens / venons / venez

EXAMPLE PHRASES

Elle ne **viendra** pas cette année.   She won't be coming this year.
Fatou et Malik **viennent** du Sénégal.   Fatou and Malik come from Senegal.
Je **viens** de manger.   I've just eaten.

je/j' = I tu = you il = he/it elle = she/it on = we/one nous = we vous = you ils/elles = they

voir (to see)

	PRESENT			PRESENT SUBJUNCTIVE
je	vois		je	voie
tu	vois		tu	voies
il/elle/on	voit		il/elle/on	voie
nous	voyons		nous	voyions
vous	voyez		vous	voyiez
ils/elles	voient		ils/elles	voient

	PERFECT			IMPERFECT
j'	ai vu		je	voyais
tu	as vu		tu	voyais
il/elle/on	a vu		il/elle/on	voyait
nous	avons vu		nous	voyions
vous	avez vu		vous	voyiez
ils/elles	ont vu		ils/elles	voyaient

	FUTURE			CONDITIONAL
je	verrai		je	verrais
tu	verras		tu	verrais
il/elle/on	verra		il/elle/on	verrait
nous	verrons		nous	verrions
vous	verrez		vous	verriez
ils/elles	verront		ils/elles	verraient

PRESENT PARTICIPLE

voyant

PAST PARTICIPLE

vu

IMPERATIVE

vois / voyons / voyez

EXAMPLE PHRASES

Venez me **voir** quand vous serez à Paris.   Come and see me when you're in Paris.

Je ne **vois** rien sans mes lunettes.   I can't see anything without my glasses.

Est-ce que tu l'**as vu**?   Did you see him? *or* Have you seen him?

Est-ce que cette tache **se voit**?   Does that stain show?

je/j' = I **tu** = you **il** = he/it **elle** = she/it **on** = we/one **nous** = we **vous** = you **ils/elles** = they

vouloir (to want)

	PRESENT		**PRESENT SUBJUNCTIVE**
je	veux	je	veuille
tu	veux	tu	veuilles
il/elle/on	veut	il/elle/on	veuille
nous	voulons	nous	voulions
vous	voulez	vous	vouliez
ils/elles	veulent	ils/elles	veuillent

	PERFECT		**IMPERFECT**
j'	ai voulu	je	voulais
tu	as voulu	tu	voulais
il/elle/on	a voulu	il/elle/on	voulait
nous	avons voulu	nous	voulions
vous	avez voulu	vous	vouliez
ils/elles	ont voulu	ils/elles	voulaient

	FUTURE		**CONDITIONAL**
je	voudrai	je	voudrais
tu	voudras	tu	voudrais
il/elle/on	voudra	il/elle/on	voudrait
nous	voudrons	nous	voudrions
vous	voudrez	vous	voudriez
ils/elles	voudront	ils/elles	voudraient

PRESENT PARTICIPLE

voulant

PAST PARTICIPLE

voulu

IMPERATIVE

veuille / veuillons / veuillez

EXAMPLE PHRASES

Elle **veut** un vélo pour Noël.   She wants a bike for Christmas.
Ils **voulaient** aller au cinéma.   They wanted to go to the cinema.
Est-ce que tu **voudrais** une tasse de thé?   Would you like a cup of tea?

je/j' = I tu = you il = he/it elle = she/it on = we/one nous = we vous = you ils/elles = they

French verb forms

	PRESENT	PERFECT	IMPERFECT	FUTURE	PRESENT SUBJUNCTIVE
1 acheter to buy	j' achète	j' ai acheté	j' achetais	j' achèterai	j' achète
	tu achètes	tu as acheté	tu achetais	tu achèteras	tu achètes
	il/elle achète	il/elle a acheté	il/elle achetait	il/elle achètera	il/elle achète
	nous achetons	nous avons acheté	nous achetions	nous achèterons	nous achetions
	vous achetez	vous avez acheté	vous achetiez	vous achèterez	vous achetiez
	ils/elles achètent	ils/elles ont acheté	ils/elles achetaient	ils/elles achèteront	ils/elles achètent
2 acquérir to acquire	j' acquiers	j' ai acquis	j' acquérais	j' acquerrai	j' acquière
	tu acquiers	tu as acquis	tu acquérais	tu acquerras	tu acquières
	il/elle acquiert	il/elle a acquis	il/elle acquérait	il/elle acquerra	il/elle acquière
	nous acquérons	nous avons acquis	nous acquérions	nous acquerrons	nous acquérions
	vous acquérez	vous avez acquis	vous acquériez	vous acquerrez	vous acquériez
	ils/elles acquièrent	ils/elles ont acquis	ils/elles acquéraient	ils/elles acquerront	ils/elles acquièrent
3 aller to go	see full verb table page 629				
4 appeler to call	j' appelle	j' ai appelé	j' appelais	j' appellerai	j' appelle
	tu appelles	tu as appelé	tu appelais	tu appelleras	tu appelles
	il/elle appelle	il/elle a appelé	il/elle appelait	il/elle appellera	il/elle appelle
	nous appelons	nous avons appelé	nous appelions	nous appellerons	nous appelions
	vous appelez	vous avez appelé	vous appeliez	vous appellerez	vous appeliez
	ils/elles appellent	ils/elles ont appelé	ils/elles appelaient	ils/elles appelleront	ils/elles appellent
5 arriver to arrive	j' arrive	je suis arrivé(e)	j' arrivais	j' arriverai	j' arrive
	tu arrives	tu es arrivé(e)	tu arrivais	tu arriveras	tu arrives
	il/elle arrive	il/elle est arrivé(e)	il/elle arrivait	il/elle arrivera	il/elle arrive
	nous arrivons	nous sommes arrivé(e)s	nous arrivions	nous arriverons	nous arrivions
	vous arrivez	vous êtes arrivé(e)(s)	vous arriviez	vous arriverez	vous arriviez
	ils/elles arrivent	ils/elles sont arrivé(e)s	ils/elles arrivaient	ils/elles arriveront	ils/elles arrivent
6 s'asseoir to sit down	see full verb table page 630				
7 attendre to wait	j' attends	j' ai attendu	j' attendais	j' attendrai	j' attende
	tu attends	tu as attendu	tu attendais	tu attendras	tu attendes
	il/elle attend	il/elle a attendu	il/elle attendait	il/elle attendra	il/elle attende
	nous attendons	nous avons attendu	nous attendions	nous attendrons	nous attendions
	vous attendez	vous avez attendu	vous attendiez	vous attendrez	vous attendiez
	ils/elles attendent	ils/elles ont attendu	ils/elles attendaient	ils/elles attendront	ils/elles attendent
8 avoir to have	see full verb table page 631				
9 battre to beat	je bats	j' ai battu	je battais	je battrai	je batte
	tu bats	tu as battu	tu battais	tu battras	tu battes
	il/elle bat	il/elle a battu	il/elle battait	il/elle battra	il/elle batte
	nous battons	nous avons battu	nous battions	nous battrons	nous battions
	vous battez	vous avez battu	vous battiez	vous battrez	vous battiez
	ils/elles battent	ils/elles ont battu	ils/elles battaient	ils/elles battront	ils/elles battent
10 boire to drink	je bois	j' ai bu	je buvais	je boirai	je boive
	tu bois	tu as bu	tu buvais	tu boiras	tu boives
	il/elle boit	il/elle a bu	il/elle buvait	il/elle boira	il/elle boive
	nous buvons	nous avons bu	nous buvions	nous boirons	nous buvions
	vous buvez	vous avez bu	vous buviez	vous boirez	vous buviez
	ils/elles boivent	ils/elles ont bu	ils/elles buvaient	ils/elles boiront	ils/elles boivent
11 bouillir to boil	je bous	j' ai bouilli	je bouillais	je bouillirai	je bouille
	tu bous	tu as bouilli	tu bouillais	tu bouilliras	tu bouilles
	il/elle bout	il/elle a bouilli	il/elle bouillait	il/elle bouillira	il/elle bouille
	nous bouillons	nous avons bouilli	nous bouillions	nous bouillirons	nous bouillions
	vous bouillez	vous avez bouilli	vous bouilliez	vous bouillirez	vous bouilliez
	ils/elles bouillent	ils/elles ont bouilli	ils/elles bouillaient	ils/elles bouilliront	ils/elles bouillent

Letters in bold indicate a significant change in spelling from the infinitive form.

	PRESENT	PERFECT	IMPERFECT	FUTURE	PRESENT SUBJUNCTIVE
12 commencer to start	je commence	j' ai commencé	je commençais	je commencerai	je commence
	tu commences	tu as commencé	tu commençais	tu commenceras	tu commences
	il/elle commence	il/elle a commencé	il/elle commençait	il/elle commencera	il/elle commence
	nous commençons	nous avons commencé	nous commencions	nous commencerons	nous commencions
	vous commencez	vous avez commencé	vous commenciez	vous commencerez	vous commenciez
	ils/elles commencent	ils/elles ont commencé	ils/elles commençaient	ils/elles commenceront	ils/elles commencent
13 conclure to conclude	je conclus	j' ai conclu	je concluais	je conclurai	je conclue
	tu conclus	tu as conclu	tu concluais	tu concluras	tu conclues
	il/elle conclut	il/elle a conclu	il/elle concluait	il/elle conclura	il/elle conclue
	nous concluons	nous avons conclu	nous concluions	nous conclurons	nous concluions
	vous concluez	vous avez conclu	vous concluiez	vous conclurez	vous concluiez
	ils/elles concluent	ils/elles ont conclu	ils/elles concluaient	ils/elles concluront	ils/elles concluent
14 connaître to know	je connais	j' ai connu	je connaissais	je connaîtrai	je connaisse
	tu connais	tu as connu	tu connaissais	tu connaîtras	tu connaisses
	il/elle connaît	il/elle a connu	il/elle connaissait	il/elle connaîtra	il/elle connaisse
	nous connaissons	nous avons connu	nous connaissions	nous connaîtrons	nous connaissions
	vous connaissez	vous avez connu	vous connaissiez	vous connaîtrez	vous connaissiez
	ils/elles connaissent	ils/elles ont connu	ils/elles connaissaient	ils/elles connaîtront	ils/elles connaissent
15 coudre to sew	je couds	j' ai cousu	je cousais	je coudrai	je couse
	tu couds	tu as cousu	tu cousais	tu coudras	tu couses
	il/elle coud	il/elle a cousu	il/elle cousait	il/elle coudra	il/elle couse
	nous cousons	nous avons cousu	nous cousions	nous coudrons	nous cousions
	vous cousez	vous avez cousu	vous cousiez	vous coudrez	vous cousiez
	ils/elles cousent	ils/elles ont cousu	ils/elles cousaient	ils/elles coudront	ils/elles cousent
16 courir to run	je cours	j' ai couru	je courais	je courrai	je coure
	tu cours	tu as couru	tu courais	tu courras	tu coures
	il/elle court	il/elle a couru	il/elle courait	il/elle courra	il/elle coure
	nous courons	nous avons couru	nous courions	nous courrons	nous courions
	vous courez	vous avez couru	vous couriez	vous courrez	vous couriez
	ils/elles courent	ils/elles ont couru	ils/elles couraient	ils/elles courront	ils/elles courent
17 craindre to fear	je crains	j' ai craint	je craignais	je craindrai	je craigne
	tu crains	tu as craint	tu craignais	tu craindras	tu craignes
	il/elle craint	il/elle a craint	il/elle craignait	il/elle craindra	il/elle craigne
	nous craignons	nous avons craint	nous craignions	nous craindrons	nous craignions
	vous craignez	vous avez craint	vous craigniez	vous craindrez	vous craigniez
	ils/elles craignent	ils/elles ont craint	ils/elles craignaient	ils/elles craindront	ils/elles craignent
18 créer to create	je crée	j' ai créé	je créais	je créerai	je crée
	tu crées	tu as créé	tu créais	tu créeras	tu crées
	il/elle crée	il/elle a créé	il/elle créait	il/elle créera	il/elle crée
	nous créons	nous avons créé	nous créions	nous créerons	nous créions
	vous créez	vous avez créé	vous créiez	vous créerez	vous créiez
	ils/elles créent	ils/elles ont créé	ils/elles créaient	ils/elles créeront	ils/elles créent
19 crier to cry	je crie	j' ai crié	je criais	je crierai	je crie
	tu cries	tu as crié	tu criais	tu crieras	tu cries
	il/elle crie	il/elle a crié	il/elle criait	il/elle criera	il/elle crie
	nous crions	nous avons crié	nous criions	nous crierons	nous criions
	vous criez	vous avez crié	vous criiez	vous crierez	vous criiez
	ils/elles crient	ils/elles ont crié	ils/elles criaient	ils/elles crieront	ils/elles crient
20 croire to believe	see full verb table page 632				
21 croître to grow	je croîs	j' ai crû	je croissais	je croîtrai	je croisse
	tu croîs	tu as crû	tu croissais	tu croîtras	tu croisses
	il/elle croît	il/elle a crû	il/elle croissait	il/elle croîtra	il/elle croisse
	nous croissons	nous avons crû	nous croissions	nous croîtrons	nous croissions
	vous croissez	vous avez crû	vous croissiez	vous croîtrez	vous croissiez
	ils/elles croissent	ils/elles ont crû	ils/elles croissaient	ils/elles croîtront	ils/elles croissent
22 cueillir to pick	je cueille	j' ai cueilli	je cueillais	je cueillerai	je cueille
	tu cueilles	tu as cueilli	tu cueillais	tu cueilleras	tu cueilles
	il/elle cueille	il/elle a cueilli	il/elle cueillait	il/elle cueillera	il/elle cueille
	nous cueillons	nous avons cueilli	nous cueillions	nous cueillerons	nous cueillions
	vous cueillez	vous avez cueilli	vous cueilliez	vous cueillerez	vous cueilliez
	ils/elles cueillent	ils/elles ont cueilli	ils/elles cueillaient	ils/elles cueilleront	ils/elles cueillent

Letters in bold indicate a significant change in spelling from the infinitive form.

	PRESENT	PERFECT	IMPERFECT	FUTURE	PRESENT SUBJUNCTIVE
23 cuire to cook	je cuis	j' ai cuit	je cuisais	je cuirai	je cuise
	tu cuis	tu as cuit	tu cuisais	tu cuiras	tu cuises
	il/elle cuit	il/elle a cuit	il/elle cuisait	il/elle cuira	il/elle cuise
	nous cuisons	nous avons cuit	nous cuisions	nous cuirons	nous cuisions
	vous cuisez	vous avez cuit	vous cuisiez	vous cuirez	vous cuisiez
	ils/elles cuisent	ils/elles ont cuit	ils/elles cuisaient	ils/elles cuiront	ils/elles cuisent
24 descendre to go down	je descends	je suis descendu(e)/ j' ai descendu	je descendais	je descendrai	je descende
	tu descends	tu es descendu(e)/ tu as descendu	tu descendais	tu descendras	tu descendes
	il/elle descend	il/elle est descendu(e)/ il/elle a descendu	il/elle descendait	il/elle descendra	il/elle descende
	nous descendons	nous sommes descendu(e)s/ nous avons descendu	nous descendions	nous descendrons	nous descendions
	vous descendez	vous êtes descendu(e)(s)/ vous avez descendu	vous descendiez	vous descendrez	vous descendiez
	ils/elles descendent	ils/elles sont descendu(e)s/ ils/elles ont descendu	ils/elles descendaient	ils/elles descendront	ils/elles descendent
25 devenir to become	je deviens	je suis devenu(e)	je devenais	je deviendrai	je devienne
	tu deviens	tu es devenu(e)	tu devenais	tu deviendras	tu deviennes
	il/elle devient	il/elle est devenu(e)	il/elle devenait	il/elle deviendra	il/elle devienne
	nous devenons	nous sommes devenu(e)s	nous devenions	nous deviendrons	nous devenions
	vous devenez	vous êtes devenu(e)(s)	vous deveniez	vous deviendrez	vous deveniez
	ils/elles deviennent	ils/elles sont devenu(e)s	ils/elles devenaient	ils/elles deviendront	ils/elles deviennent
26 devoir to have to; to owe	see full verb table page 633				
27 dire to say	see full verb table page 634				
28 donner to give	see full verb table page 635				
29 dormir to sleep	je dors	j' ai dormi	je dormais	je dormirai	je dorme
	tu dors	tu as dormi	tu dormais	tu dormiras	tu dormes
	il/elle dort	il/elle a dormi	il/elle dormait	il/elle dormira	il/elle dorme
	nous dormons	nous avons dormi	nous dormions	nous dormirons	nous dormions
	vous dormez	vous avez dormi	vous dormiez	vous dormirez	vous dormiez
	ils/elles dorment	ils/elles ont dormi	ils/elles dormaient	ils/elles dormiront	ils/elles dorment
30 écrire to write	j' écris	j' ai écrit	j' écrivais	j' écrirai	j' écrive
	tu écris	tu as écrit	tu écrivais	tu écriras	tu écrives
	il/elle écrit	il/elle a écrit	il/elle écrivait	il/elle écrira	il/elle écrive
	nous écrivons	nous avons écrit	nous écrivions	nous écrirons	nous écrivions
	vous écrivez	vous avez écrit	vous écriviez	vous écrirez	vous écriviez
	ils/elles écrivent	ils/elles ont écrit	ils/elles écrivaient	ils/elles écriront	ils/elles écrivent
31 émouvoir to move	j' ém**eu**s	j' ai ému	j' émouvais	j' émouvrai	j' ém**eu**ve
	tu ém**eu**s	tu as ému	tu émouvais	tu émouvras	tu ém**eu**ves
	il/elle ém**eu**t	il/elle a ému	il/elle émouvait	il/elle émouvra	il/elle ém**eu**ve
	nous émouvons	nous avons ému	nous émouvions	nous émouvrons	nous émouvions
	vous émouvez	vous avez ému	vous émouviez	vous émouvrez	vous émouviez
	ils/elles ém**eu**vent	ils/elles ont ému	ils/elles émouvaient	ils/elles émouvront	ils/elles ém**eu**vent
32 entrer to come in; to go in	j' entre	je suis entré(e)/ j' ai entré	j' entrais	j' entrerai	j' entre
	tu entres	tu es entré(e)/ tu as entré	tu entrais	tu entreras	tu entres
	il/elle entre	il/elle est entré(e)/ il/elle a entré	il/elle entrait	il/elle entrera	il/elle entre
	nous entrons	nous sommes entré(e)s/ nous avons entré	nous entrions	nous entrerons	nous entrions
	vous entrez	vous êtes entré(e)(s)/ vous avez entré	vous entriez	vous entrerez	vous entriez
	ils/elles entrent	ils/elles sont entré(e)s/ ils/elles ont entré	ils/elles entraient	ils/elles entreront	ils/elles entrent

Letters in bold indicate a significant change in spelling from the infinitive form.

	PRESENT	**PERFECT**	**IMPERFECT**	**FUTURE**	**PRESENT SUBJUNCTIVE**
33 envoyer to send	j' envoie tu envoies il/elle envoie nous envoyons vous envoyez ils/elles envoient	j' ai envoyé tu as envoyé il/elle a envoyé nous avons envoyé vous avez envoyé ils/elles ont envoyé	j' envoyais tu envoyais il/elle envoyait nous envoyions vous envoyiez ils/elles envoyaient	j' enverrai tu enverras il/elle enverra nous enverrons vous enverrez ils/elles enverront	j' envoie tu envoies il/elle envoie nous envoyions vous envoyiez ils/elles envoient
34 espérer to hope	j' espère tu espères il/elle espère nous espérons vous espérez ils/elles espèrent	j' ai espéré tu as espéré il/elle a espéré nous avons espéré vous avez espéré ils/elles ont espéré	j' espérais tu espérais il/elle espérait nous espérions vous espériez ils/elles espéraient	j' espérerai tu espéreras il/elle espérera nous espérerons vous espérerez ils/elles espéreront	j' espère tu espères il/elle espère nous espérions vous espériez ils/elles espèrent
35 être to be	see full verb table page 636				
36 faire to do; to make	see full verb table page 637				
37 falloir to have to	il faut	il a fallu	il fallait	il faudra	il faille
38 finir to finish	see full verb table page 638				
39 fuir to flee; to drip	je fuis tu fuis il/elle fuit nous fuyons vous fuyez ils/elles fuient	j' ai fui tu as fui il/elle a fui nous avons fui vous avez fui ils/elles ont fui	je fuyais tu fuyais il/elle fuyait nous fuyions vous fuyiez ils/elles fuyaient	je fuirai tu fuiras il/elle fuira nous fuirons vous fuirez ils/elles fuiront	je fuie tu fuies il/elle fuie nous fuyions vous fuyiez ils/elles fuient
40 haïr to hate	je hais tu hais il/elle hait nous haïssons vous haïssez ils/elles haïssent	j' ai haï tu as haï il/elle a haï nous avons haï vous avez haï ils/elles ont haï	je haïssais tu haïssais il/elle haïssait nous haïssions vous haïssiez ils/elles haïssaient	je haïrai tu haïras il/elle haïra nous haïrons vous haïrez ils/elles haïront	je haïsse tu haïsses il/elle haïsse nous haïssions vous haïssiez ils/elles haïssent
41 jeter to throw (away)	je jette tu jettes il/elle jette nous jetons vous jetez ils/elles jettent	j' ai jeté tu as jeté il/elle a jeté nous avons jeté vous avez jeté ils/elles ont jeté	je jetais tu jetais il/elle jetait nous jetions vous jetiez ils/elles jetaient	je jetterai tu jetteras il/elle jettera nous jetterons vous jetterez ils/elles jetteront	je jette tu jettes il/elle jette nous jetions vous jetiez ils/elles jettent
42 joindre to join	je joins tu joins il/elle joint nous joignons vous joignez ils/elles joignent	j' ai joint tu as joint il/elle a joint nous avons joint vous avez joint ils/elles ont joint	je joignais tu joignais il/elle joignait nous joignions vous joigniez ils/elles joignaient	je joindrai tu joindras il/elle joindra nous joindrons vous joindrez ils/elles joindront	je joigne tu joignes il/elle joigne nous joignions vous joigniez ils/elles joignent
43 lever to raise	je lève tu lèves il/elle lève nous levons vous levez ils/elles lèvent	j' ai levé tu as levé il/elle a levé nous avons levé vous avez levé ils/elles ont levé	je levais tu levais il/elle levait nous levions vous leviez ils/elles levaient	je lèverai tu lèveras il/elle lèvera nous lèverons vous lèverez ils/elles lèveront	je lève tu lèves il/elle lève nous levions vous leviez ils/elles lèvent
44 lire to read	je lis tu lis il/elle lit nous lisons vous lisez ils/elles lisent	j' ai lu tu as lu il/elle a lu nous avons lu vous avez lu ils/elles ont lu	je lisais tu lisais il/elle lisait nous lisions vous lisiez ils/elles lisaient	je lirai tu liras il/elle lira nous lirons vous lirez ils/elles liront	je lise tu lises il/elle lise nous lisions vous lisiez ils/elles lisent
45 manger to eat	je mange tu manges il/elle mange nous mangeons vous mangez ils/elles mangent	j' ai mangé tu as mangé il/elle a mangé nous avons mangé vous avez mangé ils/elles ont mangé	je mangeais tu mangeais il/elle mangeait nous mangions vous mangiez ils/elles mangeaient	je mangerai tu mangeras il/elle mangera nous mangerons vous mangerez ils/elles mangeront	je mange tu manges il/elle mange nous mangions vous mangiez ils/elles mangent

Letters in bold indicate a significant change in spelling from the infinitive form.

	PRESENT	PERFECT	IMPERFECT	FUTURE	PRESENT SUBJUNCTIVE
46 maudire to curse	je maudis	j' ai maudit	je maudissais	je maudirai	je maudisse
	tu maudis	tu as maudit	tu maudissais	tu maudiras	tu maudisses
	il/elle maudit	il/elle a maudit	il/elle maudissait	il/elle maudira	il/elle maudisse
	nous maudissons	nous avons maudit	nous maudissions	nous maudirons	nous maudissions
	vous maudissez	vous avez maudit	vous maudissiez	vous maudirez	vous maudissiez
	ils/elles maudissent	ils/elles ont maudit	ils/elles maudissaient	ils/elles maudiront	ils/elles maudissent
47 mettre to put	see full verb table page 639				
48 monter to go up	je monte	je suis monté(e)/ j' ai monté	je montais	je monterai	je monte
	tu montes	tu es monté(e)/ tu as monté	tu montais	tu monteras	tu montes
	il/elle monte	il/elle est monté(e)/ il/elle a monté	il/elle montait	il/elle montera	il/elle monte
	nous montons	nous sommes monté(e)s/ nous avons monté	nous montions	nous monterons	nous montions
	vous montez	vous êtes monté(e)(s)/ vous avez monté	vous montiez	vous monterez	vous montiez
	ils/elles montent	ils/elles sont monté(e)s/ ils/elles ont monté	ils/elles montaient	ils/elles monteront	ils/elles montent
49 mordre to bite	je mords	j' ai mordu	je mordais	je mordrai	je morde
	tu mords	tu as mordu	tu mordais	tu mordras	tu mordes
	il/elle mord	il/elle a mordu	il/elle mordait	il/elle mordra	il/elle morde
	nous mordons	nous avons mordu	nous mordions	nous mordrons	nous mordions
	vous mordez	vous avez mordu	vous mordiez	vous mordrez	vous mordiez
	ils/elles mordent	ils/elles ont mordu	ils/elles mordaient	ils/elles mordront	ils/elles mordent
50 moudre to grind	je mouds	j' ai moulu	je moulais	je moudrai	je moule
	tu mouds	tu as moulu	tu moulais	tu moudras	tu moules
	il/elle moud	il/elle a moulu	il/elle moulait	il/elle moudra	il/elle moule
	nous moulons	nous avons moulu	nous moulions	nous moudrons	nous moulions
	vous moulez	vous avez moulu	vous mouliez	vous moudrez	vous mouliez
	ils/elles moulent	ils/elles ont moulu	ils/elles moulaient	ils/elles moudront	ils/elles moulent
51 mourir to die	je m**eur**s	je suis mort(e)	je mourais	je mourrai	je m**eur**e
	tu m**eur**s	tu es mort(e)	tu mourais	tu mourras	tu m**eur**es
	il/elle m**eur**t	il/elle est mort(e)	il/elle mourait	il/elle mourra	il/elle m**eur**e
	nous mourons	nous sommes mort(e)s	nous mourions	nous mourrons	nous mourions
	vous mourez	vous êtes mort(e)(s)	vous mouriez	vous mourrez	vous mouriez
	ils/elles m**eur**ent	ils/elles sont mort(e)s	ils/elles mouraient	ils/elles mourront	ils/elles m**eur**ent
52 naître to be born	je nais	je suis né(e)	je naissais	je naîtrai	je naisse
	tu nais	tu es né(e)	tu naissais	tu naîtras	tu naisses
	il/elle naît	il/elle est né(e)	il/elle naissait	il/elle naîtra	il/elle naisse
	nous naissons	nous sommes né(e)s	nous naissions	nous naîtrons	nous naissions
	vous naissez	vous êtes né(e)(s)	vous naissiez	vous naîtrez	vous naissiez
	ils/elles naissent	ils/elles sont né(e)s	ils/elles naissaient	ils/elles naîtront	ils/elles naissent
52 nettoyer to clean	je netto**i**e	j' ai nettoyé	je nettoyais	je netto**i**erai	je netto**i**e
	tu netto**i**es	tu as nettoyé	tu nettoyais	tu netto**i**eras	tu netto**i**es
	il/elle netto**i**e	il/elle a nettoyé	il/elle nettoyait	il/elle netto**i**era	il/elle netto**i**e
	nous nettoyons	nous avons nettoyé	nous nettoyions	nous netto**i**erons	nous nettoyions
	vous nettoyez	vous avez nettoyé	vous nettoyiez	vous netto**i**erez	vous nettoyiez
	ils/elles netto**i**ent	ils/elles ont nettoyé	ils/elles nettoyaient	ils/elles netto**i**eront	ils/elles netto**i**ent
54 offrir to offer	j' offre	j' ai offert	j' offrais	j' offrirai	j' offre
	tu offres	tu as offert	tu offrais	tu offriras	tu offres
	il/elle offre	il/elle a offert	il/elle offrait	il/elle offrira	il/elle offre
	nous offrons	nous avons offert	nous offrions	nous offrirons	nous offrions
	vous offrez	vous avez offert	vous offriez	vous offrirez	vous offriez
	ils/elles offrent	ils/elles ont offert	ils/elles offraient	ils/elles offriront	ils/elles offrent
55 ouvrir to open	see full verb table page 640				

Letters in bold indicate a significant change in spelling from the infinitive form.

	PRESENT	**PERFECT**	**IMPERFECT**	**FUTURE**	**PRESENT SUBJUNCTIVE**
56 paraître to seem	je parais	j' ai paru	je paraissais	je paraîtrai	je paraisse
	tu parais	tu as paru	tu paraissais	tu paraîtras	tu paraisses
	il/elle paraît	il/elle a paru	il/elle paraissait	il/elle paraîtra	il/elle paraisse
	nous paraissons	nous avons paru	nous paraissions	nous paraîtrons	nous paraissions
	vous paraissez	vous avez paru	vous paraissiez	vous paraîtrez	vous paraissiez
	ils/elles paraissent	ils/elles ont paru	ils/elles paraissaient	ils/elles paraîtront	ils/elles paraissent
57 partir to leave	see full verb table page 641				
58 passer to pass	je passe	j' ai passé/ je suis passé(e)	je passais	je passerai	je passe
	tu passes	tu as passé/ tu es passé(e)	tu passais	tu passeras	tu passes
	il/elle passe	il/elle a passé/ il/elle est passé(e)	il/elle passait	il/elle passera	il/elle passe
	nous passons	nous avons passé/ nous sommes passé(e)s	nous passions	nous passerons	nous passions
	vous passez	vous avez passé/ vous êtes passé(e)(s)	vous passiez	vous passerez	vous passiez
	ils/elles passent	ils/elles ont passé/ ils/elles sont passé(e)s	ils/elles passaient	ils/elles passeront	ils/elles passent
59 payer to pay	je paie *or* paye	j' ai payé	je payais	je paierai	je paie *or* paye
	tu paies *or* payes	tu as payé	tu payais	tu paieras	tu paies *or* payes
	il/elle paie *or* paye	il/elle a payé	il/elle payait	il/elle paiera	il/elle paie *or* paye
	nous payons	nous avons payé	nous payions	nous paierons	nous payions
	vous payez	vous avez payé	vous payiez	vous paierez	vous payiez
	ils/elles paient *or* payent	ils/elles ont payé	ils/elles payaient	ils/elles paieront	ils/elles paient *or* payent
60 peindre to paint	je peins	j' ai peint	je peignais	je peindrai	je peigne
	tu peins	tu as peint	tu peignais	tu peindras	tu peignes
	il/elle peint	il/elle a peint	il/elle peignait	il/elle peindra	il/elle peigne
	nous peignons	nous avons peint	nous peignions	nous peindrons	nous peignions
	vous peignez	vous avez peint	vous peigniez	vous peindrez	vous peigniez
	ils/elles peignent	ils/elles ont peint	ils/elles peignaient	ils/elles peindront	ils/elles peignent
61 perdre to lose	je perds	j' ai perdu	je perdais	je perdrai	je perde
	tu perds	tu as perdu	tu perdais	tu perdras	tu perdes
	il/elle perd	il/elle a perdu	il/elle perdait	il/elle perdra	il/elle perde
	nous perdons	nous avons perdu	nous perdions	nous perdrons	nous perdions
	vous perdez	vous avez perdu	vous perdiez	vous perdrez	vous perdiez
	ils/elles perdent	ils/elles ont perdu	ils/elles perdaient	ils/elles perdront	ils/elles perdent
62 plaire to please	je plais	j' ai plu	je plaisais	je plairai	je plaise
	tu plais	tu as plu	tu plaisais	tu plairas	tu plaises
	il/elle plaît	il/elle a plu	il/elle plaisait	il/elle plaira	il/elle plaise
	nous plaisons	nous avons plu	nous plaisions	nous plairons	nous plaisions
	vous plaisez	vous avez plu	vous plaisiez	vous plairez	vous plaisiez
	ils/elles plaisent	ils/elles ont plu	ils/elles plaisaient	ils/elles plairont	ils/elles plaisent
63 pleuvoir to rain	il pleut	il a plu	il pleuvait	il pleuvra	il pleuve
64 pouvoir to be able	see full verb table page 642				
65 prendre to take	see full verb table page 643				
66 protéger to protect	je protège	j' ai protégé	je protégeais	je protégerai	je protège
	tu protèges	tu as protégé	tu protégeais	tu protégeras	tu protèges
	il/elle protège	il/elle a protégé	il/elle protégeait	il/elle protégera	il/elle protège
	nous protégeons	nous avons protégé	nous protégions	nous protégerons	nous protégions
	vous protégez	vous avez protégé	vous protégiez	vous protégerez	vous protégiez
	ils/elles protègent	ils/elles ont protégé	ils/elles protégeaient	ils/elles protégeront	ils/elles protègent
67 recevoir to receive	je reçois	j' ai reçu	je recevais	je recevrai	je reçoive
	tu reçois	tu as reçu	tu recevais	tu recevras	tu reçoives
	il/elle reçoit	il/elle a reçu	il/elle recevait	il/elle recevra	il/elle reçoive
	nous recevons	nous avons reçu	nous recevions	nous recevrons	nous recevions
	vous recevez	vous avez reçu	vous receviez	vous recevrez	vous receviez
	ils/elles reçoivent	ils/elles ont reçu	ils/elles recevaient	ils/elles recevront	ils/elles reçoivent

Letters in bold indicate a significant change in spelling from the infinitive form.

	PRESENT	PERFECT	IMPERFECT	FUTURE	PRESENT SUBJUNCTIVE
68 rentrer to come in	je rentre	je suis rentré(e)/ j' ai rentré	je rentrais	je rentrerai	je rentre
	tu rentres	tu es rentré(e)/ tu as rentré	tu rentrais	tu rentreras	tu rentres
	il/elle rentre	il/elle est rentré(e)/ il/elle a rentré	il/elle rentrait	il/elle rentrera	il/elle rentre
	nous rentrons	nous sommes rentré(e)s/ nous avons rentré	nous rentrions	nous rentrerons	nous rentrions
	vous rentrez	vous êtes rentré(e)(s)/ vous avez rentré	vous rentriez	vous rentrerez	vous rentriez
	ils/elles rentrent	ils/elles sont rentré(e)s/ ils/elles ont rentré	ils/elles rentraient	ils/elles rentreront	ils/elles rentrent
69 répondre to answer	je réponds	j' ai répondu	je répondais	je répondrai	je réponde
	tu réponds	tu as répondu	tu répondais	tu répondras	tu répondes
	il/elle répond	il/elle a répondu	il/elle répondait	il/elle répondra	il/elle réponde
	nous répondons	nous avons répondu	nous répondions	nous répondrons	nous répondions
	vous répondez	vous avez répondu	vous répondiez	vous répondrez	vous répondiez
	ils/elles répondent	ils/elles ont répondu	ils/elles répondaient	ils/elles répondront	ils/elles répondent
70 résoudre to resolve	je résous	j' ai résolu	je résolvais	je résoudrai	je résolve
	tu résous	tu as résolu	tu résolvais	tu résoudras	tu résolves
	il/elle résout	il/elle a résolu	il/elle résolvait	il/elle résoudra	il/elle résolve
	nous résolvons	nous avons résolu	nous résolvions	nous résoudrons	nous résolvions
	vous résolvez	vous avez résolu	vous résolviez	vous résoudrez	vous résolviez
	ils/elles résolvent	ils/elles ont résolu	ils/elles résolvaient	ils/elles résoudront	ils/elles résolvent
71 rester to stay	je reste	je suis resté(e)	je restais	je resterai	je reste
	tu restes	tu es resté(e)	tu restais	tu resteras	tu restes
	il/elle reste	il/elle est resté(e)	il/elle restait	il/elle restera	il/elle reste
	nous restons	nous sommes resté(e)s	nous restions	nous resterons	nous restions
	vous restez	vous êtes resté(e)(s)	vous restiez	vous resterez	vous restiez
	ils/elles restent	ils/elles sont resté(e)s	ils/elles restaient	ils/elles resteront	ils/elles restent
72 retourner to go back	je retourne	je suis retourné(e)/ j' ai retourné	je retournais	je retournerai	je retourne
	tu retournes	tu es retourné(e)/ tu as retourné	tu retournais	tu retourneras	tu retournes
	il/elle retourne	il/elle est retourné(e)/ il/elle a retourné	il/elle retournait	il/elle retournera	il/elle retourne
	nous retournons	nous sommes retourné(e)s/ nous avons retourné	nous retournions	nous retournerons	nous retournions
	vous retournez	vous êtes retourné(e)(s)/ vous avez retourné	vous retourniez	vous retournerez	vous retourniez
	ils/elles retournent	ils/elles sont retourné(e)s/ ils/elles ont retourné	ils/elles retournaient	ils/elles retourneront	ils/elles retournent
73 revenir to come back	je reviens	je suis revenu(e)	je revenais	je reviendrai	je revienne
	tu reviens	tu es revenu(e)	tu revenais	tu reviendras	tu reviennes
	il/elle revient	il/elle est revenu(e)	il/elle revenait	il/elle reviendra	il/elle revienne
	nous revenons	nous sommes revenu(e)s	nous revenions	nous reviendrons	nous revenions
	vous revenez	vous êtes revenu(e)(s)	vous reveniez	vous reviendrez	vous reveniez
	ils/elles reviennent	ils/elles sont revenu(e)s	ils/elles revenaient	ils/elles reviendront	ils/elles reviennent
74 rire to laugh	je ris	j' ai ri	je riais	je rirai	je rie
	tu ris	tu as ri	tu riais	tu riras	tu ries
	il/elle rit	il/elle a ri	il/elle riait	il/elle rira	il/elle rie
	nous rions	nous avons ri	nous riions	nous rirons	nous riions
	vous riez	vous avez ri	vous riiez	vous rirez	vous riiez
	ils/elles rient	ils/elles ont ri	ils/elles riaient	ils/elles riront	ils/elles rient
75 rompre to break	je romps	j' ai rompu	je rompais	je romprai	je rompe
	tu romps	tu as rompu	tu rompais	tu rompras	tu rompes
	il/elle rompt	il/elle a rompu	il/elle rompait	il/elle rompra	il/elle rompe
	nous rompons	nous avons rompu	nous rompions	nous romprons	nous rompions
	vous rompez	vous avez rompu	vous rompiez	vous romprez	vous rompiez
	ils/elles rompent	ils/elles ont rompu	ils/elles rompaient	ils/elles rompront	ils/elles rompent
76 savoir to know	see full verb table page 644				

Letters in bold indicate a significant change in spelling from the infinitive form.

	PRESENT	PERFECT	IMPERFECT	FUTURE	PRESENT SUBJUNCTIVE
77 sentir to smell; to feel	je sens tu sens il/elle sent nous sentons vous sentez ils/elles sentent	j' ai senti tu as senti il/elle a senti nous avons senti vous avez senti ils/elles ont senti	je sentais tu sentais il/elle sentait nous sentions vous sentiez ils/elles sentaient	je sentirai tu sentiras il/elle sentira nous sentirons vous sentirez ils/elles sentiront	je sente tu sentes il/elle sente nous sentions vous sentiez ils/elles sentent
78 servir to serve	je sers tu sers il/elle sert nous servons vous servez ils/elles servent	j' ai servi tu as servi il/elle a servi nous avons servi vous avez servi ils/elles ont servi	je servais tu servais il/elle servait nous servions vous serviez ils/elles servaient	je servirai tu serviras il/elle servira nous servirons vous servirez ils/elles serviront	je serve tu serves il/elle serve nous servions vous serviez ils/elles servent
79 sortir to go out	je sors tu sors il/elle sort nous sortons vous sortez ils/elles sortent	je suis sorti(e)/ j' ai sorti tu es sorti(e)/ tu as sorti il/elle est sorti(e)/ il/elle a sorti nous sommes sorti(e)s/ nous avons sorti vous êtes sorti(e)(s)/ vous avez sorti ils/elles sont sorti(e)(s)/ ils/elles ont sorti	je sortais tu sortais il/elle sortait nous sortions vous sortiez ils/elles sortaient	je sortirai tu sortiras il/elle sortira nous sortirons vous sortirez ils/elles sortiront	je sorte tu sortes il/elle sorte nous sortions vous sortiez ils/elles sortent
80 suffire to be enough	je suffis tu suffis il/elle suffit nous suffisons vous suffisez ils/elles suffisent	j' ai suffi tu as suffi il/elle a suffi nous avons suffi vous avez suffi ils/elles ont suffi	je suffisais tu suffisais il/elle suffisait nous suffisions vous suffisiez ils/elles suffisaient	je suffirai tu suffiras il/elle suffira nous suffirons vous suffirez ils/elles suffiront	je suffise tu suffises il/elle suffise nous suffisions vous suffisiez ils/elles suffisent
81 suivre to follow	je suis tu suis il/elle suit nous suivons vous suivez ils/elles suivent	j' ai suivi tu as suivi il/elle a suivi nous avons suivi vous avez suivi ils/elles ont suivi	je suivais tu suivais il/elle suivait nous suivions vous suiviez ils/elles suivaient	je suivrai tu suivras il/elle suivra nous suivrons vous suivrez ils/elles suivront	je suive tu suives il/elle suive nous suivions vous suiviez ils/elles suivent
82 se taire to stop talking	see full verb table page 645				
83 tenir to hold	je tiens tu tiens il/elle tient nous tenons vous tenez ils/elles tiennent	j' ai tenu tu as tenu il/elle a tenu nous avons tenu vous avez tenu ils/elles ont tenu	je tenais tu tenais il/elle tenait nous tenions vous teniez ils/elles tenaient	je tiendrai tu tiendras il/elle tiendra nous tiendrons vous tiendrez ils/elles tiendront	je tienne tu tiennes il/elle tienne nous tenions vous teniez ils/elles tiennent
84 tomber to fall	je tombe tu tombes il/elle tombe nous tombons vous tombez ils/elles tombent	je suis tombé(e) tu es tombé(e) il/elle est tombé(e) nous sommes tombé(e)s vous êtes tombé(e)(s) ils/elles sont tombé(e)s	je tombais tu tombais il/elle tombait nous tombions vous tombiez ils/elles tombaient	je tomberai tu tomberas il/elle tombera nous tomberons vous tomberez ils/elles tomberont	je tombe tu tombes il/elle tombe nous tombions vous tombiez ils/elles tombent
85 traire to milk	je trais tu trais il/elle trait nous trayons vous trayez ils/elles traient	j' ai trait tu as trait il/elle a trait nous avons trait vous avez trait ils/elles ont trait	je trayais tu trayais il/elle trayait nous trayions vous trayiez ils/elles trayaient	je trairai tu trairas il/elle traira nous trairons vous trairez ils/elles trairont	je traie tu traies il/elle traie nous trayions vous trayiez ils/elles traient

Letters in bold indicate a significant change in spelling from the infinitive form.

	PRESENT	PERFECT	IMPERFECT	FUTURE	PRESENT SUBJUNCTIVE
86 vaincre to defeat; to overcome	je vaincs	j' ai vaincu	je vainquais	je vaincrai	je vainque
	tu vaincs	tu as vaincu	tu vainquais	tu vaincras	tu vainques
	il/elle vainc	il/elle a vaincu	il/elle vainquait	il/elle vaincra	il/elle vainque
	nous vainquons	nous avons vaincu	nous vainquions	nous vaincrons	nous vainquions
	vous vainquez	vous avez vaincu	vous vainquiez	vous vaincrez	vous vainquiez
	ils/elles vainquent	ils/elles ont vaincu	ils/elles vainquaient	ils/elles vaincront	ils/elles vainquent
87 valoir to be worth	je vaux	j' ai valu	je valais	je vaudrai	je vaille
	tu vaux	tu as valu	tu valais	tu vaudras	tu vailles
	il/elle vaut	il/elle a valu	il/elle valait	il/elle vaudra	il/elle vaille
	nous valons	nous avons valu	nous valions	nous vaudrons	nous valions
	vous valez	vous avez valu	vous valiez	vous vaudrez	vous valiez
	ils/elles valent	ils/elles ont valu	ils/elles valaient	ils/elles vaudront	ils/elles vaillent
88 vendre to sell	see full verb table page 646				
89 venir to come	see full verb table page 647				
90 vêtir to dress	je vêts	j' ai vêtu	je vêtais	je vêtirai	je vête
	tu vêts	tu as vêtu	tu vêtais	tu vêtiras	tu vêtes
	il/elle vêt	il/elle a vêtu	il/elle vêtait	il/elle vêtira	il/elle vête
	nous vêtons	nous avons vêtu	nous vêtions	nous vêtirons	nous vêtions
	vous vêtez	vous avez vêtu	vous vêtiez	vous vêtirez	vous vêtiez
	ils/elles vêtent	ils/elles ont vêtu	ils/elles vêtaient	ils/elles vêtiront	ils/elles vêtent
91 vivre to live	je vis	j' ai vécu	je vivais	je vivrai	je vive
	tu vis	tu as vécu	tu vivais	tu vivras	tu vives
	il/elle vit	il/elle a vécu	il/elle vivait	il/elle vivra	il/elle vive
	nous vivons	nous avons vécu	nous vivions	nous vivrons	nous vivions
	vous vivez	vous avez vécu	vous viviez	vous vivrez	vous viviez
	ils/elles vivent	ils/elles ont vécu	ils/elles vivaient	ils/elles vivront	ils/elles vivent
92 voir to see	see full verb table page 648				
93 vouloir to want	see full verb table page 649				

Letters in bold indicate a significant change in spelling from the infinitive form.